A⁄Z LONDON Street Atlas

CONTENTS

REFERENCE

Motorway	M25 ═ M25	Church or Chapel	†
Dual Carriageway		Disabled Toilet	♿
'A' Road	A24	Fire Station	■
'B' Road	B243	Hospital	⊞
One Way 'A' Roads Traffic flow is indicated by a heavy line to the Drivers Left	→	House Numbers 'A' and 'B' Roads only	113 98
Map Continuation	61 Enlarged Central Area 140	Information Centre	🄸
Docklands Light Railway Stations	─DLR─	National Grid Reference	⁵10
British Rail Line	Level Crossing ✕ ■	Police Station	▲
Underground Stations	●	Post Office	★

SCALE

Map Pages 4-137 1:22,000 (2.88 inches to 1 Mile)	Central Area pages 138-149 1:14,080 (4.5 inches to 1 Mile)
0 ¼ ½ Mile	0 ⅛ ¼ ⅜ Mile
0 250 500 750 Metres	0 250 500 Metres

Geographers' A-Z Map Co. Ltd.

Head Office :
Fairfield Road, Borough Green,
Sevenoaks, Kent. TN15 8PP
Telephone 01732 781000
Showrooms :
44 Gray's Inn Road, London, WC1X 8HX
Telephone 0171 242 9246

© Edition 3 1995

Copyright of the Publishers

P9-DDL-672

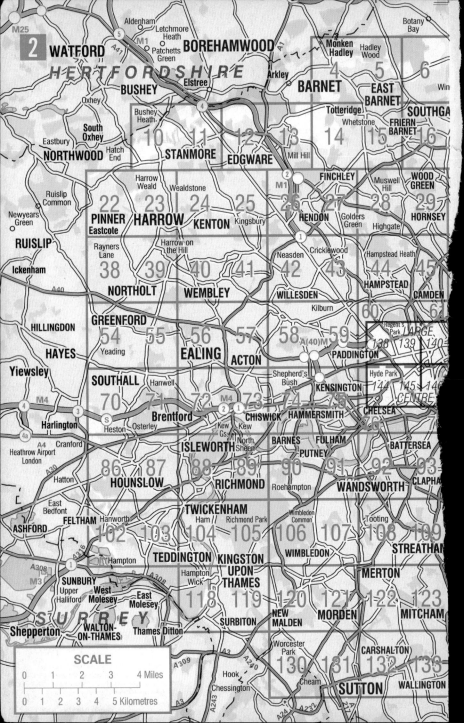

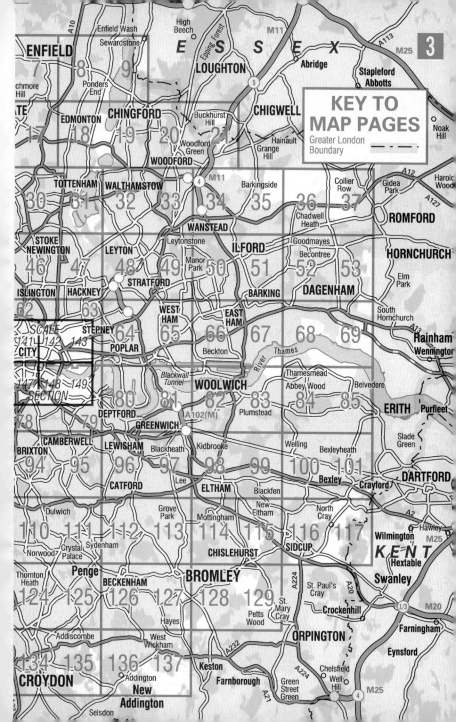

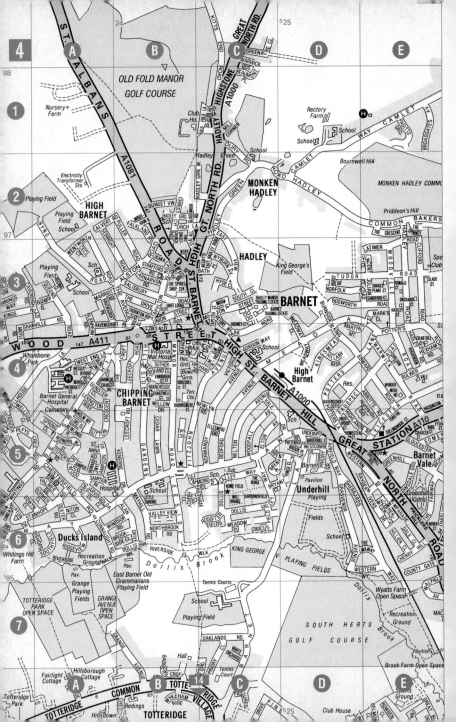

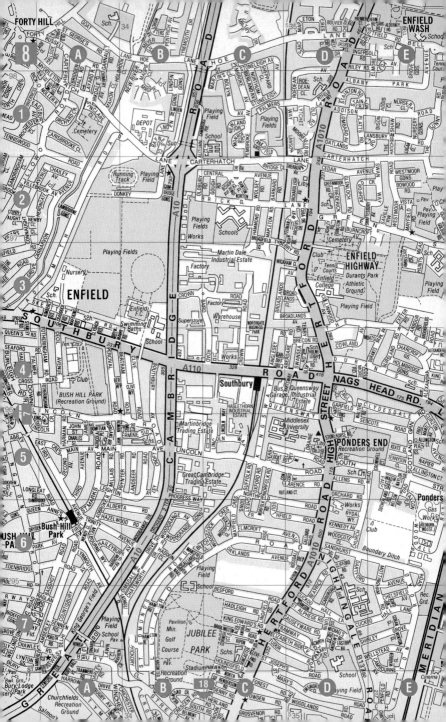

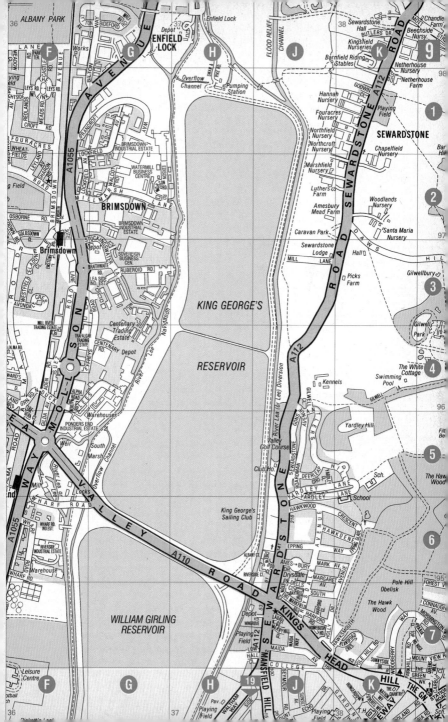

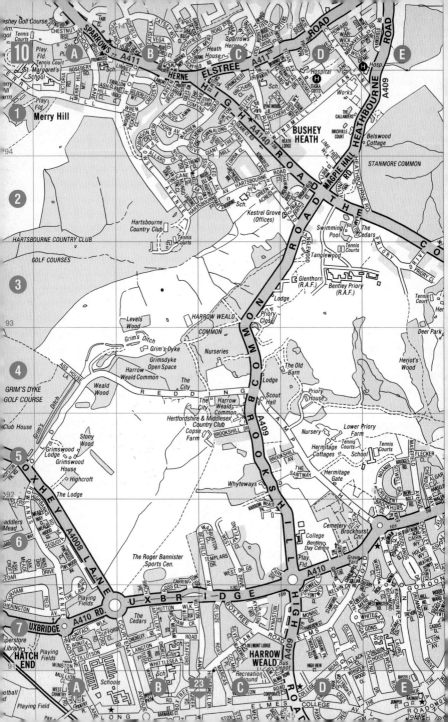

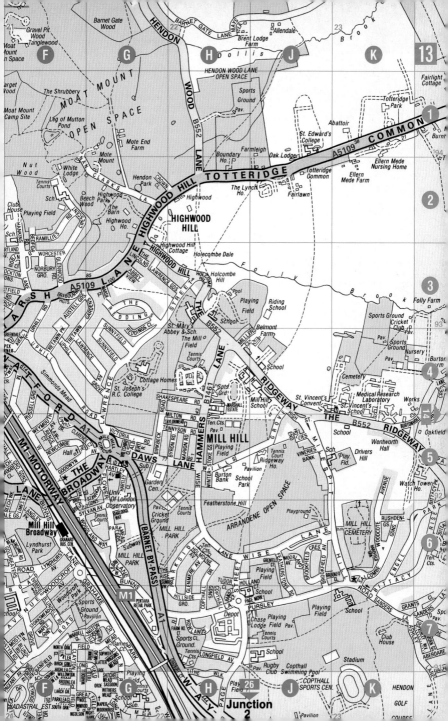

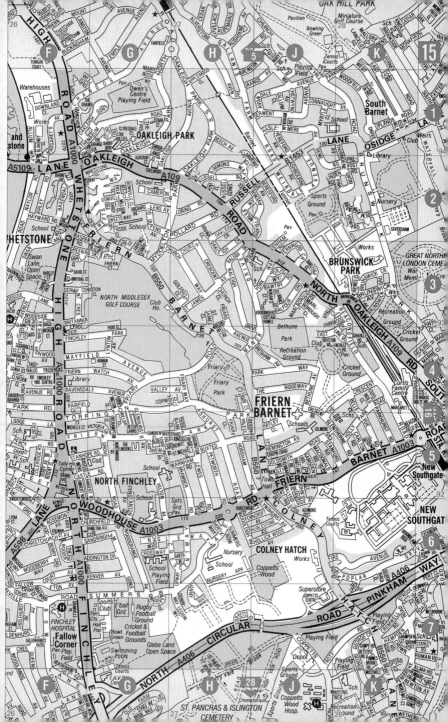

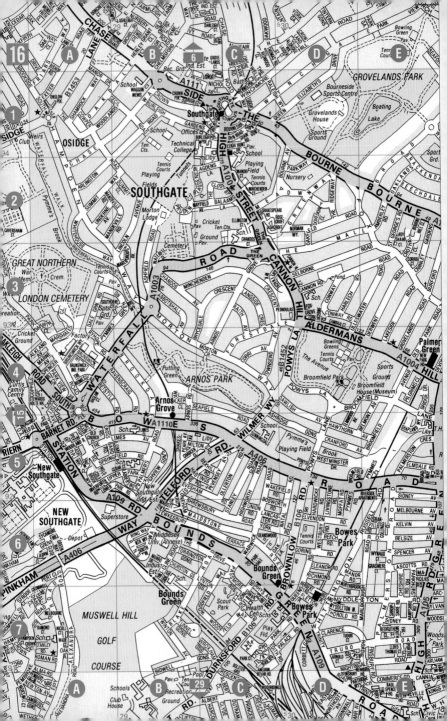

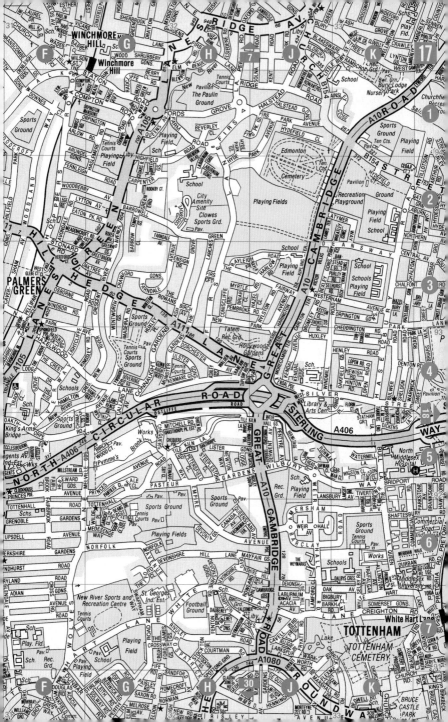

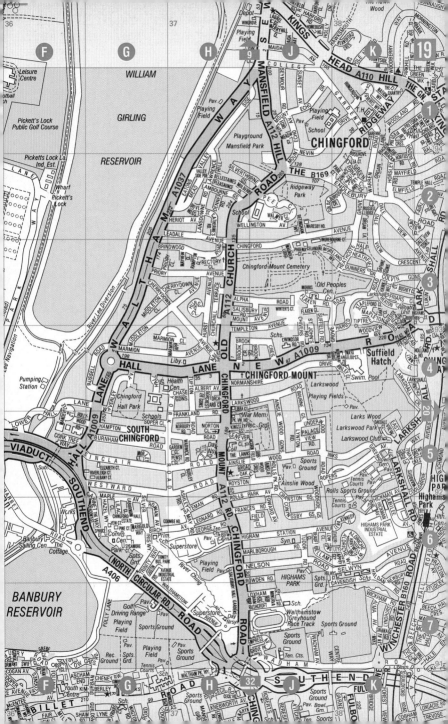

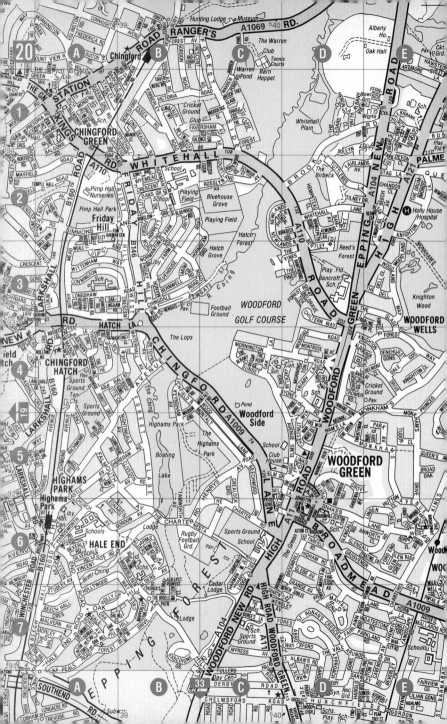

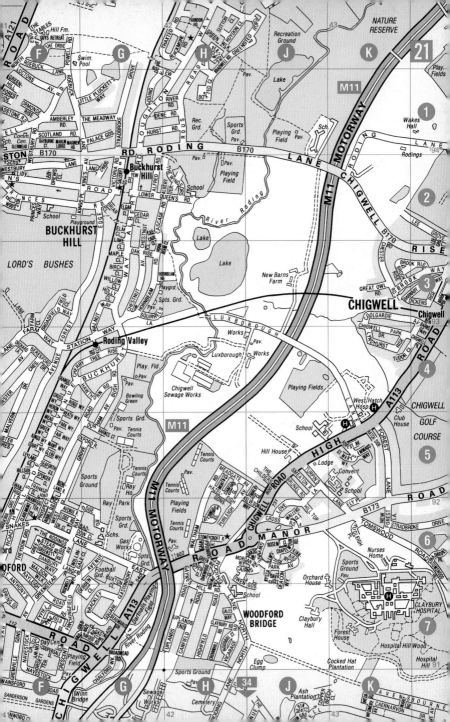

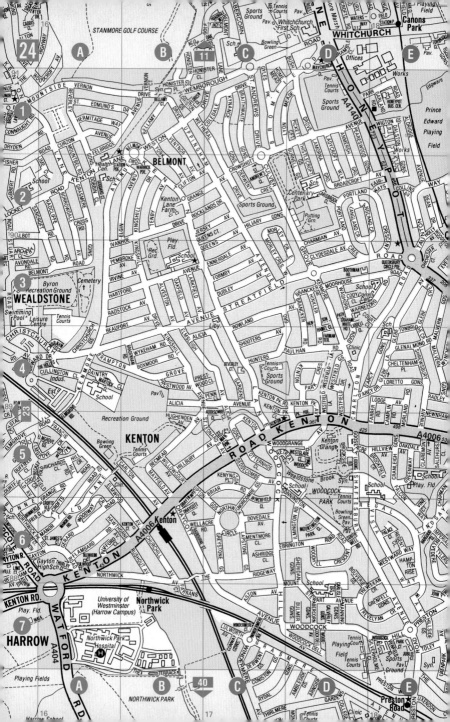

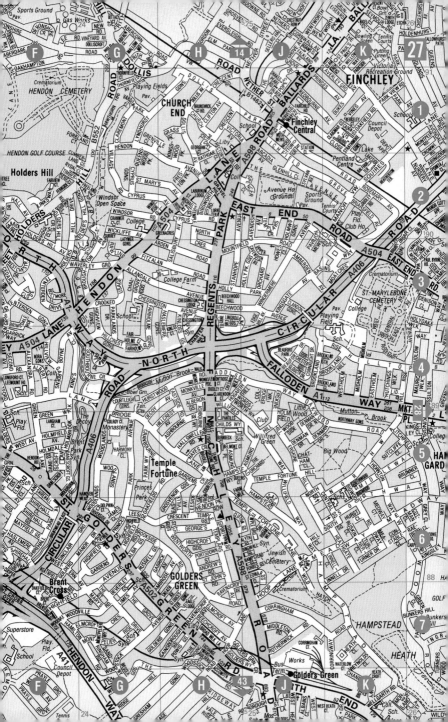

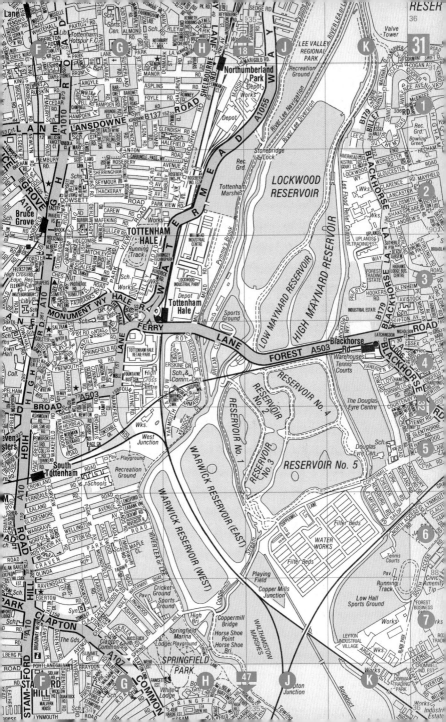

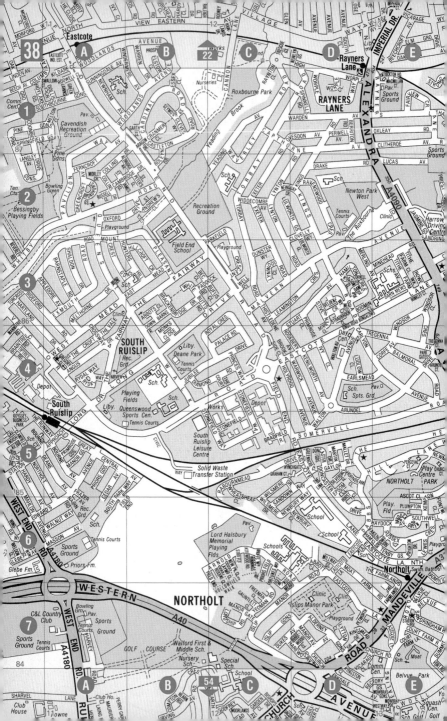

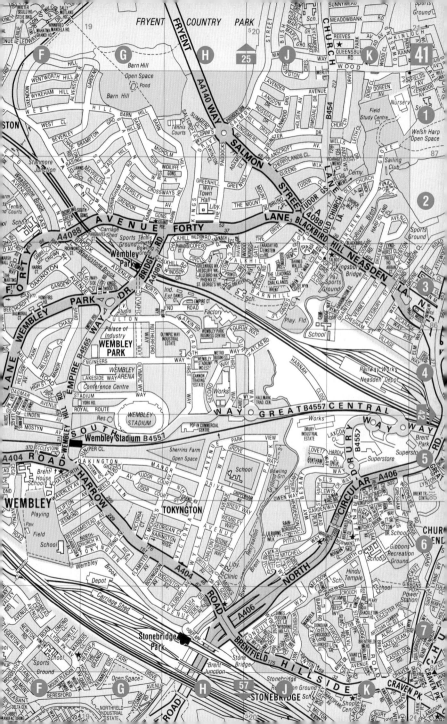

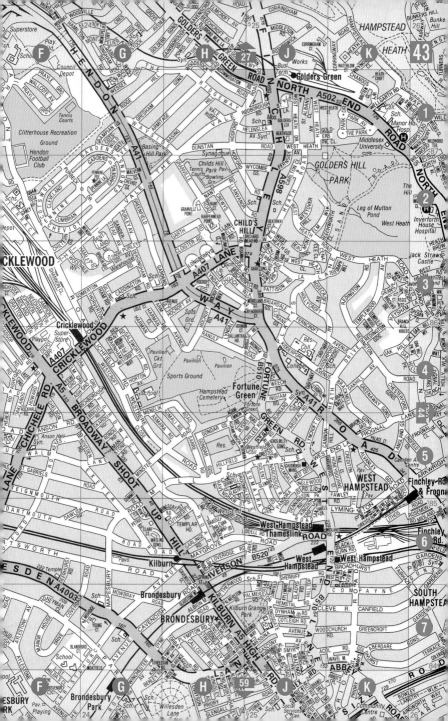

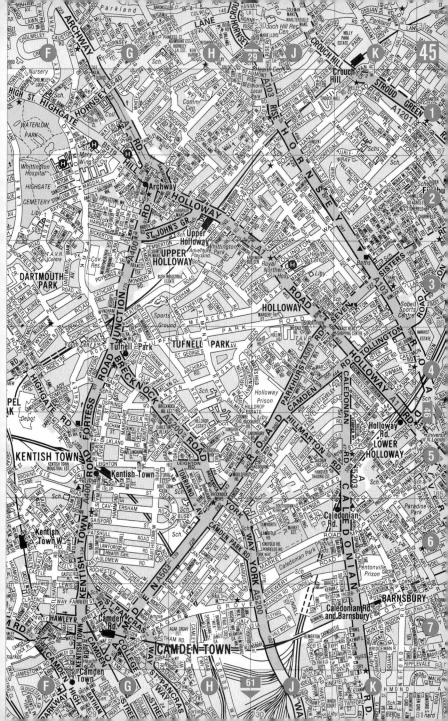

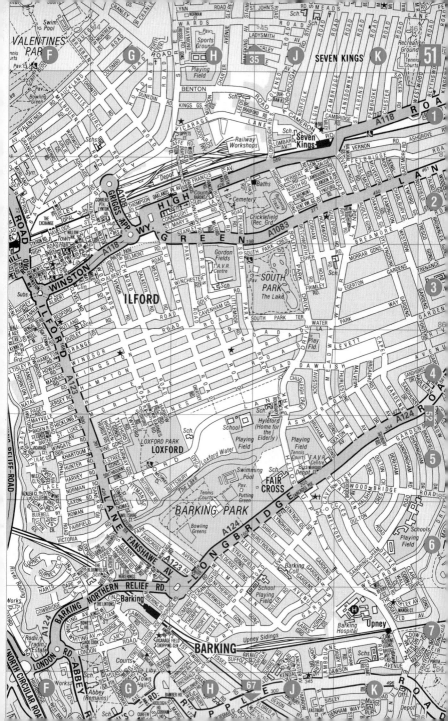

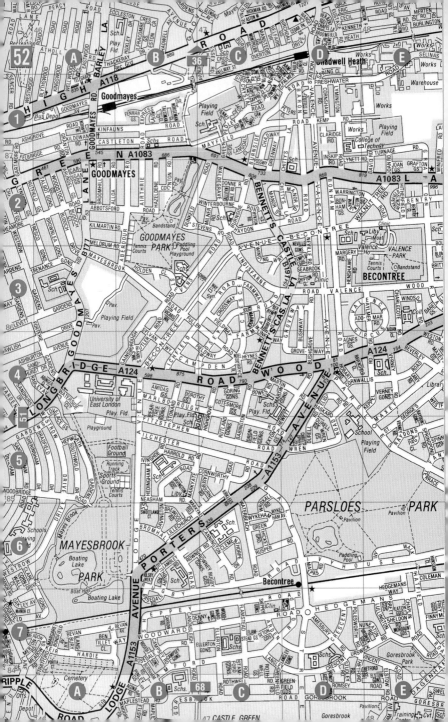

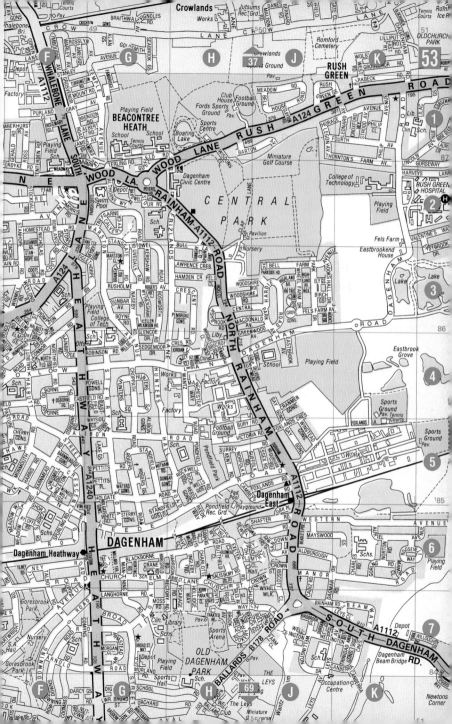

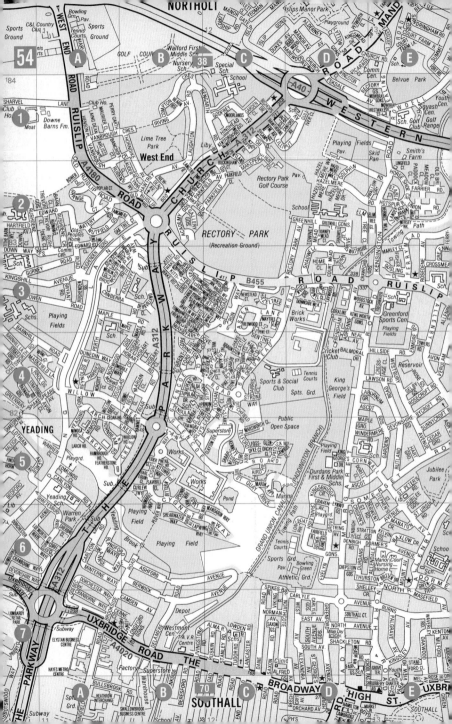

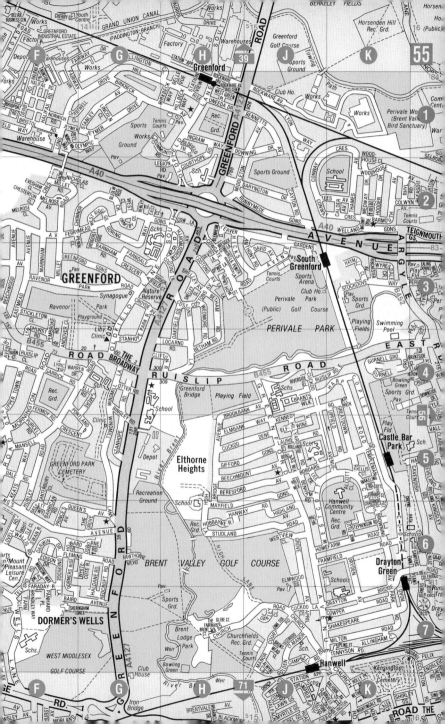

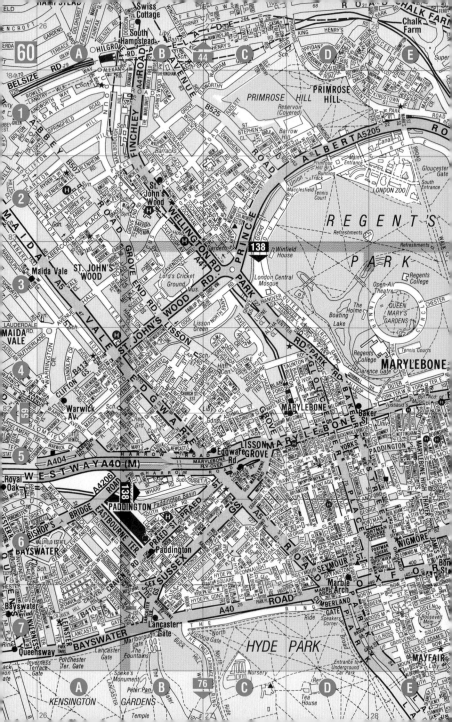

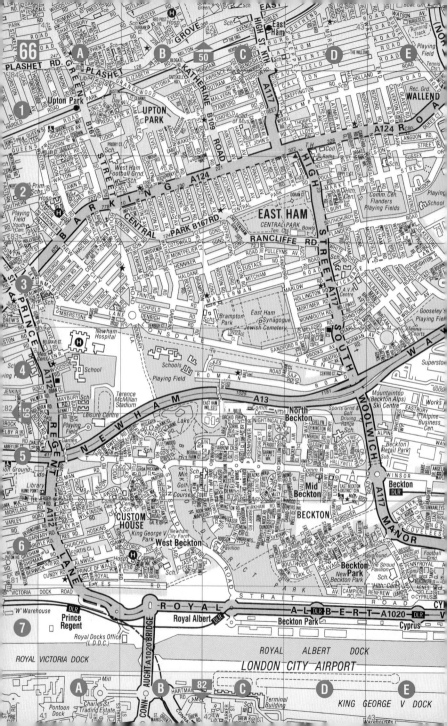

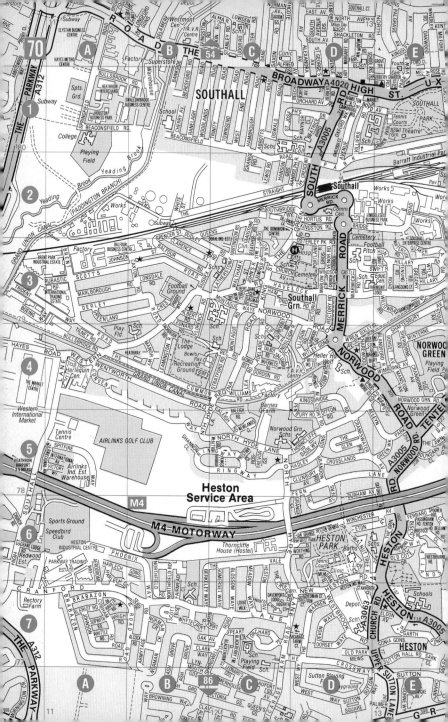

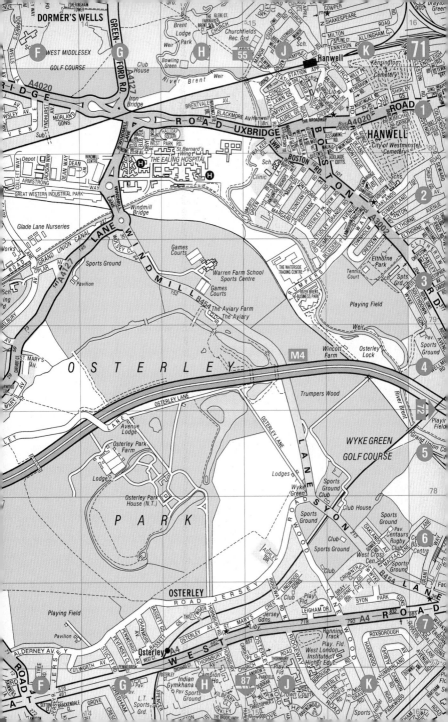

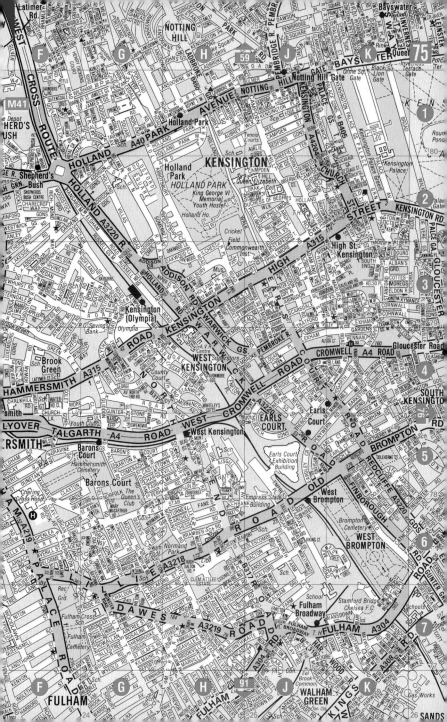

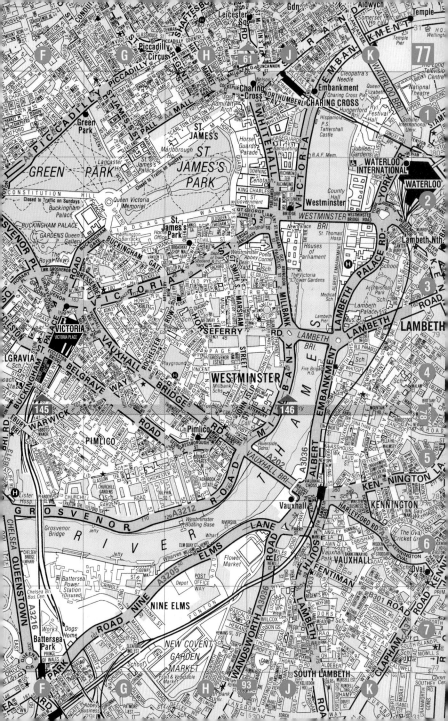

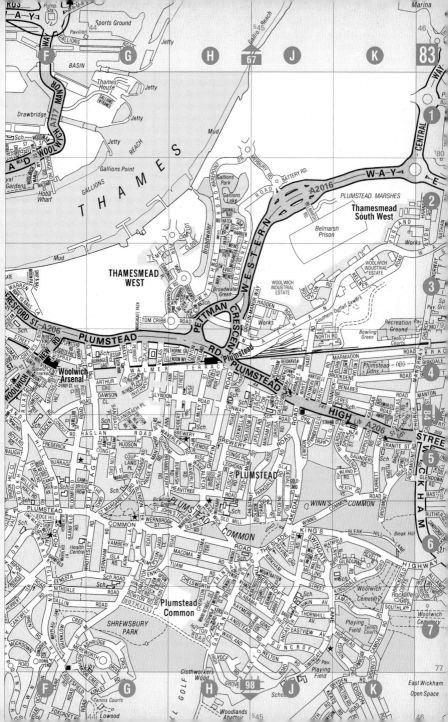

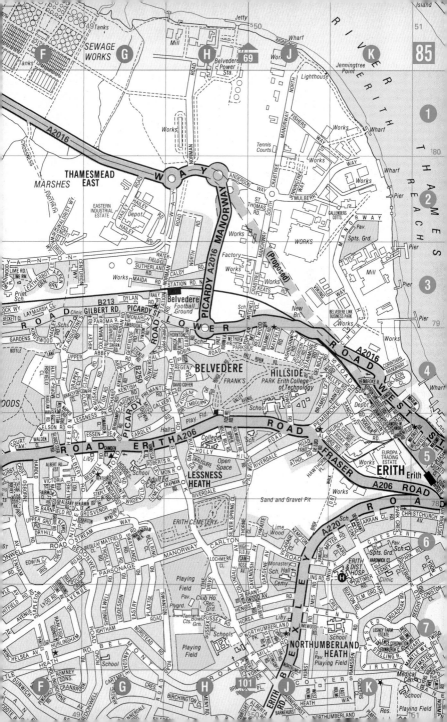

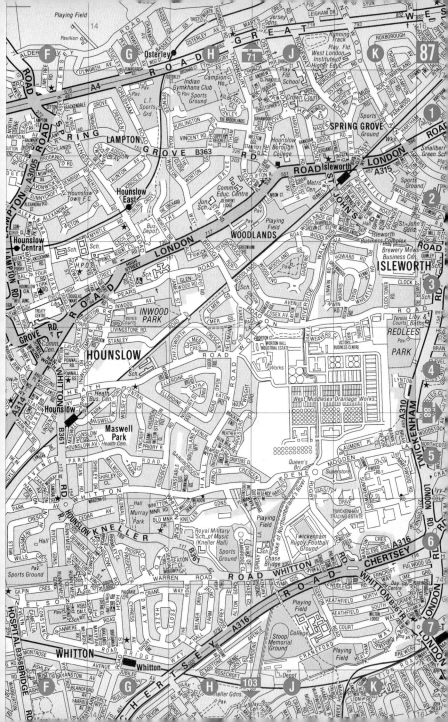

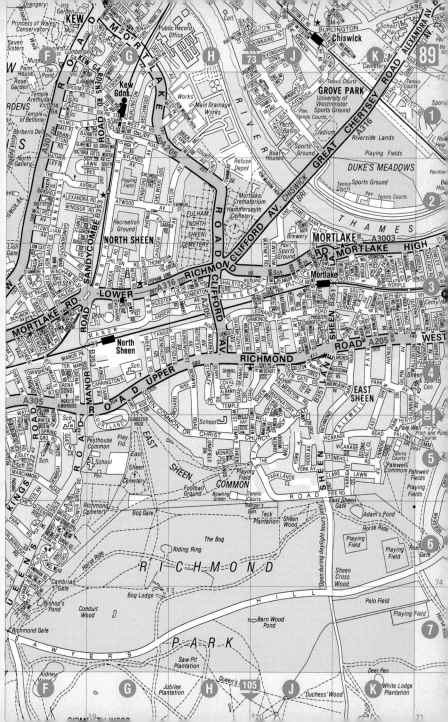

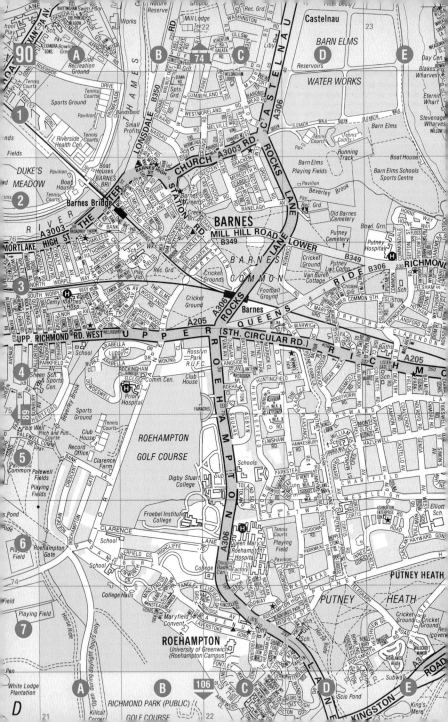

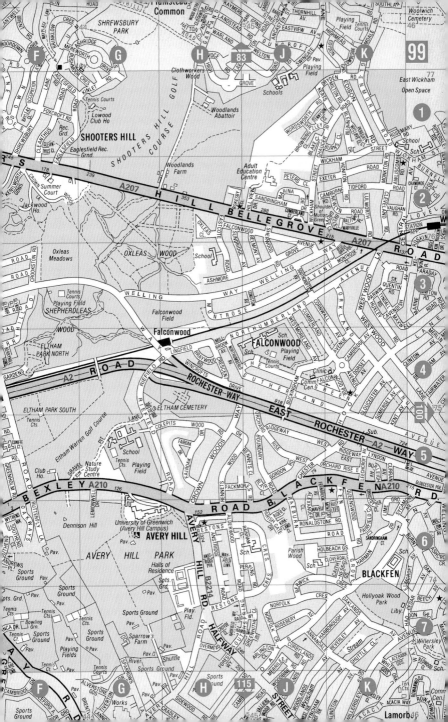

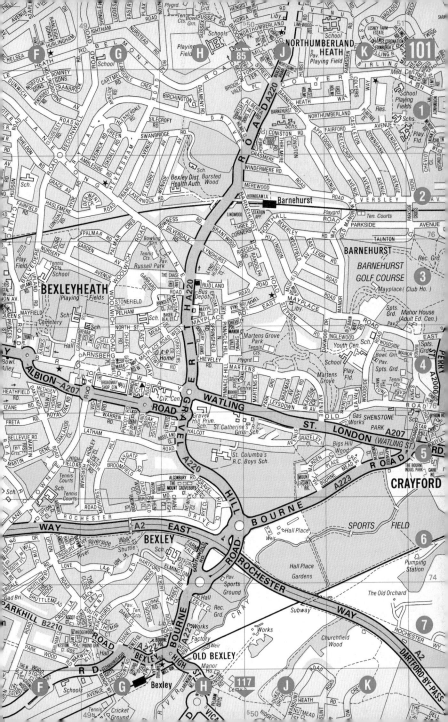

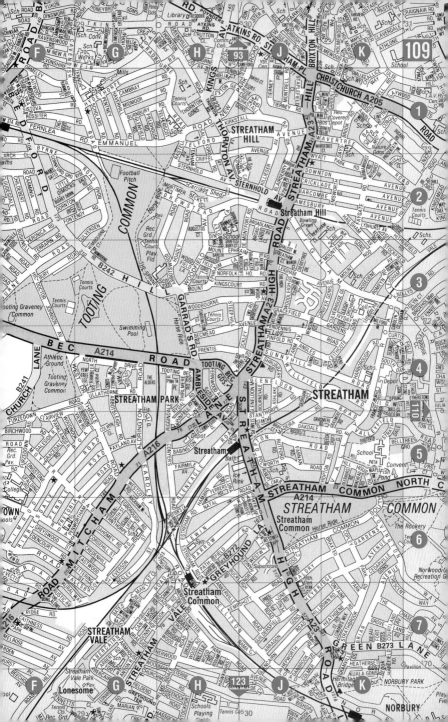

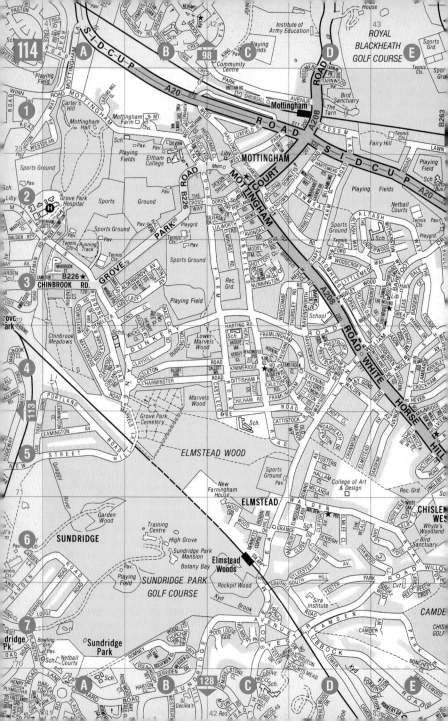

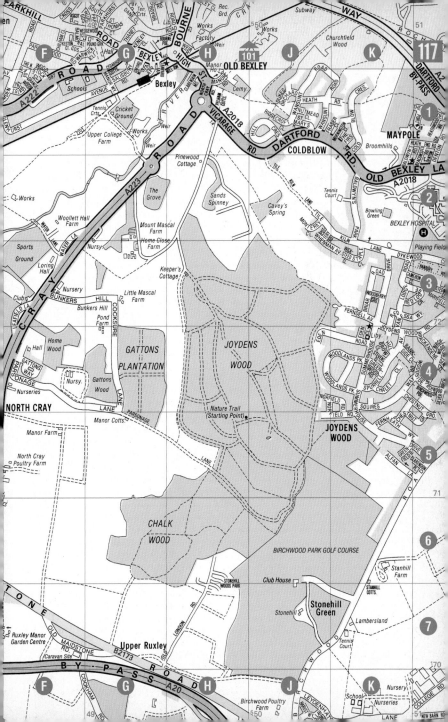

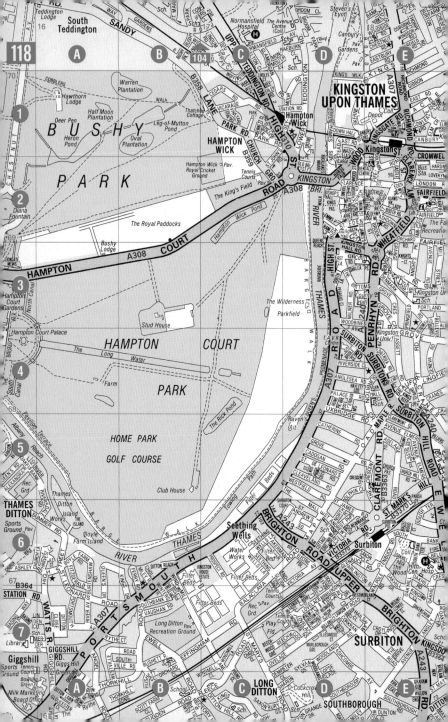

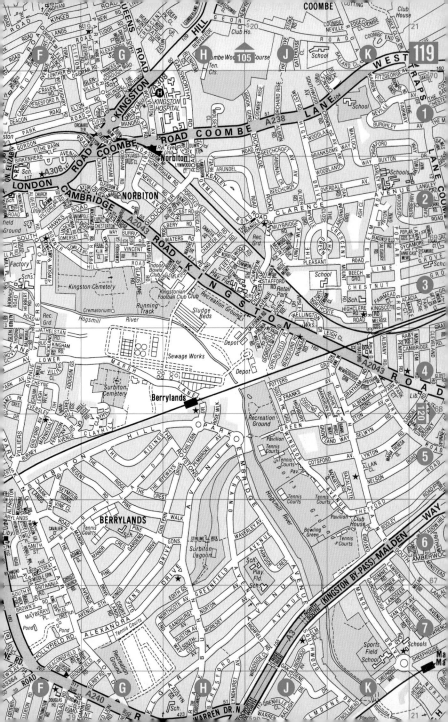

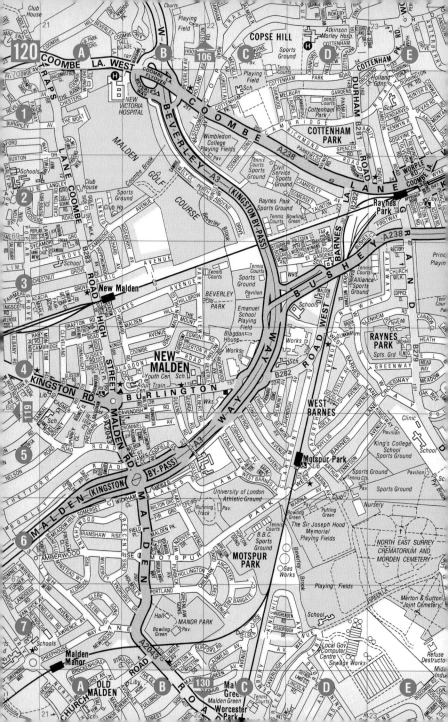

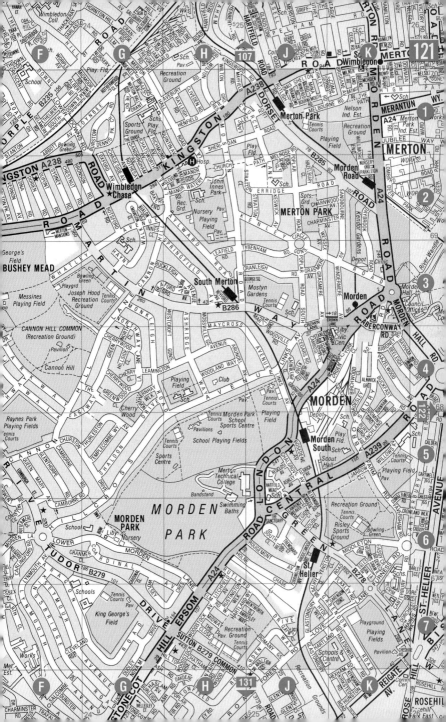

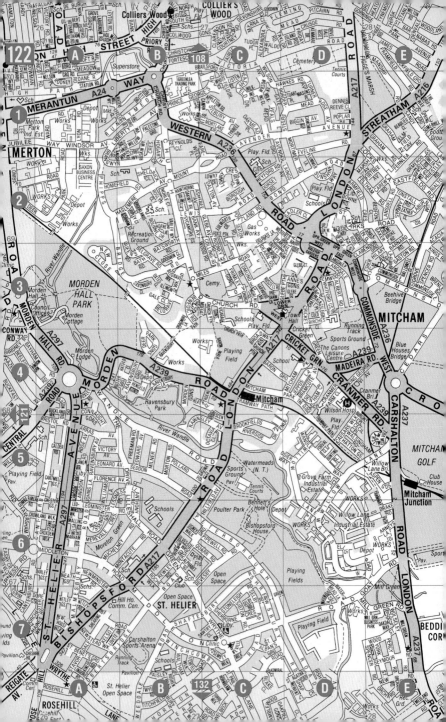

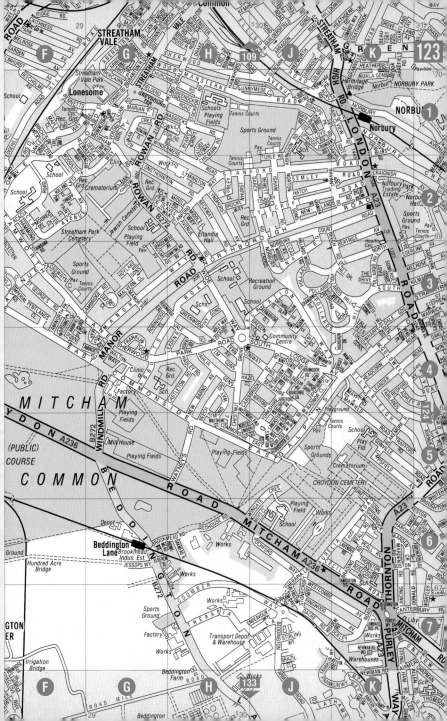

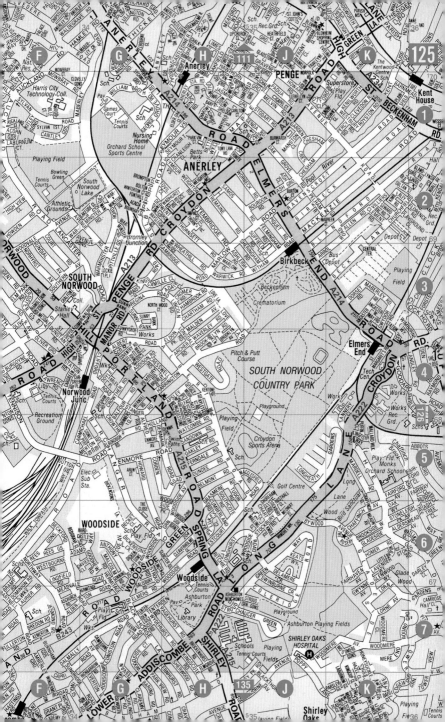

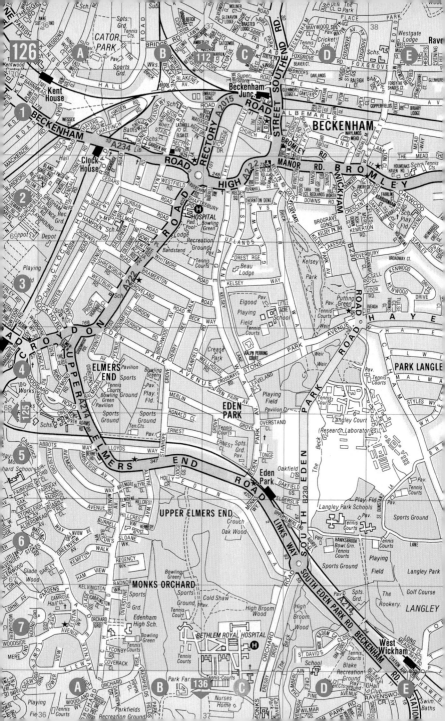

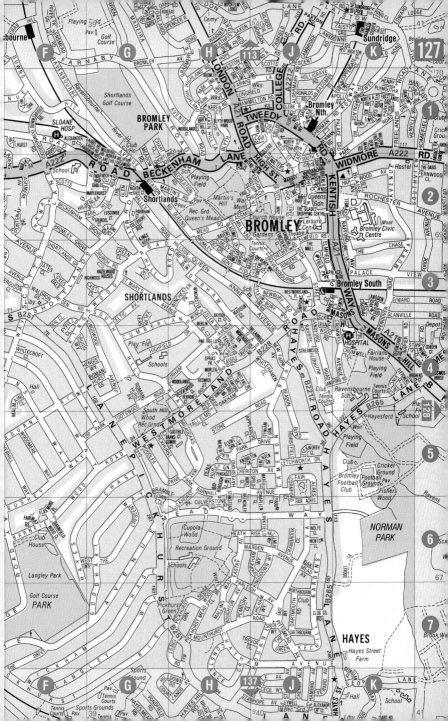

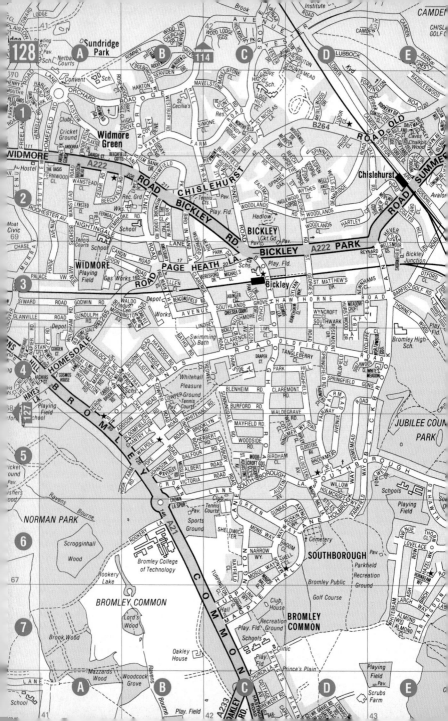

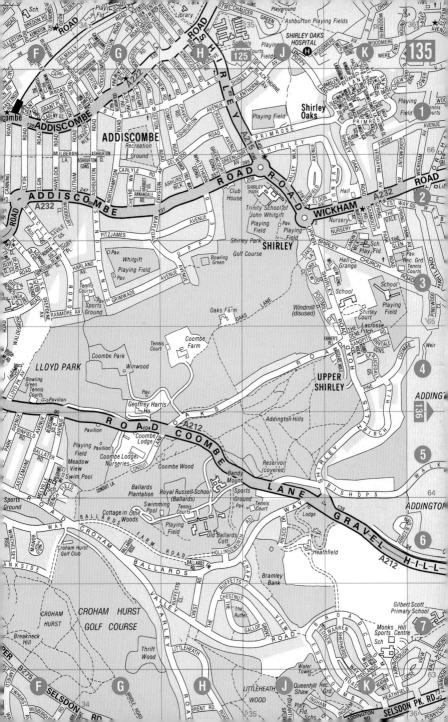

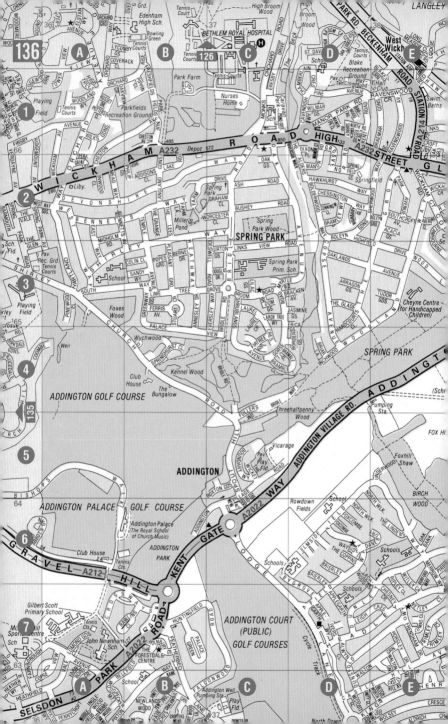

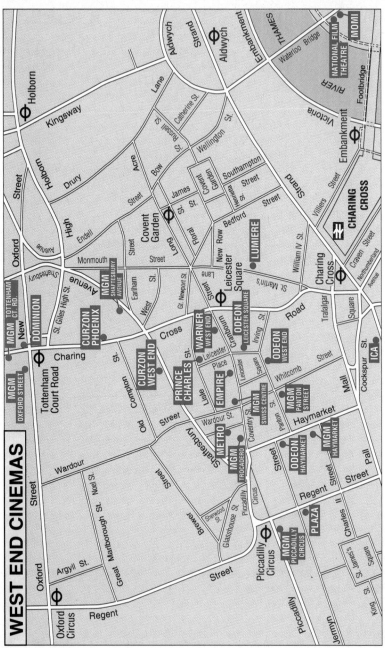

WEST END CINEMAS

150

© Copyright: Geographers' A-Z Map Company Ltd.

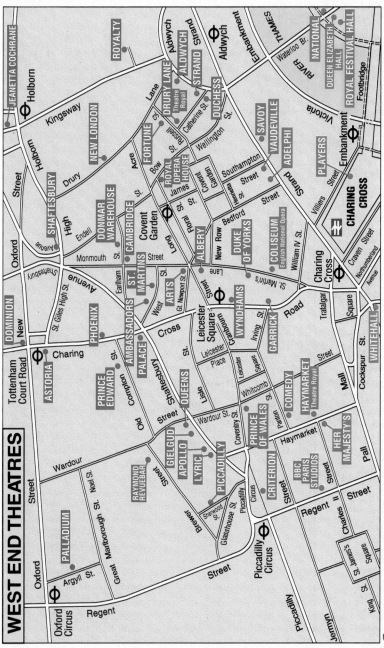

WEST END THEATRES

PALLADIUM
DOMINION
ASTORIA
PRINCE EDWARD
RAYMOND REVUEBAR
GIELGUD
APOLLO
LYRIC
PICCADILLY
CRITERION
BBC PARIS STUDIOS
PRINCE OF WALES
HER MAJESTY'S
COMEDY
HAYMARKET Theatre Royal
WHITEHALL
WYNDHAMS
GARRICK
PHOENIX
AMBASSADORS
PALACE
ARTS
ST. MARTINS
QUEENS
SHAFTESBURY
DONMAR WAREHOUSE
CAMBRIDGE
ALBERY
DUKE OF YORKS
COLISEUM English National Opera
NEW LONDON
FORTUNE
ROYAL OPERA HOUSE
DRURY LANE Theatre Royal
ALDWYCH
STRAND
DUCHESS
SAVOY
VAUDEVILLE
ADELPHI
PLAYERS
ROYALTY
NATIONAL
QUEEN ELIZABETH HALL
ROYAL FESTIVAL HALL

© Copyright: Geographers' A-Z Map Company Ltd.

151

INDEX TO STREETS

HOW TO USE THIS INDEX

1. Each street name is followed by its Postal District (or, if outside the London Postal District, by its Posttown or Postal Locality), and then by its map reference; e.g. Abberley M. SW4 —3F **93** is in the South West 4 Postal District and is to be found in square 3F on page **93**. The page number being shown in bold type.
A strict alphabetical order is followed in which Av., Rd., St., etc. (though abbreviated) are read in full and as part of the street name; e.g. Abbotstone Rd. appears after Abbots Ter. but before Abbot St.

2. Streets and a selection of Subsidiary names not shown on the Maps, appear in the index in *Italics* with the thoroughfare to which it is connected shown in brackets; e.g. *Abchurch Yd. EC4* —7D **43** *(off Abchurch La.)*

3. The page references shown in brackets indicate those streets that appear on the enlarged scale map pages 138-149; e.g. Abbey Orchard St. SW1 —3H **77** (6A **146**) appears in square 3H on page **77** and also appears in the enlarged section in square 6A on page **146**.

4. With the now general usage of Postcodes for addressing mail, it is not recommended that this index is used for such a purpose.

GENERAL ABBREVIATIONS

All: Alley	Chyd: Churchyard	Gdns: Gardens	Mans: Mansions	Sq: Square
App: Approach	Circ: Circle	Ga: Gate	Mkt: Market	Sta: Station
Arc: Arcade	Cir: Circus	Gt: Great	M: Mews	St: Street
Av: Avenue	Clo: Close	Grn: Green	Mt: Mount	Ter: Terrace
Bk: Back	Comn: Common	Gro: Grove	N: North	Up: Upper
Boulevd: Boulevard	Cotts: Cottages	Ho: House	Pal: Palace	Vs: Villas
Bri: Bridge	Ct: Court	Ind: Industrial	Pde: Parade	Wlk: Walk
B'way: Broadway	Cres: Crescent	Junct: Junction	Pk: Park	W: West
Bldgs: Buildings	Dri: Drive	La: Lane	Pas: Passage	Yd: Yard
Bus: Business	E: East	Lit: Little	Pl: Place	
Cen: Centre	Embkmt: Embankment	Lwr: Lower	Rd: Road	
Chu: Church	Est: Estate	Mnr: Manor	S: South	

POSTTOWN AND POSTAL LOCALITY ABBREVIATIONS

Bark: Barking	Croy: Croydon	Har W: Harrow Weald	N Har: North Harrow	S'leigh: Stoneleigh
B'side: Barkingside	Dag: Dagenham	H End: Hatch End	N'holt: Northolt	Sun: Sunbury-on-Thames
B'hurst: Barnehurst	Dart: Dartford	Hay: Hayes (Middlesex)	N Hth: Northumberland Heath	Surb: Surbiton
Barn: Barnet	Dit H: Ditton Hill	Hayes: Hayes (Bromley)	Orp: Orpington	Sutt: Sutton
Beck: Beckenham	Eastc: Eastcote	H Bar: High Barnet	Pet W: Petts Wood	Swan: Swanley
Bedd: Beddington	E Mol: East Molesey	Houn: Hounslow	Pinn: Pinner	Tedd: Teddington
Belv: Belvedere	Edgw: Edgware	Ilf: Ilford	Purf: Purfleet	Th Dit: Thames Ditton
Bex: Bexley	Els: Elstree	Iswth: Isleworth	Purl: Purley	T Hth: Thornton Heath
Bexh: Bexleyheath	Enf: Enfield	Kent: Kenton	Rain: Rainham	Twic: Twickenham
Bren: Brentford	Eps: Epsom	Kes: Keston	Rich: Richmond	Wall: Wallington
Brom: Bromley	Eri: Erith	Kew: Kew	Romf: Romford	W'stone: Wealdstone
Buck H: Buckhurst Hill	Ewe: Ewell	King T: Kingston Upon Thames	Ruis: Ruislip	Well: Welling
Bush: Bushey	Felt: Feltham	L Hth: Little Heath	Rush: Rush Green	Wemb: Wembley
Cars: Carshalton	Gnfd: Greenford	Lou: Loughton	St P: St Pauls Cray	W Wick: West Wickham
Chad: Chadwell Heath	Hack: Hackbridge	Mawn: Mawneys	Short: Shortlands	Whit: Whitton
Cheam: Cheam	Ham: Ham	Mitc: Mitcham	Sidc: Sidcup	Wilm: Wilmington
Chig: Chigwell	Hamp: Hampton	Mit J: Mitcham Junction	S'hall: Southall	Wfd G: Woodford Green
Chst: Chislehurst	Hamp H: Hampton Hill	Mord: Morden	S Croy: South Croydon	Wor Pk: Worcester Park
Cockf: Cockfosters	Hamp W: Hampton Wick	New Ad: New Addington	S Harr: South Harrow	
Col R: Collier Row	Hanw: Hanworth	New Bar: New Barnet	S Ruis: South Ruislip	
Cray: Crayford	Harr: Harrow	N Mald: New Malden	Stan: Stanmore	

INDEX TO STREETS

Abberley M. SW4 —3F **93**	Abbey Gdns. NW8 —2A **60**	Abbey Rd. NW10 —2H **57**	Abbotsbury Rd. W14 —2G **75**	Abbot's Rd. E6 —1B **66**
Abbess Clo. E6 —5C **66**	Abbey Gdns. SE16 —4G **79**	Abbey Rd. SW19 —7A **108**	Abbotsbury Rd. Brom —2H **137**	Abbots Rd. Edgw —7D **12**
Abbess Clo. SW2 —1B **110**	Abbey Gdns. W6 —6G **75**	Abbey Rd. Bark —7F **51**	Abbotsbury Rd. Mord —5K **121**	Abbots Ter. N8 —6J **29**
Abbeville M. SW4 —4H **93**	Abbey Gro. SE2 —4B **84**	Abbey Rd. Belv —4D **84**	Abbots Clo. N1 —6C **46**	Abbotstone Rd. SW15 —3E **90**
Abbeville Rd. N8 —4H **29**	Abbey Hill Rd. Sidc —2C **116**	Abbey Rd. Bexh —4E **100**	Abbots Clo. Orp —7G **129**	Abbot St. E8 —6F **47**
Abbeville Rd. SW4 —6G **93**	Abbey La. E15 —2E **64**	Abbey Rd. Croy —3B **134**	Abbots Clo. Ruis —3B **38**	Abbots Way. Beck —5A **126**
Abbey Av. Wemb —2E **56**	Abbey La. Beck —7C **112**	Abbey Rd. Enf —5K **7**	Abbots Dri. Harr —2E **38**	Abbotswell Rd. SE4 —5B **96**
Abbey Bus. Cen. SW8 —1G **93**	Abbey La. Commercial Est. E15	Abbey Rd. Ilf —5H **35**	Abbotsford Av. N15 —4C **30**	Abbotswood Clo. Belv —3E **84**
Abbey Clo. N'holt —3D **54**	—2G **65**	Abbey St. E13 —4J **65**	Abbotsford Gdns. Wfd G —7D **20**	Abbotswood Gdns. Ilf —3D **34**
Abbey Clo. Pinn —3A **22**	Abbey Life Ct. E16 —5K **65**	Abbey St. SE1 —3E **78** (6D **148**)	Abbotsford Rd. Ilf —2A **52**	Abbotswood Rd. SW16 —3H **109**
Abbey Ct. Hamp —7E **102**	Abbey Manufacturing Est. Wemb	Abbey Ter. SE2 —4C **84**	Abbots Gdns. N2 —4B **28**	Abbotswood Way. Hay —1A **70**
Abbey Cres. Belv —4G **85**	—1F **57**	Abbey Trading Est. SE26 —5B **112**	Abbotshall Av. N14 —3B **16**	Abbott Av. SW20 —1F **121**
Abbeydale Rd. Wemb —1F **57**	Abbey M. E17 —5C **32**	Abbey View. NW7 —3G **13**	Abbotshall Rd. SE6 —1F **113**	Abbott Clo. Hamp —6C **102**
Abbey Dri. SW17 —5E **108**	Abbey Orchard St. SW1	Abbey Wharf Ind. Est. Bark —3H **67**	Abbots La. SE1 —1E **78** (3D **148**)	Abbott Clo. N'holt —6D **38**
Abbey Est. NW8 —1K **59**	—3H **77** (6A **146**)	Abbey Wood Rd. SE2 —4B **84**	Abbotsleigh Clo. Sutt —7K **131**	Abbott Rd. E14 —5E **64**
Abbeyfield Est. SE16 —4J **79**	Abbey Pde. W5 —3F **57**	Abbotsbury Clo. E15 —2E **64**	Abbotsleigh Rd. SW16 —4G **109**	(in two parts)
Abbeyfield Rd. SE16 —4J **79**	Abbey Pk. Beck —7C **112**	Abbotsbury Clo. W14 —2H **75**	Abbot's Mnr. SW1 —5F **77**	Abbotts Clo. Romf —3H **37**
(in two parts)	Abbey Rd. E15 —2F **65**	Abbotsbury Gdns. Pinn —7A **22**	Abbots Pk. SW2 —1A **110**	Abbotts Cres. E4 —4A **20**
Abbeyfields Clo. NW10 —2G **57**	Abbey Rd. NW6 & NW8 —7K **43**	Abbotsbury M. SE15 —3J **95**	Abbot's Pl. NW6 —1K **59**	Abbotts Cres. Enf —2G **7**

152

Abbotts Dri. Wemb —2B 40
Abbott's Grn. Croy —6K 135
Abbottsmede Clo. Twic —2K 103
Abbotts Pk. Rd. E10 —7E 32
Abbotts Rd. Barn —4E 4
Abbotts Rd. Mitc —4G 123
Abbotts Rd. S'hall —1C 70
Abbotts Rd. Sutt —4G 131
(in two parts)
Abbott's Wlk. Bexh —7D 84
Abchurch La. EC4 —7D 62 (9B 142)
Abchurch Yd. EC4 —7D 62 (9A 142)
(off Abchurch La.)
Abdale Rd. W12 —1D 74
Abel Ho. SE11 —6A 78
Aberavon Rd. E3 —3A 64
Abercairn Rd. SW16 —1G 123
Aberconway Rd. Mord —4K 121
Abercorn Clo. NW7 —7B 14
Abercorn Clo. NW8 —3A 60
Abercorn Commercial Cen. Wemb
 —1D 56
Abercorn Cres. Harr —1F 39
Abercorn Gdns. Harr —7D 24
Abercorn Gdns. Romf —6B 36
Abercorn Pl. NW8 —3A 60
Abercorn Rd. NW7 —7B 14
Abercorn Rd. Stan —7H 11
Abercorn Way. SE1 —5G 79
Abercrombie St. SW11 —2C 92
Aberdare Clo. W Wick —2E 136
Aberdare Gdns. NW6 —7K 43
Aberdare Gdns. NW7 —7A 14
Aberdare Rd. Enf —4D 8
Aberdeen La. N5 —5C 46
Aberdeen Pde. N18 —5C 18
(off Angel Rd.)
Aberdeen Pk. N5 —5C 46
Aberdeen Pl. NW8
 —4B 60 (4A 138)
Aberdeen Rd. N5 —4C 46
Aberdeen Rd. N18 —5C 18
Aberdeen Rd. NW10 —5B 42
Aberdeen Rd. Croy —4D 134
Aberdeen Rd. Harr —2K 23
Aberdeen Ter. SE3 —2F 97
Aberdour Rd. Ilf —3B 52
Aberdour St. SE1 —4E 78 (7C 148)
Aberfeldy Ho. SE5 —7B 78
Aberfeldy St. E14 —6E 64
(in two parts)
Aberford Gdns. SE18 —1C 98
Aberfoyle Rd. SW16 —7H 109
Abergeldie Rd. SE12 —6K 97
Abernethy Rd. SE13 —4G 97
Abersham Rd. E8 —5F 47
Abery St. SE18 —4J 83
Abingdon Clo. NW1 —6H 45
Abingdon Clo. SE1 —5F 79
(off Bushwood Dri.)
Abingdon Clo. SW19 —6A 108
Abingdon Ct. W8 —3J 75
(off Abingdon Vs.)
Abingdon Gdns. W8 —3J 75
Abingdon Lodge. W8 —3J 75
Abingdon Rd. N3 —2A 28
Abingdon Rd. SW16 —2J 123
Abingdon Rd. W8 —3J 75
Abingdon St. SW1 —3J 77 (6C 146)
Abingdon Vs. W8 —3J 75
Abinger Av. Sutt —7E 130
Abinger Clo. Bark —4A 52
Abinger Clo. Brom —3C 128
Abinger Clo. Wall —5J 133
Abinger Ct. Wall —5J 133
Abinger Gdns. Iswth —3J 87
Abinger Gro. SE8 —6B 80
Abinger M. W9 —4J 59

Abinger Rd. W4 —3A 74
Ablett St. SE16 —5J 79
Abney Gdns. N16 —2F 47
Aboyne Dri. SW20 —2C 120
Aboyne Rd. NW10 —3A 42
Aboyne Rd. SW17 —3B 108
Abridge Way. Bark —2B 68
Abyssinia Clo. SW11 —4C 92
Acacia Av. N17 —7J 17
Acacia Av. Bren —7B 72
Acacia Av. Rich —2F 89
Acacia Av. Wemb —5E 40
Acacia Bus. Cen. E11 —3G 49
(off Howard Rd.)
Acacia Clo. SE20 —2G 125
Acacia Clo. Orp —5H 129
Acacia Clo. Stan —6D 10
Acacia Ct. Harr —5F 23
Acacia Dri. Sutt —1J 131
Acacia Gdns. NW8 —2B 60
Acacia Gdns. W Wick —2E 136
Acacia Gro. SE21 —2D 110
Acacia Gro. N Mald —3K 119
Acacia Ho. N22 —1A 30
(off Douglas Rd.)
Acacia Pl. NW8 —2B 60
Acacia Rd. E11 —2G 49
Acacia Rd. E17 —6A 32
Acacia Rd. N22 —1A 30
Acacia Rd. NW8 —2B 60
Acacia Rd. SW16 —1K 123
Acacia Rd. W3 —7J 57
Acacia Rd. Beck —3B 126
Acacia Rd. Enf —1J 7
Acacia Rd. Hamp —6E 102
Acacia Rd. Mitc —2E 122
Acacias, The. Barn —5G 5
Acacia Way. Sidc —1K 115
Academy Bldgs. N1 —3E 62 (1C 142)
(off Fanshaw St.)
Academy Gdns. Croy —1F 135
Academy Gdns. N'holt —2B 54
Academy Pl. SE18 —1D 98
Academy Rd. SE18 —1D 98
Acanthus Dri. SE1 —5G 79
Acanthus Rd. SW11 —3E 92
Accommodation Rd. NW11 —1H 43
Accommodation Rd. Wor Pk
 —5C 130
A.C. Court. Th Dit —6A 118
Acfold Rd. SW6 —1K 91
Achilles Clo. SE1 —5G 79
Achilles Rd. NW6 —5J 43
Achilles St. SE14 —7B 80
Achilles Way. W1 —1E 76 (3H 145)
Acklam Rd. W10 —5G 59
Acklington Dri. NW9 —1A 26
Ackmar Rd. SW6 —1J 91
Ackroyd Dri. E3 —5B 64
Ackroyd Rd. SE23 —7K 95
Acland Clo. SE18 —7H 83
Acland Cres. SE5 —3D 94
Acland Ho. SW9 —2K 93
Acland Rd. NW2 —6D 42
Acol Cres. Ruis —5A 38
Acol Rd. NW6 —7J 43
Aconbury Rd. Dag —1B 68
Acorn Clo. E4 —5J 19
Acorn Clo. Chst —6G 115
Acorn Clo. Enf —1G 7
Acorn Clo. Hamp —6F 103
Acorn Clo. Stan —7G 11
Acorn Ct. E6 —7C 50
Acorn Ct. Ilf —6J 35
Acorn Gdns. SE19 —1F 125
Acorn Gdns. W3 —5K 57
Acorn Pde. SE15 —7H 79
Acorn Wlk. SE16 —1A 80

Acorn Way. SE23 —3K 111
(off Belle Vue Est.)
Acrefield Ho. NW4 —4F 27
(off Belle Vue Est.)
Acre La. SW2 —4J 93
Acre La. Cars & Wall —4E 132
Acre Path. N'holt —6C 38
(off Arnold Rd.)
Acre Rd. SW19 —6B 108
Acre Rd. Dag —7H 53
Acre Rd. King T —1E 118
Acris St. SW18 —5A 92
Acton Clo. N9 —2B 18
Acton La. NW10 —3J 57
Acton La. W3 —2J 73
Acton La. W4 & W3 —4J 73
(in three parts)
Acton M. E8 —1F 63
Acton Pk. Ind. Est. W3 —2K 73
Acton St. WC1 —3K 61 (2E 140)
Acuba Rd. SW18 —2K 107
Acworth Clo. N9 —7D 8
Ada Gdns. E14 —6F 65
Ada Gdns. E15 —1H 65
Adair Clo. SE25 —3H 125
Adair Rd. W10 —4G 59
Adam and Eve Ct. W1
 (off Oxford St.) —6G 61 (7M 139)
Adam and Eve M. W8 —3J 75
Adam Ct. SW7 —4A 76
(off Gloucester Rd.)
Adams Clo. N3 —7D 14
Adams Clo. NW9 —2H 41
Adams Clo. Surb —6F 119
Adams Ct. E17 —6A 32
Adams Ct. EC2 —6E 62 (7B 142)
Adams Gdns. Est. SE16 —2J 79
Adamson Ct. N2 —3C 28
Adamson Rd. E16 —6J 65
Adamson Rd. NW3 —7B 44
Adams Pl. E14 —1D 80
(off N. Colonnade)
Adams Rd. N17 —2D 30
Adams Rd. Beck —5A 126
Adam's Row. W1 —7E 60 (1H 145)
Adams Sq. Bexh —3E 100
Adams Wlk. King T —2E 118
Adams Way. Croy —6F 125
Adam Wlk. SW6 —7E 74
(off Crabtree La.)
Ada Pl. E2 —1H 63
Adare Wlk. SW16 —3K 109
Ada Rd. SE5 —7E 78
Ada Rd. Wemb —3D 40
Ada St. E8 —1H 63
Ada Workshops. E8 —1H 63
Adderley Gdns. SE9 —4E 114
Adderley Gro. SW11 —5E 92
Adderley Rd. Harr —1K 23
Adderley St. E14 —6E 64
Addington Ct. SW14 —3K 89
Addington Dri. N12 —6G 15
Addington Gro. SE26 —4A 112
Addington Rd. E3 —3C 64
Addington Rd. E16 —4G 65
Addington Rd. N4 —6A 30
Addington Rd. Croy & W Wick
 —4E 133
Addington Rd. S Croy —7K 135
Addington Sq. SE5 —6D 78
Addington St. SE1 —2K 77 (5F 146)

Addington Village Rd. Croy —6B 136
(in two parts)
Addis Clo. Enf —1E 8
Addiscombe Av. Croy —1G 135
Addiscombe Clo. Harr —5C 24
Addiscombe Ct. Rd. Croy —1E 134
Addiscombe Gro. Croy —2E 134
Addiscombe Rd. Croy —2E 134
Addison Av. N14 —6A 6
Addison Av. W11 —1G 75
Addison Av. Houn —1G 87
Addison Bri. Pl. W14 —4H 75
Addison Clo. Orp —6G 129
Addison Ct. E2 —2G 63
(off Pritchard's Rd.)
Addison Dri. SE12 —5K 97
Addison Gdns. W14 —3F 75
Addison Gdns. Surb —4F 119
Addison Gro. W4 —3A 74
Addison Pl. SE25 —4G 125
Addison Pl. W11 —1G 75
Addison Pl. S'hall —7E 54
Addison Rd. E11 —6J 33
Addison Rd. E17 —5D 32
Addison Rd. SE25 —4G 125
Addison Rd. W14 —2G 75
Addison Rd. Brom —5B 128
Addison Rd. Enf —1D 8
Addison Rd. Ilf —1G 35
Addison Rd. Tedd —6B 104
Addisons Clo. Croy —2B 136
Addison Ter. W4 —4J 73
(off Chiswick Rd.)
Addison Way. NW11 —4H 27
Addle Hill. EC4 —6B 62 (8K 141)
Addle St. EC2 —6C 62 (7M 141)
Addlestone Ho. W10 —5F 59
(off Sutton Way)
Adela Av. N Mald —5D 120
Adelaide Av. SE4 —4B 96
Adelaide Clo. Enf —1K 7
Adelaide Clo. Stan —4F 11
Adelaide Cotts. W7 —2K 71
Adelaide Ct. Beck —7B 112
Adelaide Gdns. Romf —6E 36
Adelaide Gro. W12 —1C 74
Adelaide Ho. E15 —2H 65
Adelaide Ho. SE5 —2E 94
Adelaide Rd. E10 —3E 48
Adelaide Rd. NW3 —7B 44
Adelaide Rd. SW18 —5J 91
Adelaide Rd. W13 —1A 72
Adelaide Rd. Chst —5F 115
Adelaide Rd. Houn —1C 86
Adelaide Rd. Ilf —2F 51
Adelaide Rd. Rich —4F 89
Adelaide Rd. S'hall —4C 70
Adelaide Rd. Surb —5E 118
Adelaide Rd. Tedd —6K 103
Adelaide St. WC2 —7J 61 (1C 146)
Adelaide Ter. Bren —5D 72
Adelaide Wlk. SW9 —4A 94
Adela St. W10 —4G 59
Adelina Gro. E1 —5J 63
Adelina M. SW12 —1H 109
Adeline Pl. WC1 —5H 61 (6B 140)
Adelphi Ct. W4 —6K 73
Adelphi Ter. WC2 —7J 61 (1D 146)
Adeney Clo. W6 —6F 75
Aden Gro. N16 —4D 46
Adenmore Rd. SE6 —7C 96
Aden Rd. Enf —4F 9
Aden Rd. Ilf —7F 35
Aden Ter. N16 —4D 46
Adeyfield Ho. EC1 —3D 62 (2B 142)
(off Cranwood St.)
Adie Rd. W6 —3E 74
Adine Rd. E13 —4K 65

Adler St. E1 —6G 63
Adley St. E5 —5A 48
Admaston Rd. SE18 —7G 83
Admiral Ct. SW10 —1A 92
(off Thames Av.)
Admiral Ct. Cars —1C 132
Admiral Hyson Ind. Est. SE16
 —5H 79
Admiral M. W10 —4F 59
Admiral Pl. SE16 —1A 80
Admirals Clo. E18 —4K 33
Admiral Seymour Rd. SE9 —4D 98
Admiral Sq. SW10 —1A 92
Admiral St. SE8 —1C 96
Admirals Wlk. NW3 —3A 44
Admirals Way. E14 —2C 80
Admiralty Clo. SE8 —7C 80
Admiralty Rd. Tedd —6K 103
Admiral Wlk. W9 —5J 59
Adolf St. SE6 —4D 112
Adolphus Rd. N4 —2B 46
Adolphus St. SE8 —7B 80
Adpar St. W2 —5B 60 (5A 138)
Adrian Av. NW2 —1D 42
Adrian Ho. N1 —1K 61
(off Barnsbury Est.)
Adrian M. SW10 —6K 75
Adrienne Av. S'hall —4D 54
Advance Rd. SE27 —4C 110
Adys Lawn. NW2 —6D 42
Ady's Rd. SE15 —3F 95
Aerodrome Rd. NW9 & NW4 —2B 26
Aerodrome Way. Houn —6A 70
Aeroville. NW9 —2A 26
Affleck St. N1 —2K 61
Afghan Rd. SW11 —2C 92
Agamemnon Rd. NW6 —5H 43
Agar Gro. NW1 —7G 45
Agar Gro. Est. NW1 —7H 45
Agar Pl. NW1 —7G 45
Agar St. WC2 —7J 61 (1C 146)
Agate Clo. E16 —6B 66
Agate Rd. W6 —3E 74
Agatha Clo. E1 —1H 79
Agaton Rd. SE9 —2G 115
Agave Rd. NW2 —4E 42
Agdon St. EC1 —4B 62 (3J 141)
Agincourt Rd. NW3 —4D 44
Agnes Av. Ilf —4E 50
Agnes Clo. E6 —7E 66
Agnes Gdns. Dag —4D 52
Agnes Rd. W3 —1B 74
Agnes St. E14 —6B 64
Agnew Rd. SE23 —7K 95
Agricola Pl. Enf —5A 8
Aidan Clo. Dag —3E 52
Aigburth Mans. SW9 —7A 78
(off Mowll St.)
Aileen Wlk. E15 —7H 49
Ailsa Av. Twic —5A 88
Ailsa Rd. Twic —5B 88
Ailsa St. E14 —5E 64
Ainger M. NW3 —7D 44
(off Ainger Rd.)
Ainger Rd. NW3 —7D 44
Ainsdale Clo. Orp —7H 129
Ainsdale Cres. Pinn —3E 22
Ainsdale Rd. W5 —4D 56
Ainsley Av. Romf —6H 37
Ainsley Clo. N9 —1K 17
Ainsley St. E2 —3H 63
Ainslie Wlk. SW12 —7F 93
Ainslie Wood Cres. E4 —5J 19
Ainslie Wood Gdns. E4 —4J 19
Ainslie Wood Rd. E4 —5H 19
Ainsty Est. SE16 —2K 79
Ainsty St. SE16 —2J 79

Ainsworth Clo. NW2 —3C **42**
Ainsworth Rd. E9 —7J **47**
Ainsworth Rd. Croy —2D **124**
Ainsworth Way. NW8 —1K **59**
Aintree Av. E6 —1C **66**
Aintree Cres. Ilf —2G **35**
Aintree Est. SW6 —7G 75
(off Aintree St.)
Aintree Rd. Gnfd —2B **56**
Aintree St. SW6 —7G **75**
Airbourne Ho. Wall —4G 133
(off Maldon Rd.)
Airdrie Clo. N1 —7K **45**
Airdrie Clo. Hay —5C **54**
Airedale Av. W4 —4B **74**
Airedale Av. S. W4 —5B **74**
Airedale Rd. SW12 —7D **92**
Airedale Rd. W5 —3C **72**
Airlie Gdns. W8 —1J **75**
Airlie Gdns. Ilf —1F **51**
Airlinks Ind. Est. Houn —5A **70**
Air St. W1 —7G **61** (1M **145**)
Airthrie Rd. Ilf —2B **52**
Aisgill Av. W14 —5H **75**
Aisher Rd. SE28 —7C **68**
Aislibie Rd. SE12 —4G **97**
Aitken Clo. E8 —1G **63**
Aitken Rd. SE6 —2D **112**
Ajax Av. NW9 —3A **26**
Ajax Rd. NW6 —5H **43**
Akehurst St. SW15 —6C **90**
Akenside Rd. NW3 —5B **44**
Akerman Rd. SW9 —2B **94**
Akerman Rd. Surb —6C **118**
Alabama St. SE18 —7H **83**
Alacross Rd. W5 —2C **72**
Alan Barclay Clo. N15 —6F **31**
Aland Ct. SE16 —3A **80**
Alan Dri. Barn —6B **4**
Alan Gdns. Romf —7G **37**
Alan Hocken Way. E15 —2G **65**
Alan Rd. SW19 —5G **107**
Alanthus Clo. SE12 —6J **97**
Alaska St. SE1 —1A **78** (3G **147**)
Alba Clo. Hay —4B **54**
Albacore Cres. SE13 —6D **96**
Alba Gdns. NW11 —6G **27**
Alban Highwalk. EC2
(in two parts) —5C **62** (6M **141**)
Albany. N12 —6E **14**
Albany. W1 —7G **61** (1L **145**)
Albany Clo. N15 —4B **30**
Albany Clo. SW14 —4H **89**
Albany Clo. Bex —7C **100**
Albany Ct. E4 —5G **19**
Albany Ct. E10 —7C **32**
Albany Ct. NW9 —1K **25**
Albany Ct. Yd. W1 —7G 61 (1M 145)
(off Piccadilly)
Albany Cres. Edgw —7B **12**
Albany M. N1 —7A **46**
Albany M. SE5 —6C **78**
Albany M. Brom —6J **113**
Albany M. King T —6D **104**
Albany M. Sutt —5K **131**
Albany Pde. Bren —6E **72**
Albany Pk. Av. Enf —1D **8**
Albany Pk. Rd. King T —6D **104**
Albany Pas. Rich —5E **88**
Albany Pl. N7 —4A **46**
Albany Pl. Bren —6D **72**
Albany Rd. E10 —7C **32**
Albany Rd. E12 —4B **50**
Albany Rd. E17 —6A **32**
Albany Rd. N4 —6A **30**
Albany Rd. N18 —5C **18**
Albany Rd. SE5 —6C **78**
Albany Rd. SW19 —5K **107**

Albany Rd. W13 —7B **56**
Albany Rd. Belv —6F **85**
Albany Rd. Bex —7C **100**
Albany Rd. Bren —6D **72**
Albany Rd. Chst —5F **115**
Albany Rd. N Mald —4K **119**
Albany Rd. Rich —5F **89**
Albany Rd. Romf —6F **37**
Albany St. NW1 —2F **61**
Albany Ter. NW1 —4F 61 (4K 139)
(off Marylebone Rd.)
Albany, The. Wfd G —4C **20**
Albany View. Buck H —1D **20**
Alba Pl. W11 —6H **59**
Albatross. NW9 —2B **26**
Albatross St. SE18 —7J **83**
Albatross Way. SE16 —2K **79**
Albemarle. SW19 —2F **105**
Albemarle App. Ilf —6F **35**
Albemarle Av. Twic —1D **102**
Albemarle Gdns. Ilf —6F **35**
Albemarle Gdns. N Mald —4K **119**
Albemarle Pk. Stan —5H **11**
Albemarle Rd. Beck —1D **126**
Albemarle Rd. E Barn —6H **5**
Albemarle St. W1 —7F **61** (1K **145**)
Albemarle Way. EC1
—4B **62** (4J **141**)
Albermarle App. Ilf —6F **35**
Albermarle Av. Twic —1D **102**
Albermarle Gdns. Ilf —6F **35**
Albermarle Ho. Sw9 —3A **94**
Alberon Gdns. NW11 —4H **27**
Alberta Av. Sutt —4G **131**
Alberta Est. SE17 —5B **78**
Alberta Rd. Enf —6A **8**
Alberta Rd. Eri —1J **101**
Alberta St. SE17 —5B **78**
Albert Av. E4 —4H **19**
Albert Av. SW8 —7K **77**
Albert Bigg Point. E15 —1E 64
(off Godfrey St.)
Albert Bri. SW3 & SW11 —6C **76**
Albert Bri. Rd. SW11 —7C **76**
Albert Carr Gdns. SW16 —5J **109**
Albert Clo. E9 —1H **63**
Albert Clo. N22 —1H **29**
Albert Ct. E7 —4J **49**
Albert Ct. SW7 —2B **76** (5A **144**)
Albert Cres. E4 —4H **19**
Albert Dri. SW19 —2G 107
Albert Embkmt. SE1 —5J **77**
Albert Gdns. E1 —6K **63**
Albert Ga. SW1 —2D **76** (4F **144**)
Albert Gro. SW20 —1F **121**
Albert Hall Mans. SW7
—2B **76** (5A **144**)
Albert Ho. E18 —3K 33
(off Albert Rd.)
Albert M. N4 —1K **45**
Albert M. W8 —3A **76**
Albert Pl. N3 —1J **27**
Albert Pl. N17 —3F **31**
Albert Pl. W8 —2K **75**
Albert Rd. E10 —2E **48**
Albert Rd. E16 —1C **82**
Albert Rd. E17 —5C **32**
Albert Rd. E18 —3K **33**
Albert Rd. N4 —1K **45**
Albert Rd. N15 —6E **30**
Albert Rd. N22 —1G **29**
Albert Rd. NW4 —4F **27**
Albert Rd. NW6 —2H **59**
Albert Rd. NW7 —5G **13**
Albert Rd. SE9 —3C **114**
Albert Rd. SE20 —6K **111**
Albert Rd. SE25 —4G **125**
Albert Rd. W5 —4B **56**
Albert Rd. Barn —4F **5**
Albert Rd. Belv —5F **85**

Albert Rd. Bex —6G **101**
Albert Rd. Brom —5B **128**
Albert Rd. Buck H —2G **21**
Albert Rd. Dag —1G **53**
Albert Rd. Hamp —5G **103**
Albert Rd. Harr —3G **23**
Albert Rd. Houn —4E **86**
Albert Rd. Ilf —3F **51**
Albert Rd. King T —2F **119**
Albert Rd. Mitc —3D **122**
Albert Rd. N Mald —4B **120**
Albert Rd. Rich —5E **88**
Albert Rd. S'hall —3B **70**
Albert Rd. Sutt —5B **132**
Albert Rd. Tedd —6K **103**
Albert Rd. Twic —1K **103**
Albert Rd. Est. Belv —5F **85**
Albert Sq. E15 —5G **49**
Albert Sq. SW8 —7K **77**
Albert St. N12 —5F **15**
Albert St. NW1 —6F **61**
Albert Studios. SW11 —1D **92**
Albert Ter. NW1 —1E **60**
Albert Ter. NW10 —1J **57**
Albert Ter. Buck H —2H **21**
Albert Ter. M. NW1 —1E **60**
Albert Victoria Ho. N22 —1A 30
(off Pellatt Gro.)
Albert Wlk. E16 —2E **82**
Albert Whicker Ho. E17 —4E **32**
Albert Westcott Ho. SE17 —5B **78**
Albert Yd. SE19 —6F **111**
Albion Av. N10 —1E **28**
Albion Av. SW8 —2H **93**
Albion Clo. W2 —7C **60** (9D **138**)
Albion Clo. Romf —6K **37**
Albion Dri. E8 —7F **47**
Albion Est. SE16 —2K **79**
Albion Gdns. W6 —4D **74**
Albion Gro. N16 —4E **46**
Albion Ho. E16 —1E 83
(off Church St.)
Albion M. N1 —1A **62**
Albion M. NW6 —7H **43**
Albion M. W2 —7C **60** (9D **138**)
Albion M. W6 —4D **74**
Albion Pl. EC1 —5B **62** (5J **141**)
Albion Pl. EC2 —5D **62** (6B **142**)
Albion Pl. SE25 —3G **125**
Albion Pl. W6 —4D **74**
Albion Rd. E17 —3E **32**
Albion Rd. N16 —4D **46**
Albion Rd. N17 —2F **31**
Albion Rd. Bexh —4F **101**
Albion Rd. Houn —4E **86**
Albion Rd. King T —1J **119**
Albion Rd. Sutt —6B **132**
Albion Rd. Twic —1J **103**
Albion Sq. E8 —7F **47**
Albion St. SE16 —2J **79**
Albion St. W2 —6C **60** (8D **138**)
Albion St. Croy —1B **134**
Albion Ter. E8 —7F **47**
Albion Vs. Rd. SE26 —3J **111**
Albion Way. EC1 —5C **62** (6L **141**)
Albion Way. SE13 —4E **96**
Albion Way. Wemb —3G **41**
Albion Yd. N1 —2J **61**
Albrighton Rd. SE22 —3E **94**
Albuhera Clo. Enf —1F **7**
Albury Av. Bexh —2E **100**
Albury Av. Iswth —7K **71**
Albury Clo. Hamp —6F **103**
Albury Ct. Sutt —4A **132**
Albury Dri. Pinn —1A **22**
Albury St. SE8 —6C **80**

Albyfield. Brom —4D **128**
Albyn St. SE8 —1C **96**
Alcester Cres. E5 —2H **47**
Alcester Rd. Wall —4F **133**
Alcock Clo. Wall —7H **133**
Alcock Rd. Houn —7B **70**
Alconbury. Bexh —5H **101**
Alconbury Rd. E5 —2G **47**
Alcorn Clo. Sutt —2J **131**
Alcott Clo. W7 —5K **55**
Alcuin Ct. Stan —7H **11**
Aldam Pl. N16 —2F **47**
Aldborough Rd. Dag —6J **53**
Aldborough Rd. N. Ilf —5K **35**
Aldborough Rd. S. Ilf —1J **51**
Aldbourne Rd. W12 —1B **74**
Aldburgh M. W1 —6E **60** (7H **139**)
(in two parts)
Aldbury Av. Wemb —7H **41**
Aldbury M. N9 —7J **7**
Aldebert Ter. SW8 —7J **77**
Aldeburgh Clo. E5 —2H **47**
Aldeburgh Pl. Wfd G —4D **20**
Alden Av. E15 —4H **65**
Alden Ct. Croy —3E **134**
Aldenham St. NW1 —2G **61**
Aldensley Rd. W6 —3D **74**
Alderbrook Rd. SW12 —6F **93**
Alderburgh St. SE10 —5J **81**
Alderbury Rd. SW13 —6C **74**
Alder Clo. SE15 —6F **79**
Alder Gro. NW2 —2C **42**
Aldergrove Gdns. Houn —2C **86**
Alderholt Way. SE15 —7E **78**
Alder Lodge. SW6 —1F **91**
Alderman Av. Bark —3A **68**
Aldermanbury. EC2
—6C **62** (7M **141**)
Aldermanbury Sq. EC2
—5C **62** (6M **141**)
Alderman Judge Mall. King T
—2E **118**
Aldermans Hill. N13 —4D **16**
Aldermans Wlk. EC2
—5E **62** (6C **142**)
Aldermary Rd. Brom —1J **127**
Alder M. N19 —2G **45**
Alderminster Rd. SE1 —5G **79**
Aldermoor Rd. SE6 —3B **112**
Alderney Av. Houn —7F **71**
Alderney Gdns. N'holt —7D **38**
Alderney Ho. Enf —1E **8**
Alderney Rd. E1 —4K **63**
Alderney St. SW1 —4F **77** (9K **145**)
Alder Rd. SW14 —3K **89**
Alder Rd. Sidc —3K **115**
Alders Av. Wfd G —6B **20**
Aldersbrook Av. Enf —2K **7**
Aldersbrook Dri. King T —6F **105**
Aldersbrook La. E12 —3D **50**
Aldersbrook Rd. E11 & E12 —2K **49**
Alders Clo. E11 —2K **49**
Alders Clo. W5 —3D **72**
Alders Clo. Edgw —5D **12**
Aldersey Gdns. Bark —6H **51**
Aldersford Clo. SE4 —5K **95**
Aldersgate St. EC1 —5C **62** (5L **141**)
Aldersgrove Av. SE9 —3B **114**
Aldershot Rd. NW6 —1H **59**
Aldersmead Av. Croy —6K **125**
Aldersmead Rd. Beck —7A **112**
Alderson Pl. S'hall —1G **71**
Alderson St. W10 —4G **59**
Alders Rd. Edgw —5D **12**
Alders, The. N21 —6G **7**
Alders, The. SW16 —4G **109**
Alders, The. Felt —4C **102**

Alders, The. Houn —6D **70**
Alders, The. W Wick —2D **136**
Alderton Clo. NW10 —3K **41**
Alderton Cres. NW4 —5D **26**
Alderton Rd. SE24 —3C **94**
Alderton Rd. Croy —7F **125**
Alderton Way. NW4 —5D **26**
Alderville Rd. SW6 —2H **91**
Alderwick Dri. Houn —3H **87**
Alderwood Rd. SE9 —6H **99**
Aldford St. W1 —1E **76** (2G **145**)
Aldgate. EC3 —6E **62** (8E **142**)
Aldgate Av. E1 —6F **63** (7E **142**)
Aldgate Barrs. E1 —6F **63** (7F **142**)
Aldgate High St. EC3
—6F **63** (8E **142**)
Aldine Ct. W12 —2E 74
(off Aldine St.)
Aldine Pl. W12 —2E **74**
Aldine St. W12 —2E **74**
Aldington Clo. Dag —1C **52**
Aldington Ct. E8 —7G **47**
Aldington Rd. SE18 —3B **82**
Aldis M. SW17 —5C **108**
Aldis St. SW17 —5C **108**
Aldred Rd. NW6 —5J **43**
Aldren Rd. SW17 —3A **108**
Aldrich Cres. New Ad —7E **136**
Aldriche Way. E4 —6K **19**
Aldrich Ter. SW18 —2A **108**
Aldridge Av. Edgw —3C **12**
Aldridge Av. Ruis —2A **38**
Aldridge Av. Stan —1E **24**
Aldridge Rise. N Mald —7A **120**
Aldridge Rd. Vs. W11 —5H **59**
Aldridge Wlk. N14 —7D **6**
Aldrington Rd. SW16 —5G **109**
Aldsworth Clo. W9 —4K **59**
Aldwick Clo. SE9 —3H **115**
Aldwick Rd. Croy —3K **133**
Aldworth Gro. SE13 —6E **96**
Aldworth Rd. E15 —7G **49**
Aldwych. WC2 —6K **61** (9E **140**)
Aldwych Av. Ilf —4G **35**
Alers Rd. Bexh —5D **100**
Alestan Beck Rd. E16 —6B **66**
Alexa Ct. W8 —4K **75**
Alexa Ct. Sutt —6J **131**
Alexander Av. NW10 —7D **42**
Alexander Clo. Barn —4G **5**
Alexander Clo. Brom —1J **137**
Alexander Clo. Sidc —6J **99**
Alexander Clo. S'hall —1G **71**
Alexander Clo. Twic —2K **103**
Alexander Ct. SE16 —1B **80**
Alexander Ct. Beck —1F **127**
Alexander Ct. Stan —3F **25**
Alexander Evans M. SE23 —2K **111**
Alexander M. W2 —6K **59**
Alexander Pl. SW7 —4C **76** (8C **144**)
Alexander Rd. N19 —3J **45**
Alexander Rd. Bexh —2D **100**
Alexander Rd. Chst —6F **115**
Alexander Sq. SW3 —4C **76**
Alexandra Av. N22 —1H **29**
Alexandra Av. SW11 —1E **92**
Alexandra Av. W4 —7A **73**
Alexandra Av. Harr —1D **38**
Alexandra Av. S'hall —7D **54**
Alexandra Av. Sutt —3J **131**
Alexandra Clo. Harr —3E **38**
Alexandra Cotts. SE14 —1B **96**
Alexandra Ct. N14 —5B **6**
Alexandra Ct. Houn —2F **87**
Alexandra Cres. Brom —6H **113**
Alexandra Dri. SE19 —5E **110**
Alexandra Dri. Surb —7G **119**

154

Alexandra Gdns. N10 —4F **29**
Alexandra Gdns. W4 —7A **74**
Alexandra Gdns. Cars —7E **132**
Alexandra Gdns. Houn —2F **87**
Alexandra Gro. N4 —1B **46**
Alexandra Gro. N12 —5E **14**
Alexandra M. N2 —3D **28**
Alexandra M. SW19 —6H **107**
Alexandra Pal. Way. N22 —4G **29**
Alexandra Pk. Rd. N10 —2F **29**
Alexandra Pk. Rd. N22 —1G **29**
Alexandra Pl. NW8 —1A **60**
Alexandra Pl. SE25 —5D **124**
Alexandra Rd. Croy —1E **134**
Alexandra Rd. E6 —3E **66**
Alexandra Rd. E10 —3E **48**
Alexandra Rd. E17 —6B **32**
Alexandra Rd. E18 —3K **33**
Alexandra Rd. N8 —3A **30**
Alexandra Rd. N9 —7C **8**
Alexandra Rd. N10 —1F **29**
Alexandra Rd. N15 —5D **30**
Alexandra Rd. NW4 —4F **27**
Alexandra Rd. NW8 —1A **60**
Alexandra Rd. SE26 —6K **111**
Alexandra Rd. SW14 —3K **89**
Alexandra Rd. SW19 —6H **107**
Alexandra Rd. W4 —2K **73**
Alexandra Rd. Bren —6D **72**
Alexandra Rd. Chad —6E **36**
Alexandra Rd. Croy —1E **134**
Alexandra Rd. Enf —4E **8**
Alexandra Rd. Houn —2F **87**
Alexandra Rd. King T —7G **105**
Alexandra Rd. Mitc —7C **108**
Alexandra Rd. Rich —2F **89**
Alexandra Rd. Th Dit —5A **118**
Alexandra Rd. Twic —6C **88**
Alexandra Rd. / Alma Rd. Ind. Est. Enf
—4E **8**
Alexandra Sq. SW3 —4C **76** (8C **144**)
Alexandra Sq. Mord —5G **121**
Alexandra St. E16 —5J **65**
Alexandra St. SE14 —7A **80**
Alexandra Wlk. SE19 —5E **110**
Alexandra Yd. E9 —1K **63**
Alexandria Rd. W13 —7A **56**
Alexis St. SE16 —4G **79**
Alfan La. Dart —5K **117**
Alfearn Rd. E5 —4J **47**
Alford Grn. New Ad —6F **137**
Alford Ho. N6 —6G **29**
Alford Pl. N1 —2C **62**
Alford Rd. Eri —5J **85**
Alfoxton Av. N15 —4B **30**
Alfreda St. SW11 —1F **93**
Alfred Finlay Ho. N22 —2B **30**
Alfred Gdns. S'hall —7C **54**
Alfred Ho. E9 —5A **48**
(off Homerton Rd.)
Alfred La. Felt —2A **102**
Alfred M. W1 —5H **61** (5A **140**)
Alfred Pl. WC1 —5H **61** (5A **140**)
Alfred Pl. SE25 —5G **125**
Alfred Rd. SW8 —1H **93**
Alfred Rd. W2 —5J **59**
Alfred Rd. W3 —1J **73**
Alfred Rd. Belv —5F **85**
Alfred Rd. Buck H —2G **21**
Alfred Rd. King T —3E **118**
Alfred Rd. Sutt —5A **132**
Alfred's Gdns. Bark —2J **67**
Alfred St. E3 —3B **64**
Alfreds Way. Bark —3F **67**
Alfred's Way Ind. Est. Bark —2A **68**
Alfreton Clo. SW19 —3F **107**

Alfriston. Surb —6F **119**
Alfriston Av. Croy —7J **123**
Alfriston Av. Harr —6E **22**
Alfriston Clo. Surb —5F **119**
Alfriston Rd. SW11 —5D **92**
Algar Clo. Iswth —3A **88**
Algar Clo. Stan —5E **10**
Algar Ho. SE1 —2B **78** (5J **147**)
(off Webber Row)
Algar Rd. Iswth —3A **88**
Algarve Rd. SW18 —1K **107**
Algernon Rd. NW4 —6C **26**
Algernon Rd. NW6 —1J **59**
Algernon Rd. SE13 —4D **96**
Algiers Rd. SE13 —4C **96**
Alibon Gdns. Dag —5G **53**
Alibon Rd. Dag —5F **53**
Alice Burrell Cen. E10 —2E **48**
(off Sidmouth Rd.)
Alice Ct. SW15 —4H **91**
Alice Gilliat Ct. W14 —6H **75**
(off Star Rd.)
Alice La. E3 —1B **64**
Alice M. Tedd —5K **103**
Alice Thompson Clo. SE12 —2A **114**
Alice Walker Clo. SE24 —4B **94**
Alice Way. Houn —4F **87**
Alicia Av. Harr —4B **24**
Alicia Clo. Harr —5C **24**
Alicia Gdns. Harr —4B **24**
Alicia Rd. Ilf —2A **52**
Alie St. E1 —6F **63** (8F **142**)
Alington Cres. NW9 —7J **25**
Alington Gro. Wall —7G **133**
Alison Clo. E6 —6E **66**
Alison Clo. Croy —1K **135**
Aliwal Rd. SW11 —4C **92**
Alkerden Rd. W4 —5A **74**
Alkham Rd. N16 —2F **47**
Allan Clo. N Mald —5K **119**
Allandale Av. N3 —3G **27**
Allan Way. W3 —5J **57**
Allard Cres. Bush —1B **10**
Allard Gdns. SW4 —5H **93**
Allardyce St. SW4 —4K **93**
Allbrook Clo. Tedd —5J **103**
Allcroft Rd. NW5 —5E **44**
Allenby Av. S Croy —7C **134**
Allenby Clo. Gnfd —3E **54**
Allenby Rd. SE23 —3A **112**
Allenby Rd. S'hall —6E **54**
Allen Ct. E17 —6C **32**
(off Yunus Khan Clo.)
Allen Ct. Gnfd —5K **39**
Allendale Av. S'hall —6E **54**
Allendale Clo. SE5 —2D **94**
Allendale Clo. SE26 —5K **111**
Allendale Rd. Gnfd —6B **40**
Allen Edwards Dri. SW8 —1J **93**
Allen Rd. E3 —1B **64**
Allen Rd. N16 —4E **46**
Allen Rd. Beck —2K **125**
Allen Rd. Croy —1A **134**
Allensbury Pl. NW1 —7H **45**
Allens Rd. Enf —5D **8**
Allen St. W8 —3J **75**
Allenswood Rd. SE9 —3C **98**
Allerford Ct. Harr —5G **23**
Allerford Rd. SE6 —3D **112**
Allerton Ho. N1 —2D **62**
(off Provost Est.)
Allerton Rd. N16 —2C **46**
Allerton Wlk. N7 —2K **45**
Allestree Rd. SW6 —7G **75**
Alleyn Cres. SE21 —2D **110**
Alleyndale Rd. Dag —2C **52**
Alleyn Pk. SE21 —2D **110**

Alleyn Pk. S'hall —5E **70**
Alleyn Rd. SE21 —3D **110**
Allfarthing La. SW18 —6K **91**
Allgood Clo. Mord —6F **121**
Allgood St. E2 —2F **63**
Allhallows La. EC4 —7D **62** (1A **148**)
Allhallows Rd. E6 —5C **66**
All Hallows Rd. N17 —1E **30**
Alliance Clo. Wemb —4D **40**
Alliance Rd. E13 —5A **66**
Alliance Rd. SE18 —6A **84**
Alliance Rd. W3 —4H **57**
Allied Ind. Est. W3 —2A **74**
Allingham Clo. W7 —7K **55**
Allingham St. N1 —2C **62**
Allington Av. N17 —6K **17**
Allington Clo. SW19 —5F **107**
Allington Clo. Gnfd —7G **39**
Allington Ct. Enf —5E **8**
Allington Rd. NW4 —5D **26**
Allington Rd. W10 —3G **59**
Allington Rd. Harr —5G **23**
Allington Rd. Orp —7J **129**
Allington St. SW1 —3F **77** (7K **145**)
Allison Clo. SE10 —1E **96**
Allison Gro. SE21 —1E **110**
Allison Rd. N8 —5A **30**
Allison Rd. W3 —6J **57**
Allitsen Rd. NW8 —2C **60**
Allnutt Way. SW4 —5H **93**
Alloa Rd. SE8 —5K **79**
Alloa Rd. Ilf —2A **52**
Alloway Rd. E3 —3A **64**
All Saints Clo. N9 —2A **18**
All Saints Clo. Houn —1B **86**
(off Springwell Rd.)
Alpha St. SE15 —2G **95**
Alphea Clo. SW19 —7C **108**
Alpine Bus. Cen. E6 —5E **66**
Alpine Clo. Croy —3E **134**
Alpine Copse. Brom —2E **128**
Alpine Rd. SE16 —4K **79**
(in two parts)
Alpine View. Sutt —5C **132**
Alpine Wlk. Stan —2D **10**
Alpine Way. E6 —5E **66**
Alric Av. NW10 —7K **41**
Alric Av. N Mald —3A **120**
Alroy Rd. N4 —7A **30**
Alsace Rd. SE17 —5E **78**
Alscot Rd. SE1 —4F **79** (8E **148**)
(in three parts)
Alscot Way. SE1 —4F **79** (8E **148**)
Alsike Rd. Eri —4D **84**
Alsom Av. Wor Pk —4C **130**
Alston Clo. Surb —7B **118**
Alston Rd. N18 —5C **18**
Alston Rd. SW17 —4B **108**
Alston Rd. Barn —3B **4**
Altair Clo. N17 —6A **18**
Altash Way. SE9 —2D **114**
Altenburg Av. W13 —3B **72**
Altenburg Gdns. SW11 —4D **92**
Alt Gro. SW19 —7H **107**
Altham Rd. Pinn —1C **22**
Althea St. SW6 —2K **91**
Althorne Gdns. E18 —4H **33**
Althorne Way. Dag —2G **53**
Althorpe M. SW11 —1B **92**
(in two parts)
Althorpe Rd. Harr —5G **23**
Althorp Rd. SW17 —1D **108**
Altior Ct. N6 —6G **29**
Altmore Av. E6 —7D **50**
Alton Av. Stan —7E **10**
Alton Clo. Bex —1E **116**
Alton Clo. Iswth —2K **87**

Almer Rd. SW20 —7C **106**
Almington St. N4 —1K **45**
Almond Av. W5 —3D **72**
Almond Av. Cars —2D **132**
Almond Clo. SE15 —2G **95**
Almond Clo. Brom —7E **128**
Almond Gro. Bren —7B **72**
Almond Rd. N17 —7B **18**
Almond Rd. SE16 —4H **79**
Almonds Av. Buck H —2D **20**
Almondsbury Ct. SE15 —7E **78**
(off Lynbrook Clo.)
Almond Way. Brom —7E **128**
Almond Way. Harr —2F **23**
Almond Way. Mitc —5K **123**
Almorah Rd. N1 —7D **46**
Almorah Rd. Houn —1B **86**
Alnwick. N17 —7C **18**
Alnwick Gro. Mord —4K **121**
Alnwick Rd. E16 —6A **66**
Alnwick Rd. SE12 —7K **97**
Alperton La. Gnfd & Wemb —3C **56**
Alperton St. W10 —4H **59**
Alphabet Gdns. Cars —6B **122**
Alphabet Sq. E3 —5C **64**
Alpha Bus. Cen. E17 —5B **32**
Alpha Clo. NW1 —4C **60** (2D **138**)
Alpha Gro. E14 —2C **80**
Alpha Pl. NW6 —2J **59**
Alpha Pl. SW3 —6C **76**
Alpha Rd. E4 —3H **19**
Alpha Rd. N18 —6B **18**
Alpha Rd. SE14 —1B **96**
Alpha Rd. Croy —1E **134**
Alpha Rd. Enf —4F **9**
Alpha Rd. Surf —6F **119**
Alpha Rd. Tedd —5H **103**

Alton Gdns. Beck —7C **112**
Alton Gdns. Twic —7H **87**
Alton Rd. N17 —3D **30**
Alton Rd. SW15 —1C **106**
Alton Rd. Croy —3A **134**
Alton Rd. Rich —4E **88**
Alton St. E14 —6D **64**
Altyre Clo. Beck —5B **126**
Altyre Rd. Croy —2D **134**
Altyre Way. Beck —5B **126**
Alvanley Gdns. NW6 —5K **43**
Alverstone Av. SW19 —2J **107**
Alverstone Av. Barn —7H **5**
Alverstone Gdns. SE9 —1G **115**
Alverstone Ho. SE11 —6A **78**
Alverstone Rd. E12 —4E **50**
Alverstone Rd. NW2 —7E **42**
Alverstone Rd. N Mald —4B **120**
Alverstone Rd. Wemb —1F **41**
Alverston Gdns. SE25 —5E **124**
Alverton St. SE8 —5B **80**
(in two parts)
Alveston Av. Harr —3B **24**
Alvey St. SE17 —5E **78**
Alvia Gdns. Sutt —4A **132**
Alvington Cres. E8 —5F **47**
Alwold Cres. SE12 —6K **97**
Alwyn Av. W4 —5K **73**
Alwyn Clo. New Ad —7D **136**
Alwyne La. N1 —7B **46**
Alwyne Pl. N1 —6C **46**
Alwyne Rd. N1 —7C **46**
Alwyne Rd. SW19 —6H **107**
Alwyne Rd. W7 —7J **55**
Alwyne Sq. N1 —6C **46**
Alwyne Vs. N1 —7B **46**
Alwyn Gdns. NW4 —4C **26**
Alwyn Gdns. W3 —6H **57**
Alyth Gdns. NW11 —6J **27**
Amalgamated Dri. Bren —6A **72**
Amar Ct. SE18 —4K **83**
Amar Deep Ct. SE18 —5K **83**
Amazon St. E1 —6G **63**
Ambassador Clo. Houn —2C **86**
Ambassador Gdns. E6 —5D **66**
Ambassador's Ct. SW1
—1G **77** (3M **145**)
(off St James' Pal.)
Ambassador Sq. E14 —4D **80**
Amber Av. E17 —1A **32**
Amberden Av. N3 —3J **27**
Ambergate St. SE17 —5B **78**
Amberley Clo. Pinn —3D **22**
Amberley Ct. Beck —7B **112**
Amberley Ct. Sidc —5C **116**
Amberley Gdns. Enf —7K **7**
Amberley Gdns. Eps —4B **130**
Amberley Gro. SE26 —5H **111**
Amberley Gro. Croy —7F **125**
Amberley Rd. E10 —7C **32**
Amberley Rd. N13 —2E **16**
Amberley Rd. SE2 —6D **84**
Amberley Rd. W9 —5J **59**
Amberley Rd. Buck H —1F **21**
Amberley Rd. Enf —7A **8**
Amberley Way. Houn —5A **86**
Amberley Way. Mord —7H **121**
Amberley Way. Romf —4H **37**
Amber St. E15 —7F **49**
Amberwood Rise. N Mald —6A **120**
Amblecote Clo. SE12 —3K **113**
Amblecote Meadows. SE12 —3K **113**
Amblecote Rd. SE12 —3K **113**
Ambler Rd. N4 —3B **46**
Ambleside. Brom —6F **113**
Ambleside Av. SW16 —4H **109**
Ambleside Av. Beck —5A **126**

Ambleside Clo. E9 —5J 47
Ambleside Clo. E10 —7D 32
Ambleside Cres. Enf —3E 8
Ambleside Gdns. SW16 —5H 109
Ambleside Gdns. Ilf —4C 34
Ambleside Gdns. Sutt —6A 132
Ambleside Gdns. Wemb —1D 40
Ambleside Point. SE15 —7J 79
  (off Tustin Est.)
Ambleside Rd. NW10 —1A 58
Ambleside Rd. Bexh —2G 101
Ambrooke Rd. Belv —3G 85
Ambrosden Av. SW1
                    —3G 77 (7M 145)
Ambrose Av. NW11 —7G 27
Ambrose Clo. E6 —5D 66
Ambrose M. SW11 —2D 92
Ambrose St. SE16 —4H 79
Ambrose Wlk. E3 —2C 64
AMC Bus. Cen. NW10 —3H 57
Amelia St. SE17 —5B 78
Amen Corner. EC4 —6B 62 (8K 141)
Amen Corner. SW17 —6E 108
Amen Ct. EC4 —6B 62 (8K 141)
America Sq. EC3 —7F 63 (9E 142)
America St. SE1 —1C 78 (3L 147)
Amerland Rd. SW18 —5H 91
Amersham Av. N18 —6J 17
Amersham Gro. SE14 —7B 80
Amersham Rd. SE14 —1B 96
Amersham Rd. Croy —6C 124
Amersham Vale. SE14 —7B 80
Amery Gdns. NW10 —1D 58
Amery Rd. Harr —2A 40
Amesbury Av. SW2 —2J 109
Amesbury Clo. Wor Pk —1E 130
Amesbury Ct. Enf —2F 7
Amesbury Dri. E4 —6J 9
Amesbury Rd. Brom —3B 128
Amesbury Rd. Dag —7D 52
Amesbury Rd. Felt —2B 102
Amesbury Tower. SW8 —2G 93
Amethyst Rd. E15 —4F 49
Amherst Av. W13 —6C 56
Amherst Dri. Orp —4K 129
Amherst Rd. W13 —6C 56
Amhurst Gdns. Iswth —2K 87
Amhurst Pk. N16 —7D 30
Amhurst Pas. E8 —5G 47
Amhurst Rd. E8 —5H 47
Amhurst Rd. N16 & E8 —4F 47
Amhurst Ter. E8 —4G 47
Amhurst Wlk. SE28 —1A 84
Amidas Gdns. Dag —4B 52
Amiel St. E1 —4J 63
Amies St. SW11 —3D 92
Amina Way. SE16 —3G 79
Amity Gro. SW20 —1D 120
Amity Rd. E15 —1H 65
Ammanford Grn. NW9 —6A 26
Amner Rd. SW11 —6E 92
Amor Rd. W6 —3E 74
Amos Est. E16 —1K 79
Amott Rd. SE15 —3G 95
Amoy Pl. E14 —7C 64
Ampere Way. Bedd —1K 133
Ampthill Est. WC2 —6J 61
Ampton Pl. WC1 —3K 61 (2E 140)
Ampton St. WC1 —3K 61 (2E 140)
Amroth Clo. SE23 —1H 111
Amroth Grn. NW9 —6A 26
Amsterdam Rd. E14 —3E 80
Amunsden Ho. NW10 —7K 41
  (off Stonebridge Pk.)
Amwell Clo. E4 —5J 7
Amwell Ct. Est. N4 —2C 46
Amwell St. EC1 —3A 62 (1G 141)

Amyand Cotts. Twic —6B 88
Amyand La. Twic —7B 88
Amyand Pk. Gdns. Twic —7B 88
Amyand Pk. Rd. Twic —7A 88
Amy Johnson. Edgw —2H 25
Amyruth Rd. SE4 —5C 96
Anatola Rd. N19 —2G 45
Ancaster Cres. N Mald —6C 120
Ancaster M. Beck —3K 125
Ancaster Rd. Beck —3K 125
Ancaster St. SE18 —7J 83
Anchorage Clo. SW19 —5J 107
Anchor Brewhouse. SE1
                    —1F 79 (3E 148)
Anchor Ct. Enf —5K 7
Anchor & Hope La. SE7 —3K 81
Anchor M. SW12 —6F 93
Anchor St. SE16 —4H 79
Anchor Yd. EC1 —4C 62 (3M 141)
Ancill Clo. W6 —6F 75
Ancona Rd. NW10 —2C 58
Ancona Rd. SE18 —5H 83
Andace Pk. Gdns. Brom —2A 128
Andalus Rd. SW9 —3J 93
Ander Clo. Wemb —4D 40
Anderson Clo. W3 —6K 57
Anderson Ct. NW2 —1E 42
Anderson Ho. Bark —2H 67
Anderson Pl. Houn —4F 87
Anderson Rd. E9 —6K 47
Anderson Rd. Wfd G —3K 34
Anderson St. SW3 —5D 76
Anderson Way. Belv —2H 85
Anderton Clo. SE5 —3D 94
Anderton Ct. N22 —2H 29
Andorra Ct. Brom —1A 128
Andover Av. E16 —6B 66
Andover Clo. Gnfd —4F 55
Andover Pl. NW6 —2K 59
Andover Rd. N7 —2K 45
Andover Rd. Orp —7J 129
Andover Rd. Twic —1H 103
Andoversford Ct. SE15 —6E 78
  (off Bibury Clo.)
Andreck Ct. Beck —2D 126
Andre St. E8 —5G 47
Andrew Borde St. WC1 —6H 61
Andrew Borde St. WC2
                    —6H 61 (7B 140)
Andrew Clo. Dart —5K 101
Andrew Ct. SE23 —2K 111
Andrewes Clo. E6 —6C 66
Andrewes Highwalk. EC2
  (off Barbican)   —5C 62 (6M 141)
Andrewes Ho. EC2 —5C 62 (6M 141)
  (off Barbican)
Andrewes Ho. Sutt —4J 131
Andrew Pl. SW8 —1H 93
Andrews Clo. Buck H —2F 21
Andrews Clo. Harr —7H 23
Andrews Clo. Wor Pk —2F 131
Andrews Crosse. WC2
  (off Chancery La.) —6A 62 (8G 141)
Andrews Pl. SE9 —6F 99
Andrew's Rd. E8 —1H 63
Andrew St. E14 —6E 64
Andrews Wlk. SE17 —6B 78
Andwell Clo. SE2 —2B 84
Anerley Gro. SE19 —7F 111
Anerley Hill. SE19 —6F 111
Anerley Pk. SE20 —7G 111
Anerley Pk. Rd. SE20 —7H 111
Anerley Rd. SE19 & SE20 —7G 111
Anerley Sta. Rd. SE20 —1H 125
Anerley St. SW11 —2D 92
Anerley Vale. SE19 —7F 111
Anerdurin Bevan Ct. NW2 —2D 42
Aneurin Bevan Ho. N11 —7C 16

Anfield Clo. SW12 —7G 93
Angela Davies Ind. Est. SW9 —4B 94
Annetts Cres. N1 —7C 46
Angel All. E1 —6F 63
Angel Clo. N18 —4A 18
Angel Corner Pde. N18 —5B 18
Angel Ct. EC2 —6D 62 (7B 142)
Angel Ct. SW1 —1G 77 (3M 145)
Angelfield. Houn —5F 87
Angel Ga. EC1 —3B 62 (1K 141)
Angel Hill. Sutt —3K 131
Angel Hill Dri. Sutt —3K 131
Angelica Dri. E6 —5E 66
Angelica Gdns. Croy —1K 135
Angel La. E15 —6F 49
Angell Pk. Gdns. SW9 —3A 94
Angell Rd. SW9 —2A 94
Angel M. N1 —2A 62
Angel Pas. EC4 —7D 62 (1A 148)
Angel Pl. SE1 —2D 78 (4A 148)
Angel Pl. SW1 —2D 78
Angel Rd. N18 —5B 18
Angel Rd. Harr —6J 23
Angel Rd. Th Dit —7A 118
Angel Sq. N1 —2A 62
Angel St. EC1 —6C 62 (7L 141)
Angel Wlk. W6 —4E 74
Angel Way. Romf —5K 37
Angerstein La. SE3 —1H 97
Angle Grn. Dag —1C 52
Anglers Clo. Rich —4C 104
Angler's La. NW5 —6F 45
Anglesea Av. SE18 —4F 83
Anglesea Rd. SE18 —4F 83
Anglesea Rd. King T —4D 118
Anglesey Ct. Rd. Cars —6E 132
Anglesey Gdns. Cars —6E 132
Anglesey Rd. Enf —4C 8
Anglesmede Cres. Pinn —3E 22
Anglesmede Way. Pinn —3E 22
Angles Rd. SW16 —4J 109
Anglia Wlk. E6 —1E 66
  (off Napier Rd.)
Anglo Rd. E3 —2B 64
Angrave Ct. E8 —1F 63
Angrave Pas. E8 —1F 63
Angus Dri. Ruis —4A 38
Angus Gdns. NW9 —1K 25
Angus Ho. SW2 —7H 93
Angus Rd. E13 —3A 66
Angus St. SE14 —7A 80
Anhalt Rd. SW11 —7C 76
Ankerdine Cres. SE18 —7F 83
Anlaby Rd. Tedd —5J 103
Anley Rd. W14 —2F 75
Anmersh Gro. Stan —1D 24
Annabel Clo. E14 —6D 64
Anna Clo. E8 —1F 63
Annandale Rd. SE10 —6H 81
Annandale Rd. W4 —5A 74
Annandale Rd. Croy —2G 135
Annandale Rd. Sidc —7J 99
Anna Neagle Clo. E7 —4J 49
Annan Way. Romf —1K 37
Anne Boleyn's Wlk. King T —5E 104
Anne Boleyn's Wlk. Sutt —7F 131
Anne Case M. N Mald —3A 120
Annesley Av. NW9 —3K 25
Annesley Clo. NW10 —3A 42
Annesley Dri. Croy —3B 136
Annesley Rd. SE3 —1K 97
Annesley Wlk. N19 —2G 45
Anne St. E13 —4J 65
Annette Clo. Harr —2J 23

Annette Rd. N7 —3K 45
Annie Besant Clo. E3 —1B 64
Annie Taylor Ho. E12 —4E 50
  (off Walton Rd.)
Anning St. EC2 —4E 62 (3D 142)
Annington Rd. N2 —3D 28
Annis Rd. E9 —6A 48
Ann La. SW10 —6B 76
Ann Moss Way. SE16 —3J 79
Ann's Clo. SW1 —2D 76 (5F 144)
  (off Kinnerton St.)
Ann's Pl. E1 —5F 63 (6E 142)
  (off Wentworth St.)
Ann St. SE18 —5G 83
  (in two parts)
Annsworth Av. T Hth —3D 124
Annsworthy Cres. SE25 —2D 124
Ansdell Rd. SE15 —2J 95
Ansdell St. W8 —3K 75
Ansdell Ter. W8 —3K 75
Ansell Gro. Cars —1E 132
Ansell Rd. SW17 —3C 108
Anselm Clo. Croy —3F 135
Anselm Rd. SW6 —6J 75
Anselm Rd. Pinn —1D 22
Ansford Rd. Brom —5E 112
Ansleigh Pl. W11 —7F 59
Anson Clo. Romf —2H 37
Anson Rd. N7 —4G 45
Anson Rd. NW2 —4D 42
Anson Ter. N'holt —6F 39
Anstey Ct. W3 —2H 73
Anstey Rd. SE15 —3G 95
Anstey Wlk. N15 —4B 30
Anstice Clo. W4 —7A 74
Anstridge Path. SE9 —6H 99
Anstridge Rd. SE9 —6H 99
Antelope Rd. SE18 —3D 82
Anthony Cope Ct. N1
  (off Chart St.) —3D 62 (1B 142)
Anthony Rd. SE25 —6G 125
Anthony Rd. Gnfd —3J 55
Anthony Rd. Well —1A 100
Anthony St. E1 —6H 63
Antigua Wlk. SE19 —5D 110
Antill Rd. E3 —3A 64
Antill Rd. N15 —4G 31
Antill Ter. E1 —6K 63
Antlers Hill. E4 —5J 9
Anton Cres. Sutt —3J 131
Antoneys Clo. Pinn —2B 22
Anton St. E8 —5G 47
Antrim Gro. NW3 —6D 44
Antrim Rd. NW3 —6D 44
Antrobus Clo. Sutt —5H 131
Antrobus Rd. W4 —4J 73
Anworth Clo. Wfd G —6E 20
Apeldoorn Dri. Wall —7J 133
Apex Clo. Beck —1D 126
Apex Corner. NW7 —4F 13
Apex Ct. W13 —7A 56
Aplin Way. Iswth —1J 87
Apollo Av. Brom —1K 127
Apollo Ho. N6 —7D 28
Apollo Pl. SW10 —7B 76
Apollo Pl. E11 —2G 49
Apollo Way. SE28 —3H 83
Apothecary St. EC4 —6B 62 (8J 141)
Appach Rd. SW2 —6A 94
Appleby Clo. E4 —6K 19
Appleby Clo. N15 —5D 30
Appleby Clo. Twic —2H 103
Appleby Rd. E8 —7G 47
Appleby Rd. E16 —6H 65
Appleby St. E2 —2F 63
Appledore Av. Bexh —1J 101
Appledore Av. Ruis —3A 38

Appledore Clo. Brom —5J 127
Appledore Clo. Edgw —1G 25
Appledore Cres. Sidc —3J 115
Appleford Rd. W10 —4G 59
Apple Garth. Bren —4D 72
Applegarth. New Ad —7D 136
  (in two parts)
Applegarth Dri. Ilf —4K 35
Applegarth Rd. SE28 —1B 84
Applegarth Rd. W14 —3F 75
Apple Gro. Enf —3K 7
Apple Mkt. King T —2D 118
Appleton Gdns. N Mald —6C 120
Appleton Rd. SE9 —3C 98
Appleton Sq. Mitc —1C 122
Appletree Gdns. Barn —4H 5
Apple Tree Yd. SW1
                    —1G 77 (2M 145)
Applewood Clo. N20 —1H 15
Applewood Clo. NW2 —3D 42
Appold St. EC2 —5E 62 (5C 142)
Apprentice Way. E5 —4H 47
Approach Clo. N16 —4E 46
Approach Rd. E2 —2J 63
Approach Rd. SW20 —2E 120
Approach Rd. Barn —4G 5
Approach, The. NW4 —5F 27
Approach, The. W3 —6K 57
Approach, The. Enf —2C 8
Aprey Gdns. NW4 —4E 26
April Clo. W7 —7J 55
April Glen. SE23 —3K 111
April St. E8 —4F 47
Apsley Clo. Harr —5G 23
Apsley Rd. SE25 —4H 125
Apsley Rd. N Mald —3J 119
Apsley Way. NW8 —2B 60
Apsley Way. W1 —2E 76 (4H 145)
Aquila St. NW8 —2B 60
Aquinas St. SE1 —1A 78 (3H 147)
Arabella Dri. SW15 —4A 90
Arabia Clo. E4 —7K 9
Arabin Rd. SE4 —4A 96
Aragon Av. Th Dit —5A 118
Aragon Clo. Brom —7D 128
Aragon Clo. Enf —1E 6
Aragon Dri. Ruis —1B 38
Aragon M. E1 —1G 79
Aragon Rd. King T —5E 104
Aragon Rd. Mord —6F 121
Aragon Rd. Twic —7A 88
Aragon Tower. SE8 —4B 80
Arandora Cres. Romf —7B 36
Aran Dri. Stan —4H 11
Arbery Rd. E3 —3A 64
Arbinger Ct. W5 —7C 56
Arbor Clo. Beck —2D 126
Arbor Ct. N16 —2D 46
Arbor Rd. E4 —3A 20
Arbour Rd. Enf —4E 8
Arbour Sq. E1 —6K 63
Arbroath Rd. SE9 —3C 98
Arbuthnot La. Bex —6E 100
Arbuthnot Rd. SE14 —2K 95
Arbutus St. E8 —1F 63
Arcade Pl. Romf —5K 37
Arcade, The. E14 —6D 64
Arcade, The. EC2 —5E 62 (6C 142)
Arcade, The. E17 —4C 32
Arcade, The. SE9 —5E 82 (6C 142)
  (off Liverpool St.)
Arcade, The. Bark —7G 51
Arcadia Av. N3 —1J 27
Arcadian Av. Bex —6E 100
Arcadian Clo. Bex —6E 100
Arcadian Gdns. N22 —7E 16
Arcadian Rd. Bex —6E 100
Arcadia St. E14 —6C 64
Archangel St. SE16 —2K 79

Archbishop's Pl. SW2 —7K 93
Archdale Rd. SE22 —5F 95
Archel Rd. W14 —6H 75
Archer Clo. King T —7E 104
Archer M. Hamp —6G 103
Archer Rd. SE25 —4H 125
Archer Rd. Orp —5K 129
Archers Ct. Brom —4K 127
Archers Dri. Enf —2D 8
Archer St. W1 —7H 61 (9A 140)
Archers Wlk. SE15 —1F 95
  (off Exeter Rd.)
Archer Tower. SE14 —6A 80
Archery Clo. W2 —6C 60 (8D 138)
  (off Villiers Rd.)
Archery Rd. SE9 —5D 98
Arches, The. WC2 —1J 77 (2D 146)
  (off Villiers St.)
Arches, The. Harr —2F 39
Archibald M. SW6 —7J 75
Archibald Rd. N7 —4H 45
Archibald St. E3 —3C 64
Arch St. SE1 —3C 78 (7L 147)
Archway Bus. Cen. N19 —3H 45
Archway Clo. N19 —2G 45
Archway Clo. SW19 —3K 107
Archway Clo. W10 —5F 59
Archway Clo. Wall —3J 133
Archway Mall. N19 —2G 45
Archway Rd. N6 & N19 —6E 28
Archway St. SW13 —3A 90
Arcola St. E8 —5F 47
Arcon Ter. N9 —7B 8
Arctic St. NW5 —5E 44
Arcus Rd. Brom —6G 113
Ardbeg Rd. SE24 —5D 94
Arden Clo. Harr —3H 39
Arden Ct. Gdns. N2 —6B 28
Arden Cres. E14 —4D 80
Arden Cres. Dag —7C 52
Arden Est. N1 —2E 62
Arden Grange. N12 —4F 15
Arden Ho. SW9 —2J 93
  (off Grantham Rd.)
Arden M. E17 —5D 32
Arden Mhor. Pinn —4A 22
Arden Rd. N3 —3H 27
Arden Rd. W13 —7C 56
Ardent Clo. SE25 —3E 124
Arderne Av. SW16 —3A 124
Ardfillan Rd. SE6 —1F 113
Ardgowan Rd. SE6 —7G 97
  (in two parts)
Ardilaun Rd. N5 —4C 46
Ardleigh Gdns. Sutt —7J 121
Ardleigh Ho. Bark —1G 67
Ardleigh M. Ilf —3F 51
Ardleigh Rd. E17 —1B 32
Ardleigh Rd. N1 —6E 46
Ardleigh Ter. E17 —1B 32
Ardley Clo. NW10 —3A 42
Ardley Clo. SE6 —3A 112
Ardlui Rd. SE27 —2C 110
Ardmay Gdns. Surb —5E 118
Ardmere Rd. SE13 —6F 97
Ardmore La. Buck H —1E 20
Ardoch Rd. SE6 —2F 113
Ardra Rd. N9 —3E 18
Ardrossan Gdns. Wor Pk —3C 130
Ardshiel Clo. SW15 —3F 91
Ardwell Av. Ilf —5G 35
Ardwell Rd. SW2 —2J 109
Ardwick Rd. NW2 —4J 43
Arena Bus. Cen. N4 —6C 30
Argall Ho. Eri —3E 84
  (off Kale Rd.)
Argall Av. E10 —7K 31

Argon M. SW6 —7J 75
Argosy Ho. SE8 —4A 80
Argus Clo. Romf —1H 37
Argus Way. W3 —3H 73
Argus Way. N'holt —3C 54
Argyle Av. Houn —6E 86
Argyle Av. S'hall —1F 71
Argyle Clo. W13 —4A 56
Argyle Pl. W6 —4D 74
Argyle Rd. E1 —4K 63
Argyle Rd. E15 —4G 49
Argyle Rd. E16 —6K 65
Argyle Rd. N12 —5E 14
Argyle Rd. N17 —1G 31
Argyle Rd. N18 —4B 18
Argyle Rd. Barn —3G 5
Argyle Rd. Gnfd & W13 —3K 55
Argyle Rd. Harr —6F 23
Argyle Rd. Houn —5F 87
Argyle Rd. Ilf —2E 50
Argyle Sq. WC1 —3J 61 (1D 140)
Argyle St. WC1 —3J 61 (1C 140)
Argyle Wlk. WC1 —3J 61 (2C 140)
Argyll Clo. SW9 —3K 93
Argyll Gdns. Edgw —2H 25
Argyll Mans. SW3 —6B 76
Argyll Rd. W8 —2J 75
Argyll St. W1 —6G 61 (8L 139)
Arica Rd. SE4 —4A 96
Aricola Pl. Enf —5A 8
Ariel Rd. NW6 —6J 43
Ariel Way. W12 —1E 74
Aristotle Rd. SW4 —3H 93
Arkell Gro. SE19 —7B 110
Arkindale Rd. SE6 —3E 112
Arkley Cres. E17 —5B 32
Arkley Rd. E17 —5B 32
Arklow Rd. SE14 —6B 80
Arkwright Ho. SW2 —7J 93
  (off Streatham Pl.)
Arkwright Rd. NW3 —5A 44
Arkwright Rd. S Croy —7F 134
Arlesey Clo. SW15 —5G 91
Arlesford Rd. SW9 —3J 93
Arlingford Rd. SW2 —5A 94
Arlington. N12 —3D 14
Arlington Av. N1 —1C 62
Arlington Clo. Sidc —7J 99
Arlington Clo. Sutt —2J 131
Arlington Clo. Twic —6C 88
Arlington Dri. Cars —2D 132
Arlington Gdns. W4 —5J 73
Arlington Gdns. Ilf —1E 50
Arlington Lodge. SW2 —4K 93
Arlington M. Twic —6C 88
Arlington Pk. Mans. W4 —5J 73
  (off Sutton La. N.)
Arlington Pas. Tedd —4K 103
Arlington Pl. SE10 —7E 80
Arlington Rd. N14 —2A 16
Arlington Rd. NW1 —1F 61
Arlington Rd. W13 —6B 56
Arlington Rd. Rich —2D 104
Arlington Rd. Surb —6D 118
Arlington Rd. Tedd —4K 103
Arlington Rd. Twic —6C 88
Arlington Rd. Wfd G —7D 20
Arlington Sq. N1 —1C 62
Arlington St. SW1 —1G 77 (2L 145)
Arlington Way. EC1
                  —3A 62 (1H 141)
Arliss Way. N'holt —1A 54
Arlow Rd. N21 —1F 17
Armada Ct. SE8 —6C 80
Armadale Clo. N17 —4H 31
Armadale Rd. SW6 —6J 75
Armada Way. E6 —7F 67
Armagh Rd. E3 —1B 64

Armfield Cres. Mitc —2D 122
Armfield Rd. Enf —1J 7
Arminger Rd. W12 —1D 74
Armitage Rd. NW11 —1G 43
Armitage Rd. SE10 —5H 81
Armitage Rd. Houn —7B 70
Armour Clo. N7 —6K 45
Armoury Rd. SE8 —2D 96
Armoury Way. SW18 —5J 91
Armstead Wlk. Dag —7G 53
Armstrong Av. Wfd G —6B 20
Armstrong Clo. E6 —6D 66
Armstrong Clo. Dag —7D 36
Armstrong Cres. Barn —3G 5
Armstrong Rd. SW7
                  —3B 76 (7A 144)
Armstrong Rd. W3 —1B 74
Armstrong Rd. Felt —5C 102
Armstrong Way. S'hall —2F 71
Arnal Cres. SW18 —7G 91
Arndale Cen., The. SW18 —6K 91
Arndale Wlk. SW18 —5K 91
Arne Ho. SE11 —5K 77
  (off Tyers St.)
Arne St. WC2 —6J 61 (8D 140)
Arne Wlk. SE3 —4H 97
Arneways Av. Romf —3D 36
Arneway St. SW1 —3H 77 (7B 146)
Arnewood Clo. SW15 —1C 106
Arneys La. Mitc —6E 122
Arngask Rd. SE6 —7F 97
Arnhem Way. SE22 —5E 94
Arnold Cir. E2 —3F 63 (2E 142)
Arnold Clo. Harr —7F 25
Arnold Ct. N22 —7D 16
Arnold Cres. Iswth —5H 87
Arnold Est. SE1 —2F 79 (5F 148)
Arnold Gdns. N13 —5G 17
Arnold Ho. SE17 —5B 78
Arnold Rd. E3 —3C 64
Arnold Rd. N15 —3F 31
Arnold Rd. SW17 —7D 108
Arnold Rd. N'holt —6C 38
Arnold Rd. Dag —7F 53
Arnos Gro. N14 —4C 16
Arnos Gro. Ct. N11 —5B 16
  (off Palmer's Rd.)
Arnos Rd. N11 —4B 16
Arnot Ho. SE5 —7C 78
  (off Comber Gro.)
Arnott Clo. SE28 —1C 84
Arnott Clo. W4 —4A 73
Arnould Av. SE5 —4D 94
Arnsberg Way. Bexh —4G 101
Arnside Gdns. Wemb —1D 40
Arnside Rd. Bexh —1G 101
Arnside St. SE17 —6D 78
Arnulf St. SE6 —4D 112
Arnulls Rd. SW16 —6B 110
Arodene Rd. SW2 —6K 93
Arragon Gdns. SW16 —7J 109
Arragon Gdns. W Wick —3D 136
Arragon Rd. E6 —1B 66
Arragon Rd. Twic —1K 103
Arragon Rd. SW18 —1J 107
Arran Clo. Eri —6K 85
Arran Clo. Wall —4F 133
Arran Ct. NW9 —2B 26
Arran Dri. E12 —1B 50
Arran M. W5 —1E 72
Arran Rd. SE6 —2D 112
Arran Wlk. N1 —7C 46
Arras Av. Mord —5A 122
Arrel Rd. SE1 —3C 78 (7M 147)
Arrol Rd. Beck —3J 125
Arrowhead Ct. E11 —6F 33
Arrow Rd. E3 —3D 64
Arrowscout Wlk. N'holt —3C 54

Arrowsmith Ho. SE11 —5K 77
  (off Tyers St.)
Arsenal Rd. SE9 —2D 98
Arterberry Rd. SW20 —7E 106
Arteris Rd. Wfd G —7E 20
Artesian Clo. NW10 —7K 41
Artesian Rd. W2 —6J 59
Arthingworth St. E15 —1G 65
Arthur Ct. W10 —6F 59
  (off Silchester Rd.)
Arthurdon Rd. SE4 —5C 96
Arthur Gro. SE18 —4G 83
Arthur Rd. E6 —2D 66
Arthur Rd. N7 —4K 45
Arthur Rd. N9 —2A 18
Arthur Rd. SW19 —4J 107
Arthur Rd. King T —7G 105
Arthur Rd. N Mald —5D 120
Arthur Rd. Romf —6C 36
Arthur St. EC4 —7D 62 (1B 148)
Artichoke Hill. E1 —7H 63
Artichoke M. SE5 —1D 94
  (off Artichoke Pl.)
Artichoke Pl. SE5 —1D 94
Artillery Clo. Ilf —6G 35
Artillery Ho. E15 —6G 49
Artillery La. E1 —5E 62 (6D 142)
Artillery Pas. E1 —5E 62 (6D 142)
  (off Artillery La.)
Artillery Pl. SE18 —4E 82
Artillery Pl. SW1 —3H 77 (7A 146)
Artillery Pl. Harr —7B 10
Artillery Rd. W12 —6C 58
Artillery Row. SW1 —3H 77 (7A 146)
Artizan St. E1 —6E 62 (7D 142)
  (off Harrow Pl.)
Arun Ct. SE25 —5G 125
Arundel Av. Mord —4H 121
Arundel Bldgs. SE1 —3E 78 (7D 148)
  (off Swan Mead)
Arundel Clo. E15 —4G 49
Arundel Clo. SW11 —5C 92
Arundel Clo. Bex —6F 101
Arundel Clo. Croy —3B 134
Arundel Clo. Hamp —5F 103
Arundel Ct. N12 —6H 15
Arundel Ct. N17 —1G 31
Arundel Ct. Short —2G 127
Arundel Ct. S Harr —4E 38
Arundel Dri. Harr —4D 38
Arundel Dri. Wfd G —7D 20
Arundel Gdns. N21 —1F 17
Arundel Gdns. W11 —7H 59
Arundel Gdns. Edgw —7E 12
Arundel Gdns. Ilf —2A 52
Arundel Gro. N16 —5E 46
Arundel Mans. SW6 —1H 91
  (off Kelvedon Rd.)
Arundel Pl. N1 —6A 46
Arundel Rd. Barn —3H 5
Arundel Rd. Croy —6D 124
Arundel Rd. Houn —3A 86
Arundel Rd. King T —2H 119
Arundel Rd. Sutt —7H 131
Arundel Sq. N7 —6A 46
Arundel St. WC2 —7K 61 (9F 140)
Arundel Ter. SW13 —6D 74
Arvon Rd. N5 —5A 46
Ascalon St. SW8 —7G 77
Ascham Dri. E4 —7J 19
Ascham End. E17 —1A 32
Ascham St. NW5 —5G 45
Aschurch Rd. Croy —7F 125
Ascot Clo. N'holt —5E 38
Ascot Gdns. S'hall —5D 54
Ascot Ct. Bex —7F 101
Ascot M. Wall —7G 133
Ascot Pl. Stan —5H 11

Ascot Rd. E6 —3D 66
Ascot Rd. N15 —5D 30
Ascot Rd. N18 —4B 18
Ascot Rd. SW17 —6E 108
Ascot Rd. Orp —4K 129
Ascott Av. W5 —2E 72
Ashbourne Av. E18 —4K 33
Ashbourne Av. N20 —2J 15
Ashbourne Av. NW11 —5H 27
Ashbourne Av. Bexh —7E 84
Ashbourne Av. Harr —1H 39
Ashbourne Clo. N12 —4E 14
Ashbourne Clo. W5 —5G 57
Ashbourne Ct. E5 —4A 48
Ashbourne Ct. N12 —4E 14
  (off Ashbourne Clo.)
Ashbourne Gro. NW7 —5E 12
Ashbourne Gro. SE22 —4F 95
Ashbourne Gro. W4 —5A 74
Ashbourne Pde. W5 —4F 57
Ashbourne Rd. W5 —4F 57
Ashbourne Rd. Mitc —7E 108
Ashbourne Ter. SW19 —7J 107
Ashbourne Way. NW11 —4H 27
Ashbridge Rd. E11 —7G 33
Ashbridge St. NW8 —4C 60 (4C 138)
Ashbrook Rd. N19 —1H 45
Ashbrook Rd. Dag —3H 53
Ashburn Gdns. SW7 —4A 76
Ashburnham Av. Harr —6K 23
Ashburnham Clo. N2 —3B 28
Ashburnham Ct. Beck —2E 126
Ashburnham Ct. Pinn —3B 22
Ashburnham Gdns. Harr —6K 23
Ashburnham Gro. SE10 —7D 80
Ashburnham Retreat. SE10 —7D 80
Ashburnham Rd. NW10 —3E 58
Ashburnham Rd. SW10 —7A 76
Ashburnham Rd. Belv —4J 85
Ashburnham Rd. Rich —3B 104
Ashburnham Tower. SW10 —7B 76
  (off Worlds End Est.)
Ashburn M. SW7 —4A 76
Ashburn Pl. SW7 —4A 76
Ashburton Av. Croy —1H 135
Ashburton Av. Ilf —5J 51
Ashburton Clo. Croy —1G 135
Ashburton Enterprise Cen. SW15
                  —6E 90
Ashburton Gdns. Croy —2G 135
Ashburton Gro. N7 —4A 46
Ashburton Memorial Homes. Croy
                  —7H 125
Ashburton Rd. E16 —6J 65
Ashburton Rd. Croy —2G 135
Ashburton Ter. E13 —2J 65
Ashbury Gdns. Romf —5D 36
Ashbury Rd. SW11 —3D 92
Ashby Gro. N1 —7C 46
Ashby Ho. SW9 —2B 94
Ashby M. SE4 —2B 96
Ashby Rd. N15 —5G 31
Ashby Rd. SE4 —2B 96
Ashby St. EC1 —3B 62 (2K 141)
Ashby Wlk. Croy —6C 124
Ashchurch Gro. W12 —3C 74
Ashchurch Pk. Vs. W12 —3C 74
Ashchurch Ter. W12 —3C 74
Ash Clo. SE20 —2J 125
Ash Clo. Cars —2D 132
Ash Clo. Edgw —4D 12
Ash Clo. N Mald —2K 119
Ash Clo. Orp —5H 129
Ash Clo. Romf —1H 37
Ash Clo. Sidc —3B 116
Ash Clo. Stan —6F 11
Ashcombe Av. Surb —7D 118

157

Baldwin Ter. N1 —2C **62**
Baldwyn Gdns. W3 —7K **57**
Baldwyn's Pk. Bex —2K **117**
Baldwyn's Rd. Bex —2K **117**
Bales Ter. N9 —3A **18**
Balfern Gro. W4 —5A **74**
Balfern St. SW11 —2C **92**
Balfe St. N1 —2J **61**
Balforn Tower. E14 —6E **64**
Balfour Av. W7 —1K **71**
Balfour Bus. Cen. S'hall —3A **70**
Balfour Gro. N20 —3J **15**
Balfour M. N9 —3B **18**
Balfour M. W1 —1E **76** (2H **145**)
Balfour Pl. SW15 —4D **90**
Balfour Pl. W1 —7E **60** (1H **145**)
Balfour Rd. N5 —4C **46**
Balfour Rd. SE25 —4G **125**
Balfour Rd. SW19 —7K **107**
Balfour Rd. W3 —5J **57**
Balfour Rd. W13 —2A **72**
Balfour Rd. Brom —5B **128**
Balfour Rd. Cars —7D **132**
Balfour Rd. Harr —5K **23**
Balfour Rd. Houn —3F **87**
Balfour Rd. Ilf —2F **51**
Balfour Rd. S'hall —3B **70**
Balfour St. SE17 —4D **78** (8A **148**)
Balfour Ter. N3 —2K **27**
Balgonie Rd. E4 —1A **20**
Balgowan Clo. N Mald —5A **120**
Balgowan Rd. Beck —2A **126**
Balgowan St. SE18 —4K **83**
Balham Continental Mkt. SW12
—1F **109**
(off Shipka Rd.)
Balham Gro. SW12 —7E **92**
Balham High Rd. SW17 & SW12
—3E **108**
Balham Hill. SW12 —7F **93**
Balham New Rd. SW12 —7F **93**
Balham Pk. Rd. SW12 —1D **108**
Balham Rd. N9 —2B **18**
Balham Sta. Rd. SW12 —1F **109**
Balkan Wlk. E1 —7H **63**
Ballamore Rd. Brom —3J **113**
Ballance Rd. E9 —6K **47**
Ballantrae Ho. NW2 —4H **43**
Ballard Clo. King T —7K **105**
Ballards Clo. Dag —1H **69**
Ballards Farm Rd. S Croy & Croy
—6F **135**
Ballards La. N3 & N12 —1J **27**
Ballards Rise. S Croy —6G **135**
Ballards Rd. NW2 —2C **42**
Ballards Rd. Dag —2H **69**
Ballards Way. S Croy & Croy
—6G **135**
Ballards Yd. Edgw —6B **12**
Ballast Quay. SE10 —5F **81**
Ballater Rd. SW2 —4J **93**
Ballater Rd. S Croy —5F **135**
Ballatine St. SW18 —4A **92**
Ball Ct. EC3 —6D **62** (8B **142**)
(off Cornhill)
Ballina St. SE23 —7K **95**
Ballingdon Rd. SW11 —6E **92**
Balliol Av. E4 —4B **20**
Balliol Rd. N17 —1E **30**
Balliol Rd. W10 —6E **58**
Balliol Rd. Well —2B **100**
Balloch Rd. SE6 —1F **113**
Ballogie Av. NW10 —4A **42**
Ballow Clo. SE5 —7E **78**
Ball's Pond Pl. N1 —6D **46**
Balls Pond Rd. N1 —6D **46**
Balmain Clo. W5 —1D **72**
Balmain Ct. Houn —1F **87**
Balmer Rd. E3 —2B **64**

Balmes Rd. N1 —1D **62**
Balmoral Av. Beck —4A **126**
Balmoral Clo. SW15 —6F **91**
Balmoral Ct. SE12 —4K **113**
Balmoral Ct. SE27 —4C **110**
Balmoral Ct. Sutt —7J **131**
Balmoral Dri. S'hall —4D **54**
Balmoral Gdns. W13 —3A **72**
Balmoral Gdns. Bex —1F **117**
Balmoral Gdns. Ilf —1K **51**
Balmoral Gro. N7 —6K **45**
Balmoral M. W12 —3B **74**
Balmoral Rd. E7 —4A **50**
Balmoral Rd. E10 —2D **48**
Balmoral Rd. NW2 —6D **42**
Balmoral Rd. Harr —4E **38**
Balmoral Rd. King T —4F **119**
Balmoral Rd. Wor Pk —3D **130**
Balmore Cres. Barn —5K **5**
Balmore St. N19 —2F **45**
Balmuir Gdns. SW15 —4E **90**
Balnacraig Av. NW10 —4A **42**
Balniel Ga. SW1 —5H **77**
Baltic Cen. Bren —5D **72**
Baltic Clo. SW19 —7B **108**
Baltic Ct. SE16 —2K **79**
Baltic Ho. SE5 —2C **94**
Baltic St. EC1 —4C **62** (4L **141**)
Baltimore Ho. SE11 —5A **78**
(off Hotspur St.)
Baltimore Pl. Well —2K **99**
Balvaird Pl. SW1 —6H **77**
Balvernie Gro. SW18 —7H **91**
Bamber Ho. Bark —1G **67**
Bamborough Gdns. W12 —2E **74**
Bamburgh. N17 —7C **18**
Bamford Av. Wemb —1F **57**
Bamford Rd. Bark —6G **51**
Bamford Rd. Brom —5E **112**
Bampfylde Clo. Wall —3G **133**
Bampton Rd. SE23 —3K **111**
Banavie Gdns. Beck —1E **126**
Banbury Clo. Enf —1G **7**
Banbury Ct. SW8 —7J **77**
(off Long Acre)
Banbury Ct. Sutt —7J **131**
Banbury Ho. E9 —7K **47**
Banbury Rd. E9 —7K **47**
Banbury Rd. E17 —7E **18**
Banbury St. SW11 —2C **92**
Banbury Wlk. N'holt —2E **54**
(off Brabazon Rd.)
Banchory Rd. SE3 —7K **81**
Bancroft Av. N2 —5C **28**
Bancroft Av. Buck H —2D **20**
Bancroft Clo. N'holt —1A **54**
Bancroft Ct. SW8 —7J **77**
(off Allen Edwards Dri.)
Bancroft Gdns. Harr —1G **23**
Bancroft Gdns. Orp —7K **129**
Bancroft Rd. E1 —3K **63**
Bancroft Rd. Harr —2G **23**
Bandon Rise. Wall —5H **133**
Bangalore St. SW15 —3E **90**
Bangor Clo. N'holt —7F **39**
Banim St. W6 —4D **74**
Banister Ho. E9 —5K **47**
Banister Rd. W10 —3F **59**
Bank Av. Mitc —2B **122**
Bank End. SE1 —1C **78** (2M **147**)
Bankfoot Rd. Brom —4G **113**
Bankhurst Rd. SE6 —7B **96**
Bank La. SW15 —5A **90**
Bank La. King T —7E **104**
Bank M. Sutt —6A **132**
Banksian Wlk. Iswth —1J **87**

Bankside. SE1 —7C **62** (1L **147**)
Bankside. Enf —1G **7**
Bankside. S'hall —1B **70**
Bankside. S Croy —6F **135**
Bankside Clo. Bex —4K **117**
Bankside Clo. Cars —6C **132**
Bankside Way. SE19 —6E **110**
Banks La. Bexh —4F **101**
Bank, The. N6 —1F **45**
Bankton Rd. SW2 —4A **94**
Bankwell Rd. SE13 —4G **97**
Bannerman Ho. SW8 —6K **77**
Banner St. EC1 —4C **62** (4M **141**)
Banning St. SE10 —5G **81**
Bannister Clo. SW2 —1A **110**
Bannister Clo. Gnfd —5H **39**
Bannockburn Rd. SE18 —4J **83**
Banstead Gdns. N9 —3K **17**
Banstead Rd. Cars —7B **132**
Banstead Rd. S. Sutt —7B **132**
Banstead St. SE15 —3J **95**
Banstead Way. Wall —5J **133**
Banstock Rd. Edgw —6C **12**
Banting Ho. NW2 —3C **42**
Banton Clo. Enf —2C **8**
Bantry St. SE5 —7D **78**
Banwell Rd. Bex —6D **100**
Banyard Rd. SE16 —3H **79**
Baptist Gdns. NW5 —6E **44**
Barandon Wlk. W11 —7F **59**
Barbara Brosnan Ct. NW8 —2B **60**
Barbara Hucklesby Clo. N22 —2B **30**
Barbauld Rd. N16 —3E **46**
Barber Ho. N21 —7F **7**
Barbers All. E13 —3K **65**
Barbers Rd. E15 —2D **64**
Barbican. EC2 —5C **62** (6M **141**)
Barbican Rd. Gnfd —6F **55**
Barb M. W6 —3E **74**
Barbon Clo. WC1 —5K **61** (5D **140**)
Barbot Clo. N9 —3B **18**
Barchard St. SW18 —5K **91**
Barchester Clo. W7 —1K **71**
Barchester Rd. Harr —2H **23**
Barchester St. E14 —5D **64**
Barclay Clo. SW6 —7J **75**
Barclay Oval. Wfd G —4D **20**
Barclay Path. E17 —5E **32**
Barclay Rd. E11 —1H **49**
Barclay Rd. E13 —4A **66**
Barclay Rd. E17 —5E **32**
Barclay Rd. N18 —6J **17**
Barclay Rd. SW6 —7J **75**
Barclay Rd. Croy —3D **134**
Barclay Way. SE22 —1G **111**
Barden St. SE18 —7J **83**
Bardfield Av. Romf —3D **36**
Bardney Rd. Mord —4K **121**
Bardolph Av. Croy —7A **136**
Bardolph Rd. N7 —4J **45**
Bardolph Rd. Rich —3F **89**
Bard Rd. W10 —7F **59**
Bardsey Wlk. N1 —6C **46**
Bardsley Clo. Croy —3F **135**
Bardsley La. SE10 —6E **80**
Barfett St. W10 —4H **59**
Barfield Av. N20 —2J **15**
Barfield Rd. E11 —1H **49**
Barfield Rd. Brom —3E **128**
Barfleur Ho. SE8 —5B **80**
Barford Clo. NW4 —2C **26**
Barford St. N1 —1A **62**
Barforth Rd. SE15 —3H **95**
Barfreston Way. SE20 —1H **125**
Bargate Clo. SE18 —5K **83**
Bargate Clo. N Mald —7C **120**

Barge Ho. Rd. E16 —2F **83**
Barge Ho. St. SE1 —1A **78** (2H **147**)
Bargery Rd. SE6 —1D **112**
Barge Wlk. King T —1D **118**
Bargrove Clo. SE20 —7G **111**
Bargrove Cres. SE6 —2B **112**
Barham Clo. Brom —7C **128**
Barham Clo. Chst —5F **115**
Barham Clo. Romf —2H **37**
Barham Clo. Wemb —6B **40**
Barham Rd. SW20 —7C **106**
Barham Rd. Chst —5F **115**
Barham Rd. S Croy —5C **134**
Baring Clo. SE12 —2J **113**
Baring Rd. SE12 —7J **97**
Baring Rd. Barn —4G **5**
Baring Rd. Croy —1G **135**
Baring St. N1 —1D **62**
Barker Dri. NW1 —7G **45**
Barkers Arc. W8 —2K **75**
Barker's Row. EC1 —4A **62**
Barker St. SW10 —6A **76**
Barker Wlk. SW16 —3H **109**
Barker Way. SE22 —7G **95**
Barkham Rd. N17 —7J **17**
Barking Northern Relief Rd. Bark
—7F **51**
Barking Rd. E16, E13 & E6 —5H **65**
Barkis Way. SE16 —5H **79**
Bark Pl. W2 —7K **59**
Barkston Gdns. SW5 —4K **75**
Barkway Ct. N4 —2C **46**
Barkwood Clo. Romf —5J **37**
Barkworth Rd. SE16 —5H **79**
Barlborough St. SE14 —7K **79**
Barlby Gdns. W10 —4F **59**
Barlby Rd. W10 —5E **58**
Barleycorn Way. E14 —7B **64**
Barleyfields Clo. Romf —6B **36**
Barley La. Ilf & Romf —7A **36**
Barleymow Pas. EC1
(off Long La.) —5B **62** (6K **141**)
Barley Mow Pas. W4 —5K **73**
Barlow Clo. Wall —6J **133**
Barlow Ho. N1 —3D **62** (1A **142**)
(off Provost Est.)
Barlow Pl. W1 —7F **61**
Barlow Rd. NW6 —6H **43**
Barlow Rd. W3 —1H **73**
Barlow Rd. Hamp —7E **102**
Barlow St. SE17 —4D **78**
Barlow Way. Rain —5K **69**
Barmeston Rd. SE6 —2D **112**
Barmor Clo. Harr —2F **23**
Barmouth Av. Gnfd —2K **55**
Barmouth Rd. SW18 —6A **92**
Barmouth Rd. Croy —2K **135**
Barnabas Ct. N21 —5G **7**
Barnabas Rd. E9 —5K **47**
Barnaby Clo. Harr —2G **39**
Barnaby Ct. NW9 —3A **26**
Barnaby Pl. SW7 —4B **76** (9A **144**)
(off Brompton Rd.)
Barnaby Way. Chig —3K **21**
Barnard Clo. SE18 —3E **82**
Barnard Clo. Chst —1H **129**
Barnard Clo. Wall —7H **133**
Barnard Gdns. Hay —4A **54**
Barnard Gdns. N Mald —4C **120**
Barnard Gro. E15 —7H **49**
Barnard Hill. N10 —1F **29**
Barnard Lodge. New Bar —4F **5**
Barnard M. SW11 —4C **92**
Barnardo Dri. Ilf —4G **35**
Barnardo Gdns. E1 —7K **63**
Barnardo St. E1 —6K **63**
Barnardos Village. B'side —3G **35**
Barnard Rd. SW11 —4C **92**

Barnard Rd. Enf —2C **8**
Barnard Rd. Mitc —3E **122**
Barnard's Inn. EC1 —6A **62** (7H **141**)
(off Fetter La.)
Barnards Pl. S Croy —7B **134**
Barnby Sq. E15 —1G **65**
Barnby St. E15 —1G **65**
Barnby St. NW1 —2G **61**
Barn Clo. N'holt —2A **54**
Barn Cres. Stan —6H **11**
Barnehurst Av. Eri & Bexh —1J **101**
Barnehurst Clo. Eri —1J **101**
Barnehurst Rd. Bexh —2J **101**
Barn Elms Pk. SW15 —3E **90**
Barnes Av. SW13 —7C **74**
Barnes Av. S'hall —4D **70**
Barnes Clo. E12 —4B **50**
Barnes Ct. E16 —5A **66**
Barnes Ct. Wfd G —5G **21**
Barnes End. N Mald —5C **120**
Barnes High St. SW13 —2B **90**
Barnes Ho. Bark —1H **67**
Barnes Pikle. W5 —7D **56**
Barnes Rd. N18 —4D **18**
Barnes Rd. Ilf —5G **51**
Barnes St. E14 —6A **64**
Barnes Wallis Ct. Wemb —3J **41**
Barnet Ga. La. Barn —1H **13**
Barnet Gro. E2 —3G **63**
Barnet Hill. Barn —4C **4**
Barnet Ho. N20 —2F **15**
Barnet La. N20 & Barn —1C **14**
Barnet Trading Est. H Bar —3C **4**
Barnetts Ct. Harr —3F **39**
Barnett St. E1 —6H **63**
Barnet Way. NW7 —3E **12**
Barnet Wood Rd. Brom —2K **137**
Barney Clo. SE7 —5A **82**
Barn Field. NW3 —5D **44**
Barnfield. N Mald —6A **120**
Barnfield Av. Croy —2J **135**
Barnfield Av. King T —4D **104**
Barnfield Av. Mitc —3F **123**
Barnfield Clo. N4 —7J **29**
Barnfield Clo. SW17 —3B **108**
Barnfield Gdns. King T —4E **104**
Barnfield Pl. E14 —4C **80**
Barnfield Rd. SE18 —6F **83**
(in two parts)
Barnfield Rd. W4 —4C **56**
Barnfield Rd. Belv —6F **85**
Barnfield Rd. Edgw —1J **25**
Barnfield Rd. S Croy —7E **134**
Barnfield Wood Clo. Beck —6F **127**
Barnfield Wood Rd. Beck —6F **127**
Barnham Rd. Gnfd —3G **55**
Barnham St. SE1 —2E **78** (4D **148**)
Barnhill. Pinn —5A **22**
Barn Hill. Wemb —1G **41**
Barnhill Av. Brom —5H **127**
Barnhill La. Hay —4A **54**
Barnhill Rd. Hay —3A **54**
Barnhill Rd. Wemb —3J **41**
Barningham Way. NW9 —6K **25**
Barnlea Clo. Felt —2C **102**
Barnmead Gdns. Dag —5F **53**
Barnmead Rd. Beck —1K **125**
Barnmead Rd. Dag —5F **53**
Barn M. S Harr —3E **38**
Barn Rise. Wemb —1G **41**
Barnsbury Clo. N Mald —4J **119**
Barnsbury Est. N1 —1A **62**
Barnsbury Gro. N7 —7K **45**
Barnsbury Pk. N1 —7A **46**
Barnsbury Rd. N1 —2A **62**
Barnsbury Sq. N1 —7A **46**
Barnsbury St. N1 —7A **46**

Barnsbury Ter. N1 —7K **45**
Barnscroft. SW20 —3D **120**
Barnsdale Av. E14 —4D **80**
Barnsdale Rd. W9 —4H **59**
Barnsley St. E1 —4H **63**
Barnstaple Rd. Ruis —3A **38**
Barn St. N16 —2E **46**
Barn Way. Wemb —1G **41**
Barnwell Rd. SW2 —5A **94**
Barnwood Clo. W9 —4K **59**
Barnwood Ct. E16 —1K **81**
Baron Clo. N1 —2A **62**
Baroness Rd. E2 —3F **63** (1F **142**)
Baronet Gro. N17 —1G **31**
Baronet Rd. N17 —1G **31**
Baron Gdns. Ilf —3G **35**
Baron Gro. Mitc —4C **122**
Baron Rd. Dag —1D **52**
Baronsclere Ct. N6 —7G **29**
Barons Ct. Ilf —2H **51**
Barons Ct. Wall —3H **133**
Baron's Ct. Rd. W14 —5G **75**
Baronsfield Rd. Twic —6B **88**
Barons Ga. Barn —6H **5**
Barons Keep. W14 —5G **75**
Barons Mead. Harr —4J **23**
Baronsmead Rd. SW13 —1C **90**
Baronsmede. W5 —2F **73**
Baronsmere Ct. Barn —4B **4**
Baronsmere Rd. N2 —4C **28**
Baron's Pl. SE1 —2A **78** (5H **147**)
Barons, The. Twic —6B **88**
Baron St. N1 —2A **62**
Baron's Wlk. Croy —6A **126**
Baron Wlk. E16 —5H **65**
Baron Wlk. Mitc —4C **122**
Barque M. SE8 —6C **80**
Barrack Rd. Houn —4B **86**
Barrack Yd. SW1 —2E **76**
Barratt Av. N22 —2K **29**
Barratt Ind. Pk. E3 —4E **64**
Barratt Way. Harr —2H **23**
Barrenger Rd. N10 —1D **28**
Barrets Grn. Rd. NW10 —3J **57**
Barrett Ho. SE17 —5C **78**
(off Browning St.)
Barrett Ho. SW9 —3K **93**
(off Benedict Rd.)
Barrett Rd. E17 —4E **32**
Barretts Gro. N16 —5E **46**
Barrett St. W1 —6E **60** (8H **139**)
Barrhill Rd. SW2 —2J **109**
Barrie Ct. New Bar —5F **5**
(off Lyonsdown Rd.)
Barriedale. SE14 —2A **96**
Barrie Est. W2 —7B **60** (9A **138**)
Barrier App. SE7 —3B **82**
Barrington Sq. SW17 —4E **108**
Barrington Clo. NW5 —5E **44**
Barrington Clo. Ilf —1D **34**
Barrington Ct. NW5 —5E **44**
Barrington Rd. E12 —6E **50**
Barrington Rd. N8 —5H **29**
Barrington Rd. SW9 —3B **94**
Barrington Rd. Bexh —2D **100**
Barrington Rd. Sutt —2J **131**
Barrington Vs. SE18 —1E **98**
Barrosa Dri. Hamp —7E **102**
Barrow Av. Cars —7D **132**
Barrow Clo. N21 —3G **17**
Barrowdene Clo. Pinn —2C **22**
Barrowell Grn. N21 —2G **17**
Barrowfield Clo. N9 —3C **18**
Barrowgate Rd. W4 —5J **73**
Barrow Hedges Clo. Cars —7C **132**
Barrow Hedges Way. Cars —7C **132**
Barrowhill. Wor Pk —2A **130**

Barrowhill Clo. Wor Pk —2A **130**
Barrow Hill Est. NW8 —2C 60
(off Barrow Hill Rd.)
Barrow Hill Rd. NW8 —2C **60**
Barrow Point Av. Pinn —2C **22**
Barrow Point La. Pinn —2C **22**
Barrow Rd. SW16 —6H **109**
Barrow Rd. Croy —5A **134**
Barrow Wlk. Bren —6C **72**
Barrs Rd. NW10 —7K **41**
Barry Av. N15 —6F **31**
Barry Av. Bexh —7E **84**
Barrydene. N20 —1G **15**
Barry Rd. E6 —6C **66**
Barry Rd. NW10 —7J **41**
Barry Rd. SE22 —6G **95**
Barset Rd. SE15 —3J **95**
(in three parts)
Barson Clo. SE20 —7J **111**
Barston Rd. SE27 —3C **110**
Barstow Cres. SW2 —1K **109**
Barter St. WC1 —5J **61** (6D **140**)
Barters Wlk. Pinn —3C **22**
Bartholomew Clo. EC1
(in two parts) —5C **62** (6K **141**)
Bartholomew Clo. SW18 —4A **92**
Bartholomew Ct. E1
(off Old St.) —4C 62 (3M 141)
Bartholomew La. EC2
—6D **62** (8B **142**)
Bartholomew Pl. EC1
—5C 62 (6L 141)
(off Bartholomew Clo.)
Bartholomew Rd. NW5 —6G **45**
Bartholomew Sq. E1 —4H **63**
Bartholomew Sq. EC1
—4C **62** (3M **141**)
Bartholomew St. SE1
—3D **78** (7B **148**)
Bartholomew Vs. NW5 —6G **45**
Barth Rd. SE18 —4J **83**
Bartle Av. E6 —2C **66**
Bartle Rd. W11 —6G **59**
Bartlett Clo. E14 —6C **64**
Bartlett Ct. EC4 —6A **62** (7H **141**)
Bartlett Houses. Dag —7H 53
(off Vicarage Rd.)
Bartlett St. S Croy —5D **134**
Bartlow Gdns. Romf —1K **37**
Barton Av. Romf —1H **53**
Barton Clo. E6 —6D **66**
Barton Clo. E9 —5J **47**
Barton Clo. SE15 —3H **95**
Barton Clo. Bexh —5E **100**
Barton Grn. N Mald —2K **119**
Barton Ho. SW6 —3K 91
(off Wandsworth Bri. Rd.)
Barton Meadows. Ilf —4F **35**
Barton Rd. W14 —5G **75**
Barton Rd. Sidc —6E **116**
Barton St. SW1 —3J **77** (6C **146**)
Bartram Rd. SE4 —5A **96**
Bartrams La. Barn —1F **5**
Barville Clo. SE4 —4A **96**
Barwick Rd. E7 —4K **49**
Barwood Av. W Wick —1D **136**
Basden Gro. Felt —2E **102**
Basden Ho. Felt —2E **102**
Basedale Rd. Dag —7B **52**
Baseing Clo. E6 —7E **66**
Bashley Rd. NW10 —4K **57**
Basil Av. E6 —3D **66**
Basildene Rd. Houn —3B **86**
Basildon Av. Ilf —1E **34**
Basildon Clo. Sutt —7K **131**
Basildon Rd. SE2 —5A **84**
Basil Gdns. Croy —1K **135**
Basilon Rd. Bexh —2E **100**

Basil Spence Ho. N22 —1K **29**
Basil St. SW3 —3D **76** (6E **144**)
Basing Clo. Th Dit —7A **118**
Basing Ct. SE15 —1F **95**
Basingdon Way. SE5 —4D **94**
Basing Dri. Bex —6F **101**
Basinghall Av. EC2 —6D **62** (7A **142**)
Basinghall Gdns. Sutt —7K **131**
Basinghall St. EC2 —6D **62** (7M **141**)
Basing Hill. NW11 —1H **43**
Basing Hill. Wemb —2F **41**
Basing Ho. Bark —1H 67
(off St Margarets)
Basing Ho. Yd. E2 —3E **62** (1D **142**)
Basing Pl. E2 —3E **62** (1D **142**)
Basing St. W11 —6H **59**
Basing Way. N3 —3J **27**
Basing Way. Th Dit —7A **118**
Basire St. N1 —1C **62**
Baskerville Rd. SW18 —7C **92**
Basket Gdns. SE9 —5C **98**
Baslow Clo. Harr —1H **23**
Baslow Wlk. E5 —4K **47**
Basnett Rd. SW11 —3E **92**
Bassano St. SE22 —5F **95**
Bassant Rd. SE18 —6K **83**
Bassein Pk. Rd. W12 —2B **74**
Bassett Gdns. Iswth —7G **71**
Bassett Rd. E7 —4B **50**
Bassett Rd. W10 —6F **59**
Bassett St. NW5 —6E **44**
Bassett Way. Gnfd —6F **55**
Bassingham Rd. SW18 —7A **92**
Bassingham Rd. Wemb —6D **40**
Basswood Clo. SE15 —3H **95**
Bastable Av. Bark —2J **67**
Basterfield Ho. EC1 —4C **62** (4L **141**)
(off Golden La. Est.)
Bastion Highwalk. EC2
(off London Wall) —5D 62 (6A 142)
Bastion Rd. SE2 —5C **84**
Bastion Ho. EC2 —5C 62 (6M 141)
(off London Wall)
Baston Mnr. Rd Kes —3K **137**
Baston Mnr. Rd. Brom —3K **137**
Baston Rd. Brom —2K **137**
Bastwick St. EC1 —4C **62** (3L **141**)
Basuto Rd. SW6 —1J **91**
Batavia M. SE14 —7A **80**
Batavia Rd. N19 —2J **45**
Batavia Rd. SE14 —7A **80**
Batchelor St. N1 —1A **62**
Bateman Clo. Bark —6G **51**
Bateman Rd. E4 —6H **19**
Bateman's Bldgs. W1
(off Bateman St.) —6H 61 (8A 140)
Bateman's Row. EC2
—4E **62** (3D **142**)
Bates Cres. SW16 —7G **109**
Bates Cres. Croy —5A **134**
Bateson St. SE18 —4J **83**
Bates Point. E13 —1J 65
(off Pelly Rd.)
Bate St. E14 —7B **64**
Bath Clo. SE15 —1J **95**
Bath Ct. EC1 —4A 62 (4G 141)
(off St Lukes Est.)
Bath Ct. EC1 —3E 62 (2C 142)
(off Bath Pl.)
Bathgate Rd. SW19 —3F **107**
Bath Ho. Rd. Bedd —1J **133**
Bath Pas. King T —2D **118**
Bath Pl. EC2 —3E **62** (2C **142**)
Bath Pl. W6 —5E 74
(off Square, The)
Bath Pl. Barn —3C **4**

Bath Rd. E7 —6B **50**
Bath Rd. N9 —2C **18**
Bath Rd. W4 —4A **74**
Bath Rd. Houn —1A **86**
Bath Rd. Mitc —3B **122**
Bath Rd. Romf —6E **36**
Baths Rd. Brom —4B **128**
Bath St. EC1 —3C **62** (2M **141**)
Bath Ter. SE1 —3C **78** (7L **147**)
Bathurst Av. SW19 —1K **121**
Bathurst Gdns. NW10 —2D **58**
Bathurst M. W2 —7B **60** (9B **138**)
Bathurst Rd. Ilf —1F **51**
Bathurst St. W2 —7B **60** (9B **138**)
Bathway. SE18 —4E **82**
Batley Pl. N16 —3F **47**
Batley Rd. N16 —3F **47**
Batley Rd. Enf —1H **7**
Batman Clo. W12 —1D **74**
Batoum Gdns. W6 —3E **74**
Batson St. W12 —2C **74**
Batsworth Rd. Mitc —3B **122**
Battenberg Wlk. SE19 —6E **110**
Batten Clo. E6 —6D **66**
Batten Ho. SW4 —5G **93**
Batten St. SW11 —3C **92**
Battersby Rd. SE6 —2F **113**
Battersea Bri. SW3 & SW11 —7B **76**
Battersea Bri. Rd. SW11 —7C **76**
Battersea Chu. Rd. SW11 —1B **92**
Battersea High St. SW11 —1B **92**
Battersea Pk. Rd. SW11 & SW8
—2C **92**
Battersea Rise. SW11 —5C **92**
Battersea Sq. SW11 —1B **92**
Battery Rd. SE28 —2J **83**
Batteson St. SE11 —4J **83**
Battishill St. N1 —7B **46**
Battis, The. Romf —6K **37**
Battlebridge Ct. N1 —2J 61
(off Wharfdale Rd.)
Battle Bri. La. SE1 —1E **78** (3C **148**)
Battle Bri. Rd. NW1 —2J **61**
Battle Clo. SW19 —6A **108**
Battledean Rd. N5 —5B **46**
Battle Rd. Belv & Erii —4J **85**
Batty St. E1 —6G **63**
Baudwin Rd. SE6 —2G **113**
Baugh Rd. Sidc —5C **116**
Baulk, The. SW18 —7J **91**
Bavant Rd. SW16 —2J **123**
Bavaria Rd. N19 —2J **45**
Bavent Rd. SE5 —2C **94**
Bawdale Rd. SE22 —5F **95**
Bawdsey Av. Ilf —4K **35**
Bawtree Rd. SE14 —7A **80**
Bawtry Rd. N20 —3J **15**
Baxendale. N20 —2F **15**
Baxendale St. E2 —3G **63**
Baxter Rd. E16 —6A **66**
Baxter Rd. N1 —6D **46**
Baxter Rd. N18 —4C **18**
Baxter Rd. Ilf —5F **51**
Bayard Ct. Bexh —4H **101**
Bay Ct. W5 —3E **72**
Baydon Ct. Short —3H **127**
Bayer Ho. EC1 —4C 62 (4L 141)
(off Golden La.)
Bayes Clo. SE26 —5J **111**
Bayfield Rd. SE9 —4B **98**
Bayford Rd. NW10 —3F **59**
Bayford St. E8 —7H **47**
Bayham Pl. NW1 —1G **61**
Bayham Rd. W4 —3K **73**
Bayham Rd. Mord —4K **121**
Bayham St. NW1 —1G **61**
Bayley St. WC1 —5H **61** (6A **140**)
Bayley Wlk. SE2 —5E **84**

Baylin Rd. SW18 —6K **91**
Baylis Rd. SE1 —2A **78** (5G **147**)
Bayliss Av. SE28 —7D **68**
Bayne Clo. E6 —6D **66**
Baynes Clo. Enf —1B **8**
Baynes M. NW3 —6B **44**
Baynes Pl. NW1 —7G **45**
Baynes St. NW1 —7G **45**
Baynham Clo. Bex —6F **101**
Bayonne Rd. W6 —6G **75**
Bays Ct. Edgw —5C **12**
Bayston Rd. N16 —3F **47**
Bayswater Rd. W2 —7K **59**
Bay Tree Clo. Brom —1B **128**
Baytree Clo. Sidc —1J **115**
Baytree Ct. SW2 —4K **93**
Baytree Ho. E4 —7J **9**
Baytree Rd. SW2 —4K **93**
Bazalgette Clo. N Mald —5K **119**
Bazalgette Gdns. N Mald —5K **119**
Bazely St. E14 —7E **64**
Bazile Rd. N21 —6F **7**
Beacham Clo. SE7 —5B **82**
Beachborough Rd. Brom —4E **112**
Beachcroft Rd. E11 —3G **49**
Beachcroft Way. N19 —1H **45**
Beach Gro. Felt —2E **102**
Beach Ho. Felt —2E **102**
Beachy Rd. E3 —7C **48**
Beacon Gro. Cars —4E **132**
Beacon Hill. N7 —5J **45**
Beacon Rd. SE13 —6F **97**
Beacons Clo. E6 —5C **66**
Beaconsfield Clo. N11 —5K **15**
Beaconsfield Clo. SE3 —6J **81**
Beaconsfield Clo. W4 —5J **73**
Beaconsfield Pde. SE9 —4C **114**
Beaconsfield Rd. E10 —3E **48**
Beaconsfield Rd. E16 —4H **65**
Beaconsfield Rd. E17 —6B **32**
Beaconsfield Rd. N9 —3B **18**
Beaconsfield Rd. N11 —3K **15**
Beaconsfield Rd. N15 —4E **30**
Beaconsfield Rd. NW10 —6B **42**
Beaconsfield Rd. SE3 —7H **81**
Beaconsfield Rd. SE9 —2C **114**
Beaconsfield Rd. SE17 —5D **78**
Beaconsfield Rd. SW19 —6J **107**
Beaconsfield Rd. W4 —3K **73**
Beaconsfield Rd. W5 —2C **72**
Beaconsfield Rd. Bex —2K **117**
Beaconsfield Rd. Brom —3B **128**
Beaconsfield Rd. Croy —6D **124**
Beaconsfield Rd. Hay —1A **70**
Beaconsfield Rd. N Mald —2K **119**
Beaconsfield Rd. S'hall —1B **70**
Beaconsfield Rd. Surb —7F **119**
Beaconsfield Rd. Twic —6B **88**
Beaconsfield Ter. Romf —6D **36**
Beaconsfield Ter. Rd. W14 —3G **75**
Beaconsfield Wlk. E6 —6E **66**
Beaconsfield Wlk. SW6 —1H **91**
Beacontree Av. E17 —1F **33**
Beacontree Rd. E11 —7H **33**
Beadle's Pde. Dag —6J **53**
Beadlow Clo. Cars —6B **122**
Beadman Pl. SE27 —4B **110**
Beadman St. SE27 —4B **110**
Beadnell Rd. SE23 —1K **111**
Beadon Rd. W6 —4E **74**
Beadon Rd. Brom —4J **127**
Beaford Gro. SW20 —3G **121**
Beak St. W1 —7G **61** (9M **139**)
Beal Clo. Well —1A **100**
Beale Clo. N13 —5G **17**
Beale Pl. E3 —2B **64**
Beale Rd. E3 —1B **64**
Beal Rd. Ilf —2E **50**
Beam Av. Dag —1H **69**

Beaminster Gdns. Ilf —2F 35
Beaminster Ho. SW8 —7K 77
(off Dorset Rd.)
Beamish Dri. Bush —1B 10
Beamish Ga. NW1 —7H 45
Beamish N9 —1B 18
Beam Vs. Dag —2K 69
Beanacre Clo. E9 —6B 48
Bean Rd. Bexh —4D 100
Beanshaw. SE9 —4E 114
Beansland Gro. Romf —3E 36
Bear All. EC4 —6B 62 (7J 141)
Bear Clo. Romf —6H 37
Beardell St. SE19 —6F 111
Beardow Gro. N14 —6B 6
Beard Rd. King T —5F 105
Beardsfield. E13 —2J 65
Beard's Hill. Hamp —7E 102
Beardsley Way. W3 —3F 57
Bearfield Rd. King T —7E 104
Bear Gdns. SE1 —1C 78 (2L 147)
Bear La. SE1 —1B 78 (2K 147)
Bear Rd. Felt —4B 102
Bearsted Rise. SE4 —5B 96
Bearsted Ter. Beck —1C 126
Bear St. WC2 —7H 61 (9B 140)
Beatrice Av. SW16 —3K 123
Beatrice Av. Wemb —5E 40
Beatrice Clo. E13 —4J 65
Beatrice Pl. W8 —3K 75
Beatrice Rd. E17 —5C 32
Beatrice Rd. N4 —3A 30
Beatrice Rd. N9 —7D 8
Beatrice Rd. SE1 —4G 79
Beatrice Rd. Rich —5F 89
Beatrice Rd. S'hall —1D 70
Beatson Wlk. SE16 —1A 80
Beattock Rise. N10 —4F 29
Beatty Ho. E14 —2C 80
(off Admirals Way)
Beatty Rd. N16 —4E 46
Beatty Rd. Stan —6H 11
Beatty St. NW1 —2G 61
Beattyville Gdns. Ilf —4E 34
Beauchamp Clo. W4 —3J 73
Beauchamp Ct. Stan —5H 11
Beauchamp Pl. SW3
—3C 76 (6D 144)
Beauchamp Rd. E7 —7K 49
Beauchamp Rd. SE19 —1D 124
Beauchamp Rd. SW11 —4C 92
Beauchamp Rd. Sutt —4J 131
Beauchamp Rd. Twic —7A 88
Beauchamp St. EC1
—5A 62 (6G 141)
Beauchamp Ter. SW15 —3D 90
Beauclerc Rd. W6 —3D 74
Beauclerk Clo. Felt —1A 102
Beaufort. E6 —6G 67
Beaufort Av. Harr —4A 24
Beaufort Clo. E4 —6J 19
Beaufort Clo. SW15 —7D 90
Beaufort Clo. W5 —5F 57
Beaufort Clo. Romf —4J 37
Beaufort Ct. N11 —5A 16
(off Limes Av., The)
Beaufort Ct. New Bar —5F 5
Beaufort Ct. Rich —4C 104
Beaufort Dri. NW11 —4J 27
Beaufort Gdns. NW4 —6E 26
Beaufort Gdns. SW3
—3C 76 (6D 144)
Beaufort Gdns. SW16 —7K 109
Beaufort Gdns. Houn —1C 86
Beaufort Gdns. Ilf —1E 50
Beaufort M. SW6 —6H 75
Beaufort Pk. NW11 —4J 27

Beaufort Rd. W5 —5F 57
Beaufort Rd. King T —4E 118
Beaufort Rd. Rich —4C 104
Beaufort Rd. Twic —7C 88
Beaufort St. SW3 —6B 76
Beaufort Way. Eps —7C 130
Beaufoy Rd. SE27 —3B 110
Beaufoy Rd. N17 —7K 17
Beaufoy Wlk. SE11 —4K 77 (9F 146)
Beaulieau Gdns. N21 —7H 7
Beaulieu Av. SE26 —4H 111
Beaulieu Clo. NW9 —4A 26
Beaulieu Clo. SE5 —3D 94
Beaulieu Clo. Houn —5D 86
Beaulieu Clo. Mitc —1E 122
Beaulieu Clo. Twic —6D 88
Beaulieu Dri. Pinn —6B 22
Beaulieu Pl. W4 —3J 73
Beaumanor Gdns. SE9 —4E 114
Beaumaris Dri. Wfd G —7G 21
Beaumaris Grn. NW9 —6A 26
(off Pendragon Wlk.)
Beaumont Av. W14 —5H 75
Beaumont Av. Harr —6F 23
Beaumont Av. Rich —3F 89
Beaumont Av. Wemb —5C 40
Beaumont Clo. King T —7G 105
Beaumont Ct. E5 —3H 47
Beaumont Ct. W4 —5J 73
Beaumont Cres. W14 —5H 75
Beaumont Gdns. NW3 —3J 43
Beaumont Gro. E1 —4K 63
Beaumont Ho. E10 —7D 32
Beaumont Ho. E15 —1H 65
(off John St.)
Beaumont M. W1 —5E 60 (5H 139)
Beaumont Pl. W1 —4G 61 (3M 139)
Beaumont Pl. Barn —1C 4
Beaumont Pl. Iswth —5K 87
Beaumont Rise. N19 —1H 45
Beaumont Rd. E10 —7D 32
Beaumont Rd. E13 —3K 65
Beaumont Rd. SE19 —6C 110
Beaumont Rd. SW19 —7G 91
Beaumont Rd. W4 —3J 73
Beaumont Rd. Orp —6H 129
Beaumont Sq. E1 —5K 63
Beaumont St. W1 —5E 60 (5H 139)
Beaumont Wlk. NW3 —7D 44
Beauvais Ter. N'holt —3B 54
Beauval Rd. SE22 —6F 95
Beav Callender Clo. SW8 —3F 93
Beaverbank Rd. SE9 —1H 115
Beaver Clo. SE20 —7G 111
Beaver Clo. Hamp —7F 103
Beavercote Wlk. Belv —5F 85
Beaver Ct. Beck —7D 112
Beaver Gro. N'holt —3C 54
Beavers Cres. Houn —4A 86
Beavers La. Houn —2A 86
Beavers Lodge. Sidc —4K 115
Beaverwood Rd. Chst —5J 115
Bede Clo. Pinn —1B 22
Bedefield. E15 —3J 61 (2D 140)
Bedens Rd. Sidc —6E 116
Bede Rd. Romf —6C 36
Bedfont Clo. Mitc —2E 122
Bedford Av. WC1 —5H 61 (6B 140)
Bedford Av. Barn —5C 4
Bedford Av. Hay —5A 54
Bedfordbury. WC2 —7J 61 (1C 146)
Bedford Clo. N10 —7K 15
Bedford Corner. W4 —4A 74
(off South Pde.)
Bedford Ct. WC2 —7J 61 (1C 146)
Bedford Ct. Wemb —3F 41
Bedford Gdns. W8 —1J 75
Bedford Hill. SW12 & SW16 —1F 109
Bedford Ho. SW4 —4J 93
(off Solon New Rd. Est.)

Beckenham. Beck —1K 125
Beckenham Rd. W Wick —7E 126
Beckers, The. N16 —3G 47
Becket Av. E6 —3E 66
Becket Clo. SE25 —6G 125
Becket Clo. SW19 —1K 121
(off High Path)
Becket Fold. Harr —5K 23
Becket Ho. SE1 —2D 78 (5A 148)
(off Tabard St.)
Becket Rd. N18 —4D 18
Becket St. SE1 —3D 78 (6A 148)
Beckett Clo. NW10 —6A 42
Beckett Clo. SW16 —2H 109
Beckett Clo. Belv —3F 85
Beckett Ho. SW9 —2J 93
Becketts Ho. Ilf —3E 50
Becketts Pl. Hamp W —1D 118
Beckford Dri. Orp —7H 129
Beckford Rd. N16 —5E 46
Beckford Pl. SE17 —5C 78
Beckford Rd. Croy —6F 125
Becklow Gdns. W12 —1C 74
(off Becklow Rd.)
Becklow Rd. W12 —2B 74
Beck River Pk. Beck —1C 126
Beck Rd. E8 —1H 63
Becks Rd. Sidc —3A 116
Beckton Retail Pk. E6 —5E 66
Beckton Rd. E16 —5H 65
Beck Way. Beck —3B 126
Beckway Rd. SW16 —2H 123
Beckway St. SE17 —4E 78 (9B 148)
(in two parts)
Beckwith Rd. SE24 —5D 94
Beclands Rd. SW17 —6E 108
Becmead Av. SW16 —4H 109
Becmead Av. Harr —5B 24
Becondale Rd. SE19 —5E 110
Becontree Av. Dag —4B 52
Bective Pl. SW15 —4F 91
Bective Rd. E7 —4J 49
Bective Rd. SW15 —4H 91
Becton Pl. Eri —7H 85
Bedale Rd. Enf —1H 7
Bedale St. SE1 —1D 78 (3A 148)
Beddalls Farm Ct. E6 —5C 66
Beddington Farm Rd. Bedd —7J 123
Beddington Farm Rd. Croy —7J 123
Beddington Gdns. Cars & Wall —6E 132
Beddington Grn. Orp —1K 129
Beddington Gro. Wall —5H 133
Beddington La. Croy —5G 123
Beddington Pk. Cotts. Wall —3H 133
Beddington Path. St P —1K 129
Beddington Rd. Ilf —7K 35
Beddington Rd. Orp —1J 129
Beddington Ter. Croy —7K 123
Bede St. E17 —3F 33
Bedivere Rd. Brom —3J 113
Bedlow Way. Croy —4K 133
Bedonwell Rd. Bexh & Belv —1F 101
Bedser Clo. T Hth —3C 124
Bedser Dri. Gnfd —5H 39
Bedwardine Rd. SE19 —7E 110
Bedwell Ct. Romf —7D 36
(off Broomfield Rd.)
Bedwell Ho. SW9 —2A 94
Bedwell Rd. N17 —1E 30
Bedwell Rd. Belv —5G 85
Bedwin Way. SE16 —5H 79
Beeby Rd. E16 —5K 65
Beech Av. N20 —1H 15
Beech Av. W3 —1A 74
Beech Av. Bren —7B 72
Beech Av. Buck H —2E 20
Beech Av. Ruis —1A 38
Beech Av. Sidc —7A 100
Beech Clo. N9 —6B 8
Beech Clo. SE8 —6C 80
Beech Clo. SW15 —7C 90
Beech Clo. SW19 —6E 106
Beech Clo. Cars —2D 132
Beech Clo. Houn —7C 70
Beech Ct. E17 —3F 33
Beech Ct. Beck —7B 112
Beech Ct. Surb —7D 118
Beech Cres. Ct. N5 —4B 46

Bedford Pk. W4 —3A 74
Bedford Pk. Croy —1C 134
Bedford Pk. Corner. W4 —4A 74
Bedford Pk. Mans. W4 —4K 73
Bedford Pas. SW6 —7G 75
(off Dawes Rd.)
Bedford Pas. W1 —5G 61 (5M 139)
Bedford Pl. W1 —5G 61
Bedford Pl. WC1 —5J 61 (5C 140)
Bedford Pl. Croy —1D 134
Bedford Rd. E6 —1E 66
Bedford Rd. E17 —2C 32
Bedford Rd. E18 —2J 33
Bedford Rd. N2 —3C 28
Bedford Rd. N8 —6H 29
Bedford Rd. N9 —7C 8
Bedford Rd. N15 —4E 30
Bedford Rd. N22 —1J 29
Bedford Rd. NW7 —2F 13
Bedford Rd. SW4 —4J 93
Bedford Rd. W4 —3K 73
Bedford Rd. W13 —7B 56
Bedford Rd. Harr —6G 23
Bedford Rd. Sidc —3J 115
Bedford Rd. Twic —3H 103
Bedford Rd. Wor Pk —2E 130
Bedford Row. WC1 —5K 61 (5F 140)
Bedford Sq. WC1 —5H 61 (6B 140)
Bedford St. WC2 —7J 61 (9C 140)
Bedford Way. WC1 —4H 61 (4B 140)
Bedgebury Gdns. SW19 —2G 107
Bedgebury Rd. SE9 —4B 98
Bedlow Way. Croy —4K 133
Bedonwell Rd. Bexh & Belv —1F 101
Bedser Clo. T Hth —3C 124
Bedser Dri. Gnfd —5H 39
Bedwardine Rd. SE19 —7E 110
Bedwin Way. SE16 —5H 79
Beeby Rd. E16 —5K 65
Beech Av. N20 —1H 15
Beech Av. W3 —1A 74
Beech Copse. Brom —2D 128
Beech Copse. S Croy —5E 134
Beech Ct. E17 —3F 33
Beech Ct. Beck —7B 112
Beech Ct. Surb —7D 118
Beech Cres. Ct. N5 —4B 46

Beechdale Rd. SW2 —6K 93
Beech Dri. N2 —2D 28
Beechen Cliff Way. Iswth —2K 87
Beechen Gro. Pinn —3D 22
Beechen Pl. SE23 —2K 111
Beeches Av. Cars —7C 132
Beeches Clo. SE20 —1J 125
Beeches Rd. SW17 —3C 108
Beeches Rd. Sutt —1G 131
Beeches, The. E12 —7D 50
Beeches, The. Houn —1F 87
Beeches, The. S Croy —5D 134
Beeches Wlk. Cars —7B 132
Beechcroft Cotts. Brom —2A 128
Beechfield Gdns. Romf —7J 37
Beechfield Rd. N4 —6C 30
Beechfield Rd. SE6 —1B 112
Beechfield Rd. Brom —2A 128
Beechfield Rd. Eri —7K 85
Beech Gdns. EC2 —5C 62 (5L 141)
(off Beech St.)
Beech Gdns. W5 —2E 72
Beech Gdns. Dag —7J 53
Beech Gro. Mitc —5H 123
Beech Gro. N Mald —3K 119
Beech Hale Cres. E4 —7A 20
Beech Hall Rd. E4 —7K 19
Beech Hill. Barn —1G 5
Beech Hill Av. Barn —1F 5
Beech Ho. Roy. Croy —3D 134
Beechhill Rd. SE9 —5E 98
Beech La. Buck H —2E 20
Beech Lawns. N12 —5G 15
Beechmont Clo. Brom —5G 113
Beechmore Gdns. Sutt —2F 131
Beechmore Rd. SW11 —1D 92
Beechmount Av. W7 —5H 55
Beecholme. N12 —4E 14
Beecholme Av. Mitc —1F 123
Beecholme Est. E5 —3H 47
Beech Rd. N11 —6D 16
Beech Rd. SW16 —2K 123
Beech Row. Ham —4E 104
Beech St. EC2 —5C 62 (5L 141)
Beech St. Romf —4J 37
Beech Tree Clo. Stan —5H 11
Beech Tree Glade. E4 —1C 20
Beech Tree Pl. Sutt —5J 131
Beechvale Clo. N12 —5H 15
Beech Wlk. NW7 —6F 13
Beech Way. NW10 —7K 41
Beechway. Bex —6D 100
Beech Way. Twic —3E 102
Beechwood Av. N3 —3H 27
Beechwood Av. Gnfd —3F 55
Beechwood Av. Harr —3F 39
Beechwood Av. Rich —1G 89
Beechwood Av. T Hth —4B 124
Beechwood Circ. Harr —3F 39
Beechwood Clo. N2 —4D 28
(off Western Rd.)
Beechwood Clo. NW7 —5F 13
Beechwood Clo. Surb —7C 118
Beechwood Ct. SE19 —5F 111
Beechwood Ct. W4 —6K 73
Beechwood Ct. Cars —4D 132
Beechwood Cres. Bexh —3D 100
Beechwood Dri. Wfd G —5C 20
Beechwood Gdns. NW10 —3F 57
Beechwood Gdns. Harr —3F 39
Beechwood Gdns. Ilf —5D 34
Beechwood Gro. W3 —7A 58
Beechwood Gro. Surb —7C 118
Beechwood Hall. N3 —3H 27
Beechwood M. N9 —2B 18
Beechwood Pk. E18 —3J 33

Beresford Rd. N2 —3C **28**
Beresford Rd. N5 —5D **46**
Beresford Rd. N8 —5A **30**
Beresford Rd. Harr —5H **23**
Beresford Rd. King T —1F **119**
Beresford Rd. N Mald —4J **119**
Beresford Rd. S'hall —1B **70**
Beresford St. SE18 —4H **83**
Beresford Sq. SE18 —4F **83**
Beresford St. SE18 —3F **83**
Beresford Ter. N5 —5C **46**
Berestede Rd. W6 —5B **74**
Bere St. E1 —7K **63**
Bergen Sq. SE16 —3A **80**
Berger Clo. Orp —6H **129**
Berger Rd. E9 —6K **47**
Berghem M. W14 —3F **75**
Bergholt Av. Ilf —5C **34**
Bergholt Cres. N16 —7E **30**
Bergholt M. NW1 —7G **45**
Bering Wlk. E16 —6B **66**
Berkeley Av. Bexh —1D **100**
Berkeley Av. Gnfd —6J **39**
Berkeley Av. Ilf —2E **34**
Berkeley Av. Romf —1J **37**
Berkeley Clo. Bren —6A **72**
Berkeley Clo. King T —7E **104**
Berkeley Clo. Orp —7J **129**
Berkeley Ct. N3 —1K **27**
Berkeley Ct. NW11 —7H 27
(off Ravenscroft Av.)
Berkeley Ct. Surb —7D **118**
Berkeley Ct. Wall —3G **133**
Berkeley Cres. Barn —5G **5**
Berkeley Gdns. N21 —7J **7**
Berkeley Gdns. W8 —1J **75**
Berkeley Ho. Bren —6D 72
(off Albany Rd.)
Berkeley M. W1 —6D **60** (8F **138**)
Berkeley Pl. SW19 —6F **107**
Berkeley Rd. E12 —5C **50**
Berkeley Rd. N8 —5H **29**
Berkeley Rd. N15 —6D **30**
Berkeley Rd. NW9 —4G **25**
Berkeley Rd. SW13 —1C **90**
Berkeley Sq. W1 —7F **61** (1K **145**)
Berkeley St. W1 —7F **61** (1K **145**)
Berkeley Wlk. N7 —2K 45
(off Durham Rd.)
Berkeley Waye. Houn —6B **70**
Berkhampstead Rd. Belv —5G **85**
Berkhamsted Av. Wemb —6F **41**
Berkley Gro. NW1 —7D **44**
Berkley Rd. NW1 —7D **44**
Berkshire Gdns. N13 —6F **17**
Berkshire Gdns. N18 —5C **18**
Berkshire Rd. E9 —6B **48**
Berkshire Sq. Mitc —4J **123**
Berkshire Way. Mitc —4J **123**
Bermans Way. NW10 —4A **42**
Bermondsey Sq. SE1

       —3E **78** (6D **148**)
Bermondsey St. SE1

       —1E **78** (3C **148**)
Bermondsey Trading Est. SE16

       —5J **79**
Bermondsey Wall E. SE16 —2G **79**
Bermondsey Wall W. SE16 —2G **79**
Bernal Clo. SE28 —7D **68**
Bernard Ashley Dri. SE7 —5K **81**
Bernard Av. W13 —3B **72**
Bernard Cassidy St. E16 —5H **65**
Bernard Gdns. SW19 —5H **107**
Bernard Rd. N15 —5F **31**
Bernard Rd. Romf —7J **37**
Bernard Rd. Wall —4F **133**
Bernard St. WC1 —4J **61** (4C **140**)
Bernays Clo. Stan —6H **11**

Bernay's Gro. SW9 —4K **93**
Bernel Dri. Croy —3B **136**
Berne Rd. T Hth —5C **124**
Berners Dri. W13 —7A **56**
Berners M. W1 —5G **61** (6M **139**)
Berners Pl. W1 —6G **61** (7M **139**)
Berners Rd. N1 —1B **62**
Berners Rd. N22 —1A **30**
Berners St. W1 —5G **61** (6M **139**)
Berney Ho. Beck —5A **126**
Berney Rd. Croy —7D **124**
Bernville Way. Harr —5F **25**
Bernwell Rd. E4 —3B **20**
Berridge Grn. Edgw —7B **12**
Berridge M. NW6 —5J 43
(off Hillfield Rd.)
Berridge Rd. SE19 —5D **110**
Berriman Rd. N7 —3K **45**
Berriton Rd. Harr —1D **38**
Berrybank Clo. E4 —2K **19**
Berry Clo. N21 —1G **17**
Berry Clo. NW10 —7A **42**
Berry Ct. Houn —5D **86**
Berrydale Rd. Hay —4C **54**
Berryfield Clo. E17 —4D **32**
Berryfield Clo. Brom —1C **128**
Berryfield Rd. SE17 —5B **78**
Berryhill. SE9 —4F **99**
Berry Hill. Stan —4J **11**
Berryhill Gdns. SE9 —4F **99**
Berrylands. SW20 —4E **120**
Berrylands. Surb —6F **119**
(in two parts)
Berrylands Rd. Surb —6F **119**
Berry La. SE21 —4D **110**
Berryman Clo. Dag —3C **52**
Berryman's La. SE26 —4K **111**
Berrymead Gdns. W3 —1J **73**
Berrymede Rd. W4 —3K **73**
Berry Pl. EC1 —3B **62** (2K **141**)
Berry St. EC1 —4B **62** (3K **141**)
Berry Way. W5 —3E **72**
Bertal Rd. SW17 —4B **108**
Berthon St. SE8 —7C **80**
Bertie Rd. NW10 —6C **42**
Bertie Rd. SE26 —6K **111**
Bertram Cotts. SW19 —7J **107**
Bertram Rd. NW4 —6C **26**
Bertram Rd. Enf —4B **8**
Bertram Rd. King T —7G **105**
Bertram St. N19 —3F **45**
Bertrand St. SE13 —3D **96**
Bertrand Way. SE28 —7B **68**
Bert Rd. T Hth —5C **124**
Bert Way. Enf —4A **8**
Berwick Av. Hay —6B **54**
Berwick Clo. Stan —6E **10**
Berwick Cres. Sidc —6J **99**
Berwick Ho. N2 —2B **28**
Berwick Rd. E16 —6K **65**
Berwick Rd. N22 —1B **30**
Berwick Rd. Well —1B **100**
Berwick St. W1 —6G **61** (7M **139**)
Berwick Tower. SE14 —6A **80**
Berwick Way. Orp —7K **129**
Berwyn Av. Houn —1F **87**
Berwyn Rd. SE24 —1B **110**
Berwyn Rd. Rich —4H **89**
Beryl Av. E6 —5C **66**
Beryl Rd. W6 —5F **75**
Berystede. King T —7H **105**
Besant Ct. N1 —5D **46**
Besant Rd. NW2 —4G **43**
Besant Wlk. N7 —2K **45**
Besant Way. NW10 —5J **41**
Besley St. SW16 —6G **109**
Bessborough Gdns. SW1 —5H **77**
Bessborough Pl. SW1 —5H **77**

Bessborough Rd. SW15 —1C **106**
Bessborough Rd. Harr —1H **39**
Bessborough St. SW1 —5H **77**
Bessemer Rd. SE5 —2C **94**
Bessie Lansbury Clo. E6 —6E **66**
Besson St. SE14 —1J **95**
Bessy St. E2 —3J **63**
Bestwood St. SE8 —4K **79**
Beswick M. NW6 —6K **43**
Betchworth Clo. Sutt —5B **132**
Betchworth Rd. Ilf —2J **51**
Betchworth Way. New Ad —7E **136**
Bethal Est. SE1 —1E 78 (3D 148)
(off Tooley St.)
Betham Rd. Gnfd —4H **55**
Bethecar Rd. Harr —5J **23**
Bethell Av. E16 —4H **65**
Bethell Av. Ilf —7E **34**
Bethel Rd. Well —3C **100**
Bethersden Clo. Beck —7B **112**
Bethnal Grn. Rd. E1 & E2

       —4F **63** (3E **142**)
Bethune Av. N11 —4J **15**
Bethune Clo. N16 —1E **46**
Bethune Rd. N16 —7D **30**
Bethune Rd. NW10 —4K **57**
Bethwin Rd. SE5 —7B **78**
Betjeman Clo. Pinn —4E **22**
Betony Clo. Croy —1K **135**
Betoyne Av. E4 —4B **20**
Betstyle Cir. N11 —4A **16**
Betstyle Ho. N10 —7K **15**
Betstyle Rd. N11 —4A **16**
Betterton Dri. Sidc —2E **116**
Betterton Rd. Rain —3K **69**
Betterton St. WC2 —6J **61** (8D **140**)
Bettons Pk. E15 —1G **65**
Bettridge Rd. SW6 —2H **91**
Betts Clo. Beck —2A **126**
Betts M. E17 —6B **32**
Betts Rd. E16 —7K **65**
Betts St. E1 —7H **63**
Betts Way. SE20 —1H **125**
Betts Way. Surb —7B **118**
Beulah Av. T Hth —2C **124**
Beulah Clo. Edgw —3C **12**
Beulah Cres. T Hth —2C **124**
Beulah Gro. Croy —6C **124**
Beulah Hill. SE19 —6B **110**
Beulah Path. E17 —5E **32**
Beulah Rd. E17 —5D **32**
Beulah Rd. SW19 —7H **107**
Beulah Rd. Sutt —4J **131**
Beulah Rd. T Hth —2C **124**
Bevan Av. Bark —1A **52**
Bevan Ct. Croy —5A **134**
Bevan Rd. SE2 —5B **84**
Bevan Rd. Barn —4J **5**
Bevan St. N1 —1C **62**
Bev Callender Clo. SW8 —3F **93**
Bevenden St. N1 —3D **62** (1B **142**)
Beveridge Rd. NW10 —7A **42**
Beverley Av. SW20 —1B **120**
Beverley Av. Houn —4D **86**
Beverley Av. Sidc —7K **99**
Beverley Clo. N21 —1H **17**
Beverley Clo. SW11 —4B **92**
Beverley Clo. SW13 —2C **90**
Beverley Clo. Enf —4K **7**
Beverley Ct. N14 —7B **6**
Beverley Ct. SE4 —3B **96**
Beverley Ct. W4 —5J **73**
Beverley Ct. Harr —3D **23**
Beverley Ct. Houn —4D **86**
Beverley Ct. Kent —4C **24**
Beverley Cres. Wfd G —1K **33**

Beverley Dri. Edgw —3G **25**
Beverley Gdns. NW11 —7G **27**
Beverley Gdns. SW13 —3B **90**
Beverley Gdns. Stan —1A **24**
Beverley Gdns. Wemb —1F **41**
Beverley Gdns. Wor Pk —1C **130**
Beverley La. SW15 —3B **106**
Beverley La. King T —7A **106**
Beverley M. E4 —6A **20**
Beverley Path. SW13 —2B **90**
Beverley Rd. E4 —6A **20**
Beverley Rd. E6 —3B **66**
Beverley Rd. SE20 —2H **125**
Beverley Rd. SW13 —3B **90**
Beverley Rd. W4 —5B **74**
Beverley Rd. Bexh —2J **101**
Beverley Rd. Dag —4E **52**
Beverley Rd. King T —1C **118**
Beverley Rd. Mitc —4H **123**
Beverley Rd. N Mald —4C **120**
Beverley Rd. Ruis —3A **38**
Beverley Rd. S'hall —4C **70**
Beverley Rd. Wor Pk —2E **130**
Beverley Way. N Mald & SW20

       —1B **120**
Beversbrook Rd. N19 —3H **45**
Beverstone Rd. SW2 —5K **93**
Beverstone Rd. T Hth —4A **124**
Bevill Allen Clo. SW17 —5D **108**
Bevin Clo. SE16 —1A **80**
Bevington Rd. W10 —5G **59**
Bevington Rd. Beck —2D **126**
Bevington St. SE16 —2G **79**
Bevin Way. WC1 —2A **62** (1G **141**)
Bevis Marks. EC3 —6E **62** (7D **142**)
Bewcastle Gdns. Enf —4D **6**
Bew Ct. SE22 —7G **95**
Bewdley St. N1 —7A **46**
Bewick St. SW8 —2F **93**
Bewley St. E1 —7J **63**
Bewlys Rd. SE27 —5B **110**
Bexhill Clo. Felt —2C **102**
Bexhill Rd. N11 —5C **16**
Bexhill Rd. SE4 —6B **96**
Bexhill Rd. SW14 —3J **89**
Bexhill Wlk. E15 —1G **65**
Bexley Clo. Dart —5K **101**
Bexley Gdns. N9 —3J **17**
Bexley High St. Bex —7G **101**
Bexley La. Dart —5K **101**
Bexley La. Sidc —4C **116**
Bexley Rd. SE9 —5F **99**
Bexley Rd. Eri —7J **85**
(in two parts)
Beynon Rd. Cars —5D **132**
Bianca Rd. SE15 —6G **79**
Bibsworth Rd. N3 —2H **27**
Bibury Clo. SE15 —6E **78**
Bicester Rd. Rich —3G **89**
Bickenhall St. W1 —5D **60** (5F **138**)
Bickersteth Rd. SW17 —6D **108**
Bickerton Rd. N19 —2G **45**
Bickley Cres. Brom —4C **128**
Bickley Pk. Rd. Brom —3C **128**
Bickley Rd. E10 —7D **32**
Bickley Rd. Brom —2B **128**
Bickley St. SW17 —5C **108**
Bicknell Rd. SE5 —3C **94**
Bicknoller Rd. Enf —1K **7**
Bicknor Rd. Orp —7J **129**
Bidborough Clo. Brom —5H **127**
Bidborough St. WC1

       —3J **61** (2C **140**)
Biddenden Way. SE9 —4E **114**
Bidder St. E16 —5G **65**
(in two parts)
Biddestone Rd. N7 —4K **45**
Biddulph Ho. SE18 —4D **82**

Biddulph Mans. W9 —3K **59**
(off Elgin Av.)
Biddulph Rd. W9 —3K **59**
Bideford Av. Gnfd —2B **56**
Bideford Clo. Edgw —1G **25**
Bideford Clo. Felt —3D **102**
Bideford Gdns. Enf —7K **7**
Bideford Rd. Brom —3H **113**
Bideford Rd. Enf —1G **9**
Bideford Rd. Ruis —3A **38**
Bideford Rd. Well —7B **84**
Bidwell Gdns. N11 —7B **16**
Bidwell St. SE15 —1H **95**
Bigbury Clo. N17 —7J **17**
Biggerstaff Rd. E15 —1E **64**
Biggerstaff St. N4 —2A **46**
Biggin Av. Mitc —1D **122**
Biggin Hill. SE19 —7B **110**
Biggin Way. SE19 —7B **110**
Bigginwood Rd. SW16 —7B **110**
Biggs Row. SW15 —3F **91**
Big Hill. E5 —1H **47**
Bigland St. E1 —6H **63**
Bignell Rd. SE18 —5F **83**
Bignold Rd. E7 —4J **49**
Bigwood Ct. NW11 —5K **27**
Bigwood Rd. NW11 —5K **27**
Billet Clo. Romf —3D 36
Billet Rd. E17 —1K **31**
Billet Rd. Romf —3B **36**
Bill Hamling Clo. SE9 —2D **114**
Billingford Clo. SE4 —4K **95**
Billing Pl. SW10 —7K **75**
Billing Rd. SW10 —7K **75**
Billingsgate Rd. E14 —7C **64**
Billing St. SW10 —7K **75**
Billington Rd. SE14 —7K **79**
Billiter Sq. EC3 —6E 62 (8D 142)
(off Fenchurch Av.)
Billiter St. EC3 —6E **62** (8D **142**)
Billson St. E14 —4E **80**
Bilsby Gro. SE9 —4B **114**
Bilsby Lodge. Wemb —3J 41
(off Chalklands)
Bilton Rd. Gnfd —1A **56**
Bilton Way. Enf —1F **9**
Bina Gdns. SW5 —4A **76**
Bincote Rd. Enf —3E **6**
Binden Rd. W12 —3B **74**
Bindon Grn. Mord —4K **121**
Binfield Rd. SW4 —1J **93**
Binfield Rd. S Croy —5F **135**
Bingfield St. N1 —1J **61**
(in two parts)
Bingham Pl. W1 —5E **60** (5G **139**)
Bingham Rd. Croy —1G **135**
Bingham St. N1 —6D **46**
Bingley Rd. E16 —6A **66**
Bingley Rd. Gnfd —4G **55**
Binney St. W1 —6E **60** (8H **139**)
Binns Rd. W4 —5A **74**
Binsey Wlk. SE2 —2C **84**
Binyon Cres. Stan —5E **10**
Birbetts Rd. SE9 —2D **114**
Birchanger Rd. SE25 —5G **125**
Birch Av. N13 —3H **17**
Birch Clo. E16 —5H **65**
Birch Clo. N19 —2G **45**
Birch Clo. SE15 —2G **95**
Birch Clo. Bren —7B **72**
Birch Clo. Buck H —3G **21**
Birch Clo. Romf —3H **37**
Birch Clo. Tedd —5A **104**
Birch Clo. Wall —4F **133**
Birchdale Gdns. Romf —7D **36**
Birchdale Rd. E7 —5A **50**
Birchdene Dri. SE28 —1A **84**
Birchen Clo. NW9 —2K **41**

irchend Clo. S Croy —6D **134**
irches Grn. NW9 —2K **41**
irches Clo. Mitc —3D **122**
irches Clo. Pinn —5C **22**
irches, The. N21 —6E **6**
irches, The. SE7 —6K **81**
irches, The. Pinn —7D **86**
irchfield St. E14 —7C **64**
irch Gdns. Dag —3J **53**
irch Grn. NW9 —7F **13**
irch Gro. SE12 —7H **97**
irch Gro. W3 —1G **73**
irch Gro. Well —4A **100**
irch Hill. Croy —5K **135**
Birch Ho. SW2 —6A **94**
  (off Tulse Hill)
irchington Clo. Bexh —1H **101**
irchington Ho. E5 —5H **47**
irchington Rd. N8 —6H **29**
irchington Rd. NW6 —1J **59**
irchington Rd. Surb —7F **119**
irchin La. EC3 —6D **62** (8B **142**)
irchlands Av. SW12 —7D **92**
irchmead Av. Pinn —4A **22**
irchmere Row. SE3 —2H **97**
irch Row. Brom —7E **128**
irch Tree Av. W Wick —5G **137**
irch Tree Way. Croy —2H **135**
irch Wlk. Eri —6J **85**
irch Wlk. Mitc —1F **123**
irchwood Av. N10 —3E **28**
irchwood Av. Beck —4B **126**
irchwood Av. Sidc —3B **116**
irchwood Av. Wall —3E **132**
irchwood Clo. Mord —4K **121**
irchwood Ct. Edgw —2J **25**
irchwood Dri. NW3 —3K **43**
irchwood Dri. Dart —4K **117**
irchwood Gro. Hamp —6E **102**
irchwood Pde. Wilm —4K **117**
irchwood Rd. SW17 —5F **109**
irchwood Rd. Orp —1H **129**
irchwood Rd. Swan & Dart
  —7J **117**
irdbrook Clo. Dag —7J **53**
irdbrook Rd. SE3 —3A **98**
irdcage Wlk. SW1 —2G **77** (5L **145**)
irdham Clo. Brom —5C **128**
irdhurst Av. S Croy —4D **134**
irdhurst Gdns. S Croy —4D **134**
irdhurst Rise. S Croy —5E **134**
irdhurst Rd. SW18 —5A **92**
irdhurst Rd. SW16 —6C **108**
irdhurst Rd. S Croy —5E **134**
ird in Bush Rd. SE15 —7G **79**
ird in Hand La. Brom —2B **128**
ird-in-Hand Pas. SE23 —2J **111**
Bird in Hand Yd. NW3 —4A **44**
  (off Hampstead High St.)
irdlington Rd. N9 —7C **8**
irdlip Clo. SE15 —6E **78**
irdlip Clo. SE15 —6E **78**
irds Farm Av. Romf —1H **37**
irdsfield La. E3 —1B **64**
ird St. W1 —6E **60** (8H **139**)
ird Wlk. Twic —1D **102**
irdwood Clo. Tedd —4J **103**
irkbeck Av. W3 —7J **57**
irkbeck Av. Gnfd —1G **55**
irkbeck Gdns. Wfd G —2D **20**
irkbeck Gro. W3 —2K **73**
irkbeck Hill. SE21 —1B **110**
irkbeck M. E8 —5F **47**

Birkbeck Pl. SE21 —2C **110**
Birkbeck Rd. E8 —5F **47**
Birkbeck Rd. N8 —4J **29**
Birkbeck Rd. N12 —5F **15**
Birkbeck Rd. N17 —1F **31**
Birkbeck Rd. NW7 —5G **13**
Birkbeck Rd. SW19 —5K **107**
Birkbeck Rd. W3 —1K **73**
Birkbeck Rd. W5 —4C **72**
Birkbeck Rd. Beck —2J **125**
Birkbeck Rd. Enf —1J **7**
Birkbeck Rd. Ilf —3H **35**
Birkbeck Rd. Romf —1K **53**
Birkbeck Rd. Sidc —3A **116**
Birkbeck St. E2 —3H **63**
Birkbeck Way. Gnfd —1H **55**
Birkdale Av. Pinn —3E **22**
Birkdale Clo. Orp —7H **129**
Birkdale Gdns. Croy —4A **135**
Birkdale Rd. SE2 —4A **84**
Birkdale Rd. W5 —4E **56**
Birkenhead Av. King T —2F **119**
Birkenhead St. WC1 —3J **61** (1D **140**)
Birkhall Rd. SE6 —1F **113**
Birkwood Clo. SW12 —1H **93**
Birley Rd. N20 —2F **15**
Birley St. SW11 —2E **92**
Birling Rd. Eri —7K **85**
Birnam Rd. N4 —2K **45**
Birnbeck Ct. NW11 —5H **27**
Birnbeck Ct. Barn —4A **4**
Birrell Ho. SW9 —2K **93**
  (off Stockwell Rd.)
Birse Cres. NW10 —3A **42**
Birstall Rd. N15 —5E **30**
Biscay Rd. W6 —5F **75**
Biscoe Clo. Houn —6E **70**
Biscoe Way. SE13 —3F **97**
Bisenden Rd. Croy —2E **134**
Bisham Clo. Cars —1D **132**
Bisham Gdns. N6 —1E **44**
Bishop Clo. W4 —5J **73**
Bishop Ct. N12 —4E **14**
Bishop Ken Rd. Harr —2K **23**
Bishop King's Rd. W14 —4G **75**
Bishop Rd. N14 —7A **6**
Bishop's Av. E13 —1K **65**
Bishop's Av. SW6 —2F **91**
Bishops Av. Brom —2A **128**
Bishops Av. Romf —6C **36**
Bishops Av., The. N2 —6B **28**
Bishop's Bri. Rd. W2 —6K **59**
Bishops Clo. E17 —4D **32**
Bishop's Clo. N19 —3G **45**
Bishop's Clo. SE9 —2G **115**
Bishops Clo. Barn —6A **4**
Bishops Clo. Enf —2C **8**
Bishops Clo. Rich —3D **104**
Bishops Clo. Sutt —3J **131**
Bishop's Ct. EC4 —6B **62** (7J **141**)
  (off Old Bailey)
Bishop's Ct. WC2 —6A **62** (7G **141**)
  (off Star Yd.)
Bishops Ct. Rich —3E **88**
Bishops Dri. N'holt —1C **54**
Bishopsford Rd. Mord —7A **122**
Bishopsgate. EC2 —6E **62** (8C **142**)
Bishopsgate Arc. EC2
  (off Bishopsgate) —5E **62** (6D **142**)
Bishopsgate Chu. Yd. EC2
  —5E **62** (7C **142**)
Bishops Grn. Brom —1A **128**
  (off Up. Park Rd.)
Bishops Gro. N2 —6C **28**
Bishops Gro. Hamp —4D **102**
Bishop's Hall. King T —2D **118**
Bishop's Mans. SW6 —1G **91**
  (in two parts)

Bishop's Pk. Rd. SW6 —2F **91**
Bishops Pk. Rd. SW16 —1J **123**
Bishops Rd. N6 —6E **28**
Bishop's Rd. SW6 —1G **91**
Bishop's Rd. SW11 —7C **76**
Bishops Rd. W7 —2J **71**
Bishop's Rd. Croy —7B **124**
Bishop's Ter. SE11 —4A **78** (8H **147**)
Bishopsthorpe Rd. SE26 —4K **111**
Bishop St. N1 —1C **62**
Bishops Wlk. Chst —1G **129**
Bishops Wlk. Croy —5K **135**
Bishops Wlk. Pinn —3C **22**
Bishop's Way. E2 —2H **63**
Bishopswood Rd. N6 —7D **28**
Bishop Way. NW10 —7A **42**
Bishop Wilfred Wood Clo. SE15
  —2H **95**
Bisley Clo. Wor Pk —1E **130**
Bison Ct. Felt —7A **86**
Bispham Rd. NW10 —3F **57**
Bisson Rd. E15 —2E **64**
Bisterne Av. E17 —3F **33**
Bittacy Clo. NW7 —6A **14**
Bittacy Ct. NW7 —7B **14**
Bittacy Hill. NW7 —6A **14**
Bittacy Pk. Av. NW7 —6A **14**
Bittacy Rise. NW7 —6K **13**
Bittacy Rd. NW7 —6A **14**
Bittern Clo. Hay —5B **54**
Bittern Ct. NW9 —2A **26**
Bittern Ct. SE8 —6C **80**
Bittern Pl. N22 —2K **29**
Bittern St. SE1 —2C **78** (5L **147**)
Bittoms, The. King T —3D **118**
Bixley Clo. S'hall —4D **70**
Blackall St. EC2 —4E **62** (3C **142**)
Blackberry Farm Clo. Houn —7C **70**
Blackbird Ct. NW9 —2K **41**
Blackbird Hill. NW9 —2J **41**
Blackbird Yd. E2 —3F **63**
Blackborne La. Brom —5E **128**
Blackburn. NW9 —2B **26**
Blackburne's M. W1
  —7E **60** (9G **139**)
Blackburn Rd. NW6 —6K **43**
Blackbush Av. Romf —5D **36**
Blackbush Clo. Sutt —7K **131**
Blackett St. SW15 —3F **91**
Black Fan Clo. Enf —1H **7**
Blackfen Pde. Sidc —6A **100**
Blackfen Rd. Sidc —5J **99**
Blackford Clo. S Croy —7B **134**
Blackford's Path. SW15 —7C **90**
Blackfriars Bri. SE1 & EC4
  —7B **62** (1J **147**)
Blackfriars Ct. EC4 —7B **62** (9J **141**)
  (off New Bridge St.)
Black Friars La. EC4
  —7B **62** (9J **141**)
Blackfriars Pas. EC4
  —7B **62** (9J **141**)
Blackfriars Rd. SE1 —2B **78** (5J **147**)
Blackfriars Underpass. EC4
  —7B **62** (9J **141**)
Black Gates. Pinn —3D **22**
Blackheath Av. SE10 —7F **81**
Blackheath Gro. SE3 —2H **97**
Blackheath Hill. SE10 —1E **96**
Blackheath Pk. SE3 —3H **97**
Blackheath Rise. SE13 —2E **96**
Blackheath Rd. SE10 —1D **96**
Blackheath Vale. SE3 —2H **97**
Blackheath Village. SE3 —2H **97**
Black Horse Ct. SE1 —3D **78** (7B **148**)
  (off Gt. Dover St.)

Blackhorse La. E17 —2K **31**
Black Horse La. Croy —7G **125**
Blackhorse M. E17 —3K **31**
Blackhorse Rd. E17 —4K **31**
Blackhorse Rd. SE8 —6A **80**
Blackhorse Rd. Sidc —4A **116**
Blacklands Rd. SE6 —4E **112**
Blacklands Ter. SW3
  —4D **76** (9F **144**)
Black Lion La. W6 —4C **74**
Black Lion M. W6 —4C **74**
Blackmore Av. S'hall —1H **71**
Blackmore Ho. N1 —1K **61**
  (off Barnsbury Est.)
Blackmore Rd. Buck H —1H **21**
Blackmore's Gro. Tedd —6A **104**
Black Path. E10 —7K **31**
Blackpool Rd. SE15 —2H **95**
Black Prince Rd. SE1 & SE11
  —4K **77** (9E **146**)
Blackshaw Pl. N1 —7E **46**
Blackshaw Rd. SW17 —4A **108**
Blacksmiths Clo. Romf —6C **36**
Blacks Rd. W6 —5E **74**
Blackstock M. N4 —2B **46**
Blackstock Rd. N4 & N5 —2B **46**
Blackstone Est. E8 —7H **47**
Blackstone Rd. NW2 —5E **42**
Black Swan Yd. SE1
  —2E **78** (4C **148**)
Blackthorn Ct. Houn —7C **70**
Blackthorn Av. Croy —1J **135**
Blackthorne Ct. SE1 —7F **79**
  (off Cator St.)
Blackthorn Dri. E4 —4A **20**
Blackthorn Gro. Bexh —3E **100**
Blackthorn St. E3 —4C **64**
Blacktree M. SW9 —3A **94**
Blackwall La. SE10 —5G **81**
  (in two parts)
Blackwall Trading Est. E14 —5F **65**
Blackwall Tunnel. E14 & SE10
  —1F **81**
Blackwall Tunnel App. E14 —7E **64**
Blackwall Tunnel Northern App. E3 &
  E14 —2D **64**
Blackwall Tunnel Southern App. SE10
  —3G **81**
Blackwall Way. E14 —1E **80**
  (in two parts)
Blackwater Clo. E7 —5H **49**
Blackwater Clo. Rain —5K **69**
Blackwater St. SE22 —5F **95**
Blackwell Clo. E5 —4K **47**
Blackwell Clo. Harr —7C **10**
Blackwell Gdns. Edgw —3B **12**
Blackwood St. SE17 —5D **78**
Blade M. SW15 —4H **91**
Blades Ct. SW15 —4H **91**
Blades Ho. SE11 —6A **78**
  (off Kennington Oval)
Bladindon Dri. Bex —7C **100**
Bladon Ct. SW16 —6J **109**
Bladon Gdns. Harr —6F **23**
Blagdens Clo. N14 —2C **16**
Blagdens La. N14 —2C **16**
Blagdon Rd. SE13 —6D **96**
Blagdon Rd. N Mald —4B **120**
Blagdon Wlk. Tedd —6C **104**
Blagrove Rd. W10 —5G **59**
Blair Av. NW9 —7A **26**
Blair Clo. N1 —6C **46**
Blair Clo. Sidc —5J **99**
Blair Ct. Beck —1D **126**
Blairderry Rd. SW2 —2J **109**
Blair Ho. SW9 —2K **93**
Blair St. E14 —6E **64**
Blake Av. Bark —1J **67**

Blake Clo. W10 —5E **58**
Blake Clo. Cars —1C **132**
Blake Clo. Well —1J **99**
Blake Gdns. SW6 —1K **91**
Blake Hall Cres. E11 —1J **49**
Blake Hall Rd. E11 —7J **33**
Blakehall Rd. Cars —6D **132**
Blake Ho. E14 —2D **80**
  (off Admirals Way)
Blakeley Cotts. SE10 —2F **81**
Blakemore Rd. SW16 —3J **109**
Blakemore Rd. T Hth —5K **123**
Blakemore Way. Belv —3E **84**
Blakeney Av. Beck —1B **126**
Blakeney Clo. E8 —5G **47**
Blakeney Clo. N20 —1F **15**
Blakeney Clo. NW1 —7H **45**
Blakeney Rd. Beck —7B **112**
Blakenham Rd. SW17 —4D **108**
Blake Rd. E16 —4H **65**
Blake Rd. N11 —7B **16**
Blake Rd. Croy —2E **134**
Blake Rd. Mitc —3C **122**
Blaker Rd. E15 —1E **64**
Blakes Av. N Mald —5B **120**
Blake's Grn. W Wick —1E **136**
Blakes La. N Mald —5B **120**
Blakesley Av. W5 —6C **56**
Blakesley Wlk. SW20 —2H **121**
Blake's Rd. SE15 —7H **78**
Blakes Ter. N Mald —5C **120**
Blakeswarre Gdns. N9 —7J **7**
Blakewood Clo. Felt —4A **102**
Blanchard Clo. SE9 —3C **114**
Blanchard Way. E8 —6G **47**
Blanch Clo. SE15 —7J **79**
Blanchedowne. SE5 —4D **94**
Blanch St. E16 —4H **65**
Blanchland Rd. Mord —5K **121**
Blandfield Rd. SW12 —7E **92**
Blandford Av. Beck —2A **126**
Blandford Av. Twic —1F **103**
Blandford Clo. N2 —4A **28**
Blandford Clo. Croy —3J **133**
Blandford Clo. Romf —4G **37**
Blandford Ct. NW6 —7G **43**
Blandford Cres. E4 —7K **9**
Blandford Rd. W4 —3A **74**
Blandford Rd. W5 —2D **72**
Blandford Rd. Beck —2A **126**
Blandford Rd. S'hall —4E **70**
Blandford Rd. Tedd —5H **103**
Blandford Sq. NW1
  —4C **60** (4D **138**)
Blandford St. W1 —6D **60** (7F **138**)
Blandford Waye. Hay —6A **54**
Bland Ho. SE11 —5K **77**
  (off Vauxhall St.)
Bland St. SE9 —4B **98**
Blaney Cres. E6 —3F **67**
Blanmerle Rd. SE9 —1F **115**
Blann Clo. SE9 —6B **98**
Blantyre St. SW10 —7B **76**
Blantyre Wlk. SW10 —7B **76**
  (off Worlds End Est.)
Blashford St. SE13 —7F **97**
Blasker Wlk. E14 —5D **80**
Blawith Rd. Harr —4J **23**
Blaxland Ho. W12 —7D **58**
  (off White City Est.)
Blaydon Clo. N17 —7C **18**
Bleak Hill La. SE18 —6K **83**
Blean Gro. SE20 —7J **111**
Bleasdale Av. Gnfd —2A **56**
Blechynden St. W10 —7F **59**
Bleddyn Clo. Sidc —6C **100**
Bledlow Clo. SE28 —7C **68**
Bledlow Rise. Gnfd —2G **55**

Bleeding Heart Yd. EC1
(off Greville St.) —5A **62 (6H 141)**
Blegborough Rd. SW16 —6G **109**
Blendon Dri. Bex —6D **100**
Blendon Path. Brom —7H **113**
Blendon Rd. Bex —6D **100**
Blendon Ter. SE18 —5G **83**
Blendworth Way. SE15 —7E **78**
Blenheim Av. Ilf —6E **34**
Blenheim Clo. N21 —1H **17**
Blenheim Clo. SW20 —3E **120**
Blenheim Clo. Gnfd —2H **55**
Blenheim Clo. Romf —4J **37**
Blenheim Clo. Wall —7G **133**
Blenheim Ct. N19 —2J **45**
Blenheim Ct. Kent —6A **24**
Blenheim Ct. Sidc —3H **115**
Blenheim Ct. Sutt —6A **132**
Blenheim Cres. W11 —7G **59**
Blenheim Cres. S Croy —7C **134**
Blenheim Dri. Well —1K **99**
Blenheim Gdns. NW2 —6E **42**
Blenheim Gdns. SW2 —6K **93**
Blenheim Gdns. King T —7H **105**
Blenheim Gdns. Wall —6G **133**
Blenheim Gdns. Wemb —3E **40**
Blenheim Gro. SE15 —2G **95**
Blenheim Ho. Houn —3E **86**
Blenheim Pk. Rd. S Croy —7C **134**
Blenheim Pas. NW8 —2A **60**
(off Carlton Hill)
Blenheim Pl. NW8 —2A **60**
Blenheim Rise. N15 —4F **31**
Blenheim Rd. E6 —3B **66**
Blenheim Rd. E15 —4G **49**
Blenheim Rd. E17 —3K **31**
Blenheim Rd. NW8 —2A **60**
Blenheim Rd. SE20 —7J **111**
Blenheim Rd. SW20 —3E **120**
Blenheim Rd. W4 —3A **74**
Blenheim Rd. Barn —3A **4**
Blenheim Rd. Brom —4C **128**
Blenheim Rd. Harr —6F **23**
Blenheim Rd. N'holt —6F **39**
Blenheim Rd. Sidc —1C **116**
Blenheim Rd. Sutt —3J **131**
Blenheim Shopping Cen. SE20
—7J **111**
Blenheim St. W1 —6F **61 (8J 139)**
Blenheim Ter. NW8 —2A **60**
Blenkarne Rd. SW11 —6D **92**
Bleriot. NW9 —2B **26**
(off Belvedere Strand)
Bleriot Rd. Houn —7A **70**
Blessbury Rd. Edgw —1J **25**
Blessington Clo. SE13 —3F **97**
Blessington Rd. SE13 —4F **97**
Bletchingley Clo. T Hth —4B **124**
Bletchley St. N1 —2C **62**
Bletsoe Wlk. N1 —2C **62**
Blewbury Ho. SE2 —2D **84**
Blincoe Clo. SW19 —2F **107**
Bliss Cres. SE13 —2D **96**
Blissett St. SE10 —1E **96**
Blisworth Clo. Hay —4C **54**
Blithbury Rd. Dag —6B **52**
Blithdale Rd. SE2 —4A **84**
Blithfield St. W8 —3K **75**
Blockley Rd. Wemb —2B **40**
Bloemfontein Av. W12 —1D **74**
Bloemfontein Rd. W12 —7D **58**
Blomfield Rd. W9 —5K **59**
Blomfield St. EC2 —5D **62 (6B 142)**
Blomfield Vs. W2 —5K **59**
Blomville Rd. Dag —3E **52**
Blondel St. SW11 —2E **92**
Blondin Av. W5 —4C **72**
Blondin St. E3 —2C **64**

166

Bloomburg St. SW1
—4H **77 (9M 145)**
Bloomfield Ct. N6 —6E **28**
Bloomfield Cres. Ilf —6F **35**
Bloomfield Pl. W1 —7F **61 (9K 139)**
(off Grosvenor Hill)
Bloomfield Rd. N6 —6E **28**
Bloomfield Rd. SE18 —5F **83**
Bloomfield Rd. Brom —5B **128**
Bloomfield Rd. King T —3E **118**
Bloomfields, The. Bark —6G **51**
Bloomfield Ter. SW1 —5E **76**
Bloom Gro. SE27 —3B **110**
Bloomhall Rd. SE19 —5D **110**
Bloom Pk. Rd. SW6 —7H **75**
Bloomsbury Clo. W5 —7F **57**
Bloomsbury Ct. WC1
(off Barter St.) —5J **61 (6D 140)**
Bloomsbury Ct. Pinn —3D **22**
Bloomsbury Ho. SW4 —6H **93**
Bloomsbury Pl. SW18 —5A **92**
Bloomsbury Pl. WC1
—5J **61 (6D 140)**
Bloomsbury Sq. WC1
—5J **61 (6D 140)**
Bloomsbury St. WC1
—5H **61 (6B 140)**
Bloomsbury Way. WC1
—5J **61 (6C 140)**
Blore Clo. SW8 —1H **93**
Blore Ct. SW8 —1H **93**
Blore Ct. W1 —7H **61 (9A 140)**
(off Berwick St.)
Blossom Clo. W5 —2E **72**
Blossom Clo. Dag —1F **69**
Blossom Clo. S Croy —5F **135**
Blossom La. Enf —1H **7**
Blossom St. E1 —4E **62 (5D 142)**
Blossom Waye. Houn —6C **70**
Blount St. E14 —6A **64**
Bloxhall Rd. E10 —1B **48**
Bloxham Cres. Hamp —7D **102**
Bloxham Gdns. SE9 —5C **98**
Bloxworth Clo. Wall —3G **133**
Bloxworth Gro. N1 —1K **61**
Blucher Rd. SE5 —7C **78**
Blue Anchor All. Rich —4E **88**
Blue Anchor La. SE16 —4G **79**
Blue Anchor Yd. E1 —7G **63**
Blue Ball Yd. SW1 —1G **77 (3L 145)**
Bluebell Av. E12 —5B **50**
Bluebell Clo. SE26 —4F **111**
Bluebell Clo. Wall —1F **133**
Bluebell Way. Ilf —6F **51**
Bluebird Wlk. Wemb —3H **41**
Bluefield Clo. Hamp —5E **102**
Bluegates. Ewe —7C **130**
Bluehouse Rd. E4 —3B **20**
Blue Riband Ind. Est. Croy —2B **134**
Blundell Ho. SE14 —7A **80**
Blundell Rd. Edgw —1K **25**
Blundell St. N7 —7J **45**
Blunden Clo. Dag —1C **52**
Blunt Rd. S Croy —5D **134**
Blunts Rd. SE9 —5E **98**
Blurton Rd. E5 —4J **47**
Blydon Ho. N21 —5E **6**
(off Chaseville Pk. Rd.)
Blyth Clo. E14 —4F **81**
Blyth Clo. Twic —6K **87**
Blythe Clo. SE6 —7B **96**
Blythe Hill. SE6 —7B **96**
Blythe Hill. Orp —1K **129**
Blythe Hill La. SE6 —7B **96**
Blythe Ho. SE11 —6A **78**
Blythe M. W14 —3F **75**
Blythe Rd. W14 —3F **75**
Blythe St. E2 —3H **63**

Blythe Vale. SE6 —1B **112**
Blyth Rd. E17 —7B **32**
Blyth Rd. SE28 —7C **68**
Blyth Rd. Brom —1H **127**
Blythswood Rd. Ilf —1A **52**
Blythwood. Pinn —1B **22**
Blyth Wood Pk. Brom —1H **127**
Blythwood Rd. N4 —7J **29**
Blythwood Rd. Pinn —1B **22**
Boades M. NW3 —4B **44**
Boadicea St. N1 —1K **61**
Boakes Clo. NW9 —4J **25**
Boardman Av. E4 —5J **9**
Boarhound. NW9 —2B **26**
(off Further Acre)
Boathouse Wlk. SE15 —7G **79**
Boat Lifter Way. SE16 —3A **80**
Bob Anker Clo. E13 —3J **65**
Bobbin Clo. SW4 —3G **93**
Bob Marley Way. SE24 —4A **94**
Bockhampton Rd. King T —7F **105**
Bocking St. E8 —1H **63**
Boddicott Clo. SW19 —2G **107**
Bodeney Ho. SE5 —1E **94**
(off Peckham Rd.)
Bodiam Clo. Enf —2K **7**
Bodiam Rd. SW16 —7H **109**
Bodley Clo. N Mald —5A **120**
Bodley Mnr. Way. SW2 —7A **94**
Bodley Rd. N Mald —6K **119**
Bodmin. NW9 —2B **26**
(off Further Acre)
Bodmin Gro. Mord —5K **121**
Bodmin St. SW18 —1J **107**
Bodnant Gdns. SW20 —3C **120**
Bodney Rd. E8 —5H **47**
Boeing Way. S'hall —3A **70**
Boevey Path. Belv —5F **85**
Bognor Rd. Well —1D **100**
Bohemia Pl. E8 —6J **47**
Bohun Gro. Barn —6H **5**
Boileau Pde. W5 —6F **57**
(off Boileau Rd.)
Boileau Rd. SW13 —7C **74**
Boileau Rd. W5 —6F **57**
Bolden St. SE8 —2D **96**
Bolderwood Way. W Wick —2D **136**
Boldmere Rd. Pinn —7A **22**
Boleyn Av. Enf —1C **8**
Boleyn Clo. E17 —4C **32**
Boleyn Ct. Buck H —1D **20**
Boleyn Dri. Ruis —2B **38**
Boleyn Gdns. Dag —7J **53**
Boleyn Gdns. W Wick —2D **136**
Boleyn Gro. W Wick —2E **136**
Boleyn Rd. E6 —2B **66**
Boleyn Rd. E7 —7J **49**
Boleyn Rd. N16 —5E **46**
Boleyn Way. Barn —3F **5**
Bolina Rd. SE16 —5J **79**
Bolingbroke Gro. SW11 —4C **92**
Bolingbroke Rd. W14 —3F **75**
Bolingbroke Wlk. SW11 —1B **92**
Bollo Bri. Rd. W3 —3H **73**
Bollo La. W3 & W4 —2H **73**
Bolney Ga. SW7 —2C **76 (5C 144)**
Bolney St. SW8 —7K **77**
Bolney Way. Felt —3C **102**
Bolsover St. W1 —4F **61 (4K 139)**
Bolstead Rd. Mitc —1F **123**
Bolster Gro. N22 —1H **29**
Bolt Ct. EC4 —6A **62 (8H 141)**
Boltmore Clo. NW4 —3F **27**
Bolton Clo. SE20 —2G **125**
Bolton Cres. SE5 —7B **78**
Bolton Gdns. NW10 —2F **59**
Bolton Gdns. SW5 —5K **75**

Bolton Gdns. Brom —6H **113**
Bolton Gdns. Tedd —6A **104**
Bolton Gdns. M. SW10 —5A **76**
Bolton Ho. SE10 —5G **81**
(off Trafalgar Rd.)
Bolton Rd. E15 —6H **49**
Bolton Rd. N18 —5A **18**
Bolton Rd. NW8 —1K **59**
Bolton Rd. NW10 —1A **58**
Bolton Rd. W4 —7J **73**
Bolton Rd. Harr —4G **23**
Boltons, The. SW10 —5A **76**
Boltons, The. Wemb —4K **39**
Bolton St. W1 —1F **77 (2K 145)**
Bolton Wlk. N7 —2K **45**
(off Durham Rd.)
Bombay St. SE16 —4H **79**
Bomore Rd. W11 —7G **59**
Bonar Pl. Chst —7C **114**
Bonar Rd. SE15 —7G **79**
Bonchester Clo. Chst —7E **114**
Bonchurch Clo. Sutt —7K **131**
Bonchurch Rd. W10 —5G **59**
Bonchurch Rd. W13 —1B **72**
Bondfield Clo. E6 —5D **66**
Bond Gdns. Wall —4G **133**
Bonding Yd. Wlk. SE16 —3A **80**
Bond Rd. E15 —1D **64**
Bond Rd. Mitc —2C **122**
Bond St. E15 —5G **49**
Bond St. W4 —4K **73**
Bond St. W5 —7D **56**
Bondway. SW8 —6J **77**
Boneta Rd. SE18 —3D **82**
Bonfield Rd. SE13 —4E **96**
Bonham Gdns. Dag —2D **52**
Bonham Rd. SW2 —5K **93**
Bonham Rd. Dag —2D **52**
Bonheur Rd. W4 —2K **73**
Bonhill St. EC2 —4D **62 (4B 142)**
Boniface Gdns. Harr —7A **10**
Boniface Wlk. Harr —7A **10**
Bon Marche Ter. SE27 —4E **110**
Bonner Hill Rd. King T —2F **119**
Bonner Rd. E2 —2J **63**
Bonnersfield Clo. Harr —6K **23**
Bonnersfield La. Harr —6K **23**
Bonner St. E2 —2K **63**
Bonneville Gdns. SW4 —6G **93**
Bonnington Sq. SW8 —6K **77**
Bonny St. NW1 —7G **45**
Bonser Rd. Twic —2K **103**
Bonsor St. SE5 —7E **78**
Bonville Gdns. NW4 —4D **26**
Bonville Rd. Brom —5H **113**
Bookbinders Cottage Homes. N20
—3J **15**
Booker Clo. E14 —5B **64**
Booker Rd. N18 —5B **18**
Book M. WC2 —6H **61 (8B 140)**
Boone Ct. N9 —3D **18**
Boones Rd. SE13 —4G **97**
Boone St. SE13 —4G **97**
Boord St. SE10 —3G **81**
Boothby Ct. E4 —3K **19**
Boothby Rd. N19 —2H **45**
Booth Clo. SE28 —1B **84**
Booth La. EC4 —7C **62 (9L 141)**
(off Baynard St.)
Boothman Ho. Kent —3D **24**
Booth Rd. NW9 —2K **25**
Booth Rd. Croy —2B **134**
Booth's Pl. W1 —5G **61 (6M 139)**
Boot Pde. Edgw —6B **12**
(off High St. Edgware)
Boot St. N1 —3E **62 (2C 142)**
Bordars Rd. W7 —5J **55**
Bordars Wlk. W7 —5J **55**

Borden Av. Enf —6J **7**
Border Cres. SE26 —5H **111**
Border Gdns. Croy —4D **136**
Bordergate. Mitc —1D **122**
Border Rd. SE26 —5H **111**
Bordesley Rd. Mord —4K **121**
Bordon Wlk. SW15 —7C **90**
Boreas Wlk. N1 —2B **62**
(off Nelson Pl.)
Boreham Av. E16 —6J **65**
Boreham Clo. E11 —1E **48**
Boreham Rd. N22 —2C **30**
Borgard Rd. SE18 —4D **82**
Borland Rd. SE15 —4J **95**
Borland Rd. Tedd —7B **104**
Borneo St. SW15 —3E **90**
Borough High St. SE1
—2C **78 (5M 147)**
Borough Hill. Croy —3B **134**
Borough Rd. SE1 —3B **78 (6J 147)**
Borough Rd. Iswth —1J **87**
Borough Rd. King T —1G **119**
Borough Rd. Mitc —2C **122**
Borough Sq. SE1 —2C **78 (5L 147)**
(off MacColl Way)
Borrett Clo. SE17 —5C **78**
Borrodaile Rd. SW18 —6K **91**
Borrowdale Av. Harr —2A **24**
Borrowdale Clo. Ilf —4C **34**
Borthwick M. E15 —4G **49**
Borthwick Rd. E15 —4G **49**
Borthwick Rd. NW9 —6B **26**
Borthwick St. SE8 —5C **80**
Borwick Av. E17 —3B **32**
Bosbury Rd. SE6 —3E **112**
Boscastle Rd. NW5 —3F **45**
Boscobel Pl. SW1 —4E **76 (8H 145)**
Boscobel St. NW8 —4B **60 (4B 138)**
Boscombe Av. E10 —7F **33**
Boscombe Clo. E5 —5A **48**
Boscombe Gdns. SW16 —6J **109**
Boscombe Rd. SW17 —6E **108**
Boscombe Rd. SW19 —1J **121**
Boscombe Rd. W12 —1C **74**
Boscombe Rd. Wor Pk —1E **130**
Bosgrove. E4 —2K **19**
Boss St. SE1 —2F **79 (4E 148)**
Bostall Hill. SE2 —6C **84**
Bostall Hill. SE2 —5A **84**
Bostall La. SE2 —5B **84**
Bostall Mnr. SE2 —4B **84**
Bostall Pk. Av. Bexh —7E **84**
Bostall Rd. Orp —7B **116**
Bostal Row. Bexh —3F **101**
Bostock Ho. Houn —6E **70**
Boston Gdns. W4 —6A **74**
Boston Gdns. W7 —4A **72**
Boston Gdns. Bren —4A **72**
Boston Mnr. Rd. Bren —4A **72**
Boston Pde. W7 —4A **72**
Boston Pk. Rd. Bren —5C **72**
Boston Pl. NW1 —4D **60 (3E 138)**
Boston Rd. E6 —3C **66**
Boston Rd. E17 —6C **32**
Boston Rd. W7 —1J **71**
Boston Rd. Croy —6K **123**
Boston Rd. Edgw —7D **12**
Bostonthorpe Rd. W7 —2J **71**
Boston Vale. W7 —4A **72**
Boswell Ct. WC1 —5J **61 (5D 140)**
Boswell Rd. T Hth —4C **124**
Boswell St. WC1 —5J **61 (5D 140)**
Bosworth Clo. E17 —1B **32**
Bosworth Rd. N11 —6C **16**
Bosworth Rd. W10 —4G **59**
Bosworth Rd. Barn —3D **4**
Bosworth Rd. Dag —3G **53**
Botany Bay La. Chst —2G **129**

Botany Clo. New Bar —4H **5**
Boteley Clo. E4 —2A **20**
Botham Clo. Edgw —7D **12**
Botha Rd. E13 —5K **65**
Bothwell Clo. E16 —5H **65**
Bothwell St. W6 —6F **75**
Bothwick St. SE8 —5C **80**
Botolph All. EC3 —7E **62** *(9C 142)*
(off Botolph La.)
Botolph La. EC3 —7E **62** (1C **148**)
Botsford Rd. SW20 —2G **121**
Botts M. W2 —6J **59**
Boucher Clo. Tedd —5K **103**
Boughton Av. Brom —7H **127**
Boughton Rd. SE28 —3J **83**
Boulcott St. E1 —6K **63**
Boulevard, The. SW17 —2E **108**
Boulevard, The. Pinn —4E **22**
(in two parts)
Boulogne Rd. Croy —6C **124**
Boulton Ho. Bren —5E **72**
Boulton Rd. Dag —2E **52**
Boultwood Rd. E6 —6D **66**
Bounaparte M. SW1 —5H **77**
Bounces La. N9 —2C **18**
Bounces Rd. N9 —2C **18**
Boundaries Rd. SW12 —2D **108**
Boundaries Rd. Felt —1A **102**
Boundary Av. E17 —7B **32**
Boundary Clo. SE20 —2G **125**
Boundary Clo. Ilf —4J **51**
Boundary Clo. King T —3H **119**
Boundary Clo. S'hall —5E **70**
Boundary Ct. N18 —6A 18
(off Snells Pk.)
Boundary Ho. SE5 —7C **78**
Boundary La. E13 —4B **66**
Boundary La. SE5 & SE17 —6C **78**
Boundary La. SE17 —6C **78**
(in two parts)
Boundary Pas. E2 —4F **63** (3E **142**)
Boundary Rd. E13 —2A **66**
Boundary Rd. E17 —7B **32**
Boundary Rd. N2 —1B **28**
Boundary Rd. N9 —6D **8**
Boundary Rd. N22 —3B **30**
Boundary Rd. NW8 —1K **59**
Boundary Rd. SW19 —6B **108**
Boundary Rd. Bark —2G **67**
(in two parts)
Boundary Rd. Cars —6F **133**
Boundary Rd. Pinn —7B **22**
Boundary Rd. Sidc —3J **99**
Boundary Rd. Wemb —3D **40**
Boundary Row. SE1 —2B **78** (4J **147**)
Boundary St. E2 —3F **63** (2E **142**)
(in two parts)
Boundary Way. Croy —5C **136**
Boundfield Rd. SE6 —3G **113**
Bounds Grn. Ct. N11 —6C 16
(off Bounds Grn. Rd.)
Bounds Grn. Ind. Est. N11 —6B **16**
Bounds Grn. Rd. N11 & N22 —6B **16**
Bourbon Ho. SE6 —5E **112**
Bourchier St. W1 —7H **61** (9A **140**)
Bourdon Pl. W1 —7F 61 (9K 139)
(off Bourdon St.)
Bourdon Rd. SE20 —2J **125**
Bourdon St. W1 —7F **61** (1J **145**)
Bourke Clo. NW10 —6A **42**
Bourke Clo. SW4 —6J **93**
Bourlet Clo. W1 —5G **61** (6L **139**)
Bourn Av. N15 —4D **30**
Bournbrook Rd. SE3 —3B **98**
Bourne Av. N14 —2D **16**
Bourne Av. Barn —5G **5**
Bourne Av. Ruis —5A **38**
Bourne Ct. W4 —6J **73**

Bourne Ct. S Ruis —5A **38**
Bourne Dri. Mitc —2B **122**
Bourne Est. EC1 —5A **62** (5G **141**)
Bourne Gdns. E4 —4J **19**
Bourne Hill. N13 —2E **16**
Bourne Hill Clo. N13 —2E **16**
Bourne Ind. Pk., The. Dart —5K **101**
Bourne Mead. Bex —5K **101**
Bournemouth Rd. SE15 —2G **95**
Bournemouth Rd. SW19 —1J **121**
Bourne Pde. Bex —7H **101**
Bourne Pl. W4 —5K **73**
Bourne Rd. E7 —3H **49**
Bourne Rd. N8 —6J **29**
Bourne Rd. Bex & Dart —7H **101**
Bourne Rd. Brom —4B **128**
Bournes Ho. N15 —6E 30
(off Chisley Rd.)
Bourneside Cres. N14 —1C **16**
Bourneside Gdns. SE6 —5E **112**
Bourne St. SW1 —4E **76**
Bourne St. Croy —2B **134**
Bourne Ter. W2 —5K **59**
Bourne, The. N14 —1C **16**
Bourne Vale. Brom —1H **137**
Bournevale Rd. SW16 —4J **109**
Bourne View. Gnfd —6K **39**
Bourneville Rd. SE6 —7C **96**
Bourne Way. Brom —2H **137**
Bourne Way. Sutt —5H **131**
Bournewood Rd. SE18 —7A **84**
Bournwell Clo. Barn —3J **5**
Bousefield Rd. SE14 —2K **95**
Boutflower Rd. SW11 —4C **92**
Bouverie Gdns. Harr —6D **24**
Bouverie M. N16 —2E **46**
Bouverie Pl. W2 —6B **60** (7B **138**)
Bouverie Rd. N16 —2E **46**
Bouverie Rd. Harr —6G **23**
Bouverie St. EC4 —6A **62** (8H **141**)
Bouvier Rd. Enf —1D **8**
Boveney Rd. SE23 —7K **95**
Bovill Rd. SE23 —7K **95**
Bovingdon Av. Wemb —6G **41**
Bovingdon Clo. N19 —2G **45**
Bovingdon La. NW9 —1A **26**
Bovingdon Rd. SW6 —1K **91**
Bovingdon Sq. Mitc —4J **123**
Bowater Clo. NW9 —5K **25**
Bowater Clo. SW2 —6J **93**
Bowater Ho. EC1 —4C 62 (4L 141)
(off Golden La. Est.)
Bowater Pl. SE3 —7K **81**
Bowater Rd. SE18 —3B **82**
Bow Bri. Est. E3 —3D **64**
Bow Chyd. EC4 —6C 62 (8M 141)
(off Cheapside)
Bow Comn. La. E3 —4A **64**
Bowden St. SE11 —5A **78**
Bowditch. SE8 —4B **80**
Bowdon Rd. E17 —7C **32**
Bowen Dri. SE21 —3E **110**
Bowen Rd. Harr —7G **23**
Bowen St. E14 —6D **64**
Bower Av. SE10 —1G **97**
Bower Clo. N'holt —2A **54**
Bower Clo. Romf —1K **37**
Bowerdean St. SW6 —1K **91**
Bowerman Av. SE14 —6A **80**
Bowerman Ct. N19 —2H 45
(off St Johns Way)
Bower St. E1 —6K **63**
Bowers Wlk. E6 —6D **66**
Bowes Clo. Sidc —6B **100**
Bowe's Ho. Bark —7F **51**
Bowes Rd. N11 & N13 —5B **16**
Bowes Rd. W3 —7A **58**
Bowes Rd. Dag —4C **52**

Bowfell Rd. W6 —6E **74**
Bowford Av. Bexh —1E **100**
Bowhill Clo. SW9 —7A **78**
Bowie Clo. SW4 —7H **93**
Bow Ind. Pk. E15 —7C **48**
Bowland Rd. SW4 —4H **93**
Bowland Rd. Wfd G —5F **21**
Bowland Yd. SW1 —2D 76 (5F 144)
(off Kinnerton St.)
Bow La. EC4 —6C **62** (8M **141**)
Bow La. N12 —7F **15**
Bow La. Mord —6G **121**
Bowl Ct. EC2 —4E **62** (4D **142**)
Bowles Rd. SE1 —6G **79**
Bowley Clo. SE19 —6F **111**
Bowley Ho. SE16 —3G **79**
Bowley La. SE19 —5F **111**
Bowling Grn. Clo. SW15 —7D **90**
Bowling Grn. Ct. Wemb —2F **41**
Bowling Grn. La. EC1

—4A **62** (4H **141**)
Bowling Grn. Pl. SE1

—2D **78** (4A **148**)
Bowling Grn. Rd. E3 —1C **64**
Bowling Grn. Row. SE18 —3D **82**
Bowling Grn. St. SE11 —6A **78**
Bowling Grn. Wlk. N1

—3E **62** (1C **142**)
Bowls Clo. Stan —5G **11**
Bowman Av. E16 —7H **65**
Bowman M. SW18 —1H **107**
Bowmans Clo. W13 —1B **72**
Bowmans Lea. SE23 —7J **95**
Bowmans Meadow. Wall —3F **133**
Bowmans M. E1 —7G **63**
Bowman's N. N7 —3J **45**
Bowman's Pl. N7 —3J **45**
Bowmead. SE9 —2D **114**
Bowmore Wlk. NW1 —7H **45**
Bowness Clo. E8 —6H 47
(off Beechwood Rd.)
Bowness Cres. SW15 —5A **106**
Bowness Dri. Houn —4C **86**
Bowness Ho. SE15 —7J 79
(off Hillbeck Clo.)
Bowness Rd. SE6 —7D **96**
Bowness Rd. Bexh —2H **101**
Bowood Rd. SW11 —5E **92**
Bowood Rd. Enf —2E **8**
Bow Rd. E3 —3B **64**
Bowrons Av. Wemb —7D **40**
Bow St. E15 —5G **49**
Bow St. WC2 —6J **61** (8D **140**)
Bow Triangle Bus. Cen. E3 —4C **64**
Bowyer Clo. E6 —5D **66**
Bowyer Ct. E4 —1K 19
(off Ridgeway, The.)
Bowyer Ho. N1 —1E 62
(off Whitmore Est.)
Bowyer Pl. SE5 —7C **78**
Bowyer St. SE5 —7C **78**
Boxall Rd. SE21 —6E **94**
Boxgrove Rd. SE2 —3C **84**
Box La. Bark —2B **68**
Boxley Rd. Mord —4A **122**
Boxley St. E16 —1K **81**
Boxmoor Ho. W11 —1F 75
(off Queensdale Cres.)
Boxmoor Rd. Harr —4B **24**
Boxoll Rd. Dag —4F **53**
Boxted Clo. Buck H —1H **21**
Boxtree La. Harr —1G **23**
Boxtree Rd. Harr —7C **10**
Boxworth Gro. N1 —1K **61**
Boyard Rd. SE18 —5F **83**
Boyce St. SE1 —1A 78 (3G 147)
(off Mepham St.)
Boyce Way. E13 —4J **65**

Boycroft Av. NW9 —6J **25**
Boyd Av. S'hall —1D **70**
Boyd Clo. King T —7G **105**
Boydell Ct. NW8 —1B **60**
Boyden Ho. E17 —3E **32**
Boyd Rd. SW19 —6B **108**
Boyd St. E1 —6G **63**
Boyfield St. SE1 —2B **78** (5K **147**)
Boyland Rd. Brom —5H **113**
Boyle Av. Stan —6F **11**
Boyle Farm Rd. Th Dit —6A **118**
Boyle St. W1 —7G **61** (9L **139**)
Boyne Av. NW4 —4F **27**
Boyne Rd. SE13 —3E **96**
Boyne Rd. Dag —3G **53**
Boyne Ter. M. W11 —1H **75**
Boyseland Ct. Edgw —2D **12**
Boyson Rd. SE17 —6D **78**
Boyson Wlk. SE17 —6D **78**
Boythorn Rd. SE16 —5H **79**
Boythorn Way. SE16 —5H **79**
Boyton Clo. E1 —4J **63**
Boyton Clo. N8 —3J **29**
Boyton Rd. N8 —3J **29**
Brabant Ct. EC3 —7E 62 (9C 142)
(off Philpot La.)
Brabant Rd. N22 —2K **29**
Brabazon Av. Wall —7J **133**
Brabazon Rd. Houn —7A **70**
Brabazon Rd. N'holt —2E **54**
Brabazon St. E14 —6D **64**
Brabourne Clo. SE19 —5E **110**
Brabourne Cres. Bexh —6F **85**
Brabourne Heights. NW7 —3F **13**
Brabourne Rise. Beck —5E **126**
Brabourn Gro. SE15 —2J **95**
Brabrook Ct. Wall —4F **133**
Bracer Ho. N1 —2E 62
(off Whitmore Est.)
Bracewell Av. Gnfd —5K **39**
Bracewell Rd. W10 —5E **58**
Bracewood Gdns. Croy —3F **135**
Bracey St. N4 —2J **45**
Bracken Av. SW12 —6E **92**
Bracken Av. Croy —3D **136**
Brackenbridge Dri. Ruis —3B **38**
Brackenbury. N4 —1A 46
(off Osborne Rd.)
Brackenbury Gdns. W6 —3D **74**
Brackenbury Rd. N2 —3A **28**
Brackenbury Rd. W6 —3D **74**
Bracken Clo. E6 —5D **66**
Bracken Clo. Twic —7E **86**
Brackendale. N21 —2E **16**
Brackendale Clo. Houn —1F **87**
Brackendene. Dart —4K **117**
Bracken End. Iswth —5H **87**
Brackenfield Clo. E5 —3H **47**
Bracken Gdns. SW13 —2C **90**
Bracken Hill Clo. Brom —1H **127**
Bracken Ind. Est. Ilf —1K **35**
Bracken M. E4 —1K **19**
Bracken M. Romf —6H **37**
Brackens, The. Enf —7K **7**
Bracken, The. E4 —2K **19**
Brackley Clo. Wall —7J **133**
Brackley Rd. W4 —5A **74**
Brackley Rd. Beck —7B **112**
Brackley Sq. Wfd G —7G **21**
Brackley St. EC1 —4C **62** (5M **141**)
Brackley Ter. W4 —5A **74**
Bracklyn Ct. N1 —2D **62**
Bracklyn St. N1 —2D **62**
Bracknell Clo. N22 —1A **30**
Bracknell Gdns. NW3 —4K **43**

Bracknell Ga. NW3 —5K **43**
Bracknell Way. NW3 —4K **43**
Bracondale Rd. SE2 —4A **84**
Bradbourne Rd. Bex —7G **101**
Bradbourne St. SW6 —2J **91**
Bradbury Clo. S'hall —4D **70**
Bradbury St. N16 —5E **46**
Braddon Rd. Rich —3F **89**
Braddyll St. SE10 —5G **81**
Bradenham Av. Well —4A **100**
Bradenham Rd. Harr —4B **24**
Braden St. W9 —4K **59**
Bradfield Dri. Bark —5A **52**
Bradfield Rd. E16 —2J **81**
Bradfield Rd. Ruis —5C **38**
Bradford Clo. SE26 —4H **111**
Bradford Dri. Eps —6B **130**
Bradford Rd. W3 —2A **74**
Bradford Rd. Ilf —1H **51**
Bradgate Rd. SE6 —6D **96**
Brading Cres. E11 —2K **49**
Brading Rd. SW2 —7K **93**
Brading Rd. Croy —6K **123**
Bradiston Rd. W9 —3H **59**
Bradley Clo. N7 —6J **45**
Bradley Ho. SE16 —4J 79
(off Raymouth Rd.)
Bradley M. SW17 —1D **108**
Bradley Rd. N22 —2K **29**
Bradley Rd. SE19 —6C **110**
Bradley Rd. Enf —1F **9**
Bradley's Clo. N1 —2A **62**
Bradman Row. Edgw —7D **12**
Bradmead. SW8 —7F **77**
Bradmore Pk. Rd. W6 —4D **74**
Bradshaws Clo. SE25 —3G **125**
Bradstock Ho. E9 —7A **48**
Bradstock Rd. Eps —5C **130**
Bradstock Rd. E9 —6K **47**
Bradstone Rd. Rich —1F **89**
Brad St. SE1 —1A **78** (3H **147**)
Bradwell Av. Dag —2G **53**
Bradwell Clo. E18 —4H **33**
Bradwell M. N18 —4B **18**
Bradwell Rd. Buck H —1H **21**
Bradymead. E6 —6E **66**
Brady St. E1 —4H **63**
Braeburn Ct. Barn —4H **5**
Braemar Av. N22 —1J **29**
Braemar Av. NW10 —3K **41**
Braemar Av. SW19 —3J **107**
Braemar Av. Bexh —4J **101**
Braemar Av. S Croy —7C **134**
Braemar Av. T Hth —3B **124**
Braemar Av. Wemb —7D **40**
Braemar Gdns. NW9 —1K **25**
Braemar Gdns. Sidc —3H **115**
Braemar Gdns. W Wlck —1E **136**
Braemar Rd. E13 —4H **65**
Braemar Rd. N15 —5E **30**
Braemar Rd. Bren —6D **72**
Braemar Rd. Wor Pk —3D **130**
Braeside. Beck —5C **112**
Braeside Av. SW19 —1G **121**
Braeside Clo. Pinn —1E **22**
Braeside Cres. Bexh —4J **101**
Braeside Rd. SW16 —7G **109**
Braes St. N1 —7B **46**
Braesyde Clo. Belv —4F **85**
Brafferton Rd. Croy —4C **134**
Braganza St. SE17 —5B **78**
Braham Ho. SE11 —5K **77**
Braham St. E1 —6F **63** (8F **142**)
Braid Av. W3 —6A **58**
Braid Clo. Felt —2D **102**
Braidwood Pas. EC1 —5C 62 (6L 141)
(off Aldersgate St.)

Braidwood Rd. SE6 —1F 113
Braidwood St. SE1 —1E 78 (3C 148)
Brailsford Rd. SW2 —5A 94
Brainton Av. Felt —7A 86
Braintree Av. Ilf —4C 34
Braintree Rd. Dag —3J 53
Braintree Rd. Ruis —4A 38
Braintree St. E2 —3J 63
Braithwaite Av. Romf —7G 37
Braithwaite Gdns. Stan —1C 24
Braithwaite Ho. E14 —6F 65
Braithwaite Rd. Enf —3G 9
Bramah Grn. SW9 —1A 94
Bramalea Clo. N6 —6E 28
Bramall Clo. E15 —5H 49
Bramall Ct. N7 —6K 45
(off Georges Rd.)
Bramber. WC1 —3J 61 (2C 140)
(off Cromer St.)
Bramber Ct. W5 —4E 72
Bramber Ct. Bren —4E 72
Bramber Rd. N12 —5H 15
Bramber Rd. W14 —6H 75
Brambleacres. Sutt —7J 131
(off Overton Rd.)
Bramblebury Rd. SE18 —5G 83
Bramble Clo. N15 —4G 31
Bramble Clo. Croy —4C 136
Bramble Clo. Stan —7J 11
Bramble Croft. Eri —4J 85
Brambledown Clo. W Wick —5G 137
Brambledown Rd. Cars & Wall
—7E 132
Brambledown Rd. S Croy —7E 134
Bramble Gdns. W12 —7B 58
Bramble La. Hamp —6D 102
Brambles. The. E4 —4A 20
Bramblewood Clo. Cars —1C 132
Bramblings, The. E4 —4A 20
Bramcote Av. Mitc —4D 122
Bramcote Gro. SE16 —5J 79
Bramcote Rd. SW15 —4D 90
Bramdean Cres. SE12 —1J 113
Bramdean Gdns. SE12 —1J 113
Bramerton Rd. Beck —3B 126
Bramerton St. SW3 —6C 76
Bramfield Ct. N4 —3C 46
(off Queens Dri.)
Bramfield Rd. SW11 —6C 92
Bramford Rd. SW18 —4A 92
Bramham Gdns. SW5 —5K 75
Bramham Ho. SE22 —4E 94
Bramhope La. SE7 —6A 82
Bramlands Clo. SW11 —3C 92
Bramley Clo. E17 —2A 32
Bramley Clo. N14 —5A 6
Bramley Clo. Orp —7F 129
Bramley Clo. S Croy —5C 134
Bramley Clo. Twic —6G 87
Bramley Ct. Barn —4H 5
Bramley Ct. Well —1B 100
Bramley Cres. SW8 —7H 77
Bramley Cres. Ilf —6E 34
Bramley Hill. S Croy —5B 134
Bramley Ho. W10 —6F 59
Bramley Pde. N14 —4B 6
Bramley Rd. N14 —4A 6
Bramley Rd. W5 —3C 72
Bramley Rd. W10 —7F 59
Bramley Rd. Cheam —7F 131
Bramley Rd. Sutt —5B 132
Bramley St. W10 —6F 59
Bramley Way. Houn —5D 86
Bramley Way. W Wick —2D 136
Brampton Clo. E5 —2H 47
Brampton Gdns. N15 —5C 30
Brampton Gro. NW4 —4D 26

Brampton Gro. Harr —4A 24
Brampton Gro. Wemb —1F 41
Brampton La. NW4 —4E 26
Brampton Pk. Rd. N22 —3A 30
Brampton Rd. E6 —3B 66
Brampton Rd. N15 —5C 30
Brampton Rd. NW9 —4G 25
Brampton Rd. Bexh & SE2 —3D 100
Brampton Rd. Croy —6F 125
Bramshaw Rise. N Mald —6A 120
Bramshaw Rd. E9 —6K 47
Bramshill Gdns. NW5 —3F 45
Bramshill Rd. NW10 —2A 58
Bramshot Av. SE7 —6J 81
Bramston Rd. NW10 —2C 58
Bramston Rd. SW17 —3A 108
Bramwell Ho. SE1 —3D 78 (7M 147)
Brancaster Rd. E12 —4D 50
Brancaster Rd. SW16 —3J 109
Brancaster Rd. Ilf —6G 35
Brancepeth Gdns. Buck H —2D 20
Branch Hill. NW3 —3A 44
Branch Hill Ho. NW3 —3K 43
Branch Pl. N1 —1D 62
Branch Rd. E14 —7A 64
Brancker Clo. Wall —7J 133
Brancker Rd. Harr —3D 24
Brancroft Way. Enf —1F 9
Brandlehow Rd. SW15 —4H 91
Brandon. NW9 —2B 26
(off Further Acre)
Brandon Est. SE17 —6B 78
Brandon M. EC2 —5D 62 (6A 142)
(off Barbican)
Brandon Rd. E17 —4E 32
Brandon Rd. N7 —7J 45
Brandon Rd. S'hall —5D 70
Brandon Rd. Sutt —4K 131
Brandon St. SE17 —4C 78 (9M 147)
(in three parts)
Brandram Rd. SE13 —3G 97
Brandreth Ct. Harr —6K 23
Brandreth Rd. E6 —6D 66
Brandreth Rd. SW17 —2F 109
Brandries, The. Wall —3H 133
Brand St. SE10 —7E 80
Brandville Gdns. Ilf —4F 35
Brandy Way. Sutt —7J 131
Brangbourne Rd. Brom —5E 112
Brangton Rd. SE11 —5A 78
Brangwyn Cres. SW19 —1A 122
Branksea St. SW6 —7G 75
Branksome Av. N18 —6A 18
Branksome Rd. SW2 —5J 93
Branksome Rd. SW19 —1J 121
Branksome Way. Harr —6F 25
Branksome Way. N Mald —1J 119
Branksone Ct. N2 —3A 28
Branscombe Ct. Brom —5H 127
Branscombe Gdns. N21 —7F 7
Branscombe St. SE13 —3D 96
Bransdale Clo. NW6 —1J 59
Bransgrove Rd. Edgw —1F 25
Branston Cres. Orp —7H 129
Branstone Rd. Rich —1F 89
Brants Wlk. W7 —4J 55
Brantwood Av. Eri —7J 85
Brantwood Av. Iswth —4A 88
Brantwood Clo. E17 —3E 32
Brantwood Gdns. Enf —4D 6
Brantwood Gdns. Ilf —4C 34
Brantwood Ho. N17 —6B 18
Brantwood Rd. SE24 —5C 94
Brantwood Rd. Bexh —2H 101
Brantwood Rd. S Croy —7C 134
Brasher Clo. Gnfd —3H 39
Brassett Point. E15 —1G 65
(off Abbey Rd.)

Brassey Rd. NW6 —6H 43
Brassey Sq. SW11 —3E 92
Brassie Av. W3 —6A 58
Brass Tally All. SE16 —2K 79
Brasted Clo. SE26 —4J 111
Brasted Clo. Bexh —5D 100
Brasted Lodge. SE20 —7C 112
Brasted Rd. Eri —7K 85
Brathway Rd. SW18 —7K 91
Bratley St. E1 —4G 63
Bratten Ct. Croy —6D 124
Braund Av. Gnfd —4F 55
Braundton Av. Sidc —1K 115
Braunston Dri. Hay —4C 54
Bravington Pl. W9 —4H 59
Bravington Rd. W9 —3H 59
Braxfield Rd. SE4 —4A 96
Braxted Pk. SW16 —6K 109
Brayards Rd. SE15 —2H 95
Brayards Rd. Est. SE15 —2J 95
(off Brayards Rd.)
Braybourne Dri. Iswth —7K 71
Braybrook St. W12 —5B 58
Brayburne Av. SW4 —2G 93
Bray Clo. SW16 —5J 109
Bray Cres. SE16 —2K 79
Braydon Rd. N16 —1G 47
Bray Dri. E16 —7H 65
Brayfield Ter. N1 —7A 46
Brayford Sq. E1 —6J 63
Bray Pas. E16 —7J 65
Bray Pl. SW3 —4D 76
Bray Rd. NW7 —6A 14
Brayton Gdns. Enf —4C 6
Braywood Rd. SE9 —4H 99
Brazil Clo. Bedd —7J 123
Breach La. Dag —3G 69
Bread St. EC4 —6C 62 (9M 141)
Breakspears Dri. Orp —7A 116
Breakspears M. SE4 —2B 96
Breakspears Rd. SE4 —4B 96
Bream Clo. N17 —4H 31
Bream Gdns. E6 —3E 66
Breamore Clo. SW15 —1C 106
Breamore Rd. Ilf —2K 51
Bream's Bldgs. EC4
—6A 62 (7G 141)
Bream St. E3 —7C 48
Bream St. E9 —7C 48
Breamwater Gdns. Rich —3B 104
Brearley Clo. Edgw —7D 12
Breasley Clo. SW15 —4E 90
Brechin Pl. SW7 —4A 76
Brecknock M. N7 —5H 45
Brecknock Rd. N19 & N7 —4G 45
Brecknock Rd. Est. N19 —4G 45
Breckonmead. Brom —2A 128
Brecon Clo. Mitc —3J 123
Brecon Clo. Wor Pk —2C 130
Brecon Grn. NW9 —6A 26
Brecon Rd. W6 —6G 75
Brecon Rd. Enf —4D 8
Brede Clo. E6 —3E 66
Bredgar Rd. N19 —2G 45
Bredhurst Clo. SE20 —6J 111
Bredo Ho. Bark —3B 68
Bredon Rd. Croy —7F 125
Breer St. SW6 —3K 91
Breezer's Hill. E1 —7G 63
Brember Rd. Harr —2G 39
Bremner Rd. SW7 —3A 76
Brenchley Clo. Brom —6H 127
Brenchley Clo. Chst —1E 128
Brenchley Gdns. SE23 —6J 95
Brenchley Rd. Orp —2K 129
Brenda Rd. SW17 —2D 108
Brendon Av. NW10 —5A 42

Brendon Gdns. Harr —4F 39
Brendon Gdns. Ilf —5J 35
Brendon Rd. SE9 —2H 115
Brendon Rd. Dag —1F 53
Brendon St. W1 —6C 60 (7D 138)
Brendon Vs. N21 —1H 17
Brendon Way. Enf —7K 7
Brenley Clo. Mitc —3E 122
Brenley Gdns. SE9 —4B 98
Brennand Ct. N19 —3G 45
Brent Clo. Bex —1E 116
Brentcot Clo. W13 —4B 56
Brent Ct. NW11 —7F 27
Brent Ct. W7 —7H 55
Brent Cres. NW10 —2F 57
Brent Cross Fly-Over. NW2 —7F 27
Brent Cross Shopping Cen. NW4
—7E 26
Brentfield. NW10 —7H 41
Brentfield Clo. NW10 —6K 41
Brentfield Gdns. NW2 —7F 27
Brentfield Ho. NW10 —7K 41
Brentfield Rd. NW10 —6K 41
Brentford Bus. Cen. Bren —7C 72
Brentford Clo. Hay —4B 54
Brentford Ho. Twic —7B 88
Brent Grn. NW4 —5E 26
Brent Grn. Wlk. Wemb —3J 41
Brentham Way. W5 —4D 56
Brenthouse Rd. E9 —6J 47
Brenthurst Rd. NW10 —6B 42
Brent Lea. Bren —7C 72
Brentmead Clo. W7 —7J 55
Brentmead Gdns. NW10 —2F 57
Brentmead Pl. NW11 —6F 27
Brent New Enterprise Cen. NW10
—6B 42
Brenton St. E14 —6A 64
Brent Pk. Ind. Est. W7 —3A 70
Brent Pk. Rd. NW9 & NW4 —7C 26
(in two parts)
Brent Pl. Barn —5C 4
Brent Rd. E16 —6J 65
Brent Rd. SE18 —7F 83
Brent Rd. Bren —6C 72
Brent Rd. S'hall —3A 70
Brent Rd. S Croy —7H 135
Brent Side. Bren —6C 72
Brentside Clo. W13 —4A 56
Brentside Executive Pk. Bren —6C 72
Brent St. NW4 —4E 26
Brent Ter. NW2 —1E 42
Brent Trading Cen. NW10 —5A 42
Brentvale Av. S'hall —1H 71
Brentvale Av. Wemb —6F 57
Brent View Rd. NW9 —6C 26
Brentwater Bus. Pk. Bren —7C 72
Brent Way. N3 —6D 14
Brent Way. Bren —7D 72
Brent Way. Wemb —6H 41
Brentwick Gdns. Bren —4E 72
Brentwood Clo. SE9 —1G 115
Brentwood Lodge. NW4 —5F 27
(off Holmdale Gdns.)
Brereton Rd. N17 —7A 18
Bressenden Pl. SW1
—3F 77 (6K 145)
Bressey Gro. E18 —2H 33
Breton Highwalk. EC2
(off Golden La.) —5C 62 (5M 141)
Breton Ho. EC2 —5C 62 (5M 141)
(off Barbican)
Brett Clo. N16 —2E 46
Brett Clo. N'holt —3B 54
Brett Ct. N9 —2D 18
Brett Cres. NW10 —1K 57
Brettell St. SE17 —5D 78
Brettenham Av. E17 —1C 32

Brettenham Rd. E17 —2C 32
Brettenham Rd. N18 —4B 18
Brett Gdns. Dag —7E 52
Brett Ho. Clo. SW15 —7F 91
Brett Pas. E8 —5H 47
Brett Rd. E8 —5H 47
Brewers Grn. SW1 —3G 77 (6M 145)
(off Buckingham Ga.)
Brewer's Hall Garden. EC2
(off London Wall) —5C 62 (6M 141)
Brewers La. Rich —5D 88
Brewer St. W1 —7G 61 (1M 145)
Brewery Clo. Wemb —5A 40
Brewery La. Twic —7K 87
Brewery M. Bus. Cen. Iswth —3K 87
Brewery Rd. N7 —7J 45
Brewery Rd. SE18 —5H 83
Brewery Rd. Brom —7C 128
Brewery Sq. SE1 —1F 79 (3E 148)
(off Horselydown La.)
Brewhouse La. E1 —1H 79
Brewhouse Rd. SE18 —4D 82
Brewhouse St. SW15 —3G 91
Brewhouse Wlk. SE16 —1A 80
Brewhouse Yd. EC1 —4B 62 (3J 140)
Brewood Rd. Dag —6B 52
Brewster Gdns. W10 —5E 58
Brewster Rd. E10 —1D 48
Brian Rd. Romf —5C 36
Briant Ho. SE1 —3K 77 (7F 146)
(off Hercules Rd.)
Briants Clo. Pinn —2D 22
Briant St. SE14 —1K 95
Briar Av. SW16 —7K 109
Briarbank Rd. W13 —6A 56
Briar Clo. N2 —3K 27
Briar Clo. N13 —3H 17
Briar Clo. Buck H —2G 21
Briar Clo. Hamp —5D 102
Briar Clo. Iswth —5K 87
Briar Ct. E8 —7F 47
Briar Ct. Sutt —4E 130
Briar Cres. N'holt —6F 39
Briardale Gdns. NW3 —3J 43
Briarfield Av. N3 —2K 27
Briar Gdns. Brom —1H 137
Briar La. Cars —7E 132
Briar La. Croy —4D 136
Briar Rd. NW2 —4E 42
Briar Rd. SW16 —3J 123
Briar Rd. Bex —3K 117
Briar Rd. Harr —5C 24
Briar Rd. Twic —1J 103
Briars Clo. N17 —7C 18
Briars, The. Bush —1D 10
Briar Wlk. SW15 —4D 90
Briar Wlk. W10 —4G 59
Briar Wlk. Edgw —7D 12
Briarwood Clo. NW9 —6J 25
Briarwood Rd. SW4 —5H 93
Briarwood Rd. Eps —6C 130
Briary Clo. NW3 —7C 44
Briary Ct. Sidc —5B 116
Briary Gdns. Brom —5K 113
Briary Gro. Edgw —2H 25
Briary La. N9 —3A 18
Briary Lodge. Beck —1E 126
Brick Ct. EC4 —6A 62 (8G 141)
Brick Farm Clo. Rich —1H 89
Brickfield Clo. Bren —7C 72
Brickfield Cotts. SE18 —6K 83
Brickfield Rd. SW19 —4K 107
Brickfield Rd. T Hth —1B 124
Brickfields. Harr —2H 39
(in two parts)
Brick La. E1 —4F 63
Brick La. E2 —3F 63 (2F 142)
Brick La. Enf —2C 8

ick La. Stan —7J 11
ick St. W1 —1F 77 (3J 145)
ickwood Clo. SE26 —3H 111
ickwood Rd. Croy —2E 134
ide Ct. EC4 —6B 62 (8J 141)
(off Bride La.)
ide La. EC4 —6B 62 (8J 141)
ide St. N7 —6K 45
idewell Pl. E1 —1H 79
idewell Pl. EC4 —6B 62 (8J 141)
idford M. W1 —5F 61 (5K 139)
idge App. NW1 —7E 44
idge Av. W6 —4E 74
idge Av. W7 —5H 55
idge Clo. Enf —2C 8
idge Clo. Tedd —4K 103
idge Ct. E10 —1B 48
idge Dri. N13 —4E 16
idge End. E17 —1E 32
idgefield Rd. Sutt —6J 131
idgefoot. SE1 —5J 77
idge Ga. N21 —7H 7
idge Ho. E9 —6K 47
(off Homerton High St.)
idge Ho. Sutt —6K 131
(off Bridge Rd.)
idge Ho. Quay. E14 —1E 80
idgeland Rd. E16 —7J 65
idge La. NW11 —5G 27
idge La. SW11 —1C 92
idgeman Rd. N1 —7K 45
idgeman Rd. Tedd —6A 104
idgeman St. NW8 —2C 60
idge Meadows. SE14 —6K 79
idgend Rd. SW18 —4A 92
idgenhall Rd. Enf —1A 8
idgen Rd. Bex —7E 100
idgepark. SW18 —5J 91
idge Pl. SW1 —4F 77 (8K 145)
idge Pl. Croy —1D 134
idgeport Pl. E1 —1G 79
idge Rd. E6 —7D 50
idge Rd. E15 —7F 49
idge Rd. E17 —7B 32
idge Rd. N9 —3B 18
idge Rd. N22 —1J 29
idge Rd. NW10 —6A 42
idge Rd. Beck —7B 112
idge Rd. Bexh —2E 100
idge Rd. Houn & Iswth —3H 87
idge Rd. Romf —6K 37
idge Rd. S'hall —2D 70
idge Rd. Sutt —6K 131
idge Rd. Twic —6B 88
idge Rd. Wall —5G 133
idge Rd. Wemb —3G 41
idge Row. Croy —1D 134
idges Ct. SW11 —2B 92
(in two parts)
idges La. Croy —4J 133
idges Pl. SW6 —1H 91
idges Rd. SW19 —6K 107
idges Rd. Stan —5E 10
idges Rd. M. SW19 —6K 107
idge St. SW1 —2J 77 (5C 146)
idge St. W4 —4K 73
idge St. Pinn —3C 22
idge St. Rich —5D 88
idge Ter. E15 —7F 49
(in two parts)
idge, The. Harr —4K 23
idgetown Clo. SE19 —5E 110
idge View. W6 —5E 74
idgewater Clo. Chst —3J 129
idgewater Gdns. Edgw —2F 25
idgewater Rd. E15 —1E 64
idgewater Rd. Wemb —6C 40
idgewater Sq. EC2 —5C 62 (5L 141)
Bridgewater St. EC2
—5C 62 (5L 141)
Bridge Way. N11 —3B 16
Bridge Way. NW11 —5H 27
Bridgeway. Bark —7K 51
Bridge Way. Twic —7G 87
Bridge Way. Wemb —7E 40
Bridgeway St. NW1 —2G 61
Bridge Wharf. E3 —2K 63
Bridge Wharfe Rd. Iswth —3B 88
Bridge Wharf Rd. Iswth —3B 88
Bridgewood Clo. SE20 —7H 111
Bridgewood Rd. SW16 —7H 109
Bridgewood Rd. Wor Pk —4C 130
Bridge Yd. SE1 —1D 78 (2B 148)
Bridgford St. SW18 —3A 108
Bridgman Rd. W4 —3J 73
Bridle Clo. King T —4D 118
Bridle La. W1 —7G 61 (9M 139)
Bridle Path. Croy —3J 133
Bridle Path, The. E4 —7B 20
Bridle Rd. Croy —3C 136
(in two parts)
Bridle Rd. Pinn —6A 22
Bridle Rd. S Croy —7G 135
Bridle Way. Croy —4C 136
Bridleway, The. Wall —5G 133
Bridlington Rd. N9 —7C 8
Bridport Av. Romf —6H 37
Bridport Ho. N1 —1D 62
(off Colville Est.)
Bridport Pl. N1 —1D 62
(in three parts)
Bridport Rd. N18 —5K 17
Bridport Rd. T Hth —3A 124
Bridport Ter. SW8 —1H 93
Bridstow Pl. W2 —6J 59
Brief St. SE5 —1B 94
Brierley. New Ad —6D 136
(in two parts)
Brierley Av. N9 —1D 18
Brierley Clo. SE25 —4G 125
Brierley Rd. E11 —4F 49
Brierley Rd. SW12 —2G 109
Brierly Gdns. E2 —2J 63
Brigade Clo. Harr —2H 39
Brigade St. SE3 —2H 97
Brigadier Av. Enf —1H 7
Brigadier Hill. Enf —1H 7
Briggeford Clo. E5 —2G 47
Bright Clo. Belv —4D 84
Brightfield Rd. SE12 —5G 97
Brightling Rd. SE4 —6B 96
Brightlingsea Pl. E14 —7B 64
Brightman Rd. SW18 —1B 108
Brighton Av. E17 —5B 32
Brighton Bldgs. SE1
—3E 78 (7C 148)
(off Tower Bri. Rd.)
Brighton Dri. N'holt —6E 38
Brighton Gro. SE14 —1A 96
Brighton Rd. E6 —3E 66
Brighton Rd. N2 —2A 28
Brighton Rd. N16 —4E 46
Brighton Rd. S Croy —5C 134
Brighton Rd. Surb —6C 118
Brighton Rd. Sutt —7K 131
Brighton Ter. SW9 —4K 93
Brightside Rd. SE13 —6F 97
Brightside, The. Enf —1F 9
Bright St. E14 —6D 64
Brightwell Cres. SW17 —5D 108
Brig M. SE8 —6C 80
Brigstock Ho. SE5 —2C 94
Brigstock Rd. Belv —4H 85
Brigstock Rd. T Hth —5A 124
Brill Pl. NW1 —2H 61
Brim Hill. N2 —4A 28
Brimpsfield Clo. SE2 —3B 84
Brimsdon Ind. Est. Enf —2G 9
Brimsdown Av. Enf —2F 9
Brimsdown Ind. Est. Enf —1G 9
Brindle Ga. Sidc —1J 115
Brindley Clo. Bexh —3H 101
Brindley St. SE14 —1B 96
Brindley Way. Brom —5J 113
Brindley Way. S'hall —7F 55
Brindwood Rd. E4 —3G 19
Brinkburn Clo. SE2 —4A 84
Brinkburn Clo. Edgw —3H 25
Brinkburn Gdns. Edgw —3G 25
Brinkley Rd. Wor Pk —2D 130
Brinklow Cres. SE18 —7F 83
Brinkworth Rd. Ilf —3C 34
Brinkworth Way. E9 —6B 48
Brinsdale Rd. NW4 —3F 27
Brinsley Rd. Harr —2H 23
Brinsley St. E1 —6H 63
Brinsworth Clo. Twic —2H 103
Brinsworth Ho. Twic —2H 103
Brinton Wlk. SE1 —1B 78 (3J 147)
(off Chancel St.)
Brion Pl. E14 —5E 64
Brisbane Av. SW19 —1K 121
Brisbane Rd. E10 —2D 48
Brisbane Rd. W13 —2A 72
Brisbane Rd. Ilf —7F 35
Brisbane St. SE5 —7D 78
Briscoe Clo. E11 —3H 49
Briscoe Rd. SW19 —6B 108
Briset Rd. SE9 —3B 98
Briset St. EC1 —5B 62 (5J 141)
Briset Way. N7 —2K 45
Bristol Gdns. SW15 —7E 90
Bristol Gdns. W9 —4K 59
Bristol Ho. Bark —7A 52
(off Margaret Bondfield Av.)
Bristol M. W9 —4K 59
Bristol Pk. Rd. E17 —4A 32
Bristol Rd. E7 —6A 50
Bristol Rd. Gnfd —1F 55
Bristol Rd. Mord —5A 122
Briston Gro. N8 —6J 29
Bristow Rd. SE19 —5E 110
Bristow Rd. Bexh —1E 100
Bristow Rd. Croy —4J 133
Bristow Rd. Houn —3G 87
Britannia Clo. SW4 —4H 93
Britannia Clo. N'holt —3B 54
Britannia La. Twic —7G 87
Britannia Rd. E14 —4C 80
Britannia Rd. N12 —3F 15
Britannia Rd. SW6 —7K 75
Britannia Rd. Ilf —3F 51
Britannia Rd. Surb —7F 119
Britannia Row. N1 —1B 62
Britannia St. WC1 —3K 61 (1E 140)
Britannia Wlk. N1 —2D 62
(in two parts)
Britannia Way. NW10 —4H 57
Britannia Way. SW6 —7K 75
Britannic Highwalk. EC2
(off Moor La.) —5D 62 (6A 142)
Britannic Ho. EC2 —5D 62 (5A 142)
(off Finsbury Cir.)
British Gro. W4 —5B 74
British Gro. W6 —5B 74
British Gro. S. W6 —5C 74
British Legion Rd. E4 —2C 20
British St. E3 —3B 64
Brittain Ho. SE9 —1C 114
Brittain Rd. Dag —3E 52
Brittany Point. SE11
—4A 78 (9G 147)
Britten Clo. NW11 —1K 43
Britten Ct. E15 —2F 65
Britten Dri. S'hall —6E 54
Britten St. SW3 —5C 76
Britton St. EC1 —4B 62 (4J 141)
Brixham Gdns. Ilf —5J 51
Brixham Rd. Well —1D 100
Brixham St. E16 —1E 82
Brixton Est. Edgw —2H 25
Brixton Hill. SW2 —7J 93
Brixton Hill Ct. SW2 —5K 93
Brixton Hill Pl. SW2 —7J 93
Brixton Oval. SW2 —4A 94
Brixton Rd. SW9 & SE11 —4A 94
Brixton Sta. Rd. SW9 —3A 94
Brixton Water La. SW2 —5K 93
Broadbent Clo. N6 —1F 45
Broadbent St. W1 —7F 61 (9J 139)
Broadbridge Clo. SE3 —7J 81
Broadbury Ct. N18 —6C 18
Broad Comn. Est. N16 —1G 47
(off Osbaldeston Rd.)
Broadcoombe. S Croy —7J 135
Broad Ct. WC2 —6J 61 (8D 140)
Broadcroft Av. Stan —2D 24
Broadcroft Rd. Orp —7H 129
Broadfield Clo. NW2 —3E 42
Broadfield Clo. Croy —2J 133
Broadfield Ct. Bush —2D 10
Broadfield Ct. N Har —1F 23
(off Broadfields)
Broadfield Heights. NW7 —4C 12
Broadfield La. NW1 —7H 45
Broadfield Rd. SE6 —7G 97
Broadfields. Harr —2F 23
Broadfields Av. N21 —7F 7
Broadfields Av. Edgw —4C 12
Broadfields Cen. Edgw —1C 12
Broadfield Sq. Enf —2C 8
Broadfields Way. NW10 —5B 42
Broadfield Way. Buck H —3F 21
Broadgate. EC2 —4E 62 (5C 142)
Broadgate Circ. EC2
(off Broadgate) —5E 62 (6C 142)
Broadgate Cir. EC2 —5E 62
Broadgate Ct. EC2 —5E 62 (5C 142)
Broadgate Rd. E16 —6B 66
Broadgates Av. Barn —1E 4
Broadgates Ct. SE11 —5A 78
(off Cleaves St.)
Broadgates Rd. SW18 —1B 108
Broad Grn. Av. Croy —7B 124
Broadhead Strand. NW9 —1B 26
Broadheath Dri. Chst —5D 114
Broadhinton Rd. SW4 —3F 93
Broadhurst Av. Edgw —4C 12
Broadhurst Av. Ilf —4K 51
Broadhurst Clo. NW6 —6A 44
Broadhurst Clo. Rich —5F 89
Broadhurst Gdns. NW6 —6K 43
Broadhurst Gdns. Ruis —2A 38
Broadlands. E17 —3A 32
Broadlands Av. SW16 —2J 109
Broadlands Av. Enf —3C 8
Broadlands Clo. N6 —7E 28
Broadlands Clo. SW16 —2J 109
Broadlands Clo. Enf —3D 8
Broadlands Ct. Rich —7G 73
(off Kew Gdns. Rd.)
Broadlands Lodge. N6 —7D 28
Broadlands Rd. N6 —7D 28
Broadlands Rd. Brom —4K 113
Broadlands, The. Felt —3E 102
Broadlands Way. N Mald —6B 120
Broad La. N8 —5K 29
Broad La. N15 —4F 31
Broad La. Hamp —7D 102
Broad Lawn. SE9 —2E 114
Broadlawns Ct. Harr —1K 23
Broadley St. NW8 —5B 60 (5B 138)
Broadley Ter. NW1 —4C 60 (4D 138)
Broadmead. SE6 —3C 112
Broadmead Av. Wor Pk —7C 120
Broadmead Clo. Hamp —6E 102
Broadmead Clo. Pinn —1C 22
Broadmead Ct. Wfd G —6D 20
Broadmead Rd. Hay & N'holt —4C 54
Broadmead Rd. Wfd G —6D 20
Broad Oak. Wfd G —5E 20
Broad Oak Clo. E4 —5H 19
Broad Oak Clo. Orp —2K 129
Broadoak Rd. Eri —7K 85
Broadoaks Way. Brom —5H 127
Broad Sanctuary. SW1
—2H 77 (5B 146)
Broadstone Pl. W1 —5E 60 (6G 139)
Broad St. Dag —7G 53
Broad St. Tedd —6K 103
Broad St. Av. EC2 —5E 62 (6C 142)
Broad St. Mkt. Dag —7H 53
Broad St. Pl. EC2 —5D 62 (6B 142)
(off Blomfield St.)
Broad View. NW9 —6G 25
Broadview Rd. SW16 —7H 109
Broadwalk. E18 —3H 33
Broad Wlk. N21 —2E 16
Broad Wlk. NW1 —1E 60
Broad Wlk. SE3 —2A 98
Broad Wlk. W2 & W1
—7D 60 (1F 144)
Broad Wlk. Houn —1B 86
Broadwalk. N Har —5E 22
Broad Wlk. Rich —7F 73
Broad Wlk. La. NW11 —7H 27
Broadwalk Shopping Cen. Edgw
—6C 12
Broad Wlk., The. W8 —1K 75
Broad Wlk., The. E Mol —4A 118
Broadwall. SE1 —1A 78 (2H 147)
Broadwater Farm Est. N17 —2D 30
Broadwater Rd. N17 —1E 30
Broadwater Rd. SE28 —3H 83
Broadwater Rd. SW17 —4C 108
Broadway. E13 —2K 65
Broadway. E15 —7F 49
(in two parts)
Broadway. NW9 —7C 26
Broadway. SW1 —3H 77 (6A 146)
Broadway. Bark —1G 67
Broadway. Bexh —4E 100
Broadway Arc. W6 —4E 74
(off Hammersmith B'way.)
Broadway Av. Croy —5D 124
Broadway Av. Twic —6B 88
Broadway Clo. Wfd G —6E 20
Broadway Ct. SW19 —6J 107
Broadway Ct. Beck —3E 126
Broadway Gdns. Mitc —4C 122
Broadway Mkt. E8 —1H 63
Broadway M. E5 —7F 31
Broadway M. N13 —5E 16
Broadway M. N21 —1G 17
Broadway Pde. N8 —6J 29
Broadway Pde. Harr —5F 23
Broadway Pl. SW19 —6H 107
Broadway Rd. Hay & N'holt —4C 54
Broadway Shopping Cen. Bexh
—4G 101
Broadway Shopping Mall. SW1
—3H 77 (6A 146)
Broadway, The. E4 —6A 20
Broadway, The. N8 —6J 29
Broadway, The. N9 —3B 18
Broadway, The. N22 —2A 30
Broadway, The. NW7 —5F 13
Broadway, The. SW13 —2A 90
Broadway, The. SW19 —7J 107
Broadway, The. W3 —2G 73

Broadway, The. W5 —7D 56
Broadway, The. W7 & W13 —1J 71
(in two parts)
Broadway, The. Cheam —6G 131
Broadway, The. Croy —4J 133
Broadway, The. Dag —2F 53
Broadway, The. Eps —5C 130
Broadway, The. Gnfd —4G 55
Broadway, The. S'hall —1C 70
Broadway, The. Stan —5H 11
Broadway, The. Sutt —5A 132
Broadway, The. W'stone —2J 23
Broadway, The. Wemb —3E 40
Broadwell. SE1 —1A 78
Broadwell Ct. Houn —1B 86
(off Springwell Rd.)
Broadwick St. W1 —7G 61 (9M 139)
Broad Yd. EC1 —4B 62 (4J 141)
Brocas Clo. NW3 —7C 44
Brockdish Av. Bark —5K 51
Brockenhurst Av. Wor Pk —1A 130
Brockenhurst Gdns. NW7 —5F 13
Brockenhurst Gdns. Ilf —5G 51
Brockenhurst Rd. Croy —7H 125
Brockenhurst Way. SW16 —2H 123
Brocket Ho. SW8 —2H 93
Brockham Clo. SW19 —5H 107
Brockham Cres. New Ad —7F 137
Brockham Dri. SW2 —7K 93
Brockham Dri. Ilf —6F 35
Brockham Ho. SW2 —7K 93
(off Brockham Dri.)
Brockham St. SE1 —3C 78 (6M 147)
Brockhurst Clo. Stan —6E 10
Brockill Cres. SE4 —4A 96
Brocklebank Ho. E16 —1E 82
(off Glenister St.)
Brocklebank Rd. SE7 —4K 81
Brocklebank Rd. SW18 —7A 92
Brocklebank Rd. Ind. Est. SE7 —4J 81
Brocklehurst St. SE14 —7K 79
Brocklesby Rd. SE25 —4H 125
Brockley Av. N. Stan —3K 11
Brockley Av. S. Stan —3K 11
Brockley Clo. Stan —4K 11
Brockley Cres. Romf —1J 37
Brockley Cross. SE4 —3A 96
Brockley Cross Bus. Cen. SE4
—3A 96
Brockley Footpath. SE4 —5A 96
Brockley Footpath. SE15 —4J 95
Brockley Gdns. SE4 —2B 96
Brockley Gro. SE4 —5B 96
Brockley Hall Rd. SE4 —5A 96
Brockley Hill. Stan —1H 11
Brockley Pk. SE23 —7A 96
Brockley Rise. SE23 —1A 112
Brockley Rd. SE4 —3B 96
Brockley Side. Stan —4K 11
Brockley View. SE23 —7A 96
Brockley Way. SE4 —5K 95
Brockman Rise. Brom —4F 113
Brock Pl. E3 —4D 64
Brock Rd. E13 —5K 65
Brocks Dri. Sutt —3G 131
Brockshot Clo. Bren —5D 72
Brock St. SE15 —3J 95
Brockway Clo. E11 —2G 49
Brockwell Clo. Orp —5K 129
Brockwell Ct. SW2 —5A 94
Brockwell Pk. Gdns. SE24 —7B 94
Brockworth Clo. SE15 —6E 78
Broderick Gro. SE2 —4B 84
Brodia Rd. N16 —3E 46
Brodie Rd. E4 —1K 19
Brodie Rd. Enf —1H 7
Brodie St. SE1 —5F 79

Brodlove La. E1 —7K 63
Brodrick Rd. SW17 —2C 108
Brograve Gdns. Beck —2D 126
Broken Wharf. EC4 —7C 62 (9L 141)
Brokesley St. E3 —3B 64
Broke Wlk. E8 —1G 63
Bromar Rd. SE5 —3E 94
Bromefield. Stan —1C 24
Brome Rd. SE9 —3D 98
Bromfelde Rd. SW4 —3H 93
Bromfelde Wlk. SW4 —2H 93
Bromfield St. N1 —2A 62
Bromhall Rd. Dag —6B 52
Bromhedge. SE9 —3D 114
Bromholm Rd. SE2 —3B 84
Bromleigh Ct. SE23 —2H 111
Bromley Av. Brom —7G 113
Bromley Comn. Brom —4A 128
Bromley Cres. Brom —3H 127
Bromley Gdns. Brom —3H 127
Bromley Gro. Brom —2F 127
Bromley Hall Rd. E14 —5E 64
Bromley High St. E3 —3D 64
Bromley Hill. Brom —6G 113
Bromley La. Chst —7G 115
Bromley Pk. Brom —1H 127
Bromley Pl. W1 —5G 61 (5L 139)
Bromley Rd. E10 —6D 32
Bromley Rd. E17 —3C 32
Bromley Rd. N17 —1F 31
Bromley Rd. N18 —3J 17
Bromley Rd. SE6 & Brom —1D 112
Bromley Rd. Beck & Brom —1D 126
Bromley Rd. Chst —1F 129
Bromley St. E1 —5K 63
Brompton Arc. SW3
—2D 76 (5F 144)
(off Brompton Rd.)
Brompton Clo. SE20 —2G 125
Brompton Clo. Houn —5D 86
Brompton Gro. N2 —4C 28
Brompton Pk. Cres. SW6 —6K 75
Brompton Pl. SW3 —3C 76 (6D 144)
Brompton Rd. SW3, SW7 & SW1
—4C 76 (8C 144)
Brompton Sq. SW3 —3C 76 (6C 144)
Brompton Ter. SE18 —1D 98
Bromwells Rd. SW4 —4G 93
Bromwich Av. N6 —2E 44
Bromyard Av. W3 —7A 58
Brondesbury M. NW6 —7J 43
Brondesbury Pk. NW2 & NW6
—6D 42
Brondesbury Rd. NW6 —2H 59
Brondesbury Vs. NW6 —2H 59
Bronsart Rd. SW6 —7G 75
Bronson Rd. SW20 —2F 121
Bronte Clo. E7 —4J 49
Bronte Clo. Ilf —4E 34
Bronte Ho. N16 —5E 46
Bronte Ho. SW4 —7G 93
Bronti Clo. SE17 —5C 78
Bronze St. SE8 —7C 80
Brook Av. Dag —7H 53
Brook Av. Edgw —5C 12
Brook Av. Wemb —3F 41
Brookbank Av. W7 —4H 55
Brookbank Rd. SE13 —3C 96
Brodrick Rd. NW7 —7B 14
Brook Clo. SW20 —3D 120
Brook Clo. W3 —1G 73
Brook Ct. E11 —3G 49
Brook Ct. E15 —5D 48
(off Clays La.)
Brook Ct. E17 —3A 32
Brook Ct. Edgw —5C 12
Brook Cres. E4 —4H 19
Brook Cres. N9 —4C 18

Brookdale. N11 —4B 16
Brookdale Rd. E17 —3C 32
Brookdale Rd. SE6 —7D 96
Brookdale Rd. Bex —6E 100
Brookdene Rd. SE18 —4K 83
Brook Dri. SE11 —3A 78 (7H 147)
Brook Dri. Harr —4G 23
Brooke Av. Harr —3G 39
Brooke Clo. Bush —1B 10
Brookehowse Rd. SE6 —2C 112
Brookend Rd. Sidc —1J 115
Brooke Rd. E5 —3G 47
Brooke Rd. E17 —4E 32
Brooke Rd. N16 —3F 47
Brooke's Ct. EC1 —5A 62 (6G 141)
Brooke St. EC1 —5A 62 (6G 141)
Brooke Way. Bush —1B 10
Brookfield. N6 —3E 44
Brookfield Av. E17 —4E 32
Brookfield Av. NW7 —6J 13
Brookfield Av. W5 —4D 56
Brookfield Av. Sutt —4C 132
Brookfield Clo. NW7 —6J 13
Brookfield Ct. Gnfd —3G 55
Brookfield Cres. NW7 —6J 13
Brookfield Cres. Harr —5E 24
Brookfield Path. E4 —5H 45
Brookfield Rd. E9 —6A 48
Brookfield Rd. N9 —3B 18
Brookfield Rd. W4 —2K 73
Brookfields. Enf —4E 8
Brookfields Av. Mitc —5C 122
Brook Gdns. E4 —4J 19
Brook Gdns. SW13 —3B 90
Brook Gdns. King T —1J 119
Brook Ga. W1 —7D 60 (1F 144)
Brook Grn. W6 —3F 75
Brook Hill Clo. SE18 —5F 83
Brookhill Clo. Barn —5H 5
Brookhill Rd. SE18 —5F 83
Brookhill Rd. Barn —5H 5
Brookhouse Gdns. E4 —4B 20
Brooking Rd. E7 —5J 49
Brookland Clo. NW11 —4J 27
Brookland Garth. NW11 —4J 27
Brookland Hill. NW11 —4K 27
Brookland Rise. NW11 —4J 27
Brooklands App. Romf —4K 37
Brooklands Av. SW19 —2K 107
Brooklands Av. Sidc —2H 115
Brooklands Clo. Romf —4K 37
Brooklands Ct. N21 —5J 7
Brooklands Ct. Mitc —2B 122
Brooklands Dri. Gnfd —1D 56
Brooklands La. Romf —4K 37
Brooklands Pk. SE3 —3J 97
Brooklands Rd. Romf —4K 37
Brooklands, The. Iswth —1H 87
Brook La. SE3 —2K 97
Brook La. Bex —6D 100
Brook La. Brom —6J 113
Brook La. N. Bren —5D 72
(in two parts)
Brook La. Trading Cen. Bren —5D 72
Brooklea Clo. NW9 —1A 26
Brooklyn Av. SE25 —4H 125
Brooklyn Clo. Cars —2C 132
Brooklyn Gro. SE25 —4H 125
Brooklyn Rd. SE25 —4H 125
Brooklyn Rd. Brom —5B 128
Brook Mead. Eps —6A 130
Brookmead Av. Brom —5D 128

Brookmead Ind. Est. Croy —6G 123
Brook Meadow. N12 —3E 14
Brook Meadow Clo. E4 —6B 20
Brookmead Rd. Croy —6G 123
Brook M. N. W2 —7A 60
Brookmead Rd. SE8 —1C 96
Brook Pde. Chig —3K 21
Brook Pk. Clo. N21 —6G 7
Brook Pas. SW6 —7J 75
Brook Pl. Barn —5D 4
Brook Rise. Chig —3K 21
Brook Rd. N2 —7H 15
Brook Rd. N8 —4J 29
Brook Rd. N22 —3K 29
Brook Rd. NW2 —2B 42
Brook Rd. Buck H —2D 20
Brook Rd. Ilf —6J 35
Brook Rd. T Hth —4C 124
Brook Rd. Twic —6A 88
Brook Rd. S. Bren —6D 72
Brooks Av. E6 —4D 66
Brooksbank St. E9 —6K 47
Brooksby M. N1 —7A 46
Brooksby St. N1 —7A 46
Brooksby's Wlk. E9 —5K 47
Brooks Clo. SE9 —2E 114
Brookscroft Rd. E17 —1D 32
(in two parts)
Brookshill. Harr —5C 10
Brookshill Av. Harr —5C 10
Brookshill Dri. Harr —5C 10
Brookside. N21 —6E 6
Brookside. Barn —6H 5
Brookside. Cars —5E 132
Brookside. Orp —7K 129
Brookside Clo. Barn —6B 4
Brookside Clo. Kent —5D 24
Brookside Clo. S Harr —4C 38
Brookside Cres. Wor Pk —1C 130
Brookside Rd. N9 —4C 18
Brookside Rd. N19 —2G 45
Brookside Rd. NW11 —6G 27
Brookside Rd. Hay —7A 54
Brookside S. Barn —7K 5
Brookside Wlk. N12 —6D 14
Brookside Way. Croy —6K 125
Brooks La. W4 —6G 73
Brooks M. W1 —7F 61 (9J 139)
Brooks Rd. E13 —1J 65
Brooks Rd. W4 —5G 73
Brookstone Ct. SE15 —4H 95
Brook St. N17 —2F 31
Brook St. W1 —7F 61 (9H 139)
Brook St. W2 —7B 60 (9B 138)
Brook St. Belv & Eri —5H 85
Brook St. King T —2E 118
Brooksville Av. NW6 —1G 59
Brooks Wlk. N3 —3G 27
Brook Vale. Eri —1H 101
Brookview Ct. Enf —5K 7
Brookview Rd. SW16 —5G 109
Brookville Rd. SW6 —7H 75
Brook Wlk. N2 —1B 28
Brook Wlk. Edgw —6E 12
Brookway. SE3 —3J 97
Brook Way. Chig —3K 21
Brookwood Av. SW13 —2B 90
Brookwood Clo. Brom —4H 127
Brookwood Rd. SW18 —1H 107
Brookwood Rd. Houn —2F 87
Broom Clo. Brom —6C 128
Broom Clo. Tedd —7D 104
Broome Rd. Hamp —7D 102
Broome Way. SE5 —7D 78
Broomfield. E17 —7B 32
Broomfield Av. N13 —5E 16
Broomfield Ct. SE16 —3G 79
(off John Roll Way)

Broomfield Ho. Stan —3F 11
(off Stanmore Hill)
Broomfield La. N13 —4D 16
Broomfield Pl. W13 —1B 72
Broomfield Rd. N13 —5D 16
Broomfield Rd. W13 —1B 72
Broomfield Rd. Beck —3B 126
Broomfield Rd. Bexh —5G 101
Broomfield Rd. Rich —1F 89
Broomfield Rd. Romf —7D 36
Broomfield Rd. Surb —7F 119
Broomfield Rd. Tedd —6C 104
Broomfield St. E14 —5C 64
Broom Gdns. Croy —3C 136
Broomgrove Gdns. Edgw —1G 25
Broomgrove Rd. SW9 —2K 93
Broomhall Rd. S Croy —7D 134
Broomhill Ct. Wfd G —6D 20
Broom Hill Rise. Bexh —5G 101
Broomhill Rd. Ilf —2A 52
Broomhill Rd. Orp —7K 129
Broomhill Rd. Wfd G —6D 20
(in two parts)
Broomhill Wlk. Wfd G —7C 20
Broomhouse La. SW6 —2J 91
Broomhouse Rd. SW6 —2J 91
Broomloan La. Sutt —2J 131
Broom Lock. Tedd —6C 104
Broom Mead. Bexh —5G 101
Broom Pk. Tedd —7D 104
Broom Rd. Croy —3C 136
Broom Rd. Tedd —5B 104
Broomsleigh Bus. Pk. SE26 —5B 112
(off Worsley Bri. Rd.)
Broomsleigh St. NW6 —5H 43
Broom Water. Tedd —6C 104
Broom Water W. Tedd —5C 104
Broomwood Rd. SW11 —6D 92
Broseley Gro. SE26 —5A 112
Broster Gdns. SE25 —3F 125
Brougham Rd. E8 —1G 63
Brougham Rd. W3 —6J 57
Brougham St. SW11 —2D 92
Brough Clo. SW8 —7J 77
Brough St. SW8 —7J 77
Broughton Av. N3 —3G 27
Broughton Av. Rich —3B 104
Broughton Ct. W13 —7B 56
Broughton Dri. SW9 —4B 94
Broughton Gdns. N6 —6G 29
Broughton Rd. SW6 —2K 91
Broughton Rd. W13 —7B 56
Broughton Rd. T Hth —6A 124
Broughton St. SW8 —2E 92
Brouncker Rd. W3 —2J 73
Browells La. Felt —2A 102
Brown Bear Ct. Felt —4B 102
Brown Clo. Wall —7J 133
Brownfield St. E14 —6D 64
Brown Hart Gdns. W1
—7E 60 (9H 139)
Brownhill Rd. SE6 —7D 96
Browning Av. W7 —6K 55
Browning Av. Sutt —4C 132
Browning Av. Wor Pk —1D 130
Browning Clo. W9 —4A 60
Browning Clo. Col R —1F 37
Browning Clo. Hamp —4D 102
Browning Clo. Well —1J 99
Browning M. W1 —5F 61 (6H 139)
Browning Rd. E11 —7H 33
Browning Rd. E12 —5D 50
Browning Rd. Enf —1J 7
Browning St. SE17 —5C 78
Browning Way. Houn —1B 86
Brownlea Gdns. Ilf —2A 52
Brownlow Ct. N2 —5B 28

Brownlow Ct. N11 —6D 16
(off Brownlow Rd.)
Brownlow Ho. SE16 —2G 79
(off George Row)
Brownlow M. WC1 —4K 61 (4F 140)
Brownlow Rd. E7 —4J 49
Brownlow Rd. E8 —1G 63
Brownlow Rd. N3 —7E 14
Brownlow Rd. N11 —6D 15
Brownlow Rd. NW10 —7A 42
Brownlow Rd. W13 —1A 72
Brownlow Rd. Croy —4E 134
Browns Arc. W1 —7G 61 (1M 145)
(off Regent St.)
Brown's Bldgs. EC3
—6E 62 (8D 142)
Brownspring Dri. SE9 —4F 115
Browns Rd. E17 —3C 32
Browns Rd. Surb —7F 119
Brown St. W1 —6D 60 (7E 138)
Brownswell Rd. N2 —2B 28
Brownswood Rd. N4 —3B 46
Broxash Rd. SW11 —6E 92
Broxbourne Av. E18 —4K 33
Broxbourne Rd. E7 —3J 49
Broxbourne Rd. Orp —7K 129
Broxholme Ho. SW6 —1K 91
(off Harwood Rd.)
Broxholm Rd. SE27 —3A 110
Broxted Rd. SE6 —2B 112
Broxwood Way. NW8 —1C 60
Bruce Castle Ct. N17 —1F 31
(off Lordship La.)
Bruce Castle Rd. N17 —1F 31
Bruce Clo. W10 —5F 59
Bruce Clo. Well —1B 100
Bruce Ct. Sidc —4K 115
Bruce Gdns. N20 —3J 15
Bruce Gro. N17 —1E 30
Bruce Hall M. SW17 —4E 108
Bruce Rd. E3 —3D 64
Bruce Rd. NW10 —7K 41
Bruce Rd. SE25 —4D 124
Bruce Rd. Barn —3B 4
Bruce Rd. Harr —2J 23
Bruce Rd. Mitc —7E 108
Brudenell Rd. SW17 —3D 108
Bruffs Meadow. N'holt —6C 38
Bruges Pl. NW1 —7G 45
Brummel Clo. Bexh —3J 101
Brumwill Rd. W5 —2E 56
Brunel Clo. SE19 —6F 111
Brunel Clo. N'holt —3D 54
Brunel Est. W2 —5J 59
Brunel Pl. S'hall —7F 55
Brunel Rd. SE16 —2J 79
Brunel Rd. W3 —5A 58
Brunel Rd. Wfd G —5J 21
Brunel St. E16 —6H 65
Brunel Wlk. N15 —4E 30
Brunel Wlk. Twic —7E 86
Brune St. E1 —5F 63 (6E 142)
Brunner Clo. NW11 —5K 27
Brunner Ho. SE6 —4E 112
Brunner Rd. E17 —5A 32
Bruno Pl. NW9 —2J 41
Brunswick Av. N11 —3K 15
(in two parts)
Brunswick Cen. WC1
—4J 61 (3D 140)
Brunswick Clo. Bexh —4D 100
Brunswick Clo. Pinn —6C 22
Brunswick Clo. Twic —3H 103
Brunswick Clo. Est. EC1
(off Wyclif St.) —3B 62 (2J 141)

Brunswick Ct. SE1 —2E 78 (5D 148)
Brunswick Ct. Barn —5G 5
Brunswick Ct. Sutt —4K 131
Brunswick Cres. N11 —3K 15
Brunswick Gdns. W5 —4E 56
Brunswick Gdns. W8 —1J 75
Brunswick Gro. N11 —3K 15
Brunswick Ho. N3 —1H 27
Brunswick Ind. Pk. N11 —4A 16
Brunswick M. SW16 —6H 109
Brunswick Pk. SE5 —1E 94
Brunswick Pk. Gdns. N11 —2K 15
Brunswick Pk. Rd. N11 —2K 15
Brunswick Pl. N1 —3D 62 (2B 142)
Brunswick Pl. SE19 —7G 111
Brunswick Quay. SE16 —3K 79
Brunswick Rd. E10 —1E 48
Brunswick Rd. E14 —6E 64
Brunswick Rd. N15 —4E 30
(in two parts)
Brunswick Rd. W5 —4D 56
Brunswick Rd. Bexh —4D 100
Brunswick Rd. King T —1G 119
Brunswick Rd. Sutt —4K 131
Brunswick Sq. N17 —6A 18
Brunswick Sq. WC1
—4J 61 (3D 140)
Brunswick St. E17 —5E 32
Brunswick Vs. SE5 —1E 94
Brunswick Way. N11 —4A 16
Brunton Pl. E14 —6A 64
Brushfield St. E1 —5E 62 (6D 142)
Brussells Rd. SW11 —4B 92
Bruton Clo. Chst —7D 114
Bruton La. W1 —7F 61 (1K 145)
Bruton Pl. W1 —7F 61 (1K 145)
Bruton Rd. Mord —4A 122
Bruton St. W1 —7F 61 (1K 145)
Bruton Way. W13 —5A 56
Bryan Av. NW10 —7D 42
Bryan Ho. SE16 —3B 80
Bryan Rd. SE16 —2B 80
Bryanston Av. Twic —1F 103
Bryanston Clo. S'hall —4D 70
Bryanston Ct. Sutt —4A 132
Bryanston Rd. N8 —6H 29
Bryanston M. E. W1
—5D 60 (6E 138)
Bryanston M. W. W1
—5D 60 (6E 138)
Bryanston Pl. W1 —5D 60 (6E 138)
Bryanston Sq. W1 —6D 60 (6E 138)
Bryanston St. W1 —6D 60 (6E 138)
Bryant Clo. Barn —5C 4
Bryant Ct. E2 —2F 63
(off Whiston Rd.)
Bryant Rd. N'holt —3A 54
Bryant St. E15 —7F 49
Bryantwood Rd. N7 —5A 46
Brycedale Cres. N14 —4C 16
Bryce Rd. Dag —4C 52
Bryden Clo. SE26 —5A 112
Brydges Pl. WC2 —7J 61 (1C 146)
Brydges Rd. E15 —5F 49
Brydon Wlk. N1 —1J 61
Bryer Ct. EC2 —5C 62 (5L 141)
(off Barbican)
Bryett Rd. N7 —3J 45
Brymay Clo. E3 —2C 64
Brynmaer Rd. SW11 —1D 92
Brynmawr Rd. Enf —4A 8
Bryony Rd. W12 —7C 58
Buccleugh Ho. E5 —7G 31
Buchanan Gdns. NW10 —2D 58
Buchan Rd. SE15 —3J 95
Bucharest Rd. SW18 —7A 92

Buckden Clo. N2 —4D 28
Buckden Clo. SE12 —6H 97
Bucklast Rd. Mord —4K 121
Bucklast St. E2 —3G 63
Buck Hill Wlk. W2 —7B 60 (1B 144)
Buckhold Rd. SW18 —6J 91
Buckhurst Av. Cars —1C 132
Buckhurst Ho. N7 —5H 45
Buckhurst St. E1 —4H 63
Buckhurst Way. Buck H —4G 21
Buckingham Arc. WC2
(off Strand) —7J 61 (1D 146)
Buckingham Av. N20 —7F 5
Buckingham Av. Gnfd —1A 56
Buckingham Av. T Hth —1A 124
Buckingham Av. Well —4J 99
Buckingham Clo. Enf —2K 7
Buckingham Clo. Gnfd —5C 56
Buckingham Clo. Hamp —5D 102
Buckingham Clo. Orp —7J 129
Buckingham Ct. NW4 —3C 26
Buckingham Ct. N'holt —2C 54
Buckingham Dri. Chst —5G 115
Buckingham Gdns. Edgw —7A 12
Buckingham Gdns. T Hth —2A 124
Buckingham Ga. SW1
—3G 77 (6L 145)
Buckingham La. SE23 —7A 96
Buckingham Mans. NW6 —5K 43
(off W. End La.)
Buckingham M. N1 —6D 46
Buckingham M. NW10 —2B 58
Buckingham M. SW1
(off Stafford Pl.) —3G 77 (6L 145)
Buckingham Pal. Rd. SW1
—4F 77 (9J 145)
Buckingham Pde. Stan —5H 11
Buckingham Pl. SW1
—3G 77 (6L 145)
Buckingham Rd. E10 —3D 48
Buckingham Rd. E11 —5A 34
Buckingham Rd. E15 —5H 49
Buckingham Rd. E18 —1H 33
Buckingham Rd. N1 —6E 46
Buckingham Rd. N22 —1J 29
Buckingham Rd. NW10 —2B 58
Buckingham Rd. Edgw —7A 12
Buckingham Rd. Hamp —4D 102
Buckingham Rd. Harr —5H 23
Buckingham Rd. Ilf —2H 51
Buckingham Rd. King T —4F 119
Buckingham Rd. Mitc —5J 123
Buckingham Rd. Rich —2D 104
Buckingham St. WC2
—1J 77 (1D 146)
Buckingham Way. Wall —7G 133
Buckland Ct. N1 —2E 62
(off St Johns Est.)
Buckland Cres. NW3 —7B 44
Buckland Rise. Pinn —1A 22
Buckland Rd. E10 —2E 48
Bucklands Rd. Tedd —6C 104
Buckland St. N1 —2D 62
Buckland Wlk. W3 —2J 73
Buckland Wlk. Mord —4A 122
Buckland Way. Wor Pk —1E 130
Buck La. NW9 —5K 25
Buckleigh Av. SW20 —3G 121
Buckleigh Rd. SW16 —6H 109
Buckleigh Way. SE19 —7F 111
Buckler Gdns. SE9 —3D 114
Bucklers All. SW6 —6H 75
Bucklersbury. EC4 —6D 62 (8A 142)
(in two parts)
Buckler's Way. Cars —3D 132
Buckles Ct. Belv —4D 84
Buckle St. E1 —6F 63
Buckley Rd. NW6 —7H 43

Buckley St. SE1 —1A 78 (3G 147)
(off Mepham St.)
Buckmaster Ho. N7 —4K 45
Buckmaster Rd. SW11 —4C 92
Bucknall St. WC2 —6J 61 (7B 140)
Bucknall Clo. SW2 —4K 93
Buckner Rd. SW2 —4K 93
Buckner St. W10 —3G 59
Buckrell Rd. E4 —2A 20
Buckstone Clo. SE23 —6J 95
Buckstone Rd. N18 —5B 18
Buck St. NW1 —7F 45
Buckters Rents. SE16 —1A 80
Buckthorne Rd. SE4 —5A 96
Buckwheat Ct. Eri —3D 84
Budd Clo. N12 —4E 14
Buddings Circ. Wemb —3J 41
Budd's All. Twic —5C 88
Budge Row. EC4 —7D 62 (9A 142)
Budge's Wlk. W2 —1A 76
(off North Wlk.)
Budleigh Cres. Well —1C 100
Budoch Ct. Ilf —2J 52
Budoch Dri. Ilf —2A 52
Buer Rd. SW6 —2G 91
Bugsby's Way. SE10 & SE7 —4H 81
Bulganak Rd. T Hth —4C 124
Bulinga St. SW1 —4J 77 (9C 146)
Bullace Row. SE5 —1D 94
Bull All. SE1 —7A 62 (1H 147)
Bull All. Well —3B 100
Bullard's Pl. E2 —3K 63
Bullbanks Rd. Belv —4J 85
Bulleid Way. SW1 —4F 77 (9K 145)
Bullen St. SW11 —2C 92
Buller Clo. SE15 —7G 79
Buller Rd. N17 —2G 31
Buller Rd. N22 —2A 30
Buller Rd. NW10 —3F 59
Buller Rd. Bark —7J 51
Buller Rd. T Hth —2D 124
Bullers Clo. Sidc —5E 116
Bullers Wood Dri. Chst —7D 114
Bullescroft Rd. Edgw —3B 12
Bullingham Mans. W8 —2J 75
(off Pitt St.)
Bull Inn Ct. WC2 —7J 61 (1D 146)
(off Strand)
Bullivant St. E14 —6E 64
Bull La. N18 —5K 17
Bull La. Chst —7H 115
Bull La. Dag —3H 53
Bull Rd. E15 —2H 65
Bull's All. SW14 —2K 89
Bullsbridge Rd. S'hall —4A 70
Bullsbrook Rd. Hay —1A 70
Bulls Gdns. SW3 —4C 76 (8D 144)
Bulls Head Pas. EC3
—6E 62 (8C 142)
(off Gracechurch St.)
Bull Yd. SE15 —1G 95
Bulmer Gdns. Harr —7D 24
Bulmer M. W11 —7J 59
Bulmer Pl. W11 —1J 75
Bulow Est. SW6 —1K 91
(off Pearscroft Rd.)
Bulstrode Av. Houn —2D 86
Bulstrode Gdns. Houn —3E 86
Bulstrode Pl. W1 —5E 60 (6H 139)
Bulstrode Rd. Houn —3E 86
Bulstrode St. W1 —6E 60 (7H 139)
Bulwer Ct. E11 —1F 49
Bulwer Ct. Rd. E11 —1F 49
Bulwer Gdns. Barn —4F 5
Bulwer Rd. E11 —7F 33
Bulwer Rd. N18 —4K 17
Bulwer Rd. Barn —4E 4
Bulwer St. W12 —1E 74

Bunce's La. Wfd G —7C 20
Bungalow Rd. SE25 —4E 124
Bungalows, The. E10 —6E 32
Bungalows, The. SW16 —7F 109
Bungalows, The. Ilf —4D 52
Bunhill Row. EC1 —4D 62 (3A 142)
Bunhouse Pl. SW1 —5E 76
Bunkers Hill. NW1 —7A 28
Bunkers Hill. Belv —4G 85
Bunkers Hill. Sidc —3F 117
Bunning Way. N7 —7J 45
Bunns La. NW7 —6F 13
(in two parts)
Bunsen St. E3 —2A 64
Buntingbridge Rd. Ilf —5H 35
Bunting Clo. N9 —1E 18
Bunting Clo. Mitc —5D 122
Bunting Ct. NW9 —2A 26
Bunton St. SE18 —3E 82
Bunyan Ct. EC2 —5C 62 (5L 141)
(off Barbican)
Bunyan Rd. E17 —3A 32
Buonaparte M. SW1 —5H 77
Burbage Clo. SE1 —3D 78 (7A 148)
Burbage Ho. N1 —1D 62
(off Poole St.)
Burbage Rd. SE24 & SE21 —6C 94
Burberry Clo. N Mald —2A 120
Burbridge Way. N17 —2G 31
Burcham St. E14 —6D 64
Burcharbro Rd. SE2 —6D 84
Burchell Ct. Bush —1B 10
Burchell Ho. SE11 —5K 77
(off Jonathan St.)
Burchell Rd. E10 —1D 48
Burchell Rd. SE15 —1H 95
Burchett Way. Romf —6F 37
Burchwall Clo. Romf —1J 37
Burcote Rd. SW18 —7B 92
Burden Clo. Bren —5C 72
Burdenshott Av. Rich —4H 89
Burden Way. E11 —2K 49
Burder Clo. N1 —6E 46
Burder Rd. N1 —6E 46
Burdett M. W2 —6K 59
Burdett Av. SW20 —1C 120
Burdett Clo. W7 —1K 71
(off Silverdale Clo.)
Burdett Clo. Sidc —5E 116
Burdett M. NW3 —6B 44
Burdett M. W2 —6K 59
Burdett Rd. E3 & E14 —4A 64
Burdett Rd. Croy —6D 124
Burdett Rd. Rich —2F 89
Burdetts Rd. Dag —1F 69
Burdett St. SE1 —3A 78 (6G 147)
Burdock Clo. Croy —1K 135
Burdock Rd. N17 —3G 31
Burdon La. Sutt —7G 131
Bure Ct. New Bar —5E 4
Burfield Clo. SW17 —4B 108
Burford Clo. Dag —3C 52
Burford Clo. Ilf —4G 35
Burford Gdns. N13 —3E 16
Burford Ho. Bren —5E 72
Burford Rd. E6 —3C 66
Burford Rd. E15 —1F 65
Burford Rd. SE6 —2B 112
Burford Rd. Bren —5E 72
Burford Rd. Brom —4C 128
Burford Rd. Sutt —2J 131
Burford Rd. Wor Pk —7B 120
Burford Wlk. SW6 —7A 75
Burford Way. New Ad —6E 136
Burge St. E7 —4B 50
Burges Rd. E6 —7C 50
Burgess Av. NW9 —6K 25
Burgess Clo. Felt —4C 102

Burgess Ct. E6 —7E **50**
Burgess Hill. NW2 —4J **43**
Burgess Ind. Pk. SE5 —7D **78**
Burgess Pk. Ind. Est. SE5 —7D **78**
Burgess Rd. E15 —4G **49**
Burgess Rd. Sutt —4K **131**
Burgess St. E14 —5C **64**
Burge St. SE1 —3D **78** (7B **148**)
Burghill Rd. SE26 —4A **112**
Burghley Av. N Mald —1K **119**
Burghley Pl. Mitc —5D **122**
Burghley Rd. E11 —1G **49**
Burghley Rd. N8 —3A **30**
Burghley Rd. NW5 —4F **45**
Burghley Rd. SW19 —4F **107**
Burgh St. N1 —2B **62**
Burgon St. EC4 —6B **62** (8K **141**)
Burgos Gro. SE10 —1D **96**
Burgoyne Rd. N4 —6B **30**
Burgoyne Rd. SE25 —4F **125**
Burgoyne Rd. SW9 —3K **93**
Burham Clo. SE20 —7J **111**
Burhill Gro. Pinn —2C **22**
Burke Clo. SW15 —4A **90**
Burke Lodge. E13 —3K **65**
Burke St. E16 —5H **65**
Burland Rd. SW11 —5D **92**
Burleigh Av. Sidc —5K **99**
Burleigh Av. Wall —3E **132**
Burleigh Gdns. N14 —1B **16**
Burleigh Pde. N14 —1C **16**
Burleigh Pl. SW15 —5F **91**
Burleigh Rd. Enf —4K **7**
Burleigh Rd. Sutt —1G **131**
Burleigh St. WC2 —7K **61** (9E **140**)
Burleigh Wlk. SE6 —1E **112**
Burleigh Way. Enf —3J **7**
Burley Clo. E4 —5H **19**
Burley Clo. SW16 —2H **123**
Burley Rd. E16 —6A **66**
Burlington Arc. W1
—7G **61** (1L **145**)
Burlington Av. Rich —1G **89**
Burlington Av. Romf —6H **37**
Burlington Clo. E6 —6C **66**
Burlington Clo. W9 —4J **59**
Burlington Gdns. W1
—7G **61** (1L **145**)
Burlington Gdns. W3 —1J **73**
Burlington Gdns. W4 —5J **73**
Burlington Gdns. Romf —7E **36**
Burlington La. W4 —7J **73**
Burlington M. W3 —1J **73**
Burlington Pl. SW6 —2G **91**
Burlington Pl. Wfd G —3E **20**
Burlington Rise. Barn —7H **5**
Burlington Rd. N10 —3E **28**
Burlington Rd. N17 —1G **31**
Burlington Rd. SW6 —2G **91**
Burlington Rd. W4 —5J **73**
Burlington Rd. Enf —1J **7**
Burlington Rd. Iswth —1H **87**
Burlington Rd. N Mald —4B **120**
Burlington Rd. T Hth —2C **124**
Burma M. N16 —4D **46**
Burma Rd. N16 —4D **46**
Burmarsh Ct. SE20 —1J **125**
Burmester Rd. SW17 —3A **108**
Burnaby Cres. W4 —6J **73**
Burnaby Gdns. W4 —6H **73**
Burnaby St. SW10 —7A **76**
Burnage Ct. SE26 —4H **111**
Burnard Pl. N7 —5K **45**
Burnaston Ho. E5 —3G **47**
Burnbrae Clo. N12 —6E **14**
Burnbury Rd. SW12 —1G **109**
Burncroft Av. Enf —2D **8**

*Burne Jones Ho. W14 —4G **75***
(off North End Rd.)
Burnell Av. Rich —5C **104**
Burnell Av. Well —2A **100**
Burnell Gdns. Stan —2D **24**
Burnell Rd. Sutt —4K **131**
*Burnell Wlk. SE1 —5F **79***
(off Abingdon Clo.)
Burnels Av. E6 —3E **66**
Burness Clo. N7 —6K **45**
Burne St. NW1 —5C **60** (5C **138**)
Burnett Clo. E9 —5J **47**
Burney Av. Surb —5F **119**
Burney St. SE10 —7E **80**
Burnfoot Av. SW6 —1G **91**
Burnham Clo. SE1 —5F **79**
Burnham Clo. Enf —1K **7**
Burnham Clo. W'stone —4A **24**
Burnham Cres. E11 —4A **34**
Burnham Dri. Wor Pk —2F **131**
Burnham Gdns. Croy —7F **125**
Burnham Rd. E4 —5G **19**
Burnham Rd. Dag —7B **52**
Burnham Rd. Mord —4K **121**
Burnham Rd. Romf —3K **37**
Burnham Rd. Sidc —2E **116**
Burnham St. E2 —3J **63**
Burnham St. King T —1G **119**
Burnham Way. SE26 —5B **112**
Burnham Way. W13 —4B **72**
Burhhill Rd. Beck —2C **126**
Burnley Rd. NW10 —5B **42**
Burnley Rd. SW9 —2K **93**
Burnsall St. SW3 —5C **76**
Burns Av. Chad —7C **36**
Burns Av. Sidc —6B **100**
Burns Av. S'hall —7E **54**
Burnsbury Ho. SW4 —6H **93**
Burns Clo. E17 —4E **33**
Burns Clo. Well —1K **99**
Burns Clo. SW16 —6H **109**
Burnside. SE27 —4D **110**
*Burns Ho. SE17 —5B **78***
(off Doddington Gro.)
Burn Side. N9 —3D **18**
Burnside Clo. SE16 —1K **79**
Burnside Clo. Barn —3D **4**
Burnside Clo. Twic —6A **88**
Burnside Cres. Wemb —1D **56**
Burnside Rd. Dag —2C **52**
Burns Rd. NW10 —1B **58**
Burns Rd. SW11 —2D **92**
Burns Rd. W13 —2B **72**
Burns Rd. Wemb —2E **56**
Burns Way. Houn —2B **86**
Burnt Ash Hill. SE12 —6H **97**
(in two parts)
Burnt Ash La. Brom —7J **113**
Burnt Ash Rd. SE12 —5H **97**
Burnthwaite Rd. SW6 —7H **75**
*Burnt Oak B'way. Edgw —1C **12***
Burnt Oak Fields. Edgw —1J **25**
Burnt Oak La. Sidc —6A **100**
Burntwood Clo. SW18 —1C **108**
Burntwood Grange Rd. SW18
—1B **108**
Burntwood La. SW17 —3A **108**
Burntwood View. SE19 —5F **111**
Buross St. E1 —6H **63**
Burrage Gro. SE18 —4G **83**
Burrage Pl. SE18 —5F **83**
Burrage Rd. SE18 —5G **83**
Burrard Rd. E16 —6K **65**
Burrard Rd. NW6 —5J **43**
Burr Clo. E1 —1G **79**
Burr Clo. Bexh —3F **101**
Burrel Clo. Edgw —2C **12**
Burrell Clo. Croy —6A **126**
Burrell Row. Beck —2C **126**
Burrell St. SE1 —1B **78** (2J **147**)

Burrell's Wharf Sq. E14 —5D **80**
Burritt Rd. King T —2G **119**
Burroughs Gdns. NW4 —4D **26**
Burroughs Pde. NW4 —4D **26**
Burroughs, The. NW4 —4D **26**
*Burrow Ho. SW9 —2K **93***
(off Stockwell Pk. Rd.)
Burrows M. SE1 —2B **78** (4J **147**)
Burrows Rd. NW10 —3E **58**
Burrow Wlk. SE21 —7C **94**
Burr Rd. SW18 —1J **107**
*Bursar St. SE1 —1E **78** (3C **148**)*
(off Tooley St.)
Bursdon Clo. Sidc —2K **115**
Bursland Rd. Enf —4E **8**
Burslem St. E1 —6G **63**
Burstock Rd. SW15 —4G **91**
Burston Rd. SW15 —5F **91**
Burstow Rd. SW20 —1G **121**
Burtenshaw Rd. Th Dit —7A **118**
Burtley Clo. N4 —1C **46**
Burton Clo. Chst —6J **115**
Burton Gdns. Houn —1D **86**
Burton Gro. SE17 —5D **78**
Burtonhole Clo. NW7 —4A **14**
Burtonhole La. NW7 —5K **13**
Burton La. SW9 —2A **94**
(in two parts)
Burton M. SW1 —4E **76** (9H **145**)
Burton Pl. WC1 —4H **61** (3B **140**)
Burton Rd. E18 —3K **33**
Burton Rd. NW6 —7H **43**
Burton Rd. SW9 —2A **94**
(in two parts)
Burton Rd. King T —7E **104**
Burtons Ct. E15 —7F **49**
Burton's Rd. Hamp —4F **103**
Burton St. WC1 —3H **61** (2B **140**)
*Burtonwood Ho. N4 —7D **30***
Burt Rd. E16 —1A **82**
Burtwell La. SE27 —4D **110**
Burwash Rd. SE18 —5H **83**
Burwell Av. Gnfd —6J **39**
Burwell Clo. E1 —6H **63**
Burwell Rd. E10 —1A **48**
Burwell Wlk. E3 —4C **64**
Burwood Av. Brom —2K **137**
Burwood Av. Pinn —5A **22**
Burwood Pl. W2 —6C **60** (7D **138**)
Bury Clo. SE16 —1K **79**
Bury Ct. EC3 —6E **62** (7D **142**)
Bury Gro. Mord —5K **121**
Bury Hall Vs. N9 —1A **18**
Bury Pl. WC1 —5J **61** (6C **140**)
Bury Rd. E4 —1B **20**
Bury Rd. N22 —2A **30**
Bury Rd. Dag —6H **53**
Bury St. N9 —7A **8**
Bury St. SW1 —1G **77** (2M **145**)
Bury St. W. N9 —7J **7**
Bury Wlk. SW3 —4C **76** (9C **144**)
Busby M. NW5 —6H **45**
Busby Pl. NW5 —6H **45**
Busby St. E2 —4F **63**
Bushberry Rd. E9 —6A **48**
Bush Clo. Ilf —5H **35**
Bush Cotts. SW18 —5J **91**
Bush Ct. N14 —1C **16**
*Bush Ct. W12 —2F **75***
(off Shepherd's Bush Grn.)
Bushell Clo. SW2 —2K **109**
Bushell Grn. Bush —2C **10**
Bushell St. E1 —1G **79**
Bushell Way. Chst —5E **114**
Bushey Av. E18 —3H **33**
Bushey Av. Orp —7H **129**
Bushey Clo. E4 —3K **19**

Bushey Ct. SW20 —2D **120**
Bushey Down. SW12 —2F **109**
Bushey Hill Rd. SE5 —1E **94**
Bushey La. Sutt —4J **131**
Bushey Rd. E13 —2A **66**
Bushey Rd. N15 —6E **30**
Bushey Rd. SW20 —3D **120**
Bushey Rd. Croy —2C **136**
Bushey Rd. Sutt —4J **131**
Bushey Way. Beck —6F **127**
Bush Fair Ct. N14 —6A **6**
Bushfield Clo. Edgw —2C **12**
Bushfield Cres. Edgw —2C **12**
Bush Gro. NW9 —7J **25**
Bush Gro. Stan —7J **11**
Bushgrove Rd. Dag —4D **52**
Bush Hill. N21 —7H **7**
Bush Hill Rd. N21 —6J **7**
Bush Hill Rd. Harr —6F **25**
Bush Ind. Est. NW10 —4K **57**
Bush La. EC4 —7D **62** (9A **142**)
Bushmead Clo. N15 —4F **31**
Bushmoor Cres. SE18 —7F **83**
Bushnell Rd. SW17 —2F **109**
Bush Rd. E8 —1H **63**
Bush Rd. E11 —7H **33**
Bush Rd. SE8 —4K **79**
Bush Rd. Buck H —6G **21**
Bush Rd. Rich —6F **73**
Bushway. Dag —4D **52**
Bushwood. E11 —7H **33**
*Bushwood Dri. SE1 —4F **79** (9H **148**)*
Bushwood Rd. Rich —6G **73**
*Bushy Ct. King T —1C **118***
(off Up. Teddington Rd.)
Bushy Lees. Sidc —6K **99**
Bushy Pk. Gdns. Tedd —5H **103**
Bushy Pk. Rd. Tedd —7B **104**
(in two parts)
Bushy Rd. Tedd —6K **103**
Butcher Row. E14 & E1 —7K **63**
Butchers Rd. E16 —6J **65**
Bute Av. Rich —2E **104**
Bute Ct. Wall —5G **133**
Bute Gdns. W6 —4F **75**
Bute Gdns. Wall —5G **133**
Bute Gdns. W. Wall —5G **133**
Bute Rd. Croy —1A **134**
Bute Rd. Ilf —5F **35**
Bute Rd. Wall —4G **133**
Bute St. SW7 —4B **76** (8A **144**)
Bute Wlk. N1 —6D **46**
*Butler Av. Harr —7H **23***
Butler Ct. Wemb —4A **40**
*Butler Pl. SW1 —3H **77** (6A **146**)*
(off Palmer St.)
Butler Rd. NW10 —7A **42**
Butler Rd. Dag —4B **52**
Butler Rd. Harr —7G **23**
Butiers Dri. E4 —1K **9**
Butler St. E2 —3J **63**
*Butlers Wharf. SE1 —2F **79** (4E **148**)*
(off Shad Thames)
Butterfield Clo. SE16 —2H **79**
Butterfield Clo. Twic —6K **87**
Butterfields. E17 —5E **32**
Butterfield Sq. E6 —6D **66**
Butterfly La. SE9 —6F **99**
Butterfly Wlk. SE5 —2D **94**
Butter Hill. Wall —3E **132**
Butteridges Clo. Dag —1F **69**
Buttermere Clo. SE1
—4F **79** (9E **148**)
Buttermere Clo. Mord —6F **121**
Buttermere Dri. SW15 —5G **91**
Buttermere Wlk. E8 —6F **47**
Butterwick. W6 —4E **74**
Butterworth Wlk. Wfd G —5D **20**

Buttesland St. N1 —3D **62** (1B **142**)
Buttfield Clo. Dag —6H **53**
Buttmarsh Clo. SE18 —5F **83**
*Buttsbury Rd. Ilf —5G **51***
(in two parts)
Butts Cotts. Felt —3C **102**
Butts Cres. Felt —3E **102**
Butts Rd. Brom —5G **113**
Butts, The. Bren —6D **72**
Buxted Clo. E8 —7F **47**
Buxted Rd. N12 —5H **15**
Buxton Clo. Wfd G —6G **21**
*Buxton Ct. N1 —3C **62** (1M **141**)*
(off Thoresby St.)
Buxton Cres. Sutt —4G **131**
Buxton Dri. E11 —4G **33**
Buxton Dri. N Mald —2K **119**
Buxton Gdns. W3 —7H **57**
Buxton Ho. E11 —4G **33**
Buxton Rd. E4 —1A **20**
Buxton Rd. E6 —3C **66**
Buxton Rd. E15 —5G **49**
Buxton Rd. E17 —4A **32**
Buxton Rd. N19 —1H **45**
Buxton Rd. NW2 —6D **42**
Buxton Rd. SW14 —3A **90**
Buxton Rd. Eri —7K **85**
Buxton Rd. Ilf —6J **35**
Buxton Rd. T Hth —5B **124**
Buxton St. E1 —4F **63**
Buzzard Creek Ind. Est. Bark —5A **68**
Byam St. SW6 —2A **92**
Byards Croft. SW16 —1H **123**
Byatt Wlk. Hamp —6C **102**
Bychurch End. Tedd —5K **103**
Bycroft Rd. S'hall —4E **54**
Bycroft St. SE20 —7K **111**
Bycullah Av. Enf —3G **7**
Bycullah Rd. Enf —2G **7**
Byefield Pas. Iswth —2A **88**
Byefield Rd. Iswth —3A **88**
Byegrove Rd. SW19 —6B **108**
Byelands Clo. SE16 —1K **79**
Bye, The. W3 —6A **58**
Byeways. Twic —3F **103**
Byeways, The. Surb —5G **119**
Byeway, The. SW14 —3J **89**
*Bye Way, The. Harr —1K **23***
Byfeld Gdns. SW13 —1C **90**
Byford Clo. E15 —7G **49**
Byford Ho. Barn —4A **4**
Bygrove. New Ad —6C **136**
Bygrove St. E14 —6D **64**
Byland Clo. N21 —7E **6**
Bylands Clo. SE2 —3B **84**
Byne Rd. SE26 —6J **111**
Byne Rd. Cars —2C **132**
Bynes Rd. S Croy —7D **134**
Byng Pl. WC1 —4H **61** (4B **140**)
Byng Rd. Barn —2A **4**
Byng St. E14 —2C **80**
Bynon Av. Bexh —3F **101**
Byre Rd, The. N14 —6A **6**
Byre Rd. N14 —6A **6**
Byrne Rd. SW12 —1F **109**
Byron Av. E12 —6C **50**
Byron Av. E18 —3H **33**
Byron Av. NW9 —4H **25**
Byron Av. N Mald —5C **120**
Byron Av. Sutt —4B **132**
Byron Av. E. Sutt —4B **132**
Byron Clo. E8 —1G **63**
Byron Clo. SE20 —3H **125**
Byron Clo. SE26 —5A **112**
Byron Clo. SE28 —1C **84**
Byron Clo. Hamp —4D **102**
Byron Ct. Harr —6K **23**
Byron Dri. N2 —6B **28**

Byron Gdns. Sutt —4B.132
Byron Hill Rd. Harr —1H 39
Byron Ho. Dart —5K 101
Byron Rd. E10 —1D 48
Byron Rd. E17 —3C 32
Byron Rd. NW2 —2D 42
Byron Rd. NW5 —1F 13
Byron Rd. W5 —1F 73
Byron Rd. Harr —6J 23
Byron Rd. W'stone —2K 23
Byron Rd. Wemb —2C 40
Byron St. E14 —6E 64
Byron Ter. N9 —6D 8
Byron Way. N'holt —3C 54
Bysouth Clo. Ilf —1F 35
Bythorn St. SW9 —3K 93
Byton Rd. SW17 —6D 108
Byward Av. Felt —6A 85
Byward St. EC3 —7E 62 (1D 148)
Bywater Pl. SE16 —1A 80
Bywater St. SW3 —5D 76
Byway. E11 —5A 34
Byway, The. Eps —4B 130
Byway, The. Sutt —7B 132
Bywell Pl. W1 —5G 61 (6L 139)
  (off Wells St.)
Bywood Av. Croy —6J 125
Byworth Wlk. N19 —1J 45

Cabbell St. NW1 —5C 60 (6C 138)
Cabinet Way. E4 —5G 19
Cable Pl. SE10 —1E 96
Cable St. E1 —7G 63
Cabot Sq. E14 —1C 80
Cabot Way. E6 —1B 66
Cabul Rd. SW11 —2C 92
Cactus Wlk. W12 —6B 58
Cadbury Clo. Iswth —1A 88
Cadbury Way. SE16 —4F 79 (8F 148)
Caddington Clo. Barn —5H 5
Caddington Rd. NW2 —3G 43
Caddis Clo. Stan —7E 10
Cadell Clo. E2 —2F 63
Cade Rd. SE10 —1F 97
Cader Rd. SW18 —6A 92
Cadet Dri. SE1 —5F 79
Cadet Pl. SE10 —5G 81
Cadiz Rd. Dag —7J 53
Cadiz St. SE17 —5C 78
Cadmer Clo. N Mald —4A 120
Cadmus Clo. SW4 —3H 93
Cadogan Clo. Beck —1F 127
Cadogan Clo. Harr —4F 39
Cadogan Clo. Tedd —5J 103
Cadogan Ct. Sutt —6K 131
Cadogan Gdns. E18 —3K 33
Cadogan Gdns. N3 —1K 27
Cadogan Gdns. N21 —5F 7
Cadogan Gdns. SW3
  —4D 76 (8F 144)
Cadogan Ga. E9 —7B 48
Cadogan Ga. SW1 —4D 76 (8F 144)
Cadogan La. SW1 —3E 76 (7G 145)
Cadogan Pl. SW1 —3D 76 (6F 144)
Cadogan Rd. Surb —5D 118
Cadogan Sq. SW1 —3D 76 (7E 144)
Cadogan St. SW3 —4D 76 (9F 144)
Cadogan Ter. E9 —6B 48
Cadoxton Av. N15 —6F 31
Cadwallon Rd. SE9 —2F 115
Caedmon Rd. N7 —4K 45
Caerleon Clo. Sidc —5C 116
Caerlon Ter. SE2 —4B 84
Caernarvon Clo. Mitc —3J 123

Caernarvon Dri. Ilf —1E 34
Caesars Wlk. Mitc —5D 122
Cahill St. EC1 —4C 62 (4A 142)
Cahir St. E14 —4D 80
Caird St. W10 —3G 59
Cairn Av. W5 —1D 72
Cairndale Clo. Brom —7H 113
Cairnfield Av. NW2 —3A 42
Cairngorm Clo. Tedd —5A 104
Cairns Av. Wfd G —6H 21
Cairns Rd. SW11 —5C 92
Cairn Way. Stan —6E 10
Cairo New Rd. Croy —2B 134
Cairo Rd. E17 —4C 32
Caister M. SW12 —7F 93
Caister Pk. Rd. E15 —1H 65
Caistor Rd. SW12 —7F 93
Caithness Gdns. Sidc —6K 99
Caithness Ho. N1 —1K 61
  (off Bemerton Est.)
Caithness Rd. W14 —3F 75
Caithness Rd. Mitc —7F 109
Calabria Rd. N5 —6B 46
Calais Ga. SE5 —1B 94
Calais St. SE5 —1B 94
Calbourne Rd. SW12 —7D 92
Calcott Wlk. SE9 —4C 114
Caldbeck Av. Wor Pk —2D 130
Caldecote Gdns. Bush —1D 10
Caldecot Rd. SE5 —2C 94
Caldecott Way. E5 —3K 47
Calder Av. Gnfd —2K 55
Calder Clo. Enf —3K 7
Calder Gdns. Edgw —3G 25
Calderon Pl. W10 —5E 58
Calderon Rd. E11 —4E 48
Calder Rd. Mord —5A 122
Caldervale Rd. SW4 —5H 93
Calderwood St. SE18 —4E 82
Caldew St. SE5 —7D 78
Caldicot Grn. NW9 —6A 26
Caldwell St. SW9 —7K 77
Caldy Rd. Belv —3H 85
Caldy Wlk. N1 —6C 46
Caleb St. SE1 —2C 78 (4J 147)
Caledonian Clo. Ilf —1B 52
Caledonian Rd. N1 & N7 —2J 61
Caledonian Rd. N7 —4K 45
Caledonia St. N1 —2J 61
Caledon Rd. E6 —1D 66
Caledon Rd. Wall —4E 132
Cale St. SW3 —5C 76
Caletock Way. SE10 —5H 81
Caliban Tower. N1 —2E 62
  (off Purcell St.)
Calico Row. SW11 —3A 92
Calidore Clo. SW2 —6K 93
California La. Bush —1C 10
California Rd. N Mald —3J 119
California St. N Mald —3A 119
Callaghan Clo. SE13 —4G 97
Callanby Ter. N1 —6D 46
Callander Rd. SE6 —2D 112
Callanders, The. Bush —1D 10
Callard Av. N13 —4G 17
Callcott Rd. NW6 —7H 43
Callcott St. W8 —1J 75
Callendar Rd. SW7 —3B 76 (6A 144)
Callenders Cotts. Belv —2K 85
Callingham Clo. E14 —5B 64
Callis Rd. E17 —6B 32
Callonfield. E17 —4A 32
Callow St. SW3 —6B 76
Calmington Rd. SE5 —6E 78
Calmont Rd. Brom —6F 113

Calne Av. Ilf —1F 35
Calonne Rd. SW19 —4F 107
Calshot St. N1 —2K 61
Calshot Way. Enf —3G 7
Calstock Ho. SE11 —5A 78
  (off Kennings Way)
Calthorpe Gdns. Edgw —5K 11
Calthorpe Gdns. Sutt —3A 132
Calthorpe St. WC1 —4K 61 (3F 140)
Calton Av. SE21 —6E 94
Calton Rd. Barn —6F 5
Calvary Gdns. SW15 —5H 91
Calverley Clo. Beck —6D 112
Calverley Cres. Dag —2G 53
Calverley Gdns. Harr —7D 24
Calverley Gro. N19 —1H 45
Calverley Rd. Eps —6C 130
Calvert Av. E2 —3F 63 (2D 142)
Calvert Clo. Belv —4G 85
Calvert Clo. Sidc —6E 116
Calverton. SE17 —6E 78
  (off Albany Rd.)
Calverton Rd. E6 —1E 66
Calvert Rd. SE10 —5H 81
Calvert Rd. Barn —2A 4
Calvert's Bldgs. SE1
  —1D 78 (3A 148)
  (off Southwark St.)
Calvert St. NW1 —1E 60
Calvin St. E1 —4F 63 (4E 142)
Calydon Rd. SE7 —5K 81
Calypso Way. SE16 —3B 80
Camac Rd. Twic —1H 103
Cambalt Rd. SW15 —5F 91
Camber Ho. SE15 —6J 79
Camberley Av. SW20 —2D 120
Camberley Av. Enf —4K 7
Camberley Clo. Sutt —3F 131
Cambert Way. SE3 —4K 97
Camberwell Chu. St. SE5 —1D 94
Camberwell Glebe. SE5 —1E 94
Camberwell Grn. SE5 —1D 94
Camberwell Gro. SE5 —1D 94
Camberwell New Rd. SE5 —6A 78
Camberwell Pl. SE5 —1C 94
Camberwell Rd. SE17 & SE5 —6C 78
Camberwell Sta. Rd. SE5 —1C 94
Camberwell Trading Est. SE5 —1C 94
Cambeys Rd. Dag —5H 53
Camborne Av. W13 —2B 72
Camborne M. W11 —6G 59
Camborne Rd. SW18 —7J 91
Camborne Rd. Croy —7G 125
Camborne Rd. Mord —5F 121
Camborne Rd. Sidc —3C 116
Camborne Rd. Sutt —7J 131
Camborne Rd. Well —2K 99
Camborne Way. Houn —1E 86
Cambourne Av. N9 —7E 8
Cambourne Wlk. Rich —6D 88
Cambrai Ct. N13 —3D 16
Cambray Rd. SW12 —1G 109
Cambray Rd. Orp —7K 129
Cambria Clo. Houn —4E 86
Cambria Clo. Sidc —1H 115
Cambria Ct. Felt —7A 86
Cambrian Av. Ilf —5J 35
Cambrian Grn. NW9 —5A 26
  (off Snowden Dri.)
Cambrian Rd. E10 —7C 32
Cambrian Rd. Rich —6F 89
Cambria Rd. SE5 —3C 94
Cambria St. SW6 —7K 75
Cambridge Av. NW6 —2J 59
Cambridge Av. Gnfd —5K 39
Cambridge Av. N Mald —3A 120
  (in two parts)
Cambridge Av. Well —4K 99

Cambridge Barracks Rd. SE18
  —4D 82
Cambridge Cir. WC2
  —6H 61 (8B 140)
Cambridge Clo. N22 —1A 30
Cambridge Clo. NW10 —3K 41
Cambridge Clo. SW20 —1D 120
Cambridge Clo. Houn —4C 86
Cambridge Cotts. Rich —6G 73
Cambridge Ct. N16 —7E 30
  (off Amhurst Pk.)
Cambridge Cres. E2 —2H 63
Cambridge Cres. Tedd —5A 104
Cambridge Dri. SE12 —5J 97
Cambridge Dri. Ruis —2A 38
Cambridge Gdns. N10 —1E 28
Cambridge Gdns. N17 —7J 17
Cambridge Gdns. N21 —7J 7
Cambridge Gdns. NW6 —2J 59
Cambridge Gdns. W10 —6F 59
Cambridge Gdns. Enf —2B 8
Cambridge Gdns. King T —2G 119
Cambridge Ga. NW1
  —4F 61 (3J 139)
Cambridge Ga. M. NW1
  —4F 61 (3K 139)
Cambridge Grn. SE9 —1F 115
Cambridge Gro. SE20 —1H 125
Cambridge Gro. W6 —4D 74
Cambridge Gro. Rd. King T —3G 119
Cambridge Heath Rd. E1 & E2
  —4H 63
Cambridge Lodge Vs. E8 —1H 63
Cambridge Pde. Enf —1B 8
Cambridge Pk. E11 —7J 33
Cambridge Pk. Twic —6C 88
Cambridge Pk. Ct. Twic —7D 88
Cambridge Pk. Rd. E11 —7H 33
Cambridge Pl. NW6 —3J 59
Cambridge Pl. W8 —2K 75
Cambridge Rd. E4 —1A 20
Cambridge Rd. E11 —6H 33
Cambridge Rd. NW6 —2J 59
  (in two parts)
Cambridge Rd. SE20 —3H 125
Cambridge Rd. SW11 —1D 92
Cambridge Rd. SW13 —2B 90
Cambridge Rd. SW20 —1C 120
Cambridge Rd. W7 —2K 71
Cambridge Rd. Bark —7G 51
Cambridge Rd. Brom —7J 102
Cambridge Rd. Cars —6C 132
Cambridge Rd. Hamp —7D 102
Cambridge Rd. Harr —5E 22
Cambridge Rd. Houn —4C 86
Cambridge Rd. Ilf —1J 51
Cambridge Rd. King T —2F 119
Cambridge Rd. Mitc —3G 123
Cambridge Rd. N Mald —4A 120
Cambridge Rd. Rich —7G 73
Cambridge Rd. Sidc —4J 115
Cambridge Rd. S'hall —1D 70
Cambridge Rd. Tedd —4K 103
Cambridge Rd. Twic —6D 88
Cambridge Rd. N. W4 —5H 73
Cambridge Rd. S. W4 —5H 73
Cambridge Row. SE18 —5F 83
Cambridge Sq. W2 —6C 60 (7C 138)
Cambridge St. SW1 —4F 77 (9K 145)
Cambridge Ter. N9 —7A 8
Cambridge Ter. NW1
  —3F 61 (2J 139)
Cambridge Ter. M. NW1
  —3F 61 (2K 139)
Cambus Clo. Hay —5C 54
Cambus Rd. E16 —5J 65
Cam Ct. SE15 —6F 79
  (off Bibury Clo.)

Camdale Rd. SE18 —7K 83
Camden Av. Felt —1A 102
Camden Av. Hay —7B 54
Camden Ct. Belv —5G 85
Camden Est. SE15 —1F 95
Camden Gdns. NW1 —7F 45
Camden Gdns. Sutt —5K 131
Camden Gdns. T Hth —3B 124
Camden Gro. Chst —6F 115
Camden High St. NW1 —7F 45
Camden Hill Rd. SE19 —6E 110
Camden Ho. SE8 —5B 80
Camdenhurst St. E14 —6A 64
Camden La. N7 —5H 45
Camden Lock Pl. NW1 —7F 45
Camden M. NW1 —7G 45
Camden Pk. Rd. NW1 —6H 45
Camden Pk. Rd. Chst —7D 114
Camden Pas. N1 —1B 62
Camden Rd. E11 —6K 33
Camden Rd. E17 —6B 32
Camden Rd. N7 —4J 45
Camden Rd. NW1 & N7 —7G 45
Camden Rd. Bex —1F 117
Camden Rd. Cars —4D 132
Camden Rd. Sutt —5K 131
Camden Row. SE3 —2G 97
Camden Row. Pinn —3A 22
Camden Sq. NW1 —6H 45
Camden Sq. SE15 —1F 95
Camden St. NW1 —7G 45
Camden Ter. NW1 —6H 45
Camden Wlk. N1 —1B 62
Camden Way. Chst —7D 114
Camden Way. T Hth —3B 124
Camelford Ct. SW12 —7J 93
Camelford Ct. W11 —6G 59
  (off Albert Embkmt.)
Camelford Wlk. W11 —6G 59
Camellia Pl. Twic —7F 87
Camellia St. SW8 —7J 77
Camelot Clo. SE28 —2H 83
Camelot Clo. SW19 —4J 107
Carnel Rd. E16 —1B 82
Camera Pl. SW10 —6B 76
Cameron Clo. N18 —4C 18
Cameron Clo. N20 —2G 15
Cameron Clo. Bex —3K 117
Cameron Ho. SE5 —7C 78
Cameron Pl. E1 —6H 63
Cameron Rd. SE6 —2B 112
Cameron Rd. Brom —5J 127
Cameron Rd. Croy —6B 124
Camerton Clo. E8 —6F 47
Camilla Rd. SE16 —4H 79
Camille Clo. SE25 —3G 125
Camlan Rd. Brom —4H 113
Camlet St. E2 —4F 63 (3E 142)
Camlet Way. Barn —2D 4
Camley St. NW1 —7H 45
Camm Gdns. King T —2F 119
Camomile Av. Mitc —1D 122
Camomile St. EC3 —6E 62 (7C 142)
Campana Rd. SW6 —1J 91
Campbell Av. Ilf —4F 35
Campbell Clo. SE18 —1E 98
Campbell Clo. SW16 —4H 109
Campbell Clo. Twic —1H 103
Campbell Ct. N17 —1F 31
Campbell Ct. SE22 —1G 111
Campbell Croft. Edgw —5B 12
Campbell Ho. W12 —7D 58
  (off White City Est.)

Campbell Rd. E3 —3C 64
Campbell Rd. E6 —1C 66
Campbell Rd. E15 —1H 49
Campbell Rd. E17 —4B 32
Campbell Rd. N17 —1F 31
Campbell Rd. W7 —7J 55
Campbell Rd. Croy —7B 124
Campbell Rd. Twic —2H 103
Campbell Wlk. N1 —1J 61
(off Outram Pl.)
Campdale Rd. N7 —3H 45
Campden Clo. SW19 —2G 107
Campden Cres. Dag —4B 52
Campden Cres. Wemb —3B 40
Campden Gro. W8 —2J 75
Campden Hill. W8 —2J 75
Campden Hill Gdns. W8 —1J 75
Campden Hill Ga. W8 —2J 75
Campden Hill Pl. W11 —1H 75
Campden Hill Rd. W8 —1J 75
Campden Hill Sq. W8 —1H 75
Campden Rd. S Croy —5E 134
Campden St. W8 —1J 75
Campe Ho. N10 —7K 15
Camperdown St. E1 —6F 63
Campfield Rd. SE9 —7B 98
Campion Clo. E6 —7D 66
Campion Clo. Croy —4E 134
Campion Clo. Harr —6F 25
Campion Ct. Wemb —2E 56
Campion Pl. SE28 —1A 84
Campion Rd. SW15 —4E 90
Campion Rd. Iswth —1K 87
Campion Ter. NW2 —3F 43
Camplin Rd. Harr —5E 24
Camplin St. SE14 —7K 79
Camp Rd. SW19 —5E 106
Campsbourne Rd. N8 —3J 29
(in two parts)
Campsbourne, The. N8 —4J 29
Campsey Gdns. Dag —7B 52
Campsey Rd. Dag —7B 52
Campsfield Rd. N8 —3J 29
Campshill Pl. SE13 —5E 96
Campshill Rd. SE13 —5E 96
Campus Rd. E17 —6B 32
Camp View. SW19 —5D 106
Cam Rd. E15 —1F 65
Camrose Av. Edgw —2F 25
Camrose Av. Eri —6H 85
Camrose Av. Felt —4A 102
Camrose Clo. Croy —7A 126
Camrose Clo. Mord —4J 121
Camrose St. SE2 —5A 84
Canada Av. N18 —6H 17
Canada Cres. W3 —4J 57
Canada Est. SE16 —3J 79
Canada Gdns. SE13 —5E 96
Canada Rd. W3 —5J 57
Canada Sq. E14 —1D 80
Canada St. SE16 —2K 79
Canada Way. W12 —7D 58
Canadian Av. SE6 —7D 96
Canal App. SE8 —6A 80
Canal Clo. E1 —4A 64
Canal Gro. SE15 —6G 79
Canal Head. SE15 —1G 95
Canal Rd. E3 —4A 64
Canalside. SE28 —7D 68
Canal St. SE5 —6D 78
Canal Wlk. N1 —1D 62
Canal Wlk. SE26 —5J 111
Canal Wlk. Croy —6F 125
Canal Way. W10 —4F 59
Canberra Clo. NW4 —3C 26
Canberra Clo. Dag —1K 69
Canberra Cres. Dag —7K 53
Canberra Dri. N'holt —3A 54

Canberra Rd. E6 —1D 66
Canberra Rd. SE7 —7A 82
Canberra Rd. W13 —1A 72
Canberra Rd. Bexh —6D 84
Canbury Av. King T —1F 119
Canbury M. SE26 —3G 111
Canbury Pk. Rd. King T —1E 118
Canbury Pas. King T —1D 118
Canbury Path. Orp —4K 129
Canbury Pl. King T —1E 118
Cancell Rd. SW9 —1A 94
Candahar Rd. SW11 —2C 92
Candler St. N15 —6D 30
Candover St. W1 —5G 61 (6L 139)
Candy St. E3 —1B 64
Cane Clo. Wall —7J 133
Caney M. NW2 —2F 43
Canfield Dri. Ruis —5A 38
Canfield Gdns. NW6 —7K 43
Canfield Pl. NW6 —6A 44
Canfield Rd. Wfd G —7H 21
Canford Av. N'holt —1D 54
Canford Clo. Enf —2F 7
Canford Gdns. N Mald —6A 120
Canford Rd. SW11 —5E 92
Canham Rd. SE25 —3E 124
Canham Rd. W3 —2A 74
Canmore Gdns. SW16 —7G 109
Cann Hall Rd. E11 —4G 49
Canning Cres. N22 —1K 29
Canning Cross. SE5 —2E 94
Canning Ho. W12 —7D 58
(off White City Est.)
Canning Pas. W8 —3A 76
Canning Pl. W8 —3A 76
Canning Pl. M. W8 —3A 76
(off Canning Pl.)
Canning St. E2 —2F 65
Canning Rd. E17 —4A 32
Canning Rd. N5 —3B 46
Canning Rd. Croy —2F 135
Canning Rd. Harr —3J 23
Cannington Rd. Dag —6C 52
Cannizaro Rd. SW19 —6E 106
Cannock Ho. N4 —7C 30
Cannon Clo. SW20 —4E 120
Cannon Clo. Hamp —6F 103
Cannon Dri. E14 —7C 64
Cannon Hill. N14 —3D 16
Cannon Hill. NW6 —5J 43
Cannon Hill La. SW20 —5F 121
Cannon Hill M. N14 —3D 16
Cannon La. NW3 —3A 44
Cannon La. Pinn —5C 22
Cannon Pl. NW3 —3B 44
Cannon Pl. SE7 —5C 82
Cannon Rd. N14 —3D 16
Cannon Rd. Bexh —1E 100
Cannon St. EC4 —6C 62 (8L 141)
Cannon St. Rd. E1 —6H 63
Cannon Trading Est. Wemb —4H 41
Cannon Wharf Bus. Pk. SE8 —4A 80
Canon Av. Romf —5C 36
Canon Beck Rd. SE16 —2J 79
Canonbie Rd. SE23 —7J 95
Canonbury Cres. N1 —7C 46
Canonbury Gro. N1 —7C 46
Canonbury La. N1 —7B 46
Canonbury Pk. N. N1 —6C 46
Canonbury Pk. S. N1 —6C 46
Canonbury Pl. N1 —6B 46
Canonbury Rd. N1 —6B 46
Canonbury Rd. Enf —1K 7
Canonbury Sq. N1 —7B 46
Canonbury St. N1 —7C 46

Canonbury Vs. N1 —7B 46
Canon Mohan Clo. N14 —6K 5
Canon Mohan Clo. N14 —6A 6
Canon Murnane Rd. SE1
(off Grange Rd.) —3F 79 (7E 148)
Canon Rd. Brom —3A 128
Canon Row. SW1 —2J 77 (4C 146)
Canon's Clo. N2 —7B 28
Canons Clo. Edgw —6A 12
Canons Corner. Edgw —4K 11
Canons Ct. Edgw —6K 11
Canonsleigh Rd. Dag —7B 52
Canons Pk. Stan —6J 11
Canon St. N1 —1C 62
Canon's Wlk. Croy —3K 135
Canrobert St. E2 —2H 63
Cantelowes Rd. NW1 —6H 45
Canterbury Av. Ilf —7C 34
Canterbury Clo. E6 —6D 66
Canterbury Clo. Beck —1D 126
Canterbury Clo. Gnfd —5F 55
Canterbury Ct. NW9 —2A 26
Canterbury Ct. SE12 —3K 113
Canterbury Cres. SW9 —3A 94
Canterbury Gro. SE27 —4A 110
Canterbury Ho. SE1 —3K 77 (6F 146)
Canterbury Ho. SW9 —7A 76
Canterbury Pl. SE17
—4B 78 (9K 147)
Canterbury Rd. E10 —7E 32
Canterbury Rd. NW6 —2J 59
Canterbury Rd. Croy —7K 123
Canterbury Rd. Felt —2C 102
Canterbury Rd. Harr —5F 23
Canterbury Rd. Mord —7K 121
Canterbury Ter. NW6 —2J 59
Cantley Gdns. SE19 —1F 125
Cantley Gdns. Ilf —6G 35
Cantley Rd. W7 —3A 72
Canton St. E14 —6C 64
Cantrell Rd. E3 —4B 64
Cantwell Rd. SE18 —7F 83
Canvey St. SE1 —1C 78 (2L 147)
Cape Clo. Bark —7F 51
Capel Av. Wall —5K 133
Capel Clo. N20 —3F 15
Capel Clo. Brom —7C 128
Capel Ct. SE20 —1J 125
Capel Gdns. Ilf —4K 51
Capel Gdns. Pinn —4D 22
Capel Rd. E7 & E12 —4K 49
Capel Rd. Barn —6H 5
Capener's Clo. SW1 —2E 76 (5G 145)
(off Kinnerton St.)
Capern Rd. SW18 —1A 108
Cape Rd. N17 —3G 31
Cape Yd. E1 —7G 63
Capital Bus. Cen. W3 —5H 57
Capital Bus. Cen. Wemb —2D 56
Capital Interchange Way. Bren
—5G 73
Capital Pl. Croy —5K 133
Capitol Ind. Pk. NW9 —3J 25
Capitol Way. NW9 —3J 25
Capland St. NW8 —4B 60 (3B 138)
Caple Rd. NW10 —2B 58
Capper St. WC1 —4G 61 (4M 139)
Capri Rd. Croy —1F 135
Capstan Clo. Romf —6B 36
Capstan Ride. Enf —2F 7
Capstan Rd. SE8 —4B 80
Capstan Sq. E14 —2E 80
Capstan Way. SE16 —1A 80

Capstone Rd. Brom —4H 113
Capthorne Av. Harr —1C 38
Capuchin Clo. Stan —6G 11
Capworth St. E10 —1C 48
Caradoc Clo. W2 —6J 59
Caradoc Evans Clo. N11 —5A 16
(off Springfield Rd.)
Caradoc St. SE10 —5G 81
Caradon Clo. E11 —1G 49
Caradon Way. N15 —4D 30
Carage Clo. Eri —6J 85
Caravel M. SE8 —6C 80
Caraway Clo. E13 —5K 65
Carberry Rd. SE19 —6E 110
Carbery Av. W3 —2F 73
Carbis Clo. E4 —1A 20
Carbis Rd. E14 —6B 64
Carbuncle Pas. Way. N17 —2G 31
Carburton St. W1 —5F 61 (5K 139)
Cardale St. E14 —2E 80
Carden Rd. SE15 —3H 95
Cardiff Rd. W7 —3A 72
Cardiff Rd. Enf —4C 8
Cardiff St. SE18 —7J 83
Cardigan Gdns. Ilf —2A 52
Cardigan Rd. E3 —2B 64
Cardigan Rd. SW13 —2C 90
Cardigan Rd. SW19 —6A 108
Cardigan Rd. Rich —6E 88
Cardigan St. SE11 —5A 78
Cardigan Wlk. N1 —7C 46
(off Ashby Gro.)
Cardinal Av. King T —5E 104
Cardinal Av. Mord —6G 121
Cardinal Bourne St. SE1
(off Burge St.) —3D 78 (7B 148)
Cardinal Cap All. SE1
—1C 78 (2L 147)
Cardinal Clo. Chst —1J 129
Cardinal Clo. Mord —6G 121
Cardinal Clo. Wor Pk —4C 130
Cardinal Cres. N Mald —2J 119
Cardinal Pl. SW15 —4F 91
Cardinal Rd. Felt —1A 102
Cardinal Rd. Ruis —1B 38
Cardinals Wlk. Hamp —7G 103
Cardinals Way. N19 —1H 45
Cardine M. SE15 —7H 79
Cardington Sq. Houn —4B 86
Cardington St. NW1
—3G 61 (1M 139)
Cardozo Rd. N7 —5J 45
Cardrew Av. N12 —5G 15
Cardrew Clo. N12 —5H 15
Cardrew Ct. N12 —5G 15
Cardross St. W6 —3D 74
Cardwell Rd. N7 —4J 45
Cardwell Rd. SE18 —4C 82
Carew Clo. N7 —2K 45
Carew Ct. Sutt —7K 131
Carew Mnr. Cotts. Wall —3H 133
Carew Rd. N17 —2G 31
Carew Rd. W13 —2C 72
Carew Rd. Mitc —2E 122
Carew Rd. T Hth —4B 124
Carew Rd. Wall —6G 133
Carew St. SE5 —2C 94
Carey Ct. Bexh —5H 101
Carey Gdns. SW8 —1G 93
Carey La. EC2 —6C 62 (7L 141)
Carey Pl. SW1 —4H 77 (9A 146)
Carey Rd. Dag —4E 52
Carey St. WC2 —6K 61 (8F 140)
Carfax Pl. SW4 —4H 93
Carfree Clo. N1 —7A 46
Cargill Rd. SW18 —1K 107

Cargreen Pl. SE25 —4F 125
Cargreen Rd. SE25 —4F 125
Cargrey Ho. Stan —5H 11
Carholme Rd. SE23 —1B 112
Carlton Clo. NW3 —2J 43
Carina M. SE27 —4C 110
Carisbrook Clo. Stan —2D 24
Carisbrooke Av. Bex —1D 116
Carisbrooke Clo. Enf —1A 8
Carisbrooke Ct. N'holt —1D 54
(off Eskdale Av.)
Carisbrooke Gdns. SE15 —7F 79
Carisbrooke Rd. E17 —4A 32
Carisbrooke Rd. Brom —4A 128
Carisbrooke Rd. Mitc —4H 123
Carker's La. NW5 —5F 45
Carleton Av. Wall —7H 133
Carleton Gdns. N19 —5G 45
Carleton Rd. N7 —5H 45
Carleton Vs. NW5 —5G 45
Carlile Clo. E3 —2B 64
Carlingford Gdns. Mitc —7E 108
Carlingford Rd. N15 —3B 30
Carlingford Rd. NW3 —4B 44
Carlingford Rd. Mord —6F 121
Carlisle Av. EC3 —6F 63 (8E 142)
Carlisle Av. W3 —6A 58
Carlisle Clo. King T —1G 119
Carlisle Gdns. Harr —7D 24
Carlisle Gdns. Ilf —6C 34
Carlisle La. SE1 —3H 77 (7F 146)
Carlisle M. NW8 —5B 60 (5B 138)
Carlisle M. King T —1G 119
Carlisle Pl. N11 —4A 16
Carlisle Pl. SW1 —3G 77 (7L 145)
Carlisle Rd. E10 —1C 48
Carlisle Rd. N4 —7A 30
Carlisle Rd. NW6 —1G 59
Carlisle Rd. NW9 —3J 25
Carlisle Rd. Hamp —7F 103
Carlisle Rd. Sutt —6H 131
Carlisle St. W1 —6H 61 (8A 140)
Carlisle Wlk. E8 —6F 47
Carlisle Way. SW17 —5E 108
Carlos Pl. W1 —7E 60 (1H 145)
Carlow St. NW1 —2G 61
Carlton Av. N14 —5C 6
Carlton Av. Felt —6A 86
Carlton Av. Harr —5A 24
Carlton Av. S Croy —7E 134
Carlton Av. E. Wemb —2D 40
Carlton Av. W. Wemb —2B 40
Carlton Clo. NW3 —2J 43
Carlton Clo. Edgw —5B 12
Carlton Clo. N'holt —5G 39
Carlton Clo. SE20 —1H 125
Carlton Clo. SW9 —1B 94
Carlton Ct. Ilf —3H 35
Carlton Cres. Sutt —4G 131
Carlton Dri. SW15 —5F 91
Carlton Dri. Ilf —3H 35
Carlton Gdns. SW1 —1H 77 (3A 146)
Carlton Gdns. W5 —6C 56
Carlton Gro. SE15 —1H 95
Carlton Hill. NW8 —2K 59
Carlton Ho. Ter. SW1
—1H 77 (3A 146)
Carlton Lodge. N4 —7A 30
(off Carlton Rd.)
Carlton Pk. Av. SW20 —2F 121
Carlton Rd. E11 —1H 49
Carlton Rd. E12 —4B 50
Carlton Rd. E17 —1A 32
Carlton Rd. N4 —7A 30
Carlton Rd. N11 —5K 15
Carlton Rd. SW14 —3J 89
Carlton Rd. W4 —2K 73
Carlton Rd. W5 —7C 56

Carlton Rd. Eri —6H 85
Carlton Rd. N Mald —2A 120
Carlton Rd. Sidc —5K 115
Carlton Rd. S Croy —6D 134
Carlton Rd. Well —3B 100
Carlton Sq. E1 —4K 63
(in two parts)
Carlton St. SW1 —7H 61 (1A 145)
Carlton Ter. E7 —7A 50
Carlton Ter. E11 —5K 33
Carlton Ter. N18 —3J 17
Carlton Ter. SE26 —3J 111
Carlton Tower Pl. SW1
(off Cadogan Pl.) —4D 76 (8F 144)
Carlton Vale. NW6 —2H 59
Carlwell St. SW17 —5C 108
Carlyle Av. Brom —3B 128
Carlyle Av. S'hall —7D 54
Carlyle Clo. N2 —6A 28
Carlyle Clo. NW10 —1K 57
Carlyle Ct. SW6 —1K 91
(off Maltings Pl.)
Carlyle Ct. SW10 —1A 92
(off Chelsea Harbour)
Carlyle Gdns. S'hall —7D 54
Carlyle Pl. SW15 —4F 91
Carlyle Rd. E12 —4C 50
Carlyle Rd. SE28 —7B 68
Carlyle Rd. W5 —5C 72
Carlyle Rd. Croy —2G 135
Carlyle Sq. SW3 —5B 76
Carlyon Av. Harr —4D 38
Carlyon Clo. Wemb —1E 56
Carlyon Rd. Hay —5A 54
(in two parts)
Carlyon Rd. Wemb —2E 56
Carmalt Gdns. SW15 —4E 90
Carmarthen Grn. NW9 —5A 26
(off Snowden Dri.)
Carmarthen Pl. SE1 —2E 78 (4C 148)
Carmel Ct. W8 —2K 75
(off Holland St.)
Carmelite Clo. Harr —1G 23
Carmelite Rd. Harr —1G 23
Carmelite St. EC4 —7A 62 (9H 141)
Carmelite Wlk. Harr —1G 23
Carmelite Way. Harr —2G 23
Carmen St. E14 —6D 64
Carmichael Clo. SW11 —3B 92
Carmichael M. SW18 —6B 92
Carmichael Rd. SE25 —5G 125
Carminia Rd. SW17 —2F 109
Carnaby St. W1 —6G 61 (8L 139)
Carnac St. SE27 —4D 110
Carnanton Rd. E17 —1F 33
Carnarvon Av. Enf —3A 8
Carnarvon Rd. E10 —5E 32
Carnarvon Rd. E15 —6H 49
Carnarvon Rd. E18 —1H 33
Carnarvon Rd. Barn —3B 4
Carnation St. SE2 —5B 84
Carnbrook Rd. SE3 —3B 98
Carnecke Gdns. SE9 —5C 98
Carnegie Pl. SW19 —3F 107
Carnegie Rd. Harr —7K 23
Carnegie St. N1 —1K 61
Carnforth Rd. SW16 —7H 109
Carnie Hall. SW17 —3F 109
Carnoustie Dri. N1 —7J 45
(in two parts)
Carnwath Rd. SW6 —3J 91
Carolina Clo. E15 —5G 49
Carolina Rd. T Hth —2B 124
Caroline Clo. N10 —2F 29
Caroline Clo. SW16 —3K 109
Caroline Clo. W2 —7K 59
(off Bayswater Rd.)
Caroline Clo. Croy —4E 134

Caroline Clo. Iswth —7H 71
Caroline Ct. Stan —6F 11
Caroline Gdns. E2 —3E 62 (1D 142)
Caroline Gdns. SE15 —7G 79
Caroline Pl. SW11 —2E 92
Caroline Pl. W2 —7K 59
Caroline Pl. M. W2 —7K 59
Caroline Rd. SW19 —7H 107
Caroline St. E1 —6K 63
Caroline Ter. SW1 —4E 76 (9G 145)
Caroline Wlk. W6 —6G 75
Carol St. NW1 —1G 61
Carpenter Gdns. N21 —2G 17
Carpenter Ho. NW11 —6A 28
Carpenters Ct. Twic —2J 103
Carpenters M. N7 —5J 45
Carpenters Pl. SW4 —4H 93
Carpenter's Rd. E15 —6C 48
Carpenter St. W1 —7F 61 (1J 145)
Carrara Wlk. SW9 —4A 94
Carr Gro. SE18 —4C 82
Carr Ho. Dart —5K 101
Carriage Dri. E. SW11 —7E 76
Carriage Dri. N. SW11 —7D 76
Carriage Dri. S. SW11 —1D 92
Carriage Dri. W. SW11 —7D 76
Carrick Clo. Iswth —3A 88
Carrick Dri. Ilf —1G 35
Carrick Gdns. N17 —7K 17
Carrick Ho. N7 —6K 45
(off Caledonian Rd.)
Carrick Ho. SE11 —5B 78
Carrick M. SE8 —6C 80
Carrill Way. Belv —3D 84
Carrington Av. Houn —5F 87
Carrington Clo. Croy —7A 126
Carrington Gdns. E7 —4J 49
Carrington Pl. W1 —1F 77
Carrington Rd. Rich —4G 89
Carrington Sq. Harr —6B 10
Carrington St. W1 —1F 77 (3J 145)
Carrol Clo. NW5 —4F 45
Carroll Clo. E15 —5H 49
Carron Clo. E14 —6D 64
Carroun Rd. SW8 —7K 77
Carroway La. Gnfd —3H 55
Carrow Rd. Dag —7B 52
Carr Rd. E17 —2B 32
Carr Rd. N'holt —6E 38
Carrs La. N21 —5H 7
Carr St. E14 —5A 64
(in two parts)
Carshalton Gro. Sutt —4B 132
Carshalton Pk. Rd. Cars —5D 132
Carshalton Pl. Cars —5E 132
Carshalton Rd. Mitc —4E 122
Carshalton Rd. Sutt & Cars —5A 132
Carslake Rd. SW15 —6E 90
Carson Rd. E16 —4J 65
Carson Rd. SE21 —2D 110
Carson Rd. Barn —4J 5
Carstairs Rd. SE6 —3E 112
Carston Clo. SE12 —5H 97
Carswell Clo. Ilf —4B 34
Carswell Rd. SE6 —7E 96
Cartaret St. SW1 —2H 77
Carter Clo. Romf —1G 37
Carter Clo. Wall —7H 133
Carter Ct. EC4 —6B 62 (8K 141)
(off Carter La.)
Carter Dri. Romf —1H 37
Carteret St. SW1 —2H 77 (5A 146)
Carteret Way. SE8 —4A 80
Carterhatch La. Enf —1A 8
Carterhatch Rd. Enf —2D 8
Carter La. EC4 —6B 62 (8K 141)
Carter Pl. SE17 —5C 78
Carter Rd. E13 —1K 65

Carter Rd. SW19 —6B 108
Carters Clo. Wor Pk —1F 131
Carters Hill Clo. SE9 —1A 114
Carters La. SE23 —2A 112
Carter St. SE17 —6C 78
Carter's Yd. SW18 —5J 91
Carthew Rd. W6 —3D 74
Carthew Vs. W6 —3D 74
Carthusian St. EC1 —5C 62 (5L 141)
Cartier Circ. E14 —1D 80
Carting La. WC2 —7J 61 (1D 146)
Cart La. E4 —1B 20
Cartmel Clo. N17 —7C 18
Cartmel Gdns. Mord —5A 122
Cartmel Rd. Bexh —1G 101
Carton Ho. SE16 —3G 79
(off Marine St.)
Cartwright Gdns. WC1
—3J 61 (2C 140)
Cartwright Rd. Dag —7F 53
Cartwright St. E1 —7F 63
Carvelle Gdns. N'holt —3B 54
Carver Rd. SE24 —6C 94
Carville Cres. Bren —4E 72
Cary Rd. E11 —4G 49
Carysfort Rd. N8 —5H 29
Carysfort Rd. N16 —3D 46
Cascade Av. N10 —4G 29
Cascade Clo. Buck H —2G 21
Cascade Rd. Buck H —2G 21
Cascades Tower. E14 —1B 80
Casella Rd. SE14 —7K 79
Casewick Rd. SE27 —5A 110
Casimir Rd. E5 —2J 47
Casino Av. SE24 —5C 94
Caspian St. SE5 —7D 78
Caspian Wlk. E16 —6B 66
Cassandra Clo. N'holt —4H 39
Cassell Ho. SW9 —2K 93
(off Stockwell Rd.)
Cassidy Rd. SW6 —7J 75
Cassilda Rd. SE2 —4A 84
Cassilis Rd. Twic —5B 88
Cassiobury Rd. E17 —5A 32
Cassland Rd. E9 —7K 47
Cassland Rd. T Hth —4D 124
Casslee Rd. SE6 —7B 96
Casson St. E1 —5G 63
Castalia Sq. E14 —2E 80
Castellain Mans. W9 —4K 59
(off Castellain Rd.)
Castellain Rd. W9 —4K 59
Castellane Clo. Stan —7E 10
Castellano Av. SW15 —5E 90
Castelnau. SW13 —1C 90
Castelnau Gdns. SW13 —6D 74
Castelnau Pl. SW13 —6D 74
Castelnau Row. SW13 —6D 74
Casterbridge Rd. SE3 —3J 97
Casterton St. E8 —6H 47
Castile Rd. SE18 —4E 82
Castillon Rd. SE6 —2G 113
Castlands Rd. SE6 —2B 112
Castle Av. E4 —5A 20
Castle Av. Eps —7D 130
Castlebar Ct. W5 —5C 56
Castlebar Hill. W5 —5C 56
Castlebar M. W5 —5C 56
Castlebar Pk. Gnfd —4B 56
Castlebar Rd. W5 —5C 56
Castle Baynard St. EC4
—7B 62 (9K 141)
Castle Clo. E9 —5A 48
Castle Clo. SW19 —3F 107
Castle Clo. W3 —2H 73
Castle Clo. Brom —3G 127
Castlecombe Dri. SW19 —7F 91

Castlecombe Rd. SE9 —4C 114
Castle Ct. EC3 —6D 62 (8B 142)
(off Birchin La.)
Castle Ct. SE26 —4A 112
Castledine Rd. SE20 —7H 111
Castle Dri. Ilf —6C 34
Castleford Av. SE9 —1F 115
Castlegate. Rich —3F 89
Castlehaven Rd. NW1 —7F 45
Castle Hill Av. New Ad —7D 136
Castle Ind. Est. SE17
—4C 78 (8L 147)
Castle La. SW1 —3G 77 (6L 145)
Castleleigh Ct. Enf —5J 7
Castlemaine Av. Eps —7D 130
Castlemaine Av. S Croy —5F 135
Castle Mead. SE17 —7C 78
Castle M. N12 —5F 15
Castle M. NW1 —6F 45
Castle Pde. Eps —7C 130
Castle Pl. NW1 —6F 45
Castle Pl. W4 —4A 74
Castle Point. E13 —2A 66
(off Boundary Rd.)
Castlereagh St. W1 —6C 60 (7E 138)
Castle Rd. N12 —5F 15
Castle Rd. NW1 —6F 45
Castle Rd. Dag —1B 68
Castle Rd. Enf —1F 9
Castle Rd. N'holt —6F 39
Castle Rd. S'hall —3D 70
Castle Row. W4 —5K 73
Castle St. E6 —2A 66
Castle St. King T —2E 118
Castleton Av. Bexh —1K 101
Castleton Av. Wemb —4E 40
Castleton Gdns. Wemb —3E 40
Castleton Rd. E17 —2F 33
Castleton Rd. SE9 —4B 114
Castleton Rd. Ilf —1A 52
Castleton Rd. Mitc —4H 123
Castleton Rd. Ruis —1B 38
Castletown Rd. W14 —5G 75
Castleview Gdns. Ilf —6C 34
Castlewood Dri. SE9 —2D 98
Castlewood Rd. N15 & N16 —6G 31
Castlewood Rd. Barn —3G 5
Castle Way. Felt —4A 102
Castle Yd. SE1 —1B 78 (2K 147)
Castle Yd. Rich —5D 88
Castor La. E14 —7D 64
Caterham Av. Ilf —2D 34
Caterham Rd. SE13 —3E 96
Catesby St. SE17 —4D 78 (9B 148)
Catford B'way. SE6 —7D 96
Catford Hill. SE6 —2B 112
Catford M. SE6 —7D 96
Catford Rd. SE6 —7C 96
Cathall Rd. E11 —2F 49
Cathay Ho. SE16 —2H 79
Cathay St. SE16 —2H 79
Cathay Wlk. N'holt —2E 54
(off Brabazon St.)
Cathcart Dri. Orp —7J 129
Cathcart Hill. N19 —3G 45
Cathcart Rd. SW10 —6K 75
Cathcart St. NW5 —6F 45
Cathedral Pl. EC4 —6C 62 (8L 141)
(off Paternoster Row)
Cathedral Piazza. SW1
—3G 77 (7L 145)
Cathedral St. SE1 —1D 78 (2A 148)
Catherall Rd. N5 —3C 46
Catherine Clo. N14 —5B 6
Catherine Ct. SW19 —5H 107

Catherine Ct. Ilf —6G 35
Catherine Gdns. Houn —4H 87
Catherine Gro. SE10 —1D 95
Catherine Ho. N1 —1E 62
(off Whitmore Est.)
Catherine Pl. SW1 —3G 77 (6L 145)
Catherine Rd. Surb —5D 118
Catherine Rd. Romf —5K 61 (9E 140)
Catherine Wheel All. E1
—5E 62 (6D 142)
Catherine Wheel Rd. Bren —7D 72
Catherine Wheel Yd. SW1
—1G 77 (3L 145)
(off Lit. St James's St.)
Catherwood Ct. N1 —3D 62 (1A 142)
(off Murray Gro.)
Cat Hill. Barn —6H 5
Cathles Rd. SW12 —6F 93
Cathnor Hall Ct. W12 —2D 74
Cathnor Rd. W12 —2D 74
Catling Clo. SE23 —3J 111
Catlin's La. Pinn —3A 22
Catlin St. SE16 —5G 79
Cator La. Beck —1B 126
Cato Rd. SW4 —3H 93
Cator Rd. SE26 —6K 111
Cator Rd. Cars —5D 132
Cator St. SE15 —6F 79
(in two parts)
Cato St. W1 —6C 60 (6D 138)
Catsey La. Bush —1B 10
Catsey Wood. Bush —1B 10
Cattistock Rd. SE9 —5D 114
Cattistock Rd. SE12 —5C 114
Catton St. WC1 —5K 61 (6E 140)
Caulfield Rd. E6 —1C 66
Caulfield Rd. SE15 —2H 95
Causeway, The. N2 —4C 28
Causeway, The. SW18 —4K 91
Causeway, The. SW19 —5E 106
Causeway, The. Cars —2E 132
Causeway, The. Felt & Houn —3A 86
Causeway, The. Sutt —7A 132
Causeway, The. Tedd —6K 103
Causeyware Rd. N9 —7D 8
Causton Rd. N6 —7F 29
Causton St. SW1 —4H 77 (9B 146)
Cautley Av. SW4 —5G 93
Cavalier Clo. Romf —4D 36
Cavalier Ct. Surb —6F 119
Cavalry Cres. Houn —4B 86
Cavaye Pl. SW10 —5A 76
Cavell Dri. Enf —2F 7
Cavell Rd. N17 —7J 17
Cavell St. E1 —5H 63
Cavendish Av. N3 —2J 27
Cavendish Av. NW8 —2B 60
Cavendish Av. W13 —5A 56
Cavendish Av. Eri —6J 85
Cavendish Av. Harr —4H 39
Cavendish Av. N Mald —5D 120
Cavendish Av. Ruis —5A 38
Cavendish Av. Sidc —7A 100
Cavendish Av. Well —3K 99
Cavendish Av. Wfd G —1K 33
Cavendish Clo. N18 —5C 18
Cavendish Clo. NW6 —6H 43
Cavendish Clo. NW8
—3B 60 (1B 138)
Cavendish Ct. EC3 —6E 62 (7D 142)
(off Devonshire Row)
Cavendish Dri. E11 —1F 49
Cavendish Dri. Edgw —6A 12
Cavendish Gdns. Bark —5J 51
Cavendish Gdns. Ilf —1E 50
Cavendish Gdns. Romf —5E 36
Cavendish Mans. NW6 —5J 43

Cavendish M. N. W1
　—5F 61 (5K 139)
Cavendish M. S. W1 —5F 61
Cavendish Pl. W1 —6F 61 (7K 139)
Cavendish Rd. E4 —5K 19
Cavendish Rd. N4 —6B 30
Cavendish Rd. N18 —5C 18
Cavendish Rd. NW6 —7G 43
Cavendish Rd. SW12 —6F 93
Cavendish Rd. SW19 —7B 108
Cavendish Rd. W4 —1J 89
Cavendish Barn —3A 4
Cavendish Rd. Croy —1B 134
Cavendish N Mald —4B 120
Cavendish Rd. Sutt —7A 132
Cavendish Sq. W1 —6F 61 (7K 139)
Cavendish St. N1 —2D 62
Cavendish Way. W Wick —1D 136
Cavenham Gdns. Ilf —3H 51
Caverleigh Way. Wor Pk —1C 130
Cave Rd. E13 —3K 65
Cave Rd. Rich —4C 104
Caversham Av. N13 —3F 17
Caversham Av. Sutt —2G 131
Caversham Ct. N11 —2K 15
Caversham Ho. N15 —4C 30
　(off Caversham Rd.)
Caversham M. SW3 —6D 76
Caversham Rd. N15 —4C 30
Caversham Rd. NW5 —6G 45
Caversham Rd. King T —2F 119
Caverswall St. W12 —6E 58
Caveside Clo. Chst —1E 128
Cawdor Cres. W7 —4A 72
Cawnpore St. SE19 —5E 110
Caxton Gro. E3 —3C 64
Caxton M. Bren —6D 72
Caxton Pl. Ilf —3E 50
Caxton Rd. N22 —2K 29
Caxton Rd. SW19 —5A 108
Caxton Rd. W12 —2F 75
Caxton St. S'hall —3B 70
Caxton St. N. E16 —7H 77 (6M 145)
Caxton St. N. E16 —6H 65
Caxton St. S. E16 —7J 65
Caxton Wlk. WC2 —6H 61 (8B 140)
Cayenne Ct. SE1 —2F 79 (4F 148)
　(off Lafone St.)
Caygill Clo. Brom —4H 127
Cayley Clo. Wall —7J 133
Cayton Pl. EC1 —3D 62 (2A 142)
　(off Cayton St.)
Cayton Rd. Gnfd —2J 55
Cayton St. EC1 —3D 62 (2A 142)
Cazenove Rd. E17 —1C 32
Cazenove Rd. N16 —2F 47
Cearns Ho. E6 —1B 66
Cecil Av. Bark —7H 51
Cecil Av. Enf —4A 8
Cecil Av. Wemb —5F 41
Cecil Clo. W5 —5D 56
Cecil Ct. WC2 —7J 61 (1C 140)
Cecil Ct. Barn —3A 4
Cecile Pk. N8 —6J 29
Cecil Ho. E17 —1C 32
Cecilia Clo. N2 —3A 28
Cecil Rd. E8 —5H 47
Cecil Pk. Pinn —4C 22
Cecil Pl. Mitc —5D 122
Cecil Rd. E11 —3H 49
Cecil Rd. E13 —1J 65
Cecil Rd. E17 —1C 32
Cecil Rd. N10 —2F 29
Cecil Rd. N14 —1B 16
Cecil Rd. NW9 —3A 26
Cecil Rd. NW10 —1A 58
Cecil Rd. SW19 —7K 107

Cecil Rd. W3 —5J 57
Cecil Rd. Croy —6K 123
Cecil Rd. Enf —4H 7
Cecil Rd. Harr —3H 23
Cecil Rd. Houn —2G 87
Cecil Rd. Ilf —4F 51
Cecil Rd. Romf —7D 36
Cecil Rd. Sutt —6H 131
Cecil Rosen Ct. Wemb —3B 40
Cecil Way. Brom —1J 137
Cedar Av. Barn —7H 5
Cedar Av. Enf —2D 8
Cedar Av. Romf —5E 36
Cedar Av. Ruis —5A 38
Cedar Av. Sidc —7A 109
Cedar Av. Twic —6F 87
Cedar Clo. SE21 —1C 110
Cedar Clo. SW15 —4K 105
Cedar Clo. Buck H —2G 21
Cedar Clo. Cars —6D 132
Cedar Clo. Romf —4J 37
Cedar Copse. Brom —2D 128
Cedar Ct. E8 —7F 47
Cedar Ct. E18 —1J 33
Cedar Ct. N1 —7C 46
Cedar Ct. N10 —2E 28
Cedar Ct. N11 —5B 16
Cedar Ct. N20 —1G 15
Cedar Ct. SW19 —3F 107
Cedar Ct. Bren —6D 72
　(off Boston Mnr. Rd.)
Cedar Dri. N2 —4C 28
Cedar Dri. Pinn —6A 16
Cedar Gdns. Sutt —6A 132
Cedar Grange. Enf —5K 7
Cedar Gro. W5 —3E 72
Cedar Gro. Bex —6D 100
Cedar Gro. S'hall —6E 54
Cedar Heights. Rich —1E 104
Cedar Ho. N22 —1A 30
　(off Acacia Rd.)
Cedar Ho. W8 —3K 75
　(off Marloes Rd.)
Cedar Ho. Hay —4A 54
Cedarhurst. Brom —7G 113
Cedarhurst Cotts. Bex —1G 117
Cedarhurst Dri. SE9 —5A 98
Cedarland Ter. SW20 —7D 106
Cedar Lawn Av. Barn —5A 4
Cedar Mt. SE9 —1B 114
Cedarne Rd. SW6 —7K 75
Cedar Pk. Gdns. Romf —7D 36
Cedar Pk. Rd. Enf —1H 7
Cedar Pl. SE7 —5A 82
Cedar Rise. N14 —7K 5
Cedar Rd. N17 —1F 31
Cedar Rd. NW2 —4E 42
Cedar Rd. Brom —2A 128
Cedar Rd. Croy —2E 134
Cedar Rd. Enf —1G 7
Cedar Rd. Houn —2A 86
Cedar Rd. Romf —4J 37
Cedar Rd. Sutt —6A 132
Cedar Rd. Tedd —5A 104
Cedars Av. E17 —5C 32
Cedars Av. Mitc —4E 122
Cedars Clo. NW4 —3F 27
Cedars Ct. N9 —2K 17
Cedars Ho. E17 —3D 32
Cedars M. SW4 —4F 93
Cedars Rd. E15 —6G 49
Cedars Rd. N9 —2B 18
Cedars Rd. N21 —2G 17
Cedars Rd. SW4 —3F 93
Cedars Rd. SW13 —2C 90
Cedars Rd. W4 —6J 73
Cedars Rd. Beck —2A 126
Cedars Rd. Croy —3J 133

Cedars Rd. King T —1C 118
Cedars Rd. Mord —4J 121
Cedars, The. W13 —6C 56
Cedars, The. Buck H —1D 20
Cedars, The. Tedd —6K 103
Cedars, The. Wall —4G 133
Cedar Ter. Rich —4E 88
Cedar Tree Gro. SE27 —5B 110
Cedarville Gdns. SW16 —6K 109
Cedar Vista. Rich —2E 88
Cedar Way. NW1 —7H 45
Cedra Ct. N16 —1G 47
Cedric Rd. SE9 —3G 115
Celadon Clo. Enf —3F 9
Celandine Clo. E3 —5C 64
Celandine Ct. E4 —3J 19
Celandine Dri. SE28 —1B 84
Celandine Way. E15 —3G 65
Celbridge M. W2 —6K 59
　(off Porchester Rd.)
Celebridge M. W2 —5K 59
Celestial Gdns. SE13 —4F 97
Celia Ho. N1 —2E 62
　(off Arden Est.)
Celia Rd. N19 —4G 45
Celtic Av. Brom —3G 127
Celtic St. E14 —5D 64
Cemetery La. SE7 —6C 82
Cemetery Rd. E7 —4H 49
Cemetery Rd. N17 —7K 17
Cemetery Rd. SE2 —7B 84
Cenacle Clo. NW3 —3J 43
Centaurs Bus. Cen. Iswth —6A 72
Centaur St. SE1 —3K 77 (6F 146)
Centenary Rd. Enf —4G 9
Centenary Trading Est. Enf —4G 9
Central Av. E11 —2F 49
Central Av. N2 —2B 28
Central Av. N9 —3K 17
Central Av. SW11 —7D 76
Central Av. Enf —2C 8
Central Av. Houn —4G 87
Central Av. Pinn —6D 22
Central Av. Wall —5J 133
Central Av. Well —2K 99
Central Bus. Cen. NW10 —5A 42
Central Cir. NW4 —5D 26
Central Hill. SE19 —6D 110
Central Ho. E15 —2E 64
Central Mans. NW4 —6D 26
　(off Watford Way)
Central Markets. EC1 —5B 62 (6J 141)
　(off Charterhouse St.)
Central Pde. E17 —4C 32
Central Pde. SE20 —7K 111
　(off High St. Penge)
Central Pde. W3 —2H 73
Central Pde. Felt —7A 86
Central Pde. Gnfd —3A 56
Central Pde. Harr —5K 23
Central Pk. Av. Dag —3H 53
Central Pk. Est. Houn —5B 86
Central Pk. Rd. E6 —2B 66
Central Rd. Mord —6J 121
Central Rd. Wemb —5B 40
Central Rd. Wor Pk —1C 130
Central School Path. SW14 —3J 89
Central Sq. NW11 —6J 27
Central Sq. Wemb —5E 40
Central St. EC1 —3C 62 (1L 141)
Central Ter. Beck —3K 125
Central Way. SE28 —1A 84
Central Way. Cars —7C 132
Central Way. Felt —5A 86
Centre Av. N2 —2C 28
Centre Av. W3 —1K 73

Centre Comn. Rd. Chst —6G 115
Centre Ct. W2 —7A 60
　(off Princes Sq.)
Centre Ct. Shopping Cen. SW19
　—6H 107
Centre Dri. E7 —4A 50
Centre Rd. E11 & E7 —2J 49
Centre Rd. Dag —2H 69
Centre St. E2 —2H 63
Centre Way. E17 —7K 19
Centre Way. N9 —2D 18
Centre Way. Ilf —2G 51
Centric Clo. NW1 —1E 60
Centro Ct. E6 —4D 66
Centurion Clo. N7 —7K 45
Centurion La. E3 —2B 64
Centurion Way. Eri —3F 85
Century Ho. SW15 —4F 91
Century Rd. E17 —3A 32
Cephas Av. E1 —4J 63
Cephas St. E1 —4J 63
Ceres Rd. SE18 —4K 83
Cerise Rd. SE15 —1G 95
Cerne Clo. Hay —7A 54
Cerne Rd. Mord —6A 122
Cervantes Ct. W2 —6K 59
Cester St. E2 —1G 63
Ceylon Rd. W14 —3F 75
Chadacre Av. Ilf —3D 34
Chadacre Ct. E13 —1J 65
　(off Vicars Clo.)
Chadacre Rd. Eps —6D 130
Chadbourn St. E14 —5D 64
Chadbury Ct. NW7 —7H 13
Chadd Dri. Brom —3C 128
Chad Grn. E13 —1J 65
　(in two parts)
Chadville Gdns. Romf —5D 36
Chadway. Dag —1C 52
Chadwell Av. Romf —7B 36
Chadwell Heath La. Chad —4B 36
Chadwell St. EC1 —3A 62 (1H 141)
Chadwick Av. E4 —4A 20
Chadwick Clo. W7 —6K 55
Chadwick Clo. Tedd —6A 104
Chadwick Rd. E11 —7G 33
Chadwick Rd. NW10 —1B 58
Chadwick Rd. SE15 —2F 95
Chadwick Rd. Ilf —3F 51
Chadwick St. SW1 —3H 77 (7A 146)
Chadwick Way. SE28 —7D 68
Chadwin Rd. E13 —5K 65
Chadworth Ho. N4 —1C 46
Chaffinch Av. Croy —6K 125
Chaffinch Clo. N9 —1E 18
Chaffinch Clo. Croy —5K 125
Chaffinch Rd. Beck —1A 125
Chafford Way. Romf —4C 36
Chagford St. NW1 —4D 60 (4E 138)
Chailey Av. Enf —2A 8
Chailey Clo. Houn —1B 86
Chailey St. E5 —3J 47
Chalbury Wlk. N1 —2A 62
Chalcombe Rd. SE2 —3B 84
Chalcot Clo. Sutt —7J 131
Chalcot Cres. NW1 —1D 60
Chalcot Gdns. NW3 —6D 44
Chalcot M. SW16 —3J 109
Chalcot Rd. NW1 —7E 44
Chalcot Sq. NW1 —7E 44
Chalcroft Rd. SE13 —5G 97
Chaldon Ct. SE19 —1D 124
Chaldon Rd. SW6 —7G 75
Chale Rd. SW2 —6J 93
Chalet Clo. Bex —4K 117
Chale Wlk. Sutt —7K 131
Chalfont Av. Wemb —6H 41
Chalfont Ct. NW9 —3B 26

Chalfont Ct. Harr —6K 23
　(off Northwick Pk. Rd.)
Chalfont Grn. N9 —3K 17
Chalfont Ho. N9 —3K 17
Chalfont Rd. SE25 —3F 125
Chalfont Wlk. Pinn —2A 22
Chalfont Way. W13 —3B 72
Chalford Rd. SE21 —4D 110
Chalford Wlk. Wfd G —1B 34
Chalgrove Av. Mord —5J 121
Chalgrove Cres. Ilf —2C 34
Chalgrove Gdns. N3 —3G 27
Chalgrove Rd. E9 —6J 47
Chalgrove Rd. N17 —1H 31
Chalgrove Rd. Sutt —7B 132
Chalice Clo. Wall —6H 133
Chalice Ct. N2 —4C 28
Chalkenden Clo. SE20 —7H 111
Chalk Farm Rd. NW1 —7E 44
Chalkhill Rd. W6 —4F 75
Chalkhill Rd. Wemb —3G 41
Chalklands. Wemb —3J 41
Chalk La. Barn —3J 5
Chalkley Clo. Mitc —2D 122
Chalk Pit Caravan Site. Sidc —7F 11
Chalk Pit Way. Sutt —6A 132
Chalk Rd. E13 —5K 65
Chalkstone Clo. Well —1A 100
Chalkwell Pk. Av. Enf —4K 7
Challenge Way. SW2 —1K 109
Challin St. SE20 —1J 125
Challis Rd. Bren —5D 72
Challoner Clo. N2 —2B 28
Challoner Cres. W14 —5H 75
Challoner St. W14 —5H 75
Chalmers Ho. E17 —5D 32
Chalmers Ho. E17 —5D 32
Chalmer's Wlk. SE17 —6B 78
　(off Hillingdon St.)
Chalsey Rd. SE4 —4B 96
Chalton Dri. N2 —6B 28
Chalton St. NW1 —2G 61
Chamberlain Clo. SE28 —3H 83
Chamberlain Cotts. SE5 —1D 94
Chamberlain Cres. W Wick —1D 136
Chamberlain Pl. E17 —3A 32
Chamberlain Rd. N2 —2A 28
Chamberlain Rd. N9 —3B 18
Chamberlain Rd. W13 —2A 72
Chamberlain St. NW1 —7D 44
Chamberlain Way. Felt —4C 102
Chamberlain Way. Pinn —3A 22
Chamberlain Way. Surb —7E 118
Chamberlayne Rd. NW10 —7E 42
Chambers Gdns. N2 —1B 28
Chambers La. NW10 —7D 42
Chambers Rd. N7 —4J 45
Chambers St. SE16 —2G 79
Chamber St. E1 —7F 63
Chambers Wharf. SE16 —2G 79
Chambord St. E2 —3F 63 (2F 142)
Chamomile Ct. E17 —6C 32
　(off Yunus Khan Clo.)
Champion Cres. SE26 —4A 112
Champion Gro. SE5 —3D 94
Champion Hill. SE5 —3D 94
Champion Hill Est. SE5 —3E 94
Champion Pk. SE5 —2D 94
Champion Rd. SE26 —4A 112
Champlain Ho. W12 —7D 58
　(off White City Est.)
Champness Clo. SE27 —4D 110
Champneys Clo. Sutt —7H 131
Chancel Ind. Est. NW10 —6B 42
Chancellor Gdns. S Croy —7B 134
Chancellor Gro. SE21 —2C 110
Chancellor Pas. E14 —1C 80
Chancellors Ct. WC1 —5K 61 (5E 140)
　(off Olde Hall St.)

176

Chancellor's Rd. W6 —5E 74
Chancellor's St. W6 —5E 74
Chancellors Wharf. W6 —5E 74
Chancelot Rd. SE2 —4B 84
Chancel St. SE1 —1B 78 (3J 147)
Chancery La. WC2 —6A 62 (6F 140)
Chancery La. Beck —2D 126
Chance St. E2 & E1 —4F 63 (3E 142)
Chanctonbury Clo. SE9 —3F 115
Chanctonbury Gdns. Sutt —7K 131
Chanctonbury Way. N12 —6G 14
Chandler Av. E16 —5J 65
Chandler Clo. Hamp —7E 102
Chandlers. M. E14 —2C 80
Chandler St. E1 —1H 79
Chandlers Way. SW2 —7A 94
Chandos Av. E17 —2C 32
Chandos Av. N14 —3B 16
Chandos Av. N20 —1F 15
Chandos Av. W5 —4C 72
Chandos Clo. Buck H —2E 20
Chandos Ct. N14 —2C 16
Chandos Ct. Edgw —7A 12
Chandos Cres. Edgw —7A 12
Chandos Pde. Edgw —7A 12
Chandos Pl. WC2 —7J 61 (1C 146)
Chandos Rd. E15 —5F 49
Chandos Rd. N2 —2B 28
Chandos Rd. N17 —2E 30
Chandos Rd. NW2 —5E 42
Chandos Rd. NW10 —4A 58
Chandos Rd. Harr —5G 23
Chandos Rd. Pinn —7B 22
Chandos St. W1 —5F 61 (6K 139)
Chandos Way. NW11 —1K 43
Change All. EC3 —6D 62 (8B 142)
Channel Clo. Houn —1E 86
Channelsea Rd. E15 —1F 65
Chantree Grn. W4 —4J 73
Chantry Rd. SW9 —3K 93
Chantry Clo. Enf —1H 7
Chantry Clo. Harr —5F 25
Chantry Clo. Sidc —5G 116
Chantry La. Brom —5B 128
Chantry Pl. Harr —1F 23
Chantry Rd. Harr —1F 23
Chantry Sq. W8 —3K 75
Chantry St. N1 —1B 62
Chantry, The. E4 —1K 19
Chantry Way. Rain —2K 69
Chant Sq. E15 —7F 49
Chant St. E15 —7F 49
Chanute Gdns. SE15 —4K 79
Chapel Ct. N2 —3C 28
Chapel Ct. SE1 —2D 78 (4A 148)
(off Borough High St.)
Chapel Ct. SW1 —2D 78
Chapel Farm Rd. SE9 —3D 114
Chapel Hill. N2 —2C 28
Chapel Hill. Dart —5K 101
Chapel Ho. St. E14 —5D 80
Chapel La. Pinn —3B 22
Chapel La. Romf —7D 36
Chapel Mkt. N1 —2A 62
Chapelmount Rd. Wfd G —6J 21
Chapel Path. E11 —6J 33
(off Woodbine Pl.)
Chapel Pl. EC2 —3E 62 (2C 142)
Chapel Pl. N1 —2A 62
Chapel Pl. N17 —7A 18
Chapel Pl. W1 —6F 61 (8J 139)
Chapel Rd. SE27 —4B 110
Chapel Rd. W13 —1B 72
Chapel Rd. Bexh —4G 101
Chapel Rd. Houn —3F 87
Chapel Rd. Ilf —3E 50
Chapel Rd. Twic —7B 88

Chapel Side. W2 —7K 59
Chapel Stones. N17 —1F 31
Chapel St. NW1 —5C 60 (6C 138)
Chapel St. SW1 —3E 76 (6H 145)
Chapel St. Enf —3J 7
Chapel View. S Croy —6J 135
Chapel Wlk. NW4 —4D 26
(in two parts)
Chapel Wlk. Croy —2C 134
Chapel Way. N7 —3K 45
Chaplin Clo. SE1 —2B 78 (4H 147)
Chaplin Gro. Wemb —6D 40
Chaplin Rd. E15 —2H 65
Chaplin Rd. N17 —3F 31
Chaplin Rd. NW2 —6C 42
Chaplin Rd. Dag —7E 52
Chaplin Rd. Wemb —6C 40
Charleston St. SE17
—4C 78 (9M 147)
Chapman Cres. Harr —6E 24
Chapman Rd. E9 —6B 48
Chapman Rd. Belv —5H 85
Chapman Rd. Croy —1A 134
Chapman's La. SE2 & Belv —4D 84
Chapman St. E1 —7H 63
Chapone Pl. W1 —6H 61 (8A 140)
(off Dean St.)
Chara Pl. W4 —3J 73
Charcroft Ct. W14 —2F 75
(off Minford Gdns.)
Charcroft Gdns. Enf —4E 8
Chardin Rd. W4 —4A 74
Chardmore Rd. N16 —1G 47
Chardwell Clo. E6 —6D 66
Charecroft Way. W12 —2F 75
Charfield Ct. W9 —4K 59
(off Shirland Rd.)
Charford Rd. E16 —5J 65
Chargeable La. E13 —4H 65
Chargeable St. E16 —4H 65
Chargrove Clo. SE16 —2K 79
Charing Ct. Short —2G 127
Charlbert St. NW8 —2C 60
Charlbury Av. Stan —5J 11
Charlbury Gdns. Ilf —2K 51
Charlbury Gro. W5 —6C 56
Charldane Rd. SE9 —3F 115
Charlecote Gro. SE26 —3H 111
Charlecote Rd. Dag —3E 52
Charlemont Rd. E6 —3D 66
Charles Barry Clo. SW4 —3G 93
Charles Bradlaugh Ho. N17 —7C 18
(off Haynes Clo.)
Charles Clo. Sidc —4B 116
Charles Cres. Harr —7H 23
Charle Sevright Dri. NW7 —5A 14
Charlesfield. SE9 —3A 114
Charles Gardner Ct. N1
—3D 62 (1B 142)
(off Haberdasher St.)
Charles Grinling Wlk. SE18 —4E 82
Charles Ho. N15 —7A 18
(off Love La.)
Charles La. NW8 —2C 60
Charles Pl. NW1 —3G 61 (2M 139)
Charles Rd. E7 —7A 50

Charles Rd. SW19 —1J 121
Charles Rd. W13 —6A 56
Charles Rd. Dag —6K 53
Charles Rd. Romf —6D 36
Charles II Pl. SW3 —5C 76
Charles II St. SW1 —1H 77 (2A 146)
Charles Sq. N1 —3D 62 (2B 142)
Charles Sq. Est. N1 —3D 62 (2B 142)
(off Charles Sq.)
Charles St. E16 —1A 82
Charles St. SW13 —2A 90
Charles St. W1 —1F 77 (2J 145)
Charles St. Croy —3C 134
Charles St. Enf —5A 8
Charles St. Houn —2E 86
Charles St. Trading Est. E16 —1A 82
Charleston Ct. SE17
—4C 78 (9M 147)
Charleville Cir. SE26 —5G 111
Charleville Mans. W14 —5G 75
(off Charleville Rd.)
Charleville Rd. Eri —7J 85
Charleville Rd. W14 —5G 75
Charlmont Rd. SW17 —6C 108
Charlotte Clo. Bexh —5E 100
Charlotte Ct. N8 —6H 29
Charlotte Ct. Ilf —6D 34
Charlotte Despard Av. SW11 —1E 92
Charlotte M. W1 —5G 61 (5M 139)
Charlotte M. W14 —4G 75
Charlotte Pl. NW9 —5J 25
Charlotte Pl. SW1 —4G 77 (9L 145)
Charlotte Pl. W1 —5G 61 (6M 139)
Charlotte Rd. EC2 —3E 62 (2C 142)
Charlotte Rd. SW13 —1B 90
Charlotte Rd. Dag —6H 53
Charlotte Rd. Wall —6G 133
Charlotte Row. SW4 —3G 93
Charlotte Sq. Rich —6F 89
Charlotte St. W1 —5G 61 (5M 139)
Charlotte Ter. N1 —1K 61
Charlow Clo. SW6 —2A 92
Charlton Chu. La. SE7 —5A 82
Charlton Ct. E2 —1F 63
Charlton Cres. Bark —2K 67
Charlton Dene. SE7 —7A 82
Charlton Ho. Bren —6E 72
Charlton King's Rd. NW5 —5F 45
Charlton La. SE7 —4B 82
Charlton Pk. La. SE7 —7B 82
Charlton Pk. Rd. SE7 —6B 82
Charlton Pl. N1 —2B 62
Charlton Rd. N9 —1E 18
Charlton Rd. NW10 —1A 58
Charlton Rd. SE3 & SE7 —7J 81
Charlton Rd. Harr —4D 24
Charlton Rd. Wemb —1F 41
Charlton Way. SE3 —1G 97
Charlwood. Croy —7B 136
Charlwood Clo. Harr —6D 10
Charlwood Pl. SW1
—4G 77 (9M 145)
Charlwood Rd. SW15 —4F 91
Charlwood St. SW1 —5G 77
Charlwood Ter. SW15 —4F 91
Charminster Av. SW19 —2J 121
Charminster Ct. Surb —7D 118
Charminster Rd. SE9 —4B 114
Charminster Rd. Wor Pk —1F 131
Charmouth Ct. Rich —5F 89
Charmouth Ho. SW8 —7K 77
Charmouth Rd. Well —1C 100
Charnock Rd. E5 —3H 47
Charnwood Av. SW19 —2J 121
Charnwood Clo. N Mald —4A 120
Charnwood Dri. E18 —3K 33

Charnwood Gdns. E14 —4C 80
Charnwood Pl. N20 —3F 15
Charnwood Rd. SE25 —5D 124
Charnwood St. E5 —2H 47
Charrington Rd. Croy —2C 134
Charrington St. NW1 —2H 61
Charsley Rd. SE6 —2D 112
Chart Clo. Brom —1G 127
Chart Clo. Croy —6J 125
Charter Av. Ilf —1H 51
Charter Ct. N4 —1A 46
Charter Ct. N Mald —3A 120
Charter Ct. Shall —1E 70
Charter Cres. Houn —4C 86
Charter Dri. Bex —7E 100
Charterhouse Av. Wemb —5C 40
Charterhouse Bldgs. EC1
—4B 62 (4L 141)
Charterhouse M. EC1
—5B 62 (5K 141)
Charterhouse Sq. EC1
—5B 62 (5K 141)
Charterhouse St. EC1
—5A 62 (6H 141)
Charteris Rd. N4 —1A 46
Charteris Rd. NW6 —1H 59
Charteris Rd. Wfd G —7F 20
Charter Rd. King T —3H 119
Charter Rd., The. Wfd G —6B 20
Charters Clo. SE19 —5E 110
Charter Sq. King T —1H 119
Charter Way. N3 —4H 27
Charter Way. N14 —6B 6
Chartfield Av. SW15 —5D 90
Chartfield Sq. SW15 —5F 91
Chartham Ct. SW9 —3A 94
(off Canterbury Cres.)
Chartham Gro. SE27 —3B 110
Chartham Rd. SE25 —3H 125
Chartley Av. NW2 —3A 42
Chartley Av. Stan —6E 10
Charton Clo. Belv —6G 85
Chart St. N1 —3D 62 (1B 142)
Chartwell Clo. SE9 —2H 115
Chartwell Clo. Croy —1D 134
Chartwell Clo. Gnfd —1F 55
Chartwell Ct. Barn —4B 4
Chartwell Ct. Wfd G —7C 20
Chartwell Gdns. Sutt —4G 131
Chartwell Pl. Harr —2H 39
Chartwell Pl. Sutt —3H 131
Chartwell Way. SE20 —1H 125
Charville Ct. Harr —6K 23
Char Wood. SW16 —4A 110
Chase Bank Ct. N14 —6B 6
(off Avenue Rd.)
Chase Ct. Iswth —2A 88
Chase Ct. Gdns. Enf —3H 7
Chase Cross Rd. Romf —1J 37
Chasefield Rd. SW17 —4D 108
Chase Gdns. E4 —4H 19
Chase Gdns. Twic —7H 87
Chase Grn. Enf —3H 7
Chase Grn. Av. Enf —2G 7
Chase Hill. Enf —3H 7
Chase La. Ilf —5H 35
(in two parts)
Chaseley Dri. W4 —5H 73
Chaseley St. E14 —6A 64
Chasemore Gdns. Croy —5A 134
Chase Ridings. Enf —2F 7
Chase Rd. N14 —5B 6
Chase Rd. NW10 —4K 57
Chase Rd. Trading Est. NW10
—4K 57
Chase Side. N14 —5K 5
Chase Side. Enf —2H 7

Chaseside Av. SW20 —2G 121
Chase Side Av. Enf —2H 7
Chase Side Cres. Enf —1H 7
Chase Side Pl. Enf —3H 7
Chase Side Works Ind. Est. N14
—7C 6
Chase, The. E12 —4B 50
Chase, The. SW4 —4F 93
Chase, The. SW16 —7K 109
Chase, The. SW20 —1G 121
Chase, The. Bexh —3H 101
Chase, The. Brom —3K 127
Chase, The. Chad —6A 38
Chase, The. Eastc —6A 22
Chase, The. Edgw —1H 25
Chase, The. Pinn —4D 22
Chase, The. Romf —3K 37
Chase, The. Stan —6F 11
Chase, The. Sun —7A 102
Chase, The. Wall —5K 133
Chaseville Pde. N21 —5E 6
Chaseville Pk. Rd. N21 —5D 6
Chase Way. N14 —2A 16
Chaseways Vs. Romf —1F 37
Chasewood Av. Enf —2G 7
Chasewood Ct. NW7 —5E 12
Chasewood Pk. Harr —3J 39
Chaston St. NW5 —5E 44
(off Grafton Ter.)
Chatfield Rd. SW11 —3A 92
Chatfield Rd. Croy —1B 134
Chatham Av. Brom —7H 127
Chatham Clo. NW11 —5J 27
Chatham Clo. Sutt —7H 121
Chatham Pl. E9 —6J 47
Chatham Rd. E17 —3A 32
Chatham Rd. E18 —2H 33
Chatham Rd. SW11 —6D 92
Chatham Rd. King T —2G 119
Chatham St. SE17 —4D 78 (8A 148)
Chatsfield Pl. W5 —6E 56
Chatsworth Av. NW4 —2E 26
Chatsworth Av. SW20 —1G 121
Chatsworth Av. Brom —4K 113
Chatsworth Av. Sidc —1A 116
Chatsworth Av. Wemb —5F 41
Chatsworth Ct. NW4 —2E 26
Chatsworth Clo. NW4 —6J 73
Chatsworth Clo. W Wick —1H 137
Chatsworth Ct. Stan —5H 11
Chatsworth Cres. Houn —4H 87
Chatsworth Dri. Enf —7B 8
Chatsworth Est. E5 —4K 47
Chatsworth Gdns. W3 —1H 73
Chatsworth Gdns. Harr —1F 39
Chatsworth Gdns. N Mald —5B 120
Chatsworth Pde. Orp —5G 129
Chatsworth Pl. Mitc —3D 122
Chatsworth Pl. Tedd —4A 104
Chatsworth Rise. W5 —4F 57
Chatsworth Rd. E5 —3J 47
Chatsworth Rd. E15 —5H 49
Chatsworth Rd. NW2 —6E 42
Chatsworth Rd. W4 —6J 73
Chatsworth Rd. W5 —4F 57
Chatsworth Rd. Croy —4D 134
Chatsworth Rd. Hay —4A 54
Chatsworth Rd. Sutt —5F 131
Chatsworth Way. SE27 —3B 110
Chatterton Ct. Rich —2F 89
Chatterton Rd. N4 —3B 46
Chatterton Rd. Brom —4B 128
Chatto Rd. SW11 —5D 92
Chaucer Av. Rich —3G 89
Chaucer Clo. N11 —5B 16
Chaucer Ct. New Bar —5E 4
Chaucer Dri. SE1 —4F 79 (9F 148)
Chaucer Gdns. Sutt —3J 131

Chaucer Grn. Croy —7H 125
Chaucer Ho. Barn —4A 4
Chaucer Ho. Sutt —3J 131
(off Chaucer Gdns.)
Chaucer Rd. E7 —6J 49
Chaucer Rd. E11 —6J 33
Chaucer Rd. E17 —2E 32
Chaucer Rd. SE24 —5A 94
Chaucer Rd. W3 —1J 73
Chaucer Rd. Sidc —1C 116
Chaucer Rd. Sutt —4J 131
Chaucer Rd. Well —1J 99
Chaucer Way. SW19 —6B 108
Chaulden Ho. EC1 —3D 62 (2B 142)
(off Cranwood St.)
Chauncey Clo. N9 —3B 18
Chaundrye Clo. SE9 —6D 98
Chaville Ho. N11 —4K 15
Cheam Comn. Rd. Wor Pk —2D 130
Cheam Pk. Way. Sutt —6G 131
Cheam Rd. Cheam —7F 131
Cheam Rd. Sutt —6H 131
Cheam St. SE15 —3J 95
Cheapside. EC2 —6C 62 (7L 141)
Cheapside. N13 —4J 17
Cheddington Rd. N18 —3K 17
Chedworth Clo. E16 —6H 65
Cheeseman Clo. Hamp —6C 102
Cheesemans Ter. W14 —5H 75
Chelford Rd. Brom —5F 113
Chelmer Cres. Bark —2B 68
Chelmer Rd. E9 —5K 47
Chelmsford Clo. E6 —6D 66
Chelmsford Clo. W6 —6F 75
Chelmsford Ct. N14 —7C 6
(off Ivy Rd.)
Chelmsford Gdns. IIf —7C 34
Chelmsford Ho. N7 —7K 61
(off Holloway Rd.)
Chelmsford Rd. E11 —1F 49
Chelmsford Rd. E17 —6C 32
Chelmsford Rd. E18 —1H 33
Chelmsford Rd. N14 —7B 6
Chelmsford Sq. NW10 —1E 58
Chelsea Bri. SW1 & SW8 —6F 77
Chelsea Bri. Bus. Cen. SW8 —7F 77
Chelsea Bri. Rd. SW1 —5E 76
Chelsea Bri. Wharf. SW8 —6F 77
Chelsea Cloisters. SW3
—4C 76 (9D 144)
Chelsea Clo. NW10 —1K 57
Chelsea Clo. Edgw —2G 25
Chelsea Clo. Hamp —5G 103
Chelsea Clo. Wor Pk —7C 120
Chelsea Ct. Brom —4C 128
Chelsea Cres. SW10 —1A 92
Chelsea Embkmt. SW3 —6C 76
Chelsea Garden Mkt. SW10 —1A 92
Chelsea Harbour. SW10 —1A 92
Chelsea Harbour Dri. SW10 —1A 92
Chelsea Mnr. Ct. SW3 —6C 76
Chelsea Mnr. Gdns. SW3 —5C 76
Chelsea Mnr. St. SW3 —5C 76
Chelsea Pk. Gdns. SW3 —6B 76
Chelsea Reach Tower. SW10 —7B 76
(off Worlds End Est.)
Chelsea Sq. SW3 —5B 76
Chelsea Towers. SW3 —6C 76
(off Chelsea Mnr. Gdns.)
Chelsfield Av. N9 —7F 8
Chelsfield Gdns. SE26 —3J 111
Chelsfield Grn. N9 —7F 8
Chelsham Rd. SW4 —3H 93
Chelsham Rd. S Croy —7D 134
Chelster Ct. Sidc —4K 115
Chelsworth Dri. SE18 —6H 83

Cheltenham Av. Twic —7A 88
Cheltenham Clo. N Mald —3J 119
Cheltenham Clo. N'holt —6E 39
Cheltenham Ct. Stan —5H 11
(off Marsh La.)
Cheltenham Gdns. E6 —2C 66
Cheltenham Pl. W3 —1H 73
Cheltenham Pl. Harr —4C 24
Cheltenham Rd. E10 —6E 32
Cheltenham Rd. SE15 —4J 95
Cheltenham Ter. SW3 —5D 76
Chelverton Rd. SW15 —4F 91
Chelwood. N20 —2G 15
Chelwood Clo. E4 —6J 9
Chelwood Gdns. Rich —2G 89
Chelwood Gdns. Pas. Rich —2G 89
Chelwood Wlk. SE4 —4A 96
Chenappa Clo. E13 —3J 65
Chenduit Way. Stan —5E 10
Cheney Ct. SE23 —1K 111
Cheney Rd. NW1 —2J 61
Cheney Row. E17 —1B 32
Cheneys Rd. E11 —3G 49
Cheney St. Pinn —4A 22
Chenies M. WC1 —4H 61 (4A 140)
Chenies Pl. NW1 —2H 61
Chenies St. WC1 —5H 61 (5A 140)
Chenies, The. Orp —6J 129
Cheniston Gdns. W8 —3K 75
Chepstow Clo. SW15 —5G 91
Chepstow Cres. W11 —7J 59
Chepstow Cres. IIf —6J 35
Chepstow Gdns. S'hall —6D 54
Chepstow Pl. W2 —6J 59
Chepstow Rise. Croy —3E 134
Chepstow Rd. W2 —6J 59
Chepstow Rd. W7 —3A 72
Chepstow Rd. Croy —3E 134
Chepstow Vs. W11 —7H 59
Chepstow Way. SE15 —1F 95
Chequers. Buck H —1E 20
Chequers Clo. Orp —4K 129
Chequers La. Dag —5F 69
Chequers Pde. N13 —5H 17
Chequers Pde. Dag —1F 69
Chequers, The. Pinn —3B 22
Chequer St. EC1 —4C 62 (4M 141)
(in two parts)
Chequers Way. N13 —5G 17
Cherbury Clo. SE28 —6D 68
Cherbury Ct. N1 —2D 62
(off St Johns Est.)
Cherbury St. N1 —2D 62
Cherchefelle M. Stan —5G 11
Cherington Rd. W7 —1J 71
Cheriton Av. Brom —5H 127
Cheriton Av. IIf —2D 34
Cheriton Clo. W5 —5C 56
Cheriton Ct. SE12 —7J 97
Cheriton Dri. SE18 —7H 83
Cheriton Sq. SW17 —2E 108
Cherry Av. S'hall —1B 70
Cherry Clo. E17 —5D 32
Cherry Clo. SW2 —7A 94
Cherry Clo. W5 —3D 72
Cherry Clo. Cars —2D 132
Cherry Clo. Mord —4G 121
Cherry Ct. W3 —1A 74
Cherry Cres. Bren —7B 72
Cherrycroft Gdns. Pinn —1D 22
Cherrydown Av. E4 —3G 19
Cherrydown Clo. E4 —3H 19
Cherrydown Rd. Sidc —2D 116
Cherrydown Wlk. Romf —2H 37
Cherry Gdns. Dag —6F 53
Cherry Gdns. N'holt —7F 39
Cherry Garden St. SE16 —2H 79
Cherry Garth. Bren —5D 72

Cherry Hill. Barn —6E 4
Cherry Hill. Harr —6E 10
Cherry Hill Gdns. Croy —4K 133
Cherrylands Clo. NW9 —2J 41
Cherry Laurel Wlk. SW2 —6K 93
Cherry Orchard. SE7 —6A 82
Cherry Orchard Gdns. Croy —1E 134
Cherry Orchard Rd. Croy —2D 134
Cherry Rd. Enf —1D 8
Cherry St. Romf —5K 37
Cherry Tree Clo. Wemb —4A 40
Cherry Tree Ct. NW9 —4J 25
Cherrytree Dri. SW16 —3J 109
Cherry Tree Hill. N2 —5C 28
Cherry Tree Rise. Buck H —4F 21
Cherry Tree Rd. E15 —4G 49
Cherry Tree Rd. N2 —4D 28
Cherry Tree Wlk. EC1
—4C 62 (4M 141)
Cherry Tree Wlk. Beck —4B 126
Cherry Tree Wlk. W Wick —4H 137
Cherrytree Way. Stan —6G 11
Cherry Wlk. Brom —1J 137
Cherry Wood Clo. King T —7G 105
Cherrywood Ct. Tedd —5A 104
Cherrywood Dri. SW15 —5F 91
Cherrywood La. Mord —4G 121
Cherry Wood Way. W5 —5G 57
Chertsey Dri. Sutt —2G 131
Chertsey Rd. E11 —2F 49
Chertsey Rd. IIf —4H 51
Chertsey Rd. Twic —2F 103
Chertsey St. SW17 —5E 108
Chervil M. SE28 —1B 84
Cheryls Clo. SW6 —1K 91
Cheseman St. SE26 —3H 111
Chesfield Rd. King T —7E 104
Chesham Av. Orp —6F 129
Chesham Clo. SW1 —3E 76 (7G 145)
(off Lyall St.)
Chesham Clo. Romf —4K 37
Chesham Cres. SE20 —1J 125
Chesham M. SW1 —3E 76 (6G 145)
(off Belgrave M. W.)
Chesham Pl. SW1 —3E 76 (7G 145)
(in two parts)
Chesham Rd. SE20 —2J 125
Chesham Rd. SW19 —5B 108
Chesham Rd. King T —2G 119
Chesham St. NW10 —3K 41
Chesham St. SW1 —3E 76 (7G 145)
Chesham Ter. W13 —2B 72
Cheshire Clo. SE4 —2B 96
Cheshire Clo. Mitc —3J 123
Cheshire Ho. Mord —7K 121
Cheshire Rd. N22 —7E 16
Cheshire St. E2 —4F 63
Cheshir Ho. NW4 —4E 26
Chesholm Rd. N16 —3E 46
Cheshunt Rd. E7 —6K 49
Chesil Ct. E2 —2J 63
Chesil Ct. SW3 —6C 76
Chesilton Rd. SW6 —1H 91
Chesley Gdns. E6 —2B 66
Chesney Cres. New Ad —7E 136
Chesney St. SW11 —1E 92
Chesnut Gro. N17 —3F 31
Chesnut Rd. N17 —3F 31
Chessing Ct. N2 —3D 28
(off Fortis Grn.)
Chessington Av. N3 —3G 27
Chessington Av. Bexh —7E 84
Chessington Ct. N3 —3H 27
(off Charter Way)
Chessington Ho. SW8 —2H 93
Chessington Lodge. N3 —3H 27
Chessington Mans. E10 —7C 32

Chessington Mans. E11 —7G 33
Chessington Rd. Eps —7A 130
Chessington Way. W Wick —2D 136
Chesson Rd. W14 —6H 75
Chesswood Way. Pinn —2B 22
Chester Av. Rich —2F 89
Chester Av. Twic —1D 102
Chester Clo. SW1 —2F 77 (5J 145)
Chester Clo. SW15 —3D 90
Chester Clo. Sutt —2J 131
Chester Clo. N. NW1
—3F 61 (1K 139)
Chester Clo. S. NW1
—3F 61 (2K 139)
Chester Cotts. SW1 —4E 76 (9G 145)
(off Bourne St.)
Chester Ct. NW1 —3F 61 (1K 139)
Chester Cres. E8 —5F 47
Chester Dri. Harr —6D 22
Chesterfield Clo. SE13 —2F 97
Chesterfield Flats. Barn —5A 4
(off Bells Hill)
Chesterfield Gdns. N4 —5B 30
Chesterfield Gdns. W1
—1F 77 (2J 146)
Chesterfield Gro. SE22 —5F 95
Chesterfield Hill. W1
—1F 77 (2J 146)
Chesterfield Lodge. N21 —7E 6
(off Church Hill)
Chesterfield Rd. E10 —6E 32
Chesterfield Rd. N3 —6D 14
Chesterfield Rd. W4 —6J 73
Chesterfield Rd. Barn —5A 4
Chesterfield St. W1 —1F 77 (2J 146)
Chesterfield Wlk. SE10 —1F 97
Chesterfield Way. SE15 —7J 79
Chesterford Gdns. NW3 —4K 43
Chesterford Rd. E12 —5D 50
Chester Gdns. W13 —6B 56
Chester Gdns. Enf —6C 8
Chester Gdns. Mord —6A 122
Chester Ga. NW1 —3F 61 (2J 139)
Chester M. SW1 —3F 77 (6J 145)
Chester Pl. NW1 —3F 61 (1J 139)
Chester Rd. E7 —7B 50
Chester Rd. E11 —6K 33
Chester Rd. E16 —4G 65
Chester Rd. E17 —5K 31
Chester Rd. N9 —1C 18
Chester Rd. N17 —3D 30
Chester Rd. N19 —2F 45
Chester Rd. NW1 —3E 60 (2H 139)
Chester Rd. SW19 —6E 106
Chester Rd. Chig —3K 21
Chester Rd. Houn —3A 86
Chester Rd. IIf —1K 51
Chester Rd. Sidc —5J 99
Chester Row. SW1 —4E 76 (8H 145)
Chester Sq. SW1 —4E 76 (8H 145)
Chester Sq. M. SW1 —3F 77 (7J 145)
(off Chester Sq.)
Chesters, The. N Mald —1A 120
Chester St. E2 —4G 63
Chester St. SW1 —3E 76 (6H 145)
Chester Ter. NW1 —3F 61 (1J 139)
Chester Ter. Bark —6H 51
Chesterton Clo. SW18 —5J 91
Chesterton Clo. Gnfd —2F 55
Chesterton Clo. W3 —5D 56
Chesterton Rd. E13 —3J 65
Chesterton Rd. W10 —5F 59
Chesterton Sq. W8 —4H 75
Chesterton Ter. E13 —3J 65
Chesterton Ter. King T —2G 119
Chester Way. SE11 —4A 78 (9H 147)

Chesthunte Rd. N17 —1C 30
Chestnut All. SW6 —6H 75
Chestnut Av. E7 —4K 49
Chestnut Av. N8 —5J 29
Chestnut Av. SW14 —3K 89
Chestnut Av. Bren —4D 72
Chestnut Av. Buck H —3G 21
Chestnut Av. E Mol & Tedd —3A 118
Chestnut Av. Edgw —6K 11
Chestnut Av. Eps —4A 130
Chestnut Av. Hamp —7E 102
Chestnut Av. Wemb —5B 40
Chestnut Av. W Wick —5G 137
Chestnut Av. N. E17 —4F 33
Chestnut Av. S. E17 —5E 32
Chestnut Clo. N14 —5C 6
Chestnut Clo. N16 —2D 46
Chestnut Clo. SE6 —5E 112
Chestnut Clo. SW16 —4A 110
Chestnut Clo. Buck H —3G 21
Chestnut Clo. Cars —1D 132
Chestnut Ct. N8 —5J 29
Chestnut Ct. SW6 —6H 75
Chestnut Ct. Felt —5B 102
Chestnut Dri. E11 —6J 33
Chestnut Dri. Bexh —3D 100
Chestnut Dri. Harr —7E 10
Chestnut Dri. Pinn —6B 22
Chestnut Gro. SE20 —7H 111
Chestnut Gro. SW12 —7E 92
Chestnut Gro. W5 —3D 72
Chestnut Gro. Barn —5J 5
Chestnut Gro. Dart —5K 117
Chestnut Gro. Iswth —4A 88
Chestnut Gro. Mitc —5H 123
Chestnut Gro. N Mald —3K 119
Chestnut Gro. S Croy —7H 135
Chestnut Gro. Wemb —5B 40
Chestnut La. N20 —1B 14
Chestnut Lodge. SE12 —3K 113
Chestnut Rise. SE18 —6H 83
Chestnut Rise. Bush —1A 10
Chestnut Rd. SE27 —3B 110
Chestnut Rd. SW20 —2F 121
Chestnut Rd. Belv —5G 85
Chestnut Rd. King T —7E 104
Chestnut Rd. Twic —2J 103
Chestnut Row. N3 —7D 14
Chestnuts, The. N5 —4C 46
(off Highbury Grange)
Chestnuts, The. Pinn —1D 22
Chestnut Ter. Sutt —4K 131
Chestnut Wlk. Wfd G —5D 20
Chestnut Way. Felt —3A 102
Cheston Av. Croy —2A 136
Chettle Clo. SE1 —3D 78 (6A 148)
(off Spurgeon St.)
Chettle Ct. N8 —6A 30
Chetwode Rd. SW17 —3D 108
Chetwood Wlk. E6 —5C 66
(off Greenwich Cres.)
Chetwynd Av. Barn —1J 15
Chetwynd Rd. NW5 —4F 45
Cheval Pl. SW7 —3C 76 (6D 144)
Cheval St. E14 —3C 80
Cheveney Wlk. Brom —3J 127
Chevening Rd. NW6 —2F 59
Chevening Rd. SE10 —5H 81
Chevening Rd. SE19 —6D 110
Chevenings, The. Sidc —3C 116
Cheverton Rd. N19 —1H 45
Chevet St. E9 —5A 48
Cheviot. N17 —7C 18
Cheviot Clo. Bexh —2K 101
Cheviot Clo. Enf —2J 7
Cheviot Clo. Sutt —7B 132
Cheviot Ct. S'hall —4F 71
Cheviot Gdns. NW2 —2F 43

Cheviot Gdns. SE27 —4B 110
Cheviot Ga. NW2 —2G 43
Cheviot Rd. SE27 —5A 110
Cheviot Way. Ilf —5J 35
Chevron Clo. E16 —6J 65
Chevy Rd. S'hall —1G 71
Chewton Rd. E17 —4A 32
Cheyne Av. E18 —3H 33
Cheyne Clo. NW4 —5E 26
Cheyne Ct. SW3 —6D 76
Cheyne Gdns. SW3 —6C 76
Cheyne Hill. Surb —4F 119
Cheyne M. SW3 —6C 76
Cheyne Path. SW7 —6K 55
Cheyne Pl. SW3 —6D 76
Cheyne Row. SW3 —6C 76
Cheyne Wlk. N21 —6G 7
Cheyne Wlk. NW4 —6E 26
Cheyne Wlk. SW10 & SW3 —7B 76
(in three parts)
Cheyne Wlk. Croy —2G 135
Cheyneys Av. Edgw —6J 11
Chichele Gdns. Croy —4E 134
Chichele Rd. NW2 —5F 43
Chicheley Gdns. Harr —7B 10
(in two parts)
Chicheley Rd. Harr —7B 10
Chicheley St. SE1 —2K 77 (4F 146)
Chichester Bldgs. SE1
(off Swan Mead) —3E 78 (7C 148)
Chichester Clo. E6 —6C 66
Chichester Clo. SE3 —1A 98
Chichester Clo. Hamp —6D 102
Chichester Ct. Edgw —6B 12
(off Whitchurch La.)
Chichester Ct. Eps —7B 130
Chichester Ct. Stan —9E 84
Chichester Gdns. Ilf —7C 34
Chichester M. SE27 —4A 110
Chichester Rents. WC2
(off Chancery La.) —6A 62 (7G 141)
Chichester Rd. E11 —3G 49
Chichester Rd. N9 —1B 18
Chichester Rd. NW6 —2J 59
Chichester Rd. W2 —5A 59
Chichester Rd. Croy —3E 134
Chichester St. SW1 —5G 77
Chichester Way. E14 —4F 81
Chicksand St. E1 —5F 63
Chiddingfold. N12 —3D 14
Chiddingstone Av. Bexh —7F 85
Chiddingstone St. SW6 —2J 91
Chieveley Pde. Bexh —4H 101
Chieveley Rd. Bexh —4H 101
Chignell Pl. W13 —1A 72
Chigwell Hill. E1 —7H 63
Chigwell Hurst Ct. Pinn —3B 22
Chigwell Pk. Chig —4K 21
Chigwell Pk. Dri. Chig —4K 21
Chigwell Rise. Chig —2K 21
Chigwell Rd. E18 & Wfd G —3K 33
Chilcot Clo. E14 —6D 64
Childebert Rd. SW17 —2F 109
Childeric Rd. SE14 —7A 80
Childerley St. SW6 —1G 91
Childers St. SE8 —6A 80
Childers, The. Wfd G —5J 21
Childs Hill Wlk. NW2 —3H 43
(off Cricklewood La.)
Child's La. SE19 —6E 110
Child's Pl. SW5 —4J 75
Child's St. SW5 —4J 75
Child's Wlk. SW5 —4J 75
Childs Way. NW11 —5H 27
Chilerton Rd. SW17 —5E 108
Chilham Clo. Bex —7F 101

Chilham Clo. Gnfd —2A 56
Chilham Ho. SE1 —3D 78 (6B 148)
Chilham Rd. SE9 —4C 114
Chilham Way. Brom —7J 127
Chillingworth Gdns. Twic —3K 103
Chillingworth Rd. N7 —5A 46
Chilmark Gdns. N Mald —6C 120
Chilmark Rd. SW16 —2H 123
Chiltern Av. Twic —1E 102
Chiltern Clo. Bexh —1K 101
Chiltern Clo. Croy —3E 134
Chiltern Clo. Wor Pk —2E 130
Chiltern Ct. N10 —2E 28
Chiltern Ct. Harr —5H 23
Chiltern Ct. New Bar —5F 5
Chiltern Dene. Enf —4E 6
Chiltern Dri. Surb —6G 119
Chiltern Gdns. NW2 —3F 43
Chiltern Gdns. Brom —4H 127
Chiltern Ho. W5 —5E 56
Chiltern Rd. E3 —4C 64
Chiltern Rd. Ilf —5J 35
Chiltern Rd. Pinn —5A 22
Chiltern St. W1 —5E 60 (5G 139)
Chiltern Way. Wfd G —3D 20
Chilthorne Clo. SE6 —7B 96
Chilton Av. W5 —4D 72
Chilton Ct. N22 —7D 16
(off Truro Rd.)
Chilton Gro. SE8 —4K 79
Chilton Rd. Edgw —6B 12
Chilton Rd. Rich —3G 89
Chilton St. E2 —4F 63
Chilver St. SE10 —5H 81
Chilworth Ct. SW19 —1F 107
Chilworth Gdns. Sutt —3A 132
Chilworth M. W2 —6B 60 (8A 138)
Chilworth St. W2 —6A 60
Chimes Av. N13 —5F 17
China Wharf. SE1 —2G 79
(off Mill St.)
Chinbrook Cres. SE12 —3K 113
Chinbrook Rd. SE12 —3K 113
Chinchilla Dri. Houn —2A 86
Chine, The. N10 —4G 29
Chine, The. N21 —6G 7
Chine, The. Wemb —5C 40
Chingdale Rd. E4 —3B 20
Chingford Av. E4 —3H 19
Chingford Hall Est. E4 —6G 19
Chingford La. Wfd G —4B 20
Chingford Mt. Rd. E4 —4H 19
Chingford Rd. E4 —6H 19
Chingford Rd. E17 —1D 32
Chingley Clo. Brom —6G 113
Chinnery Clo. Enf —1A 8
Chinnor Cres. Gnfd —2F 55
Chipka St. E14 —2E 80
Chipley St. SE14 —6A 80
Chipmunk Gro. N'holt —3C 54
Chippendale St. E5 —3K 47
Chippenham Av. Wemb —5H 41
Chippenham Gdns. NW6 —3J 59
Chippenham M. W9 —4J 59
Chippenham Rd. W9 —4J 59
Chipperfield Rd. Orp —7A 116
Chipping Clo. Barn —3B 4
Chipstead Av. T Hth —4B 124
Chipstead Clo. SE19 —7F 111
Chipstead Clo. Sutt —7K 131
Chipstead Gdns. NW2 —2D 42
Chipstead St. SW6 —1J 91
Chip St. SW4 —3H 93
Chirk Clo. Hay —4C 54
Chisenhale Rd. E3 —2A 64
Chisholm Rd. Croy —2E 135
Chisholm Rd. Rich —6F 89

Chisledon Wlk. E9 —6B 48
(off Eastway)
Chislehurst Av. N12 —7F 15
Chislehurst Rd. Brom & Chst
—2B 128
Chislehurst Rd. Chst —1D 128
Chislehurst Rd. Orp —4J 129
Chislehurst Rd. Rich —5E 88
Chislehurst Rd. Sidc —5A 116
Chislet Clo. Beck —7C 112
Chisley Rd. N15 —6E 30
Chiswell Sq. SE3 —2K 97
Chiswell St. EC1 —5D 62 (5M 141)
Chiswick Bri. SW14 & W4 —2J 89
Chiswick Clo. Croy —3K 133
Chiswick Comn. Rd. W4 —4K 73
Chiswick Ct. Pinn —3D 22
Chiswick High Rd. Bren & W4
(in two parts) —5G 73
Chiswick La. N. W4 —5A 74
Chiswick La. S. W4 —6B 74
Chiswick Mall. W4 & W6 —6B 74
Chiswick Plaza. W4 —6J 73
Chiswick Quay. W4 —1J 89
Chiswick Rd. N9 —2B 18
Chiswick Rd. W4 —4J 73
Chiswick Sq. W4 —6A 74
Chiswick Staithe. W4 —1H 73
Chiswick Ter. W4 —4J 73
Chiswick Village. W4 —6G 73
Chiswick Wharf. W4 —6B 74
Chitty's La. Dag —2D 52
Chitty St. W1 —5G 61 (5M 139)
Chivalry Rd. SW11 —5C 92
Chive Clo. Croy —1K 135
Chivers Rd. E4 —4J 19
Chiver St. SE10 —5H 81
Choats Mnr. Way. Dag —2F 69
Choats Rd. Dag —3E 68
Chobham Gdns. SW19 —2F 107
Chobham Rd. E15 —5F 49
Cholmeley Cres. N6 —7F 29
Cholmeley Lodge. N6 —1F 45
Cholmeley Pk. N6 —1F 45
Cholmley Gdns. NW6 —5J 43
Cholmley Rd. Th Dit —6B 118
Cholmondeley Av. NW10 —2C 58
Cholmondeley Wlk. Rich —5C 88
Choppin's Ct. E1 —1H 79
Chopwell Clo. E15 —7G 49
Chorleywood Cres. Orp —2K 129
Choumert Gro. SE15 —2G 95
Choumert Rd. SE15 —3F 95
Choumert Sq. SE15 —2G 95
Chrisp St. E14 —5D 64
(in two parts)
Christchurch Av. N12 —6F 15
Christchurch Av. NW6 —1F 59
Christchurch Av. Eri —6K 85
Christchurch Av. Harr —4K 23
Christchurch Av. Tedd —5A 104
Christchurch Av. Wemb —6E 40
Christchurch Clo. N12 —7G 15
Christchurch Clo. SW19 —7B 108
Christchurch Ct. NW10 —1A 58
Christchurch Gdns. Harr —4A 24
Christchurch Grn. Wemb —6E 40
Christchurch Hill. NW3 —3B 44
Christchurch Ho. SW2 —1K 109
(off Christchurch Rd.)
Christchurch La. Barn —2B 4
Christchurch Pk. Sutt —7A 132
Christchurch Pas. NW3 —3A 44
Christchurch Pas. H Bar —2B 4
Christchurch Pl. SW8 —2H 93
Christchurch Rd. N8 —6J 29
Christchurch Rd. SW2 —1K 109
Christ Chu. Rd. SW14 —5H 89

Christchurch Rd. SW19 —7B 108
Christ Chu. Rd. Beck —2C 126
Christchurch Rd. Ilf —1F 51
Christchurch Rd. Sidc —4K 115
Christchurch Rd. Surb —6F 119
Christchurch Sq. E9 —1J 63
Christchurch St. SW3 —6D 76
Christchurch Ter. SW3 —6D 76
(off Christchurch St.)
Christchurch Way. SE10 —5G 81
Christian Ct. SE16 —1B 80
Christian Fields. SW16 —7A 110
Christian St. E1 —6G 63
Christie Ct. N19 —2J 45
Christie Gdns. Chad —6B 36
Christie Rd. E9 —6A 48
Christina Sq. N4 —1B 46
Christina St. EC2 —4E 62 (3C 142)
Christopher Av. W7 —3A 72
Christopher Clo. SE16 —2K 79
Christopher Clo. Sidc —6K 99
Christopher Gdns. Dag —5D 52
Christopher Ho. Sidc —2A 116
(off Longlands Rd.)
Christopher Pl. NW1
—3H 61 (1B 140)
Christopher Rd. S'hall —4A 70
Christopher St. EC2 —4D 62 (5B 142)
Chryssell Rd. SW9 —7A 78
Chubworthy St. SE14 —6A 80
Chudleigh. Sidc —4B 116
Chudleigh Cres. Ilf —4J 51
Chudleigh Gdns. Sutt —3A 132
Chudleigh Rd. NW6 —7F 43
Chudleigh Rd. SE4 —5B 96
Chudleigh Rd. Twic —6J 87
Chudleigh St. E1 —6K 63
Chulsa Rd. SE26 —5H 111
Chumleigh St. SE5 —6E 78
Chumleigh Wlk. Surb —4F 119
Church All. Croy —1A 134
Church App. SE21 —3D 110
Church Av. E4 —6A 20
Church Av. N2 —2B 28
Church Av. NW1 —6F 45
Church Av. SW14 —3K 89
Church Av. Beck —1C 126
Church Av. N'holt —7D 38
Church Av. Pinn —6C 22
Church Av. Sidc —5A 116
Church Av. S'hall —3C 70
Churchbank. E17 —4C 32
(off Teresa M.)
Churchbury Clo. Enf —2K 7
Churchbury La. Enf —3J 7
Churchbury Rd. SE9 —7B 98
Churchbury Rd. Enf —2K 7
Church Cloisters. EC3
(off Lovat La.) —7E 62 (1C 148)
Church Clo. N20 —3H 15
Church Clo. W8 —2K 75
Church Clo. Edgw —5D 12
Church Ct. Rich —5D 88
Church Ct. Wfd G —6F 21
Church Cres. E9 —7K 47
Church Cres. N3 —1H 27
Church Cres. N10 —4F 29
Church Cres. N20 —3H 15
Churchcroft Clo. SW12 —7E 92
Churchdown. Brom —4G 113
Church Dri. NW9 —1K 41
Church Dri. Harr —6E 22
Church Dri. W Wick —3G 137
Church Elm La. Dag —6G 53
Church End. E17 —4D 32
Church End. NW4 —3D 26
Church Entry. EC4 —6B 62 (8K 141)
(off Carter La.)

Church Farm La. Sutt —6G 131
Churchfield Av. N12 —6G 15
Churchfield Clo. Harr —4G 23
Churchfield Rd. W3 —1J 73
Churchfield Rd. W7 —2J 71
Churchfield Rd. W13 —1B 72
Churchfield Rd. Well —3A 100
Churchfields. E18 —1J 33
Churchfields. SE10 —6E 80
Churchfields Av. Felt —3D 102
Churchfields Rd. Beck —2K 125
Churchfields Way. N12 —6F 15
Church Gdns. W5 —2D 72
Church Gdns. Wemb —4A 40
Church Ga. SW6 —3G 91
Church Gro. SE13 —5D 96
Church Gro. King T —1C 118
Church Hill. E17 —4C 32
Church Hill. N21 —7E 6
Church Hill. SE18 —3D 82
Church Hill. SW19 —5H 107
Church Hill. Cars —5D 132
Church Hill. Dart —4K 101
Church Hill. Harr —1J 39
Church Hill Rd. E17 —4D 32
Church Hill Rd. Barn —6H 5
Church Hill Rd. Surb —5E 118
Church Hill Rd. Sutt —1F 131
Church Hill Wood. Orp —5K 129
Church Hyde. SE18 —6J 83
Churchill Av. Harr —6B 24
Churchill Ct. N4 —7A 30
Churchill Ct. W5 —4F 57
Churchill Ct. N'holt —5E 38
Churchill Ct. S Harr —5F 23
Churchill Gdns. SW1 —5G 77
Churchill Gdns. SW7
—3B 76 (7A 144)
Churchill Gdns. W3 —6G 57
Churchill Gdns. Rd. SW1 —5F 77
Churchill M. Wfd G —6C 20
Churchill Pl. E14 —1D 80
Churchill Pl. Harr —4J 23
Churchill Rd. E16 —6A 66
Churchill Rd. NW2 —6D 42
Churchill Rd. NW5 —4F 45
Churchill Rd. Edgw —6A 12
Churchill Rd. S Croy —7C 134
Churchills M. Wfd G —6C 20
Churchill Ter. E4 —4H 19
Churchill Wlk. E9 —5J 47
Churchill Way. Brom —3J 127
Church La. E11 —1G 49
Church La. E17 —4D 32
Church La. N2 —3B 28
Church La. N8 —4K 29
Church La. N9 —2B 18
Church La. N17 —1E 30
Church La. NW9 —6J 25
Church La. SW17 —4F 109
Church La. SW19 —1J 121
Church La. W5 —2C 72
Church La. Brom —7C 128
Church La. Chst —1G 129
Church La. Dag —7J 53
Church La. Enf —3J 7
Church La. Harr —1K 23
Church La. Pinn —3C 22
Church La. Rich —1E 104
Church La. Romf —4K 37
Church La. Tedd —5K 103
Church La. Th Dit —6A 118
Church La. Twic —1A 104
Church La. Wall —3H 133
Churchley Rd. SE26 —4H 111
Church Manorway. SE2 —4A 84

Church Manorway. Eri —4K 85
Churchmead Clo. Barn —6H 5
Churchmead Rd. NW10 —6C 42
Churchmore Rd. SW16 —1G 123
Church Mt. N2 —5B 28
Church Pas. Surb —5E 118
Church Pas. Twic —1B 104
Church Path. E11 —5J 33
Church Path. E17 —4D 32
Church Path. N5 —5B 46
(Highbury New Pk.)
Church Path. N5 —4C 46
(Highbury Pl.)
Church Path. N17 —1E 30
Church Path. N20 —4F 15
Church Path. NW10 —7A 42
Church Path. SW14 —3K 89
(in two parts)
Church Path. SW19 —2H 121
Church Path. W4 & W3 —3J 73
Church Path. W7 —1J 71
Church Path. Bark —1G 67
Church Path. Barn —4B 4
Church Pas. Croy —2C 134
Church Path. Mitc —3C 122
Church Path. Romf —5K 37
Church Path. S'hall —1E 70
Church Path. S'hall —3D 70
(Southall Green)
Church Pl. SW1 —7G 61 (1M 145)
Church Pl. W5 —2D 72
Church Pl. Mitc —3C 122
Church Rise. SE23 —2K 111
Church Rd. E10 —1C 48
Church Rd. E12 —5C 50
Church Rd. E17 —2A 32
Church Rd. N6 —6E 28
Church Rd. N17 —1E 30
Church Rd. NW4 —4D 26
Church Rd. NW10 —7A 42
Church Rd. SE19 —1E 124
Church Rd. SW13 —2B 90
Church Rd. SW19 & Mitc —1B 122
(Merton)
Church Rd. SW19 —5G 107
(Wimbledon)
Church Rd. W3 —1J 73
Church Rd. W7 —7H 55
Church Rd. Bark —6G 51
Church Rd. Bexh —2F 101
Church Rd. Brom —2J 127
Church Rd. Buck H —1E 20
Church Rd. Cran —6A 70
Church Rd. Croy —3C 134
(in two parts)
Church Rd. Enf —6D 8
Church Rd. Eri —5K 85
Church Rd. Ewe —7A 130
Church Rd. Felt —5B 102
Church Rd. Ham —4D 104
Church Rd. Houn —7E 70
Church Rd. Ilf —6J 35
Church Rd. Iswth —1H 87
Church Rd. King T —2F 119
Church Rd. N'holt —2B 54
Church Rd. Rich —4E 88
Church Rd. Short —3G 127
Church Rd. Sidc —4A 116
Church Rd. Stan —5G 11
Church Rd. Sutt —6G 131
Church Rd. Tedd —4J 103
Church Rd. Wall —3H 133
Church Rd. Well —2B 100
Church Rd. Wor Pk —1A 130
Church Rd. N2 —2B 28
Church Rd. S. N2 —2B 28
Church Row. NW3 —4A 44
Church Row. Chst —1G 129

Church Row. M. Chst —7G 115
Church St. E15 —1G 65
Church St. E16 —1F 83
Church St. N9 —7J 7
Church St. W2 & NW8
  —5B 60 (5B 138)
Church St. W4 —6B 74
Church St. Croy —2B 134
Church St. Dag —6H 53
Church St. Enf —3H 7
Church St. Ewe —7C 130
Church St. Hamp —7G 103
Church St. Iswth —3B 88
Church St. King T —2D 118
Church St. Sutt —5K 131
Church St. Twic —1A 104
Church St. Est. NW8
  —4B 60 (4B 138)
Church St. N. E15 —1G 65
Church St. Pas. E15 —1G 65
Church Stretton Rd. Houn —5G 87
Church Ter. NW4 —3D 26
Church Ter. SE13 —3G 97
Church Ter. Rich —5D 88
Church Vale. N2 —3D 28
Church Vale. SE23 —2K 111
Church View. Rich —5E 88
Churchview Rd. Twic —1H 103
Church Wlk. N6 —3E 44
Church Wlk. N16 —3D 46
Church Wlk. NW2 —3H 43
Church Wlk. NW4 —3E 26
Church Wlk. NW9 —2K 41
Church Wlk. SW13 —1C 90
Church Wlk. SW15 —5D 90
Church Wlk. SW16 —2G 123
Church Wlk. SW20 —3E 120
Church Wlk. Bren —6C 72
(in two parts)
Church Wlk. Rich —5D 88
Church Wlk. Th Dit —1A 130
Churchward Ho. W14 —5H 75
(off Ivatt Pl.)
Church Way. N20 —3H 15
Churchway. NW1 —3H 61 (1B 140)
Church Way. Barn —4J 5
Church Way. Edgw —6B 12
Churchwell Path. E9 —5J 47
Churchwood Gdns. Wfd G —4D 20
Churchyard Pas. SE5 —1D 94
Churchyard Row. SE11
  —4B 78 (8K 147)
Churnfield. N4 —2A 46
Churston Av. E13 —1K 65
Churston Clo. SW2 —1A 110
Churston Dri. Mord —5F 121
Churston Gdns. N11 —6B 16
Churton Pl. SW1 —4G 77 (9M 145)
Churton St. SW1 —4G 77 (9M 145)
Chusan Pl. E14 —6B 64
Chute Ho. SW9 —2A 94
(off Stockwell Pk. Rd.)
Chyngton Clo. Sidc —3K 115
Cibber Rd. SE23 —2K 111
Cicada Rd. SW18 —6A 92
Cicely Rd. SE15 —1G 95
Clifton Pl. W2 —7B 60 (9B 138)
Cinderford Way. Brom —4G 113
Cinnamon Row. SW11 —3A 92
Cinnamon St. E1 —1H 79
Cintra Pk. SE19 —7F 111
Circle Gdns. SW19 —2J 121
Circle, The. NW2 —3A 42
Circle, The. NW7 —6E 12
Circuits, The. Pinn —4A 22
Circular Rd. N2 —2B 28
Circular Rd. N17 —3F 31
Circular Way. SE18 —6D 82

Circus M. W1 —5D 60 (5E 138)
(off Enford St.)
Circus Pl. EC2 —5D 62 (6B 142)
Circus Rd. NW8 —3B 60 (1A 138)
Circus St. SE10 —7E 80
Cirencester St. W2 —5K 59
Cissbury Ho. SE26 —3G 111
Cissbury Ring N. N12 —5C 14
Cissbury Ring S. N12 —5C 14
Cissbury Rd. N15 —5D 30
Citadel Pl. SE11 —5K 77
Citizen Rd. N7 —4A 46
City Garden Row. N1 —2B 62
City Ho. Wall —1E 132
(off Corbet Clo.)
City Rd. EC1 —2B 62
Civic Way. Ilf —4G 35
Clabon M. SW1 —3D 76 (7E 144)
Clack St. SE16 —2J 79
Clacton Rd. E6 —3B 66
Clacton Rd. E17 —6A 32
Clacton Rd. N17 —2F 31
Claigmar Gdns. N3 —1K 27
Claire Ct. N12 —4F 15
Claire Ct. NW2 —6G 43
Claire Ct. Bush —1C 10
Claire Ct. Pinn —1D 22
Claire Gdns. Stan —5H 11
Claire Ho. Edgw —2J 25
(off Burnt Oak B'way.)
Claire Pl. E14 —3C 80
Clairvale Rd. Houn —1C 86
Clairview Rd. SW16 —5F 109
Clairville Gdns. W7 —1J 71
Clamp Hill. Stan —4C 10
Clancarty Rd. SW6 —2J 91
Clandeboye Ho. E15 —1H 65
(off John St.)
Clandon Clo. W3 —2H 73
Clandon Clo. Eps —6B 130
Clandon Gdns. N3 —3J 27
Clandon Rd. Ilf —2J 51
Clandon St. SE8 —2C 96
Clanfield Way. SE15 —7F 79
Clanricarde Gdns. W2 —7J 59
Clapham Comn. N. Side. SW4
  —4D 92
Clapham Comn. S. Side. SW4
  —6F 93
Clapham Comn. W. Side. SW4
  —4D 92
Clapham Cres. SW4 —4H 93
Clapham High St. SW4 —4H 93
Clapham Junc. App. SW11 —4C 92
Clapham Mnr. St. SW4 —3G 93
Clapham Pk. Est. SW4 —6H 93
Clapham Pk. Rd. SW4 —4H 93
Clapham Rd. SW9 —3J 93
Clapham Rd. SW4 —3J 93
Clap La. Dag —2H 53
Claps Ga. La. E6 & Bark —4F 67
(in two parts)
Clapton Comn. E5 —7F 31
Clapton Pk. Est. E5 —4K 47
Clapton Sq. E5 —5J 47
Clapton Ter. N16 —1G 47
Clapton Way. E5 —4G 47
Clara Nehab Ho. NW11 —5H 27
(off Leeside Cres.)
Clara Pl. SE18 —4E 82
Clare Clo. N2 —3A 28
Clare Corner. SE9 —7F 99
Claredale St. E2 —2G 63
Clare Gdns. W11 —6G 59
Clare Gdns. E7 —4J 49
Clare Gdns. Bark —6K 51
Clare La. N1 —7C 46

Clare Lawn Av. SW14 —5K 89
Clare Mkt. WC2 —6K 61 (8F 140)
Clare M. SW6 —7K 75
Claremont Av. Harr —5E 24
Claremont Av. N Mald —5C 120
Claremont Clo. E16 —1E 82
Claremont Clo. N1 —2A 62
Claremont Clo. SW2 —1J 109
Claremont Gdns. Ilf —2J 51
Claremont Gdns. Surb —5E 118
Claremont Gro. W4 —7A 74
Claremont Gro. Wfd G —6F 21
Claremont Pk. N3 —1G 27
Claremont Rd. E7 —5K 49
Claremont Rd. E11 —3F 49
Claremont Rd. E17 —2A 32
Claremont Rd. N6 —7G 29
Claremont Rd. NW2 —7F 27
Claremont Rd. W9 —2G 59
Claremont Rd. W13 —5A 56
Claremont Rd. Brom —4C 128
Claremont Rd. Croy —1G 135
Claremont Rd. Harr —2J 23
Claremont Rd. Surb —5E 118
Claremont Rd. Tedd —5K 103
Claremont Rd. Twic —7B 88
Claremont Sq. N1 —2A 62
Claremont St. E16 —2E 82
Claremont St. N18 —6D 18
Claremont St. SE10 —6D 80
Claremont Way. NW2 —1E 42
(in two parts)
Claremont Way Ind. Est. NW2
  —1E 42
Clarence Av. SW4 —7H 93
Clarence Av. Brom —4C 128
Clarence Av. Ilf —6E 34
Clarence Av. N Mald —2J 119
Clarence Clo. Bush —1E 10
Clarence Ct. NW7 —5G 13
Clarence Cres. SW4 —6H 93
Clarence Cres. Sidc —3B 116
Clarence Gdns. NW1
  —3F 61 (2K 139)
Clarence Ga. Gdns. NW1
  (off Chagford St.) —4D 60 (4F 138)
Clarence La. SW15 —6A 90
Clarence M. E5 —5H 47
Clarence Pas. NW1 —2J 61
Clarence Pl. E5 —5H 47
Clarence Rd. E12 —5B 50
Clarence Rd. E16 —4G 65
Clarence Rd. E17 —2K 31
Clarence Rd. N15 —5C 30
Clarence Rd. N22 —7D 16
Clarence Rd. NW6 —7H 43
Clarence Rd. SE9 —2C 114
Clarence Rd. SW19 —6K 107
Clarence Rd. W4 —5G 73
Clarence Rd. Bexh —4E 100
Clarence Rd. Brom —3B 128
Clarence Rd. Croy —7D 124
Clarence Rd. Enf —5D 8
Clarence Rd. Rich —1F 89
Clarence Rd. Sidc —3B 116
Clarence Rd. Sutt —5K 131
Clarence Rd. Tedd —6K 103
Clarence Rd. Wall —5F 133
Clarence St. King T —2D 118
Clarence St. Rich —4E 88
Clarence St. S'hall —3D 70
Clarence Ter. NW1 —4D 60 (3F 138)
Clarence Ter. Houn —4F 87
Clarence Wlk. SW4 —2J 93
Clarence Way. NW1 —7F 45
Clarence Yd. SE17 —5C 78
(off Penton Pl.)

Clarendon Clo. W2 —7C 60 (9C 138)
Clarendon Clo. St P —3K 129
Clarendon Ct. NW11 —4H 27
Clarendon Ct. Beck —1D 126
(off Albemarle Rd.)
Clarendon Ct. Rich —1F 89
Clarendon Cres. W11 —7G 59
Clarendon Cres. Twic —3H 103
Clarendon Dri. SW15 —4E 90
Clarendon Gdns. NW4 —3C 26
Clarendon Gdns. W9 —4A 60
Clarendon Gdns. Ilf —7D 34
Clarendon Gdns. Wemb —3D 40
Clarendon Grn. Orp —4K 129
Clarendon Gro. NW1
  —3H 61 (1A 140)
Clarendon Gro. Mitc —3D 122
Clarendon Gro. St P —4K 129
Clarendon M. W2 —7C 60 (9C 138)
Clarendon M. Bex —1H 117
Clarendon Path. St P —4K 129
(in two parts)
Clarendon Pl. W2 —7C 60 (9C 138)
Clarendon Pl. Wilm —5K 117
Clarendon Rise. SE13 —4E 96
Clarendon Rd. E11 —1F 49
Clarendon Rd. E17 —6D 32
Clarendon Rd. E18 —3J 33
Clarendon Rd. N8 —4K 29
Clarendon Rd. N15 —4C 30
Clarendon Rd. N18 —6B 18
Clarendon Rd. N22 —2K 29
Clarendon Rd. SW19 —7C 108
Clarendon Rd. W5 —4E 56
Clarendon Rd. W11 —7G 59
Clarendon Rd. Croy —2B 134
Clarendon Rd. Harr —6J 23
Clarendon Rd. Wall —6G 133
Clarendon St. SW1 —5F 77
Clarendon Ter. W9 —4A 60
Clarendon Way. N21 —6H 7
Clarendon Way. Chst & St M
  —3K 129
Clarens St. SE6 —2B 112
Clare Pl. SW15 —7B 90
Clare Rd. E11 —6F 33
Clare Rd. NW10 —7C 42
Clare Rd. SE14 —2B 96
Clare Rd. Gnfd —6H 39
Clare Rd. Houn —3D 86
Clare St. E2 —2H 63
Claret Gdns. SE25 —3E 124
Clareville Gdns. SW7 —4A 76
Clareville Gro. M. SW7 —4A 76
Clareville St. SW7 —4A 76
Clare Way. Bexh —1E 100
Clarewood Wlk. SW9 —4A 94
Clarges M. W1 —1F 77 (2J 145)
Clarges St. W1 —1F 77 (2K 145)
Claribel Rd. SW9 —2B 94
Clarice Way. Wall —7J 133
Claridge Rd. Dag —1D 52
Clarissa Rd. Romf —7D 36
Clarissa St. E8 —1F 63
Clarke M. N'holt —7J 41
Clarke Mans. Bark —7K 51
(off Upney La.)
Clarke Path. N16 —1G 47
Clarkes Av. Wor Pk —1F 131
Clarke's M. W1 —5E 60 (5H 139)
(off Beaumont St.)
Clark's La. WC2 —6K 61 (8E 140)
Clarks Mead. Bush —1B 10
Clarkson Row. NW1 —2G 61
(off Mornington Ter.)
Clarkson Rd. E16 —6H 65
Clarksons, The. Bark —2G 67
Clarkson St. E2 —3H 63

Clovelly Clo. Pinn —3A **22**
Clovelly Gdns. SE19 —1F **125**
Clovelly Gdns. Enf —1K **7**
Clovelly Gdns. Romf —1H **37**
Clovelly Rd. N8 —4H **29**
Clovelly Rd. W4 —2K **73**
Clovelly Rd. W5 —2C **72**
Clovelly Rd. Bexh —6E **84**
Clovelly Rd. Houn —2E **86**
Clovelly Way. Orp —6K **129**
Clovelly Clo. S Harr —2D **38**
Clover Clo. E11 —2F **49**
Cloverdale Gdns. Sidc —6K **99**
Clover M. SW3 —6D **76**
Clover Way. Wall —1E **132**
Clove St. E13 —4J **65**
Clowders Rd. SE6 —3B **112**
Clowser Clo. Sutt —5A **132**
Cloysters Grn. E1 —1G **79**
Cloyster Wood. Edgw —7J **11**
Club Gdns. Rd. Hayes —7J **127**
Club Row. E2 & E1 —4F **63** (3E **142**)
Clunbury Av. S'hall —5D **70**
Clunbury St. N1 —2D **62**
Cluny Est. SE1 —3E **78** (6C **148**)
Cluny M. SW5 —4J **75**
Cluny Pl. SE1 —3E **78** (6C **148**)
Clutton St. E14 —5D **64**
Clydach Rd. Enf —4A **8**
Clyde Cir. N15 —4E **30**
Clyde Ho. SE15 —7G **79**
 (off Sumner Est.)
Clyde Pl. E10 —7D **32**
Clyde Rd. N15 —4E **30**
Clyde Rd. N22 —1H **29**
Clyde Rd. Croy —2F **135**
Clyde Rd. Sutt —5J **131**
Clyde Rd. Wall —6G **133**
Clydesdale. Enf —4E **8**
Clydesdale Av. Stan —3D **24**
Clydesdale Ct. N20 —1G **15**
Clydesdale Gdns. Rich —4H **89**
Clydesdale Ho. Eri —2E **84**
 (off Kale Rd.)
Clydesdale Rd. W11 —6H **59**
Clyde St. SE8 —6B **80**
Clyde Ter. SE23 —2J **111**
Clyde Vale. SE23 —2J **111**
Clyde Way. Romf —1K **37**
Clyde Wharf. E16 —1K **81**
Clydon Clo. Eri —6K **85**
Clynes Ho. Dag —3G **53**
 (off Uvedale Rd.)
Clyston St. SW8 —2G **93**
Cmabrian Clo. SE27 —3B **110**
Coach & Horses Yd. W1
 —7G **61** (9L **139**)
Coach Ho. La. N5 —4B **46**
Coach Ho. La. SW19 —4F **107**
Coach Ho. M. SE20 —7H **111**
Coach Ho. M. SE23 —6K **95**
Coach Ho. Yd. NW3 —4A **44**
 (off Hampstead High St.)
Coach Ho. Yd. SW18 —4K **91**
Coaldale Wlk. SE21 —7C **94**
Coalecroft Rd. SW15 —4E **90**
Coalport Ho. SE11 —4A **78** (8G **147**)
 (off Walnut Tree Wlk.)
Coal Wharf Rd. W12 —1F **75**
Coates Hill Rd. Brom —2E **128**
Coates Rd. E15 —1J **11**
Coate St. E2 —2G **63**
Coates Wlk. Bren —5E **72**
Cobalt Sq. SW8 —6K **77**
 (off S. Lambeth Rd.)
Cobbett Rd. SE9 —3C **98**
Cobbett Rd. Twic —1E **102**

Cobbetts Av. Ilf —5B **34**
Cobbett St. SW8 —7K **77**
Cobblers Wlk. Hamp & Tedd
 —7G **103**
Cobblestone Pl. Croy —1C **134**
Cobbold Est. NW10 —6B **42**
Cobbold M. W12 —2B **74**
Cobbold Rd. E11 —3H **49**
Cobbold Rd. NW10 —6B **42**
Cobbold Rd. W12 —2A **74**
Cobb's Ct. EC4 —6B **62** (8K **141**)
 (off Carter La.)
Cobb's Rd. Houn —4D **86**
Cobb St. E1 —5F **63** (6E **142**)
Cobden Ct. Brom —4A **128**
Cobden Rd. E11 —3G **49**
Cobden Rd. SE25 —5G **125**
Cobden St. E14 —5D **64**
Cobham Av. N Mald —5C **120**
Cobham Clo. SW11 —6C **92**
Cobham Clo. Brom —7C **128**
Cobham Clo. Sidc —6B **100**
Cobham Clo. Wall —6J **133**
Cobham Clo. Mitc —2B **122**
Cobham Ho. Bark —1G **67**
 (in two parts)
Cobham M. NW1 —7H **45**
Cobham Pl. Bexh —4E **100**
Cobham Rd. E17 —1E **32**
Cobham Rd. N22 —3B **30**
Cobham Rd. Houn —7A **70**
Cobham Rd. Ilf —2J **51**
Cobland Rd. SE12 —4A **114**
Coborn Rd. E3 —3B **64**
Coborn St. E3 —3B **64**
Cobourg Rd. SE5 —6F **79**
Cobourg St. NW1 —3G **61** (2B **139**)
Coburg Clo. SW1 —4G **77** (8M **145**)
 (off Windsor Pl.)
Coburg Cres. SW2 —1K **109**
Coburg Gdns. Ilf —2B **34**
Coburg Rd. N22 —3K **29**
Cochrane Clo. E14 —2C **80**
 (off Admirals Way)
Cochrane Clo. NW8 —2B **60**
 (off Cochrane St.)
Cochrane M. NW8 —2B **60**
Cochrane Rd. SW19 —7H **107**
Cochrane St. NW8 —2B **60**
Cockayne Way. SE8 —4A **80**
Cockfosters Pde. Barn —4K **5**
Cockfosters Rd. Barn —1H **5**
Cock Hill. E1 —5E **62** (6D **142**)
Cockhill Rd. SE2 —3B **84**
Cock La. EC1 —5B **62** (6J **141**)
Cockpit Steps. SW1
 —2H **77** (5B **146**)
 (off Birdcage Wlk.)
Cockpit Yd. WC1 —5K **61** (5F **140**)
Cocks Cres. N Mald —4B **120**
Cockspur Ct. SW1 —1H **77** (2B **146**)
Cockspur St. SW1 —1H **77** (2B **146**)
Cocksure La. Sidc —3G **117**
Code St. E1 —4F **63**
Codicote Ter. N4 —2C **46**
Codling Clo. E1 —1G **79**
Codling Way. Wemb —4D **40**
Codrington Hill. SE23 —7A **96**
Codrington M. W11 —6G **59**
Cody Clo. Harr —3D **24**
Cody Clo. Wall —7H **133**
Cody Rd. E16 —4F **65**
Coe Av. SE25 —6G **125**
Coe's All. Barn —4B **4**
Cofers Circ. Wemb —3H **41**
Cogan Av. E17 —1A **32**
Coin St. SE1 —1A **78** (2G **147**)

Coity Rd. NW5 —6E **44**
Cokers La. SE21 —1D **110**
Coke St. E1 —6G **63**
Colas M. NW6 —1J **59**
Colbeck M. SW7 —4K **75**
Colbeck Rd. Harr —7G **23**
Colberg Pl. N16 —7F **31**
Colborne Way. Wor Pk —3E **130**
Colburn Way. Sutt —3B **132**
Colby M. SE19 —5E **110**
Colby Rd. SE19 —5E **110**
Colchester Av. E12 —4D **50**
Colchester Dri. Pinn —5B **22**
Colchester Rd. E10 —7E **32**
Colchester Rd. E17 —6C **32**
Colchester Rd. Edgw —7D **12**
Colchester St. E1 —6F **63**
Coldbath Sq. EC1 —4A **62** (3G **141**)
Coldbath St. SE13 —1D **96**
Cold Blow Cres. Bex —1K **117**
Cold Blow La. SE14 —6K **79**
Cold Blows. Mitc —3D **122**
Coldershaw Rd. W13 —1A **72**
Coldfall Av. N10 —2E **28**
Coldham Ct. N22 —1B **30**
Coldharbour. E14 —2E **80**
Coldharbour La. SW9 & SE5 —4A **94**
Coldharbour Pl. SE5 —2C **94**
Coldharbour Rd. Croy —5A **134**
Coldharbour Way. Croy —5A **134**
Coldstream Gdns. SW18 —6H **91**
Colebeck M. N1 —6B **46**
Colebert Av. E1 —4J **63**
Colebrook Clo. SW15 —7F **91**
Colebrooke Av. W13 —6B **56**
Colebrooke Ct. Sidc —4B **116**
 (off Granville Rd.)
Colebrooke Dri. E11 —7K **33**
Colebrooke Pl. N1 —1B **62**
Colebrooke Rise. Brom —2G **127**
Colebrooke Row. N1 —2B **62**
 (in two parts)
Colebrook Rd. SW16 —1J **123**
Colebrook Way. N11 —5A **16**
Coleby Path. SE5 —7D **78**
Cole Clo. SE28 —1B **84**
Cole Ct. Twic —7A **88**
Coledale Dri. Stan —1C **24**
Coleford Rd. SW18 —5A **92**
Colegrave Rd. E15 —5F **49**
Colegrove Rd. SE15 —6F **79**
Coleherne Ct. SW5 —5K **75**
Coleherne M. SW10 —5K **75**
Coleherne Rd. SW10 —5K **75**
Colehill Gdns. SW6 —1G **91**
Colehill La. SW6 —1G **91**
Cole Ho. SE1 —2A **78** (5G **147**)
 (off Baylis Rd.)
Coleman Fields. N1 —1C **62**
Coleman Mans. N8 —7J **29**
Coleman Rd. SE5 —7E **78**
Coleman Rd. Belv —4G **85**
Coleman Rd. Dag —6E **52**
Coleman's Bldgs. EC2
 (off Colman St.) —6D **62** (7A **142**)
Colemans Heath. SE9 —3E **114**
Coleman St. EC2 —6D **62** (7A **142**)
Colenso Rd. E5 —4J **47**
Colenso Rd. Ilf —1J **51**
Cole Pk. Gdns. Twic —6A **88**
Cole Pk. Rd. Twic —6A **88**
Cole Pk. View. Twic —6A **88**
Colepits Wood Rd. SE9 —5H **99**
Coleraine Rd. N8 —3A **30**
Coleraine Rd. SE3 —6H **81**
Coleridge Av. E12 —6C **50**
Coleridge Av. Sutt —4C **132**

Coleridge Clo. SW8 —2F **93**
Coleridge Ct. New Bar —5E **4**
 (off Station Rd.)
Coleridge Gdns. NW6 —7A **44**
Coleridge Ho. SE17 —5C **78**
 (off Browning St.)
Coleridge La. N8 —6J **29**
Coleridge Rd. E17 —4B **32**
Coleridge Rd. N4 —2A **46**
Coleridge Rd. N8 —6H **29**
Coleridge Rd. N12 —5F **15**
Coleridge Rd. Croy —7J **125**
Coleridge Sq. W13 —6A **56**
Coleridge Wlk. NW11 —4J **27**
Cole Rd. Twic —6A **88**
Colesbourne Ct. SE15 —7E **78**
 (off Birdlip Clo.)
Colesburg Rd. Beck —3B **126**
Coles Cres. Harr —2F **39**
Coles Grn. Bush —1B **10**
Coles Grn. Ct. NW2 —2C **42**
Coles Grn. Rd. NW2 —1C **42**
Coleshill Rd. Tedd —6J **103**
Colestown St. SW11 —2C **92**
Cole St. SE1 —2C **78** (5M **147**)
Colesworth Ho. Edgw —2J **25**
 (off Burnt Oak B'way.)
Colet Clo. N13 —6G **17**
Colet Gdns. W14 —4F **75**
Colet Ho. SE17 —5B **78**
 (off Doddington Gro.)
Coley St. WC1 —4K **61** (4F **140**)
Colfe Rd. SE23 —1A **112**
Colina M. N15 —4B **30**
Colina Rd. N15 —5B **30**
Colin Clo. NW9 —4A **26**
Colin Clo. Croy —3B **136**
Colin Clo. W Wick —3H **137**
Colin Cres. NW9 —4B **26**
Colindale Av. NW9 —3K **25**
Colindale Bus. Pk. NW9 —3J **25**
Colindeep Gdns. NW4 —4C **26**
Colindeep La. NW9 & NW4 —3A **26**
Colin Dri. NW9 —5B **26**
Colinette Rd. SW15 —4E **90**
Colin Gdns. NW9 —4B **26**
Colin Pde. NW9 —4A **26**
Colin Pk. Rd. NW9 —4A **26**
Colin Rd. NW10 —6C **42**
Colinton Rd. Ilf —2B **52**
Colin Winter Ho. E1 —4J **63**
 (off Nicholas Rd.)
Coliston Pas. SW18 —7J **91**
Coliston Rd. SW18 —7J **91**
Collamore Av. SW18 —1C **108**
Collapit Clo. Harr —6F **23**
College App. SE10 —6E **80**
College Av. Harr —1J **23**
College Clo. E9 —5J **47**
College Clo. N18 —5A **18**
College Clo. Harr —7D **10**
College Clo. Twic —1H **103**
College Ct. SW3 —5D **76**
 (off West Rd.)
College Ct. W5 —7E **56**
College Ct. W6 —5E **74**
 (off Queen Caroline St.)
College Ct. Enf —4D **8**
College Cres. NW3 —6A **44**
 (in two parts)
College Cross. N1 —7A **46**
College Dri. E9 —5F **63** (6F **142**)
College Fields Bus. Cen. SW19
 —1B **122**
College Gdns. E4 —7J **9**
College Gdns. N18 —5A **18**
College Gdns. SE21 —1E **110**
College Gdns. SW17 —2C **108**

College Gdns. Ilf —5C **34**
College Gdns. N Mald —5B **120**
College Gdns. Enf —1J **7**
College Grn. SE19 —7E **110**
College Gro. NW1 —1G **61**
College Hill. EC4 —7C **62** (9M **141**)
College Hill Rd. Harr —7D **10**
College La. NW5 —4F **45**
College M. SW1 —3J **77** (7C **146**)
 (off Gt. College St.)
College M. SW18 —5K **91**
College Pk. Clo. SE13 —4F **97**
College Pk. Rd. N17 —6A **18**
College Pl. E17 —4G **33**
College Pl. NW1 —1G **61**
College Pl. SW10 —7A **76**
College Point. E15 —6H **49**
College Rd. E17 —5E **32**
College Rd. N17 —6A **18**
College Rd. N21 —2F **17**
College Rd. NW10 —2E **58**
College Rd. SE19 —5F **111**
College Rd. SE21 & SE19 —7E **94**
College Rd. SE19 —6B **108**
College Rd. W13 —6B **56**
College Rd. Brom —1J **127**
College Rd. Croy —2D **134**
College Rd. Harr —6J **23**
College Rd. Har W —1J **23**
College Rd. Iswth —1K **87**
College Rd. Swan —7K **117**
College Rd. Wemb —1D **40**
College Roundabout. King T
 —3E **11**
College Row. E9 —5K **47**
College Slip. Brom —1J **127**
College St. EC4 —7C **62** (9M **141**)
College Ter. E3 —3B **64**
College Ter. N3 —2H **27**
College View. SE9 —1B **114**
College Wlk. King T —3E **118**
Collent St. E9 —6J **47**
Colleraine Rd. SE3 —6H **81**
Colless Rd. N15 —5F **31**
Collett Rd. SE16 —3H **79**
Collett Way. S'hall —2F **71**
Collier Dri. Edgw —2G **25**
Collier Row La. Romf —1H **37**
Collier Row Rd. Romf —1F **37**
Colliers Ct. Croy —4D **134**
Collier St. N1 —2K **61**
Colliers Water La. T Hth —5A **124**
Collindale Av. Eri —7H **85**
Collindale Av. Sidc —1A **116**
Collingbourne Rd. W12 —1D **74**
Collingham Gdns. SW5 —4K **75**
Collingham Pl. SW5 —4K **75**
Collingham Rd. SW5 —4K **75**
Collings Clo. N13 —6E **16**
Collington St. SE10 —5F **81**
Collingtree Rd. SE26 —4J **111**
Collingwood Av. N10 —3E **28**
Collingwood Av. Surb —7J **119**
Collingwood Clo. SE20 —1H **125**
Collingwood Clo. Twic —7E **86**
Collingwood Ct. New Bar —5E **4**
Collingwood Rd. E17 —6C **32**
Collingwood Rd. N15 —4E **30**
Collingwood Rd. Mitc —3C **122**
Collingwood Rd. Sutt —3J **131**
Collingwood St. E1 —4H **63**
Collins Av. Stan —2E **24**
Collins Ct. E8 —6G **47**
Collins Dri. Ruis —2A **38**
Collins Ho. E15 —1H **65**
 (off John St.)
Collinson St. SE1 —2C **78** (5L **147**)
Collinson Wlk. SE1 —2C **78** (5L **147**)

Collins Path. Hamp —6D **102**
Collin Rd. N5 —4C **46**
Collins St. SE3 —3G **97**
Collin's Yd. N1 —1B **62**
Collinwood Av. Enf —3D **8**
Collinwood Gdns. Ilf —5D **34**
Collis All. Twic —1J **103**
Collis Rd. SE15 —1J **95**
Collyer Av. Croy —4J **133**
Collyer Pl. SE15 —1G **95**
Collyer Rd. Bedd —4J **133**
Colman Ct. N12 —6F **15**
Colman Ct. Stan —6G **11**
Colman Rd. E16 —5A **66**
Colmar Clo. E1 —4K **63**
Colmer Pl. Harr —7C **10**
Colmore M. SE15 —1H **95**
Colmore Rd. Enf —4D **8**
Colnbrook St. SE1 —3B **78** (7J **147**)
Colne Rd. E5 —4A **48**
Colne Rd. N21 —7J **7**
Colne St. E13 —3J **65**
Colney Hatch La. N11 & N10 —6J **15**
Cologne Rd. Croy —4B **134**
Colombo Rd. Ilf —7G **35**
Colombo St. SE1 —1B **78** (3J **147**)
Colomb St. SE10 —5G **81**
Colonel's Wlk. Enf —3G **7**
Colonial Av. Twic —5G **87**
Colonial Dri. W4 —4J **73**
Colonnade. WC1 —4J **61** (4D **140**)
Colonnades, The. W2 —6K **59**
Colonnade, The. SE8 —4B **80**
Colonnade Wlk. SW1
—4F **77** (9J **145**)
Colosseum Ter. NW1
*(off Albany St.) —3F **61** (2K **139**)*
*Colour Ct. SW1 —1G **77** (3M **145**)*
(off St James' Pal.)
Colroy Ct. NW11 —5G **27**
Colson Rd. Croy —2E **134**
Colson Way. SW16 —4G **109**
Colsterworth Rd. N15 —4F **31**
(in two parts)
Colston Av. Cars —4C **132**
Colston Ct. Cars —4D 132
(off West Cl.)
Colston Rd. E7 —6B **50**
Colston Rd. SW14 —4J **89**
Coltness Cres. SE2 —5B **84**
Colton Gdns. N17 —3C **30**
Colton Rd. Harr —5J **23**
Columbia Av. Edgw —1H **25**
Columbia Av. Ruis —1A **38**
Columbia Av. Wor Pk —7B **120**
Columbia Rd. E2 —3F **63** (1E **142**)
Columbia Rd. E13 —4H **65**
Columbia Row. E2 —3F **63**
Columbia Sq. SW14 —4J **89**
Columbia Wharf. SE16 —1B **80**
Columbine Av. E6 —5C **66**
Columbine Av. S Croy —7B **134**
Columbine Way. SE13 —2E **96**
Columbus Courtyard. E14 —1C 80
(off Whitmore Rd.)
Colva Wlk. NW19 —2F **45**
Colvestone Cres. E8 —5F **47**
Colview Ct. SE9 —1B **114**
Colville Est. N1 —1E 62
(off Whitmore Rd.)
Colville Gdns. W11 —6H **59**
Colville Houses. W11 —6H **59**
Colville Pl. W1 —5G **61** (6M **139**)
Colville Rd. E11 —3E **48**
Colville Rd. E17 —2A **32**
Colville Rd. N9 —1C **18**

Colville Rd. W3 —3H **73**
Colville Rd. W11 —6H **59**
Colville Sq. W11 —6H **59**
Colville Sq. M. W11 —6H **59**
Colville Ter. W11 —6H **59**
Colvin Clo. SE26 —5J **111**
Colvin Gdns. E4 —3K **19**
Colvin Gdns. E11 —4K **33**
Colvin Gdns. Ilf —1G **35**
Colvin Rd. E6 —7C **50**
Colvin Rd. T Hth —5A **124**
Colwell Rd. SE22 —5F **95**
Colwick Clo. N6 —7H **29**
Colwith Rd. W6 —6E **74**
Colwood Gdns. SW19 —7B **106**
Colworth Gro. SE17
—4C **78** (9M **147**)
Colworth Rd. E11 —6G **33**
Colworth Rd. Croy —1G **135**
Colwyn Av. Gnfd —2K **55**
Colwyn Clo. SW16 —5G **109**
Colwyn Cres. Houn —1G **87**
Colwyn Grn. NW9 —6A 26
(off Snowden Dri.)
Colwyn Rd. NW2 —3D **42**
Colwyn Way. N18 —5B **18**
Colyer Clo. N1 —2K **61**
Colyer Clo. SE9 —2F **115**
Colyers Clo. Eri —1K **101**
Colyers La. Eri —1J **101**
Colyers Wlk. Eri —1K **101**
Colyton Clo. Well —1D **100**
Colyton Clo. Wemb —6C **40**
Colyton Rd. SE22 —5H **95**
Combe Av. SE3 —7H **81**
Combedale Rd. SE10 —5J **81**
Combe Lodge. SE7 —6A **82**
Combemartin Rd. SW18 —7G **91**
Combe M. SE3 —7H **81**
Comber Clo. NW2 —3D **42**
Comber Gro. SE5 —7C **78**
Comber Ho. SE5 —7C **78**
Combermere Rd. SW9 —3K **93**
Combermere Rd. Mord —6K **121**
Comberton Rd. E5 —2H **47**
Combeside. SE18 —7K **83**
Combe, The. NW1 —3G **61** (2L **139**)
Combwell Cres. SE2 —3A **84**
Comely Bank Rd. E17 —5E **32**
Comeragh M. W14 —5G **75**
Comeragh Rd. W14 —5G **75**
Comerell Pl. SE10 —5H **81**
Comerford Rd. SE4 —4A **96**
Comet Pl. SE8 —7C **80**
Comet St. SE8 —7C **80**
Commerce Rd. N22 —1K **29**
Commerce Rd. Bren —7C **72**
Commerce Way. Croy —2K **133**
Commercial Rd. E1 & E14 —6G **63**
Commercial Rd. N18 —6K **17**
Commercial Rd. Ind. Est. SE1
—6A **18**
Commercial St. E1 —4F **63** (4E **142**)
Commercial Way. NW10 —2H **57**
Commercial Way. SE15 —7H **79**
Commerell St. SE10 —5G **81**
Commodity Quay. E1 —7F **63**
Commodore Sq. SW10 —1A **92**
Commodore St. E1 —4A **64**
Commondale. SW15 —3E **90**
Commonfield La. SW17 —5C **108**
Common Rd. SW13 —3D **90**
Common Rd. Stan —4C **10**
Commonside E. Mitc —3E **122**
Commonside W. Mitc —3D **122**
Common, The. W5 —1E **72**
Common, The. S'hall —4B **70**
Common, The. Stan —3E **10**

Commonwealth Av. W12 —7D **58**
(in three parts)
Commonwealth Av. N17 —7B **18**
Commonwealth Way. SE2 —5B **84**
Community La. N7 —5H **45**
Community Rd. E15 —5F **49**
Community Rd. Gnfd —1G **55**
Como Rd. SE23 —2A **112**
Como St. Romf —5K **37**
Compass Hill. Rich —6D **88**
Compayne Gdns. NW6 —7K **43**
Compton Av. E6 —2B **66**
Compton Av. N1 —6B **46**
Compton Av. N6 —7C **28**
Compton Clo. NW1 —3F 61 (2K 139)
(off Robert St.)
Compton Clo. W13 —6A **56**
Compton Clo. Edgw —7D **12**
Compton Ct. SE19 —6E **110**
Compton Ct. Sutt —4A **132**
Compton Cres. N17 —7H **17**
Compton Cres. W4 —6J **73**
Compton Cres. N'holt —1B **54**
Compton Pas. EC1 —4B 62 (3K 141)
(off Compton St.)
Compton Pl. EC1 —4B **62**
Compton Pl. WC1 —4J **61** (3C **140**)
Compton Rise. Pinn —5C **22**
Compton Rd. N1 —6B **46**
Compton Rd. N21 —1F **17**
Compton Rd. NW10 —3F **59**
Compton Rd. SW19 —6H **107**
Compton Rd. Croy —1H **135**
Compton St. EC1 —4B **62** (3J **141**)
Compton Ter. N1 —6B **46**
Compton Ter. N21 —1F **17**
Comreddy Clo. N16 —1E **7**
Comus Pl. SE17 —4E **78** (9C **148**)
Comyn Rd. SW11 —4C **92**
Comyns Clo. E16 —5H **65**
Comyns Rd. Dag —7G **53**
Comyns, The. Bush —1B **10**
Conant M. E1 —7G **63**
Concanon Rd. SW2 —4K **93**
Concert Hall App. SE1
—1K **77** (3F **146**)
Concord Bus. Cen. W3 —4H **57**
Concord Clo. N'holt —3B **54**
Concorde Clo. Houn —2F **87**
Concorde Dri. E6 —5D **66**
Concord Ho. N17 —7A 18
(off Park La.)
Concord Rd. W3 —4H **57**
Concord Rd. Enf —5C **8**
Concourse, The. NW9 —1B **26**
Condell Rd. SW8 —1G **93**
Conder St. E14 —6A **64**
Condover Cres. SE18 —7F **83**
Condray Pl. SW11 —7C **76**
Conduit Ct. WC2 —7J **61** (9C **140**)
(off Floral St.)
Conduit La. Croy —5G **135**
Conduit La. Enf —7F **9**
Conduit La. S Croy & Croy —5G **135**
Conduit M. W2 —6B **60** (8A **138**)
Conduit Pas. W2 —6B 60 (8A 138)
(off Conduit Pl.)
Conduit Pl. W2 —6B **60** (8A **138**)
Conduit Rd. SE18 —5F **83**
Conduit St. W1 —7F **61** (9K **139**)
Conduit Way. NW10 —7J **41**
Conewood St. N5 —3B **46**
Coney Acre. SE21 —1C **110**
Coney Burrows. E4 —2B **20**
Coneygrove Path. N'holt —6C 38
(off Arnold Rd.)
Coney Hall Pde. W Wick —3G **137**
Coney Hill Rd. W Wick —2G **137**

Coney Way. SW8 —6K **77**
Conference Clo. E4 —2K **19**
Conference Rd. SE2 —4C **84**
Congleton Gro. SE18 —5G **83**
Congo Rd. SE18 —5H **83**
Congress Rd. SE2 —4C **84**
Congreve Ct. SE11 —4A **78** (9H **147**)
Congreve Ho. N16 —5E **46**
Congreve Rd. SE9 —3D **98**
Congreve St. SE17 —4E **78** (8C **148**)
Congreve Wlk. E16 —5B 66
(off Stansfield Rd.)
Conical Corner. Enf —2H **7**
Conifer Gdns. SW16 —3K **109**
Conifer Gdns. Enf —6K **7**
Conifer Gdns. Sutt —2K **131**
Conifer Gdns. Sutt —2B **132**
Conifer Way. Wemb —3C **40**
Coniger Rd. SW6 —2J **91**
Coningham Rd. W12 —1C **74**
Coningham Rd. W12 —2D **74**
Coningsby Cotts. W5 —2D **72**
Coningsby Gdns. E4 —6J **19**
Coningsby Rd. N4 —7B **30**
Coningsby Rd. W5 —2D **72**
Coningsby Rd. S Croy —7C **134**
Conington Rd. SE13 —2D **96**
Conisbee Ct. N14 —5B **6**
Conisborough Cres. SE6 —3E **112**
Coniscliffe Clo. Chst —1E **128**
Coniscliffe Rd. N13 —3H **17**
Coniston Av. Bark —7J **51**
Coniston Av. Gnfd —3B **56**
Coniston Av. Well —3J **99**
Coniston Clo. N20 —3G **15**
Coniston Clo. SW13 —7B **74**
Coniston Clo. SW20 —6F **121**
Coniston Clo. W4 —7J **73**
Coniston Clo. Bark —7J **51**
Coniston Clo. Bexh —1J **101**
Coniston Clo. Brom —6G **113**
Coniston Clo. Croy —7G **125**
Coniston Clo. Eri —6F **87**
Coniston Dri. W10 —4G **59**
Conlan St. W10 —4G **59**
Conley Rd. NW10 —6A **42**
Conley St. SE10 —5G **81**
Connaught Av. E4 —7K **9**
Connaught Av. SW14 —3J **89**
Connaught Av. Barn —1J **15**
Connaught Av. Enf —2K **7**
Connaught Av. Houn —4C **86**
Connaught Bri. E16 —1B **82**
Connaught Bus. Cen. NW9 —5B **26**
Connaught Clo. E10 —2A **48**
Connaught Clo. W2 —6C 60 (8D 138)
(off Connaught St.)
Connaught Clo. Enf —2K **7**
Connaught Clo. Sutt —2B **132**
Connaught Dri. NW11 —4J **27**
Connaught Gdns. N10 —5F **29**
Connaught Gdns. N13 —4G **17**
Connaught Gdns. Mord —4A **122**
Connaught La. Ilf —2G **51**
Connaught Lodge. N4 —7A 30
(off Connaught Rd.)
Connaught M. SE18 —5E **82**

Connaught M. W2 —6D **60** (8E **138**)
Connaught Pl. W2 —7D **60** (9E **138**)
Connaught Rd. E4 —1B **20**
Connaught Rd. E11 —1F **49**
Connaught Rd. E16 —1B **82**
Connaught Rd. E17 —5C **32**
Connaught Rd. N4 —7A **30**
Connaught Rd. NW10 —1A **58**
Connaught Rd. SE18 —5E **82**
Connaught Rd. W13 —7B **56**
Connaught Rd. Barn —4A **4**
Connaught Rd. Harr —1K **23**
Connaught Rd. If —2H **51**
Connaught Rd. N Mald —4A **120**
Connaught Rd. Rich —5F **89**
Connaught Rd. Sutt —2B **132**
Connaught Rd. Tedd —5H **103**
Connaught Sq. W2 —6D **60** (8E **138**)
Connaught Sq. W2 —6C **60** (8D **138**)
Connaught Way. N13 —4G **17**
Connell Cres. W5 —4F **57**
Connington Cres. E4 —3A **20**
Connor Rd. Dag —4F **53**
Connor St. E9 —1K **63**
Conolly Rd. W7 —1J **71**
Conrad Dri. Wor Pk —1E **130**
Conrad Ho. N16 —5E 46
(off Mayville Est.)
Consfield Av. N Mald —4C **120**
Consort M. Iswth —5H **87**
Consort Rd. SE15 —1H **95**
Cons St. SE1 —2A **78** (4H **147**)
Constable Clo. NW11 —6K **27**
Constable Ct. W4 —5H 73
(off Chaseley Dri.)
Constable Cres. N15 —5G **31**
Constable Gdns. Edgw —1G **25**
Constable Gdns. Iswth —5H **87**
Constable Ho. E16 —6B **66**
Constable Wlk. SE21 —3E **110**
Constance Cres. Brom —7H **127**
Constance Rd. Croy —7B **124**
Constance Rd. Enf —6K **7**
Constance Rd. Sutt —4A **132**
Constance Rd. Twic —7F **87**
Constance St. E16 —1C **82**
Constantine Rd. NW3 —4C **44**
Constitution Hill. SW1
—2F **77** (4J **145**)
Constitution Rise. SE18 —1E **98**
Content St. SE17 —4D **78** (9A **148**)
Convair Wlk. N'holt —3B **54**
Convent Gdns. W5 —4C **72**
Convent Gdns. W11 —6G **59**
Convent Hill. SE19 —6C **110**
Convent Way. S'hall —4A **70**
Conway Clo. Stan —6F **11**
Conway Cres. Gnfd —2J **55**
Conway Cres. Romf —6C **36**
Conway Dri. Sutt —6K **131**
Conway Gdns. Enf —1K **7**
Conway Gdns. Mitc —4J **123**
Conway Gdns. Wemb —7C **24**
Conway Gro. W3 —5K **57**
Conway Ho. E17 —5A 32
(off Mission Gro.)
Conway M. W1 —4G 61 (4L 139)
(off Conway St.)
Conway Rd. N14 —3D **16**
Conway Rd. N15 —5B **30**
Conway Rd. NW2 —2E **42**
Conway Rd. SE18 —4H **83**
Conway Rd. SW20 —1E **120**
Conway Rd. Felt —6B **102**
Conway Rd. Houn —7D **86**
Conway St. W1 —4G **61** (4L **139**)
(in two parts)
Conway Wlk. Hamp —6D **102**

183

Conybeare. NW3 —7C 44
Conyers Clo. Wfd G —6B 20
Conyer's Rd. SW16 —5H 109
Conyer St. E3 —2A 64
Cooden Clo. Brom —7K 113
Cookes Clo. E11 —2H 49
Cookes La. Sutt —6G 131
Cookham Cres. SE16 —2K 79
Cookham Dene Clo. Chst —1H 129
Cookham Rd. Swan —7G 117
Cookhill Rd. SE2 —2B 84
Cook's Clo. Romf —1J 37
Cooks Hole Rd. Enf —1H 7
Cook's Rd. E15 —2D 64
Cook's Rd. SE17 —6B 78
Coolfin Rd. E16 —6J 65
Coolgardie Av. E4 —5A 20
Coolgardie Av. Chig —3K 21
Coolhurst Rd. N8 —6H 29
Cool Oak La. NW9 —1A 42
Coomassie Rd. W9 —4H 59
Coombe Av. Croy —4E 134
Coombe Bank. King T —1A 120
Coombe Clo. Edgw —2F 25
Coombe Clo. Houn —4E 86
Coombe Corner. N21 —1G 17
Coombe Cres. Hamp —7D 102
Coombe Dri. Ruis —1A 38
Coombe End. King T —7K 105
Coombefield Clo. N Mald —5A 120
Coombe Gdns. SW20 —2C 120
Coombe Gdns. N Mald —4B 120
Coombe Hill Glade. King T —7A 106
Coombe Hill Rd. King T —7A 106
Coombe Ho. E4 —6G 19
Coombe Ho. N7 —5H 45
Coombe Ho. Chase. N Mald —1K 119
Coombehurst Clo. Barn —2J 5
Coombe La. SW20 —2E 120
Coombe La. Croy —5H 135
Coombe La. King T —1H 119
Coombe La. Flyover. King T —1B 120
Coombe La. W. King T —1H 119
Coombe Lea. Brom —3C 128
Coombe Neville. King T —7K 105
Coombe Pk. King T —5J 105
Coomber Ho. SW6 —3K 91
(off Wandsworth Bri. Rd.)
Coombe Ridings. King T —5J 105
Coombe Rise. King T —1J 119
Coombe Rd. N22 —2A 30
Coombe Rd. NW10 —3K 41
Coombe Rd. SE26 —4H 111
Coombe Rd. W4 —5A 74
Coombe Rd. W13 —3B 72
Coombe Rd. Croy —4D 134
Coombe Rd. Hamp —6D 102
Coombe Rd. King T —1G 119
Coombe Rd. N Mald —2A 120
Coomber Way. Croy —7H 123
Coombes Rd. Dag —1F 69
Coombe Wlk. Sutt —3K 131
Coombe Wood Dri. Romf —6F 37
Coombewood Rd. King T —5J 105
Coombs St. N1 —2B 62
Coomer M. SW6 —6H 75
Coomer Pl. SW6 —6H 75
Coomer Rd. SW6 —6H 75
Cooms Wlk. Edgw —1J 25
Cooperage Clo. N17 —6A 18
Cooper Av. E17 —1A 32
Cooper Clo. E15 —5D 48
Cooper Cres. Cars —3D 132
Cooper Ho. Houn —3D 86
Cooper Rd. NW4 —6F 27
Cooper Rd. NW10 —5B 42
Cooper Rd. Croy —5A 134

Coopersale Clo. Wfd G —7F 21
Coopersale Rd. E9 —5K 47
Coopers Clo. E1 —4J 63
Coopers Clo. Dag —6H 53
Coopers Ct. Iswth —2K 87
(off Woodlands Rd.)
Coopers La. E10 —1D 48
Coopers La. NW1 —2H 61
Coopers La. SE12 —2K 113
Cooper's Rd. SE17 —5F 79
Cooper's Row. EC3 —7F 63 (9E 142)
Cooper St. E16 —5H 65
Coopers Wlk. E15 —5G 49
Cooper's Yd. SE19 —6E 110
Coote Gdns. Dag —3F 53
Coote Rd. Bexh —1F 101
Coote Rd. Dag —3F 53
Copeland Dri. E14 —4C 80
Copeland Ho. SE11 —3K 77 (7F 146)
(off Lambeth Wlk.)
Copeland Rd. E17 —6D 32
Copeland Rd. SE15 —2H 95
Copeman Clo. SE26 —5J 111
Copenhagen Gdns. W4 —2K 73
Copenhagen Ho. N1 —1A 62
(off Barnsbury Est.)
Copenhagen Pl. E14 —6B 64
Copenhagen St. N1 —1J 61
Cope Pl. W8 —3J 75
Copers Cope Rd. Beck —7B 112
Cope St. SE16 —4K 79
Copford Clo. Wfd G —6H 21
Copford Wlk. N1 —1C 62
(off Popham St.)
Copinger Wlk. Edgw —1H 25
Copland Av. Wemb —5D 40
Copland Clo. Wemb —5C 40
Copland Rd. Wemb —6E 40
Copleston M. SE15 —2F 95
Copleston Pas. SE15 —2F 95
Copleston Rd. SE15 —3G 95
Copley Clo. SE17 —6C 78
Copley Clo. W7 —4K 55
Copley Dene. Brom —1B 128
Copley Pk. SW16 —6K 109
Copley Rd. Stan —5H 11
Copley St. E1 —5K 63
Copner Way. SE15 —7F 79
Coppelia Rd. SE3 —4H 97
Coppen Rd. Dag —7F 37
Copperas St. SE8 —6D 80
Copperbeech Clo. NW3 —5B 44
Copper Beech Clo. Ilf —1D 34
Copper Beeches Ct. Iswth —1H 87
Copper Clo. SE19 —7F 111
Copperfield Dri. N15 —4F 31
Copperfield M. N18 —4K 17
Copperfield Rd. E3 —4A 64
Copperfield Rd. SE28 —6C 68
Copperfields. Beck —1E 126
Copperfields. Harr —7J 23
Copperfields Ct. W3 —2G 73
Copperfield St. SE1 —2B 78 (4K 147)
Copperfield Way. Chst —6G 115
Copperfield Way. Pinn —4D 22
Coppergate Clo. Brom —1K 127
Copper Mead Clo. NW2 —3E 42
Copper Mill Dri. Iswth —2K 87
Copper Mill La. SW17 —4A 108
Copper Row. SE1 —1F 79 (3E 148)
(off Horselydown La.)
Coppetts Cen. N11 —7J 15
Coppetts Clo. N12 —7H 15
Coppetts Rd. N10 —7J 15
Coppice Clo. SW20 —3E 120
Coppice Clo. Stan —6E 10
Coppice Dri. SW15 —6D 90

Coppice, The. Enf —4G 7
Coppice, The. New Bar —6E 4
(off Gt. North Rd.)
Coppice Wlk. N20 —3D 14
Coppice Way. E18 —4H 33
Coppies Gro. N11 —4K 15
Copping Clo. Croy —4E 134
Coppins, The. Harr —6D 10
Coppins, The. New Ad —6D 136
Coppock Clo. SW11 —2C 92
Copse Av. W Wick —3D 136
Copse Clo. SE7 —6K 81
Copse Glade. Surb —7D 118
Copse Hill. SW20 —1C 120
Copse Hill. Sutt —7K 131
Copse, The. E4 —1C 20
Copse, The. N2 —3D 28
Copse View. S Croy —7K 135
Coptefield Dri. Belv —3D 84
Copthall Av. EC2 —6D 62 (7B 142)
Copthall Bldgs. EC2
(off Copthall Av.) —6D 62 (7B 142)
Copthall Clo. EC2 —6D 62 (7A 142)
Copthall Dri. NW7 —7H 13
Copthall Gdns. NW7 —7H 13
Copthall Gdns. Twic —1K 103
Copthorne Av. SW12 —7H 93
Coptic St. WC1 —5J 61 (6C 140)
Copwood Clo. N12 —4G 15
Coral Clo. Romf —4C 36
Coraline Clo. S'hall —3D 54
Coralline Wlk. SE2 —2C 84
Coral Row. SW11 —3A 92
Coral St. SE1 —2A 78 (5H 147)
Coram Ho. W4 —5A 74
(off Wood St.)
Coram St. WC1 —4J 61 (4C 140)
Coran Clo. N9 —7E 8
Corban Rd. Houn —3E 86
Corbar Clo. Barn —1G 5
Corbet Clo. Wall —1E 132
Corbet Ct. EC3 —6D 62 (8B 142)
Corbet Pl. E1 —5F 63 (5E 142)
Corbett Ct. SE26 —4B 112
Corbett Gro. N22 —7D 16
Corbett Rd. E11 —6A 34
Corbett Rd. E17 —3E 32
Corbetts La. SE16 —4J 79
(in two parts)
Corbett W. E11 —6A 34
Corbicum. E11 —7G 33
Corbiere Ct. SW19 —6F 107
Corbins La. Harr —3F 39
Corbridge. N17 —7C 18
Corbridge Cres. E2 —2H 63
Corby Cres. Enf —4G 6
Corbylands Rd. Sidc —1J 115
Corbyn St. N4 —1J 45
Corby Rd. NW10 —2K 57
Corby Way. E3 —4C 64
Cordelia Clo. SE24 —4B 94
Cordelia Ho. N1 —2E 62
(off Arden Est.)
Cordelia St. E14 —6D 64
Cordell Ho. N15 —5F 31
(off Newton St.)
Cording St. E14 —5D 64
Cordova Rd. E3 —3A 64
Cordwainers Wlk. E13 —2J 65
Cord Way. E14 —3C 80
Cordwell Rd. SE13 —5G 97
Corelli Rd. SE3 —2C 98
Corfe Av. Harr —4E 38
Corfe Clo. Hay —6A 54
Corfe Ho. SW8 —7K 77
(off Dorset Rd.)
Corfe Tower. W3 —2J 73
Corfield Rd. E23 —2H 63

Corfton Rd. W5 —6E 56
Coriander Av. E14 —6F 65
Corinium Clo. Wemb —4F 41
Corinne Rd. N19 —4G 45
Corinthian Manorway. Eri —4K 85
Corinthian Rd. Eri —4K 85
Corkran Rd. Surb —7D 118
Corkscrew Hill. W Wick —2E 136
Cork Sq. E1 —1H 79
Cork St. W1 —7G 61 (1L 145)
Cork St. M. W1 —7G 61 (1L 145)
(off Cork St.)
Cork Tree Ho. SE27 —5B 110
(off Lakeview Rd.)
Cork Tree Way. E4 —5F 19
Corlett St. NW1 —5C 60 (5C 138)
Cormont Rd. SE5 —1B 94
Cormorant Clo. E17 —7E 18
Cormorant Rd. E7 —5H 49
Cornbury Rd. Edgw —7J 11
Cornel Ho. Sidc —3A 116
Cornelia St. N7 —6K 45
Cornell Clo. Sidc —6E 116
Cornell Ho. S Harr —3D 38
Corner Fielde. SW2 —1K 109
Corner Grn. SE3 —2J 97
Corner Ho. St. WC2 —1J 77 (2C 146)
(off Lit. Britain)
Corner Mead. NW9 —7G 13
Cornerstone Ho. Croy —7C 124
Corney Rd. W4 —6A 74
Cornflower La. Croy —1K 135
Cornflower Ter. SE22 —6H 95
Cornford Clo. Brom —5J 127
Cornford Gro. SW12 —2F 109
Cornhill. EC3 —6D 62 (8B 142)
Cornish Ct. N9 —7C 8
Cornish Gro. SE20 —1H 125
(in two parts)
Cornish Ho. Bren —5F 73
Corn Mill Dri. Orp —7K 129
Cornmill La. SE13 —3E 96
Cornrow Dri. NW10 —5B 42
Cornshaw Rd. Dag —1D 52
Cornthwaite Rd. E5 —3J 47
Cornwall Av. E2 —3J 63
Cornwall Av. N3 —7D 14
Cornwall Av. N22 —1J 29
Cornwall Av. S'hall —6D 54
Cornwall Av. Well —3J 99
Cornwall Clo. Bark —6K 51
Cornwall Ct. Pinn —1D 22
Cornwall Cres. W11 —6G 59
Cornwall Dri. Orp —7C 116
Cornwall Gdns. NW10 —6D 42
Cornwall Gdns. SW7 —3K 75
Cornwall Gdns. Wlk. SW7 —3K 75
Cornwall Gdns. W. SW7 —3K 75
Cornwall Ga. Purf —4J 85
Cornwall Gro. W4 —5A 74
Cornwallis Av. N9 —2C 18
Cornwallis Av. SE9 —2H 115
Cornwallis Ct. SW8 —1J 93
(off Lansdowne Grn.)
Cornwallis Gro. N9 —2C 18
Cornwallis Ho. W12 —7D 58
(off White City Est.)
Cornwallis Rd. E17 —4K 31
Cornwallis Rd. N9 —2C 18
Cornwallis Rd. N19 —2J 45
Cornwallis Rd. Dag —4D 52
Cornwallis Sq. N19 —2J 45
Cornwallis Wlk. SE9 —3D 98
Cornwall M. S. SW7 —3A 76
Cornwall M. W. SW7 —3K 75
Cornwall Rd. N4 —7A 30

Cornwall Rd. N15 —5D 30
Cornwall Rd. N18 —5B 18
Cornwall Rd. SE1 —1A 78 (2G 147)
Cornwall Rd. Croy —2B 134
Cornwall Rd. Harr —6G 23
Cornwall Rd. Pinn —1D 22
Cornwall Rd. Sutt —7H 131
Cornwall Rd. Twic —7A 88
Cornwall St. E1 —7H 63
Cornwall Ter. NW1 —4D 60 (4F 138)
Cornwall Ter. M. NW1
(off Allsop Pl.) —4D 60 (4F 138)
Cornwell Cres. E7 —4A 50
Cornwood Clo. N2 —5B 28
Cornwood Dri. E1 —6J 63
Cornworthy Rd. Dag —5C 52
Corona Rd. SE12 —7J 97
Coronation Av. N16 —4F 47
Coronation Clo. Bex —6D 100
Coronation Clo. Ilf —4G 35
Coronation Ct. E15 —6H 49
Coronation Ct. Eri —7K 85
Coronation Rd. E13 —3A 66
Coronation Rd. NW10 —3F 57
Coronation Wlk. Twic —1E 102
Coronet St. N1 —3E 62 (2C 142)
Corporate Ho. Har W —1J 23
Corporation Av. Houn —4C 86
Corporation Row. EC1
—4A 62 (3H 141)
Corporation St. E15 —2G 65
Corporation St. N7 —5J 45
Corrance Rd. SW2 —4J 93
Corri Av. N14 —4C 16
Corrib Ct. N13 —3E 16
Corrib Dri. Sutt —5C 132
Corringham Ct. NW11 —7J 27
Corringham Rd. NW11 —7J 27
Corringham Rd. Wemb —2G 41
Corringway. NW11 —7K 27
Corringway. W5 —5F 57
Corris Grn. NW9 —6A 26
Corronade Pl. SE28 —3G 83
Corscombe Clo. King T —5J 105
Corsehill St. SW16 —6G 109
Corsham St. N1 —3D 62 (2B 142)
Corsica St. N5 —6B 46
Corsley Way. E9 —6B 48
Cortayne Ct. Twic —2J 103
Cortayne Rd. SW6 —2H 91
Cortis Rd. SW15 —6D 90
Cortis Ter. SW15 —6D 90
Corunna Rd. SW8 —1G 93
Corunna Ter. SW8 —1G 93
Corvette Sq. SE10 —6F 81
Coryton Path. W9 —4H 59
Cosbycote Av. SE24 —5C 94
Cosdach Av. Wall —7H 133
Cosedge Cres. Croy —5A 134
Cosgrove Clo. N21 —2H 17
Cosgrove Clo. Hay —4C 54
Cosmo Pl. WC1 —5J 61 (5D 140)
Cosmos Ho. Brom —4A 128
Cosmur Clo. W12 —3B 74
Cossall Wlk. SE15 —2H 95
Cosser St. SE1 —3A 78 (6G 147)
Costa St. SE15 —2G 95
Costons Av. Gnfd —3H 55
Costons La. Gnfd —3H 55
Cosway St. NW1 —5C 60 (5D 138)
Cotall St. E14 —5C 64
Coteford St. SW17 —4D 108
Cotelands. Croy —3E 134
Cotesbach Rd. E5 —3J 47
Cotesmore Gdns. Dag —4C 52
Cotford Rd. T Hth —4C 124
Cotham St. SE17 —4C 78 (9M 147)
Cotherstone Rd. SW2 —1K 109

184

Cotleigh Av. Bex —2D 116
Cotleigh Rd. NW6 —7J 43
Cotleigh Rd. Romf —6K 37
Cotman Clo. NW11 —6A 28
Cotman Clo. SW15 —6F 91
Cotman Gdns. Edgw —2G 25
Coton Rd. Well —3A 100
Cotsford Av. N Mald —5J 119
Cotswold Clo. N11 —4K 15
Cotswold Clo. Bexh —2K 101
Cotswold Clo. King T —6J 105
Cotswold Gdns. E6 —3B 66
Cotswold Gdns. NW2 —2F 43
Cotswold Gdns. Ilf —7H 35
Cotswold Ga. NW2 —1G 43
Cotswold Grn. Enf —4E 6
Cotswold M. SW11 —1B 92
Cotswold Rise. Orp —6K 129
Cotswold Rd. Hamp —6E 102
Cotswold St. SE27 —4B 110
Cotswold Way. Enf —3E 6
Cotswold Way. Wor Pk —2E 130
Cottage Av. Brom —7C 128
Cottage Field Clo. Sidc —1C 116
Cottage Grn. SE5 —7D 78
Cottage Gro. SW9 —3J 93
Cottage Gro. Surb —6D 118
Cottage Pl. SW3 —3C 76 (6C 144)
Cottage Rd. Eps —7A 130
Cottage St. E14 —7D 64
Cottage Wlk. N16 —3F 47
Cottage Wlk. SW15 —1F 95
Cottage Wlk. SW1 —3D 76 (6F 144)
Cottenham Dri. SW20 —7D 106
Cottenham Pk. Rd. SW20 —1C 120
(in two parts)
Cottenham Pl. SW20 —7D 106
Cottenham Rd. E17 —4B 32
Cotterill Rd. Surb —7F 119
Cottesbrook St. SE14 —7A 80
Cottesmore Av. Ilf —2E 34
Cottesmore Gdns. W8 —3K 75
Cottingham Rd. SE20 —7K 111
Cottingham Rd. SW8 —7K 77
Cottington Clo. SE11 —5B 78
Cottington Rd. Felt —4B 102
Cottington St. SE11 —5B 78
Cotton Av. W3 —6K 57
Cottongrass Clo. Croy —1K 135
Coton Hill. Brom —4E 112
Coton Ho. SW12 —7J 93
Cotton Row. SW11 —3B 92
Cottons App. Romf —5K 37
Cottons Cen. SE1 —1E 78 (2C 148)
Cottons Ct. Romf —5K 37
Cotton's Gdns. E2 —3E 62 (1D 142)
Cottons La. SE1 —1D 78 (2B 148)
Cotton St. E14 —7E 64
Cotts Clo. W7 —5K 55
Couchmore Av. Ilf —2D 34
Couldridge La. Eri —3D 84
Coulgate St. SE4 —3A 96
Coulson Clo. Dag —1C 52
Coulson St. SW3 —5D 76
Coulter Clo. Hay —4C 54
Coulter Rd. W6 —3D 74
Councillor St. SE5 —7C 78
Counter Ct. SE1 —1D 78 (3A 148)
(off Borough High St.)
Counter St. SE1 —1E 78 (3C 148)
(off Hays La.)
Countess Rd. NW5 —5G 45
Countisbury Av. Enf —7A 8
Country Ga. SE9 —3G 115
Country Way. Felt —6A 102
County Gdns. Bark —2J 67
County Ga. Barn —6E 4
County Gro. SE5 —1C 94

County Pde. Bren —7D 72
County Rd. E6 —5F 67
County Rd. T Hth —2B 124
County St. SE1 —3C 78 (7M 147)
Coupland Pl. SE18 —5G 83
Courcy Rd. N8 —3A 30
Courland Gro. SW8 —1H 93
Courland St. SW8 —1H 93
(in two parts)
Course, The. SE9 —3E 114
Courtauld Clo. SE28 —1A 84
Courtauld Rd. N19 —1J 45
Court Av. Belv —5F 85
Court Clo. Harr —3D 24
Court Clo. Wall —7H 133
Court Clo. Av. Twic —3F 103
Court Downs Rd. Beck —2D 126
Court Dri. Croy —4K 133
Court Dri. Stan —4K 11
Court Dri. Sutt —4C 132
Courtenay Av. N6 —7C 28
Courtenay Av. Harr —7B 10
Courtenay Av. Sutt —7J 131
Courtenay Dri. Beck —2F 127
Courtenay Gdns. Harr —2G 23
Courtenay M. E17 —5A 32
Courtenay Pl. E17 —5A 32
Courtenay Rd. E11 —3H 49
Courtenay Rd. E17 —4K 31
Courtenay Rd. SE20 —6K 111
Courtenay Rd. Wemb —3D 40
Courtenay Rd. Wor Pk —3E 130
Courtenay Sq. SE11 —5A 78
Courtenay St. SE11 —5A 78
Courtens M. Stan —7H 11
Court Farm Av. Eps —5A 130
Court Farm La. N'holt —7E 38
Court Farm Rd. SE9 —2B 114
Court Farm Rd. N'holt —7E 38
Courtfield. W5 —5C 56
Courtfield Av. Harr —5K 23
Courtfield Cres. Harr —5K 23
Courtfield Gdns. SW5 —4K 75
Courtfield Gdns. W13 —6A 56
Courtfield M. SW5 —4A 76
Courtfield M. SW7 —4A 76
Courtfield Rise. W Wick —3F 137
Coverack Clo. N14 —6B 6
Coverack Clo. Croy —7A 125
Court Gdns. N1 —6B 46
Courthill Rd. SE13 —4E 96
Courthope Rd. NW3 —4D 44
Courthope Rd. SW19 —5G 107
Courthope Rd. Gnfd —2H 55
Courthope Vs. SW19 —7G 107
Court Ho. Gdns. N3 —6D 14
Courthouse Rd. N12 —6E 14
Courtland Av. E4 —2C 20
Courtland Av. NW7 —2E 12
Courtland Av. SW16 —7K 109
Courtland Av. Ilf —2D 50
Courtland Gro. SE28 —7D 68
Courtlands. Rich —5G 89
Courtlands Av. SE12 —5K 97
Courtlands Av. Brom —1G 137
Courtlands Av. Hamp —6D 102
Courtlands Av. Rich —1H 89
Courtlands Dri. Eps —6A 130
Courtlands Rd. Surb —7G 119
Court La. SE21 —6E 94
Court La. Gdns. SE21 —7E 94
Courtleet Dri. Eri —1H 101
Courtleigh. NW11 —5H 27
Courtleigh Gdns. NW11 —4G 27
Courtman Rd. N17 —7H 17
Court Mead. N'holt —3D 54
Courtmead Clo. SE24 —6C 94

Courtnell St. W2 —6J 59
Courtney Clo. SE19 —6E 110
Courtney Ct. N7 —5A 46
Courtney Cres. Cars —7D 132
Courtney Ho. NW4 —3E 26
(off Mulberry Clo.)
Courtney Pl. Croy —3A 134
Courtney Rd. N7 —5A 46
Courtney Rd. SW19 —7C 108
Courtney Rd. Croy —3A 134
Courtral Rd. SE23 —6A 96
Court Rd. SE9 —6D 98
Court Rd. SE25 —2F 125
Court Rd. S'hall —4D 70
Court, The. Ruis —4C 38
Courtside. N8 —6H 29
Courtside. SE26 —3H 111
Court St. E1 —5H 63
Court St. Brom —2J 127
Courtyard, The. N1 —7K 45
Courtyard, The. NW1 —7E 44
Cousin La. EC4 —7D 62 (1A 148)
Couthurst Rd. SE3 —7K 81
Coutt's Cres. NW5 —3E 44
Coval Gdns. SW14 —4H 89
Coval La. SW14 —4H 89
Coval Pas. SW14 —4J 89
Coval Rd. SW14 —4J 89
Covelees Wall. E6 —6E 66
Covell Ct. SE8 —7C 80
Covell Ct. Enf —1E 6
Coventry Rd. SE25 —4G 125
Covent Garden. WC2
—7J 61 (9D 140)
Coventry Clo. E6 —6D 66
Coventry Clo. NW6 —2J 59
Coventry Cross. E3 —4E 64
Coventry Rd. E1 & E2 —4H 63
Coventry Rd. SE25 —4G 125
Coventry Rd. Ilf —2F 51
Coventry St. W1 —7H 61 (1A 146)
Coverack Clo. N14 —6B 6
Coverack Clo. Croy —7A 125
Coverdale Clo. Stan —5G 11
Coverdale Gdns. Croy —3F 135
Coverdale Rd. NW2 —7F 43
Coverdale Rd. W12 —2D 74
Coverdales, The. Bark —2H 67
Coverley Clo. E1 —5G 63
Coverton Rd. SW17 —5C 108
Covert, The. Orp —6J 129
Covert Way. Barn —2F 5
Covet Wood Clo. Orp —6K 129
Covington Gdns. SW16 —7B 110
Covington Way. SW16 —6K 109
(in two parts)
Cowan Clo. E6 —5C 66
Cowbridge La. Bark —7F 51
Cowbridge Rd. Harr —4F 25
Cowcross St. EC1 —5B 62 (5J 141)
Cowdenbeath Path. N1 —1K 61
Cowden Rd. Orp —7K 129
Cowden St. SE6 —4C 112
Cowdrey Clo. Enf —2K 7
Cowdrey Rd. SW19 —5K 107
Cowdry Rd. E9 —6A 48
Cowen Av. Harr —2H 39
Cowgate Rd. Gnfd —3H 55
Cowick Rd. SW17 —4D 108
Cowings Mead. N'holt —6C 38
Cowland Av. Enf —4D 8

Cow La. Gnfd —2H 55
Cow Leaze. E6 —6E 66
Cowleaze Rd. King T —1E 118
Cowley La. E11 —3G 49
Cowley Pl. NW4 —5E 26
Cowley Rd. E11 —3K 33
Cowley Rd. SW9 —1A 94
Cowley Rd. SW14 —3A 90
Cowley Rd. W3 —1B 74
Cowley Rd. Ilf —7D 34
Cowley St. SW1 —3J 77 (7C 146)
Cowling Clo. W11 —7G 59
Cowper Av. E6 —7C 50
Cowper Av. Sutt —4B 132
Cowper Clo. Brom —4B 128
Cowper Clo. Well —5A 100
Cowper Gdns. N14 —6A 6
Cowper Gdns. Wall —6G 133
Cowper Ho. SE17 —5C 78
(off Browning St.)
Cowper Rd. N14 —1A 16
Cowper Rd. N16 —5E 46
Cowper Rd. N18 —5B 18
Cowper Rd. SW19 —6A 108
Cowper Rd. W3 —1K 73
Cowper Rd. W7 —7K 55
Cowper Rd. Belv —4G 85
Cowper Rd. Brom —4B 128
Cowper Rd. King T —5F 105
Cowper's Ct. EC3 —6D 62 (8B 142)
(off Birchin La.)
Cowper St. EC2 —4D 62 (3B 142)
Cowper Ter. W10 —5F 59
Cowslip Rd. E18 —2K 33
Cowthorpe Rd. SW8 —1H 93
Cox Ho. W6 —6G 75
(off Field Rd.)
Coxmount Rd. SE7 —5B 82
Coxson Way. SE1 —2F 79 (5E 148)
Cox's Ct. E1 —5F 63 (6E 142)
(off Bell La.)
Coxwell Rd. SE18 —5H 83
Coxwell Rd. SE19 —7E 110
Crab Hill. Beck —7F 113
Crabtree Av. Romf —4D 36
Crabtree Av. Wemb —2E 56
Crabtree Ct. E15 —5D 48
Crabtree Ct. New Bar —4E 4
Crabtree La. SW6 —7E 74
(in two parts)
Crabtree Manorway N. Belv —2J 85
Crabtree Manorway S. Belv —3J 85
Crabtree Wlk. SE15 —1F 95
(off Exeter Rd.)
Crabtree Wlk. Croy —1G 135
Crace St. NW1 —3H 61 (1A 140)
Craddock Rd. Enf —3A 8
Craddock St. NW5 —6E 44
Cradley Rd. SE9 —1H 115
Craigen Av. Croy —1H 135
Craigerne Rd. SE3 —7K 81
Craig Gdns. E18 —2H 33
Craigholm. SE18 —2E 98
Craigmuir Pk. Wemb —1F 57
Craignair Rd. SW2 —7A 94
Craigmish Av. SW16 —2K 123
Craig Pk. Rd. N18 —5C 18
Craig Rd. Rich —4C 104
Craig's Ct. SW1 —1J 77 (2C 146)
Craigton Rd. SE9 —4D 98
Craigwell Clo. Stan —5J 11
Craigwell Dri. Stan —5J 11
Crailey Av. Enf —2A 8
Crail Row. SE17 —4D 78 (9B 148)
Cramer St. W1 —5E 60 (6H 139)
Crammond Clo. W6 —6G 75

Cramonde Ct. Well —2A 100
Crampton Rd. SE20 —6J 111
Crampton St. SE17 —4C 78 (9L 147)
Cranberry Clo. N'holt —2B 54
Cranberry La. E16 —4G 65
Cranborne Av. S'hall —4E 70
Cranborne Rd. Bark —1H 67
Cranborne Waye. Hay —7A 54
Cranbourn All. WC2 —7H 61 (9B 140)
(off Cranbourn St.)
Cranbourne Av. E11 —4K 33
Cranbourne Clo. SW16 —3J 123
Cranbourne Dri. Pinn —5B 22
Cranbourne Gdns. NW11 —5G 27
Cranbourne Gdns. Ilf —3G 35
Cranbourne Rd. E12 —5C 50
Cranbourne Rd. E15 —4E 48
Cranbourne Rd. N10 —2F 29
Cranbourne Waye. Hay —6A 54
Cranbourn Pl. SE16 —2H 79
Cranbourn St. WC2 —7H 61 (9B 140)
Cranbrook Clo. Brom —6J 127
Cranbrook Ct. Bren —6D 72
(off Somerset Rd.)
Cranbrook Dri. Twic —1F 103
Cranbrook Est. E2 —2K 63
Cranbrook M. E17 —5B 32
Cranbrook Pk. N22 —1A 30
Cranbrook Point. E16 —1J 81
Cranbrook Rise. Ilf —6D 34
Cranbrook Rd. SE8 —1C 96
Cranbrook Rd. SW19 —7G 107
Cranbrook Rd. W4 —5A 74
Cranbrook Rd. Barn —6G 5
Cranbrook Rd. Bexh —1F 101
Cranbrook Rd. Houn —0D 86
Cranbrook Rd. Ilf —7E 34
Cranbrook Rd. T Hth —2C 124
Cranbrook St. E2 —2K 63
Cranbury Rd. SW6 —2K 91
Crandley Ct. SE8 —4A 80
Crane Av. W3 —7J 57
Crane Av. Iswth —5A 88
Cranebrook. Twic —2G 103
Crane Clo. Dag —6G 53
Crane Ct. EC4 —6A 62 (8H 141)
Cranford Clo. Twic —7J 87
Crane Gro. N7 —6A 46
Crane Ho. Felt —3E 102
Crane Lodge Rd. Houn —6A 70
Cranemead. SE16 —4K 79
Crane Mead Ct. Twic —7K 87
Crane Pk. Rd. Twic —2F 103
Crane Rd. Twic —1J 103
Cranes Dri. Surb —4F 119
Cranes Pk. Surb —4E 118
Cranes Pk. Av. Surb —4E 118
Cranes Pk. Cres. Surb —4F 119
Crane St. SE10 —5F 81
Craneswater Pk. S'hall —5D 70
Crane Way. Twic —7G 87
Cranfield Clo. SE27 —3C 110
Cranfield Dri. NW9 —7F 13
Cranfield Rd. SE4 —3B 96
Cranfield Rd. E. Cars —7E 132
Cranfield Rd. W. Cars —7E 132
Cranfield Row. SE1 —3A 78 (6H 147)
(off Gerridge St.)
Cranford Av. N13 —5D 16
Cranford Clo. SW20 —7D 106
Cranford La. Houn —7A 70
Cranford St. E1 —7K 63
Cranford Way. N8 —4K 29
Cranhurst Rd. NW2 —5E 42
Cranleigh Clo. SE20 —1H 125
Cranleigh Clo. Bex —6H 101

Cranleigh Gdns. N21 —5F 7
Cranleigh Gdns. SE25 —3E 124
Cranleigh Gdns. Bark —7H 51
Cranleigh Gdns. Harr —5E 24
Cranleigh Gdns. King T —6F 105
Cranleigh Gdns. S'hall —6D 54
Cranleigh Gdns. Sutt —2K 131
Cranleigh M. SW11 —2C 92
Cranleigh Rd. N15 —5C 30
Cranleigh Rd. SW19 —3J 121
Cranleigh St. NW1 —2G 61
Cranley Dene Ct. N10 —4F 29
Cranley Dri. Ilf —7G 35
Cranley Gdns. N10 —4F 29
Cranley Gdns. N13 —3E 16
Cranley Gdns. SW7 —5A 76
Cranley Gdns. Wall —7G 133
Cranley M. SW7 —5A 76
Cranley Pde. SE9 —4C 114
Cranley Pl. SW7 —4B 76 (9A 144)
Cranley Rd. E13 —5K 65
Cranley Rd. Ilf —6G 35
Cranmer Av. W13 —3B 72
Cranmer Clo. Mord —6F 121
Cranmer Clo. Ruis —1B 38
Cranmer Clo. Stan —7H 11
Cranmer Ct. N3 —2G 27
Cranmer Ct. SW3 —4C 76 (9D 144)
Cranmer Ct. SW4 —3H 93
Cranmere Ct. Enf —2F 7
Cranmer Farm Clo. Mitc —4D 122
Cranmer Gdns. Dag —4J 53
Cranmer Rd. E7 —4K 49
Cranmer Rd. SW9 —7A 78
Cranmer Rd. Croy —3B 134
Cranmer Rd. Edgw —3C 12
Cranmer Rd. Hamp —5F 103
Cranmer Rd. King T —5E 104
Cranmer Rd. Mitc —4D 122
Cranmer St. W1 —5E 60
Cranmer Ter. SW17 —5B 108
Cranmore Av. Iswth —7G 71
Cranmore Rd. Brom —3H 113
Cranmore Rd. Chst —5D 114
Cranmore Way. N10 —4G 29
Cranston Clo. Houn —2C 86
Cranston Est. N1 —2D 62
Cranston Gdns. E4 —6J 19
Cranston Rd. SE23 —1A 110
Cranswick Rd. SE16 —5H 79
Crantock Rd. SE6 —2D 112
Cranwell Clo. E3 —4D 64
Cranwich Av. N21 —7J 7
Cranwich Rd. N16 —7D 30
Cranwood Ct. EC1 —3D 62 (2B 142)
 (off Vince St.)
Cranwood St. EC1 —3D 62 (2B 142)
Cranworth Cres. E4 —1A 20
Cranworth Gdns. SW9 —1A 94
Craster Rd. SW2 —7K 93
Crathie Rd. SE12 —6K 97
Craven Av. W5 —7C 56
Craven Clo. N16 —7G 31
Craven Ct. NW10 —1A 58
Craven Ct. Romf —6E 36
Craven Gdns. SW19 —5J 107
Craven Gdns. Bark —2J 67
Craven Gdns. Ilf —2H 35
Craven Hill. W2 —7A 60
Craven Hill Gdns. W2 —7A 60
Craven Hill M. W2 —7A 60
Craven M. SW11 —3E 92
Craven Pk. NW10 —1K 57
Craven Pk. Rd. N15 —6F 31
Craven Pk. Rd. NW10 —1A 58
Craven Pas. WC2 —1J 77 (2C 146)
 (off Craven St.)

Craven Rd. NW10 —1K 57
Craven Rd. W2 —7A 60
Craven Rd. W5 —7C 56
Craven Rd. Croy —1H 135
Craven Rd. King T —1F 119
Craven St. WC2 —1J 77 (2C 146)
Craven Ter. W2 —7A 60
Craven Wlk. N16 —7G 31
Crawford Av. Wemb —5D 40
Crawford Clo. Iswth —2J 87
Crawford Gdns. N13 —3G 17
Crawford Gdns. N'holt —5E 42
Crawford M. W1 —5D 60 (6E 138)
Crawford Pas. EC1 —4A 62 (4H 141)
Crawford Pl. W1 —6C 60 (7D 138)
Crawford Point. E16 —6H 65
 (off Wouldham Rd.)
Crawford Rd. SE5 —1C 94
Crawford St. W1 —5C 60 (6D 138)
Crawley Rd. E10 —1D 48
Crawley Rd. N22 —2C 30
Crawley Rd. Enf —7K 7
Crawshay Ct. SW9 —1A 94
Crawthew Gro. SE22 —4F 95
Craybrooke Rd. Sidc —4B 116
Craybury End. SE9 —2G 115
Crayford Clo. E6 —6C 66
Crayford Rd. N7 —4H 45
Cray Rd. Belv —6G 85
Cray Rd. Sidc —6C 116
Cray Valley Rd. Orp —5K 129
Crealock Gro. Wfd G —5C 20
Crealock St. SW18 —6K 91
Creasy Est. SE1 —3E 78 (7C 148)
Creasy St. SE1 —3E 78 (7C 148)
Crebor St. SE22 —6G 95
Credenhall Dri. Brom —7D 128
Credenhill St. SW15 —7H 79
Credenhill St. SW16 —6B 109
Crediton Hill. NW6 —5K 43
Crediton Rd. E16 —6J 65
Crediton Rd. NW10 —1F 59
Credon Rd. E13 —2A 66
Credon Rd. SE16 —5H 79
Creechurch La. EC3
 —6E 62 (8D 142)
Creechurch Pl. EC3 —6E 62 (8D 142)
 (off Creechurch La.)
Creed La. EC4 —6B 62 (8K 141)
 (off Ludgate Hill)
Creed La. EC4 —6B 62 (8K 141)
Creek Rd. SE8 & SE10 —6C 80
Creek Rd. Bark —3K 67
Creekside. SE8 —7D 80
Creeland Gro. SE6 —1B 112
Crefeld Clo. W6 —6G 75
Creffield Rd. W5 & W3 —7F 57
Creighton Av. E6 —2B 66
Creighton Av. N2 & N10 —3C 28
Creighton Clo. W12 —7C 58
Creighton Rd. N17 —7K 17
Creighton Rd. NW6 —2F 59
Creighton Rd. W5 —3D 72
Cremer St. E2 —2F 63
Cremorne Est. SW10 —6B 76
Cremorne Rd. SW10 —7A 76
Crescent. EC3 —7F 63 (9E 142)
Crescent Ct. Surb —5D 118
Crescent Ct. Bus. Cen. E3 —4F 65
Crescent Dri. Orp —6F 129
Crescent E. Barn —1F 5
Crescent Gdns. SW19 —3J 107
Crescent Gdns. Ruis —7A 22
Crescent Gro. SW4 —4G 93
Crescent Gro. Mitc —5C 122
Crescent Ho. EC1 —4C 62 (4L 141)
 (off Golden La. Est.)

Crescent La. SW4 —4G 93
Crescent M. N22 —1J 29
Crescent Pl. SW3 —4C 76 (8D 144)
Crescent Rise. N22 —1H 29
Crescent Rise. Barn —5H 5
Crescent Rd. E4 —1B 20
Crescent Rd. E6 —1A 66
Crescent Rd. E10 —2D 48
Crescent Rd. E13 —1J 65
Crescent Rd. E18 —1A 34
Crescent Rd. N3 —1H 27
Crescent Rd. N8 —6H 29
Crescent Rd. N9 —1B 18
Crescent Rd. N11 —4J 15
Crescent Rd. N15 —3B 30
Crescent Rd. N22 —1H 29
Crescent Rd. SE18 —5F 83
Crescent Rd. SW20 —1F 121
Crescent Rd. Barn —6G 5
Crescent Rd. Beck —2D 126
Crescent Rd. Brom —7J 113
Crescent Rd. Dag —3F 53
Crescent Rd. Enf —4G 7
Crescent Rd. King T —7G 105
Crescent Rd. Sidc —3K 115
Crescent Row. EC1 —4C 62 (4L 141)
Crescent Stables. SW15 —5G 91
Crescent St. N1 —7K 45
Crescent, The. E17 —5A 32
Crescent, The. N9 —2C 18
Crescent, The. N11 —4K 15
Crescent, The. NW2 —3D 42
Crescent, The. SW13 —2C 90
Crescent, The. SW19 —3J 107
Crescent, The. W3 —6A 58
Crescent, The. Barn —2E 4
Crescent, The. Beck —1C 126
Crescent, The. Croy —6D 124
Crescent, The. Harr —5J 23
Crescent, The. Ilf —6E 34
Crescent, The. N Mald —2K 119
Crescent, The. Sidc —4K 115
Crescent, The. S'hall —2D 70
Crescent, The. Surb —5E 118
Crescent, The. Sutt —5B 132
Crescent, The. Wemb —2B 40
Crescent, The. W Wick —6G 127
Crescent Way. N12 —6H 15
Crescent Way. SE4 —3C 96
Crescent Way. SW16 —6K 109
Crescent W. Barn —1F 5
Crescent Wharf. E16 —2K 81
Crescent Wood Rd. SE26 —3G 111
Cresford Rd. SW6 —1K 91
Crespigny Rd. NW4 —6D 26
Cressage Clo. S'hall —4E 54
Cressage Ho. Bren —6E 72
 (off Ealing Rd.)
Cresset Rd. E9 —6J 47
Cresset St. SW4 —3H 93
Cressfield Clo. NW5 —5E 44
Cressida Rd. N19 —1G 45
Cressingham Gdns. Est. SW2
 —7A 94
Cressingham Gro. Sutt —4A 132
Cressingham Rd. SE13 —3E 96
Cressingham Rd. Edgw —6E 12
Cressington Clo. N16 —5E 46
Cresswell. NW9 —2B 26
Cresswell Gdns. SW5 —5A 76
Cresswell Pk. SE3 —3H 97
Cresswell Pl. SW10 —5A 76
Cresswell Rd. SE25 —4G 125
Cresswell Rd. Felt —3C 102
Cresswell Rd. Twic —6D 88
Cresswell Way. N21 —7F 7

Cressy Ct. E1 —5J 63
Cressy Ct. W6 —3D 74
Cressy Houses. E1 —5J 63
 (off Hannibal Rd.)
Cressy Pl. E1 —5J 63
Cressy Rd. NW3 —5D 44
Crestbrook Av. N13 —3G 17
Crestbrook Pl. N13 —3G 17
 (off Green Lanes)
Crest Ct. NW4 —5E 26
Crest Dri. Enf —1D 8
Crestfield St. WC1 —3J 61 (1D 140)
Crest Gdns. Ruis —3A 38
Creston Way. Wor Pk —1F 131
Crest Rd. NW2 —2C 42
Crest Rd. Brom —7H 127
Crest Rd. S Croy —7H 135
Crest, The. N13 —4F 17
Crest, The. NW4 —6F 27
Crest, The. Surb —5G 119
Crest View. Pinn —4B 22
Crest View Dri. Pet W —5F 129
Crestway. SW15 —6C 90
Crestwood Way. Houn —5D 86
Creswick Rd. W3 —7H 57
Creswick Wlk. E3 —3C 64
Creswick Wlk. NW11 —4H 27
Creton St. SE18 —3E 82
Crewdson Rd. SW9 —7A 78
Crewe Pl. NW10 —3B 58
Crews St. E14 —4C 80
Crewys Rd. NW2 —2H 43
Crewys Rd. SE15 —2H 95
Crichton Av. Wall —5H 133
Crichton Gdns. Romf —7G 37
Crichton Rd. Sidc —6D 116
Crichton Rd. Cars —7D 132
Cricketers Clo. N14 —7B 6
Cricketers Clo. Eri —5K 85
Cricketer's Ct. SE11
 —4B 78 (9J 147)
Cricketers Rd. Enf —2H 7
Cricketfield Rd. E5 —4H 47
Cricket Grn. Mitc —3D 122
Cricket Ground Rd. Chst —1F 129
Cricket La. Beck —5A 112
Cricklade Av. SW2 —2J 109
Cricklewood B'way. NW2 —3E 42
Cricklewood La. NW2 —4F 43
Cricklewood Trading Est. NW2
 —3G 43
Cridland St. E15 —1H 65
Crieff Ct. Tedd —7C 104
Crieff Rd. SW18 —6A 92
Criffel Av. SW2 —2H 109
Crimscott St. SE1 —3E 78 (7D 148)
Crimsworth Rd. SW8 —1H 93
Crinan St. N1 —2J 61
Cringle St. SW8 —7G 77
Cripplegate St. EC2
 —5C 62 (5M 141)
Cripps Grn. Hay —4A 54
Crispe Ho. N1 —1K 61
 (off Barnsbury Est.)
Crispen Rd. Felt —4C 102
Crispian Clo. NW10 —4A 42
Crispin Clo. Croy —2J 133
Crispin Cres. Croy —3H 133
Crispin Lodge. NW1 —5J 15
Crispin Rd. Edgw —6D 12
Crispin St. E1 —5F 63 (6E 142)
Crisp Rd. W6 —5E 74
Cristowe Rd. SW6 —2H 91
Criterion M. N19 —2H 45
Crockerton Rd. SW17 —2D 108
Crockham Way. SE9 —4E 114
Crocus Clo. Croy —1K 135

Crocus Field. Barn —6C 4
Croft Av. W Wick —1E 136
Croft Clo. NW7 —3F 13
Croft Clo. Belv —5F 85
Croft Clo. Chst —5D 114
Croft Ct. SE13 —6E 96
Croftdown Rd. NW5 —3E 44
Crofters Clo. Iswth —5H 87
Crofters Mead. Croy —7B 136
Crofters Way. NW1 —1H 61
Croft Gdns. W7 —2A 72
Croft Ho. E17 —4D 32
Croft Lodge Clo. Wfd G —6E 20
Crofton Av. W4 —7K 73
Crofton Av. Bex —7D 100
Croftongate Way. SE4 —5A 96
Crofton La. Orp —7H 128
Crofton Pk. Rd. SE4 —6B 96
Crofton Rd. E13 —4K 65
Crofton Rd. SE5 —1E 94
Crofton Ter. E5 —5A 48
Crofton Ter. Rich —4F 89
Crofton Way. Barn —6E 4
Crofton Way. Enf —2F 7
Croft Rd. SW16 —1A 124
Croft Rd. SW19 —7A 108
Croft Rd. Brom —6J 113
Croft Rd. Enf —1F 9
Croft Rd. Sutt —5C 132
Crofts Rd. Harr —6A 24
Crofts St. E1 —7G 63
Croft St. SE8 —4A 80
Crofts Vs. Harr —6A 24
Croft, The. NW10 —2B 58
Croft, The. W5 —5E 56
Croft, The. Barn —4A 4
Croft, The. Houn —7C 70
Croft, The. Pinn —7D 22
Croft, The. Ruis —4A 38
Croft, The. Wemb —5C 40
Croftway. NW3 —4J 43
Croftway. Rich —3B 104
Croft Way. Sidc —3J 115
Crogsland Rd. NW1 —7E 44
Croham Clo. S Croy —7E 134
Croham Mnr. Rd. S Croy —7E 134
Croham Pk. Av. S Croy —5F 135
Croham Rd. S Croy —5E 134
Croham Valley Rd. S Croy —6G 135
Croindene Rd. SW16 —1J 123
Crokesley Ho. Edgw —2J 25
 (off Burnt Oak B'way.)
Cromartie Rd. N19 —7H 29
Cromarty Ct. SW2 —5K 93
Cromarty Rd. Edgw —2C 12
Cromberdale Ct. N17 —1G 31
 (off Spencer Rd.)
Crombie Clo. Ilf —5D 34
Crombie M. SW11 —2C 92
Crombie Rd. Sidc —1H 115
Cromer Pl. Orp —7H 129
Cromer Rd. E10 —7F 33
Cromer Rd. N17 —2G 31
Cromer Rd. SE25 —3H 125
Cromer Rd. SW17 —6E 108
Cromer Rd. Barn —4F 5
Cromer Rd. Chad —6E 36
Cromer Rd. Romf —6J 37
Cromer Rd. Wfd G —4D 20
Cromer Rd. WC1 —3J 61 (2C 140)
Cromer Ter. E8 —5G 47
Cromer Vs. Rd. SW18 —6H 91
Cromford Path. E5 —4K 47
Cromford Rd. SW18 —5J 91
Cromford Way. N Mald —2K 119
Cromlix Clo. Chst —2F 129
Crompton St. W2 —4B 60 (4A 138)

omwell Av. N6 —1F 45
omwell Av. W6 —5D 74
omwell Av. Brom —4K 127
omwell Av. N Mald —5B 120
omwell Cen. NW10 —3K 57
omwell Clo. E1 —1G 79
omwell Clo. N2 —4B 28
omwell Clo. W3 —1J 73
omwell Clo. Brom —4K 127
omwell Ct. Enf —5E 8
omwell Cres. SW5 —4J 75
omwell Gdns. SW7
   —3B 76 (7B 144)
romwell Highwalk. EC2
romwell Ind. Est. E10 —1A 48
omwell Lodge. Bexh —5E 100
omwell M. SW7 —4B 76 (8B 144)
omwell Pl. EC2 —5C 62 (5M 141)
(off Barbican)
omwell Pl. N6 —1F 45
romwell Pl. SW7 —4B 76 (8B 144)
romwell Pl. SW14 —3J 89
omwell Rd. E7 —7A 50
omwell Rd. E17 —5E 32
omwell Rd. N3 —1A 28
omwell Rd. N10 —7K 15
(in two parts)
omwell Rd. SW5 & SW7 —4J 75
romwell Rd. SW9 —1B 94
romwell Rd. SW19 —5J 107
omwell Rd. Beck —2A 126
omwell Rd. Croy —7D 124
romwell Rd. Felt —1A 102
romwell Rd. Houn —4E 86
romwell Rd. King T —1E 118
romwell Rd. Tedd —6A 104
omwell Rd. Wemb —2E 56
romwell Rd. Wor Pk —3A 130
omwell Rd. S. Houn —4E 86
romwell Tower. EC2
(off Barbican) —5C 62 (5M 141)
rondace Rd. SW6 —1J 91
rondall Ct. N1 —2D 62
(off St Johns Est.)
rondall St. N1 —2D 62
rooked Billet. SW19 —6E 106
rooked Billet Yd. E2
   —3E 62 (1D 142)
rooked Usage. N3 —3G 27
rooke Rd. SE8 —5A 80
rookham Rd. SW6 —1H 91
rook Log. Bexh —3D 100
rookston Rd. SE9 —3E 98
roombs Rd. E16 —5A 66
room's Hill. SE10 —7E 80
room's Hill Gro. SE10 —7E 80
ropley St. N1 —2D 62
roppath Rd. Dag —4G 53
ropthorne Ct. W9 —3A 60
(off Maida Vale)
rosbie. NW9 —2B 26
rosbie Ho. E17 —3E 32
(off Prospect Hill.)
rosby Clo. Felt —3C 102
rosby Ct. SE1 —2D 78 (4A 148)
(off Crosby Row)
rosby Ho. E7 —6J 49
rosby Rd. E7 —6J 49
rosby Rd. Dag —2H 69
rosby Row. SE1 —2D 78 (5A 148)
rosby Row. SW1 —2D 78
rosby Sq. EC3 —6E 62 (8C 142)
rosby Wlk. E8 —6F 47
rosby Wlk. SW2 —7A 94
rosland. SW11 —3E 92
ross Av. SE10 —6F 81

Crossbrook Rd. SE3 —3C 98
Cross Deep. Twic —2K 103
Cross Deep Gdns. Twic —2K 103
Crossfield Rd. N17 —3C 30
Crossfield Rd. NW3 —6B 44
Crossfield St. SE8 —7C 80
Crossford St. SW9 —2K 93
Cross Ga. Edgw —3B 12
Crossgate. Gnfd —6B 40
Cross Keys Clo. W1
   —5E 60 (6H 139)
Cross Keys Clo. EC1 —5C 62 (6L 141)
(off St Nicholas Way)
Cross Lances Rd. Houn —4F 87
Crossland Rd. T Hth —6B 124
Crosslands Av. W5 —1F 73
Crosslands Av. S'hall —5D 70
Cross La. EC3 —7E 62 (1C 148)
Cross La. N8 —3K 29
(in two parts)
Cross La. Bex —7F 101
Crosslet St. SE17 —4D 78 (8B 148)
Crosslet Vale. SE10 —1D 96
Crossley St. N7 —6A 46
Crossmead. SE9 —1D 114
Crossmead Av. Gnfd —3E 54
Crossness Footpath. Eri —1F 85
Crossness La. SE28 —7D 68
Crossness Rd. Bark —3K 67
Cross Rd. E4 —1B 20
Cross Rd. N11 —5A 16
Cross Rd. N22 —7F 17
Cross Rd. SW19 —7J 107
Cross Rd. Chad —7C 36
Cross Rd. Croy —1D 134
Cross Rd. Enf —4K 7
Cross Rd. Felt —4C 102
Cross Rd. Harr —4H 23
Cross Rd. King T —7F 105
Cross Rd. Mawn —4G 37
Cross Rd. Sidc —4B 116
Cross Rd. S Harr —3F 39
Cross Rd. Sutt —5B 132
Cross Rd. W'stone —2A 24
Cross Rd. Wfd G —6J 21
Cross St. N1 —1B 62
Cross St. N18 —5B 18
Cross St. SE5 —3D 94
Cross St. SW13 —2A 90
Cross St. Hamp —5G 103
Crosshwaite Av. SE5 —4D 94
Crosswall. EC3 —7F 63 (9E 142)
Crossway. N12 —6G 15
Crossway. N16 —5E 46
Crossway. NW9 —4B 26
Crossway. SE28 —7C 68
Crossway. SW20 —4E 120
Crossway. W13 —4A 56
Crossway. Dag —3C 52
Crossway. Enf —7K 7
Crossway. Orp —4H 129
Crossway. Ruis —4A 38
Cross Way. Wfd G —4F 21
Crossway Ct. SE4 —2A 96
Crossways. N21 —6H 7
Crossways. S Croy —7A 136
Crossways. Sutt —7B 132
Crossways Rd. Beck —4C 126
Crossways Rd. Mitc —3F 123
Crossways, The. Houn —7D 70
Crossways, The. Surb —7H 119
Crossways, The. Wemb —2G 41
Crossway, The. N22 —7G 17
Crossway, The. SE9 —2B 114
Cross Way, The. Harr —2J 23
Croston St. E8 —1G 63
Crothall Clo. N13 —3E 16

Crouch. Sidc —5B 116
Crouch Av. Bark —2B 68
Crouch Clo. Beck —6C 112
Crouch Croft. SE9 —3E 114
Crouch End Hill. N8 —7H 29
Crouch Hall Ct. N19 —1J 45
Crouch Hall Rd. N8 —6H 29
Crouch Hill. N8 & N4 —6J 29
Crouchman's Clo. SE26 —3F 111
Crouch Rd. NW10 —7K 41
Crowborough Rd. SW17 —6E 108
Crowbourne Ct. Sutt —4K 131
(off St Nicholas Way)
Crowden Way. SE28 —7C 68
Crowder St. E1 —7H 63
Crowfield Ho. N5 —4C 46
Crowhurst Clo. SW9 —2A 94
Crowhurst Ho. SW9 —2K 93
(off Aytoun Rd.)
Crowland Gdns. N14 —7D 6
Crowland Rd. N15 —5F 31
Crowland Rd. T Hth —4D 124
Crowlands Av. Romf —6H 37
Crowland Ter. N1 —7D 46
Crowland Wlk. Mord —6K 121
Crow La. Romf —7F 37
Crowley Cres. Croy —5A 134
Crowlin Wlk. N1 —6D 46
Crowmarsh Gdns. SE23 —7J 95
Crown Arc. King T —2D 118
Crownbourne Ct. Sutt —4K 131
Crown Clo. E3 —1C 64
Crown Clo. NW6 —6K 43
Crown Clo. NW7 —2G 13
Crown Cotts. Romf —1F 37
Crown Ct. EC2 —6C 62 (8M 141)
(off Cheapside)
Crown Ct. N10 —7K 15
Crown Ct. SE12 —6K 97
Crown Ct. WC2 —6J 61 (8D 140)
Crown Dale. SE19 —6B 110
Crowndale Rd. NW1 —2G 61
Crownfield Av. Ilf —6J 35
Crownfield Rd. E15 —4F 49
Crown Hill. Croy —2C 134
Crown Hill Rd. NW10 —1B 58
Crownhill Rd. Wfd G —7H 21
Crown La. N14 —1B 16
Crown La. SW16 —5A 110
Crown La. Brom —5B 128
Crown La. Chst —1G 129
Crown La. Mord —4J 121
Crown La. Gdns. SW16 —5A 110
Crown La. Spur. Brom —6B 128
Crownmead Way. Romf —4H 37
Crown M. E13 —1A 66
Crown M. W6 —4C 74
Crown Office Row. EC4
   —7A 62 (9G 141)
Crown Pde. N14 —1B 16
Crown Pde. SE19 —6B 110
Crown Pas. SW1 —1G 77 (3M 145)
Crown Pas. King T —2D 118
Crown Pl. NW5 —6F 45
Crown Pl. SW1 —1G 77
Crown Rd. N10 —7K 15
Crown Rd. Enf —4B 8
Crown Rd. Ilf —4H 35
Crown Rd. Mord —4K 121
Crown Rd. N Mald —1J 119
Crown Rd. Sutt —4K 131
Crown Rd. Twic —6B 88
Crownstone Rd. SW2 —5A 94
Crownstone Rd. SW2 —5A 94
Crown St. SE5 —7C 78
Crown St. W3 —1H 73
Crown St. Dag —6J 53
(in two parts)

Crown St. Harr —1H 39
Crown Ter. Rich —4F 89
Crowntree Clo. Iswth —6K 71
Crown Wlk. Wemb —3F 41
Crown Woods La. SE9 —5H 99
Crown Woods Way. SE9 —5H 99
Crown'd. Houn —3G 87
Crowshott Av. Stan —2C 24
Crows Rd. E15 —3F 65
Crowther Av. Bren —4E 72
Crowther Rd. SE25 —4G 125
Crowthorne Clo. SW18 —7H 91
Crowthorne Rd. W10 —6F 59
Croxden Clo. Edgw —3G 25
Croxden Wlk. Mord —6A 122
Croxford Gdns. N22 —7E 17
Croxford Way. Romf —1K 53
Croxley Grn. Orp —7B 116
Croxley Rd. W9 —3H 59
Croxted Clo. SE21 —7C 94
Croxted Rd. SE24 & SE21 —6C 94
Croxteth Ho. SW8 —2H 93
Croyde Av. Gnfd —3G 55
Croyde Clo. Sidc —7H 99
Croydon. N17 —2D 30
(off Gloucester Rd.)
Croydon Flyover, The. Croy —3C 134
Croydon Gro. Croy —1B 134
Croydon Rd. E13 —4H 65
Croydon Rd. SE20 —2H 125
Croydon Rd. Beck —4K 125
Croydon Rd. Mitc & Croy —4E 122
Croydon Rd. Wall & Croy —4F 133
Croydon Rd. W Wick & Brom
   —3G 137
Croyland Rd. N9 —1B 18
Croylands Dri. Surb —7E 118
Crozier Ter. E9 —5K 47
Crucible Clo. Romf —6B 36
Crucifix La. SE1 —2E 78 (4C 148)
Cruden St. N1 —1B 62
Cruikshank Rd. E15 —4G 49
Cruikshank St. WC1
   —3A 62 (1G 141)
Crummock Gdns. NW9 —5A 26
Crumpsall St. SE2 —4C 84
Crundale Av. NW9 —5G 25
Crunden St. S Croy —7D 134
Crusader Gdns. Croy —3E 134
Crusoe Rd. Eri —5K 85
Crusoe Rd. Mitc —7D 108
Crutched Friars. EC3
   —7E 62 (9D 142)
Crutchley Rd. SE6 —2G 113
Crystal Pal. Pde. SE19 —6F 111
Crystal Pal. Pk. Rd. SE26 —5G 111
Crystal Pal. Rd. SE22 —6F 95
Crystal Pal. Sta. Rd. SE19 —6G 111
Crystal Ter. SE19 —6D 110
Crystal Way. Dag —1C 52
Crystal Way. Harr —5K 23
Cuba Dri. Enf —2D 8
Cuba St. E14 —2C 80
Cubitt Ho. SW4 —6G 93
Cubitt Sq. S'hall —1G 71
Cubitt Steps. E14 —1C 80
Cubitt St. WC1 —3K 61 (2F 140)
Cubitt St. Croy —5K 133
Cubitt's Yd. WC2 —7J 61 (9D 140)
(off James St.)
Cubitt Ter. SW4 —3G 93
Cuckoo Av. W7 —4H 55
Cuckoo Dene. W7 —5H 55
Cuckoo Hall La. N9 —7D 8
Cuckoo Hall Rd. N9 —7D 8
Cuckoo Hill. Pinn —3A 22

Cuckoo Hill Dri. Pinn —3A 22
Cuckoo Hill Rd. Pinn —4A 22
Cuckoo La. W7 —7J 55
Cudas Clo. Eps —4B 130
Cuddington Av. Wor Pk —3B 130
Cuddington Ct. Sutt —7F 131
Cudham St. SE6 —7E 96
Cudworth St. E1 —4H 63
Cuff Cres. SE9 —6B 98
Culford Gdns. SW3 —4D 76 (9F 144)
Culford Gro. N1 —6E 46
Culford M. N1 —6E 46
Culford Rd. N1 —7E 46
Culgaith Gdns. Enf —4D 6
Cullen Way. NW10 —4J 57
Culling Rd. SE16 —3J 79
Cullington Clo. Harr —4A 24
Cullingworth Rd. NW10 —5C 42
Culloden Rd. Enf —2G 7
Culloden St. E14 —6E 64
Cullum St. EC3 —7E 62 (9C 142)
Culmington Rd. W13 —1C 72
Culmington Rd. S Croy —7C 134
Culmore Rd. SE15 —7H 79
Culmstock Rd. SW11 —5E 92
Culpepper Ct. SE11 —4A 78 (8G 147)
(off Kennington Rd.)
Culross Clo. N15 —4C 30
Culross St. W1 —7E 60 (1G 145)
Culverden Rd. SW12 —2G 109
Culver Gro. Stan —2C 24
Culverhouse Gdns. SW16 —3K 109
Culverlands Clo. Stan —4G 11
Culverley Rd. SE6 —1D 112
Culvers Av. Cars —2D 132
Culvers Retreat. Cars —2D 132
Culverstone Clo. Hayes —6H 127
Culvers Way. Cars —2D 132
Culvert Pl. SW11 —2E 92
Culvert Rd. N15 —5E 30
Culvert Rd. SW11 —2D 92
Culworth St. NW8 —2C 60
Cumberland Av. NW10 —3H 57
Cumberland Av. Well —3J 99
Cumberland Bus. Cen. NW10
   —4H 57
Cumberland Clo. E8 —6F 47
Cumberland Clo. SW20 —7F 107
Cumberland Clo. Ilf —1G 35
Cumberland Clo. Twic —6B 88
Cumberland Ct. Harr —3J 23
(off Princes Dri.)
Cumberland Ct. Well —2J 99
Cumberland Cres. W14 —4G 75
Cumberland Dri. Bexh —7E 84
Cumberland Gdns. NW4 —1F 27
Cumberland Gdns. WC1
   —3A 62 (1G 141)
Cumberland Ga. W1
   —7D 60 (9E 138)
Cumberland Ho. N9 —1D 18
(off Cumberland Rd.)
Cumberland Ho. King T —7H 105
Cumberland Mkt. NW1
   —3F 61 (1K 139)
Cumberland Mills Sq. E14 —5F 81
Cumberland Pk. W3 —7J 57
Cumberland Pk. Ind. Est. NW10
   —3C 58
Cumberland Pl. NW1
   —3F 61 (1J 139)
Cumberland Pl. SE6 —7H 97
Cumberland Rd. E12 —4B 50
Cumberland Rd. E13 —5K 65
Cumberland Rd. E17 —2A 32

Cumberland Rd. N9 —1D **18**
Cumberland Rd. N22 —2K **29**
Cumberland Rd. SE25 —6H **125**
Cumberland Rd. SW13 —1B **90**
Cumberland Rd. W3 —7J **57**
Cumberland Rd. W7 —2K **71**
Cumberland Rd. Brom —4G **127**
Cumberland Rd. Harr —5F **23**
Cumberland Rd. Rich —7G **73**
Cumberland Rd. Stan —9F **25**
Cumberland St. SW1 —5F **77**
Cumberland Ter. NW1 —2F **61**
Cumberland Ter. M. NW1 —2F **61**
(in three parts)
Cumberland Vs. W3 —7J 57
(off Cumberland Rd.)
Cumberlow Av. SE25 —3F **125**
Cumberton Rd. N17 —1D **30**
Cumbrian Gdns. NW2 —2F **43**
Cumming St. N1 —2K **61**
Cumnor Gdns. Eps —6C **130**
Cumnor Rd. Sutt —6A **132**
Cunard Pl. EC3 —6E **62** (8D **142**)
Cunard Rd. NW10 —3K **57**
Cunard St. SE5 —6E **78**
Cunard Wlk. SE5 —1E **94**
Cundy Rd. E16 —6A **66**
Cundy St. SW1 —4E **76** (9H **145**)
Cunliffe Rd. Eps —4B **130**
Cunliffe St. SW16 —6G **109**
Cunningham Clo. Romf —5C **36**
Cunningham Clo. W Wick —2D **136**
Cunningham Pk. Harr —5G **23**
Cunningham Pl. NW8
　　　　—4B **60** (3A **138**)
Cunningham Rd. N15 —4G **31**
Cunnington St. W4 —4J **73**
Cupar Rd. SW11 —1E **92**
Cupola Clo. Brom —5K **113**
Cureton St. SW1 —4H **77** (9B **146**)
Curfew Ho. Bark —1G **67**
Curie Gdns. NW9 —2A **26**
Curlew Clo. SE28 —7D **68**
Curlew St. SE1 —2F **79** (4F **148**)
Curlew Way. Hay —5B **54**
Cumick's La. SE27 —4C **110**
Curran Av. Sidc —5K **99**
Curran Av. Wall —3E **132**
Currey Rd. Gnfd —6H **39**
Curricle St. W3 —1A **74**
Currie Hill Clo. SW19 —4H **107**
Curry Rise. NW7 —6A **14**
Cursitor St. EC4 —6A **62** (7G **141**)
Curtain Pl. EC2 —4E 62 (3D 142)
(off Curtain Rd.)
Curtain Rd. EC2 —4E **62** (2D **142**)
(in two parts)
Curthwaite Gdns. Enf —4C **6**
Curtis Dri. W3 —6K **57**
Curtis Field Rd. SW16 —4K **109**
Curtis Ho. SE17 —5D 78
(off Morecambe St.)
Curtis La. Wemb —5E **40**
Curtis Rd. Houn —7D **86**
Curtis St. SE1 —4F **79** (8E **148**)
Curtis Way. SE1 —4F **79** (8E **148**)
Curtis Way. SE28 —7B **68**
Curtlington Ho. Edgw —2J 25
(off Burnt Oak B'way.)
Curve, The. W12 —7C **58**
Curwen Av. E7 —4K **49**
Curwen Rd. W12 —2C **74**
Curzon Av. Stan —1A **24**
Curzon Ct. SW6 —1K 91
(off Maltings Pl.)
Curzon Cres. NW10 —7A **42**
Curzon Cres. Bark —2K **67**

Curzon Ga. W1 —1E **76** (3H **145**)
Curzon Pl. W1 —1E **76** (3H **145**)
Curzon Pl. Pinn —5A **22**
Curzon Rd. N10 —2F **29**
Curzon Rd. W4 —4B **56**
Curzon Rd. T Hth —6A **124**
Curzon St. W1 —1E **76** (3H **145**)
Cusack Clo. Twic —4K **103**
Custance Ho. N1 —2D 62
(off Provost Est.)
Custom Ho. Wlk. EC3
　　　　—7E **62** (1C **148**)
(off Lwr. Thames St.)
Custonm Ho. Reach. SE16 —2B **80**
Cutbush Ho. N7 —5H **45**
Cutcombe Rd. SE5 —2C **94**
Cuthbert Gdns. SE25 —3E **124**
Cuthbert Harrowing Ho. EC1
　　　　—4C **62** (4L **141**)
(off Golden La. Est.)
Cuthbert Rd. E17 —3E **32**
Cuthbert Rd. N18 —5B **18**
Cuthbert Rd. Croy —2B **134**
Cuthberts Rd. NW2 —6H **43**
Cuthbert St. W2 —5B **60** (4A **138**)
Cuthill Wlk. SE5 —1D **94**
Cutlers Gdns. E1 —6E 62 (7D 142)
(off Cutlers St.)
Cutlers Sq. E14 —4C **80**
Cutler St. E1 —6E **62** (7D **142**)
Cut, The. SE1 —2B **78** (4J **147**)
Cutthroat All. Rich —2C **104**
Cuxton. Pet W —5G **129**
Cuxton Clo. Bexh —5F **100**
Cyclamen Clo. Hamp —6E **102**
Cyclops M. E14 —4C **80**
Cygnet Av. Felt —7A **86**
Cygnet Clo. NW10 —5K **41**
Cygnets, The. Felt —4C **102**
Cygnet St. E1 —4F **63** (3F **142**)
Cygnet Way. Hay —5B **54**
Cygnus Bus. Cen. NW10 —6B **42**
Cymbeline Ct. Harr —6K 23
(off Gayton Rd.)
Cynthia St. N1 —2K **61**
Cyntra Pl. E8 —7H **47**
Cypress Av. Twic —7G **87**
Cypress Pl. W1 —4G **61** (4M **139**)
Cypress Rd. SE25 —2E **124**
Cypress Rd. Harr —2H **23**
Cyprus Av. N3 —2G **27**
Cyprus Gdns. N3 —2G **27**
Cyprus Pl. E2 —2J **63**
Cyprus Pl. E6 —7E **66**
Cyprus Rd. N3 —2H **27**
Cyprus Rd. N9 —2A **18**
Cyprus St. E2 —2J **63**
(in two parts)
Cyrena Rd. SE22 —6F **95**
Cyril Lodge. Sidc —4A **116**
Cyril Mans. SW11 —1D **92**
Cyril Rd. Bexh —2E **100**
Cyril Rd. Orp —7K **129**
Cyrus St. EC1 —4B **62** (3K **141**)
Czar St. SE8 —6C **80**

Dabbs Hill La. N'holt —6D **38**
Dabin Cres. SE10 —1E **96**
Dacca St. SE8 —6B **80**
Dace Rd. E3 —1C **64**
Dacre Av. Ilf —2E **34**
Dacre Clo. Gnfd —2F **55**
Dacre Gdns. SE13 —4G **97**
Dacre Pk. SE13 —3G **97**
Dacre Pl. SE13 —3G **97**
Dacre Rd. E11 —1H **49**
Dacre Rd. E13 —1K **65**

Dacre Rd. Croy —7J **123**
Dacres Est. SE23 —3K **111**
Dacres Ho. SW4 —6F **77**
Dacres Rd. SE23 —2K **111**
Dacre St. SW1 —3H **77** (6A **146**)
Dade Way. S'hall —5D **70**
Daffodil Clo. Croy —1K **135**
Daffodil Gdns. Ilf —5F **51**
Daffodil Pl. Hamp —6E **102**
Daffodil St. W12 —7B **58**
Dafforne Rd. SW17 —3E **108**
Dagenham Av. Dag —1E **68**
(in two parts)
Dagenham Rd. E10 —1B **48**
Dagenham Rd. Rain —7K **53**
Dagenham Rd. Romf —7K **37**
Dagmar Av. Wemb —4F **41**
Dagmar Ct. E14 —3E **80**
Dagmar Gdns. NW10 —2F **59**
Dagmar M. S'hall —3C 70
(off Dagmar Rd.)
Dagmar Pas. N1 —1B 62
(off Cross St.)
Dagmar Rd. N4 —7A **30**
Dagmar Rd. N15 —4D **30**
Dagmar Rd. N22 —1H **29**
Dagmar Rd. SE5 —1E **94**
Dagmar Rd. SE25 —5E **124**
Dagmar Rd. Dag —7J **53**
Dagmar Rd. King T —1F **119**
Dagmar Rd. S'hall —3C **70**
Dagmar Ter. N1 —1B **62**
Dagnall Pk. SE25 —6D **124**
Dagnall Rd. SE25 —6E **124**
Dagnall St. SW11 —2D **92**
Dagnan Rd. SW12 —7F **93**
Dagonet Gdns. Brom —3J **113**
Dagonet Rd. Brom —3J **113**
Dahlia Gdns. Ilf —6F **51**
Dahlia Gdns. Mitc —4H **123**
Dahlia Rd. SE2 —4B **84**
Dahomey Rd. SW16 —6G **109**
Daimler Way. Wall —7J **133**
Daines Clo. E12 —3D **50**
Dainford Clo. Brom —5F **113**
Dainton Clo. Brom —1K **127**
Daintry Clo. Harr —4A **24**
Daintry Way. E9 —6B **48**
Dairsie Ct. Brom —2A **128**
Dairsie Rd. SE9 —3E **98**
Dairy Clo. T Hth —2C **124**
Dairy La. SE18 —4D **82**
Dairy M. SW9 —3J **93**
Dairy Wlk. SW19 —4G **107**
Daisy Clo. Croy —1K **135**
Daisy Dobbins Wlk. N19 —7J 29
(off Jessie Blythe La.)
Daisy La. SW6 —3J **91**
Daisy Rd. E16 —4G **65**
Daisy Rd. E18 —2K **33**
Dakota Gdns. N'holt —3C **54**
Dalberg Rd. SW2 —4A **94**
Dalberg Way. SE2 —3D **84**
Dalby Rd. SW18 —4A **92**
Dalby St. NW5 —6F **45**
Dalbys Cres. N17 —6K **17**
Dalcross Rd. Houn —2C **86**
Dale Av. Edgw —1F **25**
Dale Av. Houn —3C **86**
Dalebury Rd. SW17 —2D **108**
Dale Clo. SE3 —3J **97**
Dale Clo. Barn —6E **4**
Dale Gdns. Wfd G —4E **20**
Dale Grn. Rd. N11 —3A **16**
Dale Gro. N12 —5F **15**
Daleham Gdns. NW3 —5B **44**
Daleham M. NW3 —6B **44**

Dale Lodge. N6 —6G **29**
Dale Pk. Av. Cars —2D **132**
Dale Pk. Rd. SE19 —1D **124**
Dale Rd. NW5 —5E **44**
Dale Rd. SE17 —6B **78**
Dale Rd. Gnfd —5F **55**
Dale Rd. Sutt —4H **131**
Dale Row. W11 —6G **59**
Daleside Rd. SW16 —5F **109**
Daleside Rd. Eps —6A **130**
Dale St. W4 —5A **74**
Dale View Av. E4 —2K **19**
Dale View Cres. E4 —2K **19**
Dale View Gdns. E4 —3A **20**
Daleview Rd. N15 —6E **30**
Dalewood Gdns. Wor Pk —2D **130**
Dale Wood Rd. Orp —7J **129**
Daley St. E9 —6K **47**
Daley Thompson Way. SW8 —3F **93**
Dalgarno Gdns. W10 —5E **58**
Dalgarno Way. W10 —4E **58**
Dalgleish St. E14 —6A **64**
Daling Way. E3 —2A **64**
Dalkeith Gro. Stan —5J **11**
Dalkeith Rd. SE21 —1C **110**
Dalkeith Rd. Ilf —3G **51**
Dallas Rd. NW4 —7C **26**
Dallas Rd. SE26 —3H **111**
Dallas Rd. W5 —5F **57**
Dallas Rd. Sutt —6G **131**
Dallinger Rd. SE12 —6H **97**
Dalling Rd. W6 —4D **74**
Dallington St. EC1 —4B **62** (3K **141**)
Dallin Rd. SE18 —7F **83**
Dallin Rd. Bexh —4D **100**
Dalmain Rd. SE23 —1K **111**
Dalmally Rd. Croy —7F **125**
Dalmeny Av. N7 —4H **45**
Dalmeny Av. SW16 —2A **124**
Dalmeny Clo. Wemb —6C **40**
Dalmeny Cres. Houn —4H **87**
Dalmeny Rd. N7 —3H **45**
Dalmeny Rd. Barn —6F **5**
Dalmeny Rd. Cars —7E **132**
Dalmeny Rd. Eri —1H **101**
Dalmeny Rd. Wor Pk —3D **130**
Dalmeyer Rd. NW10 —6B **42**
Dalmore Rd. SE21 —2C **110**
Dalrymple Clo. N14 —7C **6**
Dalrymple Rd. SE4 —4A **96**
Dalston Cross Shopping Cen. E8
　　　　—6F **47**
Dalston Gdns. Stan —1E **24**
Dalston La. E8 —6F **47**
Dalton Av. Mitc —2C **122**
Dalton Rd. W'stone —2H **23**
Dalton St. SE27 —2B **110**
Dalwood St. SE5 —1E **94**
Daly Ct. E15 —5D **48**
Dalyell Rd. SW9 —3J **93**
Damascene Wlk. SE21 —1C **106**
Damask Cres. E16 —4G **65**
Damer Ter. SW10 —7A **76**
Dames Rd. E7 —3J **49**
Dame St. N1 —2C **62**
Damien St. E1 —6H **63**
Damon Clo. Sidc —3B **116**
Damsonwood Rd. S'hall —3E **70**
Danbrook Rd. SW16 —1J **123**
Danbury Clo. Romf —3D **36**
Danbury Mans. Bark —7F 51
(off Whiting Av.)
Danbury M. Wall —4F **133**
Danbury St. N1 —2B **62**
Danbury Way. Wfd G —6F **21**
Danby Ct. Enf —3H 7
(off Horshoe La.)
Danby St. SE15 —3F **95**
Dancer Rd. SW6 —1H **91**

Dancer Rd. Rich —3G **89**
Dando Cres. SE3 —3K **97**
Dandridge Clo. SE10 —5H **81**
Danebury. New Ad —6D **136**
Danebury Av. SW15 —6A **90**
(in two parts)
Daneby Rd. SE6 —3D **112**
Dane Clo. Bex —7G **101**
Danecourt Gdns. Croy —3F **135**
Danecroft Rd. SE24 —5C **94**
Danehill Wlk. Sidc —3A **116**
Dane Ho. N14 —7C **6**
Danehurst Gdns. Ilf —5C **34**
Danehurst St. SW6 —1G **91**
Daneland. Barn —6J **5**
Danemead Gro. N'holt —5F **39**
Danemere St. SW15 —3E **90**
Dane Pl. E3 —2B 64
Dane Rd. N18 —4D **18**
Dane Rd. SW19 —1A **122**
Dane Rd. W13 —1C **72**
Dane Rd. Ilf —5G **51**
Dane Rd. S'hall —7C **54**
Danesbury Rd. Felt —1A **102**
Danescombe. SE12 —1J **113**
Danes Ct. Wemb —3H **41**
Danescourt Cres. Sutt —2A **132**
Danescroft. NW4 —5F **27**
Danescroft Av. NW4 —5F **27**
Danescroft Gdns. NW4 —5F **27**
Danesdale Rd. E9 —6A **48**
Danesfield. SE17 —6E 78
(off Albany Rd.)
Danes Ga. Harr —3J **23**
Danes Rd. Romf —7J **37**
Dane St. WC1 —5K **61** (6E **140**)
Daneswood Av. SE6 —3E **112**
Danethorpe Rd. Wemb —6D **40**
Danette Gdns. Dag —2G **53**
Daneville Rd. SE5 —1D **94**
Daniel Bolt Clo. E14 —5D 64
Daniel Clo. N18 —4D **18**
Daniel Clo. SW17 —6C **108**
Daniel Ct. NW9 —1A **26**
Daniel Gdns. SE15 —7F **79**
Daniel Ho. N1 —2D **62**
(off Cranston Est.)
Daniel Pl. NW4 —7C **26**
Daniel Rd. W5 —7F **57**
Daniels Rd. SE15 —3J **95**
Danleigh Ct. N14 —7C **6**
Dan Leno Wlk. SW6 —7K **75**
Dansey Pl. W1 —7H 61 (9A 140)
(off Wardour St.)
Dansington Rd. Well —4A **100**
Danson Cres. Well —3B **100**
Danson La. Well —4B **100**
Danson Mead. Well —3C **100**
Danson Rd. Bex & Bexh —5D **100**
(in two parts)
Danson Underpass. Sidc —6C **100**
Dante Pl. SE11 —4B 78 (9K 147)
(off Dante Rd.)
Dante Rd. SE11 —4B **78** (8J **147**)
Danube St. SW3 —5C **76**
Danvers Rd. N8 —4H **29**
Danvers St. SW3 —6B **76**
Daphne Gdns. E4 —3K **19**
Daphne Ho. N22 —1A 30
(off Acacia Rd.)
Daphne St. SW18 —6A **92**
Daplyn St. E1 —5G **63**
D'Arblay St. W1 —6G **61** (8M **139**)
Darcy Av. Wall —4G **133**
Darcy Clo. N20 —2G **15**
D'Arcy Dri. Harr —4D **24**
Darcy Gdns. Dag —1F **69**

D'Arcy Gdns. Harr —4D 24
Darcy Rd. SW16 —2J 123
D'Arcy Rd. Sutt —4F 131
Dare Ct. E10 —7E 32
Dare Gdns. Dag —3E 52
Darell Rd. Rich —3G 89
Darenth Rd. N16 —7F 31
Darenth Rd. Well —1A 100
Darfield Rd. SE4 —5B 96
Darfield Way. W10 —6F 59
Darfur St. SW15 —3F 91
Dargate Clo. SE19 —7F 111
Darien Rd. SW11 —3B 92
Dark Ho. Wharf. EC3
—7D 62 (1B 148)
Darlan Rd. SW6 —7H 75
Darlaston Rd. SW19 —7F 107
Darley Clo. Croy —6A 126
Darley Dri. N Maid —2C 119
Darley Gdns. Mord —6A 122
Darley Ho. SE11 —5K 77
(off Laud St.)
Darley Rd. N9 —1A 18
Darley Rd. SW11 —6D 92
Darling Rd. SE4 —3C 96
Darling Row. E1 —4H 63
Darlington Rd. SE27 —5B 110
Darmaine Clo. S Croy —7C 134
Darnay Ho. SE16 —3G 79
Darnley Rd. E9 —6J 47
Darnley Rd. Wfd G —1J 33
Darnley Ter. W11 —1F 75
Darrell Rd. SE22 —5G 95
Darren Clo. N4 —7K 29
Darris Clo. Hay —4C 54
Darsley Dri. SW8 —1H 93
Dartford. N9 —6D 8
Dartford By-Pass. Bex & Dart
—1K 117
Dartford Rd. Bex —1J 117
Dartford St. SE17 —6C 78
Dartington Ho. SW8 —2H 93
(off Union Gro.)
Dartmoor Wlk. E14 —4C 80
(off Charnwood Gdns.)
Dartmouth Clo. W11 —6J 59
Dartmouth Ct. SE10 —1F 97
Dartmouth Gro. SE10 —1E 96
Dartmouth Hill. SE10 —1E 96
Dartmouth Pk. Av. NW5 —3F 45
Dartmouth Pk. Hill. N19 & NW5
—1F 45
Dartmouth Pk. Rd. NW5 —4F 45
Dartmouth Pl. SE23 —2J 111
Dartmouth Pl. W4 —6A 74
Dartmouth Rd. NW2 —6F 43
Dartmouth Rd. NW4 —6C 26
Dartmouth Rd. SE26 & SE23
—3H 111
Dartmouth Rd. Brom —7J 127
Dartmouth Row. SE10 —1E 96
Dartmouth St. SW1 —2H 77 (5B 146)
Dartmouth Ter. SE10 —1F 97
Dartnell Rd. Croy —7F 125
Darton Ct. W3 —1J 73
Dartrey Tower. SW10 —7A 76
(off Worlds End Est.)
Dartrey Wlk. SW10 —7B 76
Dart St. W10 —3G 59
Darville Rd. N16 —3F 47
Darwell Clo. E6 —2E 66
Darwin Clo. N11 —3A 16
Darwin Dri. S'hall —6F 55
Darwin Rd. N22 —1B 30
Darwin Rd. W5 —5C 72
Darwin Rd. Well —3K 99
Darwin St. SE17 —4D 78 (8B 148)
(in two parts)

Daryngton Dri. Gnfd —2J 55
Dashwood Clo. Bexh —5G 101
Dashwood Rd. N8 —6K 29
Dassett Rd. SE27 —5B 110
Datchelor Pl. SE5 —1D 94
Datchet Rd. SE6 —2B 112
Datchworth Ct. Enf —5K 7
Date St. SE17 —5D 78
Daubeney Gdns. N17 —7H 17
Daubeney Rd. E5 —4A 48
Daubeney Rd. N17 —7H 17
Dault Rd. SW18 —6A 92
Dauncey Ho. SE1 —2B 78 (5J 147)
(off Webber Row)
Davema Clo. Chst —1E 128
Davenant Rd. N19 —2H 45
Davenant Rd. Croy —4B 134
Davenant St. E1 —5G 63
Davenport Clo. Tedd —6A 104
Davenport Ho. SE11
—4A 78 (8G 147)
(off Walnut Tree Wlk.)
Davenport Lodge. Houn —7C 70
Davenport Rd. SE6 —6D 96
Davenport Rd. Sidc —2E 116
Daventer Dri. Stan —7E 10
Daventry Av. E17 —6C 32
Daventry St. NW1 —5C 60 (5C 138)
Daver Ct. SW3 —5C 76
Davern Clo. SE10 —4H 81
Davey Clo. N7 —6K 45
Davey Rd. E9 —7C 48
Davey's Ct. WC2 —7J 61 (9C 140)
(off Bedfordbury)
Davey St. SE15 —6F 79
David Av. Gnfd —3J 55
David Coffer Ct. Belv —4H 85
David Ho. Sidc —3A 116
David Lee Point. E15 —1G 65
(off Leather Gdns.)
David M. W1 —5D 60 (5G 139)
David Rd. Dag —2E 52
Davidson Gdns. SW8 —7J 77
Davidson La. Harr —7K 23
Davidson Rd. Croy —7E 124
Davidson Ter. E7 —5K 49
(off Claremont Rd.)
Davidson Ter. E7 —5K 49
(off Windsor Rd.)
David's Rd. SE23 —1J 111
David St. E15 —6F 49
David's Way. Ilf —1J 35
Davies La. E11 —2G 49
Davies M. W1 —7F 61 (9J 139)
Davies St. W1 —6F 61 (8J 139)
Davington Gdns. Dag —5B 52
Davington Rd. Dag —6B 52
Davinia Clo. Wfd G —6J 21
Davis Rd. W3 —1B 74
Davis St. E13 —2K 65
Davisville Rd. W12 —2C 74
Davmor Ct. Bren —5C 72
Dawes Av. Iswth —5A 88
Dawes Rd. SW6 —7G 75
Dawes St. SE17 —5D 78
Dawlish Av. N13 —4D 16
Dawlish Av. SW18 —2K 107
Dawlish Av. Gnfd —2A 56
Dawlish Dri. Ilf —4J 51
Dawlish Dri. Pinn —5C 22
Dawlish Rd. E10 —1E 48
Dawlish Rd. N17 —3G 31
Dawlish Rd. NW2 —6F 43

Dawnay Gdns. SW18 —2B 108
Dawnay Rd. SW18 —2A 108
Dawn Clo. Houn —3C 86
Dawn Cres. E15 —1F 65
Dawpool Rd. NW2 —2B 42
Daws Hill. E4 —2K 9
Daws La. NW7 —5G 13
Dawson Av. Bark —7J 51
Dawson Clo. SE18 —4G 83
Dawson Gdns. Bark —7K 51
Dawson Pl. W2 —7J 59
Dawson Rd. NW2 —5E 42
Dawson Rd. King T —3F 119
Dawson St. E2 —2F 63
Dawson Ter. N9 —7D 8
Daybrook Rd. SW19 —2K 121
Daylesford Av. SW15 —4C 90
Daymer Gdns. Pinn —4A 22
Daysbrook Rd. SW2 —1K 109
Days La. Sidc —7J 99
Dayton Gro. SE15 —1J 95
Deaconess Ct. N15 —4F 31
(off Tottenham Grn. E.)
Deacon Est., The. E4 —6G 19
Deacon Rd. NW2 —5C 42
Deacon Rd. King T —1F 119
Deacons Clo. Pinn —2A 22
Deacons Ct. Twic —2K 103
Deacons Wlk. Hamp —4E 102
Deacon Way. SE17 —4C 78 (8L 147)
Deacon Way. Wfd G —6J 21
Deal Porters Way. SE16 —3J 79
Deal Rd. SW17 —6E 108
Deal's Gateway. SE10 —1C 96
Deal St. E1 —5G 63
Dealtry Rd. SW15 —4E 90
Deal Wlk. SW9 —7A 78
Dean Bradley St. SW1
—3J 77 (7C 146)
Dean Clo. E9 —5J 47
Dean Clo. SE16 —1K 79
Dean Ct. Edgw —6C 12
Dean Ct. Romf —5K 37
Dean Ct. Wemb —3E 40
Deancross St. E1 —6J 63
Dean Dri. Stan —2E 24
Deane Av. Ruis —5A 38
Deane Croft Rd. Pinn —6A 22
Deanery Clo. N2 —4C 28
Deanery M. W1 —1E 76 (2H 145)
(off Deanery St.)
Deanery Rd. E15 —7G 49
Deanery St. W1 —1E 76 (2H 145)
Dean Farrar St. SW1
—3H 77 (6B 146)
Dean Gdns. E17 —4F 33
Deanhill Ct. SW14 —4H 89
Deanhill Rd. SW14 —4H 89
Dean Rd. NW2 —6E 42
Dean Rd. Croy —4D 134
Dean Rd. Hamp —5E 102
Dean Rd. Houn —5F 87
Dean Ryle St. SW1 —4J 77 (8C 146)
Deansbrook Clo. Edgw —7D 12
Deansbrook Rd. Edgw —7C 12
Dean's Bldgs. SE17 —4D 78 (9A 148)
Deans Clo. W4 —6H 73
Deans Clo. Croy —3F 135
Deans Clo. Edgw —6D 12
Deans Ct. EC4 —6B 62 (8K 141)
Deanscroft Av. NW9 —1J 41
Deans Dri. N13 —6G 17
Deans Dri. NW7 —5E 12
Deans Dri. Edgw —5E 12
Deans Ga. Clo. SE23 —3K 111
Deans La. W4 —6H 73
(off Deans Clo.)

Deans La. Edgw —6D 12
Dean's M. W1 —6F 61 (7K 139)
Dean's Pl. SW1 —5H 77
Deans Rd. W7 —1K 71
Deans Rd. Sutt —3K 131
Dean Stanley St. SW1
—3J 77 (7C 146)
Deanston Wharf. E16 —2K 81
Dean St. E7 —5J 49
Dean St. W1 —6H 61 (7A 140)
Deansway. N2 —4B 28
Deansway. N9 —3K 17
Deans Way. Edgw —5D 12
Deanswood. N11 —6C 16
Dean's Yd. SW1 —3H 77 (6B 146)
(off Sanctuary, The)
Dean Trench St. SW1
—3J 77 (7C 146)
Dean Wlk. Edgw —6D 12
Dearne Clo. Stan —5F 11
Dearn Gdns. Mitc —3C 122
Deason St. E15 —1E 64
Deauville Ct. SW4 —6G 93
De Barowe M. N5 —4B 46
Debden. N7 —20 30
(off Gloucester Rd.)
Debden Clo. Wfd G —7F 21
De Beauvoir Cres. N1 —1E 62
De Beauvoir Est. N1 —1E 62
De Beauvoir Pl. N1 —6E 46
De Beauvoir Rd. N1 —1E 62
De Beauvoir Sq. N1 —7E 46
Debnams Rd. SE16 —4J 79
De Bohun Av. N14 —6A 6
Deborah Clo. Iswth —1J 87
Deborah Ct. E18 —3K 33
(off Victoria Rd.)
Deborah Lodge. Edgw —1H 25
Debrabant Clo. Eri —6K 85
De Bruin Ct. E14 —5E 80
De Burgh Rd. SW19 —7A 108
Debussy. NW9 —2B 26
Decima St. SE1 —3E 78 (6C 148)
Deck Clo. SE16 —1K 79
Decoy Av. NW11 —5G 27
De Crespigny Pk. SE5 —2D 94
Deeley Rd. SW8 —1H 93
Deena Clo. W3 —6F 57
Deepdale. SW19 —4F 107
Deepdale Av. Brom —4H 127
Deepdene. W5 —4F 57
Deepdene Av. Croy —3F 135
Deepdene Clo. E11 —4J 33
Deepdene Ct. N21 —6G 7
Deepdene Gdns. SW2 —7K 93
Deepdene Rd. SE5 —4D 94
Deepdene Rd. Well —3A 100
Deepwell Clo. Iswth —1A 88
Deepwood La. Gnfd —3H 55
Deerbrook Rd. SE24 —1B 110
Deerdale Rd. SE24 —4C 94
Deerhurst Rd. NW2 —6F 43
Deerhurst Rd. SW16 —5K 109
Deerleap Gro. E4 —5J 9
Dee Rd. Rich —4F 89
Deer Pk. Clo. King T —7H 105
Deer Pk. Gdns. Mitc —4B 122
Deer Pk. Rd. SW19 —2K 121
Deer Pk. Way. W Wick —2H 137
Deeside Rd. SW17 —3B 108
Dee St. E14 —6E 64
Defiance Wlk. SE18 —3D 82
Defoe Av. Rich —7G 73

Defoe Clo. SE16 —2B 80
Defoe Clo. SW17 —6C 108
Defoe Ho. EC2 —5C 62 (5L 141)
(off Barbican)
Defoe Pl. EC2 —5C 62 (5M 141)
(off Beech St.)
Defoe Rd. N16 —3E 46
De Frene Rd. SE26 —4K 111
Degema Rd. Chst —5F 115
Dehar Cres. NW9 —7B 26
Dehavilland Clo. N'holt —3B 54
De Havilland Rd. Edgw —2H 25
De Havilland Rd. Houn —7A 70
De Havilland Rd. Wall —7J 133
Dekker Rd. SE21 —6E 94
Delacourt Rd. SE3 —7K 81
Delafield Rd. SE7 —5K 81
Delaford Rd. SE16 —5H 79
Delaford St. SW6 —7G 75
Delamere Cres. Croy —6J 125
Delamere Gdns. NW7 —6E 12
Delamere Rd. SW20 —1F 121
Delamere Rd. W5 —2E 72
Delamere Rd. Hay —7B 54
Delamere Ter. W2 —5K 59
Delancey Pas. NW1 —1F 61
(off Delancey St.)
Delancey St. NW1 —1F 61
De Laune St. SE17 —5B 78
Delaware Mans. W9 —4K 59
(off Delaware Rd.)
Delaware Rd. W9 —4K 59
Delawyk Cres. SE24 —6C 94
Delcombe Av. Wor Pk —1E 130
Delderfield Ho. Romf —2K 37
(off Portnoi Clo.)
Delft Way. SE22 —5E 94
Delhi Rd. Enf —7A 8
Delhi St. N1 —1J 61
Delia St. SW18 —7K 91
Delia Path. E5 —3G 47
Dell Clo. E15 —1F 65
Dell Clo. Wall —4H 133
Dell Clo. Wfd G —3E 20
Dellfield Clo. Beck —1E 126
Dell La. Eps —5C 130
Dellors Clo. Barn —5A 4
Dellow Clo. Ilf —7H 35
Dellow St. E1 —7H 63
Dell Rd. Enf —1D 8
Dell Rd. Eps —6C 130
Dells Clo. E4 —7J 9
Dell's M. SW1 —4G 77 (9M 145)
(off Churton Pl,)
Dell, The. SE2 —5A 84
Dell, The. SE19 —1F 125
Dell, The. Bex —1K 117
Dell, The. Bren —6C 72
Dell, The. Pinn —2B 22
Dell, The. Wemb —5B 40
Dell, The. Wfd G —3E 20
Dell Wlk. N Mald —2A 120
Dell Way. W13 —6C 56
Dellwood Gdns. Ilf —3E 34
Delmare Clo. SW9 —4K 93
Delme Cres. SE3 —2K 97
Delmey Clo. Croy —3F 135
Delorme St. W6 —6F 75
Delroy Ct. N20 —7F 5
Delta Bus. Pk. SW18 —4K 91
Delta Cen. Wemb —1F 57
Delta Clo. Wor Pk —3B 130
Delta Ct. NW2 —2C 42
Delta Gro. N'holt —3B 54
Delta Rd. Wor Pk —3A 130
Delta St. E2 —3G 63
De Luci Rd. Eri —5J 85
De Lucy St. SE2 —4B 84

Delvan Clo. SE18 —7E 82
Delvers Mead. Dag —4J 53
Delverton Rd. SE17 —5B 78
Delvino Rd. SW6 —1J 91
Demead Way. SE15 —7F 79
(off Pentridge St.)
Demesne Rd. Wall —4H 133
Demeta Clo. Wemb —3J 41
De Montfort Rd. SW16 —2J 109
De Morgan Rd. SW6 —3K 91
Dempster Clo. Surb —7C 118
Dempster Rd. SW18 —5A 92
Denbar Pde. Romf —4J 37
Denberry Dri. Sidc —3B 116
Denbigh Clo. NW10 —7A 42
Denbigh Clo. W11 —7H 59
Denbigh Clo. Chst —6D 114
Denbigh Clo. S'hall —5H 131
Denbigh Ct. E6 —3B 66
Denbigh Gdns. Rich —5F 89
Denbigh M. SW1 —4G 77 (9L 145)
(off Denbigh St.)
Denbigh Pl. SW1 —5G 77
Denbigh Rd. E6 —3B 66
Denbigh Rd. W11 —7H 59
Denbigh Rd. W13 —7B 56
Denbigh Rd. Houn —2F 87
Denbigh Rd. S'hall —6D 54
Denbigh Rd. SW1 —4G 77 (9L 145)
Denbigh Ter. W11 —7H 59
Denbridge Rd. Brom —2D 128
Denby Ct. SE11 —4K 77 (8F 146)
(off Lambeth Wlk.)
Denchworth Ho. SW9 —2A 94
Den Clo. Beck —3F 127
Dene Av. Houn —3D 86
Dene Av. Sidc —7B 100
Dene Clo. SE4 —3A 96
Dene Clo. Brom —1H 137
Dene Clo. Wor Pk —2B 130
Dene Ct. W5 —5C 56
Dene Gdns. Stan —5H 11
Denehurst Gdns. NW4 —6E 26
Denehurst Gdns. W3 —1H 73
Denehurst Gdns. Rich —4G 89
Denehurst Gdns. Twic —7H 87
Denehurst Gdns. Wfd G —4E 20
Dene Rd. N11 —1J 15
Dene Rd. Buck H —1G 21
Denesmead. SE24 —5C 94
Dene, The. W13 —6B 56
Dene, The. Croy —4K 135
Dene, The. Wemb —4E 40
Denewood. Barn —4F 5
Denewood Rd. N6 —6D 28
Denford St. SE10 —5H 81
Dengarth Rd. N'holt —1C 54
Dengie Wlk. N1 —1C 62
(off Basire St.)
Denham Clo. Well —3C 100
Denham Ct. SE26 —3H 111
Denham Cres. Mitc —4D 122
Denham Dri. Ilf —6G 35
Denham Ho. W12 —7D 58
(off White City Est.)
Denham Rd. N20 —3J 15
Denham Rd. Felt —7A 86
Denham St. SE10 —5J 81
Denham Way. Bark —1J 67
Denholme Rd. W9 —3H 59
Denison Clo. N2 —3A 28
Denison Rd. SW19 —6B 108
Denison Rd. W5 —4C 56
Deniston Av. Bex —1E 116
Denis Way. SW4 —3H 93
Denleigh Gdns. N21 —1F 17
Denman Dri. NW11 —5J 27

Denman Dri. N. NW11 —5J 27
Denman Dri. S. NW11 —5J 27
Denman Rd. SE15 —1F 95
Denman St. W1 —7H 61
Denmark Av. SW19 —7G 107
Denmark Ct. Mord —6J 121
Denmark Gdns. Cars —3D 132
Denmark Gro. N1 —2A 62
Denmark Hill. SE5 —1D 94
Denmark Hill Dri. NW9 —4C 26
Denmark Hill Est. SE5 —4D 94
Denmark Path. SE25 —5H 125
Denmark Pl. WC2 —6H 61 (7B 140)
Denmark Rd. N8 —4A 30
Denmark Rd. NW6 —2H 59
(in two parts)
Denmark Rd. SE5 —1C 94
Denmark Rd. SE25 —5G 125
Denmark Rd. SW19 —6F 107
Denmark Rd. W13 —7B 56
Denmark Rd. Brom —1K 127
Denmark Rd. Cars —3D 132
Denmark Rd. King T —3E 118
Denmark Rd. Twic —3H 103
Denmark St. E11 —3G 49
Denmark St. E13 —5K 65
Denmark St. N17 —1H 31
Denmark St. WC2 —6H 61 (8B 140)
Denmark Ter. N2 —3D 28
Denmark Wlk. SE27 —4C 110
Denmead Rd. Croy —1B 134
Dennan Rd. Surb —7F 119
Denner Rd. E4 —2H 19
Denne Ter. E8 —1F 63
Dennett Rd. Croy —1A 134
Dennetts Gro. SE14 —1J 95
Dennett's Rd. SE14 —2K 95
Denning Av. Croy —4A 134
Denning Clo. NW8 —3A 60
Denning Clo. Hamp —5D 102
Denning Rd. NW3 —4B 44
Dennington Clo. E5 —2J 47
Dennington Pk. Rd. NW6 —6J 43
Denningtons, The. Wor Pk —2A 130
Dennis Av. Wemb —5F 41
Dennis Gdns. Stan —5H 11
Dennis Ho. Sutt —4K 131
Dennis La. Stan —3G 11
Dennison Gro. SE14 —3K 89
Dennison Point. E15 —7E 48
Dennis Pde. N14 —1C 16
Dennis Pk. Cres. SW20 —1G 121
Dennis Reeve Clo. Mitc —1D 122
Dennis Rd. E Mol —4H 117
Denny Clo. E6 —5C 66
Denny Cres. SE11 —5A 78
Denny Gdns. Dag —7C 52
Denny Rd. N9 —1C 18
Denny St. SE11 —5A 78
Den Rd. Brom —3F 127
Densham Rd. E15 —1G 65
Densole Clo. Beck —1A 126
Densworth Gro. N9 —2D 18
Denton Rd. N8 —5K 29
Denton Rd. N18 —4K 17
Denton Rd. NW10 —7J 41
Denton Rd. Bex —1K 117
Denton Rd. Twic —6D 88
Denton Rd. Well —7C 84
Denton St. SW18 —6K 91
Denton Ter. Bex —2K 117
Denton Way. E5 —3K 47
Dents Rd. SW11 —6D 92
Denver Clo. Orp —6J 129
Denver Rd. N16 —7E 30
Denyer St. SW3 —4C 76 (9D 144)
Denzil Rd. NW10 —5B 42
Deodara Clo. N20 —3H 15
Deodar Rd. SW15 —4G 91

Depot App. N3 —1K 27
Depot App. NW2 —4F 43
Depot App. NW10 —7H 41
Depot Rd. Houn —3H 87
Depot St. SE5 —6D 78
Deptford B'way. SE8 —1C 96
Deptford Church St. SE8 —6C 80
Deptford Ferry Rd. E14 —4C 80
Deptford Grn. SE8 —6C 80
Deptford High St. SE8 —6C 80
Deptford Pk. Bus. Cen. SE8 —5A 80
Deptford Strand. SE8 —4B 80
Deptford Wharf. SE8 —4B 80
De Quincey Rd. N17 —1D 30
Derby Av. N12 —5F 15
Derby Av. Harr —1H 23
Derby Av. Romf —6J 37
Derby Est. Houn —4F 87
Derby Ga. SW1 —2J 77 (4C 146)
Derby Hill. SE23 —2J 111
Derby Hill Cres. SE23 —2J 111
Derby Ho. SE11 —4A 78 (8G 147)
(off Walnut Tree Wlk.)
Derby Rd. E7 —7B 50
Derby Rd. E9 —1K 63
Derby Rd. E18 —1H 33
Derby Rd. N18 —5D 18
Derby Rd. SW14 —4H 89
Derby Rd. SW19 —7J 107
Derby Rd. Croy —1B 134
Derby Rd. Enf —5C 8
Derby Rd. Gnfd —1F 55
Derby Rd. Houn —4F 87
Derby Rd. Surb —7G 119
Derby Rd. Sutt —6H 131
Derbyshire St. E2 —3G 63
Derby St. W1 —1E 76 (3H 145)
Dereham Pl. EC2 —3E 62 (2D 142)
Dereham Rd. Bark —5K 51
Derek Av. Wall —4F 133
Derek Av. Wemb —7H 41
Derek Walcott Clo. SE24 —5B 94
Dericote St. E8 —1H 63
Derifall Clo. E6 —5D 66
Dering Pl. Croy —4C 134
Dering Rd. Croy —4C 134
Dering St. W1 —6F 61 (8J 139)
Dering Yd. W1 —6F 61 (8K 139)
Derinton Rd. SW17 —4D 108
Derley Rd. S'hall —3A 70
Dermody Gdns. SE13 —5F 97
Dermody Rd. SE13 —5F 97
Deronda Est. SW2 —1B 110
Deronda Rd. SE24 —1B 110
Deroy Clo. Cars —6D 132
Derrick Gdns. SE7 —4A 82
Derrick Rd. Beck —3B 126
Derry Rd. Croy —3J 133
Derry St. W8 —2K 75
Dersingham Av. E12 —4D 50
Dersingham Rd. NW2 —3G 43
Derwent Av. N18 —5J 17
Derwent Av. NW7 —6E 12
Derwent Av. NW9 —5A 26
Derwent Av. SW15 —4A 106
Derwent Av. Barn —1J 15
Derwent Clo. N20 —3F 15
Derwent Cres. Bexh —2G 101
Derwent Cres. Stan —2C 24
Derwent Dri. Orp —7H 129
Derwent Gdns. Ilf —4C 34
Derwent Gdns. Wemb —7C 24
Derwent Gro. SE22 —4F 95
Derwent Ho. SE20 —2H 125
(off Derwent Rd.)
Derwent Lodge. Iswth —2H 87

Derwent Lodge. Wor Pk —2D 130
Derwent Rise. NW9 —6A 26
Derwent Rd. N13 —4E 16
Derwent Rd. SE20 —2G 125
Derwent Rd. SW20 —5F 121
Derwent Rd. W5 —3C 72
Derwent Rd. S'hall —6E 54
Derwent Rd. Twic —6F 87
Derwent St. SE10 —5G 81
Derwent Wlk. Wall —7F 133
Derwentwater Rd. W3 —1J 73
Derwent Yd. W5 —3C 72
(off Derwent Rd.)
Desborough Ho. W14 —6H 75
(off North End Rd.)
Desenfans Rd. SE21 —6E 94
Desford Rd. E16 —4G 65
Desmond Ho. Barn —6H 5
Desmond St. SE14 —7A 80
Desmond Tutu Ho. Wemb —7F 25
Despard Rd. N19 —1G 45
Detling Rd. Brom —5J 113
Detling Rd. Eri —7K 85
Detmold Rd. E5 —2J 47
Devalls Clo. E6 —7F 67
Devana End. Cars —3D 132
Devas Rd. SW20 —1E 120
Devas St. E3 —4D 64
Devenay Rd. E15 —7H 49
Devenish Rd. SE2 —2A 84
Deventer Cres. SE22 —5E 94
De Vere Gdns. W8 —2A 76
De Vere Gdns. Ilf —2D 50
Deverell St. SE1 —3D 78 (7A 148)
De Vere M. W8 —3A 76
(off De Vere Gdns.)
Devereux Ct. WC2 —6A 62 (8G 141)
(off Essex St.)
Devereux Rd. SW11 —6D 92
Deveron Way. Romf —1K 37
Devon Av. Twic —1G 103
Devon Clo. N17 —3F 31
Devon Clo. Buck H —2E 20
Devon Clo. Gnfd —1C 56
Devon Ct. Hamp —7E 102
Devoncroft Gdns. Twic —7A 88
Devon Gdns. N4 —6B 30
Devonhurst Pl. W4 —5K 73
Devonia Gdns. N18 —6H 17
Devonia Rd. N1 —2B 62
Devonport Gdns. Ilf —6D 34
Devonport M. W12 —2D 74
Devonport Rd. W12 —1D 74
Devonport St. E1 —6K 63
Devon Rise. N2 —4B 28
Devon Rd. Bark —1J 67
Devon Rd. Sutt —7G 131
Devons Est. E3 —3D 64
Devonshire Av. Sutt —7A 132
Devonshire Clo. E15 —4G 49
Devonshire Clo. N13 —3F 17
Devonshire Clo. W1 —5F 61 (5J 139)
Devonshire Ct. Pinn —1D 22
(off Devonshire Rd.)
Devonshire Cres. NW7 —7A 14
Devonshire Dri. SE10 —7D 80
Devonshire Gdns. N17 —6H 17
Devonshire Gdns. N21 —7H 7
Devonshire Gdns. W4 —7J 73
Devonshire Gro. SE15 —6H 79
Devonshire Hill La. N17 —6H 17
Devonshire Ho. Sutt —7A 132
Devonshire M. N13 —4F 17
Devonshire M. W4 —5A 74
Devonshire M. N. W1
      —5F 61 (5J 139)
Devonshire M. S. W1
      —5F 61 (5J 139)

Devonshire M. W. W1
      —4E 60 (4H 139)
Devonshire Pas. W4 —5A 74
Devonshire Pl. NW2 —3J 43
Devonshire Pl. W1 —4E 60 (4H 139)
Devonshire Pl. W4 —5A 74
Devonshire Pl. W8 —3K 75
Devonshire Pl. M. W1
      —5E 60 (5H 139)
Devonshire Rd. E15 —4G 49
Devonshire Rd. E16 —6K 65
Devonshire Rd. E17 —6C 32
Devonshire Rd. N9 —1D 18
Devonshire Rd. N13 —4E 16
Devonshire Rd. N17 —6H 17
Devonshire Rd. NW7 —7A 14
Devonshire Rd. SE9 —2C 114
Devonshire Rd. SE23 —1J 111
Devonshire Rd. SW19 —7C 108
Devonshire Rd. W4 —5A 74
Devonshire Rd. W5 —3C 72
Devonshire Rd. Bexh —4E 100
Devonshire Rd. Cars —4E 132
Devonshire Rd. Croy —7D 124
Devonshire Rd. Eastc —6A 22
Devonshire Rd. Felt —3C 102
Devonshire Rd. Harr —6H 23
Devonshire Rd. Ilf —7J 35
Devonshire Rd. Orp —7K 129
Devonshire Rd. Pinn —1D 22
Devonshire Rd. S'hall —5E 54
Devonshire Rd. Sutt —7A 132
Devonshire Row. EC2
      —5E 62 (6D 142)
Devonshire Row M. W1
      —4F 61 (4K 139)
(off Devonshire St.)
Devonshire Sq. E1 —6E 62 (7D 142)
Devonshire Sq. EC2
      —6E 62 (7D 142)
Devonshire Sq. Brom —4K 127
Devonshire St. W1 —5E 60 (5H 139)
Devonshire St. W4 —5A 74
Devonshire Ter. W2 —6A 60
Devonshire Way. Croy —2A 136
Devonshire Way. Hay —6A 54
Devons Rd. E3 —5C 64
Devon St. SE15 —6H 79
Devon Waye. Houn —7D 70
De Walden St. W1 —5E 60 (6H 139)
Dewar St. SE15 —3G 95
Dewberry Gdns. E6 —5C 66
Dewberry St. E14 —5E 64
Dewey Rd. N1 —2A 62
Dewey Rd. Dag —6H 53
Dewey St. SW17 —5D 108
Dewhurst Rd. W14 —3F 75
Dewsbury Clo. Pinn —6C 22
Dewsbury Ct. W4 —4J 73
Dewsbury Gdns. Wor Pk —3C 130
Dewsbury Rd. NW10 —5C 42
Dewsbury Ter. NW1 —1F 61
Dexter Ho. Eri —3E 84
(off Kale Rd.)
Dexter Rd. Barn —6A 4
Deyncourt Rd. N17 —1C 30
Deynecourt Gdns. E11 —4A 34
D'Eynsford Rd. SE5 —1D 94
Diadem Ct. W1 —6H 61 (8A 140)
(off Dean St.)
Dial Wlk., The. W8 —2K 75
(off Broad Wlk., The)
Diameter Rd. Orp —6G 129
Diamond Clo. Dag —1C 52
Diamond Est. SW17 —3C 108
Diamond Rd. Ruis —4B 38
Diamond St. SE15 —7E 78
Diamond Ter. SE10 —1E 96

Dovedale Av. Harr —6C 24
Dovedale Av. Ilf —2E 34
Dovedale Clo. Well —2A 100
Dovedale Rise. Mitc —7D 108
Dovedale Rd. SE22 —6E 94
Dovedon Clo. N14 —2D 16
Dove Ho. Gdns. E4 —2H 19
Dovehouse Mead. Bark —2H 67
Dovehouse St. SW3 —5B 76
Dove M. SW5 —4A 76
Dove Pk. Pinn —1E 22
Dover Clo. Romf —2J 37
Dovercourt Av. T Hth —4A 124
Dovercourt Est. N1 —6D 46
Dovercourt Gdns. Stan —5K 11
Dovercourt La. Sutt —3A 132
Dovercourt Rd. SE22 —6E 94
Doverfield Rd. SW2 —7J 93
Dover Flats. SE1 —4E 78 (9D 148)
Dover Ho. SE15 —6J 79
Dover Ho. Rd. SW15 —4C 90
Doveridge Gdns. N13 —4G 17
Dove Rd. N1 —6D 46
Dove Row. E2 —1G 63
Dover Pk. Dri. SW15 —6D 90
Dover Rd. E12 —2A 50
Dover Rd. N9 —2D 18
Dover Rd. SE19 —6D 110
Dover Rd. Romf —6E 36
Dovers Gdns. Cars —3D 132
Dover St. W1 —7F 61 (1K 145)
Dover Yd. W1 —1G 77 (2L 145)
(off Berkeley St.)
Dovet Ct. SW8 —1K 93
Doveton Rd. S Croy —5D 134
Doveton St. E1 —4J 63
Dove Wlk. SW1 —5E 76
Dowanhill Rd. SE6 —1F 113
Dowdeswell Clo. SW15 —4A 90
Dowding Ho. N6 —7E 28
(off Hillcrest)
Dowding Pl. Stan —6F 11
Dowend Ct. SE15 —6E 78
(off Longhope Clo.)
Dower Av. Wall —7F 133
Dowgate Hill. EC4 —7D 62 (9A 142)
Dowland St. W10 —3G 59
Dowlas St. SE5 —7E 78
Dowman Clo. SW19 —1K 121
Downage. NW4 —3E 26
Downalong. Bush —1C 10
Downbank Av. Bexh —1K 101
Down Barns Rd. Ruis —3B 38
Downbury M. SW18 —5J 91
Down Clo. N'holt —2A 54
Downderry Rd. Brom —3F 113
Downe Clo. Well —7C 84
Down End. SE18 —7F 83
Downe Rd. Mitc —2D 122
Downers Cotts. SW4 —4G 93
Downes Ct. N21 —1F 17
Downes Pl. SE15 —6G 79
Downe Ter. Rich —6E 88
Downfield. Wor Pk —1B 130
Downfield Clo. W9 —4K 59
Down Hall Rd. King T —1D 118
Downham Clo. Romf —1G 37
Downham La. Brom —5F 113
Downham Rd. N1 —7D 46
Downham Way. Brom —5F 113
Downhills Av. N17 —3D 30
Downhills Pk. Rd. N17 —3C 30
Downhills Way. N17 —3C 30
Downhurst Av. NW7 —5E 12
Downhurst Ct. NW4 —3E 26
Downing Clo. Harr —3G 23
Downing Dri. Gnfd —1H 55

Downing Rd. Dag —7F 53
Downings. E6 —6E 66
Downing St. SW1 —2J 77 (4C 145)
Downland Clo. N20 —1F 15
Downleys Clo. SE9 —2C 114
Downman Rd. SE9 —3C 98
Down Pl. W6 —4D 74
Down Rd. Tedd —6B 104
Downs Av. Chst —5D 114
Downs Av. Pinn —6C 22
Downsbridge Rd. Beck —1F 127
Downsell Rd. E15 —4E 48
Downsfield Rd. E17 —6A 32
Downshall Av. Ilf —6J 35
Downs Hill. Beck —7F 113
Downshire Hill. NW3 —4B 44
Downside. Twic —3K 103
Downside Clo. SW19 —6A 108
Downside Cres. NW3 —5C 44
Downside Cres. W13 —4A 56
Downside Rd. Sutt —6B 132
Downside Wlk. N'holt —3D 54
Downs La. E5 —4H 47
Downs Pk. Rd. E8 & E5 —5F 47
Downs Rd. E5 —4G 47
Downs Rd. Beck —2D 126
Downs Rd. Enf —4K 7
Downs Rd. T Hth —1C 124
Downs. The. SW20 —7F 107
Down St. W1 —1F 77 (3J 145)
Down St. M. W1 —1F 77 (3J 145)
Downs View. Iswth —1K 87
Downsview Gdns. SE19 —7B 110
Downsview Rd. SE19 —7C 110
Downsway, The. Sutt —7A 132
Downton Av. SW2 —2J 109
Downtown Rd. SE16 —2A 80
Downway. N12 —7H 15
Down Way. N'holt —3A 54
Dowrey St. N1 —1A 62
Dowsett Rd. N17 —2F 31
Dowson Clo. SE5 —4D 94
Doyce St. SE1 —2C 78 (4L 147)
Doyle Gdns. NW10 —1C 58
Doyle Rd. SE25 —4G 125
D'Oyley St. SW1 —4E 76 (8G 145)
Doynton St. N19 —2F 45
Draco St. SE17 —6C 78
Dragmire La. Mitc —4B 122
Dragonfly Clo. E13 —3K 65
Dragon Yd. WC1 —6J 61 (7D 140)
(off High Holborn)
Dragoon Rd. SE8 —5B 80
Dragor Rd. NW10 —4J 57
Drake Clo. SE16 —2K 79
Drake Cres. SE28 —6C 68
Drakefell Rd. SE14 & SE4 —2K 95
Drakefield Rd. SW17 —3E 108
Drakeley Ct. N5 —4B 46
Drake Rd. SE4 —3C 96
Drake Rd. Croy —7K 123
Drake Rd. Harr —2D 38
Drake Rd. Mitc —6E 122
Drakes Courtyard. NW6 —7H 43
Drake St. WC1 —5K 61 (6E 140)
Drake St. Enf —1J 7
Drakes Wlk. E6 —1D 66
(in two parts)
Drakewood Rd. SW16 —7H 109
Draper Clo. Belv —4F 85
Draper Clo. Brom —4C 128
Draper Ho. SE1 —4C 78 (8L 147)
(off Elephant & Castle)
Drapers Gdns. EC2 —6D 62 (7B 142)
Drapers Rd. E15 —4F 49
Drapers Rd. N17 —3F 31
Drapers Rd. Enf —2G 7
Drappers Way. SE16 —4G 79

Drawdock Rd. SE10 —2F 81
Drawell Clo. SE18 —5J 83
Drax Av. SW20 —7C 106
Draxmont App. SW19 —6G 107
Draycot Rd. E11 —6K 33
Draycott Av. SW3 —4C 76 (8D 144)
Draycott Av. Harr —6B 24
Draycott Clo. Harr —6B 24
Draycott Pl. SW3 —4D 76 (9E 144)
Draycott Ter. SW3 —4D 76 (9F 144)
Dray Ct. Wor Pk —2C 130
Drayford Clo. W9 —4H 59
Dray Gdns. SW2 —5K 93
Drayson M. W8 —2J 75
Drayton Av. W13 —7A 56
Drayton Av. Orp —7F 129
Drayton Bri. Rd. W7 & W13 —7K 55
Drayton Clo. Houn —5D 86
Drayton Clo. Ilf —1H 51
Drayton Gdns. N21 —7G 7
Drayton Gdns. SW10 —5A 76
Drayton Gdns. W13 —7A 56
Drayton Grn. W13 —7A 56
Drayton Grn. Rd. W13 —7B 56
Drayton Gro. W13 —7A 56
Drayton Ho. E11 —1F 49
Drayton Pk. N5 —4A 46
Drayton Pk. M. N5 —5A 46
Drayton Rd. E11 —1F 49
Drayton Rd. N17 —2E 30
Drayton Rd. NW10 —1B 58
Drayton Rd. Croy —2B 134
Drayton Waye. Harr —6B 24
Dreadnought St. SE10 —3G 81
Dresden Clo. NW6 —6K 43
Dresden Rd. N19 —1G 45
Dressington Av. SE4 —6C 96
Drew Av. NW7 —6B 14
Drew Gdns. Gnfd —6K 39
Drew Rd. E16 —1B 82
(in three parts)
Drewstead Rd. SW16 —2H 109
Driffield Ct. NW9 —1A 26
(off Pageant Av.)
Driffield Rd. E3 —2A 64
Driftway, The. Mitc —1E 122
Drinkwater Rd. Harr —2F 39
Drive Mans. SW6 —2G 91
(off Fulham Rd.)
Drive, The. E4 —1A 20
Drive, The. E17 —4D 32
Drive, The. E18 —3J 33
Drive, The. N3 —7D 14
Drive, The. N6 —5D 28
Drive, The. N7 —6K 45
Drive, The. N11 —6C 16
Drive, The. NW10 —1B 58
Drive, The. NW11 —7G 27
Drive, The. SW16 —3K 123
Drive, The. SW20 —7E 106
Drive, The. W3 —6J 57
Drive, The. Bark —7K 51
Drive, The. Beck —1C 126
Drive, The. Bex —7D 100
Drive, The. Buck H —1F 21
Drive, The. Chst —3K 129
Drive, The. Col R —1K 37
Drive, The. Edgw —5C 12
Drive, The. Enf —1J 7
Drive, The. Eps —6B 130
Drive, The. Eri —7H 85
Drive, The. Felt —7A 86
Drive, The. Harr —7E 22
Drive, The. H Bar —3B 4
Drive, The. Houn & Iswth —2H 87
Drive, The. Ilf —7D 34
Drive, The. King T —7J 105
Drive, The. Mord —5B 122

Drive, The. New Bar —6F 5
Drive, The. Sidc —4B 116
Drive, The. Surb —7E 118
Drive, The. T Hth —4D 124
Drive, The. Wemb —2J 41
Drive, The. W Wick —7F 127
Droitwich Clo. SE26 —3G 111
Dromey Gdns. Harr —7E 10
Dromore Rd. SW15 —6G 91
Dronfield Gdns. Dag —5C 52
Droop St. W10 —3F 59
Drovers Pl. SE15 —7J 79
Drovers Rd. S Croy —5D 134
Druce Rd. SE21 —6E 94
Druid St. SE1 —2E 78 (4D 148)
Druids Way. Brom —4F 127
Druid Tower. SE14 —6A 80
Drumaline Ridge. Wor Pk —2A 130
Drummond Av. Romf —4K 37
Drummond Cen. Croy —2C 134
Drummond Cres. NW1
 —3H 61 (1A 140)
Drummond Dri. Stan —7E 10
Drummond Ga. SW1 —5H 77
Drummond Pl. Croy —2C 134
Drummond Pl. Twic —6B 88
Drummond Rd. E11 —6A 34
Drummond Rd. SE16 —3H 79
Drummond Rd. Croy —2C 134
Drummond Rd. Romf —4K 37
Drummonds, The. Buck H —2E 20
Drummond St. NW1
 —4G 61 (3L 139)
Drum St. E1 —6F 63
Drury Cres. Croy —2A 134
Drury Ind. Est. NW10 —5J 41
Drury La. WC2 —6J 61 (7D 140)
Drury Rd. Harr —7G 23
Drury Way. NW10 —5K 41
Dryad St. SW15 —3F 91
Dryburgh Gdns. NW9 —3G 25
Dryburgh Rd. SW15 —3D 90
Dryden Av. W7 —6K 55
Dryden Ct. SE11 —4B 78
Dryden Rd. SW19 —6A 108
Dryden Rd. Enf —6K 7
Dryden Rd. Harr —1K 23
Dryden Rd. Well —1K 99
Dryden St. WC2 —6J 61 (8D 140)
Dryfield Clo. NW10 —6J 41
Dryfield Rd. Edgw —6D 12
Dryfield Wlk. SE8 —6C 80
Dryhill Rd. Belv —6F 85
Drylands Rd. N8 —6J 29
Drysdale Av. E4 —7J 9
Drysdale Ho. N1 —3E 62 (1D 142)
(off Drysdale St.)
Drysdale Pl. N1 —3E 62 (1D 142)
Drysdale St. N1 —3E 62 (2D 142)
Dublin Av. E8 —1G 63
Dublin Ct. S Harr —2H 39
Du Burstow Ter. W7 —2J 71
Ducal St. E2 —3F 63 (2F 142)
Du Cane Clo. W12 —6E 58
(off Wood La.)
Du Cane Ct. SW12 —1E 108
Du Cane Rd. W12 —6B 58
Ducavel Ho. SW2 —1K 109
Duchess M. W1 —5F 61 (6K 139)
Duchess of Bedford's Wlk. W8
 —2J 75
Duchess St. W1 —5F 61 (6K 139)
Duchy Pl. SE1 —1A 78 (2H 147)
Duchy Rd. Barn —1G 5
Duchy St. SE1 —1A 78 (2H 147)
Ducie St. SW4 —4K 93
Duckett Rd. N4 —6A 30
Duckett St. E1 —4K 63

Duck La. W1 —6H 61 (8A 140)
(off Broadwick St.)
Duck Lees La. Enf —4F 9
Ducks Wlk. Twic —5C 88
Du Cros Dri. Stan —6J 11
Du Cros Rd. W3 —1A 74
Dudden Hill La. NW10 —4B 42
Dudden Hill Pde. NW10 —4A 42
Duddington Clo. SE9 —4B 114
Dudley Av. Harr —3C 24
Dudley Ct. NW11 —4H 27
Dudley Dri. Mord —1G 131
Dudley Dri. Ruis —5A 38
Dudley Gdns. W13 —2B 72
Dudley Gdns. Harr —1H 39
Dudley Rd. E17 —2C 32
Dudley Rd. N3 —2K 27
Dudley Rd. NW6 —2G 59
Dudley Rd. SW19 —6J 107
Dudley Rd. Harr —2G 39
Dudley Rd. Ilf —4F 51
Dudley Rd. King T —3F 119
Dudley Rd. Rich —2F 89
Dudley Rd. S'hall —2B 70
Dudley St. W2 —5B 60 (6A 138)
Dudlington Rd. E5 —2J 47
Dudmaston M. SW3 —5B 76
(off Fulham Rd.)
Dudsbury Rd. Sidc —6B 116
Duffell Ho. SE11 —5K 77
(off Loughborough St.)
Dufferin Av. EC1 —4D 62 (4A 142)
(off Loughborough St.)
Dufferin St. EC1 —4C 62 (4M 141)
Duffield Clo. Harr —5K 23
Duffield Dri. N15 —4F 31
Duff St. E14 —6D 64
Dufour's Pl. W1 —6G 61 (8M 139)
Duke Gdns. Ilf —4H 35
Duke Humphrey Rd. SE3 —1G 97
(in two parts)
Duke of Cambridge Clo. Twic
 —6H 8
Duke of Edinburgh Rd. Sutt —2B 13
Duke of Wellington Pl. SW1
 —2E 76 (5H 145)
Duke of York St. SW1
 —1G 77 (2M 145)
Duke Rd. W4 —5K 73
Duke Rd. Ilf —4H 35
Dukes Av. N3 —1K 27
Duke's Av. N10 —3F 29
Duke's Av. W4 —5K 73
Duke's Av. Edgw —6A 12
Dukes Av. Harr —4J 23
Dukes Av. Houn —4C 86
Dukes Av. N Mald —3B 120
Dukes Av. N Har —6D 22
Dukes Av. N'holt —7C 38
Dukes Av. Rich & King T —4C 104
Dukes Clo. Hamp —5D 102
Dukes Ct. E6 —1E 66
Dukes Ct. SE13 —2E 96
Dukes Head Pas. Hamp —7G 103
Duke Shore Pl. E14 —7B 64
Duke's La. W8 —2K 75
Dukes M. N10 —3F 29
Duke's M. W1 —6E 60 (7H 139)
(off Duke St.)
Dukes Orchard. Bex —1J 117
Duke's Pas. E17 —4E 32
Duke's Pl. EC3 —6E 62 (8D 142)
Dukes Rd. E6 —1E 66
Dukes Rd. W3 —4G 57
Duke's Rd. WC1 —3H 61 (2B 140)
Dukesthorpe Rd. SE26 —4K 111
Duke St. SW1 —1G 77
Duke St. W1 —6E 60 (7H 139)

Duke St. Rich —4D **88**
Duke St. Sutt —4B **132**
Duke St. Hill. SE1 —1D **78** (2B **148**)
Duke St. St James's. SW1
　　　　　—1G **77** (2M **145**)
Dukes Way. W Wick —3G **137**
Duke's Yd. W1 —7E **60** (9H **139**)
Dulas St. N4 —1A **46**
Dulford St. W11 —7G **59**
Dulka Rd. SW11 —5D **92**
Dulverton Mans. WC1
　　　　　—4K **61** (4F **140**)
(off Grays Inn Rd.)
Dulverton Rd. SE9 —2G **115**
Dulwich Comn. SE21 & SE22
　　　　　—1E **110**
Dulwich Lawn Clo. SE22 —5F **95**
Dulwich Oaks Pl. SE21 —3F **111**
Dulwich Rise Gdns. SE22 —5F **95**
Dulwich Rd. SE24 —5A **94**
Dulwich Village. SE21 —6E **94**
Dulwich Wood Av. SE19 —4E **110**
Dulwich Wood Pk. SE19 —4E **110**
Dumbarton Ct. SW2 —7J **93**
Dumbarton Rd. SW2 —6J **93**
Dumbleton Clo. King T —1H **119**
Dumbreck Rd. SE9 —4D **98**
Dumont Rd. N16 —3E **46**
Dumpton Pl. NW1 —7E **44**
Dunbar Av. SW16 —2A **124**
Dunbar Av. Beck —4A **126**
Dunbar Av. Dag —3G **53**
Dunbar Gdns. Dag —5G **53**
Dunbar Rd. E7 —6J **49**
Dunbar Rd. N22 —1A **30**
Dunbar Rd. N Mald —4J **119**
Dunbar St. SE27 —3C **110**
Dunblane Clo. Edgw —2C **12**
Dunblane Rd. SE9 —3C **98**
Dunboyne Rd. NW3 —5D **44**
Dunbridge St. E2 —4G **63**
Duncan Clo. Barn —4F **5**
Duncan Gro. W3 —6A **58**
Duncannon St. WC2
　　　　　—7J **61** (1C **146**)
Duncan Rd. E8 —1H **63**
Duncan Rd. Rich —4E **88**
Duncan St. N1 —2B **62**
Duncan Ter. N1 —2B **62**
Duncombe Hill. SE23 —7A **96**
Duncombe Rd. N19 —1H **45**
Duncrievie Rd. SE13 —6F **97**
Duncroft. SE18 —7J **83**
Dundalk Rd. SE4 —3A **96**
Dundas Rd. SE15 —2J **95**
Dundee Rd. E13 —2K **65**
Dundee Rd. SE25 —5H **125**
Dundee St. E1 —1H **79**
Dundela Gdns. Wor Pk —4D **130**
Dundonald Clo. E6 —6C **66**
Dundonald Rd. NW10 —1F **59**
Dundonald Rd. SW19 —7G **107**
Dundry Ho. SE26 —3G **111**
Dunedin Rd. E10 —3D **48**
Dunedin Rd. Ilf —1G **51**
Dunelm Gro. SE27 —3C **110**
Dunelm St. E1 —6K **63**
Dunfield Gdns. SE6 —5D **112**
Dunfield Rd. SE6 —5D **112**
(in two parts)
Dunford Ct. Pinn —1D **22**
Dunford Rd. N7 —4K **45**
Dungarvan Av. SW15 —4C **90**
Dunheved Clo. T Hth —6A **124**
Dunheved Rd. N. T Hth —6A **124**
Dunheved Rd. S. T Hth —6A **124**
Dunheved Rd. W. T Hth —6A **124**

Dunholme Grn. N9 —3A **18**
Dunholme La. N9 —3A **18**
Dunholme Rd. N9 —3A **18**
Dunkeld Rd. SE25 —4D **124**
Dunkeld Rd. Dag —2B **52**
Dunkery Rd. SE9 —4B **114**
Dunkirk St. SE27 —4C **110**
Dunlace Rd. E5 —4J **47**
Dunleary Clo. Houn —7D **86**
Dunley Dri. New Ad —7D **136**
Dunloe Av. N17 —3D **30**
Dunloe Ct. E2 —2F **63**
Dunloe St. E2 —2F **63**
Dunlop Pl. SE16 —3F **79**
Dunlop Point. E16 —1K **81**
Dunmore Rd. NW6 —1G **59**
Dunmore Rd. SW20 —1E **120**
Dunmow Clo. Felt —3C **102**
Dunmow Clo. Romf —5C **35**
*Dunmow Ho. SE11 —5K **77***
(off Newburn St.)
Dunmow Rd. E15 —4F **49**
*Dunmow Wlk. N1 —1C **62***
(off Popham St.)
Dunn Mead. NW9 —7G **13**
Dunnock Clo. N9 —1E **18**
Dunnock Rd. E6 —6C **66**
*Dunn's Pas. WC1 —6J **61** (7D **140**)*
(off High Holborn)
Dunn St. E8 —5F **47**
Dunollie Pl. NW5 —5G **45**
Dunollie Rd. NW5 —5G **45**
*Dunoon Ho. N1 —1K **61***
(off Bemerton Est.)
Dunoon Rd. SE23 —7J **95**
Dunraven Dri. Enf —2F **7**
Dunraven Rd. W12 —1C **74**
Dunraven St. W1 —7D **60** (9F **138**)
Dunsany Rd. W14 —3F **75**
Dunsbury Clo. Sutt —7K **131**
Dunsdale Rd. SE3 —6H **81**
Dunsfold Way. New Ad —7D **136**
Dunsmore Clo. Hay —4C **54**
Dunsmore Rd. N16 —1E **46**
Dunspring La. Ilf —2F **35**
Dunstable M. W1 —5E **60** (5H **139**)
Dunstable Rd. Rich —4E **88**
Dunstall Rd. SW20 —6D **105**
Dunstall Welling Est. Well —2B **100**
Dunstan Clo. N2 —3A **28**
*Dunstan Glade. Orp —6H **129***
*Dunstan Houses. E1 —5J **63***
(off Stepney Grn.)
Dunstan Rd. E8 —1F **63**
Dunstan Rd. NW11 —1H **43**
Dunstan's Gro. SE22 —6H **95**
Dunstan's Rd. SE22 —7G **95**
Dunster Av. Mord —1F **131**
Dunster Clo. Barn —4A **4**
Dunster Clo. Romf —2J **37**
Dunster Ct. EC3 —7E **62** (9D **142**)
Dunster Dri. NW9 —1J **41**
Dunster Gdns. NW6 —7H **43**
Dunster Ho. SE6 —3E **112**
Dunsterville Way. SE1
　　　　　—2D **78** (5B **148**)
Dunsterville Way. SW1 —2D **78**
Dunster Way. Harr —3C **38**
Dunston Rd. E8 —1F **63**
Dunston Rd. SW11 —2E **92**
Dunston St. E8 —1F **63**
Dunton Clo. Surb —7E **118**
Dunton Ct. SE23 —2H **111**
Dunton Rd. E10 —7D **32**
Dunton Rd. SE1 —5F **79**
Dunton Rd. Romf —4K **37**
Duntshill Rd. SW18 —1K **107**
Dunvegan Rd. SE9 —4D **98**

Dunwich Rd. Bexh —1F **101**
Dunworth M. W11 —6H **59**
Duplex Ride. SW1 —2D **76** (5F **144**)
Duplex Rd. SW1 —2D **76**
Dupont Rd. SW20 —2F **121**
Dupont St. E14 —6A **64**
Duppas Av. Croy —4B **134**
Duppas Hill La. Croy —4B **134**
Duppas Hill Rd. Croy —4A **134**
Duppas Hill Ter. Croy —3B **134**
Duppas Rd. Croy —3A **134**
Dupree Rd. SE7 —5K **81**
Duraden Clo. Beck —7D **112**
Durand Clo. Cars —1D **132**
Durand Gdns. SW9 —1K **93**
Durands Wlk. SE16 —2B **80**
Durand Way. NW10 —7J **41**
Durants Pk. Av. Enf —4E **8**
Durants Rd. Enf —4D **8**
Durant St. E2 —2G **63**
Durban Gdns. Dag —7J **53**
Durban Rd. E15 —3G **65**
Durban Rd. E17 —1B **32**
Durban Rd. N17 —6K **17**
Durban Rd. SE27 —4C **110**
Durban Rd. Beck —2B **126**
Durban Rd. Ilf —1J **51**
Durdans Rd. S'hall —6D **54**
Durell Gdns. Dag —5D **52**
Durell Rd. Dag —5D **52**
Durford Cres. SW15 —1D **106**
Durham Av. Brom —4H **127**
Durham Av. Houn —5D **70**
Durham Av. Wfd G —5G **21**
Durham Clo. SW20 —2D **120**
Durham Ct. Tedd —4H **103**
Durham Hill. Brom —4H **113**
Durham Ho. Bark —7A **52**
*Durham Ho. WC2 —7J **61** (1D **146**)*
(off John Adam St.)
*Durham Ho. Bark —7A **52***
(off Margaret Bondfield Av.)
Durham Ho. Dag —5J **53**
Durham Pl. SW3 —5D **76**
Durham Pl. Ilf —4G **51**
Durham Rise. SE18 —5G **83**
Durham Rd. E12 —4B **50**
Durham Rd. E16 —4G **65**
Durham Rd. N2 —3C **28**
Durham Rd. N7 —2K **45**
Durham Rd. N9 —2B **18**
Durham Rd. SW20 —1D **120**
Durham Rd. W5 —3D **72**
Durham Rd. Brom —3H **127**
Durham Rd. Dag —5J **53**
Durham Rd. Felt —7A **86**
Durham Rd. Harr —5F **23**
Durham Rd. Sidc —5B **116**
Durham Row. E1 —5K **63**
Durham St. SE11 —6K **77**
Durham Ter. W2 —6K **59**
Durham Wharf. Bren —7C **72**
Durham Yd. E2 —3H **63**
Durley Av. Pinn —7C **22**
Durley Rd. N16 —7E **30**
Durlston Rd. E5 —2G **47**
Durlston Rd. King T —6E **104**
Durnford Ho. SE6 —3E **112**
Durnford St. N15 —5E **30**
Durnford St. SE10 —6E **80**
Durning Rd. SE19 —5D **110**
Durnsford Av. SW19 —2J **107**
Durnsford Rd. N11 —1H **29**
Durnsford Rd. SW19 —2J **107**
Durrant Way. Orp —5H **137**
Durrell Rd. SW6 —2H **91**
Durrington Av. SW20 —7E **106**
Durrington Pk. Rd. SW20 —1E **120**

Durrington Rd. E5 —4A **48**
Durrington Tower. SW8 —2G **93**
*Durrisdeer Ho. NW2 —4H **43***
(off Lyndale)
Dursley Clo. SE3 —2A **98**
*Dursley Ct. SE15 —6E **78***
(off Lydney Clo.)
Dursley Gdns. SE3 —1B **98**
Dursley Rd. SE3 —2A **98**
Durward St. E1 —5H **63**
*Durweston M. W1 —5D **60** (5F **138**)*
(off Crawford St.)
Durweston St. W1 —5D **60** (6H **138**)
Dury Falls Ct. Romf —2J **37**
Dury Rd. Barn —1C **4**
Dutch Gdns. King T —6H **105**
Dutch Yd. SW18 —5J **91**
Duthie St. E14 —7E **64**
Dutton St. SE10 —1E **96**
Duxberry Clo. Brom —5C **128**
*Duxford Ho. SE2 —2D **84***
(off Wolvercote Rd.)
Dye Ho. La. E3 —1C **64**
Dyer's Bldgs. EC1 —5A **62** (6G **141**)
Dyers Hall Rd. E11 —2G **49**
Dyers La. SW15 —4D **90**
Dyke Cl. E17 —5B **32**
Dykes Way. Brom —3H **127**
Dykewood Clo. Bex —3K **117**
Dylan Rd. SE24 —4B **94**
Dylan Rd. Belv —3G **85**
Dylan Thomas Ho. N8 —4K **29**
Dylways. SE5 —4D **94**
Dymchurch Clo. Ilf —2E **34**
Dymes Path. SW19 —2F **107**
*Dymock Ct. SE15 —6E **78***
(off Lydney Cl...)
Dymock St. SW6 —3K **91**
Dyneley Rd. SE12 —3A **114**
Dyne Rd. NW6 —7G **43**
Dynevor Rd. N16 —3E **46**
Dynevor Rd. Rich —5E **88**
Dynham Rd. NW6 —7J **43**
Dyott St. WC1 —6H **61** (7B **140**)
Dysart Av. King T —5C **104**
Dysart St. EC2 —4D **62** (4C **142**)
Dyson Ct. NW2 —7E **26**
Dyson Ct. Wemb —2A **40**
*Dyson Ho. SE10 —5H **81***
(off Blackwall La.)
Dyson Rd. E11 —6G **33**
Dyson Rd. E15 —6H **49**
Dysons Rd. N18 —5C **18**

Eade Rd. N4 —7C **30**
Eagans Clo. N2 —3B **28**
Eagle Av. Romf —6E **36**
Eagle Clo. Enf —4D **8**
Eagle Ct. EC1 —5B **62** (5J **141**)
Eagle Ct. N1 —6E **46**
Eagle Dri. NW9 —2A **26**
Eagle Hill. SE19 —6D **110**
Eagle La. E11 —4J **33**
Eagle Lodge. NW11 —7H **27**
*Eagle Pl. SW1 —7G **61** (1M **145**)*
(off Piccadilly)
*Eagle Pl. SW7 —5A **76***
(off Rolandway)
Eagle Rd. Wemb —7D **40**
Eaglesfield Rd. SE18 —1F **99**
Eagle St. WC1 —5K **61** (6E **140**)
Eagle Ter. Wfd G —7E **20**
*Eagle Wharf E. E14 —7A **64***
(off Narrow St.)
Eagle Wharf Rd. N1 —2C **62**
*Eagle Wharf W. E14 —7A **64***
(off Narrow St.)

Ealdham Sq. SE9 —4A **98**
Ealing B'way. Cen. W5 —7D **56**
Ealing Downs Ct. Gnfd —3A **56**
Ealing Grn. W5 —1D **72**
Ealing Pk. Gdns. W5 —4C **72**
Ealing Rd. Bren —4D **72**
Ealing Rd. N'holt —1E **54**
Ealing Rd. Wemb —6E **40**
Ealing Village. W5 —6E **56**
Eamont St. NW8 —2C **60**
Eardley Cres. SW5 —5J **75**
Eardley Rd. SW16 —5G **109**
Eardley Rd. Belv —5G **85**
Earldom Rd. SW15 —4E **90**
Earle Gdns. King T —7E **104**
Earlham Gro. E7 —5H **49**
Earlham Gro. N22 —7E **16**
Earlham St. WC2 —6J **61** (8B **140**)
Earl Rise. SE18 —4H **83**
Earl Rd. SE1 —5F **79**
Earl Rd. SW14 —4J **89**
Earls Ct. Gdns. SW5 —4K **75**
Earl's Ct. Rd. W8 & SW5 —3J **75**
Earls Ct. Sq. SW5 —5K **75**
Earls Cres. Harr —4J **23**
Earlsferry Way. N1 —7K **45**
Earlsfield Rd. SW18 —1A **108**
Earlshall Rd. SE9 —4D **98**
Earlsmead. Harr —4D **38**
Earlsmead Rd. N15 —5F **31**
Earlsmead Rd. NW10 —3E **58**
Earls Ter. W8 —3H **75**
Earlsthorpe M. SW12 —6E **92**
Earlsthorpe Rd. SE26 —4K **111**
Earlstoke St. EC1 —3B **62** (1J **141**)
Earlston Gro. E9 —1H **63**
Earl St. EC2 —5D **62** (5G **142**)
Earl's Wlk. Dag —4E **52**
Earlswood Av. T Hth —5A **124**
Earlswood Clo. SE10 —6G **81**
Earlswood Gdns. Ilf —3E **34**
Earlswood St. SE10 —5G **81**
Early M. NW1 —1F **61**
Earne Rd. W4 —6G **73**
Earnshaw St. WC2 —6H **61** (7B **140**)
Earsby St. W14 —4G **75**
Easby Cres. Mord —6K **121**
Easebourne Rd. Dag —5C **52**
*Easley's M. W1 —6E **60** (7H **139**)*
(off Wigmore St.)
Easirsdown Ho. Bark —2H **67**
Eastbourne Av. W3 —6K **57**
Eastbourne M. W2 —6A **60**
Eastbourne Bldgs. SE1
　　　　　—3E **78** (7C **148**)
Eastbourne Gdns. SW14 —3J **89**
Eastbourne M. W2 —6A **60**
Eastbourne Rd. E6 —3E **66**
Eastbourne Rd. E15 —1G **65**
Eastbourne Rd. N15 —6E **30**
Eastbourne Rd. SW17 —6E **108**
Eastbourne Rd. W4 —6J **73**
Eastbourne Rd. Bren —5C **72**
Eastbourne Rd. Felt —2B **102**
Eastbourne Ter. W2 —6A **60**
Eastbournia Av. N9 —3C **18**

Edmunds Wlk. N2 —4C 28
Edna Rd. SW20 —2F 121
Edna St. SW11 —1C 92
Edred Ho. E9 —4A 48
(off King's Mead Way)
Edrich Ho. SW4 —1J 93
Edrick Rd. Edgw —6D 12
Edrick Wlk. Edgw —6D 12
Edric Rd. SE14 —7K 79
Edridge Rd. Croy —3C 134
Edward Av. E4 —6J 19
Edward Av. Mord —5B 122
Edward Clo. N9 —7A 8
Edward Clo. Hamp —5G 103
Edward Clo. N'holt —2A 54
Edward Ct. E16 —5J 65
Edward Dodd Ct. N1 —3D 62 (1B 142)
(off Chart St.)
Edwardes Pl. W8 —3H 75
Edwardes Sq. W8 —3H 75
Edward Gro. Barn —5G 5
Edward Ho. SE11 —5K 7
(off Newburn St.)
Edward M. NW1 —3F 61 (1K 139)
Edward M. W1 —6E 60
Edward Pl. SE8 —6B 80
Edward Rd. E17 —4K 31
Edward Rd. SE20 —6K 111
Edward Rd. Barn —5G 5
Edward Rd. Brom —7K 113
Edward Rd. Chst —5F 115
Edward Rd. Croy —7E 124
Edward Rd. Hamp —5G 103
Edward Rd. Harr —3G 23
Edward Rd. N'holt —2A 54
Edward Rd. Romf —6E 36
Edward's Av. Ruis —6A 38
Edwards Clo. Wor Pk —2F 131
Edwards Cotts. N1 —6B 46
Edwards Dri. N11 —7C 16
Edwards La. N16 —2E 46
Edwards Mans. Bark —7K 51
(off Upney La.)
Edwards M. W1 —6E 60 (8G 139)
Edward Sq. N1 —1K 61
Edwards Rd. Belv —4G 85
Edward St. E16 —4J 65
Edward St. SE8 —6B 80
Edward St. SE14 —7A 80
Edward Temme Av. E15 —7H 49
Edwina Gdns. Ilf —5C 34
Edwin Arnold Ct. Sidc —4K 115
Edwin Av. E6 —2E 66
(in two parts)
Edwin Clo. Bexh —6F 85
Edwin Pl. Croy —1E 134
Edwin Rd. Edgw —6E 12
Edwin Rd. Twic —1J 103
Edwin's Mead. E9 —4A 48
Edwinstray Ho. Felt —3E 102
Edwin St. E1 —4J 63
Edwin St. E16 —5J 65
Edwin Ware Ct. Pinn —2A 22
Edwis Ho. SE15 —7G 79
Edwyn Clo. Barn —6A 4
Eel Pie Island. Twic —1A 104
Effie Pl. SW6 —7J 75
Effie Rd. SW6 —7J 75
Effingham Clo. Sutt —7K 131
Effingham Rd. N8 —5A 30
Effingham Rd. SE12 —5G 97
Effingham Rd. Croy —7K 123
Effingham Rd. Surb —7B 118
Effort St. SW17 —5C 108
Effra Ct. SW2 —5K 93
(off Brixton Hill)

Effra Pde. SW2 —5A 94
Effra Rd. SW2 —4A 94
Effra Rd. SW19 —6K 107
Egan Way. SE16 —5H 79
Egbert St. NW1 —1E 60
Egbwerts Way. E14 —1K 19
Egerton Ct. E11 —7F 33
Egerton Cres. SW3 —4C 76 (8D 144)
Egerton Dri. SE10 —1D 96
Egerton Gdns. NW4 —4D 26
Egerton Gdns. NW10 —1E 58
Egerton Gdns. SW3 —3C 76 (7C 144)
Egerton Gdns. W13 —6B 56
Egerton Gdns. Ilf —3K 51
Egerton Gdns. M. SW3 —3C 76 (7D 144)
Egerton M. SW3 —3C 76
Egerton Pl. SW3 —3C 76 (7D 144)
Egerton Rd. N16 —7F 31
Egerton Rd. SE25 —3E 124
Egerton Rd. N Mald —4B 120
Egerton Rd. Twic —7J 87
Egerton Rd. Wemb —7F 41
Egerton Ter. SW3 —3C 76 (7D 144)
Eggardon Ct. N'holt —6G 39
Eggerton Rd. —4H 59
Egham Clo. SW19 —2G 107
Egham Clo. Sutt —2G 131
Egham Cres. Sutt —3F 131
Egham Rd. E13 —5K 65
Eglantine Rd. SW18 —5A 92
Egleston Rd. Mord —6K 121
Eglington Ct. SE17 —6C 78
Eglington Rd. E4 —1A 20
Eglinton Hill. SE18 —6F 83
Eglinton Rd. SE18 —6E 82
Egliston M. SW15 —3E 90
Egliston Rd. SW15 —3E 90
Eglon M. NW1 —7D 44
Egmont Av. Surb —7F 119
Egmont Rd. N Mald —4B 120
Egmont Rd. Surb —7F 119
Egmont Rd. Sutt —7A 132
Egmont St. SE14 —7K 79
Egremont Rd. SE27 —3A 110
Egret Way. Hay —6K 54
Eider Clo. E7 —5H 49
Eider Clo. Hay —5B 54
Eighteenth Rd. Mitc —4J 123
Eighth Av. E12 —4D 50
Eileen Rd. SE25 —5D 124
Eisenhower Dri. E6 —5C 66
Elaine Gro. NW5 —5E 44
Elam Clo. SE5 —2B 94
Elam St. SE5 —2B 94
Eland Pl. Croy —3B 134
Eland Rd. SW11 —3D 92
Eland Rd. Croy —3B 134
Elba Pl. SE17 —4C 78 (8M 147)
Elberon Av. Croy —6G 123
Elbe St. SW6 —2A 92
Elborough Rd. SE25 —5G 125
Elborough St. SW18 —1J 107
Elbury Dri. E16 —6J 65
Elcho St. SW11 —7C 76
Elcot Av. SE15 —7H 79
Elder Av. N8 —5J 29
Elderberry Gro. SE27 —4C 110
Elderberry Rd. W5 —2E 72
Elder Ct. Bush —2D 10
Elderfield Rd. E5 —4J 47
Elderfield Wlk. E11 —5K 33
Elder Oak Clo. SE20 —1H 125
Elder Oak Ct. SE20 —1G 125
Elder Rd. SE27 —4C 110
Elderslie Clo. Beck —6D 126

Elderslie Rd. SE9 —5E 98
Elder St. E1 —4F 63 (5E 142)
Elderton Rd. SE26 —4A 112
Eldertree Pl. Mitc —1G 123
Eldertree Way. Mitc —1G 123
Elderwood Pl. SE27 —5C 110
Eldon Av. Croy —2J 135
Eldon Av. Houn —7E 70
Eldon Gro. NW3 —5B 44
Eldon Pk. SE25 —4H 125
Eldon Rd. E17 —4B 32
Eldon Rd. N9 —1D 18
Eldon Rd. N22 —1B 30
Eldon Rd. W8 —3K 75
Eldon St. EC2 —5D 62 (6B 142)
Eldon Way. NW10 —3H 57
Eldred Rd. Bark —1J 67
Eldridge Ct. SE16 —3G 79
Eleanor Clo. N15 —3F 31
Eleanor Clo. SE16 —2K 79
Eleanor Cres. NW7 —5A 14
Eleanor Gdns. Barn —5A 4
Eleanor Gdns. Dag —2F 53
Eleanor Gro. SW13 —3A 90
Eleanor Rd. E8 —6H 47
Eleanor Rd. E15 —6H 49
Eleanor Rd. N11 —6D 16
Eleanor St. E3 —3C 64
Eleanor Wlk. SE18 —4C 82
Electric Av. SW9 —4A 94
Electric La. SW9 & SW2 —4A 94
(in two parts)
Electric Pde. Surb —6D 118
Elephant & Castle. SE1 —4B 78 (8K 147)
Elephant La. SE16 —2J 79
Elephant Rd. SE17 —4C 78 (8L 147)
Elers Rd. W13 —2C 72
Eley Ind. Est. N18 —4E 18
(in two parts)
Eley Rd. N18 —4D 18
Elfindale Rd. SE24 —5C 94
Elfin Gro. Tedd —5K 103
Elford Clo. SE3 —4K 97
Elford M. SW4 —5G 93
Elfort Rd. N5 —4A 46
Elfrida Cres. SE6 —4C 112
Elf Row. E1 —7J 63
Elfwine Rd. W7 —5J 55
Elgar. N8 —3J 29
(off Boyton Clo.)
Elgar Av. NW10 —6K 41
(in two parts)
Elgar Av. SW16 —3J 123
Elgar Av. W5 —2E 72
Elgar Av. Surb —7G 119
Elgar Clo. E13 —2A 66
Elgar Clo. SE8 —7C 80
Elgar Clo. Buck H —2G 21
Elgar Clo. Els —1H 11
Elgar St. SE16 —3A 80
Elgin Av. W9 —4H 59
Elgin Av. Harr —2B 24
Elgin Cres. W11 —7G 59
Elgin M. N. W9 —3K 59
Elgin M. S. W9 —3K 59
Elgin Rd. N22 —2G 29
Elgin Rd. Croy —2F 135
Elgin Rd. Ilf —1J 51
Elgin Rd. Sutt —3A 132
Elgin Rd. Wall —6G 133
Elgood Clo. W11 —7G 59
Elham Clo. Brom —7B 114
Elham Ho. E5 —5H 47
Elia M. N1 —2B 62
Elias Pl. SW8 —6A 78

Elia St. N1 —2B 62
Elibank Rd. SE9 —4D 98
Elim Est. SE1 —3E 78 (6B 148)
Elim St. SE1 —3D 78 (6B 148)
(in two parts)
Elim Way. E13 —3H 65
Eliot Bank. SE23 —2H 111
Eliot Cotts. SE3 —2G 97
Eliot Dri. Harr —2F 39
Eliot Hill. SE13 —2E 96
Eliot Pk. SE13 —2E 96
Eliot Pl. SE3 —2G 97
Eliot Rd. Dag —4D 52
Eliot Vale. SE3 —2F 97
Elizabeth Av. N1 —1C 62
Elizabeth Av. Enf —3G 7
Elizabeth Av. Ilf —2H 51
Elizabeth Blackwell Ho. N22 —1A 30
(off Progress Way)
Elizabeth Bri. SW1 —4F 77 (9J 145)
Elizabeth Clo. E14 —6D 64
Elizabeth Clo. W9 —4A 60
Elizabeth Clo. Barn —3A 4
Elizabeth Clo. Romf —1H 37
Elizabeth Clyde Clo. N15 —4E 30
Elizabeth Cotts. Rich —1F 89
Elizabeth Ct. E4 —5G 19
Elizabeth Ct. SW1 —3H 77 (7B 146)
(off Milmans Ct.)
Elizabeth Ct. Eri —7K 85
(off Valence Rd.)
Elizabeth Ct. Tedd —5J 103
Elizabeth Fry Rd. E8 —7H 47
Elizabeth Gdns. W3 —1B 74
Elizabeth Gdns. Stan —6H 11
Elizabeth Garrett Anderson Ho. Belv —3G 85
Elizabeth Ho. SE11 —4A 78 (9H 147)
(off Reedworth St.)
Elizabeth M. NW3 —6C 44
Elizabeth M. Harr —6J 23
Elizabeth Newcomen Ho. SE1 —2D 78 (4A 148)
(off Newcomen St.)
Elizabeth Pl. N15 —4D 30
Elizabeth Ride. N9 —7C 8
Elizabeth Rd. E6 —1B 66
Elizabeth Rd. N15 —5E 30
Elizabeth St. SE1 —2F 79
Elizabeth St. SW1 —4E 76 (8H 145)
Elizabeth Ter. SE9 —6D 98
Elizabeth Way. SE19 —7D 110
Elizabeth Way. Felt —4A 102
Elkington Rd. E13 —4K 65
Elkstone Ct. SE15 —6E 78
(off Birdlip Clo.)
Elkstone Rd. W10 —5H 59
Ellaline Rd. W6 —6F 75
Ellanby Cres. N18 —4C 18
Elland Rd. SE15 —4J 95
Ella Rd. N8 —7J 29
Ellement Clo. Pinn —5B 22
Ellena Ct. N14 —3D 16
(off Conway Rd.)
Ellenborough Ho. W12 —7D 58
(off White City Est.)
Ellenborough Pl. SW15 —4C 90
Ellenborough Rd. N22 —1C 30
Ellenborough Rd. Sidc —5D 116
Ellenbridge Way. S Croy —7E 134
Ellen Clo. Brom —3B 128
Ellen Ct. E4 —1K 19
(off Ridgeway, The.)
Ellen Ct. N9 —2D 18
Ellen St. E1 —6G 63
Ellen Wilkinson Ho. Dag —3G 53
Elleray Rd. Tedd —6K 103
Ellerby St. SW6 —1F 91

Ellerdale Clo. NW3 —4A 44
Ellerdale Rd. NW3 —5A 44
Ellerdale St. SE13 —4D 96
Ellerdine Rd. Houn —4G 87
Ellerker Gdns. Rich —6E 88
Ellerman Av. Twic —1D 102
Ellerslie Gdns. NW10 —1C 58
Ellerslie Rd. W12 —1D 74
Ellerslie Sq. Ind. Est. SW2 —5J 93
Ellerton Gdns. Dag —7C 52
Ellerton Rd. SW13 —1C 90
Ellerton Rd. SW18 —1B 108
Ellerton Rd. SW20 —7C 106
Ellerton Rd. Dag —7C 52
Ellerton Rd. Surb —7F 119
Ellery Ho. SE17 —4D 78 (9B 148)
Ellery Rd. SE19 —7D 110
Ellery St. SE15 —2H 95
Ellesmere Av. NW7 —3E 12
Ellesmere Av. Beck —2E 126
Ellesmere Clo. E11 —5H 33
Ellesmere Ct. W4 —6K 73
Ellesmere Gdns. Ilf —5C 34
Ellesmere Gro. Barn —5C 4
Ellesmere Rd. E3 —2A 64
Ellesmere Rd. NW10 —5C 42
Ellesmere Rd. W4 —6J 73
Ellesmere Rd. Gnfd —4G 55
Ellesmere Rd. Twic —6C 88
Ellesmere St. E14 —6D 64
Elleswood Ct. Surb —7D 118
Ellingfort Rd. E8 —7H 47
Ellingham Rd. E15 —4F 49
Ellingham Rd. W12 —2C 74
Ellington Ct. N14 —2C 16
Ellington Ho. SE1 —3C 78 (7M 147)
Ellington Rd. N10 —4F 29
Ellington Rd. Houn —2F 87
Ellington St. N7 —6A 46
Elliot Clo. E15 —7G 49
Elliot Gdns. SW15 —4C 90
Elliot Rd. NW4 —6D 26
Elliot Rd. SW9 —7B 78
Elliot Rd. W4 —4A 74
Elliot Rd. Brom —4B 128
Elliot Rd. Stan —6F 11
Elliot Rd. T Hth —4B 124
Elliot's Pl. N1 —1B 62
Elliot Sq. NW3 —7C 44
Elliots Row. SE11 —4B 78 (8K 147)
Ellis Clo. SE9 —2G 115
Elliscombe Rd. SE7 —6A 82
Ellis Ct. W7 —5K 55
Ellisfield Dri. SW15 —7C 90
Ellis Ho. SE17 —5D 78
Ellis M. SE7 —6A 82
Ellison Gdns. S'hall —4D 70
Ellison Rd. SW13 —2B 90
Ellison Rd. SW16 —7H 109
Ellison Rd. Sidc —1H 115
Ellis Rd. Mitc —6D 122
Ellis Rd. S'hall —1G 71
Ellis St. SW1 —4E 76 (8F 144)
Ellora Rd. SW16 —5H 109
Ellsworth St. E2 —3H 63
Ellwood Ct. W9 —4K 59
(off Clearwell Dri.)
Elmar Rd. N15 —4D 30
Elm Av. W5 —1E 72
Elm Av. Ruis —7A 22
Elm Bank. N14 —7D 6
Elm Bank Av. Barn —4A 4
Elm Bank Dri. Brom —2A 128
Elm Bank Gdns. SW13 —2A 90
Elmbank Way. W7 —5H 55
Elmbourne Dri. Belv —4H 85
Elmbourne Rd. SW17 —3F 109

Elmbridge Av. Surb —5H 119
Elmbridge Wlk. E8 —7G 47
Elmbrook Gdns. SE9 —4C 98
Elmbrook Rd. Sutt —4H 131
Elm Clo. E11 —6K 33
Elm Clo. N19 —2G 45
Elm Clo. NW4 —5F 27
Elm Clo. SW20 —4E 120
Elm Clo. Buck H —2G 21
Elm Clo. Cars —1D 132
Elm Clo. Harr —6F 23
Elm Clo. Romf —1H 37
Elm Clo. S Croy —6E 134
Elm Clo. Surb —7J 119
Elm Clo. Twic —2F 103
Elmcote. Pinn —2B 22
Elm Ct. EC4 —7A 62 (9G 141)
(off Terrace, The)
Elmcourt Rd. SE27 —2B 110
Elm Cres. W5 —7E 56
Elm Cres. King T —1E 118
Elmcroft. N6 —7G 29
Elmcroft Av. E11 —5K 33
Elmcroft Av. N9 —6C 8
Elmcroft Av. NW11 —7H 27
Elmcroft Av. Sidc —7K 99
Elmcroft Clo. E11 —4K 33
Elmcroft Clo. W5 —6D 56
Elmcroft Cres. NW11 —7G 27
Elmcroft Cres. Harr —3E 22
Elmcroft Gdns. NW9 —4G 25
Elmcroft Ho. N8 —5K 29
Elmcroft St. E5 —4J 47
Elmdale Rd. N13 —5F 16
Elmdene. Surb —7J 119
Elmdene Clo. Beck —6B 126
Elmdene Rd. SE18 —5F 83
Elmdon Rd. Houn —2C 86
Elm Dri. Harr —6F 23
Elmer Clo. Enf —3E 6
Elmer Gdns. Edgw —7C 12
Elmer Gdns. Iswth —3H 87
Elmer Rd. SE6 —7E 96
Elmers Dri. Tedd —6B 104
Elmers End Rd. SE20 & Beck
—2J 125
Elmerside Rd. Beck —4A 126
Elmers Rd. SE25 —7G 125
Elmfield Av. N8 —5J 29
Elmfield Av. Mitc —1E 122
Elmfield Av. Tedd —5K 103
Elmfield Clo. Harr —2J 39
Elmfield Ct. Well —1B 100
Elmfield Ho. N2 —2B 28
(off Grange, The)
Elmfield Pk. Brom —3J 127
Elmfield Rd. E4 —2K 19
Elmfield Rd. E17 —6K 31
Elmfield Rd. N2 —3B 28
Elmfield Rd. SW17 —2E 108
Elmfield Rd. Brom —2J 127
Elmfield Rd. S'hall —3C 70
Elmfield Way. S Croy —7F 135
Elm Friars Wlk. NW1 —7H 45
Elm Gdns. N2 —3A 28
Elm Gdns. Enf —1J 7
Elm Gdns. Mitc —4H 123
Elmgate Av. Felt —3A 102
Elmgate Gdns. Edgw —5D 12
Elm Grn. W3 —6A 58
Elm Grn. Clo. E15 —1G 65
Elm Gro. N8 —6J 29
Elm Gro. NW2 —4F 43
Elm Gro. SE15 —2F 95
Elm Gro. SW19 —7G 107
Elm Gro. Eri —7K 85
Elm Gro. Harr —7E 22
Elm Gro. King T —1E 118

Elm Gro. Sutt —4K 131
Elm Gro. Wfd G —5C 20
Elmgrove Cres. Harr —5K 23
Elmgrove Gdns. Harr —5A 24
Elm Gro. Pde. Wall —3E 132
Elm Gro. Rd. SW13 —1C 90
Elm Gro. Rd. W5 —2E 72
Elmgrove Rd. Croy —7H 125
Elmgrove Rd. Harr —5K 23
Elmgrove Rd. Kent —5A 24
Elm Hall Gdns. E11 —6K 33
(in two parts)
Elm Hatch. Pinn —1D 22
(off Westfield Pk.)
Elmhurst. Belv —6E 84
Elmhurst Av. N2 —3B 28
Elmhurst Av. Mitc —7F 109
Elmhurst Dri. E18 —2J 33
Elmhurst Lodge. Sutt —7A 132
Elmhurst Mans. SW4 —3H 93
Elmhurst Rd. E7 —7K 49
Elmhurst Rd. N17 —2F 31
Elmhurst Rd. SE9 —2C 114
Elmhurst Rd. SW4 —3H 93
Elmhurst St. SW4 —3H 93
Elmira St. SE13 —3D 96
Elm La. SE6 —2B 112
Elmlee Clo. Chst —6D 114
Elmley Clo. E6 —5C 66
Elmley St. SE18 —5H 83
Elm Lodge. SW6 —1F 91
Elm M. Rich —6F 89
Elmore Clo. Wemb —2E 56
Elmore Ho. SW9 —2B 94
Elmore Rd. E11 —3E 48
Elmore Rd. Enf —1E 8
Elmore St. N1 —7C 46
Elm Pde. Sidc —4A 116
Elm Pk. SW2 —6K 93
Elm Pk. Stan —5G 11
Elm Pk. Av. N15 —5F 31
Elm Pk. Ct. Pinn —3A 22
Elm Pk. Gdns. NW4 —5F 27
Elm Pk. Gdns. SW10 —5B 76
Elm Pk. La. SW3 —5B 76
Elm Pk. Mans. SW10 —6A 76
(off Park Wlk.)
Elm Pk. Rd. E10 —1A 48
Elm Pk. Rd. N3 —7C 14
Elm Pk. Rd. N21 —7H 7
Elm Pk. Rd. SE25 —3F 125
Elm Pk. Rd. SW3 —6B 76
Elm Pk. Rd. Pinn —2A 22
Elm Pas. Barn —4C 4
Elm Pl. SW7 —5B 76
Elm Quay Ct. SW8 —6H 77
Elm Rd. E7 —6H 49
Elm Rd. E11 —2F 49
Elm Rd. E17 —5E 32
Elm Rd. N22 —1B 30
Elm Rd. SW14 —3J 89
Elm Rd. Barn —4C 4
Elm Rd. Beck —2B 126
Elm Rd. Eps —6B 130
Elm Rd. King T —1F 119
Elm Rd. N Mald —4K 119
Elm Rd. Romf —2H 37
Elm Rd. Sidc —4A 116
Elm Rd. T Hth —4D 124
Elm Rd. Wall —1E 132
Elm Rd. Wemb —5E 40
Elm Rd. W. Sutt —7H 121
Elm Row. NW3 —3A 44
Elms Av. N10 —3F 29
Elms Av. NW4 —5F 27

Elmscott Gdns. N21 —6H 7

Elmscott Rd. Brom —5G 113
Elms Ct. Wemb —4A 40
Elms Cres. SW4 —6G 93
Elmsdale Rd. E17 —4B 32
Elms Gdns. Dag —4F 53
Elms Gdns. Wemb —4A 40
Elmshaw Rd. SW15 —5C 90
Elmshurst Cres. N2 —4B 28
Elmside. New Ad —6D 136
Elmside Rd. Wemb —3G 41
Elmsleigh Av. Harr —4B 24
Elmsleigh Ct. Sutt —3K 131
Elmsleigh Ho. Twic —2H 103
(off Staines Rd.)
Elmsleigh Rd. Twic —2H 103
Elmslie Clo. Wfd G —6J 21
Elms M. W2 —7B 60 (9A 138)
Elms Pk. Av. Wemb —4A 40
Elms Rd. SW4 —5G 93
Elms Rd. Harr —7D 10
Elmstead Av. Chst —5D 114
Elmstead Av. Wemb —1E 40
Elmstead Clo. N20 —2D 14
Elmstead Clo. Eps —5A 130
Elmstead Gdns. Wor Pk —3C 130
Elmstead Glade. Chst —6D 114
Elmstead La. Chst —7C 114
Elmstead Rd. Eri —1K 101
Elmstead Rd. Ilf —2J 51
Elmstead Cres. Well —6C 84
Elms, The. SW13 —3B 90
Elmstone Rd. SW6 —1J 91
Elm St. WC1 —4K 61 (4F 140)
Elmsworth Av. Houn —2F 87
Elm Ter. NW2 —3J 43
Elm Ter. NW3 —4C 44
Elm Ter. SE9 —6E 98
Elm Ter. Harr —1H 23
Elm Ter. Stan —5H 11
Elmton Way. E5 —3G 47
Elm Tree Clo. NW8 —3B 60 (1A 138)
Elm Tree Clo. N'holt —2D 54
Elm Tree Rd. NW8 —3B 60 (1A 138)
Elmtree Rd. Tedd —4J 103
Elm Wlk. NW3 —2J 43
Elm Wlk. SW20 —4E 120
Elm Way. N11 —6K 15
Elm Way. NW10 —4A 42
Elm Way. Eps —5A 130
Elmwood Av. Felt —3A 102
Elmwood Av. N13 —5D 16
Elmwood Av. Harr —5K 23
Elmwood Clo. Eps —7C 130
Elmwood Clo. Wall —2F 133
Elmwood Ct. E10 —1C 48
(off Goldsmith Rd.)
Elmwood Ct. Wemb —3A 40
Elmwood Cres. NW9 —4J 25
Elmwood Dri. Bex —7E 100
Elmwood Dri. Eps —6C 130
Elmwood Gdns. W7 —6J 55
Elmwood Rd. SE24 —5D 94
Elmwood Rd. W4 —6J 73
Elmwood Rd. Croy —7B 124
Elmwood Rd. Mitc —3D 122
Elmworth Gro. SE21 —2D 110
Elnathan M. W9 —4K 59
Elphinstone Ct. SW16 —6J 109
Elphinstone Rd. E17 —2B 32
Elphinstone St. N5 —4B 46
Elrington Rd. E8 —6G 47
Elsa Ct. Beck —1B 126
Elsa Rd. Well —2B 100
Elsa St. E1 —5A 64
Elsdale St. E9 —6J 47
Elsden M. E2 —2J 63

Elsden Rd. N17 —1F 31
Elsenham Rd. E12 —5E 50
Elsenham St. SW18 —1H 107
Elsham Rd. E11 —3G 49
Elsham Rd. W14 —2G 75
Elsham Ter. W14 —3G 75
(off Elsham Rd.)
Elsiedene Rd. N21 —7H 7
Elsiemaud Rd. SE4 —5B 96
Elsie Rd. SE22 —4F 95
Elsinore Gdns. NW2 —3G 43
Elsinore Rd. SE23 —1A 112
Elsinore Way. Rich —3H 89
Elsley Rd. SW11 —3D 92
Elspeth Rd. SW11 —4D 92
Elspeth Rd. Wemb —5E 40
Elsrick Av. Mord —5J 121
Elstan Way. Croy —7A 126
Elstead Ct. Sutt —1G 131
Elstead Ho. SW2 —7K 93
(off Redlands Way)
Elsted St. SE17 —4D 78 (9B 148)
Elstow Clo. SE9 —5E 98
(in two parts)
Elstow Clo. Ruis —7B 22
Elstow Gdns. Dag —1E 68
Elstow Glade. Chst —6D 114
Elstow Rd. Dag —1E 68
Elstree Gdns. N9 —1C 18
Elstree Gdns. Belv —4E 84
Elstree Gdns. Ilf —5G 51
Elstree Hill. Brom —7G 113
Elstree Hill S. Els —1J 11
Elstree Rd. Bush & Borwd —1C 10
Elswick Rd. SE13 —2D 96
Elswick St. SW6 —2A 92
Elsworth Clo. Felt —1A 102
Elsworthy. Th Dit —6A 118
Elsworthy Rise. NW3 —7C 44
Elsworthy Rd. NW3 —1C 60
Elsworthy Ter. NW3 —7C 44
Elsynge Rd. SW18 —5B 92
Eltham Grn. SE9 —5B 98
Eltham Grn. Rd. SE9 —4A 98
Eltham High St. SE9 —6D 98
Eltham Hill. SE9 —5B 98
Eltham Pal. Rd. SE9 —6A 98
Eltham Pk. Gdns. SE9 —4E 98
Eltham Rd. SE12 & SE9 —5J 97
Elthiron Rd. SW6 —1J 91
Elthorne Av. W7 —2K 71
Elthorne Ct. Felt —1A 102
Elthorne Pk. Rd. W7 —2K 71
Elthorne Rd. N19 —2H 45
Elthorne Rd. NW9 —7K 25
Elthorne Way. NW9 —6K 25
Elthruda Rd. SE13 —6F 97
Eltisley Rd. Ilf —4F 51
Elton Av. Barn —5C 4
Elton Av. Gnfd —6J 39
Elton Av. Wemb —5B 40
Elton Clo. King T —7C 104
Elton Pl. N16 —5E 46
Elton Rd. King T —1F 119
Eltringham St. SW18 —4A 92
Elvaston M. SW7 —3A 76
Elvaston Pl. SW7 —3A 76
Elveden Ho. SE24 —5B 94
Elveden Pl. NW10 —2G 57
Elveden Rd. NW10 —2G 57
Elvendon Rd. N13 —6D 16
Elver Gdns. E2 —3G 63
Elverson Rd. SE8 —2D 96
Elverton St. SW1 —4H 77 (8A 146)
Elvington Grn. Brom —5H 127
Elvington La. NW9 —1A 26
Elvino Rd. SE26 —5A 112
Elvis Rd. NW2 —6E 42
Elwill Way. Beck —4E 126
Elwin St. E2 —3G 63
Elwood St. N5 —3B 46

Elwyn Gdns. SE12 —7J 97
Ely Clo. SW20 —2B 120
Ely Cotts. SW8 —7K 77
Ely Ct. EC1 —5A 62 (6H 141)
(off Ely Pl.)
Ely Gdns. Dag —3J 53
Ely Gdns. Ilf —7C 34
Elyne Rd. N4 —6A 30
Ely Pl. EC1 —5A 62 (6H 141)
Ely Pl. Wfd G —6K 21
Ely Rd. E10 —6E 32
Ely Rd. Croy —5D 124
Ely Rd. Houn —3A 86
Elysian Av. Orp —6K 129
Elysium Pl. SW6 —2H 91
(off Elysium St.)
Elysium St. SW6 —2H 91
Elysan Bus. Cen. Hay —7A 54
Elystan Clo. Wall —7G 133
Elystan Pl. SW3 —5C 76
Elystan St. SW3 —4C 76 (9C 144)
Elystan Wlk. N1 —1A 62
Emanuel Av. W3 —6J 57
Embankment. SW15 —2F 91
Embankment Gdns. SW3 —6D 76
Embankment Pl. WC2
—1J 77 (2D 146)
Embankment, The. Twic —1A 104
Embassy Ct. N11 —6C 16
(off Bounds Grn. Rd.)
Embassy Ct. NW8 —2B 60
(off Wellington Rd.)
Embassy Ct. Sidc —3B 116
Embassy Ct. Well —3B 100
Embassy Gdns. Beck —1B 126
Emba St. SE16 —2G 79
Ember Clo. Orp —7G 129
Ember Ct. NW9 —2B 26
Emberton. SE17 —6E 78
(off Albany Rd.)
Embleton Rd. SE13 —4D 96
Embleton Wlk. Hamp —5D 102
Embley Point. E5 —4H 47
(off Tiger Way)
Embry Clo. Stan —4F 11
Embry Dri. Stan —6E 11
Embry Way. Stan —5F 11
Emden St. SW6 —1K 91
Emerald Clo. E16 —6B 66
Emerald Gdns. Dag —1G 53
Emerald St. WC1 —5K 61 (5E 140)
Emerson Gdns. Harr —6F 25
Emerson Rd. Ilf —7E 34
Emerson St. SE1 —1C 78 (2L 147)
Emerton Clo. Bexh —4E 100
Emery Hill St. SW1
—3G 77 (7M 145)
Emery St. SE1 —3A 78 (6H 147)
Emes Rd. Eri —7J 85
Emily Pl. N7 —4A 46
Emily St. E16 —6H 65
(off Jude St.)
Emlyn Gdns. W12 —2A 74
Emlyn Rd. W12 —2A 74
Emmanuel Ct. E10 —7D 32
Emmanuel Rd. SW12 —1G 109
Emma Rd. E13 —2H 65
Emma St. E2 —2H 63
Emmaus Way. Chig —5K 21
Emmott Av. Ilf —5G 35
Emmott Clo. E1 —4A 64
Emmott Clo. NW11 —6A 28
Emms Pl. King T —2D 118
Emperor's Ga. SW7 —3K 75
Empire Av. N18 —5H 17
Empire Ct. Wemb —3H 41
Empire Pde. N18 —6J 17
Empire Pde. Wemb —3G 41

Empire Rd. Gnfd —1C **56**
Empire Way. Wemb —4F **41**
Empire Wharf Rd. E14 —4F **81**
Empire Yd. N7 —3J **45**
Empress Av. E4 —7J **19**
Empress Av. E12 —2A **50**
Empress Av. Ilf —2D **50**
Empress Av. Wfd G —7C **20**
Empress Dri. Chst —6F **115**
Empress Pde. E4 —7J **19**
Empress Pl. SW6 —5J **75**
Empress St. SE17 —6C **78**
Empson St. E3 —4D **64**
Emsworth Clo. N9 —1D **18**
Emsworth Ct. SW16 —3J **109**
Emsworth Rd. Ilf —2F **35**
Emsworth St. SW2 —2K **109**
Emu Rd. SW8 —2F **93**
Ena Rd. SW16 —3J **123**
Enbrook St. W10 —3G **59**
Endale Clo. Cars —2D **132**
Endeavour Way. SW19 —4K **107**
Endeavour Way. Bark —2A **68**
Endeavour Way. Croy —7J **123**
Endell St. WC2 —6J **61** (7C **140**)
Enderby St. SE10 —5G **81**
Enderley Clo. Harr —2J **23**
Enderley Rd. Harr —1J **23**
Endersleigh Gdns. NW4 —4C **26**
Endlebury Rd. E4 —2K **19**
Endlesham Rd. SW12 —7E **92**
Endsleigh Gdns. WC1
           —4H **61** (3A **140**)
Endsleigh Gdns. Ilf —2D **50**
Endsleigh Gdns. Surb —6C **118**
Endsleigh Pl. WC1 —4H **61** (3B **140**)
Endsleigh Rd. W13 —7A **56**
Endsleigh Rd. S'hall —4C **70**
Endsleigh St. WC1 —4H **61** (3A **140**)
End Way. Surb —7G **119**
Endwell Rd. SE4 —2A **96**
Endymion Rd. N4 —7A **30**
Endymion Rd. SW2 —5K **93**
Enfield Ho. SW9 —2J **93**
  (off Stockwell Rd.)
Enfield Rd. N1 —7E **46**
Enfield Rd. W3 —2H **73**
Enfield Rd. Bren —5D **72**
Enfield Rd. Enf —4C **6**
Enfield Wlk. Bren —5D **72**
Enford St. W1 —5D **60** (5E **138**)
Engadine Clo. Croy —3F **135**
Engadine St. SW18 —1J **107**
Engate St. SE13 —4E **96**
Engel Pk. NW7 —6K **13**
Engine Ct. SW1 —1G **77** (3M **145**)
  (off St James' Palace)
Engineer Clo. SE18 —6E **82**
Engineers Way. Wemb —4G **41**
England's La. NW3 —6D **44**
Englefield Clo. Croy —6C **124**
Englefield Clo. Enf —2F **7**
Englefield Rd. Orp —4K **129**
Englefield Cres. Orp —4K **129**
Englefield Path. Orp —4K **129**
Englefield Rd. N1 —7D **46**
Engleheart Rd. SE6 —7D **96**
Englewood Rd. SW12 —6F **93**
English Grounds. SE1
           —1E **78** (3D **148**)
English St. E3 —4B **64**
Enid St. SE16 —3F **79** (6E **148**)
Enmore Av. SE25 —5G **125**
Enmore Gdns. SW14 —5K **89**
Enmore Rd. SE25 —5G **125**
Enmore Rd. SW15 —4E **90**
Enmore Rd. S'hall —4E **54**

Ennerdale Av. Stan —3C **24**
Ennerdale Clo. Sutt —4H **131**
Ennerdale Dri. NW9 —5A **26**
Ennerdale Gdns. Wemb —1C **40**
Ennerdale Rd. Bexh —1G **101**
Ennerdale Rd. Rich —2F **89**
Ennersdale Rd. SE13 —5F **97**
Ennismore Av. W4 —4B **74**
Ennismore Av. Gnfd —6J **39**
Ennismore Gdns. SW7
           —2C **76** (5C **144**)
Ennismore Gdns. M. SW7
           —3C **76** (6C **144**)
Ennismore M. SW7 —3C **76** (6C **144**)
Ennismore St. SW7
           —3C **76** (6C **144**)
Ennis Rd. N4 —1A **46**
Ennis Rd. SE18 —6G **83**
Ennor Ct. Sutt —4E **130**
Ensign Dri. N13 —3H **17**
Ensign Ind. Cen. E1 —7G **63**
  (off Ensign St.)
Ensign St. E1 —7G **63**
Enslin Rd. SE9 —7E **98**
Ensor M. SW7 —5B **76**
Enstone Rd. Enf —3F **9**
Enterprise Bus. Pk. E14 —2C **80**
Enterprise Clo. Croy —1A **134**
Enterprise Ho. Bark —3K **67**
Enterprise Ind. Est. SE16 —5J **79**
Enterprise Way. NW10 —3B **58**
Enterprise Way. SW18 —4J **91**
Enterprise Way. Tedd —6K **103**
Enterprize Way. SE8 —4B **80**
Epcot M. NW10 —2C **58**
Epirus M. SW6 —7J **75**
Epirus Rd. SW6 —7H **75**
Epping Clo. E14 —4C **80**
Epping Clo. Romf —3H **37**
Epping Glade. E4 —6K **9**
Epping New Rd. Buck H & Lou
           —2E **20**
Epping Pl. N1 —6A **46**
Epping Way. E4 —6J **9**
Epple Rd. SW6 —1H **91**
Epsom Clo. Bexh —3H **101**
Epsom Clo. N'holt —5D **38**
Epsom Rd. E10 —6E **32**
Epsom Rd. Croy —4A **134**
Epsom Rd. Ilf —6K **35**
Epsom Rd. Sutt & Mord —7H **121**
Epstein Rd. SE28 —1A **84**
Epworth Rd. Iswth —7B **72**
Epworth St. EC2 —4D **62** (4B **142**)
Erasmus St. SW1 —4H **77** (9B **146**)
Erconwald St. W12 —6B **58**
Eresby Dri. Beck —1C **136**
Eresby Pl. NW6 —7J **43**
Erica Gdns. Croy —3D **136**
Erica St. W12 —7C **58**
Eric Clo. E7 —4J **49**
Ericsson Clo. SW18 —5J **91**
Eric Rd. E7 —4J **49**
Eric Rd. NW10 —6B **42**
Eric Rd. Romf —7D **36**
Eric St. E3 —4B **64**
Eridge Rd. W4 —3K **73**
Erin Clo. Brom —7G **113**
Erindale. SE18 —6H **83**
Erindale Ter. SE18 —6H **83**
Erith Cres. Romf —1J **37**
Erith Rd. Belv & Eri —5G **85**
Erith Rd. Bexh & N Hth —5G **85**
Erlanger Rd. SE14 —1K **95**
Erlesmere Gdns. W13 —3A **72**
Ermine Clo. Houn —2A **86**

Ermine Rd. N15 —6F **31**
Ermine Rd. SE13 —4D **96**
Ermine Side. Enf —5B **8**
Ermington Rd. SE9 —2G **115**
Ernald Av. E6 —2C **66**
Erncroft Way. Twic —6K **87**
Ernest Av. SE27 —4B **110**
Ernest Clo. Beck —5C **126**
Ernest Gdns. W4 —6H **73**
Ernest Gro. Beck —5B **126**
Ernest Rd. King T —2H **119**
Ernest Sq. King T —2H **119**
Ernle Rd. SW20 —7D **106**
Ernshaw Pl. SW15 —5G **91**
Erpingham Rd. SW15 —3E **90**
Erridge Rd. SW19 —2J **121**
Errington Rd. W9 —4H **59**
Errol Gdns. Hay —4A **54**
Errol Gdns. N Mald —4C **120**
Errol St. EC1 —4C **62** (4M **141**)
Erskine Clo. Sutt —3C **132**
Erskine Cres. N17 —4H **31**
Erskine Hill. NW11 —4J **27**
Erskine M. NW3 —7D **44**
  (off Erskine Rd.)
Erskine Rd. E17 —4B **32**
Erskine Rd. NW3 —7D **44**
Erskine Rd. Sutt —4B **132**
Erwood Rd. SE7 —5C **82**
Esam Way. SW16 —5A **110**
Escott Gdns. SE9 —4C **114**
Escreet Gro. SE18 —4E **82**
Esher Av. Romf —6J **37**
Esher Av. Sutt —3F **131**
Esher Clo. Bex —1E **116**
Esher Gdns. SW19 —2F **107**
Esher M. Mitc —3E **122**
Esher Rd. Ilf —3J **51**
Eskdale Av. N'holt —1D **54**
Eskdale Clo. Wemb —2D **40**
Eskdale Rd. Bexh —2G **101**
Eskmont Ridge. SE19 —7E **110**
Esk Rd. E13 —4J **65**
Esk Way. Romf —1K **37**
Esmar Cres. NW9 —7C **26**
Esmeralda Rd. SE1 —4G **79**
Esmond Gdns. W4 —4K **73**
Esmond Rd. NW6 —1H **59**
Esmond Rd. W4 —4K **73**
Esmond St. SW15 —4G **91**
Esparto St. SW18 —7K **91**
Essan Ho. N12 —7F **15**
Essenden Rd. Belv —5G **85**
Essenden Rd. S Croy —7E **134**
Essendine Rd. W9 —4J **59**
Essex Av. Iswth —3J **87**
Essex Clo. E17 —4A **32**
Essex Clo. Mord —7F **121**
Essex Clo. Romf —4H **37**
Essex Clo. Ruis —1B **38**
Essex Ct. EC4 —6A **62** (8G **141**)
  (off Temple)
Essex Ct. SW13 —2B **90**
Essex Gdns. N4 —6B **30**
Essex Gro. SE19 —6D **110**
Essex Hall. E17 —1K **31**
Essex Mans. E11 —7F **33**
Essex Pk. N3 —6E **14**
Essex Pk. M. W3 —1A **74**
Essex Pl. W4 —4J **73**
Essex Pl. Sq. W4 —4K **73**
Essex Rd. E4 —1B **20**
Essex Rd. E10 —6E **32**
Essex Rd. E12 —5C **50**
Essex Rd. E17 —6A **32**
Essex Rd. E18 —2K **33**
Essex Rd. N1 —1B **62**
Essex Rd. NW10 —7A **42**

Essex Rd. W3 —7J **57**
Essex Rd. W4 —4K **73**
Essex Rd. Bark —7H **51**
Essex Rd. Chad —7C **36**
Essex Rd. Dag —5J **53**
Essex Rd. Enf —4J **7**
Essex Rd. Romf —4H **37**
Essex Rd. S. E11 —7F **33**
Essex St. E7 —5J **49**
Essex St. WC2 —7A **62** (8G **141**)
Essex Vs. W8 —2J **75**
Essex Wharf. E5 —2K **47**
Essian St. E1 —5A **64**
Essoldo Way. Edgw —3F **25**
Estate Way. E10 —1B **48**
Estcourt Rd. SE25 —6H **125**
Estcourt Rd. SW6 —7H **75**
Estella Av. N Mald —4D **120**
Estelle Rd. NW3 —4D **44**
Esterbrooke St. SW1
           —4H **77** (9A **146**)
Este Rd. SW11 —3C **92**
Esther Clo. N21 —7F **7**
Esther Rd. E11 —7G **33**
Estreham Rd. SW16 —6H **109**
Estridge Clo. Houn —4E **86**
Eswyn Rd. SW17 —4D **108**
Etchingham Ct. N3 —7F **15**
Etchingham Pk. Rd. N3 —7E **14**
Etchingham Rd. E15 —4E **48**
Eternit Wlk. SW6 —1F **91**
Etfield Gro. Sidc —5B **116**
Ethelbert Clo. Brom —2J **127**
Ethelbert Gdns. Ilf —5D **34**
Ethelbert Rd. SW20 —1F **121**
Ethelbert Rd. Brom —3J **127**
Ethelbert Rd. Eri —7J **85**
Ethelbert St. SW12 —1F **109**
Ethelburga St. SW11 —1C **92**
Etheldene Av. N10 —4G **29**
Ethelden Rd. W12 —1D **74**
Ethel Rd. E16 —6K **65**
Ethel St. SE17 —4C **78** (9M **147**)
Etheridge Rd. NW4 —7E **26**
Etherley Rd. N15 —5C **30**
Etherow St. SE22 —6G **95**
Etherstone Grn. SW16 —4A **110**
Etherstone Rd. SW16 —4A **110**
Ethnard Rd. SE15 —6H **79**
Ethronvi Rd. Bexh —3E **100**
Etloe Rd. E10 —2C **48**
Eton Av. N12 —7F **15**
Eton Av. NW3 —7B **44**
Eton Av. Barn —6H **5**
Eton Av. Houn —6D **70**
Eton Av. N Mald —5K **119**
Eton Av. Wemb —4D **40**
Eton Clo. SW18 —7K **91**
Eton College Rd. NW3 —6D **44**
Eton Ct. Wemb —4D **40**
Eton Garages. NW3 —6C **44**
Eton Gro. NW9 —3G **25**
Eton Gro. SE13 —3G **97**
Eton Ho. N5 —4B **46**
  (off Leigh Rd.)
Eton Pl. NW3 —7E **44**
Eton Rise. NW3 —6D **44**
Eton Rd. NW3 —7D **44**
Eton Rd. Ilf —4G **51**
Eton Rd. Hay —6H **69**
Eton St. Rich —5E **88**
Eton Vs. NW3 —6D **44**
Etta St. SE8 —6A **80**
Ettrick St. E14 —6E **64**
  (in two parts)
Etwell Pl. Surb —6F **119**
Eugenia Rd. SE16 —4J **79**
Eureka Rd. King T —2G **119**
Eurolink Bus. Cen. SW2 —5A **94**

Europa Pl. EC1 —3C **62** (2L **141**)
Europa Trading Est. Eri —5K **85**
Europe Rd. SE18 —3D **82**
Eustace Pl. SE18 —4D **82**
Eustace Rd. E6 —3C **66**
Eustace Rd. SW6 —7J **75**
Eustace Rd. Romf —7D **36**
Euston Gro. NW1 —3H **61** (2A **140**)
  (off Euston Sq.)
Euston Rd. NW1 —4F **61** (4K **139**)
Euston Rd. Croy —1A **134**
Euston Sq. NW1 —3H **61** (2A **140**)
Euston Sta. Colonnade. NW1
           —3H **61** (2A **140**)
Euston St. NW1 —3G **61** (3M **139**)
Evandale Rd. SW9 —2A **94**
Evangelist Rd. NW5 —4F **45**
Evans Clo. E8 —6F **47**
Evans Gro. Felt —2E **102**
Evans Ho. W12 —7D **58**
  (off Whilte City Est.)
Evans Ho. Felt —2E **102**
Evans Rd. SE6 —2G **113**
Evanston Av. E4 —7K **19**
Evanston Gdns. Ilf —6C **34**
Eva Rd. Romf —7C **36**
Evelina Mans. SE5 —7D **78**
Evelina Rd. SE15 —3H **95**
Evelina Rd. SE20 —7J **111**
Eveline Rd. Mitc —1D **122**
Evelyn Av. NW9 —4K **25**
Evelyn Clo. Twic —7F **87**
Evelyn Ct. E8 —4G **47**
Evelyn Denington Rd. E6 —5D **66**
Evelyn Dri. Pinn —1B **22**
Evelyn Fox Ct. W10 —5F **58**
Evelyn Gdns. SW7 —5A **76**
Evelyn Gdns. Rich —4E **88**
Evelyn Gro. W5 —1F **73**
Evelyn Gro. S'hall —6D **54**
Evelyn Ho. W12 —2B **74**
  (off Cobbold Rd.)
Evelyn Lowe Est. SE16 —3G **79**
Evelyn Rd. E16 —1K **81**
Evelyn Rd. E17 —4E **32**
Evelyn Rd. SW19 —5K **107**
Evelyn Rd. W4 —3K **73**
Evelyn Rd. Barn —4J **5**
Evelyn Rd. Ham —3C **104**
Evelyn Rd. Rich —3E **88**
Evelyn St. SE8 —4A **80**
Evelyn Ter. Rich —3E **88**
Evelyn Wlk. N1 —2D **62**
Evelyn Way. Wall —4H **133**
Evelyn Yd. W1 —6H **61** (7A **140**)
Evening Hill. Beck —7E **112**
Evenwood Clo. SW15 —5G **91**
Everall Av. SW6 —2K **91**
Everard Av. Brom —1J **137**
Everard Ct. N13 —3E **16**
  (off Crothall Clo.)
Everard Way. Wemb —3E **40**
Everatt Clo. SW18 —6H **91**
Everdon Rd. SW13 —6C **74**
Everest Pl. E14 —5E **64**
Everest Rd. SE9 —5D **98**
Everett Wlk. Belv —5F **85**
Everglade Strand. NW9 —1B **26**
Everilda St. N1 —1K **61**
Evering Rd. N16 & E5 —3F **47**
Everington Rd. N10 —2D **28**
Everington St. W6 —6F **75**
Everitt Rd. NW10 —3K **57**
Everleigh St. N4 —1K **45**
Eve Rd. E11 —4G **49**
Eve Rd. E15 —2G **65**
Eve Rd. N17 —3E **30**
Eve Rd. Iswth —4A **88**

Eversfield Gdns. NW7 —6F 13
Eversfield Rd. Rich —2F 89
Eversholt St. NW1 —2G 61
Evershot Rd. N4 —1K 45
Eversleigh Rd. E6 —1B 66
Eversleigh Rd. N3 —7C 14
Eversleigh Rd. SW11 —3D 92
Eversleigh Rd. Barn —5F 5
Eversley Av. Bexh —2K 101
Eversley Av. Wemb —2G 41
Eversley Clo. N21 —6E 6
Eversley Cres. N21 —6F 7
Eversley Cres. Iswth —1H 87
Eversley Mt. N21 —6E 6
Eversley Pk. Rd. N21 —6E 6
Eversley Rd. SE7 —6K 81
Eversley Rd. SE19 —7D 110
Eversley Rd. Surb —4F 119
Eversley Way. Croy —3C 136
Everthorpe Rd. SE15 —3F 95
Everton Bldgs. NW1
   —3G 61 (2L 139)
Everton Dri. Stan —3E 24
Everton Rd. Croy —1G 135
Evesham Av. E17 —2C 32
Evesham Clo. Gnfd —2F 55
Evesham Clo. Sutt —7J 131
Evesham Grn. Mord —6K 121
Evesham Rd. E15 —7H 49
Evesham Rd. N11 —5B 16
Evesham Rd. Mord —6K 121
Evesham St. W11 —7F 59
Evesham Wlk. SE5 —2D 94
Evesham Wlk. SW9 —2A 94
Evesham Way. SW11 —3E 92
Evesham Way. IIf —3E 34
Evry Rd. Sidc —6C 116
Ewald Rd. SW6 —2H 91
Ewanrigg Ter. Wfd G —5F 21
Ewart Gro. N22 —1A 30
Ewart Pl. E3 —2B 64
Ewart Rd. SE23 —7K 95
Ewe Clo. N7 —6J 45
Ewell By-Pass. Eps —7C 130
Ewell Ct. Av. Ewe —5A 130
Ewellhurst Rd. IIf —2C 34
Ewell Pk. Way. Eps —6C 130
Ewell Rd. Dit H —7B 118
Ewell Rd. Surb —6E 118
Ewell Rd. Sutt —7F 131
Ewelme Rd. SE23 —1J 111
Ewen Cres. SW2 —1A 110
Ewen Ho. N1 —1K 61
   (off Barnsbury Est.)
Ewer St. SE1 —1C 78 (3L 147)
Ewhurst Av. S Croy —7F 135
Ewhurst Clo. Sutt —7E 130
Ewhurst Rd. SE4 —6B 96
Exbury Ho. E9 —6J 47
Exbury Rd. SE6 —2C 112
Excel Ct. WC2 —7H 61 (1B 146)
   (off Whitcomb St.)
Excelsior Clo. King T —2G 119
Excelsior Gdns. SE13 —2E 96
Exchange Arc. EC2 —5E 62 (5D 142)
Exchange Ct. WC2 —7J 61 (1D 146)
Exchange Mans. NW11 —7H 27
Exchange Pl. EC2 —5E 62 (5D 142)
Exchange Sq. EC2 —5E 62 (5D 142)
Exchange St. Romf —5K 37
Exchange, The. IIf —2F 51
Exeter Clo. E6 —6D 66
Exeter Gdns. IIf —1C 50
Exeter Ho. Bark —7A 52
   (off Margaret Bondfield Av.)
Exeter Ho. Felt —2C 102
   (off Watermill Way)

Exeter M. NW6 —6K 43
Exeter Rd. E16 —5J 65
Exeter Rd. E17 —5C 32
Exeter Rd. N9 —2D 18
Exeter Rd. N14 —1A 16
Exeter Rd. NW2 —5G 43
Exeter Rd. SE15 —7F 79
Exeter Rd. Croy —7E 124
Exeter Rd. Dag —6H 53
Exeter Rd. Enf —3E 8
Exeter Rd. Felt —3D 102
Exeter Rd. Harr —2C 38
Exeter Rd. Well —6K 99
Exeter St. WC2 —7J 61 (9D 140)
Exeter Way. SE14 —7B 80
Exford Gdns. SE12 —1K 113
Exford Rd. SE12 —2K 113
Exhibition Clo. W12 —7E 58
Exhibition Rd. SW7 —2B 76 (5B 144)
Exmoor Clo. IIf —1F 35
Exmoor St. W10 —5F 59
Exmouth Mkt. EC1 —4A 62 (3G 141)
Exmouth M. NW1 —3G 61 (2M 139)
Exmouth Pl. E8 —7H 47
Exmouth Rd. E17 —5B 32
Exmouth Rd. Brom —3K 127
Exmouth Rd. Ruis —3A 38
Exmouth Rd. Well —1C 100
Exmouth St. E1 —6J 63
Exning Rd. E16 —4H 65
Exon St. SE17 —5E 78
Express Dri. IIf —1B 52
Exton Cres. NW10 —7J 41
Exton Gdns. Dag —6C 52
Exton St. SE1 —1A 78 (3G 147)
Eybright Clo. Croy —1K 135
Eyhurst Clo. NW2 —2C 42
Eylewood Rd. SE27 —5C 110
Eynella Rd. SE22 —7F 95
Eynham Rd. W12 —6E 58
Eynsford Clo. Orp —7G 129
Eynsford Cres. Bex —1C 116
Eynsford Rd. IIf —2J 51
Eynsham Dri. SE2 —4A 84
Eynswood Dri. Sidc —5B 116
Eyot Gdns. W6 —5B 74
Eyot Grn. W4 —5B 74
Eyre Ct. NW8 —2B 60
Eyre St. Hill. EC1 —4A 62 (4G 141)
Eysdown Rd. SE9 —2C 114
Eysham Ct. New Bar —5E 4
Eythorne Rd. SW9 —1A 94
Ezra St. E2 —3F 63

Fairby Rd. SE12 —5K 97
Faircharm Trading Est. SE8 —7D 80
Fairchild Clo. SW11 —2B 92
Fairchild Ho. N3 —1J 27
Fairchild Pl. EC2 —4E 62 (4D 142)
   (off Gt. Eastern St.)
Fairchild St. EC2 —4E 62 (4D 142)
Fair Clo. Bush —1A 10
Fairclough St. E1 —6G 63
Faircroft. N22 —1J 29
Faircroft Ct. Tedd —6A 104
Faircross Av. Bark —6G 51
Faircross Av. Romf —1K 37
Faircross Pde. Bark —6J 51
Fairdale Gdns. SW15 —4D 90
Fairdale Gdns. Eps —7D 130
Fairfax. Eps —7D 130
Fairfax Gdns. SE3 —1A 98
Fairfax Pl. NW6 —7A 44
Fairfax Rd. N8 —4A 30
Fairfax Rd. NW6 —7A 44
Fairfax Rd. W4 —3A 74
Fairfax Rd. Tedd —6A 104
Fairfax Way. N10 —7E 14
Fairfield Av. NW4 —6D 26
Fairfield Av. Edgw —6C 12
Fairfield Av. Twic —1F 103
Fairfield Clo. N12 —4F 15
Fairfield Clo. Enf —4E 8
Fairfield Clo. Ewe —5A 130
Fairfield Clo. Mitc —7C 108
Fairfield Clo. Sidc —6K 99
Fairfield Ct. NW10 —1C 58
Fairfield Cres. Edgw —6C 12
Fairfield Dri. SW18 —5K 91
Fairfield Dri. Gnfd —1C 56
Fairfield Dri. Harr —3G 23
Fairfield E. King T —2E 118
Fairfield Gdns. N8 —5J 29
Fairfield Gro. SE7 —6B 82
Fairfield N. King T —2E 118
Fairfield Path. Croy —3D 134
Fairfield Pl. King T —3E 118
Fairfield Rd. E3 —2C 64
Fairfield Rd. E17 —2A 32
Fairfield Rd. N8 —5J 29
Fairfield Rd. N18 —4B 18
Fairfield Rd. Beck —2C 126
Fairfield Rd. Bexh —2F 101
Fairfield Rd. Brom —7J 113
Fairfield Rd. Croy —3D 134
Fairfield Rd. IIf —6F 51
Fairfield Rd. King T —2E 118
Fairfield Rd. Orp —6H 129
Fairfield Rd. S'hall —5D 54
Fairfield Rd. Wfd G —6D 20
Fairfield S. King T —3E 118
Fairfields Clo. NW9 —5J 25
Fairfields Cres. NW9 —5J 25
Fairfield St. SW18 —5K 91
Fairfield Way. Barn —5D 4
Fairfield Way. Eps —5A 130
Fairfield W. King T —2E 118
Fairfoot Rd. E3 —4C 64
Fairford Av. Bexh —1K 101
Fairford Av. Croy —5K 125
Fairford Clo. Croy —5K 125
Fairford Ct. Sutt —7K 131
Fairford Gdns. Wor Pk —3B 130
Fairford Ho. SE11 —4A 78 (9H 147)
Fairgreen. Barn —3J 5
Fairgreen Ct. Barn —5K 5
Fairgreen E. Barn —3J 5
Fairgreen Rd. T Hth —5B 124
Fairhaven Av. Croy —6K 125
Fairhazel Gdns. NW6 —6K 43
Fairholme. Felt —1F 101
Fairholme Clo. N3 —4G 27
Fairholme Gdns. N3 —3G 27
Fairholme Rd. W14 —5G 75

Fairholme Rd. Croy —7A 124
Fairholme Rd. Harr —5K 23
Fairholme Rd. IIf —2D 50
Fairholme Rd. Sutt —6H 131
Fairholt Clo. N16 —1E 46
Fairholt Rd. N16 —1D 46
Fairholt St. SW7 —3C 76 (6D 144)
Fairland Rd. E15 —6H 49
Fairlands Av. Buck H —2D 20
Fairlands Av. Sutt —2J 131
Fairlands Av. T Hth —4K 123
Fairlands Ct. SE9 —6E 98
Fairlawn. SE7 —6A 82
Fairlawn Av. N2 —4C 28
Fairlawn Av. Bexh —2D 100
Fairlawn Av. W4 —4J 73
Fairlawn Clo. N14 —6B 6
Fairlawn Clo. Felt —4D 102
Fairlawn Clo. King T —6J 105
Fairlawn Ct. SE7 —6A 82
Fairlawn Ct. W4 —4J 73
Fairlawn Dri. Wfd G —7D 20
Fairlawn Gro. W4 —4J 73
Fairlawn Mans. SE14 —1K 95
Fairlawn Pk. SE26 —5A 112
Fairlawn Rd. SW19 —7H 107
Fairlawns. Pinn —2B 22
Fairlawns. Twic —6C 88
Fairlawns. Wall —5F 133
Fairlea Pl. W5 —4D 56
Fairlie Gdns. SE23 —7J 95
Fairlight Av. E4 —2A 20
Fairlight Av. NW10 —2A 58
Fairlight Av. Wfd G —6D 20
Fairlight Clo. E4 —2A 20
Fairlight Clo. Wor Pk —4E 130
Fairlight Ct. NW10 —2A 58
Fairlight Rd. SW17 —4B 108
Fairline Ct. Beck —2E 126
Fairlop Ct. E11 —1F 49
Fairlop Gdns. IIf —1G 35
Fairlop Pl. NW8 —3B 60 (2B 138)
Fairlop Rd. E11 —7F 33
Fairlop Rd. IIf —2G 35
Fairman Ter. Kent —4D 24
Fairmead. Brom —4D 128
Fairmead Clo. Brom —4D 128
Fairmead Clo. Houn —7B 70
Fairmead Clo. N Mald —3K 119
Fairmead Ct. Rich —2H 89
Fairmead Cres. Edgw —3D 12
Fairmead Gdns. IIf —5C 34
Fairmead Ho. E9 —4A 48
Fairmead Rd. N19 —3H 45
Fairmead Rd. Croy —7K 123
Fairmile Av. SW16 —5H 109
Fairmont Clo. Belv —5F 85
Fairmount Rd. SW2 —6K 93
Fairoak Clo. Orp —7F 129
Fairoak Dri. SE9 —5H 99
Fairoak Gdns. Romf —2K 37
Fairseat Clo. Bush —2D 10
Fairstead Wlk. N1 —1C 62
   (off Popham St.)
Fair St. SE1 —2E 78 (4D 148)
Fair St. Houn —3G 87
Fairthorn Rd. SE7 —6J 81
Fairview Av. Wemb —6D 40
Fairview Clo. E17 —1A 32
Fairview Ct. NW4 —2F 27
Fairview Cres. Harr —1E 38
Fairview Gdns. Wfd G —1K 33
Fairview Ho. SW2 —7K 93
Fairview Ind. Pk. Rain —5K 69
Fairview Pl. SW2 —7K 93
Fairview Rd. N15 —5F 31
Fairview Rd. SW16 —1K 123
Fairview Rd. Enf —1F 7

Fairview Rd. Sutt —5C 132
Fairview Way. Edgw —4B 12
Fairwall Ho. SE5 —1E 94
Fairwater Av. Well —4A 100
Fairwater Clo. N15 —4E 30
Fairway. SW20 —3E 120
Fairway. Bexh —5E 100
Fairway. Orp —5H 129
Fair Way. Wfd G —5F 21
Fairway Av. NW9 —3H 25
Fairway Clo. NW11 —7A 28
Fairway Clo. Croy —5A 126
Fairway Clo. Houn —5A 86
Fairway Clo. NW7 —5E 13
Fairway Ct. New Bar —6E 4
Fairway Dri. Gnfd —1F 55
Fairway Gdns. Beck —6F 127
Fairway Gdns. IIf —5G 51
Fairways. Stan —2E 24
Fairways. Tedd —7D 104
Fairways Bus. Pk. E10 —2B 48
Fairway, The. N13 —3J 17
Fairway, The. N14 —6B 6
Fairway, The. NW7 —3E 12
Fairway, The. W3 —6A 58
Fairway, The. W7 —7H 55
Fairway, The. Barn —6E 4
Fairway, The. Brom —5D 128
Fairway, The. N Mald —1K 119
Fairway, The. N'holt —6G 39
Fairway, The. Ruis —4A 38
Fairway, The. Wemb —2B 40
Fairweather Clo. N15 —4E 30
Fairweather Rd. N16 —6G 31
Fairwyn Rd. SE26 —4A 112
Fakenham Clo. N'holt —6D 38
Fakruddin St. E1 —4G 63
Falconberg Ct. W1 —6H 61 (7B 140)
Falconberg M. W1 —6H 61 (7A 140)
Falcon Clo. SE1 —1B 78 (2K 147)
Falcon Clo. W4 —6J 73
Falcon Ct. E18 —3K 33
   (off Albert Rd.)
Falcon Ct. EC4 —6A 62 (8H 141)
Falcon Ct. N1 —2B 62
   (off City Garden Row)
Falcon Ct. SE1 —1B 78
Falcon Ct. New Bar —4F 5
Falcon Cres. Enf —5E 8
Falconer Ct. N17 —7H 17
Falconer Wlk. N7 —2K 45
Falcon Gro. SW11 —3C 92
Falcon La. SW11 —3D 92
Falcon Point. SE1 —1B 78 (2K 147)
Falcon Rd. SW11 —2C 92
Falcon Rd. Enf —5E 8
Falcon Rd. Hamp —7D 102
Falcon St. E13 —4H 65
Falcon Ter. SW11 —3C 92
Falcon Way. E11 —4J 33
Falcon Way. E14 —4D 80
Falcon Way. NW9 —2A 26
Falcon Way. Harr —5E 24
Falconwood Av. Well —2H 99
Falconwood Ct. SE3 —2H 97
Falconwood Pde. Well —4K 99
Falconwood Rd. Croy —7B 136
Falcourt Clo. Sutt —5K 131
Falkirk St. N1 —2E 62
Falkland Av. N3 —7D 14
Falkland Av. N11 —4A 16
Falkland Ho. W8 —3K 75
Falkland Pk. Av. SE25 —3E 124
Falkland Pl. NW5 —5G 45
Falkland Rd. N8 —4A 30
Falkland Rd. NW5 —5G 45
Falkland Rd. Barn —2B 4

Fernside. NW11 —2J 43
Fernside. Buck H —1E 20
Fernside Av. NW7 —3E 12
Fernside Av. Felt —4A 102
Fernside Ct. NW4 —2F 27
Fernside Rd. SW12 —1D 108
Ferns Rd. E15 —6H 49
Fern St. E3 —4C 64
Fernthorpe Rd. SW16 —6G 109
Ferntower Rd. N5 —5D 46
Fernways. Ilf —4F 51
Fernwood. Croy —7A 136
Fernwood Av. SW16 —4H 109
Fernwood Av. Wemb —6C 40
Fernwood Clo. Brom —2A 128
Fernwood Cres. N20 —3J 15
Ferny Hill. Barn —1K 5
Ferranti Clo. SE18 —4B 82
Ferrard Clo. Houn —6E 72
Ferrers Av. Wall —4H 133
Ferrers Rd. SW16 —5H 109
Ferrestone Rd. N8 —4K 29
Ferriby Clo. N1 —7A 46
Ferrier Point. E16 —5J 65
  (off Forty Acre La.)
Ferrier St. SW18 —4K 91
Ferring Clo. Harr —1G 39
Ferrings. SE21 —3E 110
Ferris Av. Croy —3B 136
Ferris Rd. SE22 —4G 95
Ferron Rd. E5 —3H 47
Ferry App. SE18 —3E 82
Ferrybridge Ho. SE11
          —3K 77 (7F 146)
  (off Lambeth Wlk.)
Ferrydale Lodge. NW4 —4E 26
  (off Church Rd.)
Ferry Ho. E5 —1H 47
  (off Harrington Hill)
Ferry La. N17 —4G 31
Ferry La. SW13 —6B 74
Ferry La. Bren —6E 72
Ferry La. Rain —6K 69
Ferry La. Rich —6F 73
Ferrymead Av. Gnfd —3E 54
Ferrymead Dri. Gnfd —2E 54
Ferrymoor. Rich —3B 104
Ferry Pl. SE18 —3E 82
Ferry Rd. SW13 —7C 74
Ferry Rd. Tedd —5B 104
Ferry Rd. Th Dit —6B 118
Ferry Rd. Twic —1B 104
Ferry Sq. Bren —7E 72
Ferry St. E14 —5E 80
Festing Rd. SW15 —3F 91
Festival Clo. Bex —1D 116
Festival Wlk. Cars —5D 132
Fetter La. EC4 —6A 62 (8H 141)
  (in two parts)
Ffinch St. SE8 —7C 80
Field Clo. E4 —6J 19
Field Clo. Brom —2A 128
Field Clo. Buck H —3F 21
Field Clo. Houn —2A 86
Field Ct. SW19 —3J 107
Field Ct. WC1 —5K 61 (6F 140)
Field End. N'holt —6C 38
Field End. Ruis —6A 38
Field End. Twic —4K 103
Fieldend Rd. SW16 —1G 123
Field End Rd. Eastc & Ruis —6A 22
Fielders Clo. Enf —4J 7
Fielders Clo. Harr —1G 39
Fieldfare Rd. SE28 —7C 68
Fieldgate La. Mitc —2C 122
Fieldgate St. E1 —5G 63
Fieldhouse Rd. SW12 —1G 109
Fielding Av. Twic —3G 103

Fielding Ho. W4 —6A 74
  (off Devonshire Rd.)
Fielding Rd. W4 —3K 73
Fielding Rd. W14 —3F 75
Fieldings, The. SE23 —1J 111
Fielding St. SE17 —6C 78
Fielding Ter. W5 —7F 57
Field La. Bren —7C 72
Field La. Tedd —5A 104
Field Mead. NW9 & NW7 —7F 13
Field Pl. N Mald —6B 120
Field Point. E7 —4J 49
Field Rd. E7 —4J 49
Field Rd. N17 —3D 30
Field Rd. W6 —5G 75
Field Rd. Felt —6A 86
Fieldsend Rd. Sutt —5G 131
Fields Est. E8 —7G 47
Fieldside Rd. Brom —5F 113
Fields Pk. Cres. Romf —5D 36
Field St. WC1 —3K 61 (1E 140)
Fieldsway Ho. N5 —5A 46
Fieldview. SW18 —1B 108
Field Way. NW10 —7J 41
Fieldway. Dag —3C 52
Field Way. Gnfd —1F 55
Field Way. New Ad —7D 136
Fieldway. Orp —6H 129
Fieldway Cres. N5 —5A 46
Fiennes Clo. Dag —1C 52
Fife Rd. E16 —5J 65
Fife Rd. N22 —7G 17
Fife Rd. SW14 —5A 89
Fife Rd. King T —2E 118
Fife Ter. N1 —2K 61
Fifield Path. SE23 —3K 111
Fifth Av. E12 —4D 50
Fifth Av. W10 —3G 59
Fifth Cross Rd. Twic —2H 103
Fifth Way. Wemb —4H 41
Figges Rd. Mitc —7E 108
Fig Tree Clo. NW10 —1A 58
Filey Av. N16 —1G 47
Filey Clo. Sutt —7A 132
Fillebrook Av. Enf —2K 7
Fillebrook Rd. E11 —1G 49
Filmer Rd. SW6 —1G 91
Filston Rd. Eri —5J 85
Filton Ct. SE15 —6E 78
  (off Brockworth Clo.)
Finborough Rd. SW10 —5K 75
Finborough Rd. SW17 —6D 108
Finchale Rd. SE2 —3A 84
Finch Av. SE27 —4D 110
Finch Clo. NW10 —6K 41
Finch Clo. Barn —5D 4
Finch Clo. Sidc —3B 116
Finchdean Way. SE15 —7F 79
Finch Dri. Felt —7B 86
Finchingfield Av. Wfd G —7F 21
Finch La. EC3 —6D 62 (8B 142)
Finchley Ct. N3 —6E 14
Finchley Ind. Est. N12 —4F 15
Finchley La. NW4 —4E 26
Finchley Pk. N12 —4F 15
Finchley Pl. NW8 —2B 60
Finchley Rd. NW3 —4J 43
Finchley Rd. NW8 —1B 60
Finchley Rd. NW11 & NW2 —4H 27
Finchley Way. N3 —7D 14
Finch's Ct. E14 —7D 64
Finck St. SE1 —2K 77 (5F 146)
Finden Rd. E7 —5A 50
Findhorn Av. Hay —5A 54
Findhorn St. E14 —6E 64
Findon Clo. SW18 —6J 91
Findon Clo. Harr —3F 39
Findon Rd. N9 —1C 18

Findon Rd. W12 —2C 74
Fingal St. SE10 —5H 81
Finland Rd. SE4 —3A 96
Finland St. SE16 —3A 80
Finlay St. SW6 —1F 91
Finmere Ho. N4 —7C 30
Finnis St. E2 —3H 63
Finnymore Rd. Dag —7E 52
Finsbury Av. EC2 —5D 62 (6B 142)
Finsbury Av. Sq. EC2
  (off Finsbury Av.) —5E 62 (5C 142)
Finsbury Cir. EC2 —5D 62 (6B 142)
Finsbury Cotts. N22 —7D 16
Finsbury Est. EC1 —3A 62 (2H 141)
Finsbury Ho. N22 —1J 29
Finsbury Mkt. EC2 —4E 62 (4C 142)
  (in two parts)
Finsbury Pk. Av. N4 —6C 30
Finsbury Pk. Rd. N4 —2B 46
Finsbury Pavement. EC2
          —5D 62 (5B 142)
Finsbury Rd. N22 —7E 16
Finsbury Sq. EC2 —4D 62 (5B 142)
Finsbury St. EC2 —5D 62 (5A 142)
Finsbury Way. Bex —6F 101
Finsen Rd. SE5 —4C 94
Finstock Rd. W10 —6F 59
Finucane Rise. Bush —2B 10
Firbank Clo. E16 —5B 66
Firbank Clo. Enf —4H 7
Firbank Rd. SE15 —2H 95
Fircroft Gdns. Harr —3J 39
Fircroft Rd. SW17 —2D 108
Fire Bell La. Surb —6E 118
Firecrest Dri. NW3 —3K 43
Firefly Clo. Wall —7J 133
Fire Sta. All. H Bar —3B 4
Fire Sta. M. Beck —1D 126
Fir Gro. N Mald —6B 120
Fir Rd. Felt —5B 102
Fir Rd. Sutt —1H 131
Firs Av. N10 —3E 28
Firs Av. N11 —6J 15
Firs Av. SW14 —4J 89
Firs Av. Croy —1K 135
Firsby Rd. N16 —1G 47
Firs Clo. N10 —4E 28
Firs Clo. SE23 —7A 96
Firs Clo. Mitc —1F 123
Firs Croft. N13 —3H 17
Firs Ho. N22 —1A 30
  (off Acacia Rd.)
Firside Gro. Sidc —1K 115
Firs La. N13 & N21 —3H 17
Firs La. N21 —7H 7
Firs Pk. Av. N21 —1J 17
Firs Pk. Gdns. N21 —1J 17
First Av. E12 —4C 50
First Av. E13 —3J 65
  (in two parts)
First Av. E17 —5C 32
First Av. N18 —4D 18
First Av. N21 —6A 8
First Av. NW4 —4E 26
First Av. SW14 —3A 90
First Av. W3 —1B 74
First Av. W10 —4H 59
First Av. Bexh —7C 84
First Av. Dag —2H 69
First Av. Enf —5A 8
First Av. Eps —7A 130
First Av. Romf —5C 36
First Av. Wemb —2D 40
First Cross Rd. Twic —2J 103
Firs, The. E6 —7C 50
Firs, The. N20 —1G 15
Firs, The. W5 —5D 56

Firs, The. Bex —1K 117
Firs, The. Sidc —3K 115
First St. SW3 —4C 76 (8D 144)
Firstway. SW20 —2E 120
First Way. Wemb —4H 41
Firs Wlk. Wfd G —5D 20
Firth Gdns. SW6 —1G 91
Firtree Av. Mitc —2E 122
Firtree Clo. SW16 —5G 109
Fir Tree Clo. W5 —6E 56
Fir Tree Clo. Ewe —4B 130
Fir Tree Clo. Romf —3K 37
Fir Tree Gdns. Croy —4C 136
Fir Tree Gro. Cars —7D 132
Fir Tree Rd. Houn —4C 86
Fir Trees Clo. SE16 —1A 80
Fir Tree Wlk. Dag —3J 53
Fir Tree Wlk. Enf —3J 7
Fir Wlk. Sutt —6F 131
Fisher Clo. Croy —1F 135
Fisher Clo. Gnfd —3E 54
Fisher Ho. N1 —1A 62
  (off Barnsbury Est.)
Fisherman Clo. Rich —4C 104
Fishermans Dri. SE16 —2K 79
Fisherman's Pl. W4 —6B 74
Fisherman's Wlk. E14 —1C 80
Fisher Rd. Harr —2C 23
Fishers Ct. SE14 —1K 95
Fisher's La. W4 —4K 73
Fisher St. E16 —5J 65
Fisher St. WC1 —5K 61 (6E 140)
Fishers Way. Belv —1J 85
Fisherton St. NW8 —4B 60 (4A 138)
Fishmongers Hall Wharf. EC4
  (off Swan La.) —7D 62 (1B 148)
Fishponds Rd. SW17 —4C 108
Fish St. Hill. EC3 —7D 62 (1B 148)
Fish Wharf. EC3 —7D 62 (1B 148)
  (off Lwr. Thames St.)
Fiske Ct. N17 —1G 31
Fiske Ct. Bark —2H 67
Fisons Rd. E16 —1J 81
Fitzalan Rd. N3 —3G 27
Fitzalan St. SE11 —4A 78 (8F 146)
Fitzgeorge Av. W14 —4G 75
Fitzgeorge Av. N Mald —1K 119
Fitzgerald Av. SW14 —3A 90
Fitzgerald Ho. SW9 —2A 94
Fitzgerald Rd. E11 —5J 33
Fitzgerald Rd. SW14 —3K 89
Fitzgerald Rd. Th Dit —6A 118
Fitzhardinge St. W1
          —6E 60 (7G 139)
Fitzhugh Gro. SW18 —6B 92
Fitzjames Av. W14 —4G 75
Fitzjames Av. Croy —2G 135
Fitzjohn Av. Barn —5B 4
Fitzjohn's Av. NW3 —4A 44
Fitzmaurice Pl. W1 —1F 77 (2K 145)
Fitzneal St. W12 —6B 58
Fitzroy Clo. N6 —1D 44
Fitzroy Ct. N6 —6D 28
Fitzroy Ct. W1 —4G 61 (4M 139)
  (off Tottenham Ct. Rd.)
Fitzroy Cres. W4 —7K 73
Fitzroy Gdns. SE19 —7E 110
Fitzroy M. W1 —4G 61 (4L 139)
  (off Cleveland St.)
Fitzroy Pk. N6 —1D 44
Fitzroy Rd. NW1 —1E 60
Fitzroy Sq. W1 —4G 61 (4L 139)
Fitzroy St. W1 —4G 61 (4L 139)
  (in two parts)
Fitzstephen Rd. Dag —5B 52
Fitzwarren Gdns. N19 —1G 45
Fitzwilliam Av. Rich —2F 89

Fitzwilliam Heights. SE23 —2J 111
Fitzwilliam Ho. Rich —4D 88
Fitzwilliam Rd. SW4 —3G 93
Fitzwygram Clo. Hamp —5G 103
Five Acre. NW9 —2B 26
Fiveacre Clo. T Hth —6A 124
Five Elms Rd. Brom —2K 137
Five Elms Rd. Dag —3F 53
Fiveways Rd. SW9 —2A 94
Flack Ct. E10 —7D 32
Fladbury Rd. N15 —6D 30
Fladgate Rd. E11 —6G 33
Flag Clo. Croy —1K 135
Flambard Rd. Harr —6A 24
Flamborough Ho. SE15 —1G 95
  (off Oliver Goldsmith Est.)
Flamborough St. E14 —6A 64
Flamingo Gdns. N'holt —3C 54
Flamstead Gdns. Dag —7C 52
Flamstead Rd. Dag —7C 52
Flamsted Av. Wemb —6G 41
Flamsted Rd. SE7 —5C 82
Flanchford Rd. W12 —3B 74
Flanders Ct. E17 —6A 32
Flanders Cres. SW17 —7D 108
Flanders Mans. W4 —4B 74
Flanders Rd. E6 —2D 66
Flanders Rd. W4 —4A 74
Flanders Way. E9 —6K 47
Flank St. E1 —7G 63
Flask Wlk. NW3 —4A 44
Flaxen Clo. E4 —3J 19
Flaxen Rd. E4 —3J 19
Flaxley Rd. Mord —7K 121
Flaxman Ct. W1 —6H 61 (8A 140)
  (off Flaxman Ct.)
Flaxman Ct. Belv —5G 85
  (off Hoddesdon Rd.)
Flaxman Ho. W4 —5A 74
  (off Devonshire St.)
Flaxman Rd. SE5 —3B 94
Flaxman Ter. WC1 —3H 61 (2B 140)
Flaxmore Pl. Beck —6F 127
Flaxton Rd. SE18 —7J 83
Flecker Clo. Stan —5E 10
Fleece Rd. Surb —7C 118
Fleece Wlk. N7 —6J 45
Fleeming Clo. E17 —2B 32
Fleeming Rd. E17 —2B 32
Fleet Bldgs. EC4 —6B 62 (7J 141)
  (off Shoe Pl.)
Fleet Pl. EC4 —6B 62 (7J 141)
  (off Old Fleet La.)
Fleet Rd. NW3 —5C 44
Fleet Sq. WC1 —3K 61 (2F 140)
Fleet St. EC4 —6A 62 (8G 141)
Fleet St. Hill. E1 —4G 63
Fleetway Bus. Cen. NW2 —1B 42
Fleetway Bus. Pk. Gnfd —2B 56
Fleetwood Clo. E16 —5B 66
Fleetwood Clo. Croy —3F 135
Fleetwood Ct. E6 —5D 66
  (off Evelyn Dennington Rd.)
Fleetwood Rd. NW10 —5C 42
Fleetwood Rd. King T —3H 119
Fleetwood Sq. King T —3H 119
Fleetwood St. N16 —2E 46
Fleming Ct. W2 —5B 60 (5A 138)
  (off St Marys Sq.)
Fleming Ct. Croy —5A 134
Fleming Ho. N4 —1C 46
Fleming Ho. SE16 —2G 79
  (off George Row)
Fleming Ho. Wemb —3J 41
  (off Barnhill Rd.)
Fleming Mead. Mitc —7D 108
Fleming Rd. SE17 —6B 78
Fleming Rd. S'hall —6F 55

eming Way. SE28 —7D 68
eming Way. Iswth —4K 87
empton Rd. E10 —1A 48
etcher La. E10 —7E 32
etcher Path. SE16 —7C 80
etcher St. W4 —3J 73
etchers Clo. Brom —4K 127
etcher St. E1 —7G 63
etching Rd. E5 —3J 47
etching Rd. SE7 —6B 82
etton Rd. N11 —7D 16
eur-de-Lis Ct. EC4
   —6A 62 (8H 141)
eur-de-Lis St. E1 —4F 63 (4D 142)
eur Gates. SW19 —7F 91
exmere Rd. N17 —1D 30
emwell Clo. Brom —5G 113
ntmill Cres. SE3 —2C 98
nton St. SE17 —5E 78
nt. St. SE17 —4D 78 (9B 148)
xcroft St. WC2 —6H 61 (8B 140)
uckton St. SE16 —2G 79
udden Rd. SE5 —1C 94
ood La. Twic —1A 104
ood Pas. SE18 —2D 82
ood St. SW3 —5C 76
ood Wlk. SW3 —6C 76
ora Clo. E14 —6D 64
ora Gdns. W6 —4D 74
   (off Albion Gdns.)
ora Gdns. Romf —6C 36
oral Pl. N1 —5D 46
oral St. WC2 —7J 61 (9C 140)
ora St. Belv —5F 85
orence Av. Enf —3H 7
orence Av. Mord —5A 122
orence Ct. E5 —3G 47
orence Ct. E11 —4A 34
orence Ct. N1 —7B 46
   (off Florence Ct. W9 —3A 60
   (off Maida Vale)
orence Dri. Enf —3H 7
orence Gdns. W4 —6J 73
orence Mans. NW4 —5D 26
   (off Vivian Av.)
orence Rd. E6 —1A 66
orence Rd. E13 —2H 65
orence Rd. N4 —7K 29
   (in two parts)
orence Rd. SE2 —4D 84
orence Rd. SE14 —1B 96
orence Rd. SW19 —6K 107
orence Rd. W4 —3K 73
orence Rd. W5 —7E 56
orence Rd. Beck —2A 126
orence Rd. Brom —1J 127
orence Rd. Felt —1A 102
orence Rd. King T —7F 105
orence Rd. S Croy —7D 134
orence St. E16 —4G 65
orence St. N1 —7B 46
orence St. NW4 —4E 26
orence Ter. SE14 —1B 96
orence Ter. SW15 —3A 106
orfield Pas. E8 —6H 47
   (off Florfield Rd.)
orfield Rd. E8 —6H 47
orian. SE5 —1E 94
orian Av. Sutt —4B 132
orida Rd. SW15 —4G 91
orida Clo. Bush —2C 10
orida Rd. T Hth —1B 124
orida St. E2 —3G 63
orin Ct. N18 —5K 17
oriston Clo. Stan —1B 24
oriston Gdns. Stan —1B 24
oss St. SW15 —2E 90

Flower & Dean Wlk. E1 —5F 63
Flower La. NW7 —5G 13
Flowersmead. SW17 —2E 108
Forest Av. E4 —1B 20
Floyd Rd. SE7 —5A 82
Fludyer St. SE13 —4G 97
Folair Way. SE16 —5H 79
Foley St. W1 —5G 61 (6L 139)
Folgate St. E1 —5E 62 (5D 142)
Foliot St. W12 —6B 58
Folkestone Rd. E6 —2E 66
Folkestone Rd. E17 —4D 32
Folkestone Rd. N18 —4B 18
Folkington Corner. N12 —5C 14
Folland. NW9 —2B 26
   (off Hundred Acre)
Follett St. E14 —6E 64
Follingham Ct. N1 —3E 62 (1D 142)
   (off Drysdale Pl.)
Folly La. E17 —7G 19
Folly M. N19 —2G 45
Folly Wall. E14 —2E 80
Fontaine Rd. SW16 —7K 109
Fontarabia Rd. SW11 —4E 92
Fontayne Av. Romf —2K 37
Fontenelle. SE5 —1E 94
Fontenoy Pas. SE11 —4B 78 (9J 147)
   (off Cottington Clo.)
Fontenoy Rd. SW12 —2F 109
Fonteyne Gdns. Wfd G —2B 34
Fonthill Clo. SE20 —2G 125
Fonthill M. N4 —2A 46
Fonthill Rd. N4 —1K 45
Font Hills. N2 —2A 28
Fontwell Clo. Harr —7D 10
Fontwell Dri. Brom —5E 128
Football La. Harr —1K 39
Footpath, The. SW15 —5C 90
Foots Cray High St. Sidc —6C 116
Foots Cray La. Sidc —1C 116
Footscray Rd. SE9 —6E 98
Forbes Clo. NW2 —2C 42
Forbes St. E1 —6G 63
Forburg Rd. N16 —1G 47
Ford Clo. Harr —7H 23
Ford Clo. T Hth —5B 124
Ford Av. Brom —3A 128
Fordel Rd. SE6 —1F 113
Ford End. Wfd G —6E 20
Fordham Clo. Barn —3H 5
Fordham Rd. Barn —3G 5
Fordham St. E1 —6G 63
Fordhook Av. W5 —1F 73
Ford Ho. Barn —5E 4
Fordingley Rd. W9 —3H 59
Fordington Ho. SE26 —3G 111
Fordington Rd. N6 —5D 28
Fordmill Rd. SE6 —2C 112
Ford Rd. E3 —2B 64
Ford Rd. Dag —7F 53
Fords Gro. N21 —1H 17
Fords Pk. Rd. E16 —6J 65
Ford Sq. E1 —5H 63
Ford St. E3 —1A 64
Ford St. E16 —6H 65
Fordwich Clo. Orp —7K 129
Fordwych Rd. NW2 —4G 43
Fordyce Rd. SE13 —6E 96
Fordyke Rd. Dag —2F 53
Foreign St. SE5 —2B 94
Foreland Ct. NW4 —1F 27
Foreland St. SE18 —4H 83
Foreman Ct. W6 —4E 74
Foreman Ct. Twic —1K 103
Foreshore. SE8 —4B 80

Forest App. E4 —1B 20
Forest App. Wfd G —7C 20
Forest Av. E4 —1B 20
Forest Av. Chig —5K 21
Forest Bus. Pk. E17 —7A 32
Forest Clo. E11 —5J 33
Forest Clo. Chst —1E 128
Forest Clo. Wfd G —5H 65
Forest Ct. E4 —1C 20
Forest Ct. E11 —4G 33
Forest Ct. N12 —4E 14
Forest Croft. SE23 —2H 111
Forestdale. N14 —4C 16
Forestdale Cen., The. Croy —7B 136
Forest Dene Ct. Sutt —6A 132
Forest Dri. E12 —3B 50
Forest Dri. E. E11 —7F 33
Forest Dri. W. E11 —7E 32
Forest Edge. Buck H —4F 21
Forester Rd. SE15 —3H 95
Foresters Clo. Wall —7H 133
Foresters Cres. Bexh —4H 101
Foresters Dri. E17 —4F 33
Foresters Dri. Wall —7H 133
Forest Gdns. N17 —2F 31
Forest Ga. NW9 —4A 26
Forest Glade. E4 —4B 20
Forest Glade. E11 —6G 33
Forest Gro. E8 —6F 47
Forest Hill Ind. Est. SE23 —2J 111
Forest Hill Rd. SE22 & SE23 —5H 95
Forestholme Clo. SE23 —2J 111
Forest Ind. Pk. Ilf —1J 35
Forest La. E15 & E7 —6G 49
Forest La. Chig —5K 21
Forest Mt. Rd. E4 —7A 20
Forest Point. E7 —5K 49
   (off Windsor Rd.)
Fore St. EC2 —5C 62 (6M 141)
Fore St. N18 & N9 —6A 18
Fore St. Av. EC2 —5D 62 (6A 142)
Forest Ridge. Beck —3C 126
Forest Rise. E17 —5F 33
Forest Rd. E7 —4J 49
Forest Rd. E8 —6F 47
Forest Rd. E11 —7F 33
Forest Rd. N9 —1C 18
Forest Rd. N17 & E17 —4J 31
Forest Rd. Felt —2A 102
Forest Rd. Ilf —2H 35
Forest Rd. Rich —7G 73
Forest Rd. Romf —3H 37
Forest Rd. Sutt —1J 131
Forest Rd. Wfd G —3D 20
Forest Side. E4 —1C 20
Forest Side. E7 —4K 49
Forest Side. Buck H —1F 21
Forest Side. Wor Pk —1B 130
Forest St. E7 —5J 49
Forest, The. E11 —4G 33
Forest Trading Est. E17 —3K 31
Forest View. E4 —7K 9
Forest View. E11 —7H 33
Forest View Av. E10 —5F 33
Forest View Rd. E12 —4C 50
Forest View Rd. E17 —1E 32
Forest Way. E11 —7H 33
Forest Way. N19 —2G 45
Forest Way. Orp —5K 129
Forest Way. Sidc —7H 99
Forest Way. Wfd G —4E 20
Forfar Rd. N22 —1B 30
Forfar Rd. SW11 —1E 92
Forge Clo. Brom —1J 137
Forge La. Felt —5C 102
Forge La. Sutt —7G 131
Forge Pl. NW1 —6E 44

Forlong Path. N'holt —6C 38
   (off Arnold Rd.)
Forman Pl. N16 —4F 47
Formby Av. Stan —3C 24
Formby Ct. N7 —5A 46
   (off Morgan Rd.)
Formosa St. W9 —4K 59
Formunt Clo. E16 —5H 65
Forres Gdns. NW11 —6J 27
Forrester Path. SE26 —4J 111
Forrest Gdns. SW16 —3K 123
Forset St. W1 —6C 60 (7D 138)
Forstal Clo. Brom —3J 127
Forster Ho. Brom —3F 113
Forster Rd. E17 —6A 32
Forster Rd. N17 —3F 31
Forster Rd. SW2 —7J 93
Forster Rd. Beck —3A 126
Forsters Clo. Romf —6F 37
Forston St. N1 —2C 62
Forsyte Cres. SE19 —1E 124
Forsythe Shades Ct. Beck —1E 126
Forsyth Gdns. SE17 —6B 78
Forsythia Clo. Ilf —5F 51
Forsyth Pl. Enf —5A 8
Forterie Gdns. Ilf —3A 52
Fortescue Av. E8 —7H 47
Fortescue Av. Twic —3G 103
Fortescue Rd. SW19 —7B 108
Fortescue Rd. Edgw —1K 25
Fortess Gro. NW5 —5G 45
Fortess Rd. NW5 —5F 45
Fortess Wlk. NW5 —5F 45
Forthbridge Rd. SW11 —4E 92
Fortis Clo. E16 —6A 66
Fortis Ct. N10 —3E 28
Fortis Grn. N2 & N10 —4C 28
Fortis Grn. Av. N2 —3D 28
Fortis Grn. Rd. N10 —3E 28
Fortismere Av. N10 —3E 28
Fortnam Rd. N19 —2H 45
Fortnum's Acre. Stan —6E 10
Fort Rd. SE1 —4F 79 (9F 148)
Fort Rd. N'holt —7E 38
Fortrose Gdns. SW2 —1J 109
Fort St. E1 —5E 62 (6D 142)
Fort St. E16 —1K 81
Fortuna Clo. N7 —6K 45
Fortunegate Rd. NW10 —1A 58
Fortune Grn. Rd. NW6 —4J 43
Fortune Ho. SE11 —4A 78 (9G 147)
   (off Marylee Way)
Fortunes Mead. N'holt —6C 38
Fortune St. EC1 —4C 62 (4M 141)
Fortune Wlk. SE28 —3H 83
   (off Broadwater Rd.)
Fortune Way. NW10 —3C 58
Forty Acre La. E16 —5J 65
Forty Av. Wemb —3F 41
Forty Clo. Wemb —3F 41
Forty Footpath. SW14 —3J 89
Forty Hill. Enf —1K 7
Forty La. Wemb —2H 41
Forumside. Edgw —6B 12
Forum Way. Edgw —6B 12
Forval Clo. Mitc —5D 122
Forward Bus. Cen. E16 —4F 65
Forward Dri. Harr —4K 23
Fosbury M. W2 —7K 59
Foscote M. W9 —4J 59
Foscote Rd. NW4 —6D 26
Foskett Rd. SW6 —2H 91
Foss Av. Croy —5A 134
Fossdene Rd. SE7 —5K 81
Fossdyke Clo. Hay —5C 54
Fosse Way. W13 —5A 56
Fossil Rd. SE13 —3C 96

Fossington Rd. Belv —4D 84
Foss Rd. SW17 —4B 108
Fossway. Dag —2C 52
Foster Ct. NW4 —4E 26
Foster La. EC2 —6C 62 (7L 141)
Foster Rd. E13 —4J 65
Foster Rd. W3 —7A 58
Foster Rd. W4 —5K 73
Fosters Clo. E18 —1K 33
Fosters Clo. Chst —5D 114
Foster St. NW4 —4E 26
Foster Wlk. NW4 —4E 26
Fothergill Clo. E13 —2J 65
Fotheringham Rd. Enf —4A 8
Foubert's Pl. W1 —6G 61 (8L 139)
Foulden Rd. N16 —4F 47
Foulden Ter. N16 —4F 47
Foulis Ter. SW7 —5B 76
Foulser Rd. SW17 —3D 108
Foulsham Rd. T Hth —3D 124
Founders Ct. EC2 —6D 62 (7A 142)
   (off Lothbury)
Founders Gdns. SE19 —7C 110
Foundry Clo. SE16 —1A 80
Foundry M. NW1 —4G 61 (3M 139)
   (off Drummond St.)
Fountain Ct. EC4 —7A 62 (9G 141)
Fountain Ct. SE23 —2K 111
Fountain Ct. Sidc —6B 100
Fountain Dri. SE19 —4F 111
Fountain M. N5 —4C 46
   (off Highbury Grange)
Fountain Pl. SW9 —1A 94
Fountain Rd. SW17 —5B 108
Fountain Rd. T Hth —2C 124
Fountains Av. Felt —3D 102
Fountains Clo. Felt —2D 102
Fountains Cres. N14 —7D 6
Fountain Sq. SW1 —4F 77 (8K 145)
Fountains, The. N3 —7E 14
   (off Ballards La.)
Fountayne Bus. Cen. N15 —4G 31
Fountayne Rd. N15 —4G 31
Fountayne Rd. N16 —2G 47
Fount St. SW8 —7H 77
Fouracres. Enf —1F 9
Fourland Wlk. Edgw —6D 12
Fournier St. E1 —5F 63 (5E 142)
Four Seasons Cres. Sutt —2H 131
Four Sq. Ct. Houn —6E 86
Fourth Av. E12 —4D 50
Fourth Av. W10 —3G 59
Fourth Av. Romf —1K 53
Fourth Cross Rd. Twic —2H 103
Fourth Way. Wemb —4J 41
Four Wents, The. E4 —1A 20
Fowey Av. Ilf —5B 34
Fowey Clo. E1 —4H 63
Fowey Ho. SE11 —5A 78
   (off Kennings Way)
Fowler Clo. SW11 —3B 92
Fowler Rd. E7 —4J 49
Fowler Rd. N1 —1B 62
Fowler Rd. Mitc —2E 122
Fowlers Clo. Sidc —5E 116
Fowler's Wlk. W5 —4D 56
Fownes St. SW11 —3C 92
Foxberry Rd. SE4 —3A 96
Foxborough Gdns. SE4 —5C 96
Foxbourne Rd. SW17 —2E 108
Foxbury Av. Chst —6H 115
Foxbury Clo. Brom —6K 113
Foxbury Clo. Brom —6J 113
Fox Clo. E1 —4J 63
Fox Clo. E16 —5J 65
Foxcombe. New Ad —6D 136
   (in two parts)
Foxcombe Clo. E6 —2B 66

Foxcombe Rd. SW15 —1C 106
Foxcote. SE5 —5E 78
Foxcote. SE17 —5E 78
(off Albany Rd.)
Foxcroft Rd. SE18 —1F 99
Foxearth Spur. S Croy —7J 135
Foxes Dale. SE3 —3J 97
Foxes Dale. Brom —3F 127
Foxglove Ct. Wemb —2E 56
Foxglove Cres. Ilf —6F 51
Foxglove Gdns. E11 —4A 34
Foxglove St. W12 —7B 58
Foxglove Way. Wall —1F 133
Foxgrove. N14 —3D 16
Foxgrove Av. Beck —7D 112
Foxgrove Rd. Beck —7D 112
Foxham Rd. N19 —3H 45
Fox Hill. SE19 —7F 111
Fox Hill. Kes —5K 137
Fox Hill Gdns. SE19 —7F 111
Foxhole Rd. SE9 —5C 98
Fox Hollow Dri. Bexh —3D 100
Foxholt Gdns. NW10 —7J 41
Foxhome Clo. Chst —6E 114
Fox Ho. Rd. Belv —4H 85
(in two parts)
Fox & Knot St. EC1 —5B 62 (5K 141)
(off Charterhouse Sq.)
Foxlands Cres. Dag —5J 53
Foxlands La. Dag —5K 53
Foxlands Rd. Dag —5J 53
Fox La. N13 —2E 16
Fox La. W5 —4E 56
Fox La. Kes —5K 137
Foxleas Ct. Brom —7G 113
Foxlees. Wemb —4A 40
Foxley Clo. E8 —5G 47
Foxley Ct. Sutt —7A 132
Foxley Rd. SW9 —7A 78
Foxley Rd. T Hith —4B 124
Foxley Sq. SW9 —1B 94
Foxmead Clo. Enf —3E 6
Fox Rd. E16 —5H 65
Fox's Path. Mitc —2C 122
Foxton Ho. E16 —2E 82
(off Albert Rd.)
Foxwell St. SE4 —3A 96
Foxwood Rd. SE3 —4H 97
Foyle Rd. N17 —1G 31
Foyle Rd. SE3 —6H 81
Framborough Clo. Harr —7H 23
Framfield Clo. N12 —3D 14
Framfield Ct. Enf —6K 7
(off Queen Annes Gdns.)
Framfield Rd. N5 —5B 46
Framfield Rd. W7 —6J 55
Framingham Clo. E5 —2J 47
Framlingham Cres. SE9 —4C 114
Frampton Clo. Sutt —7J 131
Frampton Pk. Est. E9 —7J 47
Frampton Pk. Rd. E9 —6J 47
Frampton St. NW8 —4B 60 (4A 138)
Francemary Rd. SE4 —5C 96
Frances Ct. E17 —6C 32
Frances Rd. E4 —6H 19
Frances St. SE18 —4D 82
Franche Ct. Rd. SW17 —3A 108
Francis Av. Bexh —2G 101
Francis Av. Ilf —2H 51
Francis Barber Clo. SW16 —5K 109
Franciscan Rd. SW17 —5D 108
Francis Chichester Way. SW11
—1E 92
Francis Clo. E14 —4F 81
Francis Ct. EC1 —5B 62 (5J 141)
(off Briset St.)
Francis Gro. SW19 —6H 107

Francis Ho. E10 —1B 48
Francis Rd. E10 —1B 48
Francis Rd. N2 —4D 28
Francis Rd. Croy —7B 124
Francis Rd. Gnfd —2B 56
Francis Rd. Harr —5A 24
Francis Rd. Houn —2B 86
Francis Rd. Ilf —2H 51
Francis Rd. Pinn —5A 22
Francis Rd. Wall —6G 133
Francis St. E15 —5G 49
Francis St. SW1 —4G 77 (8L 145)
Francis St. Ilf —2H 51
Francis Ter. N19 —3G 45
Francis Wlk. N1 —1K 61
Francklyn Gdns. Edgw —3B 12
Franconia Rd. SW4 —5H 93
Frank Bailey Wlk. E12 —6E 50
Frank Burton Clo. SE7 —5K 81
Frank Dixon Clo. SE21 —1C 110
Frank Dixon Way. SE21 —1E 110
Frankel Mt. SE9 —5B 98
Frankfurt Rd. SE24 —5C 94
Frankham St. SE8 —7C 80
Frankland Clo. SE16 —4H 79
Frankland Clo. Wfd G —5F 21
Frankland Rd. E4 —5H 19
Frankland Rd. SW7 —3B 76 (7A 144)
Franklin Clo. N20 —7F 5
Franklin Clo. SE13 —1D 96
Franklin Clo. SE27 —3B 110
Franklin Clo. King T —3G 119
Franklin Cotts. Stan —4G 11
Franklin Cres. Mitc —4G 123
Franklin Pas. SE9 —3C 98
Franklin Rd. SE20 —7J 111
Franklin Rd. Bexh —1E 100
Franklins M. Harr —2G 39
Franklin Sq. W14 —5H 75
Franklin's Row. SW3 —5D 76
Franklin St. E3 —3D 64
Franklin St. N15 —6E 30
Franklin Way. Croy —7J 123
Franklyn Rd. NW10 —6B 42
Franks Av. N Mald —4A 119
Frank St. E13 —4J 65
Franks Wood Av. Orp —5F 129
Frank Welsh Ct. Pinn —4A 22
Franlaw Cres. N13 —4H 17
Fransfield Gro. SE26 —3H 111
Frans Hals Ct. E14 —3F 81
Frant Clo. SE20 —7J 111
Franthorne Way. SE6 —2D 112
Frant Rd. T Hith —5B 124
Fraser Clo. E6 —6C 66
Fraser Clo. Bex —1J 117
Fraser Ho. Bren —5F 73
Fraser Rd. E17 —5D 32
Fraser Rd. N9 —3C 18
Fraser Rd. Eri —5K 85
Fraser Rd. Gnfd —2B 57
Fraser St. W4 —5A 74
Frating Cres. Wfd G —6E 20
Frazer Av. Ruis —5A 38
Frazier St. SE1 —2A 78 (5G 147)
Frean St. SE16 —3G 79
Freda Corbett Clo. SE15 —7G 79
Frederica Rd. E4 —1A 20
Frederica St. N7 —7K 45
Frederick Clo. W2 —7C 60 (9E 138)
Frederick Clo. Sutt —4H 131
Frederick Cres. SW9 —7B 78
Frederick Cres. Enf —2D 8
Frederick Gdns. Sutt —5H 131
Frederick Pl. SE18 —5F 83
Frederick Rd. SE17 —6B 78
Frederick Rd. Rain —2K 69
Frederick Rd. Sutt —5H 131

Frederick's Pl. EC2 —6D 62 (8A 142)
Fredericks Pl. N12 —4F 15
Frederick's Row. EC1
—3B 62 (1J 141)
Frederick St. WC1 —3K 61 (2E 140)
Frederick Ter. E8 —7F 47
Frederic M. SW1 —2D 76 (5F 144)
(off Kinnerton St.)
Frederic St. E17 —5A 32
Freedom Clo. E17 —5K 47
Freedom Rd. N17 —2D 30
Freedom St. SW11 —2D 92
Freegrove Rd. N7 —5J 45
Freehold Ind. Cen. Houn —5A 86
Freeland Ct. Sidc —3A 115
Freeland Pk. NW4 —2G 27
Freeland Rd. W5 —7F 57
Freelands Av. S Croy —7K 135
Freelands Gro. Brom —1K 127
Freelands Rd. Brom —1K 127
Freeling St. N1 —7J 45
(in two parts)
Freeman Clo. N'holt —7C 38
Freeman Rd. Mord —5B 122
Freemantle Av. Enf —5E 8
Freemasons Rd. E16 —5K 65
Freemasons Rd. Croy —1E 134
Freethorpe Clo. SE19 —1E 124
Free Trade Wharf. E1 —7K 63
Freightliner Depot Rd. NW10 —3A 58
Freke Rd. SW11 —3E 92
Fremantle Rd. Belv —4G 85
Fremantle Rd. Ilf —2F 35
Fremantle St. SE17 —5E 78
Fremont St. E9 —1J 63
French Ordinary La. EC3
—7E 62 (9D 142)
(off Crutched Friars)
French Pl. E1 —4E 62 (3D 142)
Frendsbury Rd. SE4 —4A 96
Frensham Clo. S'hall —4D 54
Frensham Dri. SW15 —3B 106
Frensham Dri. New Ad —7E 136
Frensham Rd. SE9 —2H 115
Frensham St. SE15 —6G 79
Frere St. SW11 —2C 92
Freshfield Clo. SE13 —4F 97
(in two parts)
Freshfield Dri. N14 —7A 6
Freshfields. Croy —1B 136
Freshford St. SW18 —3A 108
Freshwater Clo. SW17 —6E 108
Freshwater Ct. S'hall —3E 54
Freshwater Rd. SW17 —6E 108
Freshwater Rd. Dag —1D 52
Freshwell Av. Romf —4C 36
Fresh Wharf Rd. Bark —1F 67
Freshwood Clo. Beck —1D 126
Freshwood Way. Wall —7F 133
Freston Gdns. Barn —5K 5
Freston Pk. N3 —2H 27
Freston Rd. W10 & W11 —7F 59
Freta Rd. Bexh —5F 101
Frewin Rd. SW18 —1B 108
Friar M. SE27 —3B 110
Friar Rd. Hay —4B 54
Friar Rd. Orp —5K 129
Friars Av. N20 —3H 15
Friars Av. SW15 —3B 106
Friars Clo. E4 —3K 19
Friars Clo. N'holt —3B 54
Friars Ct. E17 —1B 32
Friars Ct. SE1 —1B 78 (3K 147)
(off Bear La.)
Friars Gdns. W3 —6K 57
Friars Ga. Clo. Wfd G —4D 20
Friars La. Rich —5D 88
Friars Mead. E14 —3E 80

Friars M. SE9 —5E 98
Friars Pl. La. W3 —7K 57
Friars Rd. E6 —1B 66
Friars Stile Pl. Rich —6E 88
Friars Stile Rd. Rich —6E 88
Friar St. EC4 —6B 62 (8K 141)
Friars Wlk. N14 —7A 6
Friars Wlk. SE2 —5D 84
Friars Way. W3 —6K 57
Friarswood. Croy —7A 136
Friary Clo. N12 —5H 15
Friary Ct. SW1 —1G 77 (3M 145)
(off St James Pal.)
Friary Ct. W3 —6J 57
Friary Est. SE15 —6G 79
Friary La. Wfd G —4D 20
Friary Rd. N12 —4G 15
Friary Rd. SE15 —6G 79
Friary Rd. W3 —6J 57
Friary Way. N12 —4H 15
Friday Hill. E4 —2B 20
Friday Hill E. E4 —3B 20
Friday Hill W. E4 —2B 20
Friday Rd. Eri —5K 85
Friday Rd. Mitc —7D 108
Friday St. EC4 —7C 62 (9L 141)
Frideswide Pl. NW5 —5G 45
Friendly Pl. SE10 —1D 96
Friendly St. SE8 —2C 96
Friendly St. M. SE8 —2C 96
Friendship Wlk. N'holt —3B 54
Friends Rd. Croy —3D 134
Friend St. EC1 —3B 62 (1J 141)
Friern Barnet La. N20 & N11 —2G 15
Friern Barnet Rd. N11 —5J 15
Friern Ct. N20 —3G 15
Friern Mt. Dri. N20 —7F 5
Friern Pk. N12 —5F 15
Friern Rd. SE22 —7G 95
Friern Watch Av. N12 —4F 15
Frigate M. SE8 —6C 80
Frimley Av. Wall —5K 133
Frimley Clo. SW19 —2G 107
Frimley Clo. New Ad —7E 136
Frimley Ct. Sidc —5C 116
Frimley Cres. New Ad —7E 136
Frimley Gdns. Mitc —3C 122
Frimley Rd. Ilf —3J 51
Frimley Way. E1 —4K 63
Frinsted Rd. Eri —7K 85
Frinton Dri. Wfd G —7B 20
Frinton M. Ilf —6E 34
Frinton Rd. E6 —3B 66
Frinton Rd. N15 —6E 30
Frinton Rd. SW17 —6E 108
Frinton Rd. Romf —1F 37
Frinton Rd. Sidc —2E 116
Friston St. SW6 —2K 91
Friswell Pl. Bexh —4G 101
Fritham Clo. N Mald —6A 120
Frith Ct. NW7 —7B 14
Frith La. NW7 —7B 14
Frith Rd. E11 —4E 48
Frith Rd. Croy —2C 134
Frith St. W1 —6H 61 (8A 140)
Frithville Gdns. W12 —1E 74
Frizlands La. Dag —2H 53
Frobisher Clo. Pinn —7B 22
Frobisher Ct. NW9 —2A 26
Frobisher Ct. W12 —2E 74
(off Lime Gro.)
Frobisher Cres. EC2 —5C 62 (5M 141)
(off Barbican)
Frobisher Pas. E14 —1C 80
Frobisher Rd. E6 —6D 66
Frobisher Rd. N8 —4A 30
Frobisher St. SE10 —6G 81
Frog La. Rain —4K 69

Frogley Rd. SE22 —4F 95
Frogmore. SW18 —5J 91
Frogmore Clo. Sutt —3F 131
Frogmore Ct. S'hall —4D 70
Frogmore Gdns. Sutt —4G 131
Frogmore Ind. Est. NW10 —3J 57
Frognal. NW3 —4A 44
Frognal Av. Harr —4K 23
Frognal Av. Sidc —6A 116
Frognal Clo. NW3 —5A 44
Frognal Ct. NW3 —6A 44
Frognal Gdns. NW3 —4A 44
Frognal La. NW3 —5K 43
Frognal Pde. NW3 —6A 44
Frognal Pl. Sidc —6A 116
Frognal Rise. NW3 —3A 44
Frognal Way. NW3 —4A 44
Froissart Rd. SE9 —5B 98
Frome Ho. SE15 —4H 95
Frome Rd. N22 —3B 30
Frome St. N1 —2C 62
Fromondes Rd. Sutt —5G 131
Frostic Wlk. E1 —5G 63
Froude St. SW8 —2F 93
Fryatt Rd. N17 —7J 17
(in two parts)
Fryatt St. E14 —6G 65
Fryent Clo. NW9 —6G 26
Fryent Cres. NW9 —6A 26
Fryent Fields. NW9 —6A 26
Fryent Gro. NW9 —6A 26
Fryent Way. NW9 —5G 25
Frye's Bldgs. N1 —2A 62
Fry Ho. E6 —7A 50
Frying Pan All. E1 —5F 63 (6E 142)
(off Bell La.)
Fry Rd. E6 —7B 50
Fry Rd. NW10 —1B 58
Fryston Av. Croy —2G 135
Fuchsia St. SE2 —5B 84
Fulbeck Dri. NW9 —1A 26
Fulbeck M. N19 —4G 45
Fulbeck Rd. N19 —4G 45
Fulbeck Way. Harr —2G 23
Fulbourne Rd. E17 —1E 32
Fulbourne St. E1 —5H 63
Fulford St. SE16 —2H 79
Fulham B'way. SW6 —7J 75
Fulham High St. SW6 —2G 91
Fulham Pal. Rd. W6 & SW6 —5E 74
Fulham Pk. Gdns. SW6 —2H 91
Fulham Pk. Rd. SW6 —2H 91
Fulham Rd. SW6 —2G 91
Fulham Rd. SW10 & SW3 —6A 76
Fullbrooks Av. Wor Pk —1B 130
Fuller Rd. Dag —3B 52
Fullers Av. Wfd G —7C 20
Fullers Clo. Romf —1J 37
Fullers La. Romf —1J 37
Fuller St. E18 —1H 33
Fuller St. NW4 —4E 26
Fuller's Wood. Croy —4C 136
Fullerton Rd. SW18 —5A 92
Fullerton Rd. Cars —7C 132
Fullerton Rd. Croy —7F 125
Fullwell Av. Ilf —1D 34
Fullwood's M. N1 —3D 62 (1B 142)
Fulmar Ct. Surb —6F 119
Fulmead St. SW6 —1K 91
Fulmer Clo. Hamp —5C 102
Fulmer Rd. E16 —5B 66
Fulmer Way. W13 —3B 72
Fulready Rd. E10 —5F 33
Fulstone Clo. Houn —4D 86
Fulthorp Rd. SE3 —2H 97
Fulton M. W2 —7A 60
(off Porchester Ter.)
Fulton Rd. Wemb —3G 41

Fulwell Cross. Ilf —2H 35
Fulwell Pk. Av. Twic —2F 103
Fulwell Rd. Tedd —4H 103
Fulwood Av. Wemb —1F 57
Fulwood Ct. Kent —6A 24
Fulwood Gdns. Twic —6K 87
Fulwood Pl. WC1 —5K 61 (6F 140)
Fulwood Wlk. SW19 —1G 107
Furber St. W6 —3D 74
Furham Field. Pinn —7A 10
Furley Rd. SE15 —7G 79
Furlong Clo. Wall —1F 133
Furlong Rd. N7 —6A 46
Furmage St. SW18 —7K 91
Furneaux Av. SE27 —5B 110
Furness Rd. NW10 —2C 58
Furness Rd. SW6 —2K 91
Furness Rd. Harr —7F 23
Furness Rd. Mord —6K 121
Furnival St. EC4 —6A 62 (7G 141)
Furrow La. E9 —5J 47
Fursby Av. N3 —6D 14
Further Acre. NW9 —2B 28
Furtherfield Clo. Croy —6A 124
Further Grn. Rd. SE6 —7G 97
Furzedown Dri. SW17 —5F 109
Furzedown Rd. SW17 —5F 109
Furze Farm Clo. Romf —2E 38
Furzefield Clo. Chst —6F 115
Furzefield Rd. SE3 —7K 81
Furze Rd. T Hth —3C 124
Furze St. E3 —5C 64
Furze Foot La. EC4 —7C 62 (9L 141)
Fyfe Way. Brom —2J 127
Fyfield. N4 —2A 46
  (off Six Acres Est.)
Fyfield Clo. Brom —4F 127
Fyfield Ct. E7 —6J 49
Fyfield Rd. E17 —3F 33
Fyfield Rd. SW9 —3A 94
Fyfield Rd. Enf —3K 7
Fyfield Rd. Wfd G —7F 21
Fynes St. SW1 —4H 77 (8A 146)

Gable Clo. Pinn —1E 22
Gable Ct. SE26 —4H 111
Gables Clo. SE5 —1E 94
Gables Clo. SE12 —1J 113
Gables Lodge. Barn —1F 5
Gables, The. N10 —3E 28
  (off Fortis Grn.)
Gables, The. Bark —6G 51
Gables, The. Brom —7K 113
Gabriel Clo. Felt —4C 102
Gabriel Clo. Romf —1J 37
Gabriel Clo. Wemb —3F 41
Gabrielle Ct. NW3 —6B 44
Gabriel St. SE23 —7K 95
Gabriel's Wharf. SE1
  —1A 78 (2H 147)
Gaddesden Av. Wemb —6F 41
Gaddesden Ho. EC1 —3D 62 (2B 142)
  (off Cranwood St.)
Gadsbury Clo. NW9 —6B 26
Gadwall Clo. E16 —6K 65
Gadwall Way. SE28 —2H 83
Gage Rd. E16 —5G 65
Gage St. WC1 —5J 61 (5D 140)
Gainford St. N1 —1A 62
Gainsborough Av. E12 —5E 50
Gainsborough Clo. Beck —7C 112
Gainsborough Ct. N12 —5E 14
Gainsborough Ct. SE21 —2E 110
Gainsborough Clo. W4 —5H 73
  (off Chaseley Dri.)
Gainsborough Gdns. NW3 —3B 44
Gainsborough Gdns. NW11 —7H 27

Gainsborough Gdns. Edgw —2F 25
Gainsborough Gdns. Gnfd —5J 39
Gainsborough Gdns. Iswth —5H 87
Gainsborough Ho. Dag —4B 52
  (off Gainsborough Rd.)
Gainsborough Lodge. Harr —5K 23
  (off Hindes Rd.)
Gainsborough M. SE26 —3H 111
Gainsborough Rd. E11 —7G 33
Gainsborough Rd. E15 —3G 65
Gainsborough Rd. N12 —5E 14
Gainsborough Rd. W4 —4B 74
Gainsborough Rd. Dag —4B 52
Gainsborough Rd. N Mald —7K 119
Gainsborough Rd. Rich —2F 89
Gainsborough Rd. Wfd G —6H 21
Gainsborough Sq. Bexh —3D 100
Gainsford Rd. E17 —4B 32
Gainsford St. SE1 —2F 79 (4E 148)
Gairloch Rd. SE5 —2E 94
Gaisford St. NW5 —6G 45
Gaitskell Ho. E6 —1B 66
Gaitskell Ho. E17 —3D 32
Gaitskell Rd. SE9 —1G 115
Galahad Rd. Brom —4J 113
Galata Rd. SW13 —7C 74
Galatea Sq. SE15 —3H 95
Galba Ct. Bren —7D 72
Galbraith St. E14 —3E 80
Galdana Av. Barn —3F 5
Galeborough Av. Wfd G —7A 20
Gale Clo. Hamp —6C 102
Gale Clo. Mitc —3B 122
Galena Rd. W6 —4D 74
Galen Pl. WC1 —5J 61 (6D 140)
Galesbury Rd. SW18 —6A 92
Gales Gdns. E2 —3H 63
Gale St. E3 —5C 64
Gale St. Dag —5C 52
Gales Way. Wfd G —7H 21
Galgate Clo. SW19 —1G 107
Gallants Farm Rd. Barn —7H 5
Galleon Clo. SE16 —2K 79
Galleon Clo. Eri —4K 85
Gallery Gdns. N'holt —2B 54
Gallery Rd. SE21 —1D 110
Galleywall Rd. SE16 —4H 79
Galliard Clo. N9 —6D 8
Galliard Ct. N9 —6B 8
Galliard Rd. N9 —7B 8
Gallia Rd. N5 —5B 46
Gallions Clo. Bark —3A 68
Gallions Entrance. E16 —1G 83
Gallions Rd. E16 —7F 67
Gallions Rd. SE7 —4A 81
Galliver Pl. E5 —4H 47
Gallon Clo. SE7 —4A 82
Gallop, The. S Croy —7H 135
Gallop, The. Sutt —7B 132
Gallosson Rd. SE18 —4J 83
Galloway Rd. W12 —1C 74
Gallus Clo. N21 —6E 6
Gallus Sq. SE3 —3K 97
Galpin's Rd. T Hth —5J 123
Galsworthy Av. Romf —7B 36
Galsworthy Clo. SE28 —1B 84
Galsworthy Cres. SE3 —1A 98
Galsworthy Rd. NW2 —4G 43
Galsworthy Rd. King T —1H 119
Galsworthy Ter. N16 —3E 46
Galton St. W10 —3G 59
Galva Clo. Barn —4J 5
Galvani Way. Croy —1K 133
Galveston Rd. SW15 —5H 91
Galway Clo. SE1 —3C 62 (2M 149)
Galy. NW9 —2B 26
Gambetta St. SW8 —2F 93
Gambia St. SE1 —1B 78 (3K 147)

Gamble Rd. SW17 —4C 108
Gamien Rd. SW15 —4F 91
Gander Grn. La. Sutt —2G 131
Gandhi Clo. E17 —6C 32
Ganton St. W1 —7G 61 (9L 139)
Gantshill Cres. Ilf —5E 34
Gants Hill Cross. Ilf —6E 34
Gap Rd. SW19 —5J 107
Garage Rd. W3 —6G 57
Garbutt Pl. W1 —5E 60 (6H 139)
Garden Av. Bexh —3G 101
Garden Av. Mitc —7F 109
Garden City. Edgw —6B 12
Garden Clo. E4 —5H 19
Garden Clo. SE12 —3K 113
Garden Clo. SW15 —7E 90
Garden Clo. Hamp —5D 102
Garden Clo. N'holt —1C 54
Garden Clo. Wall —5J 133
Garden Ct. EC4 —7A 62 (9G 141)
  (off Temple)
Garden Ct. W4 —3J 73
Garden Ct. Hamp —5D 102
Garden Ct. Rich —1F 89
Garden Ct. Stan —5H 11
Gardener Gro. Felt —2D 102
Gardeners Rd. Croy —1B 134
Garden Ho. N2 —2B 28
  (off Grange, The)
Gardenia Rd. Enf —6K 7
Gardenia Way. Wfd G —5D 20
Garden La. SW2 —1K 109
Garden La. Brom —6K 113
Garden M. W2 —7J 59
Garden Rd. NW8 —3A 60
Garden Rd. SE20 —1J 125
Garden Rd. Brom —7K 113
Garden Rd. Rich —3G 89
Garden Row. SE1 —3B 78 (7J 147)
Gardens, The. N4 —3J 29
  (in two parts)
Gardens, The. SE22 —4G 95
Gardens, The. Beck —2F 127
Gardens, The. Harr —6G 23
Gardens, The. Pinn —6D 22
Garden Ter. SW1 —5H 77
Garden Ter. SW7 —2C 76 (5D 144)
  (off Trevor Pl.)
Garden View. E7 —4A 50
Garden Wlk. EC2 —3E 62 (2C 142)
Garden Wlk. Beck —1B 126
Garden Way. NW10 —6J 41
Garrison Clo. SE18 —7E 82
Garrowsfield. Barn —6C 4
Garry Way. Romf —1K 37
Garside Clo. SE28 —3H 83
Garside Clo. Hamp —6F 103
Garside Dri. Stan —3F 25
Garside Grn. SE9 —2D 98
Garsington M. SE4 —3B 96
Garter Way. SE16 —2K 79
Garth Clo. W4 —5K 73
Garth Clo. King T —5F 105
Garth Clo. Mord —7F 121
Garth Clo. Ruis —1B 38
Garth Ct. W4 —6K 73
Garth Ct. Harr —6K 23
  (off Northwick Pk. Rd.)
Garth M. W5 —5K 57
Garthorne Rd. SE23 —7K 95
Garth Rd. NW2 —2H 43
Garth Rd. W4 —5K 73
Garth Rd. King T —5F 105
Garth Rd. Mord —7E 120
Garthside. Ham —5E 104
Garth, The. Hamp —6F 103
Garth, The. Harr —6F 25
Garthway. N12 —6H 15

Garganey Wlk. SE28 —7C 68
Garibaldi St. SE18 —4J 83
Garland Dri. Houn —2F 87
Garland Rd. SE18 —7H 83
Garland Rd. Stan —1E 24
Garlick Hill. EC4 —7C 62 (9M 141)
Garlies Rd. SE23 —3A 112
Garlinge Rd. NW2 —6H 43
Garman Clo. N18 —5K 17
Garman Rd. N17 —7D 18
Garnault Rd. EC1 —3A 62 (2H 141)
  (off Rosebery Av.)
Garnault Pl. EC1 —3A 62 (2H 141)
Garnault Rd. Enf —1A 8
Garner Rd. E17 —1E 32
Garner St. E2 —2G 63
Garnet Rd. NW10 —6A 42
Garnet Rd. T Hth —4C 124
Garnet St. E1 —7J 63
Garnett Clo. SE9 —3D 98
Garnett Rd. NW3 —5D 44
Garnet Wlk. E6 —5C 66
Garnet Way. E17 —1A 32
Garnham Clo. N16 —2F 47
Garnham St. N16 —2F 47
Garnies Clo. SE15 —7F 79
Garrad's Rd. SW16 —3H 109
Garrard Clo. Bexh —3G 101
Garrard Clo. Chst —5F 115
Garrard Wlk. NW10 —6A 42
Garratt Rd. Edgw —7B 12
Garratt Clo. Croy —4J 133
Garratt Ct. SW18 —7K 91
Garratt La. SW18 & SW17 —6K 91
Garratt Ter. SW17 —4C 108
Garrett Clo. W3 —5K 57
Garrett St. EC1 —4C 62 (3M 141)
Garrick Av. NW11 —6G 27
Garrick Clo. SW18 —4A 92
Garrick Clo. Rich —5D 88
Garrick Clo. W5 —4E 56
Garrick Cres. Croy —2E 134
Garrick Dri. NW4 —2E 26
Garrick Dri. SE28 —3H 83
Garrick Ho. W4 —6A 74
Garrick Pk. NW4 —2F 27
Garrick Rd. NW9 —6B 26
Garrick Rd. Gnfd —4F 55
Garrick Rd. Rich —2G 89
Garrick St. WC2 —7J 61 (9C 140)
Garrick Way. NW4 —4F 27
Garrick Yd. WC2 —7J 61 (9C 140)
  (off St Martin's La.)
Gascoigne Gdns. Wfd G —7B 20
Gascoigne Pl. E2 —3F 63 (2E 142)
Gascoigne Rd. Bark —1G 67
Gascoigne Rd. New Ad —7F 137
Gascony Av. NW6 —7J 43
Gascoyne Ho. E9 —7A 48
Gascoyne Rd. E9 —7K 47
Gaselee St. E14 —7E 64
Gasholder Pl. SE11 —5K 77
Gaskarth Rd. SW12 —6F 93
Gaskarth Rd. Edgw —1J 25
Gaskell Rd. N6 —6D 28
Gaskell St. SW4 —2J 93
Gaskin St. N1 —1B 62
Gaspar Clo. SW5 —4K 75
  (off Courtfield Gdns.)
Gaspar M. SW5 —4K 75
Gassiot Rd. SW17 —4D 108
Gassiot Way. Sutt —3B 132
Gastein Rd. W6 —6F 75
Gaston Bell Clo. Rich —3F 89
Gaston Rd. Mitc —3E 122
Gatcombe Ct. Beck —7C 112
Gatcombe Rd. N19 —3H 45
Gateacre Ct. Sidc —4B 116
Gate Cen., The. Bren —7A 72
Gateforth St. NW8 —4C 60 (4C 138)
Gatehouse Clo. King T —7J 105
Gatehouse Sq. SE1 —1C 78 (2M 147)
  (off Porter St.)
Gateley Rd. SW9 —3K 93
Gate M. SW7 —2C 76 (5D 144)
  (off Rutland Ga.)
Gates. NW9 —2B 26
Gatesborough St. EC2
  —4E 62 (3C 142)
Gates Ct. SE17 —5C 78
Gatesden. WC1 —3J 61 (2D 140)
Gates Grn. Rd. W Wick —3H 137
Gateside Rd. SW17 —3D 108
Gatestone Rd. SE19 —6E 110
Gateway. SE17 —6C 78
Gateway Ho. Bark —1G 67
Gateway M. E8 —5F 47
Gateways Ct. Wall —5F 133
Gateways, The. SW3 —5C 76
  (off Sprimont Pl.)
Gateway Trading Est. NW10 —3B 58
Gatfield Gro. Felt —2E 102
Gatfield Ho. Felt —2E 102
Gathorne Rd. N22 —1A 30
Gathorne St. E2 —2K 63
Gatliff Rd. SW1 —5F 77
Gatling Rd. SE2 —5A 84
Gatting Clo. Edgw —7D 12
Gattis Wharf. N1 —2J 61
  (off New Wharf Rd.)
Gatton Rd. SW17 —4C 108
Gattons Way. Sidc —4F 117
Gatward Clo. N21 —6G 7
Gatward Grn. N9 —2A 18
Gatwick Rd. SW18 —7H 91
Gauden Clo. SW4 —3H 93
Gauden Rd. SW4 —2H 93
Gauntlet. NW9 —2B 26
  (off Five Acre)
Gauntlett Clo. N'holt —7C 38
Gauntlett Ct. Wemb —5B 40
Gauntlett Rd. Sutt —5B 132
Gaunt St. SE1 —3C 78 (6L 147)

Goldie Ho. N19 —7H 29
Golding Ct. Ilf —3E 50
Golding St. E1 —6G 63
Goldington Cres. NW1 —2H 61
Goldington St. NW1 —2H 61
Gold La. Edgw —6E 12
Goldman Clo. E2 —4G 63
Goldney Rd. W9 —4J 59
Goldsborough Cres. E4 —2J 19
Goldsborough Rd. SW8 —1H 93
Goldsdown Clo. Enf —2F 9
Goldsdown Rd. Enf —2E 8
Goldsmid St. SE18 —5J 83
Goldsmith Av. E12 —6C 50
Goldsmith Av. NW9 —5A 26
Goldsmith Av. W3 —7K 57
Goldsmith Av. Romf —7G 37
Goldsmith Clo. W3 —1K 73
Goldsmith Clo. Harr —1F 39
Goldsmith La. NW9 —4H 25
Goldsmith Rd. E10 —1C 48
Goldsmith Rd. E17 —2K 31
Goldsmith Rd. N11 —5J 15
Goldsmith Rd. SE15 —1G 95
Goldsmith Rd. W3 —1K 73
Goldsmith's Bldgs. W3 —1K 73
Goldsmith's Pl. NW6 —1K 59
  (off Springfield La.)
Goldsmith's Row. E2 —2G 63
Goldsmith's Sq. E2 —2G 63
Goldsmith St. EC2 —6C 62 (7M 141)
Goldsworthy Gdns. SE16 —5J 79
Goldwell Ho. SE22 —3E 94
Goldwell Rd. T Hth —4K 123
Goldwin Clo. SE14 —1J 95
Goldwing Clo. E16 —6J 65
Golf Clo. Stan —7H 11
Golfe Rd. Ilf —3H 51
Golf Rd. W5 —6F 57
Golf Rd. Brom —3E 128
Golf Side. Twic —3H 103
Golfside Clo. N20 —3H 15
Golfside Clo. N Mald —2A 120
Goliath Clo. Wall —7J 133
Gollogly Ter. SE7 —5A 82
Gomer Gdns. Tedd —6A 104
Gomer Pl. Tedd —6A 104
Gomm Rd. SE16 —3J 79
Gomshall Av. Wall —5J 133
Gondar Gdns. NW6 —5H 43
Gonson St. SE8 —6D 80
Gonston Clo. SW19 —2G 107
Gonville Cres. N'holt —6F 39
Gonville Rd. T Hth —5K 123
Gonville St. SW6 —3G 91
Gooch Ho. E5 —3H 47
Goodall Rd. E11 —3E 48
Gooden Ct. Harr —3J 39
Goodenough Rd. SW19 —7H 107
Goodfellow Gdns. King T —5J 105
Goodge Pl. W1 —5G 61 (6M 139)
Goodge St. W1 —5G 61 (6M 139)
Goodhall St. NW10 —3B 58
  (in two parts)
Goodhart Pl. E14 —7A 64
Goodhart Way. W Wick —7G 127
Goodhew Rd. Croy —6G 125
Gooding Clo. N Mald —4J 119
Goodinge Clo. N7 —6J 45
Goodman Cres. SW2 —2J 109
Goodman Rd. E10 —7E 32
Goodman's Ct. E1 —7F 63 (9E 142)
Goodmans Ct. Wemb —4D 40
Goodman's Stile. E1 —6G 63
Goodmans Yd. E1 —7F 63 (9E 142)
Goodmayes Av. Ilf —1A 52
Goodmayes La. Ilf —4A 52

Goodmayes Rd. Ilf —1A 52
Goodrich Ct. W10 —6F 59
Goodrich Rd. SE22 —6F 95
Goodson Rd. NW10 —7A 42
Goods Way. NW1 —1H 61
Goodwin Clo. SE16 —3G 79
Goodwin Clo. Mitc —3B 122
Goodwin Ct. N8 —3J 29
  (off Campsbourne Rd.)
Goodwin Ct. NW1 —2G 61
  (off Chalton St.)
Goodwin Ct. Barn —6H 5
Goodwin Ct. Mitc —7C 108
Goodwin Dri. Sidc —3D 116
Goodwin Gdns. Croy —6B 134
Goodwin Ho. N9 —1B 18
Goodwin Rd. N9 —1E 18
Goodwin Rd. W12 —2C 74
Goodwin Rd. Croy —5B 134
Goodwins Ct. WC2 —7J 61 (9C 140)
Goodwin St. N4 —2A 46
Goodwood Clo. Mord —4J 121
Goodwood Clo. Stan —5H 11
Goodwood Pde. Beck —4A 126
Goodwood Rd. SE14 —7A 80
Goodwyn Av. NW7 —5F 13
Goodwyns Vale. N10 —1E 28
Goodyers Gdns. NW4 —5F 27
Goosander Way. SE28 —3H 83
Gooseacre La. Harr —5D 24
Gooseley La. E6 —3E 66
Goose Sq. E6 —6D 66
Goossens Clo. Sutt —5A 132
Gophir La. EC4 —7D 62 (9A 142)
Gopsall St. N1 —1D 62
Gordon Av. E4 —6B 20
Gordon Av. SW14 —4A 90
Gordon Av. Stan —7E 10
Gordon Av. Twic —5A 88
Gordonbrock Rd. SE4 —5C 96
Gordon Clo. E17 —6C 32
Gordon Clo. N19 —2G 45
Gordon Ct. W12 —6E 58
Gordon Ct. Edgw —5A 12
Gordon Cres. Croy —1E 134
Gordon Gdns. Edgw —2H 25
Gordon Gro. SE5 —2B 94
Gordon Hill. Enf —1H 7
Gordon Ho. E1 —7J 63
  (off Glamis Rd.)
Gordon Ho. E1 —7J 63
  (off Highway, The)
Gordon Ho. W5 —3E 56
Gordon Ho. Rd. NW5 —4E 44
Gordon Pl. W8 —2J 75
Gordon Rd. E4 —1B 20
Gordon Rd. E11 —6J 33
Gordon Rd. E15 —4E 48
Gordon Rd. E18 —1K 33
Gordon Rd. N3 —7C 14
Gordon Rd. N9 —2C 18
Gordon Rd. N11 —7C 16
Gordon Rd. SE15 —2H 95
Gordon Rd. W4 —6H 73
Gordon Rd. W13 & W5 —7B 56
Gordon Rd. Bark —1J 67
Gordon Rd. Beck —3B 126
Gordon Rd. Belv —4J 85
Gordon Rd. Cars —6D 132
Gordon Rd. Enf —1H 7
Gordon Rd. Harr —3J 23
Gordon Rd. Houn —4G 87
Gordon Rd. Ilf —3H 51
Gordon Rd. King T —1F 119
Gordon Rd. Rich —2F 89

Gordon Rd. Romf —6F 37
Gordon Rd. Sidc —5J 99
Gordon Rd. S'hall —4C 70
Gordon Rd. Surb —7F 119
Gordon Sq. WC1 —4H 61 (3A 140)
Gordon St. E13 —3J 65
Gordon St. WC1 —4H 61 (3A 140)
Gordon Way. Barn —4C 4
Gordon Way. Brom —1J 127
Gore Ct. NW9 —5G 25
Gorefield Pl. NW6 —2J 59
Gore Rd. E9 —1J 63
Gore Rd. SW20 —2E 120
Goresbrook Rd. Dag —1B 68
Gore St. SW7 —3A 76
Gorham Pl. W11 —7G 59
Goring Clo. Romf —1J 37
Goring Gdns. Dag —4C 52
Goring Rd. N11 —6D 16
Goring Rd. Dag —6K 53
Goring St. EC3 —6E 62 (7D 142)
  (off Houndsditch)
Goring Way. Gnfd —2G 55
Gorleston Rd. N15 —5D 30
Gorleston St. W14 —4G 75
Gorman Rd. SE18 —4D 82
Gorringe Pk. Av. Mitc —7D 108
Gorse Clo. E16 —6J 65
Gorse Rise. SW17 —5E 108
Gorse Rd. Croy —4C 136
Gorseway. Romf —1K 53
Gorst Rd. NW10 —4J 57
Gorst Rd. SW11 —6D 92
Gorsuch Pl. E2 —3F 63 (1E 142)
Gorsuch St. E2 —3F 63 (1E 142)
Gosberton Rd. SW12 —1D 108
Gosfield Rd. Dag —2G 53
Gosfield St. W1 —5G 61 (5L 139)
Gosford Gdns. Ilf —5D 34
Goslett Yd. WC2 —6H 61 (8B 140)
Goslet Yd. WC2 —6H 61
Gosling Clo. Gnfd —3E 54
Gosling Way. SW9 —1A 94
Gospatrick Rd. N17 —7H 17
Gospel Oak Est. NW5 —5D 44
Gosport Rd. E17 —5B 32
Gosport Wlk. N17 —4H 31
Gosport Way. SE15 —7F 79
Gosset St. E2 —3F 63
Gosshill Rd. Chst —2E 128
Gossington Clo. Chst —4F 115
Gosterwood St. SE8 —6A 80
Gostling Rd. Twic —1E 102
Goston Gdns. T Hth —3A 124
Goswell Pl. EC1 —3B 62 (2K 141)
  (off Goswell Rd.)
Gothic Rd. Twic —2H 103
Goudhurst Rd. Brom —5G 113
Gough Rd. E15 —4H 49
Gough Rd. Enf —2C 8
Gough Sq. EC4 —6A 62 (7H 141)
Gough St. WC1 —4K 61 (3F 140)
Gough Wlk. E14 —6C 64
Gould Rd. Twic —1J 103
Gould Ter. E8 —5H 47
Goulston St. E1 —6F 63 (7E 142)
Goulton Rd. E5 —4H 47
Gourley Pl. N15 —5E 30
Gourley St. N15 —5E 30
Gourock Rd. SE9 —5E 98
Govan St. E2 —1G 63
Gover Ct. SW4 —2J 93
Govier Clo. E15 —7G 49
Gowan Av. SW6 —1G 91
Gowan Rd. NW10 —6D 42
Gower Clo. SW4 —6G 93
Gower Ct. WC1 —4H 61 (3A 140)

Gower Ho. E17 —3C 32
Gower M. WC1 —5H 61 (6B 140)
Gower Pl. WC1 —4G 61 (3M 139)
Gower Rd. E7 —6J 49
Gower Rd. Iswth —6K 71
Gower St. WC1 —4G 61 (3M 139)
Gower's Wlk. E1 —6G 63
Gowland Pl. Beck —2B 126
Gowlett Rd. SE15 —3G 95
Gowrie Rd. SW11 —3E 92
Goy Mnr. Rd. SW19 —6F 107
Grace Av. Bexh —2F 101
Gracechurch Ct. EC3
                    —7D 62 (9B 142)
  (off Gracechurch St.)
Gracechurch St. EC3
                    —7D 62 (9B 142)
Grace Clo. SE9 —3B 114
Grace Clo. Edgw —7D 12
Gracedale Rd. SW16 —5F 109
Gracefield Gdns. SW16 —3J 109
Grace Ho. SE11 —6K 77
  (off Vauxhall Rd.)
Grace Jones Clo. E8 —6G 47
Grace Path. SE26 —4J 111
Grace Pl. E3 —3D 64
Grace Rd. Croy —6C 124
Grace's All. E1 —7G 63
Graces M. NW8 —2A 60
Grace's M. SE5 —2E 94
Grace's Rd. SE5 —2E 94
Grace St. E3 —3D 64
Gradient, The. SE26 —4G 111
Graeme Rd. Enf —2J 7
Graemesdyke Av. SW14 —3H 89
Grafton Clo. W13 —6A 56
Grafton Clo. Houn —1C 102
Grafton Clo. Wor Pk —3A 130
Grafton Cres. NW1 —6F 45
Grafton Gdns. N4 —6C 30
Grafton Gdns. Dag —2E 52
Grafton M. N1 —2C 62
  (off Frome St.)
Grafton M. W1 —4G 61 (4L 139)
Grafton Pk. Rd. Wor Pk —2A 130
Grafton Pl. NW1 —3H 61 (2B 140)
Grafton Rd. NW5 —5E 44
Grafton Rd. W3 —7J 57
Grafton Rd. Croy —1A 134
Grafton Rd. Dag —2E 52
Grafton Rd. Enf —3E 6
Grafton Rd. Harr —5G 23
Grafton Rd. N Mald —3A 120
Grafton Rd. Wor Pk —3A 130
Grafton Sq. SW4 —3G 93
Graftons, The. NW2 —3J 43
Grafton St. W1 —7F 61 (1K 145)
Grafton Ter. NW5 —5D 44
Grafton Way. W1 & WC1
                    —4G 61 (4L 139)
Graham Av. W13 —2B 72
Graham Av. Mitc —1E 122
Graham Clo. Croy —2C 136
Graham Ct. N'holt —5B 38
Grahame Pk. Est. NW9 —1A 26
Grahame Pk. Way. NW7 & NW9
                    —7G 13
Grahame White Ho. Kent —3D 24
Graham Gdns. Surb —7F 118
Graham Ho. N9 —1D 18
  (off Cumberland Rd.)
Graham Lodge. NW4 —6D 26
Graham Mans. Bark —7A 52
  (off Lansbury Av.)
Graham Rd. E8 —6G 47
Graham Rd. E13 —4J 65
Graham Rd. N15 —3B 30
Graham Rd. NW4 —6D 26

Graham Rd. SW19 —7H 107
Graham Rd. W4 —3K 73
Graham Rd. Bexh —4F 101
Graham Rd. Hamp —4E 102
Graham Rd. Harr —3J 23
Graham Rd. Mitc —1E 122
Graham St. N1 —2B 62
Graham Ter. SW1 —4E 76 (9G 145)
Grainger Clo. N'holt —6G 39
Grainger Ct. SE5 —7C 78
Grainger Rd. N22 —1C 30
Grainger Rd. Iswth —2K 87
Grampian Clo. Orp —6K 129
Grampian Gdns. NW2 —1G 43
Grampians, The. W6 —2F 75
  (off Shepherd's Bush Rd.)
Granada St. SW17 —5C 108
Granard Av. SW15 —5D 90
Granard Bus. Cen. NW7 —6F 13
Granard Ho. E9 —6K 47
Granard Rd. SW12 —7D 92
Granary Clo. N9 —7D 8
Granary Rd. E1 —4H 63
Granary St. NW1 —1H 61
Granault Rd. Enf —1A 8
Granby Bldgs. SE11 —4K 77 (9E 146)
  (off Black Prince Rd.)
Granby Rd. SE9 —2D 98
Granby St. E2 —4F 63
Granby Ter. NW1 —2G 61
Grand Arc. N12 —5F 15
Grand Av. EC1 —5B 62 (5K 141)
Grand Av. N10 —4E 28
Grand Av. Surb —5H 119
Grand Av. Wemb —5G 41
Grand Av. E. Wemb —5H 41
Grand Depot Rd. SE18 —5E 82
Grand Dri. SW20 —2E 120
Granden Rd. SW16 —2J 123
Grandfield Ct. W4 —6K 73
Grandison Rd. SW11 —5D 92
Grandison Rd. Wor Pk —2E 130
Grand Pde. N4 —5B 30
Grand Pde. Wemb —2G 41
Grand Pde. M. SW15 —5G 91
Grand Union Cres. E8 —7G 47
Grand Union Ind. Est. NW10 —2H 57
Grand Wlk. E1 —4A 64
Granfield St. SW11 —1B 92
Grange Av. N12 —5F 15
Grange Av. N20 —7B 4
Grange Av. SE25 —2E 124
Grange Av. Barn —1H 15
Grange Av. Stan —2B 24
Grange Av. Twic —2J 103
Grange Av. Wfd G —6D 20
Grangecliffe Gdns. SE25 —2E 124
Grange Clo. Edgw —5D 12
Grange Clo. Houn —6D 70
Grange Clo. Sidc —3A 116
Grange Clo. Wfd G —7D 20
Grange Ct. E8 —7F 47
Grange Ct. WC2 —6K 61 (8F 140)
Grange Ct. Harr —3K 39
Grange Ct. N'holt —2A 54
Grange Ct. Pinn —3C 22
Grangecourt Rd. N16 —1E 46
Grange Cres. SE28 —6C 68
Grange Dri. Chst —4D 114
Grange Farm Clo. Harr —2G 39
Grange Gdns. N14 —1C 16
Grange Gdns. NW3 —3K 43
Grange Gdns. SE25 —2E 124
Grange Gdns. Pinn —3C 22
Grange Gro. N1 —6C 46
Grange Hill. SE25 —2E 124
Grange Hill. Edgw —5D 12

Grangehill Pl. SE9 —3D 98
Grangehill Rd. SE9 —3D 98
Grange Ho. SE1 —3F 79 (7E 148)
Grange La. SE21 —2F 111
Grange Mans. Eps —7B 130
Grangemill Rd. SE6 —3C 112
Grangemill Way. SE6 —2C 112
Grange Pk. E10 —2D 48
Grange Pk. W5 —1E 72
Grange Pk. Av. N21 —6H 7
Grange Pk. Pl. SW20 —7D 106
Grange Pk. Rd. E10 —1D 48
Grange Pk. Rd. T Hth —4D 124
Grange Pl. NW6 —7J 43
Granger Gro. SE1 —2D 78 (4B 148)
Grange Rd. E10 —1C 48
Grange Rd. E13 —3H 65
Grange Rd. E17 —5A 32
Grange Rd. N6 —6E 28
Grange Rd. N17 & N18 —6B 18
Grange Rd. NW10 —6D 42
Grange Rd. SW13 —1C 90
Grange Rd. W4 —5H 73
Grange Rd. W5 —1D 72
Grange Rd. Edgw —6E 12
Grange Rd. Ilf —4F 51
Grange Rd. King T —3E 118
Grange Rd. S Croy —7C 134
Grange Rd. S'hall —2C 70
Grange Rd. S Harr —2H 39
Grange Rd. Sutt —7J 131
Grange Rd. T Hth & SE19 —4D 124
Grange St. N1 —1E 62
Grange, The. E17 —5B 32
(off Lynmouth Rd.)
Grange, The. N2 —2B 28
Grange, The. N20 —1F 15
Grange, The. SE1 —3F 79 (7E 148)
Grange, The. SW19 —6F 107
Grange, The. Croy —2B 136
Grange, The. Wemb —7G 41
Grange, The. Wor Pk —4A 130
Grange Vale. Sutt —7K 131
Grangeview Rd. N20 —1F 15
Grange Wlk. SE1 —3E 78 (6D 148)
Grange Wlk. M. SE1 —3E 78 (7D 148)
(off Grange Wlk.)
Grange Way. N12 —4E 14
Grange Way. Harr —7J 43
Grange Way. Wfd G —4F 21
Grangeway Gdns. Ilf —5C 34
Grangeway, The. N21 —6G 7
Grangewood. Bex —1F 117
Grangewood La. Beck —6B 112
Grangewood St. E6 —1B 66
Grangewood Ter. SE25 —2D 124
Grange Yd. SE1 —3F 79 (7E 148)
Granham Gdns. N9 —2A 18
Granite St. SE18 —5H 83
Granleigh Rd. E11 —2G 49
Gransden Av. E8 —7H 47
Gransden Rd. W12 —2B 74
Grantbridge St. N1 —2B 62
Grantchester Clo. Harr —3K 39
Grant Clo. N14 —7B 6
Grantham Clo. Edgw —3K 11
Grantham Ct. Romf —7F 37
Grantham Gdns. Romf —6F 37
Grantham Pl. W1 —1F 77 (3J 145)
Grantham Rd. E12 —4E 50
Grantham Rd. SW9 —2J 93
Grantham Rd. W4 —7A 74
Grantley Rd. Houn —2A 86
Grantley St. E1 —3K 63
Grantock Rd. E17 —1F 33
Granton Rd. SW16 —1G 123

Granton Rd. Ilf —1A 52
Granton Rd. Sidc —6C 116
Grant Pl. Croy —1F 135
Grant Rd. SW11 —4B 92
Grant Rd. Croy —1F 135
Grant Rd. Harr —3K 23
Grants Clo. NW7 —7K 13
Grant St. E13 —3A 65
Grant St. N1 —2A 62
Grantully Rd. W9 —3K 59
Grant Way. Iswth —6A 72
Granville Arc. SW9 —4A 94
Granville Av. N9 —3D 18
Granville Av. Houn —5E 86
Granville Clo. Croy —2E 134
Granville Ct. N1 —1E 62
Granville Gdns. SW16 —7K 109
Granville Gdns. W5 —1E 72
Granville Gro. SE13 —3E 96
Granville M. Sidc —4A 116
Granville Pk. SE13 —3E 96
Granville Pl. N12 —7F 15
Granville Pl. W1 —6E 60 (8G 139)
Granville Pl. Pinn —3B 22
Granville Point. NW2 —2H 43
Granville Rd. E17 —6D 32
Granville Rd. E18 —2K 33
Granville Rd. N4 —6K 29
Granville Rd. N12 —7E 14
Granville Rd. N13 —6E 16
Granville Rd. N22 —1B 30
Granville Rd. NW2 —2H 43
Granville Rd. NW6 —2J 59
(in two parts)
Granville Rd. SW18 —7H 91
Granville Rd. SW19 —7J 107
Granville Rd. Barn —4A 4
Granville Rd. Ilf —1F 51
Granville Rd. Sidc —4A 116
Granville Rd. Well —3C 100
Granville Sq. SE15 —7E 78
Granville Sq. WC1 —3K 61 (2F 140)
Granville St. WC1 —3K 61 (2F 140)
Granwood Ct. Iswth —1J 87
Grape St. WC2 —6J 61 (7C 140)
Graphite Sq. SE11 —5K 77
Grasdene Rd. SE18 —7A 84
Grasmere Av. SW15 —4K 105
Grasmere Av. SW19 —3J 121
Grasmere Av. W3 —7K 57
Grasmere Av. Houn —6F 87
Grasmere Av. Wemb —7C 24
Grasmere Ct. N22 —6E 16
Grasmere Ct. SW13 —6C 74
Grasmere Gdns. Harr —2A 24
Grasmere Gdns. Ilf —5C 34
Grasmere Point. SE15 —7J 79
(off Old Kent Rd.)
Grasmere Rd. E13 —2J 65
Grasmere Rd. N10 —1F 29
Grasmere Rd. N17 —6B 18
Grasmere Rd. SE25 —5H 125
Grasmere Rd. SW16 —5N 109
Grasmere Rd. Bexh —2J 101
Grasmere Rd. Brom —1H 127
Grassington Rd. Sidc —4A 116
Grassmount. SE23 —2H 111
Grass Pk. N3 —1H 27
Grass Way. Wall —4G 133
Grasvenor Av. Barn —5D 4
Grately Way. SE15 —7F 79
Gratton Rd. W14 —3G 75
Gratton Ter. NW2 —3F 43
Gravel Hill. N3 —2H 27
Gravel Hill. Bexh —5H 101
Gravel Hill. Croy —6K 135
Gravel Hill Clo. Bexh —5H 101

Gravel La. E1 —6F 63 (7E 142)
Gravel Pit La. SE9 —5F 99
Gravel Rd. Twic —1J 103
Gravelwood Clo. Chst —3G 115
Gravenel Gdns. SW17 —5A 108
(off Nutwell St.)
Graveney Gro. SE20 —7J 111
Graveney Rd. SW17 —4C 108
Gravesend Rd. W12 —7C 58
Gray Av. Dag —1F 53
Grayham Cres. N Mald —4K 119
Grayham Rd. N Mald —4K 119
Grayland Clo. Brom —1B 128
Grayling Clo. E16 —4G 65
Grayling Rd. N16 —2D 46
Grayling Sq. E2 —3G 63
(off Nelson Gdns.)
Grayscroft Rd. SW16 —7H 109
Grays Farm Rd. Orp —7B 116
Grayshott Rd. SW11 —2E 92
Gray's Inn Pl. WC1 —5K 61 (6F 140)
Gray's Inn Rd. WC1
—3J 61 (1D 140)
Gray's Inn Sq. WC1
—5K 61 (5G 141)
Gray St. SE1 —2A 78 (5H 147)
Grayswood Gdns. SW20 —2D 120
Gray's Yd. W1 —6E 60 (7H 139)
(off James St.)
Graywood Ct. N12 —7F 15
Grazebrook Rd. N16 —2D 46
Grazeley Clo. Bexh —5J 101
Grazeley Ct. SE19 —5E 110
Gt. Acre Ct. SW4 —4H 93
Gt. Arthur Ho. EC1 —4C 62 (4L 141)
(off Golden La. Est.)
Gt. Bell All. EC2 —6D 62 (7A 142)
Gt. Brownings. SE21 —4F 111
Gt. Bushey Dri. N20 —1E 14
Gt. Cambridge Rd. N18 & N17
—5J 17
Gt. Cambridge Rd. Enf & Chesh
—1B 8
Gt. Cambridge Trading Est. Enf
—5B 8
Gt. Castle St. W1 —6F 61 (7K 139)
Gt. Central Av. Ruis —5A 38
Gt. Central St. NW1
—5D 60 (5E 138)
Gt. Central Way. Wemb & NW10
—4J 41
Gt. Chapel St. W1 —6H 61 (7A 140)
Gt. Chertsey Rd. W4 —2J 89
Gt. Chertsey Rd. Felt —3D 102
Gt. Church La. W6 —4F 75
Gt. College St. SW1 —3J 77 (6C 146)
Gt. Cross Av. SE10 —7G 81
Gt. Cumberland M. W1
—6D 60 (8E 138)
Gt. Cumberland Pl. W1
—6D 60 (7E 138)
Gt. Dover St. SE1 —2C 78 (5M 147)
Gt. Eastern Enterprise Cen. E14
—2D 80
Gt. Eastern Rd. E15 —7F 49
Gt. Eastern Rd. EC2 —3E 62 (2C 142)
Gt. Eastern Wlk. EC2
—5E 62 (6D 142)
Gt. Elms Rd. Brom —4A 128
Great Field. NW9 —1A 26
Greatfield Av. E6 —4D 66
Greatfield Clo. N19 —4G 45
Greatfield Clo. SE13 —4C 96
Greatfields Rd. Bark —1H 67
Gt. George St. SW1
—2H 77 (5B 146)

Gt. Guildford St. SE1
—1C 78 (2L 147)
Greatham Wlk. SW15 —1C 106
Gt. Harry Dri. SE9 —3E 114
Gt. James St. WC1 —5K 61 (5E 140)
Gt. Marlborough St. W1
—6G 61 (8L 139)
Gt. Maze Pond. SE1
—1D 78 (3B 148)
Gt. Maze Pond. SW1 —2D 78
Gt. Newport St. WC2
—7J 61 (9C 140)
Gt. New St. EC4 —6A 62 (7H 141)
Gt. North Rd. N2 & N6 —5C 28
Gt. North Rd. H Bar —2C 4
Gt. North Rd. New Bar —5D 4
Gt. North Way. NW4 —2D 26
Greatorex St. E1 —5G 63
Gt. Ormond St. WC1
—5J 61 (5D 140)
Gt. Owl Rd. Chig —3K 21
Gt. Percy St. WC1 —3K 61 (1F 140)
Gt. Peter St. SW1 —3H 77 (7A 146)
Gt. Portland St. W1 —4F 61 (4K 139)
Gt. Pulteney St. W1
—7G 61 (9M 139)
Gt. Queen St. WC2 —6J 61 (8D 140)
Gt. Russell St. WC1
—6H 61 (7B 140)
Gt. St Helen's. EC3 —6E 62 (7C 142)
Gt. St Thomas Apostle. EC4
—7C 62 (9M 141)
Gt. Scotland Yd. SW1
—1J 77 (3C 145)
Gt. Smith St. SW1 —3H 77 (6B 146)
Gt. South West Rd. Houn —2A 85
Gt. Spilmans. SE22 —5E 94
Gt. Strand. NW9 —1B 26
Gt. Suffolk St. SE1 —1B 78 (3K 147)
Gt. Sutton St. EC1 —4B 62 (4K 141)
Gt. Swan All. EC2 —6D 62 (7A 142)
Gt. Thrift. Orp —4G 129
Gt. Titchfield St. W1
—5F 61 (4K 139)
Gt. Tower St. EC3 —7E 62 (9C 142)
Gt. Trinity La. EC4 —7C 62 (9M 141)
Gt. Turnstile. WC1 —5K 61 (6F 140)
Gt. Western Ind. Pk. S'hall —2F 71
Gt. Western Rd. W9 & W11 —5H 59
Gt. West Rd. W4 & W6 —5B 74
Gt. West Rd. Bren —7A 72
Gt. West Rd. Houn & Iswth —2B 86
Gt. West Rd. Trading Est. Bren
—6B 72
Gt. Winchester St. EC2
—6D 62 (7B 142)
Gt. Windmill St. W1 —7H 61
Greatwood. Chst —7E 114
Great Yd. SE1 —2E 78 (4D 148)
(off Crucifix La.)
Greaves Clo. Bark —7H 51
Greaves Pl. SW17 —4C 108
Greaves Tower. SW10 —7A 76
(off Worlds End Est.)
Grebe Av. Hay —6A 54
Grebe Clo. E7 —5H 49
Grebe Clo. E17 —7F 19
Grecian Cres. SE19 —6B 110
Greek Ct. W1 —6H 61 (8B 140)
Greek St. W1 —6H 61 (8B 140)
Greenacre Clo. Barn —1C 4
Greenacre Clo. N'holt —5D 38
Greenacre Gdns. E17 —4E 32
Greenacres. N3 —2H 27
Greenacres. SE9 —6E 98
Greenacres. Bush —2C 10
Green Acres. Croy —3F 135
Greenacres. Sidc —4A 116

Greenacres Dri. Stan —7G 11
Greenacre Sq. SE16 —2K 79
Greenacre Wlk. N14 —3C 16
Green Arbour Ct. EC1
(off Old Bailey) —6B 62 (7J 141)
Green Av. NW7 —4E 12
Green Av. W13 —3B 72
Greenaway Gdns. NW3 —4K 43
Green Bank. E1 —1H 79
Greenbank. N12 —4E 14
Greenbank Av. Wemb —5A 40
Green Bank Clo. E4 —2K 19
Greenbank Cres. NW4 —4G 27
Greenbanks. Harr —4J 39
Greenbay Rd. SE7 —7B 82
Greenberry St. NW8 —2C 60
Greenbrook Av. Barn —1F 5
Green Clo. NW9 —6J 25
Green Clo. NW11 —7A 28
Green Clo. Brom —3G 127
Green Clo. Cars —2D 132
Green Clo. Felt —5C 102
Greencoat Pl. SW1
—4G 77 (8M 145)
Greencoat Row. SW1
—3G 77 (7M 145)
Greencourt Av. Croy —2H 135
Greencourt Av. Edgw —1H 25
Greencourt Gdns. Croy —2H 135
Greencourt Rd. Orp —5H 129
Greencrest Pl. NW2 —3C 42
Greencroft. Edgw —5D 12
Greencroft Av. Ruis —2A 38
Greencroft Clo. E6 —5B 66
Greencroft Gdns. NW6 —7K 43
Greencroft Gdns. Enf —3K 7
Greencroft Rd. Houn —1D 86
Green Dale. SE5 —4D 94
Green Dale. SE22 —5E 94
Greendale. Edgw —4F 13
Green Dale Clo. SE22 —5E 94
Green Dragon Ct. SE1
(off Bedale St.) —1D 78 (3A 148)
Green Dragon La. N21 —6F 7
Green Dragon La. Bren —5E 72
Green Dragon Yd. E1 —5G 63
Green Dri. S'hall —1E 70
Green End. N21 —2G 17
Greenend Rd. W4 —2A 74
Greenfell St. SE10 —3G 81
Greenfield Av. Surb —7H 119
Greenfield Gdns. NW2 —2G 43
Greenfield Gdns. Dag —1D 68
Greenfield Gdns. Orp —7H 129
Greenfield Rd. E1 —5G 63
Greenfield Rd. N15 —5E 30
Greenfield Rd. Dag —1C 68
Greenfield Rd. Dart —5K 117
Greenfield Rd. Sutt —4K 131
Greenfields. S'hall —6E 54
Greenfield Way. Harr —3F 23
Greenford. W7 —4J 55
Greenford Av. S'hall —7D 54
Greenford Gdns. Gnfd —3F 55
Greenford Grn. Gnfd —6J 39
Greenford Ind. Est. N'holt —7F 39
Greenford Rd. Harr —4J 39
Greenford Rd. S'hall & Gnfd —1G 71
Greengate. Gnfd —6B 40
Greengate Lodge. E13 —2K 65
(off Hollybush St.)
Greengate St. E13 —2K 65
Greenhalgh Wlk. N2 —4A 28
Greenham Clo. SE1
—2A 78 (5G 147)
Greenham Ho. Houn —3H 87
Greenham Rd. N10 —2E 28
Green Hedge. Twic —6C 88

Greenheys Dri. E18 —3H 33
Greenhill. NW3 —4B 44
Green Hill. SE18 —5D 82
Greenhill. Buck H —1F 21
Greenhill. Sutt —2A 132
Greenhill. Wemb —2H 41
Greenhill Gdns. N'holt —2D 54
Greenhill Gro. E12 —4C 50
Greenhill Pde. Barn —5E 4
Greenhill Pk. NW10 —1A 58
Greenhill Pk. Barn —5E 4
Greenhill Rd. NW10 —1A 58
Greenhill Rd. Harr —6J 23
Greenhill's Rents. EC1
　—5B 62 (5J 141)
Greenhills Ter. N1 —6D 46
Greenhill Ter. N'holt —2D 54
Greenhill Way. Harr —6J 23
Greenhill Way. Wemb —2H 41
Greenhithe Clo. Sidc —7J 99
Greenholm Rd. SE9 —5F 99
Green Hundred Rd. SE15 —6G 79
Greenhurst Rd. SE27 —5A 110
Greening St. SE2 —4C 84
Greenland Cres. S'hall —3A 70
Greenland M. SE8 —5K 79
Greenland Pl. NW1 —1F 61
Greenland Quay. SE16 —4A 80
Greenland Rd. NW1 —1F 61
Greenland Rd. Barn —6A 4
Greenland St. NW1 —1F 61
Green La. NW4 —4F 27
Green La. SE9 & Chst —1F 115
Green La. SE20 —7K 111
Green La. SW16 & T Hth —7K 109
Green La. W7 —2J 71
Green La. Edgw —4A 12
Green La. Felt —5C 102
Green La. Harr —3J 39
Green La. Houn —3A 86
Green La. Ilf & Dag —2H 51
Green La. Mord —6J 121
Green La. Mord —7E 120
　(Battersea Cemetery)
Green La. N Mald —5J 119
Green La. Stan —4G 11
Green La. Wor Pk —1C 130
Green La. Cotts. Stan —4G 11
Green La. Gdns. T Hth —2C 124
Green Lanes. N8, N4 & N16 —3B 30
Green Lanes. N13 & N21 —3F 17
Green Lanes. Eps —7A 130
　(in two parts)
Greenlaw Ct. W5 —6D 56
　(off Mount Pk. Rd.)
Greenlaw Gdns. N Mald —7B 120
Greenlawns. N3 —6E 14
Green Lawns. Ruis —1A 38
Greenlaw St. SE18 —3E 82
Greenleaf Clo. SW2 —7A 94
Greenleafe Dri. Ilf —3F 35
Greenleaf Rd. E6 —1A 66
Greenleaf Rd. E17 —3B 32
Greenlea Trading Pk. SW19 —1B 122
Green Man Gdns. W13 —7A 56
Green Man La. W13 —7A 56
Green Man Pas. W13 —7A 56
　(in two parts)
Greenman St. N1 —7C 46
Greenmead. Eri —3E 84
Green Moor Link. N21 —7G 7
Greenmoor Rd. Enf —2D 8
Greenoak Way. SW19 —4F 107
Greenock Rd. SW16 —1H 123
Greenock Rd. W3 —3H 73
Greenock Way. Romf —1K 37
Greenpark Ct. Wemb —7C 40
Green Point. E15 —6G 49

Green Pond Clo. E17 —3A 32
Green Pond Rd. E17 —3A 32
Greenrigg Wlk. Wemb —3H 41
Green Rd. N13 —6A 6
Green Rd. N20 —3F 15
Green's Ct. W1 —7H 61 (9A 140)
　(off Brewer St.)
Green's End. SE18 —4F 83
Greenshank Clo. E17 —7F 19
Greenshields Ind. Est. E16 —2J 81
Greenside. Bex —1E 116
Green Side. Dag —1C 52
Greenside Clo. N20 —2G 15
Greenside Clo. Chst —6F 115
Greenside Rd. W12 —3C 74
Greenside Rd. Croy —7A 124
Greenstead Av. Wfd G —7F 21
Greenstead Clo. Wfd G —6F 21
Greenstead Gdns. SW15 —5D 90
Greenstead Gdns. Wfd G —6F 21
Greensted Rd. Lou —1H 21
Greenstone M. E11 —6J 33
Green St. E7 & E13 —6K 49
Green St. W1 —7E 60 (9F 138)
Green St. Enf —2D 8
Green, The. E4 —1A 20
Green, The. E11 —6K 33
Green, The. E15 —6H 49
Green, The. N9 —2B 18
Green, The. N14 —3C 16
Green, The. N21 —1F 17
Green, The. SW19 —5F 107
Green, The. W3 —6A 58
Green, The. W5 —1D 72
Green, The. Bexh —1G 101
Green, The. Brom —3J 113
Green, The. Cars —4E 132
Green, The. Croy —7B 136
Green, The. Hayes —7J 127
Green, The. Houn —6E 70
Green, The. Mord —4G 121
Green, The. N Mald —3J 119
Green, The. Rich —5D 88
Green, The. Sidc —4A 116
Green, The. S'hall —2D 70
Green, The. St P —7B 116
Green, The. Sutt —3K 131
Green, The. Twic —1J 103
Green, The. Well —4J 99
Green, The. Wemb —2A 40
Green, The. Wfd G —5D 20
Green Vale. W5 —6F 57
Green Vale. Bexh —5D 100
Greenvale Rd. SE9 —4D 98
Green Verges. Stan —7J 11
Greenview Av. Beck —6A 126
Greenview Av. Croy —6A 126
Green Wlk. NW4 —5F 27
Green Wlk. SE1 —3E 78 (7C 148)
Green Wlk. Hamp —6D 102
Green Wlk. Lou —1H 21
Green Wlk. S'hall —5E 70
Green Wlk. Wfd G —6H 21
Green Wlk., The. E4 —1A 20
Greenway. N14 —2D 16
Greenway. N20 —2D 14
Green Way. SE9 —5B 98
Greenway. SW20 —4E 120
Green Way. Brom —6C 128
Greenway. Chst —5E 114
Greenway. Dag —2C 52
Greenway. Hay —4A 54
Greenway. Kent —5E 24
Greenway. Pinn —2A 22
Green Way. Wall —4G 133
Green Way. Wfd G —5F 21
Greenway Av. E17 —4F 33
Greenway Clo. N4 —2C 46

Greenway Clo. N11 —6A 16
Greenway Clo. N15 —4F 31
Greenway Clo. N20 —2D 14
Greenway Clo. NW9 —2K 25
Greenway Gdns. NW9 —2K 25
Greenway Gdns. Croy —3B 136
Greenway Gdns. Gnfd —3E 54
Greenway Gdns. Harr —2J 23
Greenways. Beck —3C 126
Greenways, The. Twic —6A 88
Greenway, The. NW9 —2K 25
Greenway, The. Houn —4D 86
Green Way, The. Pinn —6D 22
Green Way, The. W'stone —1J 23
Greenwell St. W1 —4F 61 (4K 139)
Greenwich Chu. St. SE10 —6E 80
Greenwich Cres. E6 —5C 66
Greenwich High Rd. SE10 —1D 96
Greenwich Pk. SE10 —6F 81
Greenwich S. St. SE10 —1D 96
Greenwich View Pl. E14 —3D 80
Greenwood Av. Dag —4H 53
Greenwood Av. Enf —2F 9
Greenwood Clo. Bush —1D 10
Greenwood Clo. Mord —4G 121
Greenwood Clo. Orp —6J 129
Greenwood Clo. Sidc —2A 116
Greenwood Ct. SW1 —5G 77
　(off Cambridge St.)
Greenwood Dri. E4 —5A 20
Greenwood Gdns. N13 —3G 17
Greenwood Gdns. Ilf —1G 35
Greenwood Ho. N22 —1A 30
Greenwood La. Hamp —5F 103
Greenwood Mans. Bark —7A 52
　(off Lansbury Av.)
Greenwood Pk. King T —7A 106
Greenwood Pl. NW5 —5F 45
Greenwood Rd. E8 —6G 47
Greenwood Rd. E13 —2J 65
Greenwood Rd. Bex —4K 117
Greenwood Rd. Croy —7B 124
Greenwood Rd. Iswth —3K 87
Greenwood Rd. Mitc —3H 123
Greenwoods, The. S Harr —2G 39
Greenwood Ter. NW10 —1K 57
Green Wrythe Cres. Cars —1C 132
Green Wrythe La. Cars —6B 122
Green Yd., The. EC3
　—6E 62 (8C 142)
　(off Leadenhall St.)
Greer Rd. Harr —1G 23
Greet St. SE1 —2A 78 (5H 147)
　(off Frazier St.)
Greg Clo. E10 —6E 32
Gregory Cres. SE9 —7B 98
Gregory M. SE3 —7J 81
Gregory Pl. W8 —2K 75
Gregory Rd. Romf —4D 36
Gregory Rd. S'hall —3E 70
Greig Clo. N8 —5J 29
Greig Ter. SE17 —6B 78
Grenaby Av. Croy —7D 124
Grenaby Rd. Croy —7D 124
Grenada Rd. SE7 —7A 82
Grenade St. E14 —7B 64
Grenadier St. E16 —1E 82
Grena Gdns. Rich —4F 89
Grena Rd. Rich —4F 89
Grendon Gdns. Wemb —2G 41
Grendon Lodge. Edgw —2D 12
Grendon St. NW8 —4C 60 (3C 138)
Grenfell Ct. NW7 —6J 13
Grenfell Gdns. Harr —7E 24
Grenfell Gdns. Ilf —5K 35
Grenfell Ho. SE5 —7C 78
Grenfell Rd. W11 —7F 59
Grenfell Rd. Mitc —6D 108

Grenfell Tower. W11 —7F 59
Grenfell Wlk. W11 —7F 59
Grennell Clo. Sutt —2B 132
Grennell Rd. Sutt —2A 132
Grenoble Gdns. N13 —6F 17
Grenville Clo. N3 —1G 27
Grenville Clo. Surb —7J 119
Grenville Gdns. Wfd G —1A 34
Grenville M. SW7 —4A 76
　(off Harrington Gdns.)
Grenville M. Hamp —5F 103
Grenville Pl. NW7 —5E 12
Grenville Pl. SW7 —3A 76
Grenville Rd. N19 —1J 45
Grenville St. WC1 —4J 61 (4D 140)
Gresham Av. N20 —4J 15
Gresham Clo. Bex —6E 101
Gresham Clo. Enf —3H 7
Gresham Dri. Romf —5B 36
Gresham Gdns. NW11 —1G 43
Gresham Lodge. E17 —5D 32
Gresham M. W4 —3J 73
Gresham Rd. E6 —2D 66
Gresham Rd. E16 —6K 65
Gresham Rd. NW10 —5K 41
Gresham Rd. SE25 —4G 125
Gresham Rd. SW9 —3A 94
Gresham Rd. Beck —2A 126
Gresham Rd. Edgw —6A 12
Gresham Rd. Hamp —6E 102
Gresham Rd. Houn —1E 87
Gresham St. EC2 —6C 62 (7L 141)
Gresham Way. SW19 —3K 107
Gresley Clo. N15 —4D 30
Gresley Rd. N19 —1G 45
Gressenhall Rd. SW18 —6H 91
Gresse St. W1 —6H 61 (6A 140)
Gresswell Clo. Sidc —3A 116
Greswell St. SW6 —1F 91
Gretton Rd. N17 —7A 18
Greville Clo. Twic —7B 88
Greville Ct. Harr —4J 39
Greville Lodge. E13 —1K 65
Greville Lodge. N12 —4E 14
Greville Lodge. Edgw —4C 12
　(off Broadhurst Av.)
Greville M. NW6 —1K 59
　(off Greville Rd.)
Greville Pl. NW6 —2K 59
Greville Rd. E17 —4E 32
Greville Rd. NW6 —2K 59
Greville Rd. Rich —6F 89
Greville St. EC1 —5A 62 (6G 141)
　(in two parts)
Grey Clo. NW11 —6A 28
Greycoat Pl. SW1 —3H 77 (7A 146)
Greycoat St. SW1 —3H 77 (7A 145)
Greycot Rd. Beck —5C 112
Grey Eagle St. E1 —4F 63 (4F 142)
Greyfell Clo. Stan —5H 11
Greyfriars Pas. EC1 —6B 62 (7K 141)
Greyhound Ct. WC2
　—7K 61 (9F 140)
Greyhound Hill. NW4 —3C 26
Greyhound La. SW16 —6H 109
Greyhound Rd. N17 —3E 30
Greyhound Rd. NW10 —3D 58
Greyhound Rd. W6 & W14 —6F 75
Greyhound Rd. Sutt —5A 132
Greyhound Rd. Mans. W14 —6G 75
　(off Greyhound Rd.)
Greyhound Ter. SW16 —1G 123
Grey Ho. W12 —7D 58
　(off White City Est.)
Greystead Rd. SE23 —7J 95
Greystoke Av. Pinn —3E 22
Greystoke Ct. W5 —4F 57
Greystoke Gdns. W5 —4E 56

Greystoke Gdns. Enf —4C 6
Greystoke Pk. Ter. W5 —3D 56
Greystoke Pk. Ter. Gnfd —2G 55
Greystoke Pl. EC4 —5A 62 (7G 141)
Greystone Gdns. Harr —6C 24
Greystone Gdns. Ilf —2G 35
Greyswood St. SW16 —6F 109
Greystone Gdns. Ilf —2G 35
Grey Turner Ho. W12 —6C 58
Grierson Rd. SE23 —7K 95
Griffin Clo. NW10 —5D 42
Griffin Ct. W4 —5B 74
Griffin Ct. Bren —6E 72
Griffin Mnr. Way. SE28 —3H 83
Griffin Rd. N17 —2E 30
Griffin Rd. SE18 —5H 83
Griffith Clo. Dag —1C 52
Griffiths Clo. Wor Pk —2D 130
Griffiths Rd. SW19 —7J 107
Griggs App. Ilf —2G 51
Grigg's Pl. SE1 —3E 78 (7D 148)
　(off Grange Rd.)
Griggs Rd. E10 —6E 32
Grilse Clo. N9 —4C 18
Grimsby St. E2 —4F 63
Grimsdyke Rd. Pinn —1D 22
Grimsell Path. SE5 —7B 78
Grimshaw Clo. N6 —7E 28
Grimston Rd. SW6 —2H 91
Grimwade Av. Croy —3G 135
Grimwood Rd. Twic —7K 87
Grindall Clo. Croy —4B 134
Grindal St. SE1 —2A 78 (5G 147)
Grinling Pl. SE8 —6C 80
Grinstead Rd. SE8 —5A 80
Grittleton Av. Wemb —6H 41
Grittleton Rd. W9 —4J 59
Grizedale Ter. SE23 —2H 111
Grocer's Hall Ct. EC2
　—6D 62 (8A 142)
Grocer's Hall Gdns. EC2
　—6D 62 (8A 142)
Grogan Clo. Hamp —6D 102
Groombridge Clo. Well —5A 100
Groombridge Rd. E9 —7K 47
Groom Cres. SW18 —7B 92
Groomfield Clo. SW17 —4E 108
Groom Pl. SW1 —3E 76 (6H 145)
Grosmont Rd. SE18 —6K 83
Grossage Rd. SE18 —5H 83
Grosse Way. SW15 —6D 90
Grosvenor Av. N5 —5C 46
Grosvenor Av. SW14 —3A 90
Grosvenor Av. Cars —6D 132
Grosvenor Av. Harr —6F 23
Grosvenor Av. Rich —5E 88
Grosvenor Cotts. SW1
　—4E 76 (8G 145)
Grosvenor Ct. E10 —1D 48
Grosvenor Ct. N14 —7B 6
Grosvenor Ct. NW6 —1F 59
Grosvenor Ct. NW7 —5E 12
　(off Hale La.)
Grosvenor Ct. W3 —1G 73
Grosvenor Ct. Barn —7B 6
Grosvenor Cres. NW9 —4G 25
Grosvenor Cres. SW1
　—2E 76 (5H 145)
Grosvenor Cres. M. SW1
　—2E 76 (5H 145)
Grosvenor Est. SW1
　—4H 77 (8B 146)
Grosvenor Gdns. E6 —3B 66
Grosvenor Gdns. N10 —3G 29
Grosvenor Gdns. N14 —5C 6
Grosvenor Gdns. NW2 —5E 42
Grosvenor Gdns. NW11 —6H 27
Grosvenor Gdns. SW1
　—3F 77 (6J 145)

Grosvenor Gdns. SW14 —3A **90**
Grosvenor Gdns. King T —6D **104**
Grosvenor Gdns. Wall —7G **133**
Grosvenor Gdns. Wfd G —6D **20**
(off Beeston Pl.)   —3F **77** (6K **145**)
Grosvenor Gdns. M. N. SW1
(off Ebury St.)   —3F **77** (7J **145**)
Grosvenor Gdns. M. S. SW1
(off Ebury St.)   —3F **77** (7K **145**)
Grosvenor Hill. SW19 —6G **107**
Grosvenor Hill. W1 —7F **61** (9J **139**)
Grosvenor Pk. SE5 —7C **78**
Grosvenor Pk. Rd. E17 —5C **32**
Grosvenor Pl. SW1 —2E **76** (4H **145**)
Grosvenor Rise. E. E17 —5D **32**
Grosvenor Rd. E6 —1B **66**
Grosvenor Rd. E7 —6K **49**
Grosvenor Rd. E10 —1E **48**
Grosvenor Rd. E11 —5K **33**
Grosvenor Rd. N3 —7C **14**
Grosvenor Rd. N9 —1C **18**
Grosvenor Rd. N10 —1F **29**
Grosvenor Rd. SE25 —4G **125**
Grosvenor Rd. SW1 —6F **77**
Grosvenor Rd. W4 —5H **73**
Grosvenor Rd. W7 —1A **72**
Grosvenor Rd. Belv —6G **85**
Grosvenor Rd. Bexh —5D **100**
Grosvenor Rd. Bren —6D **72**
Grosvenor Rd. Dag —1F **53**
Grosvenor Rd. Houn —3D **86**
Grosvenor Rd. Ilf —3G **51**
Grosvenor Rd. Orp —6J **129**
Grosvenor Rd. Rich —5E **88**
Grosvenor Rd. Romf —7K **37**
Grosvenor Rd. S'hall —3D **70**
Grosvenor Rd. Twic —1A **104**
Grosvenor Rd. Wall —6F **133**
Grosvenor Rd. W Wick —1D **136**
Grosvenor Sq. W1 —7E **60** (9H **139**)
Grosvenor St. W1 —7F **61** (9J **139**)
Grosvenor Ter. SE5 —7C **78**
Grosvenor Way. E5 —2J **47**
Grosvenor Wharf Rd. E14 —4F **81**
Grotes Bldgs. SE3 —2G **97**
Grote's Pl. SE3 —2G **97**
Groton Rd. SW18 —2K **107**
Grotto Ct. SE1 —2C **78** (4L **147**)
Grotto Pas. W1 —5E **60** (5H **139**)
Grotto Rd. Twic —2K **103**
Grove Av. N3 —7D **14**
Grove Av. W7 —6J **55**
Grove Av. Pinn —4C **22**
Grove Av. Sutt —6J **131**
Grove Av. Twic —1K **103**
Grovebury Clo. Eri —6K **85**
Grovebury Ct. Bexh —5H **101**
Grovebury Rd. SE2 —2B **84**
Grove Clo. N14 —7B **6**
Grove Clo. SE23 —1A **112**
Grove Clo. Brom —2J **137**
Grove Clo. Felt —4C **102**
Grove Clo. King T —4F **119**
Grove Cotts. W4 —6A **74**
Grove Ct. Houn —4E **86**
Grove Cres. E18 —2H **33**
Grove Cres. NW9 —4J **25**
Grove Cres. SE5 —2E **94**
Grove Cres. Felt —4C **102**
Grove Cres. King T —3E **118**
Grove Cres. Rd. E15 —6F **49**
Grovedale Rd. N19 —2H **45**
Grove Dwellings. E1 —5J **63**
Grove End. E18 —2H **33**
Grove End. NW3 —4F **45**

Grove End Rd. NW8 —2B **60**
Grove Farm Ind. Est. Mitc —5D **122**
Grovefield. N11 —4A **16**
(off Coppies Gro.)
Grove Footpath. Surb —4E **118**
Grove Gdns. E15 —6G **49**
Grove Gdns. NW4 —5C **26**
Grove Gdns. NW8 —3C **60** (2D **138**)
Grove Gdns. Dag —3J **53**
Grove Gdns. Enf —1E **8**
Grove Gdns. Rich —6E **88**
Grove Gdns. Tedd —4A **104**
Grove Grn. Rd. E11 —3E **48**
Grove Hall Ct. NW8 —3A **60**
Grove Hill. E18 —2H **33**
Grove Hill. Harr —1J **39**
Grovehill Ct. Brom —6H **113**
Grove Hill Rd. SE5 —3E **94**
Grove Hill Rd. Harr —7K **23**
Grove Ho. W5 —1C **72**
Grove Ho. Rd. N8 —4J **29**
Groveland Av. SW16 —7K **109**
Groveland Ct. EC4 —6C **62** *(8M 141)*
(off Bow La.)
Groveland Rd. Beck —3B **126**
Grovelands Clo. SE5 —2E **94**
Grovelands Clo. Harr —3F **39**
Grovelands Ct. N14 —7C **6**
Grovelands Rd. N13 —4E **16**
Grovelands Rd. N15 —6G **31**
Grovelands Rd. Orp —7A **116**
Groveland Way. N Mald —5J **119**
Grove La. SE5 —1D **94**
Grove La. SE15 —7H **79**
Grove La. King T —4E **118**
Grove La.Ter. SE5 —2D **94**
Grove Mkt. Pl. SE9 —6D **98**
Grove M. W6 —3E **74**
Grove M. W11 —6H **59**
Grove Pk. E11 —6K **33**
Grove Pk. NW9 —4J **25**
Grove Pk. SE5 —2E **94**
Grove Pk. Av. E4 —7J **19**
Grove Pk. Bri. W4 —7J **73**
Grove Pk. Gdns. W4 —7H **73**
Grove Pk. Ind. Est. NW9 —4K **25**
Grove Pk. M. W4 —7J **73**
Grove Pk. Rd. N15 —4E **30**
Grove Pk. Rd. SE9 —3A **114**
Grove Pk. Rd. W4 —7H **73**
Grove Pas. E2 —2H **63**
Grove Pl. NW3 —3B **44**
Grove Pl. W3 —1J **73**
Grove Pl. Bark —1G **67**
Grover Ct. SE13 —2D **96**
Grover Ho. SE11 —5K **77**
Grove Rd. E3 —1K **63**
Grove Rd. E4 —4K **19**
Grove Rd. E11 —7H **33**
Grove Rd. E17 —6D **32**
Grove Rd. E18 —2H **33**
Grove Rd. N11 —5A **16**
Grove Rd. N12 —5G **15**
Grove Rd. N15 —5E **30**
Grove Rd. NW2 —6E **42**
Grove Rd. SW13 —2B **90**
Grove Rd. SW19 —7A **108**
Grove Rd. W3 —1J **73**
Grove Rd. W5 —7D **56**
Grove Rd. Barn —3H **5**
Grove Rd. Belv —6F **85**
Grove Rd. Bexh —4J **101**
Grove Rd. Bren —5C **72**
Grove Rd. Edgw —6D **12**
Grove Rd. Houn —4E **86**
Grove Rd. Iswth —1J **87**
Grove Rd. L. Hth —7B **36**

Grove Rd. Mitc —3E **122**
Grove Rd. Pinn —5D **22**
Grove Rd. Rich —6F **89**
Grove Rd. Surb —5D **118**
Grove Rd. Sutt —6J **131**
Grove Rd. T Hth —4A **124**
Grove Rd. Twic —3H **103**
Grovesby Ct. N14 —7C **6**
Groveside Clo. W3 —5G **57**
Groveside Clo. Cars —2C **132**
Groveside Rd. E4 —2B **20**
Grove St. N18 —5A **18**
Grove St. SE8 —4B **80**
Grove Ter. NW5 —3E **44**
Grove Ter. S'hall —7E **54**
Grove Ter. Tedd —4A **104**
Grove Ter. M. NW5 —3F **45**
Grove, The. E15 —6G **49**
Grove, The. N3 —7D **14**
Grove, The. N4 —7K **29**
Grove, The. N6 —1E **44**
Grove, The. N8 —5H **29**
Grove, The. N13 —4F **17**
(in two parts)
Grove, The. N14 —5B **6**
Grove, The. NW9 —5K **25**
Grove, The. NW11 —7G **27**
Grove, The. W5 —7E **56**
Grove, The. Bexh —4D **100**
Grove, The. Edgw —4C **12**
Grove, The. Enf —2F **7**
Grove, The. Gnfd —6G **55**
Grove, The. Iswth —1J **87**
Grove, The. Sidc —4E **116**
Grove, The. Tedd —5A **104**
Grove, The. Twic —6B **88**
Grove, The. W Wick —2E **136**
Grove Vale. SE22 —4F **95**
Grove Vale. Chst —6E **114**
Grove Vs. E14 —7D **64**
Groveway. SW9 —1K **93**
Groveway. Dag —3D **52**
Grove Way. Wemb —5H **41**
Grovewood. Rich —1G **89**
Grummant Rd. SE15 —1F **95**
Grundy St. E14 —6D **64**
Gruneisen Rd. N3 —7E **14**
Guardian Ct. SE12 —5G **97**
Gubyon Av. SE24 —5B **94**
Guerin Sq. E3 —3B **64**
Guernsey Clo. Houn —7E **70**
Guernsey Gro. SE24 —7C **94**
Guernsey Ho. N1 —6C **46**
Guernsey Rd. E11 —1F **49**
Guest St. EC1 —4C **62** *(4M 141)*
(off Chequer St.)
Guibal Rd. SE12 —7K **97**
Guildersfield Rd. SW16 —7J **109**
Guildersome St. SE18 —6E **82**
Guilford Gro. SE10 —1D **96**
Guilford Pl. WC1 —4K **61** *(4E 140)*
Guilford Rd. E6 —6D **66**
Guilford Rd. E17 —1E **32**
Guilford Rd. SW8 —1J **93**
Guilford Rd. Croy —6D **124**
Guilford Rd. Ilf —2J **51**
Guilford St. WC1 —4J **61** *(4C 140)*
Guilford Way. Wall —5J **133**
Guildhall Bldgs. EC2
—6D **62** *(7A 142)*
(off Basinghall St.)
Guildhall Yd. EC2 —6C **62** *(7M 141)*
Guildhouse St. SW1
—4G **77** (8L **145**)
Guildown Av. N12 —4E **14**
Guild Rd. SE7 —5B **82**
Guildsway. E17 —1B **32**

Guilford Pl. WC1 —4K **61**
Guilford St. WC1 —4J **61**
Guilfoyle. NW9 —2B **26**
Guillemot Ct. SE8 —6B **80**
Guillemot Pl. N22 —2A **29**
Guilsborough Clo. NW10 —7A **42**
Guinness Clo. E9 —7A **48**
Guinness Ct. NW8 —1C **60**
Guinness Ct. SE1 —2E **78** *(4C 148)*
(off Snowsfields)
Guinness Sq. SE1 —4E **78** (8C **148**)
Guinness Trust Bldgs. SE11 —5B **78**
Guinness Trust Bldgs. SE17 —5B **78**
Guinness Trust Bldgs. W6 —5F **75**
(off Fulham Pal. Rd.)
Guinness Trust Est. N16 —1E **46**
Guion Rd. SW6 —2H **91**
Gulland Wlk. N1 —6C **46**
(off Oronsay Wlk.)
Gull Clo. Wall —7J **133**
Gulliver Clo. N'holt —1D **54**
Gulliver Rd. Sidc —2H **115**
Gulliver St. SE16 —3A **80**
Gulliver's Ho. EC1 —4C **62** *(4L 141)*
(off Goswell Rd.)
Gulliver St. SE16 —3A **80**
Gulston Wlk. SW3 —4D **76** *(9F 144)*
(off Blackland Ter.)
Gumleigh Rd. W5 —4C **72**
Gumley Gdns. Iswth —3A **88**
Gunderson Corner. Mitc —3D **122**
Gundulph Rd. Brom —3A **128**
Gunmaker's La. E3 —1A **64**
Gunnell Clo. SE26 —4G **111**
Gunner La. SE18 —5E **82**
Gunnersbury Av. W5, W3 & W4
—1F **73**
Gunnersbury Clo. W4 —5H **73**
Gunnersbury Ct. W3 —2H **73**
Gunnersbury Cres. W3 —2G **73**
Gunnersbury Dri. W5 —2F **73**
Gunnersbury Gdns. W3 —2G **73**
Gunnersbury La. W3 —3G **73**
Gunnersbury M. W4 —5H **73**
Gunners Gro. E4 —3K **19**
Gunners Rd. SW18 —2B **108**
Gunning St. SE18 —4J **83**
Gunpowder Sq. EC4
(off Gough Sq.)   —6A **62** *(7H 141)*
Gunstor Rd. N16 —4E **46**
Gun St. E1 —5F **63** (6E **142**)
Gunter Gro. SW10 —6A **76**
Gunter Gro. Edgw —1K **25**
Gunterstone Rd. W14 —4G **75**
Gunthorpe St. E1 —5F **63**
Gunton Rd. E5 —3H **47**
Gunton Rd. SW17 —6E **108**
Gunwhale Clo. SE16 —1K **79**
Gurdon Rd. SE7 —5J **81**
Gurenne Ct. E4 —1K **19**
Gurnell Gro. W13 —4K **55**
Gurney Clo. E15 —5G **49**
Gurney Clo. E17 —1K **31**
Gurney Clo. Bark —6F **51**
Gurney Cres. Croy —1K **133**
Gurney Dri. N2 —4A **28**
Gurney Rd. E15 —5G **49**
Gurney Rd. Cars —4E **132**
Gurney Rd. N'holt —3A **54**
Guthrie Ct. SE1 —2A **78** *(5H 147)*
(off Morley St.)
Guthrie St. SW3 —5B **76**
Gutter La. EC2 —6C **62** *(7M 141)*
Guyatt Gdns. Mitc —2E **122**
Guy Barnett Gro. SE3 —3J **97**
Guy Rd. Wall —3H **133**
Guyscliff Rd. SE13 —5E **96**
Guys Retreat. Buck H —1F **21**

Guy St. SE1 —2D **78** (4B **148**)
Guy St. SW1 —2D **78**
Gwalior Rd. SW15 —3F **91**
Gwendolen Av. SW15 —4F **91**
Gwendolen Clo. SW15 —5F **91**
Gwendoline Av. E13 —1K **65**
Gwendwr Rd. W14 —5G **75**
Gweneth Cotts. Edgw —6B **12**
Gwillim Clo. Sidc —5A **100**
Gwydor Rd. Beck —3K **125**
Gwydyr Rd. Brom —3H **127**
Gwyn Clo. SW6 —7A **76**
Gwynne Av. Croy —7K **125**
Gwynne Pk. Av. Wfd G —6J **21**
Gwynne Pl. WC1 —3K **61** (2F **140**)
Gwynne Rd. SW11 —2B **92**
Gylcote Clo. SE5 —4D **94**
Gyles Pk. Stan —1C **24**
Gyllyngdune Gdns. Ilf —2K **51**

Haarlem Rd. W14 —3F **75**
Haberdasher Est. N1
—3D **62** (1B **142**)
Haberdasher Pl. N1
—3D **62** (1C **142**)
Haberdasher St. N1
—3D **62** (1B **142**)
Haccombe Rd. SW19 —6A **108**
Hackbridge Grn. Wall —2E **132**
Hackbridge Pk. Cars —2D **132**
Hackbridge Pk. Gdns. Cars —2D **132**
Hackbridge Rd. Wall —2E **132**
Hackford Rd. SW9 —1K **93**
Hackford Wlk. SW9 —1K **93**
Hackington Cres. Beck —6C **112**
Hacklington Ct. New Bar —5E **4**
Hackney Gro. E8 —6H **47**
Hackney Rd. E2 —3F **63** (2D **142**)
Hadden Rd. SE28 —3J **83**
Hadden Way. Gnfd —6H **39**
Haddington Rd. Brom —3F **113**
Haddo Clo. Enf —6B **8**
Haddo Clo. N Mald —5B **120**
Haddonfield. SE8 —4K **79**
Haddon Gro. Sidc —7K **99**
Haddon Rd. Sutt —4K **131**
Haddo St. SE10 —6E **80**
Haden Ct. N4 —2A **46**
Hadleigh Clo. E1 —4J **63**
Hadleigh Ct. E4 —1B **20**
Hadleigh Rd. N9 —7C **8**
Hadleigh St. E2 —3J **63**
Hadleigh Wlk. E6 —6C **66**
Hadley Clo. N21 —6F **7**
Hadley Comn. Barn —2F **4**
Hadley Ct. N16 —1G **47**
Hadley Ct. New Bar —3E **4**
Hadley Gdns. W4 —5K **73**
Hadley Gdns. S'hall —5D **70**
Hadley Grn. Rd. Barn —2C **4**
Hadley Grn. W. Barn —2C **4**
Hadley Gro. Barn —2B **4**
Hadley Highstone. Barn —1C **4**
Hadley Mnr. Trading Est. Barn —3C **4**
Hadley Ridge. Barn —3C **4**
Hadley Rd. Barn —2E **4**
Hadley Rd. Barn & Enf —1J **5**
(Hadley Wood)
Hadley Rd. Belv —4F **85**
Hadley Rd. Mitc —4H **123**
Hadley St. NW1 —6F **45**
Hadley Way. N21 —6F **7**
Hadley Wood Rd. Barn —2F **5**
Hadlow Pl. SE19 —7G **111**
Hadlow Rd. Sidc —4A **116**
Hadlow Rd. Well —7C **84**
Hadrian Clo. Wall —7J **133**

Hanbury Ct. Harr —6K **23**
Hanbury M. N1 —1C **62**
Hanbury Rd. N17 —2H **31**
Hanbury Rd. W3 —2H **73**
Hanbury St. E1 —5F **63** (5E **142**)
Hanbury Wlk. Bex —3H **117**
Hancock Rd. E3 —3E **64**
Hancock Rd. SE19 —6D **110**
Handa Wlk. N1 —6D **46**
Hand Cl. WC1 —5K **61** (6F **140**)
Handcroft Rd. Croy —7B **124**
Handel Clo. Edgw —6A **12**
Handel Pde. Edgw —7B **12**
  (off Whitchurch La.)
Handel Pl. NW10 —6K **41**
Handel St. WC1 —4J **61** (3C **140**)
Handel Way. Edgw —7B **12**
Handen Rd. SE12 —5G **97**
Handforth Rd. SW9 —7A **78**
Handforth Rd. Ilf —3F **51**
Handley Rd. E9 —1J **63**
Handowe Clo. NW4 —4C **26**
Handside Clo. Wor Pk —1F **131**
Hands Wlk. E16 —6J **65**
Handsworth Av. E4 —6A **20**
Handsworth Rd. N17 —3D **30**
Handtrough Way. Bark —2F **67**
Hanford Clo. SW18 —1J **107**
Hanford Row. SW19 —6E **106**
Hanger Grn. W5 —4G **57**
Hanger La. W5 —2E **56**
Hanger Vale La. W5 —6F **57**
Hanger View Way. W3 —6G **57**
Hanging Sword All. EC4
  —6A **62** (8H **141**)
  (off Hood Ct.)
Hankey Pl. SE1 —2D **78** (5B **148**)
Hankins La. NW7 —2F **13**
Hanley Pl. Beck —7C **112**
Hanley Rd. N4 —1J **45**
Hanmer Wlk. N7 —2K **45**
Hannah Clo. NW10 —4J **41**
Hannah Clo. Beck —3E **126**
Hannah Mary Way. SE1 —4G **79**
Hannah M. Wall —7G **133**
Hannay La. N8 —7H **29**
Hannay Wlk. SW16 —2H **109**
Hannell Rd. SW6 —7G **75**
Hannen Rd. SE27 —3B **110**
Hannibal Rd. E1 —5J **63**
Hannibal Way. Croy —5K **133**
Hannington Point. E9 —6B **48**
  (off Eastway)
Hannington Rd. SW4 —3F **93**
Hanover Clo. Rich —7G **73**
Hanover Clo. Sutt —4G **131**
Hanover Ct. NW9 —3A **26**
Hanover Ct. SW15 —4B **90**
Hanover Ct. W12 —1C **74**
  (off Uxbridge Rd.)
Hanover Dri. Chst —4G **115**
Hanover Est. N22 —3K **29**
Hanover Gdns. SE11 —6A **78**
Hanover Gdns. Ilf —1G **35**
Hanover Ga. NW1 —3C **60** (2D **138**)
Hanover Ho. SW9 —3A **94**
Hanover Mead. NW11 —5G **27**
Hanover Pk. SE15 —1G **95**
Hanover Pl. WC2 —6J **61** (8D **140**)
Hanover Rd. N15 —4F **31**
Hanover Rd. NW10 —7E **42**
Hanover Rd. SW19 —7A **108**
Hanover Sq. W1 —6F **61** (8K **139**)
Hanover St. W1 —6F **61** (8K **139**)
Hanover St. Croy —3B **134**
Hanover Ter. NW1 —3C **60** (2E **138**)
Hanover Ter. Iswth —1A **88**
Hanover Ter. M. NW1
  —3C **60** (2D **138**)

Hanover Trading Est. N7 —5J **45**
Hanover Way. Bexh —3D **100**
Hanover W. Ind. Est. NW10 —3K **57**
Hanover Yd. N1 —2C **62**
  (off Noel Rd.)
Hansard M. W14 —2F **75**
Hansart Way. Enf —1F **7**
Hans Cres. SW1 —3D **76** (6E **144**)
Hanselin Clo. Stan —5E **10**
Hanshaw Dri. Edgw —1K **25**
Hansler Rd. SE22 —5F **95**
Hansol Rd. Bexh —5E **100**
Hanson Clo. SW12 —7F **93**
Hanson Clo. SW14 —3J **89**
Hanson Clo. Beck —6D **112**
Hanson Ct. E17 —6D **32**
Hanson Gdns. S'hall —2C **70**
Hanson St. W1 —5G **61** (5L **139**)
Hans Pl. SW1 —3D **76** (6F **144**)
Hans Rd. SW3 —3D **76** (6E **144**)
Hans St. SW1 —3D **76** (7F **144**)
Hanway Pl. W1 —6H **61**
Hanway Rd. W7 —6H **55**
Hanway St. W1 —6H **61**
Hanworth Ho. SE5 —7B **78**
Hanworth Rd. Felt —1A **102**
Hanworth Rd. Hamp —4D **102**
Hanworth Rd. Houn —1C **102**
Hanworth Ter. Houn —4F **87**
Hanworth Trading Est. Felt —3C **102**
Hapgood Clo. Gnfd —5H **39**
Harad's Pl. E1 —7G **63**
Harben Rd. NW6 —7A **44**
Harberson Rd. E15 —1H **65**
Harberson Rd. SW12 —1F **109**
Harberton Rd. N19 —1G **45**
Harbet Rd. N18 —5E **18**
Harbet Rd. W2 —5B **60** (6B **138**)
Harbex Clo. Bex —7H **101**
Harbinger Rd. E14 —4D **80**
Harbledown Rd. SW6 —1J **91**
Harbord Clo. SE5 —2D **94**
Harbord St. SW6 —1F **91**
Harborough Av. Sidc —7K **99**
Harborough Rd. SW16 —4K **109**
Harbour Av. SW10 —1A **92**
Harbour Exchange Sq. E14 —2D **80**
Harbour Quay. E14 —1E **80**
Harbour Rd. SE5 —3C **94**
Harbour Yd. SW10 —1A **92**
Harbridge Av. SW15 —7B **90**
Harbury Rd. Cars —7C **132**
Harbut Rd. SW11 —4B **92**
Harcombe Rd. N16 —3E **46**
Harcourt Av. E12 —4D **50**
Harcourt Av. Edgw —3D **12**
Harcourt Av. Sidc —6C **100**
Harcourt Av. Wall —4F **133**
Harcourt Bldgs. EC4
  (off Temple) —7A **62** (9G **141**)
Harcourt Clo. Iswth —3A **88**
Harcourt Field. Wall —4F **133**
Harcourt Lodge. Wall —4F **133**
Harcourt Rd. E15 —2H **65**
Harcourt Rd. N22 —1H **29**
Harcourt Rd. SE4 —3B **96**
Harcourt Rd. SW19 —7J **107**
Harcourt Rd. Bexh —4E **100**
Harcourt Rd. T Hth —6K **123**
Harcourt Rd. Wall —4F **133**
Harcourt St. W1 —5C **60** (6D **138**)
Harcourt Ter. SW10 —5K **75**
Hardcastle Clo. Croy —6G **125**
Hardcourts Clo. W Wick —3D **136**
Hardel Rise. SW2 —1B **110**
Hardel Wlk. SW2 —7A **94**
Harden Ho. SE5 —2E **94**
Harden's Mnr. Way. SE7 —4B **82**

Harden St. SE18 —4C **82**
Harders Rd. SE15 —2H **95**
Hardess St. SE24 —3C **94**
Hardie Clo. NW10 —5K **41**
Hardie Rd. Dag —3J **53**
Harding Clo. SE17 —6C **78**
Harding Rd. N18 —6K **17**
Harding Rd. NW10 —1D **58**
Hardinge St. E1 —6J **63**
Harding Rd. Bexh —2F **101**
Hardings La. SE20 —6K **111**
Hardwick Clo. Stan —5H **11**
Hardwick Ct. Eri —6K **85**
Hardwick Av. Houn —1E **86**
Hardwicke Rd. N13 —6D **16**
Hardwicke Rd. W4 —4K **73**
Hardwicke Rd. Rich —4C **104**
Hardwicke St. Bark —1G **67**
Hardwick Grn. W13 —5B **56**
Hardwick St. EC1 —3A **62** (2H **141**)
Hardwicks Way. SW18 —5J **91**
Hardwidge St. SE1 —2E **78** (4C **148**)
Hardy Av. Ruis —5A **38**
Hardy Clo. SE16 —2K **79**
Hardy Clo. Barn —6B **4**
Hardy Clo. Pinn —7B **22**
Hardy Ho. SW4 —1G **109**
Hardying Ho. E17 —4A **32**
Hardy Rd. SE3 —6H **81**
Hardy Rd. SW19 —7K **107**
Hardy Way. Enf —1F **7**
Harebell Dri. E6 —5E **66**
Hare & Billet Rd. SE3 —1F **97**
Harecastle Clo. Hay —4C **54**
Hare Ct. EC4 —6A **62** (8G **141**)
Harecourt Rd. N1 —6C **46**
Haredale Rd. SE24 —4C **94**
Haredon Clo. SE23 —7K **95**
Harefield Clo. Enf —1F **7**
Harefield Grn. NW7 —6K **13**
Harefield M. SE4 —3B **96**
Harefield Rd. N8 —5H **29**
Harefield Rd. SE4 —3B **96**
Harefield Rd. SW16 —7K **109**
Harefield Rd. Sidc —3D **116**
Hare Marsh. E2 —4G **63**
Hare Pl. EC4 —6A **62** (8H **141**)
  (off Pleydell St.)
Hare Row. E2 —2H **63**
Haresfield Rd. Dag —6G **53**
Hare St. SE18 —3E **82**
Hare Wlk. N1 —2E **62**
Harewood Av. NW1
  —4C **60** (4D **138**)
Harewood Av. N'holt —7D **38**
Harewood Clo. N'holt —7D **38**
Harewood Pl. W1 —6F **61** (8K **139**)
Harewood Rd. N'holt —5D **108**
Harewood Rd. SW19 —6C **108**
Harewood Rd. Iswth —7K **71**
Harewood Rd. S Croy —6E **134**
Harewood Row. NW1
  —5C **60** (5D **138**)
Harewood Ter. S'hall —4D **70**
Harfield Gdns. SE5 —3E **94**
Harford Clo. E4 —7J **9**
Harford Rd. E4 —7J **9**
Harford St. E1 —4A **64**
Harford Wlk. N2 —4B **28**
Hargood Clo. Harr —6E **24**
Hargood Rd. SE3 —1H **98**
Hargrave Mans. N19 —2H **45**
Hargrave Pk. N19 —2G **45**
Hargrave Pl. N7 —5H **45**
Hargrave Rd. N19 —2G **45**

Hargraves Ho. W12 —7D **58**
  (off White City Est.)
Hargwyne St. SW9 —3K **93**
Haringey Pk. N8 —6J **29**
Haringey Rd. N8 —4J **29**
Haringey Technopark. N17 —3G **31**
Harington Ter. N9 —3J **17**
Harkett Clo. Harr —2K **23**
Harkett Ct. W'stone —2K **23**
Harland Av. Croy —3G **135**
Harland Av. Sidc —3H **115**
Harland Rd. SE12 —1J **113**
Harlech Gdns. Houn —6A **70**
Harlech Rd. N14 —3D **16**
Harlech Tower. W3 —2J **73**
Harlequin Av. Bren —6A **72**
Harlequin Clo. Hay —5B **54**
Harlequin Clo. Iswth —5J **87**
Harlequin Ct. NW10 —6K **41**
  (off Mitchellbrook Way)
Harlequin Ho. Eri —3E **84**
  (off Kale Rd.)
Harlequin Rd. Tedd —7B **104**
Harlescott Rd. SE15 —4K **95**
Harlesden Gdns. NW10 —1B **58**
Harlesden La. NW10 —1C **58**
Harlesden Rd. NW10 —1C **58**
Harleston Clo. E5 —2J **47**
Harley Clo. Wemb —6D **40**
Harley Ct. E11 —7J **33**
Harley Ct. N20 —3F **15**
Harley Ct. Harr —4H **23**
Harley Cres. Harr —4H **23**
Harleyford. Brom —1A **128**
Harleyford Ct. SE11 —6K **77**
  (off Harleyford Rd.)
Harleyford Rd. SE11 —6K **77**
Harleyford St. SE11 —6A **78**
Harley Gdns. SW10 —5A **76**
Harley Gro. E3 —3B **64**
Harley Ho. E11 —7F **33**
Harley Pl. W1 —5F **61** (6J **139**)
Harley Rd. NW3 —7B **44**
Harley Rd. NW10 —2A **58**
Harley Rd. Harr —4H **23**
Harley St. W1 —4F **61** (4J **139**)
Harlington Rd. Bexh —3E **100**
Harlington Rd. E. Felt —7A **86**
Harlington Rd. W. Felt —7A **86**
Harlowe Clo. E8 —1G **63**
Harlow Mans. Bark —7F **51**
  (off Whiting Av.)
Harlow Rd. N13 —3J **17**
Harman Av. Wfd G —6C **20**
Harman Clo. E4 —4A **20**
Harman Clo. NW2 —3G **43**
Harman Dri. NW2 —3G **43**
Harman Dri. Sidc —6K **99**
Harman Rd. Enf —5A **8**
Harmond Ho. SE8 —4B **80**
Harmony Clo. NW11 —5G **27**
Harmony Clo. Wall —7J **133**
Harmood Gro. NW1 —7F **45**
Harmood Ho. NW1 —7F **45**
Harmood St. NW1 —6F **45**
Harmsworth St. SE17 —6B **78**
Harmsworth Way. N20 —1C **14**
Harness Rd. SE28 —2A **84**
Harold Av. Belv —5F **85**
Harold Est. SE1 —3E **78** (7D **148**)
Harold Pl. SE11 —5A **78**
Harold Rd. E4 —4K **19**
Harold Rd. E11 —1G **49**
Harold Rd. E13 —1K **65**
Harold Rd. N8 —5K **29**
Harold Rd. N15 —5F **31**
Harold Rd. NW10 —3K **57**

Harold Rd. SE19 —7D **110**
Harold Rd. Sutt —4B **132**
Harold Rd. Wfd G —1J **33**
Haroldstone Rd. E17 —5K **31**
Harold Wilson Ho. SE28 —1B **84**
Harp All. EC4 —6B **62** (7J **141**)
Harp Bus. Cen. NW2 —2C **42**
  (off Apsley Way)
Harpenden Rd. E12 —2A **50**
Harpenden Rd. SE27 —3B **110**
Harpenmead Point. NW2 —2H **43**
Harper Ho. SW9 —3B **94**
Harper Rd. E6 —6D **66**
Harper Rd. SE1 —3C **78** (6L **147**)
Harper's Yd. N17 —1F **31**
Harp Island Clo. NW10 —2K **41**
Harp La. EC3 —7E **62** (1C **148**)
Harpley Sq. E1 —4K **63**
Harpour Rd. Bark —6G **51**
Harp Rd. W7 —4K **55**
Harpsden St. SW11 —1E **92**
Harpur M. WC1 —5K **61** (5E **140**)
Harpur St. WC1 —5K **61** (5E **140**)
Harraden Rd. SE3 —1A **98**
Harrier M. SE28 —2H **83**
Harrier Rd. NW9 —2A **26**
Harriers Clo. W5 —7E **56**
Harrier Way. E6 —5D **66**
Harries Rd. Hay —4A **54**
Harriet Clo. E8 —1G **63**
Harriet Gdns. Croy —2G **135**
Harriet St. SW1 —2D **76** (5F **144**)
Harriet Wlk. SW1 —2D **76** (5F **144**)
Harriet Way. Bush —1C **10**
Harringay Gdns. N8 —4B **30**
Harringay Rd. N15 —5B **30**
Harrington Clo. NW10 —3K **41**
Harrington Clo. Croy —2J **133**
Harrington Gdns. SW7 —4K **75**
Harrington Hill. E5 —1H **47**
Harrington Rd. E11 —1G **49**
Harrington Rd. SE25 —4H **125**
Harrington Rd. SW7
  —4B **76** (8A **144**)
Harrington Sq. NW1 —2G **61**
Harrington St. NW1 —2G **61**
Harrington Way. SE18 —3B **82**
Harriott Clo. SE10 —4H **81**
Harris Clo. Houn —1E **86**
Harris Clo. Enf —1G **7**
Harris Cotts. E15 —1H **65**
  (off Gift La.)
Harris Ct. Wemb —3F **41**
Harris Ho. SW9 —3A **94**
  (off St James's Cres.)
Harrison Rd. Dag —6H **53**
Harrisons Rise. Croy —3B **134**
Harrison St. WC1 —3J **61** (2D **140**)
Harris Rd. Bexh —1E **100**
Harris Rd. Dag —5F **53**
Harris St. E17 —7B **32**
Harris St. SE5 —7D **78**
Harrogate Ct. SE12 —7J **97**
Harrold Rd. Dag —5B **52**
Harrovian Bus. Village. Harr —7J **23**
Harrow Av. Enf —6A **8**
Harroway Rd. SW11 —2B **92**
Harrow Bri. Rd. W2 —5A **60**
Harrowby St. W1 —6C **60** (7D **138**)
Harrowdene Clo. Wemb —4D **40**
Harrowdene Gdns. Tedd —7A **104**
Harrowdene Rd. Wemb —3D **40**
Harrow Dri. N9 —1A **18**
Harrowes Meade. Edgw —3H **12**
Harrow Fields Gdns. Harr —3J **39**
Harrowgate Ho. E9 —6K **47**
Harrowgate Rd. E9 —6A **48**
Harrow Grn. E11 —3G **49**

Harrow La. E14 —7E 64
Harrow Mnr. Way. SE2 —2C 84
Harrow Pk. Harr —2J 39
Harrow Pas. King T —2D 118
Harrow Pl. E1 —6E 62 (7D 142)
Harrow Rd. E6 —1C 66
Harrow Rd. E11 —3G 49
Harrow Rd. NW10 —3C 58
Harrow Rd. W2 —5K 59
Harrow Rd. W10 & W9 —4F 59
Harrow Rd. Bark —1J 67
Harrow Rd. Cars —6C 132
Harrow Rd. Ilf —4G 51
Harrow Rd. Wemb —5G 41
Harrow Rd. Wemb —4K 39
(Sudbury)
Harrow View. Harr —2G 23
Harrow View Rd. W4 —4B 56
Harrow Weald Pk. Harr —6C 10
Harry Lambourn Ho. SE15 —7H 79
(off Gervase St.)
Hart Ct. E6 —7E 50
Harte Rd. Houn —2D 86
Hartfield Av. N'holt —2A 54
Hartfield Cres. SW19 —7H 107
Hartfield Cres. W Wick —3J 137
Hartfield Gro. SE20 —1H 125
Hartfield Rd. SW19 —7H 107
Hartfield Rd. W Wick —4J 137
Hartfield Ter. E3 —2C 64
Hartford Av. Harr —3A 24
Hartford Rd. Bex —6G 101
Hart Gro. W5 —1G 73
Hart Gro. S'hall —5E 54
Hart Gro. Ct. W5 —1G 73
Hartham Clo. N7 —5J 45
Hartham Clo. Iswth —1A 88
Hartham Rd. N7 —5J 45
Hartham Rd. N17 —2F 31
Hartham Rd. Iswth —1K 87
Harting Rd. SE9 —3C 114
Hartington Clo. Harr —4J 39
Hartington Ct. SW8 —1J 93
Hartington Ct. W4 —7H 73
Hartington Rd. E16 —6K 65
Hartington Rd. E17 —6A 32
Hartington Rd. SW8 —1J 93
Hartington Rd. W4 —7H 73
Hartington Rd. W13 —7B 56
Hartington Rd. S'hall —3C 70
Hartington Rd. Twic —7B 88
Hartismere Rd. SW6 —7H 75
Hartlake Rd. E9 —6K 47
Hartland Clo. Edgw —2B 12
Hartland Dri. Edgw —2B 12
Hartland Dri. Ruis —3A 38
Hartland Rd. E15 —7H 49
Hartland Rd. N11 —5J 15
Hartland Rd. NW1 —7F 45
Hartland Rd. NW6 —2H 59
Hartland Rd. Hamp —4F 103
Hartland Rd. Iswth —3A 88
Hartland Rd. Mord —7J 121
Hartlands Clo. Bex —6F 101
Hartland Way. Croy —3A 136
Hartland Way. Mord —7H 121
Hartley Av. E6 —1C 66
Hartley Av. NW7 —5G 13
Hartley Clo. NW7 —5G 13
Hartley Clo. Brom —2D 128
Hartley Rd. E11 —1H 49
Hartley Rd. Croy —7C 124
Hartley Rd. Well —7C 84
Hartley St. E2 —3J 63
(in two parts)
Hart Lodge. H Bar —3B 4
Hartman Rd. E16 —1B 82
Hartnoll St. N7 —5K 45

Harton Clo. Brom —1B 128
Harton Rd. N9 —2C 18
Harton St. SE8 —1C 96
Hartop Point. SW6 —7G 75
(off Pellant Rd.)
Hartsbourne Av. Bush —2B 10
Hartsbourne Clo. Bush —2C 10
Hartsbourne Rd. Bush —2C 10
Harts Gro. Wfd G —5D 20
Hartshorn All. EC3 —6E 62 (8D 142)
(off Leadenhall St.)
Hartshorn Gdns. E6 —4E 66
Hart's La. SE14 —1A 96
Harts La. Bark —7F 51
Hartslock Dri. SE2 —2D 84
Hartsmead Rd. SE9 —2D 114
Hart St. EC3 —7E 62 (9D 142)
Hartsway. Enf —4D 8
Hartswood Gdns. W12 —3B 74
Hartswood Rd. W12 —2B 74
Hartsworth Clo. E13 —2H 65
Hartville Rd. SE18 —4J 83
Hartwell Dri. E4 —6K 19
Hartwell St. E8 —6F 47
Harwood Grn. Bush —2C 10
Harvard Ct. NW6 —5J 43
Harvard Hill. W4 —6H 73
Harvard La. W4 —5J 73
Harvard Rd. SE13 —5E 96
Harvard Rd. W4 —5H 73
Harvard Rd. Iswth —1J 87
Harvel Clo. Orp —3K 129
Harvel Cres. SE2 —5D 84
Harvest Bank Rd. W Wick —3H 137
Harvesters Clo. Iswth —5H 87
Harvest La. Th Dit —6A 118
Harvey Ct. E17 —5C 32
Harvey Gdns. E11 —1H 49
Harvey Gdns. SE7 —4B 82
Harvey Ho. N1 —1D 62
(off Colville Est.)
Harvey Ho. Bren —5E 72
Harvey Ho. Romf —4D 36
Harvey Point. E16 —5J 65
(off Fife Rd.)
Harvey Rd. E11 —1G 49
Harvey Rd. N8 —5K 29
Harvey Rd. SE5 —1D 94
(in two parts)
Harvey Rd. Houn —7D 86
Harvey Rd. Ilf —5F 51
Harvey Rd. N'holt —7A 38
Harvey's Bldgs. WC2 —7J 61 (1D 146)
Harveys La. Romf —2K 53
Harvey St. N1 —1D 62
Harvill Rd. Sidc —5E 116
Harvington Wlk. E8 —7G 47
Harvist Est. N7 —4A 46
Harvist Rd. NW6 —2F 59
Harvst Way. Swan —7J 117
Harwell Pas. N2 —4D 28
Harwich La. EC2 —5E 62 (5D 142)
Harwood Av. Brom —2K 127
Harwood Av. Mitc —3C 122
Harwood Clo. Wemb —4D 40
Harwood Clo. N1 —1D 62
(off Colville Est.)
Harwood Rd. SW6 —7J 75
Harwoods Yd. N21 —7F 7
Harwood Ter. SW6 —1K 91
Haselbury Rd. N18 & N9 —4K 17
Haseley End. SE23 —7J 95
Haselrigge Rd. SW4 —4H 93
Haseltine Rd. SE26 —4B 112
Haselwood Dri. Enf —4G 7
Haskard Rd. Dag —4D 52
Hasker St. SW3 —4C 76 (8D 144)

Haslam Av. Sutt —1G 131
Haslam Clo. N1 —7A 46
Haslam St. N11 —4A 16
Haslemere Av. NW4 —6F 27
Haslemere Av. SW18 —2K 107
Haslemere Av. W7 & W13 —3A 72
Haslemere Av. Barn —1J 15
Haslemere Av. Houn —2A 86
Haslemere Av. Mitc —2B 122
Haslemere Clo. Hamp —5D 102
Haslemere Clo. Wall —5J 133
Haslemere Gdns. N3 —3H 27
Haslemere Rd. N8 —7H 29
Haslemere Rd. N21 —2G 17
Haslemere Rd. Bexh —2F 101
Haslemere Rd. Ilf —2K 51
Haslemere Rd. T Hth —5B 124
Hasler Clo. SE28 —7B 68
Haslemere Ind. Est. Enf —4C 8
Hasluck Gdns. Barn —6F 5
Hassard St. E2 —2F 63
Hassendean Rd. SE3 —6K 81
Hassett Rd. E9 —6K 47
Hassocks Clo. SE26 —3H 111
Hassocks Rd. SW16 —1H 123
Hassop Rd. NW2 —4F 43
Hassop Wlk. SE9 —4C 114
Hasted Rd. SE7 —5B 82
Hastings Av. Ilf —4G 35
Hastings Bldgs. SE1 —3E 78 (7C 148)
(off Swan Mead)
Hastings Clo. SE15 —7G 79
Hastings Clo. Barn —4F 5
Hastings Ct. Tedd —5H 103
Hastings Ho. W12 —7D 58
(off White City Est.)
Hastings Ho. W13 —7B 56
Hastings Rd. N11 —5C 16
Hastings Rd. N17 —3E 30
Hastings Rd. W13 —7B 56
Hastings Rd. Brom —1C 128
Hastings Rd. Croy —1F 135
Hastings St. WC1 —3J 61 (2C 140)
Hastingwood Ct. E17 —5D 32
Hastingwood Trading Est. N18 —6E 18
Hastoe Clo. Hay —4C 54
Hat and Mitre Ct. EC1 —4B 62 (4K 141)
(off St John St.)
Hatcham Pk. M. SE14 —1K 95
Hatcham Pk. Rd. SE14 —1K 95
Hatcham Rd. SE15 —6J 79
Hatchard Rd. N19 —2H 45
Hatchcliffe St. SE10 —5H 81
Hatchcroft. NW4 —3D 26
Hatchfield Ho. N15 —6E 30
(off Albert Rd.)
Hatch Gro. Romf —4E 36
Hatch La. E4 —4A 20
(in two parts)
Hatch Pl. King T —5F 105
Hatch Rd. SW16 —2J 123
Hatch Side. Chig —5K 21
Hatch, The. Enf —1E 8
Hatchwood Clo. Wfd G —4C 20
Hatcliffe Clo. SE3 —3H 97
Hatfield Clo. SE14 —7K 79
Hatfield Clo. Ilf —3F 35
Hatfield Clo. Mitc —4B 122
Hatfield Mead. Mord —5J 121
Hatfield Rd. E15 —5G 49
Hatfield Rd. W4 —2K 73
Hatfield Rd. W13 —1A 72
Hatfield Rd. Dag —6F 53
Hatfields. SE1 —1A 78 (2H 147)
Hathaway Clo. Stan —5F 11
Hathaway Cres. E12 —6D 50
Hathaway Gdns. W13 —5A 56

Hathaway Gdns. Romf —5D 36
Hathaway Ho. N1 —2E 62
Hathaway Rd. Croy —7B 124
Hatherleigh Clo. Mord —4J 121
Hatherley Cres. Sidc —2A 116
Hatherley Gdns. E6 —3B 66
Hatherley Gdns. N8 —6J 29
Hatherley Gro. W2 —6K 59
Hatherley Ho. E17 —4C 32
Hatherley M. E17 —4C 32
Hatherley Rd. E17 —4B 32
Hatherley Rd. Rich —2F 89
Hatherley Rd. Sidc —4A 116
Hatherley St. SW1 —4G 77 (9M 145)
Hathern Gdns. SE9 —4E 114
Hatherop Rd. Hamp —7D 102
Hathersage Ct. N1 —5D 46
Hathway St. SE15 —2K 95
Hatley Av. Ilf —4G 35
Hatley Clo. N11 —5J 15
Hatley Rd. N4 —2K 45
Hatteraick St. SE16 —2J 79
Hattersfield Clo. Belv —4F 85
Hatton Clo. SE18 —7H 83
Hatton Garden. EC1 —5A 62 (5H 141)
Hatton Gdns. Mitc —5D 122
Hatton Pl. EC1 —5A 62 (5H 141)
Hatton Rd. Croy —1A 134
Hatton Row. NW8 —4B 60 (4B 138)
(off Hatton St.)
Hatton St. NW8 —4B 60 (4B 138)
Hatton Wall. EC1 —5A 62 (5H 141)
Haughmond. N12 —4E 14
Haughton Clo. E8 —6F 47
Haunch of Venison Yd. W1 —6F 61 (8J 139)
Havana Rd. SW19 —2J 107
Havannah St. E14 —2C 80
Havant Rd. E17 —3E 32
Havant Way. SE15 —7F 79
Havelock Clo. W12 —7D 58
(off White City Est.)
Havelock Pl. Harr —6J 23
Havelock Rd. N17 —2G 31
Havelock Rd. SW19 —5A 108
Havelock Rd. Belv —4F 85
Havelock Rd. Brom —4A 128
Havelock Rd. Croy —2F 135
Havelock Rd. Harr —3J 23
Havelock Rd. S'hall —3C 70
Havelock St. N1 —1J 61
Havelock St. Ilf —2F 51
Havelock Ter. SW8 —7F 77
Havelock Wlk. SE23 —1J 111
Haven Clo. SE9 —3D 114
Haven Clo. SW19 —3F 107
Haven Clo. Sidc —6C 116
Haven Ct. Beck —2E 126
Haven Grn. W5 —6D 56
Haven Grn. Ct. W5 —6D 56
Havenhurst Rise. Enf —2F 7
Haven La. W5 —6E 56
Haven Lodge. Enf —5K 7
(off Village Rd.)
Haven M. E3 —5B 64
Haven Pl. W5 —7D 56
Haven St. NW1 —7F 45
Haven, The. Rich —3G 89
Haven Wood. Wemb —3H 41
Haverfield Gdns. Rich —7G 73
Haverfield Rd. E3 —3A 64
Haverford Way. Edgw —1F 25
Haverhill Rd. E4 —1K 19
Haverhill Rd. SW12 —1G 109
Havering Dri. Romf —4K 37
Havering Gdns. Romf —5C 36
Havering St. E1 —6K 63
Havering Way. Bark —3B 68

Haversham Clo. Twic —6D 88
Haversham Ho. SE16 —2G 79
Haverstock Hill. NW3 —5C 44
Haverstock Rd. NW5 —5E 44
Haverstock St. N1 —2B 62
Havil St. SE5 —7E 78
Havisham Pl. SW16 & SE19 —6B 110
Hawarden Gro. SE24 —7C 94
Hawarden Hill. NW2 —3C 42
Hawarden Rd. E17 —4K 31
Hawbridge Rd. E11 —1F 49
Hawes Clo. N'wd —1E 22
Hawes La. W Wick —1E 136
Hawes Rd. Brom —1K 127
Hawes Rd. N18 —6C 18
(in two parts)
Hawes St. N1 —7B 46
Hawgood St. E3 —5C 64
Hawkdene. E4 —6J 9
Hawke Pk. Rd. N22 —3B 30
Hawke Pl. SE16 —2K 79
Hawker. NW9 —1B 26
Hawker Clo. Wall —7J 133
Hawke Rd. SE19 —6D 110
Hawkesbury Rd. SW15 —5D 90
Hawkesfield Rd. SE23 —2A 112
Hawkesley Clo. Twic —4A 104
Hawks Rd. Mitc —1C 122
Hawke Tower. SE14 —6A 80
Hawkfield Ct. Iswth —2J 87
Hawkhurst Rd. SW16 —1H 123
Hawkhurst Way. N Mald —5K 119
Hawkhurst Way. W Wick —2D 136
Hawkinge. N17 —2D 30
(off Gloucester Rd.)
Hawkins Clo. NW7 —5E 12
Hawkins Clo. Harr —7H 23
Hawkins Ct. SE18 —4C 82
Hawkins Rd. Tedd —6B 104
Hawkley Gdns. SE27 —2B 110
Hawkridge Clo. Romf —6C 36
Hawksbrook La. Beck —6D 126
Hawkshaw Clo. SW2 —1J 109
Hawkshead Clo. Brom —7G 113
Hawkshead Rd. NW10 —7B 42
Hawkshead Rd. W4 —2A 74
Hawkslade Rd. SE15 —5K 95
Hawksley Rd. N16 —3E 46
Hawks M. SE10 —7E 80
Hawksmoor Clo. E6 —6C 66
Hawksmoor M. E1 —7H 63
Hawksmoor St. W6 —6F 75
Hawksmouth. E4 —7K 9
Hawks Rd. King T —2F 119
Hawkstone Rd. SE16 —4J 79
Hawkwell Ct. E4 —3K 19
Hawkwell Wlk. N1 —1C 62
(off Basire St.)
Hawkwood Cres. E4 —6J 9
Hawkwood La. Chst —1G 129
Hawkwood Mt. E5 —1H 47
Hawlands Dri. Pinn —7C 22
Hawley Clo. Hamp —6D 102
Hawley Cres. NW1 —7F 45
Hawley M. NW1 —7F 45
Hawley Rd. N18 —5E 18
Hawley Rd. NW1 —7F 45
Hawley St. NW1 —7F 45
Hawstead Rd. SE6 —6D 96
Hawsted. Buck H —1E 20
Hawthordene Rd. Beck —2H 137
Hawthorn Av. Rich —2E 88
Hawthorn Cen. Harr —4K 23
Hawthorn Clo. Hamp —5E 102
Hawthorn Clo. Orp —6H 129
Hawthorn Ct. Pinn —2A 22
(off Rickmansworth Rd.)

Heddon Ct. Pde. Barn —5K 5
Heddon Rd. Barn —5K 5
Heddon St. W1 —7G 61 (9L 139)
Hedge Hill. Enf —1G 7
Hedge La. N13 —3G 17
Hedgemans Rd. Dag —7D 52
Hedgemans Way. Dag —6E 52
Hedgerley Gdns. Gnfd —2G 55
Hedgers Gro. E9 —6A 48
Hedge Wlk. SE6 —4D 112
Hedgewood Gdns. Ilf —5E 34
Hedgley. Ilf —4D 34
Hedgley St. SE12 —5H 97
Hedingham Clo. N1 —7C 46
Hedingham Rd. Dag —5B 52
Hedley Rd. Twic —7E 86
Hedley Row. N5 —5D 46
Heenan Clo. Bark —6G 51
Heene Rd. Enf —1J 7
Heigham Rd. E6 —7B 50
Heighton Gdns. Croy —5B 134
Heights Clo. SW20 —7D 106
Heights, The. SE7 —5B 82
Heights, The. Beck —7E 112
Heights, The. N'holt —5E 38
Heiron St. SE17 —6B 78
Helby Rd. SW4 —6H 93
Heldar Ct. SE1 —2D 78 (5B 148)
  (off Kipling Est.)
Helder Ct. SE1 —2D 78
Helder Gro. SE12 —7H 97
Helder St. S Croy —6D 134
Heldmann Clo. Houn —4H 87
Helena Clo. Wall —7K 133
Helena Ct. W5 —5D 56
Helena Pl. E9 —1H 63
Helena Rd. E13 —2H 65
Helena Rd. E17 —5C 32
Helena Rd. NW10 —5D 42
Helena Rd. W5 —5D 56
Helen Clo. N2 —3A 28
Helenslea Av. NW11 —1J 43
Helen's Pl. E2 —3J 63
Helen St. SE18 —4F 83
Helix Gdns. SW2 —6K 93
Helix Rd. SW2 —6K 93
Hellings St. E1 —1G 79
Helme Clo. SW19 —5H 107
Helmet Row. EC1 —4C 62 (3M 141)
Helmsdale Clo. Hay —4C 54
Helmsdale Rd. SW16 —1H 123
Helmsley Pl. E8 —7H 47
Helmsley St. E8 —7H 47
Helsinki Sq. SE16 —3A 80
Helston Clo. Pinn —1D 22
Helston Ct. N15 —5E 30
  (off Culvert Rd.)
Helston Ho. SE11 —5A 78
  (off Kennings Way)
Helvetia St. SE6 —2B 112
Hemans St. SW8 —7H 77
Hemans St. Est. SW8 —7H 77
Hemberton Rd. SW9 —3J 93
Hemery Rd. Gnfd —5H 39
Hemingford Rd. N1 —1K 61
Hemingford Rd. Sutt —4E 130
Heming Rd. Edgw —7C 12
Hemington Av. N11 —5J 15
Hemlock Rd. W12 —7B 58
Hemming Clo. Hamp —7E 102
Hemming St. E1 —4G 63
Hempstead Clo. Buck H —2D 20
Hempstead Rd. E17 —2F 33
Hemp Wlk. SE17 —4D 78 (8B 148)
Hemstal Rd. NW6 —7J 43
Hemsted Rd. Eri —7K 85
Hemswell Dri. NW9 —1A 26
Hemsworth Ct. N1 —2E 62

Hemsworth St. N1 —2E 62
Hemus Pl. SW3 —5C 76
Henchman St. W12 —6B 58
Hendale Av. NW4 —3C 26
Henderson Clo. NW10 —6J 41
Henderson Dri. NW8
  —4B 60 (3A 138)
Henderson Ho. Dag —3G 53
  (off Kershaw Rd.)
Henderson Rd. E7 —6A 50
Henderson Rd. N9 —1C 18
Henderson Rd. SW18 —7C 92
Henderson Rd. Croy —6D 124
Hendham Rd. SW17 —2C 108
Hendon Av. N3 —1G 27
Hendon Hall Ct. NW4 —3F 27
Hendon Ho. NW4 —5F 27
Hendon La. N3 —3G 27
Hendon Lodge. NW4 —3D 26
Hendon Pk. Mans. NW4 —5E 26
Hendon Pk. Row. NW11 —6H 27
Hendon Rd. N9 —2B 18
Hendon Urban Motorway. Edgw &
  NW7 —1K 11
Hendon Way. NW4 & NW2 —6D 26
Hepworth Ct. NW3 —5C 44
Hendon Wood La. NW7 —1G 13
Hendren Clo. Gnfd —5H 39
Hendre Rd. SE1 —4E 78 (9D 148)
Hendrick Av. SW12 —7D 92
Hendy Ct. Enf —3J 7
Heneage La. EC3 —6E 62 (8D 142)
Herald Gdns. Wall —2F 133
Heneage Pl. EC3 —6E 62 (8D 142)
Heneage St. E1 —5F 63
Henfield Clo. N19 —1G 45
Henfield Clo. Bex —6G 101
Henfield Rd. SW19 —1H 121
Hengelo Gdns. Mitc —4B 122
Hengist Rd. SE12 —7K 97
Hengist Rd. Eri —7H 85
Hengist Way. Brom —4G 127
Hengrave Rd. SE23 —7J 95
Hengrove Ct. Bex —1E 116
Henham Ct. Romf —2J 37
Henley Av. Sutt —3G 131
Henley Clo. Gnfd —2G 55
Henley Clo. Iswth —1K 87
Henley Ct. N14 —7B 6
Henley Dri. SE1 —4F 79 (8F 148)
Henley Dri. King T —7B 106
Henley Gdns. Romf —5E 36
Henley Rd. E16 —2D 82
Henley Rd. N18 —4K 17
Henley Rd. NW10 —1E 58
Henley Rd. Ilf —4G 51
Henley Rd. W. Felt —5B 102
Henley St. SW11 —2E 92
Hennel Clo. SE23 —3J 111
Henniker Gdns. E6 —3B 66
Henniker M. SW3 —6B 76
Henniker Rd. E15 —5F 49
Henningham Rd. N17 —1D 30
Henning St. SW11 —1C 92
Henrietta Ho. N15 —6E 30
  (off St Ann's Rd.)
Henrietta Ho. W6 —5E 74
  (off Queen Caroline St.)
Henrietta M. WC1 —4J 61 (3D 140)
Henrietta Pl. W1 —6F 61 (8J 139)
Henrietta St. E15 —5E 48
Henrietta St. WC2 —7J 61 (9D 140)
Henriques St. E1 —6G 63
Henry Cooper Way. SE9 —3B 114
Henry Darlot Dri. NW7 —5A 14
Henry Dickens Ct. W11 —7F 59
Henry Hatch Wlk. Sutt —7A 132
Henry Jackson Rd. SW15 —3F 91
Henry Rd. E6 —2C 66
Henry Rd. N4 —1C 46

Henry Rd. Barn —5G 5
Henrys Av. Wfd G —5C 20
Henryson Rd. SE4 —5C 96
Henry St. Brom —1K 127
Henry's Wlk. Ilf —1H 35
Hensford Gdns. SE26 —4H 111
Henshall St. N1 —6D 46
Henshawe Rd. Dag —3D 52
Henshaw St. SE17 —4D 78 (8A 148)
Henslowe Rd. SE22 —5G 95
Henson Av. NW2 —5E 42
Henson Path. Harr —3D 24
Henson Pl. N'holt —1A 54
Henstridge Pl. NW8 —2C 60
Henty Clo. SW11 —7C 76
Henty Wlk. SW15 —5D 90
Henville Rd. Brom —1K 127
Henwick Rd. SE9 —3B 98
Henwood Rd. SE16 —3J 79
Hepburn Gdns. Brom —1G 137
Hepburn M. SW11 —5D 92
Hepple Clo. Iswth —2B 88
Hepplestone Clo. SW15 —6D 90
Hepscott Rd. E9 —6C 48
Hepworth Ct. NW3 —5C 44
Hepworth Gdns. Bark —5A 52
Hepworth Rd. SW16 —7J 109
Heracles. NW9 —1B 26
  (off Five Acre)
Herald St. E2 —4H 63
Herald St. E2 —4H 63
Herbal Hill. EC1 —4A 62 (4H 141)
Herbal Pl. EC1 —4A 62 (4H 141)
  (off Herbal Hill)
Herbert Cres. SW1 —3D 76 (6F 144)
Herbert Gdns. NW10 —2D 58
Herbert Gdns. W4 —6H 73
Herbert Gdns. Romf —7D 36
Herbert Pl. SE18 —6F 83
Herbert Rd. E12 —4C 50
Herbert Rd. E17 —7B 32
Herbert Rd. N11 —7D 16
Herbert Rd. N15 —5F 31
Herbert Rd. NW9 —6C 26
Herbert Rd. SE18 —7E 82
Herbert Rd. SW19 —7H 107
  (in two parts)
Herbert Rd. Bexh —2E 100
Herbert Rd. Brom —5B 128
Herbert Rd. Ilf —2J 51
Herbert Rd. King T —3F 119
Herbert Rd. S'hall —1D 70
Herbert St. E13 —2J 65
Herbert St. NW5 —6E 44
Herbert Ter. SE18 —7F 83
Herbrand St. WC1 —4J 61 (3C 140)
Hercules Pl. N7 —3J 45
  (in two parts)
Hercules Rd. SE1 —3K 77 (7F 146)
Hercules St. N7 —3J 45
Hercules Tower. SE14 —6A 80
Hercules Yd. N7 —3J 45
Hereford Av. Barn —1J 15
Hereford Ct. Harr —3J 23
Hereford Ct. Sutt —7J 131
Hereford Gdns. Ilf —7C 34
Hereford Gdns. Pinn —5C 22
Hereford Gdns. Twic —1G 103
Hereford Ho. NW6 —2J 59
Hereford M. W2 —6J 59
Hereford Pl. SE14 —7B 80
Hereford Retreat. SE15 —7G 79
Hereford Rd. E11 —5K 33
Hereford Rd. W2 —6J 59
Hereford Rd. W3 —7H 57

Hereford Rd. W5 —3C 72
Hereford Rd. Felt —1A 102
Hereford Sq. SW7 —4A 76
Hereford St. E2 —4G 63
Herent Dri. Ilf —4C 34
Hereward Gdns. N13 —5F 17
Hereward Rd. SW17 —4D 108
Herga Ct. Harr —3J 39
Herga Rd. Harr —4K 23
Heriot Av. E4 —2H 19
Heriot Rd. NW4 —5E 27
Heriots Clo. Stan —4F 11
Heritage Hill. Kes —5K 137
Heritage View. Harr —3K 39
Herlwyn Gdns. SW17 —4D 108
Hermes Point. W9 —4J 59
  (off Chippenham Rd.)
Hermes St. N1 —2A 62
Hermes Wlk. N'holt —2E 54
Hermitage. The. N'holt —1H 133
Herm Ho. N1 —6C 46
Herm Ho. Enf —1E 8
Hermiston Av. N8 —5J 29
Hermitage Clo. E18 —4H 33
Hermitage Clo. Enf —2G 7
Hermitage Ct. E18 —4J 33
Hermitage Ct. NW2 —3J 43
Hermitage Gdns. NW2 —3J 43
Hermitage Gdns. SE19 —7C 110
Hermitage Grn. SW16 —1J 123
Hermitage La. N18 —5J 17
Hermitage La. NW2 —3J 43
Hermitage La. SE25 —6G 125
  (in two parts)
Hermitage La. SW16 —7K 109
Hermitage La. Croy & SE25 —7G 125
Hermitage Path. SW16 —1J 123
Hermitage Rd. N4 & N15 —7C 30
Hermitage Rd. SE19 —7C 110
Hermitage Row. E8 —5F 47
Hermitage St. W2 —5B 60 (6A 138)
Hermitage, The. SE23 —1J 111
Hermitage, The. SW13 —1B 90
Hermitage, The. Rich —5E 88
Hermitage Wlk. E18 —4H 33
Hermitage Wall. E1 —1G 79
Hermitage Way. Stan —1A 24
Hermit Pl. NW6 —1K 59
Hermit Rd. E16 —5H 65
Hermit St. EC1 —3B 62 (1J 141)
Hermon Hill. E11 & E18 —5J 33
Herndon Rd. SW18 —5A 92
Herne Clo. NW10 —5K 41
Herne Ct. Bush —1B 10
Herne Hill. SE24 —6C 94
Herne Hill Ho. SE24 —6B 94
  (off Railton Rd.)
Herne Hill Rd. SE24 —3C 94
Herne M. N18 —4B 18
Herne Pl. SE24 —5B 94
Heron Clo. E17 —2B 32
Heron Clo. NW10 —6A 42
Heron Clo. Buck H —1D 20
Heron Cres. Sidc —3J 115
Herondale Av. SW18 —1B 108
Herongate Clo. Enf —2A 8
Herongate Rd. E12 —2A 50
Heron Hill. Belv —5F 85
Heron Ho. E6 —7C 50
Heron Ho. W13 —4A 56
Heron Ind. Est. E15 —1D 64
Heron M. Ilf —2F 51
Heron Pl. SE16 —1A 80
Heron Quay. E14 —1C 80
Heron Quays Development. E14
  —1D 80
Heron Rd. SE24 —4C 94
Heron Rd. Croy —2E 134

Heron Rd. Twic —4A 88
Heronsforde. W13 —6C 56
Herons Ga. Edgw —5B 12
Heronslea Dri. Stan —5K 11
Heron's Pl. Iswth —3B 88
Heron Sq. Rich —5D 88
Herons, The. E11 —6H 33
Heron Way. Wfd G —4F 21
Herrick Rd. N5 —3C 46
Herrick St. SW1 —4H 77 (9B 146)
Herries St. W10 —3G 59
Herringham Rd. SE7 —3A 82
Herring St. SE5 —6E 78
Herron Ct. Short —4H 127
Hersant Clo. NW10 —1C 58
Herschell Rd. SE23 —7A 96
Hersham Clo. SW15 —7C 90
Hertford Av. SW14 —5K 89
Hertford Clo. Barn —3F 5
Hertford Ct. E6 —3D 66
  (off Vicarage La.)
Hertford Ct. N13 —3F 17
Hertford Pl. W1 —4G 61 (4L 139)
Hertford Rd. N1 —1E 62
  (in two parts)
Hertford Rd. N2 —3C 28
Hertford Rd. N9 —2C 18
Hertford Rd. Bark —7E 50
Hertford Rd. Barn —3F 5
Hertford Rd. Enf —4D 8
Hertford Rd. Ilf —6J 35
Hertford Sq. Mitc —4J 123
Hertford St. W1 —1F 77 (3J 145)
Hertford Wlk. Belv —5G 85
Hertford Way. Mitc —4J 123
Hertslet Rd. N7 —3K 45
Hertsmere Rd. E14 —1C 80
Hervey Clo. N3 —1J 27
Hervey Pk. Rd. E17 —4A 32
Hervey Rd. SE3 —1K 97
Hervey Way. N3 —1J 27
Hesketh Pl. W11 —7G 59
Hesketh Rd. E7 —3J 49
Heslop Rd. SW12 —1D 108
Hesper M. SW5 —4K 75
Hesperus Cres. E14 —4D 80
Hessel Rd. W13 —2A 72
Hessel St. E1 —6H 63
Hestercombe Av. SW6 —2G 91
Hester Rd. N18 —5B 18
Hester Rd. SW11 —7C 76
Heston Av. Houn —6C 70
Heston Grange. Houn —6D 70
Heston Grange La. Houn —6D 70
Heston Ind. Cen. Houn —6A 70
Heston Ind. Mall. Houn —7D 70
Heston Rd. Houn —7E 70
Heston St. SE14 —1C 96
Hetherington Rd. SW4 —4J 93
Hetley Gdns. SE19 —7F 111
Hetley Ho. W12 —2D 74
  (off Hetley Rd.)
Hetley Rd. W12 —1D 74
Heton Gdns. NW4 —4D 26
Hevelius Clo. SE10 —5H 81
Hever Croft. SE9 —4E 114
Hever Gdns. Brom —2E 128
Heversham Rd. Bexh —2G 101
Hewer St. W10 —5F 59
Hewett Clo. Stan —4G 11
Hewett Rd. Dag —4D 52
Hewett St. EC2 —4E 62 (4D 142)
Hewish Rd. N18 —4K 17
Hewison St. E3 —2B 64
Hewitt Av. N22 —2B 30
Hewitt Rd. N8 —5A 30

214

Hewlett Rd. E3 —2A 64
Hexagon, The. N6 —1D 44
Hexal Rd. SE6 —3G 113
Hexham Gdns. Iswth —7A 72
Hexham Rd. SE27 —2C 110
Hexham Rd. Barn —4E 4
Hexham Rd. Mord —1K 131
Heybourne Rd. N17 —7C 18
Heybridge Av. SW16 —1J 109
Heybridge Dri. Ilf —2H 35
Heybridge Way. E10 —7A 32
Heyford Av. SW8 —7J 77
Heyford Av. SW20 —3H 121
Heyford Rd. Mitc —2C 122
Heygate Sq. E3 —3B 64
Heygate St. SE17 —4C 78 (9L 147)
Heylyn Sq. E3 —3B 64
Heynes Rd. Dag —4C 52
Heysham La. NW3 —3K 43
Heysham Rd. N15 —6D 30
Heythorp St. SW18 —1H 107
Heywood, Stan —5H 11
Heywood Av. NW9 —1A 26
Heyworth Rd. E5 —4H 47
Heyworth Rd. E15 —4H 49
Hibbert Rd. E17 —7B 32
Hibbert Rd. Harr —2K 23
Hibbert St. SW11 —3B 92
Hibernia Gdns. Houn —4E 86
Hibernia Point. SE2 —2D 84
(off Wolvercote Rd.)
Hibernia Rd. Houn —4E 86
Hichisson Rd. SE15 —5J 95
Hickey's Almshouses. Rich —4F 89
Hickin Clo. SE7 —4B 82
Hickin St. E14 —3E 80
Hickling Rd. Ilf —5F 51
Hickman Av. E4 —6K 19
Hickman Clo. E16 —5B 66
Hickman Rd. Romf —7C 36
Hickmore Wlk. SW4 —3H 93
Hickory Clo. N9 —1B 18
Hicks Av. Gnfd —3H 55
Hicks Clo. SW11 —3C 92
Hicks St. SE8 —5A 80
Hidcote Gdns. SW20 —3D 120
Hide. E6 —6E 66
Hide Pl. SW1 —4H 77 (9A 146)
Hide Rd. Harr —4G 23
Hides St. N7 —6K 45
Higgs Ind. Est. SE24 —3B 94
High Acres. Enf —3G 7
Higham Hill Rd. E17 —1A 32
Higham Pk. Ind. Est. E4 —6K 19
Higham Path. E17 —3A 32
Higham Pl. E17 —3A 32
Higham Rd. N17 —3D 30
Higham Rd. Wfd G —6D 20
Highams Ct. E4 —3A 20
Highams Lodge Bus. Cen. E17
—3K 31
Higham Sta. Av. E4 —6H 19
Higham St. E17 —3A 32
Highbanks Clo. Well —7B 84
Highbanks Rd. Pinn —6A 10
Highbarrow Rd. Croy —1G 135
High Beech. N21 —6E 6
High Beech. S Croy —7C 134
High Beeches. Sidc —5E 116
High Birch Ct. New Bar —4H 5
(off Park Rd.)
High Bri. SE10 —5F 81
Highbridge Rd. Bark —1F 67
Highbrook Rd. SE3 —3B 98
High Broom Cres. W Wick —7D 126
Highbury Av. T Hth —2A 124
Highbury Barn. N5 —4B 46
Highbury Clo. N Mald —4J 119

Highbury Clo. W Wick —2D 136
Highbury Cres. N5 —5B 46
Highbury Est. N5 —5C 46
Highbury Gdns. Ilf —2J 51
Highbury Grange. N5 —4C 46
Highbury Gro. N5 —5B 46
Highbury Hill. N5 —3A 46
Highbury M. N7 —6A 46
Highbury New Pk. N5 —5C 46
Highbury Pk. N5 —3B 46
Highbury Pk. M. N5 —4C 46
Highbury Pl. N5 —5B 46
Highbury Quadrant. N5 —3C 46
Highbury Rd. SW19 —5G 107
Highbury Sta. Rd. N1 —6A 46
Highbury Ter. N5 —5B 46
Highbury Ter. M. N5 —5B 46
High Cedar Dri. SW20 —7E 106
Highclere Rd. N Mald —3K 119
Highclere St. SE26 —4A 112
Highcliffe. W13 —5B 56
(off Clivedon Ct.)
Highcliffe Dri. SW15 —6B 90
Highcliffe Gdns. Ilf —5C 34
Highcombe. SE7 —6K 81
Highcombe Clo. SE9 —1B 114
High Coombe Pl. King T —7K 105
High Croft. NW9 —5A 26
Highcroft Av. Wemb —7G 41
Highcroft Est. N19 —7J 29
Highcroft Gdns. NW11 —6H 27
Highcroft Rd. N19 —7J 29
High Cross Rd. N17 —3G 31
Highcross Way. SW15 —1C 106
Highdaun Dri. SW16 —4K 123
Highdown. Wor Pk —2A 130
Highdown Rd. SW15 —6D 90
High Dri. N Mald —1J 119
High Elms. Wfd G —5D 20
Highfield Av. NW9 —5J 25
Highfield Av. NW11 —7F 27
Highfield Av. Eri —6H 85
Highfield Av. Gnfd —5J 39
Highfield Av. Pinn —5D 22
Highfield Av. Wemb —3F 41
Highfield Clo. NW9 —5J 25
Highfield Clo. Surb —7C 118
Highfield Ct. N14 —6B 6
Highfield Ct. NW11 —6G 27
Highfield Dri. Brom —4G 127
Highfield Dri. Eps —6B 130
Highfield Dri. W Wick —2D 136
Highfield Gdns. NW11 —6G 27
Highfield Hill. SE19 —7D 110
Highfield Rd. N21 —2G 17
Highfield Rd. NW11 —6G 27
Highfield Rd. W3 —5H 57
Highfield Rd. Bexh —5F 101
Highfield Rd. Brom —4D 128
Highfield Rd. Chst —3K 129
Highfield Rd. Iswth —1K 87
Highfield Rd. Surb —7J 119
Highfield Rd. Sutt —5C 132
Highfield Rd. Wfd G —7H 21
Highfields. Sutt —2J 131
Highfields Gro. N6 —1D 44
High Gables. Brom —7G 137
Highgate Av. N6 —7F 29
Highgate Clo. N6 —7E 28
Highgate Edge. N2 —5C 28
Highgate Heights. N6 —6G 29
Highgate High St. N6 —1E 44
Highgate Hill. N6 & N19 —1F 45
Highgate Rd. NW5 —3E 44
Highgate Spinney. N8 —6H 29
Highgate Wlk. SE23 —2J 111
Highgate W. Hill. N6 —2E 44

High Gro. SE18 —7H 83
High Gro. Brom —1B 128
Highgrove Clo. Chst —1C 128
Highgrove Ct. Beck —7C 112
Highgrove Rd. Dag —5C 52
High Hill Est. E5 —1H 47
High Hill Ferry. E5 —1H 47
High Holborn. WC1
—6J 61 (7C 140)
Highland Av. W7 —6J 55
Highland Av. Dag —3J 53
Highland Cotts. Wall —4F 133
Highland Ct. E18 —1K 33
Highland Croft. Beck —5D 112
Highland Dri. Bush —1A 10
Highland Rd. SE19 —6E 110
Highland Rd. Bexh —5G 101
Highland Rd. Brom —1H 127
Highlands Av. W3 —7J 57
Highlands Clo. N4 —7J 29
Highlands Clo. Houn —1F 87
Highlands Ct. SE19 —6E 110
Highlands Gdns. Ilf —1D 50
Highlands Heath. SW15 —7E 90
Highlands Rd. Barn —5D 4
Highlands, The. Edgw —2H 25
High La. W7 —5H 55
Highlea Clo. NW9 —7F 13
High Level Dri. SE26 —4G 111
Highlever Rd. W10 —5E 58
Highmead. SE18 —7J 83
High Mead. Harr —5J 23
High Mead. W Wick —2F 137
Highmead Cres. Wemb —7F 41
High Meadow Clo. Pinn —4A 22
High Meadow Cres. NW9 —5K 25
High Meads Rd. E16 —6B 66
Highmore Rd. SE3 —7G 81
High Mt. NW4 —6C 26
High Oaks. Enf —1E 6
High Pk. Av. Rich —1G 89
High Pk. Rd. Rich —1G 89
High Path. SW19 —1K 121
Highpoint. N6 —7E 28
High Point. SE9 —3F 115
High Ridge Pl. Enf —1E 6
High Rd. E18 —1J 33
High Rd. N11 —5A 16
High Rd. N15 & N17 —5F 31
High Rd. N22 —1K 29
High Rd. NW10 —6A 42
High Rd. Buck H & Lou —2E 20
High Rd. Bush —1C 10
High Rd. Chig —5K 21
High Rd. Harr —7D 10
High Rd. Ilf & Romf —3F 51
(in five parts)
High Rd. Wfd G —6C 20
High Rd. E. Finchley. N2 —1B 28
High Rd. Leyton. E10 & E15 —6D 32
High Rd. Leytonstone. E11 & E15
—4G 49
High Rd. N. Finchley. N12 —5F 15
High Rd. Whetstone. N20 —7F 5
High Sheldon. N6 —5D 28
Highshore Rd. SE15 —2F 95
Highstead Cres. Eri —1K 101
Highstone Av. E11 —6J 33
Highstone Ct. E11 —6H 33
(off New Wanstead)
High St. Acton, W3 —1H 73
High St. Barkingside, Ilf —3G 35
High St. Barnet, Barn —3B 4
High St. Beckenham, Beck —2C 126

High St. Brentford, Bren —7C 72
High St. Bromley, Brom —2J 127
High St. Carshalton, Cars —4E 132
High St. Chislehurst, Chst —6F 115
High St. Colliers Wood, SW19
—7B 108
High St. Cranford, Cran —6A 70
High St. Croydon, Croy —3C 134
High St. Ealing, W5 —7D 56
High St. Edgware, Edgw —6B 12
High St. Ewell, Eps —7B 130
High St. Hampton, Hamp —7G 103
High St. Hampton Hill, Hamp H
—6G 103
High St. Hampton Wick, King T
—1C 118
High St. Harlesden, NW10 —2B 58
High St. Harrow, Harr —1J 39
High St. Hornsey, N8 —4J 29
High St. Hounslow, Houn —3F 87
High St. Kingston upon Thames,
King T —3D 118
High St. M. SW19 —5G 107
High St. New Malden, N Mald
—4A 120
High St. Orpington, Orp —7K 129
High St. Penge, SE20 —6J 111
High St. Pinner, Pinn —3C 22
High St. Plaistow, E13 —2J 65
High St. Ponders End, Enf —6D 8
High St. Romford, Romf —5K 37
High St. S. E6 —2D 66
High St. Southall, S'hall —1D 70
High St. Southgate, N14 —1C 16
High St. South Norwood, SE25
—4F 125
High St. Stratford, E15 —2E 64
High St. Sutton, Sutt —4K 131
High St. Teddington, Tedd —5K 103
High St. Thames Ditton, Th Dit
—6A 118
High St. Thornton Heath, T Hth
—4C 124
High St. Walthamstow, E17 —5A 32
High St. Wanstead, E11 —5J 33
High St. Wealdstone, W'stone
—2J 23
High St. Wembley, Wemb —4F 41
High St. Whitton, Twic —7G 87
High St. Wimbledon, SW19 —5F 107
High St. Woolwich, SE18 —3E 82
High, The. SW16 —3J 109
High Timber St. EC4
—7C 62 (9L 141)
High Tor Clo. Brom —7K 113
High Trees. SW2 —1A 110
High Trees. Barn —5H 5
High Trees. Croy —1A 136
Highview. N6 —6G 29
Highview. NW7 —3E 12
Highview Av. Edgw —4D 12
Highview Av. Wall —5K 133
High View Clo. SE19 —2F 125
High View Rd. E18 —3H 33
Highview Gdns. N3 —3G 27
Highview Gdns. N11 —5B 16
Highview Gdns. Edgw —4D 12
Highview Ho. Romf —4E 36
High View Rd. E18 —2H 33
High View Rd. N2 —1D 28
Highview Rd. SE19 —6D 110
Highview Rd. W13 —5A 56
Highview Rd. Sidc —4B 116
Highway, The. E1 —7J 63
Highway, The. Stan —7F 11
Highway, The. Sutt —7A 132

Highway Trading Cen., The. E1
(off Heckford St.) —7K 63
Highwood. Short —3G 127
Highwood Av. N12 —4F 15
Highwood Ct. N12 —3F 15
Highwood Clo. SE22 —5D 34
Highwood Gdns. Ilf —5D 34
Highwood Gro. NW7 —5E 12
Highwood Hill. NW7 —2G 13
Highwood Rd. N19 —3J 45
High Worple. Harr —7D 22
Highworth Rd. N11 —6C 16
Hilary Av. Mitc —3E 122
Hilary Clo. E11 —5J 33
Hilary Clo. SW6 —7K 75
Hilary Clo. Eri —1H 101
Hilary Rd. W12 —7B 58
Hilbert Rd. Sutt —3F 131
Hilborough Ct. E8 —1F 63
Hilda Ct. Surb —7D 118
Hilda Rd. E6 —7B 50
Hilda Rd. E16 —4G 65
Hilda Ter. SW9 —2A 94
Hildenborough Gdns. Brom —6G 113
Hildenborough Ho. Beck —7B 112
(off Bethersden Clo.)
Hildenlea Pl. Brom —2G 127
Hildreth St. SW12 —1F 109
Hildyard Rd. SW6 —6J 75
Hiley Rd. NW10 —3E 58
Hilgrove Rd. NW6 —7A 44
Hiliary Gdns. Stan —2C 24
Hillary Rise. Barn —4D 4
Hillary Rd. S'hall —3E 70
Hilbeck Clo. SE15 —7J 79
Hillbeck Way. Gnfd —1H 55
Hillboro Ct. E11 —7F 33
Hillborough Clo. SW19 —7A 108
Hillbrook Rd. SW17 —3D 108
Hill Brow. Brom —1B 128
Hillbrow. N Mald —3B 120
Hill Brow Clo. Bex —4K 117
Hill Brow Rd. Brom —7G 113
Hillbury Av. Harr —5B 24
Hillbury Rd. SW17 —3F 109
Hill Clo. NW2 —3D 42
Hill Clo. NW11 —6J 27
Hill Clo. Chst —5F 115
Hill Clo. Harr —3J 39
Hill Clo. Stan —4G 11
Hillcote Av. SW16 —7A 110
Hill Ct. Barn —4H 5
Hillcourt Av. N12 —6E 14
Hillcourt Est. N16 —1D 46
Hillcourt Rd. SE22 —6H 95
Hill Cres. N20 —2E 14
Hill Cres. Bex —1J 117
Hill Cres. Harr —5A 24
Hill Cres. Surb —5F 119
Hill Cres. Wor Pk —2E 130
Hillcrest. N6 —7E 28
Hillcrest. N21 —7F 7
Hillcrest. SE25 —4D 94
Hillcrest. Sidc —7A 100
Hillcrest Av. NW11 —5G 27
Hillcrest Av. Edgw —4C 12
Hillcrest Av. Pinn —4B 22
Hillcrest Clo. SE26 —4G 111
Hillcrest Clo. Beck —6B 126
Hillcrest Ct. Sutt —6B 132
Hillcrest Gdns. N3 —4G 27
Hillcrest Gdns. NW2 —3C 42
Hillcrest Rd. E17 —2F 33
Hillcrest Rd. E18 —2J 33
Hillcrest Rd. W3 —1G 73
Hillcrest Rd. W5 —5E 56
Hillcrest Rd. Brom —5J 113
Hillcrest View. Beck —6B 126

215

Hillcroft Av. Pinn —6D **22**
Hillcroft Cres. W5 —6E **56**
Hillcroft Cres. Ruis —3B **38**
Hillcroft Cres. Wemb —4F **41**
Hillcroft Rd. E6 —5F **67**
Hillcroome Rd. Sutt —6B **132**
Hillcross Av. Mord —6F **121**
Hilldale Rd. Sutt —4H **131**
Hilldown Rd. SW16 —7J **109**
Hilldown Rd. Brom —1G **137**
Hill Dri. NW9 —1J **41**
Hill Dri. SW16 —3K **123**
Hilldrop Cres. N7 —5H **45**
Hilldrop Est. N7 —4H **45**
Hilldrop La. N7 —5H **45**
Hilldrop Rd. N7 —5H **45**
Hilldrop Rd. Brom —6K **113**
Hillend. SE18 —1E **98**
Hillersdon Av. SW13 —2C **90**
Hillersdon Av. Edgw —5A **12**
Hillery Clo. SE17 —4D **78** (9B **148**)
Hill Farm Rd. W10 —5E **58**
Hillfield Av. N8 —5J **29**
Hillfield Av. NW9 —5A **26**
Hillfield Av. Mord —6C **122**
Hillfield Av. Wemb —7E **40**
Hillfield Clo. Harr —4G **23**
Hillfield Ct. NW3 —5C **44**
Hillfield Pk. N5 —5C **46**
Hillfield Pk. N10 —4F **29**
Hillfield Pk. N21 —2F **17**
Hillfield Pk. M. N10 —4F **29**
Hillfield Rd. NW6 —5H **43**
Hill Field Rd. Hamp —7D **102**
Hillfoot Av. Romf —1J **37**
Hillfoot Rd. Romf —1J **37**
Hillgate Pl. SW12 —7F **93**
Hillgate Pl. W8 —1J **75**
Hillgate St. W8 —1J **75**
Hill Gro. Romf —3K **37**
Hill Ho. E5 —1H 47
(off Harrington Hill)
Hillhouse Av. Stan —7E **10**
Hill Ho. Clo. N21 —7F **7**
Hill Ho. Rd. SW16 —5K **109**
Hilliards Ct. E1 —1J **79**
Hillier Clo. Barn —6E **4**
Hillier Gdns. Croy —5A **134**
Hillier Lodge. Tedd —5H **103**
Hillier Rd. SW11 —6D **92**
Hilliers La. Croy —3J **133**
Hillingdon Rd. Bexh —2J **101**
Hillingdon St. SE5 & SE17 —6B **78**
Hillingdon St. SE17 —6C **78**
Hillington Gdns. Wfd G —2B **34**
Hillman St. E8 —6H **47**
Hillmarton Rd. N7 —5J **45**
Hillmead Dri. SW9 —4B **94**
Hillmore Gro. SE26 —5A **112**
Hill Path. SW16 —5K **109**
Hillreach. SE18 —5D **82**
Hill Rise. N9 —6C **8**
Hill Rise. NW11 —4K **27**
Hill Rise. SE23 —1H **111**
Hill Rise. Gnfd —7G **39**
Hill Rise. Rich —5D **88**
Hillrise Mans. N19 —7J 29
(off Warltersville Rd.)
Hillrise Rd. N19 —7J **29**
Hill Rd. N10 —1D **28**
Hill Rd. NW8 —3A **60**
Hill Rd. Cars —6C **132**
Hill Rd. Harr —5A **24**
Hill Rd. Mitc —1F **123**
Hill Rd. Pinn —5C **22**
Hill Rd. Sutt —5K **131**
Hill Rd. Wemb —3B **40**
Hillsborough Rd. SE22 —5E **94**

Hillside. N8 —6H **29**
Hillside. NW5 —3E **44**
Hillside. NW9 —4K **25**
Hillside. NW10 —7J **41**
Hillside. SW19 —6F **107**
Hillside. Barn —5F **5**
Hillside Av. N11 —6J **15**
Hillside Av. Wemb —4F **41**
Hillside Av. Wfd G —6F **21**
Hillside Clo. NW6 —2K **59**
Hillside Clo. NW8 —2K **59**
Hillside Clo. Mord —4G **121**
Hillside Clo. Wfd G —5F **21**
Hillside Cres. Enf —1J **7**
Hillside Cres. Harr —1G **39**
Hillside Dri. Edgw —6B **12**
Hillside Est. N15 —6F **31**
Hillside Gdns. E17 —3F **33**
Hillside Gdns. N6 —6F **29**
Hillside Gdns. N11 —6B **16**
Hillside Gdns. SW2 —2A **110**
Hillside Gdns. Barn —4B **4**
Hillside Gdns. Edgw —4A **12**
Hillside Gdns. Harr —7E **24**
Hillside Gdns. Wall —7G **133**
Hillside Gro. N14 —7C **6**
Hillside Gro. NW7 —7H **13**
Hillside La. Brom —2H **137**
(in two parts)
Hillside Pas. SW16 —2K **109**
Hillside Rd. N15 —7E **30**
Hillside Rd. SW2 —2K **109**
Hillside Rd. W5 —5E **56**
Hillside Rd. Brom —3H **127**
Hillside Rd. Croy —5B **134**
Hillside Rd. Pinn —1A **22**
Hillside Rd. S'hall —4E **54**
Hillside Rd. Surb —4G **119**
Hillside Rd. Sutt —7H **131**
Hillsleigh Rd. W8 —1H **75**
Hills M. W5 —7E **56**
Hills Pl. W1 —6G **61** (8L **139**)
Hills Rd. Buck H —1E **20**
Hillstowe St. E5 —3J **47**
Hill St. W1 —1E **76** (2H **145**)
Hill St. Rich —5D **88**
Hilltop. NW11 —4K **27**
Hill Top. Mord —6J **121**
Hill Top. Sutt —7H **121**
Hill Top. Wfd G —6J **21**
Hilltop Gdns. NW4 —2D **26**
Hilltop Rd. NW6 —7J **43**
Hilltop Way. Stan —3F **11**
Hillview. SW20 —7D **106**
Hillview Av. Harr —5E **24**
Hill View Cres. Ilf —6D **34**
Hill View Dri. Well —2J **99**
Hillview Gdns. NW4 —4F **27**
Hill View Gdns. NW9 —5K **25**
Hillview Gdns. Harr —3E **22**
Hillview Rd. NW7 —4A **14**
Hillview Rd. Chst —5E **114**
Hillview Rd. Pinn —1D **22**
Hillview Rd. Sutt —3A **132**
Hill View Rd. Twic —6A **88**
Hillway. N6 —2E **44**
Hillway. NW9 —1A **42**
Hillworth. Beck —2D **126**
Hillworth Rd. SW2 —7A **94**
Hillyard Rd. W7 —5J **55**
Hillyard St. SW9 —1A **94**
Hillyfield. E17 —2A **32**
Hilly Fields Cres. SE4 —3C **96**
Hilsea St. E5 —4J **47**
Hilton Av. N12 —5G **15**
Hilversum Cres. SE22 —5E **94**
Himley Rd. SW17 —5C **108**
Hinchcliffe Clo. Wall. N133

Hinckley Rd. SE15 —4G **95**
Hind Ct. EC4 —6A **62** (8H **141**)
Hind Cres. N Hth —6K **85**
Hinde M. W1 —6E 60 (7H 139)
(off Marylebone La.)
Hindes Rd. Harr —5H **23**
Hinde St. W1 —6E **60** (7H **139**)
Hind Gro. E14 —6C **64**
Hindhead Clo. N16 —1E **46**
Hindhead Gdns. N'holt —1C **54**
Hindhead Way. Wall —5J **133**
Hindlip Ho. SW8 —1H **93**
Hindmans Rd. SE22 —5G **95**
Hindmans Way. Dag —4F **69**
Hindmarsh Clo. E1 —7G **63**
Hindrey Rd. E5 —5H **47**
Hindsley's Pl. SE23 —2J **111**
Hinkler Clo. Wall —7J **133**
Hinkler Rd. Harr —3D **24**
Hinksey Path. SE2 —3D **84**
Hinstock Rd. SE18 —6G **83**
Hinton Av. Houn —4B **86**
Hinton Clo. SE9 —1C **114**
Hinton Rd. N18 —4K **17**
Hinton Rd. SE24 —3B **94**
Hinton Rd. Wall —6G **133**
Hippodrome M. W11 —7G **59**
Hippodrome Pl. W11 —7G **59**
Hiroshima Promenade. SE7 —3A **82**
Hisocks Ho. NW10 —7J **41**
Hitcham Rd. E17 —7B **32**
Hitchin Sq. E3 —2A **64**
Hitherfield Rd. SW16 —3K **109**
Hitherfield Rd. Dag —2E **52**
Hither Grn. La. SE13 —5E **96**
Hitherwell Dri. Harr —1H **23**
Hitherwood Dri. SE19 —4F **111**
Hive Clo. Bush —2C **10**
Hive Rd. Bush —2C **10**
Hoadly Rd. SW16 —3H **109**
Hobart Clo. N20 —2H **15**
Hobart Clo. Hay —4B **54**
Hobart Dri. Hay —4B **54**
Hobart Gdns. T Hth —3D **124**
Hobart La. Hay —4B **54**
Hobart Pl. SW1 —3F **77** (7J **145**)
Hobart Pl. Rich —7F **89**
Hobart Rd. Dag —4D **52**
Hobart Rd. Hay —4B **54**
Hobart Rd. Ilf —2G **35**
Hobart Rd. Wor Pk —3D **130**
Hobbayne Rd. W7 —6H **55**
Hobbes Wlk. SW15 —5D **90**
Hobbs Grn. N2 —3A **28**
Hobbs M. Ilf —2K **51**
Hobbs Pl. N1 —1E **62**
Hobbs Pl. Est. N1 —1E 62
(off Hobbs Pl.)
Hobbs Rd. SE27 —4C **110**
Hobday St. E14 —6D **64**
Hobill Wlk. Surb —6F **119**
Hoblands End. Chst —6J **115**
Hobsons Pl. E1 —5G **63**
Hobury St. SW10 —6B **76**
Hocker St. E2 —3F **63** (2E **142**)
Hockett Clo. SE8 —4A **80**
Hockley Av. E6 —2C **66**
Hockley Ct. E18 —1J **33**
Hocroft Av. NW2 —3H **43**
Hocroft Ct. NW2 —3H **43**
Hocroft Rd. NW2 —3H **43**
Hocroft Wlk. NW2 —3H **43**
Hodder Dri. Gnfd —2K **55**
Hoddesdon Rd. Belv —5G **85**
Hodford Rd. NW11 —1H **43**
Hodgkin Clo. SE28 —7D **68**
Hodister Clo. SE5 —7C **78**
Hodnet Gro. SE16 —4K **79**

Hodson Clo. Harr —3D **38**
Hoecroft Ct. Enf —1D 8
(off Hoe La.)
Hoe La. Enf —1B **8**
Hoe St. E17 —4C **32**
Hoever Ho. SE6 —4E **112**
Hofland Rd. W14 —3G **75**
Hogan M. W2 —5A **60** (5A **138**)
Hogan Way. E5 —2G **47**
Hogarth Clo. E16 —5B **66**
Hogarth Clo. W5 —5E **56**
Hogarth Ct. EC3 —6E **62** (8D **142**)
Hogarth Ct. SE19 —4F **111**
Hogarth Ct. Houn —7C **70**
Hogarth Cres. SW19 —1B **122**
Hogarth Cres. Croy —7C **124**
Hogarth Gdns. Houn —7E **70**
Hogarth Hill. NW11 —4H **27**
Hogarth Ind. Est. NW10 —4C **58**
Hogarth La. W4 —6A **74**
Hogarth Pl. SW5 —4K 75
(off Hogarth Rd.)
Hogarth Rd. SW5 —4K **75**
Hogarth Rd. Edgw —2G **25**
Hogarth Ter. W4 —6A **74**
Hog Hill Rd. Romf —1F **37**
Hogshead Pas. E1 —7H 63
(off Pennington St.)
Holbeach Gdns. Sidc —6K **99**
Holbeach Rd. SE6 —7D **96**
Holbeck Row. SE15 —7G **79**
Holbein M. SW1 —5E **76**
Holbein Pl. SW1 —4E **76** (9G **145**)
Holberton Gdns. NW10 —3D **58**
Holborn. EC1 —5A **62** (6G **141**)
Holborn Cir. EC1 —5A **62** (6H **141**)
Holborn Pl. WC1 —5K 61 (6E 140)
(off High Holborn)
Holborn Rd. E13 —5K **65**
Holborn Viaduct. EC1
—5B **62** (6H **141**)
Holborough M. SW12 —1F **109**
Holbroke Cl. N7 —3J **45**
Holbrook Clo. N19 —1F **45**
Holbrook Clo. Enf —1A **8**
Holbrooke Pl. Rich —5D **88**
Holbrook Ho. Chst —1H **129**
Holbrook La. Chst —7H **115**
Holbrook Rd. E15 —2H **65**
Holbrook Way. Brom —6D **128**
Holburne Clo. SE3 —1A **98**
Holburne Gdns. SE3 —1B **98**
Holburne Rd. SE3 —1A **98**
Holcombe Hill. NW7 —3H **13**
Holcombe Ho. SW9 —3J 93
(off Landor Rd.)
Holcombe Rd. N17 —3F **31**
(in two parts)
Holcombe Rd. Ilf —7E **34**
Holcombe St. W6 —4D **74**
Holcote Clo. Belv —3E **84**
Holcroft Rd. E9 —7J **47**
Holden Av. N12 —5E **14**
Holden Av. NW9 —1J **41**
Holdenby Rd. SE4 —5A **96**
Holden Clo. Dag —3B **52**
Holdenhurst Av. N12 —7F **15**
Holden Rd. N12 —5E **14**
Holden St. SW11 —2E **92**
Holdernesse Rd. SW17 —3D **108**
Holdernesse Way. SE27 —5B **110**
Holder's Hill Av. NW4 —2F **27**
Holders Hill Cir. NW7 —7B **14**
Holders Hill Cres. NW4 —2F **27**
Holders Hill Dri. NW4 —3F **27**
Holder's Hill Gdns. NW4 —2G **27**
Holders Hill Rd. NW4 & NW7 —2F **27**
Holford Pl. WC1 —3K **61** (1F **140**)

Holford Rd. NW3 —3A **44**
Holford St. WC1 —3K **61** (1G **141**)
Holford Yd. WC1 —3A **62** (1G **141**)
Holgate Av. SW11 —3B **92**
Holgate Gdns. Dag —6G **53**
Holgate Rd. Dag —5G **53**
Holgate St. SE7 —3B **82**
Hollam Ho. N8 —4K **29**
Holland Av. SW20 —1B **120**
Holland Av. Sutt —7J **131**
Holland Clo. Barn —7G **5**
Holland Clo. Brom —2H **137**
Holland Clo. Romf —5J **37**
Holland Clo. Stan —5G **11**
Holland Ct. E17 —4E 32
(off Evelyn Rd.)
Holland Ct. NW7 —6H **13**
Holland Dri. SE23 —3A **112**
Holland Gdns. W14 —3G **75**
Holland Gro. SW9 —7A **78**
Holland Ho. E4 —4A **20**
Holland La. W14 —3H **75**
Holland Pk. W11 —1G **75**
Holland Pk. Av. W11 —2F **75**
Holland Pk. Av. Ilf —6J **35**
Holland Pk. Gdns. W14 —2G **75**
Holland Pk. M. W11 —1G **75**
Holland Pk. Rd. W14 —3H **75**
Holland Pas. N1 —1C 62
(off Basire St.)
Holland Pl. W8 —2K 75
(off Kensington Church St.)
Holland Pl. Chambers. W8 —2K 75
(off Holland St.)
Holland Rise Ho. SW9 —7K 77
(off Clapham Rd.)
Holland Rd. E6 —1D **66**
Holland Rd. E15 —3G **65**
Holland Rd. NW10 —1C **58**
Holland Rd. SE25 —5G **125**
Holland Rd. W14 —2F **75**
Holland Rd. Wemb —6D **40**
Hollands, The. Felt —4B **102**
Hollands, The. Wor Pk —1B **130**
Holland St. SE1 —1B **78** (2K **147**)
Holland St. W8 —2J **75**
Holland Vs. Rd. W14 —2G **75**
Holland Wlk. N19 —1H **45**
Holland Wlk. W8 —1H **75**
Holland Wlk. Stan —5F **11**
Holland Way. Brom —2H **137**
Hollar Rd. N16 —3F **47**
Hollen St. W1 —6H **61** (7A **140**)
Holles Clo. Hamp —6E **102**
Holles Ho. SW9 —2A **94**
Holles St. W1 —6F **61**
Holley Rd. W3 —2A **74**
Hollick Wood Av. N12 —6J **15**
Holliday Sq. SW11 —3B 92
(off Fowler Clo.)
Hollidge Way. Dag —7H **53**
Hollies Av. Sidc —2K **115**
Hollies Clo. SW16 —6A **110**
Hollies Clo. Twic —2K **103**
Hollies End. NW7 —5J **13**
Hollies Rd. W5 —4C **72**
Hollies St. W1 —6F **61** (7K **139**)
Hollies, The. N20 —1G **15**
Hollies, The. Harr —4A **24**
Hollies Way. SW12 —7E **92**
Holligrave Rd. Brom —1J **127**
Hollingbourne Av. Bexh —1F **101**
Hollingbourne Gdns. W13 —5B **56**
Hollingbourne Rd. SE24 —5C **94**
Hollingsworth Ct. Surb —7D **118**
Hollingsworth Rd. Croy —6H **135**
Hollington Ct. Chst —6F **115**
Hollington Cres. N Mald —6B **120**

Hollington Rd. E6 —3D 66
Hollington Rd. N17 —2G 31
Hollingworth Rd. Orp —7F 129
Hollins. N7 —4J 45
Hollman Gdns. SW16 —6B 110
Holloway Ho. NW2 —3E 42
Holloway Rd. E6 —3D 66
Holloway Rd. E11 —3G 49
Holloway Rd. N7 —4K 45
Holloway Rd. N19 & N7 —2H 45
Holloway St. Houn —3F 87
Hollowfield Wlk. N'holt —7C 38
Hollows, The. Wfd G —4C 20
Holly Av. Stan —2E 24
Hollybank Clo. Hamp —5E 102
Hollyberry La. NW3 —4A 44
Hollybrake Clo. Chst —7H 115
Hollybush Clo. E11 —5J 33
Hollybush Clo. Harr —1J 23
Hollybush Gdns. E2 —3H 63
Hollybush Hill. E11 —4G 33
Hollybush Hill. NW3 —4A 44
Hollybush Ho. E2 —3H 63
Holly Bush La. Hamp —7D 102
Hollybush Pl. E2 —3H 63
Hollybush Rd. King T —5E 104
Hollybush Steps. NW3 —4A 44
  (off Holly Mt.)
Hollybush St. E13 —2K 65
Holly Bush Vale. NW3 —4A 44
Hollybush Wlk. SW9 —4B 94
Holly Clo. NW10 —7A 42
Holly Clo. Buck H —3K 21
Holly Clo. Felt —5C 102
Holly Clo. Wall —7F 133
Holly Ct. N15 —4E 30
Holly Ct. Sutt —7J 131
Holly Cres. Beck —5B 126
Holly Cres. Wfd G —7A 20
Hollycroft Av. NW3 —3J 43
Hollycroft Av. Wemb —2F 41
Hollydale Rd. SE15 —1J 95
Holly Dene. SE15 —1H 95
Hollydown Way. E11 —3F 49
Holly Dri. E4 —7J 9
Holly Farm Rd. S'hall —5C 70
Hollyfield Av. N11 —5J 15
Hollyfield Rd. Surb —7F 119
Holly Gro. NW9 —7J 25
Holly Gro. SE15 —2F 95
Hollygrove. Bush —1C 10
Holly Gro. Pinn —1C 22
Hollyhead Clo. E3 —3C 64
Holly Hedge Ter. SE13 —5F 97
Holly Hill. N21 —6E 6
Holly Hill. NW3 —4A 44
Holly Hill Rd. Belv & Eri —5H 85
Holly Ho. Iswth —6C 72
Holly Lodge. Harr —5H 23
Hollymead. Cars —3D 132
Holly M. SW10 —5A 76
  (off Drayton Gdns.)
Holly Mt. NW3 —4A 44
Hollymount Clo. SE10 —1E 96
Holly Pk. N3 —3H 27
Holly Pk. N4 —7J 29
  (in two parts)
Holly Pk. Est. N4 —7K 29
Holly Pk. Gdns. N3 —3J 27
Holly Pk. Rd. N11 —5K 15
Holly Pk. Rd. W7 —1K 71
Holly Pl. NW3 —4A 44
  (off Holly Berry La.)
Holly Rd. E11 —7H 33
Holly Rd. W4 —4K 73
Holly Rd. Hamp —6G 103

Holly Rd. Houn —4F 87
Holly Rd. Twic —1K 103
Holly St. E8 —7F 47
Holly St. Est. E8 —7F 47
Holly Ter. N6 —1E 44
Holly Ter. N20 —2F 15
Holly Tree Clo. SW19 —1F 107
Holly View Clo. NW4 —6C 26
Holly Village. N6 —2F 45
Holly Wlk. NW3 —4A 44
Holly Wlk. Enf —3H 7
Holly Way. Mitc —4H 123
Hollywood M. SW10 —6A 76
Hollywood Rd. E4 —5F 19
Hollywood Rd. SW10 —6A 76
Hollywood Way. Wfd G —7A 20
Holman Ct. Ewe —7C 130
Holman Hunt Ho. W6 —5G 75
  (off Field Rd.)
Holman Rd. SW11 —2B 92
Holmbridge Gdns. Enf —4E 8
Holmbrook Dri. NW4 —5F 27
Holmbury Clo. Bush —2D 10
Holmbury Ct. SW17 —3D 108
Holmbury Ct. S Croy —5E 134
Holmbury Gro. Croy —7B 136
Holmbury Ho. SW24 —5B 94
Holmbury Mnr. Sidc —4A 116
Holmbury Pk. Brom —7C 114
Holmbury View. E5 —1H 47
Holmbush Rd. SW15 —6G 91
Holmcote Gdns. N5 —5C 46
Holmcroft Ho. E17 —4D 32
Holmcroft Way. Brom —5D 128
Holmdale Gdns. NW4 —5F 27
Holmdale Rd. NW6 —5J 43
Holmdale Rd. Chst —5G 115
Holmdale Ter. N15 —7E 30
Holmdene. N12 —5E 14
Holmdene Av. NW7 —6H 13
Holmdene Av. SE24 —5C 94
Holmdene Av. Harr —3F 23
Holmdene Clo. Beck —2E 126
Holmead Rd. SW6 —7K 75
Holme Lacey Rd. SE12 —6H 97
Holmeleigh Ct. Enf —4D 8
Holme Oak M. SW4 —5J 93
Holme Rd. E6 —1C 66
Holmes Av. E17 —3B 32
Holmes Av. NW7 —5B 14
Holmesdale Av. SW14 —3H 89
Holmesdale Clo. SE25 —3F 125
Holmesdale Rd. N6 —7F 29
Holmesdale Rd. Bexh —2D 100
Holmesdale Rd. Croy & SE25
  —5D 124
Holmesdale Rd. Rich —1F 89
Holmesdale Rd. Tedd —6C 104
Holmesley Rd. SE23 —6A 96
Holmes Pl. SW10 —6A 76
Holmes Rd. NW5 —5F 45
Holmes Rd. SW19 —7A 108
Holmes Rd. Twic —2K 103
Holmes Ter. SE1 —2A 78 (4G 147)
  (off Waterloo Rd.)
Holmeswood Ct. N22 —2A 30
Holme Way. Stan —6E 10
Holmewood Gdns. SW2 —7K 93
Holmewood Rd. SE25 —3E 124
Holmewood Rd. SW2 —7K 93
Holmfield. NW11 —4J 27
Holmfield Av. NW4 —5F 27
Holmfield Ct. NW3 —6C 44
Holmhurst Rd. Belv —5H 85
Holmleigh Rd. N16 —1E 46
Holmleigh Rd. Est. N16 —1E 46
Holmoak Clo. SW15 —6H 91
Holmoaks Ho. Beck —2E 126

Holmsdale Gro. Bexh —2K 101
Holmsdale Ho. N11 —4A 16
  (off Coppies Gro.)
Holmshaw Clo. SE26 —4A 112
Holmside Rd. SW12 —6E 92
Holmsley Clo. N Mald —6B 120
Holmstall Av. Edgw —3J 25
Holmstall Pde. Edgw —2J 25
Holm Wlk. SE3 —2J 97
Holmwood Clo. Harr —3G 23
Holmwood Clo. N'holt —6F 39
Holmwood Clo. Sutt —7F 131
Holmwood Gdns. N3 —2J 27
Holmwood Gdns. Wall —6F 133
Holmwood Gro. NW7 —5E 12
Holmwood Rd. Ilf —2J 51
Holmwood Rd. Sutt —7E 130
Holmwood Vs. SE7 —5J 81
Holne Chase. N2 —6A 28
Holne Chase. Mord —6H 121
Holness Rd. E15 —6H 49
Holroyd Rd. SW15 —4E 90
Holstein Way. Eri —3D 84
Holstock Rd. Ilf —2G 51
Holsworth Clo. Harr —5G 23
Holsworthy Sq. WC1
  —4K 61 (4F 140)
  (off Elm St.)
Holt Clo. N10 —4E 28
Holt Clo. SE28 —7B 68
Holt Ct. E15 —5E 48
Holt Ho. SW2 —6A 94
Holton St. E1 —4K 63
Holt Rd. E16 —1C 82
Holt Rd. Wemb —3B 40
Holt, The. Wall —4G 133
Holtwhites Av. Enf —2H 7
Holtwhite's Hill. Enf —1G 7
Holwell Pl. Pinn —4C 22
Holwood Pl. SW4 —4H 93
Holybourne Av. SW15 —7C 90
Holylake Ct. SE16 —2B 80
Holyoake Wlk. N2 —3A 28
Holyoake Wlk. W4 —4C 56
Holyoak Rd. SE11 —4B 78 (8J 147)
Holyport Rd. SW6 —7F 75
Holyrood Av. Harr —4C 38
Holyrood Gdns. Edgw —3H 25
Holyrood Rd. Barn —6F 5
Holyrood St. SE1 —1E 78 (3C 148)
Holywell Clo. SE3 —6J 81
Holywell La. EC2 —4E 62 (3D 142)
Holywell Row. EC2 —4E 62 (4C 142)
Homan Ct. N12 —4G 15
Homebush Ho. E4 —7J 9
Home Clo. Cars —2D 132
Home Clo. N'holt —3D 54
Homecroft Rd. N22 —1C 30
Homecroft Rd. SE26 —5J 111
Homefarm Rd. W7 —6J 55
Homefield Rd. W4 —4B 74
Homefield Clo. NW10 —7J 41
Homefield Clo. Hay —4B 54
Homefield Ct. SW16 —3J 109
Homefield Gdns. N2 —3B 28
Homefield Gdns. Mitc —2A 122
Homefield Pk. Sutt —6K 131
Homefield Rise. Orp —7K 129
Homefield Rd. SW19 —6G 107
Homefield Rd. W4 —4B 74
Homefield Rd. Brom —1A 128
Homefield Rd. Edgw —6E 12
Homefield Rd. Wemb —4A 40
Homefield St. N1 —2E 62
Homefirs Ho. Wemb —3F 41
Home Gdns. Dag —3J 53
Homeland Dri. Sutt —7K 131
Homelands Dri. SE19 —7E 110

Homeleigh Rd. SE15 —5K 95
Home Mead. Stan —1C 24
Homemead Rd. Brom —5D 128
Homemead Rd. Croy —6H 123
Home Pk. Rd. SW19 —4H 107
Home Pk. Wlk. King T —4D 118
Homer Clo. Bexh —1J 101
Homer Dri. E14 —4C 80
Home Rd. SW11 —2C 92
Homer Rd. E9 —6A 48
Homer Rd. Croy —6K 125
Homer Row. W1 —5C 60 (6D 138)
Homersham Rd. King T —2G 119
Homer St. W1 —5C 60 (6D 138)
Homerton Gro. E9 —5K 47
Homerton High St. E9 —5K 47
Homerton Rd. E9 —5A 48
Homerton Row. E9 —6J 47
Homerton Ter. E9 —6J 47
Homesdale Clo. E11 —5J 33
Homesdale Rd. Brom —4A 128
Homesdale Rd. Orp —7J 129
Homestall Rd. SE22 —5J 95
Homestead, The. Dag —2F 53
Homestead Paddock. N14 —5A 6
Homestead Pk. NW2 —3D 42
Homestead Rd. SW6 —7H 75
Homestead Rd. Dag —2F 53
Homestead, The. N11 —4A 16
Homewillow Clo. N21 —6G 7
Homewood Clo. Hamp —6D 102
Homewood Cres. Chst —6J 115
Homewoods. SW12 —7G 93
Hamilton Ho. SE26 —3G 111
Honduras St. EC1 —4C 62 (3L 141)
Honeybourne Rd. NW6 —5K 43
Honeybourne Way. Orp —7H 129
Honeybrook Rd. SW12 —7G 93
Honey Clo. Dag —6H 53
Honeyden Rd. Sidc —6E 116
Honey La. EC2 —6C 62 (8M 141)
  (off Trump St.)
Honeyman Clo. NW6 —7F 43
Honeypot Bus. Cen. Stan —1E 24
Honeypot Clo. NW9 —4F 25
Honeypot La. Stan & NW9 —7J 11
Honeysett Rd. N17 —2F 31
Honeysuckle Gdns. Croy —7K 125
Honeysuckle La. N22 —2C 30
Honeywell Rd. SW11 —6D 92
Honeywood Rd. NW10 —2B 58
Honeywood Rd. Iswth —4A 88
Honeywood Wlk. Cars —4D 132
Honister Clo. Stan —1B 24
Honister Gdns. Stan —7G 11
Honister Pl. Stan —1B 24
Honiton Rd. NW6 —2H 59
Honiton Rd. Romf —6K 37
Honiton Rd. Well —2K 99
Honley Rd. SE6 —7D 96
Honnor Gdns. Iswth —2H 87
Honor Oak Pk. SE23 —6J 95
Honor Oak Rise. SE23 —6J 95
Honor Oak Rd. SE23 —1J 111
Hood Av. N14 —6A 6
Hood Av. SW14 —5J 89
Hood Clo. Croy —1B 134
Hoodcote Gdns. N21 —7G 7
Hood Ct. EC4 —6A 62 (8H 141)
  (off Fleet St.)
Hood Rd. SW20 —7B 106
Hood Wlk. Romf —1H 37
Hookers Rd. E17 —3K 31
Hook Farm Rd. Brom —5B 128
Hooking Grn. Harr —5F 23
Hook La. Well —5K 99
Hooks Clo. SE15 —1H 95
Hookshall Dri. Dag —3J 53
Hookstone Way. Wfd G —7G 21

Hooks Way. SE22 —1G 111
Hook, The. Barn —6G 5
Hook Wlk. Edgw —6D 12
Hook Wlk. Edgw —6D 12
Hooper Rd. E16 —6J 65
Hooper's Ct. SW3 —2D 76 (5E 144)
Hooper St. E1 —6G 63
Hoop La. NW11 —7H 27
Hope Clo. N1 —6C 46
Hope Clo. SE12 —3K 113
Hope Clo. Sutt —5A 132
Hope Clo. Wfd G —6F 21
Hope Ct. SE12 —3K 113
Hopedale Rd. SE7 —6K 81
Hopefield Av. NW6 —2G 59
Hope Pk. Brom —7H 113
Hope St. SW11 —3B 92
Hopetown St. E1 —5F 63
Hopewell St. SE5 —7D 78
Hop Gdns. WC2 —7J 61 (1C 146)
Hopgood St. W12 —2E 74
Hopkinsons Pl. NW1 —1E 60
Hopkins St. W1 —6G 61 (8R 139)
Hopper's M. W3 —1J 73
Hoppers Rd. N13 & N21 —2F 17
Hoppett Rd. E4 —2B 20
Hopping La. N1 —6B 46
Hoppingwood Av. N Mald —3A 120
Hopton Ct. Hayes —1J 137
Hopton Gdns. N Mald —6C 120
Hopton Rd. SW16 —5K 109
Hopton's Gdns. SE1
  (off Hopton St.) —1B 78 (2K 147)
Hopton St. SE1 —1B 78 (2K 147)
Hopwood Rd. SE17 —6D 78
Hopwood Wlk. E8 —7G 47
Horace Av. Romf —1J 53
Horace Rd. E7 —4K 49
Horace Rd. Ilf —3G 35
Horace Rd. King T —3F 119
Horatio St. E2 —2G 63
Horatius Way. Croy —5K 133
Horbury Cres. W11 —7J 59
Horbury M. W11 —7H 59
Horder Rd. SW6 —1G 91
Hordle Promenade E. SE15 —7F 79
Hordle Promenade N. SE15 —7E 78
Hordle Promenade S. SE15 —7F 78
Hordle Promenade W. SE15 —7E 78
Horizon Way. SE7 —4K 81
Horle Wlk. SE5 —2B 94
Horley Clo. Bexh —5G 101
Horley Rd. SE9 —4C 114
Hormead Rd. W9 —4H 59
Hornbeam Clo. SE11
  —4A 78 (8G 147)
Hornbeam Clo. Buck H —3G 21
Hornbeam Clo. N'holt —5D 38
Hornbeam Cres. Bren —7B 72
Hornbeam Gro. E4 —3B 20
Hornbeam Ho. Buck H —3G 21
Hornbeam La. Bexh —2J 101
Hornbeam Rd. Buck H —3G 21
Hornbeam Rd. Hay —5A 54
Hornbeams Rise. N11 —6K 15
Hornbeam Wlk. Rich —3F 105
Hornbeam Way. Brom —6E 128
Hornblower Clo. SE16 —3A 80
Hornbuckle Clo. Harr —2H 39
Hornby Clo. NW3 —7B 44
Hornby Ho. SE11 —6A 78
  (off Clayton St.)
Horncastle Clo. SE12 —7J 97
Horncastle Rd. SE12 —7J 97
Hornchurch. N17 —2D 30
  (off Gloucester Rd.)
Horndon Clo. SW15 —1C 106
Horndon Clo. Romf —1J 37

Horndon Grn. Romf —1J 37
Horndon Rd. Romf —1J 37
Horner Ho. N1 —2E 62
(off Whitmore Est.)
Horner La. Mitc —2B 122
Horne Way. SW15 —2E 90
Hornfair Rd. SE7 —6B 82
Horniman Dri. SE23 —1H 111
Horning Clo. SE9 —4C 114
Horn La. SE10 —4J 81
Horn La. W3 —1J 73
Horn La. Wfd G —6D 20
Hornpark Clo. SE12 —5K 97
Hornpark La. SE12 —5K 97
Horns End Pl. Pinn —4A 22
Hornsey La. N6 —1F 45
Hornsey La. Est. N19 —7H 29
Hornsey La. Gdns. N6 —7G 29
Hornsey Pk. Rd. N8 —3K 29
Hornsey Rise. N19 —7H 29
Hornsey Rise Gdns. N19 —7H 29
Hornsey Rd. N19 & N7 —1J 45
Hornsey St. N7 —5K 45
Hornshay St. SE15 —6J 79
Horns Rd. Ilf —5G 35
Hornton Pl. W8 —2K 75
Hornton St. W8 —2J 75
Horsa Clo. Wall —7J 133
Horsa Rd. SE12 —7A 98
Horsa Rd. Eri —7H 85
Horsebridge Clo. Dag —1E 68
Horsecroft Rd. Edgw —7E 12
Horse & Dolphin Yd. W1
—7H 61 (9B 140)
(off Macclesfield St.)
Horse Fair. King T —2D 118
Horseferry Pl. SE10 —6E 80
Horseferry Rd. E14 —7A 64
Horseferry Rd. SW1
—3H 77 (7A 146)
Horseguards Av. SW1
—1J 77 (3C 146)
Horse Guards Rd. SW1
—1H 77 (3B 146)
Horse Leaze. E6 —6E 66
Horsell Rd. N5 —5A 46
Horsell Rd. Orp —7B 116
Horseydown La. SE1
—2F 79 (4E 148)
Horsenden Av. Gnfd —5J 39
Horsenden Cres. Gnfd —5K 39
Horsenden La. Gnfd —6J 39
Horsenden La. N. Gnfd —6K 39
Horsenden La. S. Gnfd —1A 56
Horse Ride. SW1 —2G 77 (4L 145)
(off Mall, The.)
Horseshoe Clo. E14 —5E 80
Horseshoe Clo. NW2 —2D 42
Horse Shoe Cres. N'holt —2E 54
Horse Shoe Grn. Sutt —2K 131
Horseshoe La. N20 —1A 14
Horseshoe La. Enf —3H 7
Horse Shoe Yd. W1 —7F 61 (9K 139)
(off Brook St.)
Horse Yd. N1 —1B 62
(off Essex Rd.)
Horsfeld Gdns. SE9 —5C 98
Horsfeld Rd. SE9 —5B 98
Horsford Rd. SW2 —5K 93
Horsham Av. N12 —5H 15
Horsham Ct. N17 —1G 31
(off Lansdowne Rd.)
Horsham Rd. Bexh —5G 101
Horsleydown La. SE1 —2F 79
Horsleydown Sq. SE1
—1F 79 (3E 148)
Horsley Dri. New Ad —7E 136
Horsley Rd. E4 —2K 19

Horsley Rd. Brom —1K 127
Horsley St. SE17 —6D 78
Horsman St. SE5 —6C 78
Horsmonden Clo. Orp —7K 129
Horsmonden Rd. SE4 —5B 96
Hortensia Rd. SW10 —7A 76
Horticultural Pl. W4 —5K 73
Horton Av. NW2 —4G 43
Horton Ho. SE15 —6J 79
Horton Ho. SW6 —7K 77
Horton Ho. W6 —5G 75
(off Field Rd.)
Horton Rd. E8 —6H 47
Horton St. SE13 —3D 96
Hortus Rd. E4 —2K 19
Hortus Rd. S'hall —2D 70
Hosack Rd. SW17 —2E 108
Hoser Av. SE12 —2J 113
Hoskins Clo. E16 —6A 66
Hoskins St. SE10 —5G 81
Hospital Bridge Rd. Twic —7F 87
Hospital Rd. E9 —5K 47
Hospital Rd. Houn —3E 86
Hotham Rd. SW15 —3E 90
Hotham Rd. SW19 —7A 108
Hotham Rd. M. SW19 —7A 108
Hotham St. E15 —1G 65
Hothfield Pl. SE16 —3J 79
Hotspur Ind. Est. N17 —6C 18
Hotspur Rd. N'holt —2E 54
Hotspur St. SE11 —5A 78
Houblon Rd. Rich —5E 88
Houghton Clo. E8 —6F 47
Houghton Clo. Hamp —6C 102
Houghton Rd. N15 —4F 31
Houghton St. WC2 —6K 61 (8F 140)
Houlder Cres. Croy —6B 134
Houndsditch. EC3 —6E 62 (7D 142)
Houndsfield Rd. N9 —7C 8
Hounslow Av. Houn —5F 87
Hounslow Bus. Pk. Houn —4E 86
Hounslow Cen. Houn —3F 87
Hounslow Gdns. Houn —5F 87
Hounslow Rd. Hanw —4B 102
Hounslow Rd. Twic —6F 87
Houseman Way. SE5 —7D 78
Houston Bus. Pk. Hay —1A 70
Houston Rd. SE23 —2A 112
Houstoun Ct. Houn —7D 70
Hove Av. E17 —6B 32
Hoveden Rd. NW2 —5G 43
Hove Gdns. Sutt —1K 131
Hoveton Rd. SE28 —7C 68
Howard Av. Bex —1C 116
Howard Clo. N11 —2A 16
Howard Clo. NW2 —4G 43
Howard Clo. W3 —6H 57
Howard Clo. Bush —1D 10
Howard Clo. Hamp —7G 103
Howard Ct. Bark —1H 67
Howard Ho. SW9 —3B 94
(off Barrington Rd.)
Howard M. N5 —4B 46
Howard Rd. E6 —2D 66
Howard Rd. E11 —3G 49
Howard Rd. E17 —3C 32
Howard Rd. N15 —6E 30
Howard Rd. N16 —4D 46
Howard Rd. NW2 —4F 43
Howard Rd. SE20 —1J 125
Howard Rd. SE25 —5G 125
Howard Rd. Bark —1H 67
Howard Rd. Brom —7J 113
Howard Rd. Ilf —4F 51
Howard Rd. Iswth —3K 87
Howard Rd. N Mald —3A 120

Howard Rd. S'hall —6F 55
Howard Rd. Surb —6F 119
Howards Clo. Pinn —2A 22
Howards Crest Clo. Beck —2E 126
Howard's La. SW15 —4D 90
Howards Rd. E13 —3J 65
Howard St. Th Dit —7B 118
Howard Wlk. N2 —4A 28
Howard Way. SE22 —1G 111
Howard Way. Barn —5A 4
Howarth Rd. SE2 —5A 84
Howberry Clo. Edgw —6J 11
Howberry Rd. Stan & Edgw —6J 11
Howberry Rd. T Hth —1D 124
Howbury Rd. SE15 —3J 95
Howcroft Cres. N3 —7D 14
Howcroft La. Gnfd —3H 55
Howden Clo. SE28 —7D 68
Howden Ho. Houn —7C 86
Howden Rd. SE25 —2F 125
Howden St. SE15 —3G 95
Howe Clo. Romf —1G 37
Howell Clo. Romf —5D 36
Howell Ct. E10 —1D 48
Howell Wlk. SE17 —4B 78 (9K 147)
Howes Clo. N3 —3J 27
Howfield Pl. N17 —3F 31
Howgate Rd. SW14 —3K 89
Howick Pl. SW1 —3G 77 (7M 145)
Howie St. SW11 —7C 76
Howitt Clo. NW3 —6C 44
Howitt Rd. NW3 —6C 44
Howland Est. SE16 —3J 79
Howland M. E. W1 —5G 61 (5M 139)
Howland St. W1 —5G 61 (5L 139)
Howland Way. SE16 —2A 80
Howlett's Rd. SE24 —6C 94
Howley Pl. W2 —5A 60
Howley Rd. Croy —3B 134
Howsman Rd. SW13 —6C 74
Howson Rd. SE4 —4A 96
Howson Ter. Rich —6E 88
How's St. E2 —2F 63
Howton Pl. Bush —1C 10
Hoxton Mkt. N1 —3E 62 (2C 142)
(off Boot St.)
Hoxton Sq. N1 —3E 62 (2C 142)
Hoxton St. N1 —1E 62
Hoylake Gdns. Mitc —3G 123
Hoylake Gdns. Ruis —1A 38
Hoylake Rd. W3 —6A 58
Hoyland Clo. SE15 —7G 79
Hoyle Rd. SW17 —5C 108
Hoy St. E16 —6H 65
Hubbard Rd. SE27 —4C 110
Hubbard St. E15 —1G 65
Hubert Gro. SW9 —3J 93
Hubert Rd. E6 —3B 66
Huddart St. E3 —5B 64
(in two parts)
Huddleston Clo. E2 —2J 63
Huddlestone Rd. E7 —4H 49
Huddlestone Rd. NW2 —6D 42
Huddleston Rd. N7 —3G 45
Hudson. NW9 —1B 26
(off Near Acre)
Hudson Clo. W12 —7D 58
(off White City Est.)
Hudson Pl. SE18 —5G 83
Hudson Rd. Bexh —2F 101
Hudson's Pl. SW1 —4G 77 (8L 145)
(off Bridge Pl.)
Huggin Ct. EC4 —7C 62 (9M 141)
(off Huggin Hill)
Huggin Hill. EC4 —7C 62 (9M 141)
Hughan Rd. E15 —5F 49
Hugh Dalton Av. SW6 —6H 75
(off Clem Attlee Ct.)

Hughenden Av. Harr —5B 24
Hughenden Gdns. N'holt —3A 54
Hughenden Rd. Wor Pk —7C 120
Hughendon. New Bar —4E 4
Hughendon Ter. E15 —4E 48
Hughes Cl. N7 —5H 45
Hughes M. SW11 —5D 92
Hughes Rd. SE20 —7H 111
Hughes Ter. E16 —5H 65
(off Clarkson Rd.)
Hughes Wlk. Croy —7C 124
Hugh Gaitskell Ho. N16 —2F 47
Hugh Gaitskell Ho. SW6 —6H 75
(off Clem Attlee Ct.)
Hugh M. SW1 —4F 77 (9H 145)
Hugh St. SW1 —4F 77 (9H 145)
Hugon Rd. SW6 —3K 91
Hugo Rd. N19 —4G 45
Huguenot Pl. E1 —5F 63
Huguenot Pl. SW18 —5A 92
Huguenot Sq. SE15 —3H 95
Hullbridge M. N1 —1D 62
Hull Clo. SE16 —2K 79
Hull St. EC1 —3C 62 (2L 141)
Hulme Pl. SE1 —2C 78 (5M 147)
Hulse Av. Bark —6H 51
Hulse Av. Romf —1H 37
Humber Rd. NW2 —2D 42
Humber Rd. SE3 —6H 81
Humberstone Rd. E13 —3A 66
Humberton Clo. E9 —5A 48
Humbolt Rd. W6 —6G 75
Hume Point. E16 —5A 66
Humes Av. W7 —3J 71
Hume Ter. E16 —6K 65
Humphrey Clo. Ilf —1D 34
Humphrey St. SE1 —5F 79
Humphries Clo. Dag —4F 53
Hundred Acre. NW9 —2B 26
Hungerdown. E4 —1K 19
Hungerford La. WC2
(off Craven St.) —1J 77 (2C 146)
Hungerford Rd. N7 —6H 45
Hunsdon Clo. Dag —6E 52
Hunsdon Rd. SE14 —7K 79
Hunslett St. E2 —3J 63
Hunston Rd. Mord —1K 131
Hunt Ct. N14 —7A 6
Hunter Clo. SE1 —3D 78 (7B 148)
Hunter Rd. SW20 —1E 120
Hunter Rd. Ilf —5F 51
Hunter Rd. T Hth —3D 124
Hunters Clo. SW12 —1E 108
Hunters Ct. Rich —5D 88
Hunters Gro. Harr —4C 24
Hunters Hall Rd. Dag —4G 53
Hunters Hill. Ruis —3A 38
Hunters Meadow. SE19 —4E 110
Hunters Sq. Dag —4G 53
Hunter St. WC1 —4J 61 (3D 140)
Hunter's Way. Croy —4E 134
Hunters Way. Enf —1F 7
Hunter Wlk. E13 —2J 65
Huntingdon Clo. Mitc —3J 123
Huntingdon Gdns. W4 —7J 73
Huntingdon Gdns. Wor Pk —3E 130
Huntingdon Rd. N2 —3C 28
Huntingdon Rd. N9 —1D 18
Huntingdon St. E16 —6H 65
Huntingfield. Croy —7B 135
Huntingfield Rd. SW15 —4C 90
Hunting Ga. Clo. Enf —3F 7
Hunting Ga. M. Sutt —3K 131
Hunting Ga. M. Twic —1J 103
Huntings Rd. Dag —6G 53
Huntley Dri. N3 —6D 14
Huntley St. WC1 —4G 61 (4M 139)

Huntley Way. SW20 —2C 120
Huntly Rd. SE25 —4E 124
Hunton St. E1 —5G 63
Hunt Rd. S'hall —3E 70
Hunt's Clo. SE3 —2J 97
Hunt's Ct. WC2 —7H 61 (1B 146)
Hunts La. E15 —2E 64
Huntsman St. SE17 —4E 78 (9C 148)
Hunts Mead. Enf —3E 8
Huntsmead Clo. Chst —1D 128
Huntspill St. SW17 —3A 108
Hunts Slip Rd. SE21 —3E 110
Hunt St. W11 —1F 75
Huntsworth M. NW1
—4D 60 (3E 138)
Hunt Way. SE22 —1G 111
Hurdwick Pl. NW1 —2G 61
(off Harrington Sq.)
Hurley Ct. W5 —6C 56
Hurley Cres. SE16 —2K 79
Hurley Rd. Gnfd —6F 55
Hurlingham Bus. Pk. SW6 —3J 91
Hurlingham Ct. SW6 —3H 91
Hurlingham Gdns. SW6 —3H 91
Hurlingham Rd. SW6 —2H 91
Hurlingham Rd. Bexh —7F 85
Hurlingham Sq. SW6 —3J 91
Hurlock St. N5 —3B 46
Hurlstone Rd. SE25 —5E 124
Hurn Ct. Houn —2B 86
Hurn Ct. Rd. Houn —2B 86
Huron Rd. SW17 —2E 108
Hurren Clo. SE3 —3G 97
Hurry Clo. E15 —7G 49
Hurst Av. E4 —4H 19
Hurst Av. N6 —6G 29
Hurstbourne Gdns. Bark —6J 51
Hurstbourne Rd. SE23 —1A 112
Hurst Clo. E4 —4H 19
Hurst Clo. NW11 —6K 27
Hurst Clo. Brom —1H 137
Hurst Clo. N'holt —5D 38
Hurst Ct. Sidc —2A 116
Hurstcourt Rd. Sutt —2K 131
Hurstdene Av. Brom —1H 137
Hurstdene Gdns. N15 —7E 30
Hurstfield. Brom —5J 127
Hurst La. SE2 —5D 84
Hurst La. Est. SE2 —5D 84
Hurstleigh Gdns. Ilf —1D 34
Hurstmead Ct. Edgw —4C 12
Hurst Rise. Barn —3D 4
Hurst Rd. E17 —3D 32
Hurst Rd. N21 —1F 17
Hurst Rd. Buck H —1G 21
Hurst Rd. Croy —4D 134
Hurst Rd. Eri —1J 101
Hurst Rd. Sidc & Bex —2A 116
Hurst Springs. Bex —1E 116
Hurst St. SE24 —6B 94
Hurstview Grange. S Croy —7B 134
Hurst View Rd. S Croy —7E 134
Hurst Way. S Croy —6E 134
Hurstway Wlk. W11 —7F 59
Hurstwood Av. E18 —4K 33
Hurstwood Av. Bex —1E 116
Hurstwood Ct. N12 —6H 15
Hurstwood Ct. NW11 —4H 27
Hurstwood Dri. Brom —3D 128
Hurstwood Rd. NW11 —4G 27
Huson Clo. NW3 —7C 44
Husseywell Cres. Brom —1J 137
Hutchings St. E14 —2C 80
Hutchings Wlk. NW11 —4K 27
Hutchins Clo. E15 —7E 48
Hutchinson Ct. Romf —4D 36
Hutchinson Ter. Wemb —3D 40
Hutton Clo. Gnfd —5H 39

Joseph Powell Clo. SW12 —6F 93
Joseph Ray Rd. E11 —2G 49
Joseph St. E3 —4B 64
Joshua St. E14 —6E 64
Joubert St. SW11 —2D 92
Jowett St. SE15 —7F 79
Joyce Av. N18 —5A 18
Joyce Butler Ho. N22 —1K 29
Joyce Dawson Way. SE28 —7A 68
Joyce Page Clo. SE7 —6B 82
Joyce Wlk. SW2 —6A 94
Joydens Wood Rd. Bex —4K 117
Joydon Dri. Romf —6B 36
Joyners Clo. Dag —4F 53
Joystone Ct. New Bar —4H 5
(off Park Rd.)
Jubb Powell Ho. N15 —6E 30
Jubilee Av. E4 —6K 19
Jubilee Av. Romf —5H 37
Jubilee Av. Twic —1G 103
Jubilee Clo. NW9 —6K 25
Jubilee Clo. King T —1C 118
Jubilee Clo. Pinn —2A 22
Jubilee Clo. Romf —5H 37
Jubilee Ct. Harr —7E 24
Jubilee Cres. E14 —3E 80
Jubilee Cres. N9 —1B 18
Jubilee Gdns. S'hall —5E 54
Jubilee Ho. SE11 —4A 78 (9H 147)
(off Reedworth St.)
Jubilee Ho. WC1 —4K 61 (3E 140)
(off Gray's Inn Rd.)
Jubilee Pl. SW3 —5C 76
Jubilee Rd. Gnfd —1B 56
Jubilee Rd. Sutt —7F 131
Jubilee St. E1 —6J 63
Jubilee Ter. N1 —2D 62
Jubilee Way. SW19 —1K 121
Jubilee Way. Sidc —2A 116
Judd St. WC1 —3J 61 (1C 140)
Jude St. E16 —6H 65
Judges Wlk. NW3 —3A 44
Juer St. SW11 —7C 76
Juglans Rd. Orp —7K 129
Julia Ct. E17 —5D 32
Julia Gdns. Bark —2D 68
Julian Av. W3 —7H 57
Julian Clo. Barn —3E 4
Julian Hill. Harr —2J 39
Julian Pl. E14 —5D 80
Julian Taylor Path. SE23 —2H 111
Julia St. NW5 —4E 44
Julien Rd. W5 —4C 72
Juliet Ho. N1 —2E 62
(off Arden Est.)
Juliette Rd. E13 —2J 65
Junction App. SE13 —3E 96
Junction App. SW11 —3C 92
Junction M. W2 —6C 60 (7C 138)
Junction Pl. W2 —6C 60 (7C 138)
(off Praed St.)
Junction Rd. E13 —2K 65
Junction Rd. N9 —1B 18
Junction Rd. N17 —3G 31
Junction Rd. N19 —4G 45
Junction Rd. W5 —4C 72
Junction Rd. Harr —5J 23
Junction Rd. S Croy —5D 134
Junction Rd. E. Romf —7E 36
Junction Rd. W. Romf —7E 36
Junction Wharf. N1 —2C 62
Juniper Clo. Barn —5A 4
Juniper Clo. Wemb —5G 41
Juniper Ct. W8 —3K 75
(off St. Marys Pl.)
Juniper Ct. Harr —1K 23
Juniper Gdns. SW16 —1G 123

Juniper La. E6 —5C 66
Juniper Rd. Ilf —3E 50
Juniper St. E1 —7J 63
Juno Way. SE14 —6K 79
Jupiter Way. N7 —6K 45
Jupp Rd. E15 —7F 49
Jupp Rd. W. E15 —1F 65
Justice Wlk. SW3 —6C 76
(off Lawrence St.)
Justin Clo. Bren —7D 72
Justin Rd. E4 —6G 19
Jute La. Enf —3F 9
Jutland Clo. N19 —1J 45
Jutland Rd. E13 —4J 65
Jutland Rd. SE6 —7E 96
Jutsums Av. Romf —6H 37
Jutsums Ct. Romf —6H 37
Jutsums La. Romf —6H 37
Juxon Clo. Harr —1F 23
Juxon St. SE11 —4K 77 (8F 146)
JVC Bus. Pk. NW2 —1C 42

Kale Rd. Eri —2E 84
Kambala Rd. SW11 —3B 92
Kangley Bri. Rd. SE26 —5B 112
Kangley Bus. Cen. SE26 —6B 112
Karen Ct. Brom —1H 127
Karen Ter. E11 —2H 49
Kashgar Rd. SE18 —4K 83
Kashmir Rd. SE7 —7B 82
Kassala Rd. SW11 —1D 92
Katharine St. Croy —3C 134
Katherine Gdns. SE9 —4B 98
Katherine Gdns. Ilf —1G 35
Katherine Rd. E7 & E6 —5A 50
Katherine Rd. Twic —7A 88
Katherine Sq. W11 —1G 75
Kathleen Av. W3 —5J 57
Kathleen Av. Wemb —7E 40
Kathleen Godfree Ct. SW19 —5J 107
Kathleen Rd. SW11 —3D 92
Kayemoor Rd. Sutt —6B 132
Kay Rd. SW9 —2J 93
Kay St. E2 —2G 63
Kay St. E15 —7F 49
Kay St. Well —1B 100
Kean Ho. SE17 —6B 78
Kean St. WC2 —6K 61 (8E 140)
Keat's Clo. NW3 —4C 44
Keat's Clo. SE1 —4F 79 (9E 148)
Keats Clo. E11 —5K 33
Keats Clo. SW19 —6B 108
Keats Clo. Enf —5E 8
Keat's Gro. NW3 —4C 44
Keats Ho. EC2 —5D 62 (6A 142)
(off Moorgate)
Keats Rd. Belv —3J 85
Keats Rd. Well —1J 99
Keats Way. Croy —6J 125
Keats Way. Gnfd —5F 55
Kebbell Ter. E7 —5K 49
(off Claremont Rd.)
Keble Clo. N'holt —5G 39
Keble Clo. Wor Pk —1B 130
Keble St. SW17 —4A 108
Kechill Gdns. Brom —7J 127
Kedeston Ct. Sutt —1K 131
Kedleston Dri. Orp —5K 129
Kedleston Wlk. E2 —3H 63
Kedyngton Ho. Edgw —2J 25
(off Burnt Oak B'way.)
Keedonwood Rd. Brom —5G 113
Keel Clo. SE16 —1K 79
Keeley Rd. Croy —2C 134
Keeley St. WC2 —6K 61 (8E 140)
Keeling Rd. SE9 —5B 98
Keely Clo. Barn —5H 5

Keemor Clo. SE18 —7E 82
Keens Clo. SW16 —5H 109
Keens Rd. Croy —4C 134
Keen's Yd. N1 —6B 46
Keep, The. SE3 —2J 97
Keep, The. King T —5F 105
Keeton's Rd. SE16 —3H 79
Keevil Dri. SW19 —7F 91
Keighley Clo. N7 —5J 45
Keightley Dri. SE9 —1G 115
Keildon Rd. SW11 —4D 92
Keir Hardie Est. E5 —1H 47
Keir Hardie Ho. N19 —7H 29
Keir Hardie Way. Bark —7A 52
Keith Connor Clo. SW8 —3F 93
Keith Gro. W12 —2C 74
Keith Rd. E17 —1B 32
Keith Rd. Bark —2H 67
Kelbrook Rd. SE3 —2C 98
Kelby Path. SE9 —3F 115
Kelceda Clo. NW2 —2C 42
Kelfield Ct. W10 —6F 59
Kelfield Gdns. W10 —6E 58
Kelfield M. W10 —6F 59
Kelland Clo. N8 —5H 29
Kelland Rd. E13 —4J 65
Kellaway Rd. SE3 —2B 98
Kellerton Rd. SE13 —5G 97
Kellett Ho. N1 —1E 62
(off Colville Est.)
Kellett Rd. SW2 —4A 94
Kelling Gdns. Croy —7B 124
Kelling Rd. SE9 —5B 98
Kellino St. SW17 —4D 108
Kellner Rd. SE28 —3K 83
Kell St. SE1 —3B 78 (6K 147)
Kelmore Gro. SE22 —4G 95
Kelmscott Clo. E17 —1B 32
Kelmscott Gdns. W12 —3C 74
Kelmscott Rd. SW11 —5C 92
Kelross Pas. N5 —4C 46
Kelross Rd. N5 —4C 46
Kelsall Clo. SE3 —2K 97
Kelsey La. Beck —2C 126
Kelsey Pk. Av. Beck —2D 126
Kelsey Pk. Rd. Beck —2C 126
Kelsey Sq. Beck —2C 126
Kelsey St. E2 —4G 63
Kelsey Way. Beck —3C 126
Kelson Ho. E14 —3E 81
Kelso Pl. W8 —3K 75
Kelso Rd. Cars —7J 121
Kelston Rd. Ilf —2F 35
Kelvedon Clo. King T —5G 105
Kelvedon Ho. SW8 —1J 93
Kelvedon Rd. SW6 —7H 75
Kelvedon Way. Wfd G —6J 21
Kelvin Av. N13 —6E 16
Kelvin Clo. Eps —6G 129
Kelvin Cres. Harr —7D 10
Kelvin Dri. Twic —6B 88
Kelvin Gdns. Croy —7K 123
Kelvin Gdns. S'hall —6E 54
Kelvin Gro. SE26 —3H 111
Kelvington Clo. Croy —7A 126
Kelvington Rd. SE15 —5K 95
Kelvin Rd. N5 —4C 46
Kelvin Rd. Well —3A 100
Kember St. N1 —7K 45
Kemble Ct. SE15 —7E 78
(off Ludney Rd.)
Kemble Ho. SW9 —3B 94
(off Barrington Rd.)

Kemble Rd. N17 —1G 31
Kemble Rd. SE23 —1K 111
Kemble Rd. Croy —3B 134
Kemble St. WC2 —6K 61 (8E 140)
Kemerton Rd. SE5 —3C 94
Kemerton Rd. Beck —2D 126
Kemerton Rd. Croy —7F 125
Kemeys St. E9 —5A 48
Kemnal Rd. Chst —7G 115
Kemp, NW9 —1B 26
(off Concourse, The)
Kemp Ct. SW8 —7J 77
(off Hartington Rd.)
Kempe Rd. NW6 —2F 59
Kemp Gdns. Croy —6C 124
Kemp Ho. E6 —6E 50
Kempis Way. SE22 —5E 94
Kemplay Rd. NW3 —4B 44
Kemp Rd. Dag —1D 52
Kemps Dri. E14 —7C 64
Kempsford Gdns. SW5 —5J 75
Kempsford Rd. SE11
—4A 78 (9H 147)
Kemps Gdns. SE13 —5E 96
Kempshott Rd. SW16 —7H 109
Kempson Rd. SW6 —1J 91
Kempthorne Rd. SE8 —4B 80
Kempton Av. N'holt —6E 38
Kempton Av. S'hall —7A 102
Kempton Clo. Eri —6J 85
Kempton Clo. S'hall —7A 102
Kempton Rd. E6 —1D 66
Kempton Wlk. Croy —6A 126
Kempt St. SE18 —6E 82
Kemsing Clo. Bex —7E 100
Kemsing Clo. Brom —2H 137
Kemsing Clo. T Hth —4C 124
Kemsing Rd. SE10 —5J 81
Kenbury St. SE5 —2C 94
Kenchester Clo. SW8 —7J 77
Kencot Way. Eri —2F 85
Kendal Av. N18 —4J 17
Kendal Av. W3 —4G 57
(in two parts)
Kendal Av. Bark —1J 67
Kendal Clo. SW9 —7B 78
Kendal Clo. Wfd G —2C 20
Kendal Ct. W3 —5G 57
Kendale Rd. Brom —5G 113
Kendal Gdns. N18 —4J 17
Kendal Gdns. Sutt —2A 132
Kendale Av. Beck —2A 126
Kendall Av. S Croy —7D 134
Kendall Pl. W1 —5E 60
Kendall Rd. Beck —2A 126
Kendall Rd. Iswth —2A 88
Kendalmere Clo. N10 —1F 29
Kendal Pde. N18 —4J 17
Kendal Pl. SW15 —5H 91
Kendal Pl. W1 —5E 60 (6G 139)
Kendal Rd. NW10 —4C 42
Kendal St. W2 —6C 60 (8D 138)
Kender St. SE14 —7J 79
Kendoa Rd. SW4 —4H 93
Kendon Clo. E11 —5K 33
Kendra Hall Rd. S Croy —7B 134
Kendrey Gdns. Twic —7J 87
Kendrick M. SW7 —4B 76 (8A 144)
Kendrick Pl. SW7 —4B 76 (9A 144)
Kenelm Clo. Harr —3A 40
Kenerne Dri. Barn —5B 4
Kenilford Rd. SW12 —7F 93
Kenilworth Av. E17 —2C 32
Kenilworth Av. SW19 —5J 107
Kenilworth Av. Harr —4D 38
Kenilworth Clo. Barn —5F 5

Kenilworth Gdns. SE18 —2F 99
Kenilworth Gdns. Ilf —2K 51
Kenilworth Gdns. S'hall —3D 54
Kenilworth Rd. E3 —2A 64
Kenilworth Rd. NW6 —1H 59
Kenilworth Rd. SE20 —1K 125
Kenilworth Rd. W5 —1E 72
Kenilworth Rd. Edgw —3D 12
Kenilworth Rd. Eps —5C 130
Kenilworth Rd. Orp —6G 129
Kenley Av. NW9 —1A 26
Kenley Clo. Barn —4H 5
Kenley Clo. Bex —7G 101
Kenley Clo. Chst —3J 129
Kenley Gdns. T Hth —4B 124
Kenley Rd. SW19 —2J 121
Kenley Rd. King T —2H 119
Kenley Rd. Twic —6B 88
Kenley Wlk. W11 —7G 59
Kenley Wlk. Sutt —4F 131
Kenlor Rd. SW17 —5B 108
Kenmare Dri. Mitc —7D 108
Kenmare Gdns. N13 —4H 17
Kenmare Rd. T Hth —6A 124
Kenmere Gdns. Wemb —1G 57
Kenmere Rd. Well —2C 100
Kenmore Av. Harr —4A 24
Kenmore Clo. Rich —7G 73
Kenmore Gdns. Edgw —2H 25
Kenmore Rd. Harr —3D 24
Kenmore Rd. E8 —5H 47
Kenmure Yd. E8 —5H 47
Kennard Rd. E15 —7F 49
Kennard Rd. N11 —5J 15
Kennard St. E16 —1D 82
Kennard St. SW11 —1E 92
Kennedy Av. Enf —6D 8
Kennedy Clo. E13 —2J 65
Kennedy Clo. Mitc —2E 122
Kennedy Clo. Orp —7H 129
Kennedy Clo. Pinn —6D 10
Kennedy Ct. Beck —6B 126
Kennedy Ct. Bush —2C 10
Kennedy Clo. Croy —6B 126
Kennedy Ho. SE11 —5K 77
(off Vauxhall Wlk.)
Kennedy Path. W7 —4K 55
Kennedy Rd. W7 —5J 55
Kennedy Rd. Bark —1J 67
Kennedy Wlk. SE17 —4D 78 (9B 148)
(off Tisdall Pl.)
Kennet Clo. SW11 —4B 92
Kenneth Av. Ilf —4F 51
Kenneth Ct. SE11 —4A 78 (8H 147)
Kenneth Cres. NW2 —5D 42
Kenneth Gdns. Stan —6F 11
Kenneth More Rd. Ilf —3F 51
Kenneth Rd. Romf —7D 36
Kenneth Robbins Ho. N17 —7C 18
Kennet Rd. Iswth —3K 87
Kennet Sq. Mitc —1C 122
Kennet St. E1 —1G 79
Kennett Ct. W4 —7H 73
Kennett Dri. Hay —6C 54
Kenninghall Rd. E5 —3G 47
Kenninghall Rd. N18 —5D 18
Kenning St. SE16 —2J 79
Kennings Way. SE11 —5A 78
Kenning Ter. N1 —1E 62
Kennington Grn. SE11 —5A 78
Kennington Gro. SE11 —6K 77
Kennington La. SE11 —5K 77
Kennington Oval. SE11 —6K 77
Kennington Pal. Ct. SE11 —5A 78
(off Sancroft St.)
Kennington Pk. Gdns. SE11 —6B 78
Kennington Pk. Pl. SE11 —6A 78
Kennington Pk. Rd. SE11 —6A 78

King George's Dri. S'hall —5D 54
King George VI Av. Mitc —4D 122
King George Sq. Rich —6F 89
King George St. SE10 —7E 80
Kingham Clo. W11 —2G 75
King Harolds Way. Bexh —7D 84
King Henry's Dri. New Ad —7D 136
King Henry's Rd. NW3 —7D 44
King Henry's Rd. King T —3H 119
King Henry St. N16 —5E 46
King Henry's Wlk. N1 —6E 46
Kinghorn St. EC1 —5C 62 (6L 141)
King James St. SE1
      —2B 78 (5K 147)
King John St. EC2 —4G 62 (3D 142)
King John's Wlk. SE9 —1B 114
Kinglake Est. SE17 —5E 78
Kinglake St. SE17 —5E 78
Kingly Ct. W1 —7G 61 (9M 139)
   (off Beak St.)
Kingly St. W1 —6G 61 (8H 139)
King & Queen St. SE17 —5C 78
Kingsand Rd. SE12 —2J 113
Kings Arbour. S'hall —5C 70
King's Arms All. Bren —6D 72
Kings Arms Yd. EC2
      —6D 62 (7A 142)
Kingsash Dri. Hay —4C 54
King's Av. N10 —3E 28
Kings Av. N21 —1G 17
King's Av. SW12 & SW4 —1H 109
Kings Av. W5 —6D 56
Kings Av. Brom —6H 113
King's Av. Buck H —2G 21
King's Av. Cars —7C 132
Kings Av. Gnfd —5F 55
Kings Av. Houn —1F 87
Kings Av. N Mald —4A 120
Kings Av. Romf —6F 37
King's Av. Wfd G —6E 20
King's Bench St. SE1
      —2B 78 (4K 147)
King's Bench Wlk. EC4
      —7A 62 (9H 141)
Kingsbridge Av. W3 —2F 73
Kingsbridge Cres. S'hall —5D 54
Kingsbridge Rd. W10 —6E 58
Kingsbridge Rd. Bark —2H 67
Kingsbridge Rd. Mord —7F 121
Kingsbridge Rd. S'hall —4D 70
Kingsbury Circ. NW9 —5G 25
Kingsbury Rd. N1 —6E 46
Kingsbury Rd. NW9 —5G 25
Kingsbury Ter. N1 —6E 46
Kingsbury Trading Est. NW9 —6K 25
Kingsclere Clo. SW15 —7C 90
Kingsclere Ct. N12 —5H 15
Kingscliffe Gdns. SW19 —1H 107
Kings Clo. E10 —7D 32
King's Clo. NW4 —4F 27
King's Clo. Dart —4K 101
King's College Rd. NW3 —7C 44
Kingscote Rd. W4 —3K 73
Kingscote Rd. Croy —7H 125
Kingscote Rd. N Mald —3K 119
Kingscote St. EC4 —7B 62 (9J 141)
King's Ct. E13 —1K 65
King's Ct. SE1 —2B 78 (4K 147)
Kings Ct. W6 —4C 74
   (off King St.)
Kings Ct. N. SW3 —5C 76
Kings Ct. S. SW3 —5C 76
   (off King's Rd.)
King's Cres. N4 —3C 46
Kings Cres. Est. N4 —2C 46
Kingscroft. SW4 —6J 93

Kingscroft Rd. NW2 —6H 43
King's Cross Bri. N1 —3J 61 (1D 140)
   (off Gray's Inn Rd.)
King's Cross Rd. WC1
      —3K 61 (1E 140)
Kingsdale Gdns. W11 —1F 75
Kingsdale Rd. SE18 —7K 83
Kingsdale Rd. SE20 —7K 111
Kingsdown Av. W3 —7A 58
Kingsdown Av. W13 —2B 72
Kingsdown Av. S Croy —7C 134
Kingsdown Clo. W10 —6F 59
Kingsdowne Rd. Surb —7E 118
Kingsdown Rd. E11 —3G 49
Kingsdown Rd. N19 —2J 45
Kingsdown Rd. Sutt —5G 131
Kingsdown Way. Brom —6J 127
King's Dri. Edgw —4A 12
King's Dri. Surb —7G 119
Kings Dri. Tedd —5H 103
Kings Dri. Th Dit —6B 118
Kings Dri. Wemb —2H 41
Kings Farm Av. Rich —4G 89
Kingsfield Av. Harr —4F 23
Kingsfield Rd. Harr —7H 23
Kingsfield Ter. Harr —1H 39
Kingsford St. NW5 —5D 44
Kingsford Way. E6 —5D 66
King's Gdns. NW6 —7J 43
Kings Gdns. Ilf —1H 51
Kings Garth M. SE23 —2J 111
Kingsgate. Wemb —3J 41
Kingsgate Av. N3 —3J 27
Kingsgate Clo. Bexh —1E 100
Kingsgate Est. N1 —6E 46
Kingsgate Ho. SW9 —1A 94
Kingsgate Pde. SW1
   (off Victoria St.) —3G 77 (7M 145)
Kingsgate Pl. NW6 —7J 43
Kingsgate Rd. NW6 —7J 43
Kingsgate Rd. King T —1E 118
Kingsground. SE9 —7B 98
King's Gro. SE15 —1H 95
   (in two parts)
Kings Hall Rd. Beck —7A 112
Kings Head Ct. EC3 —7D 62 (1B 148)
   (off Pudding La.)
Kings Head Hill. E4 —7J 9
Kings Head Pas. SW4 —4H 93
   (off Clapham Pk. Rd.)
King's Head Yd. SE1
      —1D 78 (3A 148)
King's Highway. SE18 —6J 83
Kingshill Av. Harr —4B 24
Kingshill Av. N'holt —3A 54
Kingshill Av. Wor Pk —7C 120
Kingshill Ct. Barn —4B 4
Kingshill Dri. Harr —3B 24
Kingshold Rd. E9 —7J 47
Kingsholm Gdns. SE9 —4B 98
Kings Ho. SW8 —7J 77
   (off South Lambeth Rd.)
Kingshurst Rd. SE12 —7J 97
Kings Keep. Brom —3G 127
Kings Keep. King T —4E 118
Kingsland Grn. E8 —6E 46
Kingsland Gro. N16 —6E 46
Kingsland High St. E8 —6F 47
Kingsland Pas. E8 —6E 46
Kingsland Rd. E2 & E8
      —3E 62 (2D 142)
Kingsland Rd. E13 —3A 66
Kings La. Sutt —5B 132
Kingslawn Clo. SW15 —5D 90
Kingsleigh Pl. Mitc —3D 122
Kingsleigh Wlk. Brom —4H 127

Kingsley Av. W13 —6A 56
Kingsley Av. Houn —2G 87
Kingsley Av. S'hall —7E 54
Kingsley Av. Sutt —4B 132
Kingsley Clo. N2 —5A 28
Kingsley Clo. Dag —4H 53
Kingsley Ct. Bexh —5G 101
Kingsley Ct. Edgw —2C 12
Kingsley Ct. Sutt —7K 131
Kingsley Ct. Wor Pk —2B 130
   (off Avenue, The)
Kingsley Dri. Wor Pk —2B 130
Kingsley Flats. SE1 —4E 78 (8C 148)
Kingsley Gdns. E4 —5H 19
Kingsley M. E1 —7H 63
Kingsley M. W8 —3K 75
Kingsley Pl. N6 —7E 28
Kingsley Rd. E7 —7J 49
Kingsley Rd. E17 —2E 32
Kingsley Rd. N13 —4F 17
Kingsley Rd. NW6 —1H 59
Kingsley Rd. SW19 —5K 107
Kingsley Rd. Croy —1A 134
Kingsley Rd. Harr —4G 39
Kingsley Rd. Houn —1F 87
Kingsley Rd. Ilf —1G 35
Kingsley Rd. Pinn —4D 22
Kingsley St. SW11 —3D 92
Kingsley Way. N2 —6A 28
Kingsley Wood Dri. SE9 —3D 114
Kingslyn Cres. SE19 —2E 124
Kings Mall. W6 —4E 74
Kingsman Pde. SE18 —3D 82
Kingsman St. SE18 —3D 82
Kingsmead. Barn —4D 4
Kings Mead. Rich —6F 89
Kingsmead Av. N9 —1C 18
Kingsmead Av. NW9 —7K 25
Kingsmead Av. Mitc —3G 123
Kingsmead Av. Wor Pk —2D 130
Kingsmead Clo. Eps —7A 130
Kingsmead Clo. Sidc —2A 116
Kingsmead Clo. Tedd —6B 104
Kingsmead Ct. N6 —7H 29
Kingsmead Dri. N'holt —7D 38
Kingsmead Ho. E9 —4A 48
Kingsmeadow. King T —3H 119
Kingsmead Rd. SW2 —2A 110
King's Mead Way. E9 —4A 48
Kingsmere Clo. SW15 —3F 91
Kingsmere Pk. NW9 —1H 41
Kingsmere Rd. SW19 —2F 107
King's M. SW4 —5J 93
King's M. WC1 —4K 61 (4F 140)
Kingsmill Gdns. Dag —5F 53
Kingsmill Rd. Dag —5F 53
Kingsmill Ter. NW8 —2B 60
Kingsnorth Ho. W10 —6F 59
Kingsnympton Pk. King T —6H 105
King's Orchard. SE9 —6C 98
King's Paddock. Hamp —7G 103
Kingspark Ct. E18 —3J 33
Kings Pas. King T —2D 118
King's Pl. SE1 —2C 78 (5L 147)
King's Pl. W4 —5J 73
Kings Pl. Buck H —2F 21
Kings Sq. EC1 —3C 62 (2L 141)
King's Quay. SW10 —1A 92
   (off Chelsea Harbour)
Kings Reach Tower. SE1
   (off Stamford St.) —1B 78 (2J 147)
Kings Ride Ga. Rich —4G 89
Kingsridge. SW19 —2G 107
Kings Rd. E4 —1A 20
King's Rd. E6 —1A 66
Kings Rd. E11 —7G 33
King's Rd. N17 —1F 31
King's Rd. N18 —5B 18

Kings Rd. N22 —1K 29
King's Rd. NW10 —7D 42
Kings Rd. SE25 —3G 125
King's Rd. SW3 —6B 76
King's Rd. SW6 & SW10 —7K 75
Kings Rd. SW14 —3K 89
Kings Rd. SW19 —6J 107
Kings Rd. W5 —5D 56
Kings Rd. Bark —7G 51
Kings Rd. Barn —3A 4
Kings Rd. Felt —1A 102
Kings Rd. Harr —2D 38
King's Rd. King T —1E 118
Kings Rd. Mitc —3E 122
Kings Rd. Rich —6F 89
King's Rd. Surb —7C 118
King's Rd. Tedd —5H 103
Kings Rd. Twic —6B 88
Kings Rd. Bungalows. S Harr —3D 38
King's Scholars' Pas. SW1
   (off Carlisle Pl.) —3G 77 (7L 145)
King Stairs Clo. SE16 —2H 79
King's Ter. NW1 —1G 61
King's Ter. Iswth —4A 88
Kingston Av. Sutt —3G 131
Kingston Bri. King T —2D 118
Kingston By-Pass. SW15 & SW20
      —5A 106
Kingston Clo. N'holt —1D 54
Kingston Clo. Romf —3E 35
Kingston Clo. Tedd —6B 104
Kingston Cres. Beck —1B 126
Kingston Gdns. Croy —3J 133
Kingston Hall Rd. King T —3D 118
Kingston Hill. King T —1G 119
Kingston Hill Av. Romf —2E 35
Kingston Hill Pl. King T —4K 105
Kingston Ho. Est. Surb —6C 118
Kingston La. Tedd —5A 104
Kingston Pl. Harr —7E 10
Kingston Rd. N9 —2B 18
Kingston Rd. SW15 —2C 106
Kingston Rd. SW20 & SW19
      —2E 120
Kingston Rd. Barn —5G 5
Kingston Rd. Eps —7B 130
Kingston Rd. Ilf —4F 51
Kingston Rd. King T & N Mald
      —3H 119
Kingston Rd. S'hall —2D 70
Kingston Rd. Tedd —5B 104
Kingston Rd. Wor P —4A 130
Kingston Sq. SE19 —5D 110
Kingston Vale. SW15 —4K 105
Kingstown St. NW1 —1E 60
King St. E13 —4J 65
King St. EC2 —6C 62 (8M 141)
King St. N2 —3B 28
King St. N17 —1F 31
King St. SW1 —1G 77 (3M 145)
King St. W3 —1H 73
King St. W6 —4C 74
King St. WC2 —7J 61 (9C 140)
King St. Rich —5D 88
King St. S'hall —3C 70
King St. Twic —1A 104
King's Wlk. King T —1D 118
Kingswater Pl. SW11 —7C 76
Kingsway. N12 —6F 15
Kingsway. WC2 —6K 61 (7E 140)
King's Way. Croy —5K 133
Kingsway. Enf —6C 8
Kings Way. Harr —4J 23
Kingsway. N Mald —5E 120
Kingsway. Orp —5H 129
Kingsway. Wemb —4E 40

Kings Way. Wfd G —5F 21
Kingsway. W Wick —3G 137
Kingsway Bus. Pk. Hamp —7D 102
Kingsway Cres. Harr —4G 23
Kingsway Rd. Sutt —7G 131
Kingswear Rd. NW5 —3F 45
Kingswood Av. NW6 —1G 59
Kingswood Av. Belv —4F 85
Kingswood Av. Brom —4G 127
Kingswood Av. Hamp —6F 103
Kingswood Av. Houn —2D 86
Kingswood Av. T Hth —5A 124
Kingswood Clo. N20 —7F 5
Kingswood Clo. SW8 —7J 77
Kingswood Clo. Enf —5K 7
Kingswood Clo. N Mald —6B 120
Kingswood Clo. Orp —7H 129
Kingswood Clo. Surb —7E 118
Kingswood Dri. SE19 —4E 110
Kingswood Dri. Cars —1D 132
Kingswood Dri. Sutt —7K 131
Kingswood Est. SE21 —4E 110
Kingswood Pk. N3 —1H 27
Kingswood Pl. SE13 —4G 97
Kingswood Rd. E11 —7G 33
Kingswood Rd. SE20 —6J 111
Kingswood Rd. SW2 —6J 93
Kingswood Rd. SW19 —7H 107
Kingswood Rd. W4 —3J 73
Kingswood Rd. Brom —4F 127
Kingswood Rd. Ilf —1A 52
Kingswood Rd. Wemb —3G 41
Kingswood Way. Wall —5J 133
Kingsworth Clo. Beck —5A 126
Kingsworthy Clo. King T —3F 119
Kingthorpe Rd. NW10 —7K 41
Kingthorpe Ter. NW10 —2B 58
   (off Rucklidge Av.)
Kingwell Rd. Barn —1G 5
King William IV Gdns. SE20 —6J 111
King William La. SE10 —5G 81
King William St. EC4
      —6D 62 (9B 142)
King William Wlk. SE10 —6E 80
   (in two parts)
Kingwood Rd. SW6 —1G 91
Kinlet Rd. SE18 —1G 99
Kinloch Dri. NW9 —7K 25
Kinloch St. N7 —3K 45
Kinloss Ct. N3 —4H 27
Kinloss Gdns. N3 —3H 27
Kinloss Rd. Cars —7A 122
Kinnaird Av. W4 —7J 73
Kinnaird Av. Brom —6H 113
Kinnaird Clo. Brom —6H 113
Kinnaird Way. Wfd G —6J 21
Kinnear Rd. W12 —2B 74
Kinnerton Pl. N. SW1
   (off Kinnerton St.) —2D 76 (5F 144)
Kinnerton Pl. S. SW1
   (off Kinnerton St.) —2D 76 (5F 144)
Kinnerton St. SW1 —2E 76 (5G 145)
Kinnerton Yd. SW1 —2E 76 (5G 145)
   (off Kinnerton St.)
Kinnoul Rd. W6 —6G 75
Kinross Av. Wor Pk —2C 130
Kinross Clo. Edgw —2C 12
Kinross Clo. Harr —5E 24
Kinsale Rd. SE15 —3G 95
Kintore Way. SE1 —4F 79 (8E 148)
Kintyre Clo. SW16 —2K 123
Kintyre Ct. SW2 —7J 93
Kinveachy Gdns. SE7 —5C 82
Kinver Rd. SE26 —4J 111
Kipling Ct. W7 —7K 55
Kipling Dri. SW19 —6B 108
Kipling Est. SE1 —2D 78 (5B 148)
   (off Kipling St.)
Kipling Est. SW1 —2D 78

Kipling Pl. Stan —6E 10
Kipling Rd. Bexh —1E 100
Kipling St. SE1 —2D 78 (5B 148)
Kipling St. SW1 —2D 78
Kipling Ter. N9 —3J 17
Kippington Dri. SE9 —1B 114
Kirby Clo. Eps —5B 130
Kirby Clo. Lou —1H 21
Kirby Est. SE16 —3H 79
Kirby Gro. SE1 —2E 78 (4C 148)
Kirby St. EC1 —5A 62 (5H 141)
Kirchen Rd. W13 —7B 56
Kirkdale. SE26 —2H 111
Kirkdale Rd. E11 —1G 49
Kirkham Rd. E6 —6C 66
Kirkham St. SE18 —6J 83
Kirkland Av. Ilf —2E 34
Kirkland Clo. Sidc —6J 99
Kirkland Wlk. E8 —6F 47
Kirk La. SE18 —6G 83
Kirkleas Rd. Surb —7E 118
Kirklees Rd. Dag —5C 52
Kirklees Rd. T Hth —5A 124
Kirkley Rd. SW19 —1J 121
Kirkly Clo. S Croy —7E 134
Kirkman Pl. W1 —5H 61 (6A 140)
  (off Tottenham Ct. Rd.)
Kirkmichael Rd. E14 —6E 64
Kirk Rise. Sutt —3K 131
Kirk Rd. E17 —6B 32
Kirkside Rd. SE3 —6J 81
Kirk's Pl. E14 —5B 64
Kirkstall Av. N17 —4D 30
Kirkstall Gdns. SW2 —1J 109
Kirkstall Rd. SW2 —1H 109
Kirksted Rd. Mord —1K 131
Kirkstone Way. Brom —7G 113
Kirk St. WC1 —4K 61 (4F 140)
  (off Northington St.)
Kirkton Rd. N15 —4E 30
Kirkwall Pl. E2 —3J 63
Kirkwood La. NW1 —7E 44
Kirkwood Rd. SE15 —2H 95
Kirtley Rd. SE26 —4A 112
Kirtling St. SW8 —7G 77
Kirton Clo. W4 —4K 73
Kirton Gdns. E2 —3F 63 (2F 142)
Kirton Rd. E13 —2A 66
Kirton Wlk. Edgw —7D 12
Kirwyn Way. SE5 —7C 78
Kitcat Ter. E3 —3C 64
Kitchener Rd. E7 —6K 49
Kitchener Rd. E17 —1D 32
Kitchener Rd. N2 —3C 28
Kitchener Rd. N17 —3E 30
Kitchener Rd. Dag —6J 53
Kitchener Rd. T Hth —3D 124
Kite Pl. E2 —3G 63
  (off Lampern St.)
Kite Yd. SW11 —1D 92
Kitley Gdns. SE19 —1F 125
Kitson Rd. SE5 —7D 78
Kitson Rd. SW13 —1C 90
Kittiwake Rd. N'holt —3B 54
Kittiwake Way. Hay —5B 54
Kitto Rd. SE14 —2K 95
Kitts End Rd. Barn —1C 4
Kiver Rd. N19 —2H 45
Klea Av. SW4 —6G 93
Knaersborough Pl. SW5 —4K 75
Knapdale Clo. SE23 —2H 111
Knapmill Rd. SE6 —2C 112
Knapmill Way. SE6 —2D 112
Knapp Clo. NW10 —6A 42
Knapp Rd. E3 —4C 64
Knapton M. SW17 —6E 108
Knaresborough Pl. SW5 —4K 75
Knatchbull Rd. NW10 —1K 57

Knatchbull Rd. SE5 —2B 94
Knebworth Av. E17 —1C 32
Knebworth Ho. SW8 —1H 93
Knebworth Rd. N16 —4E 46
Knee Hill. SE2 —4C 84
Kneehill Cres. SE2 —4C 84
Kneller Gdns. Iswth —6H 87
Kneller Rd. SE4 —4A 96
Kneller Rd. N Mald —7A 120
Kneller Rd. Twic —6G 87
Knighten St. E1 —1H 79
Knighthead Point. E14 —2C 80
Knighthorpe Rd. NW10 —7K 41
Knightland Rd. E5 —2H 47
Knighton Clo. Romf —6K 37
Knighton Clo. S Croy —7B 134
Knighton Clo. Wfd G —4E 20
Knighton Dri. Wfd G —4E 20
Knighton La. Buck H —2E 20
Knighton Pk. Rd. SE26 —5K 111
Knighton Rd. E7 —3J 49
Knighton Rd. Romf —6J 37
Knightrider Ct. EC4 —7C 62 (9L 141)
  (off Knightrider St.)
Knightrider St. EC4 —6B 62 (9K 141)
Knight's Arc. SW1 —2D 76 (5E 144)
  (off Knightsbridge)
Knights Av. W5 —2E 72
Knightsbridge. SW7 & SW1
  —2C 76 (5C 144)
Knightsbridge Ct. SW1
  (off Sloane St.) —2D 76 (5F 144)
Knightsbridge Gdns. Romf —5K 37
Knightsbridge Grn. SW1
  —2D 76 (5E 144)
Knights Clo. E9 —5J 47
Knights Ct. Brom —3H 113
Knights Ct. King T —3E 118
Knights Hill. SE27 —5B 110
Knight's Hill Sq. SE27 —4B 110
Knights La. N9 —3B 18
Knight's Pk. King T —3E 118
Knight's Rd. E16 —2J 81
Knights Rd. Stan —4H 11
Knights Wlk. SE11 —4B 78 (9J 147)
Knightswood Clo. Edgw —2D 12
Knightswood Ct. N6 —7H 29
Knightwood Cres. N Mald —6A 120
Knivet Rd. SW6 —6J 75
Knobs Hill Rd. E15 —1D 64
Knockholt Rd. SE9 —5B 98
Knolls Clo. Wor Pk —3D 130
Knoll, The. W5 —5C 56
Knoll, The. Beck —1D 126
Knoll, The. Brom —1J 137
Knollys Clo. SW16 —3A 110
Knollys Rd. SW16 —3A 110
Knottisford St. E2 —3J 63
Knotts Grn. Rd. E10 —6D 32
Knowle Av. Bexh —7E 84
Knowle Clo. SW9 —3A 94
Knowle Rd. Twic —1J 103
Knowles Ct. Harr —6K 23
  (off Gayton Rd.)
Knowles Hill Cres. SE13 —5F 97
Knowles Wlk. SW4 —3G 93
Knowlton Grn. Brom —5H 127

Knowlton Ho. SW9 —1B 94
  (off Cowley Rd.)
Knowsley Av. S'hall —1F 71
Knowsley Rd. SW11 —2D 92
Knox Ct. SW4 —2J 93
Knox Rd. E7 —6H 49
Knox St. W1 —5D 60 (5E 138)
Knoyle St. SE14 —6A 80
Koblenz Ho. N8 —3J 29
  (off Newland Rd.)
Kohat Rd. SW19 —5K 107
Komeheather Ho. Ilf —5D 34
Kossuth St. SE10 —5G 81
Kotree Way. SE1 —4G 79
Kramer M. SW5 —5J 75
Kreisel Wlk. Rich —6F 73
Kristina Ct. Sutt —7J 131
  (off Overton Rd.)
Krupnik Pl. EC2 —4E 62 (3D 142)
  (off Krupnik Pl.)
Kuala Gdns. SW16 —1K 123
Kuhn Way. E7 —5J 49
Kydbrook Clo. Orp —7G 129
Kylemore Clo. E6 —2B 66
Kylemore Rd. NW6 —7J 43
Kymberley Rd. Harr —6J 23
Kymes Ct. S Harr —2H 39
Kynance Gdns. Stan —1C 24
Kynance M. SW7 —3K 75
Kynance Pl. SW7 —3A 76
Kynaston Av. N16 —3F 47
Kynaston Av. T Hth —5C 124
Kynaston Clo. Harr —7C 10
Kynaston Cres. T Hth —5C 124
Kynaston Rd. N16 —3E 45
Kynaston Rd. Brom —5J 113
Kynaston Rd. Enf —1J 7
Kynaston Rd. T Hth —5C 124
Kynaston Wood. Harr —7C 10
Kynnersley Clo. Cars —3D 132
Kynoch Rd. N18 —4D 18
Kyrle Rd. SW11 —6E 92
Kyverdale Rd. N16 —1F 47

Laburnam Av. N9 —2A 18
Laburnum Av. N17 —7J 17
Laburnam Av. Sutt —3C 132
Laburnum Clo. E4 —6G 19
Laburnum Clo. N11 —6A 16
Laburnum Clo. SE15 —7J 79
Laburnum Ct. E2 —1F 63
Laburnam Ct. SE16 —2J 79
  (off Albion St.)
Laburnum Ct. SE19 —1F 125
Laburnum Ct. Harr —6F 23
Laburnum Ct. Stan —4H 11
Laburnum Cres. Sun —7A 102
Laburnum Gdns. N21 —2H 17
Laburnum Gdns. Croy —1K 135
Laburnum Gro. N21 —2H 17
Laburnum Gro. NW9 —7J 25
Laburnum Gro. Houn —4D 86
Laburnum Gro. N Mald —2K 119
Laburnum Gro. S'hall —4D 54
Laburnum Ho. Brom —1G 127
Laburnum Lodge. N3 —2H 27
Laburnum Rd. SW19 —7A 108
Laburnum Rd. Mitc —2E 122
Laburnum St. E2 —1F 63
Laburnum Way. Brom —7E 128

Lacon Rd. SE22 —4G 95
Lacy Rd. SW15 —4F 91
Ladas Rd. SE27 —4C 110
Ladbroke Cres. W11 —6G 59
Ladbroke Gdns. W11 —7H 59
Ladbroke Gro. W10 & W11 —4F 59
Ladbroke M. W11 —1G 75
Ladbroke Rd. W11 —1H 75
Ladbroke Rd. Enf —6A 8
Ladbroke Sq. W11 —7H 59
Ladbroke Ter. W11 —7H 59
Ladbroke Wlk. W11 —1H 75
Ladbrook Clo. Pinn —5D 22
Ladbrook Ct. SE13 —3D 116
Ladbrook Rd. SE25 —4D 124
Ladderstile Ride. King T —5H 105
Ladderswood. N11 —5B 16
Lady Booth Rd. King T —2E 118
Ladycroft Rd. SE13 —3D 96
Ladycroft Wlk. Stan —1D 24
Lady Dock Wlk. SE16 —2A 80
Ladygrove. Croy —7A 136
Lady Hay. Wor Pk —2B 130
Lady Margaret Rd. NW5 & N19
  —5G 45
Lady Margaret Rd. S'hall —7D 54
Lady Shaw Ct. N13 —2E 16
Ladyship Ter. SE22 —7G 95
Ladysmith Av. E6 —2C 66
Ladysmith Av. Ilf —7H 35
Ladysmith Rd. E16 —3H 65
Ladysmith Rd. N17 —2G 31
Ladysmith Rd. N18 —5C 18
Ladysmith Rd. SE9 —6E 98
Ladysmith Rd. Enf —3K 7
Ladysmith Rd. Harr —2J 23
Lady Somerset Rd. NW5 —4F 45
Ladywell Clo. SE4 —5C 96
Ladywell Heights. SE4 —6B 96
Ladywell Rd. SE13 —5C 96
Ladywell St. E15 —1H 65
Ladywood Av. Orp —5J 129
Lafone Av. Felt —2A 102
Lafone St. SE1 —2F 79 (4E 148)
Lagado M. SE16 —1K 79
Lagan Ho. SE15 —7G 79
  (off Sumner Est.)
Laing Dean. N'holt —1A 54
Laing Ho. SE5 —7C 78
Laings Av. Mitc —2D 122
Lainlock Pl. Houn —1F 87
Lainson St. SW18 —7J 91
Lairdale Clo. SE21 —1C 110
Lairs Clo. N7 —5J 45
Laitwood Rd. SW12 —1F 109
Lake Av. Brom —6J 113
Lake Bus. Cen. N17 —7B 18
Lakedale Rd. SE18 —6J 83
Lake Dri. Bush —2B 10
Lakefield Rd. N22 —2B 30
Lake Footpath. SE2 —2D 84
Lake Gdns. Dag —5G 53
Lake Gdns. Rich —2B 104
Lake Gdns. Wall —3F 133
Lakehall Gdns. T Hth —5B 124
Lakehall Rd. T Hth —5B 124
Lake Ho. Rd. E11 —3J 49
Lakehurst Rd. Eps —5A 130
Lakeland Clo. Harr —6C 10
Lakenheath. N14 —5B 6
Laker Ct. SW4 —1J 93
Lake Rd. SW19 —5H 107
Lake Rd. Croy —2B 136
Lake Rd. Romf —4D 36
Laker Pl. SW15 —6H 91
Lakeside. N3 —2K 27
Lakeside. SE2 —3D 84
Lakeside. W13 —6C 56

Lakeside. Beck —3D 126
Lakeside. Enf —4C 6
Lakeside. Eps —6A 130
Lakeside. Wall —4F 133
Lakeside Av. Ilf —4B 34
Lakeside Clo. SE25 —2G 125
Lakeside Clo. Sidc —5C 100
Lakeside Ct. N4 —2C 46
Lakeside Cres. Barn —5J 5
Lakeside Rd. N13 —4E 16
Lakeside Rd. W14 —3F 75
Lakeside Ter. EC2 —5C 62 (5M 141)
  (off Barbican)
Lakeside Way. Wemb —4G 41
Lakeswood Rd. Orp —6G 129
Lake, The. Bush —1C 10
Lake View. Edgw —5A 12
Lake View Est. E3 —2A 64
Lakeview Rd. SE27 —5A 110
Lakeview Rd. Well —4B 100
Lakis Clo. NW3 —4A 44
Laleham Av. NW7 —3E 12
Laleham Rd. SE6 —7E 96
Lalor St. SW6 —2G 91
Lambarde Av. SE9 —4E 114
Lamberhurst Rd. SE27 —4A 110
Lamberhurst Rd. Dag —1F 53
Lambert Av. Rich —3G 89
Lambert Jones M. EC2
  (off Barbican) —5C 62 (5L 141)
Lambert Lodge. Bren —5D 72
  (off Layton Rd.)
Lambert Rd. E16 —6K 65
Lambert Rd. N12 —5G 15
Lambert Rd. SW2 —5J 93
Lambert's Pl. Croy —1D 134
Lamberts Rd. Surb —5F 119
Lambert St. N1 —7A 46
Lambert Wlk. Wemb —3D 40
Lambert Way. N12 —5F 15
Lambeth Bri. SW1 & SE1
  —4J 77 (8D 146)
Lambeth High St. SE1
  —4K 77 (9E 146)
Lambeth Hill. EC4 —7C 62 (9L 141)
Lambeth Pal. Rd. SE1
  —3K 77 (7E 146)
Lambeth Rd. SE1 —3K 77 (8E 146)
Lambeth Rd. Croy —1A 134
Lambeth Wlk. SE11 —4K 77 (8F 146)
Lambfold Ho. N7 —6J 45
Lamb La. E8 —7H 47
Lamble St. NW5 —5E 44
Lambley Rd. Dag —6B 52
Lambolle Pl. NW3 —6C 44
Lambolle Rd. NW3 —6C 44
Lambourn Clo. W7 —2K 71
Lambourne Av. SW19 —4H 107
Lambourne Gdns. E4 —2H 19
Lambourne Gdns. Bark —7K 51
Lambourne Gdns. Enf —2A 8
Lambourne Ho. SE16 —4K 79
Lambourne Pl. SE3 —1K 97
Lambourne Rd. E11 —7E 32
Lambourne Rd. Bark —7J 51
Lambourne Rd. Ilf —2J 51
Lambourn Gro. King T —2H 119
Lambourn Rd. SW4 —3F 93
Lamb Pas. Bren —6F 73
Lambrook Ho. SE15 —1G 95
Lambrook Ter. SW6 —1G 91
Lamb's Bldgs. EC1 —4D 62 (4A 142)
Lamb's Clo. N9 —2B 18
Lamb's Conduit Pas. WC1
  —5K 61 (5E 140)
Lamb's Conduit St. WC1
  (in three parts) —4K 61 (4E 140)
Lambscroft Av. SE9 —3A 114

224

Lambs Meadow. Wfd G —2B **34**
Lamb's M. N1 —1B **62**
Lamb's Pas. EC1 —4D **62** (5A **142**)
Lambs Ter. N9 —2J **17**
Lamb St. E1 —5F **63** (5E **142**)
Lamb's Wlk. Enf —2H **7**
Lambton Pl. W11 —7H **59**
Lambton Rd. N19 —1J **45**
Lambton Rd. SW20 —1E **120**
Lamerock Rd. Brom —4H **113**
Lamerton Rd. Ilf —2F **35**
Lamerton St. SE8 —6C **80**
Lamford Clo. N17 —7J **17**
Lamington St. W6 —4D **74**
Lamlash St. SE11 —4B **78** (8J **147**)
Lammas Av. Mitc —2E **122**
Lammas Grn. SE26 —3H **111**
Lammas Pk. Gdns. W5 —1C **72**
Lammas Pk. Rd. W5 —2D **72**
Lammas Rd. E9 —7K **47**
Lammas Rd. E10 —2A **48**
Lammas Rd. Rich —4C **104**
Lammermuir Rd. SW12 —7F **93**
Lamont Rd. SW10 —6A **76**
Lamont Rd. Pas. SW10 —6B **76**
(off Lamont Rd.)
Lamorbey Clo. Sidc —1K **115**
Lamorna Clo. Orp —7K **129**
Lamorna Gro. Stan —1D **24**
Lampard Gro. N16 —1F **47**
Lampern Sq. E2 —3G **63**
Lampeter Sq. W6 —6G **75**
Lamplighter Clo. E1 —4J **63**
Lampmead Rd. SE12 —4H **97**
Lamp Office Ct. WC1
    —4K **61** (4E **140**)
Lamport Clo. SE18 —4D **82**
Lamps Ct. SE5 —7C **78**
Lampton Av. Houn —1F **87**
Lampton Ct. Houn —1F **87**
Lampton Ho. Clo. SW19 —4F **107**
Lampton Pk. Rd. Houn —2F **87**
Lampton Rd. Houn —2F **87**
Lanacre Av. NW9 —1K **25**
Lanark Clo. W5 —5C **56**
Lanark Ho. SE1 —5G **79**
(off Old Kent Rd.)
Lanark Pl. W9 —4A **60**
Lanark Rd. W9 —2K **59**
Lanark Sq. E14 —3D **80**
Lanata Wlk. Hay —4B **54**
(off Alba Clo.)
Lanbury Rd. SE15 —4K **95**
Lancashire Ct. W1 —7F **61** (9K **139**)
(off New Bond St.)
Lancaster Av. E18 —4K **33**
Lancaster Av. SE27 —2B **110**
Lancaster Av. SW19 —5F **107**
Lancaster Av. Bark —7J **51**
Lancaster Av. Barn —1F **5**
Lancaster Av. Mitc —5J **123**
Lancaster Clo. N1 —7E **46**
Lancaster Clo. Brom —4H **127**
Lancaster Clo. Croy —2J **133**
Lancaster Clo. King 1 —5D **104**
Lancaster Cotts. Rich —6E **88**
Lancaster Clo. SW6 —7H **75**
Lancaster Clo. Sutt —7J **131**
(off Mulgrave Rd.)
Lancaster Dri. E14 —1E **80**
Lancaster Dri. NW3 —6C **44**
Lancaster Gdns. SW19 —5G **107**
Lancaster Gdns. King 1 —5D **104**
Lancaster Ga. W2 —7A **60**
Lancaster Gro. NW3 —6B **44**

Lancaster Ho. Enf —1J **7**
Lancaster M. SW18 —5K **91**
Lancaster M. W2 —7A **60**
Lancaster M. Rich —6E **88**
Lancaster Pk. Rich —5E **88**
Lancaster Pl. SW19 —5F **107**
Lancaster Pl. WC2 —7K **61** (9E **140**)
Lancaster Pl. Houn —2B **86**
Lancaster Pl. Ilf —4G **51**
Lancaster Pl. Twic —6A **88**
Lancaster Rd. E7 —7J **49**
Lancaster Rd. E11 —2G **49**
Lancaster Rd. E17 —2K **31**
Lancaster Rd. N4 —7K **29**
Lancaster Rd. N11 —6C **16**
Lancaster Rd. N18 —5A **18**
Lancaster Rd. NW10 —5C **42**
Lancaster Rd. SE25 —2F **125**
Lancaster Rd. SW19 —5F **107**
Lancaster Rd. W11 —6G **59**
Lancaster Rd. Barn —4G **5**
(in two parts)
Lancaster Rd. Enf —1J **7**
Lancaster Rd. Harr —5E **22**
Lancaster Rd. N'holt —6G **39**
Lancaster Rd. S'hall —7C **54**
Lancaster Stables. NW3 —6C **44**
Lancaster St. SE1 —2B **78** (5J **147**)
Lancaster St. SE18 —7J **83**
Lancaster Ter. W2 —7B **60** (9A **138**)
Lancaster Wlk. W2 —1A **76**
Lancefield St. SE15 —3H **95**
Lancefield St. W10 —2G **59**
(in two parts)
Lancell St. N16 —2E **46**
Lancelot Av. Wemb —4D **40**
Lancelot Cres. Wemb —4D **40**
Lancelot Gdns. Barn —7K **5**
Lancelot Pl. SW7 —2D **76** (5E **144**)
Lancelot Rd. Well —4A **100**
Lancelot Rd. Wemb —4D **40**
Lance Rd. Harr —7G **23**
Lancer Sq. W8 —2K **75**
Lancey Clo. SE7 —4C **82**
Lanchester Rd. N6 —5D **28**
Lancing Gdns. N9 —1A **18**
Lancing Rd. W13 —7B **56**
Lancing Rd. Croy —7K **123**
Lancing Rd. Ilf —6H **35**
Lancing St. NW1 —3H **61** (2A **140**)
Lancresse Ct. N1 —1E **62**
(off De Beauvoir Est.)
Landcroft Rd. SE22 —5F **95**
Landells Rd. SE22 —6F **95**
Landford Rd. SW15 —3E **90**
Landgrove Rd. SW19 —5J **107**
Landmann Way. E14 —5K **79**
Landon Pl. SW1 —3D **76** (6E **144**)
London's Clo. E14 —1E **80**
Landon Wlk. E14 —7D **64**
Landor Rd. SW9 —3J **93**
Landor Wlk. W12 —2C **74**
Landport Way. SE15 —7F **79**
Landra Gdns. N21 —6G **7**
Landridge Rd. SW6 —2H **91**
Landrock Rd. N8 —6J **29**
Landscape Rd. Wfd G —7E **20**
Landseer Av. E12 —5E **50**
Landseer Clo. SW19 —1A **122**
Landseer Clo. Edgw —2G **25**
Landseer Rd. N19 —3J **45**
Landseer Rd. Enf —5B **8**
Landseer Rd. N Mald —7K **119**
Landseer Rd. Sutt —6J **131**
Landstead Rd. SE18 —7H **83**
Landulph Ho. SE11 —5A **78**
(off Kennings Way)
Lane App. NW7 —5B **14**

Lane Clo. NW2 —3D **42**
Lane End. Bexh —3H **101**
Lane Gdns. Bush —1D **10**
Lane M. E12 —3D **50**
Lanercost Clo. SW2 —2A **110**
Lanercost Gdns. N14 —7D **6**
Lanercost Rd. SW2 —2A **110**
Lanesborough Pl. SW1
    —2E **76** (4H **145**)
(off Grosvenor Pl.)
Laneside. Chst —5G **115**
Laneside. Edgw —5D **12**
Laneside Av. Dag —7F **37**
Lane, The. NW8 —2A **60**
Lane, The. SE3 —3J **97**
Laneway. SW15 —5D **90**
Lanfranc Ct. Harr —3K **39**
Lanfranc Rd. E3 —2A **64**
Lanfrey Pl. W14 —5H **75**
Langbourne Av. N6 —2E **44**
Langbrook Rd. SE3 —3B **98**
Langcroft Clo. Cars —3D **132**
Langdale Av. Mitc —3D **122**
Langdale Clo. SE17 —6C **78**
Langdale Clo. SW14 —4H **89**
Langdale Clo. Dag —1C **52**
Langdale Cres. Bexh —7G **85**
Langdale Gdns. Gnfd —3B **56**
Langdale Pde. Mitc —3D **122**
Langdale Rd. SE10 —7E **80**
Langdale Rd. T Hth —4A **124**
Langdale St. E1 —6H **63**
Langdon Ct. NW10 —1A **58**
Langdon Cres. E6 —2E **66**
Langdon Dri. NW9 —1J **41**
Langdon Pk. N6 —7G **29**
Langdon Pl. SW14 —3J **89**
Langdon Rd. E6 —1E **66**
Langdon Rd. Brom —3K **127**
Langdon Rd. Mord —5A **122**
Langdons Ct. S'hall —3E **70**
Langdon Shaw. Sidc —5K **115**
Langdon Wlk. Mord —5A **122**
Langdon Way. SE1 —4G **79**
Langford Clo. E8 —5G **47**
Langford Clo. N15 —6E **30**
Langford Clo. NW8 —2A **60**
Langford Cres. Barn —4J **5**
Langford Grn. SE5 —3E **94**
Langford Pl. NW8 —2A **60**
Langford Pl. Sidc —3A **116**
Langford Rd. SW6 —2K **91**
Langford Rd. Barn —4J **5**
Langford Rd. Wfd G —6F **21**
Langfords. Buck H —2G **21**
Langham Ct. NW4 —5F **27**
Langham Dri. Romf —6B **36**
Langham Gdns. N21 —5F **7**
Langham Gdns. W13 —7B **56**
Langham Gdns. Edgw —7D **12**
Langham Gdns. Rich —4C **104**
Langham Gdns. Wemb —2C **40**
Langham Ho. Clo. Rich —4D **104**
Langham Mans. SW5 —5K **75**
(off Earl's Ct. Sq.)
Langham Pl. N15 —3B **30**
Langham Pl. W1 —5F **61** (6K **139**)
Langham Pl. W4 —6A **74**
Langham Rd. N15 —3B **30**
Langham Rd. SW20 —1E **120**
Langham Rd. Edgw —6D **12**
Langham Rd. Tedd —5B **104**
Langham St. W1 —5F **61** (6K **139**)
Langhedge Clo. N18 —6A **18**
Langhedge La. N18 —6A **18**
Langhedge La. Ind. Est. N18 —6A **18**
Langholm Clo. SW12 —7H **93**
Langholme. Bush —1B **10**

Langhorne Rd. Dag —7G **53**
Langland Cres. Stan —2D **24**
Langland Dri. Pinn —1C **22**
Langland Gdns. NW3 —5K **43**
Langland Gdns. Croy —2B **136**
Langler Rd. NW10 —2E **58**
Langley Av. Ruis —2A **38**
Langley Av. Surb —7D **118**
Langley Av. Wor Pk —2F **131**
Langley Ct. WC2 —7J **61** (9C **140**)
Langley Cres. E11 —7A **34**
Langley Cres. Dag —7C **52**
Langley Cres. Edgw —3D **12**
Langley Dri. E11 —7K **33**
Langley Dri. W3 —2H **73**
Langley Gdns. Brom —4A **128**
Langley Gdns. Dag —7D **52**
Langley Gdns. Orp —6F **129**
Langley Gro. N Mald —2A **120**
Langley La. SW8 —6J **77**
Langley Mans. SW8 —6K **77**
(off Langley La.)
Langley Pk. NW7 —6F **13**
Langley Pk. Rd. Sutt —5A **132**
Langley Rd. SW19 —1H **121**
Langley Rd. Beck —4A **126**
Langley Rd. Iswth —2K **87**
Langley Rd. Surb —7E **118**
Langley Rd. Well —6C **84**
Langley St. WC2 —6J **61** (8C **140**)
Langley Way. W Wick —1F **137**
Langmead Dri. Bush —1D **10**
Langmead St. SE27 —4C **110**
Langmore Ct. Bexh —3D **100**
Langport Ho. SW9 —2B **94**
Langroyd Rd. SW17 —2D **108**
Langside Av. SW15 —4C **90**
Langside Cres. N14 —3C **16**
Langston Hughes Clo. SE24 —4B **94**
Lang St. E1 —4J **63**
Langthorn Ct. EC2 —6D **62** (7B **142**)
Langthorne Rd. E11 —3E **48**
Langthorne St. SW6 —7F **75**
Langton Av. E6 —3E **66**
Langton Av. N20 —7F **5**
Langton Clo. WC1 —4K **61** (3F **140**)
Langton Rise. SE23 —7H **95**
Langton Rd. NW2 —3E **42**
Langton Rd. SW9 —7B **78**
Langton Rd. Harr —7B **10**
Langton St. SW10 —6A **76**
Langton Way. SE3 —1H **97**
Langton Way. Croy —4E **134**
Langtry Rd. NW8 —1K **59**
Langtry Rd. N'holt —2B **54**
Langtry Wlk. NW8 —1K **59**
Langwood Chase. Tedd —6C **104**
Lanhill Rd. W9 —4J **59**
Lanier Rd. SE13 —6F **97**
Lanigan Dri. Houn —5F **87**
Lankaster Gdns. N2 —1B **28**
Lankers Dri. Harr —6D **22**
Lankton Clo. Beck —1E **126**
Lannoy Point. SW6 —7G **75**
(off Pellant Rd.)
Lannoy Rd. SE9 —1G **115**
Lanrick Rd. E14 —6F **65**
Lanridge Rd. SE2 —3D **84**
Lansbury Av. N18 —5J **17**
Lansbury Av. Bark —7A **52**
Lansbury Av. Felt —6A **86**
Lansbury Av. Romf —5E **36**
Lansbury Clo. NW10 —5J **41**
Lansbury Est. E14 —6D **64**
Lansbury Gdns. E14 —6F **65**
Lansbury Rd. Enf —1E **8**
Lansbury Way. N18 —5K **17**
Lanscombe Wlk. SW8 —1J **93**

Lansdell Ho. SW2 —5A **94**
(off Tulse Hill)
Lansdell Rd. Mitc —2E **122**
Lansdown Av. Bexh —7D **84**
Lansdowne Av. Orp —7F **129**
Lansdowne Clo. SW20 —7F **107**
Lansdowne Clo. Twic —1K **103**
Lansdowne Ct. Wor Pk —2C **130**
Lansdowne Cres. W11 —7G **59**
Lansdowne Dri. E8 —6G **47**
Lansdowne Gdns. SW8 —1J **93**
Lansdowne Gro. NW10 —4A **42**
Lansdowne Hill. SE27 —3B **110**
Lansdowne La. SE7 —5B **82**
Lansdowne M. SE7 —5B **82**
Lansdowne M. W11 —1H **75**
Lansdowne Pl. SE1 —3D **78** (6B **148**)
Lansdowne Pl. SE19 —7F **111**
Lansdowne Rise. W11 —7G **59**
Lansdowne Rd. E4 —2H **19**
Lansdowne Rd. E11 —2H **49**
Lansdowne Rd. E17 —6C **32**
Lansdowne Rd. E18 —3J **33**
Lansdowne Rd. N3 —7D **14**
Lansdowne Rd. N10 —2G **29**
Lansdowne Rd. N17 —1G **31**
Lansdowne Rd. SW20 —7E **106**
Lansdowne Rd. W11 —7G **59**
Lansdowne Rd. Brom —7J **113**
Lansdowne Rd. Croy —2D **134**
Lansdowne Rd. Harr —7J **23**
Lansdowne Rd. Houn —3F **87**
Lansdowne Rd. Ilf —1K **51**
Lansdowne Rd. Stan —6H **11**
Lansdowne Row. W1
    —1F **77** (2K **145**)
Lansdowne Ter. WC1
    —4J **61** (4D **140**)
Lansdowne Wlk. W11 —1H **75**
Lansdowne Way. SW8 —1H **93**
Lansdowne Wood Clo. SE27 —3B **110**
Lansdown Rd. E7 —7A **50**
Lansdown Rd. Sidc —3B **116**
Lansfield Av. N18 —4B **18**
Lantern Clo. SW15 —4C **90**
Lantern Clo. Wemb —5D **40**
Lanterns Ct. E14 —3C **80**
Lant St. SE1 —2C **78** (4L **147**)
Lanvanor Rd. SE15 —2J **95**
Lanyard Ho. SE8 —4B **80**
Lapford Clo. W9 —4H **59**
Lapponum Wlk. Hay —4B **54**
Lapse Wood Wlk. SE23 —1H **111**
Lapstone Gdns. Harr —6C **24**
Lapwing Way. Hay —6B **54**
Lapworth. N11 —4A **16**
(off Coppies Gro.)
Lara Clo. SE13 —6E **96**
Larbert Rd. SW16 —7G **109**
Larch Av. W3 —1A **74**
Larch Clo. N11 —7K **15**
Larch Clo. N19 —2G **45**
Larch Clo. SE8 —6B **80**
Larch Clo. SW12 —2F **109**
Larch Cres. Hay —5A **54**
Larch Dri. W4 —5G **73**
Larches Av. SW14 —4K **89**
Larches, The. N13 —3H **17**
Larch Grn. NW9 —1A **26**
Larch Gro. Sidc —1J **115**
Larch Ho. Brom —1G **127**
Larch Ho. Hay —5A **54**
Larch Rd. NW2 —4E **42**
Larch Tree Way. Croy —3C **136**
Larchvale Ct. Sutt —7K **131**
Larch Way. Brom —7E **128**
Larchwood Rd. SE9 —2F **115**
Larcombe Clo. Croy —4F **135**

Larcombe Ct. Sutt —7K 131
(off Worcester Rd.)
Larcom St. SE17 —4C 78 (9L 147)
Larden Rd. W3 —1A 74
Larissa St. SE17 —5D 78
Larkbere Rd. SE26 —4A 112
Larken Clo. Bush —1B 10
Larken Dri. Bush —1B 10
Larkfield Av. Harr —3B 24
Larkfield Clo. Brom —2H 137
Larkfield Rd. Rich —4E 88
Larkfield Rd. Sidc —3K 115
Larkhall La. SW4 —2H 93
Larkhall Rise. SW4 —3G 93
Lark Row. E2 —1J 63
Larksfield Gro. Enf —1C 8
Larks Gro. Bark —7J 51
Larkshall Ct. Romf —2J 37
Larkshall Cres. E4 —4K 19
Larkshall Rd. E4 —5K 19
Larkspur Clo. E6 —5C 66
Larkspur Clo. N17 —7J 17
Larkspur Lodge. Sidc —3B 116
Larkswood Ct. E4 —5A 20
Larkswood Rise. Pinn —4A 22
Larkswood Rd. E4 —4H 19
Larkway Clo. NW9 —4K 25
Larnach Rd. W6 —6F 75
Larpent Av. SW15 —5E 90
Larshall Rd. E4 —3A 20
Larwood Clo. Gnfd —5H 39
Lascelles Av. Harr —7H 23
Lascelles Clo. E11 —2F 49
Lascotts Rd. N22 —6E 16
Lassa Rd. SE9 —5C 98
Lassell St. SE10 —5F 81
Latchett Rd. E18 —1K 33
Latchingdon Ct. E17 —4K 31
Latchingdon Gdns. Wfd G —6H 21
Latchmere Clo. Rich —5E 104
Latchmere La. King T —6F 105
Latchmere Pas. SW11 —2C 92
Latchmere Rd. SW11 —2D 92
Latchmere Rd. King T —7E 104
Latchmere St. SW11 —2D 92
Lateward Rd. Bren —6D 72
Latham Clo. E6 —5C 66
Latham Clo. Twic —7A 88
Latham Rd. Bexh —5G 101
Latham Rd. Twic —7K 87
Latham's Way. Croy —1J 133
Lathkill Clo. Enf —7B 8
Lathkill Ct. Beck —1B 126
Lathom Rd. E6 —7C 50
Latimer Av. E6 —1D 66
Latimer Clo. Wor Pk —4D 130
Latimer Clo. Pinn —1A 22
Latimer Gdns. Pinn —1A 22
Latimer Ho. E9 —6K 47
Latimer Ind. Est. W10 —6E 58
Latimer Pl. W10 —6E 58
Latimer Rd. E7 —4K 49
Latimer Rd. N15 —6E 30
Latimer Rd. SW19 —6K 107
Latimer Rd. W10 —5E 58
Latimer Rd. Barn —3E 4
Latimer Rd. Croy —3B 134
Latimer Rd. Tedd —5K 103
Latona Rd. SE15 —6G 79
Latymer Ct. W6 —4F 75
Latymer Gdns. N3 —2G 27
Latymer Rd. N9 —1A 18
Latymer Way. N9 —2K 17
Lauder Clo. N'holt —2B 54
Lauder Ct. N14 —7D 6
Lauderdale Dri. Rich —3D 104
Lauderdale Mans. W9 —3K 59
(off Lauderdale Rd.)

Lauderdale Pl. EC2 —5C 62 (5L 141)
(off Barbican)
Lauderdale Rd. W9 —3K 59
Lauderdale Tower. EC2
(off Barbican) —5C 62 (5L 141)
Laud St. SE11 —5K 77
Laud St. Croy —3C 134
Laughton Rd. N'holt —1B 54
Launcelot Rd. Brom —4J 113
Launcelot St. SE1 —2A 78 (5G 147)
Launceston Gdns. Gnfd —1C 56
Launceston Pl. W8 —3A 76
Launceston Rd. Gnfd —1C 56
Launch St. E14 —3E 80
Laundry La. N1 —7C 46
Laundry Rd. W6 —6G 75
Laura Clo. E11 —5A 34
Laura Clo. Enf —5K 7
Lauradale Rd. N2 —4D 28
Laura Pl. E5 —4J 47
Laurel Av. Twic —1K 103
Laurel Bank Gdns. SW6 —2H 91
Laurel Bank Rd. SE9 —2C 114
Laurel Bank Vs. W7 —1J 71
(off Lwr. Boston Rd.)
Laurelbrook. SE6 —3G 113
Laurel Clo. N19 —2G 45
Laurel Clo. SW17 —5C 108
Laurel Clo. Sidc —3A 116
Laurel Ct. E8 —6F 47
Laurel Ct. Wemb —2E 56
Laurel Cres. Croy —3C 136
Laurel Cres. Romf —1K 53
Laurel Dri. N21 —7F 7
Laurel Gdns. E4 —7J 9
Laurel Gdns. NW7 —3E 12
Laurel Gdns. W7 —1J 71
Laurel Gdns. Houn —4C 86
Laurel Gro. SE20 —7J 111
Laurel Gro. SE26 —4K 111
Laurel Ho. Brom —1G 127
Laurel Pk. Harr —7E 10
Laurel Rd. SW13 —2C 90
Laurel Rd. SW20 —1D 120
Laurel Rd. Hamp —5H 103
Laurels, The. Brom —3J 127
Laurel St. E8 —6F 47
Laurel View. N12 —3E 14
Laurel Way. E18 —4H 33
Laurel Way. N20 —3A 14
Laurence Ct. E10 —7D 32
Laurence M. W12 —2C 74
Laurence Pountney Hill. EC4
—7D 62 (9A 142)
Laurence Pountney La. EC4
—7D 62 (1A 148)
Laurie Gro. SE14 —1A 96
Laurie Rd. W7 —5J 55
Laurier Rd. NW5 —3F 45
Laurier Rd. Croy —7F 125
Laurimel Clo. Stan —6G 11
Laurino Pl. Bush —2B 10
Lauriston Rd. E9 —7J 47
Lauriston Rd. SW19 —6F 107
Lausanne Rd. N8 —4A 30
Lausanne Rd. SE15 —1J 95
Lavell St. N16 —4D 46
Lavender Av. NW9 —1J 41
Lavender Av. Mitc —1C 122
Lavender Av. Wor Pk —3E 130
Lavender Clo. SW3 —6C 76
Lavender Clo. Cars —4F 133
Lavender Ct. Felt —6A 86
Lavender Gdns. SW11 —4D 92
Lavender Gdns. Enf —1G 7
Lavender Gro. E8 —7G 47
Lavender Gro. Mitc —1C 122
Lavender Hill. SW11 —4C 92

Lavender Hill. Enf —1F 7
Lavender Pl. Ilf —5F 51
Lavender Rd. SE16 —1A 80
Lavender Rd. SW11 —3B 92
Lavender Rd. Cars —4E 133
Lavender Rd. Croy —6K 123
Lavender Rd. Enf —1J 7
Lavender Rd. Sutt —4B 132
Lavender St. E15 —6G 49
Lavender Sweep. SW11 —4D 92
Lavender Ter. SW11 —3C 92
Lavender Vale. Wall —6H 133
Lavender Wlk. SW11 —4D 92
Lavender Wlk. Mitc —3E 122
Lavender Way. Croy —6K 125
Lavengro Rd. SE27 —2C 110
Lavenham Rd. SW18 —2H 107
Lavernock Rd. Bexh —2G 101
Lavers Rd. N16 —3E 46
Laverstoke Gdns. SW15 —7B 90
Laverton M. SW5 —4K 75
Laverton Pl. SW5 —4K 75
Lavidge Rd. SE9 —2C 114
Lavina Gro. N1 —2K 61
Lavington Rd. W13 —1B 72
Lavington Rd. Croy —3K 133
Lavington St. SE1 —1B 78 (3K 147)
Lavinia Gro. N1 —2K 61
Lawdons Gdns. Croy —4B 134
Lawford Clo. Wall —7J 133
Lawford Rd. N1 —7E 46
Lawford Rd. NW5 —6G 45
Lawford Rd. W4 —7J 73
Law Ho. Bark —2A 68
Lawless St. E14 —7D 64
Lawley Rd. N14 —7A 6
Lawley St. E5 —4J 47
Lawn Clo. N9 —7A 8
Lawn Clo. Brom —7K 113
Lawn Clo. N Mald —2A 120
Lawn Cres. Rich —2G 89
Lawn Dri. E7 —4B 50
Lawn Farm Gro. Romf —4E 36
Lawn Gdns. W7 —1J 71
Lawn Ho. Clo. E14 —2E 80
Lawn La. SW8 —6J 77
Lawn Pl. SE15 —1F 95
Lawn Rd. NW3 —5D 44
Lawn Rd. Beck —7B 112
Lawns Ct. Wemb —2F 41
Lawns, The. SE3 —4H 97
Lawns, The. SE19 —1D 124
Lawns, The. SW19 —5H 107
Lawns, The. Pinn —7A 10
Lawns, The. Sidc —4C 116
Lawns, The. Sutt —7G 131
Lawnsway. Romf —1J 37
Lawn Ter. SE3 —3G 97
Lawn, The. S'hall —5E 70
Lawn Vale. Pinn —2C 22
Lawrence Av. E12 —4E 50
Lawrence Av. E17 —1K 31
Lawrence Av. N13 —4G 17
Lawrence Av. NW7 —4F 13
Lawrence Av. N Mald —6K 119
Lawrence Bldgs. N16 —3F 47
Lawrence Campe Clo. N20 —3G 15
Lawrence Clo. E3 —3C 64
Lawrence Clo. N15 —3E 30
Lawrence Clo. W12 —7D 58
(off White City Est.)
Lawrence Ct. NW7 —5F 13
Lawrence Cres. Dag —3H 53
Lawrence Cres. Edgw —2G 25
Lawrence Gdns. NW7 —3G 13
Lawrence Hill. E4 —2H 19

Lawrence La. EC2 —6C 62 (8M 141)
Lawrence Pl. N1 —1J 61
(off Brydon Wlk.)
Lawrence Rd. E6 —1C 66
Lawrence Rd. E13 —1K 65
Lawrence Rd. N15 —4E 30
Lawrence Rd. N18 —4C 18
Lawrence Rd. SE25 —4F 125
Lawrence Rd. W5 —4C 72
Lawrence Rd. Hamp —7D 102
Lawrence Rd. Houn —4A 86
Lawrence Rd. Pinn —6B 22
Lawrence Rd. Rich —4C 104
Lawrence Rd. W Wick —4J 137
Lawrence St. E16 —5H 65
Lawrence St. NW7 —4G 13
Lawrence St. SW3 —6C 76
Lawrence Way. NW10 —3K 41
Lawrence Weaver Clo. Mord
—6J 121
Lawrence Yd. N15 —4E 30
Lawrie Pk. Av. SE26 —5H 111
Lawrie Pk. Cres. SE26 —5H 111
Lawrie Pk. Gdns. SE26 —4H 111
Lawrie Pk. Rd. SE26 —6H 111
Lawson Clo. E16 —5A 66
Lawson Clo. SW19 —3F 107
Lawson Ct. N4 —1K 45
(off Lorne Rd.)
Lawson Ct. Surb —7D 118
Lawson Gdns. Pinn —3A 22
Lawson Ho. W12 —7D 58
(off White City Est.)
Lawson Rd. Enf —1D 8
Lawson Rd. S'hall —4E 54
Law St. SE1 —3D 78 (6B 148)
Lawton Rd. E3 —3A 64
(in two parts)
Lawton Rd. E10 —1E 48
Lawton Rd. Barn —3G 5
Laxcon Clo. NW10 —5K 41
Laxley Clo. SE5 —7B 78
Laxton Pl. NW1 —4F 61 (3K 139)
Layard Rd. SE16 —4H 79
Layard Rd. Enf —1A 8
Layard Rd. T Hth —2D 124
Layard Sq. SE16 —4H 79
Laybourne Ho. E14 —2D 80
(off Admirals Way)
Laybrook Lodge. E18 —4H 33
Laycock St. N1 —6A 46
Layer Gdns. W3 —7G 57
Layfield Clo. NW4 —7D 26
Layfield Cres. NW4 —7D 26
Layfield Rd. NW4 —7D 26
Layhams Rd. W Wick & Kes
—4G 137
Laymarsh Clo. Belv —3F 85
Laymead Clo. N'holt —6C 38
Laystall St. EC1 —4A 62 (4G 141)
Layton Ct. Bren —5D 72
Layton Cres. Croy —5A 134
Layton Rd. N1 —2A 62
Layton Rd. Bren —5D 72
Layton Rd. Houn —4F 87
Layton's Bldgs. SE1
—2D 78 (4A 148)
Laytons Bldgs. SW1 —2D 78
Layzell Wlk. SE9 —1B 114
Lazar Wlk. N7 —2K 45
Lazenby Ct. WC2 —7J 61 (9C 140)
(off Floral St.)
Leabank Clo. Harr —3J 39
Leabank Sq. E9 —6C 48
Leabank View. N15 —6G 31
Leabourne Rd. N16 —7G 31
Lea Bri. Rd. E5 & E10 E17 —3J 47
Lea Ct. E4 —2K 19

Lea Ct. E13 —3J 65
Leacroft Av. SW12 —7D 92
Leadale Av. E4 —2H 19
Leadale Rd. N15 & N16 —6G 31
Leadbetter Ct. NW10 —7K 41
(off Melville Rd.)
Leadenhall Mkt. EC3 —6E 62 (8C 142)
(off Leadenhall Pl.)
Leadenhall Pl. EC3 —6E 62 (8C 142)
Leadenhall St. EC3 —6E 62 (8C 142)
Leadenham Ct. E3 —4C 64
Leader Av. E12 —5E 50
Leadings, The. Wemb —3J 41
Leaf Gro. SE27 —5A 110
Leafield Clo. SW16 —6B 110
Leafield La. Sidc —3F 117
Leafield Rd. SW20 —3H 121
Leafield Rd. Sutt —2J 131
Leafy Gro. Kes —5K 137
Leafy Oak Rd. SE12 —4A 114
Leafy Way. Croy —2F 135
Lea Gdns. Wemb —5F 41
Leagrave St. E5 —3J 47
Lea Hall Rd. E10 —1C 48
Leahurst Rd. SE13 —5F 97
Leake Clo. SE1 —2K 77
Leake Ct. SE1 —2K 77 (5F 146)
Leake St. SE1 —2K 77 (4F 146)
Lealand Rd. N15 —6F 31
Leamington Av. E17 —5C 32
Leamington Av. Brom —5A 114
Leamington Av. Mord —4G 121
Leamington Clo. E12 —5C 50
Leamington Clo. Brom —4B 114
Leamington Clo. Houn —5G 87
Leamington Cres. Harr —3C 38
Leamington Gdns. Ilf —2K 51
Leamington Ho. Edgw —5A 12
Leamington Pk. W3 —5K 57
Leamington Rd. S'hall —4B 70
Leamington Rd. Vs. W11 —5H 59
Leamore St. W6 —4E 74
Leamouth Rd. E6 —5C 66
Leamouth Rd. E14 —6F 65
Leander Ct. SE8 —1C 96
Leander Ct. SE16 —1B 80
Leander Ct. Surb —7D 118
Leander Rd. SW2 —6K 93
Leander Rd. N'holt —2E 54
Leander Rd. T Hth —4K 123
Leapold M. E9 —1J 63
Lea Rd. Beck —2C 126
Lea Rd. Enf —1J 7
Lea Rd. S'hall —4C 70
Learoyd Gdns. E6 —7E 66
Leary Ho. SE11 —5K 77
Leas Dale. SE9 —3E 114
Leas Grn. Chst —6K 115
Leaside Av. N10 —3E 28
Lea Side Ind. Est. Enf —3G 9
Leaside Mans. N10 —3E 28
(off Fortis Grn.)
Leaside Rd. E5 —1J 47
Leasowes Rd. E10 —1C 48
Leathart Rd. Houn —4F 87
Leatherbottle Grn. Eri —3F 85
Leather Bottle La. Belv —4E 84
Leather Clo. Mitc —2E 122
Leatherdale St. E1 —4J 63
(in two parts)
Leather Gdns. E15 —1G 65
Leatherhead Clo. N16 —1F 47
Leather La. EC1 —5A 62 (5G 141)
(in two parts)
Leathermarket St. SE1
—2E 78 (5C 148)
Leathersellers Clo. Barn —3B 4
Leathsail Rd. Harr —3F 39
Leathwaite Rd. SW11 —4D 92

226

Liberty St. SW9 —1K 93
Libra Ct. E4 —4H 19
Libra Rd. E3 —1B 64
Libra Rd. E13 —2J 65
Library Pl. E1 —7H 63
Library St. SE7 —2B 78 (5J 147)
Library Way. Twic —7G 87
Lichfield Gdns. Rich —4E 88
Lichfield Gro. N3 —1J 27
Lichfield M. E3 —3A 64
Lichfield Rd. E3 —3A 64
Lichfield Rd. E6 —3B 66
Lichfield Rd. N9 —2B 18
Lichfield Rd. NW2 —4G 43
Lichfield Rd. Dag —4B 52
Lichfield Rd. Houn —3A 86
Lichfield Rd. Rich —1F 89
Lichfield Rd. Wfd G —4B 20
Lichfield Sq. Rich —4E 88
Lickey Ho. W14 —6H 75
(off North End Rd.)
Lidbury Rd. NW7 —6B 14
Lidcote Gdns. SW9 —2A 94
Liddell Clo. Harr —3D 24
Liddell Gdns. NW10 —2E 58
Liddell Rd. NW6 —6J 43
Lidding Rd. Harr —5D 24
Liddington Rd. E15 —1H 65
Liddon Rd. E13 —3K 65
Liddon Rd. Brom —3A 128
Liden Clo. E17 —7B 32
Lidfield Rd. N16 —4D 46
Lidiard Rd. SW18 —2A 108
Lidlington Pl. NW1 —2G 61
Lido Sq. N17 —2D 30
Lidyard Rd. N19 —1G 45
Liffler Rd. SE18 —5J 83
Liffords Pl. SW13 —2B 90
Lifford St. SW15 —4F 91
Light App. NW9 —2B 26
Lightcliffe Rd. N13 —4F 17
Lightermans Rd. E14 —2C 80
Lightfoot Rd. N8 —5J 29
Light Horse Ct. SW3 —5E 76
(off Royal Hospital Rd.)
Lightley Clo. Wemb —1E 56
Ligonier St. E2 —4F 63 (3E 142)
Lilac Clo. E4 —6G 19
Lilac Ct. E13 —1A 66
Lilac Ct. Tedd —4K 103
Lilac Gdns. W5 —3D 72
Lilac Gdns. Croy —3C 136
Lilac Gdns. Iff —5F 51
Lilac Gdns. Romf —1K 53
Lilac Pl. SE11 —4K 77 (9E 146)
Lilac St. W12 —7C 58
Lilburne Gdns. SE9 —5C 98
Lilburne Rd. SE9 —5C 98
Lilburne Wlk. NW10 —6J 41
Lile Cres. W7 —5J 55
Lilestone St. NW8 —4C 60 (3C 138)
Lilford Ho. SE5 —2C 94
Lilford Rd. SE5 —2B 94
Lilian Barker Clo. SE12 —5J 97
Lilian Board Way. Gnfd —5H 39
Lilian Clo. N16 —3E 46
Lilian Gdns. Wfd G —1K 33
Lilian Rd. SW16 —1G 123
Lillechurch Rd. Dag —6B 52
Lilleshall Rd. Mord —6B 122
Lillian Av. W3 —2G 73
Lillian Rd. SW13 —6C 74
Lillie Rd. SW6 —6F 75
Lillieshall Rd. SW4 —3F 93
Lillie Yd. SW6 —6J 75
Lillington Gdns. Est. SW1
—4G 77 (9M 145)
(off Vauxhall Bri. Rd.)

Lilliput Av. N'holt —1C 54
Lilliput Ct. SE12 —5K 97
Lilliput Rd. Romf —7K 37
Lily Clo. W14 —4F 75
(in two parts)
Lily Gdns. Wemb —2C 56
Lily Pl. EC1 —5A 62 (5H 141)
Lily Rd. E17 —6C 32
Lilyville Rd. SW6 —1H 91
Limbourne Av. Dag —7F 37
Limburg Rd. SW11 —4C 92
Limeburner La. EC4
—6B 62 (8J 141)
Lime Clo. E1 —1G 79
Lime Clo. Buck H —2G 21
Lime Clo. Cars —2D 132
Lime Clo. Harr —2A 24
Lime Clo. Romf —4J 37
Lime Ct. E11 —2G 49
(off Trinity Clo.)
Lime Ct. E17 —5E 32
Lime Ct. SE9 —2F 115
Lime Ct. Harr —6K 23
Lime Ct. Mitc —2B 122
Limecroft Clo. Eps —7A 130
Limedene Clo. Pinn —1B 22
Lime Gro. N20 —1C 14
Lime Gro. W12 —2E 74
Lime Gro. N Mald —3K 119
Lime Gro. Sidc —6K 99
Lime Gro. Twic —6K 87
Limeharbour. E14 —3D 80
Limeharbour Ct. E14 —3D 80
Limehouse Causeway. E14 —7B 64
Limehouse Fields Est. E14 —5A 64
Limehouse Link. E14 —7B 64
Limerick Clo. SW12 —7G 93
Lime Rd. Eri —3F 85
Lime Rd. Rich —4F 89
Lime Row. Eri —3F 85
Limerston St. SW10 —6A 76
Limes Av. E11 —4K 33
Limes Av. E12 —3C 50
Limes Av. N12 —4F 15
Limes Av. NW7 —6F 13
Limes Av. NW11 —7G 27
Limes Av. SE20 —7H 111
Limes Av. SW13 —2B 90
Limes Av. Cars —1D 132
Limes Av. Croy —3A 134
Limes Av., The. N11 —5A 16
Limes Clo. N11 —5B 16
Limesdale Gdns. Edgw —2J 25
Limes Field Rd. SW14 —3A 90
Limesford Rd. SE15 —4K 95
Limes Gdns. SW18 —6J 91
Limes Gro. SE13 —4E 96
Limes Pl. Croy —7D 124
Limes Rd. Beck —2D 126
Limes Rd. Croy —7D 124
Limes, The. W2 —7J 59
(off Linden Gdns.)
Limestone Wlk. Eri —2D 84
Lime St. E17 —4A 32
Lime St. EC3 —7E 62 (9C 142)
Lime St. Pas. EC3 —6E 62 (9C 142)
Limes Wlk. SE15 —4J 95
Limes Wlk. W5 —2D 72
Lime Ter. W7 —7J 55
Limetree Clo. SW2 —1K 109
Lime Tree Gro. Croy —3B 136
Lime Tree Pl. Mitc —1F 122
Lime Tree Rd. Houn —1F 87
Lime Tree Ter. SE6 —1B 112
Lime Tree Wlk. Bush —1D 10
Lime Tree Wlk. Enf —1H 7
Lime Tree Wlk. W Wick —4H 137

Lime Wlk. E15 —1G 65
Limewood Clo. W13 —6B 56
Limewood Ct. Iff —5D 34
Limewood Rd. Eri —7J 85
Limpsfield Av. SW19 —2F 107
Limpsfield Av. T Hth —5K 123
Linacre Rd. NW2 —6D 42
Linberry Wlk. SE8 —4B 80
Linchmere Rd. SE12 —7H 97
Lincoln Av. N14 —3B 16
Lincoln Av. SW19 —3F 107
Lincoln Av. Romf —2K 53
Lincoln Av. Twic —2G 103
Lincoln Clo. SE25 —6G 125
Lincoln Clo. Gnfd —1G 55
Lincoln Clo. Harr —5D 22
Lincoln Ct. N16 —7D 30
Lincoln Ct. Romf —4J 37
Lincoln Cres. Enf —5K 7
Lincoln Gdns. Iff —7C 34
Lincoln Ho. SW9 —7A 78
Lincoln M. NW6 —1H 59
Lincoln M. SE21 —2D 110
Lincoln Rd. E7 —6B 50
Lincoln Rd. E13 —4K 65
Lincoln Rd. E18 —1H 33
Lincoln Rd. N2 —3C 28
Lincoln Rd. SE25 —3H 125
Lincoln Rd. Enf —4K 7
Lincoln Rd. Felt —3D 102
Lincoln Rd. Harr —5D 22
Lincoln Rd. Mitc —5J 123
Lincoln Rd. N Mald —3J 119
Lincoln Rd. Sidc —5B 116
Lincoln Rd. Wemb —6D 40
Lincoln Rd. Wor Pk —1D 130
Lincoln's Inn Fields. WC2
—6K 61 (7E 140)
Lincolns, The. NW7 —3G 13
Lincoln St. E11 —2G 49
Lincoln St. SW3 —4D 76 (9E 144)
Lincoln Way. Enf —5C 8
Lincombe Rd. Brom —3H 113
Lindal Cres. Enf —4D 6
Lindal Rd. SE4 —5B 96
Lindbergh Rd. Wall —7J 133
Linden Av. NW10 —2F 59
Linden Av. Enf —1B 8
Linden Av. Houn —5F 87
Linden Av. Ruis —1A 38
Linden Av. T Hth —4B 124
Linden Av. Wemb —5F 41
Linden Clo. N14 —6B 6
Linden Clo. Stan —6G 11
Linden Clo. Th Dit —7A 118
Linden Ct. W12 —1E 74
Linden Ct. Sidc —4J 115
Linden Cres. Gnfd —6K 39
Linden Cres. King T —2F 119
Linden Cres. Wfd G —6E 20
Lindenfield. Chst —2F 129
Linden Gdns. SW2 —7J 59
Linden Gdns. W4 —5A 74
Linden Gdns. Enf —1B 8
Linden Gro. SE15 —3H 95
Linden Gro. SE26 —6J 111
Linden Gro. N Mald —3A 120
Linden Gro. Tedd —5K 103
Linden Ho. SE15 —3H 95
Linden Ho. Hamp —6F 103
Linden Lawns. Wemb —4F 41
Linden Lea. N2 —5A 28
Linden Lea. Pinn —1D 22
Linden Leas. W Wick —2F 137
Linden M. N1 —5D 46
Linden M. W2 —7J 59
Linden Rd. N10 —4F 29
Linden Rd. N11 —2J 15

Linden Rd. N15 —4C 30
Linden Rd. Hamp —7E 102
Lindens, The. N12 —5G 15
Lindens, The. W4 —1J 89
Lindens, The. New Ad —6E 136
Linden St. Romf —4K 37
Linden Wlk. N19 —2G 45
Linden Way. N14 —6B 6
Lindeth Clo. Stan —6G 11
Lindfield Gdns. NW3 —5K 43
Lindfield Rd. W4 —4C 56
Lindfield Rd. Croy —6F 125
Lindfield St. E14 —6C 64
Lindholme Ct. NW9 —1A 26
(off Pageant Av.)
Lindisfarne Rd. SW20 —7C 106
Lindisfarne Rd. Dag —3C 52
Lindisfarne Way. E9 —4A 48
Lindley Est. SE15 —7G 79
Lindley Rd. E10 —2E 48
Lindley St. E1 —5J 63
Lindore Rd. SW11 —4D 92
Lindores Rd. Cars —1A 132
Lindo St. SE15 —2J 95
Lind Rd. Sutt —5A 132
Lindrop St. SW6 —2A 92
Lindsay Dri. Harr —6E 24
Lindsay Rd. Hamp —4F 103
Lindsay Rd. Wor Pk —2D 130
Lindsay Sq. SW1 —5H 77
Lindsell St. SE10 —1E 96
Lindsey Clo. Brom —3B 128
Lindsey Clo. Mitc —4J 123
Lindsey Ct. N13 —3F 17
(off Green Lanes)
Lindsey M. N1 —7C 46
Lindsey Rd. Dag —4C 52
Lindsey St. EC1 —5B 62 (5K 141)
Lind St. SE8 —2C 96
Lindum Rd. Tedd —7C 104
Lindway. SE27 —5B 110
Linford Rd. E17 —3E 32
Linford St. SW8 —1G 93
Lingards Rd. SE13 —4E 96
Lingey Clo. Sidc —2K 115
Lingfield Av. King T —4E 118
Lingfield Clo. Enf —6K 7
Lingfield Clo. N'holt —2E 54
Lingfield Cres. SE9 —4H 99
Lingfield Gdns. N9 —7C 8
Lingfield Rd. SW19 —5F 107
Lingfield Rd. Wor Pk —3E 130
Lingham St. SW9 —2J 93
Lingholm Way. Barn —5A 4
Ling Rd. E16 —5J 65
Ling Rd. Eri —6J 85
Lingrove Gdns. Buck H —2E 20
Lings Coppice. SE21 —2D 110
Lingwell Rd. SW17 —3C 108
Lingwood. Bexh —2H 101
Lingwood Gdns. Iswth —7J 71
Lingwood Rd. E5 —7G 31
Linhope St. NW1 —4D 60 (3E 138)
Linkenholt Mans. W6 —4B 74
(off Stamford Brook Av.)
Linkfield. Hayes —6J 127
Linkfield Rd. Iswth —2K 87
Link La. Wall —6H 133
Linklea Clo. NW9 —7F 13
Link Rd. N8 —3A 30
Link Rd. N11 —4K 15
Link Rd. Dag —2H 69
Link Rd. Wall —1E 132
Links Av. Mord —4J 121
Links Dri. N20 —1D 14
Links Gdns. SW16 —7A 110
Linkside. N12 —6D 14

Linkside. N Mald —2A 120
Linkside Clo. Enf —3E 6
Linkside Gdns. Enf —3E 6
Links Rd. NW2 —2B 42
Links Rd. SW17 —6E 108
Links Rd. W3 —6G 57
Links Rd. Wfd G —5D 20
Links Rd. W Wick —1E 136
Links Side. Enf —3F 7
Links, The. E17 —4A 32
Link St. E9 —6J 47
Linksview. N2 —5D 28
(off Gt. North Rd.)
Links View. N3 —7C 14
Links View Rd. Croy —3G 136
Links View Rd. Hamp —5G 103
Linksway. NW4 —2F 27
Links Way. Beck —6C 126
Link, The. W3 —6H 57
Link, The. Enf —1F 9
Link, The. N'holt —5D 38
Link, The. Pinn —7A 22
Link, The. Wemb —1C 40
Linkway. N4 —7C 30
Linkway. SW20 —4D 120
Link Way. Brom —7C 128
Linkway. Dag —4C 52
Link Way. Pinn —1B 22
Linkway. Rich —2B 104
Linkway, The. Barn —6E 4
Linkwood Wlk. NW1 —7H 45
Linley Ct. Sutt —4A 132
Linley Cres. Romf —3H 37
Linley Rd. N17 —2E 30
Linnell Clo. NW11 —6K 27
Linnell Dri. NW11 —6K 27
Linnell Rd. N18 —5B 18
Linnell Rd. SE5 —2E 94
Linnet Clo. N9 —1E 18
Linnet Clo. SE28 —7C 68
Linnet Clo. Bush —1B 10
Linnet M. SW12 —7E 92
Linnett Clo. E4 —4K 19
Linom Rd. SW4 —4J 93
Linscott Rd. E5 —4J 47
Linsdell Rd. Bark —1G 67
Linsey Ct. E10 —1C 48
(off Grange Rd.)
Linsey St. SE16 —4G 79
(in two parts)
Linslade Clo. Houn —5C 86
Linslade Ho. E2 —1G 63
Linstead St. NW6 —7J 43
Linstead Way. SW18 —7G 91
Lintaine Clo. W6 —6G 75
Linthorpe Av. Wemb —6C 40
Linthorpe Rd. N16 —7E 30
Linthorpe Rd. Barn —3H 5
Linton Clo. Well —1B 100
Linton Ct. Romf —2K 37
Linton Gdns. E6 —6C 66
Linton Gro. SE27 —5B 110
Linton Rd. Bark —7G 51
Lintons, The. Bark —7G 51
Linton St. N1 —1C 62
Linver Rd. SW6 —2J 91
Linwood Clo. SE5 —2D 94
Linwood Clo. SE5 —2F 95
Linzee Rd. N8 —4J 29
Lion Av. Twic —1K 103
Lion Clo. SE4 —6C 96
Lionel Gdns. SE9 —5B 98
Lionel M. W10 —5G 59
Lionel Rd. SE9 —5B 98
Lionel Rd. Bren —3E 72
(in two parts)
Lion Ga. Gdns. Rich —3F 89

Long Dri. W3 —6A 58
Long Dri. Gnfd —1F 55
Long Dri. Ruis —5A 38
Long Elmes. Harr —1F 23
Longfellow Rd. E3 —3A 64
Longfellow Rd. E17 —6B 32
Longfellow Rd. Wor Pk —1C 130
Longfellow Way. SE1
—4F 79 (9F 148)
Long Field. NW9 —7F 13
Longfield. Brom —1H 127
Longfield Av. E17 —4A 32
Longfield Av. NW7 —7H 13
Longfield Av. W5 —7C 56
Longfield Av. Wall —1E 132
Longfield Av. Wemb —1E 40
Longfield Cres. SE26 —3J 111
Longfield Dri. SW14 —5H 89
Longfield Dri. Mitc —1C 122
Longfield Est. SE1 —4F 79 (9F 148)
Longfield Rd. W5 —6C 56
Longfield St. SW18 —7J 91
Longfield Wlk. W5 —6C 56
Longford Av. S'hall —7F 55
Longford Clo. Hamp —4E 102
Longford Clo. Hay —7B 54
Longford Ct. NW4 —4F 27
Longford Gdns. Hay —7B 54
Longford Gdns. Sutt —3A 132
Longford Ho. Hamp —4E 102
Longford Rd. Twic —1E 102
Longford St. NW1 —4F 61 (3K 139)
Longford Wlk. SW2 —7A 94
Longhayes Av. Romf —4D 36
Longhayes Ct. Romf —4D 36
Longheath Gdns. Croy —5J 125
Long Hedges. Houn —2E 86
Longhedge St. SW11 —2E 92
Longhill Rd. SE6 —2F 113
Longhope Clo. SE15 —6E 78
Longhurst Rd. SE13 —5G 97
Longhurst Rd. Croy —6H 125
Longland Ct. SE1 —5G 79
Longland Dri. N20 —3E 14
Longlands Ct. Sidc —2K 115
Longlands Pk. Cres. Sidc —3J 115
Longlands Rd. Sidc —3J 115
Long La. EC1 —5B 62 (6K 141)
Long La. N3 & N2 —1K 27
Long La. SW1 —2D 78
Long La. Bexh —7D 84
Long La. Croy —6J 125
Longleat Rd. Enf —5K 7
Longleigh Ho. SE5 —1E 94
(off Peckham Rd.)
Longleigh La. Bexh —6C 84
Longley Av. Wemb —1F 57
Longley Ct. SW8 —1J 93
Longley Rd. SW17 —6C 108
Longley Rd. Croy —7B 124
Longley Rd. Harr —5G 23
Long Leys. E4 —6J 19
Longley St. SE1 —4G 79
Longley Way. NW2 —3E 42
Longman Ho. E8 —1F 63
Long Mark Rd. E16 —5B 66
Long Mead. NW9 —1B 26
Longmead. Chst —2E 128
Longmead Dri. Sidc —2D 116
Longmead Ho. SE27 —5C 110
Long Meadow. NW5 —5H 45
Long Meadow Clo. W Wick —7E 126
Longmeadow Rd. Sidc —1J 115
Longmead Rd. SW17 —5D 108
Longmoore St. SW1
—4G 77 (9L 145)
Longmore Av. Barn —6F 5
Longmore St. SW1 —4G 77

Longnor Est. E1 —3K 63
Longnor Rd. E1 —3K 63
Long Pond Rd. SE3 —1G 97
Longreach Ct. Bark —2H 67
Long Reach Rd. Bark —4K 67
Longridge Ho. SE1 —3C 78 (7M 147)
Longridge La. S'hall —6F 55
Longridge Rd. SW5 —4J 75
Long Ridges. N2 —3E 28
(off Fortis Grn.)
Long Rd. SW4 —4F 93
Long's Ct. WC2 —7H 61 (1B 146)
(off Orange St.)
Longs Ct. Rich —4F 89
Longshaw Rd. E4 —3A 20
Longshore. SE8 —4B 80
Longstaff Cres. SW18 —7J 91
Longstaff Rd. SW18 —6J 91
Longstone Av. NW10 —7B 42
Longstone Rd. SW17 —5F 109
Long St. E2 —3F 63 (1E 142)
(in two parts)
Longthornton Rd. SW16 —2G 123
Longton Av. SE26 —4G 111
Longton Gro. SE26 —4H 111
Longview Vs. Romf —1F 37
Longview Way. Romf —1K 37
Longville Rd. SE11 —4B 78 (8J 147)
Long Wlk. SE1 —3E 78 (6D 148)
Long Wlk. SE18 —6F 83
Long Wlk. SW13 —2B 90
Long Wlk. N Mald —3J 119
Long Wall. E15 —3F 65
Longwood Dri. SW15 —6C 90
Longwood Gdns. Ilf —4D 34
Longworth Clo. SE28 —6D 68
Long Yd. WC1 —4K 61 (4E 140)
Loning, The. NW9 —4B 26
Loning, The. Enf —1D 8
Lonsdale Av. E6 —3B 66
Lonsdale Av. Romf —6J 37
Lonsdale Av. Wemb —5E 40
Lonsdale Clo. E6 —4C 66
Lonsdale Clo. SE9 —3B 114
Lonsdale Clo. Edgw —5A 12
Lonsdale Clo. Pinn —1C 22
Lonsdale Ct. Surb —7D 118
Lonsdale Cres. Ilf —6F 35
Lonsdale Dri. Enf —4C 6
Lonsdale Gdns. T Hth —4K 123
Lonsdale M. Rich —1G 89
Lonsdale Pl. N1 —7A 46
Lonsdale Rd. E11 —7H 33
Lonsdale Rd. NW6 —2H 59
Lonsdale Rd. SE25 —4H 125
Lonsdale Rd. SW13 —1B 90
Lonsdale Rd. W4 —4B 74
Lonsdale Rd. W11 —6H 59
Lonsdale Rd. Bexh —2F 101
Lonsdale Rd. S'hall —3B 70
Lonsdale Sq. N1 —7A 46
Lonsdale Sq. W11 —7J 59
Loobert Rd. N15 —3E 30
Looe Gdns. Ilf —3F 35
Loop Rd. Chst —6G 115
Lopen Rd. N18 —4K 17
Lopez Ho. SW9 —3J 93
Lorac Ct. Sutt —7J 131
Loraine Clo. Enf —5D 8
Loraine Ct. Chst —5F 115
Loraine Ho. Wall —4F 133
Loraine Rd. N7 —4K 45
Loraine Rd. W4 —6H 73
Lord Av. Ilf —4D 34
Lord Chancellor Wlk. King T
—1K 119
Lorden Wlk. E2 —3G 63
Lord Gdns. Ilf —4D 34

Lord Hills Bri. W2 —5K 59
Lord Hills Rd. W2 —5K 59
Lord Holland La. SW9 —2A 94
Lord Napier Pl. W6 —5C 74
Lord North St. SW1 —3J 77 (7C 146)
Lord Roberts M. SW6 —7K 75
Lord Robert's Ter. SE18 —5E 82
Lord's Clo. SE21 —2C 110
Lords Clo. Felt —2C 102
Lordship Gro. N16 —2D 46
Lordship La. N22 & N17 —2A 30
Lordship La. SE22 —4F 95
Lordship La. Est. SE22 —7G 95
Lordship Pk. N16 —2C 46
Lordship Pk. M. N16 —2C 46
Lordship Pl. SW3 —6C 76
Lordship Rd. N16 —1D 46
Lordship Rd. N'holt —7C 38
Lordship Ter. N16 —2D 46
Lordsmead Rd. N17 —1E 30
Lords View. NW8 —3C 60 (2C 138)
Lord Warwick St. SE18 —3D 82
Loreburn Ho. N7 —4K 45
Lorenzo St. WC1 —3K 61 (1E 140)
Loretto Gdns. Harr —4E 24
Lorian Clo. N12 —4E 14
Loring Rd. N20 —2H 15
Loring Rd. Iswth —2K 87
Loris Rd. W6 —3E 74
Lorn Ct. SW9 —1A 94
Lorne Av. Croy —7K 125
Lorne Clo. NW8 —3C 60 (2D 138)
Lorne Gdns. E11 —4A 34
Lorne Gdns. W11 —2F 75
Lorne Gdns. Croy —7K 125
Lorne Rd. E7 —4K 49
Lorne Rd. E17 —5C 32
Lorne Rd. N4 —1K 45
Lorne Rd. Harr —2K 23
Lorne Rd. Rich —5F 89
Lorne Ter. N3 —2H 27
Lorn Rd. SW9 —2K 93
Lorraine Pk. Harr —7D 10
Lorrimore Rd. SE17 —6B 78
Lorrimore Sq. SE17 —6B 78
Losberne Way. SE16 —5G 79
Lothair Rd. W5 —2D 72
Lothair Rd. N. N4 —6B 30
Lothair Rd. S. N4 —7A 30
Lothbury. EC2 —6D 62 (7A 142)
Lothian Av. Hay —5A 54
Lothian Clo. Wemb —3A 40
Lothian Rd. SW9 —1B 94
Lothrop St. W10 —3G 59
Lots Rd. SW10 —7A 76
Lotus Clo. SE21 —3D 110
Loubet St. SW17 —6D 108
Loudon Rd. NW8 —1A 60
Loudoun Av. Ilf —5F 35
Loudoun Rd. NW8 —1A 60
Loughborough Est. SW9 —3B 94
Loughborough Pk. SW9 —4B 94
Loughborough Rd. SW9 —2A 94
Loughborough St. SE11 —5K 77
Lough La. NW9 —5J 25
Lough Rd. N7 —5A 46
Loughton Way. Buck H —1G 21
Louisa Ct. Twic —2J 103
Louisa Gdns. E1 —4K 63
Louisa St. E1 —4K 63
Louis Bennet Clo. SE24 —4B 94
Louis Clo. N10 —1F 29
Louise Ct. N22 —1A 30
Louise Rd. E15 —6G 49
Louisville Rd. SW17 —3E 108
Lousada Lodge. N14 —6B 6
(off Avenue Rd.)

Louvaine Rd. SW11 —4B 92
Lovage App. E6 —5C 66
Lovat Clo. NW2 —3B 42
Lovat La. EC3 —7E 62 (1C 148)
Lovatt Clo. Edgw —6C 12
Lovatt Wlk. Houn —7C 70
Loveday Rd. W13 —2B 72
Lovegrove St. SE1 —5G 79
Lovegrove Wlk. E14 —1E 80
Lovekyn Clo. King T —2E 118
Lovelace Av. Brom —6E 128
Lovelace Gdns. Bark —4A 52
Lovelace Gdns. Surb —7D 118
Lovelace Grn. SE9 —3D 98
Lovelace Rd. SE21 —2C 110
Lovelace Rd. Surb —7C 118
Loveland Mans. Bark —7K 51
(off Upney La.)
Love La. EC2 —6C 62 (7M 141)
Love La. N17 —7A 18
Love La. SE18 —4E 82
Love La. SE25 —3H 125
(in two parts)
Love La. Bex —6F 101
Love La. Brom —3K 127
(off Elmfield Rd.)
Love La. Mitc —3C 122
(in two parts)
Love La. Mord —7J 121
Love La. Pinn —2B 22
Love La. Sutt —6G 131
Love La. Wfd G —6J 21
Lovel Av. Well —2A 100
Lovelinch Clo. SE15 —6J 79
Lovell Pl. SE16 —3A 80
Lovell Rd. Rich —3C 104
Lovell Rd. S'hall —6F 55
Loveridge M. NW6 —6H 43
Loveridge Rd. NW6 —6H 43
Lovers Wlk. NW7 & N3 —6C 14
Lovers Wlk. SE10 —6F 81
Lovers' Wlk. W1 —1E 76 (2G 145)
(off Broad Wlk.)
Lovett Dri. Cars —7J 121
Lovett Way. NW10 —5J 41
Love Wlk. SE5 —2D 94
Lowbrook Rd. Ilf —4F 51
Low Cross Wood La. SE21 —3F 111
Lowden Rd. N9 —1C 18
Lowden Rd. SE24 —4B 94
Lowden Rd. S'hall —7C 54
Lowe Av. E16 —5J 65
Lowell St. E14 —6A 64
Lowen Rd. Rain —2K 69
Lwr. Addiscombe Rd. Croy —1E 134
Lwr. Addison Gdns. W14 —2G 75
Lwr. Belgrave St. SW1
—3F 77 (7J 145)
Lwr. Boston Rd. W7 —1J 71
Lwr. Broad St. Dag —1G 69
Lwr. Camden. Chst —7D 114
Lwr. Church St. Croy —2B 134
Lwr. Clapton Rd. E5 —3H 47
Lwr. Clarendon Wlk. W11 —6G 59
(off Clarendon Rd.)
Lwr. Common St. SW15 —3D 90
Lwr. Coombe St. Croy —4C 134
Lwr. Downs Rd. SW20 —1F 121
Lwr. Drayton Pl. Croy —2B 134
Lwr. Fosters. NW4 —5E 26
(off New Brent St.)
Lwr. George St. Rich —5D 88
Lwr. Gravel Rd. Brom —7D 128
Lwr. Green W. Mitc —3C 122
Lwr. Grosvenor Pl. SW1
—3F 77 (6K 145)
Lwr. Grove Rd. Rich —6F 89

Lwr. Hall La. E4 —5F 19
Lwr. Ham Rd. King T —5D 104
Lwr. James St. W1
—7G 61 (9M 139)
Lwr. John St. W1 —7G 61 (9M 139)
Lwr. Kenwood Av. Enf —5C 6
Lwr. Maidstone Rd. N11 —6B 16
Lwr. Mall. W6 —5D 74
Lwr. Mardyke Av. Rain —2J 69
Lwr. Marsh. SE1 —2A 78 (5G 147)
Lwr. Marsh La. King T —4F 119
Lwr. Merton Rise. NW3 —7C 44
Lwr. Morden La. Mord —6E 120
Lwr. Mortlake Rd. Rich —4E 88
Lwr. Park Rd. N11 —5B 16
Lwr. Park Rd. Belv —4G 85
Lwr. Pk. Trading Est. W5 —4J 57
Lwr. Place Bus. Cen. NW10 —2J 57
Lwr. Queen's Rd. Buck H —2G 21
Lwr. Richmond Rd. SW15 —3D 90
Lwr. Richmond Rd. Rich & SW14
—3G 89
Lower Rd. N11 —5A 16
Lower Rd. SE16 & SE8 —2J 79
(in two parts)
Lower Rd. Belv & Eri —3H 85
Lower Rd. Harr —1H 39
Lower Rd. Sutt —4A 132
Lwr. Robert St. WC2
—7J 61 (1D 146)
(off Robert St.)
Lwr. Sloane St. SW1
—4E 76 (9G 145)
Lower Sq. Iswth —3B 88
Lwr. Square, The. Sutt —5K 131
Lwr. Staithe. W4 —1J 89
Lwr. Strand. NW9 —2B 26
Lwr. Sydenham Ind. Est Beck
—5B 112
Lwr. Sydenham Ind. Est. SE26
—5B 112
Lwr. Teddington Rd. King T —1D 118
Lower Ter. NW3 —3A 44
Lower Thames St. EC3
—7D 62 (1B 148)
Lowestoft Clo. E5 —2J 47
(off Southwold Rd.)
Loweswater Clo. Wemb —2D 40
Lowfield Rd. NW6 —7J 43
Lowfield Rd. W3 —6H 57
Low Hall Clo. E4 —7J 9
Lowhall La. E17 —6A 32
Lowick Rd. Harr —4J 23
Lowlands Gdns. Romf —5H 37
Lowlands Rd. Harr —6J 23
Lowlands Rd. Pinn —7A 22
Lowman Rd. N7 —4K 45
Lowndes Clo. SW1 —3E 76 (7H 145)
Lowndes Ct. SW1 —3D 76 (6F 144)
Lowndes Ct. W1 —6G 61 (8L 139)
(off Kingly St.)
Lowndes Pl. SW1 —3E 76 (7G 145)
Lowndes Sq. SW1 —2D 76 (5F 144)
Lowndes St. SW1 —3E 76 (6F 144)
Lownds Ct. Brom —2J 127
Lowood St. E1 —7H 63
Lowry Cres. Mitc —2C 122
Lowry Ho. N17 —1F 31
(off Pembury Rd.)
Lowshoe La. Romf —1G 37
Lowther Dri. Enf —4D 6
Lowther Gdns. SW7
—3B 76 (6B 144)
Lowther Hill. SE23 —7A 96
Lowther Rd. E17 —2A 32
Lowther Rd. N7 —5A 46
Lowther Rd. SW13 —1B 90
Lowther Rd. King T —1F 119
Lowther Rd. Stan —3F 25

230

...rth Rd. SE5 —1C 94
...w Wlk. E17 —5B 32
...xford Av. E6 —2B 66
...xford La. Ilf —5G 51
...xford Rd. Bark —6F 51
...xford Ter. Bark —6G 51
...xham Rd. E4 —7J 19
...xham St. WC1 —3J 61 (2D 140)
...xley Clo. SE26 —5K 111
...xley Rd. SW18 —1B 108
...xley Rd. Hamp —4D 102
...xton Rd. SE23 —1K 111
...xwood Rd. N17 —3E 30
...bbock Rd. Chst —7D 114
...bbock St. SE14 —7J 79
...can Ho. N1 —1D 62
   (off Colville Est.)
...can Pl. SW3 —4C 76 (9C 144)
...can Rd. Barn —3B 4
...cas Av. E13 —1K 65
...cas Av. Harr —2E 38
...cas Ct. SE26 —5A 112
...cas Rd. SE20 —6J 111
...cas Sq. NW1 —1G 27
...cas St. SE8 —1C 96
...cerne Clo. N13 —3D 16
...cerne Ct. Eri —3E 84
...cerne Gro. E17 —4F 33
...cerne M. W8 —1J 75
...cerne Rd. N5 —4B 46
...cerne Rd. Orp —7K 129
...cerne Rd. T Hth —4C 124
...cey Rd. SE16 —3G 79
...cy Cres. W3 —5J 57
   (in two parts)
...cien Rd. SW17 —4E 108
...cien Rd. SW19 —2K 107
...cinda Ct. Enf —4K 7
...cknow St. SE18 —7J 83
...corn Clo. SE12 —6H 97
...ctons Av. Buck H —1F 21
...cy Cres. W3 —5J 57
...cy Gdns. Dag —3E 52
...ddesdon Rd. Eri —7G 85
...dford Clo. NW9 —2A 26
...dford Clo. Croy —3A 134
...dgate B'way. EC4
       —6B 62 (8J 141)
...dgate Cir. EC4 —6B 62 (8J 141)
...dgate Hill. EC4 —6B 62 (8J 141)
...dgate Sq. EC4 —6B 62 (8K 141)
...cham Clo. SE28 —6C 68
...dlow Clo. Brom —3J 127
...dlow Clo. Harr —4D 38
...dlow Ct. W3 —2J 73
...dlow Rd. W5 —4C 56
...dlow St. EC1 —4C 62 (3L 141)
...dlow Way. N2 —4A 28
...dovick Wlk. SW15 —4B 90
...dwick M. SE14 —7A 80
...ffield Rd. SE2 —3B 84
...ffman Rd. SE12 —3K 113
...gard Rd. SE15 —2H 95
...gg App. E12 —3E 50
...ke St. EC2 —4E 62 (3C 142)
...kin Cres. E4 —3A 20
...akin St. E1 —6J 63
...ley La. NW7 —5E 12
...llingstone Clo. Orp —7B 116
...llingstone Cres. Orp —7A 116
...llingstone Rd. Belv —6F 85
...llington Garth. N12 —5C 14
...llington Garth. Brom —7G 113
...llington Rd. SE20 —7G 111
...llington Rd. Dag —7E 52
...lot Gdns. N19 —2F 45
...lworth Av. Houn —1F 87
...lworth Av. Wemb —7C 24

Lulworth Clo. Harr —3D 38
Lulworth Cres. Mitc —2C 122
Lulworth Dri. Pinn —6B 22
Lulworth Gdns. Harr —2C 38
Lulworth Rd. Ho. SW8 —7K 77
Lulworth Rd. SE9 —2C 114
Lulworth Rd. SE15 —2H 95
Lulworth Rd. Well —2K 99
Lulworth Waye. Hay —6A 54
Lumen Rd. Wemb —2D 40
Lumley Clo. Belv —6G 85
Lumley Ct. WC2 —7J 61 (1D 145)
Lumley Gdns. Sutt —5G 131
Lumley Rd. Sutt —5G 131
Lumley St. W1 —6E 60 (8H 139)
Luna Rd. T Hth —3C 124
Lund Point. E15 —1E 64
Lunham Rd. SE19 —6E 110
Lupin Clo. SW2 —2B 110
Lupin Clo. Croy —1K 135
Lupin Gdns. Ilf —6F 51
Lupton Clo. SE12 —3K 113
Lupton St. NW5 —4G 45
Lupus St. SW1 —5F 77
Luralda Gdns. E14 —5F 81
Lurgan Av. W6 —6F 75
Lurline Gdns. SW11 —1E 92
Luscombe Ct. Short —2G 127
Luscombe Way. SW8 —7J 77
Lushington Rd. NW10 —2D 58
Lushington Rd. SE6 —4D 112
Lusitania Building. E1 —7K 63
   (off Jardine Rd.)
Lutea Ho. Sutt —7A 132
   (off Walnut M.)
Luther Clo. Edgw —2D 12
Luther King Clo. E17 —6A 32
Luther Rd. Tedd —5K 103
Luton Pl. SE10 —7E 80
Luton Rd. E13 —4J 65
Luton Rd. E17 —3B 32
Luton Rd. Sidc —3D 116
Luton St. NW8 —4B 60 (4B 138)
Lutton Ter. NW3 —4A 44
   (off Heath St.)
Luttrell Av. SW15 —5D 90
Lutwyche Rd. SE6 —2B 112
Luxborough La. Chig —3H 21
Luxborough St. W1
       —5E 60 (5G 139)
Luxemburg Gdns. W6 —4F 75
Luxfield Rd. SE9 —1C 114
Luxford St. SE16 —4K 79
Luxmore Gdns. SE4 —2B 96
Luxmore St. SE4 —1B 96
Luxor St. SE5 —3C 94
Lyall Av. SE21 —4E 110
Lyall M. SW1 —3E 76 (7G 145)
Lyall M. W. SW1 —3E 76 (7G 145)
Lyall St. SW1 —3E 76 (7G 145)
Lyal Rd. E3 —2A 64
Lycett Pl. W12 —2C 74
Lyconby Gdns. Croy —7A 126
Lydd Clo. Sidc —3J 115
Lydden Gro. SW18 —7K 91
Lydden Rd. SW18 —7K 91
Lydd Rd. Bexh —7F 85
Lydeard Rd. E6 —7D 50
Lydford Clo. N16 —5E 46
   (off Pellerin Rd.)
Lydford Rd. N15 —5D 30
Lydford Rd. NW2 —6E 42
Lydford Rd. W9 —4H 59
Lydhurst Av. SW2 —2K 109
Lydia Ct. N12 —6F 15
Lydney Clo. SE15 —7E 78
Lydney Clo. SW19 —2G 107

Lydon Rd. SW4 —3G 93
Lydstep Rd. Chst —4E 114
Lyford Rd. SW18 —7B 92
Lyford St. SE7 —4C 82
Lygon Ho. SW6 —1G 91
   (off Fulham Pal. Rd.)
Lygon Pl. SW1 —3F 77 (7J 145)
Lyham Clo. SW2 —6J 93
Lyham Rd. SW2 —5J 93
Lyle Clo. Mitc —7E 122
Lyme Farm Rd. SE12 —4J 97
Lyme Gro. E9 —7J 47
Lymer Av. SE19 —5F 111
Lyme Rd. Well —1B 100
Lymescote Gdns. Sutt —2J 131
Lyme St. NW1 —7G 45
Lyme Ter. NW1 —7G 45
Lyminge Clo. Sidc —4K 115
Lyminge Gdns. SW18 —1C 108
Lymington Av. N22 —2A 30
Lymington Clo. SW16 —2H 123
Lymington Ct. Sutt —3K 131
Lymington Gdns. Eps —5B 130
Lymington Rd. NW6 —6K 43
Lymington Rd. Dag —1D 52
Lympne. N17 —2D 30
   (off Gloucester Rd.)
Lympstone Gdns. SE15 —7G 79
Lynbridge Gdns. N13 —4G 17
Lynbrook Clo. SE15 —7E 78
Lynbrook Clo. Rain —2K 69
Lynch Wlk. SE8 —6B 80
Lynchwood. SE3 —2H 97
Lyncott Cres. SW4 —4F 93
Lyncroft Av. Pinn —5C 22
Lyncroft Gdns. NW6 —5J 43
Lyncroft Gdns. W13 —2C 72
Lyncroft Gdns. Houn —5G 87
Lyndale. NW2 —4H 43
Lyndale Av. NW2 —3H 43
Lyndale Clo. SE3 —6H 81
Lyndhurst Av. N12 —6J 15
Lyndhurst Av. NW7 —6F 13
Lyndhurst Av. SW16 —2H 123
Lyndhurst Av. Pinn —1A 22
Lyndhurst Av. S'hall —1F 71
Lyndhurst Av. Surb —7H 119
Lyndhurst Av. Twic —1D 102
Lyndhurst Clo. NW10 —3K 41
Lyndhurst Clo. Bexh —3H 101
Lyndhurst Clo. Croy —3F 135
Lyndhurst Ct. E18 —1J 33
Lyndhurst Dri. E10 —7E 32
Lyndhurst Dri. N Mald —7A 120
Lyndhurst Gdns. N3 —1G 27
Lyndhurst Gdns. NW3 —5B 44
Lyndhurst Gdns. Bark —6J 51
Lyndhurst Gdns. Enf —4K 7
Lyndhurst Gdns. Ilf —6H 35
Lyndhurst Gdns. Pinn —1A 22
Lyndhurst Gro. SE15 —2E 94
Lyndhurst Rise. Chig —4K 21
Lyndhurst Rd. E4 —7K 19
Lyndhurst Rd. N18 —4B 18
Lyndhurst Rd. N22 —6F 17
Lyndhurst Rd. NW3 —5B 44
Lyndhurst Rd. Bexh —3H 101
Lyndhurst Rd. Gnfd —4F 55
Lyndhurst Rd. T Hth —4A 124
Lyndhurst Sq. SE15 —1F 95
Lyndhurst Ter. NW3 —5B 44
Lyndhurst Way. SE15 —1F 95
Lyndhurst Way. Sutt —7J 131
Lyndon Av. Sidc —5K 99
Lyndon Av. Wall —3E 132
Lyndon Rd. Belv —4G 85
Lyne Cres. E17 —1B 32
Lyneham Wlk. E5 —5A 48

Lynette Av. SW4 —6G 93
Lynett Rd. Dag —2D 52
Lynford Clo. Edgw —1J 25
Lynford Gdns. Edgw —3C 12
Lynford Gdns. Ilf —2K 51
Lynford Ter. N9 —1A 18
Lynmere Rd. Well —2B 100
Lynmouth Av. Enf —6A 8
Lynmouth Av. Mord —6F 121
Lynmouth Gdns. Gnfd —1B 56
Lynmouth Gdns. Houn —1B 86
Lynmouth Rd. E17 —6A 32
Lynmouth Rd. N2 —3D 28
Lynmouth Rd. N16 —1F 47
Lynmouth Rd. Gnfd —1B 56
Lynn Clo. Harr —2H 23
Lynne Clo. SE23 —7B 96
Lynne Way. NW10 —6A 42
Lynne Way. N'holt —2B 54
Lynn M. E11 —2G 49
Lynn Rd. E11 —2G 49
Lynn Rd. SW12 —7F 93
Lynn Rd. Ilf —7H 35
Lynn St. Enf —1J 7
Lynscott Way. S Croy —7B 134
Lynstead Ct. Beck —2A 126
Lynsted Clo. Bexh —5H 101
Lynsted Clo. Brom —2A 128
Lynsted Ct. Beck —2A 126
Lynsted Gdns. SE9 —4B 98
Lynton Av. N12 —4G 15
Lynton Av. NW9 —4B 26
Lynton Av. W13 —6A 56
Lynton Av. Romf —1G 37
Lynton Clo. NW10 —5A 42
Lynton Clo. Iswth —4K 87
Lynton Cres. Ilf —6F 35
Lynton Est. SE1 —5G 79
Lynton Gdns. N11 —6C 16
Lynton Gdns. Enf —7K 7
Lynton Grange. N2 —3D 28
Lynton Mead. N20 —3D 14
Lynton Rd. E4 —5J 19
Lynton Rd. N8 —5H 29
   (in two parts)
Lynton Rd. NW6 —2H 59
Lynton Rd. SE1 —4F 79 (9E 148)
Lynton Rd. W3 —7G 57
Lynton Rd. Croy —6A 124
Lynton Rd. Harr —2C 38
Lynton Rd. N Mald —5K 119
Lynwood Clo. E18 —1A 34
Lynwood Clo. Harr —3C 38
Lynwood Ct. King T —2H 119
Lynwood Dri. Wor Pk —2C 130
Lynwood Gdns. Croy —4K 133
Lynwood Gdns. S'hall —6D 54
Lynwood Gro. N21 —1F 17
Lynwood Gro. Orp —7J 129
Lynwood Rd. SW17 —3D 108
Lynwood Rd. W5 —3E 55
Lyon Bus. Pk. Bark —2J 67
Lyon Ind. Est. NW2 —2D 42
Lyon Meade. Stan —1C 24
Lyon Pk. Av. Wemb —6E 40
   (in two parts)
Lyon Rd. SW19 —1A 122
Lyon Rd. Harr —6K 23
Lyonsdown Av. Barn —6F 5
Lyonsdown Rd. Barn —6F 5
Lyons Pl. NW8 —4B 60 (4A 138)
Lyon St. N1 —7K 45
Lyons Wlk. W14 —4G 75
Lyon Way. Gnfd —1J 55
Lyric Dri. Gnfd —4F 55
Lyric Rd. SW13 —1B 90
Lysander Gro. N19 —1H 45
Lysander Rd. Croy —6K 133

Lysias Rd. SW12 —6F 93
Lysia St. SW6 —7F 75
Lysons Wlk. SW15 —4C 90
Lytchet Rd. Brom —7K 113
Lytchet Way. Enf —1D 8
Lytchgate Clo. S Croy —7E 134
Lytcott Gro. SE22 —5E 94
Lytham Gro. W5 —3F 57
Lytham St. SE17 —6D 78
Lyttelton Clo. NW3 —7C 44
Lyttelton Ct. N2 —5A 28
Lyttelton Rd. E10 —3D 48
Lyttelton Rd. N2 —5A 28
Lyttleton Rd. N8 —3A 30
Lytton Av. N13 —2F 17
Lytton Av. Enf —1F 9
Lytton Clo. N2 —6B 28
Lytton Clo. N'holt —7D 38
Lytton Gdns. Wall —4H 133
Lytton Gro. SW15 —5F 91
Lytton Rd. E11 —7G 33
Lytton Rd. Barn —4F 5
Lytton Rd. Pinn —1C 22
Lytton Strachey Path. SE28 —7B 68
Lyveden Rd. SE3 —7K 81
Lyveden Rd. SW17 —6D 108

Maberley Cres. SE19 —7G 111
Maberley Rd. SE19 —1G 125
Maberley Rd. Beck —3K 125
Mabledon Pl. WC1 —3H 61 (2B 140)
Mablethorpe Rd. SW6 —7G 75
Mabley St. E9 —5A 48
Mablin Lodge. Buck H —1F 21
McAdam Dri. Enf —2G 7
Macaret Clo. N20 —7E 4
Macarthur Clo. E7 —6J 49
Macarthur Ter. SE7 —6B 82
Macaulay Ct. SW4 —3F 93
   (off Macaulay Rd.)
Macaulay Rd. E6 —2B 66
Macaulay Rd. SW4 —3F 93
Macaulay Sq. SW4 —4F 93
Macaulay Way. SE28 —1B 84
McAuley Clo. SE1 —3A 78 (6G 147)
McAuley Clo. SE9 —5E 98
Macauley M. SE13 —1E 96
Macbean St. SE18 —3F 83
Macbeth Ho. N1 —2E 62
Macbeth St. W6 —5D 74
McCall Clo. SW4 —2J 93
McCall Cres. SE7 —5C 82
McCall Ho. N7 —4J 45
McCarthy Rd. Felt —5B 102
Macclesfield Rd. EC1
       —3C 62 (1L 141)
Macclesfield Rd. SE25 —5J 125
Macclesfield St. W1
       —7H 61 (9B 140)
McCoid Way. SE1 —2C 78 (5L 147)
McConnell Rd. NW1
       —3H 61 (2A 140)
McCrone M. NW3 —6B 44
McCullum Rd. E3 —1B 64
McDermott Clo. SW11 —3C 92
McDermott Rd. SE15 —3G 95
Macdonald Av. Dag —3H 53
Macdonald Rd. E7 —4J 49
Macdonald Rd. E17 —2E 32
Macdonald Rd. N11 —5J 15
Macdonald Rd. N19 —2G 45
Macdonald Rd. Dag —3H 53
McDowall Clo. E16 —5H 65
McDowall Rd. SE5 —1C 94
Macduff Rd. SW11 —1E 92
Mace Clo. E1 —1H 79
McEntee Av. E17 —1A 32

anningtree Rd. Ruis —4A 38
anningtree St. E1 —6G 63
annin Rd. Rœml —7B 36
annock Rd. N22 —3B 30
ann's Clo. Iswth —5K 87
anns Rd. Edgw —6B 12
anoel Rd. Twic —3G 103
anor Av. E7 —4A 50
anor Av. SE4 —2B 96
anor Av. Houn —3B 86
anor Av. N'holt —7D 38
anor Brook. SE3 —4J 97
anor Clo. E17 —2A 32
anor Clo. NW7 —5E 12
anor Clo. NW9 —5H 25
anor Clo. SE28 —7C 68
anor Clo. Barn —4B 4
anor Clo. Cray —4K 101
anor Clo. Dag —6K 53
anor Clo. Wor Pk —1A 130
anor Cotts. N2 —2A 28
anor Cotts. App. N2 —2A 28
anor Ct. E4 —1B 20
anor Ct. E10 —1D 48
anor Ct. N20 —3J 15
(off Aylmer Rd.)
anor Ct. N14 —2C 16
anor Ct. N20 —3J 15
(off York Way)
anor Ct. SW2 —5K 93
anor Ct. SW16 —3J 109
anor Ct. W3 —4G 73
anor Ct. Bark —7K 51
anor Ct. Bexh —5H 101
anor Ct. Harr —6K 23
anor Ct. Twic —2G 103
anor Ct. W Wick —1D 136
anor Ct. Rd. W7 —7J 55
anor Cres. Surb —6G 119
anor Deerfield Cotts. NW9 —5B 26
anor Dene. SE26 —6C 68
anordene Rd. SE28 —6D 68
anor Dri. N14 —1A 16
anor Dri. N20 —4H 15
anor Dri. NW7 —5E 12
anor Dri. Eps —6A 130
anor Dri. Felt —5B 102
anor Dri. Surb —6F 119
anor Dri. Wemb —4F 41
anor Dri. N. N Mald & Wor Pk
—7K 119
anor Dri., The. Wor Pk —1A 130
anor Est. SE16 —4H 79
anor Farm Ct. E6 —3D 66
(off Holloway Rd.)
anor Farm Dri. E4 —3B 20
anor Farm Rd. SW16 —2A 124
anor Farm Rd. Wemb —2D 56
anorfield Clo. N19 —4G 45
(off Fulbeck M.)
anor Fields. SW15 —6F 91
anorfields Clo. Chst —3K 129
anor Gdns. N7 —3J 45
anor Gdns. SW20 —2H 121
anor Gdns. W3 —4G 73
anor Gdns. W4 —5A 74
anor Gdns. Hamp —7F 103
anor Gdns. Rich —5A 88
anor Gdns. Ruis —5A 38
anor Gdns. S Croy —6F 135
anor Ga. N'holt —7C 38
anorgate Rd. King T —1G 119
anor Gro. SE15 —6J 79
anor Gro. Beck —2D 126
anor Gro. Rich —4G 89
anor Hall Av. NW4 —2F 27
anor Hall Dri. NW4 —2F 27

Manorhall Gdns. E10 —1C 48
Manor Ho. Dri. NW6 —7F 43
Manor Ho. Est. Stan —5G 11
Manor Ho. Way. Iswth —3B 88
Manor La. SE13 & SE12 —5G 97
Manor La. Sutt —5A 132
Manor La. Ter. SE13 —4G 97
Manor M. SE4 —2B 96
Manor Mt. SE23 —1J 111
Manor Pde. Harr —6K 23
Manor Pk. SE13 —4G 97
Manor Pk. Chst —2H 129
Manor Pk. Rich —4F 89
Manor Pk. Clo. W Wick —1D 136
Manor Pk. Cres. Edgw —6B 12
Manor Pk. Dri. Harr —3F 23
Manor Pk. Gdns. Edgw —5B 12
Manor Pk. Rd. E12 —4B 50
Manor Pk. Rd. N2 —3A 28
Manor Pk. Rd. NW10 —1B 58
Manor Pk. Rd. Chst —1G 129
Manor Pk. Rd. Sutt —5A 132
Manor Pk. Rd. W Wick —1D 136
Manor Pl. SE17 —5B 78
Manor Pl. Chst —2H 129
Manor Pl. Mitc —3G 123
Manor Pl. Sutt —4K 131
Manor Rd. E10 —7C 32
Manor Rd. E15 & E16 —2G 65
Manor Rd. E17 —2A 32
Manor Rd. N16 —2D 46
Manor Rd. N17 —1G 31
Manor Rd. N22 —6D 16
Manor Rd. SE25 —4G 125
Manor Rd. SW20 —2H 121
Manor Rd. W13 —7A 56
Manor Rd. Bark —7K 51
Manor Rd. Barn —4B 4
Manor Rd. Beck —2D 126
Manor Rd. Bex —1H 117
Manor Rd. Chad —6D 36
Manor Rd. Dag —6J 53
Manor Rd. Dart —4K 101
Manor Rd. Enf —2H 7
Manor Rd. Harr —6A 24
Manor Rd. Mitc —4G 123
Manor Rd. Rich —4G 89
Manor Rd. Sidc —3A 116
Manor Rd. Sutt —7H 131
Manor Rd. Tedd —5A 104
Manor Rd. Twic —2G 103
Manor Rd. Wall —4F 133
Manor Rd. Wfd G & Chig —6J 21
Manor Rd. W Wick —2D 136
Manor Rd. N. N Mald —6A 120
Manor Rd. N. Wall —4F 133
Manorside. Barn —4B 4
Manorside Clo. SE2 —4C 84
Manor Sq. Dag —2C 52
Manor Vale. Bren —5C 72
Manor View. N3 —2K 27
Manor Way. E4 —4A 20
Manor Way. NW9 —4A 26
Manor Way. SE3 —4H 97
Manor Way. Beck —2C 126
Manor Way. Bex —1G 117
Manor Way. Bexh —3K 101
Manor Way. Brom —6C 128
Manorway. Enf —7K 7
Manor Way. Harr —4F 23
Manor Way. Mitc —3G 123
Manor Way. Orp —4G 129
Manor Way. Rain —6K 69
(in two parts)
Manor Way. S'hall —4B 70
Manor Way. S Croy —6E 134
Manor Way. Wfd G —5F 21
Manor Way. Wor Pk —1A 130

Manor Way, The. Wall —4F 133
Manresa Rd. SW3 —5C 76
Mansard Beeches. SW17 —5E 108
Mansard Clo. Pinn —3B 22
Mansel Gro. E17 —1C 32
Mansell Rd. W3 —2K 73
Mansell Rd. Gnfd —5F 55
Mansell St. E1 —6F 63 (8F 142)
Mansel Rd. SW19 —6G 107
Mansergh Clo. SE18 —7C 82
Manse Rd. N16 —3F 47
Manser Rd. Rain —3K 69
Mansfield Av. N15 —4D 30
Mansfield Av. Barn —6J 5
Mansfield Clo. N9 —6B 8
Mansfield Heights. N2 —5D 28
Mansfield Hill. E4 —7J 9
Mansfield M. W1 —5F 61 (6J 139)
Mansfield Pl. NW3 —4A 44
Mansfield Rd. E11 —6K 33
Mansfield Rd. E17 —4B 32
Mansfield Rd. NW3 —5D 44
Mansfield Rd. W3 —4H 57
Mansfield Rd. Ilf —2E 50
Mansfield Rd. S Croy —6D 134
Mansfield St. W1 —5F 61 (6J 139)
Mansford St. E2 —2G 63
Manship Rd. Mitc —7E 108
Mansion Gdns. NW3 —3K 43
Mansion Ho. Pl. EC4
—6D 62 (8A 142)
Mansion Ho. St. EC2
(off Victoria St.) —6D 62 (8A 142)
Mansions, The. SW5 —5K 75
Manson M. SW7 —4A 76
Manson Pl. SW7 —4B 76 (9A 144)
Mansted Gdns. Romf —7C 36
Manston. N17 —2D 30
(off Adams Rd.)
Manston Av. S'hall —4E 70
Manston Clo. SE20 —1J 125
Manstone Rd. NW2 —5G 43
Manthorp Rd. SE18 —5G 83
Mantilla Rd. SW17 —4E 108
Mantle Rd. SE4 —3A 96
Mantlet Clo. SW16 —7G 109
Manton Av. W7 —2K 71
Manton Rd. SE2 —4A 84
Mantua St. SW11 —3B 92
Mantus Clo. E1 —4J 63
Mantus Rd. E1 —4J 63
Manus Way. N20 —2F 15
Manville Gdns. SW17 —3F 109
Manville Rd. SW17 —2E 108
Manwood Rd. SE4 —5B 96
Manwood St. E16 —1D 82
Manygates. SW12 —2F 109
Mapesbury Rd. NW2 —7G 43
Mape St. E2 —4H 63
Maple Av. E4 —5G 19
Maple Av. W3 —1A 74
Maple Av. Harr —2F 39
Maple Clo. N16 —6G 31
Maple Clo. SW4 —6H 93
Maple Clo. Buck H —3G 21
Maple Clo. Hamp —6D 102
Maple Clo. Hay —3B 54
Maple Clo. Mitc —1F 123
Maple Clo. Orp —5H 129
Maple Ct. E6 —5E 66
Maple Ct. N Mald —3K 119
Maple Cres. Sidc —6A 100
Maplecroft Clo. E6 —6B 66
Mapledale Av. Croy —2G 135
Mapledene. Chst —5G 115
Mapledene Est. E8 —7G 47
Mapledene Rd. E8 —7G 47
Maple Gdns. Edgw —7F 13

Maple Gro. NW9 —7J 25
Maple Gro. W5 —3D 72
Maple Gro. Bren —7B 72
Maple Gro. S'hall —5D 54
Maple Ho. E17 —6D 32
Maplehurst. Brom —7G 137
Maplehurst Clo. King T —4E 118
Maple Leaf Dri. Sidc —1K 115
Mapleleafe Gdns. Ilf —3F 35
Maple Leaf Sq. SE16 —2K 79
Maple M. NW6 —2K 59
Maple M. SW16 —5K 109
Maple Pl. W1 —4G 61 (4M 139)
Maple Pl. Bans —7B 72
Maple SE20 —1H 125
Maple Hay —3A 54
Maple Rd. E11 —6G 33
Maple Rd. SE20 —1H 125
Maple Rd. Surb —6B 118
Maple St. E2 —5H 63
Maple St. Romf —4J 37
Maple St. W1 —5G 61 (5L 139)
Maplethorpe Rd. T Hth —4B 124
Mapleton Clo. Brom —6J 127
Mapleton Cres. SW18 —6K 91
Mapleton Cres. Enf —1D 8
Mapleton Rd. E4 —3K 19
Mapleton Rd. SW18 —6J 91
(in two parts)
Maplin Clo. N21 —6E 6
Maplin Wlk. W10 —3F 59
Maplin Rd. E16 —6J 65
Maplin St. E3 —4B 64
Mapperley Clo. E11 —6H 33
Mapperley Dri. Wfd G —7B 20
Maran Way. Eri —3D 84
Marban Rd. W9 —3H 59
Marble Arch. W1 —7D 60 (9E 138)
Marble Clo. W3 —1H 73
Marble Hill Clo. Twic —7B 88
Marble Hill Gdns. Twic —7B 88
Marble Quay. E1 —1G 79
Marbrook Ct. SE12 —3A 114
March. NW9 —18 26
(off Concourse, The)
Marchant Rd. E11 —2F 49
Marchant St. SE14 —6B 80
Marchbank Rd. W14 —6H 75
Marchmont Rd. Rich —5F 89
Marchmont Rd. Wall —7G 133
Marchmont St. WC1
—4J 61 (3C 140)
March Rd. Twic —3C 102
Marchside Clo. Houn —1B 86
Marchwood Clo. SE5 —7E 78
Marchwood Cres. W5 —6C 56
Marcia Rd. SE1 —4E 78 (9D 148)
Marcilly Rd. SW18 —5B 92
Marcon Ct. E8 —5H 47
(off Amhurst Rd.)
Marconi Way. S'hall —6F 55
Marcon Pl. E8 —5H 47
Marco Rd. W6 —3E 74
Marcourt Lawns. W5 —4E 56
Marcus Ct. E15 —1G 65
Marcus Garvey Way. SE24 —4A 94
Marcus St. E15 —1G 65
Marcus St. SW18 —6K 91
Marcus Ter. SW18 —6K 91
Mardale Dri. NW9 —5K 25
Mardell Rd. Croy —5K 125
Marden Av. Brom —6J 127
Marden Ct. SE8 —6C 80
Marden Cres. Bex —5J 101

Marden Cres. Croy —6K 123
Marden Ho. E8 —5H 47
Marden Rd. N17 —2E 30
Marden Rd. Croy —6K 123
Marden Sq. SE16 —3H 79
Marder Rd. W13 —2A 72
Marechal Neil Av. Sidc —3H 115
Marechal Niel Pde. Sidc —3H 115
(off Main Rd.)
Maresby Ho. E4 —2J 19
Mares Field. Croy —3E 134
Maresfield Gdns. NW3 —5A 44
Mare St. E8 —1H 63
Marfleet Clo. Cars —2C 132
Margaret Av. E4 —6J 9
Margaret Bondfield Av. Bark —7A 52
Margaret Bldgs. N16 —1F 47
Margaret Ct. W1 —6G 61 (7L 139)
(off Margaret St.)
Margaret Ct. Barn —4G 5
Margaret Gardner Dri. SE9 —2D 114
Margaret Rd. N16 —1F 47
Margaret Rd. Barn —4G 5
Margaret Rd. Bex —6D 100
Margaret St. W1 —6F 61 (7K 139)
Margaretta Ter. SW3 —6C 76
Margaretting Rd. E12 —1A 50
Margaret Way. Ilf —6C 34
Margate Rd. SW2 —5J 93
Margery Fry Ct. N7 —3J 45
Margery Pk. Rd. E7 —6J 49
Margery Rd. Dag —3D 52
Margery St. WC1 —3A 62 (2G 141)
Margin Dri. SW19 —5F 107
Margravine Gdns. W6 —5F 75
Margravine Rd. W6 —6F 75
Marham Gdns. SW18 —1C 108
Marham Gdns. Mord —6A 122
Maria Clo. SE1 —4H 79
Marian Clo. Hay —4B 54
Marian Ct. E9 —6J 47
Marian Ct. Sutt —5K 131
Marian Pl. E2 —2H 63
Marian Rd. SW16 —1G 123
Marian St. E2 —2H 63
Marian Way. W10 —7B 42
Maria Ter. E1 —4K 63
Maria Theresa Clo. N Mald —5K 119
Maricas Av. Harr —1H 23
Marie Lloyd Gdns. N19 —7J 29
Marie Lloyd Wlk. E8 —6F 47
Mariette Way. Wall —7J 133
Marigold All. SE1 —7B 62 (1J 147)
(off Up. Ground)
Marigold Rd. N17 —7D 18
Marigold St. SE16 —2H 79
Marigold Way. E4 —6G 19
Marigold Way. Croy —1K 135
Marina App. Hay —5C 54
Marina Av. N Mald —5D 120
Marina Clo. Brom —3J 127
Marina Dri. Well —2J 99
Marina Gdns. Romf —6H 37
Marina Way. Tedd —7D 104
Marine Dri. SE18 —4D 82
Marinefield Rd. SW6 —2K 91
Marinel Ho. SE5 —7C 78
Mariner Gdns. Rich —3C 104
Mariner Rd. E12 —4E 50
Mariners M. E14 —4F 81
Marine St. SE16 —3G 79
Marion Clo. Ilf —1H 35
Marion Gro. Wfd G —5B 20
Marion Rd. NW7 —5H 13
Marion Rd. T Hth —5C 124
Marion Sq. E2 —2H 63
Marischal Rd. SE13 —3F 97
Maritime St. E3 —4B 64

Marius Pas. SW17 —2E **108**
Marius Rd. SW17 —2E **108**
Marjorie Gro. SW11 —4D **92**
Marjorie M. E1 —6K **63**
Mark Av. E4 —6J **9**
Mark Clo. Bexh —1E **100**
Market Cen., The. S'hall —4A **70**
Market Ct. W1 —6G 61 (7L 139)
 (off Market Pl.)
Market Entrance. SW8 —7G **77**
Market Est. N7 —6J **45**
Market Hill. SE18 —3E **82**
Market La. Edgw —1J **25**
Market Link. Romf —4K **37**
Market M. W1 —1F **77** (3J **145**)
Market Pde. Sidc —4B **116**
Market Pl. E10 —3C **48**
Market Pl. N2 —3C **28**
Market Pl. NW11 —4K **27**
Market Pl. SE16 —4G **79**
Market Pl. W1 —6G 61 (7L 139)
Market Pl. W3 —1J **73**
Market Pl. Bexh —4G **101**
Market Pl. Bren —7C **72**
Market Pl. Enf —3J **7**
Market Pl. King T —2D **118**
Market Pl. Romf —5K **37**
Market Pl. S'hall —1D **70**
Market Rd. N7 —6J **45**
Market Rd. Rich —3G **89**
Market Row. SW9 —4A **94**
Market Sq. E14 —6D **64**
Market Sq. N9 —2C **18**
Market Sq. Brom —2J **127**
Market St. E6 —2D **66**
Market St. SE18 —4E **82**
Market Ter. Bren —6E 72
 (off Albany Rd.)
Market Way. E14 —6D **64**
Market Way. Wemb —5E **40**
Markfield Gdns. E4 —7J **9**
Markfield Rd. N15 —4G **31**
Markham Ho. Dag —3G 53
 (off Uvedale Rd.)
Markham Pl. SW3 —5D **76**
Markham Sq. SW3 —5D **76**
Markham St. SW3 —5C **76**
Markhole Clo. Hamp —7D **102**
Markhouse Av. E17 —6A **32**
Markhouse Pas. E17 —6B 32
 (off Markhouse Rd.)
Markhouse Rd. E17 —6B **32**
Mark La. EC3 —7E **62** (9D **142**)
Markmanor Av. E17 —7A **32**
Mark Rd. N22 —1B **30**
Marksbury Av. Rich —3G **89**
Marks Lodge. Romf —5K **37**
Mark St. E15 —7G **49**
Mark St. EC2 —4E **62** (3C **142**)
Markwell Clo. SE26 —4H **111**
Markyate Rd. Dag —5B **52**
Marlands Rd. Ilf —3C **34**
Marlborough Av. E8 —1G **63**
 (in two parts)
Marlborough Av. N14 —3B **16**
Marlborough Av. Edgw —3C **12**
Marlborough Bldgs. SW3
 (off Walton St.) —4C 76 (8D 144)
Marlborough Clo. N20 —2J **15**
Marlborough Clo. SE17
 —4C **78** (9K **147**)
Marlborough Clo. SW19 —6C **108**
Marlborough Clo. Orp —6K **129**
Marlborough Ct. W1
 (off Kingly St.) —7G 61 (9L 139)
Marlborough Ct. Enf —5K **7**
Marlborough Ct. Harr —4H **23**

Marlborough Cres. W4 —3K **73**
Marlborough Dri. Ilf —3C **34**
Marlborough Gdns. N20 —3J **15**
Marlborough Gdns. Surb —7D **118**
Marlborough Ga. Stables. W2
 (off Elms M.) —7B 60 (9A 138)
Marlborough Gro. SE1 —5G **79**
Marlborough Hill. NW8 —2A **60**
Marlborough Hill. Harr —4H **23**
Marlborough La. SE7 —7A **82**
Marlborough Mans. NW6 —5K 43
 (off Cannon Hill)
Marlborough Pk. Av. Sidc —7A **100**
Marlborough Pl. NW8 —2A **60**
Marlborough Rd. E4 —6J **19**
Marlborough Rd. E7 —7A **50**
Marlborough Rd. E15 —4G **49**
Marlborough Rd. E18 —2J **33**
Marlborough Rd. N9 —1A **18**
Marlborough Rd. N19 —2H **45**
Marlborough Rd. N22 —7D **16**
Marlborough Rd. SW1
 —1G **77** (3M **145**)
Marlborough Rd. SW19 —6C **108**
Marlborough Rd. W4 —5J **73**
Marlborough Rd. W5 —2D **72**
Marlborough Rd. Bexh —3D **100**
Marlborough Rd. Brom —4A **128**
Marlborough Rd. Dag —4B **52**
Marlborough Rd. Felt —2B **102**
Marlborough Rd. Hamp —6E **102**
Marlborough Rd. Iswth —1B **88**
Marlborough Rd. Rich —6F **89**
Marlborough Rd. Romf —4G **37**
Marlborough Rd. S'hall —3A **70**
Marlborough S. Croy —7C **134**
Marlborough Rd. Sutt —3J **131**
Marlborough St. SW3
 —4C **76** (9C **144**)
Marlborough Yd. N19 —2H **45**
Marler Rd. SE23 —1A **112**
Marley Av. Bexh —6D **84**
Marley Clo. Gnfd —3E **54**
Marley Wlk. NW2 —5E **42**
Marlingdene Clo. Hamp —6E **102**
Marlings Clo. Chst —4J **129**
Marlings Pk. Av. Chst —4J **129**
Marlins Clo. Sutt —5A **132**
Marloes Clo. Wemb —4D **40**
Marloes Rd. W8 —3K **75**
Marlow Clo. SE20 —3H **125**
Marlow Ct. N14 —7B 6
 (off Chase Side)
Marlow Ct. NW9 —3B **26**
Marlow Cres. Twic —6K **87**
Marlow Dri. Sutt —2F **131**
Marlowe Clo. Chst —6H **115**
Marlowe Clo. Ilf —1G **35**
Marlowe Gdns. SE9 —6E **98**
Marlowe Rd. E17 —4E **32**
Marlowe Sq. Mitc —4G **123**
Marlowes, The. NW8 —1B **60**
Marlowes, The. Dart —4K **101**
Marlow Rd. E6 —3D **66**
Marlow Rd. SE20 —3H **125**
Marlow Rd. S'hall —3D **70**
Marlow Way. SE16 —2K **79**
Marlton St. SE10 —5H **81**
Marmadon Rd. SE18 —4K **83**
Marmion App. E4 —4H **19**
Marmion Av. E4 —4G **19**
Marmion Clo. E4 —4G **19**
Marmion M. SW11 —3E **92**
Marmion Rd. SW11 —4E **92**
Marmont Rd. SE15 —1G **95**
Marmora Rd. SE22 —6J **95**
Marmot Rd. Houn —3B **86**
Marne Av. N11 —4A **16**

Marne Av. Well —3A **100**
Marne Ho. SE15 —7G 79
 (off Sumner Est.)
Marnell Way. Houn —3B **86**
Marne St. W10 —3G **59**
Marney Rd. SW11 —4E **92**
Marnham Av. NW2 —4G **43**
Marnham Ct. Wemb —5C **40**
Marnham Cres. Gnfd —3F **55**
Marnock Rd. SE4 —5B **96**
Maroon St. E14 —5A **64**
Maroons Way. SE6 —5C **112**
Marquess Rd. N1 —6D **46**
Marquis Clo. Wemb —7F **41**
Marquis Ct. N4 —7A 30
 (off Marquis Rd.)
Marquis Ct. Bark —5J **51**
Marquis Rd. N4 —1K **45**
Marquis Rd. N22 —6E **16**
Marquis Rd. NW1 —6H **45**
Marriett Ho. SW5 —4C **90**
Marriett Ho. SE6 —4E **112**
Marrilyne Av. Enf —1G **9**
Marriott Rd. E15 —1G **65**
Marriott Rd. N4 —1K **45**
Marriott Rd. N10 —1D **28**
Marriott Rd. Barn —3A **4**
Marriotts Clo. NW9 —6B **26**
Marryat Pl. SW19 —4G **107**
Marryat Rd. SW19 —5F **107**
Marsala Rd. SE13 —4D **96**
Marsden Rd. N9 —2C **18**
Marsden Rd. SE15 —3F **95**
Marsden St. NW5 —6E **44**
Marshall Clo. SW18 —6A **92**
Marshall Clo. Harr —7H **23**
Marshall Clo. Houn —5D **86**
Marshall Est. NW7 —4H **13**
Marshall Ho. N1 —2D 62
 (off Cranston Est.)
Marshall Ho. Eri —2D **84**
Marshall Path. SE28 —7B **68**
Marshall Rd. N17 —1D **30**
Marshalls Clo. N11 —4A **16**
Marshalls Dri. Romf —3K **37**
Marshalls Gro. SE18 —4C **82**
Marshall's Pl. SE16 —3F **79** (7F **148**)
Marshalls Rd. Romf —4K **37**
Marshall's Rd. Sutt —4A **131**
Marshall St. W1 —6G **61** (8M **139**)
Marshalsea Rd. SE1
 —2C **78** (4M **147**)
Marsham Clo. Chst —5F **115**
Marsham Ct. SW1 —4H **77** (8B **146**)
Marsham St. SW1 —3H **77** (7B **145**)
Marsh Av. Mitc —2D **122**
Marshbrook Clo. SE3 —3B **98**
Marsh Clo. NW7 —3G **13**
Marsh Ct. E8 —7G **47**
Marsh Dri. NW9 —6B **26**
Marsh Farm Rd. Twic —1K **103**
Marshfield St. E14 —3E **80**
Marsh Ga. Bus. Cen. E15 —2E **64**
Marshgate La. E15 —7D **48**
Marshgate Path. SE18 —3G **83**
Marshgate Trading Est. E15 —7D **48**
Marsh Grn. Rd. Dag —1G **69**
Marsh Hall. Wemb —3F **41**
Marsh Hill. E9 —5A **48**
Marsh La. E10 —2B **48**
Marsh La. N17 —1H **31**
Marsh La. NW7 —3F **13**
Marsh La. Stan —5H **11**
Marsh Rd. Pinn —4C **22**
Marsh Rd. Wemb —3D **56**
Marsh St. E14 —4D **80**
Marsh Wall. E14 —1C **80**
Marsh Way. Rain —6K **69**

Marsland Clo. SE17 —5B **78**
Marsom Ho. N1 —3D 62 (1A 142)
 (off Provost Est.)
Marston Av. Dag —2G **53**
Marston Clo. NW6 —7A **44**
Marston Clo. Dag —3G **53**
Marston Ho. SW9 —2A **94**
Marston Rd. Ilf —1C **34**
Marston Rd. Tedd —5B **104**
Marston Way. SE19 —7B **110**
Marsworth Av. Pinn —1B **22**
Marsworth Clo. Hay —5C **54**
Martaban Rd. N16 —2F **47**
Martello St. E8 —7H **47**
Martello Ter. E8 —7H **47**
Martell Rd. SE21 —3D **110**
Martel Pl. E8 —6F **47**
Marten Rd. E17 —2C **32**
Martens Av. Bexh —4H **101**
Martens Clo. Bexh —4J **101**
Martha Ct. E2 —2H **63**
Martham Clo. SE28 —7D **68**
Martha Rd. E15 —6G **49**
Martha St. E1 —6J **63**
Marthorne Cres. Harr —2H **23**
Martin Bowes Rd. SE9 —3D **98**
Martindale. SW14 —5J **89**
Martindale Av. E16 —7J **65**
Martin Dale Ind. Est. Enf —3C **8**
Martindale Rd. SW12 —7F **93**
Martindale Rd. Houn —3C **86**
Martin Dene. Bexh —5F **101**
Martin Dri. N'holt —5D **38**
Martineau Est. E1 —6J **63**
Martineau M. N5 —4B **46**
Martineau Rd. N5 —4B **46**
Martingales Clo. Rich —3D **104**
Martin Gdns. Dag —4C **52**
Martin Gro. Mord —4J **121**
Martin Ho. SE1 —3C **78** (7H **147**)
Martin La. EC4 —7D **62** (9B **142**)
Martin Rise. Bexh —5F **101**
Martin Rd. Dag —4C **52**
Martins Clo. W Wick —2F **137**
Martinside. NW9 —1B 26
 (off Concourse, The)
Martins Mt. Barn —4D **4**
Martin's Pl. SE14 —1K **95**
Martin's Rd. Brom —2H **127**
Martins, The. Wemb —3F **41**
Martins. N10 —1E **28**
Martin Way. SW20 & Mord —3G **121**
Martlesham. N17 —2E 30
 (off Adams Rd.)
Martlet Gro. N'holt —3B **54**
Martlett Ct. WC2 —6J **61** (8D **140**)
Martley Dri. Ilf —5F **35**
Martock Clo. Harr —4A **24**
Marton Clo. SE6 —3C **112**
Marton Rd. N16 —2E **46**
Mart St. WC2 —7J **61** (9D **140**)
Marvels Clo. SE12 —2K **113**
Marvels La. SE12 —2K **113**
Marville Rd. SW6 —7H **75**
Marvin St. E8 —6H **47**
Marwell Clo. W Wick —2H **137**
Marwood Clo. Well —3B **100**
Marwood Way. SE16 —5H **79**
Mary Adelaide Clo. SW15 —4A **106**
Mary Ann Gdns. SE8 —6C **80**
Maryatt Av. Harr —2F **39**
Mary Bank. SE18 —4D **82**
Mary Clo. Stan —4F **25**
Mary Datchelor Clo. SE5 —1D **94**
Maryfield Clo. Bex —3K **117**

Mary Grn. NW8 —1K **59**
Maryland Ho. E15 —6G 49
 (off Manbey Pk. Rd.)
Maryland Pk. E15 —5G **49**
Maryland Rd. E15 —5F **49**
Maryland Rd. N22 —6E **16**
Maryland Rd. T Hth —1B **124**
Maryland Sq. E15 —5G **49**
Marylands Rd. W9 —4J **59**
Maryland St. E15 —5F **49**
Maryland Wlk. N1 —1C 62
 (off Popham St.)
Mary Lawrenson Pl. SE3 —7J **81**
Marylebone Fly-Over. W2 —5C **60**
Marylebone High St. W1
 —5E **60** (5H **139**)
Marylebone La. W1 —5E **60** (6H **139**)
Marylebone M. W1 —5F **61** (6J **139**)
Marylebone Pas. W1
 —6G **61** (7M **139**)
Marylebone Rd. NW1
 —5C **60** (5D **138**)
Marylebone St. W1 —5E **60** (6H **139**)
Marylee Way. SE11 —4K **77** (9F **146**)
Mary Macarthur Ho. W6 —6G **75**
Mary Macarthur Ho. Dag —3G 53
 (off Wythenshawe Rd.)
Maryon Gro. SE7 —4C **82**
Maryon M. NW3 —4C **44**
Maryon Rd. SE7 —4C **82**
Maryon Rd. SE18 —4C **82**
Mary Peters Dri. Gnfd —5H **39**
Mary Pl. W11 —7G **59**
Mary Rose Clo. Hamp —7E **102**
Mary Rose Mall. E6 —5D **66**
Mary Rose Way. N20 —1G **15**
Mary Seacole Clo. E8 —1F **63**
Mary's Ter. Twic —7A **88**
Mary St. E16 —5H **65**
Mary St. N1 —1C **62**
Mary Ter. NW1 —1F **61**
Maryville. Well —2K **99**
Marzena Ct. Houn —6G **87**
Masbro Rd. W14 —3F **75**
Mascalls Rd. SE7 —6A **82**
Mascotte Rd. SW15 —4F **91**
Mascotts Clo. NW2 —3D **42**
Masefield Av. S'hall —7E **54**
Masefield Av. Stan —5E **10**
Masefield Ct. New Bar —4F **5**
Masefield Ct. Surb —7D **118**
Masefield Cres. N14 —6B **6**
Masefield Gdns. E6 —4E **66**
Masefield La. Hay —4A **54**
Masefield Rd. Hamp —4D **102**
Mashie Rd. W3 —6A **58**
Mashiters Hill. Romf —1K **37**
Maskall Clo. SW2 —1A **110**
Maskani Wlk. SW16 —7G **109**
Maskell Rd. SW17 —3A **108**
Maskelyne Clo. SW11 —1C **92**
Mason Clo. E16 —7J **65**
Mason Clo. SE16 —5G **79**
Mason Clo. Bexh —3H **101**
Mason Rd. Wfd G —4B **20**
Mason's Arms M. W1
 —6F **61** (8K **139**)
Mason's Av. EC2 —6D **62** (7A **142**)
Masons Av. Croy —3C **134**
Masons Av. Harr —4K **23**
Masons Grn. La. W3 —4G **57**
Masons Hill. SE18 —4F **83**
Masons Hill. Brom —3K **127**
Mason's Pl. EC1 —3C **62** (1L **141**)
Masons Pl. Mitc —1D **122**
Mason St. SE17 —4D **78** (8B **148**)
Mason's Yd. SW1 —1G **77** (2M **145**)
Mason's Yd. SW19 —5F **107**

234

Medcroft Gdns. SW14 —4J 89
Medebourne Clo. SE3 —3J 97
Medesenge Way. N13 —6G 17
Medfield St. SW15 —7C 90
Medhurst Clo. E3 —2A 64
Median Rd. E5 —5J 47
Medina Gro. N7 —3A 46
Medina Rd. N7 —3A 46
Medland Clo. Wall —1E 132
Medlar Clo. N'holt —2B 54
Medlar Ho. Sidc —3A 116
Medley Rd. NW6 —6J 43
Medora Rd. SW2 —7K 93
Medora Rd. Romf —4K 37
Medusa Rd. SE6 —6D 96
Medway Clo. Croy —6J 125
Medway Clo. Ilf —5G 51
Medway Dri. Gnfd —2K 55
Medway Gdns. Wemb —4A 40
Medway M. E3 —2A 64
Medway Pde. Gnfd —2K 55
Medway Rd. E3 —2A 64
Medway St. SW1 —3H 77 (7A 146)
Medwin St. SW4 —4K 93
Meek Clo. E8 —1H 63
Meerbrook Rd. SE3 —3A 98
Meeson Rd. E15 —1H 65
Meeson St. E5 —4A 48
Meeting Field Path. E9 —6J 47
Meetinghouse All. E1 —1H 79
Meeting Ho. La. SE15 —1H 95
Mehetabel Rd. E9 —6J 47
Meister Clo. Ilf —1H 51
Melancholy Wlk. Rich —2C 104
Melanda Clo. Chst —5D 114
Melanie Clo. Bexh —1E 100
Melba Way. SE13 —1D 96
Melbourne Av. N13 —6E 16
Melbourne Av. W13 —1A 72
Melbourne Av. Pinn —3F 23
Melbourne Clo. SE20 —7G 111
Melbourne Clo. Orp —7J 129
Melbourne Clo. Wall —5G 133
Melbourne Ct. N10 —7A 16
Melbourne Gdns. Romf —5E 36
Melbourne Gro. SE22 —4E 94
Melbourne M. SE6 —7E 96
Melbourne M. SW9 —1A 94
Melbourne Pl. WC2 —6K 61 (9F 140)
Melbourne Rd. E6 —2D 66
Melbourne Rd. E10 —7D 32
Melbourne Rd. E17 —4A 32
Melbourne Rd. SW19 —1J 121
Melbourne Rd. Ilf —1F 51
Melbourne Rd. Tedd —6C 104
Melbourne Rd. Wall —5F 133
Melbourne Sq. SW9 —1A 94
Melbourne Ter. Enf —6A 8
Melbury Av. S'hall —3F 71
Melbury Clo. Chst —6D 114
Melbury Ct. W8 —3H 75
Melbury Dri. SE5 —7E 78
Melbury Gdns. SW20 —1C 120
Melbury Rd. W14 —3H 75
Melbury Rd. Harr —5F 25
Melbury Ter. NW1 —4C 60 (4D 138)
Melchester Ho. N19 —3H 45
(off Wedmore St.)
Melcombe Gdns. Harr —6F 25
Melcombe Pl. NW1 —5D 60 (5E 138)
Melcombe St. NW1 —4D 60 (4F 138)
Meldon Clo. SW6 —1K 91
Meldrum Rd. Ilf —2A 52
Melfield Gdns. SE6 —4E 112
Melford Av. Bark —6J 51
Melford Ct. SE22 —1G 111
Melford Rd. E6 —3D 66

Melford Rd. E11 —2G 49
Melford Rd. E17 —4A 32
Melford Rd. SE22 —7G 95
Melford Rd. Ilf —2H 51
Melfort Av. T Hth —3B 124
Melfort Rd. T Hth —3B 124
Melgund Rd. N5 —5A 46
Melina Ct. SW15 —3C 90
Melina Pl. NW8 —3B 60 (2A 138)
Melina Rd. W12 —2D 74
Melior Ct. N6 —6G 29
Melior Pl. SE1 —2E 78
Melior St. SE1 —2E 78 (4C 148)
Meliot Rd. SE6 —2F 113
Meller Clo. Croy —3J 133
Melling St. SE18 —6J 83
Mellish Clo. Bark —1K 67
Mellish Gdns. Wfd G —5D 20
Mellish Ind. Est. SE18 —3B 82
Mellish St. E14 —3C 80
Mellison Rd. SW17 —5C 108
Mellitus St. W12 —5B 58
Mellor Pl. SE1 —2E 78 (4C 148)
Mellows Rd. Ilf —3D 34
Mellows Rd. Wall —5H 133
Mells Cres. SE9 —4D 114
Mell St. SE10 —5G 81
Melody Rd. SW18 —5A 92
Melon Pl. W8 —2J 75
Melon Rd. E15 —1G 65
Melon Rd. SE15 —1G 95
Melrose Av. N22 —1B 30
Melrose Av. NW2 —5D 42
Melrose Av. SW16 —3A 124
Melrose Av. SW19 —2H 107
Melrose Av. Gnfd —2F 55
Melrose Av. Mitc —7F 109
Melrose Av. Twic —7F 87
Melrose Clo. SE12 —1J 113
Melrose Clo. Gnfd —2F 55
Melrose Dri. S'hall —1E 70
Melrose Gdns. W6 —3E 74
Melrose Gdns. Edgw —3H 25
Melrose Gdns. N Mald —3K 119
Melrose Rd. SW13 —2B 90
Melrose Rd. SW18 —6H 91
Melrose Rd. SW19 —1J 121
Melrose Rd. W3 —3J 73
Melrose Rd. Pinn —4D 22
Melrose Ter. W6 —3E 74
Melrose Tudor. Wall —5J 133
(off Plough La.)
Melsa Rd. Mord —6A 122
Meltham Way. SE16 —5H 79
Melthorne Dri. Ruis —3A 38
Methorpe Gdns. SE3 —1C 98
Melton Clo. Ruis —7A 22
Melton Ct. SW7 —4B 76 (9B 144)
Melton Ct. Sutt —7A 132
Melton Fields. Eps —7A 130
Melton Pl. Eps —7A 130
Melville Av. SW20 —7C 106
Melville Av. Gnfd —5K 39
Melville Av. S Croy —5F 135
Melville Ct. SE8 —4A 80
Melville Ct. W12 —2D 74
(off Goldhawk Rd.)
Melville Gdns. N13 —5G 17
Melville Ho. New Bar —5G 5
Melville Pl. N1 —7C 46
Melville Rd. E17 —3B 32
Melville Rd. NW10 —7K 41
Melville Rd. SW13 —1C 90
Melville Rd. Romf —1H 37
Melville Rd. Sidc —2C 116
Melville St. N1 —7C 46
Melvin Rd. SE20 —1J 125
Melyn Clo. N7 —4G 45

Memel Ct. EC1 —4C 62 (4L 141)
(off Memel St.)
Memel St. EC1 —4C 62 (4L 141)
Memess Path. SE18 —6E 82
Memorial Av. E15 —3G 65
Memorial Clo. Houn —6D 70
Mendip Clo. SE26 —4J 111
Mendip Clo. SW19 —2G 107
Mendip Clo. Wor Pk —2E 130
Mendip Dri. NW2 —2G 43
Mendip Houses. E2 —3J 63
(off Welwyn St.)
Mendip Rd. SW11 —3A 92
Mendip Rd. Bexh —1K 101
Mendip Rd. Ilf —5J 35
Mendora Rd. SW6 —7G 75
Menelik Rd. NW2 —4G 43
Menlo Gdns. SE19 —7D 110
Menlo Lodge. N13 —3E 16
(off Crothall Clo.)
Menotti St. E2 —4G 63
Mentmore Clo. Harr —6C 24
Mentmore Ter. E8 —7H 47
Meon Ct. Iswth —2J 87
Meon Rd. W3 —2J 73
Meopham Rd. Mitc —1G 123
Mepham Cres. Harr —7B 10
Mepham Gdns. Harr —7B 10
Mepham St. SE1 —1K 77 (3F 146)
Mera Dri. Bexh —4G 101
Merantun Way. SW19 —1K 121
Merbury Clo. SE13 —5F 97
Merbury Rd. SE28 —2J 83
Mercator Rd. SE13 —4F 97
Mercer Clo. Th Dit —7A 118
Merceron Houses. E2 —3J 63
(off Globe Rd.)
Merceron St. E1 —4H 63
Mercer Pl. Pinn —2A 22
Mercers Clo. SE10 —4H 81
Mercers Pl. W6 —4E 74
Mercers Rd. N19 —3H 45
Mercer St. WC2 —6J 61 (8C 140)
Merchant Ind. Est. NW10 —4J 57
Merchant St. E3 —3B 64
Merchiston Rd. SE6 —2F 113
Merchland Rd. SE9 —1G 115
Mercia Gro. SE13 —4E 96
Mercier Rd. SW15 —5G 91
Mercury. NW9 —1B 26
(off Concourse, The)
Mercury Ho. Bren —6C 72
(off Glenhurst Rd.)
Mercury Rd. Bren —6C 72
Mercury Way. SE14 —6K 79
Mercy Ter. SE13 —5D 96
Merebank La. Croy —5K 133
Mere Clo. SW15 —7F 91
Meredith Av. NW2 —5E 42
Meredith Clo. Pinn —1B 22
Meredith Ho. N16 —5E 46
Meredith St. E13 —3J 65
Meredith St. EC1 —3B 62 (2J 141)
Meredyth Rd. SW13 —2C 90
Mere End. Croy —7K 125
Meretone Clo. SE4 —4A 96
Merevale Cres. Mord —6A 122
Mereway Rd. Twic —1H 103
Merewood Clo. Brom —2E 128
Merewood Rd. Bexh —2J 101
Mereworth Clo. Brom —5H 127
Mereworth Dri. SE18 —7F 83
Mereworth Ho. SE15 —6J 79
Merganser Gdns. SE28 —3H 83
Meriden Clo. Brom —7B 114
Meriden Clo. Ilf —1G 35
Meriden Ct. SW3 —5C 76
(off Chelsea Manor St.)

Meridian Ga. E14 —2E 80
Meridian Rd. SE7 —7B 82
Meridian Wlk. N17 —6K 17
Meridian Way. N18 —5D 18
Meridian Way. N18, N9 & Enf —5D 18
Marifield Rd. SE9 —4A 98
Merino Clo. E11 —4A 34
Merino Pl. Sidc —6A 100
Merivale Rd. SW15 —4G 91
Merivale Rd. Harr —7G 23
Merlewood Dri. Chst —1D 128
Merlewood Pl. SE9 —6D 98
Merley Ct. NW9 —1J 41
Merlin Clo. Croy —4E 134
Merlin Clo. N'holt —3A 54
Merlin Ct. SE8 —6B 80
Merlin Ct. Short —3H 127
Merlin Cres. Edgw —1F 25
Merlin Gdns. Brom —3J 113
Merlin Gro. Beck —4B 126
Merlin Rd. E12 —2B 50
Merlin Rd. Well —4A 100
Merlin Rd. N. Well —4A 100
Merlins Av. Harr —3D 38
Merlin St. WC1 —3A 62 (2G 141)
Mermaid Ct. SE1 —2D 78 (4A 148)
(off Borough High St.)
Mermaid Ct. SE16 —1B 80
Mermaid Ct. SW1 —2D 78
Merredene St. SW2 —6K 93
Merrick Ho. SE8 —4B 80
Merrick Rd. S'hall —3D 70
Merrick Sq. SE1 —3D 78 (6A 148)
Merridene. N21 —6J 7
Merrielands Cres. Dag —2F 69
Merrilands Rd. Wor Pk —1E 130
Merrilees Rd. Sidc —7J 99
Merriman Rd. SE3 —1A 98
Merrington Rd. SW6 —6J 75
Merrion Av. Stan —5J 11
Merritt Rd. SE4 —5B 96
Merritt's Bldgs. EC2 —4E 62 (4C 142)
(off Worship St.)
Merrivale. N14 —6C 6
Merrivale Av. Ilf —4B 34
Merrow Rd. Sutt —7F 131
Merrow St. SE17 —5D 78
Merrow Wlk. SE17 —5D 78
Merrow Way. New Ad —6E 136
Merrydown Way. Chst —1C 128
Merryfield. SE3 —2H 97
Merryfield Gdns. Stan —5H 11
Merryfields Way. SE6 —7D 96
Merryhill Clo. E4 —7J 9
Merry Hill Mt. Bush —1A 10
Merry Hill Rd. Bush —1A 10
Merryhills Ct. N14 —5B 6
Merryhills Dri. Enf —4C 6
Merryweather Ct. N19 —3G 45
Mersey Rd. E17 —3B 32
Mersey Wlk. N'holt —2E 54
Mersham Dri. NW9 —5G 25
Mersham Pl. SE20 —1H 125
Mersham Rd. T Hth —3D 124
Merten Rd. Romf —7E 36
Merthyr Ter. SW13 —6D 74
Merton Av. W4 —4B 74
Merton Av. N'holt —5G 39
Merton Ct. Ilf —6C 34
Merton Ct. Well —2B 100
Merton Gdns. Orp —5F 129
Merton Hall Gdns. SW20 —1G 121
Merton Hall Rd. SW19 —1G 107
Merton High St. SW19 —7K 107
Merton La. N6 —2D 44
Merton Lodge. New Bar —5F 5

Merton Mans. SW20 —2F 121
Merton Pk. Ind. Est. SW19 —1K 121
Merton Rise. NW3 —7C 44
Merton Rd. E17 —5E 32
Merton Rd. SE25 —5G 125
Merton Rd. SW18 —6J 91
Merton Rd. SW19 —7K 107
Merton Rd. Bark —7K 51
Merton Rd. Enf —1J 7
Merton Rd. Harr —1G 39
Merton Rd. Ilf —7K 35
Merttins Rd. SE15 & SE4 —5K 95
Meru Clo. NW5 —4E 44
Mervan Rd. SW2 —4A 94
Mervyn Av. SE9 —3G 115
Mervyn Rd. W13 —3A 72
Messaline Av. W3 —6J 57
Messent Rd. SE9 —5A 98
Messeter Pl. SE9 —6E 98
Messina Av. NW6 —7J 43
Messiter Ho. N1 —1K 61
(off Barnsbury Est.)
Metcalf Wlk. Felt —4C 102
Meteor St. SW11 —4E 92
Meteor Way. Wall —7J 133
Metheringham Way. NW9 —1A 26
Methley St. SE11 —5A 78
Methuen Clo. Edgw —7B 12
Methuen Pk. N10 —3F 29
Methuen Rd. Belv —4H 85
Methuen Rd. Bexh —4F 101
Methuen Rd. Edgw —7B 12
Methwold Rd. W10 —5F 59
Metro Bus. Pk. Wemb —4H 41
Mews Pl. Wfd G —4D 20
Mews St. E1 —1G 79
Mews, The. N1 —1C 62
Mews, The. Ilf —5B 34
Mews, The. Romf —4K 37
Mews, The. Sidc —4A 116
Mews, The. Twic —6B 88
Mexfield Rd. SW15 —5H 91
Meyer Grn. Enf —1B 8
Meyer Rd. Eri —6K 85
Meymott St. SE1 —1B 78 (3J 147)
Meynell Cres. E9 —7K 47
Meynell Gdns. E9 —7K 47
Meynell Rd. E9 —7K 47
Meyrick Rd. NW10 —6C 42
Meyrick Rd. SW11 —3B 92
Miall Wlk. SE26 —4A 112
Micawber Ho. SE16 —2G 79
(off Llewellyn St.)
Micawber St. N1 —3C 62 (1M 141)
Michael Gaynor Clo. W7 —1K 71
Michael Manley Ind. Est. SW8
—2H 93
Michael Rd. E11 —1G 49
Michael Rd. SE25 —3E 124
Michael Rd. SW6 —1K 91
Michael's Clo. SE13 —4G 97
Michael's Row. Rich —4E 88
Michael Stewart Ho. SW6 —6H 75
(off Clem Attlee Ct.)
Micheldever Rd. SE12 —6H 97
Michelham Gdns. Twic —3K 103
Michelle Ct. N12 —5F 15
Michel's Row. Rich —4E 88
Michigan Av. E12 —4D 50
Michigan Ho. E14 —4C 80
Mickleham Down. N12 —4C 14
Mickleham Clo. Orp —2K 129
Mickleham Gdns. Sutt —6G 131
Mickleham Rd. Orp —1K 129
Mickleham Way. New Ad —7F 137
Micklethwaite Rd. SW6 —6J 75
Midas Metropolitan Ind. Est. Mord
—7E 12(?)

Middle Dene. NW7 —3E 12
Middle Field. NW8 —1B 60
Middlefielde. W13 —5B 56
Middlefield Gdns. Ilf —6F 35
Middlefields. Croy —7A 136
Middle Grn. Clo. Surb —6F 119
Middleham Gdns. N18 —6B 18
Middleham Rd. N18 —6B 18
Middle La. N8 —5J 29
Middle La. Tedd —6K 103
Middle La. M. N8 —5J 29
Middle Path. Harr —1H 39
Middle Rd. E13 —2J 65
Middle Rd. SW16 —2H 123
Middle Rd. Barn —6H 5
Middle Rd. Harr —2H 39
Middle Row. W10 —4G 59
Middlesborough Rd. N18 —6B 18
Middlesex Bus. Pk. S'hall —2D 70
Middlesex Ct. W4 —5B 74
Middlesex Pas. EC1 —5B 62 (6K 141)
(off Bartholomew Clo.)
Middlesex Rd. Mitc —5J 123
Middlesex St. E1 —5E 62 (6D 142)
Middlesex Wharf. E5 —2J 47
Middle St. EC1 —5C 62 (5L 141)
Middle St. Croy —3C 134
(in two parts)
Middle Temple La. EC4
—6A 62 (8G 141)
Middleton Av. E4 —4G 19
Middleton Av. Gnfd —2H 55
Middleton Av. Sidc —6B 116
Middleton Bldgs. W1
(off Langham St.) —5G 61 (6L 139)
Middleton Clo. E4 —3G 19
Middleton Dri. SE16 —2K 79
Middleton Gdns. Ilf —6F 35
Middleton Gro. N7 —5J 45
Middleton M. N7 —5J 45
Middleton Rd. E8 —7F 47
Middleton Rd. NW11 —7J 27
Middleton Rd. Mord & Cars —6K 121
Middleton Rd. N Mald —2J 119
Middleton St. E2 —3H 63
Middleton Way. SE13 —4F 97
Middleway. NW11 —5K 27
Middle Way. SW16 —2H 123
Middle Way. Hay —4A 54
Middle Way. The. Harr —2K 23
Middle Yd. SE1 —1E 78
Midfield Av. Bexh —3J 101
Midfield Pl. Bexh —3J 101
Midfield Way. Orp —7B 116
Midford Ho. NW4 —4F 27
(off Belle Vue Est.)
Midford Pl. W1 —4G 61 (4M 139)
Midholm. Wemb —1G 41
Midholm Clo. N2 —4K 27
Midholm Clo. NW11 —4K 27
Midholm Rd. Croy —2A 136
Midhope St. WC1 —3J 61 (2D 140)
Midhurst. SE26 —6J 111
Midhurst Av. N10 —3E 28
Midhurst Av. Croy —7A 124
Midhurst Hill. Bexh —6G 101
Midhurst Pde. N10 —3E 28
(off Fortis Grn.)
Midhurst Rd. W13 —2A 72
Midland Cres. NW3 —6A 44
Midland Pde. NW6 —6K 43
Midland Pl. E14 —5E 80
Midland Rd. E10 —7E 32
Midland Rd. NW1 —2H 61
Midland Ter. NW2 —3F 43
Midland Ter. NW10 —4A 58
Midlothian Rd. E3 —5B 64

Middle Rd. SW12 —1G 109
Midmoor Rd. SW19 —1G 121
Midship Clo. SE16 —1K 79
Midship Point. E14 —2C 80
(off Quarterdeck, The.)
Midstrath Rd. NW10 —4A 42
Midsummer Av. Houn —4D 86
Midway. Sutt —7H 121
Midwood Clo. NW2 —3D 42
Mid Yd. SE1 —1E 78 (2C 148)
Miers Clo. E6 —1E 66
Mighell Av. Ilf —5B 34
Milborne Gro. SW10 —5A 76
Milborne St. E9 —6J 47
Milborough Cres. SE12 —6G 97
Milcote St. SE1 —2B 78 (5J 147)
Mildenhall Rd. E5 —4J 47
Mildmay Av. N1 —6D 46
Mildmay Gro. N1 —5D 46
Mildmay Pk. N1 —5D 46
Mildmay Pl. N16 —5E 46
Mildmay Rd. N1 —5D 46
Mildmay Rd. Ilf —3F 51
Mildmay Rd. Romf —5J 37
Mildmay St. N1 —6D 46
Mildred Av. N'holt —5F 39
Mildred Av. Eri —5K 85
Mildura Ct. N8 —4K 29
Mile End Pl. E1 —4K 63
Mile End Rd. E1 & E3 —5J 63
Mile End, The. E17 —1K 31
Mile Rd. Wall —1F 133
Miles Lodge. Harr —5H 23
Milespit Hill. NW7 —5J 13
Miles Pl. NW8 —5C 60 (5C 138)
(off Broadley St.)
Miles Pl. Surb —4F 119
Miles Rd. N8 —3J 29
Miles Rd. Mitc —3C 122
Miles St. SW8 —6J 77
Milestone Clo. Sutt —7B 132
Milestone Rd. SE19 —6F 111
Miles Way. N20 —2H 15
Milfoil St. W12 —7C 58
Milford Clo. SE2 —6E 84
Milford Gdns. Edgw —7B 12
Milford Gdns. Wemb —4D 40
Milford Gro. Sutt —4A 132
Milford La. WC2 —7A 62 (9G 141)
Milford M. SW16 —3K 109
Milford Rd. W13 —1B 72
Milford Rd. S'hall —7E 54
Milford Towers. SE6 —7D 96
Milford Way. SE15 —1F 95
Milk St. E16 —1F 83
Milk St. EC2 —6C 62 (8M 141)
Milk St. Brom —6K 113
Milkwell Gdns. Wfd G —7E 20
Milkwell Yd. SE5 —1C 94
Milkwood Rd. SE24 —5B 94
Milk Yd. E1 —7J 63
Millais Av. E12 —5E 50
Millais Gdns. Edgw —2G 25
Millais Rd. E11 —4F 48
Millais Rd. Enf —5A 8
Millais Rd. N Mald —7A 120
Millard Clo. N16 —5E 46
Millard Ter. Dag —6G 53
Millbank. SW1 —3J 77 (7C 146)
Millbank Way. SE12 —5J 97
Millbourne Rd. Felt —4C 102
Mill Bri. Barn —6C 4
Millbrook Av. Well —4H 99
Millbrook Gdns. Chad —6F 37
Millbrook Pas. SW9 —3B 94
Millbrook Pl. NW1 —2G 61
(off Hampstead Rd.)
Millbrook Rd. N9 —1C 18

Millbrook Rd. SW9 —3B 94
Mill Clo. Cars —2E 132
Mill Corner. Barn —1C 4
Mill Ct. E10 —3E 48
Milledge Corner. SE16 —5H 79
Millender Wlk. SE16 —4J 79
Millennium Pl. E2 —2H 63
Miller Clo. Pinn —2A 22
Miller Rd. SW19 —6B 108
Miller Rd. Croy —1K 133
Miller's Av. E8 —5F 47
Millers Clo. NW7 —4H 13
Miller's Ct. W6 —5B 74
Millers Ct. Wemb —2E 56
(off Vicars Bri. Clo.)
Millers Grn. Clo. Enf —3G 7
Miller's Ter. E8 —5F 47
Miller St. NW1 —2G 61
Millers Way. W6 —2E 74
Miller Wlk. SE1 —1A 78 (3H 147)
Millet Rd. Gnfd —3F 55
Mill Farm Clo. Pinn —2A 22
Mill Farm Cres. Houn —1C 102
Millfield. N4 —2A 46
Millfield Av. E17 —1A 32
Millfield La. N6 —1C 44
Millfield Pl. N6 —2E 44
Millfield Rd. Edgw —2J 25
Millfield Rd. Houn —1C 102
Millfields Rd. E5 —4J 47
Mill Gdns. SE26 —3H 111
Mill Grn. Mitc —7E 122
Mill Grn. Bus. Pk. Mitc —7E 122
Mill Grn. Rd. Mitc —7E 122
Millgrove St. SW11 —1E 92
Millharbour. E14 —2D 80
Millhaven Clo. Romf —6B 36
Mill Hill Cir. NW7 —5G 13
Mill Hill Gro. W3 —1H 73
Mill Hill Rd. SW13 —2C 90
Mill Hill Rd. W3 —2H 73
Mill Hill Ter. W3 —1H 73
Mill Hill Yd. W3 —2G 73
Millhouse Pl. SE27 —4B 110
Millicent Fawcett Ct. N17 —1F 31
Millicent Rd. E10 —1B 48
Milligan St. E14 —7B 64
Milling Rd. Edgw —7E 12
Millington Ho. N16 —3D 46
Mill La. E4 —3J 9
Mill La. NW6 —5H 43
Mill La. SE18 —5E 82
Mill La. Cars —4D 132
Mill La. Croy —3K 133
Mill La. Eps —7B 130
Mill La. Romf —6E 36
Mill La. Wfd G —5C 20
Mill Plat. Iswth —2A 88
(in two parts)
Mill Plat Av. Iswth —2A 88
Millpond Est. SE16 —2H 79
Mill Ridge. Edgw —5A 12
Mill River Trading Est. Enf —4F 9
Mill Rd. E16 —1K 81
Mill Rd. SE13 —3E 96
Mill Rd. SW19 —7A 108
Mill Rd. Eri —7J 85
Mill Rd. Ilf —3E 50

Mill Rd. Twic —2G 103
Mill Row. N1 —1E 62
Mill Row. Bex —7H 101
Mill Shot Clo. SW6 —1E 90
Millside. Cars —2D 132
Millside Pl. Iswth —2B 88
Millson Clo. N20 —2G 15
Mills Row. W4 —4K 73
Millstream Clo. N13 —5F 17
Millstream Rd. SE1 —2F 79 (5E 148)
Mill St. SE1 —2F 79 (5F 148)
Mill St. W1 —7F 61 (9L 139)
Mill St. King T —3E 118
Mill Vale. Brom —2H 127
Mill View Clo. Ewe —7B 130
Mill View Gdns. Croy —3K 135
Millwall Dock Rd. E14 —3C 80
Millway. NW7 —4F 13
Mill Way. Felt —5A 86
Millway Gdns. N'holt —6D 38
Millwood Rd. Houn —5G 87
Millwood St. W10 —5G 59
Mill Yd. E1 —7G 63
Milman Clo. Pinn —3B 22
Milman Rd. NW6 —2F 59
Milman's St. SW10 —6B 76
Milne Felid. Pinn —7A 10
Milne Gdns. SE9 —5C 98
Milne Ho. SE18 —4D 82
(off Ogilby St.)
Milner Dri. Twic —7H 87
Milner Pl. N1 —1A 62
Milner Pl. Cars —4E 132
Milner Rd. E15 —3G 65
Milner Rd. SW19 —1K 121
Milner Rd. Dag —2C 52
Milner Rd. King T —3D 118
Milner Rd. Mord —5B 122
Milner Rd. T Hth —3D 124
Milner Sq. N1 —7B 46
Milner St. SW3 —4D 76 (8E 144)
Milner Wlk. Sidc —2H 115
Milnthorpe Rd. W4 —6K 73
Milo Gdns. SE22 —6F 95
Milo Rd. SE22 —6F 95
Milroy Wlk. SE1 —1B 78 (2J 147)
Milson Rd. W14 —3F 75
Milstead Ho. E5 —5H 47
Milton Av. E6 —7B 50
Milton Av. N6 —7G 29
Milton Av. NW9 —3J 25
Milton Av. NW10 —1J 57
Milton Av. Barn —5C 4
Milton Av. Croy —7D 124
Milton Av. Sutt —3B 132
Milton Clo. N2 —5A 28
Milton Clo. SE1 —4F 79 (9E 148)
Milton Clo. Sutt —3B 132
Milton Ct. EC2 —5D 62 (5A 142)
Milton Ct. Rd. SE14 —6A 80
Milton Cres. Ilf —7F 35
Milton Garden Est. N16 —4E 46
Milton Gro. N11 —5B 16
Milton Gro. N16 —4D 46
Milton Ho. E17 —4C 32
Milton Ho. Sutt —3J 131
Milton Lodge. Twic —7K 87
Milton Pk. N6 —7G 29
Milton Pl. N7 —5A 46
Milton Rd. E17 —4C 32
Milton Rd. N6 —7G 29

Milton Rd. N15 —4B 30
Milton Rd. NW7 —5H 13
Milton Rd. NW9 —7C 26
Milton Rd. SE24 —5B 94
Milton Rd. SW14 —3K 89
Milton Rd. SW19 —6A 108
Milton Rd. W3 —1K 73
Milton Rd. W7 —7K 55
Milton Rd. Belv —4G 85
Milton Rd. Croy —7D 124
Milton Rd. Hamp —7E 102
Milton Rd. Harr —4J 23
Milton Rd. Mitc —7E 108
Milton Rd. Sutt —3J 131
Milton Rd. Wall —6G 133
Milton Rd. Well —1K 99
Milton St. EC2 —5D 62 (5A 142)
Milverton Gdns. Ilf —2K 51
Milverton Ho. SE23 —3A 112
Milverton Rd. NW6 —7E 42
Milverton St. SE11 —5A 78
Milverton Way. SE9 —4E 114
Milward Wlk. E1 —5H 63
Milward Wlk. SE18 —6E 82
Mimosa Ho. Hay —5A 54
Mimosa Lodge. NW10 —5B 42
Mimosa Rd. Hay —5A 54
Mimosa St. SW6 —1H 91
Minard Rd. SE6 —7G 97
(in two parts)
Mina Rd. SE17 —5E 78
Mina Rd. SW19 —1J 121
Minchenden Ct. N14 —2C 16
Minchenden Cres. N14 —3B 16
Mincing La. EC3 —7E 62 (9C 142)
Minden Rd. SE20 —1H 125
Minden Rd. Sutt —2H 131
Minehead Rd. SW16 —5K 109
Minehead Rd. Harr —3E 38
Mineral St. SE18 —4J 83
Minera M. SW1 —4E 76 (8H 145)
Minerva Clo. SW9 —7A 78
Minerva Clo. Sidc —3J 115
Minerva Rd. E4 —7J 19
Minerva Rd. NW10 —4J 57
Minerva Rd. King T —2F 119
Minerva St. E2 —2H 63
Minet Av. NW10 —2A 58
Minet Gdns. NW10 —2A 58
Minet Rd. SW9 —2B 94
Minford Gdns. W14 —2F 75
Mingard Wlk. N7 —2K 45
Ming St. E14 —7C 64
Ministry Way. SE9 —2D 114
Miniver Pl. EC4 —7C 62 (9M 141)
(off Garlick Hill)
Miniver St. SE1 —2B 78 (5K 147)
(off Boyfield St.)
Mink Ct. Houn —2A 86
Minniedale. Surb —5F 119
Minnow Wlk. SE17 —4E 78 (9D 148)
Minoco Wharf. E16 —2A 82
Minories. EC3 —6F 63 (8E 142)
Minshaw Ct. Sidc —4A 116
Minshill St. SW8 —1H 93
Minshull Pl. Beck —7C 112
Minson Rd. E9 —1K 63
Minstead Gdns. SW15 —7B 90
Minstead Way. N Mald —6A 120
Minster Av. Sutt —2J 131
Minster Ct. EC3 —7E 62 (9D 142)
(off Mincing La.)
Minster Dri. Croy —4E 134
Minster Pavement. EC3
(off Mincing La.) —7E 62 (9D 142)
Minster Rd. NW2 —5G 43
Minster Rd. Brom —7K 113
Minster Wlk. N8 —4J 29
Minstrel Gdns. Surb —4F 119

Mintern Clo. N13 —3G 17
Minterne Av. S'hall —4E 70
Minterne Rd. Harr —5F 25
Minterne Waye. Hay —6A 54
Mintern St. N1 —2D 62
Minton Ho. SE11 —4A 78 (8G 147)
  (off Walnut Tree Wlk.)
Minton M. NW6 —6K 43
Mint Rd. Wall —4F 133
Mint St. SE1 —2C 78 (4L 147)
Mint Wlk. Croy —3C 134
Minverva Rd. NW10 —4J 57
Mirabel Rd. SW6 —7H 75
Miranda Clo. E1 —5J 63
Miranda Rd. N19 —1G 45
Mirfield St. SE7 —4B 82
Miriam Rd. SE18 —5J 83
Mirren Clo. Harr —4D 38
Mirror Path. SE9 —3A 114
Missenden. SE17 —5D 78
  (off Roland Way)
Missenden Gdns. Mord —6A 122
Mission Gro. E17 —5A 32
Mission Pl. SE15 —1G 95
Mission Sq. Bren —6E 72
Mistletoe Clo. Croy —1K 135
Mitcham Garden Village. Mitc
  —5E 122
Mitcham Ho. SE5 —1C 94
Mitcham La. SW16 —6G 109
Mitcham Pk. Mitc —4C 122
Mitcham Rd. E6 —3C 66
Mitcham Rd. SW17 —5D 108
Mitcham Rd. Croy —6J 123
Mitcham Rd. Ilf —7K 35
Mitcheldean Ct. SE15 —7E 78
  (off Newent Clo.)
Mitchell. NW9 —1B 26
  (off Concourse, The)
Mitchellbrook Way. NW10 —6K 41
Mitchell Clo. SE2 —4C 84
Mitchell Clo. Belv —3J 85
Mitchell Ho. W12 —7D 58
  (off White City Est.)
Mitchell Rd. N13 —5H 17
Mitchell St. EC1 —4C 62 (3L 141)
Mitchell Wlk. E6 —5B 66
  (off Neats Ct. Rd.)
Mitchell Way. NW10 —6J 41
Mitchell Way. Brom —1J 127
Mitchison Rd. N1 —6D 46
Mitchley Rd. N17 —3G 31
Mitford Rd. N19 —2J 45
Mitre Bri. Ind. Pk. W10 —4D 58
Mitre Clo. Brom —2H 127
Mitre Clo. Sutt —7A 132
Mitre Ct. EC2 —6C 62 (7M 141)
  (off Wood St.)
Mitre Ct. EC4 —6A 62 (8H 141)
Mitre Rd. E15 —2G 65
Mitre Rd. SE1 —2A 78 (4H 147)
Mitre Sq. EC3 —6E 62 (8D 142)
Mitre Sq. EC3 —6E 62 (8D 142)
Mitre, The. E14 —7B 64
Mitre Way. NW10 —5D 58
Mitre Yd. SW3 —4C 76 (8D 144)
Moat Ct. Sidc —3K 115
Moat Cres. N3 —3K 27
Moat Croft. Well —3C 100
Moat Dri. E13 —2A 66
Moat Dri. Harr —4G 23
Moat Farm Rd. N'holt —6D 38
Moatfield. NW6 —7G 43
Moat Gdns. SE28 —7C 68
Moat Pl. SW9 —2X 93
Moat Pl. W3 —6H 57
Moatside. Enf —4E 8
Moatside. Felt —4A 102

Moat, The. N Mald —1A 120
Moberley Rd. SW4 —7H 93
Modbury Gdns. NW5 —6E 44
Modder Pl. SW15 —4F 91
Model Bldgs. WC1 —3K 61 (2F 140)
  (off Cubitt St.)
Model Cotts. SW14 —4J 89
Model Cotts. W13 —2B 72
Model Farm Clo. SE9 —3C 114
Modern Ct. EC4 —6B 62 (7J 141)
  (off Farringdon St.)
Modern Wharf Rd. SE10 —3G 81
Moelwyn. N7 —5H 45
Moelyn M. Harr —5A 24
Moffat Clo. SW19 —5J 107
Moffat Gdns. Mitc —3C 122
Moffat Ho. SE5 —7C 78
Moffat Rd. N13 —6D 16
Moffat Rd. SW17 —4D 108
Moffat Rd. T Hth —2C 124
Mogden La. Iswth —5K 87
Moiety Rd. E14 —2C 80
Moineau. NW9 —1B 26
  (off Concourse, The)
Moira Clo. N17 —2E 30
Moira Rd. SE9 —4D 98
Moir Clo. S Croy —7G 135
Mokswell Ct. N10 —1E 28
Moland Mead. SE16 —5K 79
Molescroft. SE9 —3G 115
Molesey Dri. Sutt —2G 131
Molesford Rd. SW6 —1J 91
Molesworth St. SE13 —3E 96
Moliner Ct. Beck —7C 112
Mollison Dri. Wall —7H 133
Mollison Way. Edgw —2F 25
Molly Huggins Clo. SW12 —7G 93
Molton Ho. N1 —1K 61
  (off Barnsbury Est.)
Molyneux St. W1 —5C 60 (6D 138)
Monarch Cl. W Wick —4H 137
Monarch Clo. W Wick —4H 137
Monarch Ct. N2 —5B 28
Monarch Dri. E16 —5B 66
Monarch M. SW16 —5A 110
Monarch Rd. Belv —3G 85
Mona Rd. SE15 —2J 95
Monastery Gdns. Enf —2J 7
Mona St. E16 —5H 65
Monck St. SW1 —3H 77 (7B 146)
Monclar Rd. SE5 —4D 94
Moncorvo Clo. SW7
  —2C 76 (5C 144)
Moncrieff Clo. E6 —6C 66
Moncrieff St. SE15 —2G 95
  (in two parts)
Monega Rd. E7 & E12 —6A 50
Moneyer Ho. N1 —3D 62 (1A 142)
  (off Provost Est.)
Monfitchet. E6 —6F 67
Monica Ct. Enf —5K 7
Monica James Ho. Sidc —3A 116
Monier Rd. E3 —7C 48
Monivea Rd. Beck —7B 112
Monk Dri. E16 —7J 65
Monkfrith Av. N14 —6A 6
Monkfrith Clo. N14 —7A 6
Monkfrith Way. N14 —7K 5
Monkham's Av. Wfd G —5E 20
Monkham's Dri. Wfd G —5E 20
Monkham's La. Buck H —2E 20
Monkham's La. Wfd G —5D 20
Monkleigh Rd. Mord —3G 121
Monk Pas. E16 —7J 65
  (off Monk Dri.)
Monks Av. Barn —6F 5
Monks Clo. SE2 —4D 84
Monks Clo. Enf —2H 7

Monks Clo. Harr —2E 38
Monks Clo. Ruis —4B 38
Monksdene Gdns. Sutt —3K 131
Monks Dri. W3 —5G 57
Monks Orchard Rd. Beck —1C 136
Monks Pk. Wemb —6H 41
Monks Pk. Gdns. Wemb —7H 41
Monks Rd. Enf —2H 7
Monk St. SE18 —4E 82
Monks Way. NW11 —4H 27
Monks Way. Beck —6C 126
Monks Way. Orp —7G 129
Monkswood Gdns. Ilf —3E 34
Monkton Ho. E5 —5H 47
Monkton Rd. Well —2K 99
Monkton St. SE11 —4A 78 (8H 147)
Monkville Av. NW11 —4H 27
Monkville Pde. NW11 —4H 27
Monkwell Sq. EC2 —5C 62 (6M 141)
Monmouth Av. E18 —3K 33
Monmouth Av. King T —7C 104
Monmouth Clo. Mitc —4J 123
Monmouth Clo. Well —4A 100
Monmouth Gro. Bren —4E 72
Monmouth Pl. W2 —6K 59
  (off Monmouth Rd.)
Monmouth Rd. E6 —3D 66
Monmouth Rd. N9 —2C 18
Monmouth Rd. W2 —6J 59
Monmouth Rd. Dag —5F 53
Monmouth St. WC2
  —6J 61 (8C 140)
Monnery Rd. N19 —3G 45
Monnow Rd. SE1 —4G 79
Monoux Almshouses. E17 —4D 32
Monoux Gro. E17 —1C 32
Monroe Cres. Enf —1C 8
Monroe Dri. SW14 —5H 89
Monro Gdns. Harr —7D 10
Monsell Rd. N4 —3B 46
Monson Rd. NW10 —2C 58
Monson Rd. SE14 —7A 79
Mons Way. Brom —6C 128
Montacute Rd. SE6 —7B 96
Montacute Rd. Bush —1D 10
Montacute Rd. Mord —6B 122
Montacute Rd. New Ad —7E 136
Montagu Cres. N18 —4C 18
Montague Av. SE4 —4B 96
Montague Av. W7 —1K 71
Montague Clo. SE1 —1D 78 (2A 148)
Montague Gdns. W3 —7G 57
Montague Pl. EC1 —5C 62 (6L 141)
Montague Pl. WC1 —5H 61 (5B 140)
Montague Rd. E8 —5G 47
Montague Rd. E11 —2H 49
Montague Rd. N8 —5K 29
Montague Rd. N15 —4G 31
Montague Rd. SW19 —7K 107
Montague Rd. W7 —1K 71
Montague Rd. W13 —6B 56
Montague Rd. Croy —1B 134
Montague Rd. Houn —3F 87
Montague Rd. Rich —6E 88
Montague Rd. S'hall —4C 70
Montague Sq. SE15 —7J 79
Montague St. WC1 —5J 61 (5C 140)
Montague Ter. Brom —3H 127
Montague Waye. S'hall —3C 70
Montagu Gdns. N18 —4C 18
Montagu Gdns. Wall —4G 133
Montagu Mans. W1
  —5D 60 (5F 138)
Montagu M. N. W1 —5D 60 (6F 138)
Montagu M. S. W1 —6D 60 (7F 138)
Montagu M. W. W1 —6D 60 (7F 138)
Montagu Pl. W1 —5D 60 (6E 138)

Montagu Rd. N18 & N9 —5C 18
Montagu Rd. NW4 —6C 26
Montagu Rd. Ind. Est. N18 —4D 18
Montagu Row. W1 —5D 60 (6F 138)
Montagu Sq. W1 —5D 60 (6F 138)
Montagu St. W1 —6D 60 (7F 138)
Montalt Rd. Wfd G —5C 20
Montana Rd. SW17 —3E 108
Montana Rd. SW20 —1E 120
Montbelle Rd. SE9 —3F 115
Montcalm Clo. Brom —6J 127
Montcalm Ho. E14 —4B 80
Montcalm Rd. SE7 —7B 82
Montclare St. E2 —4F 63 (2E 142)
Monteagle Av. Bark —6G 51
Monteagle Ct. N1 —2E 62
Monteagle Way. E5 —3G 47
Monteagle Way. SE15 —3H 95
Montefiore St. SW8 —2F 93
Monteith Rd. E3 —1B 64
Montem Rd. SE23 —7B 96
Montem Rd. N Mald —4A 120
Montem St. N4 —1K 45
Montenotte Rd. N8 —5G 29
Monterey Clo. Bex —2J 117
Montesole Ct. Pinn —2A 22
Montesquieu Ter. E16 —6H 65
  (off Clarkson Rd.)
Montford Pl. SE11 —5A 78
Montford Rd. Sun —3J 118
Montfort Pl. SW19 —1F 107
Montgolfier Wlk. N'holt —3C 54
Montgomery Clo. Mitc —4J 123
Montgomery Clo. Sidc —6K 99
Montgomery Rd. W4 —4J 73
Montgomery Rd. Edgw —6A 12
Montholme Rd. SW11 —6D 92
Monthope Rd. E1 —5G 63
Montolieu Gdns. SW15 —5D 90
Montpelier Av. W5 —5C 56
Montpelier Av. Bex —2D 116
Montpelier Clo. W5 —5D 56
Montpelier Gdns. E6 —3B 66
Montpelier Gdns. Romf —7C 36
Montpelier Gro. NW5 —5G 45
Montpelier M. SW7
  —3C 76 (6D 144)
Montpelier Pl. SW7
  —3C 76 (6D 144)
Montpelier Rise. NW11 —7G 27
Montpelier Rise. Wemb —1D 40
Montpelier Rd. N3 —1A 28
Montpelier Rd. SE15 —1H 95
Montpelier Rd. W5 —5D 56
Montpelier Rd. Sutt —4A 132
Montpelier Row. SE3 —2H 97
Montpelier Row. Twic —7C 88
Montpelier Sq. SW7
  —2C 76 (5D 144)
Montpelier St. SW7
  —3C 76 (6D 144)
Montpelier Ter. SW7
  —2C 76 (5D 144)
Montpelier Vale. SE3 —2H 97
Montpelier Wlk. SW7
  —3C 76 (6D 144)
Montpelier Way. NW11 —7G 27
Montrave Rd. SE20 —6J 111
Montreal Pl. WC2 —7K 61 (9E 140)
Montreal Rd. Ilf —6G 35
Montrell Rd. SW2 —1J 109
Montrose Av. NW6 —2G 59
Montrose Av. Edgw —2J 25
Montrose Av. Sidc —7A 100
Montrose Av. Twic —7F 87
Montrose Av. Well —3H 99
Montrose Av. Well —3K 99
Montrose Clo. Wfd G —4D 20
Montrose Clo. NW9 —2J 25

Montrose Ct. NW11 —4H 27
Montrose Ct. SW7 —2B 76 (5B 144)
Montrose Ct. Harr —5F 23
Montrose Cres. N12 —6F 15
Montrose Cres. Wemb —6E 40
Montrose Gdns. Mitc —2D 122
Montrose Gdns. Sutt —2K 131
Montrose Ho. E14 —3C 80
Montrose Pl. SW1 —2E 76 (5H 145)
Montrose Rd. Harr —2J 23
Montrose Wlk. Stan —6G 11
Montrose Way. SE23 —1K 111
Montserrat Av. Wfd G —7A 20
Montserrat Clo. SE19 —5D 110
Montserrat Rd. SW15 —4G 91
Monument Gdns. SE13 —5E 96
Monument St. EC3 —7D 62 (1B 148)
Monument Way. N17 —3F 31
Monza St. E1 —7J 63
Moodkee St. SE16 —3J 79
Moody St. E1 —3K 63
Moon Ct. SE12 —4J 97
Moon La. Barn —3C 4
Moon St. N1 —1B 62
Moorcroft Gdns. Brom —5C 128
Moorcroft Rd. SW16 —3J 109
Moorcroft Way. Pinn —5C 22
Moordown. SE18 —1E 98
Moore Clo. SW14 —3J 89
Moore Clo. Mitc —2F 123
Moore Clo. Wall —7J 133
Moore Cres. Dag —1B 68
Moore Ho. N8 —4J 29
  (off Pembroke Rd.)
Mooreland Rd. Brom —7H 113
Moore Pk. Rd. SW6 —7J 75
Moore St. SW3 —4D 76 (8E 144)
Moore Wlk. E7 —4J 49
Moore Way. Sutt —7J 131
Moorey Clo. E15 —1H 65
Moorfield Av. W5 —4D 56
Moorfield Rd. N17 —2F 31
Moorfield Rd. Enf —1D 8
Moorfields. EC2 —5D 62 (6A 142)
Moorfields Highwalk. EC2
  (off Fore St.) —5D 62 (6A 142)
Moorgate. EC2 —6D 62 (7A 142)
Moorgate Pl. EC2 —6D 62 (7A 142)
  (off Swan All.)
Moorhead Way. SE3 —3K 97
Moorhouse. NW9 —1B 26
Moorhouse Rd. W2 —6J 59
Moorhouse Rd. Harr —3D 24
Moorings, The. E16 —5A 66
  (off Prince Regent La.)
Moorland Clo. Romf —1H 37
Moorland Clo. Twic —7E 86
Moorland Rd. SW9 —4B 94
Moorlands. N'holt —1C 54
Moorlands Av. NW7 —6J 13
Moor La. EC2 —5D 62 (6A 142)
Moor La. EC2 —5D 62 (6A 142)
Moor Mead Rd. Twic —6A 88
Moor Pk. Gdns. King T —7A 106
Moor Pl. EC2 —5D 62 (6A 142)
Moorside Rd. Brom —3G 113
Moor St. W1 —6H 61 (8B 140)
Moot Ct. NW9 —5G 25
Morant Pl. N22 —1K 29
Morant St. E14 —7C 64
Mora Rd. NW2 —4E 42
Mora St. EC1 —3C 62 (2M 141)
Morat St. SW9 —1K 93
Moravian Clo. SW10 —6B 76
Moravian Pl. SW10 —6B 76
Moravian St. E2 —2J 63
Moray Clo. Edgw —2C 12

Moray Clo. Romf —1K 37
Moray M. N7 —2K 45
Moray Rd. N4 —2K 45
Moray Way. Romf —1K 37
Mordaunt Gdns. Dag —7E 52
Mordaunt Rd. NW10 —1K 57
Mordaunt St. SW9 —3K 93
Morden Ct. Mord —4K 121
Morden Ct. Pde. Mord —4K 121
Morden Gdns. Gnfd —5K 39
Morden Gdns. Mitc —4B 122
Morden Hall Rd. Mord —3K 121
Morden Hill. SE13 —2E 96
Morden La. SE13 —1E 96
Morden Rd. SE3 —2J 97
Morden Rd. SW19 —1K 121
Morden Rd. Mord & Mitc —4A 122
Morden Rd. Romf —7E 36
Morden M. SE3 —2J 97
Morden St. SE13 —1D 96
Morden Way. Sutt —7J 121
Morden Wharf Rd. SE10 —3G 81
Mordon Rd. Ilf —7K 35
Mordred Rd. SE6 —2G 113
Morecambe Clo. E1 —5K 63
Morecambe Gdns. Stan —4J 11
Morecambe St. SE17
    —5C 78 (9M 147)
Morecambe Ter. N18 —4J 17
More Clo. E16 —6H 65
More Clo. W14 —4F 75
Morecoombe Clo. King T —7H 105
Moree Way. N18 —4B 18
Moreland Ct. NW2 —3J 43
Moreland Rd. EC1 —3B 62 (1K 141)
Moreland Way. E4 —3J 19
Morella Rd. SW12 —7D 92
Moremead Rd. SE6 —4B 112
Morena St. SE6 —7D 96
Moresby Av. Surb —7H 119
Moresby Rd. E5 —1H 47
Moresby Wlk. SW8 —2G 93
More's Gdns. SW3 —6B 76
    (off Cheyne Wlk.)
Moreton Av. Iswth —1J 87
Moreton Clo. E5 —2H 47
Moreton Clo. N15 —6D 30
Moreton Gdns. Wfd G —5H 21
Moreton Pl. SW1 —5G 77
Moreton Rd. N15 —6D 30
Moreton Rd. S Croy —5D 134
Moreton Rd. Wor Pk —2C 130
Moreton Ter. SW1 —5G 77
Moreton Ter. M. N. SW1 —5G 77
Moreton Ter. M. S. SW1 —5G 77
Moreton Tower. W3 —1H 73
Morfe Way. N18 —4B 18
Morford Clo. Ruis —7A 22
Morford Way. Ruis —7A 22
Morgan Av. E17 —4F 33
Morgan Clo. Dag —7G 53
Morgan Mans. N7 —5A 46
    (off Morgan Rd.)
Morgan Rd. N7 —5A 45
Morgan Rd. W10 —5H 59
Morgan Rd. Brom —7J 113
Morgan Rd. Tedd —6J 103
Morgan's La. SE1 —1E 78 (3C 148)
Morgan St. E3 —3A 64
Morgan St. E16 —5H 65
Morgan Way. Wfd G —6H 21
Moriatry Clo. N7 —4J 45
Morie St. SW18 —5K 91
Morieux Rd. E10 —1B 48
Moring Rd. SW17 —4E 108
Morkyns Wlk. SE21 —3E 110
Morland Av. Croy —1E 134

Morland Clo. NW11 —1K 43
Morland Clo. Hamp —5D 102
Morland Clo. Mitc —3C 122
Morland Est. E8 —7G 47
Morland Gdns. NW10 —7K 41
Morland Gdns. S'hall —1F 71
Morland M. N1 —7A 46
Morland Rd. E17 —5K 31
Morland Rd. SE20 —6K 111
Morland Rd. Croy —1E 134
Morland Rd. Dag —7G 53
Morland Rd. Harr —5E 24
Morland Rd. Ilf —2F 51
Morland Rd. Sutt —5A 132
Morley Av. E4 —7A 20
Morley Av. N18 —4B 18
Morley Av. N22 —2A 30
Morley Ct. E4 —5G 19
Morley Ct. Short —4H 127
Morley Cres. Edgw —2D 12
Morley Cres. Ruis —2A 38
Morley Cres. E. Stan —2C 24
Morley Cres. W. Stan —3C 24
Morley Hill. Enf —1J 7
Morley Ho. N16 —2G 47
Morley Rd. E10 —1E 48
Morley Rd. E15 —2H 65
Morley Rd. SE13 —4E 96
Morley Rd. Bark —1H 67
Morley Rd. Chst —1G 129
Morley Rd. Romf —5E 36
Morley Rd. Sutt —1H 131
Morley Rd. Twic —6D 88
Morley St. SE1 —3A 78 (6H 147)
Morna Rd. SE5 —2C 94
Morning La. E9 —6J 47
Morningside Rd. Wor Pk —2E 130
Mornington Av. W14 —4H 75
Mornington Av. Brom —3A 128
Mornington Av. Ilf —7E 34
Mornington Clo. Wfd G —4D 20
Mornington Ct. Bex —1K 117
Mornington Cres. NW1 —2G 61
Mornington Cres. Houn —1A 86
Mornington Gro. E3 —3C 64
Mornington M. SE5 —1C 94
Mornington Pl. NW1 —2F 61
Mornington Rd. E4 —7K 9
Mornington Rd. E11 —7H 33
Mornington Rd. SE8 —7B 80
Mornington Rd. Gnfd —5F 55
Mornington Rd. Wfd G —4C 20
Mornington St. NW1 —2F 61
Mornington Ter. NW1 —1F 61
Mornington Wlk. Rich —4C 104
Morocco St. SE1 —2E 78 (5C 148)
Morpeth Gro. E9 —1K 63
Morpeth Rd. E9 —1J 63
Morpeth St. E2 —3K 63
Morpeth Ter. SW1
    —3G 77 (7L 145)
Morpeth Wlk. N17 —7C 18
Morrab Gdns. Ilf —3K 51
Morrell Clo. New Bar —3E 5
Morris Av. E12 —5D 50
Morris Blitz Ct. N16 —4F 47
Morris Clo. Croy —6A 126
Morris Ct. E4 —3J 19
Morris Gdns. SW18 —7J 91
Morris Ho. SE16 —2H 79
    (off Cherry Garden St.)
Morrish Rd. SW2 —7J 93
Morrison Av. N17 —3E 30
Morrison Rd. Bark —2E 68
Morrison St. SW11 —3E 92
Morris Pl. N4 —2A 46
Morris Rd. E14 —5D 64
Morris Rd. E15 —4G 49

Morris Rd. Dag —2F 53
Morris Rd. Iswth —3K 87
Morris St. E1 —6H 63
Morse Clo. E13 —3J 65
Morshead Mans. W9 —3K 59
    (off Morshead Rd.)
Morshead Rd. W9 —3J 59
Morson Rd. Enf —6F 9
Morston Gdns. SE9 —4D 114
Morten Clo. SW4 —6H 93
Morteyne Rd. N17 —1D 30
Mortgramit Sq. SE18 —3E 82
Mortham St. E15 —1G 65
Mortimer Clo. NW2 —2H 43
Mortimer Clo. SW16 —2H 109
Mortimer Cres. NW6 —1K 59
Mortimer Cres. Wor Pk —3A 130
Mortimer Dri. Enf —5K 7
Mortimer Est. NW6 —1K 59
    (off Mortimer Pl.)
Mortimer M. W11 —1F 75
    (off Queensdale Cres.)
Mortimer Mkt. WC1
    —4G 61 (4M 139)
Mortimer Pl. NW6 —1K 59
Mortimer Rd. E6 —3D 66
Mortimer Rd. N1 —7E 46
Mortimer Rd. NW10 —3E 58
Mortimer Rd. W13 —6C 56
Mortimer Rd. Eri —6K 85
Mortimer Rd. Mitc —1D 122
Mortimer Sq. W11 —7F 59
Mortimer St. W1 —6G 61 (7K 139)
Mortimer Ter. NW5 —4F 45
Mortlake Clo. Croy —3J 133
Mortlake Dri. Mitc —1C 122
Mortlake High St. SW14 —3K 89
Mortlake Rd. E16 —6K 65
Mortlake Rd. Ilf —4G 51
Mortlake Rd. Rich —7G 73
Mortlock Clo. SE15 —1H 95
Morton Clo. E14 —6E 64
Morton Cres. N14 —4C 16
Morton Gdns. Wall —5G 133
Morton M. SW5 —4K 75
Morton Pl. SE1 —3A 78 (7G 147)
Morton Rd. E15 —7H 49
Morton Rd. N1 —7C 46
Morton Rd. Mord —5B 122
Morton Way. N14 —3B 16
Morvale Clo. Belv —4F 85
Morval Rd. SW2 —5A 94
Morven Rd. SW17 —3D 108
Morville St. E3 —2C 64
Morwell St. WC1 —5H 61 (6A 140)
Moscow Pl. W2 —7K 59
Moscow Rd. W2 —7J 59
Moselle Av. N22 —2A 30
Moselle Clo. N8 —3K 29
Moselle Ho. N17 —7A 18
    (off William St.)
Moselle Pl. N17 —7A 18
Moselle St. N17 —7A 18
Mossborough Clo. N12 —6E 14
Mossbury Rd. SW11 —3C 92
Moss Clo. E1 —5G 63
Moss Clo. Pinn —2D 22
Mossdown Clo. Belv —4G 85
Mossford Ct. Ilf —2F 35
Mossford Grn. Ilf —2F 35
Mossford La. Ilf —2F 35
Mossford St. E3 —4B 64
Moss Gdns. S Croy —7K 135
Moss Hall Ct. N12 —6E 14
Moss Hall Cres. N12 —6E 14
Moss Hall Gro. N12 —6E 14
Mossington Gdns. SE16 —4J 79
Moss La. Pinn —1C 22

Mosslea Rd. SE20 —6J 111
    (in two parts)
Mosslea Rd. Brom —5B 128
Mossop St. SW3 —4C 76 (8D 144)
Moss Rd. Dag —7G 53
Mossville Gdns. Mord —3H 121
Mosswell Ho. N10 —1E 28
Mostyn Av. Wemb —5F 41
Mostyn Gdns. NW10 —2F 59
Mostyn Gro. E3 —2C 64
Mostyn Rd. SW9 —1A 94
Mostyn Rd. SW19 —1H 121
Mostyn Rd. Edgw —7F 13
Mosul Way. Brom —6C 128
Motcomb St. SW1 —3E 76 (6G 145)
Mothers Sq. E5 —4J 47
Motley Av. EC2 —4E 62 (3C 142)
    (off Christina St.)
Motley St. SW8 —2G 93
Motspur Pk. N Mald —6B 120
Mottingham Gdns. SE9 —1B 114
Mottingham La. SE12 & SE9
    —1A 114
Mottingham Rd. N9 —6E 8
Mottingham Rd. SE9 —2C 114
Mottisfont Rd. SE2 —3A 84
Mott St. E4 & Lou —1K 9
Moules Ct. SE5 —7C 78
Moulins Rd. E9 —7J 47
Moulsford Ho. N7 —5H 45
Moulton Av. Houn —2C 86
Moundfield Rd. N16 —6G 31
Mound, The. SE9 —3E 114
Mountacre Clo. SE26 —4F 111
Mt. Adon Pk. SE22 —7G 95
Mountague Pl. E14 —7E 64
Mountain Ho. SE11 —5K 77
Mt. Angelus Rd. SW15 —7B 90
Mt. Ararat Rd. Rich —5E 88
Mt. Arlington. Short —2G 127
    (off Park Hill Rd.)
Mt. Ash Rd. SE26 —3H 111
Mount Av. E4 —3H 19
Mount Av. W5 —5C 56
Mount Av. S'hall —6E 54
Mountbatten Clo. SE18 —6J 83
Mountbatten Clo. SE19 —5E 110
Mountbatten Ho. N6 —7E 28
    (off Hillcrest)
Mountbatten M. SW18 —7A 92
Mountbel Rd. Stan —1A 24
Mount Clo. W5 —5C 56
Mount Clo. Barn —4K 5
Mount Clo. Brom —1C 128
Mount Clo. Cars —7E 132
Mountcombe Clo. Surb —7E 118
Mount Ct. SW15 —3G 91
Mount Ct. W Wick —2G 137
Mt. Culver Av. Sidc —6D 116
Mount Dri. Bexh —5E 100
Mount Dri. Harr —5D 22
Mount Dri. Wemb —2J 41
Mountearl Gdns. SW16 —3K 109
Mt. Echo Av. E4 —1J 19
Mt. Echo Dri. E4 —1J 19
Mt. Ephraim La. SW16 —3H 109
Mt. Ephraim Rd. SW16 —3H 109
Mountfield Rd. E6 —2E 66
Mountfield Rd. N3 —3H 27
Mountfield Rd. W5 —6D 56
Mountford Rd. E8 —5G 47
Mountfort Cres. N1 —7A 46
Mountfort Ter. N1 —7A 46
Mount Gdns. SE26 —3H 111
Mount Gro. Edgw —3D 12
Mountgrove Rd. N5 —3B 46
Mounthurst Rd. Brom —7H 127

Mountington Pk. Clo. Harr —6D 24
Mountjoy Clo. EC2 —5C 62 (6M 141)
    (off Thomas More Highwalk.)
Mountjoy Clo. SE2 —2B 84
Mountjoy Ho. EC2 —5C 62 (6M 141)
    (off Barbican)
Mt. Lodge. N6 —6G 29
Mt. Mills. EC1 —3B 62 (2K 141)
Mt. Nod Rd. SW16 —3K 109
Mount Pde. Barn —4H 5
Mount Pk. Cars —7E 132
Mount Pk. Av. Harr —2H 39
Mount Pk. Av. S Croy —7B 134
Mount Pk. Cres. W5 —6D 56
Mount Pk. Rd. W5 —5D 56
Mount Pk. Rd. Harr —3H 39
Mount Pl. W3 —1H 73
Mt. Pleasant. N14 —1C 16
    (off Wells, The.)
Mt. Pleasant. SE27 —4C 110
Mt. Pleasant. WC1 —4A 62 (4G 141)
Mt. Pleasant. Barn —4H 5
Mt. Pleasant. Ruis —2A 38
Mt. Pleasant. Wemb —1E 56
Mt. Pleasant Cres. N4 —1K 45
Mt. Pleasant Hill. E5 —2H 47
Mt. Pleasant La. E5 —2H 47
Mt. Pleasant Rd. E17 —2A 32
Mt. Pleasant Rd. N17 —2E 30
Mt. Pleasant Rd. NW10 —7E 42
Mt. Pleasant Rd. SE13 —6D 96
Mt. Pleasant Rd. W5 —4C 56
Mt. Pleasant Rd. N Mald —3J 119
Mt. Pleasant Vs. N4 —7K 29
Mt. Pleasant Wlk. Bex —5J 101
Mount Rd. NW2 —3D 42
Mount Rd. NW4 —6C 26
Mount Rd. SW19 —2J 107
Mount Rd. Barn —5H 5
Mount Rd. Bexh —5D 100
Mount Rd. Dag —1F 53
Mount Rd. Felt —3C 102
Mount Rd. Ilf —5F 51
Mount Rd. Mitc —2B 122
Mount Rd. N Mald —3K 119
Mount Row. W1 —7F 61 (1J 145)
Mountsfield Ct. SE13 —6F 97
Mountside. Stan —1K 23
Mounts Pond Rd. SE3 —2F 97
    (in two parts)
Mount Sq., The. NW3 —3A 44
Mt. Stewart Av. Harr —7D 24
Mount St. SE18 —4F 83
Mount St. W1 —7E 60 (1G 145)
Mount Ter. E1 —5H 63
Mount, The. E5 —2H 47
Mount, The. N20 —2F 15
Mount, The. NW3 —4A 44
Mount, The. W3 —1H 73
Mount, The. Bexh —5H 101
Mount, The. N Mald —3B 120
Mount, The. Wemb —2J 41
Mount, The. Wor Pk —4D 130
Mt. Vernon. NW3 —4A 44
Mount View. NW7 —3E 12
Mount View. W5 —4D 56
Mount View. Enf —1E 6
Mount View. Felt —1E 6
Mountview Ct. N15 —4B 30
Mt. View Rd. E4 —7K 9
Mt. View Rd. N4 —7J 29
Mt. View Rd. NW9 —5K 25
Mountview Rd. Orp —7K 129
    (in two parts)
Mount Vs. SE27 —3B 110
Mount Way. Cars —7E 132
Movers La. Bark —1H 67
Mowat Ct. Wor Pk —2B 130
    (off Avenue, The.)

239

Mowatt Clo. N19 —2H 45
Mowbray Ct. N22 —1A 30
Mowbray Ct. SE19 —7F 111
Mowbray Gdns. N'holt —1E 54
Mowbray Ho. N2 —2B 28
  (off Grange, The)
Mowbray Pde. Edgw —4B 12
Mowbray Pde. N'holt —1E 54
Mowbray Rd. NW6 —7G 43
Mowbray Rd. SE19 —1F 125
Mowbray Rd. Barn —4F 5
Mowbray Rd. Edgw —4B 12
Mowbray Rd. Rich —3C 104
Mowbrays Clo. Romf —1J 37
Mowbrays Rd. Romf —2J 37
Mowlem St. E2 —2H 63
Mowlem Trading Est. N17 —7D 18
Mowll St. SW9 —7A 78
Moxon Clo. E13 —2H 65
Moxon St. W1 —5E 60 (6G 139)
Moxon St. Barn —3C 4
Moye Clo. E2 —2G 63
Moyers Rd. E10 —7E 32
Moylan Rd. W6 —6G 75
Moyne Ho. SE24 —5B 94
Moyne Pl. NW10 —2G 57
Moys Clo. Croy —6J 123
Moyser Rd. SW16 —5F 109
Mozart St. W10 —3H 59
Mozart Ter. SW1 —4E 76 (9H 145)
Muchelney Rd. Mord —6A 122
Mudlarks Way. SE10 & SE7 —3H 81
Muggeridge Rd. Dag —4H 53
Muirdown Av. SW14 —4K 89
Muirfield. W3 —6A 58
Muirfield Cres. E14 —3D 80
Muirkirk Rd. SE6 —1E 112
Muir Rd. E5 —4G 47
Muir St. E16 —1C 82
Mulberry Bus. Pk. SE16 —2K 79
Mulberry Clo. E4 —2H 19
Mulberry Clo. NW3 —4B 44
Mulberry Clo. NW4 —3E 26
Mulberry Clo. SE22 —5G 95
Mulberry Clo. SW3 —6B 76
Mulberry Clo. SW16 —4G 109
Mulberry Clo. Barn —4G 5
Mulberry Clo. N'holt —2C 54
Mulberry Ct. Bark —7K 51
Mulberry Ct. Surb —7D 118
Mulberry Ct. Twic —3K 103
Mulberry Ho. Short —2G 127
Mulberry La. Croy —1F 135
Mulberry M. Wall —6G 133
Mulberry Pl. W6 —5C 74
Mulberry St. E1 —6G 63
Mulberry Wlk. SW3 —6B 76
Mulberry Way. E18 —2K 33
Mulberry Way. Belv —2J 85
Mulberry Way. Ilf —4G 35
Mulgrave Ct. Sutt —6K 131
  (off Mulgrave Rd.)
Mulgrave Rd. NW10 —4B 42
Mulgrave Rd. SW6 —6H 75
Mulgrave Rd. W5 —3D 56
Mulgrave Rd. Croy —3D 134
Mulgrave Rd. Harr —2A 40
Mulgrave Rd. Sutt —7H 131
Mulhaney Way. SE1 —2D 78 (5B 148)
Mulkern Rd. N19 —1H 45
Muller Rd. SW4 —6H 93
Mullet Gdns. E2 —3G 63
Mullins Path. SW14 —3K 89
Mullion Clo. Harr —1F 23
Mull Wlk. N1 —6C 46
  (off Clephane Rd.)

Mulready St. NW8 —4C 60 (4C 138)
Multi Way. W3 —2A 74
Multon Rd. SW18 —7B 92
Mumford Ct. EC2 —6C 62 (7M 141)
Mumford Rd. SE24 —5B 94
Muncaster Rd. SW11 —5D 92
Muncies M. SE6 —2E 112
Mundania Rd. SE22 —6H 95
Munday Rd. E16 —7J 65
Munden St. W14 —4G 75
Mundford Rd. E5 —2J 47
Mundon Gdns. Ilf —1H 51
Mund St. W14 —5H 75
Mundy St. N1 —3E 62 (1C 142)
Mungo Pk. Clo. Bush —2B 10
Munnings Gdns. Iswth —5H 87
Munro Dri. N11 —6B 16
Munro Rd. SW18 —7A 78 (5G 147)
Munro M. W10 —5G 59
Munster Av. Houn —5C 86
Munster Gdns. N13 —4G 17
Munster Rd. SW6 —7G 75
Munster Rd. Tedd —6C 104
Munster Sq. NW1 —3F 61 (2K 139)
Munton Rd. SE17 —4C 78 (8M 147)
Murchison Av. Bex —1D 116
Murchison Rd. E10 —2E 48
Murdock Clo. E16 —6H 65
Murdock St. SE15 —6H 79
Murlett Clo. SW9 —2G 107
Muriel Ct. E10 —7D 32
Muriel St. N1 —2K 61
  (in two parts)
Murillo Rd. SE13 —4F 97
Murphy St. SE1 —2A 78 (5G 147)
Murray Av. Brom —3K 127
Murray Av. Houn —5F 87
Murray Ct. Harr —6K 23
Murray Ct. Twic —2H 103
Murray Cres. Pinn —1B 22
Murray Gro. N1 —2C 62
Murray Ho. SE18 —4D 82
  (off Rideout St.)
Murray M. NW1 —7H 45
Murray Rd. SW19 —6F 107
Murray Rd. W5 —4C 72
Murray Rd. Rich —2C 104
Murray Sq. E16 —6J 65
Murray St. NW1 —7G 45
Murray Ter. NW3 —4A 44
Mursell Est. SW8 —1K 93
Musard Rd. W6 —6G 75
Musbury St. E1 —6J 63
Muscatel Pl. SE5 —7E 78
Muschamp Rd. SE15 —3F 95
Muschamp Rd. Cars —2C 132
Muscovy Ho. Eri —2E 84
  (off Kale Rd.)
Muscovy St. EC3 —7E 62 (1D 148)
Museum Path. E2 —3J 63
Museum St. WC1 —5J 61 (5C 140)
Musgrave Clo. Barn —1F 5
Musgrave Cres. SW6 —7J 75
Musgrave Rd. Iswth —1K 87
Musgrove Rd. SE14 —1K 95
Musjid Rd. SW11 —2B 92
Musquash Way. Houn —2A 86
Muston Rd. E5 —2H 47
Mustow Pl. SW6 —2H 91
Muswell Av. N10 —1F 29
Muswell Hill. N6 & N10 —6E 28
Muswell Hill. N10 —3F 29
Muswell Hill B'way. N10 —3F 29
Muswell Hill Pl. N10 —4F 29
Muswell M. N10 —3F 29
Muswell Rd. N10 —3F 29
Mutrix Rd. NW6 —1J 59

Mutton Pl. NW1 —6E 44
Muybridge Rd. N Mald —2J 119
Myatt Rd. SW9 —1B 94
Mycenae Rd. SE3 —7J 81
Myddelton Clo. Enf —1A 8
Myddelton Gdns. N21 —7H 7
Myddelton Pk. N20 —3G 15
Myddelton Pas. EC1
                —3A 62 (1H 141)
Myddelton Rd. N8 —3J 29
Myddelton Sq. EC1 —3A 62 (1H 141)
Myddelton St. EC1 —3A 62 (2H 141)
Myddleton Av. Enf —1K 7
Myddleton Rd. N22 —7D 16
Myddleton Rd. N22 —7D 16
Myers Clo. SE14 —6K 79
Mylis Clo. SE26 —4H 111
Mylne Clo. W6 —5C 74
Mylne St. EC1 —3A 62 (1G 141)
Myra St. SE2 —4A 84
Myrdle St. E1 —5G 63
Myrna Clo. SW19 —7C 108
Myron Pl. SE13 —3E 96
Myrtleberry Clo. E8 —6F 47
  (off Beechwood Rd.)
Myrtle Clo. Barn —1J 15
Myrtledene Rd. SE2 —5A 84
Myrtle Gdns. W7 —1J 71
Myrtle Gro. Enf —1J 7
Myrtle Gro. N Mald —2J 119
Myrtle Rd. E6 —1C 66
Myrtle Rd. E17 —6A 32
Myrtle Rd. N13 —3H 17
Myrtle Rd. W3 —1J 73
Myrtle Rd. Croy —3C 136
Myrtle Rd. Hamp —6G 103
Myrtle Rd. Houn —2G 87
Myrtle Rd. Ilf —2F 51
Myrtle Rd. Sutt —5A 132
Myrtle Wlk. N1 —2E 62
Mysore Rd. SW11 —4D 92
Myton Rd. SE21 —3D 110

Nadine Ct. Wall —7G 133
Nadine St. SE7 —5A 82
Nagasaki Wlk. SE7 —3K 81
Nagle Clo. E17 —2F 33
Nags Head Ct. EC1 —4C 62 (4M 141)
  (off Golden La.)
Nags Head La. Well —3B 100
Nags Head Rd. Enf —4D 8
Nags Head Shopping Cen. N7
                —4K 45
Nailsworth Ct. SE15 —6E 78
  (off Birdlip Clo.)
Nainby Ho. SE11 —4A 78 (9G 147)
  (off Hotspur St.)
Nairne Gro. SE24 —5D 94
Nairn Rd. Ruis —6A 38
Nairn St. E14 —5E 64
Naish Ct. N1 —1J 45
  (in two parts)
Naldera Gdns. SE3 —6J 81
Nallhead Rd. Felt —5A 102
Namton Dri. T Hth —4K 123
Nan Clark's La. NW7 —2F 13
Nankin St. E14 —6C 64
Nansen Ho. NW10 —7K 41
  (off Stonebridge Pk.)
Nansen Rd. SW11 —3E 92
Nansen Village. N12 —4E 14
Nant Ct. NW2 —2H 43
Nant Clo. SW18 —4A 92
Nantes Pas. E1 —5F 63 (5E 142)
Nant Rd. NW2 —2H 43

Nant St. E2 —3H 63
Napier. NW9 —1B 26
Napier Av. E14 —5C 80
Napier Av. SW6 —3H 91
Napier Clo. SE8 —7B 80
Napier Clo. W14 —3G 75
Napier Ct. SW6 —3H 91
  (off Ranelagh Gdns.)
Napier Gro. N1 —2C 62
Napier Pl. W14 —3H 75
Napier Rd. E6 —1E 66
Napier Rd. E11 —4G 49
Napier Rd. E15 —2G 65
  (in two parts)
Napier Rd. N17 —3E 30
Napier Rd. NW10 —3D 58
Napier Rd. SE25 —4H 125
Napier Rd. W14 —3G 75
Napier Rd. Belv —4F 85
Napier Rd. Brom —4K 127
Napier Rd. Enf —4F 8
Napier Rd. Iswth —4A 88
Napier Rd. S Croy —7D 134
Napier Rd. Wemb —5D 40
Napier Ter. N1 —7B 46
Napoleon Rd. E5 —3H 47
Napoleon Rd. Twic —7B 88
Napton Clo. Hay —4C 54
Narbonne Av. SW4 —5G 93
Narborough St. SW6 —2K 91
Narcissus Rd. NW6 —5J 43
Nardini. NW9 —1B 26
  (off Concourse, The)
Naresby Fold. Stan —6H 11
Narford Rd. E5 —3G 47
Narrow St. E14 —7A 64
Narrow St. W3 —1H 73
Narrow Way. Brom —6C 128
Nascot St. W12 —6E 58
Naseby Clo. NW6 —7A 44
Naseby Clo. Iswth —1J 87
Naseby Ct. Sidc —4K 115
Naseby Rd. SE19 —6D 110
Naseby Rd. Dag —3G 53
Naseby Rd. Ilf —1D 34
Nash Grn. Brom —6J 113
Nash Ho. E17 —4D 32
Nash La. Kes —7J 137
Nash Pl. E14 —1D 80
Nash Rd. N9 —2D 18
Nash Rd. SE4 —4A 96
Nash Rd. Romf —4D 36
Nash St. NW1 —3F 61 (1K 139)
Nasmyth St. W6 —3C 74
Nassau Path. SE28 —1C 84
Nassau Rd. SW13 —1B 90
Nassau St. W1 —5G 61 (6L 139)
Nassington Rd. NW3 —4C 44
Natal Rd. N11 —6D 16
Natal Rd. SW16 —6H 109
Natal Rd. Ilf —4F 51
Natal Rd. T Hth —3D 124
Nathan Ct. N9 —7D 8
  (off Causeyware Rd.)
Nathan Ho. SE11 —4A 78 (9H 147)
  (off Reedworth St.)
Nathaniel Clo. E1 —5F 63 (6F 142)
Nathaniel Ct. E17 —6A 32
Nathans Rd. Wemb —1C 40
Nathan Way. SE28 —4J 83
Nation Way. E4 —1K 19
Naval Row. E14 —7E 64
Naval Wlk. Brom —2J 127
Navarino Gro. E8 —6G 47
Navarino Mans. E8 —6G 47
Navarino Rd. E8 —6G 47
Navarre Rd. E6 —2C 66
Navarre St. E2 —4F 63 (3E 142)

Navenby Wlk. E3 —4C 64
Navestock Clo. E4 —3K 19
Navestock Cres. Wfd G —7F 21
Navestock Ho. Bark —2B 68
Navy St. SW4 —3H 93
Naylor Gro. Enf —5E 8
Naylor Rd. N20 —2F 15
Naylor Rd. SE15 —7H 79
Nazrul St. E2 —3F 63 (1E 142)
Neagle Clo. E7 —4J 49
Neagle Ho. NW2 —3E 42
  (off Stoll Clo.)
Neal Av. S'hall —4D 54
Nealden St. SW9 —3K 93
Neale Clo. N2 —3A 28
Neal St. WC2 —6J 61 (8C 140)
Neal's Yd. WC2 —6J 61 (8C 140)
Near Acre. NW9 —1B 26
Neasden Clo. NW10 —5A 42
Neasden La. NW10 —3A 42
Neasden La. N. NW10 —3K 41
Neasham Rd. Dag —5B 52
Neate St. SE5 —6E 78
Neath Gdns. Mord —6A 122
Neath Ho. SE24 —6B 94
  (off Dulwich Rd.)
Neathouse Pl. SW1 —4G 77 (8L 145)
Neatscourt Rd. E6 —5B 66
Nebraska St. SE1 —2D 78 (5A 148)
Nebraska St. SW1 —2D 78
Neckinger. SE16 —3F 79 (6F 148)
Neckinger Est. SE1 —3F 79 (6F 148)
Neckinger Est. SE16 —3F 79
Neckinger St. SE1 —2F 79
Nectarine Way. SE13 —2D 96
Needham Ho. SE11 —4A 78 (9G 147)
  (off Tracey St.)
Needham Rd. W11 —6J 59
Needham Ter. NW2 —3F 43
Needleman St. SE16 —2K 79
Needwood Ho. N4 —1C 46
Neeld Cres. NW4 —5D 26
Neeld Cres. Wemb —5G 41
Neil Wates Cres. SW2 —1A 110
Nelgarde Rd. SE6 —7C 96
Nella Rd. W6 —6F 75
Nelldale Rd. SE16 —4J 79
Nello James Gdns. SE27 —4D 110
Nelson Clo. Croy —1B 134
Nelson Clo. Romf —1H 37
Nelson Ct. SE1 —2B 78 (4K 147)
  (off Suffolk St.)
Nelson Gdns. E2 —3G 63
Nelson Gdns. Houn —6E 86
Nelson Gro. Rd. SW19 —1A 122
Nelson Ind. Est. SW19 —1K 121
Nelson Mandela Rd. N10 —2E 28
Nelson Mandella Rd. SE3 —3A 98
Nelson Pas. EC1 —3C 62 (2M 141)
Nelson Pl. N1 —2B 62
Nelson Pl. Sidc —4A 116
Nelson Rd. E4 —6J 19
Nelson Rd. E11 —4J 33
Nelson Rd. N8 —5K 29
Nelson Rd. N9 —2C 18
Nelson Rd. N15 —4E 30
Nelson Rd. SE10 —6E 80
Nelson Rd. SW19 —7A 108
Nelson Rd. Belv —5F 85
Nelson Rd. Brom —4A 128
Nelson Rd. Enf —6E 8
Nelson Rd. Harr —1H 39
Nelson Rd. Houn —6E 86
Nelson Rd. N Mald —5K 119
Nelson Rd. Sidc —4A 116
Nelson Rd. Stan —6H 11
Nelson Rd. Twic —6E 86
Nelson Sq. SE1 —2B 78 (4J 147)

Nelson's Row. SW4 —4H **93**
Nelson St. E1 —6H **63**
Nelson St. E6 —2D **66**
(in two parts)
Nelson St. E16 —7H **65**
(in two parts)
Nelsons Yd. NW1 —2G **61**
Nelson Ter. N1 —2B **62**
Nelson Wlk. SE16 —1A **80**
Nemoure Rd. W3 —7J **57**
Nene Gdns. Felt —2D **102**
Nepal Rd. SW11 —3C **92**
Nepean St. SW15 —6C **90**
Neptune Rd. Harr —6H **23**
Neptune St. SE16 —3J **79**
Nero Ct. Bren —7D **72**
Nesbit Rd. SE9 —4B **98**
Nesbitt Clo. SE3 —3G **97**
Nesbitts All. Barn —3C **4**
Nesbitt Sq. SE19 —7E **110**
Nesham St. E1 —1G **79**
Ness St. SE16 —3G **79**
Nesta Rd. Wfd G —6B **20**
Nestor Av. N21 —6G **7**
Netheravon Rd. W7 —1K **71**
Netheravon Rd. N. W4 —4B **74**
Netheravon Rd. S. W4 —5B **74**
Netherbury Rd. W5 —3D **72**
Netherby Gdns. SW5 —4A **76**
Netherby Gdns. Enf —4D **6**
Netherby Rd. SE23 —7J **95**
Nether Clo. N3 —7D **14**
Nethercourt Av. N3 —6D **14**
Netherfield Gdns. Bark —7H **51**
Netherfield Rd. N12 —5E **14**
Netherfield Rd. SW17 —3E **108**
Netherford Rd. SW4 —2G **93**
Netherhall Gdns. NW3 —6A **44**
Netherhall Way. NW3 —5A **44**
Netherlands Rd. Barn & N20 —6G **5**
Netherleigh Clo. N19 —1F **45**
Nether St. N3 & N12 —1J **27**
Nether St. N12 —5F **15**
Netherton Gro. SW10 —6A **76**
Netherton Rd. N15 —6D **30**
Netherton Rd. Twic —5A **88**
Netherwood. N2 —2B **28**
Netherwood Rd. W14 —3F **75**
Netherwood St. NW6 —7H **43**
Netley Clo. New Ad —7E **136**
Netley Clo. Sutt —5F **131**
Netley Gdns. Mord —7A **122**
Netley Rd. E17 —5B **32**
Netley Rd. Bren —6E **72**
Netley Rd. Ilf —5H **35**
Netley Rd. Mord —7A **122**
Netley St. NW1 —3G **61** (2L **139**)
Nettlecombe Clo. Sutt —7K **131**
Nettleden Av. Wemb —6G **41**
Nettlefold Pl. SE27 —3B **110**
Nettlestead Clo. Beck —7B **112**
Nettleton Ct. EC2 —5C **62** (6L **141**)
(off London Wall)
Nettleton Rd. SE14 —1K **95**
Nettlewood Rd. SW16 —7H **109**
Neuchatel Rd. SE6 —2B **112**
Nevada Clo. N Mald —4J **119**
Nevada St. SE10 —6E **80**
Nevern Mans. SW5 —4J **75**
(off Warwick Rd.)
Nevern Pl. SW5 —4J **75**
Nevern Rd. SW5 —4J **75**
Nevern Sq. SW5 —4J **75**
Nevil Ho. SW9 —2B **94**
(off Rupert Gdns.)
Nevill Clo. W3 —2J **73**
Neville Av. N Mald —1K **119**

Neville Clo. E11 —3H **49**
Neville Clo. NW1 —2H **61**
Neville Clo. NW6 —2H **59**
Neville Clo. SE15 —1G **95**
Neville Clo. Houn —2F **87**
Neville Clo. Sidc —4K **115**
Neville Dri. N2 —6A **28**
Neville Gdns. Dag —3D **52**
Neville Gill Clo. SW18 —6J **91**
Neville Ho. N11 —4K **15**
Neville Ho. N22 —6E **16**
(off Neville Pl.)
Neville Pl. N22 —1K **29**
Neville Rd. E7 —7J **49**
Neville Rd. NW6 —2H **59**
Neville Rd. W5 —4D **56**
Neville Rd. Croy —7D **124**
Neville Rd. Dag —2D **52**
Neville Rd. Ilf —1G **35**
Neville Rd. King T —2G **119**
Neville Rd. Rich —3C **104**
Nevilles Ct. NW2 —3C **42**
Neville St. SW7 —5B **76**
Neville Ter. SW7 —5B **76**
Neville Wlk. Cars —7C **122**
Nevin Dri. E4 —1J **19**
Nevis Rd. SW17 —2E **108**
Nevitt Ho. N1 —2D **62**
(off Cranston Est.)
Newark Cres. NW10 —3K **57**
Newarke Ho. SW9 —2B **94**
Newark Knok. E6 —6E **66**
Newark Pde. NW4 —3C **26**
Newark Rd. S Croy —6D **134**
Newark St. E1 —5H **63**
(in two parts)
Newark Way. NW4 —4C **26**
New Ash Clo. N2 —3B **28**
New Barn Rd. Swan —7K **117**
New Barns Av. Mitc —4H **123**
New Barn St. E13 —4J **65**
New Barns Way. Chig —3K **21**
Newbolt Av. Sutt —5E **130**
Newbolt Ho. SE17 —5D **78**
(off Brandon Est.)
Newbolt Rd. Stan —5E **10**
New Bond St. W1 —6F **61** (8J **139**)
Newborough Grn. N Mald —4A **119**
New Brent St. NW4 —5E **26**
New Bridge St. EC4 —6B **62** (8J **141**)
New Broad St. EC2 —5E **62** (6B **142**)
New Broadway. W5 —7D **56**
New Broadway. Hamp —5H **103**
Newburgh Rd. W3 —1J **73**
Newburgh St. W1 —6G **61** (8L **139**)
New Burlington M. W1
—7G **61** (9L **139**)
New Burlington Pl. W1
—7G **61** (9L **139**)
New Burlington St. W1
—7G **61** (9L **139**)
Newburn Ho. SE11 —5K **77**
(off Newburn St.)
Newburn St. SE11 —5K **77**
Newbury Clo. N'holt —6D **38**
Newbury Ct. Sidc —4K **115**
Newbury Gdns. Eps —4B **130**
Newbury Ho. N22 —1J **29**
Newbury Ho. SW9 —2B **94**
Newbury M. NW5 —6E **44**
Newbury Rd. E4 —6K **19**
Newbury Rd. Brom —3J **127**
Newbury Rd. Ilf —6J **35**
Newbury St. EC1 —5C **62** (6L **141**)
Newbury Way. N'holt —6C **38**
New Business Cen., The. NW10
—3B **58**

New Butt La. SE8 —7C **80**
New Butt La. N. SE8 —7C **80**
(off Reginald Rd.)
Newby Clo. Enf —2K **7**
Newby Pl. E14 —7E **64**
Newby St. SW8 —3F **93**
New Caledonian Wharf. SE16
—3B **80**
Newcastle Clo. EC4 —6B **62** (7J **141**)
Newcastle Ct. EC4 —7C **62** (9M **141**)
(off College Hill.)
Newcastle Pl. W2 —5B **60** (5B **138**)
Newcastle Row. EC1
—4A **62** (4H **141**)
New Cavendish St. W1
—5E **60** (6H **139**)
New Change. EC4 —6C **62** (8L **141**)
New Church Rd. SE5 —7C **78**
(in two parts)
New City Rd. E13 —3A **66**
New Clo. SW19 —3A **122**
New Clo. Felt —5C **102**
New Colebrooke Ct. Cars —7E **132**
(off Stanley Rd.)
New College Ct. NW3 —6A **44**
(off College Cres.)
New College M. N1 —7A **46**
New College Pde. NW3 —6B **44**
(off College Cres.)
Newcombe Gdns. SW16 —4J **109**
Newcombe Pk. NW7 —5F **13**
Newcombe Pk. Wemb —1F **57**
Newcombe St. W8 —1J **75**
Newcomen Rd. E11 —3H **49**
Newcomen Rd. SW11 —3B **92**
Newcomen St. SE1 —2D **78** (4A **148**)
Newcomen St. SW1 —2D **78**
New Compton St. WC2
—6H **61** (8B **140**)
New Concordia Wharf. SE1 —2G **79**
New Ct. EC4 —7A **62** (9G **141**)
(off Temple)
Newcourt St. NW8 —2C **60**
New Covent Garden Mkt. SW8
—7H **77**
New Coventry St. W1
—7H **61** (1B **146**)
New Crane Pl. E1 —1J **79**
New Cross Rd. SE15 & SE14 —7J **79**
Newdales Clo. N9 —2B **18**
Newdene Av. N'holt —2B **54**
Newell St. E14 —6B **64**
New End. NW3 —3A **44**
New End Sq. NW3 —4B **44**
Newent Clo. SE15 —7E **78**
New Era Est. N1 —1E **62**
(off Phillipp St.)
New Farm Av. Brom —4J **127**
New Fetter La. EC4 —6A **62** (7H **141**)
Newfield Clo. Hamp —1E **102**
Newfield Rise. NW2 —3D **42**
New Forest La. Chig —6K **21**
Newgale Gdns. Edgw —1F **25**
Newgate. Croy —1C **134**
Newgate Clo. Felt —3C **102**
Newgate St. E4 —3B **20**
Newgate St. EC1 —6B **62** (7K **141**)
New Globe Wlk. SE1
—1C **78** (2L **147**)
New Goulston St. E1
—6F **63** (7E **142**)
Newham's Row. SE1
—2E **78** (5D **148**)
Newham Way. E16 & E6 —5H **65**
Newhaven Gdns. SE9 —4B **98**
Newhaven Rd. SE25 —5D **124**
New Heston Rd. Houn —7D **70**
Newhouse Av. Romf —3D **36**

Newhouse Clo. N Mald —7A **120**
Newhouse Wlk. Mord —7A **122**
Newick Clo. Bex —6H **101**
Newick Rd. E5 —4H **47**
Newing Grn. Brom —7B **114**
Newington Barrow Way. N7 —3K **45**
Newington Butts. SE11 & SE1
—4B **78** (9K **147**)
Newington Causeway. SE1
—3C **78** (7K **147**)
Newington Grn. N16 & N1 —5D **46**
Newington Grn. Mans. N16 —5D **46**
Newington Grn. Rd. N1 —6D **46**
Newington Ind. Est. SE17
(off Crampton St.) —4C **78** (9L **147**)
New Inn B'way. EC2
—4E **62** (3D **142**)
New Inn Pas. WC2 —6K **61** (8F **140**)
(off Houghton St.)
New Inn Sq. EC2 —4E **62** (3D **142**)
(off Bateman's Row)
New Inn St. EC2 —4E **62** (3D **142**)
New Inn Yd. EC2 —4E **62** (3D **142**)
New Jubilee Ct. Wfd G —7D **20**
New Kent Rd. SE1 —3C **78** (7L **147**)
New Kings Rd. SW6 —2H **91**
New King St. SE8 —6C **80**
Newland Dri. Enf —1C **8**
Newland Gdns. W13 —2A **72**
Newland Ho. N8 —3J **29**
(off Newland Rd.)
Newland Rd. N8 —3J **29**
Newlands Clo. Edgw —3K **11**
Newlands Clo. S'hall —5C **70**
Newlands Clo. Wemb —6C **40**
Newlands Ct. SE9 —6E **98**
Newlands Pk. SE26 —6J **111**
Newlands Pl. Barn —5A **4**
Newlands Quay. E1 —7J **63**
Newlands Rd. SW16 —2J **123**
Newlands Rd. Wfd G —2C **20**
Newlands, The. Wall —7H **133**
Newlands Way. Chess —5C **129**
Newland St. E16 —1C **82**
Newlands Wood. New Ad —7B **136**
Newling Clo. E6 —6D **66**
New London St. EC3
(off Hart St.) —7E **62** (9D **142**)
New Lydenburg Commercial Est. SE7
—3A **82**
New Lydenburg St. SE7 —3A **82**
Newlyn Gdns. Harr —7D **22**
Newlyn Ho. Pinn —1D **22**
Newlyn Rd. N17 —1F **31**
Newlyn Rd. Barn —4C **4**
Newlyn Rd. Well —2K **99**
Newman Pas. W1 —5G **61** (6M **139**)
Newman Pl. W1 —5G **61**
Newman Rd. E13 —3K **65**
Newman Rd. E17 —5K **31**
Newman Rd. Brom —1J **127**
Newman Rd. Croy —1K **133**
Newman Rd. Hay —7A **54**
Newman Rd. Ind. Est. Croy —7K **123**
Newman's Ct. EC3 —6D **62** (8B **142**)
(off Cornhill)
Newmans La. Surb —6D **118**
Newman's Row. WC2
—5K **61** (6F **140**)
Newman's Way. Barn —1F **5**
Newman Yd. W1 —6H **61** (7A **140**)
Newmarket Av. N'holt —5E **38**
Newmarket Grn. SE9 —7B **98**
New Mill Rd. Orp —7C **116**
Newminster Rd. Mord —6A **122**
New Mount St. E15 —7F **49**
Newnes Path. SW15 —4D **90**

Newnet Clo. Cars —1D **132**
Newnham Av. Ruis —1A **38**
Newnham Clo. N'holt —6G **39**
Newnham Clo. T Hth —2C **124**
Newnham Gdns. N'holt —6G **39**
Newnham M. N22 —7F **17**
Newnham Rd. N22 —1K **29**
Newnhams Clo. Brom —3D **128**
Newnham Ter. SE1 —3A **78** (6G **147**)
Newnham Way. Harr —5E **24**
New North Pl. EC2 —4E **62** (3C **142**)
New North Rd. N1 —7C **46**
New North Rd. Ilf —1G **35**
New North St. WC1 —5K **61** (5E **140**)
Newnton Clo. N4 —7D **30**
New Oak Rd. N2 —2A **28**
New Orleans Wlk. N19 —7H **29**
New Oxford St. WC1
—6H **61** (7B **140**)
New Pk. Av. N13 —3H **17**
New Pk. Clo. N'holt —6C **38**
New Park Ho. N13 —4E **16**
New Pk. Rd. SW2 —1H **109**
New Pl. New Ad —6C **136**
New Place Sq. SE16 —3H **79**
New Plaistow Rd. E15 —1G **65**
Newport Av. E13 —4A **65**
Newport Ct. WC2 —7H **61** (9B **140**)
Newport Lodge. Enf —5K **7**
(off Village Rd.)
Newport Pl. WC2 —7H **61** (9B **140**)
Newport Rd. E10 —2E **48**
Newport Rd. E17 —4A **32**
Newport Rd. SW13 —1C **90**
Newport St. SE11 —4K **77** (9E **146**)
Newquay Cres. Harr —2C **38**
Newquay Ho. SE11 —5A **78**
Newquay Rd. SE6 —2D **112**
New Quebec St. W1
—6D **62** (8F **138**)
New Ride. SW7 & SW1
—2B **76** (5B **144**)
New River Ct. N5 —4C **46**
New River Cres. N13 —4G **17**
New River Wlk. N1 —6C **46**
New Rd. E1 —5H **63**
New Rd. E4 —4J **19**
New Rd. N8 —5J **29**
New Rd. N9 —3B **18**
New Rd. N17 —1F **31**
New Rd. N22 —1C **30**
New Rd. NW7 —1G **13**
(Highwood Hill)
New Rd. NW7 —7B **14**
(Mill Hill)
New Rd. SE2 —4D **84**
New Rd. Bren —6D **72**
New Rd. Dag & Rain —2G **69**
New Rd. Hanw —5C **102**
New Rd. Harr —4K **39**
New Rd. Houn —4F **87**
New Rd. Ilf —2J **51**
New Rd. King T —7G **105**
New Rd. Mitc —1E **132**
New Rd. Orp —7K **129**
New Rd. Rich —4C **104**
New Rd. Well —2B **100**
New Rochford St. NW5 —5D **44**
New Row. WC2 —7J **61** (9C **140**)
Newry Rd. Twic —5A **88**
Newsam Av. N15 —5D **30**
New Southgate Ind. Est. N11 —5B **16**
Spitalfields Mkt. E10 —3D **48**
New Spring Gdns. Wlk. SE11 —5J **77**
New Sq. WC2 —6K **61** (7G **141**)
Newstead Ct. N'holt —3C **54**
Newstead Rd. SE12 —7H **97**
Newstead Wlk. Cars —7J **121**

241

Newstead Way. SW19 —4F **107**
New St. EC2 —5E **62** (6D **142**)
New St. EC4 —6A **62**
New St. Hill. EC4 —6A 62 (7H 141)
  (off Printer St.)
New St. Hill. Brom —5K **113**
New St. Sq. EC4 —6A **62** (7H **141**)
Newton Av. N10 —1E **28**
Newton Av. W3 —2J **73**
Newton Gro. W4 —4A **74**
Newton Ho. E17 —3D 32
  (off Prospect Hill)
Newton Ho. SE20 —1K **125**
Newton Point. E16 —6H 65
  (off Clarkson Rd.)
Newton Rd. E15 —5F **49**
Newton Rd. NW2 —4E **42**
Newton Rd. SW19 —7G **107**
Newton Rd. W2 —6K **59**
Newton Rd. Harr —2J **23**
Newton Rd. iswth —2K **87**
Newton Rd. Well —3A **100**
Newton Rd. Wemb —7F **41**
Newton St. WC2 —6J **61** (7D **140**)
Newton's Yd. SW18 —5J **91**
Newton Wlk. Edgw —1H **25**
Newton Way. N18 —5H **17**
Newtown St. SW11 —1F **93**
  (in two parts)
New Trinity Rd. N2 —3B **28**
New Turnstile. WC1
        —5K **61** (6E **140**)
New Union Clo. E14 —3E **80**
New Union St. EC2 —5D **62** (6A **142**)
New Wanstead. E11 —6H **33**
New Way Rd. NW9 —4A **26**
New Wharf Rd. N1 —2J **61**
New Zealand Way. W12 —7D **58**
Niagara Av. W5 —4C **72**
Niagra Clo. N1 —2C **62**
Nibthwaite Rd. Harr —5J **23**
Nicholas Clo. Gnfd —2F **55**
Nicholas Gdns. W5 —2D **72**
Nicholas La. EC4 —7D **62** (9B **142**)
Nicholas Pas. EC4 —7D 62 (9B 142)
  (off Nicholas La.)
Nicholas Rd. E1 —4J **63**
Nicholas Rd. Croy —4J **133**
Nicholas Rd. Dag —2F **53**
Nicholas St. SE8 —1B **96**
Nicholay Rd. N19 —1H **45**
Nichol Clo. N14 —1C **16**
Nicholes Rd. Houn —4E **86**
Nichol La. Brom —7J **113**
Nicholl Ho. N4 —1C **46**
Nichollsfield Wlk. N7 —5K **45**
Nicholls Point. E15 —1J 65
  (off Park Gro.)
Nicholl St. E2 —1G **63**
Nichols Clo. N4 —1A 46
  (off Osborne Rd.)
Nichols Grn. W5 —5D **56**
Nicholson Ct. E17 —4A **32**
Nicholson Dri. Bush —1B **10**
Nicholson Ho. SE17 —5D **78**
Nicholson Rd. Croy —1F **135**
Nicholson St. SE1 —1B **78** (3J **147**)
Nichol's Sq. E2 —2F **63**
Nickelby Clo. SE28 —6C **68**
Nicola Clo. Harr —2H **23**
Nicola Clo. S Croy —6C **134**
Nicol Clo. N10 —7A **16**
Nicoll Ct. NW10 —1A **58**
Nicoll Rd. NW10 —1A **58**
Nicolson. NW9 —1A **26**

Nicosia Rd. SW18 —7C **92**
Niederwald Rd. SE26 —4A **112**
Nigel Clo. N'holt —1C **54**
Nigel Ct. N3 —7E **14**
Nigel M. Ilf —4F **51**
Nigel Playfair Av. W6 —5D **74**
Nigel Rd. E7 —5A **50**
Nigel Rd. SE15 —3G **95**
Nigeria Rd. SE7 —7A **82**
Nighhawk. NW9 —1B **26**
Nightingale Av. E4 —5B **20**
Nightingale Clo. E4 —4A **20**
Nightingale Clo. W4 —6J **73**
Nightingale Clo. Cars —2E **132**
Nightingale Clo. Pinn —5A **22**
Nightingale Ct. SW6 —1K 91
  (off Maltings Pl.)
Nightingale Ct. Short —2G **127**
Nightingale Gro. SE13 —5F **97**
Nightingale Ho. E1 —1G 79
  (off Thomas More St.)
Nightingale Ho. N1 —1E 62
  (off Wilmer Gdns.)
Nightingale La. E11 —5J **33**
Nightingale La. N8 —4J **29**
Nightingale La. SW12 & SW4
        —7D **92**
Nightingale La. Brom —2A **128**
Nightingale La. Rich —7E **88**
Nightingale Pl. SE18 —6E **82**
Nightingale Pl. SW10 —6A **76**
Nightingale Rd. E5 —3H **47**
Nightingale Rd. N9 —6D **8**
Nightingale Rd. N22 —7D **16**
Nightingale Rd. NW10 —2B **58**
Nightingale Rd. W7 —1K **71**
Nightingale Rd. Cars —3D **132**
Nightingale Rd. Hamp —5E **102**
Nightingale Rd. Orp —6G **129**
Nightingale Sq. SW12 —7E **92**
Nightingale Vale. SE18 —6E **82**
Nightingale Wlk. SW4 —6F **93**
Nightingale Way. E6 —5C **66**
Nile Path. SE18 —6E **82**
Nile Rd. E13 —2A **66**
Nile St. N1 —3C **62** (1M **141**)
Nile Ter. SE15 —5F **79**
Nimegen Way. SE22 —5E **94**
Nimmo Dri. Bush —1C **10**
Nimrod. NW9 —1A **26**
Nimrod Clo. N'holt —3B **54**
Nimrod Pas. N1 —6E **46**
Nimrod Rd. SW16 —6F **109**
Nine Acres Clo. E12 —5C **50**
Nine Elms La. SW8 —7G **77**
Nineteenth Rd. Mitc —4J **123**
Nithdale Rd. SE18 —7F **83**
Niton Clo. Barn —6A **4**
Niton Rd. Rich —3G **89**
Niton St. SW6 —7F **75**
Nobel Ho. SE5 —2C **94**
Nobel Rd. N18 —4D **18**
Noble Corner. Houn —1E **86**
Noble Ct. Mitc —2B **122**
Noblefield Heights. N2 —5C **28**
Noble St. EC2 —6C **62** (7L **141**)
Noel. NW9 —1A **26**
Noel Ct. Houn —3D **86**
Noel Pk. Rd. N22 —2A **30**
Noel Rd. E6 —4C **66**
Noel Rd. N1 —2B **62**
Noel Rd. W3 —7G **57**
Noel Sq. Dag —4C **52**
Noel St. W1 —6G **61** (8M **139**)
Noel Ter. SE23 —2J **111**
Noel Ter. Sidc —4B **116**
Nolan Way. E5 —4G **47**
Nolton Pl. Edgw —1F **25**

Nonsuch Wlk. Sutt —7F **131**
Noorwood Gdns. Hay —4A **54**
Nora Gdns. NW4 —4F **27**
Norbiton Av. King T —1G **119**
Norbiton Comn. Rd. King T —3H **119**
Norbiton Rd. E14 —6B **64**
Norbreck Gdns. NW10 —3F **57**
Norbreck Pde. NW10 —3E **56**
Norbroke St. W12 —7B **58**
Norburn St. W10 —5G **59**
Norbury Av. SW16 & T Hth —1K **123**
Norbury Av. Houn —4H **87**
Norbury Clo. SW16 —1A **124**
Norbury Ct. Rd. SW16 —3J **123**
Norbury Cres. SW16 —1K **123**
Norbury Cross. SW16 —3J **123**
Norbury Gdns. Romf —5D **36**
Norbury Gro. NW7 —3F **13**
Norbury Hill. SW16 —7A **110**
Norbury Rise. SW16 —3J **123**
Norbury Rd. E4 —5H **19**
Norbury Rd. T Hth —2C **124**
Norbury Trading Est. SW16 —2K **123**
Norcombe Gdns. Harr —6C **24**
Norcombe Ho. N19 —3H 45
Norcott Clo. Hay —4A **54**
Norcott Rd. N16 —2G **47**
Norcroft Gdns. SE22 —7G **95**
Norcutt Rd. Twic —1J **103**
Norfield Rd. Dart —4J **117**
Norfolk Av. N13 —6G **17**
Norfolk Av. N15 —6F **31**
Norfolk Clo. N2 —3C **28**
Norfolk Clo. N13 —6G **17**
Norfolk Clo. Barn —4K **5**
Norfolk Clo. Twic —6B **88**
Norfolk Cres. W2 —6C **60** (7C **138**)
Norfolk Cres. Sidc —7J **99**
Norfolk Gdns. Bexh —1F **101**
Norfolk Gdns. Houn —5D **86**
Norfolk Ho. Beck —1J **125**
Norfolk Ho. Rd. SW16 —3H **109**
Norfolk Pl. W2 —6B **60** (7B **138**)
Norfolk Pl. Well —2A **100**
Norfolk Rd. E6 —1D **66**
Norfolk Rd. E17 —2K **31**
Norfolk Rd. NW8 —1B **60**
Norfolk Rd. NW10 —7A **42**
Norfolk Rd. SW19 —7C **108**
Norfolk Rd. Bark —7J **51**
Norfolk Rd. Barn —3D **4**
Norfolk Rd. Dag —5H **53**
Norfolk Rd. Enf —6C **8**
Norfolk Rd. Felt —1A **102**
Norfolk Rd. Harr —5F **23**
Norfolk Rd. Ilf —1J **51**
Norfolk Rd. Romf —6J **37**
Norfolk Rd. T Hth —3C **124**
Norfolk Row. SE1 —4K **77** (8F **146**)
Norfolk Row. SE11 —4K **77** (8F **146**)
  (in two parts)
Norfolk Sq. W2 —6B **60** (8B **138**)
Norfolk Sq. M. W2 —6B 60 (8B 138)
  (off London St.)
Norfolk St. E7 —5J **49**
Nonsfolk Ter. W6 —5G **75**
Norgrove St. SW12 —7E **92**
Norhyrst Av. SE25 —3F **125**
Norland Pl. W11 —1G **75**
Noriand Rd. W11 —1F **75**
Norley Vale. SW15 —1C **106**
Noriington Rd. E10 & E11 —1E **48**
Norman Av. N22 —1B **30**
Norman Av. Felt —2C **102**

Norman Av. S'hall —7C **54**
Norman Av. Twic —7C **88**
Normanby Rd. NW10 —4A **42**
Norman Clo. N22 —1C **30**
Norman Clo. Romf —1H **37**
Norman Ct. N4 —7A **30**
Norman Ct. NW10 —7C **42**
Norman Ct. Ilf —7H **35**
Norman Cres. Houn —7B **70**
Norman Cres. Pinn —1A **22**
Normand M. W14 —6G **75**
Normand Rd. W14 —6H **75**
Normandy Av. Barn —5C **4**
Normandy Clo. SW15 —5H **91**
Normandy Rd. SW9 —1A **94**
Normandy Ter. E16 —6K **65**
Normandy Way. Eri —1K **101**
Norman Gro. E3 —2A **64**
Norman Ho. Felt —2D **102**
Normanhurst Av. Bexh —1D **100**
Normanhurst Dri. Twic —5A **88**
Normanhurst Rd. SW2 —2K **109**
Norman Rd. E6 —4D **66**
Norman Rd. E11 —2F **49**
Norman Rd. N15 —5F **31**
Norman Rd. SE10 —7D **80**
Norman Rd. SW19 —7A **108**
Norman Rd. Belv —3H **85**
Norman Rd. Ilf —5F **51**
Norman Rd. Sutt —5J **131**
Norman Rd. T Hth —6B **124**
Norman's Bldgs. EC1
        —3C **62** (2L **141**)
Norman's Clo. NW10 —6K **41**
Normansfield Av. Tedd —7C **104**
Normanshire Av. E4 —4K **19**
Normanshire Dri. E4 —4H **19**
Norman's Mead. NW10 —6K **41**
Norman St. EC1 —3C **62** (2L **141**)
Normanton Av. SW19 —2J **107**
Normanton Pk. E4 —2B **20**
Normanton Rd. S Croy —6E **134**
Normanton St. SE23 —2K **111**
Norman Way. N14 —2D **16**
Norman Way. W3 —5H **57**
Normington Clo. SW16 —5A **110**
Norrice Lea. N2 —5B **28**
Norris. NW9 —1B 26
  (off Concourse, The)
Norris St. SW1 —7H **61** (1A **146**)
Norroy Rd. SW15 —4F **91**
Norry's Clo. Barn —4J **5**
Norry's Rd. Barn —4J **5**
Norseman Clo. Ilf —1B **52**
Norseman Way. Gnfd —1F **55**
Norstead Pl. SW15 —2C **106**
N. Access Rd. E17 —6K **31**
North Acre. NW9 —1A **26**
N. Acton Rd. NW10 —2K **57**
Northall Rd. Bexh —2J **101**
Northampton Gro. N1 —5D **46**
Northampton Pk. N1 —6C **46**
Northampton Rd. EC1
        —4A **62** (3H **141**)
Northampton Rd. Croy —2G **135**
Northampton Rd. Enf —4F **9**
Northampton Row. EC1
  (off Rosoman Pl.) —4A 62 (3H 141)
Northampton Sq. EC1
        —3B **62** (2J **141**)
Northampton St. N1 —7C **46**
Northanger Rd. SW16 —6J **109**
N. Audley St. W1 —6E **60** (8G **139**)
North Av. N18 —4B **18**
North Av. W13 —5B **56**
North Av. Cars —7E **132**
North Av. Harr —6F **23**
North Av. Rich —1G **89**

North Av. S'hall —7D **54**
N. Bank. NW8 —3C **60** (2C **138**)
Northbank Rd. E17 —2E **32**
N. Birkbeck Rd. E11 —3F **49**
Northborough Rd. SW16 —3H **123**
Northbourne. Brom —7J **127**
Northbourne Rd. SW4 —5H **93**
Northbrook Rd. N22 —7D **16**
Northbrook Rd. SE13 —5G **97**
Northbrook Rd. Barn —6B **4**
Northbrook Rd. Croy —5D **124**
Northbrook Rd. Ilf —2E **50**
Northburgh St. EC1 —4B **62** (4K **141**)
N. Carriage Dri. W2 —7C 60 (9C 138)
  (off Ring, The)
Northchurch. SE17 —5D **78**
  (in two parts)
Northchurch Rd. N1 —7D **46**
Northchurch Rd. Wemb —6G **41**
Northchurch Ter. N1 —7E **46**
  (in two parts)
N. Circular Rd. N3 —4H **27**
N. Circular Rd. N12 —1B **28**
N. Circular Rd. N13 —5F **17**
N. Circular Rd. NW2 —3A **42**
N. Circular Rd. NW4 —1D **42**
N. Circular Rd. NW10 —3F **57**
N. Circular Rd. NW11 —6F **27**
Northcliffe Clo. Wor Pk —3A **130**
Northcliffe Dri. N20 —1C **14**
North Clo. Bexh —4D **100**
North Clo. Dag —1G **69**
North Clo. Mord —4G **121**
N. Colonnade. E14 —1C **80**
N. Common Rd. W5 —7E **56**
Northcote. Pinn —2A **22**
Northcote Av. W5 —7E **56**
Northcote Av. iswth —5A **88**
Northcote Av. S'hall —7C **54**
Northcote Av. Surb —7H **119**
Northcote M. SW11 —4C **92**
Northcote Rd. E17 —4A **32**
Northcote Rd. NW10 —7A **42**
Northcote Rd. SW11 —5C **92**
Northcote Rd. Croy —6D **124**
Northcote Rd. N Mald —3J **119**
Northcote Rd. Sidc —4J **115**
Northcote Rd. Twic —5A **88**
Northcott Av. N22 —1J **29**
N. Countess Rd. E17 —2B **32**
North Ct. W1 —5G **61** (5M **139**)
N. Cray Rd. Sidc & Bex —6E **116**
North Cres. E3 —4F **65**
North Cres. N3 —2H **27**
North Cres. WC1 —5H **61** (5A **140**)
Northcroft Rd. W13 —2B **72**
Northcroft Rd. Eps —7A **130**
N. Crofts. SE23 —1H **111**
N. Cross Rd. SE22 —5F **95**
N. Cross Rd. Ilf —4G **35**
North Dene. NW7 —3E **12**
North Dene. Houn —1F **87**
Northdene Gdns. N15 —6F **31**
Northdown Gdns. Ilf —5J **35**
Northdown Rd. Well —2B **100**
Northdown St. N1 —2J **61**
North Dri. SW16 —4G **109**
North Dri. Houn —2G **87**
N. East Pier. E1 —1H **79**
Northeast Pl. N1 —2A 62
  (off Chapel Mkt.)
North End. NW3 —2A **44**
North End. Buck H —1F **21**
North End. Croy —2C **134**
North End Av. NW3 —2A **44**
North End Cres. W14 —4H **75**
North End Pde. W14 —4G 75
  (off North End Rd.)

242

N. End Rd. NW11 —1J 43
North End Rd. W14 & SW6 —4G 75
N. End Rd. Wemb —3G 41
N. End Way. NW3 —2A 44
Northern Av. N9 —2K 17
Northernhay Wlk. Mord —4G 121
Northern Rd. E13 —2K 65
N. Eyot Gdns. W6 —5B 74
Northey St. E14 —7A 64
N. Feltham Trading Est. Felt —5A 86
Northfield Av. W13 & W5 —1B 72
Northfield Av. Pinn —4B 22
Northfield Clo. Brom —1C 128
Northfield Cres. Sutt —4G 131
Northfields Gdns. Dag —4F 53
Northfield Ind. Est. NW10 —3G 57
Northfield Ind. Est. Wemb —1G 57
Northfield Path. Dag —2F 53
Northfield Rd. E6 —7D 50
Northfield Rd. N16 —7E 30
Northfield Rd. W13 —2B 72
Northfield Rd. Barn —3H 5
Northfield Rd. Dag —4F 53
Northfield Rd. Enf —5C 8
Northfield Rd. Houn —6B 70
Northfields. SW18 —4J 91
Northfields Prospect Bus. Cen. SW18
　　—4J 91
Northfields Rd. W3 —5H 57
N. Flockton St. SE16 —2G 79
N. Flower Wlk. W2 —7A 60
　　(off Lancaster Wlk.)
North Gdns. SW19 —7B 108
Northgate Bus.Pk. Enf —3C 8
Northgate Dri. NW9 —6A 26
N. Glade, The. Bex —1F 117
N. Gower St. NW1 —3G 61 (2M 139)
North Grn. NW9 —7F 13
North Gro. N6 —7E 28
North Gro. N15 —5D 30
N. Hill. N6 —6D 28
N. Hill Av. N6 —6E 28
North Ho. SE8 —5B 80
N. Hyde La. S'hall & Houn —5B 70
Northiam. N12 —4D 14
　　(in two parts)
North St. E8 —1H 63
Northington St. WC1
　　—4K 61 (4F 140)
N. Kent Gro. SE18 —4D 82
Northlands St. SE5 —2C 94
North La. Tedd —6K 103
Northleach Ct. SE15 —6E 78
　　(off Birdlip Clo.)
N. Lodge. New Bar —5F 5
N. Lodge Clo. SW15 —5F 91
North Mall. N9 —2C 18
North M. WC1 —4K 61 (4F 140)
North Mt. N20 —2F 15
　　(off High Rd.)
Northolm. Edgw —4E 12
Northolme Gdns. Edgw —1G 25
Northolme Rd. N5 —4C 46
Northolt. N17 —2E 30
　　(off Griffin Rd.)
Northolt Av. Ruis —5A 38
Northolt Gdns. Gnfd —5K 39
Northolt Rd. Harr —4F 39
Northover. Brom —3H 113
North Pde. S'hall —6E 54
　　(off North Rd.)
North Pk. SE9 —6D 98
North Pl. SW18 —5J 91
North Pl. Mitc —7D 108
North Pl. Tedd —6K 103
N. Pole La. Kes —6H 137
N. Pole Rd. W10 —5E 58
Northport St. N1 —1D 62

N. Quebec St. W1 —6D 60
N. Ride. W2 —7B 60 (1B 144)
North Rd. N2 —2C 28
North Rd. N6 —7E 28
North Rd. N7 —6J 45
North Rd. N9 —1C 18
North Rd. SE18 —4J 83
North Rd. SW19 —6A 108
North Rd. W5 —3D 72
North Rd. Belv —3H 85
North Rd. Bren —6E 72
North Rd. Brom —1K 127
North Rd. Chad —5E 36
North Rd. Edgw —1H 25
North Rd. Ilf —2J 51
North Rd. Rich —3G 89
North Rd. S'hall —7E 54
North Rd. Surb —6D 118
North Rd. W Wick —1D 136
North Row. W1 —7D 60 (9F 138)
North Several. SE3 —2F 97
Northside Rd. Brom —1J 127
North-South Route. N17 —2H 31
Northspur Rd. Sutt —3J 131
North Sq. N9 —2C 18
North Sq. NW11 —5J 27
Northstead Rd. SW2 —2A 110
North St. E13 —2K 65
North St. NW4 —5E 26
North St. SW4 —3G 93
North St. Bark —6F 51
North St. Bexh —4G 101
North St. Brom —1J 127
North St. Cars —3D 132
North St. Iswth —3A 88
North St. Romf —3K 37
North St. Pas. E13 —2K 65
N. Tenter St. E1 —6F 63
North Ter. SW3 —3C 76 (7C 144)
Northumberland All. EC3
　　—6E 62 (8D 142)
Northumberland Av. E12 —1A 50
Northumberland Av. WC2
　　—1J 77 (2C 146)
Northumberland Av. Enf —1C 8
Northumberland Av. Iswth —1K 87
Northumberland Av. Well —3J 99
Northumberland Clo. Eri —7J 85
Northumberland Gdns. N9 —3A 18
Northumberland Gdns. Brom
　　—4E 128
Northumberland Gdns. Iswth —7A 72
Northumberland Gdns. Mitc
　　—5H 123
Northumberland Gro. N17 —7C 18
Northumberland Pk. N17 —7A 18
Northumberland Pk. Eri —7J 85
Northumberland Pl. W2 —6J 59
Northumberland Pl. Rich —6D 88
Northumberland Rd. E6 —6C 66
Northumberland Rd. E17 —7C 32
Northumberland Rd. Barn —6F 5
Northumberland Rd. Harr —5D 22
Northumberland Row. Twic —1J 103
Northumberland St. WC2
　　—1J 77 (2C 146)
Northumberland Way. Eri —1J 101
Northumbria St. E14 —6C 64
N. Verbena Gdns. W6 —5C 74
Northview. N7 —3J 45
N. View. SW19 —5E 106
N. View. W5 —4C 56
N. View. Ilf —1A 36
N. View. Pinn —7A 22
N. View Cres. NW10 —4B 42
Northview Dri. Wfd G —2B 34
N. View Rd. N8 —4H 29
North Vs. NW1 —6H 45

North Wlk. W2 —7K 59
　　(off Bayswater Rd.)
North Wlk. New Ad —6D 136
　　(in two parts)
North Way. N9 —2E 18
North Way. N11 —6B 16
North Way. NW9 —3H 25
Northway. NW11 —5K 27
Northway. Mord —4G 121
North Way. Pinn —4B 22
Northway. Wall —4G 133
Northway Cir. NW7 —4E 12
Northway Cres. NW7 —4E 12
Northway Gdns. NW11 —5K 27
Northway Rd. SE5 —3C 94
Northway Rd. Croy —6F 125
Northways Pde. NW3 —7B 44
　　(off College Cres.)
N. West Pier. E1 —1H 79
Northwest Pl. N1 —2A 62
N. Wharf Rd. W2 —5B 60 (6A 138)
Northwick Av. Harr —6A 24
Northwick Circ. Harr —6C 24
Northwick Clo. NW8
　　—4B 60 (3A 138)
Northwick Pk. Rd. Harr —6K 23
Northwick Rd. Wemb —1D 56
Northwick Ter. NW8
　　—4B 60 (3A 138)
Northwick Wlk. Harr —7K 23
Northwold Dri. Pinn —2A 22
Northwold Est. E5 —2G 47
Northwold Rd. N16 & E5 —2F 47
N. Wood Ct. SE25 —3G 125
Northwood Gdns. N12 —5G 15
Northwood Gdns. Gnfd —5K 39
Northwood Gdns. Ilf —4E 34
Northwood Ho. SE27 —4D 110
Northwood Pl. Eri —3F 85
Northwood Rd. N6 —7F 29
Northwood Rd. SE23 —1B 112
Northwood Rd. Cars —6E 132
Northwood Rd. T Hth —4B 124
Northwood Way. SE19 —6D 110
N. Woolwich Rd. E16 —1J 81
N. Worple Way. SW14 —3K 89
Norton Clo. E4 —5H 19
Norton Clo. Enf —2C 8
Norton Folgate. E1 —5E 62 (5D 142)
Norton Gdns. SW16 —2J 123
Norton Ho. SW9 —2K 93
　　(off Aytoun Rd.)
Norton Rd. E10 —1B 48
Norton Rd. Dag —6K 53
Norton Rd. Wemb —6D 40
Norval Rd. Wemb —2B 40
Norway Ga. SE16 —3A 80
Norway Pl. E14 —6B 64
Norway St. SE10 —6D 80
Norwich M. Ilf —1A 52
Norwich Pl. Bexh —4G 101
Norwich Rd. E7 —5J 49
Norwich Rd. Gnfd —1F 55
Norwich Rd. T Hth —3C 124
Norwich Rd. S'hall —7C 54
Norwich St. EC4 —6A 62 (7G 141)
Norwich Wlk. Edgw —7D 12
Norwood Av. Romf —7K 37
Norwood Av. Wemb —1F 57
Norwood Clo. S'hall —4D 70
Norwood Dri. Harr —6D 22
Norwood Gdns. Hay —4A 54
Norwood Gdns. S'hall —4D 70
Norwood Grn. Rd. S'hall —4E 70
Norwood High St. SE27 —3B 110
Norwood Pk. Rd. SE27 —5C 110
Norwood Rd. SE24 —1B 110

Norwood Rd. SE27 —2B 110
Norwood Rd. S'hall —3C 70
Norwood Ter. S'hall —4F 71
Noss Co. Sutt —5C 132
Notley St. SE5 —7D 78
Notson Rd. SE25 —4H 125
Notting Barn Rd. W10 —4F 59
Nottingdale Sq. W11 —1G 75
Nottingham Av. E16 —5A 66
Nottingham Ct. WC2
　　—6J 61 (8C 140)
Nottingham Pl. W1 —5E 60 (4G 139)
Nottingham Rd. E10 —6E 32
Nottingham Rd. SW17 —1D 108
Nottingham Rd. Iswth —2K 87
Nottingham Rd. S Croy —4C 134
Nottingham St. W1 —5E 60 (5G 139)
Nottingham Ter. NW1
　　—4E 60 (4G 139)
　　(off York Ter. W.)
Notting Hill Ga. W11 —1J 75
Nova M. Sutt —1G 131
Novar Clo. Orp —7K 129
Nova Rd. Croy —7B 124
Novar Rd. SE9 —1G 115
Novello St. SW6 —1J 91
Nowell Rd. SW13 —6C 74
Nower Ct. Pinn —4D 22
Nower Hill. Pinn —4D 22
Noyna Rd. SW17 —3D 108
Nuding Clo. SE13 —3C 96
Nuffield Lodge. N6 —6G 29
Nugent Rd. N19 —1J 45
Nugent Rd. SE25 —3F 125
Nugents Ct. Pinn —1C 22
Nugents Pk. Pinn —1C 22
Nugent Ter. NW8 —2A 60
Numa Ct. Bren —7D 72
Nun Ct. EC2 —6D 62 (7A 142)
　　(off Coleman St.)
Nuneaton Rd. Dag —7E 52
Nunhead Cres. SE15 —3H 95
Nunhead Est. SE15 —4H 95
Nunhead Grn. SE15 —3H 95
Nunhead Gro. SE15 —3J 95
Nunhead La. SE15 —3H 95
Nunhead Pas. SE15 —4H 95
Nunnington Clo. SE9 —3C 114
Nunns Rd. Enf —2H 7
Nupton Dri. Barn —6A 4
Nursery App. N12 —6H 15
Nursery Av. N3 —2A 28
Nursery Av. Bexh —2F 101
Nursery Av. Croy —2K 135
Nursery Clo. SW15 —4F 91
Nursery Clo. Croy —2K 135
Nursery Clo. Enf —1E 8
Nursery Clo. Orp —7K 129
Nursery Clo. Romf —6D 36
Nursery Clo. Wfd G —5E 20
Nursery Ct. N17 —7A 18
Nursery Gdns. Chst —6F 115
Nursery Gdns. Enf —1E 8
Nursery La. E7 —6J 49
Nursery La. W10 —5E 58
Nursery Rd. E9 —6J 47
Nursery Rd. N2 —1B 28
Nursery Rd. N14 —7B 6
Nursery Rd. SW9 —4K 93
Nursery Rd. SW19 —2K 121
　　(Merton)
Nursery Rd. SW19 —7G 107
　　(Wimbledon)
Nursery Rd. Pinn —3A 22
Nursery Rd. Sutt —4A 132
Nursery Rd. T Hth —4D 124
Nursery Row. Barn —3B 4
Nursery St. N17 —7A 18

Nursery Wlk. NW4 —3D 26
Nursery Wlk. Romf —7K 37
Nurstead Rd. Eri —7G 85
Nutbourne St. W10 —3G 59
Nutbrook St. SE15 —3G 95
Nutbrowne Rd. Dag —1F 69
Nutcroft Rd. SE15 —7H 79
Nutfield Clo. N18 —6A 18
Nutfield Clo. Cars —3C 132
Nutfield Gdns. Ilf —2K 51
Nutfield Gdns. N'holt —2A 54
Nutfield Rd. E15 —4E 48
Nutfield Rd. NW2 —3C 42
Nutfield Rd. SE22 —4F 95
Nutfield Rd. T Hth —4B 124
Nutford Pl. W1 —6D 60 (7D 138)
Nuthatch Gdns. SE28 —2H 83
Nuthurst Av. SW2 —2K 109
Nutley Ter. NW3 —6A 44
Nutmead Clo. Bex —1J 117
Nutmeg Clo. E16 —4G 65
Nutmeg La. E14 —6F 65
Nuttall St. N1 —2E 62
Nutter La. E11 —6A 34
Nutt Gro. Edgw —2J 11
Nutt St. SE15 —7F 79
Nutwell St. SW17 —5C 108
Nuxley Rd. Belv —6F 85
Nyanza St. SE18 —6H 83
Nye Bevan Est. E5 —3K 47
Nylands Av. Rich —1G 89
Nymans Gdns. SW20 —3D 120
Nynehead St. SE14 —7A 80
Nyon Gro. SE6 —2B 112
Nyssa Clo. Wfd G —6J 21
Nyssa Ct. E15 —3G 65
　　(off Teasel Way)
Nyton Clo. N19 —1J 45

Oak Apple Ct. SE12 —1J 113
Oak Av. N8 —4J 29
Oak Av. N10 —7A 16
Oak Av. N17 —7J 17
Oak Av. Croy —2C 135
Oak Av. Enf —1E 6
Oak Av. Hamp —5C 102
Oak Av. Houn —7B 70
Oak Bank. New Ad —6E 136
Oakbank Gro. SE24 —4C 94
Oakbrook Clo. Brom —4K 113
Oakbury Rd. SW6 —2K 91
Oak Clo. N14 —7A 6
Oak Clo. Sutt —2A 132
Oakcombe Clo. N Mald —1A 120
Oak Cottage Clo. SE6 —1H 113
Oak Cotts. W7 —2J 71
Oak Ct. SE1 —7F 79
　　(off Sumner Rd.)
Oak Cres. E16 —5G 65
Oakcroft Clo. Pinn —2A 22
Oakcroft Rd. SE13 —2F 97
Oakdale. N14 —1A 16
Oakdale Av. Harr —5K 24
Oakdale Ct. E4 —5K 19
Oakdale Rd. E7 —7K 49
Oakdale Rd. E11 —2F 49
Oakdale Rd. E18 —2K 33
Oakdale Rd. N4 —6C 30
Oakdale Rd. SE15 & SE4 —3J 95
Oakdale Rd. SW16 —5J 109
Oakdale Rd. Eps —7A 130
Oakdale Way. Mitc —7E 122
Oak Dene. SE15 —1H 95
Oakdene. W13 —5B 56
Oakdene Av. Chst —5E 114
Oakdene Av. Eri —6J 85
Oakdene Av. Th Dit —7A 118

Oakdene Clo. Pinn —1D 22
Oakdene Dri. Surb —7J 119
Oakdene M. Sutt —1H 131
Oakdene Pk. N3 —7C 14
Oakdene Rd. Orp —5K 129
Oakden St. SE11 —4A 78 (8H 147)
Oake Ct. SW15 —5G 91
Oakefield Rd. N14 —2D 16
Oakend Ho. N4 —7D 30
Oakenholt Ho. SE2 —1D 84
Oakenshaw Clo. Surb —7E 118
Oakes Clo. E6 —6D 66
Oakeshott Av. N6 —2E 44
Oakey La. SE1 —3A 78 (6G 147)
Oakfield. E4 —5J 19
Oakfield Av. Harr —3B 24
Oakfield Clo. N Mald —5B 120
Oakfield Ct. N8 —7J 29
Oakfield Ct. NW2 —7F 27
Oakfield Gdns. N18 —4K 17
Oakfield Gdns. SE19 —5E 110
(in two parts)
Oakfield Gdns. Beck —5D 126
Oakfield Gdns. Cars —1C 132
Oakfield Gdns. Gnfd —4H 55
Oakfield Lodge. Ilf —3F 51
(off Albert Rd.)
Oakfield Rd. E6 —1C 66
Oakfield Rd. E17 —2A 32
Oakfield Rd. N3 —1K 27
Oakfield Rd. N4 —6A 30
Oakfield Rd. SE20 —7H 111
Oakfield Rd. SW19 —3F 107
Oakfield Rd. Croy —1C 134
Oakfield Rd. Ilf —3F 51
Oakfield Rd. Th Dit —5A 118
Oakfields Rd. NW11 —6G 27
Oakfield St. SW10 —6A 76
Oakford Rd. NW5 —4G 45
Oak Gdns. Croy —2C 136
Oak Gro. NW2 —4F 43
Oak Gro. Ruis —7A 22
Oak Gro. W Wick —1E 136
Oak Gro. Rd. SE20 —1J 125
Oakhall Ct. E11 —6K 33
Oak Hall Rd. E11 —6K 33
Oakham Clo. SE6 —2B 112
Oakham Dri. Brom —4H 127
Oakhampton Rd. NW7 —7A 14
Oakhill. Surb —7E 118
Oak Hill. Wfd G —7A 20
Oakhill Av. NW3 —4K 43
Oakhill Av. Pinn —2C 22
Oak Hill Clo. Wfd G —7A 20
Oakhill Ct. SW19 —7F 107
Oakhill Ct. Wfd G —7B 20
Oakhill Cres. Surb —7E 118
Oakhill Dri. Surb —7E 118
Oak Hill Gdns. Wfd G —1G 33
Oakhill Gro. Surb —6E 118
Oak Hill Pk. NW3 —4K 43
Oak Hill Pk. M. NW3 —4A 44
Oakhill Path. Surb —6E 118
Oakhill Pl. SW15 —5J 91
Oakhill Rd. SW15 —5H 91
Oakhill Rd. SW16 —1K 123
Oakhill Rd. Beck —2E 125
Oakhill Rd. Surb —6E 118
Oakhill Rd. Sutt —3K 131
Oak Hill Way. NW3 —4A 44
Oak Ho. N2 —2B 28
Oakhouse Rd. Bexh —5G 101
Oakhurst Av. Barn —7H 5
Oakhurst Av. Bexh —7E 84
Oakhurst Clo. E17 —4G 33

Oakhurst Clo. Ilf —1G 35
Oakhurst Clo. Tedd —5J 103
Oakhurst Gdns. E4 —1C 20
Oakhurst Gdns. E17 —4G 33
Oakhurst Gdns. Bexh —7E 84
Oakhurst Gro. SE22 —4G 95
Oakington Av. Harr —7E 22
Oakington Av. Wemb —3F 41
Oakington Mnr. Dri. Wemb —5G 41
Oakington Rd. W9 —4J 59
Oakington Way. N8 —7J 29
Oaklands. N21 —2E 16
Oaklands. Beck —1D 126
Oaklands Av. N9 —6C 8
Oaklands Av. Iswth —6K 71
Oaklands Av. Sidc —7K 99
Oaklands Av. T Hth —4A 124
Oaklands Av. W Wick —3D 136
Oaklands Clo. Bexh —5F 101
Oaklands Clo. Orp —6J 129
Oaklands Clo. Wemb —5D 40
Oaklands Ct. NW10 —7K 41
(off Nicoll Rd.)
Oaklands Ct. Wemb —5D 40
Oaklands Dri. Twic —7G 87
Oaklands Est. SW4 —6G 93
Oaklands Gro. W12 —1C 74
Oaklands Pk. Av. Ilf —2G 51
Oaklands Pl. SW4 —4H 93
Oaklands Rd. N20 —7C 4
Oaklands Rd. NW2 —4F 43
Oaklands Rd. SW14 —3K 89
Oaklands Rd. W7 —2K 71
Oaklands Rd. Bexh —4F 101
Oaklands Rd. Brom —7G 113
Oaklands Way. Wall —7H 133
Oakland Way. Eps —6A 130
Oak La. E14 —7B 64
Oak La. N2 —2B 28
Oak La. N11 —6C 16
Oak La. Iswth —4J 87
Oak La. Twic —7A 88
Oak La. Wfd G —4C 20
Oakleafe Gdns. Ilf —3F 35
Oaklea Pas. King T —3D 118
Oakleigh Av. Edgw —2H 25
Oakleigh Av. Edgw —2H 25
Oakleigh Clo. N20 —3J 15
Oakleigh Ct. Edgw —2J 25
Oakleigh Cres. N20 —3H 15
Oakleigh Gdns. N20 —1F 15
Oakleigh Gdns. Edgw —6A 12
Oakleigh M. N20 —1F 15
Oakleigh Pk. Av. Chst —1E 128
Oakleigh Pk. N. N20 —1G 15
Oakleigh Pk. S. N20 —2H 15
Oakleigh Rd. N. N20 —2G 15
Oakleigh Rd. S. N11 —3K 15
Oakleigh Way. Mitc —1F 123
Oakley Av. W5 —7G 57
Oakley Av. Bark —7K 51
Oakley Av. Croy —4K 133
Oakley Clo. E4 —3K 19
Oakley Clo. E6 —6C 66
Oakley Clo. W7 —7J 55
Oakley Clo. Iswth —1H 87
Oakley Cres. EC1 —2B 62
Oakley Dri. SE9 —1H 115
Oakley Gdns. N8 —5K 29
Oakley Gdns. SW3 —6C 76
Oakley Grange. Harr —3G 39
Oakley Pk. Bex —7C 100
Oakley Pl. SE1 —5F 79
Oakley Rd. N1 —7D 46
Oakley Rd. SE25 —5H 125
Oakley Rd. Brom —7C 128
Oakley Rd. Harr —6J 23

Oakley Sq. NW1 —2G 61
Oakley St. SW3 —6C 76
Oakley Wlk. W6 —6F 75
Oak Lodge. E11 —6J 33
Oak Lodge. W8 —3K 75
(off Chantry Sq.)
Oak Lodge Clo. Stan —5H 11
Oak Lodge Dri. W Wick —7D 126
Oaklodge Way. NW7 —6G 13
Oakmead Av. Brom —6J 127
Oakmead Ct. Stan —4H 11
Oakmead Gdns. Edgw —4E 12
Oakmead Pl. Mitc —1C 122
Oakmead Rd. SW12 —1E 108
Oakmead Rd. Croy —6H 123
Oak Meade. Pinn —6A 10
Oakmere Rd. SE2 —6A 84
Oakmont Pl. Orp —7H 129
Oak Pk. Gdns. SW19 —1F 107
Oak Pl. SW18 —5K 91
Oakridge Dri. N2 —3B 28
Oakridge La. Brom —5F 113
Oakridge Rd. Brom —4F 113
Oak Rise. Buck H —3G 21
Oak Rd. W5 —7D 56
Oak Rd. N Mald —2K 119
Oak Rd. N Hth —7J 85
Oak Row. SW16 —2G 123
Oaks Av. SE19 —5E 110
Oaks Av. Felt —2C 102
Oaks Av. Romf —2J 37
Oaks Av. Wor Pk —3D 130
Oaksford Av. SE26 —3H 111
Oaks Gro. E4 —2B 20
Oakshade Rd. Brom —4F 113
Oakshaw Rd. SW18 —7K 91
Oaks La. Croy —3J 135
Oaks La. Ilf —5J 35
Oaks Rd. Croy —5H 135
Oak Rd. N Hth —7J 85
Oaks, The. E4 —7B 20
Oaks, The. N12 —4E 14
Oaks, The. NW10 —7D 42
Oaks, The. SE18 —5G 83
Oaks, The. Enf —3G 7
(off Bycullah Rd.)
Oak St. Romf —5J 37
Oaks Way. Cars —7D 132
Oakthorpe Ct. N18 —5H 17
Oakthorpe Rd. N13 —5F 17
Oaktree Av. N13 —3G 17
Oak Tree Clo. W5 —6C 56
Oak Tree Clo. Stan —7H 11
Oak Tree Ct. W3 —7H 57
Oak Tree Ct. N'holt —2B 54
Oak Tree Dell. NW9 —5K 25
Oak Tree Dri. N20 —1E 14
Oak Tree Gdns. Brom —5K 113
Oak Tree Rd. NW8 —3C 60 (2B 138)
Oakview Gdns. N2 —4B 28
Oakview Gro. Croy —1A 136
Oakview Lodge. NW11 —7H 27
(off Beechcroft Av.)
Oakview Rd. SE6 —5D 112
Oak Village. NW5 —4E 44
Oak Way. N14 —7A 6
Oak Way. SW20 —4C 120
Oak Way. W3 —1A 74
Oakway. Brom —2F 127
Oak Way. Croy —6K 125
Oakway Clo. Bex —6E 100
Oakways. SE9 —6F 99
Oakwood. Wall —7F 133
Oakwood Av. N14 —7C 6
Oakwood Av. Beck —2C 126
Oakwood Av. Brom —3K 127
Oakwood Av. Mitc —2B 122

Oakwood Av. S'hall —7E 54
Oakwood Bus. Pk. NW10 —4K 57
Oakwood Clo. N14 —6B 6
Oakwood Clo. Chst —6D 114
Oakwood Clo. Wfd G —6H 21
Oakwood Ct. E6 —1C 66
Oakwood Ct. W14 —3H 75
Oakwood Ct. Harr —6H 23
Oakwood Cres. N21 —6D 6
Oakwood Cres. Gnfd —6A 40
Oakwood Dri. SE19 —6D 110
Oakwood Dri. Bexh —4K 101
Oakwood Dri. Edgw —6D 12
Oakwood Dri. S'hall —7E 54
Oakwood Gdns. Ilf —2K 51
Oakwood Gdns. Orp —7J 129
Oakwood Gdns. Sutt —2J 131
Oakwood La. W14 —3H 75
Oakwood Lodge. N14 —6B 6
(off Avenue Rd.)
Oakwood Pk. Rd. N14 —7C 6
Oakwood Pl. Croy —6A 124
Oakwood Rd. NW11 —4J 27
Oakwood Rd. SW20 —1C 120
Oakwood Rd. Croy —6A 124
Oakwood View. N14 —6C 6
Oakworth Rd. W10 —5E 58
Oasis, The. Brom —2A 128
Oates Clo. Brom —3F 127
Oatfield Ho. N15 —6E 30
(off Perry Ct.)
Oatfield Rd. Orp —7K 129
Oatland Rise. E17 —2A 32
Oatlands Rd. Enf —1D 8
Oat La. EC2 —6C 62 (7M 141)
Oban Clo. E13 —4A 66
Oban Ho. Bark —2H 67
Oban Rd. E13 —3A 66
Oban Rd. SE25 —4D 124
Oban St. E14 —6F 65
Oberon Ho. N1 —2E 62
(off Arden Est.)
Oberstein Rd. SW11 —4B 92
Oborne Clo. SE24 —5B 94
Observatory Gdns. W8 —2J 75
Observatory Rd. SW14 —4J 89
Occupation La. SE18 —1F 99
Occupation La. W5 —4D 72
Occupation Rd. SE17 —5C 78
Occupation Rd. W13 —2B 72
Occupation Rd. Eps —7A 130
Ocean Est. E1 —4K 63
(in two parts)
Ocean St. E1 —5K 63
Ockendon Rd. N1 —6D 46
Ockham Dri. Orp —7A 116
Ockley Ct. Sidc —3J 115
Ockley Ct. Sutt —4A 132
Ockley Rd. SW16 —4J 109
Ockley Rd. Croy —7K 123
Octagon Arc. EC2 —5E 62 (6C 142)
Octavia Clo. Mitc —5C 122
Octavia Rd. Iswth —3J 87
Octavia St. SW11 —1C 92
Octavia Way. SE28 —7B 68
Octavius St. SE8 —7C 80
Oddmark Rd. Bark —2H 67
Odeon Ct. E16 —5J 65
Odeon Ct. NW10 —1A 58
Odessa Rd. E7 —3H 49
Odessa Rd. NW10 —2C 58
Odessa St. SE16 —3B 80
Odger St. SW11 —2D 92
Odhams Wlk. WC2 —6J 61 (8D 140)
Odin Ho. SE5 —2C 94
O'Donnell Ct. WC1 —4J 61 (3D 140)
O'Driscoll Ho. W12 —6D 58
Odyssey Bus. Pk. Ruis —5A 38
Offa's Mead. E9 —4B 48

Offenham Rd. SE9 —4D 114
Offenham Rd. SE12 —4D 114
Offerton Rd. SW4 —3G 93
Offham Slope. N12 —5C 14
Offley Rd. SW9 —7A 78
Offord Clo. N17 —6B 18
Offord Rd. N1 —7K 45
Offord St. N1 —7K 45
Ogden Ho. Felt —3C 102
Ogilby St. SE18 —4D 82
Oglander Rd. SE15 —4F 95
Ogle St. W1 —5G 61 (5L 139)
Oglethorpe Rd. Dag —3G 53
O'Grady Ho. E17 —3D 32
Ohio Cotts. Pinn —2A 22
Ohio Rd. E13 —4H 65
Okeburn Rd. SW17 —5E 108
Okehampton Clo. N12 —5G 15
Okehampton Cres. Well —1B 100
Okehampton Rd. NW10 —1E 58
Olaf St. W11 —7F 59
Oldacre M. SW12 —7F 93
Old Bailey. EC4 —6B 62 (8K 141)
Old Barge Ho. All. SE1 —7A 62 (1H 147)
(off Barge Ho. St.)
Old Barn Clo. Sutt —7G 131
Old Barn Way. Bexh —4K 101
Old Barrack Yd. SW1 —2E 76 (5G 145)
Old Barrowfield. E15 —1G 65
Oldberry Rd. Edgw —6E 12
Old Bethnal Grn. Rd. E2 —3G 63
Old Bexley La. Bex & Dart —2K 117
(in two parts)
Old Billingsgate Wlk. EC3 —7E 62 (1C 146)
Old Bond St. W1 —7G 61 (1L 145)
Oldborough Rd. Wemb —3C 40
Old Brewer's Yd. WC2 —6J 61 (8C 140)
Old Brewery M. NW3 —4B 44
Old Bri. Clo. N'holt —2E 54
Old Bri. St. Hamp W —2D 118
Old Broad St. EC2 —6D 62 (8B 142)
Old Bromley Rd. Brom —5F 113
Old Brompton Rd. SW5 & SW7 —5J 75
Old Bldgs. WC2 —6A 62 (7G 141)
(off Chancery La.)
Old Burlington St. W1 —7G 61 (9L 139)
Old Burton St. W1 —7G 61
Oldbury Pl. W1 —5E 60 (5H 139)
Oldbury Rd. Enf —2B 8
Old Castle St. E1 —6F 63 (7E 142)
Old Cavendish St. W1 —6F 61 (8K 139)
Old Change St. EC4 —6C 62 (8L 141)
(off Carter La.)
Old Chapel Pl. SW9 —2A 94
Old Chelsea M. SW3 —6C 76
Old Church Ct. N11 —5A 16
Old Church La. NW9 —2J 41
Old Church La. Stan —3A 56
Old Church La. Stan —5G 11
Old Church Rise. Romf —7K 37
Old Church Rd. E1 —6K 63
Old Church Rd. E4 —4H 19
Old Church Rd. Romf —7K 37
Old Church St. SW3 —5B 76
Old Compton St. W1 —7H 61 (9A 140)
Old Cote Dri. Houn —6E 70
Old Ct. Pl. W8 —2K 75
Old Deer Pk. Gdns. Rich —3E 88

Old Devonshire Rd. SW12 —7F 93
Old Dock Clo. Rich —6G 73
Old Dover Rd. SE3 —7J 81
Oldegate Ho. E6 —1B 66
Old Farm Av. N14 —7B 6
Old Farm Av. Sidc —1H 115
Old Farm Clo. Houn —4D 86
Old Farm Rd. N2 —1B 28
Old Farm Rd. Hamp —6D 102
Old Farm Rd. E. Sidc —2A 116
Old Farm Rd. W. Sidc —2K 115
Oldfield Clo. Brom —4D 128
Oldfield Clo. Stan —5F 11
Oldfield Farm Gdns. Gnfd —1H 55
Oldfield Gro. SE16 —4K 79
Oldfield Ho. W4 —5A 74
(off Devonshire Rd.)
Oldfield La. N. Gnfd —2H 55
Oldfield La. S. Gnfd —4G 55
Oldfield M. N6 —7G 29
Oldfield Rd. N16 —3E 46
Oldfield Rd. NW10 —7A 42
Oldfield Rd. SW19 —6G 107
Oldfield Rd. W3 —2B 74
Oldfield Rd. Bexh —2E 100
Oldfield Rd. Brom —4D 128
Oldfield Rd. Hamp —7D 102
Oldfields Cir. N'holt —6G 39
Oldfields Rd. Sutt —3H 131
Oldfields Trading Est. Sutt —3J 131
Old Fish St. Hill. EC4
(off Victoria St.) —7C 62 (9L 141)
Old Fleet La. EC4 —6B 62 (7J 141)
Old Fold Clo. Barn —1C 4
Old Fold La. Barn —1C 4
Old Fold View. Barn —3A 4
Old Ford Rd. E2 & E3 —3J 63
Old Forge Clo. Stan —4F 11
Old Forge M. W12 —2D 74
Old Forge Rd. Enf —1A 8
Old Forge Way. Sidc —4B 116
Old Gloucester St. WC1
—5J 61 (5D 140)
Old Hall Clo. Pinn —1C 22
Old Hall Dri. Pinn —1C 22
Oldham Ter. W3 —1J 73
Old Hill. Chst —1E 128
Oldhill St. N16 —1G 47
Old Homesdale Rd. Brom —4A 128
Old Hospital Clo. SW17 —1D 108
Old Ho. Clo. SW19 —5G 107
Old Ho. Gdns. Twic —6C 88
Old Jamaica Rd. SE16 —3G 79
Old James St. SE15 —3H 95
Old Jewry. EC2 —6D 62 (8A 142)
Old Kenton La. NW9 —5H 25
Old Kent Rd. SE1 & SE15
—4E 78 (8C 148)
Old Laundry, The. Chst —1G 129
Old Lodge Pl. Twic —6B 88
Old Lodge Way. Stan —5F 11
Old London Rd. Sidc —7F 117
Old Maidstone Rd. Sidc —7F 117
Old Malden La. Wor Pk —2A 130
Old Manor Dri. Iswth —6G 87
Old Manor Way. Bexh —2K 101
Old Manor Way. Chst —5D 114
Old Manor Yd. SW5 —4K 75
Old Market Sq. E2 —3F 63 (1E 142)
Old Marylebone Rd. NW1
—5C 60 (6D 138)
Oldmead Ho. Dag —6H 53
Old M. Harr —5J 23
Old Mill Clo. E18 —3A 34
Old Mill Rd. SE18 —6H 83
Old Montague St. E1 —5G 63
Old Nichol St. E2 —4F 63 (3E 142)

Old North St. WC1 —5K 61 (5E 140)
(off Theobald's Rd.)
Old Oak Common La. NW10 & W3
—5A 58
Old Oak Comn. La. W3 & NW10
—7B 58
Old Oak La. NW10 —3A 58
Old Oak Rd. W3 —7B 58
Old Orchard, The. NW3 —4C 44
Old Palace La. Rich —5C 88
Old Palace Rd. Croy —3B 134
Old Palace Ter. Rich —5D 88
Old Palace Yd. SW1
—3J 77 (6C 146)
Old Palace Yd. Rich —5C 88
Old Paradise St. SE11
—4K 77 (8E 146)
Old. Pk. Av. SW12 —6E 92
Old. Pk. Av. Enf —4H 7
Old Pk. Gro. Enf —4H 7
Old Park Ho. N13 —4E 16
(off Old Park Rd.)
Old Park La. W1 —1F 77 (3H 145)
Old. Pk. M. Houn —7D 70
Old Pk. Ridings. N21 —6G 7
Old Pk. Rd. N13 —4E 16
Old Pk. Rd. SE2 —5A 84
Old Pk. Rd. Enf —3G 7
Old Pk. Rd. S. Enf —4G 7
Old Pk. View. Enf —3F 7
Old Perry St. Chst —7J 115
Old Pye St. SW1 —3H 77 (6A 146)
Old Quebec St. W1 —6D 60 (8F 138)
Old Queen St. SW1 —2H 77 (5B 146)
Old Rectory Gdns. Edgw —6B 12
Old Redding. Harr —5A 10
Oldridge Rd. SW12 —7E 92
Old Rd. SE13 —4G 97
Old Rd. Dart —5K 101
Old Rd. Enf —1D 8
Old Royal Free Pl. N1 —1A 62
(off Liverpool Rd.)
Old Royal Free Sq. N1 —1A 62
(off Old Royal Free Pl.)
Old Ruislip Rd. N'holt —2B 54
Old Ruslip Rd. N'holt —2A 54
Old School Clo. SW19 —2J 121
Old School Clo. Beck —2A 126
Old Schools La. Eps —7B 130
Old Seacoal La. EC4
—6B 62 (8J 141)
Old South Clo. H End —1B 22
Old S. Lambeth Rd. SW8 —7J 77
Old Sq. WC2 —6K 61 (7G 141)
Old Stable M. N5 —3C 46
Oldstead Rd. Brom —4F 113
Old St. E13 —2K 65
Old St. EC1 —4C 62 (4L 141)
Old Sungate Cotts. Romf —1F 37
Old Swan Yd. Cars —4D 132
Old Town. SW4 —3G 93
Old Town. Croy —3B 134
Old Woolwich Rd. SE10 —6F 81
Old York Rd. SW18 —5K 91
O'Leary Sq. E1 —5J 63
Olga St. E3 —2A 64
Olinda Rd. N16 —6F 31
Oliphant St. W10 —3F 59
Oliver Av. SE25 —3F 125
Oliver Clo. E10 —2D 48
Oliver Clo. W4 —6H 73
Oliver Ct. SE18 —4G 83
Oliver Gdns. E6 —5C 66
Oliver Goldsmith Est. SE15 —1G 95
Oliver Gro. SE25 —4F 125
Oliver Ho. SE16 —2G 79
(off George Row)
Olive Rd. E13 —3A 66

Olive Rd. NW2 —4E 42
Olive Rd. SW19 —7A 108
Olive Rd. W5 —3D 72
Oliver Rd. E10 —2D 48
Oliver Rd. E17 —5C 32
Oliver Rd. N Mald —2J 119
Oliver Rd. Sutt —4B 132
Olivers Yd. EC1 —4D 62 (3B 142)
Olive St. Romf —5K 37
Olivette St. SW15 —3F 91
Olivia Ct. Enf —1H 7
(off Chase Side)
Ollerton Grn. E3 —1B 64
Ollerton Rd. N11 —5C 16
Olley Clo. Wall —7J 133
Ollgar Clo. W12 —1B 74
Olliffe St. E14 —3E 80
Olmar St. SE1 —6G 79
Olney Rd. SE17 —6B 78
(in two parts)
Olron Cres. Bexh —5D 100
Olven Rd. SE18 —6G 83
Olveston Wlk. Cars —6B 122
Olwen M. Pinn —2B 22
Olyffe Av. Well —1A 100
Olyffe Dri. Beck —1E 126
Olympia M. W2 —7K 59
Olympia Way. W14 —3G 75
Olympic Way. Gnfd —1G 55
Olympic Way. Wemb —3G 41
Olympus Sq. E5 —3G 47
Oman Av. NW2 —4D 42
O'Meara St. SE1 —1C 78 (3M 147)
Omega Pl. N1 —2J 61
(off Caledonian Rd.)
Omega St. SE14 —1C 96
Ommaney Rd. SE14 —1K 95
Ondine Rd. SE15 —4F 95
Onega Ga. SE16 —3K 79
O'Neill Path. SE18 —6E 82
One Tree Clo. SE23 —6J 95
Ongar Clo. Romf —5C 36
Ongar Rd. SW6 —6J 75
Onra Rd. E17 —7C 32
Onslow Av. Rich —5E 88
Onslow Clo. E4 —2K 19
Onslow Cres. Chst —1F 129
Onslow Dri. Sidc —2D 116
Onslow Gdns. E18 —3K 33
Onslow Gdns. N10 —5F 29
Onslow Gdns. N21 —5F 7
Onslow Gdns. SW7 —4B 76 (9A 144)
Onslow Gdns. Wall —6G 133
Onslow M. E. SW7 —4B 76 (9A 144)
Onslow M. W. SW7
—4B 76 (9A 144)
Onslow Pde. N14 —1A 16
Onslow Rd. Croy —7A 124
Onslow Rd. N Mald —4C 120
Onslow Rd. Rich —5E 88
Onslow Sq. SW7 —4B 76 (8B 144)
Onslow St. EC1 —4A 62 (4H 141)
Ontario St. SE1 —3B 78 (6K 147)
Ontario Way. E14 —1C 80
Opal Clo. E16 —6B 66
Opal M. NW6 —1H 59
Opal M. Ilf —2F 51
Opal St. SE11 —5B 78
Openshaw Rd. SE2 —4B 84
Openview. SW18 —1A 108
Ophelia Gdns. NW2 —3G 43
Ophir Ter. SE15 —1G 95
Opossum Way. Houn —3A 86
Oppenheim Rd. SE13 —2E 96
Oppidans M. NW3 —7D 44
Oppidans Rd. NW3 —7D 44

Orange Ct. E1 —1G 79
Orange Hill Rd. Edgw —7D 12
Orange Pl. SE16 —3J 79
Orangery La. SE9 —5D 98
Orange St. WC2 —7H 61 (1B 146)
Orange Yd. W1 —6H 61 (8B 140)
(off Manette St.)
Oratory La. SW3 —5B 76
(off Stewart's Gro.)
Orbain Rd. SW6 —7G 75
Orbel St. SW11 —1C 92
Orb St. SE17 —4D 78 (9A 148)
Orchard Av. N3 —3J 27
Orchard Av. N14 —6B 6
Orchard Av. N20 —2G 15
Orchard Av. Belv —6E 84
Orchard Av. Croy —1A 136
Orchard Av. Houn —7C 70
Orchard Av. Mitc —1E 132
Orchard Av. N Mald —3A 120
Orchard Av. S'hall —1D 70
Orchard Av. Wfd G —1H 33
Orchard Bus. Cen. SE26 —5B 112
Orchard Clo. E4 —4H 19
Orchard Clo. E11 —4K 33
Orchard Clo. N1 —7C 46
Orchard Clo. NW2 —3C 42
Orchard Clo. SE23 —6J 95
Orchard Clo. SW20 —4E 120
Orchard Clo. W10 —5H 59
Orchard Clo. Bexh —1E 100
Orchard Clo. Bush —1C 10
Orchard Clo. Edgw —6K 11
Orchard Clo. N'holt —6G 39
Orchard Clo. Surb —7B 118
Orchard Clo. Wemb —1E 56
Orchard Ct. E10 —1D 48
Orchard Ct. N14 —6B 6
Orchard Ct. Edgw —5A 12
Orchard Ct. Iswth —7H 71
Orchard Ct. New Bar —3E 4
Orchard Ct. Twic —2H 103
Orchard Ct. Wor Pk —1C 130
Orchard Cres. Edgw —5D 12
Orchard Cres. Enf —1A 8
Orchard Dri. SE3 —2F 97
Orchard Dri. Edgw —5A 12
Orchard Gdns. Sutt —5J 131
Orchard Ga. NW9 —4A 26
Orchard Ga. Gnfd —6B 40
Orchard Gro. SE20 —7G 111
Orchard Gro. Croy —7A 126
Orchard Gro. Edgw —1G 25
Orchard Gro. Harr —5F 25
Orchard Hill. SE13 —2D 96
Orchard Hill. Cars —5D 132
Orchard Ho. Dart —5K 101
Orchard Ho. SE16 —3J 79
Orchard La. SW20 —1D 120
Orchard La. Wfd G —4F 21
Orchardleigh Av. Enf —2D 8
Orchard Mead Ho. NW11 —2J 43
Orchardmede. N21 —6J 7
Orchard M. N1 —7D 46
Orchard Pl. E14 —7G 65
Orchard Pl. N17 —7A 18
Orchard Rise. Croy —1A 136
Orchard Rise. King T —1J 119
Orchard Rise. Rich —5H 89
Orchard Rise E. Sidc —5K 99
Orchard Rise W. Sidc —5J 99
Orchard Rd. N6 —7F 29
Orchard Rd. SE3 —2G 97
Orchard Rd. SE18 —4H 83
Orchard Rd. Barn —4C 4
Orchard Rd. Belv —4G 85
Orchard Rd. Bex —6C 72
Orchard Rd. Brom —1A 128

Orchard Rd. Dag —1G 69
Orchard Rd. Enf —5D 8
Orchard Rd. Hamp —7D 102
Orchard Rd. Houn —5D 86
Orchard Rd. King T —2E 118
Orchard Rd. Mitc —1E 132
Orchard Rd. Rich —3G 89
Orchard Rd. Romf —1H 37
Orchard Rd. Sidc —4J 115
Orchard Rd. Sutt —5J 131
Orchard Rd. Twic —6A 88
Orchard Rd. Well —3B 100
Orchardson St. NW8
—4B 60 (4A 138)
Orchard St. E17 —1A 32
Orchard St. W1 —6E 60 (8G 139)
Orchard, The. N14 —5A 6
Orchard, The. N21 —6J 7
Orchard, The. NW11 —5J 27
Orchard, The. SE3 —2F 97
Orchard, The. W4 —4K 73
Orchard, The. W5 —6D 56
(off Helena Rd.)
Orchard, The. Eps —7B 130
(Meadow Wlk.)
Orchard, The. Houn —2G 87
Orchard Way. Croy & Beck —7A 126
Orchard Way. Enf —3K 7
Orchard Way. Sutt —4B 132
Orchid Clo. E6 —5C 66
Orchid Grange. N14 —7B 6
Orchid Rd. N14 —7B 6
Orchid St. W12 —7C 58
Orde. NW9 —1B 26
Orde Hall St. WC1 —5K 61 (4E 140)
Ordell Rd. E3 —2B 64
Ordnance Cres. SE10 —2G 81
Ordnance Hill. NW8 —1B 60
Ordnance M. NW8 —2B 60
Ordnance Rd. E16 —5H 65
Ordnance Rd. SE18 —6E 82
Oregano Dri. E14 —6F 65
Oregon Av. E12 —4D 50.
Oregon Clo. N Mald —4J 119
Oregon Sq. Orp —7H 129
Orestes M. NW6 —5J 43
Orford Ct. SE27 —2B 110
Orford Ct. Stan —6H 11
Orford Gdns. Twic —2K 103
Orford Rd. E17 —5C 32
Orford Rd. E18 —3K 33
Orford Rd. SE6 —3D 112
Organ La. E4 —2K 19
Oriel Clo. Mitc —4H 123
Oriel Ct. NW3 —4A 44
Oriel Ct. Croy —1D 134
Oriel Dri. lif —3D 34
Oriel Pl. NW3 —4A 44
(off Heath St.)
Oriel Rd. E9 —6K 47
Oriel Way. N'holt —7F 39
Oriental Rd. E16 —1B 82
Orient Ind. Pk. E10 —2C 48
Orient St. SE11 —4B 78 (8J 147)
Orient Way. E5 —3K 47
Oriole Way. SE28 —7B 68
Orion Bus. Cen. SE14 —5K 79
Orissa Rd. SE18 —5J 83
Orkney Ho. N1 —1K 61
(off Bemerton Est.)
Orkney St. SW11 —2E 92
Orlando Rd. SW4 —3G 93
Orleans Ct. Twic —7B 88
Orleans Rd. SE19 —6D 110
Orleans Rd. Twic —7B 88
Orleston M. N7 —6A 46
Orleston Rd. N7 —6A 46

Orley Ct. Harr —4K **39**
Orley Farm Rd. Harr —3J **39**
Orlop St. SE10 —5G **81**
Ormanton Rd. SE26 —4G **111**
Orme Ct. W2 —7K **59**
Orme Ct. M. W2 —7K **59**
(off Orme La.)
Orme Ho. E8 —1F **63**
Orme La. W2 —7K **59**
Ormeley Rd. SW12 —1F **109**
Orme Rd. King T —2H **119**
Ormerod Gdns. Mitc —2E **122**
Ormesby Clo. SE28 —7D **68**
Ormesby Way. Harr —6F **25**
Orme Sq. W2 —7K **59**
Ormiston Gro. W12 —1D **74**
Ormiston Rd. SE10 —5J **81**
Ormond Av. Hamp —7F **103**
Ormond Av. Rich —5D **88**
Ormond Clo. WC1 —5J **61** (5D **140**)
Ormond Cres. Hamp —7F **103**
Ormond Dri. Hamp —7F **103**
Ormonde Ga. SW3 —5D **76**
Ormonde Pl. SW1 —4E **76** (9G **145**)
Ormonde Rise. Buck H —1F **21**
Ormonde Rd. SW14 —3J **89**
Ormonde Ter. NW8 —1D **60**
Ormond M. WC1 —4J **61** (4D **140**)
Ormond Rd. N19 —1J **45**
Ormond Rd. Rich —5D **88**
Ormond Yd. SW1 —1G **77** (2M **145**)
Ormsby Gdns. Gnfd —2G **55**
Ormsby Lodge. W4 —3A **74**
Ormsby Pl. N16 —3F **47**
Ormsby St. E2 —2F **63**
Ormside St. SE15 —6J **79**
Ornan Rd. NW3 —5C **44**
Oronsay Wlk. N1 —7C **46**
Orphen Wlk. N16 —3E **46**
Orpheus St. SE5 —1D **94**
Orpington Gdns. N18 —3K **17**
Orpington Mans. N21 —1F **17**
Orpington Rd. N21 —1G **17**
Orpington Rd. Chst —3J **129**
Orpwood Clo. Hamp —6D **102**
Orsett St. SE11 —5K **77**
Orsett Ter. W2 —6K **59**
Orsett Ter. Wfd G —7F **21**
Orsman Rd. N1 —1E **62**
Orton St. E1 —1G **79**
Orville Rd. SW11 —2B **92**
Orwell Clo. Rain —5K **69**
Orwell Ct. N5 —4C **46**
Orwell Rd. E13 —1A **66**
Osbaldeston Rd. N16 —2G **47**
Osberton Rd. SE12 —5J **97**
Osbert St. SW1 —4H **77** (9A **146**)
Osborn Clo. E8 —1G **63**
Osborne Clo. Beck —4A **126**
Osborne Clo. Felt —5B **102**
Osborne Ct. E10 —7D **32**
Osborne Ct. W5 —5C **56**
Osborne Gdns. T Hth —2C **124**
Osborne Gro. E17 —4B **32**
Osborne Gro. N4 —1A **46**
Osborne M. E17 —4B **32**
Osborne Pl. Sutt —5B **132**
Osborne Rd. E7 —5K **49**
Osborne Rd. E9 —6B **48**
Osborne Rd. E10 —3D **48**
Osborne Rd. N4 —1A **46**
Osborne Rd. N13 —3F **17**
Osborne Rd. NW2 —6D **42**
Osborne Rd. W3 —3H **73**
Osborne Rd. Belv —5F **85**
Osborne Rd. Buck H —1E **20**
Osborne Rd. Dag —5F **53**
Osborne Rd. Enf —2F **9**

Osborne Rd. Houn —3D **86**
Osborne Rd. King T —7F **104**
Osborne Rd. S'hall —6G **55**
Osborne Rd. T Hth —2C **124**
Osborne Sq. Dag —4F **53**
Osborn Gdns. NW7 —7A **14**
Osborn La. SE23 —7A **96**
Osborn St. E1 —5F **63**
Osborn Ter. SE3 —4H **97**
Osbourne Ho. Twic —2G **103**
Oscar St. SE8 —1C **96**
Oseney Cres. NW5 —5G **45**
O'Shea Gro. E3 —1B **64**
Osidge La. N14 —1K **15**
Osier Ct. Romf —6K **37**
Osiers Rd. SW18 —4J **91**
Osier St. E1 —4J **63**
Osier Way. E10 —3D **48**
Osier Way. Mitc —5D **122**
Oslac Rd. SE6 —5D **112**
Oslo Ct. NW8 —2C **60**
(off Prince Albert Rd.)
Oslo Sq. SE16 —3A **80**
Osman Clo. N15 —6D **30**
Osman Rd. N9 —3B **18**
Osman Rd. W6 —3E **74**
 Osmond Clo. Harr —2G **39**
Osmond Gdns. Wall —5G **133**
Osmund St. W12 —5B **58**
Osnaburgh St. NW1
—4F **61** (4K **139**)
Osnaburgh Ter. NW1
—4F **61** (3K **139**)
Osney Ho. SE2 —2D **84**
Osney Wlk. Cars —6B **122**
Osprey Clo. E6 —5C **66**
Osprey Clo. E11 —4J **33**
Osprey Clo. E17 —7F **19**
Osprey Ct. Beck —7C **112**
Osprey Est. SE16 —4K **79**
Osprey M. Enf —5D **8**
Ospringe Clo. SE20 —7J **111**
Ospringe Rd. NW5 —4G **45**
Osram Rd. Wemb —3D **40**
Osric Path. N1 —2E **62**
Ossian M. N4 —7K **29**
Ossian Rd. N4 —7K **29**
Ossington Bldgs. W1
—5E **60** (6G **139**)
Ossington Clo. W2 —7J **59**
Ossington St. W2 —7K **59**
Ossory Rd. SE1 —6G **79**
Ossulston St. NW1 —2H **61**
Ossulton Pl. N2 —3A **28**
Ossulton Way. N2 —4A **28**
Ostade Rd. SW2 —7K **93**
Ostend Pl. SE17 —4C **78** (8L **147**)
Osten M. SW7 —3K **75**
Osterley Av. Iswth —7H **71**
Osterley Clo. Orp —7A **116**
Osterley Ct. Iswth —1H **87**
Osterley Cres. Iswth —1J **87**
Osterley Gdns. T Hth —2C **124**
Osterley La. S'hall & Iswth —5E **70**
Osterley Lodge. Iswth —7J **71**
(off Church Rd.)
Osterley Pk. Rd. S'hall —3D **70**
Osterley Pk. View Rd. W7 —2J **71**
Osterley Rd. N16 —4E **46**
Osterley Rd. Iswth —7J **71**
Ostliffe Rd. N13 —4G **17**
Oswald Rd. S'hall —1C **70**
Oswald's Mead. E9 —4A **48**
Oswald St. E5 —3K **47**
Oswald Ter. NW2 —3E **42**
Osward. Pl. N9 —2C **18**
Osward Rd. SW17 —2D **108**
Osward Vs. N9 —2C **18**

Oswin St. SE11 —4B **78** (8K **147**)
Oswyth Rd. SE5 —2E **94**
Otford Clo. SE20 —1J **125**
Otford Clo. Bex —6H **101**
Otford Clo. Brom —3E **128**
Otford Cres. SE4 —6B **96**
Othello Clo. SE11 —5B **78**
Otho Ct. Bren —7D **72**
Otis St. E3 —3E **64**
Otley App. Ilf —6F **35**
Otley Dri. Ilf —5F **35**
Otley Ho. N5 —3B **46**
Otley Rd. E16 —6A **66**
Otley Ter. E5 —3K **47**
Ottawa Gdns. Dag —7K **53**
Ottaway Ct. E5 —3G **47**
Ottaway St. E5 —3G **47**
Otterbourne Rd. E4 —3A **20**
Otterbourne Rd. Croy —2C **134**
Otterburn Gdns. Iswth —7A **72**
Otterburn St. SW17 —6D **108**
Otterden St. SE6 —4C **112**
Otter Rd. Gnfd —4G **55**
Otto Clo. SE26 —3H **111**
Otto St. SE17 —6B **78**
Oulton Clo. E5 —2J **47**
Oulton Clo. SE28 —6C **68**
Oulton Cres. Bark —5K **51**
Oulton Rd. N15 —5D **30**
Ouseley Rd. SW12 —1D **108**
Outer Circ. NW1 —3C **60**
Outgate Rd. NW10 —7B **42**
Outram Pl. N1 —1J **61**
Outram Rd. E6 —1C **66**
Outram Rd. N22 —1H **29**
Outram Rd. Croy —2F **135**
Outwich St. EC3 —6E **62** (7D **142**)
(off Houndsditch)
Outwood Ho. SW2 —7K **93**
(off Deepdene Gdns.)
Oval Mans. SE11 —6K **77**
Oval Pl. SW8 —7K **77**
Oval Rd. NW1 —1F **61**
Oval Rd. Croy —2D **134**
Oval Rd. N. Dag —1H **69**
Oval Rd. S. Dag —2H **69**
Oval, The. E2 —2H **63**
Oval, The. Sidc —7A **100**
Oval Way. SE11 —5K **77**
Overbrae. Beck —5C **112**
Overbrook Wlk. Edgw —7B **12**
(in two parts)
Overbury Av. Beck —3D **126**
Overbury Rd. N15 —6D **30**
Overbury St. E5 —4K **47**
Overcliff Rd. SE13 —3C **96**
Overcourt Clo. Sidc —6B **100**
Overdale Av. N Mald —2K **119**
Overdale Rd. W5 —3C **72**
Overdown Rd. SE6 —4C **112**
Overhill Rd. SE22 —7G **95**
Overhill Way. Beck —5F **127**
Overlea Rd. E5 —7G **31**
Overmead. Sidc —7H **99**
Overstand Clo. Beck —5C **126**
Overstone Gdns. Croy —7B **126**
Overstone Rd. W6 —3E **74**
Overstrand Mans. SW11 —1D **92**
Overton Clo. NW10 —6J **41**
Overton Clo. Iswth —1K **87**
Overton Ct. E11 —7J **33**
Overton Ct. Sutt —7J **131**
Overton Dri. E11 —7J **33**
Overton Dri. Chad —7C **36**
Overton Rd. E10 —1A **48**
Overton Rd. N14 —5D **6**
Overton Rd. SE2 —3A **84**
Overton Rd. SW9 —2A **94**

Overton Rd. Sutt —6J **131**
Overton Rd. E. SE2 —3B **84**
Overtons Yd. Croy —3C **134**
Overy Ho. SE1 —2B **78** (5J **147**)
Ovesdon Av. Harr —1D **38**
Ovett Clo. SE19 —6E **110**
Ovex Clo. E14 —2E **80**
Ovington Gdns. SW3
—3C **76** (7D **144**)
Ovington M. SW3 —3C **76** (7D **144**)
Ovington Sq. SW3 —3C **76** (7D **144**)
Ovington St. SW3 —4C **76** (8D **144**)
Owen Clo. SE28 —1C **84**
Owen Clo. Croy —6D **124**
Owen Gdns. Wfd G —6H **21**
Owen Ho. Twic —7B **88**
Owenite St. SE2 —4B **84**
Owen Rd. N13 —5H **17**
Owen Rd. Hay —3A **54**
Owen's Ct. EC1 —3B **62** (1J **141**)
Owen's Row. EC1 —3B **62** (1J **141**)
Owen St. EC1 —2B **62**
Owens Way. SE23 —7A **96**
Owen Wlk. SE20 —7G **111**
Owen Way. NW10 —5J **41**
Owgan Clo. SE5 —7D **78**
Oxberry Av. SW6 —2G **91**
Oxendon St. SW1 —7H **61** (1A **146**)
Oxenford St. SE15 —3F **95**
Oxenpark Av. Wemb —1E **40**
Oxestall's Rd. SE8 —5A **80**
Oxford Av. NW10 —3D **58**
Oxford Av. SW20 —2G **121**
Oxford Av. Houn —5C **70**
Oxford Cir. Av. W1 —6G **61** (8L **139**)
(off Oxford St.)
Oxford Cir. W. W1 —6G **61** (8L **139**)
Oxford Clo. N9 —2C **18**
Oxford Clo. Mitc —3G **123**
Oxford Ct. EC4 —7D **62** (9A **142**)
(off Salter's Hall Ct.)
Oxford Ct. W3 —6G **57**
Oxford Ct. W4 —5H **73**
Oxford Ct. Felt —4B **102**
Oxford Cres. N Mald —6K **119**
Oxford Dri. Ruis —2A **38**
Oxford Gdns. N20 —1G **15**
Oxford Gdns. N21 —7H **7**
Oxford Gdns. W4 —5G **73**
Oxford Gdns. W10 —6E **58**
Oxford Ga. W6 —4F **75**
Oxford M. Bex —7G **101**
Oxford Rd. E15 —6F **49**
(in two parts)
Oxford Rd. N4 —1A **46**
Oxford Rd. N9 —2C **18**
Oxford Rd. NW6 —2J **59**
Oxford Rd. SE19 —6D **110**
Oxford Rd. SW15 —4G **91**
Oxford Rd. W5 —7D **56**
Oxford Rd. Cars —6C **132**
Oxford Rd. Enf —6D **8**
Oxford Rd. Harr —6G **23**
Oxford Rd. Ilf —5G **51**
Oxford Rd. Sidc —5B **116**
Oxford Rd. Tedd —5H **103**
Oxford Rd. Wall —5G **133**
Oxford Rd. W'stone —3K **23**
Oxford Rd. Wfd G —5G **21**
Oxford Sq. W2 —6C **60** (8D **138**)
Oxford Wlk. S'hall —1D **70**
Oxford Way. Felt —4B **102**
Oxgate Cen. NW2 —2D **42**

Oxgate Ct. NW2 —2C **42**
Oxgate Gdns. NW2 —3D **42**
Oxgate La. NW2 —2D **42**
Oxhawth Cres. Brom —5E **128**
Oxhey La. Harr —5A **10**
Ox La. Eps —7C **130**
Oxleas. E6 —6F **67**
Oxleas Clo. Well —2H **99**
Oxleay Rd. Harr —1E **38**
Oxleigh Clo. N Mald —5A **120**
Oxley Clo. SE1 —5F **79**
Oxleys Rd. NW2 —3D **42**
Oxlip Clo. Croy —1K **135**
Oxlow La. Dag —4F **53**
Oxmore St. SW11 —1D **92**
Oxonian St. SE22 —4F **95**
Oxted Clo. Mitc —3B **122**
Oxtoby Way. SW16 —1H **123**
Oystercatcher Clo. E16 —6K **65**
Oystergate Wlk. EC4
(off Swan La.) —7D **62** (1A **148**)
Oyster Row. E1 —6J **63**
Ozolins Way. E16 —6J **65**

Pablo Neruda Clo. SE24 —3B **94**
Pace Pl. E1 —6H **63**
Pacific Rd. E16 —6J **65**
Packington Rd. W3 —3J **73**
Packington Sq. N1 —1C **62**
Packington St. N1 —1B **62**
Packmores Rd. SE9 —5H **99**
*Padbury. SE5 —5E **78***
(off Bagshot St.)
*Padbury. SE17 —5E **78***
(off Bagshot St.)
Padbury Ct. E2 —3F **63**
Paddenswick Rd. W6 —3C **74**
Paddington Clo. Hay —4B **54**
Paddington Grn. W2
—5B **60** (5B **138**)
Paddington St. W1 —5E **60** (5G **139**)
Paddock Clo. SE3 —3J **97**
Paddock Clo. SE26 —4K **111**
Paddock Clo. N'holt —2E **54**
Paddock Clo. Wor Pk —1A **130**
Paddock Gdns. SE19 —6E **110**
*Paddock Pas. SE19 —6E **110***
(off Paddock Gdns.)
Paddock Rd. NW2 —2C **42**
Paddock Rd. Bexh —4E **100**
Paddock Rd. Ruis —3B **38**
Paddocks Clo. Harr —4F **39**
Paddocks Grn. NW9 —1H **41**
Paddocks, The. Barn —3J **5**
Paddocks, The. New Ad —5C **136**
Paddocks, The. Wemb —2H **41**
Paddock, The. NW9 —5G **25**
Paddock Way. Chst —7H **115**
Padfield Rd. SE5 —3C **94**
Padnall Ct. Romf —3D **36**
Padnall Rd. Chad —3D **36**
Padstow Rd. Enf —1G **7**
Padua Rd. SE20 —1J **125**
Pagden St. SW8 —1F **93**
Pageant Av. NW9 —1A **26**
Pageantmaster Ct. EC4
(off Ludgate Hill.) —6B **62** (8J **141**)
Pageant Wlk. Croy —3E **134**
Page Clo. Dag —5E **52**
Page Clo. Hamp —6C **102**
Page Clo. Harr —6F **25**
Page Cres. Croy —5B **134**
Page Grn. Ter. N15 —5F **31**
Page Grn Rd. N15 —5G **31**
Page Heath La. Brom —3B **128**
Page Heath Vs. Brom —3B **128**
Pagehurst Rd. Croy —7H **125**

Page Meadow. NW7 —7J **13**
Pages Hill. N10 —2E **28**
Pages La. N10 —2E **28**
Page St. NW7 —1C **26**
Page St. SW1 —4H 77 (8B **146**)
Page's Wlk. SE1 —4E 78 (8C **148**)
Pages Yd. W4 —6A **74**
Paget Av. Sutt —3B **132**
Paget Clo. Hamp —4H **103**
Paget Gdns. Chst —1F **129**
Paget La. Iswth —3H **87**
Paget Pl. King T —6J **105**
Paget Rise. SE18 —6E **82**
Paget Rd. N16 —1D **46**
Paget Rd. Ilf —4F **51**
Paget St. EC1 —3B 62 (1J **141**)
Paget Ter. SE18 —6F **83**
Pagin Ho. N15 —5E **30**
  (off Braemar Rd.)
Pagitts Gro. Barn —1E **4**
Pagnell St. SE14 —7B **80**
Pagoda Av. Rich —3F **89**
Pagoda Gdns. SE3 —2F **97**
Pagoda Vista. Rich —2F **89**
Paignton Rd. N15 —6E **30**
Paines Clo. Pinn —3C **22**
Paines La. Pinn —1C **22**
Pain's Clo. Mitc —2F **123**
Painsthorpe Rd. N16 —3E **46**
Painswick Ct. SE15 —7F **79**
  (off Daniel Gdns.)
Painters Rd. Ilf —3K **35**
Paisley Rd. N22 —1B **30**
Paisley Rd. Cars —1B **132**
Pakeman St. N7 —3K **45**
Pakenham Clo. SW12 —1E **108**
Pakenham St. WC1 —3K 61 (2F **140**)
Pakington Ho. SW9 —2J **93**
  (off Stockwell Gdns. Est.)
Palace Av. W8 —2K **75**
Palace Ct. NW3 —5K **43**
Palace Ct. W2 —7K **59**
Palace Ct. Harr —6E **24**
Palace Ct. Gdns. N10 —3G **29**
Palace Gdns. Buck H —1G **21**
Palace Gdns. Enf —4J **7**
Palace Gdns. M. W8 —1K **75**
Palace Gdns. Shopping Cen. Enf
  —4J **7**
Palace Gdns. Ter. W8 —1J **75**
Palace Ga. W8 —2K **75**
Palace Gates Rd. N22 —1H **29**
Palace Grn. W8 —1K **75**
Palace Grn. Croy —7B **136**
Palace Gro. Brom —1K **127**
Palace Gro. SE19 —7F **111**
Palace Gro. SE19 —7F **111**
Palace M. E17 —4B **32**
Palace M. SW1 —4E 76 (9H **145**)
  (off Eaton Ter.)
Palace M. SW6 —7H **75**
Palace M. Enf —3J **7**
Palace Pde. E17 —4B **32**
Palace Pl. SW1 —3G 77 (6L **145**)
Palace Pl. Mans. W8 —2K **75**
  (off Kensington Ct.)
Palace Rd. N8 —5H **29**
  (in two parts)
Palace Rd. N11 —7D **16**
Palace Rd. SE19 —7F **111**
Palace Rd. SW2 —1K **109**
Palace Rd. Brom —1K **127**
Palace Rd. King T —4D **118**
Palace Rd. Ruis —4C **38**
Palace Sq. SE19 —7F **111**
Palace St. SW1 —3G 77 (6L **145**)
Palace View. SE12 —2J **113**
Palace View. Brom —3K **127**
  (in two parts)

Palace View. Croy —4B **136**
Palace View Rd. E4 —5J **19**
Palamos Rd. E10 —1C **48**
Palatine Av. N16 —4E **46**
Palatine Rd. N16 —4E **46**
Palermo Rd. NW10 —2C **58**
Palestine Gro. SW19 —1B **122**
Palewell Comn. Dri. SW14 —5K **89**
Palewell Pk. SW14 —5K **89**
Palfrey Pl. SW8 —7K **77**
Palgrave Av. S'hall —7E **54**
Palgrave Ho. Twic —7G **87**
Palgrave Rd. W12 —3B **74**
Palissy St. E2 —3F 63 (2E **142**)
Pallant Ho. SE1 —3D 78 (7B **148**)
  (off Tabard St.)
Pallett Way. SE18 —1C **98**
Palliser Rd. W14 —5G **75**
Pall Mall. SW1 —1G 77 (3M **145**)
Pall Mall E. SW1 —1H 77 (2B **146**)
Pall Mall Pl. SW1 —1G 77 (3M **145**)
  (off Pall Mall)
Palmar Cres. Bexh —3G **101**
Palmar Rd. Bexh —2G **101**
Palm Av. Sidc —6D **116**
Palmeira Rd. Bexh —3D **100**
Palmer Av. Sutt —4E **130**
Palmer Clo. Houn —1E **86**
Palmer Clo. W Wick —2F **137**
Palmer Cres. King T —3E **118**
Palmer Gdns. Barn —5A **4**
Palmer Pl. N7 —5A **46**
Palmer Rd. E13 —4K **65**
Palmer Rd. Dag —1D **52**
Palmer's Ct. N11 —5B **16**
  (off Palmer's Rd.)
Palmers La. Enf —1C **8**
Palmers Pas. SW14 —3J **89**
Palmer's Rd. E2 —2K **63**
Palmer's Rd. N11 —5B **16**
Palmers Rd. SW14 —3J **89**
Palmers Rd. SW16 —2K **123**
Palmerston Cen. W'stone —3K **23**
Palmerston Ct. Surb —7D **118**
Palmerston Cres. N13 —5E **16**
Palmerston Cres. SE18 —6G **83**
Palmerston Gro. SW19 —7J **107**
Palmerston Rd. E7 —6K **49**
Palmerston Rd. E17 —3B **32**
Palmerston Rd. N22 —7E **16**
Palmerston Rd. NW6 —7H **43**
  (in two parts)
Palmerston Rd. SW14 —4J **89**
Palmerston Rd. SW19 —7J **107**
Palmerston Rd. W3 —3J **73**
Palmerston Rd. Buck H —2G **29**
Palmerston Rd. Cars —4D **132**
Palmerston Rd. Harr —3J **23**
Palmerston Rd. Sutt —5A **132**
Palmerston Rd. T Hth —5D **124**
Palmerston Rd. Twic —6K **87**
Palmer St. SW1 —3H 77 (6A **146**)
Palm Gro. W5 —3E **72**
Palm Rd. Romf —5J **37**
Pamela Ct. N12 —6E **14**
Pamela Gdns. Pinn —5A **22**
Pamela Wlk. E8 —1G **63**
Pampisford Rd. S Croy —7B **134**
Pam's Way. Eps —6A **130**
Pancras La. EC4 —6C 62 (8M **141**)
Pancras Rd. NW1 —2H **61**
Pandora Rd. NW6 —6J **43**
Panfield M. Ilf —6E **34**
Panfield Rd. SE2 —3A **84**
Pangbourne Av. W10 —5E **58**
Pangbourne Dri. Stan —5J **11**

Panhard Pl. S'hall —7F **55**
Pank Av. Barn —5F **5**
Pankhurst Clo. SE14 —1K **95**
Panmuir Rd. SW20 —1D **120**
Panmure Clo. N5 —4B **46**
Panmure Rd. SE26 —3H **111**
Panorama Ct. N6 —6G **29**
Pansy Gdns. W12 —7C **58**
Pantiles Clo. N13 —5G **17**
Pantiles, The. NW11 —6G **27**
Pantiles, The. Bexh —7F **85**
Pantiles, The. Brom —3C **128**
Pantiles, The. Bush —1C **10**
Panton St. SW1 —7H 61 (1A **146**)
Panyer All. EC4 —6C 62 (8L **141**)
  (off Newgate St.)
Paper Bldgs. EC4 —7A 62 (9H **141**)
  (off Temple)
Paper Mill Wharf. E14 —7A **64**
Papillons Wlk. SE3 —3J **97**
Papworth Gdns. N7 —5K **45**
Papworth Way. SW2 —7A **94**
Parade Mans. NW4 —5D **26**
Parade, The. N4 —2A **46**
Parade, The. SW11 —7D **76**
Parade, The. Hamp —5H **103**
Parade, The. Wor Pk —4B **130**
Paradise Ct. Wemb —3H **41**
Paradise Pas. N7 —5A **46**
Paradise Pl. SE18 —4C **82**
Paradise Rd. SW4 —2J **93**
Paradise Rd. Rich —5D **88**
Paradise Row. E2 —3H **63**
Paradise St. SE16 —2H **79**
Paradise Wlk. SW3 —6D **76**
Paragon All. SE1 —3E 78 (7C **148**)
Paragon Clo. E16 —6J **65**
Paragon Gro. Surb —6F **119**
Paragon M. SE1 —4D 78 (8B **148**)
Paragon Pl. SE3 —2H **97**
Paragon Pl. Surb —6F **119**
Paragon Rd. E9 —6J **47**
Paragon Row. SE17
  —4D 78 (8A **148**)
Paraside Pl. SE18 —4C **82**
Parbury Rd. SE23 —6A **96**
Parchmore Rd. T Hth —2B **124**
Parchmore Way. T Hth —2B **124**
Pardoner St. SE1 —3D 78 (6B **148**)
Pardon St. EC1 —4B 62 (3K **141**)
Parfett St. E1 —5G **63**
Parfitt Clo. NW3 —1A **44**
Parfrey St. W6 —6E **74**
Pargreaves Ct. Wemb —2G **41**
Parham Dri. Ilf —6F **35**
Parham Way. N10 —2G **29**
Paris Garden. SE1 —1B 78 (2J **147**)
Parish Cotts. Dag —2G **53**
Parish Ga. Dri. Sidc —6J **99**
Parish La. SE20 —6K **111**
Parish M. SE20 —7K **111**
Park App. SE16 —3H **79**
Park App. Well —4B **100**
Park Av. E6 —1E **66**
Park Av. E15 —6G **49**
Park Av. N3 —1K **27**
Park Av. N13 —3F **17**
Park Av. N18 —4B **18**
Park Av. N22 —2J **29**
  (in two parts)
Park Av. NW11 —1K **43**
Park Av. SW14 —4K **89**
Park Av. Bark —6G **51**

Park Av. Brom —6H **113**
Park Av. Cars —6E **132**
Park Av. Enf —5J **7**
Park Av. Houn —6F **87**
Park Av. Ilf —1E **50**
Park Av. Mitc —7F **109**
Park Av. S'hall —2D **70**
Park Av. Wfd G —5E **20**
Park Av. W Wick —2E **136**
Park Av. E. Eps —6C **130**
Park Av. M. Mitc —7F **109**
Park Av. N. N8 —4H **29**
Park Av. N. NW10 —5D **42**
Park Av. Rd. N17 —7C **18**
Park Av. S. N8 —4H **29**
Park Av. W. Eps —6C **130**
Park Bus. Cen. NW6 —3J **59**
Park Chase. Wemb —4F **41**
Park Clo. E9 —1J **63**
Park Clo. N12 —4G **15**
Park Clo. NW2 —3D **42**
Park Clo. NW10 —3F **57**
Park Clo. SE7 —5C **82**
Park Clo. SW1 —2D 76 (5E **144**)
Park Clo. W4 —5K **73**
Park Clo. W14 —3H **75**
Park Clo. Cars —6D **132**
Park Clo. Hamp —7G **103**
Park Clo. Harr —1J **23**
Park Clo. Houn —5G **87**
Park Ct. E4 —2K **19**
Park Ct. E17 —5D **32**
Park Ct. N11 —7C **16**
Park Ct. N17 —7B **18**
Park Ct. SE26 —6H **111**
Park Ct. Harr —7E **24**
Park Ct. King T —1C **118**
Park Ct. N Mald —4K **119**
Park Ct. Wemb —5E **40**
Park Cres. N3 —7E **14**
Park Cres. W1 —4F 61 (4J **139**)
Park Cres. Enf —4J **7**
Park Cres. Eri —6J **85**
Park Cres. Harr —1J **23**
Park Cres. Twic —1H **103**
Park Cres. M. E. W1
  —4F 61 (4K **139**)
Park Cres. M. W. W1
  —4F 61 (4J **139**)
Park Cres. Rd. Eri —6K **85**
Park Croft. Edgw —1J **25**
Parkcroft Rd. SE12 —7H **97**
Parkdale. N11 —6C **16**
Parkdale Cres. Wor Pk —3A **130**
Parkdale Rd. SE18 —5J **83**
Park Dri. N21 —6H **7**
Park Dri. NW11 —1K **43**
Park Dri. SE7 —6C **82**
Park Dri. SW14 —5K **89**
Park Dri. W3 —3G **73**
Park Dri. Dag —3J **53**
Park Dri. Har W —6C **10**
Park Dri. N Har —7E **22**
Park Dri. Romf —4K **37**
Park Dwellings. NW3 —5D **44**
Park End. NW3 —4C **44**
Park End. Brom —1H **127**
Park End Rd. Romf —4K **37**
Park Farm Clo. N2 —3A **28**

Park Farm Clo. Pinn —5A **22**
Park Farm Rd. Brom —1B **128**
Park Farm Rd. King T —7E **104**
Parkfield. Iswth —1J **87**
Parkfield Av. SW14 —4A **90**
Parkfield Av. Harr —2G **23**
Parkfield Av. N'holt —2B **54**
Parkfield Clo. Edgw —6C **12**
Parkfield Clo. N'holt —2C **54**
Parkfield Cres. Harr —2G **23**
Parkfield Cres. Ruis —2C **38**
Parkfield Dri. N'holt —2B **54**
Parkfield Gdns. Harr —3F **23**
Parkfield Ho. N Har —1F **23**
Parkfield Rd. NW10 —7D **42**
Parkfield Rd. SE14 —1B **96**
Parkfield Rd. Harr —3G **39**
Parkfield Rd. N'holt —2C **54**
Parkfields. SW15 —4E **90**
Parkfields. Croy —1B **136**
Parkfields Av. NW9 —1K **41**
Parkfields Av. SW20 —1D **120**
Parkfields Clo. Cars —4E **132**
Parkfields Rd. King T —5F **105**
Parkfield St. N1 —2A **62**
Parkfield Way. Brom —6D **128**
Park Gdns. E10 —1C **48**
Park Gdns. NW9 —3H **25**
Park Gdns. King T —5F **105**
Park Ga. N2 —3B **28**
Park Ga. N21 —7E **6**
Park Ga. SE3 —3H **97**
Park Ga. W5 —5D **56**
Parkgate Av. Barn —1F **5**
Park Ga. Clo. King T —6H **105**
Parkgate Cres. Barn —1F **5**
Parkgate Gdns. SW14 —5K **89**
Parkgate Rd. SW11 —7C **76**
Parkgate Rd. Wall —5E **132**
Park Gates. Harr —4E **38**
Park Gro. E15 —1J **65**
Park Gro. N11 —7C **16**
Park Gro. Bexh —4J **101**
Park Gro. Brom —1K **127**
Park Gro. Edgw —5A **12**
Park Gro. Rd. E11 —2G **49**
Parkhall Rd. N2 —4C **28**
Park Hall Rd. SE21 —3D **110**
Park Hall Trading Est. SE21 —3C **110**
Parkham Ct. Short —2G **127**
Parkham St. SW11 —1C **92**
Park Hill. SE23 —2H **111**
Park Hill. SW4 —5H **93**
Park Hill. W5 —5D **56**
Park Hill. Brom —4C **128**
Park Hill. Cars —6C **132**
Park Hill. Rich —6F **89**
Park Hill Clo. Cars —5C **132**
Park Hill Ct. SW17 —3D **108**
Park Hill Rise. Croy —2E **134**
Parkhill Rd. E4 —1K **19**
Parkhill Rd. NW3 —5D **44**
Parkhill Rd. Bex —7F **101**
Park Hill Rd. Brom —2G **127**
Park Hill Rd. Croy —4E **134**
Park Hill Rd. Sidc —3J **115**
Park Hill Rd. Wall —7F **133**
Parkhill Wlk. NW3 —5D **44**
Parkholme Rd. E8 —6G **47**
Park Ho. N21 —7E **6**
Park Ho. Gdns. Twic —5C **88**
Park Ho. Pas. N6 —7E **28**
Parkhouse St. SE5 —7D **78**
Parkhurst Gdns. Bex —7G **101**
Parkhurst Rd. E12 —4E **50**
Parkhurst Rd. E17 —4A **32**
Parkhurst Rd. N7 —4J **45**

247

Parkhurst Rd. N11 —4K 15
Parkhurst Rd. N17 —2G 31
Parkhurst Rd. N22 —6E 16
Parkhurst Rd. Bex —7G 101
Parkhurst Rd. Sutt —4B 132
Parkland Ct. E15 —5G 49
(off Maryland Pk.)
Parkland Gdns. SW19 —1F 107
Parkland Rd. N22 —2K 29
Parkland Rd. Wfd G —7D 20
Parklands. Surb —5F 119
Parklands Clo. SW14 —5J 89
Parklands Clo. Barn —1G 5
Parklands Ct. Houn —2B 86
Parklands Dri. N3 —3G 27
Parklands Pde. Houn —2B 86
Parklands Rd. SW16 —5F 109
Parklands Way. Wor Pk —2A 130
Park La. E15 —1F 65
Park La. N9 —3K 17
Park La. N17 —7A 18
Park La. W1 —7D 60 (9F 138)
Park La. Cars & Wall —4E 132
Park La. Chad —6D 36
Park La. Croy —3D 134
Park La. Harr —3F 39
Park La. Rich —4D 88
Park La. Stan —3F 11
Park La. Sutt —6G 131
Park La. Tedd —6K 103
Park La. Wemb —5E 40
Park La. Clo. N17 —7B 18
Park Lawns. Wemb —4F 41
Parklea Clo. NW9 —1A 26
Park Lee Ct. N16 —7E 30
Parkleigh Rd. SW19 —2K 121
Parkleys. Rich —4D 104
Park Mnr. Sutt —7A 132
(off Christchurch Pk.)
Park Mans. NW4 —5D 26
Park Mans. SW8 —6J 77
Parkmead. SW15 —6D 90
Park Mead. Harr —3F 39
Park Mead. Sidc —5B 100
Parkmead Gdns. NW7 —6G 13
Park M. SE24 —7C 94
Park M. Chst —6F 115
Parkmore Clo. Wfd G —4D 20
Park Pde. NW10 —2B 58
Park Pl. E14 —1C 80
Park Pl. SW1 —1G 77 (3L 145)
Park Pl. W3 —4G 73
Park Pl. W5 —1D 72
Park Pl. Hamp —6G 103
Park Pl. Wemb —4F 41
Park Pl. Gdns. W2 —5A 60
Park Pl. Vs. W2 —5A 60
Park Ridings. N8 —3A 30
Park Rise. SE23 —1A 112
Park Rise. Harr —1J 23
Park Rise Rd. SE23 —1A 112
Park Rd. E6 —1A 66
Park Rd. E10 —1C 48
Park Rd. E12 —1K 49
Park Rd. E15 —1J 65
Park Rd. E17 —5B 32
Park Rd. N2 —3B 28
Park Rd. N8 —4G 29
Park Rd. N11 —7C 16
Park Rd. N14 —1C 16
Park Rd. N15 —4B 30
Park Rd. N18 —4B 18
Park Rd. NW4 —7C 26
Park Rd. NW8 & NW1
           —3C 60 (1C 138)
Park Rd. NW9 —7K 25
Park Rd. NW10 —1A 58
Park Rd. SE25 —4E 124

Park Rd. SW19 —6B 108
Park Rd. W4 —7J 73
Park Rd. W7 —7K 55
Park Rd. Beck —7B 112
Park Rd. Brom —1K 127
Park Rd. Chst —6F 115
Park Rd. Felt —4B 102
Park Rd. Hack —2F 133
Park Rd. Hamp —4F 103
Park Rd. Hamp W —1C 118
Park Rd. H Bar —4C 4
Park Rd. Houn —5F 87
Park Rd. Ilf —3H 51
Park Rd. Iswth —1B 88
Park Rd. King T —5F 105
Park Rd. New Bar —4G 5
Park Rd. N Mald —4K 119
Park Rd. Rich —6F 89
Park Rd. Surb —5F 119
Park Rd. Sutt —6G 131
Park Rd. Tedd —6K 103
Park Rd. Twic —6G 88
Park Rd. Wall —5F 133
Park Rd. Wemb —6E 40
Park Rd. E. W3 —2J 73
Park Rd. Ho. King T —7G 105
Park Rd. Ind. Est. Swan —3A 118
Park Rd. N. W3 —2H 73
Park Rd. N. W4 —5K 73
Park Row. SE10 —5F 81
Park Royal Metro Cen. NW10
           —4H 57
Park Royal Rd. NW10 & W3 —3J 57
Parkshot. Rich —4D 88
Parkside. N3 —1K 27
Parkside. NW2 —3C 42
Parkside. NW7 —6H 13
Parkside. SW19 —3F 107
Parkside. W5 —7E 56
Parkside. Buck H —2E 20
Parkside. Hamp —5H 103
Parkside. Sidc —2B 116
Parkside. Sutt —6G 131
Parkside Av. SW19 —5F 107
Parkside Av. Bexh —2K 101
Parkside Av. Brom —4C 128
Parkside Av. Romf —3K 37
Parkside Cres. N7 —3A 46
Parkside Cres. Surb —6J 119
Parkside Cross. Bexh —2K 101
Parkside Dri. Edgw —3B 12
Parkside Est. E9 —1K 63
Parkside Gdns. SW19 —4F 107
Parkside Gdns. Barn —1J 15
Parkside Ho. Dag —3J 53
Parkside Rd. SW11 —1E 92
Parkside Rd. Belv —4H 85
Parkside Rd. Houn —5F 87
Parkside Ter. N18 —4J 17
Parkside Way. Harr —4F 23
Park Sq. E. NW1 —4F 61 (3J 139)
Park Sq. M. NW1 —4F 61 (4J 139)
(off Up. Harley St.)
Park Sq. W. NW1 —4F 61 (3J 139)
Parkstead Rd. SW15 —5C 90
Parkstone Av. N18 —6A 18
Parkstone Rd. E17 —3E 32
Parkstone Rd. SE15 —2G 95
Park St. SE1 —1C 78 (2L 147)
Park St. W1 —7E 60 (8G 139)
Park St. Croy —2C 134
Park St. Tedd —6J 103
Park Ter. Enf —1F 9
Park Ter. Wor Pk —1C 130
Park, The. N6 —6E 28
Park, The. NW11 —1K 43
Park, The. SE19 —7E 110
Park, The. SE23 —1J 111

Park, The. W5 —1D 72
Park, The. Cars —6D 132
Park, The. Sidc —5A 116
Parkthorne Clo. Harr —6F 23
Parkthorne Dri. Harr —6E 22
Parkthorne Rd. SW12 —7H 93
Park Towers. W2 —7A 60
Park View. N5 —4C 46
Park View. N21 —7E 6
Park View. W3 —5J 57
Parkview. Eri —3D 84
Park View. N Mald —3B 120
Park View. Pinn —1D 22
Park View. Romf —6D 36
Park View. Wemb —5H 41
Park View Ct. SE20 —1H 125
Parkview Ct. SW18 —5J 91
Parkview Ct. Har W —7D 10
Park View Cres. N11 —4A 16
Park View Est. E2 —2K 63
Park View Gdns. N22 —1A 30
Park View Gdns. NW4 —5E 26
Park View Gdns. Bark —2J 67
Park View Gdns. Ilf —4D 34
Park View Ho. E4 —5H 19
Parkview Ho. N9 —7C 8
Park View Ho. SE24 —6B 94
(off Hurst St.)
Park View Mans. N4 —7B 30
Park View Rd. N3 —1K 27
Park View Rd. N17 —3G 31
Park View Rd. NW10 —4B 42
Parkview Rd. SE9 —1F 115
Park View Rd. W5 —5E 56
Park View Rd. Croy —1G 135
Park View Rd. Pinn —2K 21
Park View Rd. Well —3C 100
Park Village E. NW1 —2F 61
Park Village W. NW1 —2F 61
Park Vs. Romf —6D 36
Parkville Rd. SW6 —7H 75
Park Vista. SE10 —6F 81
Park Wlk. N6 —7E 28
Park Wlk. SW10 —6A 76
Park Wlk. Barn —3G 5
Parkway. N14 —2D 16
Park Way. N20 —4J 15
Parkway. NW1 —1F 61
Park Way. NW11 —5G 27
Parkway. SW20 —4F 121
Park Way. Edgw —1H 25
Park Way. Enf —2F 7
Parkway. Eri —3E 84
Park Way. Felt —7A 86
Park Way. Ilf —3K 51
Parkway. New Ad —7D 136
Park Way. Wfd G —5F 21
Parkway, The. Hay & N'holt —1A 70
Parkway, The. Houn & S'hall —1A 86
Parkway Trading Est. Houn —6A 70
Park W. Pl. W2 —6C 60 (7D 138)
Parkwood. N20 —3J 15
Parkwood. Beck —7C 112
Parkwood M. N6 —6F 29
Parkwood Rd. SW19 —5H 107
Park Wood Rd. Bex —7F 101
Parkwood Rd. Iswth —1K 87
Parliament Ct. E1 —5E 62 (6D 142)
(off Artillery La.)
Parliament Hill. NW3 —4C 44
Parliament Sq. SW1
           —2J 77 (5C 146)
Parliament St. SW1 —2J 77 (4C 146)
Parluke Clo. E17 —5B 82
Parma Cres. SW11 —4D 92
Parmiter St. E2 —2H 63
Parndon Ho. Lou —1H 21
Parnell Clo. Edgw —4C 12

Parnell Ho. WC1 —6H 61 (7B 140)
Parnell Rd. E3 —1B 64
(in two parts)
Parnham St. E14 —6A 64
Parolles Rd. N19 —1G 45
Paroma Rd. Belv —3G 85
Parr Clo. N9 —4C 18
Parr Ct. Felt —4A 102
Parr Rd. E6 —1B 66
Parr Rd. Stan —1E 24
Parrs Clo. S Croy —7D 134
Parrs Pl. Hamp —7E 102
Parr St. N1 —2D 62
Parry Av. E6 —6D 66
Parry Clo. Eps —7D 130
Parry Rd. SE18 —4F 83
Parry Rd. SE25 —3E 124
Parry Rd. W10 —3G 59
Parry St. SW8 —6J 77
Parsifal Rd. NW6 —5J 43
Parsley Gdns. Croy —1K 135
Parsloes Av. Dag —4D 52
Parsonage Gdns. Enf —2H 7
Parsonage La. Enf —2H 7
Parsonage La. Sidc —4F 117
Parsonage Manorway. Belv —6G 85
Parsonage St. E14 —4E 80
Parson's Cres. Edgw —3B 12
Parson's Grn. SW6 —1J 91
Parson's Grn. La. SW6 —1J 91
Parson's Gro. Edgw —3B 12
Parsons Mead. Croy —1B 134
Parson's Rd. E13 —2A 66
Parson St. NW4 —4E 26
Parthenia Rd. SW6 —1J 91
Partingdale La. NW7 —5A 14
Partington Clo. N19 —1H 45
Partridge Clo. E16 —5B 66
Partridge Clo. Bush —1B 10
Partridge Ct. EC1 —4B 62 (3J 141)
(off Cyprus St.)
Partridge Grn. SE9 —3E 114
Partridge Rd. Hamp —6D 102
Partridge Rd. Sidc —4J 115
Partridge Sq. E6 —5C 66
Partridge Way. N22 —1J 29
Parvin St. SW8 —1H 93
Pascal St. SW8 —7H 77
Pascoe Rd. SE13 —5F 97
Pasley Clo. SE17 —5C 78
Pasquier Rd. E17 —3A 32
Passage, The. W6 —3E 74
Passage, The. Rich —5E 88
Passey Pl. SE9 —6D 98
Passfield Dri. E14 —5D 64
Passfield Path. SE28 —7B 68
Passfields. SE6 —3E 112
Passing All. EC1 —5B 62 (5K 141)
(off St. John St.)
Passingham Ho. Houn —6E 70
Passmore Gdns. N11 —6C 16
Passmore St. SW1 —5E 76
Pasteur Clo. NW9 —2A 26
Pasteur Gdns. N18 —5G 17
Paston Clo. E5 —3K 47
Paston Cres. SE12 —7K 97
Pastor St. N6 —6G 29
Pastor St. SE11 —4B 78 (8K 147)
Pasture Clo. Wemb —3B 40
Pasture Rd. SE6 —1H 113
Pasture Rd. Dag —4F 53
Pasture Rd. Wemb —2B 40
Pastures, The. N20 —1C 14
Patcham Ter. SW8 —1F 93
Pathway, Ct. SE15 —6E 78
(off Newent Clo.)
Paternoster Row. EC4
           —6C 62 (8L 141)

Paternoster Sq. EC4
           —6B 62 (8K 141)
Pater St. W8 —3J 75
Pathfield Rd. SW16 —6H 109
Path, The. SW19 —1K 121
Patience Rd. SW11 —2C 92
Patio Clo. SW4 —6H 93
Patmore Est. SW8 —1G 93
Patmore Ho. N16 —5E 46
Patmore Lodge. N6 —4D 28
Patmore St. SW8 —1G 93
Patmos Rd. SW9 —7B 78
Paton Clo. E3 —3C 64
Paton Ho. SW9 —2K 93
(off Stockwell Rd.)
Paton St. EC1 —3C 62 (2L 141)
Patricia Ct. Chst —1H 129
Patricia Ct. Well —7B 84
Patrick Connolly Gdns. E3 —3D 64
Patrick Pas. SW11 —2C 92
Patrick Rd. E13 —3A 66
Patriot Sq. E2 —2H 63
Patrol Pl. SE6 —6D 96
Patshull Pl. NW5 —6G 45
Patshull Rd. NW5 —6G 45
Patten All. Rich —5D 88
Pattenden Rd. SE6 —1B 112
Patten Ho. N4 —1C 46
Patten St. SW18 —7C 92
Patterdale Clo. Brom —6H 113
Patterdale Rd. SE15 —7J 79
Patterson Ct. SE19 —7F 111
Patterson Rd. SE19 —6F 111
Pattinson Point. E16 —5J 65
(off File Rd.)
Pattison Rd. NW2 —3J 43
Pattison Wlk. SE18 —5G 83
Paul Byrne Ho. N2 —3A 28
Paul Clo. E15 —1G 65
Paul Ct. Romf —6J 37
Paulet Rd. SE5 —2B 94
Paul Gdns. Croy —3F 135
Paulhan Rd. Harr —4D 24
Paulin Dri. N21 —7F 7
Pauline Cres. Twic —1G 103
Paul Julius Clo. E14 —7F 65
Paul Robeson Clo. E6 —3E 66
Paul St. E15 —1G 65
Paul St. EC2 —4D 62 (4C 142)
Paul's Wlk. EC4 —7C 62 (9K 141)
Paultons Sq. SW3 —6B 76
Paultons St. SW3 —6B 76
Pauntley St. N19 —1G 45
Paved Ct. Rich —5D 88
Paveley Dri. SW11 —7C 76
Paveley St. NW8 —3C 60 (2D 138)
Pavement M. Romf —7D 36
Pavement Sq. Croy —1G 135
Pavement, The. SW4 —4G 93
Pavement, The. W5 —3E 72
Pavet Clo. Dag —6H 53
Pavilion Lodge. Harr —1H 39
Pavilion M. N3 —2J 27
Pavilion Rd. Ilf —7D 34
Pavilion Rd. SW1 —3D 76 (7F 144)
Pavilion Way. Edgw —7C 12
Pavilion Way. Ruis —2A 38
Pawleyne Clo. SE20 —7J 111
Pawsey Clo. E13 —1K 65
Pawsons Rd. Croy —6C 124
Paxfold. Stan —6J 11
Paxford Rd. Wemb —2B 40
Paxton Pl. SE27 —4E 110
Paxton Rd. N17 —7B 18
Paxton Rd. SE23 —3A 112
Paxton Rd. W4 —6A 74
Paxton Rd. Brom —7J 113

248

Pinewood Gro. W5 —6C 56
Pinewood Lodge. Bush —1C 10
Pinewood Rd. SE2 —6D 84
Pinewood Rd. Brom —4J 127
Pinewood Rd. Felt —3A 102
Pinfold Rd. SW16 —4J 109
Pinkerton Pl. SW16 —4H 109
Pinkham Mans. W4 —5G 73
Pinkham Way. N11 —7K 15
Pinley Gdns. Dag —1B 68
Pinnacle Hill. Bexh —4H 101
Pinnacle Hill N. Bexh —4H 101
Pinnacle Pl. Stan —4G 11
Pinnell Rd. SE9 —4B 98
Pinner Ct. Pinn —4E 22
Pinner Grn. Pinn —2A 22
Pinner Hill. Pinn —1A 22
Pinner Hill. Pinn —1A 22
Pinner Hill Farm. Pinn —1A 22
Pinner Hill Rd. Pinn —1A 22
Pinner Pk. Av. Harr —3F 23
Pinner Pk. Gdns. Harr —2G 23
Pinner Rd. Harr —4E 22
Pinner Rd. Pinn —4D 22
Pinner View. Harr —4E 23
Pintail Clo. E6 —5C 66
Pintail Rd. Wfd G —7E 20
Pintail Way. Hay —5B 54
Pinter Ho. SW9 —2J 93
(off Grantham Rd.)
Pinto Way. SE3 —4K 97
Pioneer Pl. Croy —7C 136
Pioneer Way. W12 —6D 58
Piper Clo. N7 —5K 45
Piper Rd. King T —3G 119
Piper's Gdns. Croy —7A 126
Pipers Grn. NW9 —5J 25
Pipers Grn. La. Edgw —3K 11
(in two parts)
Pippenhall. Rd. Cars —6C 122
Pippin Clo. Croy —1B 136
Piquet Rd. SE20 —2J 125
Pirbright Cres. New Ad —6E 136
Pirbright Rd. SW18 —1H 107
Pirie Clo. SE5 —3D 94
Pirie St. E16 —1K 81
Pitcairn Clo. Romf —4G 37
Pitcairn Ho. E9 —7J 47
Pitcairn Rd. Mitc —7D 108
Pitchford St. E15 —7F 49
Pitfield Cres. SE28 —1A 84
Pitfield Est. N1 —3E 62 (1C 142)
Pitfield St. N1 —3E 62 (2C 142)
Pitfield Way. NW10 —6J 41
Pitfield Way. Enf —1D 8
Pitfold Clo. SE12 —6K 97
Pitfold Rd. SE12 —6J 97
Pitlake. Croy —2B 134
Pitman St. SE5 —7C 78
Pitsea Pl. E1 —6K 63
Pitsea St. E1 —6K 63
Pitshanger La. W5 —4B 56
Pitt Cres. SW19 —4K 107
Pittman Gdns. Ilf —5G 51
Pitt Rd. Harr —2G 39
Pitt Rd. T Hth —5C 124
Place Farm Av. Orp —7H 129
Plaisterers Highwalk. EC2
(off Noble St.) —5C 62 (6L 141)

Plaistow Gro. E15 —1H 65
Plaistow Gro. Brom —7K 113
Plaistow La. Brom —7J 113
(in two parts)
Plaistow Pk. Rd. E13 —2K 65
Plaistow Rd. E15 & E13 —1H 65
Plaistow Wharf. E16 —1J 81
Plane Ho. Short —2G 127
Plane St. SE26 —3H 111
Planetree Ct. W6 —4F 75
(off Brook Grn.)
Plane Tree Wlk. SE19 —6E 110
Plantagenet Clo. Wor Pk —4A 130
Plantagenet Gdns. Romf —7D 36
Plantagenet Pl. Romf —7D 36
Plantagenet Rd. Barn —4F 5
Plantain Pl. SE1 —2D 78 (4A 148)
Plantation Ho. EC3 —7E 62 (9C 142)
Plantation Pl. SW1 —2D 78
Plantation, The. SE3 —2J 97
Plasel Ct. E13 —1K 65
(off Pawsey Clo.)
Plashet Gro. E6 —1A 66
Plashet Rd. E13 —1J 65
Plassy Rd. SE6 —7D 96
Platina St. EC2 —4D 62 (3B 142)
(off Tabernacle St.)
Plato Rd. SW2 —4J 93
Platt's La. NW3 —4J 43
Platts Rd. Enf —1D 8
Platt St. NW1 —2H 61
Plawsfield Rd. Beck —1K 125
Plaxtol Clo. Brom —1A 128
Plaxtol Rd. Eri —7G 85
Plaxton Ct. E11 —3H 49
Playfair St. W6 —5E 74
Playfield Av. Romf —1J 37
Playfield Cres. SE22 —5F 95
Playfield Rd. Edgw —2J 25
Playford Rd. N4 —2K 45
(in two parts)
Playgreen Way. SE6 —3C 112
Playground Clo. Beck —2K 125
Playhouse Yd. EC4 —6B 62 (8J 141)
Plaza, The. W1 —6G 61 (7M 139)
Pleasance Rd. SW15 —5D 90
Pleasance, The. SW15 —4D 90
Pleasant Gro. Croy —3B 136
Pleasant Pl. N1 —7B 46
Pleasant Pl. S Harr —1H 39
Pleasant Row. NW1 —1F 61
Pleasant View. Eri —5K 85
Pleasant Way. Wemb —2C 56
Plender Pl. NW1 —1G 61
(off Plender St.)
Plender St. NW1 —1G 61
Pleshey Rd. N7 —4H 45
Plesman Way. Wall —7J 133
Plevna Cres. N15 —6E 30
Plevna Rd. N9 —3B 18
Plevna St. E14 —3E 80
Pleydell Av. SE19 —7F 111
Pleydell Av. W6 —4B 74
Pleydell Ct. EC4 —6A 62 (8H 141)
(off Mitre Ct.)
Pleydell Est. EC1 —3C 62 (2M 141)
(off Lever St.)
Pleydell St. EC4 —6A 62 (8H 141)
(off Bouverie St.)
Plimsoll Clo. E14 —6D 64
Plimsoll Rd. N4 —3A 46
Plough Ct. EC3 —7D 62 (9B 142)
Plough La. SE22 —6F 95
Plough La. SW19 & SW17 —5K 107
Plough La. Purl —7K 133
Plough La. Wall —4J 133
Plough La. Clo. Wall —5J 133
Ploughmans Clo. NW1 —1H 61

Ploughmans End. Iswth —5H 87
Plough Pl. EC4 —6A 62 (7H 141)
Plough Rd. SW11 —3B 92
Plough Rd. Eps —7A 130
Plough St. E1 —6G 63
Plough Ter. SW11 —4B 92
Plough Way. SE16 —4K 79
Plough Yd. EC2 —4E 62 (4D 142)
Plover Way. SE16 —3A 80
Plover Way. Hay —6B 54
Plowden Bldgs. EC4
(off Temple) —7A 62 (9G 141)
Plowman Clo. N18 —5J 17
Plowman Way. Dag —1C 52
Plumber's Row. E1 —5G 63
Plumbridge St. SE10 —1E 95
Plum Garth. Bren —4D 72
Plum La. SE18 —7F 83
Plummer La. Mitc —2D 122
Plummer Rd. SW4 —7H 93
Plumpton Clo. N'holt —6E 38
Plumpton Way. Cars —3C 132
Plums Clo. E14 —6D 64
Plumstead Comn. Rd. SE18 —6F 83
Plumstead High St. SE18 —4H 83
Plumstead Rd. SE18 —4F 83
Plumtree Clo. Dag —6H 53
Plumtree Clo. Wall —7H 133
Plumtree Ct. EC4 —6B 62 (7J 141)
Plymouth Ho. Bark —7A 52
(off Keir Hardie Way)
Plymouth Rd. E16 —5J 65
Plymouth Rd. Brom —1K 127
Plymouth Wharf. E14 —4F 81
Plympton Av. NW6 —7H 43
Plympton Clo. Belv —3E 84
Plympton Pl. NW8 —4C 60 (4C 138)
Plympton Rd. NW6 —7H 43
Plympton St. NW8 —4C 60 (4C 138)
Plymstock Rd. Well —7C 84
Pocklington Clo. NW9 —2A 26
Pocklington Clo. W12 —3C 74
(off Goldhawk Rd.)
Pocock St. SE1 —2B 78 (4J 147)
Podmore Rd. SW18 —4A 92
Poet's Rd. N5 —5D 46
Poets Way. Harr —4J 23
Pointalls Clo. N3 —2A 28
Point Clo. SE10 —1E 95
Pointer Clo. SE28 —6D 68
Pointers Clo. E14 —5D 80
Pointers Cotts. Rich —2C 104
Point Hill. SE10 —1E 96
Point Pleasant. SW18 —4J 91
Point Ter. E7 —5K 49
(off Claremont Rd.)
Poland M. W1 —6G 61
Poland St. W1 —6G 61 (7M 139)
Polebrook Rd. SE3 —3A 98
Pole Cat Aln. Brom —2H 137
Polecroft La. SE6 —2B 112
Pole Hill Rd. E4 —7K 9
Polesden Gdns. SW20 —2D 120
Polesworth Rd. Dag —7D 52
Police Sta. La. Bush —1A 10
Pollard Clo. E16 —7J 65
Pollard Clo. N7 —4K 45
Pollard Rd. N20 —2H 15
Pollard Rd. Mord —5B 122
Pollard Row. E2 —3G 63
Pollards Cres. SW16 —3J 123
Pollards Hill E. SW16 —3K 123
Pollards Hill N. SW16 —3J 123
Pollards Hill S. SW16 —3J 123
Pollards Hill W. SW16 —3K 123
Pollards Wood Rd. SW16 —3J 123
Pollard Wlk. Sidc —6C 116

Pollen St. W1 —6F 61 (8L 139)
Pollitt Dri. NW8 —4B 60 (3B 138)
Polperro Clo. Orp —6K 129
Polsted Rd. SE6 —7B 96
Polthorne Gro. SE18 —4H 83
Polworth Rd. SW16 —5J 109
Polygon Rd. NW1 —2H 61
Polygon, The. SW4 —4G 93
Polytechnic St. SE18 —4E 82
Pomell Way. E1 —6F 63 (7F 142)
Pomeroy St. SE14 —7J 79
Pomfret Rd. SE5 —3C 94
Pond Clo. SE3 —2J 97
Pond Cottage La. W Wick —1C 136
Pond Cotts. SE21 —1E 110
Pond Hill Gdns. Sutt —6G 131
Pond Mead. SE22 —6D 94
Pond Path. Chst —6F 115
Pond Pl. SW3 —4C 76 (9C 144)
Pond Rd. E15 —2G 65
Pond Rd. SE3 —2H 97
Pond Sq. N6 —1E 44
Pond St. NW3 —5C 44
Pond Way. Tedd —6C 104
Pondwood Rise. Orp —7J 129
Ponler St. E1 —6H 63
Ponsard Rd. NW10 —3D 58
Ponsford St. E9 —6J 47
Ponsonby Pl. SW1 —5H 77
Ponsonby Rd. SW15 —7D 90
Ponsonby Ter. SW1 —5H 77
Pontefract Rd. Brom —5H 113
Ponton Rd. SW8 —7H 77
Pont St. SW1 —3D 76 (7E 144)
Pont St. M. SW1 —3D 76 (7E 144)
Pontypool Pl. SE1 —2B 78 (4J 147)
Pool Clo. Beck —5C 112
Pool Ct. SE6 —2C 112
Poole Ct. Houn —2C 86
Poole Ct. Rd. Houn —2C 86
Poole Rd. E9 —6K 47
Poole Rd. Eps —7A 130
Pooles Bldgs. WC1 —4A 62 (4G 141)
(off Mt. Pleasant)
Pooles Cotts. Rich —2D 104
Pooles La. SW10 —7A 76
Pooles La. Dag —2E 68
Pooles Pk. N4 —2A 46
Poole St. N1 —1D 62
Poolmans St. SE16 —2K 79
Pool Rd. Harr —7H 23
Poolsford Rd. NW9 —4A 26
Poonah St. E1 —6J 63
Pope Clo. SW19 —6B 108
Pope Rd. Brom —5B 128
Popes Av. Twic —2J 103
Popes Ct. Twic —2J 103
Popes Dri. N3 —1J 27
Popes Gro. Croy —3B 136
Popes Gro. Twic —2K 103
Pope's Head All. EC3
—6D 62 (8B 142)
Popes La. W5 —3D 72
Pope's Rd. SW9 —3A 94
Pope St. SE1 —2E 78 (5D 148)
Popham Clo. Felt —3D 102
Popham Gdns. Rich —3G 89
Popham Rd. N1 —1C 62
Popham St. N1 —1B 62
(in two parts)
Pop-In Commercial Cen. Wemb
—5H 41

Popinjays Row. Cheam —5F 131
(off Netley Clo.)
Poplar Av. Mitc —1D 122
Poplar Av. S'hall —3F 71
Poplar Bath St. E14 —6D 64
Poplar Bus. Pk. E14 —7E 64
Poplar Clo. Pinn —1B 22
Poplar Ct. SW19 —5J 107
Poplar Ct. N'holt —2A 54
Poplar Gdns. SE28 —7C 68
Poplar Gdns. N Mald —2K 119
Poplar Gro. N11 —6K 15
Poplar Gro. W6 —2E 74
Poplar Gro. N Mald —2K 119
Poplar Gro. Wemb —3J 41
Poplar High St. E14 —7D 64
Poplar M. W12 —1E 74
(off Uxbridge Rd.)
Poplar Mt. Belv —4H 85
Poplar Pl. SE28 —7C 68
Poplar Pl. W2 —7K 59
Poplar Rd. SE24 —4C 94
Poplar Rd. SW19 —2J 121
Poplar Rd. Sutt —1H 131
Poplar Rd. S. SW19 —3J 121
Poplars Av. NW2 —6E 42
Poplars Rd. E17 —6D 32
Poplars, The. N14 —5A 6
Poplar St. Romf —4J 37
Poplar View. Wemb —2D 40
Poplar Wlk. SE24 —4C 94
Poplar Wlk. Croy —1C 134
Poplar Way. Ilf —4G 35
Poppins Ct. EC4 —6B 62 (8J 141)
Poppleton Rd. E11 —6G 33
Poppy Clo. Wall —1E 132
Poppy La. Croy —7J 125
Porchester Clo. SE5 —4D 94
Porchester Gdns. W2 —7K 59
Porchester Gdns. M. W2 —6K 59
Porchester Mead. Beck —6C 112
Porchester Pl. W2 —6K 59
Porchester Rd. W2 —6C 60 (8D 138)
Porchester Rd. King T —2H 119
Porchester Sq. W2 —6K 59
Porchester Ter. W2 —7A 60
Porchester Ter. Gdns. M. W2
—6K 59
Porchester Ter. N. W2 —6K 59
Porch Way. N20 —3J 15
Porcupine Clo. SE9 —2C 114
Porden Rd. SW2 —4K 93
Porlock Av. Harr —1G 39
Porlock Ho. SE26 —3G 111
Porlock Rd. W10 —4F 59
Porlock Rd. Enf —7A 8
Porlock St. SE1 —2D 78 (4B 148)
Porlock St. SW1 —5D 50 (5F 138)
Porrington Clo. Chst —1E 128
Porson Ct. SE13 —3D 96
Portal Clo. SE27 —3A 110
Portbury Clo. SE15 —1G 95
Port Cres. E13 —4K 65
Portcullis Lodge Rd. Enf —3J 7
Portelet Rd. E1 —3K 63
Porten Rd. W14 —3G 75
Porter Rd. E6 —6D 66
Porters Av. Dag —6B 52
Porter St. SE1 —1C 78 (2M 147)
Porter St. W1 —5D 60 (5F 138)
Porters Wlk. E1 —7H 63
(off Pennington St.)
Porters & Walters Almshouses. N22
(off Nightingale Rd.) —7E 16
Porteus Rd. W2 —5A 60 (5A 138)
Portgate Clo. W9 —4H 59
Porthcawe Rd. SE26 —4A 112

Porthkerry Av. Well —4A **100**
Portia Ct. SE11 —5B 78
(off Opal St.)
Portia Ct. Bark —7A **52**
Portia Way. E3 —4B **64**
Porticos, The. SW3 —6B 76
(off Kings Rd.)
Portinscale Rd. SW15 —5G **91**
Portland Av. N16 —1F **47**
Portland Av. N Mald —7B **120**
Portland Av. Sidc —6A **100**
Portland Clo. Romf —5E **36**
Portland Cres. SE9 —2C **114**
Portland Cres. Gnfd —4F **55**
Portland Cres. Stan —2D **24**
Portland Dri. Enf —1K **7**
Portland Gdns. N4 —6B **30**
Portland Gdns. Romf —5D **36**
Portland Gro. SW8 —1K **93**
Portland Ho. SE26 61 (8M 139)
(off Livonia St.)
Portland Pl. W1 —4F **61** (4J **139**)
Portland Rise. N4 —1B **46**
Portland Rise. Est. N4 —1C **46**
Portland Rd. N15 —4F **31**
Portland Rd. SE9 —2C **114**
Portland Rd. SE25 —4G **125**
Portland Rd. W11 —7G **59**
Portland Rd. Brom —4A **114**
Portland Rd. King T —3E **118**
Portland Rd. Mitc —2C **122**
Portland Rd. S'hall —3D **70**
Portland Sq. E1 —1H **79**
Portland St. SE17 —5D **78**
Portland Ter. Rich —4D **88**
Portland Wlk. SE17 —6D **78**
Portman Av. SW14 —3K **89**
Portman Bldgs. NW1
(off Broadley Ter.) —4C 60 (4D 138)
Portman Clo. W1 —6E **60** (7F **139**)
Portman Clo. Bex —1K **117**
Portman Clo. Bexh —3E **100**
Portman Dri. Wfd G —2B **34**
Portman Gdns. NW9 —2K **25**
Portman M. S. W1 —6E **60** (8G **139**)
Portman Pl. E2 —3J **63**
Portman Rd. King T —2F **119**
Portman Sq. W1 —6E **60** (7G **139**)
Portman St. W1 —6E **60** (8G **139**)
Portmeadow Wlk. SE2 —2D **84**
Portmeers Clo. E17 —6B **32**
Portnall Rd. W9 —2H **59**
Portnoi Clo. Romf —2K **37**
Portobello Ct. W11 —6H **59**
Portobello M. W11 —7J **59**
Portobello Rd. W10 —5G **59**
Portobello Rd. W11 —6H **59**
Portpool La. EC1 —5A **62** (5G **141**)
Portree Clo. N22 —7E **16**
Portree St. E14 —6F **65**
Portsdown. Edgw —5B **12**
Portsdown Av. NW11 —6H **27**
Portsdown M. NW11 —6H **27**
Portsea M. W2 —6C 60 (8D 138)
(off Portsea Pl.)
Portsea Pl. W2 —6C **60** (8D **138**)
Portslade Rd. SW8 —2G **93**
Portsmouth Av. Th Dit —7A **118**
Portsmouth Bldgs. SE1
(off Swan Mead) —3E 78 (7C 148)
Portsmouth Rd. SW15 —7D **90**
Portsmouth Rd. King T —4D **118**
Portsmouth St. WC2
——6K **61** (8E **140**)
Portsoken St. E1 —7F **63** (9E **142**)
Portswood Pk. SW15 —6B **90**
Portugal Gdns. Twic —2G **103**
Portugal St. WC2 —6K **61** (8E **140**)

Portway. E15 —1H **65**
Portway Gdns. SE18 —7B **82**
Postern Grn. Enf —3F **7**
Postern, The. EC2 —5C 62 (6M 141)
(off Barbican)
Post La. Twic —1H **103**
Postmill Clo. Croy —3J **135**
Post Office App. E7 —5K **49**
Post Office Ct. EC3 —6D 62 (8B 142)
(off Barbican)
Post Office Way. SW8 —6H **77**
Postway M. Ilf —3F **51**
(in two parts)
Potier St. SE1 —3D **78** (7B **148**)
Potter Clo. Mitc —2F **123**
Potteries, The. Barn —5D **4**
Potterne Clo. SW19 —7F **91**
Potters Clo. Croy —1A **136**
Pottersfield. Enf —4K 7
(off Lincoln Rd.)
Potters Fields. SE1 —1E **78** (3D **148**)
Potters Gro. N Mald —4J **119**
Potters Heights Clo. Pinn —1A **22**
Potter's La. SW16 —6H **109**
Potters La. Barn —4D **4**
Potters Rd. SW6 —2A **92**
Potter's Rd. Barn —4E **4**
Potter St. Pinn —1A **22**
Pottery La. W11 —7G **59**
Pottery Rd. Bex —2J **117**
Pottery Rd. Bren —6E **72**
Pottery St. SE16 —2H **79**
Pott St. E2 —3H **63**
Poulett Gdns. Twic —1A **104**
Poulett Rd. E6 —2D **66**
Poulner Way. SE15 —7F **79**
Poulton Av. Sutt —3B **132**
Poulton Clo. E8 —6H **47**
Poultry. EC2 —6D **62** (8A **142**)
Pound Clo. Surb —7C **118**
Pound Grn. Bex —7G **101**
Pound La. NW10 —6C **42**
Pound Pk. Rd. SE7 —4B **82**
Pound Pl. SE9 —6E **98**
Pound St. Cars —5D **132**
Pountney Rd. SW11 —3E **92**
Poverest Rd. Orp —5K **129**
Powder Mill La. Twic —1D **102**
Powell Clo. Edgw —6A **12**
Powell Clo. Wall —7J **133**
Powell Ct. E17 —3D **32**
Powell Gdns. Dag —4G **53**
Powell Rd. E5 —3H **47**
Powell Rd. Buck H —1F **21**
Powell's Wlk. W4 —6A **74**
Power Rd. W4 —4G **73**
Powers Ct. Twic —7D **88**
Powerscroft Rd. E5 —4J **47**
Powerscroft Rd. Sidc —6C **116**
Powis Gdns. NW11 —7H **27**
Powis Gdns. W11 —6H **59**
Powis M. W11 —6H **59**
Powis Pl. WC1 —4J **61** (4D **140**)
Powis Rd. E3 —3D **64**
Powis Sq. W11 —6H **59**
Powis St. SE18 —3E **82**
Powis Ter. W11 —6H **59**
Powlett Pl. NW1 —7E **44**
Pownall Gdns. Houn —4F **87**
Pownall Rd. E8 —1G **63**
Pownall Rd. Houn —4F **87**
Powster Rd. Brom —5J **113**
Powys Clo. Bexh —6D **84**
Powys Ct. N11 —5D **16**
Powys La. N14 & N13 —4D **16**
Poxon Ct. EC4 —6B **62** (8K **141**)
Poynders Ct. SW4 —6G **93**
Poynders Gdns. SW4 —7G **93**

Poynders Rd. SW4 —6G **93**
Poynings Rd. N19 —3G **45**
Poynings Way. N12 —5D **14**
Poyntell Cres. Chst —1H **129**
Poynter Ho. W11 —1F 75
(off Queensdale Cres.)
Poynter Rd. Enf —5B **8**
Poynton Rd. N17 —2G **31**
Poyntz Rd. SW11 —2D **92**
Poyser St. E2 —2H **63**
Praed M. W2 —6B **60** (7B **138**)
Praed St. W2 —6B **60** (8A **138**)
Pragel St. E13 —2A **66**
Pragnell Rd. SE12 —2K **113**
Prague Pl. SW2 —5J **93**
Prah Rd. N4 —2A **46**
Prairie St. SW8 —2E **92**
Pratt M. NW1 —1G **61**
Pratt Pas. King T —2E **118**
Pratt St. NW1 —1G **61**
Pratt Wlk. SE11 —4K **77** (8F **146**)
Prayle Gro. Nw2 —1F **43**
Prebend Gdns. W6 & W4 —3B **74**
(in two parts)
Prebend Mans. W4 —4B 74
(off Chiswick High Rd.)
Prebend St. N1 —1C **62**
Premier Corner. W9 —2H **59**
Premier Ct. Enf —1D **8**
Premier Pl. SW15 —4G **91**
Prendergast Rd. SE3 —3G **97**
Prentice Ct. SW19 —5H **107**
Prentis Rd. SW16 —4H **109**
Prentiss Ct. SE7 —4B **82**
Presburg Rd. N Mald —5A **120**
Presburg St. E5 —3K **47**
Prescelly Pl. Edgw —1F **25**
Prescot St. E1 —7F **63** (9F **142**)
Prescott Av. Orp —6F **129**
Prescott Clo. SW16 —7J **109**
Prescott Pl. SW4 —3H **93**
Presentation M. SW2 —1K **109**
Preshaw Cres. Mitc —3C **122**
President Dri. E1 —1H **79**
President St. EC1 —3C 62 (1L 141)
(off Central St.)
Press Ho. NW10 —3K **41**
Press Rd. NW10 —3K **41**
Prestbury Rd. E7 —7A **50**
Prestbury Sq. SE9 —4D **114**
Prestbury Sq. SE12 —4D **114**
Prested Rd. SW11 —4C **92**
Preston Av. E4 —6A **20**
Preston Clo. SE1 —4E **78** (8C **148**)
Preston Clo. Twic —3J **103**
Preston Ct. New Bar —4F **5**
Preston Ct. Sidc —4K 115
(off Crescent, The)
Preston Dri. E11 —5A **34**
Preston Dri. Bexh —1D **100**
Preston Dri. Eps —6A **130**
Preston Gdns. NW10 —6B **42**
Preston Gdns. Ilf —6C **34**
Preston Hill. Harr —7E **24**
Preston Ho. Dag —3G 53
(off Uvedale Rd.)
Preston Pl. NW2 —6C **42**
Preston Pl. Rich —5E **88**
Preston Rd. E11 —6G **33**
Preston Rd. SE19 —6B **110**
Preston Rd. SW20 —7B **106**
Preston Rd. Wemb & Harr —1E **40**
Preston's Rd. E14 —7E **64**
Prestons Rd. Brom —3J **137**
Preston Waye. Harr —1E **40**
Prestwick Clo. S'hall —5C **70**
Prestwood Av. Harr —4B **24**
Prestwood Clo. SE18 —7A **84**

Prestwood Clo. Harr —4B **24**
Prestwood Gdns. Croy —7C **124**
Prestwood St. N1 —2C **62**
Pretoria Av. E17 —4A **32**
Pretoria Clo. N17 —7A **18**
Pretoria Cres. E4 —1K **19**
Pretoria Rd. E4 —1K **19**
Pretoria Rd. E11 —1F **49**
Pretoria Rd. E16 —4H **65**
Pretoria Rd. N17 —7A **18**
Pretoria Rd. SW16 —6F **109**
Pretoria Rd. Ilf —5F **51**
Pretoria Rd. Romf —4J **37**
Pretoria Rd. N. N18 —6A **18**
Prevost Rd. N11 —2K **15**
Price Clo. NW7 —6B **14**
Price Clo. SW17 —3D **108**
Price Rd. Croy —5B **134**
Price's St. SE1 —1B **78** (3K **147**)
Price's Yd. N1 —1K **61**
Price Way. Hamp —6C **102**
Prichard Ct. N7 —5K **45**
Pricklers Hill. Barn —6E **4**
Prickley Wood. Brom —1H **137**
Priddy's Yd. Croy —2C **134**
Prideaux Pl. W3 —7K **57**
Prideaux Pl. WC1 —3K **61** (1F **140**)
Prideaux Rd. SW9 —3J **93**
Pridham Rd. T Hth —4D **124**
Priestfield Rd. SE23 —3A **112**
Priestlands Pk. Rd. Sidc —3K **115**
Priestley Clo. N16 —7F **31**
Priestley Gdns. Romf —6B **36**
Priestley Ho. Wemb —3J 41
(off Barnhill Rd.)
Priestley Rd. Mitc —2E **122**
Priestley Way. E17 —3K **31**
Priestley Way. NW2 —1C **42**
Priest Pk. Av. Harr —2E **38**
Priests Av. Romf —2K **37**
Priest's Bri. SW14 & SW15 —3A **90**
Priest's Ct. EC2 —6C 62 (7L 141)
(off Foster La.)
Prima Rd. SW9 —7A **78**
Primrose Av. Enf —1J **7**
Primrose Av. Romf —7B **36**
Primrose Clo. SE6 —5E **112**
Primrose Clo. Harr —3D **38**
Primrose Clo. Mitc —7F **123**
Primrose Gdns. NW3 —6C **44**
Primrose Gdns. Bush —1A **10**
Primrose Gdns. Ruis —5A **38**
Primrose Hill. EC4 —6A **62** (8H **141**)
Primrose Hill Rd. NW3 —7C **44**
Primrose La. Croy —1J **135**
Primrose Mans. SW11 —1E **92**
Primrose M. NW1 —7D 44
(off Sharpleshall St.)
Primrose Rd. E10 —1D **48**
Primrose Rd. E18 —2K **33**
Primrose St. EC2 —5E **62** (5C **142**)
Primrose Way. Wemb —2D **56**
Primula St. W12 —6C **58**
Prince Albert Rd. NW8 & NW1
——3C **60** (1C **138**)
Prince Arthur M. NW3 —4A **44**
Prince Arthur Rd. NW3 —5A **44**
Prince Charles Dri. NW4 —7E **26**
Prince Charles Rd. SE3 —2H **97**
Prince Charles Way. Wall —3F **133**
Prince Consort Dri. Chst —1H **129**
Prince Consort Rd. SW7 —3A **76**
Princedale Rd. W11 —1G **75**
Prince Edward Rd. E9 —6B **48**
Prince George Av. N14 —5C **6**
Prince George Rd. N16 —4E **46**
Prince George's Av. SW20 —2E **120**
Prince Georges Rd. SW19 —1B **122**

Prince Henry Rd. SE7 —7B **82**
Prince Imperial Rd. SE18 —1D **98**
Prince Imperial Rd. Chst —1F **129**
Prince John Rd. SE9 —5C **98**
Princelet St. E1 —5F **63** (5F **142**)
Prince of Orange La. SE10 —7E **80**
Prince of Wales Clo. NW4 —4E **26**
Prince of Wales Dri. SW11 & SW8
——1C **92**
Prince of Wales Mans. SW11 —1E **92**
Prince of Wales Pas. NW1
(off Hampstead Rd.) —3G 61 (2L 139)
Prince of Wales Rd. E16 —6A **66**
Prince of Wales Rd. NW5 —6E **44**
Prince of Wales Rd. SE3 —1H **97**
Prince of Wales Rd. Sutt —2B **132**
Prince of Wales Ter. W4 —5A **74**
Prince of Wales Ter. W8 —2K **75**
Prince Regent Ct. NW8 —2C 60
(off Avenue Rd.)
Prince Regent La. E13 & E16 —3K **65**
Prince Regent M. NW1
(off Hampstead Rd.) —3G 61 (2L 139)
Prince Regent Rd. Houn —3G **87**
Prince Rd. SE25 —5E **124**
Prince Rupert Rd. SE9 —4D **98**
Prince's Arc. SW1 —1G 77 (2M 145)
(off Piccadilly)
Princes Av. N3 —1J **27**
Princes Av. N10 —3F **29**
Princes Av. N13 —5F **17**
Princes Av. N22 —1H **29**
Princes Av. NW9 —4G **25**
Princes Av. W3 —3G **73**
Princes Av. Cars —7D **132**
Prince's Av. Gnfd —6F **55**
Princes Av. Orp —5J **129**
Princes Av. Wfd G —4E **20**
Princes Cir. WC2 —6J **61** (7C **140**)
Princes Clo. NW9 —4G **25**
Princes Clo. SW4 —3G **93**
Princes Clo. Edgw —5B **12**
Princes Clo. Sidc —3D **116**
Prince's Clo. Tedd —4H **103**
Princes Ct. Wemb —5E **40**
Princes Ct. Bus. Cen. E1 —7H **63**
Princes Dri. Harr —3J **23**
Prince's Gdns. SW7
(off Golders Grn. Rd.) —3B 76 (6B 144)
Princes Gdns. W3 —5G **57**
Princes Gdns. W5 —4C **56**
Prince's Ga. SW7 —2B **76** (5B **144**)
Prince's Ga. Ct. SW7
(off Duke St. Saint James's) —2B 76 (5B 144)
Prince's Ga. M. SW7
——3B **76** (6B **144**)
Princes La. N10 —3F **29**
Prince's M. W2 —7K **59**
Princes Pde. NW11 —6G **27**
(off Golders Grn. Rd.)
Princes Pk. Av. NW11 —6G **27**
Prince's Pl. SW1 —1G 77 (2M 145)
(off Duke St. Saint James's)
Princes Pl. W11 —1G **75**
Prince's Plain. Brom —7C **128**
Prince's Rise. SE13 —2E **96**
Princes Rd. N18 —4D **18**
Princes Rd. SE20 —6K **111**
Princes Rd. SW14 —3K **89**
Princes Rd. SW19 —6J **107**
Princes Rd. W13 —1B **72**
Princes Rd. Buck H —2F **21**
Princes Rd. Ilf —4H **35**
Princes Rd. Kew —1F **89**
Princes Rd. King T —7G **105**
Princes Rd. Rich —5F **89**

252

Prince's Rd. Tedd —4H 103
Princessa Ct. Enf —5J 7
Princess Alice Ho. W10 —4E 58
Princess Ct. N6 —7G 29
Princess Ct. SE16 —3B 80
Princess Cres. N4 —2B 45
Princess May Rd. N16 —4E 46
Princess M. NW3 —5B 44
Prince's Sq. W2 —7K 59
Princess Rd. NW1 —1E 60
Princess Rd. NW6 —2J 59
Princess Rd. Croy —6C 124
Princess St. SE1 —3B 78 (7K 147)
Prince's St. EC2 —6D 62 (8A 142)
Prince's St. N17 —6K 17
Princes St. W1 —6F 61 (8K 139)
Princes St. Bexh —3F 101
Princes St. Rich —4E 88
Princes St. Sutt —4B 132
Princes Ter. E13 —1K 65
Prince St. SE8 —6B 80
Princes Way. SW19 —7F 91
Princes Way. Buck H —2F 21
Princes Way. Ruis —4C 38
Princes Way. Croy —5K 133
Princes Way. W Wick —4H 137
Princethorpe Rd. SE26 —4K 111
Princeton Ct. SW15 —3F 91
Princeton M. King T —1G 119
Princeton St. WC1 —5K 61 (6E 140)
Pringle Gdns. SW16 —4G 109
Printer St. EC4 —6A 62 (7K 141)
Printing Ho. Yd. E2 —3F 63 (2D 142)
Priolo Rd. SE7 —5A 82
Prior Av. Sutt —7C 132
Prior Bolton St. N1 —6B 46
Prioress Rd. SE27 —3B 110
Prioress St. SE1 —3E 78 (7B 148)
Prior Rd. Ilf —3E 50
Priors Croft. E17 —2A 32
Priors Field. N'holt —6C 38
Priors Gdns. Ruis —5A 38
Priors Mead. Enf —1K 7
Prior St. SE10 —7E 80
Priory Av. E4 —5G 19
Priory Av. E17 —5C 32
Priory Av. N8 —4H 29
Priory Av. W4 —4A 74
Priory Av. Orp —6H 129
Priory Av. Sutt —4F 131
Priory Av. Wemb —4K 39
Priory Clo. E4 —3G 19
Priory Clo. E18 —1J 33
Priory Clo. N3 —1H 27
Priory Clo. N14 —5A 6
Priory Clo. N20 —7C 4
Priory Clo. SW19 —1K 121
Priory Clo. Beck —3A 126
Priory Clo. Chst —1D 128
Priory Clo. Hamp —7D 102
Priory Clo. Hay —7A 54
Priory Clo. Stan —3E 10
Priory Clo. Wemb —4K 39
Priory Ct. E6 —1B 66
Priory Ct. E9 —5K 47
Priory Ct. E17 —3E 32
Priory Ct. EC4 —6B 62 (8K 141)
(off Pilgrim St.)
Priory Ct. SW8 —1H 93
Priory Ct. Bush —1B 10
Priory Ct. Eps —7B 130
Priory Ct. Houn —3F 87
Priory Ct. Sutt —4G 131
Priory Ct. Wemb —2E 56
Priory Ct. Est. E17 —2B 32
Priory Cres. SE19 —7C 110
Priory Cres. Sutt —4F 131
Priory Cres. Wemb —3A 40

Priory Dri. SE2 —5D 84
Priory Dri. Stan —3E 10
Pryoryfield Dri. Edgw —4C 12
Priory Gdns. N6 —6F 29
Priory Gdns. SW13 —3B 90
Priory Gdns. W4 —4A 74
Priory Gdns. W5 —2E 56
Priory Gdns. Hamp —7D 102
Priory Gdns. Wemb —4A 40
Priory Grange. N2 —3D 28
(off Fortis Grn.)
Priory Grn. Est. N1 —2K 61
Priory Gro. SW8 —1J 93
Priory Gro. Barn —5D 4
Priory Hill. Wemb —4A 40
Priory La. SW15 —6A 90
Priory La. Rich —7G 73
Priory M. SW8 —1H 93
Priory Pk. SE3 —3H 97
Priory Pk. Rd. NW6 —1H 59
Priory Pk. Rd. Wemb —4A 40
Priory Rd. E6 —1B 66
Priory Rd. N8 —4G 29
Priory Rd. NW6 —1K 59
Priory Rd. SW19 —7B 108
Priory Rd. W4 —3K 73
Priory Rd. Bark —7H 51
Priory Rd. Croy —7A 124
Priory Rd. Hamp —7D 102
Priory Rd. Houn —5G 87
Priory Rd. Rich —6G 73
Priory Rd. Sutt —4F 131
Priory St. E3 —3D 64
Priory Ter. NW6 —1K 59
Priory, The. SE3 —4H 97
Priory, The. Croy —4A 134
Priory View. Bush —1D 10
Priory Vs. N11 —6J 15
(off Colney Hatch La.)
Priory Wlk. SW10 —5A 76
Priory Way. Harr —4F 23
Priory Way. S'hall —3B 70
Pritchard's Rd. E2 —1G 63
Priter Rd. SE16 —3G 79
Priter Way. SE16 —3G 79
Private Rd. Enf —5J 7
Probert Rd. SW2 —5A 94
Probyn Rd. SW2 —2B 110
Procter St. WC1 —5K 61 (6E 140)
Progress Bus. Pk., The. Croy
—2K 133
Progress Way. N22 —1A 30
Progress Way. Croy —2K 133
Progress Way. Enf —5B 8
Project Pk. E3 —4F 65
Promenade App. Rd. W4 —7A 74
Promenade Mans. Edgw —5B 12
Promenade, The. W4 —1A 90
Prospect Clo. SE26 —4H 111
Prospect Clo. Belv —4G 85
Prospect Clo. Houn —2D 86
Prospect Clo. Ruis —7B 22
Prospect Cotts. SW18 —4J 91
Prospect Cres. Twic —6G 87
Prospect Hill. E17 —4D 32
Prospect Ho. E17 —3E 32
(off Prospect Hill.)
Prospect Pl. E1 —1J 79
Prospect Pl. N2 —4B 28
Prospect Pl. N17 —7K 17
Prospect Pl. NW2 —3H 43
Prospect Pl. NW3 —4A 44
Prospect Pl. W4 —5K 73
Prospect Pl. Brom —3K 127
Prospect Pl. Romf —2J 37
Prospect Ring. N2 —3B 28
Prospect Rd. NW2 —3H 43
Prospect Rd. Barn —4D 4

Prospect Rd. Surb —6C 118
Prospect Rd. Wfd G —6F 21
Prospect St. SE16 —3H 79
Prospect Vale. SE18 —4C 82
Prospero Rd. N19 —1H 45
Protheroe Ho. N17 —3F 31
Protheroe Rd. SW6 —7G 75
Prothero Gdns. NW4 —5D 26
Prout Gro. NW10 —4A 42
Prout Rd. E5 —3H 47
Provence St. N1 —2C 62
Providence Ct. W1 —7E 60 (9H 139)
Providence Pl. N1 —1B 62
Providence Pl. Romf —2F 37
Providence Row. N1 —2K 61
(off Pentonville Rd.)
Province St. N1 —2C 62
Provost Est. N1 —2D 62 (1A 142)
Provost Rd. NW3 —7D 44
Provost St. N1 —2D 62
Prowse Av. Bush —1B 10
Prowse Pl. NW1 —7G 45
Pruden Clo. N14 —2B 16
Prudent Pas. EC2 —6C 62 (8M 141)
(off King St.)
Prusom St. E1 —1H 79
Pryors, The. NW3 —3B 44
Pudding La. EC3 —7D 62 (1B 148)
Pudding Mill La. E15 —1D 64
Puddledock. EC4 —7B 62 (9K 141)
(in two parts)
Puddledock La. Dart —5K 117
Puffin Clo. Beck —5K 125
Pulborough Rd. SW18 —7H 91
Pulborough Way. Houn —4A 86
Pulford Rd. N15 —6D 30
Pulham Av. N2 —4A 28
Puller Rd. Barn —2B 4
Pulleyns Av. E6 —3C 66
Pullman Ct. SW2 —5J 93
Pullman Gdns. SW15 —6E 90
Pulross Rd. SW9 —3K 93
Pulteney Clo. E3 —1B 64
Pulteney Rd. E18 —3K 33
Pulteney Ter. N1 —1K 61
Pulton Pl. SW6 —7J 75
Puma Ct. E1 —5F 63 (5E 142)
Pump All. Bren —7D 72
Pump Clo. N'holt —2E 54
Pump Ct. EC4 —6A 62 (8G 141)
Pumping Sta. Rd. W4 —7A 74
Pump La. SE14 —7J 79
Pump Pail N. Croy —3C 134
Pump Pail S. Croy —3C 134
Punderson's Gdns. E2 —3H 63
Purbeck Av. N Mald —6B 120
Purbeck Dri. NW2 —2F 43
Purbeck Ho. SW8 —7K 77
Purbeck St. SE1 —3E 78
Purbrook Est. SE1 —2E 78 (5D 148)
Purbrook St. SE1 —3E 78 (6D 148)
Purcell Cres. SW6 —7G 75
Purcell M. NW10 —7A 42
Purcell Ho. Gnfd —5F 55
Purcells Av. Edgw —5B 12
Purcell St. N1 —2E 62
Purchese St. NW1 —2H 61
Purdey Ct. Wor Pk —1C 130
Purdon Ho. SE15 —1G 95
(off Oliver Goldsmith Est.)
Purdy St. E3 —4D 64
Purleigh Av. Wfd G —6H 21
Purley Av. NW2 —2G 43
Purley Clo. Ilf —2E 34
Purley Pl. N1 —7B 46
Purley Rd. N9 —3K 17
Purley Rd. S Croy —7D 134

Purley Way. Croy & Purl —7K 123
Purley Way Cen., The. Croy —2A 134
Purley Way Corner. Croy —7K 123
Purley Way Cres. Croy —7K 123
Purneys Rd. SE9 —4B 98
Purrett Rd. SE18 —5K 83
Purser Ho. SW2 —6A 94
(off Tulse Hill)
Pursers Cross Rd. SW6 —1H 91
Purse Wardens Clo. W13 —1C 72
Pursley Rd. NW7 —7J 13
Purves Rd. NW10 —2D 58
Putney Bri. SW15 & SW6 —3G 91
Putney Bri. App. SW6 —3G 91
Putney Bri. Rd. SW15 & SW18
—4G 91
Putney Comn. SW15 —3E 90
Putney Exchange Shopping Cen.
SW15 —4F 91
Putney Heath. SW15 —7D 90
Putney Heath La. SW15 —6F 91
Putney High St. SW15 —4F 91
Putney Hill. SW15 —7F 91
(in two parts)
Putney Pk. Av. SW15 —4C 90
Putney Pk. La. SW15 —4D 90
Pycroft Way. N9 —4A 18
Pyecombe Corner. N12 —4C 14
Pylbrook Rd. Sutt —3J 131
Pylon Trading Est. E16 —4G 65
Pylon Way. Croy —1J 133
Pym Clo. Barn —5G 5
Pymers Mead. SE21 —1C 110
Pym Ho. SW9 —2A 94
Pymmes Brook Ho. N10 —7K 15
Pymmes Clo. N13 —5E 16
Pymmes Clo. N17 —1H 31
Pymmes Gdns. N. N9 —3A 18
Pymmes Gdns. S. N9 —3A 18
Pymmes Grn. Rd. N11 —4A 16
Pymmes Rd. N13 —6D 16
Pymms Brook Dri. Barn —4H 5
Pynfolds. SE16 —2H 79
Pynham Clo. SE2 —3B 84
Pynnacles Clo. Stan —5G 11
Pynnersmead. SE24 —5C 94
Pyramid Ho. Houn —3C 86
Pyrland Rd. N5 —5D 46
Pyrland Rd. Rich —6F 89
Pyrmont Gro. SE27 —3B 110
Pyrmont Rd. W4 —6G 73
Pytchley Cres. SE19 —6C 110
Pytchley Rd. SE22 —3E 94

Quainton St. NW10 —3K 41
Quaker La. S'hall —3E 70
Quakers Course. NW9 —1B 26
Quakers La. Iswth —7K 71
Quaker St. E1 —4F 63 (4E 142)
Quality Ct. WC2 —6A 62 (7G 141)
(off Chancery La.)
Quandrant Gro. NW5 —5F 44
Quantock Dri. Wor Pk —2E 130
Quantock Gdns. NW2 —2F 43
Quarles Clo. Romf —1G 37
Quarley Way. SE15 —7F 79
Quarrendon St. SW6 —2J 91
Quarr Rd. Cars —6C 122
Quarry Pk. Rd. Sutt —6H 131
Quarry Rise. Sutt —6H 131
Quarry Rd. SW18 —6A 92
Quarterdeck, The. E14 —2C 80
Quarter Mile La. E10 —4D 48
Quayside Ho. E14 —1C 80
Quebec M. W1 —6D 60 (8F 138)
Quebec Rd. Hay —6A 54
Quebec Rd. Ilf —7F 35
Quebec Way. SE16 —2K 79
Quedgeley Ct. SE15 —6F 79
(off Ebley Clo.)
Queen Adelaide Ct. SE20 —6J 111
Queen Adelaide Rd. SE20 —6J 111
Queen Anne Av. Brom —3H 127
Queen Anne M. W1 —5F 61 (6K 139)
Queen Anne Rd. E9 —6K 47
Queen Anne's Clo. Twic —3H 103
Queen Anne's Gdns. W4 —3A 74
Queen Anne's Gdns. W5 —2E 72
Queen Anne's Gdns. Enf —6K 7
Queen Anne's Gdns. Mitc —3D 122
Queen Anne's Ga. SW1
—2H 77 (5A 146)
Queen Anne's Gdns. Bexh —3D 100
Queen Anne's Gro. W4 —3A 74
Queen Anne's Gro. W5 —2E 72
Queen Anne's Gro. Enf —7J 7
Queen Anne's Pl. Enf —6K 7
Queen Anne St. W1 —5F 61 (7J 139)
Queen Anne's Wlk. WC1
(off Queen Sq.) —4J 61 (4D 140)
Queenborough Gdns. Chst —6H 115
Queenborough Gdns. Ilf —4E 34
Queen Caroline St. W6 —4E 74
Queen Elizabeth Bldgs. EC4
(off Temple) —7A 62 (9G 141)
Queen Elizabeth Gdns. Mord
—4J 121
Queen Elizabeth Ho. SW12 —7F 92
Queen Elizabeth Rd. E17 —3A 32
Queen Elizabeth Rd. King T —2F 119
Queen Elizabeth's Clo. N16 —2D 46
Queen Elizabeth's Dri. N14 —1D 16
Queen Elizabeth Wlk. SW13 —1C 90
Queen Elizabeth Wlk. Wall —4H 133
Queengate Ct. N12 —5E 14
Queenhithe. EC4 —7C 62 (9M 141)
Queen Margaret's Gro. N1 —5E 46
Queen Mary Av. Mord —5F 121
Queen Mary Rd. SE19 —6B 110
Queen Mary's Av. Cars —7D 132
Queen of Denmark Ct. SE16 —3B 80
Queens Acre. Sutt —7G 131
Queens Av. N3 —7F 15
Queens Av. N10 —3E 28
Queens Av. N20 —2G 15
Queens Av. N21 —1G 17
Queens Av. Felt —4A 102

Queen's Av. Gnfd —6F 55
Queen's Av. Stan —3C 24
Queen's Av. Wfd G —5E 20
Queensberry M. W. SW7
    —4B 76 (8A 144)
Queensberry Pl. SW7
    —4B 76 (8A 144)
Queensberry Way. SW7
    —4B 76 (8A 144)
Queensborough Ct. N3 —4H 27
  (off N. Circular Rd.)
Queensborough M. W2 —7A 60
Queensborough Pas. W2 —7A 60
  (off Queensborough M.)
Queensborough Studios. W2 —7A 60
  (off Queensborough M.)
Queensborough Ter. W2 —7K 59
Queensbridge Ct. E2 —1F 63
  (off Queensbridge Ct.)
Queensbridge Pk. Iswth —5J 87
Queensbridge Rd. E8 & E2 —6F 47
Queensbury Circ. Pde. Harr & Stan
    —3E 24
Queensbury Ho. Rich —5D 88
Queensbury Rd. NW9 —7K 25
Queensbury Rd. Wemb —2F 57
Queensbury Sta. Pde. Edgw —3F 25
Queensbury St. N1 —7C 46
Queen's Cir. SW8 —7F 77
Queens Clo. Edgw —5B 12
Queen's Clo. Wall —5F 133
Queen's Club Gdns. W14 —6G 75
Queens Ct. NW11 —7F 29
Queens Ct. SE23 —2J 111
Queens Ct. Rich —6F 89
Queen's Ct. W'stone —2C 24
Queenscourt. Wemb —4E 40
Queen's Cres. NW5 —6E 44
Queen's Cres. Rich —5F 89
Queenscroft Rd. SE9 —5B 98
Queensdale Cres. W11 —1F 75
Queensdale Pl. W11 —1G 75
Queensdale Rd. W11 —1F 75
Queensdale Wlk. W11 —1G 75
Queensdown Rd. E5 —4H 47
Queens Dri. E10 —7C 32
Queen's Dri. N4 —2B 46
Queens Dri. W5 & W3 —6F 57
Queen's Dri. Surb —7G 119
Queen's Dri. Th Dit —6A 118
Queen's Elm Pde. SW3 —5B 76
  (off Old Church St.)
Queen's Elm Sq. SW3 —5B 76
Queens Ferry Wlk. N17 —4H 31
Queensfield Ct. Sutt —4E 130
Queen's Gdns. NW4 —5E 26
Queen's Gdns. W2 —7A 60
Queen's Gdns. W5 —4C 56
Queen's Gdns. Houn —1C 86
Queen's Gdns. Rain —2K 69
Queen's Ga. SW7 —2A 76
Queen's Ga. Gdns. SW7 —3A 76
Queens Ga. Gdns. SW15 —4D 90
Queensgate Gdns. Chst —1H 129
Queen's Ga. M. SW7 —3A 76
Queensgate Pl. NW6 —7J 43
Queen's Ga. Pl. SW7 —3A 76
Queen's Ga. Pl. M. SW7 —3A 76
Queen's Ga. Ter. SW7 —3A 76
Queen's Gro. NW8 —1B 60
Queens Gro. Rd. E4 —1A 20
Queen's Head St. N1 —1B 62
Queen's Head Yd. SE1
    —1D 78 (3A 148)
  (off Borough High St.)
Queens Ho. Tedd —6K 103
Queensland Av. N18 —6H 17
Queensland Av. SW19 —1K 121

Queensland Ho. E16 —1E 82
  (off Rymill St.)
Queensland Pl. N7 —4A 46
Queensland Rd. N7 —4A 46
Queens La. N10 —3F 29
Queens Mkt. E13 —1A 66
Queensmead. NW8 —1B 60
Queens Mead Rd. Brom —2H 127
Queensmere Clo. SW19 —2F 107
Queensmere Ct. SW13 —6B 74
Queensmere Rd. SW19 —2F 107
Queen's M. W2 —7K 59
Queensmill Rd. SW6 —7F 75
Queens Pde. N8 —4B 30
Queens Pde. N11 —5J 15
Queens Pde. W5 —6F 57
Queens Pas. Chst —6F 115
Queens Pl. Mord —4J 121
Queen's Promenade. King T
    —4D 118
Queen Sq. WC1 —4J 61 (4D 140)
Queen Sq. Pl. WC1 —4J 61 (4D 140)
  (off Queen Sq.)
Queens Reach. King T —2D 118
Queens Ride. SW13 & SW15
    —3C 90
Queens Rise. Rich —6F 89
Queens Rd. E11 —7F 33
Queens Rd. E13 —1K 65
Queens Rd. E17 —6B 32
Queens Rd. N3 —1A 28
Queens Rd. N9 —2C 18
Queens Rd. N11 —7D 16
Queens Rd. NW4 —5E 26
Queen's Rd. SE15 & SE14 —1H 95
Queen's Rd. SW14 —3K 89
Queens Rd. SW19 —6H 107
Queen's Rd. W5 —6E 56
Queens Rd. Bark —6G 51
Queens Rd. Barn —3A 4
Queens Rd. Beck —2A 126
Queen's Rd. Brom —2J 127
Queen's Rd. Buck H —2E 20
Queens Rd. Chst —6F 115
Queens Rd. Croy —6B 124
Queen's Rd. Enf —4K 7
Queen's Rd. Felt —1A 102
Queen's Rd. Hamp —4F 103
Queen's Rd. Houn —3F 87
Queens Rd. King T —7G 105
Queens Rd. Mitc —3B 122
Queens Rd. Mord —4J 121
Queens Rd. N Mald —4B 120
Queen's Rd. Rich —7F 89
Queens Rd. S'hall —2B 70
Queen's Rd. Tedd —6K 103
Queens Rd. Th Dit —5A 118
Queens Rd. Twic —1A 104
Queens Rd. Wall —5F 133
Queen's Rd. Well —2B 100
Queen's Rd. W. E13 —2J 65
Queen's Row. SE17 —6D 78
Queens Ter. E1 —4J 63
Queen's Ter. E13 —1K 65
Queen's Ter. NW8 —2B 60
Queens Ter. Iswth —4A 88
Queen's Ter. Cotts. W7 —2J 71
Queensthorpe Rd. SE26 —4K 111
Queenstown M. SW8 —2F 93
Queenstown Rd. SW8 —6F 77
Queen St. EC4 —7C 62 (9M 141)
Queen St. N17 —6K 17
Queen St. W1 —1F 77 (2J 145)
Queen St. Bexh —3F 101
Queen St. Croy —4C 134
Queen St. Romf —6K 37
Queen St. Pl. EC4 —7C 62 (1M 147)
Queensville Rd. SW12 —7H 93

Queens Wlk. E4 —1A 20
Queens Wlk. NW9 —2J 41
Queen's Wlk. SW1 —1G 77 (2L 145)
Queen's Wlk. W5 —4C 56
Queens Wlk. Harr —4J 23
Queens Wlk. Ruis —2A 38
Queens Wlk. Ter. Ruis —3A 38
Queen's Wlk., The. SE1
    —1K 77 (2F 146)
  (off Waterloo Rd.)
Queens Way. NW4 —5E 26
Queensway. W2 —6K 59
Queensway. Croy —5K 133
Queensway. Enf —4C 8
Queens Way. Felt —4A 102
Queensway. Orp —5G 129
Queensway. W Wick —3G 137
Queensway Ind. Est. Enf —4D 8
Queenswell Av. N20 —3H 15
Queenswood Av. E17 —1E 32
Queenswood Av. Hamp —6F 103
Queenswood Av. Houn —2D 86
Queenswood Av. T Hth —5A 124
Queenswood Av. Wall —4H 133
Queenswood Ct. SE27 —4D 110
Queenswood Ct. SW4 —5J 93
Queenswood Gdns. E11 —1K 49
Queenswood Pk. N3 —2G 27
Queens Wood Rd. N10 —6F 29
Queenswood Rd. SE23 —3K 111
Queenswood Rd. Sidc —5K 99
Queen's Yd. WC1 —4G 61 (4M 139)
Queen Victoria Av. Wemb —7D 40
Queen Victoria St. EC4
    —7B 62 (9J 141)
Quemerford Rd. N7 —5K 45
Quenington Ct. SE15 —6F 79
  (off Ebley Clo.)
Quentin Pl. SE13 —3G 97
Quentin Rd. SE13 —3G 97
Quernmore Clo. Brom —6J 113
Quernmore Rd. N4 —6A 30
Quernmore Rd. Brom —6J 113
Querrin St. SW6 —2A 92
Quested Ct. E8 —5H 47
  (off Brett Rd.)
Quex M. NW6 —1J 59
Quex Rd. NW6 —1J 59
Quick Pl. N1 —1B 62
Quick Rd. W4 —5A 74
Quicksilver Pl. N22 —2K 29
Quicks Rd. SW19 —7K 107
Quick St. N1 —2B 62
Quick St. M. N1 —2B 62
Quickswood. NW3 —7C 44
Quill La. SW15 —4F 91
Quill St. W5 —3E 56
Quilp St. SE1 —2C 78 (4L 147)
Quilter St. E2 —3G 63
Quin Bldgs. SE1 —2A 78 (5H 147)
Quinta Dri. Barn —5A 4
Quintin Av. SW20 —1H 121
Quinton Clo. Beck —3E 126
Quinton Clo. Wall —4F 133
Quinton Rd. Th Dit —7A 118
Quinton St. SW18 —2A 108
Quixley St. E14 —7F 65
Quorn Rd. SE22 —4E 94

Rabbit Row. W8 —1J 75
Rabbit's Rd. E12 —4C 50
Rabournmead Dri. N'holt —5C 38
Raby Rd. N Mald —4K 119
Raby St. E14 —6A 64
Raccoon Way. Houn —2A 86
Rachel Point. E5 —4G 47
Rackham M. SW16 —6G 109

Racton Rd. SW6 —6J 75
Radbourne Av. W5 —4C 72
Radbourne Clo. E5 —4K 47
Radbourne Ct. Harr —6B 24
Radbourne Cres. E17 —2F 33
Radbourne Rd. SW12 —7G 93
Radcliffe Av. NW10 —2C 58
Radcliffe Av. Enf —1H 7
Radcliffe Gdns. Cars —7C 132
Radcliffe M. Hamp —5G 103
Radcliffe Rd. N21 —1G 17
Radcliffe Rd. Croy —2F 135
Radcliffe Rd. Harr —2A 24
Radcliffe Sq. SW15 —6F 91
Radcliffe Way. N'holt —3B 54
Radcot St. SE11 —5A 78
Raddington Rd. W10 —5G 59
Radfield Way. Sidc —7H 99
Radford Av. SE13 —6E 96
Radford Way. Bark —3K 67
Radipole Rd. SW6 —1H 91
Radland Rd. E16 —6H 65
Radlet Av. SE26 —2H 111
Radlett Clo. E7 —6H 49
Radlett Pl. NW8 —1C 60
Radley Av. Ilf —4A 52
Radley Clo. SE16 —2K 79
Radley Gdns. Harr —4E 24
Radley Ho. SE2 —2D 84
  (off Wolvercote Rd.)
Radley M. W8 —3J 75
Radley Rd. N17 —2E 30
Radley's La. E18 —2J 33
Radleys Mead. Dag —6H 53
Radley Sq. E5 —2J 47
Radley Ter. E16 —5H 65
  (off Hermit Rd.)
Radlix Rd. E10 —1C 48
Radnor Av. Harr —5J 23
Radnor Av. Well —5B 100
Radnor Clo. Chst —6J 115
Radnor Clo. Mitc —4J 123
Radnor Ct. Har W —1K 23
Radnor Cres. SE18 —7A 84
Radnor Cres. Ilf —5D 34
Radnor Gdns. Enf —1K 7
Radnor Gdns. Twic —2K 103
Radnor M. W2 —6B 60 (8B 138)
Radnor Pl. W2 —6C 60 (8C 138)
Radnor Rd. NW6 —1G 59
Radnor Rd. SE15 —7G 79
Radnor Rd. Harr —5H 23
Radnor Rd. Twic —1K 103
Radnor St. EC1 —3C 62 (2M 141)
Radnor Ter. W14 —4H 75
Radnor Wlk. E14 —4C 80
  (off Copeland Dri.)
Radnor Wlk. SW3 —5C 76
Radnor Wlk. Croy —6B 126
Radnor Way. NW10 —4H 57
Radstock Av. Harr —3A 24
Radstock St. SW11 —7C 76
Raeburn Av. Surb —7H 119
Raeburn Clo. NW11 —6A 28
Raeburn Clo. King T —7D 104
Raeburn Rd. Edgw —1G 25
Raeburn Rd. Sidc —6J 99
Raeburn St. SW2 —4J 93
Rafford Way. Brom —2K 127
Ragglewood. Chst —1E 128
Raglan Clo. Houn —5D 86
Raglan Ct. SE12 —5J 97
Raglan Ct. S Croy —5B 134
Raglan Rd. E17 —5E 32
Raglan Rd. SE18 —5G 83
Raglan Rd. Belv —4F 85
Raglan Rd. Brom —4A 128
Raglan Rd. Enf —7A 8

Raglan St. NW5 —6F 45
Raglan Ter. Gnfd —4F 39
Raglan Way. N'holt —6E 39
Ragley Clo. W3 —2J 73
Raider Clo. Romf —1G 37
Railey M. NW5 —5G 45
Railshead Rd. Iswth —4B 88
Railton Rd. SE24 —4A 94
Railway App. N4 —6A 30
Railway App. SE1 —1D 78 (3B 148)
Railway App. Harr —4K 23
Railway App. Twic —7A 88
Railway App. Wall —5F 133
Railway Av. SE16 —2J 79
Railway Cotts. Twic —6E 86
Railway M. E3 —3C 64
  (off Wellington Way)
Railway M. W11 —6G 59
Railway Pl. Belv —3G 85
Railway Rise. SE22 —4E 94
Railway Rd. Tedd —4J 103
Railway Side. SW13 —3B 90
Railway St. N1 —2J 61
Railway St. Romf —7C 36
Railway Ter. E17 —1E 32
Railway Ter. SE13 —5D 96
Rainborough Clo. NW10 —6J 41
Rainbow Av. E14 —5D 80
Rainbow St. SE5 —7E 78
Raine St. E1 —1H 79
Rainham Clo. SE9 —6J 99
Rainham Clo. SW11 —6C 92
Rainham Rd. NW10 —3E 58
Rainham Rd. N. Dag —2G 53
Rainham Rd. S. Dag —4H 53
Rainhill Way. E3 —3C 64
Rainsborough Av. SE8 —4A 80
Rainsford Clo. Stan —4H 11
Rainsford Rd. NW10 —2A 57
Rainsford St. W2 —6C 60 (7C 138)
Rainton Rd. SE7 —5J 81
Rainville Rd. W6 —6E 74
Raisins Hill. Pinn —3A 22
Raith Av. N14 —3C 16
Raleana Rd. E14 —1E 80
Raleigh Av. Hay —5A 54
Raleigh Av. Wall —4H 133
Raleigh Clo. NW4 —5E 26
Raleigh Clo. Pinn —7B 22
Raleigh Ct. Beck —1D 126
Raleigh Ct. Wall —6F 133
Raleigh Dri. N20 —3H 15
Raleigh Dri. Surb —7J 119
Raleigh Gdns. SW2 —6K 93
Raleigh Gdns. Mitc —3D 122
Raleigh Ho. E14 —2D 80
  (off Admirals Way)
Raleigh M. N1 —1B 62
  (off Queen's Head St.)
Raleigh Rd. N2 —2C 28
Raleigh Rd. N8 —4A 30
Raleigh Rd. SE20 —7K 111
Raleigh Rd. Enf —4J 7
Raleigh Rd. Rich —3F 89
Raleigh Rd. S'hall —5C 70
Raleigh St. N1 —1B 62
Raleigh Way. N14 —1C 16
Raleigh Way. Felt —5A 102
Ralph Brook Ct. N1 —3D 62 (1B 142)
  (off Haberdasher Est.)
Ralph Perring Ct. Beck —4C 126
Ralston St. SW3 —5D 76
Rama Clo. SW16 —7J 109
Rama Ct. Harr —2J 39
Ramac Way. SE7 —5K 81
Rambler Clo. SW16 —4G 109
Ramillies Clo. SW2 —6J 93

254

Ramillies Pl. W1 —6G 61 (8L 139)
Ramillies Rd. W4 —2F 13
Ramillies Rd. W4 —4K 73
Ramillies Sq. Sidc —6B 100
Ramillies St. W1 —6G 61 (8L 139)
Rampart St. E1 —6H 63
Rampton Clo. E4 —3H 19
Ram Pl. E9 —6J 47
Ram Pl. King T —2D 118
Rampton Clo. E4 —3H 19
Ramsay Pl. Harr —1J 39
Ramsay Rd. E7 —4G 49
Ramsay Rd. W3 —3J 73
Ramscroft Clo. N9 —7K 7
Ramsdale Rd. SW17 —5E 108
Ramsden Dri. Romf —1G 37
Ramsden Rd. N11 —5J 15
Ramsden Rd. SW12 —6E 92
Ramsden Rd. Eri —7K 85
Ramsey Clo. NW9 —6B 26
Ramsey Clo. Gnfd —5H 39
Ramsey Rd. T Hth —6K 123
Ramsey St. E2 —4G 63
Ramsey Wlk. N1 —6D 46
Ramsey Way. N14 —7B 6
Ramsgate St. E8 —6F 47
Ramsgill App. Ilf —4K 35
Ramsgill Dri. Ilf —5K 35
Rams Gro. Romf —4E 36
Ram St. SW18 —5K 91
Ramulis Dri. Hay —4C 54
Rancliffe Gdns. SE9 —4C 98
Rancliffe Rd. E6 —2C 66
Randall Av. NW2 —2A 42
Randall Clo. SW11 —1C 92
Randall Clo. Eri —6J 85
Randall Ct. NW7 —7H 13
Randall Pl. SE10 —7E 80
Randall Rd. SE11 —5K 77
Randall Row. SE11
   —4K 77 (9E 146)
Randell's Rd. N1 —1J 61
Randisbourne Gdns. SE6 —3D 112
Randle Rd. Rich —4C 104
Randlesdown Rd. SE6 —4C 112
   (in two parts)
Randolph App. E16 —6A 66
Randolph Av. W9 —2K 59
Randolph Clo. Bexh —3J 101
Randolph Clo. King T —5J 105
Randolph Cres. W9 —4A 60
Randolph Gdns. NW6 —2K 59
Randolph Gro. Romf —5C 36
Randolph M. W9 —4A 60
Randolph Rd. E17 —5D 32
Randolph Rd. W9 —4A 60
Randolph Rd. S'hall —2D 70
Randolph St. NW1 —7G 45
Randon Clo. Harr —2F 23
Ranelagh Av. SW6 —3H 91
Ranelagh Av. SW13 —2C 90
Ranelagh Bri. W2 —5K 59
Ranelagh Clo. Edgw —4B 12
Ranelagh Dri. Edgw —4B 12
Ranelagh Dri. Twic —5B 88
Ranelagh Gdns. E11 —5A 34
Ranelagh Gdns. SW6 —3G 91
Ranelagh Gdns. W4 —7J 73
Ranelagh Gdns. W6 —3B 74
Ranelagh Gdns. Ilf —1D 50
Ranelagh Gdns. Mans. SW6 —3G 91
   (off Ranelagh Gdns.)
Ranelagh Gro. SW1 —5E 76
Ranelagh M. W5 —2D 72
Ranelagh Pl. N Mald —5A 120
Ranelagh Rd. E6 —1E 66
Ranelagh Rd. E11 —4G 49
Ranelagh Rd. E15 —2G 65

Ranelagh Rd. N17 —3E 30
Ranelagh Rd. N22 —1K 29
Ranelagh Rd. NW10 —2B 58
Ranelagh Rd. SW1 —5G 77
Ranelagh Rd. W5 —2D 72
Ranelagh Rd. S'hall —1B 70
Ranelagh Rd. Wemb —6D 40
Ranfurly Rd. Sutt —2J 131
Rangbourne Ho. N7 —5J 45
Rangefield Rd. Brom —5G 113
Rangemoor Rd. N15 —5F 31
Ranger's Rd. E4 —1B 20
Rangeworth Pl. Sidc —3K 115
Rangoon St. EC3 —6F 63 (8E 142)
   (off Crutched Friars)
Rankin Clo. NW9 —3A 26
Ranleigh Gdns. Bexh —7F 85
Ranmere St. SW12 —1F 109
Ranmoor Clo. Harr —4H 23
Ranmoor Gdns. Harr —4H 23
Ranmore Av. Croy —3F 135
Ranmore Path. Orp —4K 129
Ranmore Rd. Sutt —7F 131
Rannoch Clo. Edgw —2C 12
Rannoch Rd. W6 —6E 74
Rannock Av. NW9 —7K 25
Ransom Rd. SE7 —5A 82
Ransom Wlk. SE7 —4A 82
Ranston St. NW1 —5C 60 (5C 138)
Ranulf Rd. NW2 —4H 43
Ranwell Clo. E3 —1B 64
Ranworth Rd. N9 —2D 18
Raphael St. SW7 —2D 76 (5E 144)
Raplace Ho. SE14 —7A 80
Rashleigh Ct. SW8 —2F 93
Rasper Rd. N20 —2F 15
Rastell Av. SW2 —2H 109
Ratcliffe Cross St. E1 —6K 63
Ratcliffe La. E14 —6A 64
Ratcliffe Orchard. E1 —7K 63
Ratcliff Ro. EC1 —3C 62 (2M 141)
Ratcliff Rd. E7 —5A 50
Rathbone Pl. W1 —5H 61 (6A 140)
Rathbone Point. E5 —4G 47
Rathbone Sq. Croy —4C 134
Rathbone St. E16 —6H 65
Rathbone St. W1 —5G 61 (6M 139)
Rathcoole Av. N8 —5K 29
Rathcoole Gdns. N8 —5K 29
Rathfern Rd. SE6 —1B 112
Rathgar Av. W13 —1B 72
Rathgar Clo. N3 —2H 27
Rathgar Rd. SW9 —3B 94
Rathlin Wlk. N1 —6C 46
Rathmell Dri. SW4 —6H 93
Rathmore Rd. SE7 —5K 81
Rattray Rd. SW2 —4A 94
Raul Rd. SE15 —2G 95
Raveley St. NW5 —4G 45
Ravenet St. SW11 —1F 93
Ravenfield Rd. SW17 —3D 108
Ravenhill Rd. E13 —2A 66
Ravenna Rd. SW15 —5F 91
Ravenor Pk. Rd. Gnfd —3F 55
Raven Rd. E18 —2A 34
Raven Row. E1 —5H 63
Ravensbourne Av. Beck & Brom
   —7F 113
Ravensbourne Gdns. W13 —5B 56
Ravensbourne Gdns. Ilf —1E 34
Ravensbourne Pk. SE6 —7C 96
Ravensbourne Pk. Cres. SE6 —7B 96
Ravensbourne Pl. SE13 —2D 96
Ravensbourne Rd. SE6 —7B 96
Ravensbourne Rd. Brom —3J 127
Ravensbourne Rd. Twic —6C 88
Ravensbury Av. Mord —5A 122

Ravensbury Gro. Mitc —4B 122
Ravensbury La. Mitc —4B 122
Ravensbury Path. Mitc —4B 122
Ravensbury Rd. SW18 —2K 107
Ravensbury Rd. Orp —4K 129
Ravensbury Ter. SW18 —2K 107
Ravenscar Rd. Brom —4G 113
Ravens Clo. NW9 —2A 26
Ravens Clo. Brom —2H 127
Ravens Clo. Enf —2K 7
Ravenscourt Av. W6 —4C 74
Ravenscourt Gdns. W6 —4C 74
Ravenscourt Pk. W6 —3C 74
Ravenscourt Pk. Barn —4A 4
Ravenscourt Pk. Mans. W6 —3D 74
   (off Paddenswick Rd.)
Ravenscourt Pl. W6 —4D 74
Ravenscourt Rd. W6 —4D 74
Ravenscourt Sq. W6 —3C 74
Ravenscraig Rd. N11 —4B 16
Ravenscroft Av. NW11 —7H 27
Ravenscroft Av. Wemb —1E 40
Ravenscroft Clo. E16 —5J 65
Ravenscroft Cotts. Barn —4D 4
Ravenscroft Cres. SE9 —3D 114
Ravenscroft Pk. Barn —3A 4
Ravenscroft Rd. E16 —5J 65
Ravenscroft Rd. W4 —4J 73
Ravenscroft Rd. Beck —2J 125
Ravenscroft St. E2 —2F 63
Ravensdale Av. N12 —4F 15
Ravensdale Gdns. SE19 —7D 110
Ravensdale Rd. N16 —7F 31
Ravensdale Rd. Houn —3C 86
Ravensdon St. SE11 —5A 78
Ravensfield Clo. Dag —4D 52
Ravensfield Gdns. Eps —5A 130
Ravenshaw St. NW6 —5H 43
Ravenshill. Chst —1F 129
Ravenshurst Av. NW4 —4E 26
Ravenside Clo. N18 —5E 18
Ravenside Retail Pk. N18 —5E 18
Ravenslea Rd. SW12 —7D 92
Ravensmead Rd. Brom —7F 113
Ravensmede Way. W4 —4B 74
Ravens M. SE12 —5J 97
Ravenstone. SE17 —5E 78
   (off Bagshot St.)
Ravenstone Rd. N8 —3A 30
Ravenstone Rd. NW9 —6B 26
Ravenstone St. SW12 —1E 108
Ravens Way. SE12 —5J 97
Ravenswood. Bex —1E 116
Ravenswood Av. W Wick —1E 136
Ravenswood Ct. King T —6H 105
Ravenswood Cres. Harr —2D 38
Ravenswood Cres. W Wick —1E 136
Ravenswood Gdns. Iswth —1J 87
Ravenswood Ind. Est. E17 —4E 32
Ravenswood Rd. E17 —4E 32
Ravenswood Rd. SW12 —7F 93
Ravenswood Rd. Croy —3B 134
Ravensworth Rd. NW10 —3D 58
Ravensworth Rd. SE9 —4D 114
Ravensworth Rd. SE12 —4D 114
Ravent Rd. SE11 —4K 77 (9F 146)
Ravey St. EC2 —4E 62 (3C 142)
Ravine Gro. SE18 —6J 83
Rawlinpindi Ho. E16 —4H 65
Rawchester Clo. SW18 —1H 107
Rawlings Clo. N3 —3G 27
Rawlins Clo. S Croy —7A 136
Rawlinson Ct. NW2 —7E 26
Rawlinson Point. E16 —5H 65
   (off Fox Rd.)
Rawnsley Ter. N17 —3F 31
Rawnsley Av. Mitc —5B 122

Rawreth Wlk. N1 —1C 62
   (off Basire St.)
Rawson St. SW11 —1E 92
   (in two parts)
Rawsthorne Clo. E16 —1D 82
Rawsthorne Ct. Houn —4D 86
Rawstone Wlk. E13 —2J 65
Rawstorne Pl. EC1 —3B 62 (1J 141)
Rawstorne St. EC1 —3B 62 (1J 141)
Rawthorn Av. N13 —5D 16
Raybell Ct. Iswth —2A 88
Rayburne Ct. W14 —3G 75
Rayburne Ct. Buck H —1F 21
Raydean Rd. Barn —4A 4
Raydons Gdns. Dag —5E 52
Raydons Rd. Dag —5E 52
Raydon St. N19 —2F 45
Rayfield Clo. Brom —6C 128
Rayford Av. SE12 —7H 97
Ray Gdns. Bark —2A 68
Ray Gdns. Stan —5G 11
Rayham Rd. W13 —7B 56
Ray Ho. N1 —1E 62
   (off Colville Est.)
Rayleas Clo. SE18 —1F 99
Rayleigh Av. Tedd —6J 103
Rayleigh Clo. N13 —3J 17
Rayleigh Ct. N22 —1C 30
Rayleigh Ct. King T —2G 119
Rayleigh Rise. S Croy —6E 134
Rayleigh Rd. N13 —3H 17
Rayleigh Rd. SW19 —1H 121
Rayleigh Rd. Wfd G —6F 21
Ray Lodge Rd. Wfd G —6F 21
Raymead. NW4 —4E 26
Raymead Av. T Hth —5A 124
Raymere Gdns. SE18 —7H 83
Raymond Av. E18 —3H 33
Raymond Av. W13 —3A 72
Raymond Bldgs. WC1
   —5K 61 (5F 140)
Raymond Clo. SE26 —5J 111
Raymond Ct. N22 —7D 16
Raymond Ct. Sutt —6K 131
Raymond Postage Ct. SE28 —7B 68
Raymond Rd. E13 —1A 66
Raymond Rd. SW19 —6G 107
Raymond Rd. Beck —4A 126
Raymond Rd. Ilf —7H 35
Raymouth Ho. SE16 —4J 79
   (off Rotherhithe New Rd.)
Raymouth Rd. SE16 —4H 79
Rayne Ct. E18 —4H 33
Rayners Clo. Wemb —5D 40
Rayners La. Pinn & Harr —5D 22
Rayners Rd. SW15 —5G 91
Raynes Av. E11 —7A 34
Raynes Pk. Bri. SW20 —2E 120
Raynham Av. N18 —6B 18
Raynham Rd. N18 —5B 18
Raynham Rd. W6 —4D 74
Raynham Ter. N18 —5B 18
Raynor Clo. S'hall —1D 70
Raynor Pl. N1 —1C 62
Raynton Clo. Harr —1C 38
Rays Av. N18 —4D 18
Rays Rd. N18 —4D 18
Rays Rd. W Wick —7E 126
Ray St. EC1 —4A 62 (4H 141)
Ray St. Bri. EC1 —4A 62 (4H 141)
   (off Farringdon Rd.)
Ray Wlk. N7 —2K 45
Reachview Clo. NW1 —7G 45
Read Ct. E17 —6C 32
Reade Wlk. NW10 —7A 42
Read Ho. SE11 —6A 78
   (off Clayton Est.)
Reading La. E8 —6H 47

Reading Rd. N'holt —5F 39
Reading Rd. Sutt —5A 132
Reading Way. NW7 —5A 14
Reads Clo. Ilf —3F 51
Reapers Clo. NW1 —1H 61
Reapers Way. Iswth —5H 87
Reardon Path. E1 —1H 79
Reardon St. E1 —1H 79
Reaston St. SE14 —7K 79
Rebecca Ter. SE16 —3J 79
Reckitt Rd. W4 —5A 74
Record St. SE15 —6J 79
Recovery St. SW17 —5C 108
Recreation Av. Romf —5J 37
Recreation Rd. SE26 —4K 111
Recreation Rd. Brom —2H 127
Recreation Rd. Sidc —3J 115
Recreation Rd. S'hall —4C 70
Recreation Way. Mitc —3J 123
Rector St. N1 —1C 62
Rectory Clo. E4 —3H 19
Rectory Clo. N3 —1H 27
Rectory Clo. SW20 —3E 120
Rectory Clo. Sidc —4B 116
Rectory Clo. Stan —6G 11
Rectory Ct. Felt —4A 102
Rectory Cres. E11 —6A 34
Rectory Farm Rd. Enf —1E 6
Rectory Field Cres. SE7 —7A 82
Rectory Gdns. N8 —4J 29
Rectory Gdns. SW4 —3G 93
Rectory Gdns. N'holt —1D 54
Rectory Grn. Beck —1B 126
Rectory Gro. SW4 —3G 93
Rectory Gro. Croy —2B 134
Rectory Gro. Hamp —4D 102
Rectory La. SW17 —6E 108
Rectory La. Edgw —6B 12
Rectory La. Sidc —4B 116
Rectory La. Stan —5G 11
Rectory La. Surb —7B 118
Rectory La. Wall —4G 133
Rectory Orchard. SW19 —4G 107
Rectory Pk. Av. N'holt —3D 54
Rectory Pl. SE18 —4E 82
Rectory Rd. E12 —5D 50
Rectory Rd. E17 —4D 32
Rectory Rd. N16 —2F 47
Rectory Rd. SW13 —2C 90
Rectory Rd. W3 —1H 73
Rectory Rd. Beck —1C 126
Rectory Rd. Dag —6H 53
Rectory Rd. Houn —2A 86
Rectory Rd. S'hall —3D 70
Rectory Rd. Sutt —3J 131
Rectory Sq. E1 —5K 63
Reculver Rd. SE16 —5K 79
Red Anchor Clo. SW3 —6B 76
Redan Pl. W2 —6K 59
Redan St. W14 —3F 75
Redan Ter. SE5 —2B 94
Red Barracks Rd. SE18 —4D 82
Redberry Gro. SE26 —3J 111
Redbourne Av. N3 —1J 27
Redbridge Gdns. SE5 —7E 78
Redbridge La. E. Ilf —6B 34
Redbridge La. W. E11 —6K 33
Redburn Ind. Est. Enf —6E 8
Redburn St. SW3 —6D 76
Redcar Clo. N'holt —5F 39
Redcar St. SE5 —7C 78
Redcastle Clo. E1 —7J 63
Red Cedars Rd. Orp —7J 129
Redchurch St. E2 —4F 63 (3E 142)
Redcliffe Clo. SW5 —5K 75
Redcliffe Gdns. SW5 & SW10
   —5K 75
Redcliffe Gdns. Ilf —1E 50

Redcliffe M. SW10 —5K **75**
Redcliffe Pl. SW10 —6A **76**
Redcliffe Rd. SW10 —5A **76**
Redcliffe Sq. SW10 —5A **76**
Redcliffe St. SW10 —6K **75**
Redcliffe Wlk. Wemb —3H **41**
Redclose Av. Mord —5J **121**
Redclyffe Rd. E6 —1A **66**
Redcourt. Croy —3E **134**
Redcroft Rd. S'hall —7G **55**
Redding. Sidc —6B **116**
Reddings Clo. NW7 —4G **13**
Reddings Rd. SE15 —7G **79**
Reddings, The. NW7 —3G **13**
Reddons Rd. Beck —7A **112**
Rede Pl. W2 —6J **59**
Redesdale Gdns. Iswth —7A **72**
Redesdale St. SW3 —6C **76**
Redfern Av. Houn —7E **86**
Redfern Ho. E13 —1H 65
 (off Redriffe Rd.)
Redfern Rd. NW10 —7A **42**
Redfern Rd. SE6 —7E **96**
Redfield La. SW5 —4J **75**
Redfield M. SW5 —4K **75**
Redford Av. T Hth —4K **123**
Redford Av. Wall —6J **133**
Redford Wlk. N1 —1C 62
 (off Popham St.)
Redgate Dri. Brom —2K **137**
Redgate Ter. SW15 —6F **91**
Redgrave Clo. Croy —6F **125**
Redgrave Rd. SW15 —3F **91**
Red Hill. Chst —5F **115**
Redhill Ct. SW2 —2A **110**
Redhill Dri. Edgw —2H **25**
Redhill St. NW1 —2F **61**
Redholm Vs. N16 —4D **46**
Red House La. Bexh —4D **100**
Redhouse Rd. Croy —6H **123**
Redington Gdns. NW3 —4K **43**
Redington Rd. NW3 —3K **43**
Redlands. N15 —4D **30**
Redlands. Tedd —6A **104**
Redlands Ct. Brom —7H **113**
Redlands Rd. Enf —1F **9**
Redlands, The. Beck —2D **126**
Redlands Way. SW2 —7K **93**
Redlaw Way. SE16 —5G **79**
Redleaf Clo. Belv —6G **85**
Redlees Clo. Iswth —4A **88**
Red Lion Clo. SE17 —6D 78
 (off Red Lion Row)
Red Lion Ct. EC4 —6A **62** (8H **141**)
Red Lion Ct. SE1 —1C **78** (2M **147**)
Red Lion Hill. N2 —2B **28**
Red Lion La. SE18 —7E **82**
Red Lion Pde. Pinn —3C **22**
Red Lion Pl. SE18 —1E **98**
Red Lion Rd. Surb —7G **119**
Red Lion Row. SE17 —6C **78**
Red Lion Sq. SW18 —5A **18**
Red Lion Sq. WC1 —5K **61** (6E **140**)
Red Lion St. WC1 —5K **61** (5E **140**)
Red Lion St. Rich —5D **88**
Red Lion Yd. W1 —1F 77 (2J 145)
 (off Waverton St.)
Red Lodge. W Wick —1E **136**
Red Lodge Cres. Bex —3K **117**
Red Lodge Rd. Bex —3K **117**
Red Lodge Rd. W Wick —1E **136**
Redman Clo. N'holt —2A **54**
Redman's Rd. E1 —5J **63**
Redmead La. E1 —1G **79**
Redmond Ho. N1 —1K 61
 (off Barnsbury Est.)
Redmore Rd. W6 —4D **74**

Redmount Clo. Buck H —2E **20**
Red Path. E9 —6A **48**
Red Pl. W1 —7E **60** (9G **139**)
Redpoll Way. Eri —3D **84**
Red Post Hill. SE24 & SE22 —4D **94**
Red Post Ho. E6 —7B **50**
Redriffe Rd. E13 —1H **65**
Redriff Est. SE16 —3B **80**
Redriff Rd. SE16 —4K **79**
Redriff Rd. Romf —2H **37**
Redroofs Clo. Beck —1D **126**
Red Rose Ind. Est. Barn —5G **5**
Redruth Clo. N22 —7E **16**
Redruth Rd. E9 —1J **63**
Redruth Rd. E9 —1J **63**
Redstart Clo. E6 —5C **66**
Redstart Clo. SE14 —7A **80**
Redston Rd. N8 —4H **29**
Redvers Rd. N22 —2A **30**
Redvers St. N1 —3E **62** (1D **142**)
Redwald Rd. E5 —4K **47**
Redway Dri. Twic —7G **87**
Redwing Path. SE28 —3H **83**
Redwood Clo. N14 —7C **6**
Redwood Clo. SE16 —1A **80**
Redwood Clo. Sidc —7A **100**
Redwood Ct. N19 —7H **29**
Redwood Ct. N'holt —3C **54**
Redwood Ct. Surb —7D **118**
Redwood Est. Houn —6A **70**
Redwood Mans. W8 —3K 75
 (off Chantry Sq.)
Redwoods. SW15 —1C **106**
Redwood Way. Barn —5A **4**
Reece M. SW7 —4B **76** (8A **144**)
Reed Clo. E16 —5J **65**
Reed Clo. SE12 —5J **97**
Reede Gdns. Dag —5H **53**
Reede Rd. Dag —6G **53**
Reedham Clo. N17 —4H **31**
Reedham St. SE15 —2G **95**
Reed Rd. N17 —2F **31**
Reed's Pl. NW1 —7G **45**
Reedworth St. SE11
 —4A **78** (9H **147**)
Reenglass Rd. Stan —4J **11**
Rees Gdns. Croy —6F **125**
Reesland Clo. E12 —5E **50**
Rees St. N1 —1C **62**
Reets Farm Clo. NW9 —6A **26**
Reeves Av. NW9 —7K **25**
Reeves Corner. Croy —2B **134**
Reeves Ho. SE1 —2A 78 (5G 147)
 (off Baylis Rd.)
Reeves M. W1 —7E **60** (1G **145**)
Reeves Rd. E3 —4D **64**
Reeves Rd. SE18 —6G **83**
Reform Row. N17 —2F **31**
Reform St. SW11 —2D **92**
Regal Clo. E1 —5G **63**
Regal Clo. W5 —5D **56**
Regal Ct. N18 —5A **18**
Regal Cres. Wall —3F **133**
Regal La. NW1 —1E **60**
Regal Pl. SW6 —7K 75
 (off Maxwell Rd.)
Regal Way. Harr —6D **24**
Regan Ho. N18 —6A **18**
Regan Way. N1 —2E **62**
Regency Clo. W5 —6E **56**
Regency Clo. Hamp —5D **102**
Regency Ct. Enf —5J **7**
Regency Ct. Sutt —4K **131**
Regency Ct. Tedd —6B **104**
Regency Cres. NW4 —2F **27**
Regency Lodge. NW3 —7B 44
 (off Adelaide Rd.)

Regency M. NW10 —6C **42**
Regency M. Beck —2E **126**
Regency M. Iswth —5J **87**
Regency Pl. SW1 —4H **77** (8B **146**)
Regency St. SW1 —4H **77** (8B **146**)
Regency Ter. SW7 —5B 76
 (off Fulham Rd.)
Regency Wlk. Croy —6B **126**
Regency Wlk. Rich —5E 88
 (off Grosvenor Av.)
Regency Way. Bexh —3D **100**
Regent Clo. N12 —5F **15**
Regent Clo. Harr —6E **24**
Regent Clo. Houn —1A **86**
Regent Ct. N3 —7E **14**
Regent Ct. N20 —2F **15**
Regent Gdns. Ilf —7A **36**
Regent Pl. SW19 —5A **108**
Regent Pl. W1 —7G **61** (9M **139**)
Regent Pl. Croy —1F **135**
Regent Rd. SE24 —6B **94**
Regent Rd. Surb —5F **119**
Regents Av. N13 —5F **17**
Regent's Bri. Gdns. SW8 —7J **77**
Regents Clo. S Croy —6E **134**
Regents Clo. Stan —4K **11**
Regents Ct. Brom —7H **113**
Regents M. NW8 —2A **60**
Regents Pk. Est. NW1
 (off Robert St.) —3G 61 (1L 139)
Regent's Pk. Gdns. M. NW1 —1D **60**
Regents Pk. Rd. N3 —3H **27**
Regent's Pk. Rd. NW1 —1D **60**
Regent's Pk. Ter. NW1 —1F **61**
Regent's Pl. SE3 —2J **97**
Regent Sq. E3 —3D **64**
Regent Sq. WC1 —3J **61** (2D **140**)
Regent Sq. Belv —4H **85**
Regent's Row. E8 —1G **63**
Regent St. NW10 —3F **59**
Regent St. SW1 —7H **61**
Regent St. W1 —6F **61** (7K **139**)
Regent St. W4 —5G **73**
Regina Clo. Barn —3A **4**
Regina Ho. SE20 —1K **125**
Reginald Rd. E7 —6J **49**
Reginald Rd. SE8 —7C **80**
Reginald Sq. SE8 —7C **80**
Regina Rd. N4 —1K **45**
Regina Rd. SE25 —3G **125**
Regina Rd. W13 —1A **72**
Regina Rd. S'hall —4C **70**
Regis Rd. NW5 —5F **45**
Regnart Bldgs. NW1
 (off Euston St.) —4G 61 (3M 139)
Reidhaven Rd. SE18 —4J **83**
Reigate Av. Sutt —1J **131**
Reigate Rd. Brom —3H **113**
Reigate Rd. Ilf —2K **51**
Reigate Way. Wall —5J **133**
Reighton Rd. E5 —3G **47**
Relay Rd. W12 —1E **74**
Relf Rd. SE15 —3G **95**
Reliance Arc. SW9 —4A **94**
Reliance Sq. EC2 —4E 62 (3D 142)
 (off Anning St.)
Relko Gdns. Sutt —5B **132**
Relton M. SW7 —3C **76** (6D **144**)
Rembrandt Clo. E14 —3F **81**
Rembrandt Clo. SW1 —5E 76
 (off Graham Ter.)
Rembrandt Rd. SE13 —4G **97**
Rembrandt Rd. Edgw —2G **25**
Rememberance Rd. E7 —4B **50**
Remington Rd. E6 —6C **66**
Remington Rd. N15 —6D **30**
Remington St. N1 —2B **62**

Remnant St. WC2 —6K **61** (7E **140**)
Rempstone M. N1 —2D **62**
Remus Rd. E3 —7C **48**
Rendlesham Rd. E5 —4G **47**
Rendlesham Rd. Enf —1G **7**
Renforth St. SE16 —2J **79**
Renfrew Clo. E6 —7E **66**
Renfrew Ct. Houn —2C **86**
Renfrew Rd. SE11 —4B **78** (8J **147**)
Renfrew Rd. Houn —2C **86**
Renfrew Rd. King T —7H **105**
Renmuir St. SW17 —6D **108**
Rennell St. SE13 —3E **96**
Rennels Way. Iswth —2J **87**
Renness Rd. E17 —3A **32**
Rennets Clo. SE9 —5J **99**
Rennets Wood Rd. SE9 —5H **99**
Rennie Ct. SE1 —1E 78
 (off Stamford St.)
Rennie Est. SE16 —4H **79**
Rennie St. SE1 —1B **78** (2J **147**)
Renown Clo. Croy —1B **134**
Renown Clo. Romf —1G **37**
Rensburg Rd. E17 —5K **31**
Renshaw Clo. Belv —6F **85**
Renters Av. NW4 —6E **26**
Renton Clo. SW2 —6K **93**
Renwick Rd. Bark —4B **68**
Repens Way. Hay —4B **54**
Rephidim St. SE1 —3E **78** (7C **148**)
Replingham Rd. SW18 —1H **107**
Reporton Rd. SW6 —7G **75**
Repository Rd. SE18 —6D **82**
Repton Av. Wemb —4C **40**
Repton Clo. Cars —5C **132**
Repton Ct. Beck —1D **126**
Repton Ct. Ilf —1D **34**
Repton Gro. Ilf —1D **34**
Repton Rd. Harr —4F **25**
Repton St. E14 —6A **64**
Repulse Clo. Romf —1H **37**
Reservoir Rd. N14 —5B **6**
Reservoir Rd. SE4 —2A **96**
Resolution Wlk. SE18 —3D **82**
Restell Clo. SE3 —6G **81**
Reston Pl. SW7 —2A **76**
Restons Cres. SE9 —6H **99**
Restormel Clo. Houn —5E **86**
Retcar Clo. NW5 —2F **45**
Retcar Pl. N19 —2F 45
 (off Retcar Clo.)
Retford St. N1 —2E **62**
Retingham Way. E4 —2J **19**
Retles Ct. Harr —7H **23**
Retreat Clo. Harr —5C **24**
Retreat Ho. E9 —6J **47**
Retreat Pl. E9 —6J **47**
Retreat Rd. Rich —5D **88**
Retreat, The. NW9 —5K **25**
Retreat, The. SW14 —3A **90**
Retreat, The. Surb —6F **119**
Retreat, The. T Hth —4D **124**
Retreat, The. Wor Pk —3D **130**
Reubens Ct. W4 —5H 73
 (off Chaseley Dri.)
Reunion Row. E1 —7H **63**
Reveley Sq. SE16 —2A **80**
Revell Rise. SE18 —6K **83**
Revell Rd. King T —2H **119**
Revell Rd. Sutt —6H **131**
Revelon Rd. SE4 —4A **96**
Revelstoke Rd. SW18 —2H **107**
Reventlow Rd. SE9 —1G **115**
Reverdy Rd. SE1 —4G **79**
Reverend Clo. Harr —3F **39**
Revesby Rd. Cars —6C **122**

Review Rd. NW2 —2B **42**
Review Rd. Dag —2H **69**
Rewell St. SW6 —7A **76**
Rewley Rd. Cars —6B **122**
Rex Clo. Romf —1H **37**
Rex Pl. W1 —7E **60** (1H **145**)
Reydon Av. E11 —6A **34**
Reynard Clo. Brom —3E **128**
Reynard Dri. SE19 —7F **111**
Reynardson Rd. N17 —7H **17**
Reynolds Av. E12 —5E **50**
Reynolds Av. Chad —7C **36**
Reynolds Clo. NW11 —7K **27**
Reynolds Clo. SW19 —1B **122**
Reynolds Clo. Cars —1D **132**
Reynolds Ct. Romf —3D **36**
Reynolds Dri. Edgw —3F **25**
Reynolds Pl. SE3 —7K **81**
Reynolds Pl. Rich —6F **89**
Reynolds Rd. SE15 —4J **95**
Reynolds Rd. W4 —3J **73**
Reynolds Rd. Hay —4A **54**
Reynolds Rd. N Mald —7K **119**
Reynolds Way. Croy —4E **134**
Rheidol M. N1 —2C **62**
Rheidol Ter. N1 —1C **62**
Rheingold Way. Wall —7J **133**
Rhein Ho. N8 —3J 29
 (off Campsbourne Rd.)
Rheola Clo. N17 —1F **31**
Rhoda St. E2 —4F **63** (3F **142**)
Rhodes Av. N22 —1G **29**
Rhodes Ho. N1 —3D 62 (1A 142)
 (off Provost Est.)
Rhodes Ho. W12 —1D 74
 (off White City Est.)
Rhodesia Rd. E11 —2F **49**
Rhodesia Rd. SW9 —2J **93**
Rhodesmoor Ho. Ct. Mord —6J **121**
Rhodes St. N7 —5K **45**
Rhodeswell Rd. E14 —5A **64**
Rhondda Gro. E3 —3A **64**
Rhyl Rd. Gnfd —2K **55**
Rhyl St. NW5 —6E **44**
Rhys Av. N11 —7C **16**
Rialto Rd. Mitc —2E **122**
Ribble Clo. Wfd G —6F **21**
Ribblesdale Av. N'holt —6F **39**
Ribblesdale Rd. N8 —4K **29**
Ribblesdale Rd. SW16 —6F **109**
Ribchester Av. Gnfd —3K **55**
Ricardo Path. SE28 —1C **84**
Ricardo St. E14 —6D **64**
Ricards Rd. SW19 —5H **107**
Riccall Ct. NW9 —1A 26
 (off Pageant Av.)
Rice Pde. Orp —5H **129**
Richard Clo. SE18 —4C **82**
Richard Fell Ho. E12 —4E 50
 (off Walton Rd.)
Richard Foster Clo. E17 —7B **32**
Richards Av. Romf —6J **37**
Richards Clo. Bush —1C **10**
Richards Clo. Harr —5A **24**
Richards Clo. Uxb —7A **38**
Richardson Ct. SW4 —2J 93
 (off Studley Rd.)
Richardson Rd. E15 —2G **65**
Richardson's M. W1
 (off Warren St.) —4G 61 (4L 139)
Richards Pl. E17 —3C **32**
Richard's Pl. SW3 —4C **76** (8D **144**)
Richard St. E1 —6H **63**
Richbell Pl. WC1 —5K **61** (5E **140**)
Richborne Ter. SW8 —7K **77**
Richborough Rd. NW2 —4G **43**
Riches Rd. Ilf —2G **51**
Richfield Rd. Bush —1B **10**

256

Richford Rd. E15 —1H 65
Richford St. W6 —2E 74
Richlands Av. Eps —4C 130
Rich La. SW5 —5K 75
Richmond Av. E4 —5A 20
Richmond Av. N1 —1K 61
Richmond Av. NW10 —6E 42
Richmond Av. SW20 —1G 121
Richmond Bri. Twic & Rich —6D 88
Richmond Bldgs. W1
       —6H 61 (8A 140)
Richmond Clo. E17 —6B 32
Richmond Cotts. W14 —4G 75
  (off Hammersmith Rd.)
Richmond Ct. Wemb —3F 41
Richmond Cres. E4 —5A 20
Richmond Cres. N1 —1K 61
Richmond Cres. N9 —1B 18
Richmond Gdns. NW4 —5C 26
Richmond Gdns. Harr —6E 10
Richmond Grn. Croy —3J 133
Richmond Gro. N1 —7B 46
Richmond Gro. Surb —6F 119
Richmond Hill. Rich —6E 88
Richmond Hill Ct. Rich —6E 88
Richmond Mans. Twic —6D 88
Richmond M. W1 —6H 61 (8A 140)
Richmond M. Tedd —5K 103
Richmond Pk. Rd. SW14 —5J 89
Richmond Pk. Rd. King T —7E 104
Richmond Pl. SE18 —4G 83
Richmond Rd. E4 —1A 20
Richmond Rd. E7 —5K 49
Richmond Rd. E8 —7F 47
Richmond Rd. E11 —2F 49
Richmond Rd. N2 —2A 28
Richmond Rd. N11 —6D 16
Richmond Rd. N15 —6E 30
Richmond Rd. SW20 —1D 120
Richmond Rd. W5 —2E 72
Richmond Rd. Barn —5E 4
Richmond Rd. Croy —3J 133
Richmond Rd. Ilf —3G 51
Richmond Rd. Iswth —3A 88
Richmond Rd. King T —5D 104
Richmond Rd. T Hth —3B 124
Richmond Rd. Twic —7B 88
Richmond St. E13 —2J 65
Richmond Ter. SW1
      —2J 77 (4C 146)
Richmond Ter. M. SW1
      —2J 77 (4C 146)
Richmond Way. E11 —2J 49
Richmond Way. W12 & W14 —2F 75
Richmount Gdns. SE3 —3J 97
Rich St. E14 —7B 64
Rickard Clo. NW4 —4D 26
Rickard Clo. SW2 —1A 110
Rickett St. SW6 —6J 75
Rickman St. E1 —4J 63
Rickmansworth Rd. Pinn —2A 22
Rickthorne Rd. N19 —2J 45
Rickyard Path. SE9 —4C 98
Ridding La. Gnfd —5K 39
Riddons Rd. SE12 —3A 114
Rideout St. SE18 —4D 82
Rider Clo. Sidc —6J 99
Ride, The. Bren —4C 72
Ride, The. Enf —4E 8
Ridgdale St. E3 —2D 64
Ridge Av. N21 —7H 7
Ridgebrook Rd. SE3 —3B 98
Ridge Clo. NW4 —2F 27
Ridge Clo. NW9 —4K 25
Ridge Ct. SE22 —7G 95
Ridge Crest. Enf —1E 6
Ridgecroft Clo. Bex —1J 117
Ridge Hill. NW11 —1G 43

Ridgemont Gdns. Edgw —4D 12
Ridgemount Av. Croy —1K 135
Ridgemount Clo. SE20 —7H 111
Ridgemount Gdns. Enf —3G 7
Ridge Rd. N8 —6K 29
Ridge Rd. N21 —1H 17
Ridge Rd. NW2 —3H 43
Ridge Rd. Mitc —7F 109
Ridge Rd. Sutt —1G 131
Ridge, The. Barn —5C 4
Ridge, The. Bex —7F 101
Ridge, The. Surb —5G 119
Ridge, The. Twic —7H 87
Ridgeview Clo. Barn —6A 4
Ridgeview Rd. N20 —3E 14
Ridgeway. Brom —2J 137
Ridge Way. Felt —3C 102
Ridge Way. Wfd G —4F 21
Ridgeway Av. Barn —6J 5
Ridgeway Ct. Pinn —1E 22
Ridgeway Dri. Brom —4K 113
Ridgeway E. Sidc —5K 99
Ridgeway Gdns. N6 —7H 29
Ridgeway Gdns. Ilf —5C 34
Ridgeway Rd. Iswth —7J 71
Ridgeway Rd. N. Iswth —7J 71
Ridgeway, The. E4 —1K 19
Ridgeway, The. N3 —7E 14
Ridgeway, The. N11 —4J 15
Ridgeway, The. N14 —2D 16
Ridgeway, The. NW7 —4J 13
Ridgeway, The. NW9 —4K 25
Ridgeway, The. NW11 —1H 43
Ridgeway, The. W3 —3G 73
Ridgeway, The. Croy —3K 133
Ridgeway, The. Enf —1E 6
Ridgeway, The. Kent —6C 24
Ridgeway, The. N Har —5D 22
  (in two parts)
Ridgeway, The. Stan —6H 11
Ridgeway, The. Sutt —6B 132
Ridgeway Wlk. N'holt —6C 38
  (off Arnold Rd.)
Ridgeway W. Sidc —5J 99
Ridgewell Clo. N1 —1C 62
Ridgewell Clo. Dag —1H 69
Ridgmount Gdns. WC1
      —5H 61 (4A 140)
Ridgmount Pl. WC1
      —5H 61 (5A 140)
Ridgmount Rd. SW18 —5K 91
Ridgmount St. WC1
      —5H 61 (5A 140)
Ridgway. SW19 —7E 106
Ridgway Gdns. SW19 —7F 107
Ridgway Pl. SW19 —6G 107
Ridgway Rd. SW9 —3B 94
Ridgwell Rd. E16 —5A 66
Riding Ho. St. W1 —5F 61 (6K 139)
Ridings Av. N21 —5H 7
Ridings Clo. N6 —7G 29
Ridings, The. W5 —5F 57
Ridings, The. Barn —7G 5
Ridings, The. Ewe —7B 130
Ridings, The. Surb —5G 119
Riding, The. NW11 —7H 27
Ridler Rd. Enf —1K 7
Ridley Av. W13 —3B 72
Ridley Ct. SW16 —6J 109
Ridley Rd. E7 —4A 50
Ridley Rd. E8 —5F 47
Ridley Rd. NW10 —2C 58
Ridley Rd. SW19 —7K 107
Ridley Rd. Brom —3H 127
Ridley Rd. Well —1B 100
Ridley Several. SE3 —2J 97
Ridsdale Rd. SE20 —1H 125

Riefield Rd. SE9 —4G 99
  (in two parts)
Riesco Dri. Croy —6J 135
Riffel Rd. NW2 —5E 42
Rifle Ct. SE11 —6A 78
Rifle Pl. W11 —1F 75
Rifle St. E14 —5D 64
Rigault Rd. SW6 —2G 91
Rigby Clo. Croy —3A 134
Rigby M. Ilf —2E 50
Rigden St. E14 —6D 64
Rigeley Rd. NW10 —3C 58
Rigg App. E10 —1K 47
Rigge Pl. SW4 —4H 93
Riggindale Rd. SW16 —5H 109
Riley Rd. SE1 —3F 79 (6E 148)
Riley Rd. Enf —1D 8
Riley St. SW10 —7B 76
Rinaldo Rd. SW12 —7F 93
Ring Clo. Brom —7K 113
Ringcroft St. N7 —5A 46
Ringers Rd. Brom —3J 127
Ringford Rd. SW18 —5H 91
Ringles Ct. E6 —1D 66
Ringmer Av. SW6 —1G 91
Ringmer Gdns. N19 —2J 45
Ringmer Pl. N21 —5J 7
Ringmer Way. Brom —5C 128
Ringmore Rise. SE23 —7H 95
Ringshall Rd. Orp —3K 129
Ringslade Rd. N22 —2A 29
Ringstead Rd. SE6 —7D 96
Ringstead Rd. Sutt —4B 132
Ring, The. W2 —1C 76 (2C 144)
Rington Rd. SW6 —6J 75
Ring Way. N11 —6B 16
Ringway. S'hall —5B 70
Ringwold Clo. Beck —7A 112
Ringwood Av. N2 —2D 28
Ringwood Av. Croy —7J 123
Ringwood Clo. Pinn —3A 22
Ringwood Gdns. E13 —4E 80
Ringwood Gdns. SW15 —1C 106
Ringwood Rd. E17 —6B 32
Ringwood Way. N21 —1G 17
Ringwood Way. Hamp —4E 102
Ripley Clo. Brom —6E 136
Ripley Clo. New Ad —6E 136
Ripley Ct. Mitc —2B 122
Ripley Gdns. SW14 —3K 89
Ripley Gdns. Sutt —4A 132
Ripley M. E11 —6G 33
Ripley Rd. E16 —6A 66
Ripley Rd. Belv —4G 85
Ripley Rd. Enf —1H 7
Ripley Rd. Hamp —7E 102
Ripley Rd. Ilf —2K 51
Ripley Vs. W5 —6C 56
Ripon Clo. N'holt —5E 38
Ripon Gdns. Ilf —7C 34
Ripon Rd. N9 —7C 8
Ripon Rd. N17 —3D 30
Ripon Rd. SE18 —6F 83
Rippersley Rd. Well —1A 100
Ripple Rd. Bark & Dag —7G 51
Rippleside Commercial Cen. Bark
      —2C 68
Ripplevale Gro. N1 —7K 45
Rippolson Rd. SE18 —5K 83
Risborough Clo. N10 —3F 29
Risborough Dri. Wor Pk —7C 120
Risborough St. SE1 —1B 78 (4K 147)
Risdon St. SE16 —2J 79
Risedale Rd. Bexh —3J 101
Riseholme St. E9 —6B 48
Riseldine Rd. SE23 —6A 96
Rise Park Pde. Romf —2K 37
Rise, The. E11 —5J 33

Rise, The. N13 —4F 17
Rise, The. NW7 —6G 13
Rise, The. NW10 —4K 41
Rise, The. Bex —7C 100
Rise, The. Buck H —1G 21
Rise, The. Edgw —5C 12
Rise, The. Gnfd —5A 40
Risinghill St. N1 —2K 61
Risingholme Clo. Bush —1A 10
Risingholme Clo. Harr —1J 23
Risingholme Rd. Harr —2J 23
Risings, The. E17 —4F 33
Rising Sun Ct. EC1 —5B 62 (6K 141)
  (off Cloth Fair)
Risley Av. N17 —1C 30
Rita Rd. SW8 —6J 77
Ritches Rd. N15 —5C 30
Ritchie Ho. N19 —1H 45
Ritchie Rd. Croy —6H 125
Ritchie St. N1 —2A 62
Ritherdon Rd. SW17 —2E 108
Ritson Ho. N1 —1K 61
  (off Barnsbury Est.)
Ritson Rd. E8 —6G 47
Ritter St. SE18 —6E 82
Ritz Pde. W5 —4F 57
Rivaz Pl. E9 —6J 47
Rivenhall Gdns. E18 —4H 33
River Av. N13 —3G 17
River Av. Th Dit —7A 118
River Bank. Barn —4E 4
River Bank. Th Dit —5A 118
Riverbank Way. Bren —6C 72
River Barge Clo. E14 —2E 80
River Brent Bus. Pk. W7 —3J 71
River Clo. E11 —6A 34
River Ct. SE1 —1B 78 (2J 147)
Rivercourt Rd. W6 —4D 74
Riverdale. SE13 —3E 96
Riverdale Ct. N21 —5J 7
Riverdale Gdns. Twic —6C 88
Riverdale Rd. SE18 —5K 83
Riverdale Rd. Bex —7F 101
Riverdale Rd. Eri —5H 85
Riverdale Rd. Felt —4C 102
Riverdale Rd. Twic —6C 88
Riverdene. Edgw —3D 12
Riverdene Rd. Ilf —3E 50
River Front. Enf —3K 7
River Gdns. Cars —2C 132
River Gdns. Felt —5A 86
River Gdns. Bus. Cen. Houn —4A 86
River Gro. Pk. Beck —1B 126
Riverhead Clo. E17 —2K 31
Riverhill. Wor Pk —4A 130
Riverholme Dri. Eps —7A 130
River Ho. SE26 —3H 111
River La. Rich —1D 104
Riverleigh Ct. E4 —5G 19
Rivermead Clo. Tedd —5B 104
Rivermead Ct. SW6 —3H 91
Rivermead Ho. E9 —5A 48
River Meads Av. Twic —3E 102
River Pk. N22 —2K 29
River Pk. Gdns. Brom —7F 113
River Pk. Trading Est. E14 —3C 80
River Pl. N1 —7C 46
River Reach. Tedd —5C 104
River Rd. Bark —2J 67
River Rd. Buck H —1H 21
Riversdale Rd. N5 —3B 46
Riversdale Rd. Romf —1H 37
Riversdale Rd. Th Dit —5A 118
Riversfield Rd. Enf —3K 7
Riverside. NW4 —7D 26
Riverside. SE7 —3A 82
Riverside. Rich —5D 88

Riverside. Twic —1B 104
Riverside Apartments. N11 —5E 16
Riverside Av. Rich —1E 88
Riverside Bus. Cen. SW18 —1K 107
Riverside Bus. Cen. Twic —1B 104
Riverside Clo. E5 —2J 47
Riverside Clo. W7 —4J 55
Riverside Clo. King T —4D 118
Riverside Clo. Wall —3F 133
Riverside Cotts. Bark —2H 67
Riverside Ct. E4 —6H 9
Riverside Ct. SE12 —4H 97
Riverside Ct. SW8 —6H 77
Riverside Ct. Iswth —2K 87
  (off Woodlands Rd.)
Riverside Dri. NW11 —6G 27
Riverside Dri. W4 —7K 73
Riverside Dri. Mitc —5C 122
Riverside Dri. Rich —2B 104
Riverside Gdns. W6 —5D 74
Riverside Gdns. Enf —2H 7
Riverside Gdns. Wemb —2E 56
Riverside Ind. Est. Bark —3A 68
Riverside Ind. Est. Enf —6F 9
Riverside Rd. E15 —2K 64
Riverside Rd. N15 —6G 31
Riverside Rd. SW17 —4K 107
Riverside Rd. Sidc —3E 116
Riverside Wlk. N12 & N20 —3E 14
Riverside Wlk. SE10 —3G 81
Riverside Wlk. SW6 —3G 91
Riverside Wlk. Barn —6A 4
Riverside Wlk. Iswth —3J 87
Riverside Wlk. King T —3D 118
Riverside Wlk. W Wick —1D 136
River St. EC1 —3A 62 (1G 141)
River Ter. W6 —5E 74
Riverton Clo. W9 —3H 59
River View. Enf —3H 7
Riverview Gdns. SW13 —6D 74
River View Gdns. Twic —2K 103
Riverview Gro. W4 —6H 73
Riverview Pk. SE6 —2C 112
Riverview Rd. W4 —7H 73
River Wlk. W6 —7E 74
Riverway. N13 —4F 17
River Way. SE10 —3H 81
River Way. Eps —5A 130
River Way. Twic —2F 103
Riverwood La. Chst —1H 129
Rivington Av. Wfd G —2B 34
Rivington Bldgs. EC2
      —3E 62 (2C 142)
Rivington Ct. NW10 —1C 58
Rivington Cres. NW7 —7G 13
Rivington Pl. EC2 —3E 62 (2D 142)
Rivington St. EC2 —3E 62 (2C 142)
Rivington Wlk. E8 —1G 63
Rivulet Rd. N17 —7H 17
Rixon St. N7 —3A 46
Rixsen Rd. E12 —5C 50
Roach Rd. E3 —7C 48
Roads Pl. N19 —2J 45
Roan St. SE10 —6E 80
Robarts Clo. Pinn —6A 22
Robb Rd. Stan —6F 11
Robert Adam St. W1
      —6E 60 (7G 139)
Roberta St. E2 —3G 63
Robert Clo. W9 —4A 60
Robert Dashwood Way. SE17
      —4C 78 (9L 147)
Robert Keen Clo. SE15 —1G 95
Robert Lowe Clo. SE14 —7K 79
Robert M. Orp —7K 129
Roberton Dri. Brom —1A 128
Robert Owen Ho. SW6 —1F 91
  (off Fulham Pal. Rd.)

Roberts All. W5 —2D 72
Robertsbridge Rd. Cars —1A 132
Roberts Clo. SE9 —1H 115
Roberts Clo. Sutt —7F 131
Roberts Ct. SE20 —1J 125
(off Maple Rd.)
Roberts M. SW1 —3E 76 (7G 145)
Robertson Rd. E15 —1E 64
Robertson St. SW8 —3F 93
Roberts Pl. EC1 —4A 62 (3H 141)
Roberts Rd. E17 —1D 32
Roberts Rd. NW7 —6B 14
Roberts Rd. Belv —5G 85
Robert St. E16 —1F 83
Robert St. NW1 —3F 61 (2K 139)
Robert St. SE18 —5H 83
Robert St. WC2 —7J 61 (1D 146)
Robert St. Croy —3C 134
Robeson St. E3 —4B 64
Robina Clo. Bexh —4D 100
Robin Clo. NW7 —6F 13
Robin Clo. Hamp —5C 102
Robin Clo. Romf —1K 37
Robin Ct. E14 —3E 80
Robin Ct. SE16 —4F 79
Robin Cres. E6 —5B 66
Robin Gro. N6 —2E 44
Robin Gro. Bren —6C 72
Robin Gro. Harr —6F 25
Robin Hill Dri. Chst —6C 114
Robinhood Clo. Mitc —4G 123
Robin Hood Dri. Harr —7E 10
Robin Hood Gdns. E14 —7E 64
(off Robin Hood La.)
Robin Hood Grn. Orp —5K 129
Robin Hood La. E14 —7E 64
Robin Hood La. SW15 —4A 106
Robin Hood La. Bexh —5E 100
Robinhood La. Mitc —3G 123
Robin Hood La. Sutt —5J 131
Robin Hood Rd. SW19 & SW15 —5C 106
Robin Hood Way. SW15 & SW20 —3A 106
Robin Hood Way. Gnfd —6K 39
Robins Ct. SE12 —3A 114
Robin's Ct. Beck —2F 127
Robinscroft M. SE10 —1D 96
Robins Gro. W Wick —3J 137
Robinson Cres. Bush —1B 10
Robinson Rd. E2 —2J 63
Robinson Rd. SW17 & SW19 —6C 108
Robinson Rd. Dag —4G 53
Robinson's Clo. W13 —5A 56
Robinson St. SW3 —6D 76
Robinwood Pl. SW15 —4K 105
Robsart St. SW9 —2K 93
Robson Av. NW10 —1C 58
Robson Clo. E6 —6C 66
Robson Clo. Enf —2G 7
Robson Rd. SE27 —3B 110
Roch Av. Edgw —2F 25
Rochdale Rd. E17 —7C 32
Rochdale Rd. SE2 —5B 84
Rochdale Way. SE8 —7C 80
Rochelle Clo. SW11 —4B 92
Rochelle St. E2 —3F 63 (2E 142)
Roche Rd. SW16 —1K 123
Rochester Av. E13 —1A 66
Rochester Av. Brom —2K 127
Rochester Clo. SE3 —3A 98
Rochester Clo. SW16 —7J 109
Rochester Clo. Enf —1K 7
Rochester Dri. Bex —6F 101
Rochester Dri. Pinn —5B 22
Rochester Gdns. Croy —3E 134

Rochester Gdns. Ilf —7D 34
Rochester M. NW1 —7G 45
Rochester Pl. NW1 —6G 45
(in two parts)
Rochester Rd. NW1 —6G 45
Rochester Rd. Cars —4D 132
Rochester Row. SW1
—4G 77 (8M 145)
Rochester Sq. NW1 —7G 45
Rochester St. SW1 —3H 77 (7A 146)
Rochester Ter. NW1 —6G 45
Rochester Wlk. SE1 —1D 78 (3A 148)
(off Stoney St.)
Rochester Way. SE3 & SE9 —1K 97
Rochester Way. Bex & Dart —6J 101
Rochester Way Relief Rd. SE3 & SE9
—1K 97
Roche Wlk. Cars —6B 122
Rochford. N17 —2E 30
(off Griffin Rd.)
Rochford Av. Romf —5C 36
Rochford Clo. E6 —2B 66
Rochford Ho. SE8 —5B 80
Rochford Wlk. E8 —7G 47
Rochford Way. Croy —6J 123
Rock Av. SW14 —3K 89
Rockbourne M. SE23 —1K 111
Rockbourne Rd. SE23 —1K 111
Rockell's Pl. SE22 —6H 95
Rockett Clo. SE8 —4A 80
Rockfield Ho. NW4 —4F 27
(off Belle Vue Est.)
Rockford Av. Gnfd —2A 56
Rock Gdns. Dag —5H 53
Rock Gro. Way. SE16 —4H 79
Rockhall Rd. NW2 —4F 43
Rockhampton Clo. SE27 —4A 110
Rockhampton Rd. SE27 —4A 110
Rockhampton Rd. S Croy —6E 134
Rock Hill. SE26 —4K 111
Rockingham Clo. SW15 —4B 90
Rockingham St. SE1
—3C 78 (7L 147)
Rockland Rd. SW15 —4G 91
Rocklands Dri. Stan —2B 24
Rockley Ct. W14 —2F 75
(off Rockley Rd.)
Rockley Rd. W14 —2F 75
Rockmount Rd. SE18 —5K 83
Rockmount Rd. SE19 —6D 110
Rocks La. SW13 —1C 90
Rock St. N4 —2A 46
Rockware Av. Gnfd —1H 55
Rockware Av. Bus. Cen. Gnfd
—1H 55
Rockwell Gdns. SE19 —5E 110
Rockwell Rd. Dag —5H 53
Rocliffe St. N1 —2B 62
Rocombe Cres. SE23 —7J 95
Rocque Ho. SW6 —7H 75
(off Estcourt Rd.)
Rocque La. SE3 —3H 97
Rodborough Rd. NW11 —1J 43
Roden Gdns. Croy —6E 124
Rodenhurst Rd. SW4 —6G 93
Roden St. N7 —3K 45
Roden St. Ilf —3E 50
Roderick Rd. NW3 —4D 44
Rodgers Ho. SW4 —7H 93
(off Clapham Pk. Est.)
Roding Av. Wfd G —6H 21
Roding Ho. N1 —1A 62
(off Barnsbury Est.)
Roding La. Buck H & Chig —1G 21
Roding La. N. Wfd G —2B 34
Roding La. S. Ilf & Wfd G —4B 34
Roding M. E1 —1G 79

Roding Rd. E5 —4K 47
Roding Rd. E6 —5F 67
Rodings, The. Wfd G —6F 21
Roding Trading Est. Bark —7F 51
Roding View. Buck H —1G 21
Rodmarton St. W1 —5D 60 (6F 138)
Rodmell Clo. Hay —4C 54
Rodmell Slope. N12 —5C 14
Rodmere St. SE10 —5G 81
Rodmill La. SW2 —7J 93
Rodney Clo. Croy —1B 134
Rodney Clo. N Mald —5A 120
Rodney Clo. Pinn —7C 22
Rodney Ct. W9 —4A 60
(off Maida Vale)
Rodney Gdns. Pinn —5A 22
Rodney Gdns. W Wick —4J 137
Rodney Pl. E17 —2A 32
Rodney Pl. SE17 —4C 78 (8M 147)
Rodney Pl. SW19 —1A 122
Rodney Rd. E11 —4K 33
Rodney Rd. SE17 —4C 78
Rodney Rd. Mitc —3C 122
Rodney Rd. N Mald —5A 120
Rodney Rd. Twic —6E 86
Rodney St. N1 —2K 61
Rodney Way. Romf —1G 37
Rodsley St. SE1 —6G 79
Rodway Rd. SW15 —7C 90
Rodway Rd. Brom —1K 127
Rodwell Clo. Ruis —1A 38
Rodwell Pl. Edgw —6B 12
Rodwell Rd. SE22 —6F 95
Rodwell Rd. N'holt —1E 54
Roe. NW9 —1B 26
Roebourne Way. E16 —1E 82
Roebuck La. N17 —6A 18
Roebuck La. Buck H —1F 21
Roedean Av. Enf —1D 8
Roedean Clo. Enf —1D 8
Roedean Cres. SW15 —6A 90
Roe End. NW9 —4J 25
Roe Grn. NW9 —5J 25
Roehampton Clo. SW15 —4C 90
Roehampton Dri. Chst —6G 115
Roehampton Ga. SW15 —6A 90
Roehampton High St. SW15 —7C 90
Roehampton La. SW15 —4C 90
Roehampton Vale. SW15 —3B 106
Roe La. NW9 —4H 25
Roe Way. Wall —6J 133
Roffey St. E14 —2E 80
Rogate Ho. E5 —3G 47
Roger Dowley Ct. E2 —2J 63
Roger Reede's Almshouses. Romf
—4K 37
Rogers Est. E2 —3J 63
Rogers Gdns. Dag —5G 53
Roger's Ho. Dag —3G 53
Rogers Rd. E16 —6H 65
Rogers Rd. SW17 —4B 108
Rogers Rd. Dag —5G 53
Roger St. WC1 —4K 61 (4F 140)
Rogers Wlk. N12 —3E 14
Rojack Rd. SE23 —1K 111
Rokeby Gdns. Wfd G —1J 33
Rokeby Pl. SW20 —7D 106
Rokeby Rd. SE4 —2B 96
Rokeby Rd. Harr —3H 23
Rokeby St. E15 —1G 65
Rokesby Clo. Well —2H 99
Rokesby Pl. Wemb —5D 40
Rokesly Av. N8 —5J 29
Roland Gdns. SW7 —5A 76
Roland M. E1 —5K 63
Roland Rd. E17 —4F 33
Roland Way. SE17 —5D 78

Roland Way. SW7 —5A 76
Roland Way. Wor Pk —2B 130
Roles Gro. Romf —4D 36
Rolfe Clo. Barn —4H 5
Rolland Ho. W7 —5J 55
Rollesby Way. SE28 —6C 68
Rolleston Av. Orp —6F 129
Rolleston Clo. Orp —7F 129
Rolleston Rd. S Croy —7D 134
Roll Gdns. Ilf —5E 34
Rollins St. SE15 —6J 79
Rollit Cres. Houn —5E 86
Rollit St. N7 —5A 46
Rolls Bldgs. EC4 —6A 62 (7H 141)
Rollscourt Av. SE24 —5C 94
Rolls Pk. Av. E4 —5H 19
Rolls Pk. Rd. E4 —5J 19
Rolls Pas. EC4 —6A 62 (7G 141)
(off Chancery La.)
Rolls Rd. SE1 —5F 79
Rolt St. SE8 —6A 80
Rolvenden Gdns. Brom —7B 114
Rolvenden Pl. N17 —1G 31
Roman Clo. W3 —2H 73
Roman Clo. Felt —5A 86
Roman Clo. Rain —2K 69
Roman Ho. EC2 —5C 62 (6M 141)
(off Wind St.)
Romanhurst Av. Brom —4G 127
Romanhurst Gdns. Brom —4G 127
Roman Ind. Est. Croy —7E 124
Roman Rise. SE19 —6D 110
Roman Rd. E2 & E3 —3J 63
Roman Rd. E6 —4C 66
Roman Rd. N10 —7A 16
Roman Rd. NW2 —3E 42
Roman Rd. W4 —4B 74
Roman Rd. Ilf —8F 51
Roman Sq. SE28 —1A 84
Roman Way. N7 —6K 45
Roman Way. SE15 —7J 79
Roman Way. Croy —2B 134
Roman Way. Enf —5A 8
Romany Gdns. E17 —1A 32
Romany Gdns. Sutt —7J 121
Romany Rd. SE27 —5D 110
Roma Read Clo. SW15 —7D 90
Roma Rd. E17 —3A 32
Romberg Rd. SW17 —3E 108
Romborough Gdns. SE13 —5E 96
Romborough Way. SE13 —5E 96
Romero Clo. SW9 —3K 93
Romero Sq. SE3 —4A 98
Romeyn Rd. SW16 —3K 109
Romford Rd. E15, E7 & E12 —7J 49
Romford Rd. Romf —1E 36
Romford St. E1 —5H 63
Romilly Rd. N4 —2B 46
Romilly St. W1 —7H 61 (9B 140)
Romily Ct. SW6 —2G 91
Rommany Rd. SE27 —4D 110
Romney Clo. NW11 —1A 44
Romney Clo. N14 —7J 79
Romney Clo. Harr —7E 22
Romney Ct. W12 —2E 74
(off Shepherd's Bush Grn.)
Romney Dri. Brom —7B 114
Romney Dri. Harr —7E 22
Romney Gdns. Bexh —1F 101
Romney M. W1 —5E 60 (5G 139)
Romney Rd. SE10 —6F 81
Romney Rd. N Mald —6K 119
Romney St. SW1 —3J 77 (7B 146)
Romola Rd. SE24 —1B 110
Romsey Gdns. Dag —1D 68
Romsey Rd. W13 —7A 56
Romsey Rd. Dag —1D 68
Romulus Ct. Bren —7D 72

Ronald Av. E15 —3G 65
Ronald Clo. Beck —5B 126
Ronald Ct. New Bar —3E 4
Ronaldshay. N4 —1A 46
Ronalds Rd. N5 —5A 46
Ronaldstone Rd. Sidc —6J 99
Ronald St. E1 —6J 63
Rona Rd. NW3 —4E 44
Ronart St. W'stone —3K 23
Rona Wlk. N1 —6D 46
(off Ramsey Wlk.)
Rondu Rd. NW2 —5G 43
Ronver Rd. SE12 —1H 113
Rood La. EC3 —7E 62 (9C 142)
Rookby Ct. N21 —2G 17
Rookeries Clo. Felt —3A 102
Rookery Clo. NW9 —5B 26
Rookery Cres. Dag —7H 53
Rookery Dri. Chst —1E 128
Rookery La. Brom —6B 128
Rookery Rd. SW4 —4G 93
Rookery Way. NW9 —5B 26
Rooke Way. SE10 —5H 81
Rookfield Av. N10 —4G 29
Rookfield Clo. N10 —4G 29
Rookstone Rd. SW17 —5D 108
Rook Wlk. E6 —6B 66
Rookwood Av. N Mald —4C 120
Rookwood Av. Wall —4H 133
Rookwood Gdns. E4 —2C 20
Rookwood Ho. Bark —2H 67
Rookwood Rd. N16 —7F 31
Roosevelt Way. Dag —6K 53
Ropemaker Rd. SE16 —2A 80
Ropemaker's Field. E14 —5B 64
Ropemaker St. EC2
—5D 62 (5A 142)
Roper La. SE1 —2E 78 (5D 148)
Ropers Av. E4 —5J 19
Ropers Orchard. SW3 —6C 76
(off Danvers St.)
Roper St. SE9 —5D 98
Ropers Wlk. SW2 —7A 94
Roper Way. Mitc —2E 122
Ropery St. E3 —4B 64
Rope St. SE16 —4A 80
Rope Wlk. Gdns. E1 —6G 63
Rope Yd. Rails. SE18 —3F 83
Ropley St. E2 —2G 63
Rosa Alba M. N5 —4C 46
Rosalind Ct. Bark —7A 52
(off Meadow Rd.)
Rosalind Ho. N1 —2E 62
(off Arden Ho.)
Rosaline Rd. SW6 —7G 75
Rosamond St. SE26 —3H 111
Rosamund Clo. S Croy —4D 134
Rosary Clo. Houn —2C 86
Rosary Gdns. SW7 —4A 76
Rosaville Rd. SW6 —7H 75
Roscoe St. EC1 —4C 62 (4M 141)
Roscoe St. Est. EC1
(off Roscoe St.)
Roscoff Clo. Edgw —1J 25
Roseacre Clo. W13 —5B 56
Roseacre Rd. Well —3B 100
Rose All. SE1 —1C 78
Rose Av. E18 —2K 33
Rose Av. Mitc —1D 122
Rose Av. Mord —5A 122
Rosebank. SE20 —7H 111
Rosebank Av. Wemb —4K 39
Rose Bank Clo. N12 —5H 15
Rosebank Gdns. E3 —2B 64
Rosebank Gro. E17 —3B 32
Rosebank Rd. E17 —6D 32
Rosebank Rd. W7 —2J 71

Rosebank Vs. E17 —4C 32
Rosebank Wlk. NW1 —7H 45
Rosebank Wlk. SE18 —4C 82
Rosebank Way. W3 —6K 57
Rose Bates Dri. NW9 —4G 25
Roseberry Av. N Mald —2B 120
Roseberry Av. T Hth —2C 124
Roseberry Gdns. N4 —6B 30
Roseberry Gdns. N8 —5J 29
Roseberry Pl. E8 —6F 47
Roseberry St. SE16 —4H 79
Rosebery Av. E12 —6C 50
Rosebery Av. N17 —2G 31
Rosebery Av. Harr —4C 38
Rosebery Av. Sidc —7J 99
Rosebery Clo. Mord —6F 121
Rosebery Ct. EC1 —4A 62 (3G 141)
  (off Rosebery Av.)
Rosebery Gdns. W13 —6A 56
Rosebery Gdns. Sutt —4K 131
Rosebery Ind. Est. N17 —2H 31
Rosebery Ind. Pk. N17 —2H 31
Rosebery M. N10 —2G 29
Rosebery Rd. N9 —3B 18
Rosebery Rd. N10 —2G 29
Rosebery Rd. SW2 —6J 93
Rosebery Rd. Bush —1A 10
Rosebery Rd. Houn —5G 87
Rosebery Rd. King T —2H 119
Rosebery Rd. Sutt —6H 131
Rosebery Sq. EC1 —4A 62 (4G 141)
  (off Rosebery Av.)
Rosebery Sq. King T —2H 119
Rosebine Av. Twic —7H 87
Rosebury Rd. SW6 —2K 91
Rose Ct. E1 —5F 63 (6E 142)
  (off Wentworth St.)
Rose Ct. S Harr —2G 39
Rose Ct. Wemb —2E 56
  (off Vicars Bri. Clo.)
Rosecourt Rd. Croy —6K 123
Rosecroft. N14 —2C 16
Rosecroft Av. NW3 —3J 43
Rosecroft Gdns. NW2 —3C 42
Rosecroft Gdns. Twic —1H 103
Rosecroft Rd. S'hall —4E 54
Rosecroft Wlk. Pinn —5B 22
Rosecroft Wlk. Wemb —5D 40
Rose & Crown Ct. EC2
  (off Foster La.) —6C 62 (7L 141)
Rose & Crown Pas. Iswth —1A 88
Rose & Crown Yd. SW1
  —1G 77 (3M 145)
Rosedale Clo. SE2 —3B 84
Rosedale Clo. W7 —2K 71
Rosedale Clo. Stan —5G 11
Rosedale Ct. N5 —4B 46
Rosedale Gdns. Dag —7B 52
Rosedale Ho. N16 —1D 46
Rosedale Rd. E7 —5A 50
Rosedale Rd. SE21 —1C 110
Rosedale Rd. Dag —7B 52
Rosedale Rd. Eps —5C 130
Rosedale Rd. Rich —4E 88
Rosedale Rd. Romf —2J 37
Rosedale Ter. W6 —3D 74
  (off Dalling Rd.)
Rosedene. NW6 —1F 59
Rosedene Av. SW16 —3K 109
Rosedene Av. Croy —7J 123
Rosedene Av. Gnfd —3E 54
Rosedene Av. Mord —5J 121
Rosedene Gdns. Ilf —4E 34
Rosedene Ter. E10 —2D 48
Rosedew Rd. W6 —6F 75
Rose End. Wor Pk —1F 131
Rosefield Clo. Cars —5C 132
Rosefield Gdns. E14 —7C 64

Roseford Ct. W12 —2F 75
  (off Shepherd's Bush Grn.)
Rose Garden Clo. Edgw —6K 11
Rose Gdns. W5 —3D 72
Rose Gdns. S'hall —4E 54
Rose Glen. NW9 —4K 25
Rose Glen. Romf —1K 53
Rosehart M. W11 —6J 59
Rosehatch Av. Romf —3D 36
Roseheath Rd. Houn —5D 86
Rosehill. Hamp —7E 102
Rose Hill. Sutt —3K 131
Rosehill Av. Sutt —1A 132
Rosehill Ct. Mord —7A 122
  (off St Helier Av.)
Rosehill Gdns. Gnfd —5K 39
Rosehill Gdns. Sutt —2K 131
Rose Hill Pk. W. Sutt —1A 132
Rosehill Rd. SW18 —6A 92
Roseland Clo. N17 —7J 17
Rose La. Romf —3D 36
Rose Lawn. Bush —1B 10
Roseleigh Av. N5 —4B 46
Roseleigh Clo. Twic —6D 88
Rosemary Av. N2 —4K 27
Rosemary Av. N3 —2K 27
Rosemary Av. N9 —1C 18
Rosemary Av. Enf —1K 7
Rosemary Av. Houn —2B 86
Rosemary Dri. E14 —6F 65
Rosemary Dri. Ilf —5B 34
Rosemary Gdns. SW14 —3J 89
Rosemary Gdns. Dag —1F 53
Rosemary Ho. N1 —1D 62
  (off Colville Est.)
Rosemary La. SW14 —3J 89
Rosemary Rd. SE15 —7F 79
Rosemary Rd. SW17 —3A 108
Rosemary Rd. Well —1K 99
Rosemary St. N1 —1D 62
Rosemead. NW9 —7B 26
Rosemead Av. Mitc —3G 123
Rosemead Av. Wemb —5E 40
Rosemont Av. N12 —6F 15
Rosemont Rd. NW3 —6A 44
Rosemont Rd. W3 —7H 57
Rosemont Rd. N Mald —3J 119
Rosemont Rd. Rich —6E 88
Rosemont Rd. Wemb —1E 56
Rosemoor St. SW3
  —4D 76 (9E 144)
Rosemount Clo. Wfd G —6J 21
Rosemount Dri. Brom —4D 128
Rosemount Rd. W13 —6A 56
Rosenau Cres. SW11 —1D 92
Rosenau Rd. SW11 —1C 92
Rosendale Rd. SE21 —3D 110
Rosendale Rd. SE24 & SE21
  —7C 94
Roseneath Av. N21 —1G 17
Roseneath Rd. SW11 —6E 92
Roseneath Wlk. Enf —4K 7
Rosen's Wlk. Edgw —3C 12
Rosenthal Rd. SE6 —6D 96
Rosenthorpe Rd. SE15 —5K 95
Rosepark Ct. Ilf —2D 34
Roserton St. E14 —2E 80
Rosery, The. Croy —6K 125
Roses, The. Wfd G —7C 20
Rose St. WC2 —7J 61 (9C 140)
Rosethorn Clo. SW12 —7H 93
Rosetta Clo. SW8 —7J 77
Roseveare Rd. SE12 —4A 114
Roseville Av. Houn —5E 86
Rosevine Rd. SW20 —1E 120
Rose Wlk. Surb —5H 119
Rose Wlk. W Wick —2E 136
Rose Way. SE12 —5J 97

Roseway. SE21 —6D 94
Rose Way. Edgw —4D 12
Rosewood Av. Gnfd —5A 40
Rosewood Clo. Sidc —3C 116
Rosewood Ct. E8 —7F 47
Rosewood Ct. Brom —1A 128
Rosewood Gdns. SE13 —2E 96
Rosewood Gro. Sutt —2A 132
Rosewood Sq. W12 —6C 58
Rosher Clo. E15 —7F 49
Roshni Ho. SW17 —6C 108
Rosina St. E9 —6K 47
Roskell Rd. SW15 —3F 91
Roslin Rd. W3 —3H 73
Roslin Way. Brom —5H 113
Roslyn Clo. Mitc —2B 122
Roslyn M. N15 —5E 30
Roslyn Rd. N15 —5D 30
Rosmead Rd. W11 —7G 59
Rosoman Pl. EC1 —4A 62 (3H 141)
Rosoman St. EC1 —3A 62 (2H 141)
Rossall Cres. NW10 —3F 57
Ross Av. NW7 —5B 14
Ross Av. Dag —1F 53
Ross Clo. Harr —7B 10
Ross Ct. NW9 —3A 26
Rossdale. Sutt —5C 132
Rossdale Dri. N9 —6D 8
Rossdale Dri. NW9 —1J 41
Rossdale Rd. SW15 —4E 90
Rosse M. SE3 —1K 97
Rossendale St. E5 —2H 47
Rossendale Way. NW1 —7G 45
Rossignol Gdns. Cars —2E 132
Rossindel Rd. Houn —5E 86
Rossington St. E5 —2G 47
Rossiter Fields. Barn —6C 4
Rossiter Rd. SW12 —1F 109
Rossland Clo. Bexh —5H 101
Rosslyn Av. E4 —2C 20
Rosslyn Av. SW13 —3A 90
Rosslyn Av. Barn —6H 5
Rosslyn Av. Dag —7F 37
Rosslyn Clo. W Wick —3H 137
Rosslyn Cres. Harr —4K 23
Rosslyn Cres. Wemb —4E 40
Rosslyn Gdns. Wemb —3E 40
  (off Rosslyn Cres.)
Rosslyn Hill. NW3 —4B 44
Rosslyn M. NW3 —4B 44
Rosslyn Pk. M. NW3 —5B 44
Rosslyn Rd. E17 —4E 32
Rosslyn Rd. Bark —7H 51
Rosslyn Rd. Twic —6C 88
Rossmore Rd. NW1 —4C 60 (4D 138)
Ross Pde. Wall —6F 133
Ross Rd. SE25 —3D 124
Ross Rd. Twic —1F 103
Ross Rd. Wall —5G 133
Ross Way. SE9 —3C 98
Rosswood Gdns. Wall —6G 133
Ross Wyld Lodge. E17 —3C 32
  (off Forest Rd.)
Rostella Rd. SW17 —4B 108
Rostrevor Av. N15 —6F 31
Rostrevor Gdns. S'hall —5C 70
Rostrevor M. SW6 —1H 91
Rostrevor Rd. SW6 —1H 91
Rostrevor Rd. SW19 —5J 107
Rotary St. SE1 —3B 78 (6J 147)
Rothbury Gdns. Iswth —7A 72
Rothbury Rd. E9 —7B 48
Rothbury Wlk. N17 —7B 18
Rotherfield Rd. Cars —4E 132
Rotherfield St. N1 —7C 46
Rotherham Wlk. SE1 —1B 78 (3J 147)
  (off Nicholson St.)
Rotherhill Av. SW16 —6H 109

Rotherhithe New Rd. SE16 —5G 79
Rotherhithe Old Rd. SE16 —4K 79
Rotherhithe St. SE16 —2J 79
Rother Ho. SE15 —4H 95
Rothermere Rd. Croy —5K 133
Rotherwick Hill. W5 —4F 57
Rotherwick Rd. NW11 —7J 27
Rotherwood Clo. SW20 —1G 121
Rotherwood Rd. SW15 —3F 91
Rothery St. N1 —1B 62
  (off St Marys Path)
Rothesay Av. SW20 —2G 121
Rothesay Av. Gnfd —6G 39
Rothesay Av. Rich —4H 89
Rothesay Ct. SE11 —6A 78
  (off Harleyford St.)
Rothesay Ct. SE12 —3K 113
Rothesay Rd. SE25 —4D 124
Rothsay Rd. E7 —7A 50
Rothsay St. SE1 —3E 78 (6C 148)
Rothsay Wlk. E14 —4C 80
  (off Charnwood Gdns.)
Rothschild Rd. W4 —4J 73
Rothschild St. SE27 —4B 110
Roth Wlk. N7 —2K 45
Rothwell Ct. Harr —5K 23
Rothwell Gdns. Dag —7G 52
Rothwell Ho. Houn —6E 70
Rothwell Rd. Dag —1C 68
Rothwell St. NW1 —1D 60
Rotten Row. NW3 —1A 44
Rotten Row. SW7 & SW1
  —2B 76 (4B 144)
Rotterdam Dri. E14 —3E 80
Rotunda, The. Romf —5K 37
  (off Yew Tree Gdns.)
Rouel Rd. SE16 —3G 79
  (in two parts)
Rougemont Av. Mord —6J 121
Roundacre. SW19 —2F 107
Roundaway Rd. Ilf —2D 34
Roundel Clo. SE4 —4B 96
Round Gro. Croy —7K 125
Roundhay Clo. SE23 —2K 111
Roundhedge Way. Enf —1E 6
Round Hill. SE26 —3J 111
Roundhill Dri. Enf —4E 6
Roundtable Rd. Brom —3H 113
Roundtree Rd. Wemb —5B 40
Roundway, The. N17 —1D 30
Roundwood. Chst —2F 129
Roundwood Rd. NW10 —6B 42
Rounton Rd. E3 —4C 64
Roupel Ho. SE15 —7G 79
  (off Sumner Est.)
Roupell Rd. SW2 —1K 109
Roupell St. SE1 —1A 78 (3H 147)
Rousden St. NW1 —7G 45
Rouse Gdns. SE21 —4E 110
Rous Rd. Buck H —1H 21
Routh Rd. SW18 —7C 92
Routh St. E6 —5D 66
Routledge Clo. N19 —1H 45
Rover Ho. N1 —1E 62
  (off Whitmore Est.)
Rowallan Rd. SW6 —7G 75
Rowan. N10 —2F 29
Rowan Av. E4 —6G 19
Rowan Clo. SW16 —1G 123
Rowan Clo. W5 —2E 72
Rowan Clo. N Mald —2A 120
Rowan Clo. Stan —6E 10
Rowan Clo. Wemb —3A 40
Rowan Ct. E8 —7F 47
Rowan Ct. E13 —2K 65
  (off High St. Plaistow)
Rowan Ct. SE15 —7F 79
  (off Garnies Clo.)

Rowan Ct. SW11 —6D 92
Rowan Cres. SW16 —1G 123
Rowan Cres. Croy —3F 135
Rowan Dri. NW9 —3C 26
Rowan Gdns. Croy —3E 135
Rowan Ho. W5 —5B 56
Rowan Ho. Hayes —2G 127
Rowan Ho. Sidc —3K 115
Rowan Rd. SW16 —2G 123
Rowan Rd. W6 —4F 75
Rowan Rd. Bexh —3E 100
Rowan Rd. Bren —7B 72
Rowans, The. N13 —3G 17
Rowan Ter. W6 —4F 75
  (off Rowan Rd.)
Rowantree Clo. N21 —1J 17
Rowantree Rd. N21 —1J 17
Rowantree Rd. Enf —2G 7
Rowan Wlk. N2 —6A 28
Rowan Wlk. N19 —2G 45
Rowan Wlk. W10 —4G 59
Rowan Way. Romf —3C 36
Rowanwood Av. Sidc —1J 115
Rowben Clo. N20 —1E 14
Rowberry Clo. SW6 —7E 74
Rowcross Pl. SE1 —5F 79
  (off Rowcross St.)
Rowcross St. SE1 —5F 79
Rowdell Rd. N'holt —1E 54
Rowden Rd. E4 —6J 19
Rowden Rd. Beck —1A 126
Rowditch La. SW11 —2E 92
Rowdon Av. NW10 —7C 42
Rowdown Cres. New Ad —7F 137
Rowdowns Rd. Dag —1F 69
Rowe Gdns. Bark —2K 67
Rowe La. E9 —5J 47
Rowena Cres. SW11 —2C 92
Rowe Wlk. Harr —3E 38
Rowfant Rd. SW17 —1E 108
Rowhill Rd. E5 —4H 47
Rowington Clo. W2 —5K 59
Rowland Av. Harr —3C 24
Rowland Ct. E16 —4H 65
Rowland Gro. SE26 —3H 111
Rowland Hill Av. N17 —7H 17
Rowland Hill Ho. SE1
  —2B 78 (4J 147)
Rowland Hill St. NW3 —5C 44
Rowlands Av. Pinn —5A 10
Rowlands Clo. N6 —6E 28
Rowlands Clo. NW7 —7H 13
Rowlands Rd. Dag —2F 53
Rowland Way. SW19 —1K 121
Rowley Av. Sidc —7B 100
Rowley Clo. Wemb —7F 41
Rowley Ct. Enf —5K 7
  (off Wellington Rd.)
Rowley Gdns. N4 —7C 30
Rowley Ho. N15 —5C 30
Rowley Way. NW8 —1K 59
Rowlls Rd. King T —3F 119
Rowney Gdns. Dag —6C 52
Rowney Rd. Dag —6B 52
Rowntree Clifford Clo. E13 —4K 65
Rowntree Path. SE28 —1B 84
Rowntree Rd. Twic —1J 103
Rowse Clo. E15 —1E 64
Rowsley Av. NW4 —3E 26
Rowstock Gdns. N7 —5H 45
Rowton Rd. SE18 —7G 83
Roxborough Av. Harr —7H 23
Roxborough Av. Iswth —7K 71
Roxborough Pk. Harr —7J 23
Roxborough Rd. Harr —5H 23
Roxbourne Clo. N'holt —6C 38
Roxburgh Rd. SE27 —5B 110
Roxby Pl. SW6 —6J 75

Roxeth Grn. Av. Harr —3F **39**
Roxeth Grn. Har —2H **39**
Roxeth Hill. Harr —2H **39**
Roxley Rd. SE13 —6D **96**
Roxton Gdns. Croy —5C **136**
Roxwell Rd. W12 —2C **74**
Roxwell Rd. Bark —2A **68**
Roxwell Trading Pk. E10 —7A **32**
Roxwell Way. Wfd G —7F **21**
Roxy Av. Romf —7C **36**
Royal Albert Way. E16 —7B **66**
Royal Arc. W1 —7G 61 (1L 145)
(off Old Bond St.)
Royal Av. SW3 —5D **76**
Royal Av. Wor Pk —2A **130**
Royal Cir. SE27 —3A **110**
Royal Clo. Ilf —7A **36**
Royal Clo. Wor Pk —2A **130**
Royal College St. NW1 —7G **45**
Royal Ct. SE16 —3B **80**
Royal Cres. W11 —1F **75**
Royal Cres. Ruis —4C **38**
Royal Cres. M. W11 —1F **75**
Royal Docks Rd. E6 & Bark —5F **67**
Royal Exchange Av. EC3
(off Finch La.) —6D **62** *(8B 142)*
Royal Exchange Bldgs. EC3
—6D **62** *(8B 142)*
(off Threadneedle St.)
Royal Gdns. W7 —3A **72**
Royal Hill. SE10 —7E **80**
Royal Hospital Rd. SW3 —6D **76**
Royal London Est., The. N17 —6C **18**
Royal London Ind. Est. NW10
—2K **57**
Royal Mint Ct. EC3 —7F **63** (1F **148**)
Royal Mint Pl. E1 —7G **63**
Royal Mint St. E1 —7F **63**
Royal Naval Pl. SE14 —7B **80**
Royal Oak Ct. SE22 —6H **95**
Royal Oak Rd. E8 —6H **47**
Royal Oak Rd. Bexh —5F **101**
Royal Opera Arc. SW1
—1H **77** (2A **146**)
Royal Orchard Clo. SW18 —7G **91**
Royal Pde. SE3 —2H **97**
Royal Pde. SW6 —7G **75**
Royal Pde. W5 —3E **56**
Royal Pde. Chst —7G **115**
Royal Pde. Dag —6H 53
(off Church St.)
Royal Pde. Rich —1G **89**
Royal Pde. M. Chst —7G 115
(off Royal Pde.)
Royal Pl. SE10 —7E **80**
Royal Rd. E16 —6A **66**
Royal Rd. SE17 —6B **78**
Royal Rd. Sidc —3D **116**
Royal Rd. Tedd —5H **103**
Royal St. SE1 —3K 77 (6F 146)
(off Dean St.)
Royal Victoria Patriotic Building.
SW18 —6B **92**
Royal Victor Pl. E3 —2K **63**
Royal Wlk. Wall —2F **133**
Roycraft Av. Bark —2K **67**
Roycroft Clo. E18 —1K **33**
Roycroft Clo. SW2 —1A **110**
Roydene Rd. SE18 —6J **83**
Roy Dennison Ho. E13 —3J **65**
Roydon Clo. Lou —1H **21**
Roy Gdns. Ilf —4J **35**
Roy Gro. Hamp —6F **103**
Royle Cres. W13 —4A **56**
Roymount Ct. Twic —3J **103**
Roy Sq. E14 —7A **64**

Royston Av. E4 —5H **19**
Royston Av. Sutt —3B **132**
Royston Av. Wall —4H **133**
Royston Ct. E13 —1J **65**
(off Stopford Rd.)
Royston Ct. SE24 —6C **94**
Royston Ct. Rich —1F **89**
Royston Gdns. Ilf —6B **34**
Royston Ho. N11 —4J **15**
Royston Pde. Ilf —6B **34**
Royston Rd. Rd. Pinn —5A **10**
Royston Rd. SE20 —1K **125**
Royston Rd. Rich —5E **88**
Roystons, The. Surb —5H **119**
Royston St. E2 —2J **63**
Rozel Ct. N1 —1E **62**
Rozel Rd. SW4 —3G **93**
Rubastic Rd. S'hall —3A **70**
Ruberoid Rd. Enf —3G **9**
Ruby M. E17 —3C **32**
Ruby Rd. E17 —3C **32**
Ruby St. SE15 —6H **79**
Ruby Triangle. SE15 —6H **79**
Ruckholt Clo. E10 —3D **48**
Ruckholt Rd. E10 —4D **48**
Rucklidge Av. NW10 —2B **58**
Rucklidge Pas. NW10 —2B **58**
(off Rucklidge Av.)
Rudall Cres. NW3 —4B **44**
Ruddstreet Clo. SE18 —4F **83**
Ruddy Way. NW7 —6G **13**
Rudgwick Ct. SE18 —4C 82
(off Woodville St.)
Rudland Rd. Bexh —3H **101**
Rudloe Rd. SW12 —7G **93**
Rudolf Pl. SW8 —6J **77**
Rudolph Rd. E13 —2H **65**
Rudolph Rd. NW6 —2J **59**
Rudyard Gro. NW7 —6D **12**
Ruffetts Clo. S Croy —7H **135**
Ruffetts, The. S Croy —7H **135**
Rufford Clo. Har —6A **24**
Rufford St. N1 —1J **61**
Rufford Tower. W3 —1H **73**
Rufforth Ct. NW9 —1A 26
(off Pageant Av.)
Rufus Clo. Ruis —3C **38**
Rufus St. N1 —3E **62** (2C **142**)
Rugby Av. N9 —1A **18**
Rugby Av. Gnfd —6H **39**
Rugby Av. Wemb —5B **40**
Rugby Clo. Harr —4J **23**
Rugby Gdns. Dag —6C **52**
Rugby La. Sutt —7F **131**
Rugby Rd. NW9 —4H **25**
Rugby Rd. W4 —2A **74**
Rugby Rd. Dag —7B **52**
Rugby Rd. Twic —5J **87**
Rugby St. WC1 —4K **61** (4E **140**)
Rugg St. E14 —7C **64**
Ruislip Clo. Gnfd —4F **55**
Ruislip Rd. N'holt & Gnfd —1A **54**
Ruislip Rd. E. Gnfd & W13 —4H **55**
Ruislip St. SW17 —4D **108**
Rumbold Rd. SW6 —7K **75**
Rum Clo. E1 —7J **63**
Rumsey Clo. Hamp —6D **102**
Rumsey M. N4 —3B **46**
Rumsey Rd. SW9 —3K **93**
Runbury Circ. NW9 —2K **41**
Runcorn Clo. N17 —4H **31**
Runcorn Pl. W11 —7G **59**
Rundell Cres. NW4 —5D **26**
Rundell Tower. SW8 —1K **93**
Runnel Field. Harr —3J **39**
Running Horse Yd. Bren —6E **72**

Runnymede. SW19 —1B **122**
Runnymede Clo. Twic —6F **87**
Runnymede Ct. SW15 —1C **106**
Runnymede Cres. SW16 —1H **123**
Runnymede Gdns. Gnfd —2J **55**
Runnymede Gdns. Twic —6F **87**
Runnymede Ho. E9 —4A **48**
Runnymede Rd. Twic —6F **87**
Runway, The. Ruis —5A **38**
Rupack St. SE16 —2J **79**
Rupert Av. Wemb —5E **40**
Rupert Ct. W1 —7H 61 (9A 140)
Rupert Gdns. SW9 —2B **94**
Rupert Ho. SE11 —4A **78** (4H **147**)
Rupert Rd. N19 —3H **45**
(in two parts)
Rupert Rd. NW6 —2H **59**
Rupert Rd. W4 —3A **74**
Rupert St. W1 —7H 61 (9A 140)
Rural Way. SW16 —7F **109**
Ruscoe Rd. E16 —6H **65**
Rusham Rd. SW12 —6D **92**
Rushbrook Cres. E17 —1B **32**
Rushbrook Rd. SE9 —2G **115**
Rushbury Ct. Hamp —7E **102**
Rushcroft Rd. E4 —7J **19**
Rushcroft Rd. SW2 —4A **94**
Rushden Clo. SE19 —7D **110**
Rushden. SE2 —3D **84**
(in two parts)
Rushdene Av. Barn —7H **5**
Rushdene Clo. N'holt —2A **54**
Rushdene Cres. N'holt —2A **54**
Rushdene Rd. Pinn —6B **22**
Rushden Gdns. NW7 —6K **13**
Rushden Gdns. Ilf —2E **34**
Rushen Wlk. Cars —1B **132**
Rushett Clo. Th Dit —7B **118**
Rushett Rd. Th Dit —7B **118**
Rushey Clo. N Mald —4K **119**
Rushey Grn. SE6 —7D **96**
Rushey Hill. Enf —4E **6**
Rushey Mead. SE4 —5C **96**
Rushford Rd. SE4 —6B **96**
Rush Grn. Gdns. Romf —1J **53**
Rush Grn. Rd. Romf —1H **53**
Rushgrove Av. NW9 —5A **26**
Rushgrove Pde. NW9 —5A **26**
Rushgrove St. SE18 —4D **82**
Rush Hill Rd. SW11 —3E **92**
Rushmead. E2 —3H **63**
Rushmead. Rich —3B **104**
Rushmead Clo. Croy —4F **135**
Rushmead Clo. Croy —4F **135**
Rushmere Ct. Wor Pk —2C **130**
Rushmere Pl. SW19 —5F **107**
Rushmoor Clo. Pinn —4A **22**
Rushmore Clo. Brom —3C **128**
Rushmore Rd. E5 —4J **47**
Rusholme Av. Dag —3G **53**
Rusholme Gro. SE19 —5E **110**
Rusholme Rd. SW15 —6F **91**
Rushout Av. Harr —6B **24**
Rushton Ho. SW8 —2H **93**
Rushton St. N1 —2D **62**
Rushworth Av. NW4 —3C **26**
Rushworth Gdns. NW4 —4C **26**
Rushworth St. SE1 —2B **78** (4K **147**)
Rushy Meadow La. Cars —3C **132**
Ruskin Av. E12 —6C **50**
Ruskin Av. Rich —7G **73**
Ruskin Av. Well —3A **100**
Ruskin Clo. NW11 —6K **27**
Ruskin Ct. N21 —7E **6**
Ruskin Ct. SE5 —3D 94
(off Champion Hill)
Ruskin Dri. Well —3A **100**

Ruskin Dri. Wor Pk —2D **130**
Ruskin Gdns. W5 —4D **56**
Ruskin Gdns. Harr —5F **25**
Ruskin Gro. Well —2A **100**
Ruskin Pk. Ho. SE5 —3D **94**
Ruskin Rd. N17 —1F **31**
Ruskin Rd. Belv —4G **85**
Ruskin Rd. Cars —5D **132**
Ruskin Rd. Croy —2B **134**
Ruskin Rd. Iswth —3K **87**
Ruskin Rd. S'hall —7C **54**
Ruskin Wlk. N9 —2B **18**
Ruskin Wlk. SE24 —5C **94**
Ruskin Wlk. Brom —6D **128**
Ruskin Way. SW19 —1B **122**
Rusland Heights. Harr —4J **23**
Rusland Pk. Rd. Harr —4J **23**
Ruslip Rd. E. W7 —4J **55**
Rusper Clo. NW2 —3E **42**
Rusper Clo. Stan —4H **11**
Rusper Ct. SW9 —2J 93
(off Clapham Rd.)
Rusper Rd. N22 & N17 —2C **30**
Rusper Rd. Dag —6C **52**
Russell Av. N22 —2A **30**
Russell Clo. NW10 —7J **41**
Russell Clo. SE7 —7A **82**
Russell Clo. W4 —6A **74**
Russell Clo. Bexh —3E **126**
Russell Clo. Bexh —4G **101**
Russell Clo. Ruis —2A **38**
Russell Ct. E10 —7D **32**
Russell Ct. N14 —6C **6**
Russell Ct. SE15 —2H 95
(off Heaton Rd.)
Russell Ct. SW1 —1G 77 (3M 145)
(off Cleveland Row)
Russell Ct. New Bar —4F 5
Russell Ct. Wall —5G 133
(off Ross Rd.)
Russell Courtyard. Chst —1E **128**
Russell Gdns. N20 —2H **15**
Russell Gdns. NW11 —6G **27**
Russell Gdns. W14 —3G **75**
Russell Gdns. Ilf —7H **35**
Russell Gdns. Rich —2C **104**
Russell Gdns. M. W14 —2G **75**
Russell Gro. NW7 —5F **13**
Russell Gro. SW9 —7A **78**
Russell Kerr Clo. W4 —7J **73**
Russell La. N20 —2H **15**
Russell Lodge. E4 —2K **19**
Russell Mead. Har W —1K **23**
Russell Pde. NW11 —6G 27
(off Golders Grn. Rd.)
Russell Pl. NW3 —5C **44**
Russell Pl. SE16 —3A **80**
Russell Rd. E4 —4G **19**
Russell Rd. E10 —6D **32**
Russell Rd. E16 —6J **65**
Russell Rd. E17 —3B **32**
Russell Rd. N8 —6H **29**
Russell Rd. N13 —6E **16**
Russell Rd. N15 —5E **30**
Russell Rd. N20 —2H **15**
Russell Rd. NW9 —6B **26**
Russell Rd. SW19 —7J **107**
Russell Rd. W14 —3G **75**
Russell Rd. Buck H —1E **20**
Russell Rd. Enf —1A **8**
Russell Rd. Mitc —3C **122**
Russell Rd. N'holt —5G **39**
Russell Rd. Twic —6K **87**
Russell's Footpath. SW16 —5J **109**
Russell Sq. WC1 —5J **61** (4C **140**)
Russell Sq. WC2 —7J **61** (9D **140**)
Russell Wlk. Rich —6F **89**
Russell Way. Sutt —5K **131**
Russell Yd. SW15 —4G **91**

Russet Cres. N7 —5K **45**
Russet Dri. Croy —1A 136
Russets Clo. E4 —4A **20**
Russettings. Pinn —1D 22
(off Westfield Pk.)
Russett Way. SE13 —2D **96**
Russett Way. Swan —7K **117**
Russia Ct. EC2 —6C 62 (8M 141)
(off Russia Row)
Russia Dock Rd. SE16 —1A **80**
Russia La. E2 —2J **63**
Russia Row. EC2 —6C **62** (8M **141**)
Russia Wlk. SE16 —2A **80**
Rusthall Av. W4 —4K **73**
Rusthall Clo. Croy —5J **125**
Rustic Av. SW16 —7F **109**
Rustic Pl. Wemb —4D **40**
Rustic Wlk. E16 —6K 65
(off Lambert Rd.)
Rustington Wlk. Mord —7H **121**
Ruston Av. Surb —7H **119**
Ruston Gdns. N14 —6A **6**
Ruston M. W11 —6G **59**
Ruston St. E3 —1B **64**
Rust Sq. SE5 —7D **78**
Rutford Rd. SW16 —5J **109**
Ruth Clo. Stan —4F **25**
Ruth Ct. E3 —2A **64**
Rutherford Clo. Sutt —6B **132**
Rutherford Ho. Wemb —3J 41
(off Barnhill Rd.)
Rutherford St. SW1
—4H **77** (8A **146**)
Rutherford Way. Bush —1C **10**
Rutherford Way. Wemb —4G **41**
Rutherglen Rd. SE2 —6A **84**
Rutherwyke Clo. Eps —6C **130**
Ruthin Clo. NW9 —6A **26**
Ruthin Rd. SE3 —6J **81**
Ruthven St. E9 —1K **63**
Rutland Av. Sidc —3A **100**
Rutland Clo. SW14 —3H **89**
Rutland Clo. SW19 —7C **108**
Rutland Clo. Bex —2D **116**
Rutland Ct. EC1 —4C 62 (4L 141)
(off Goswell Rd.)
Rutland Ct. SE5 —4D **94**
Rutland Ct. SE9 —2G **115**
Rutland Ct. W3 —6G **57**
Rutland Ct. Chst —1E **128**
Rutland Ct. Enf —5C **8**
Rutland Dri. Mord —6H **121**
Rutland Dri. Rich —1E **104**
Rutland Gdns. N4 —6B **30**
Rutland Gdns. SW7
—2C **76** (5D **144**)
Rutland Gdns. W13 —5A **56**
Rutland Gdns. Croy —4E **134**
Rutland Gdns. Dag —5C **52**
Rutland Gdns. M. SW7
—2C **76** (5D **144**)
Rutland Ga. Belv —5H **85**
Rutland Ga. Brom —4H **127**
Rutland Ga. M. SW7
(off Rutland Ga.) —2C **76** (5C **144**)
Rutland Gro. W6 —5D **74**
Rutland Ho. W8 —3K 75
(off Marloes Rd.)
Rutland M. NW8 —1K **59**
Rutland M. E. SW7 —3C 76 (6D 144)
(off Ennismore St.)
Rutland M. S. SW7 —3C 76 (6C 144)
(off Ennismore St.)
Rutland Pk. NW2 —6E **42**
Rutland Pk. SE6 —2B **112**
Rutland Pk. Mans. NW2 —6E **42**
Rutland Pl. EC1 —4B **62** (5K **141**)

260

Rutland Pt. Bush —1C 10
Rutland Rd. E7 —7B 50
Rutland Rd. E9 —1K 63
Rutland Rd. E11 —5K 33
Rutland Rd. E17 —6C 32
Rutland Rd. SW19 —7C 108
Rutland Rd. Harr —6G 23
Rutland Rd. Ilf —3F 51
Rutland Rd. S'hall —5E 54
Rutland Rd. Twic —2H 103
Rutland St. SW7 —3C 76 (6D 144)
Rutland Wlk. SE6 —2B 112
Rutley Clo. SE17 —6B 78
Rutlish Rd. SW19 —1J 121
Rutter Gdns. Mitc —4A 122
Rutt's Ter. SE14 —1K 95
Rutts, The. Bush —1C 10
Ruvigny Gdns. SW15 —3F 91
Ruxley Clo. Sidc —6D 116
Ruxley Corner Ind. Est. Sidc
  —6D 116
Ruxley La. Eps —4A 130
Ryalls Ct. N20 —3J 15
Ryan Clo. SE3 —4A 98
Ryan Ct. SW16 —7J 109
Rycott Path. SE22 —7G 95
Rycroft Way. N17 —3F 31
Ryculff Sq. SE3 —2H 97
Rydal Clo. NW4 —2F 27
Rydal Ct. Edgw —5A 12
Rydal Ct. Wemb —7F 25
Rydal Cres. Gnfd —3B 56
Rydal Dri. Bexh —1G 101
Rydal Dri. W Wick —2G 137
Rydal Gdns. NW9 —5A 26
Rydal Gdns. SW15 —5A 106
Rydal Gdns. Houn —6F 67
Rydal Gdns. Wemb —1C 40
Rydal Rd. SW16 —4H 109
Rydal Water. NW1 —3G 61 (2L 139)
Rydal Way. Enf —6D 8
Rydal Way. Ruis —4A 38
Ryde Bldgs. SE1 —3E 78 (7C 148)
  (off Swan Mead)
Ryde Pl. Twic —6D 88
Ryder Clo. Brom —5K 113
Ryder Ct. E10 —2D 48
Ryder Ct. SW1 —1G 77 (2M 145)
  (off Ryder St.)
Ryder M. E9 —5J 47
Ryder's Ter. NW8 —2A 60
Ryder St. SW1 —1G 77 (2M 145)
Ryder Yd. SW1 —1G 77 (2M 145)
Ryde Vale Rd. SW12 —2G 109
Rydons Clo. SE9 —3C 98
Rydon St. N1 —1C 62
Rydston Clo. N7 —7J 45
Rye Clo. Bexh —6H 101
Ryecotes Mead. SE21 —1E 110
Ryecroft Av. Ilf —2F 35
Ryecroft Av. Twic —7F 87
Ryecroft Lodge. SW16 —6B 110
Ryecroft Rd. SE13 —5E 96
Ryecroft Rd. SW16 —6A 110
Ryecroft Rd. Orp —6H 129
Ryecroft St. SW6 —1K 91
Ryedale. SE22 —6H 95
Ryefield Path. SW15 —1C 106
Ryefield Rd. SE19 —6C 110
Rye Hill Pk. SE15 —4J 95
Ryelands Cres. SE12 —6A 98
Rye La. SE15 —1G 95
Rye Pas. SE15 —3G 95
Rye Rd. SE15 —4K 95
Rye, The. N14 —7C 6
Rye Wlk. SW15 —5F 91
Rye Way. Edgw —6A 12
Ryfold Rd. SW19 —3J 107

Ryhope Rd. N11 —4A 16
Rylandes Rd. NW2 —3C 42
Ryland Rd. NW5 —6F 45
Rylett Cres. W12 —2B 74
Rylett Rd. W12 —2B 74
Rylston Rd. N13 —3J 17
Rylston Rd. SW6 —6H 75
Rymer Rd. Croy —7E 124
Rymer St. SE24 —6B 94
Rymill St. E16 —1E 82
Rysbrack St. SW3 —3D 76 (6E 144)
Rythe Ct. Th Dit —7A 118

Sabbarton St. E16 —6H 65
Sabella Ct. E3 —2B 64
Sabine Rd. SW11 —3D 92
Sable Clo. Houn —3A 86
Sable St. N1 —7B 46
Sach Rd. E5 —2H 47
Sackville Av. Brom —1J 137
Sackville Clo. Harr —3H 39
Sackville Gdns. Ilf —1D 50
Sackville Rd. Sutt —7J 131
Sackville St. W1 —7G 61 (1M 145)
Sackville Way. SE22 —1G 111
Saddlers Clo. Pinn —6A 10
Saddlers M. SW8 —1J 93
Saddlers M. Wemb —4K 39
Saddlescombe Way. N12 —5D 14
Saddle Yd. W1 —1F 77 (2J 145)
Sadler Clo. Mitc —2D 122
Saffron Av. E14 —7F 65
Saffron Clo. NW11 —6H 27
Saffron Clo. Croy —6J 123
Saffron Ct. E15 —5G 49
  (off Maryland Pk.)
Saffron Hill. EC1 —5A 62 (4H 141)
Saffron Rd. Romf —2K 37
Saffron St. EC1 —5A 62 (5H 141)
Sage St. E1 —7J 63
Sage Way. WC1 —3K 61 (2E 140)
  (off Cubitt St.)
Saigasso Clo. E16 —6B 66
Sail St. SE11 —4K 77 (8F 146)
Saimet. NW9 —7G 13
  (off Satchell Mead)
Sainfoin Rd. SW17 —2E 108
Sainsbury Rd. SE19 —5E 110
St Agatha's Dri. King T —6F 105
St Agatha's Gro. Cars —1D 132
St Agnes Clo. E9 —1J 63
St Agnes Pl. SE11 —6A 78
St Agnes Well. EC1 —4D 62 (3B 142)
St Aidan's Rd. SE22 —6H 95
St Aidan's Rd. W13 —2B 72
St Alban's Av. E6 —3D 66
St Alban's Av. W4 —4K 73
St Alban's Av. Felt —5B 102
St Alban's Clo. NW11 —1J 43
St Albans Clo. EC2 —6C 62 (7M 141)
  (off Wood St.)
St Alban's Cres. N22 —1A 30
St Alban's Cres. Wfd G —7D 20
St Alban's Gdns. Tedd —5A 104
St Alban's Gro. W8 —3K 75
St Alban's Gro. Cars —7C 122
St Alban's La. NW11 —1J 43
St Albans Mans. W8 —3K 75
  (off Kensington Ct. Pl.)
St Alban's M. W2 —5B 60 (5B 138)
St Alban's Pl. N1 —1B 62
St Alban's Rd. NW5 —3E 44
St Alban's Rd. NW10 —1A 58
St Albans Rd. Barn —1A 4
St Albans Rd. Ilf —1K 51
St Alban's Rd. King T —6E 104
St Alban's Rd. Sutt —4H 131
St Alban's Rd. Wfd G —7D 20

St Alban's St. SW1 —7H 61 (1A 146)
St Alban's Ter. W6 —6G 75
St Alban's Vs. NW5 —3E 44
St Alfege Pas. SE10 —6E 80
St Alfege Rd. SE7 —6B 82
St Alphage Garden. EC2
  —5C 62 (6M 141)
St Alphage Highwalk. EC2
  (off London Wall) —5C 62 (6M 141)
St Alphage Ho. EC2 —5D 62 (6A 142)
  (off Fore St.)
St Alphage Wlk. Edgw —2J 25
St Alphege Rd. N9 —7D 8
St Alphonsus Rd. SW4 —4G 93
St Amunds Clo. SE6 —4C 112
St Andrew's Av. Wemb —4A 40
St Andrew's Clo. N12 —4F 15
St Andrew's Clo. NW2 —3D 42
St Andrew's Clo. Iswth —1J 87
St Andrew's Clo. Ruis —2B 38
St Andrew's Clo. SW18 —2A 108
St Andrews Dri. Stan —1C 24
St Andrew's Gro. N16 —1D 46
St Andrew's Hill. EC4
  —7B 62 (9K 141)
St Andrews Mans. W14 —6G 75
  (off St Andrews Rd.)
St Andrew's M. N16 —1E 46
St Andrew's M. SE3 —7J 81
St Andrew's Pl. NW1
  —4F 61 (3K 139)
St Andrew's Rd. E11 —6G 33
St Andrew's Rd. E13 —3K 65
St Andrew's Rd. E17 —2K 31
St Andrew's Rd. N9 —7D 8
St Andrew's Rd. NW9 —1K 41
St Andrew's Rd. NW10 —6D 42
St Andrew's Rd. NW11 —6H 27
St Andrew's Rd. W3 —7A 58
St Andrew's Rd. W7 —2J 71
St Andrew's Rd. W14 —6G 75
St Andrew's Rd. Cars —3C 132
St Andrew's Rd. Croy —4C 134
St Andrew's Rd. Enf —3J 7
St Andrew's Rd. Ilf —7D 34
St Andrew's Rd. Romf —6K 37
St Andrew's Rd. Sidc —3D 116
St Andrew's Rd. Surb —6D 118
St Andrew Sq. EC4 —6A 62 (6H 141)
St Andrews Way. E3 —4D 64
St Andrews Wharf. SE1
  —2F 79 (4F 148)
St Anna Rd. Barn —5A 4
St Anne's Clo. N6 —3E 44
St Anne's Ct. W1 —6H 61 (8A 140)
St Anne's Gdns. NW10 —3F 57
St Anne's Pas. SW13 —3A 90
St Anne's Rd. E11 —2F 49
St Anne's Rd. Wemb —5D 40
St Anne's Row. E14 —6B 64
St Anne's St. E14 —6B 64
St Ann's. Bark —1G 67
St Ann's Clo. NW4 —3D 26
St Ann's Cres. SW18 —6A 92
St Ann's Gdns. NW5 —6E 44
St Ann's Hill. SW18 —5K 91
St Ann's La. SW1 —3H 77 (7B 146)
St Ann's Pk. Rd. SW18 —6A 92
St Ann's Pas. SW13 —3A 90
St Ann's Rd. N9 —2A 18
St Ann's Rd. N15 —5B 30
St Ann's Rd. SW13 —2B 90
St Ann's Rd. W11 —7F 59

St Ann's Rd. Bark —1G 67
St Ann's Rd. Harr —6J 23
St Ann's Shopping Cen. Harr —6J 23
St Ann's St. SW1 —3H 77 (6B 146)
St Ann's Ter. NW8 —2B 60
St Ann's Vs. W11 —1F 75
St Ann's Way. S Croy —6B 134
St Anselm's Pl. W1 —7F 61 (9J 139)
St Anthony's Av. Wfd G —6F 21
St Anthony's Clo. E1 —1G 79
St Anthony's Clo. SW17 —2C 108
St Antony's Rd. E7 —7K 49
St Arvan's Clo. Croy —3E 134
St Asaph Rd. SE4 —3K 95
St Aubins Ct. N1 —1E 62
St Aubyn's Av. SW19 —5H 107
St Aubyn's Av. Houn —5E 86
St Aubyn's Rd. SE19 —6F 111
St Audrey Av. Bexh —2G 101
St Augustine's Av. W5 —2E 56
St Augustine's Av. Brom —5C 128
St Augustine's Av. S Croy —6C 134
St Augustines Av. Wemb —3E 40
St Augustine's Rd. NW1 —7H 45
St Augustine's Rd. Belv —4F 85
St Austell Clo. Edgw —2F 25
St Awdry's Rd. Bark —7H 51
St Awdry's Wlk. Bark —7G 51
St Barnabas Clo. Beck —2C 126
St Barnabas Ct. Har W —1G 23
St Barnabas Rd. E17 —6C 32
St Barnabas Rd. Mitc —7E 108
St Barnabas Rd. Sutt —5B 132
St Barnabas Rd. Wfd G —1K 33
St Barnabas St. SW1 —5E 76
St Barnabas Ter. E9 —5K 47
St Barnabas Vs. SW8 —1J 93
St Bartholomew Pl. EC1
  (off Kinghorn St.) —5C 62 (6L 141)
St Bartholomew's Clo. SE26
  —4H 111
St Bartholomew's Ct. E6 —2C 66
  (off St Bartholomew's Rd.)
St Bartholomew's Rd. E6 —2D 66
St Benedict's Clo. SW17 —5E 108
St Benet's Clo. SW17 —2C 108
St Benet's Gro. Cars —7A 122
St Benet's Pl. EC3 —7D 62 (9B 142)
St Bernards. Croy —3E 134
St Bernard's Clo. SE27 —4D 110
St Bernard's Rd. E6 —1B 66
St Blaise Av. Brom —2K 127
St Botolph Row. EC3
  —6F 63 (8E 142)
St Botolph's Row. EC3 —6F 63
St Botolph St. EC3 —6F 63 (8E 142)
St Brelades Clo. N11 —1E 62
St Briavel's Ct. SE15 —7E 78
  (off Lynbrook Clo.)
St Bride's Av. EC4 —6B 62 (8J 141)
  (off Bride La.)
St Bride's Av. Edgw —1F 25
St Brides Clo. Eri —2D 84
St Bride's Pas. EC4 —6B 62 (8J 141)
  (off Dorset Rise)
St Bride St. EC4 —6B 62 (7J 141)
St Catherine's Clo. SW17 —2C 108
St Catherine's Ct. W4 —3A 74
St Catherine's Dri. SE14 —2K 95
St Catherines. SW3
  —4D 76 (8E 144)
St Catherine's Rd. E4 —2H 19
St Catherines Tower. E10 —7D 32
St Chads Clo. Surb —7C 118
St Chad's Gdns. Romf —7E 36
St Chad's Pl. WC1 —3K 61 (1D 140)
St Chad's Rd. Romf —7E 36
St Chad's St. WC1 —3J 61 (1D 140)

St Charles Pl. W10 —5G 59
St Charles Sq. W10 —5F 59
St Christopher's Clo. Iswth —1J 87
St Christopher's Gdns. T Hth
  —3A 124
St Christopher's M. Wall —5G 133
St Christopher's Pl. W1
  —6E 60 (7H 139)
St Clair Clo. Ilf —2D 34
St Clair Dri. Wor Pk —3D 130
St Clair Rd. E13 —2K 65
St Clair's Rd. Croy —2E 134
St Clare Bus. Pk. Hamp —6G 103
St Clare St. EC3 —6F 63 (8E 142)
St Clement's Ct. EC4
  (off Clements La.) —7D 62 (9B 142)
St Clement's Ct. N7 —6K 45
St Clement's Heights. SE26 —3G 111
St Clement's La. WC2
  —6K 61 (8F 140)
St Clements Mans. SW6 —6F 75
  (off Lillie Rd.)
St Clement St. N7 —7A 46
St Cloud Rd. SE27 —4C 110
St Columbas Ho. E17 —4D 32
St Crispin's Clo. NW3 —4C 44
St Crispin's Clo. S'hall —6D 54
St Cross St. EC1 —5A 62 (5H 141)
St Cuthbert's Rd. NW2 —6H 43
St Cuthberts Wlk. NW6 —6H 43
St Cyprian's St. SW17 —4D 108
St David's Clo. Wemb —3J 41
St David's Clo. W Wick —7D 126
St David's Dri. Edgw —1F 25
St David's Pl. NW4 —7D 26
St Denis Rd. SE27 —4D 110
St Dionis Rd. SW6 —2H 91
St Donatt's Rd. SE14 —1B 96
St Dunstans All. EC2
  —7E 62 (1C 148)
  (off St Dunstans Hill)
St Dunstan's Av. W3 —7K 57
St Dunstans Ct. EC4
  —6A 62 (8H 141)
St Dunstan's Gdns. W3 —7K 57
St Dunstans Hill. EC3
  —7E 62 (1C 148)
St Dunstan's Hill. Sutt —5G 131
St Dunstans La. EC3
  —7E 62 (1C 148)
St Dunstan's La. Beck —6E 126
St Dunstan's Rd. E7 —6A 50
St Dunstan's Rd. SE25 —4F 125
St Dunstan's Rd. W6 —5F 75
St Dunstan's Rd. W7 —2J 71
St Edmund's Clo. NW8 —1D 60
St Edmund's Clo. SW17 —2C 108
St Edmunds Clo. Eri —2D 84
St Edmund's Dri. Stan —1A 24
St Edmund's La. Twic —7F 87
St Edmund's Rd. N9 —7B 8
St Edmund's Rd. Ilf —6D 34
St Edmund's Ter. NW8 —1C 60
St Edward's Clo. NW11 —6J 27
St Edwards Ct. E10 —7D 32
St Edwards Ct. SW8 —6H 77
  (off Nine Elms La.)
St Edwards Way. Romf —5K 37
St Egberts Way. E4 —1K 19
St Elizabeth Ct. E10 —7D 32
St Elmo Rd. W12 —1B 74
St Elmos Rd. SE16 —2A 80
St Erkenwald Rd. Bark —1H 67
St Ermin's Hill. SW1
  (off Broadway) —3H 77 (6A 146)
St Ervan's Rd. W10 —5H 59
St Faith's Clo. Enf —1H 7

St Faith's Rd. SE21 —1B 110
St Fidelis Rd. Eri —5K 85
St Fillans Rd. SE6 —1E 112
St Francis Clo. Orp —6J 129
St Francis Rd. SE22 —4E 94
St Francis Rd. Eri —4K 85
St Gabriel's Clo. E11 —2K 49
St Gabriels Rd. NW2 —5F 43
St George's Av. E7 —7K 49
St George's Av. N7 —4H 45
St George's Av. NW9 —4K 25
St George's Av. W5 —2D 72
St George's Av. S'hall —7D 54
St George's Bldgs. SE1
    —2C 78 (4M 147)
St George's Cir. SE1
    —3B 78 (6J 147)
St George's Clo. NW11 —6H 27
St George's Clo. Wemb —3A 40
St George's Clo. E6 —4D 66
St Georges Ct. E17 —5F 33
St George's Ct. EC4 —6B 62 (7J 141)
St George's Ct. SW15 —4H 91
St Georges Ct. Harr —6A 24
    (off Kenton Rd.)
St George's Dri. SW1
    —4F 77 (9K 145)
St George's Fields. W2
    —6C 60 (8D 138)
St George's Gro. SW17 —3B 108
St Georges Ind. Est. N17 —7G 17
St Georges La. EC3 —7D 62 (1B 148)
    (off Pudding La.)
St George's M. NW1 —7D 44
St George's Pl. Twic —1A 104
St George's Rd. E7 —7K 49
St George's Rd. E10 —3E 48
St George's Rd. N9 —3B 18
St George's Rd. N13 —2E 16
St George's Rd. NW11 —6H 27
St George's Rd. SE1
    —3A 78 (6H 147)
St Georges Rd. SW19 —7H 107
St George's Rd. W4 —2K 73
St George's Rd. W7 —1K 71
St George's Rd. Beck —1D 126
St George's Rd. Brom —2D 128
    (in two parts)
St George's Rd. Dag —5E 52
St George's Rd. Enf —1A 8
St George's Rd. Felt —4B 102
St George's Rd. Ilf —7D 34
St George's Rd. King T —7G 105
St George's Rd. Mitc —3F 123
St George's Rd. Orp —6H 129
St Georges Rd. Rich —3F 89
St George's Rd. Sidc —6D 116
St George's Rd. Twic —5B 88
St George's Rd. Wall —5F 133
St George's Rd. W. Brom —2C 128
St George's Sq. E7 —7K 49
St Georges Sq. E14 —7A 64
St George's Sq. SE8 —4B 80
St George's Sq. SW1 —5H 77
St George's Sq. M. SW1 —5H 77
St George's Sq. N Mald —3A 120
St George's Ter. NW1 —7D 44
St George St. W1 —7F 61 (8K 139)
St George's Wlk. Croy —3C 134
St George's Wlk. Wemb —3H 41
St George's Way. SE15 —6E 78
St Gerards Clo. SW4 —5G 93
St German's Pl. SE3 —1J 97
St German's Rd. SE23 —1A 112
St Giles Av. Dag —7H 53
St Giles Cir. W1 —6H 61
St Giles Cir. WC2 —6H 61 (7B 140)
St Giles Clo. Dag —7H 53

St Giles Ct. WC2 —6J 61 (7C 140)
    (off St Giles High St.)
St Giles High St. WC2
    —6H 61 (7B 140)
St Giles Ho. New Bar —4F 5
St Giles Pas. WC2 —6H 61 (8B 140)
    (off New Compton St.)
St Giles Rd. SE5 —7E 78
St Giles Ter. EC2 —5C 62 (6M 141)
    (off Barbican)
St Gothard Rd. SE27 —4D 110
St Gregory Clo. Ruis —4A 38
St Helena Rd. SE16 —4K 79
St Helena St. WC1 —3A 62 (2G 141)
St Helen's Cres. SW16 —1K 123
St Helen's Gdns. W10 —5F 59
St Helen's Pl. EC3 —6E 62 (7C 142)
St Helen's Rd. SW16 —1K 123
St Helen's Rd. W13 —1B 72
St Helen's Rd. Eri —2D 84
St Helen's Rd. Ilf —6D 34
St Helier Av. Mord —7A 122
St Helier's Av. Houn —5E 86
St Helier's Rd. E10 —6E 32
St Hilda's Clo. NW6 —1F 59
St Hilda's Clo. SW17 —2C 108
St Hilda's Rd. SW13 —6D 74
St Hilda's Rd. SW17 —2C 108
St Hugh's Rd. SE20 —1H 125
St James Apartments. E17 —5A 32
    (off Pretoria Av.)
St James Av. N20 —3H 15
St James Av. W13 —1A 72
St James Av. Beck —3A 126
St James Av. Sutt —5J 131
St James Clo. N20 —3H 15
St James Clo. N Mald —5B 120
St James Clo. Ruis —2A 38
St James Ct. SE3 —1K 97
St James' Ct. SW1 —3G 77 (6M 145)
St James Gdns. Wemb —7E 40
St James Ga. NW1 —7H 45
St James Gro. SW11 —2D 92
St James M. E14 —3E 80
St James' Rd. E15 —5H 49
St James Rd. Cars —3C 132
St James' Rd. King T —2D 118
St James Rd. Mitc —7E 108
St James Rd. Sutt —5J 131
St James's. SE14 —1A 96
St James's App. EC2
    —4E 62 (4C 142)
St James's Av. E2 —2J 63
St James's Av. Beck —3A 126
St James's Av. Hamp —5G 103
St James's Clo. SW17 —2D 108
St James's Cotts. Rich —5D 88
St James's Ct. N18 —5B 18
    (off Fore St.)
St James's Ct. Harr —6A 24
St James's Cres. SW9 —3A 94
St James's Dri. SW17 —1D 108
St James's Gdns. W11 —1G 75
St James's La. N10 —4F 29
St James's Mkt. SW1
    —7H 61 (1A 146)
St James's Pk. Croy —7C 124
St James's Pas. EC3
    (off Duke's Pl.) —6E 62 (8D 142)
St James's Pl. SW1
    —1G 77 (3L 145)
St James's Rd. SE1 —6G 79
St James's Rd. SE16 —3G 79
St James's Rd. SW1 —1G 77
St James's Rd. Croy —7B 124
St James's Rd. Hamp —5F 103

St James's Rd. Surb —6D 118
St James's Row. EC1
    —4B 62 (4J 141)
St James's Sq. SW1
    —1G 77 (2M 145)
St James's St. SW1
    —1G 77 (2L 145)
St James's Ter. NW8 —2D 60
    (off Prince Albert Rd.)
St James's Ter. M. NW8 —1D 60
St James St. E17 —5A 32
St James St. W6 —5E 74
St James's Wlk. EC1
    —4B 62 (3J 141)
St James Wlk. SE15 —1F 95
    (off Pitt St.)
St James Way. Sidc —5E 116
St Joan's Rd. N9 —2A 18
St John's Av. N11 —5J 15
St John's Av. NW10 —1B 58
St John's av. SW15 —5F 91
St Johns Chu. Rd. E9 —5J 47
St John's Clo. N20 —3F 15
    (off Rasper Rd.)
St John's Clo. SW6 —7J 75
St John's Clo. Wemb —5E 40
St John's Cotts. SE20 —7J 111
St John's Ct. N4 —2B 46
St John's Ct. N5 —4B 46
St John's Ct. SE13 —2E 96
St John's Ct. W6 —4D 74
    (off Glenthorne Rd.)
St John's Ct. Buck H —1E 20
St John's Ct. Eri —5K 85
St John's Ct. Harr —6K 23
St John's Ct. Iswth —2K 87
St John's Cres. SW9 —3A 94
St Johns Dri. SW18 —1K 107
St John's Est. N1 —2D 62
St John's Est. SE1 —2F 79 (4E 148)
    (off Fair St.)
St John's Gdns. W11 —7G 59
St John's Gro. N19 —2G 45
St John's Gro. SW13 —2B 90
St John's Gro. Rich —4E 88
St John's Hill. SW11 —4B 92
St John's Hill Gro. SW11 —4B 92
St John's La. EC1 —4B 62 (4J 141)
St John's M. W11 —6J 59
St Johns Pde. Sidc —4B 116
    (off Sidcup High St.)
St John's Pk. SE3 —7H 81
St John's Pk. Mans. N19 —3G 45
St John's Pas. SW19 —6G 107
St John's Path. EC1 —4B 62 (4J 141)
    (off Tower Bridge Rd.)
St John's Pl. EC1 —4B 62 (4J 141)
St John's Rd. E4 —4J 19
St John's Rd. E6 —1C 66
St John's Rd. E16 —6J 65
St John's Rd. E17 —2D 32
St John's Rd. N15 —6E 30
St John's Rd. NW11 —6H 27
St John's Rd. SE20 —6J 111
St John's Rd. SW11 —4C 92
St John's Rd. SW19 —7G 107
St John's Rd. Bark —1J 67
St John's Rd. Cars —3C 132
St John's Rd. Croy —3B 134
St John's Rd. Eri —5K 85
St John's Rd. Felt —4C 102
St John's Rd. Harr —6K 23
St John's Rd. Ilf —7J 35
St John's Rd. Iswth —2J 87
St John's Rd. King T —2D 118
St John's Rd. N Mald —3J 119
St John's Rd. Orp —6H 129

St John's Rd. Rich —4E 88
St John's Rd. Sidc —4B 116
St John's Rd. S'hall —3C 70
St John's Rd. Sutt —2K 131
St John's Rd. Well —3B 100
St John's Rd. Wemb —4D 40
St John's Sq. SE1 —4B 62 (4J 141)
    (in two parts)
St John's Ter. E7 —6K 49
St John's Ter. SE18 —6G 83
St John's Ter. W10 —4F 59
St John St. EC1 —2A 62
St John's Vale. SE8 —2C 96
St John's Vs. N11 —5J 15
    (off Friern Barnet Rd.)
St John's Vs. N19 —2H 45
St John's Vs. W8 —3K 75
St John's Way. N19 —2G 45
St John's Wood Ct. NW8
    —3B 60 (2B 138)
    (off St John's Wood Rd.)
St John's Wood High St. NW8
    —2B 60
St John's Wood Pk. NW8 —1B 60
St John's Wood Rd. NW8
    —4B 60 (3A 138)
St John's Wood Ter. NW8 —2B 60
St Joseph's Clo. W10 —5G 59
St Josephs Ct. SE7 —6K 81
St Joseph's Dri. S'hall —1C 70
St Joseph's Gro. NW4 —4D 26
St Joseph's Rd. N9 —7C 8
St Joseph's St. SW8 —1F 93
St Joseph's Vale. SE3 —3F 97
St Jude's Rd. E2 —2H 63
St Jude St. N16 —5E 46
St Julian's Clo. SW16 —4A 110
St Julian's Farm Rd. SE27 —4A 110
St Julian's Rd. NW6 —1H 59
St Katharine's Precinct. NW1 —2F 61
St Katharine's Way. E1
    —1F 79 (2F 148)
St Katherine's Rd. Eri —2D 84
St Katherine's Row. EC3
    —7E 62 (9D 142)
    (off Fenchurch St.)
St Keverne Rd. SE9 —4C 114
St Kilda Rd. W13 —1A 72
St Kilda Rd. Orp —7K 129
St Kilda's Rd. N16 —1D 46
St Kilda's Rd. Harr —6J 23
St Kitts Ter. SE19 —5E 110
St Laurence Clo. NW6 —1F 59
St Lawrence Clo. Edgw —7A 12
St Lawrence Ct. N1 —1E 62
St Lawrence Dri. Pinn —5A 22
St Lawrence St. E14 —1E 80
St Lawrence Ter. W10 —5G 59
St Lawrence Way. SW9 —2A 94
St Leonard's Av. E4 —6A 20
St Leonard's Av. Harr —5C 24
St Leonard's Clo. Well —3A 100
St Leonard's Ct. N1 —3D 62 (1B 142)
    (off New North Rd.)
St Leonard's Gdns. Houn —1C 86
St Leonard's Gdns. Ilf —5G 51
St Leonard's Rd. E14 —5E 64
    (in two parts)
St Leonard's Rd. NW10 —4K 57
St Leonard's Rd. SW14 —3H 89
St Leonard's Rd. W13 —7C 56
St Leonard's Rd. Croy —3B 134
St Leonards Rd. Surb —5D 118
St Leonard's Rd. Th Dit —6A 118
St Leonards Sq. NW5 —6E 44
St Leonards Sq. Surb —5D 118
St Leonard's St. E3 —3D 64

St Leonard's Ter. SW3 —5D 76
St Leonard's Wlk. SW16 —7K 109
St Loo Av. SW3 —6C 76
St Louis Rd. SE27 —4D 110
St Loy's Rd. N17 —2E 30
St Luke's Av. SW4 —4H 93
St Luke's Av. Enf —1J 7
St Luke's Av. Ilf —5F 51
St Luke's Clo. SE25 —6H 125
St Lukes Ct. E10 —7D 32
    (off Capworth St.)
St Luke's Est. EC1 —3D 62 (3A 142)
St Luke's M. W11 —6H 59
St Luke's Pas. King T —1F 119
St Luke's Path. Ilf —5F 51
St Luke's Rd. W11 —5H 59
St Luke's Sq. E16 —6H 65
St Luke's St. SW3 —5C 76
St Luke's Yd. W9 —2H 59
St Magarets Rd. SE4 —4B 96
St Magaret's Ter. SE18 —5G 83
St Malo Av. N9 —3D 18
St Margaret's. Bark —1H 67
St Margaret's Av. N15 —4B 30
St Margaret's Av. N20 —1F 15
St Margaret's Av. Harr —3G 39
St Margaret's Av. Sidc —3H 115
St Margaret's Av. Sutt —3G 131
St Margarets Bus. Cen. Twic —6B 88
St Margaret's Ct. N11 —4K 15
St Margaret's Ct. SE1
    —1D 78 (3A 148)
St Margaret's Ct. Edgw —5C 12
St Margaret's Cres. SW15 —5D 90
St Margaret's Dri. Twic —5B 88
St Margaret's Gro. E11 —3H 49
St Margaret's Gro. SE18 —6G 83
St Margaret's Gro. Twic —6A 88
St Margaret's Pas. SE13 —3E 96
St Margaret's Rd. E12 —2A 50
St Margaret's Rd. N17 —3E 30
St Margaret's Rd. NW10 —3E 58
St Margarets Rd. SE4 —4B 96
St Margaret's Rd. W7 —2J 71
St Margaret's Rd. Beck —4K 125
St Margaret's Rd. Edgw —5C 12
St Margarets Rd. Iswth & Twic
    —4B 88
St Margaret's Sq. SE4 —4B 96
St Margaret's Ter. SE18 —5G 83
St Margaret St. SW1
    —2J 77 (5C 146)
St Margarets Vicarage. E11 —3H 49
St Mark's Clo. SE10 —7E 80
St Mark's Clo. W11 —6G 59
St Mark's Clo. Barn —3E 4
St Marks Ct. E10 —7D 32
    (off Capworth St.)
St Mark's Cres. NW1 —1E 60
St Mark's Ga. E9 —7B 48
St Mark's Gro. SW10 —6K 75
St Mark's Hill. Surb —6E 118
St Marks Ind. Est. E16 —1B 82
St Mark's Pl. SW19 —6H 107
St Mark's Pl. W11 —6G 59
St Mark's Rise. E8 —5F 47
St Mark's Rd. SE25 —4G 125
St Mark's Rd. W5 —1E 72
St Mark's Rd. W7 —2J 71
St Marks Rd. W10 —5F 59
St Mark's Rd. W11 —6G 59
St Mark's Rd. Brom —3K 127
St Marks Rd. Enf —6A 8
St Mark's Rd. Mitc —2D 122
St Mark's Sq. NW1 —1E 60
St Mark St. E1 —6F 63
St Martin's Av. E6 —2B 66

St Martin's Clo. NW1 —1G 61
St Martin's Clo. Enf —1C 8
St Martin's Clo. Enf —2D 84
St Martins Ct. N1 —1E 62
(off De Beauvoir Est.)
St Martin's Ct. WC2 —7J 61 (9C 140)
St Martins Est. SW2 —1A 110
St Martin's La. WC2
—7J 61 (9C 140)
St Martin's le Grand. EC1
—6C 62 (7L 141)
St Martin's Pl. WC2 —7J 61 (1C 146)
St Martin's Rd. N9 —2C 18
St Martin's Rd. SW9 —2K 93
St Martin's St. WC2
—7H 61 (1B 146)
St Martin's Wlk. SE1
—1D 78 (2B 148)
(off Borough High St.)
St Martins Way. SW17 —3A 108
St Mary Abbot's Ct. W14 —3H 75
(off Warwick Gdns.)
St Mary Abbot's Pl. W8 —3H 75
St Mary Abbot's Ter. W14 —3H 75
St Mary at Hill. EC3 —7E 62 (1C 148)
St Mary Av. Wall —3F 133
St Mary Axe. EC3 —6E 62 (8D 142)
St Marychurch St. SE16 —2J 79
St Mary Graces Ct. E1 —7F 63
St Mary Newington Clo. SE17
(off Surrey Sq.) —5E 78
St Mary Rd. E17 —4C 32
St Mary's. Bark —1H 67
St Mary's App. E12 —5D 50
St Mary's Av. E11 —7K 33
St Mary's Av. N3 —2G 27
St Mary's Av. Brom —3G 127
St Mary's Av. S'hall —4F 71
St Mary's Av. Tedd —6K 103
St Mary's Clo. N17 —1F 31
St Mary's Clo. Eps —7B 130
St Mary's Ct. E6 —4D 66
St Mary's Ct. SE7 —7B 82
St Mary's Ct. W5 —2D 72
St Mary's Ct. W14 —3B 74
St Mary's Ct. Wall —4G 133
St Mary's Cres. NW4 —3D 26
St Mary's Cres. Iswth —7H 71
St Mary's Gdns. SE11
—4A 78 (8H 147)
St Mary's Ga. W8 —3K 75
St Mary's Grn. N2 —2A 28
St Mary's Gro. N1 —6B 46
St Mary's Gro. SW13 —3D 90
St Mary's Gro. W4 —6H 73
St Mary's Gro. Rich —4F 89
St Mary's La. W8 —3K 75
St Mary's Mans. W2
—5B 60 (5A 138)
St Mary's M. NW6 —7K 43
St Marys M. Rich —2C 104
St Mary's Path. N1 —1B 62
St Mary's Pl. SE9 —6E 98
St Mary's Pl. W5 —2D 72
St Mary's Pl. W8 —3K 75
St Mary's Rd. E10 —3E 48
St Mary's Rd. E13 —2K 65
St Mary's Rd. N8 —4J 29
St Mary's Rd. N9 —1C 18
St Mary's Rd. NW10 —1A 58
St Mary's Rd. NW11 —7G 27
St Mary's Rd. SE15 —1J 95
St Mary's Rd. SE25 —3E 124
St Mary's Rd. SW19 —5G 107
St Mary's Rd. W5 —2D 72
St Mary's Rd. Barn —7J 5
St Mary's Rd. Bex —1J 117
St Mary's Rd. Dit H —7C 118

St Mary's Rd. Ilf —2G 51
St Mary's Rd. Surb —6D 118
St Mary's Rd. Wor Pk —2A 130
St Mary's Sq. W2 —5B 60 (5A 138)
St Mary's Sq. W5 —2D 72
St Mary's Ter. W2 —5B 60
St Mary's Vw. SE18 —4D 82
St Mary's View. Kent —5C 24
St Mary's Wlk. SE11
—4A 78 (8H 147)
St Mary's Way. Chig —5K 21
St Matthew's Av. Surb —7E 118
St Matthews Ct. E10 —7D 32
(off Capworth St.)
St Matthews Ct. N10 —2E 28
St Matthew's Dri. Brom —3D 128
St Matthew's Lodge. NW1 —2G 61
(off Oakley Sq.)
St Matthew's Rd. SW2 —4K 93
St Matthew's Rd. W5 —1E 72
St Matthew's Row. E2 —3G 63
St Matthew SW1
—3H 77 (7A 146)
St Matthias Clo. NW9 —5B 26
St Maur Rd. SW6 —1H 91
St Merryn Clo. SE18 —7H 83
St Merryn Ct. Beck —7C 112
St Michael's All. EC3
—6D 62 (8B 142)
St Michael's Av. N9 —7D 8
St Michael's Av. Enf —7D 8
St Michael's Av. Wemb —6G 41
St Michaels Clo. E16 —5B 66
St Michael's Clo. N3 —2H 27
St Michael's Clo. N12 —5H 15
St Michael's Clo. Brom —3C 128
St Michael's Clo. Eri —2D 84
St Michael's Clo. Wor Pk —2B 130
St Michaels Ct. E14 —5E 64
(off St Leonards Rd.)
St Michael's Cres. Pinn —6C 22
St Michael's Gdns. W10 —5G 59
St Michael's Rise. Well —1B 100
St Michael's Rd. NW2 —4E 42
St Michael's Rd. SW9 —2K 93
St Michael's Rd. Croy —1C 134
St Michael's Rd. Wall —6G 133
St Michael's Rd. Well —3B 100
St Michael's St. W2
—6D 62 (7B 138)
St Michael's Ter. N22 —1J 29
St Michael Tower. E17 —5B 32
St Mildred's Ct. EC2
—6D 62 (8A 142)
St Mildreds Rd. SE12 —7H 97
St Mirren Ct. New Bar —5F 5
St Nicholas Cen. Sutt —5K 131
St Nicholas Glebe. SW17 —6E 108
St Nicholas Rd. SE18 —5K 83
St Nicholas Rd. Sutt —5K 131
St Nicholas Rd. Th Dit —6A 118
St Nicholas Way. Sutt —4K 131
St Nicolas La. Chst —1C 128
St Ninian's Ct. N20 —3J 15
St Norbert Grn. SE4 —4A 96
St Norbert Rd. SE4 —5K 95
St Olaf Ho. SE1 —1D 78 (2B 148)
(off Tooley St.)
St Olaf's Rd. SW6 —7G 75
St Olaf Stairs. SE1 —1D 78 (2B 148)
(off Tooley St.)
St Olaves Ct. EC2 —6D 62 (8A 142)
St Olave's Est. SE1 —2E 78 (4D 148)
St Olave's Gdns. SE11
—4A 78 (8G 147)
St Olave's Mans. SE11
—4A 78 (8G 147)
(off Walnut Tree Wlk.)

St Olave's Rd. E6 —1E 66
St Olave's Ter. SE1 —2E 78 (4D 148)
(off Fair St.)
St Olaves Wlk. SW16 —2G 123
St Oswald's Pl. SE11 —5K 77
St Oswald's Rd. SW16 —1B 124
St Oswulf St. SW1 —4H 77 (9B 146)
(off Erasmus St.)
St Pancras Clo. N2 —2B 28
St Pancras Way. NW1 —7G 45
St Patrick's Ct. E4 —7B 20
St Patrick's Ct. E4 —7B 20
St Paulinus Ct. Dart —4K 101
(off Manor Rd.)
St Paul's All. EC4 —6B 62 (8K 141)
(off St Paul's Chu. Yd.)
St Paul's Av. NW2 —6E 42
St Paul's Av. SE16 —1K 79
St Paul's Av. Harr —4F 25
St Paul's Chyd. EC4
—6B 62 (8K 141)
St Pauls Clo. SE7 —5B 82
St Paul's Clo. W5 —2F 73
St Paul's Clo. Houn —2C 86
St Paul's Ct. Houn —3C 86
St Pauls Courtyard. SE8 —7C 80
St Paul's Cray Rd. Chst —1H 129
St Paul's Cres. NW1 —7H 45
(in two parts)
St Paul's Dri. E15 —5F 49
St Paul's M. NW1 —7H 45
St Paul's Pl. N1 —6D 46
St Paul's Rise. N13 —6G 17
St Paul's Rd. N1 —6B 46
St Paul's Rd. N11 —5A 16
St Paul's Rd. N17 —7B 18
St Paul's Rd. Bark —1G 67
St Paul's Rd. Bren —6D 72
St Paul's Rd. Eri —7J 85
St Paul's Rd. Rich —3F 89
St Paul's Rd. T Hth —3C 124
St Paul's Shrubbery. N1 —6D 46
St Paul's Sq. Brom —2H 127
St Paul's Studios. W14 —5G 75
(off Talgarth Rd.)
St Paul's Ter. SE17 —6B 78
St Paul St. N1 —1C 62
(in two parts)
St Paul's Wlk. King T —7G 105
St Paul's Way. E3 —5B 64
St Paul's Way. N3 —7E 14
St Paul's Wood Hill. Orp —2J 129
St Peter's All. EC3 —6D 62 (8B 142)
(off Cornhill)
St Peter's Av. E2 —2G 63
St Peter's Av. E17 —4G 33
St Peters Av. N2 —7H 15
St Peter's Av. N18 —4B 18
St Petersburgh M. W2 —7K 59
St Petersburgh Pl. W2 —7K 59
St Peter's Clo. E2 —2G 63
St Peter's Clo. SW17 —2C 108
St Peters Clo. Bush —1C 10
St Peter's Clo. Chst —7H 115
St Peter's Clo. Ilf —4K 35
St Peter's Clo. Ruis —2B 38
St Peter's Ct. NW4 —5E 26
St Peter's Gdns. SE27 —3A 110
St Peter's Gro. W6 —4C 74
St Peters Pl. W9 —4K 59
St Peter's Rd. N9 —1C 18
St Peter's Rd. W6 —5C 74
St Peter's Rd. Croy —4D 134
St Peter's Rd. King T —2G 119
St Peter's Rd. S'hall —5E 54

St Peter's Rd. Twic —5B 88
St Peter's Sq. E2 —2G 63
St Peter's Sq. W6 —4B 74
St Peter's St. N1 —1B 62
St Peter's St. S Croy —5D 134
St Peter's Ter. SW6 —7H 75
St Peter's Vs. W6 —4C 74
St Peter's Way. N1 —7E 46
St Peter's Way. W5 —5D 56
St Philips Av. N2 —7H 15
St Philip's Av. Wor Pk —2D 130
St Philip Sq. SW8 —2F 93
St Philip's Rd. E8 —6G 47
St Philip's Rd. Surb —6D 118
St Philip St. SW8 —2F 93
St Philip's Way. N1 —1C 62
St Phillips Rd. Surb —6D 118
St Quentin Rd. Well —3K 99
St Quentin Gdns. W10 —5E 58
St Quintin Av. W10 —5E 58
St Quintin Gdns. W10 —5E 58
St Quintin Rd. E13 —3K 65
St Raphael's Way. NW10 —5J 41
St Regis Clo. N10 —2F 29
St Regis Heights. NW3 —3K 43
St Ronan's Clo. Barn —1G 5
St Ronan's Cres. Wfd G —7D 20
St Rule St. SW8 —2G 93
St Saviours Clo. E17 —7C 32
St Saviour's College. SE17 —5D 134
St Saviours Ct. Harr —5J 23
St Saviour's Est. SE1
—3F 79 (6E 148)
St Saviour's Rd. SW2 —5K 93
St Saviour's Rd. Croy —6C 124
Saints Clo. SE27 —4B 110
Saints Dri. E7 —5B 50
St Silas Pl. NW5 —6E 44
St Simon's Av. SW15 —5E 90
St Stephen's Av. E17 —5E 32
St Stephen's Av. W12 —2D 74
St Stephen's Av. W13 —6B 56
St Stephen's Clo. E17 —5D 32
St Stephen's Clo. NW8 —1C 60
St Stephen's Clo. S'hall —5E 54
St Stephen's Ct. Enf —6K 7
St Stephen's Cres. W2 —6J 59
St Stephen's Cres. T Hth —3A 124
St Stephen's Gdns. SW15 —5H 91
St Stephen's Gdns. W2 —6J 59
St Stephen's Gdns. Twic —6C 88
St Stephens Gro. SE13 —3E 96
St Stephens Pde. E7 —7A 50
St Stephens Pde. SW1
—2J 77 (5D 146)
St Stephen's Pas. Twic —6C 88
St Stephen's Rd. E3 —1A 64
St Stephen's Rd. E6 —7A 50
St Stephen's Rd. E17 —5D 32
St Stephen's Rd. W13 —6B 56
St Stephen's Rd. Barn —5A 4
St Stephen's Rd. Houn —6E 86
St Stephen's Row. EC4
(off Walbrook) —6D 62 (8A 142)
St Stephens Ter. SW8 —7K 77
St Stephen's Wlk. SW7 —4A 76
St Swithins La. EC4
—7D 62 (9A 142)
St Swithun's Rd. SE13 —6F 97
St Thomas Clo. Surb —7F 119
St Thomas Ct. E10 —7D 32
(off Skelton's La.)
St Thomas Ct. Bex —7G 101
St Thomas Ct. Pinn —1C 22
St Thomas Dri. Orp —7G 129
St Thomas Dri. Pinn —1C 22
St Thomas Gdns. Ilf —6G 51

St Thomas Rd. E16 —6J 65
St Thomas Rd. N14 —7C 6
St Thomas Rd. W4 —6J 73
St Thomas Rd. Belv —2J 85
St Thomas's Gdns. NW5 —6E 44
St Thomas's Pl. E9 —7J 47
St Thomas's Rd. N4 —2A 46
St Thomas's Rd. NW10 —1A 58
St Thomas's Sq. E9 —7J 47
St Thomas St. SE1 —1D 78 (3A 148)
St Thomas's Way. SW6 —7H 75
St Timothys M. Brom —1K 127
St Ursula Gro. Pinn —5B 22
St Ursula Rd. S'hall —6E 54
St Vincent Clo. SE27 —5B 110
St Vincent Rd. Twic —6C 87
St Vincent St. W1 —5E 60 (6H 139)
St Wilfrid's Clo. Barn —5H 5
St Wilfrid's Rd. Barn —5H 5
St Winefride's Av. E12 —5D 50
St Winifred's Rd. Tedd —6B 104
Salamanca Pl. SE1 —4K 77 (9E 146)
Salamanca St. SE1 & SE11
—4K 77 (9E 146)
Salcombe Dri. Mord —1F 131
Salcombe Dri. Romf —6F 37
Salcombe Gdns. NW7 —6K 13
Salcombe Rd. E17 —7B 32
Salcombe Rd. N16 —5E 46
Salcott Rd. SW11 —5C 92
Salcott Rd. Croy —3J 133
Salehurst Clo. Harr —5E 24
Salehurst Rd. SE4 —6B 96
Salem Pl. Croy —3C 134
Salem Rd. W2 —7K 59
Sale Pl. W2 —6C 60 (6C 138)
Sale St. E2 —4G 63
Salford Rd. SW2 —1H 109
Salhouse Clo. SE28 —6C 68
Salisbury Av. N3 —3H 27
Salisbury Av. Bark —7H 51
Salisbury Av. Sutt —6H 131
Salisbury Clo. SE17
—4D 78 (9A 148)
Salisbury Clo. Wor Pk —3B 130
Salisbury Ct. EC4 —6B 62 (8J 141)
Salisbury Gdns. SW19 —7G 107
Salisbury Gdns. Buck H —2G 21
Salisbury Hall Gdns. E4 —6H 19
Salisbury Ho. Stan —6F 11
Salisbury Mans. N15 —5B 30
Salisbury M. SW6 —7H 75
Salisbury Pas. SW6 —7H 75
(off Dawes Rd.)
Salisbury Pl. SW9 —7B 78
Salisbury Pl. W1 —5D 60 (5F 138)
Salisbury Rd. E4 —3H 19
Salisbury Rd. E7 —6J 49
Salisbury Rd. E10 —2E 48
Salisbury Rd. E12 —5B 50
Salisbury Rd. E17 —5E 32
Salisbury Rd. N4 —5B 30
Salisbury Rd. N9 —3B 18
Salisbury Rd. N22 —1B 30
Salisbury Rd. SE25 —6G 125
Salisbury Rd. SW19 —7G 107
Salisbury Rd. W13 —2B 72
Salisbury Rd. Barn —3B 4
Salisbury Rd. Bex —1G 117
Salisbury Rd. Brom —5C 128
Salisbury Rd. Cars —6D 132
Salisbury Rd. Dag —6H 53
Salisbury Rd. Felt —1A 102
Salisbury Rd. Harr —5H 23
Salisbury Rd. Houn —3A 86
Salisbury Rd. Ilf —2J 51
Salisbury Rd. N Mald —3K 119
Salisbury Rd. Rich —4E 88

Salisbury Rd. S'hall —4C **70**
Salisbury Rd. Wor Pk —4A **130**
Salisbury Sq. EC4 —6A 62 (8H **141**)
Salisbury St. NW8 —4C 60 (4C **138**)
Salisbury St. W3 —2J **73**
Salisbury Ter. SE15 —3J **95**
Salisbury Wlk. N19 —2G **45**
Salix Ct. N3 —6D **14**
Salliesfield. Twic —6H **87**
Sally Motland Ho. Wemb —7F **25**
Salmen Rd. E13 —2H **65**
Salmond Clo. Stan —6F **11**
Salmon La. E14 —6A **64**
Salmon Rd. Belv —5G **85**
Salmons Rd. N9 —1B **18**
Salmon St. E14 —6B **64**
Salmon St. NW9 —1H **41**
Salomons Rd. E13 —5A **66**
Salop Rd. E17 —6K **31**
Saltash Clo. Sutt —4H **131**
Saltash Ho. SE11 —5B 78
(off Seaton Clo.)
Saltash Rd. Ilf —1H **35**
Saltash Rd. Well —1C **100**
Saltcoats Rd. W4 —2A **74**
Saltcroft Clo. Wemb —1H **41**
Salterford Rd. SW17 —6E **108**
Salter Rd. SE16 —1H **79**
Salters Ct. EC4 —6C 62 (8M 141)
(off Bow La.)
Salter's Hall Ct. EC4 —7D 62 (9A 142)
(off Cannon St.)
Salter's Hill. SE19 —5D **110**
Salters Rd. E17 —4F **33**
Salters Rd. W10 —4F **59**
Salter St. E14 —7C **64**
Salterton Rd. N7 —3K **45**
Saltoun Rd. SW2 —4A **94**
Saltram Clo. N15 —4F **31**
Saltram Cres. W9 —3H **59**
Saltwell St. E14 —7C **64**
Saltwood Gro. SE17 —5D **78**
Salusbury Rd. NW6 —1G **59**
Salvador. SW17 —5D **108**
Salva Gdns. Gnfd —2A **56**
Salvia Gdns. Gnfd —2A **56**
Salvin Rd. SW15 —3F **91**
Salway Clo. Wfd G —7D **20**
Salway Pl. E15 —6F **49**
Salway Rd. E15 —6F **49**
Samantha Clo. E17 —7B **32**
Sam Bartram Clo. SE7 —5A **82**
Sambrook Ho. SE11 —4A 78 (9G 147)
(off Hotspur St.)
Sambruck M. SE6 —1D **112**
Samels Ct. W6 —5C **74**
Samford Ho. N1 —1A 62
(off Barnsbury Est.)
Samford St. NW8 —4B 60 (4C **138**)
Samos Rd. SE20 —2H **125**
Sampson Av. Barn —5A **4**
Sampson Clo. Belv —3D **84**
Sampson St. E1 —1G **79**
Samsbrooke Ct. Enf —5A **8**
Samson St. E13 —2A **66**
Samuda Est. E14 —3E **80**
Samuel Clo. E8 —1F **63**
Samuel Clo. SE14 —6K **79**
Samuel Clo. SE18 —4C **82**
Samuel Johnson Clo. SW16 —4H **109**
Samuel Jones Ind. Est. SE15 —7E 78
(off Peckham Gro.)
Samuel Lewis Bldgs. N1 —6A **46**
Samuel Lewis Trust Dwellings. E8
(Amhurst Rd.) —5G **47**
Samuel Lewis Trust Dwellings. E8
(Dalston La.) —5G **47**

Samuel Lewis Trust Dwellings. N16
—6E **30**
Samuel Lewis Trust Dwellings. SE5
(off Warner Rd.) —1C **94**
Samuel Lewis Trust Dwellings. SW3
(off Ixworth Pl.) —4C 76 (9C **144**)
Samuel Lewis Trust Dwellings. SW6
(off Vanston Pl.) —7J **75**
Samuel Lewis Trust Dwellings. W14
(off Lisgar Ter.) —4H **75**
Samuel St. SE18 —4D **82**
Sancroft Clo. NW2 —3D **42**
Sancroft Ho. SE11 —5K 77
(off Sancroft St.)
Sancroft Rd. Harr —2K **23**
Sancroft St. SE11 —5K **77**
Sanctuary St. SE1 —2C 78 (4M **147**)
Sanctuary, The. SW1
—3H 77 (6B **146**)
(off Broad Sanctuary)
Sanctuary, The. Bex —6D **100**
Sanctuary, The. Mord —6J **121**
Sandale Clo. N16 —3D **46**
Sandall Clo. W5 —4E **56**
Sandall Rd. NW5 —6G **45**
Sandall Rd. W5 —4E **56**
Sandal Rd. N18 —5B **18**
Sandal Rd. N Mald —5K **119**
Sandal St. E15 —1G **65**
Sandalwood Clo. E1 —4A **64**
Sandalwood Ho. Sidc —3H **115**
Sandalwood Rd. Felt —3A **102**
Sandbach Pl. SE18 —4G **83**
Sandbourne Av. SW19 —2K **121**
Sandbourne Rd. SE4 —2A **96**
Sandbrook Clo. NW7 —6E **12**
Sandbrook Rd. N16 —3E **46**
Sandby Grn. SE9 —3C **98**
Sandcliff Rd. Eri —4K **85**
Sandcroft Clo. N13 —6G **17**
Sandell St. SE1 —2A 78 (4G **147**)
Sanderling Ct. SE28 —7C **68**
Sanders Clo. Hamp —5G **103**
Sanders La. NW7 —7K **13**
(in three parts)
Sanderson Clo. NW5 —4F **45**
Sanderson Gdns. Wfd G —1A **34**
Sanderson Shaw. SE28 —7D **68**
Sandersstead Av. NW2 —2G **43**
Sandersstead Clo. SW12 —7G **93**
Sandersstead Rd. E10 —1A **48**
Sandersstead Rd. S Croy —7D **134**
Sanders Way. N19 —1H **45**
Sandfield Gdns. T Hth —3B **124**
Sandfield Rd. T Hth —3B **124**
Sandford Av. N22 —1C **30**
Sandford Clo. E6 —4D **66**
Sandford Ct. N16 —1E **46**
Sandford Ct. New Bar —3E **4**
Sandford Rd. E6 —3C **66**
Sandford Rd. Bexh —4E **100**
Sandford Rd. Brom —4J **127**
Sandford St. SW6 —7K **75**
Sandgate Clo. Romf —7K **37**
Sandgate Ho. E5 —4H **47**
Sandgate La. SW18 —1C **108**
Sandgate Rd. Well —7C **84**
Sandgate St. SE15 —6H **79**
Sandham Ct. SW4 —1J **93**
Sandhills. Wall —4H **133**
Sandhills, The. SW10 —6A 76
(off Limerston St.)
Sandhurst Av. Harr —6F **23**
Sandhurst Av. Surb —7H **119**
Sandhurst Clo. NW9 —3G **25**
Sandhurst Clo. S Croy —7E **134**
Sandhurst Ct. SW2 —4J **93**
Sandhurst Dri. Ilf —4K **51**

Sandhurst Rd. N9 —6D **8**
Sandhurst Rd. NW9 —3G **25**
Sandhurst Rd. SE6 —1F **113**
Sandhurst Rd. Bex —5D **100**
Sandhurst Rd. Sidc —3K **115**
Sandhurst Way. S Croy —7E **134**
Sandhurst Rd. Sutt —2H **131**
Sandiland Cres. Brom —2H **137**
Sandilands. Croy —2G **135**
Sandilands Rd. SW6 —1K **91**
Sandison St. SE15 —3G **95**
Sandland St. WC1 —5K 61 (6F **140**)
Sandling Rise. SE9 —3E **114**
Sandlings, The. N22 —2B **30**
Sandmere Rd. SW4 —4J **93**
Sandown Av. Dag —6J **53**
Sandown Ct. Stan —5H **11**
Sandown Ct. Sutt —7K **131**
Sandown Dri. Cars —7E **132**
Sandown Rd. SE25 —5H **125**
Sandown Way. N'holt —6C **38**
Sandpiper Clo. E17 —7D **18**
Sandpit Rd. SE7 —5C **82**
Sandpit Rd. Brom —5G **113**
Sandpits Rd. Croy —4K **135**
Sandpits Rd. Rich —2D **104**
Sandra Clo. N22 —1C **30**
Sandra Clo. Houn —5F **87**
Sandridge Clo. Harr —4J **23**
Sandridge Ct. N4 —2C **46**
Sandridge St. N19 —2G **45**
Sandringham Av. SW20 —1G **121**
Sandringham Clo. Enf —2K **7**
Sandringham Clo. Ilf —3G **35**
Sandringham Ct. W9 —3A 60
(off Maida Vale)
Sandringham Ct. Sidc —6K **99**
Sandringham Cres. Harr —2E **38**
Sandringham Dri. Well —2J **99**
Sandringham Gdns. N8 —6J **29**
Sandringham Gdns. N12 —6G **15**
Sandringham Gdns. Ilf —3G **35**
Sandringham M. W5 —7D **56**
Sandringham Rd. E7 —5A **50**
Sandringham Rd. E8 —5F **47**
Sandringham Rd. E10 —6F **33**
Sandringham Rd. N22 —3C **30**
Sandringham Rd. NW2 —6D **42**
Sandringham Rd. NW11 —7G **27**
Sandringham Rd. Bark —6K **51**
Sandringham Rd. Brom —5J **113**
Sandringham Rd. T Hth —5C **124**
Sandringham Rd. Wor Pk —2C **130**
Sandrock Pl. Croy —4K **135**
Sandrock Rd. SE13 —3C **96**
Sand's End La. SW6 —1K **91**
Sandstone Pl. N19 —2F **45**
Sandstone Rd. SE12 —2K **113**
Sands Way. Wfd G —6J **21**
Sandtoft Rd. SE7 —6K **81**
Sandwell Cres. NW6 —6J **43**
Sandwich St. WC1 —3J 61 (2C **140**)
Sandycombe Rd. Rich —3F **89**
Sandycoombe Rd. Twic —6C **88**
Sandycroft. SE2 —6A **84**
Sandy Hill Av. SE18 —5F **83**
Sandy Hill Rd. SE18 —4E **82**
Sandyhill Rd. Ilf —4F **51**
Sandy Hill Rd. Wall —7G **133**
Sandy La. Harr —6F **25**
Sandy La. Mitc —1E **122**
Sandy La. Orp —7K **129**
Sandy La. Rich —2C **104**
Sandy La. Sidc —7D **116**
Sandy La. Sutt —7G **131**
Sandy La. Tedd & King T —7A **104**
Sandy La. N. Wall —5H **133**

Sandy La. S. Wall —7G **133**
Sandymount Av. Stan —5H **11**
Sandy Ridge. Chst —6E **114**
Sandy Rd. NW3 —2K **43**
Sandy Row. E1 —5E 62 (6D **142**)
Sandy Way. Croy —3B **136**
Sanford La. N16 —2F **47**
(in two parts)
Sanford St. SE14 —6A **80**
Sanford Ter. N16 —3F **47**
Sanford Wlk. N16 —2F **47**
Sanford Wlk. SE14 —6A **80**
Sangley Rd. SE6 —7D **96**
Sangley Rd. SE25 —4E **124**
Sangora Rd. SW11 —4B **92**
Sansom Rd. E11 —2H **49**
Sansom St. SE5 —1D **94**
Sans Wlk. EC1 —4A 62 (3H **141**)
Santley Ho. SE1 —2A 78 (5H **147**)
Santley St. SW4 —4J **93**
Santos Rd. SW18 —5J **91**
Santway, The. Stan —5D **10**
Sapcote Trading Est. NW10 —6B **42**
Saperton Wlk. SE11 —4K 77 (8F 146)
(off Juxon St.)
Sapphire Clo. E6 —6E **66**
Sapphire Clo. Dag —1C **52**
Sapphire Rd. SE8 —4A **80**
Saracen Clo. Croy —6D **124**
Saracens Head Yd. EC3
(off Jewry St.) —6F 63 (8E **142**)
Saracen St. E14 —6C **64**
Sarah St. N1 —3E 62 (1D **142**)
Saratoga Rd. E5 —4J **47**
Sardinia St. WC2 —6K 61 (8E **140**)
Sarita Clo. Harr —2H **23**
Sarjant Path. SW19 —2F 107
(off Blincoe Clo.)
Sark Clo. Houn —7E **70**
Sark Ho. Enf —1E **8**
Sark Wlk. E16 —6K **65**
Sarnes Ct. N11 —4A 16
(off Oakleigh Rd. S.)
Sarnesfield Ho. SE15 —6H 79
(off Pencraig Way)
Sarnesfield Rd. Enf —4J **7**
Sarratt Rd. NW2 —5H **43**
Sarre Rd. NW2 —5H **43**
Sarsen Av. Houn —2E **86**
Sarsfeld Rd. SW12 —1D **108**
Sarsfield Rd. Gnfd —2B **56**
Sartor Rd. SE15 —4K **95**
Sassoon. NW9 —1B **26**
Satanita Clo. E16 —6B **66**
Satchell Mead. NW9 —1B **26**
Satchwell Rd. E2 —3G **63**
Saul Ct. SE15 —6F 79
(off Daniel Gdns.)
Sauls Grn. E11 —3G **49**
Saunders Ho. W11 —1F **75**
Saunders Ness Rd. E14 —5E **80**
Saunders St. SE11 —4A 78 (8F **146**)
Saunders Way. SE28 —7B **68**
Saunderton Rd. Wemb —5B **40**
Savage Gdns. E6 —6D **66**
Savage Gdns. EC3 —7C 62 (9D **142**)
Savernake Ho. N4 —7C **30**
Savernake Rd. N9 —6B **8**
Savernake Rd. NW3 —4D **44**
Savile Clo. N Mald —5A **120**
Savile Gdns. Croy —2F **135**
Savile Row. W1 —7G 61 (9L **139**)
Saville Gdns. Croy —2F **135**
Saville Rd. E16 —1C **82**
Saville Rd. W4 —3K **73**
Saville Rd. Romf —6F **37**
Saville Rd. Twic —1K **103**
Saville Row. Brom —1H **137**

Saville Row. Enf —2E **8**
Savill Gdns. SW20 —3C **120**
Savill Ho. E16 —1F 83
(off Robert St.)
Savill Row. Wfd G —6C **20**
Savin Lodge. Sutt —7A 132
(off Walnut M.)
Savona Clo. SW19 —7F **107**
Savona St. SW8 —7G **77**
Savoy Bldgs. WC2 —7K 61 (1E 146)
(off Strand)
Savoy Clo. E15 —1G **65**
Savoy Clo. Edgw —5B **12**
Savoy Ct. NW3 —3A **44**
Savoy Ct. WC2 —7K 61 (1E **146**)
Savoy Hill. WC2 —7K 61 (1E **146**)
Savoy Pde. Enf —3K **7**
Savoy Row. WC2 —7J 61 (1D **146**)
Savoy Row. WC2 —7K 61 (9E 140)
(off Savoy St.)
Savoy Steps. WC2 —7K 61 (1E 146)
(off Savoy Row)
Savoy St. WC2 —7K 61 (9E **140**)
Savoy Way. WC2 —7K 61 (1E 146)
(off Savoy Hill)
Sawbill Clo. Hay —5B **54**
Sawkins Clo. SW19 —2G **107**
Sawley Rd. W12 —1B **74**
Sawtry Clo. Cars —7C **122**
Sawyer Clo. N9 —2B **18**
Sawyer Ct. NW10 —7K **41**
Sawyers Clo. Dag —6J **53**
Sawyers Hill. Rich —7F **89**
Sawyers Lawn. W13 —6A **56**
Sawyer St. SE1 —2C 78 (4L **147**)
Saxby Rd. SW2 —7J **93**
Saxham Rd. Bark —1J **67**
Saxlingham Rd. E4 —3A **20**
Saxon Av. Felt —2C **102**
Saxonbury Clo. Mitc —3B **122**
Saxonbury Ct. N7 —5J **45**
Saxonbury Gdns. Surb —7C **118**
Saxon Bus. Cen. SW19 —2A **122**
Saxon Clo. Surb —6D **118**
Saxon Dri. W3 —6G **57**
Saxon Gdns. S'hall —7C **54**
Saxon Ho. Felt —2D **102**
Saxon Rd. E3 —2B **64**
Saxon Rd. E6 —4D **66**
Saxon Rd. N22 —1B **30**
Saxon Rd. SE25 —5D **124**
Saxon Rd. Brom —7H **113**
Saxon Rd. Ilf —6F **51**
Saxon Rd. S'hall —7C **54**
Saxon Rd. Wemb —3J **41**
Saxon Wlk. Sidc —6C **116**
Saxon Way. N14 —6C **6**
Saxton Clo. SE13 —3F **97**
Sayers Ho. N2 —2B 28
(off Grange, The)
Sayer's Wlk. Rich —7F **89**
Sayes Ct. SE8 —5B **80**
Sayes Ct. St. SE8 —6B **80**
Scads Hill Clo. Orp —6K **129**
Scala St. W1 —5G 61 (5M **139**)
Scales Rd. N17 —3F **31**
Scampston M. W10 —6F **59**
Scandrett St. E1 —1H **79**
Scarba Wlk. N1 —6D 46
(off Marquess Rd.)
Scarborough Rd. E11 —1F **49**
Scarborough Rd. N4 —1A **46**
Scarborough Rd. N9 —7D **8**
Scarborough St. E1 —6F **63**
Scarbrook Rd. Croy —3C **134**
Scarle Rd. Wemb —6D **40**
Scarlet Rd. SE6 —3G **113**

Scarlette Mnr. Way. SW2 —7A 94
Scarsbrook Rd. SE3 —3B 98
Scarsdale Pl. W8 —3K 75
Scarsdale Rd. Harr —3G 39
Scarsdale Vs. W8 —3J 75
Scarth Rd. SW13 —3B 90
Scawen Rd. SE8 —5A 80
Scawfell St. E2 —2F 63
Sceaux Gdns. SE5 —1E 94
Sceptre Rd. E2 —3J 63
Sceynes Link. N12 —4D 14
Schofield Wlk. SE3 —7K 81
Scholars Rd. E4 —1A 20
Scholars Rd. SW12 —1G 109
Scholefield Rd. N19 —1H 45
School All. Twic —1A 104
School App. E2 —3E 62 (1D 142)
Schoolbell M. E3 —2A 64
School Ho. La. E1 —7K 63
School Ho. La. Tedd —7B 104
School La. SE23 —2H 111
School La. Bush —1A 10
School La. Well —3B 100
School La. King T —1C 118
School La. Pinn —4C 22
School Pas. King T —2P 119
School Pas. S'hall —7D 54
School Rd. E12 —4D 50
School Rd. NW10 —4K 57
School Rd. Chst —1G 129
School Rd. Dag —1G 69
School Rd. Houn —3E 87
School Rd. King T —1C 118
School Rd. Av. Hamp —6G 103
School Way. N12 —6G 15
Schooner Clo. SE16 —2K 79
Schubert Rd. SW15 —5H 91
Sclater St. E1 —4F 63 (3E 142)
Scoble Pl. N16 —4F 47
Scoles Cres. SW2 —1A 110
Scoresby St. SE1 —1B 78 (3J 147)
Scorton Av. Gnfd —2A 56
Scotch Comn. W13 —5A 56
Scoter Clo. Wfd G —7E 20
Scot Gro. Pinn —1B 22
Scotia Building. E1 —7K 63
(off Jardine Rd.)
Scotland Grn. N17 —2F 31
Scotland Grn. Rd. Enf —5E 8
Scotland Grn. Rd. N. Enf —4E 8
Scotland Pl. SW1 —1J 77 (3C 146)
Scotland Rd. Buck H —1F 21
Scotney Ho. E9 —6J 47
Scotsdale Clo. Orp —4J 129
Scotsdale Clo. Sutt —7G 131
Scotsdale Rd. SE12 —5K 97
Scotson Ho. SE11 —4A 78 (4G 147)
(off Marylee Way)
Scotswood St. EC1 —4A 62 (3H 141)
Scotswood Wlk. N17 —7B 18
Scott Clo. N16 —1K 123
Scott Ct. W3 —2K 73
Scott Cres. Harr —1F 39
Scott Ellis Gdns. NW8
—3B 60 (2A 138)
Scottes La. Dag —1D 52
Scott Farm Clo. Th Dit —7B 118
Scott Gdns. Houn —7B 70
Scott Ho. E13 —2J 65
(off Queens Rd. W.)
Scott Ho. E14 —2C 80
(off Admirals Way)
Scott Ho. NW10 —7K 41
(off Stonebridge Pk.)
Scott Lidgett Cres. SE16 —2G 79
Scott Russell Pl. E14 —5D 80

Scotts Av. Brom —2F 127
Scotts Dri. Hamp —7F 103
Scott's La. Brom —3F 127
Scotts Pas. SE18 —4F 83
Scott's Rd. E10 —1E 48
Scott's Rd. W12 —2D 74
Scotts Rd. Brom —7J 113
Scott's Rd. S'hall —3A 70
Scott St. E1 —4H 63
Scott's Yd. EC4 —7D 62 (9A 142)
(off Gophir La.)
Scottwell Dri. NW9 —5B 26
Scoulding Rd. E16 —6J 65
Scouler St. E14 —7F 65
Scout App. NW10 —4A 42
Scout La. SW4 —3G 93
Scout Way. NW7 —4E 12
Scovell Cres. SE1 —2C 78 (5L 147)
(off McCoid Way)
Scovell Rd. SE1 —2C 78 (5L 147)
Scrattons Ter. Bark —1D 68
Scriven Ct. E8 —1F 63
Scriven St. E8 —1F 63
Scrooby St. SE6 —6D 96
Scrubs La. NW10 —3C 58
Scrutton Clo. SW12 —7H 93
Scrutton St. EC2 —4E 62 (4C 142)
Scudamore La. NW9 —4J 25
Scutari Rd. SE22 —5J 95
Scylla Rd. SE15 —3G 95
(in two parts)
Seabright Pas. E2 —2G 63
Seabright St. E2 —3H 63
Seabrook Dri. W Wick —2G 137
Seabrook Gdns. Romf —7G 37
Seabrook Rd. Dag —2D 52
Seaburn Clo. Rain —3K 69
Seacole Clo. W3 —5K 57
Seacourt Rd. SE2 —2D 84
Seafield Rd. N11 —4C 16
Seaford Rd. E17 —3D 32
Seaford Rd. N15 —5D 30
Seaford Rd. W13 —1B 72
Seaford Rd. Enf —4K 7
Seaford Rd. WC1 —3J 61 (2D 140)
Seaforth Av. N Mald —5D 120
Seaforth Cres. N5 —5C 46
Seaforth Gdns. N21 —7E 6
Seaforth Gdns. Eps —4B 130
Seaforth Gdns. Wfd G —5F 21
Seaforth Pl. SW1 —3G 77 (6M 145)
(off Buckingham Ga.)
Seagar Pl. E3 —5B 64
Seagrave Clo. E1 —5K 63
Seagrave Rd. SW6 —6J 75
Seagry Rd. E11 —6J 33
Sealand Wlk. N'holt —3B 54
Seal St. E8 —4F 47
Searle Pl. N4 —1K 45
Searles Clo. SW11 —7C 76
Searles Rd. SE1 —4D 78 (8B 148)
Sears St. SE5 —7D 78
Seasprite Clo. N'holt —3B 54
Seaton Av. Ilf —5J 51
Seaton Clo. E13 —4J 65
Seaton Clo. SE11 —5B 78
Seaton Clo. SW15 —1D 106
Seaton Clo. Twic —6H 87
Seaton Pl. NW1 —4G 61 (3L 139)
(off Triton Sq.)
Seaton Point. E5 —4G 47
Seaton Rd. Mitc —2C 122
Seaton Rd. Twic —6G 87
Seaton Rd. Well —7C 84
Seaton Rd. Wemb —2E 56
Seaton St. N18 —5B 18
Sebastian St. EC1 —3B 62 (2K 141)
Sebastopol Rd. N9 —4B 18

Sebbon St. N1 —7B 45
Sebert Rd. E7 —5K 49
Sebright Rd. Barn —2A 4
Secker Cres. Harr —1G 23
Secker Ho. SW9 —2B 94
(off Rupert Gdns.)
Secker St. SE1 —1A 78 (3G 147)
Second Av. E12 —4C 50
Second Av. E13 —3J 65
Second Av. E17 —5C 32
Second Av. N18 —4D 18
Second Av. NW4 —4F 27
Second Av. SW14 —3A 90
Second Av. W3 —1B 74
Second Av. W10 —4G 59
Second Av. Dag —2H 69
Second Av. Enf —5A 8
Second Av. Romf —5C 36
Second Av. Wemb —2D 40
Second Cross Rd. Twic —2J 103
Second Way. Wemb —4H 41
Sedan Way. SE17 —5E 78
Sedcombe Clo. Sidc —4B 116
Sedcote Rd. Enf —5D 8
Sedding St. SW1 —4E 76 (8G 145)
Seddon Highwalk. EC2
—5C 62 (5L 141)
(off Barbican)
Seddon Ho. EC2 —5C 62 (5L 141)
(off Barbican)
Seddon Rd. Mord —5B 122
Seddon St. WC1 —3K 61 (2F 140)
Sedgebrook Rd. SE3 —3B 98
Sedgecombe Av. Harr —5C 24
Sedgeford Rd. W12 —1B 74
Sedgehill Rd. SE6 —4C 112
Sedgemere Av. N2 —3A 28
Sedgemere Rd. SE2 —3C 84
Sedgemoor Dri. Dag —4G 53
Sedge Rd. N17 —7D 18
Sedgeway. SE6 —1H 113
Sedgewood Clo. Brom —7H 127
Sedgmoor Pl. SE5 —7E 78
Sedgwick Rd. E10 —2E 48
Sedgwick St. E9 —5K 47
Sedleigh Rd. SW18 —6H 91
Sedlescombe Rd. SW6 —6J 75
Sedley Clo. SE26 —2H 111
Sedley Ho. SE11 —5K 77
(off Newburn St.)
Sedley Pl. W1 —6F 61 (8J 139)
Sedley Rd. SE21 —4E 110
Seelig Av. NW9 —7C 26
Seely Rd. SW17 —6E 108
Seething La. EC3 —7E 62 (9D 142)
Seething Wells La. Surb —6C 118
Sefton Av. NW7 —5E 12
Sefton Av. Harr —2H 23
Sefton Clo. Orp —4K 129
Sefton Ct. Houn —1F 87
Sefton Rd. Croy —1G 135
Sefton Rd. Orp —4K 129
Sefton St. SW15 —3E 90
Sega Ho. SW5 —4J 75
(off Cromwell Rd.)
Segal Clo. SE23 —7A 96
Sekforde St. EC1 —4B 62 (4J 141)
Sekhon Ter. Felt —3E 102
Selah Dri. Swan —7J 117
Selan Gdns. Hay —5A 54
Selbie Av. NW10 —5B 42
Selborne Av. E12 —4E 50
Selborne Av. Bex —1E 116
Selborne Gdns. NW4 —4C 26
Selborne Gdns. Gnfd —2A 56
Selborne Rd. E17 —5B 32
Selborne Rd. N14 —3D 16
Selborne Rd. N22 —1K 29
Selborne Rd. SE5 —2D 94

Selborne Rd. Croy —3E 134
Selborne Rd. Ilf —2E 50
Selborne Rd. N Mald —2A 120
Selborne Rd. Sidc —4B 116
Selborne Wlk. E17 —4B 32
Selbourne Ho. SE1 —2D 78 (5A 148)
(off Gt. Dover St.)
Selby Clo. E6 —5C 66
Selby Clo. Chst —6E 114
Selby Gdns. S'hall —4E 54
Selby Grn. Cars —7C 122
Selby Rd. E11 —3G 49
Selby Rd. E13 —5K 65
Selby Rd. SE20 —2G 125
Selby Rd. W5 —4B 56
Selby St. E1 —4G 63
Selden Rd. SE15 —2J 95
Selhurst Clo. SW19 —1F 107
Selhurst New Rd. SE25 —6E 124
Selhurst Pl. SE25 —6E 124
Selhurst Rd. N9 —3J 17
Selhurst Rd. SE25 —6E 124
Selinas La. Dag —7E 35
Selkirk Rd. SW17 —4C 108
Selkirk Rd. Twic —2G 103
Sellers Hall Clo. N3 —7D 14
Sellincourt Rd. SW17 —5C 108
Sellindge Clo. Beck —7B 112
Sellon M. SE11 —4K 77 (9E 146)
Sellons Av. NW10 —1B 58
Selsdon Av. S Croy —6D 134
Selsdon Clo. Romf —1J 37
Selsdon Clo. Surb —5E 118
Selsdon Pk. Rd. S Croy —7K 135
Selsdon Rd. E11 —7J 33
Selsdon Rd. E13 —1A 66
Selsdon Rd. NW2 —2B 42
Selsdon Rd. SE27 —3B 110
Selsdon Rd. S Croy —5D 134
Selsdon Way. E14 —3D 80
Selsea Pl. N16 —5E 46
Selsey Cres. Well —1D 100
Selsey St. E14 —5C 64
Selvage La. NW7 —5E 12
Selway Clo. Pinn —3A 22
Selwood Dri. Barn —5A 4
Selwood Pl. SW7 —5B 76
Selwood Rd. Croy —2H 135
Selwood Rd. Sutt —1H 131
Selwood Ter. SW7 —5B 76
Selworthy Clo. E11 —5J 33
Selworthy Rd. SE6 —3B 112
Selwyn Av. E4 —6K 19
Selwyn Av. Ilf —6K 35
Selwyn Av. Rich —3E 88
Selwyn Clo. Houn —4C 86
Selwyn Ct. E17 —5C 32
(off Yunus Khan Clo.)
Selwyn Ct. Edgw —7C 12
Selwyn Cres. Well —3B 100
Selwyn Rd. E3 —2B 64
Selwyn Rd. E13 —1K 65
Selwyn Rd. NW10 —7K 41
Selwyn Rd. N Mald —5K 119
Semley Ga. E9 —6A 48
Semley Pl. SW1 —4E 76 (9H 145)
Semley Rd. SW16 —2J 123
Senate St. SE15 —2J 95
Senator Wlk. SE28 —3H 83
Seneca Rd. T Hth —4C 124
Senga Rd. Wall —1E 132
Senhouse Rd. Sutt —3F 131
Senior St. W2 —5K 59
Senlac Rd. SE12 —1K 113
Sennen Rd. Enf —7A 8

Sennen Wlk. SE9 —3C 114
Senrab St. E1 —6K 63
Sentinel Clo. N'holt —4C 54
Sentinel Sq. NW4 —4E 26
September Way. Stan —6G 11
Septimus Pl. Enf —5B 8
Sequoia Clo. Bush —1C 10
Sequoia Gdns. Orp —7K 129
Sequoia Pk. Pinn —6A 10
Serbin Clo. E10 —7E 32
Sergeant Ind. Est. SW18 —6K 91
Serica Ct. SE10 —7E 80
Serjeant's Inn. EC4 —6A 62 (8H 141)
Serle St. WC2 —6K 61 (7F 140)
Sermon La. EC4 —6C 62 (8L 141)
(off Carter La.)
Serpentine Rd. W2 —1C 76 (3C 144)
Serviden Dri. Brom —1B 128
Servius Ct. Bren —7D 72
Setchell Rd. SE1 —4F 79 (8E 148)
Setchell Way. SE1 —4F 79 (8E 148)
Seth St. SE16 —2J 79
Seton Gdns. Dag —7C 52
Settle Rd. E13 —2J 65
Settles St. E1 —5G 63
Settrington Rd. SW6 —2K 91
Seven Acres. Cars —2C 132
Seven Dials. NW10 —6J 41 (8C 140)
Seven Dials. WC2
(off Short Gdns.) —6J 61 (8C 140)
Seven Kings Rd. Ilf —2K 51
Sevenoaks Clo. Bexh —4H 101
Sevenoaks Rd. SE4 —6A 96
Sevenoaks Way. Sidc & Orp
—7C 116
Seven Sisters Rd. N7, N4 & N15
—3K 45
Seven Stars Corner. W12 —3C 74
Seventh Av. E12 —4D 50
Severnake Clo. E14 —4C 80
Severn Dri. Enf —1B 8
Severn Way. NW10 —5B 42
Severus Rd. SW11 —4C 92
Seville St. SW1 —2D 76 (5F 144)
Sevington Rd. NW4 —6D 26
Sevington St. W9 —4K 59
Seward Rd. W7 —2A 72
Seward Rd. Beck —2K 125
Sewardstone Gdns. E4 —5J 9
Sewardstone Rd. E2 —2J 63
Sewardstone Rd. E4 —7J 9
Seward St. EC1 —3B 62 (3K 141)
Sewdley St. E5 —4K 47
Sewell Rd. SE2 —3A 84
Sewell St. E13 —3J 65
Sextant Av. E14 —4F 81
Seymer Rd. Romf —3K 37
Seymour Av. N17 —2G 31
Seymour Av. Eps —7D 130
Seymour Av. Mord —7F 121
Seymour Clo. EC1 —4B 62 (4J 141)
Seymour Clo. Pinn —1D 22
Seymour Ct. E4 —2C 20
Seymour Ct. N10 —2E 28
Seymour Ct. N21 —6E 6
(off Eversley Pk. Rd.)
Seymour Ct. NW2 —2D 42
Seymour Dri. Brom —7D 128
Seymour Gdns. SE4 —3A 96
Seymour Gdns. Felt —4A 102
Seymour Gdns. Ilf —1D 50
Seymour Gdns. Ruis —1B 38
Seymour Gdns. Surb —5F 119
Seymour Gdns. Twic —7B 88
Seymour M. W1 —6E 60 (7G 139)
Seymour Pl. SE25 —4H 125
Seymour Pl. W1 —5D 60 (5D 138)
Seymour Rd. E4 —1J 19

Seymour Rd. E6 —2B 66
Seymour Rd. E10 —1B 48
Seymour Rd. N3 —7E 14
Seymour Rd. N8 —5A 30
Seymour Rd. N9 —2C 18
Seymour St. SW18 —7H 91
Seymour Rd. SW19 —3F 107
Seymour Rd. W4 —4J 73
Seymour Rd. Cars —5E 132
Seymour Rd. Hamp —5G 103
Seymour King T —1D 118
Seymour Rd. Mitc —7E 122
Seymour St. W2 & W1
　　　—6D 60 (8E 138)
Seymour Ter. SE20 —1H 125
Seymour Vs. SE20 —1H 125
Seymour Wlk. SW10 —6A 76
Seyssel St. E14 —4E 80
Shaa Rd. W3 —7K 57
Shacklegate La. Tedd —4J 103
Shackleton Clo. SE23 —2H 111
Shackleton Ho. NW10 —7K 41
Shackleton Rd. S'hall —7D 54
Shacklewell Grn. E8 —4F 47
Shacklewell Ho. E8 —4F 47
Shacklewell La. E8 —5F 47
Shacklewell Rd. N16 —4F 47
Shacklewell Row. E8 —4F 47
Shacklewell St. E2 —3F 63
Shadbolt Clo. Wor Pk —2B 130
Shad Thames. SE1 —1F 79 (3E 148)
Shadwell Ct. N'holt —2D 54
Shadwell Dri. N'holt —3D 54
Shadwell Pier Head. E1 —7J 63
Shadwell Pl. E1 —7J 63
Shadybush Clo. Bush —1B 10
Shael Way. Tedd —7A 104
Shafter Rd. Dag —6J 53
Shaftesbury Av. W1 & WC2
　　　—7H 61 (9A 140)
Shaftesbury Av. Barn —4F 5
Shaftesbury Av. Enf —2E 8
Shaftesbury Av. Kent —5D 24
Shaftesbury Av. S'hall —4E 70
Shaftesbury Av. S Harr —1F 39
Shaftesbury Circ. S Harr —1G 39
Shaftesbury Ct. E6 —6E 66
　　　(off Sapphire Clo.)
Shaftesbury Ct. SE5 —4D 94
Shaftesbury Ct. SW6 —1K 91
　　　(off Maltings Pl.)
Shaftesbury Ct. SW16 —3H 109
Shaftesbury Pde. S Harr —1G 39
Shaftesbury Pl. EC2 —5C 62 (6L 141)
　　　(off Barbican)
Shaftesbury Point. E13 —2J 65
　　　(off High St. Plaistow)
Shaftesbury Rd. E4 —1A 20
Shaftesbury Rd. E7 —7A 50
Shaftesbury Rd. E10 —1C 48
Shaftesbury Rd. E17 —6D 32
Shaftesbury Rd. N18 —6K 17
Shaftesbury Rd. N19 —1J 45
Shaftesbury Rd. Beck —2B 126
Shaftesbury Rd. Cars —7B 122
Shaftesbury Rd. Rich —3E 88
Shaftesburys, The. Bark —2G 67
Shaftesbury St. N1 —2C 62
　　　(in two parts)
Shaftesbury Way. Twic —3H 103
Shaftesbury Waye. Hay —5A 54
Shafto M. SW1 —3D 76 (7F 144)
Shafton Rd. E9 —1K 63
Shafts Ct. EC3 —6E 62 (8C 142)
Shakespeare Av. N11 —5B 16
Shakespeare Av. NW10 —1K 57
Shakespeare Av. Hay —5A 54
　　　(in two parts)

Shakespeare Ct. New Bar —3E 4
Shakespeare Cres. E12 —6D 50
Shakespeare Cres. NW10 —1K 57
Shakespeare Gdns. N2 —4D 28
Shakespeare Ho. N14 —2C 16
Shakespeare Rd. E17 —2K 31
Shakespeare Rd. N3 —1J 27
Shakespeare Rd. NW7 —4G 13
Shakespeare Rd. SE24 —5B 94
Shakespeare Rd. W3 —1J 73
Shakespeare Rd. W7 —7K 55
Shakespeare Rd. Bexh —1E 100
Shakespeare Tower. EC2
　　　—5C 62 (5M 141)
　　　(off Barbican)
Shakespeare Way. Felt —4A 102
Shakspeare M. N16 —4E 46
Shakspeare Wlk. N16 —4E 46
Shalcomb St. SW10 —6A 76
Shaldon Dri. Mord —5G 121
Shaldon Dri. Ruis —3A 38
Shaldon Rd. Edgw —2F 25
Shalfleet Dri. W10 —7F 59
Shalford Ct. N1 —2B 62
　　　(off Charlton Pl.)
Shalford Ho. SE1 —3D 78 (6B 148)
Shalimar Gdns. W3 —7J 57
Shalimar Rd. W3 —7J 57
Shallons Rd. SE9 —4F 115
Shalstone Rd. SW14 —3J 89
Shalston Vs. Surb —6F 119
Shamrock Rd. Croy —6K 123
Shamrock St. SW4 —3H 93
Shamrock Way. N14 —1A 16
Shandon Rd. SW4 —6G 93
Shand St. SE1 —2E 78 (4C 148)
Shandy St. E1 —5K 63
Shanklin Rd. N8 —5H 29
Shanklin Way. SE15 —7F 79
Shannon Clo. NW2 —3F 43
Shannon Clo. S'hall —5B 70
Shannon Ct. N16 —3E 46
Shannon Gro. SW9 —4K 93
Shannon Pl. NW8 —2C 60
Shannon Way. Beck —6D 112
Shanti Ct. SW18 —1J 107
Shap Cres. Cars —1D 132
Shapland Way. N13 —5E 16
Shap St. E2 —2F 63
Shardcroft Av. SE24 —5B 94
Shardeloes Rd. SE14 —2B 96
Shard's Sq. SE15 —6G 79
Sharman Ct. Sidc —4A 116
Sharnbrooke Clo. Well —3C 100
Sharon Clo. Surb —7D 118
Sharon Gdns. E9 —1J 63
Sharon Rd. W4 —5K 73
Sharon Rd. Enf —2F 9
Sharpe Clo. W7 —5K 55
Sharp Ho. SW8 —3F 93
Sharpleshall St. NW1 —7D 44
Sharpness Clo. Hay —5C 54
Sharpness Ct. SE15 —7F 79
　　　(off Daniel Gdns.)
Sharratt St. SE15 —6J 79
Sharsted St. SE17 —5B 78
Sharvel La. N'holt —1A 54
Shaver's Pl. SW1 —7H 61 (1A 146)
　　　(off Coventry St.)
Shaw Av. Bark —2E 68
Shawbrooke Rd. SE9 —5A 98
Shawbury Rd. SE22 —5F 95
Shaw Clo. SE28 —1B 84
Shaw Clo. Bush —2D 10
Shawfield Pk. Brom —2B 128
Shawfield St. SW3 —5C 76
Shawford Ct. SW15 —7C 90
Shaw Gdns. Bark —2E 68

Shaw Ho. E16 —1E 82
　　　(off Claremont St.)
Shaw Rd. Brom —3H 113
Shaw Rd. Enf —1E 8
Shaws Path. King T —1C 118
　　　(off High St. Hampton Wick)
Shaw Sq. E17 —1A 32
Shaw Way. Wall —7J 133
Shearing Dri. Cars —7J 121
Shearling Way. N7 —6J 45
Shearman Rd. SE3 —4H 97
Shearwater Way. Hay —6B 54
Sheaveshill Av. NW9 —4A 26
Sheaveshill Ct. NW9 —4K 25
Sheaveshill Pde. NW9 —4A 26
　　　(off Sheaveshill Av.)
Sheba St. E1 —4F 63 (4F 142)
Sheen Comn. Dri. Rich —4G 89
Sheen Ct. Rd. Rich —4G 89
Sheendale Rd. Rich —4F 89
Sheenewood. SE26 —4H 111
Sheen Ga. Gdns. SW14 —4J 89
Sheen Gro. N1 —1A 62
Sheen La. SW14 —5J 89
Sheen Pk. Rich —4E 88
Sheen Rd. Orp —4K 129
Sheen Rd. Rich —5E 88
Sheen Way. Wall —5K 133
Sheen Wood. SW14 —5J 89
Sheepcote La. SW11 —2C 92
Sheepcote Rd. Harr —6K 23
Sheepcotes Rd. Romf —4E 36
Sheephouse Way. N Mald —7K 119
Sheep La. E8 —1H 63
Sheep Wlk. M. SW19 —6F 107
Sheerwater Rd. E16 —5B 66
Sheffield Sq. E3 —3B 64
Sheffield St. WC2 —6K 61 (8E 140)
Sheffield Ter. W8 —1J 75
Sheila Rd. Romf —1H 37
Shelbourne Clo. Pinn —3D 22
Shelbourne Pl. Beck —7C 112
Shelbourne Rd. N17 —2H 31
Shelburne Rd. N7 —4K 45
Shelbury Clo. Sidc —4A 116
Shelbury Rd. SE22 —5H 95
Sheldon Av. N6 —7C 28
Sheldon Av. Ilf —2F 35
Sheldon Clo. SE12 —5K 97
Sheldon Clo. SE20 —1H 125
Sheldon Ct. Barn —4E 4
Sheldon Rd. N18 —4K 17
Sheldon Rd. NW2 —4F 43
Sheldon Rd. Bexh —1F 101
Sheldon Rd. Dag —7E 52
Sheldon St. Croy —3C 134
Sheldrake Ct. E6 —2C 66
　　　(off St Bartholomew's Rd.)
Sheldrake Pl. W8 —2J 75
Sheldrick Clo. SW19 —2B 122
Sheldwich Ter. Brom —6C 128
Shelford Pl. N16 —3D 46
Shelford Rise. SE19 —7F 111
Shelford Rd. Barn —6A 4
Shelgate Rd. SW11 —5C 92
Shell Clo. Brom —6C 128
Shellduck Clo. NW9 —2A 26
Shelley. N8 —3J 29
　　　(off Boyton Rd.)
Shelley Av. E12 —6C 50
Shelley Av. Gnfd —3H 55
Shelley Clo. Edgw —4B 12
Shelley Clo. Gnfd —3H 55
Shelley Ct. N4 —1K 45
Shelley Cres. Houn —1B 86
Shelley Cres. S'hall —6D 54
Shelley Dri. Well —1J 99
Shelley Gdns. Wemb —2C 40

Shelley Rd. SW19 —6B 108
Shellness Rd. E5 —5H 47
Shell Rd. SE13 —3D 96
Shellwood Rd. SW11 —2D 92
Shelly Clo. SE15 —2H 95
Shelmerdine Clo. E3 —5C 64
Shelton Rd. SW19 —1J 121
Shelton St. WC2 —6J 61 (8C 140)
　　　(in two parts)
Shenfield Rd. Wfd G —7E 20
Shenfield St. N1 —2E 62
Shenley Rd. SE5 —1E 94
Shenley Rd. Houn —1C 86
Shenstone Clo. Dart —4K 101
Shepherdess Pl. N1
　　　—3C 62 (1A 142)
Shepherdess Wlk. N1 —2C 62
Shepherd Mkt. W1 —1F 77 (3J 145)
Shepherds Bush Cen. W12 —2F 75
Shepherd's Bush Grn. W12 —2E 74
Shepherd's Bush Mkt. W12 —2E 74
Shepherd's Bush Pl. W12 —2F 75
Shepherd's Bush Rd. W6 —4E 74
Shepherd's Clo. N6 —6F 29
Shepherds Clo. Romf —5D 36
Shepherds Ct. W12 —2F 75
　　　(off Shepherd's Bush Grn.)
Shepherds Grn. Chst —7H 115
Shepherd's Hill. N6 —6F 29
Shepherds La. E9 —6K 47
Shepherd's Path. NW3 —5B 44
　　　(off Lyndhurst Rd.)
Shepherds Path. N'holt —6C 38
　　　(off Arnold Rd.)
Shepherds Pl. W1 —7E 60 (9G 139)
Shepherd St. W1 —1F 77 (3J 145)
Shepherds Wlk. N1 —2C 62
Shepherds Wlk. NW2 —2C 42
Shepherd's Wlk. NW3 —5B 44
Shepherds Wlk. Bush —2C 10
Shepherds Way. S Croy —7K 135
Shepley Clo. Cars —3E 132
Sheppard Clo. Enf —1C 8
Sheppard Clo. King T —4E 118
Sheppard Ho. SW2 —1A 110
Sheppard St. E16 —4H 65
Shepperton Rd. N1 —1C 62
Shepperton Rd. Orp —6G 129
Sheppey Gdns. Dag —1C 52
Sheppey Rd. Dag —7B 52
Sheppey Wlk. N1 —6C 46
Shepton Houses. E2 —3J 63
　　　(off Welwyn St.)
Sherard Rd. SE9 —5C 98
Sheraton Bus. Cen. Gnfd —2C 56
Sheraton St. W1 —6H 61 (8A 140)
Sherborne Av. Enf —2D 8
Sherborne Av. S'hall —4E 70
Sherborne Clo. Hay —6A 54
Sherborne Cres. Cars —7C 122
Sherborne Gdns. NW9 —3G 25
Sherborne Gdns. W13 —5B 56
Sherborne La. EC4 —7D 62 (9A 142)
Sherborne Rd. Orp —5K 129
Sherborne Rd. Sutt —2J 131
Sherborne St. N1 —1D 62
Sherboro Rd. N15 —6F 31
Sherbourne Pl. Stan —6F 11
Sherbrooke Clo. Bexh —4G 101
Sherbrooke Rd. SW6 —7G 75
Sherbrook Gdns. N21 —7G 7
Sheredan Rd. E4 —5A 20
Shere Ho. SE1 —2D 78 (5A 148)
　　　(off Gt. Dover St.)
Shere Rd. Ilf —5E 34
Sherfield Gdns. SW15 —6B 90
Sheridan Ct. Harr —6H 23
Sheridan Ct. Houn —5C 86

Sheridan Cres. Chst —2F 129
Sheridan Gdns. Harr —6D 24
Sheridan Ho. SE11 —4A 78 (9H 147)
　　　(off Wincott St.)
Sheridan Lodge. Brom —4A 128
　　　(off Homesdale Rd.)
Sheridan Pl. SW13 —3B 90
Sheridan Pl. Hamp —7F 103
Sheridan Rd. E7 —3H 49
Sheridan Rd. E12 —5C 50
Sheridan Rd. SW19 —1H 121
Sheridan Rd. Belv —4G 85
Sheridan Rd. Bexh —3E 100
Sheridan Rd. Rich —3C 104
Sheridan St. E1 —6H 63
Sheridan Ter. N'holt —5F 39
Sheridan Wlk. NW11 —6J 27
Sheridan Wlk. Cars —5D 132
Sheridan Way. Beck —1B 126
Sheridan Pl. Harr —7J 23
Sheringham. NW8 —7B 44
Sheringham Av. E12 —4D 50
Sheringham Av. N14 —5C 6
Sheringham Av. Romf —6J 37
Sheringham Av. Twic —1D 102
Sheringham Ct. Enf —3G 7
Sheringham Dri. Bark —5K 51
Sheringham Rd. N7 —6K 45
Sheringham Rd. SE20 —3J 125
Sheringham Tower. S'hall —7F 55
Sherington Av. Pinn —7A 10
Sherington Rd. SE7 —6K 81
Sherland Rd. Twic —1K 103
Sherlock M. W1 —5E 60 (5G 139)
Sherman Rd. Brom —1J 127
Shernhall St. E17 —3E 32
Sherrard Rd. E7 & E12 —6A 50
Sherrards Way. Barn —5D 4
Sherrick Grn. Rd. NW10 —5D 42
Sherriff Rd. NW6 —6J 43
Sherringham Av. N17 —2G 31
Sherrin Rd. E10 —4D 48
Sherrock Gdns. NW4 —4C 26
Sherston Ct. SE1 —4B 78 (8K 147)
　　　(off Newington Butts)
Sherston Ct. WC1 —3A 62 (2G 141)
　　　(off Attneave St.)
Sherwin Ho. SE11 —6A 78
　　　(off Kennington Rd.)
Sherwin Rd. SE14 —1K 95
Sherwood Av. E18 —3K 33
Sherwood Av. SW16 —7H 109
Sherwood Av. Gnfd —6J 39
Sherwood Av. Hay —4A 54
Sherwood Clo. SW13 —3D 90
Sherwood Clo. W13 —1B 72
Sherwood Clo. Bex —6C 100
Sherwood Ct. S Harr —2G 39
Sherwood Gdns. Bark —7H 51
Sherwood Pk. Av. Sidc —7A 100
Sherwood Pk. Rd. Mitc —4G 123
Sherwood Pk. Rd. Sutt —5J 131
Sherwood Rd. NW4 —3E 26
Sherwood Rd. SW19 —7H 107
Sherwood Rd. Croy —7H 125
Sherwood Rd. Hamp —5G 103
Sherwood Rd. Harr —2G 39
Sherwood Rd. Ilf —4H 35
Sherwood Rd. Well —2J 99
Sherwood St. N20 —3G 15
Sherwood St. W1 —7G 61 (9M 139)
Sherwood Ter. N20 —3G 15
Sherwood Way. W Wick —2E 136
Shetland Rd. E3 —2B 64
Shield Dri. Bren —6A 72
Shieldhall St. SE2 —4C 84
Shifford Path. SE23 —3K 111

Shillibeer Pl. W1 —5C 60 (6D 138)
(off York St.)
Shillington St. N1 —7B 46
Shinfield St. W12 —6E 58
Shingle End. Bren —7C 72
Shinglewell Rd. Eri —7G 85
Shington Rd. SW6 —2H 91
Shinners Clo. SE25 —5G 125
Ship All. W4 —6G 73
Ship & Half Moon Pas. SE18
  —3F 83
Shipka Rd. SW12 —1F 109
Ship La. SW14 —3J 89
Shipman Rd. E16 —6K 65
Shipman Rd. SE23 —2K 111
Ship & Mermaid Row. SE1
(off Snowsfields) —2D 78 (4B 148)
Ship & Mermaid Row. SW1 —2D 78
Ship St. SE18 —1C 96
Ship Tavern Pas. EC3
  —7E 62 (9C 142)
Shipton Clo. Dag —3D 52
Shipton Pl. NW5 —6E 44
Shipton St. E2 —3F 63
Shipway Ter. N16 —3F 47
Shipwright Rd. SE16 —2A 80
Shipwright Yd. SE1 —1E 78 (3C 148)
Ship Yd. E14 —5D 80
Shirburn Clo. SE23 —7J 95
Shirbutt St. E14 —7D 64
Shirebrook Rd. SE3 —3B 98
Shire Ct. Eri —3D 84
Shirehall Rd. NW4 —6F 27
Shirehall Gdns. NW4 —6F 27
Shirehall La. NW4 —6F 27
Shirehall Pk. NW4 —5F 27
Shires, The. Ham —4E 104
Shirland M. W9 —3H 59
Shirland Rd. W9 —3H 59
Shirley Av. Bex —7D 100
Shirley Av. Croy —1J 135
Shirley Av. Sutt —4B 132
Shirley Av. Cheam —7H 131
Shirley Church Rd. Croy —3K 135
Shirley Clo. E17 —5D 32
Shirley Clo. Houn —5G 87
Shirley Cres. Beck —4A 126
Shirley Dri. Houn —5G 87
Shirley Gdns. W7 —1K 71
Shirley Gdns. Bark —6J 51
Shirley Gro. N9 —7D 8
Shirley Gro. SW11 —3E 92
Shirley Heights. Wall —7G 133
Shirley Ho. Dri. SE7 —7A 82
Shirley Oaks Rd. Croy —1K 135
Shirley Pk. Rd. Croy —1H 135
Shirley Rd. W4 —2K 73
Shirley Rd. Croy —7H 125
Shirley Rd. Enf —3H 7
Shirley Rd. Sidc —3J 115
Shirley Rd. Wall —7G 133
Shirley St. E16 —6H 65
Shirley Way. Croy —3A 136
Shirlock Rd. NW3 —4D 44
Shobden Rd. N17 —1D 30
Shoebury Rd. E6 —7D 50
Shoelands Ct. NW9 —3K 25
Shoe La. EC4 —6A 62 (7H 141)
Shooters Av. Harr —4C 24
Shooter's Hill. SE18 & Well —1E 96
Shooters Hill Rd. SE3 & SE18
  —1F 97
Shooters Rd. Enf —1G 7
Shoot Up Hill. NW2 —5G 43
Shore Clo. Hamp —6C 102

Shoreditch Ct. E8 —1F 63
(off Queensbridge Rd.)
Shoreditch High St. E1
  —4E 62 (2D 142)
Shore Gro. Felt —2E 102
Shoreham Clo. SW18 —5K 91
Shoreham Clo. Bex —1D 116
Shoreham Clo. Croy —5J 125
Shoreham Way. Brom —6J 127
Shore Pl. E9 —7J 47
Shore Rd. E9 —7J 47
Shorncliffe Rd. SE1 —5F 79
Shorndean St. SE6 —1E 112
Shorne Clo. Sidc —6B 100
Shornefield Clo. Brom —3E 128
Shornells Way. SE2 —5C 84
Shorrold's Rd. SW6 —7H 75
Shortcroft Rd. Eps —7B 130
Shortcrofts Rd. Dag —6F 53
Shorter St. E1 —7F 63 (1E 148)
Short Ga. N12 —4C 14
Short Hedges. Houn —1E 86
Short Hill. Harr —1J 39
Shortlands. W6 —4F 75
Shortlands Clo. N18 —3J 17
Shortlands Clo. Bexh —5E 100
Shortlands Gdns. Brom —2G 127
Shortlands Gro. Brom —3F 127
Shortlands Ho. E17 —5B 32
Shortlands Rd. E10 —7D 32
Shortlands Rd. Brom —3F 127
Shortlands Rd. King T —7F 105
Short Path. SE18 —6F 83
Short Rd. E11 —2G 49
Short Rd. E15 —1F 65
Short Rd. W4 —6A 74
Shorts Croft. NW9 —4H 25
Shorts Gdns. WC2 —6J 61 (8C 140)
Shorts Rd. Cars —4C 132
Short St. NW4 —4E 26
Short St. SE1 —2A 78 (4H 147)
Short Wall. E15 —3E 64
Short Way. N12 —6H 15
Short Way. SE9 —3B 98
Short Way. Twic —7G 87
Shotfield. Wall —6F 133
Shotfield Av. SW14 —4A 90
Shott Clo. Sutt —5A 132
Shottendane Rd. SW6 —1J 91
Shottery Clo. SE9 —3C 114
Shoulder of Mutton All. E14 —7A 64
Shouldham St. W1 —5C 60 (6D 138)
Shrapnel Clo. SE18 —7C 82
Shrapnel Rd. SE9 —3D 98
Shrewsbury Av. SW14 —4K 89
Shrewsbury Av. Harr —4F 24
Shrewsbury Cres. NW10 —1K 57
Shrewsbury Ho. SW8 —6K 77
(off Meadow Rd.)
Shrewsbury La. SE18 —1F 99
Shrewsbury Rd. E7 —5B 50
Shrewsbury Rd. N11 —6C 16
Shrewsbury Rd. W2 —6J 59
Shrewsbury Rd. Beck —3A 126
Shrewsbury Rd. Cars —7C 122
Shrewsbury Wlk. Iswth —3A 88
Shrewton Rd. SW17 —7D 108
Shroffold Rd. Brom —4G 113
Shropshire Clo. Mitc —4J 123
Shropshire Pl. WC1 —4G 61 (4M 139)
Shropshire Rd. N22 —7E 16
Shroton St. NW1 —5C 60 (5C 138)
Shrubberies, The. E18 —2J 33
Shrubbery Gdns. N21 —7G 7
Shrubbery Rd. N9 —3B 18
Shrubbery Rd. SW16 —4J 109
Shrubbery Rd. S'hall —1E 70
Shrubbery Gro. Wor Pk —3E 130

Shrubland Rd. E8 —1G 63
Shrubland Rd. E10 —7C 32
Shrubland Rd. E17 —5C 32
Shrublands Av. Croy —3C 136
Shrublands Clo. N20 —1G 15
Shrublands Clo. SE26 —3J 111
Shrubsall Clo. SE9 —1C 114
Shuna Wlk. N1 —6D 46
Shurland Av. Barn —6G 5
Shurland Gdns. SE15 —7F 79
Shuttle Clo. Sidc —7K 99
Shuttlemead. Bex —7F 101
Shuttle St. E1 —4G 63
Shuttleworth Rd. SW11 —2C 92
Sibella Rd. SW4 —2H 93
Sibley Clo. Bexh —5E 100
Sibley Gro. E12 —7C 50
Sibthorpe Rd. SE12 —6K 97
Sibton Rd. Cars —7C 122
Sicilian Av. WC1 —5J 61 (6D 140)
(off Vernon Pl.)
Sickle Corner. Dag —3H 69
Sidbury St. SW6 —1G 91
Sidcup By-Pass. Chst & Sidc
  —3H 115
Sidcup High St. Sidc —4A 116
Sidcup Hill. Sidc —4B 116
Sidcup Hill Gdns. Sidc —5C 116
Sidcup Rd. SE12 & SE9 —6A 98
Siddons La. NW1 —4D 60 (4F 138)
Siddons Rd. N17 —1G 31
Siddons Rd. SE23 —2A 112
Siddons Rd. Croy —3A 134
Side Rd. E17 —5B 32
Sidewood Rd. SE9 —1H 115
Sidford Pl. SE1 —3A 78 (7F 146)
Sidgwick Ho. SW9 —2K 93
(off Stockwell Rd.)
Sidings M. N7 —3A 46
Sidings, The. E11 —1F 49
Sidlaw Ho. N16 —1F 47
Sidmouth Av. Iswth —2J 87
Sidmouth Pde. NW10 —7E 42
Sidmouth Rd. E10 —3E 48
Sidmouth Rd. NW2 —7G 42
Sidmouth Rd. SE15 —1F 95
Sidmouth Rd. Well —7C 84
Sidmouth St. WC1 —3K 61 (2D 140)
Sidney. Sidc —6B 116
Sidney Av. N13 —5E 16
Sidney Est. E1 —5J 63
(in two parts)
Sidney Gdns. Bren —6D 72
Sidney Rd. N22 —7E 16
Sidney Rd. SE25 —5G 125
Sidney Rd. SW9 —2K 93
Sidney Rd. Beck —2A 126
Sidney Rd. Harr —3G 23
Sidney Rd. Twic —6A 88
Sidney Sq. E1 —5J 63
Sidney St. E1 —5H 63
Sidworth St. E8 —7H 47
Siebert Rd. SE3 —6J 81
Siemens Rd. SE18 —3B 82
Sigdon Pas. E8 —5G 47
Sigdon Rd. E8 —5G 47
Sigers, The. Pinn —6A 22
Silbury Av. Mitc —1C 122
Silbury Ho. SE26 —3G 111
Silbury St. N1 —3D 62 (1A 142)
Silchester Rd. W10 —6F 59
Silecroft Rd. Bexh —1G 101

Silesia Bldgs. E8 —7H 47
Silex St. SE1 —2B 78 (5K 147)
Silicone Bus. Cen. Gnfd —2C 56
Silk Clo. SE12 —5J 97
Silkfield Rd. NW9 —5A 26
Silk Ho. NW9 —3K 25
Silk Mills Path. SE13 —2E 96
Silks Ct. E11 —1H 49
Silk St. EC2 —5C 62 (5M 141)
Sillitoe Ho. N1 —1D 62
(off Colville Est.)
Silsoe Rd. N22 —2K 29
Silver Birch Av. E4 —6G 19
Silverbirch Clo. N11 —6K 15
Silver Birch Clo. Dart —4K 117
Silverbirch Ct. E8 —7F 47
Silverburn Ho. SW9 —1B 94
(off Lothian Rd.)
Silver Chase Ct. Enf —1G 7
Silvercliffe Gdns. Barn —4H 5
Silver Clo. SE14 —7A 80
Silver Clo. Harr —7C 10
Silver Cres. W4 —4H 73
Silverdale. SE26 —4J 111
Silverdale. Enf —4D 6
Silverdale Av. Ilf —3K 35
Silverdale Clo. W7 —1J 71
Silverdale Clo. N'holt —5D 38
Silverdale Clo. Sutt —4H 131
Silverdale Dri. SE9 —2C 114
Silverdale Rd. E4 —6A 20
Silverdale Rd. Bexh —2H 101
Silverdale Rd. Pet W —4G 129
Silverhall St. Iswth —3A 88
Silverholme Clo. Harr —7E 24
Silverland St. E16 —1D 82
Silver La. W Wick —2F 137
Silverleigh Rd. T Hth —4K 123
Silvermere Rd. SE6 —7D 96
Silver Pl. W1 —6G 61 (9M 139)
Silver Rd. W12 —7F 59
Silver Spring Clo. Eri —6H 85
Silverston Way. Stan —6H 11
Sliver St. N18 —4J 17
Sliver St. Enf —3J 7
Silverthorne Gdns. E4 —2H 19
Silverthorne Rd. SW8 —2F 93
Silverton Rd. W6 —6F 75
Silvertown Way. E16 —6H 65
Silvertree La. Gnfd —3H 55
Silver Wlk. SE16 —1B 80
Silver Way. Romf —3H 37
Silverwood Clo. Beck —7C 112
Silverwood Clo. Croy —7B 136
Silvester Rd. SE22 —5F 95
Silvester St. SE1 —2D 78 (5A 148)
Silvester St. SW1 —2D 78
Silwood Est. SE16 —4J 79
Silwood St. SE16 —4J 79
Simla Clo. SE14 —6A 80
Simmons Clo. N20 —1H 15
Simmons La. E4 —2A 20
Simmons Rd. SE18 —5F 83
Simmons Way. N20 —2H 15
Simmott Rd. E17 —1K 31
Simms Clo. Cars —2C 132
Simms Rd. SE1 —4G 79
Simnel Rd. SE12 —7K 97
Simon Clo. W11 —7H 59
Simonds Rd. E10 —2C 48
Simone Clo. Brom —1B 128
Simone Ct. SE26 —3J 111
Simon Peter Ct. Enf —2G 7
Simons Ct. N16 —2F 47
Simons Wlk. E15 —5F 49
Simpson Dri. W3 —6K 57

Simpson Ho. SE11 —5K 77
Simpson Rd. Houn —6D 86
Simpson Rd. Rich —4C 104
Simpson's Rd. E14 —7D 64
Simpsons Rd. Brom —3J 127
Simpson St. SW11 —2C 92
Simrose Ct. SW18 —5J 91
Sims Wlk. SE3 —4H 97
Sinclair Ct. Croy —2E 134
Sinclair Dri. Sutt —7K 131
Sinclair Gdns. W14 —2F 75
Sinclair Gro. NW11 —6F 27
Sinclair Mans. W12 —2F 75
(off Richmond Way)
Sinclair Rd. E4 —5G 19
Sinclair Rd. W14 —2F 75
Sinclare Clo. Enf —1A 8
Singapore Rd. W13 —1A 72
Singer St. EC2 —3D 62
Singleton Clo. SW17 —7D 108
Singleton Clo. Croy —7C 124
Singleton Rd. Dag —5F 53
Singleton Scarp. N12 —5D 14
Sinnott Rd. E17 —1K 31
Sion Ct. Twic —1B 104
Sion Rd. Twic —1B 104
Sippets Ct. Ilf —1H 51
Sir Alexander Clo. W3 —1B 74
Sir Alexander Rd. W3 —1B 74
Sir Cyril Black Way. SW19 —7J 107
Sirdar Rd. N22 —3B 30
Sirdar Rd. W11 —7F 59
Sirdar Rd. Mitc —6E 108
Sir Henry Floyd Ct. Stan —2G 11
Sirinham Point. SW8 —6K 77
(off Meadow Rd.)
Sirius Building. E1 —7K 63
(off Jardine Rd.)
Sir Oswald Stoll Foundation, The. SW6
(off Fulham Rd.) —7K 75
Sir William Powell's Almshouses. SW6
  —2G 91
Sise La. EC4 —6D 62 (8A 142)
(off Victoria St.)
Sisley Rd. Bark —1J 67
Sispara Gdns. SW18 —6H 91
Sissinghurst Rd. Croy —7G 125
Sister Mabel's Way. SE15 —7G 79
Sisters Av. SW11 —3D 92
Sistova Rd. SW12 —1F 109
Sisulu Pl. SW9 —3A 94
Sittingbourne Av. Enf —6J 7
Sitwell Gro. Stan —5E 10
Siverst Clo. N'holt —6F 39
Sivter Way. Dag —7H 53
Siward Rd. N17 —1D 30
Siward Rd. SW17 —3A 108
Siward Rd. Brom —3K 127
Six Acres Est. N4 —2A 46
Sixth Av. E12 —4D 50
Sixth Av. W10 —3G 59
Sixth Cross Rd. Twic —3G 103
Skardu Rd. NW2 —5G 43
Skeena Hill. SW18 —7G 91
Skeffington Rd. E6 —1D 66
Skelbrook St. SW18 —2A 108
Skelgill Rd. SW15 —4H 91
Skelley Rd. E15 —7H 49
Skelton Clo. E8 —6F 47
Skelton Rd. E7 —6J 49
Skelton's La. E10 —7D 32
Skelwith Rd. W6 —6E 74
Skerne Rd. King T —1D 118
Sketchley Gdns. SE16 —5K 79
Sketty Rd. Enf —3A 8
Skiers St. E15 —1G 65
Skiffington Clo. SW2 —1A 110
Skinner Ct. E2 —2H 63

S. Lambeth Pl. SW8 —6J 77
S. Lambeth Rd. SW8 —6J 77
Southland Rd. SE18 —7K 83
Southlands Gro. Brom —3C 128
Southlands Rd. Brom —4B 128
Southland Way. Houn —5H 87
South La. King T —3D 118
South La. N Mald —4K 119
South La. W. N Mald —4K 119
S. Lodge. Twic —7G 87
S. Lodge Av. Mitc —4J 123
S. Lodge Cres. Enf —4C 6
(in two parts)
S. Lodge Dri. N14 —4C 6
Southly Clo. Sutt —3J 131
South Mall. N9 —3B 18
South Mead. NW9 —1B 28
South Mead. Eps —7B 130
Southmead Dri. SW19 —1G 107
S. Meadows. Wemb —5F 41
S. Molton La. W1 —6F 61 (8J 139)
S. Molton Rd. E16 —6J 65
S. Molton St. W1 —6F 61 (8J 139)
Southmoor Way. E9 —6B 48
South Mt. N20 —2F 15
(off High Rd.)
S. Norwood Hill. SE19 & SE25
—2E 124
S. Oak Rd. SW16 —4K 109
Southold Rise. SE9 —3D 114
Southolme Clo. SE19 —1E 124
Southolm St. SW11 —1F 93
Southover. N12 —3D 14
Southover. Brom —5J 113
South Pde. SW3 —5B 76
South Pde. W4 —4K 73
South Pk. Ct. Beck —7C 112
S. Park Cres. SE6 —1H 113
S. Park Cres. Ilf —3H 51
South Pk. Dri. Bark & Ilf —5J 51
S. Pk. Gro. N Mald —4J 119
S. Park Hill Rd. S Croy —5D 134
S. Park M. SW6 —3K 91
S. Park Rd. SW19 —6J 107
South Pk. Rd. Ilf —3H 51
S. Pk. Ter. Ilf —3H 51
S. Park Way. Ruis —6A 38
South Pl. EC2 —5D 62 (6B 142)
South Pl. Enf —5D 8
South Pl. M. EC2 —5D 62 (6B 142)
Southport. SE18 —4H 83
South Quay Plaza. E14 —2D 80
Southridge Pl. SW20 —7F 107
S. Rise. Cars —7C 132
South Rd. N9 —1B 18
South Rd. SE23 —2K 111
South Rd. SW19 —6A 108
South Rd. W5 —4D 72
South Rd. Chad —6E 36
South Rd. Edgw —1H 25
South Rd. Felt —5B 102
South Rd. Hamp —6C 102
South Rd. L Hth —5C 36
South Rd. Twic —3H 103
South Row. SE3 —2H 97
Southsea Rd. King T —4E 118
S. Sea St. SE16 —3B 80
South Side. N15 —4F 31
S. Side. W6 —3B 74
Southside Comn. SW19 —6E 106
Southspring. Sidc —7H 99
South Sq. NW11 —6K 27
South Sq. WC1 —5A 62 (6G 141)
South St. W1 —1E 76 (2H 145)
South St. Brom —2J 127
South St. Enf —5D 8

South St. Iswth —3A 88
South St. Rain —2J 69
South St. Romf —5K 37
S. Tenter St. E1 —7F 63
South Ter. SW7 —4C 76 (8C 144)
South Ter. Surb —6E 118
Southvale. SE19 —6E 110
South Vale. Harr —4J 39
Southview. Brom —2A 128
Southview Av. NW10 —5B 42
South View Clo. Bex —6F 101
S. View Ct. SE19 —7C 110
S. View Dri. E18 —3K 33
Southview Gdns. Wall —7G 133
S. View Rd. N8 —3H 29
Southview Rd. Pinn —1A 22
Southview Rd. Brom —4F 113
South Vs. NW1 —6H 45
Southville. SW8 —1H 93
Southville Clo. Eps —7A 130
Southville Rd. Th Dit —7B 118
South Wlk. W Wick —3G 137
Southwark Bri. SE1 & EC4
—7C 62 (1M 147)
Southwark Bri. Office Village. SE1
—1C 78 (3M 147)
Southwark Bri. Rd. SE1
—3B 78 (6K 147)
Southwark Gro. SE1
—1C 78 (3L 147)
Southwark Pk. Rd. SE16
—4F 79 (8F 148)
Southwark Pk. Rd. Est. SE15 —4F 79
Southwark Pk. Rd. SE16
—4F 79 (8F 148)
Southwark Pl. Brom —3D 128
Southwark St. SE1 —1B 78 (2J 147)
Southwater Clo. E14 —6B 64
Southwater Clo. Beck —7D 112
South Way. N9 —2D 18
South Way. N11 —6B 16
Southway. N20 —2D 14
Southway. NW11 —6K 27
Southway. SW20 —4E 120
South Way. Brom —7J 127
South Way. Croy —3A 136
South Way. Harr —4E 22
Southway. Wall —4G 133
South Way. Wemb —5F 41
Southwell Av. N'holt —6E 38
Southwell Gdns. SW7 —3A 76
Southwell Gro. Rd. E11 —2G 49
Southwell Rd. SE5 —3C 94
Southwell Rd. Croy —6A 124
Southwell Rd. Kent —6D 24
S. Western Rd. Twic —6A 88
S.W. India Dock Entrance. E14
—2E 80
Southwest Rd. E11 —1F 49
S. Wharf Rd. W2 —6B 60 (7A 138)
Southwick M. W2 —6B 60 (7B 138)
Southwick Pl. W2 —6C 60 (8C 138)
Southwick St. W2 —6C 60 (7C 138)
Southwold Dri. Bark —5A 52
Southwold Rd. E5 —2H 47
Southwold Rd. Bex —6H 101
Southwood Av. N6 —7F 29
Southwood Av. King T —1J 119
Southwood Clo. Brom —4D 128
Southwood Clo. Wor Pk —1F 131
Southwood Ct. NW11 —5K 27
Southwood Dri. Surb —7J 119
S. Woodford to Barking Relief Rd.
E11 & Ilf —5B 34
Southwood Gdns. Ilf —4F 35
Southwood Hall. N6 —6F 29

Southwood Heights. N6 —7F 29
Southwood La. N6 —1E 44
Southwood Lawn Rd. N6 —7E 28
Southwood Mans. N6 —6E 28
(off Southwood La.)
Southwood Pk. N6 —7E 28
Southwood Rd. SE9 —2F 115
Southwood Rd. SE28 —1B 84
Southwood Smith St. N1 —1B 62
(off Old Royal Free Sq.)
S. Worple Av. SW14 —3A 90
S. Worple Way. SW14 —3K 89
Southwyck Ho. SW9 —4B 94
Sovereign Bus. Cen. Enf —3G 9
Sovereign Clo. E1 —7H 63
Sovereign Clo. W5 —5C 56
Sovereign Ct. Houn —3E 86
Sovereign Gro. Wemb —3D 40
Sovereign M. E2 —2F 63
Sovereign Ho. NW10 —4H 57
Sovereign Pk. Trading Est. NW10
—4H 57
Sowerby Clo. SE9 —5D 98
Spa Clo. SE19 —1E 124
Spa Ct. SW16 —4K 109
Spafield St. EC1 —4A 62 (3G 141)
Spa Grn. Est. EC1 —3B 62 (1J 141)
(off St John St.)
Spa Hill. SE19 —1D 124
Spalding Rd. NW4 —7E 26
Spalding Rd. SW17 —5F 109
Spanby Rd. E3 —4C 64
Spaniards Clo. NW11 —1B 44
Spaniards End. NW3 —1A 44
Spaniards Rd. NW3 —2A 44
Spanish Pl. W1 —6E 60 (7H 139)
Spanish Rd. SW18 —5B 92
Spanswick Lodge. N15 —4B 30
Sparkbridge Rd. Harr —4J 23
Sparkes Clo. Sidc —5B 116
Sparke Ter. E16 —6H 65
(off Clarkson Rd.)
Sparks Clo. W3 —6K 57
Sparks Clo. Hamp —6C 102
Sparrick's Row. SE1
—2D 78 (4B 148)
Sparrow Clo. Hamp —6C 102
Sparrow Dri. Orp —7G 129
Sparrow Farm Dri. Felt —7A 86
Sparrow Farm Rd. Eps —4C 130
Sparrow Grn. Dag —3H 53
Sparrows Herne. Bush —1A 10
Sparrows La. SE9 —7G 99
Sparrows Way. Bush —1B 10
Sparsholt Clo. Bark —1J 67
(off Sparsholt Rd.)
Sparsholt Rd. N19 —1J 45
Sparsholt Rd. Bark —1J 67
Sparta St. SE10 —1E 96
Speaker's Corner. W2
—7D 60 (9F 138)
Speakers Ct. Croy —1D 134
Spearman St. SE18 —6E 82
Spear M. SW5 —4J 75
Spearpoint Gdns. Ilf —5K 35
Spears Rd. N19 —1J 45
Speart La. Houn —7C 70
Spedan Clo. NW3 —3A 44
Speed Highwalk. EC2
—5C 62 (5M 141)
Speed Ho. EC2 —5D 62 (5A 142)
(off Barbican)
Speedwell Ho. N12 —5E 4
Speedwell St. SE8 —7C 80
Speedy Pl. WC1 —3J 61 (2C 140)
(off Cromer St.)
Speirs Clo. N Mald —6B 120

Speke Hill. SE9 —3D 114
Speke Rd. T Hth —2D 124
Speldhurst Clo. Brom —5J 127
Speldhurst Rd. E9 —7K 47
Speldhurst Rd. W4 —3K 73
Spellbrook Wlk. N1 —1C 62
Spelman St. E1 —5G 63
Spenbrook. Chig —3K 21
Spence Clo. SE16 —2B 80
Spencer Av. N13 —6E 16
Spencer Clo. N3 —2J 27
Spencer Clo. NW10 —3F 57
Spencer Clo. Wfd G —5F 21
Spencer Dri. N2 —6A 28
Spencer Gdns. SE9 —5D 98
Spencer Gdns. SW14 —5J 89
Spencer Hill. SW19 —6G 107
Spencer Ho. NW4 —5D 26
Spencer M. W6 —6G 75
Spencer Pk. SW18 —5B 92
Spencer Pas. E2 —2H 63
(off Coate St.)
Spencer Pl. Croy —7D 124
Spencer Rise. NW5 —4F 45
Spencer Rd. E6 —1B 66
Spencer Rd. E17 —2E 32
Spencer Rd. N8 —5K 29
(in two parts)
Spencer Rd. N11 —4A 16
Spencer Rd. N17 —1G 31
Spencer Rd. SW18 —4B 92
Spencer Rd. SW20 —1D 120
Spencer Rd. W3 —1J 73
Spencer Rd. W4 —7J 73
Spencer Rd. Brom —7H 113
Spencer Rd. Harr —2J 23
Spencer Rd. Ilf —1K 51
Spencer Rd. Iswth —1G 87
Spencer Rd. Mitc —3E 122
Spencer Rd. Mit J —7E 122
Spencer Rd. Rain —3K 69
Spencer Rd. S Croy —5E 134
Spencer Rd. Twic —3J 103
Spencer Rd. Wemb —2C 40
Spencer St. EC1 —3B 62 (2J 141)
Spencer St. S'hall —2B 70
Spencer Wlk. NW3 —4A 44
(off Hampstead High St.)
Spencer Wlk. SW15 —4F 91
Spenser Gro. N16 —5E 46
Spenser M. SE21 —2D 110
Spenser Rd. SE24 —5B 94
Spenser St. SW1 —3G 77 (6M 145)
Spensley Wlk. N16 —3D 46
Speranza St. SE18 —5K 83
Sperling Rd. N17 —2E 30
Spert St. E14 —7A 64
Spey Side. N14 —6B 6
Spey St. E14 —5B 64
Spey Way. Romf —1K 37
Spice Ct. E1 —7G 63
Spicer Clo. SW9 —2B 94
Spicer Ct. Enf —3K 7
Spice's Yd. Croy —4C 134
Spigurnell Rd. N17 —1D 30
Spikes Bri. Rd. S'hall —6C 54
Spilsby Clo. NW9 —1A 26
Spindlewood Gdns. Croy —4E 134
Spindrift Av. E14 —4C 80
Spinel Clo. SE18 —5K 83
Spinnells Rd. Harr —1D 38
Spinney Clo. N Mald —5A 120
Spinney Gdns. SE19 —5F 111
Spinney Gdns. Dag —5E 52
Spinney Oak. Brom —2C 128
Spinneys, The. Brom —2D 128
Spinney, The. N21 —7F 7

Spinney, The. SW13 —6D 74
Spinney, The. SW16 —3G 109
Spinney, The. Barn —2E 4
Spinney, The. Sidc —5E 116
Spinney, The. Stan —4K 11
Spinney, The. Sutt —4E 130
Spinney, The. Wemb —3A 40
Spires Shopping Cen., The. Barn
—3B 4
Spirit Quay. E1 —1G 79
Spital Sq. E1 —5E 62 (5D 142)
Spital St. E1 —5G 63
Spital Yd. E1 —5E 62 (5D 142)
Spitfire Way. Houn —5A 70
Spode Wlk. NW6 —5K 43
Spondon Rd. N15 —4G 31
Spoonbill Way. Hay —5B 54
Spooner Ho. Houn —6E 70
Spooner M. W3 —1K 73
Spooner Wlk. Wall —5J 133
Sportsbank St. SE6 —7E 96
Spottons Gro. N17 —1C 30
Spout Hill. Croy —5C 136
Spratt Hall Rd. E11 —6J 33
Spray La. Twic —6J 87
Spray St. SE18 —4F 83
Sprimont Pl. SW3 —4D 76
Springall St. SE15 —7H 79
Spring Bank. N21 —6E 6
Springbank Rd. SE13 —6F 97
Springbank Wlk. NW1 —7H 45
Springbourne Ct. Beck —1E 126
Spring Bri. M. W5 —7D 56
Springbridge Rd. W5 —7D 56
Spring Clo. Barn —5A 4
Spring Clo. Dag —1D 52
Spring Clo. La. Sutt —6G 131
Spring Cotts. Surb —5D 118
Spring Ct. NW6 —6H 43
Spring Ct. Eps —7B 130
Spring Ct. Rd. Enf —1F 7
Springcroft Av. N2 —4D 28
Springdale M. N16 —4D 46
Springdale Rd. N16 —4D 46
Springfield. E5 —1H 47
Springfield. Bush —1C 10
Springfield Av. N10 —3G 29
Springfield Av. SW20 —3H 121
Springfield Av. Hamp —6F 103
Springfield Clo. N12 —5E 14
Springfield Clo. Stan —3F 11
Springfield Ct. Wall —5F 133
Springfield Dri. Ilf —5G 35
Springfield Gdns. E5 —1H 47
Springfield Gdns. NW9 —5K 25
Springfield Gdns. Brom —4D 128
Springfield Gdns. Ruis —1A 38
Springfield Gdns. W Wick —2D 136
Springfield Gro. SE7 —6A 82
Springfield La. NW6 —1K 59
Springfield M. NW9 —5A 26
Springfield Pde. M. N13 —4F 17
Springfield Pl. N Mald —4J 119
Springfield Rise. SE26 —3H 111
(in two parts)
Springfield Rd. E4 —1B 20
Springfield Rd. E6 —7D 50
Springfield Rd. E15 —3G 65
Springfield Rd. E17 —6B 32
Springfield Rd. N11 —5A 16
Springfield Rd. N15 —4G 31
Springfield Rd. NW8 —1A 60
Springfield Rd. SE26 —5H 111
Springfield Rd. SW19 —5H 107
Springfield Rd. W7 —1J 71
Springfield Rd. Bexh —4H 101
Springfield Rd. Brom —4D 128

Springfield Rd. Harr —6J 23
Springfield Rd. Hay —1A 70
Springfield Rd. King T —3E 118
Springfield Rd. Tedd —5A 104
Springfield Rd. T Hth —1C 124
Springfield Rd. Twic —1E 102
Springfield Rd. Wall —5F 133
Springfield Rd. Well —3B 100
Springfields. New Bar —5E 4
(off Somerset Rd.)
Springfield Wlk. NW6 —1K 59
Springfield Wlk. Orp —7J 129
(off Andover Rd.)
Spring Gdns. N5 —5C 46
Spring Gdns. SW1 —1H 77 (2B 146)
Spring Gdns. Romf —5J 37
Spring Gdns. Wall —5G 133
Spring Gdns. Wfd G —7F 21
Spring Gro. SE19 —7F 111
Spring Gro. W4 —5G 73
Spring Gro. Mitc —1E 122
Spring Gro. Cres. Houn —1G 87
Spring Gro. Rd. Houn & Iswth
—1F 87
Spring Gro. Rd. Rich —5F 89
Spring Hill. E5 —7G 31
Spring Hill. SE26 —4J 111
Springhill Clo. SE5 —3D 94
Springhurst Clo. Croy —4B 136
Spring Lake. Stan —4G 11
Spring La. E5 —7H 31
Spring La. SE25 —6H 125
Spring M. W1 —5D 60 (5F 138)
Spring M. Eps —7B 130
Spring Pk. Av. Croy —2K 135
Spring Pk. Dri. N4 —1C 46
Springpark Dri. Beck —3E 126
Spring Pk. Rd. Croy —2K 135
Spring Path. NW3 —5B 44
Spring Pl. NW5 —5E 44
Springpond Rd. Dag —5E 52
Springrice Rd. SE13 —6F 97
Spring St. W2 —6B 60 (8A 138)
Spring St. Eps —7B 130
Spring Ter. Rich —5E 88
Spring Vale. Bexh —4H 101
Springvale Av. Bren —5E 72
Spring Vale Ter. W14 —3F 75
Spring Villa Rd. Edgw —7B 12
Spring Wlk. E1 —5G 63
Springwater Clo. SE18 —1E 98
Springway. Harr —7H 23
Springwell Av. NW10 —1B 58
Springwell Clo. SW16 —4K 109
Springwell Ct. Houn —2B 86
Springwell Rd. SW16 —4A 110
Springwell Rd. Houn —1B 86
Springwood Ct. S Croy —4E 134
Springwood Cres. Edgw —2C 12
Sprowston M. E7 —6J 49
Sprowston Rd. E7 —5J 49
Spruce Ct. E4 —6G 19
Spruce Ct. E8 —7F 47
Spruce Ct. W5 —3E 72
Sprucedale Gdns. Croy —4K 135
Sprucedale Gdns. Wall —7J 133
Spruce Hills Rd. E17 —2E 32
Spruce Pk. Short —4H 127
Sprules Rd. SE4 —2A 96
Spurgeon Av. SE19 —1D 124
Spurgeon Rd. SE19 —1D 124
Spurgeon St. SE1 —3D 78 (7A 148)
Spurling Rd. SE22 —4F 95
Spurling Rd. Dag —6F 53
Spurrell Av. Bex —4K 117
Spur Rd. N15 —4D 30
Spur Rd. SW1 —2G 77 (5L 145)
Spur Rd. Edgw —4K 11

Spur Rd. Felt —4A 86
Spur Rd. Iswth —7A 72
Spurstowe Rd. E8 —6H 47
Spurstowe Ter. E8 —5H 47
Square Rigger Row. SW11 —3A 92
Square, The. W6 —5E 74
Square, The. Cars —5E 132
Square, The. Ilf —7E 34
Square, The. Rich —5D 88
Square, The. Wfd G —5D 20
Square, The. SW17 —3A 108
Squires Ct. SW4 —1J 93
Squires La. N3 —2K 27
Squires Mt. NW3 —3B 44
Squires Way. Dart —4K 117
Squires Wood Dri. Chst —7C 114
Squirrel Clo. Houn —3A 86
Squirrel M. W13 —7K 55
Squirrels Clo. N12 —4F 15
Squirrels Ct. Wor Pk —2B 130
(off Avenue, The)
Squirrels Drey. Short —2G 127
(off Park Hill Rd.)
Squirrels Grn. Wor Pk —2B 130
Squirrel's La. Buck H —3G 21
Squirrels, The. SE13 —3F 97
Squirrels, The. Pinn —3D 22
Squirries St. E2 —3G 63
Stable Clo. N'holt —2E 54
Stable M. SE27 —5C 110
Stables, The. W10 —6F 59
(off Bassett Rd.)
Stables, The. Buck H —1F 21
Stables Way. SE11 —5A 78
Stable Wlk. N2 —1B 28
Stable Way. W10 —6E 58
Stable Yd. SW1 —2G 77 (4L 145)
(off St James Pal.)
Stable Yd. SW9 —2K 93
Stable Yd. SW15 —3E 90
Stable Yd. Rd. SW1
—2G 77 (3L 145)
Stacey Av. N18 —4D 18
Stacey Clo. E10 —5F 33
Stacey St. N7 —3A 46
Stacey St. WC2 —6H 61 (8B 140)
Stackhouse St. SW3
(off Pavilion Rd.) —3D 76 (6E 144)
Stacy Path. SE5 —7E 78
Stadbrook Clo. S Harr —3D 38
Stadium Rd. NW4 —7E 26
Stadium Rd. SE18 —7D 82
Stadium St. SW10 —7A 76
Stadium Way. Wemb —4F 41
Staffa Rd. E10 —1A 48
Stafford Clo. N14 —5B 6
Stafford Clo. NW6 —3J 59
Stafford Clo. Sutt —6G 131
Stafford Ct. SW8 —7J 77
Stafford Cripps Ho. SW6 —6H 75
(off Clem Attlee Ct.)
Stafford Gdns. Croy —5K 133
Stafford Pl. SW1 —3G 77 (6L 145)
Stafford Pl. Rich —7F 89
Stafford Rd. E3 —2B 64
Stafford Rd. E7 —7A 50
Stafford Rd. NW6 —3J 59
Stafford Rd. Harr —7B 10
Stafford Rd. H Bar —3B 4
Stafford Rd. N Mald —3J 119
Stafford Rd. Sidc —4J 115
Stafford Rd. Wall & Croy —6G 133
Staffordshire St. SE15 —1G 95
Stafford St. W1 —1G 77 (2L 145)
Stafford Ter. W8 —3J 75
Staff St. EC1 —3D 62 (2B 142)
Stag Clo. Edgw —2H 25

Stag La. SW15 —3B 106
Stag La. Buck H —2E 20
Stag La. Edgw & NW9 —2H 25
Stag Pl. SW1 —3G 77 (6L 145)
Stags Way. Iswth —7K 71
Stainbank Rd. Mitc —3F 123
Stainby Rd. N15 —4F 31
Stainer St. SE1 —1D 78 (3B 148)
Staines Av. Sutt —2F 131
Staines Rd. Felt & Houn —6A 86
Staines Rd. Ilf —4G 51
Staines Rd. Twic —3E 102
Staines Rd. E. Sun —7A 102
Staines Wlk. Sidc —6C 116
Stainforth Rd. E17 —4C 32
Stainforth Rd. Ilf —7H 35
Staining La. EC2 —6C 62 (7M 141)
Stainmore Clo. Chst —1H 129
Stainsbury St. E2 —2J 63
Stainsby Pl. E14 —6C 64
Stainsby Rd. E14 —6C 64
Stainton Rd. SE6 —6F 97
Stainton Rd. Enf —1D 8
Stalbridge St. NW1 —5C 60 (5D 138)
Stalham St. SE16 —3H 79
Stambourne Way. SE19 —7E 110
Stambourne Way. W Wick —2E 136
Stamford Brook Av. W6 —3B 74
Stamford Brook Gdns. W6 —3B 74
Stamford Brook Mans. W6 —4B 74
(off Goldhawk Rd.)
Stamford Brook Rd. W6 —3B 74
Stamford Clo. N15 —5G 31
Stamford Clo. NW3 —3A 44
(off Heath St.)
Stamford Clo. Harr —7D 10
Stamford Clo. S'hall —7E 54
Stamford Ct. W6 —4C 74
Stamford Dri. Brom —4H 127
Stamford Gdns. Dag —7C 52
Stamford Gro. E. N16 —1G 47
Stamford Gro. W. N16 —1G 47
Stamford Hill. N16 —2F 47
Stamford Lodge. N16 —7F 31
Stamford Rd. E6 —1C 66
Stamford Rd. N1 —7E 46
Stamford Rd. N15 —5G 31
Stamford Rd. Dag —1B 68
Stamford St. SE1 —1A 78 (3G 147)
Stamford Wharf. SE1
—7A 62 (1H 147)
Stamp Pl. E2 —2F 63 (1F 142)
Stanard Clo. N16 —7E 30
Stanborough Clo. Hamp —6D 102
Stanborough Pas. E8 —6F 47
Stanborough Rd. Houn —3H 87
Stanbridge Pl. N21 —3G 17
Stanbridge Rd. SW15 —3E 90
Stanbrook Rd. SE2 —2B 84
Stanbury Rd. SE15 —2H 95
(in two parts)
Stancroft. NW9 —5A 26
Standard Ind. Est. E16 —2D 82
Standard Pl. EC2 —3E 62 (2D 142)
(off Rivington St.)
Standard Rd. NW10 —4J 57
Standard Rd. Belv —5G 85
Standard Rd. Bexh —4E 100
Standard Rd. Houn —3C 86
Standen Rd. SW18 —7H 91
Standfield Gdns. Dag —6G 53
Standfield Rd. Dag —5G 53
Standish Ho. W6 —4C 74
(off St Peter's Gro.)
Standlake Point. SE23 —3K 111
Stane Clo. SW19 —7K 107
Stane Pas. SW16 —5J 109
Stane Way. SE18 —7B 82

Stanfield Rd. E3 —2A 64
Stanford Clo. Hamp —6D 102
Stanford Clo. Romf —6H 37
Stanford Clo. Wfd G —5H 21
Stanford Ct. SW6 —1K 91
Stanford Ho. Bark —2B 68
Stanford Pl. SE17 —4E 78 (9C 148)
Stanford Rd. N11 —5J 15
Stanford Rd. SW16 —2H 123
Stanford Rd. W8 —3K 75
Stanford St. SW1 —4H 77 (9A 146)
Stanford Way. SW16 —2H 123
Stangate. SE1 —3K 77 (6F 146)
(off Royal St.)
Stangate Gdns. Stan —4G 11
Stangate Lodge. N21 —7E 6
Stanger Rd. SE25 —4G 125
Stanhill Cotts. Dart —7K 117
Stanhope Av. N3 —3H 27
Stanhope Av. Brom —1H 137
Stanhope Av. Harr —1H 23
Stanhope Clo. SE16 —2K 79
Stanhope Gdns. N4 —6B 30
Stanhope Gdns. N6 —6F 29
Stanhope Gdns. NW7 —5G 13
Stanhope Gdns. SW7 —4A 76
Stanhope Gdns. Dag —3F 53
Stanhope Gdns. Ilf —1D 50
Stanhope Ga. W1 —1E 76 (3H 145)
Stanhope Gro. Beck —5B 126
Stanhope Ho. N11 —4A 16
(off Coppies Gro.)
Stanhope M. SW7 —4A 76
Stanhope M. E. SW7 —4A 76
Stanhope M. S. SW7 —4A 76
Stanhope M. W. SW7 —4A 76
Stanhope Pde. NW1
—3G 61 (1L 139)
Stanhope Pk. Rd. Gnfd —4G 55
Stanhope Pl. W2 —7D 60 (8E 138)
Stanhope Rd. E17 —5D 32
Stanhope Rd. N6 —6G 29
Stanhope Rd. N12 —5F 15
Stanhope Rd. Barn —6A 4
Stanhope Rd. Bexh —2E 100
Stanhope Rd. Cars —7E 132
Stanhope Rd. Croy —3E 134
Stanhope Rd. Dag —2F 53
Stanhope Rd. Gnfd —5G 55
Stanhope Rd. Sidc —4A 116
Stanhope Row. W1 —1F 77 (3J 145)
Stanhope St. NW1 —3G 61
Stanhope Ter. W2 —7B 60 (9B 138)
Stanier Clo. W14 —5H 75
Stanlake M. W12 —1E 74
Stanlake Rd. W12 —1E 74
Stanlake Vs. W12 —1E 74
Stanley Av. Bark —2K 67
Stanley Av. Beck —3E 126
Stanley Av. Dag —1F 53
Stanley Av. Gnfd —1G 55
Stanley Av. N Mald —6C 120
Stanley Av. Wemb —7E 40
Stanley Clo. SW8 —6K 77
Stanley Clo. Wemb —7E 40
Stanley Cres. W11 —7H 59
Stanleycroft Clo. Iswth —1J 87
Stanley Gdns. NW2 —5E 42
Stanley Gdns. W3 —2A 74
Stanley Gdns. W11 —7H 59
Stanley Gdns. Mitc —6E 108
Stanley Gdns. Wall —6G 133
Stanley Gdns. Rd. Tedd —5J 103
Stanley Gro. N17 —7A 18
Stanley Gro. SW8 —2E 92
Stanley Gro. Croy —6A 124

Stanley Horstead Tower. E10
—2D 48
Stanley Pk. Dri. Wemb —1F 57
Stanley Pk. Rd. Cars & Wall
—7D 132
Stanley Pas. NW1 —2J 61
Stanley Rd. E4 —1A 20
Stanley Rd. E10 —6D 32
Stanley Rd. E12 —5C 50
Stanley Rd. E15 —1F 65
Stanley Rd. E18 —1H 33
Stanley Rd. N2 —3B 28
Stanley Rd. N9 —1A 18
Stanley Rd. N10 —7A 16
Stanley Rd. N11 —6C 16
Stanley Rd. N15 —4B 30
Stanley Rd. NW9 —7C 26
Stanley Rd. SW14 —4H 89
Stanley Rd. SW19 —6J 107
Stanley Rd. W3 —3J 73
Stanley Rd. Brom —4A 128
Stanley Rd. Cars —7E 132
Stanley Rd. Croy —7A 124
Stanley Rd. Enf —3K 7
Stanley Rd. Harr —2G 39
Stanley Rd. Houn —4G 87
Stanley Rd. Ilf —2H 51
Stanley Rd. Mitc —7C 108
Stanley Rd. Mord —4J 121
Stanley Rd. Orp —7K 129
Stanley Rd. Sidc —3A 116
Stanley Rd. S'hall —7C 54
Stanley Rd. Sutt —6K 131
Stanley Rd. Twic & Tedd —4H 103
Stanley Rd. Wemb —6F 41
Stanley Sidings. NW5 —7F 45
Stanley Sq. Cars —7D 132
Stanley St. SE8 —7B 80
Stanley Ter. N19 —2J 45
Stanmere St. SW11 —2C 92
Stanmore Gdns. Rich —3F 89
Stanmore Gdns. Sutt —3A 132
Stanmore Hill. Stan —3F 11
Stanmore Lodge. Stan —4G 11
Stanmore Pl. NW1 —1F 61
Stanmore Rd. E11 —1H 49
Stanmore Rd. N15 —4B 30
Stanmore Rd. Belv —4J 85
Stanmore Rd. Rich —3F 89
Stanmore St. N1 —1K 61
Stanmore Ter. Beck —2C 126
Stannard Rd. E8 —6G 47
Stannary Pl. SE11 —5A 78
(off Stannary St.)
Stannary St. SE11 —6A 78
Stanning La. EC2 —6C 62
Stansfeld Rd. E16 & E6 —5B 66
Stansfield Rd. SW9 —3K 93
Stansfield Rd. Houn —2A 86
Stansgate Rd. Dag —2G 53
Stanstead Clo. Brom —6H 127
Stanstead Cres. Bex —1D 116
Stanstead Gro. SE6 —1B 112
Stanstead Mnr. Sutt —6J 131
Stanstead Rd. E11 —5K 33
Stanstead Rd. SE23 —1K 111
Stanswood Gdns. SE5 —7E 78
Stanthorpe Clo. SW16 —5J 109
Stanthorpe Rd. SW16 —5J 109
Stanton Av. Tedd —6J 103
Stanton Clo. Wor Pk —1F 131
Stanton Rd. SE26 —4B 112
Stanton Rd. SW13 —2B 90
Stanton Rd. SW20 —1F 121
Stanton Rd. Croy —7C 124
Stanton Sq. SE26 —4B 112
Stanton St. SE15 —1G 95
Stanton Way. SE26 —4B 112

Stanway Ct. N1 —2E **62**
Stanway Gdns. W3 —1G **73**
Stanway Gdns. Edgw —5D **12**
Stanway St. N1 —2E **62**
Stanwick Rd. W14 —4H **75**
Stanworth Ct. Houn —7E **70**
Stanworth St. SE1 —3F **79** (5E **148**)
Stapenhill Rd. Wemb —3B **40**
Staple Clo. Bex —3K **117**
Staplefield Clo. SW2 —1J **109**
Staplefield Clo. Pinn —1C **22**
Stapleford. N17 —2E **30**
(off Willan Rd.)
Stapleford Av. IIf —5J **35**
Stapleford Clo. E4 —3K **19**
Stapleford Clo. SW19 —7G **91**
Stapleford Clo. King T —2G **119**
Stapleford Rd. Wemb —7D **40**
Stapleford Way. Bark —3B **68**
Staplehurst Rd. SE13 —5G **97**
Staplehurst Rd. Cars —7C **132**
Staple Inn. WC1 —5A **62** (6G **141**)
(off Staple Inn Bldgs.)
Staple Inn Bldgs. WC1
—5A **62** (6G **141**)
Staples Clo. SE16 —1A **80**
Staples Ho. E6 —6E **66**
(off Savage Gdns.)
Staple St. SE1 —2D **78** (5B **148**)
Staple St. SE1 —2D **78**
Stapleton Gdns. Croy —5A **134**
Stapleton Hall Rd. N4 —1K **45**
Stapleton Rd. SW17 —3E **108**
Stapleton Rd. Bexh —7F **85**
Stapley Rd. Belv —5G **85**
Star All. EC3 —7E **62** (9D **142**)
(off Fenchurch St.)
Starboard Way. E14 —3C **80**
Starch Ho. La. IIf —2H **35**
Starcross St. NW1 —3G **61** (2M **139**)
Starfield Rd. W12 —2C **74**
Star & Garter Hill. Rich —1E **104**
Star Hill. Dart —5K **101**
Starkleigh Way. SE16 —5H **79**
Star La. E16 —4G **65**
Starling Clo. Buck H —1D **20**
Starling Clo. Pinn —3A **22**
Starling M. SE28 —2H **83**
Starling Wlk. Hamp —5C **102**
Star Path. N'holt —2E **54**
(off Brabazon Rd.)
Star Rd. W14 —6H **75**
Star Rd. Iswth —2H **87**
Star St. E16 —5H **65**
Star St. W2 —6C **60** (7B **138**)
Star Yd. WC2 —6A **62** (7G **141**)
Staten Gdns. Twic —1K **103**
Statham Gro. N16 —4D **46**
Statham Gro. N18 —5K **17**
Station App. E7 —4K **49**
Station App. E11 —5J **33**
Station App. N11 —5A **16**
Station App. N12 —4E **14**
Station App. NW10 —3B **58**
Station App. SE3 —3K **97**
Station App. SE26 —5B **112**
(Lower Sydenham)
Station App. SE26 —4J **111**
(Sydenham)
Station App. SW6 —3G **91**
Station App. SW16 —5H **109**
Station App. W7 —1J **71**
Station App. B'hurst —2J **101**
Station App. Bex —1C **126**
Station App. Bex —7G **101**
Station App. Buck H —4G **21**

Station App. Cheam —7G **131**
Station App. Chst —1E **128**
Station App. Chst —6C **114**
(Elmstead Woods)
Station App. Croy —2D **134**
Station App. Ewe —7B **130**
(Ewell West)
Station App. Hamp —7E **102**
Station App. Harr —7J **23**
Station App. Hayes —1J **137**
Station App. King T —2G **119**
Station App. New Bar —4F **5**
Station App. Pinn —3C **22**
Station App. Rich —1G **89**
Station App. S Croy —7D **134**
Station App. S Ruis —5A **38**
Station App. S'leigh —5C **130**
Station App. Well —2A **100**
(in two parts)
Station App. Wemb —6B **40**
Station App. Wor Pk —1C **130**
Station App. W Wick —7E **126**
Station App. N. Sidc —2A **116**
Station App. Rd. W4 —7J **73**
Station Av. SW9 —3B **94**
Station Av. Eps —7A **130**
Station Av. N Mald —3A **120**
Station Av. Rich —1G **89**
Station Clo. N3 —1J **27**
Station Clo. N12 —4E **14**
Station Clo. Hamp —7F **103**
Station Cres. N15 —4D **30**
Station Cres. SE3 —5J **81**
Station Cres. Wemb —6B **40**
Stationers' Hall Ct. EC4
—6B **62** (8K **141**)
Station Est. Beck —3K **125**
Station Garage M. SW16 —6H **109**
Station Gdns. W4 —7J **73**
Station Gro. Wemb —6E **40**
Station Hill. Brom —2J **137**
Station Ho. M. N9 —4B **18**
Station Pde. E11 —5J **33**
Station Pde. N14 —1C **16**
Station Pde. NW2 —6E **42**
Station Pde. W3 —6G **57**
Station Pde. W5 —1F **73**
Station Pde. Bark —7G **51**
Station Pde. Barn —4K **5**
Station Pde. Dag —6G **53**
Station Pde. Edgw —7K **11**
Station Pde. Harr —4F **39**
Station Pde. N'holt —7E **38**
Station Pde. Rich —6G **73**
Station Pde. W'stone —2A **24**
Station Pas. E18 —2K **33**
Station Pas. SE15 —1J **95**
Station Pl. N4 —2A **46**
Station Rise. SE27 —2B **110**
Station Rd. E4 —1A **20**
Station Rd. E7 —4J **49**
Station Rd. E12 —4C **50**
Station Rd. E17 —6A **32**
Station Rd. N3 —1J **27**
Station Rd. N11 —5A **16**
Station Rd. N17 —3G **31**
Station Rd. N18 —5A **18**
Station Rd. N19 —3G **45**
Station Rd. N21 —1G **17**
Station Rd. N22 —2J **29**
Station Rd. NW4 —6C **26**
Station Rd. NW7 —6F **13**
Station Rd. NW10 —2B **58**
Station Rd. SE20 —6J **111**
Station Rd. SE25 —4F **124**
Station Rd. SW13 —2B **90**

Station Rd. SW19 —1A **122**
Station Rd. W5 —6F **57**
Station Rd. W7 —1J **71**
Station Rd. B'side —3H **35**
Station Rd. Belv —3G **85**
Station Rd. Bexh —3E **100**
Station Rd. Brom —1J **127**
Station Rd. Cars —4D **132**
Station Rd. Croy —2D **134**
Station Rd. Dag & Chad —7D **36**
Station Rd. Edgw —6B **12**
Station Rd. Eri —5K **85**
Station Rd. Hamp —7E **102**
Station Rd. Hamp W —1D **118**
Station Rd. Harr —4K **23**
Station Rd. Houn —4F **87**
Station Rd. IIf —3F **51**
Station Rd. King T —1G **119**
Station Rd. New Bar —5E **4**
Station Rd. N Mald —5D **120**
Station Rd. N Har —5F **23**
Station Rd. Short —2G **127**
Station Rd. Sidc —2A **116**
Station Rd. Tedd —5K **103**
Station Rd. Th Dit —7A **118**
Station Rd. Twic —1K **103**
Station Rd. W Wick —1E **136**
Station Rd. N. Belv —3H **85**
Station Sq. Pet W —5G **129**
Station St. E15 —7F **49**
Station St. E16 —1F **83**
Station Ter. NW10 —2E **58**
Station Ter. SE5 —1C **94**
Station Ter. M. SE3 —5J **81**
Station View. Gnfd —1H **55**
Station Way. SE15 —2G **95**
Station Way. Buck H —4F **21**
Station Way. Sutt —6G **131**
Station Yd. Twic —7A **88**
Staunton Rd. King T —6E **104**
Staunton St. SE8 —6B **80**
Staveley Clo. E9 —5J **47**
Staveley Clo. N7 —4J **45**
Staveley Clo. SE15 —1J **95**
Staveley Gdns. W4 —1K **89**
Staveley Rd. W4 —6J **73**
Staverton Rd. NW2 —7E **42**
Stave Yd. Rd. SE16 —1A **80**
Stavordale Rd. N5 —4B **46**
Stavordale Rd. Cars —7A **122**
Stayner's Rd. E1 —4K **63**
Stayton Rd. Sutt —3J **131**
Steadfast Rd. King T —1D **118**
Steadman Ct. EC1 —4C **62** (3M **141**)
(off Old St.)
Steadman Ho. Dag —3G **53**
(off Uvedale Rd.)
Stead St. SE17 —4D **78** (9A **148**)
Stean St. E8 —1F **63**
Stebbing Ho. W11 —1F **75**
(off Queensdale Cres.)
Stebbing Way. Bark —2A **68**
Stebondale St. E14 —4E **80**
Stedham Pl. WC1 —6J **61** (7C **140**)
(off New Oxford St.)
Stedman Clo. Bex —3K **117**
Steedman St. SE17 —4C **78** (9L **147**)
Steeds Rd. N10 —1D **28**
Steele Ho. E15 —2G **65**
(off Eve Rd.)
Steele Rd. E11 —4G **49**
Steele Rd. N17 —3E **30**
Steele Rd. NW10 —2J **57**
Steele Rd. W4 —3J **73**
Steele Rd. Iswth —4A **88**
Steele's M. N. NW3 —6D **44**
Steele's M. S. NW3 —6D **44**
Steele's Rd. NW3 —6D **44**

Steel's La. E1 —6J **63**
Steen Way. SE22 —5E **94**
Steep Hill. SW16 —3H **109**
Steep Hill. Croy —4E **134**
Steeplands. Bush —1A **10**
Steeple Clo. SW6 —2G **91**
Steeple Clo. SW19 —5G **107**
Steeple Ct. E1 —4H **63**
Steeplestone Clo. N18 —5H **17**
Steerforth St. SW18 —2A **108**
Steers Mead. Mitc —1D **122**
Steers Way. SE16 —2A **80**
Stella Rd. SW17 —6D **108**
Stelling Rd. Eri —7K **85**
Stellman Clo. E5 —3G **47**
Stembridge Rd. SE20 —2H **125**
Stephan Clo. E8 —1G **63**
Stephendale Rd. SW6 —3K **91**
Stephen M. W1 —5H **61** (6A **140**)
Stephen Rd. Bexh —3J **101**
Stephens Ct. E16 —4H **65**
Stephenson Ho. SE1
—3C **78** (7L **147**)
Stephenson Rd. W7 —6K **55**
Stephenson Rd. Twic —7E **86**
Stephenson St. E16 —4G **65**
Stephenson St. NW10 —3A **58**
Stephenson Way. NW1
—4G **61** (3M **139**)
Stephen's Rd. E3 —2B **64**
Stephen's Rd. E15 —1G **65**
Stephen St. W1 —5H **61** (6A **140**)
Stepney Causeway. E1 —6K **63**
Stepney Grn. E1 —5J **63**
Stepney High St. E1 —5K **63**
Stepney Way. E1 —5H **63**
Sterling Av. Edgw —4A **12**
Sterling Pl. W5 —4E **72**
Sterling Rd. Enf —1J **7**
Sterling St. SW7 —3C **76** (6D **144**)
Sterling Way. N18 —5J **17**
Sterndale Rd. W14 —3F **75**
Sterne St. W12 —2F **75**
Sternhall La. SE15 —3G **95**
Sternhold Av. SW2 —2H **109**
Sterry Cres. Dag —5G **53**
Sterry Dri. Eps —4A **130**
Sterry Gdns. Dag —6G **53**
Sterry Rd. Bark —1K **67**
Sterry Rd. Dag —4G **53**
Sterry St. SE1 —2D **78** (5A **148**)
Sterry St. SW1 —2D **78**
Steucers La. SE23 —1A **112**
Steve Biko Ho. Wemb —7F **25**
Steve Biko La. SE6 —4C **112**
Steve Biko Rd. N7 —3A **46**
Steve Biko Way. Houn —3E **86**
Stevedale Rd. Well —2C **100**
Stevedore St. E1 —1H **79**
Stevenage Rd. E6 —6E **50**
Stevenage Rd. SW6 —7F **75**
Stevens Av. E9 —6J **47**
Stevens Clo. Beck —6C **112**
Stevens Clo. Bex —4K **117**
Stevens Clo. Hamp —5C **102**
Stevens Clo. Pinn —5A **22**
Stevens Grn. Bush —1B **10**
Stevenson Cres. SE16 —5H **79**
Stevens Rd. Dag —3B **52**
Stevens St. SE1 —3E **78** (6D **148**)
Steventon Rd. W12 —7B **58**
Stewards Holte Wlk. N11 —4A **16**
Steward St. E1 —5E **62** (6D **142**)
Stewart Clo. NW9 —6J **25**
Stewart Clo. Chst —5F **115**
Stewart Clo. Hamp —6C **102**
Stewart Rainbird Ho. E12 —5E **50**
(off Parkhurst Rd.)

Stewart Rd. E15 —4F **49**
Stewartsby Clo. N18 —5H **17**
Stewart's Gro. SW3 —5B **76**
Stewart's Rd. SW8 —7G **77**
Stewart St. E14 —2E **80**
Stew La. EC4 —7C **62** (9L **141**)
Steyne Rd. W3 —1H **73**
Steyning Gro. SE9 —4D **114**
Steynings Way. N12 —5D **14**
Steyning Way. Houn —4A **86**
Steynton Av. Bex —2D **116**
Stickland Rd. Belv —4G **85**
Stickleton Clo. Gnfd —3F **55**
Stilecroft Gdns. Wemb —3B **40**
Stile Hall Gdns. W4 —5G **73**
Stile Hall Pde. W4 —5G **73**
Stiles Clo. Brom —6D **128**
Stillingfleet Rd. SW13 —6C **74**
Stillington St. SW1
—4G **77** (8M **145**)
Stillness Rd. SE23 —6A **96**
Stilton Cres. NW10 —7K **41**
Stipularis Dri. Hay —4B **54**
Stirling Clo. SW16 —1G **123**
Stirling Gro. Houn —2G **87**
Stirling Rd. E13 —2K **65**
Stirling Rd. E17 —3A **32**
Stirling Rd. N17 —1G **31**
Stirling Rd. N22 —1B **30**
Stirling Rd. SW9 —2J **93**
Stirling Rd. W3 —3H **73**
Stirling Rd. Harr —3K **23**
Stirling Rd. Twic —1E **102**
Stirling Rd. Path. E17 —3A **32**
Stirling Wlk. Surb —6H **119**
Stirling Way. Croy —7J **123**
Stiven Cres. Harr —3D **38**
Stocdove Way. Gnfd —3A **55**
Stockbury Rd. Croy —6J **125**
Stockdale Rd. Dag —2F **53**
Stockdove Way. Gnfd —3K **55**
Stockfield Rd. SW16 —3K **109**
Stockholm Rd. SE16 —5J **79**
Stockholm Way. E1 —1G **79**
Stockhurst Clo. SW15 —2F **91**
Stockingswater La. Enf —3G **9**
Stockland Rd. Romf —6K **37**
Stock Orchard Cres. N7 —5K **45**
Stock Orchard St. N7 —5K **45**
Stockport Rd. SW16 —1H **123**
Stocksfield Rd. E17 —3E **32**
Stocks Pl. E14 —7B **64**
Stock St. E13 —2J **65**
Stockton Gdns. N17 —7H **17**
Stockton Gdns. NW7 —3F **13**
Stockton Ho. S Harr —1E **38**
Stockton Rd. N17 —7H **17**
Stockton Rd. N18 —6B **18**
Stockton Sq. Brom —3J **127**
Stockwell Av. SW9 —3K **93**
Stockwell Clo. Brom —2K **127**
Stockwell Gdns. SW9 —1K **93**
Stockwell Gdns. Est. SW9 —2J **93**
Stockwell Grn. SW9 —2K **93**
Stockwell Grn. Ct. SW9 —2K **93**
Stockwell La. SW9 —2K **93**
Stockwell M. SW9 —2K **93**
Stockwell Pk. Cres. SW9 —2K **93**
Stockwell Pk. Est. SW9 —2K **93**
Stockwell Pk. Rd. SW9 —1K **93**
Stockwell Pk. Wlk. SW9 —3K **93**
Stockwell Rd. SW9 —2K **93**
Stockwell St. SE10 —6E **80**
Stockwell Ter. SW9 —1K **93**
Stoddart Rd. SE20 —1J **125**
Stoddart Ho. SW8 —6K **77**
Stofield Gdns. SE9 —3B **114**
Stokenchurch St. SW6 —1K **91**

Stoke Newington Chu. St. N16
—3D 46
Stoke Newington Comn. N16 —2F 47
Stoke Newington High St. N16
—5F 47
Stoke Newington Rd. N16 —5F 47
Stoke Pl. NW10 —3B 58
Stoke Rd. King T —7J 105
Stokes Cotts. Ilf —1G 35
Stokes Ct. N2 —4C 28
Stokesley St. W12 —6B 58
Stokes Rd. E6 —4C 66
Stokes Rd. Croy —6K 125
Stokley Ct. N8 —4J 29
Stoll Clo. NW2 —3E 42
Stoms Path. SE6 —5C 112
Stonard Rd. N13 —3F 17
Stonard Rd. Dag —5B 52
Stondon Ho. E15 —1H 65
(off John St.)
Stondon Pk. SE23 —6A 96
Stondon Wlk. E6 —2B 66
Stonebridge Clo. S Harr —1E 38
Stonebridge Comn. E8 —7F 47
Stonebridge Pk. NW10 —7K 41
Stonebridge Rd. N15 —5F 31
Stonebridge Way. Wemb —6H 41
Stone Bldgs. WC2 —5K 61 (6F 140)
(off Chancery La.)
Stonechat Sq. E6 —5C 66
Stone Clo. SW4 —2G 93
Stone Clo. Dag —2F 53
Stonecot Clo. Sutt —1G 131
Stonecot Hill. Sutt —1G 131
Stonecroft Rd. Eri —7J 85
Stonecroft Way. Croy —7J 123
Stonecutter St. EC4
—6B 62 (7J 141)
Stonefield. N4 —2K 45
Stonefield Clo. Bexh —3G 101
Stonefield Clo. Ruis —5C 38
Stonefield St. N1 —1A 62
Stonefield Way. SE7 —7B 82
Stonefield Way. Ruis —5C 38
Stonegrove. Edgw —4K 11
Stone Gro. Ct. Edgw —5A 12
Stonegrove Gdns. Edgw —5A 12
Stonehall Av. Ilf —6C 34
Stonehall Pl. W8 —3K 75
Stone Hall Rd. N21 —7E 6
Stoneham Rd. N11 —5B 16
Stonehill Clo. SW14 —5K 89
Stonehill Ct. E4 —7J 9
Stonehill Rd. SW14 —5K 89
Stone Hill Rd. W4 —5G 73
Stonehills Ct. SE21 —3E 110
Stonehill Woods Pk. Sidc —6H 117
Stonehorse Rd. Enf —5D 8
Stone Ho. Ct. EC3 —6E 62 (7D 142)
(off Houndsditch)
Stoneleigh Av. Enf —1C 8
Stoneleigh Av. Wor Pk —4C 130
Stoneleigh Cres. Eps —5B 130
Stoneleigh Pk. Av. Croy —6K 125
Stoneleigh Pk. Rd. Eps —6B 130
Stoneleigh Pl. W11 —7F 59
Stoneleigh Rd. N17 —3F 31
Stoneleigh Rd. Cars —7C 122
Stoneleigh Rd. Ilf —3C 34
Stoneleigh Rd. W11 —7F 59
Stoneleigh Ter. N19 —2F 45
Stonell's Rd. SW11 —6D 92
Stonenest St. N4 —1K 45
Stone Pk. Av. Beck —4C 126
Stone Pl. Wor Pk —2C 130
Stone Rd. Brom —5H 127
Stones End St. SE1 —2C 78 (5L 147)
Stone St. Croy —5A 134

Stonewold Ct. W5 —6D 56
Stonewood Rd. Eri —5K 85
Stoney All. SE18 —2E 98
Stoneyard La. E14 —7D 64
Stoneycroft Clo. SE12 —7H 97
Stoneycroft Rd. Wfd G —6H 21
Stoneydeep. Tedd —4A 104
Stoneydown. E17 —4A 32
Stoneydown Av. E17 —4A 32
Stoneydown Ho. E17 —4A 32
(off Blackhorse Rd.)
Stoneyfields Gdns. Edgw —4D 12
Stoneyfields La. Edgw —5D 12
Stoney La. E1 —6E 62 (7D 142)
Stoney La. SE19 —6F 111
Stoney St. SE1 —1D 78 (2A 148)
Stonhouse St. SW4 —4H 93
Stonor Rd. W14 —4H 75
Stopford Clo. SW19 —7G 91
Stopford Rd. E13 —1J 65
Stopford Rd. SE17 —5B 78
Store Rd. E16 —2E 82
Storers Quay. E14 —4F 81
Store St. E15 —5F 49
Store St. WC1 —5H 61 (6A 140)
Storey Rd. E17 —4B 32
Storey Rd. N6 —6D 28
Storey's Ga. SW1 —2H 77 (5B 146)
Storey St. E16 —1E 82
Stories M. SE5 —2E 94
Stories Rd. SE5 —3E 94
Stork Rd. E7 —6J 49
Storksmead Rd. Edgw —7F 13
Stork's Rd. SE16 —3G 79
Stormont Rd. N6 —7D 28
Stormont Rd. SW11 —3E 92
Storrington Rd. Croy —1F 135
Story St. N1 —7K 45
Stothard Pl. EC2 —5E 62 (5D 142)
Stothard St. E1 —4J 63
Stoughton Av. Sutt —5F 131
Stoughton Clo. SE11
—4K 77 (9F 146)
Stoughton Clo. SW15 —1C 106
Stour Av. S'hall —3E 70
Stourcliffe St. W1 —6D 60 (8E 138)
Stourhead Clo. SW19 —7F 91
Stourhead Gdns. SW20 —3C 120
Stour Rd. E3 —7C 48
Stour Rd. Dag —2G 53
Stourton Av. Felt —4D 102
Stowage. SE8 —6C 80
Stow Cres. E17 —7F 19
Stowe Gdns. N9 —1A 18
Stowe Ho. NW11 —6A 28
Stowe Pl. N15 —3E 30
Stowe Rd. W12 —2D 74
Stoxmead. Harr —1H 23
Stracey Rd. E7 —4J 49
Stracey Rd. NW10 —1K 57
Strachan Pl. SW19 —6E 106
Stradbroke Dri. Chig —6K 21
Stradbroke Gro. Buck H —1G 21
Stradbroke Gro. Ilf —3C 34
Stradbroke Pk. Chig —6K 21
Stradbroke Rd. N5 —4C 46
Stradbrook Clo. Harr —3D 38
Stradella Rd. SE24 —6C 94
Strafford Av. Ilf —2E 34
Strafford Rd. W3 —2J 73
Strafford Rd. Barn —3B 4
Strafford Rd. Houn —3D 86
Strafford Rd. Twic —7A 88
Strafford St. E14 —2C 80
Strahan Rd. E3 —3A 64
Straightsmouth. SE10 —7E 80
Straight, The. S'hall —2C 70
Strait Rd. E6 —7C 66

Strakers Rd. SE15 —4H 95
Strale Ho. N1 —1E 62
(off Whitmore Est.)
Strand. WC2 —7J 61 (2C 146)
Strand Ct. SE18 —5J 83
Strandfield Clo. SE18 —5J 83
Strand La. WC2 —7K 61 (9F 140)
Strand on the Grn. W4 —6G 73
Strand Pl. N18 —4K 17
Strand School App. W4 —6G 73
Strangways Ter. W14 —3H 75
Stranraer Way. N1 —7K 45
Strasburg Rd. SW11 —1E 92
Stratford Av. W8 —3J 75
Stratford Cen. E15 —7F 49
Stratford Clo. Bark —7A 52
Stratford Clo. Dag —7J 53
Stratford Ct. N Mald —4K 119
Stratford Gro. SW15 —4F 91
Stratford Mkt. E15 —1F 65
Stratford Pk. Clo. N21 —7G 7
Stratford Pl. W1 —6E 60 (8J 139)
Stratford Rd. E13 —1H 65
Stratford Rd. NW4 —4E 27
Stratford Rd. W3 —2J 73
Stratford Rd. W8 —3J 75
Stratford Rd. Hay —4A 54
Stratford Rd. S'hall —4C 70
Stratford Rd. T Hth —4A 124
Stratford Vs. NW1 —7H 45
Strathan Clo. SW18 —6H 91
Strathaven Rd. SE12 —6K 97
Strathblaine Rd. SW11 —4B 92
Strathbrook Rd. SW16 —7K 109
Strathcona Rd. Wemb —2D 40
Strathdale. SW16 —5K 109
Strathdon Dri. SW17 —3B 108
Strathearn Av. Twic —1F 103
Strathearn Pl. W2 —6C 60 (9C 138)
Strathearn Rd. SW19 —5J 107
Strathearn Rd. Sutt —5J 131
Stratheden Rd. SE3 —7J 81
Strathfield Gdns. Bark —6H 51
Strathleven Rd. SW2 —5J 93
Strathmore Gdns. N3 —1K 27
Strathmore Gdns. W8 —1J 75
Strathmore Gdns. Edgw —2H 25
Strathmore Rd. SW19 —3J 107
Strathmore Rd. Croy —7D 124
Strathmore Rd. Tedd —4J 103
Strathnairn St. SE1 —4G 79
Strathray Gdns. NW3 —6C 44
Strath Ter. SW11 —4C 92
Strathville Rd. SW18 —2J 107
Strathyre Av. SW16 —3A 124
Stratton Clo. SW19 —2J 121
Stratton Clo. Bexh —3E 100
Stratton Clo. Edgw —6A 12
Stratton Clo. Houn —1E 86
Stratton Ct. Pinn —1D 22
(off Devonshire Rd.)
Strattondale St. E14 —3E 80
Stratton Dri. Bark —5J 51
Stratton Gdns. S'hall —6D 54
Stratton Rd. SW19 —2J 121
Stratton Rd. Bexh —3E 100
Stratton St. W1 —1F 77 (2K 145)
Strauss Rd. W4 —2K 73
Strawberry Fields. Swan —7K 117
Strawberry Hill. Twic —3K 103
Strawberry Hill Clo. Twic —3K 103
Strawberry Hill Rd. Twic —3K 103
Strawberry La. Cars —3E 132
Strawberry Vale. N2 —1B 28
Strawberry Vale. Twic —3A 104
Streakes Field Rd. NW2 —2C 42
Streamdale. SE2 —6B 84
Stream La. Edgw —5C 12

Streamside Clo. N9 —1A 18
Streamside Clo. Brom —4J 127
Stream Way. Belv —6F 85
Streatfield Av. E6 —1D 66
Streatfield Rd. Harr —3C 24
Streatham Clo. SW16 —2J 109
Streatham Comn. N. SW16 —5J 109
Streatham Comn. S. SW16 —6J 109
Streatham Ct. SW16 —3J 109
Streatham High Rd. SW16 —4J 109
Streatham Hill. SW2 —2J 109
Streatham Pl. SW2 —7J 93
Streatham Rd. Mitc & SW16
—1E 122
Streatham St. WC1 —6J 61 (7C 140)
Streatham Vale. SW16 —1G 123
Streathbourne Rd. SW17 —2E 108
Streatley Pl. NW3 —4A 44
Streatley Rd. NW6 —7H 43
Streeters La. Wall —3H 133
Streetfield M. SE3 —3J 97
Streimer Rd. E15 —2E 64
Strelley Way. W3 —7A 58
Stretton Rd. Croy —7E 124
Stretton Rd. Rich —2C 104
Strickland Ct. SE15 —3G 95
Strickland Row. SW18 —7B 92
Strickland St. SE8 —1C 96
Stride Rd. E13 —2H 65
Stringer Ho. N1 —1E 62
(off Whitmore Est.)
Strode Clo. N10 —7K 15
Strode Rd. E7 —4J 49
Strode Rd. N17 —2E 30
Strode Rd. NW10 —6C 42
Strode Rd. SW6 —7G 75
Strone Rd. E7 & E12 —6A 50
Strone Way. Hay —4C 54
Strongbow Cres. SE9 —5D 98
Strongbow Rd. SE9 —5D 98
Strongbridge Clo. Harr —1E 38
Stronsa Rd. W12 —2B 74
Strood Av. Romf —1K 53
Stroud Cres. SW15 —3C 106
Stroudes Clo. Wor Pk —7A 120
Stroud Field. N'holt —6C 38
Stroud Ga. Harr —4F 39
Stroud Grn. Gdns. Croy —7J 125
Stroud Grn. Rd. N4 —1K 45
Stroud Grn. Way. Croy —7H 125
Stroudley Wlk. E3 —3D 64
Stroud Rd. SE25 —6G 125
Stroud Rd. SW19 —3J 107
Strouts Pl. E2 —3F 63 (1E 142)
Strudwick Ct. SW4 —1J 93
(off Binfield Rd.)
Strutton Ground. SW1
—3H 77 (6A 146)
Strype St. E1 —5F 63 (6E 142)
Stuart Av. NW9 —7C 26
Stuart Av. W5 —1F 73
Stuart Av. Brom —1J 137
Stuart Av. Harr —3D 38
Stuart Cres. N22 —1K 29
Stuart Cres. Croy —3B 136
Stuart Evans Clo. Well —3C 100
Stuart Gro. Tedd —5J 103
Stuart Mantle Way. Eri —7K 85
Stuart Pl. Mitc —1D 122
Stuart Rd. NW6 —3J 59
Stuart Rd. SE15 —4J 95
Stuart Rd. SW19 —3J 107
Stuart Rd. W3 —1J 73
Stuart Rd. Bark —7K 51
Stuart Rd. Barn —7H 5
Stuart Rd. Harr —3K 23
Stuart Rd. Rich —2B 104
Stuart Rd. T Hth —4C 124

Stuart Rd. Well —1B 100
Stubbs Ct. W4 —5H 73
(off Chaseley Dri.)
Stubbs Point. E13 —4K 65
Stubbs Way. SW19 —1B 122
Stucley Pl. NW1 —7F 45
Studdridge St. SW6 —2J 91
Studd St. N1 —1B 62
Studholme Ct. NW3 —4J 43
Studholme St. SE15 —7H 79
Studio Pl. SW1 —2D 76 (5F 144)
(off Kinnerton St.)
Studland Clo. Sidc —3K 115
Studland Rd. SE26 —5H 111
Studland Rd. W7 —6H 55
Studland Rd. King T —6E 104
Studland St. W6 —4D 74
Studley Av. E4 —7A 20
Studley Clo. E5 —5A 48
Studley Ct. Sidc —5B 116
Studley Dri. Ilf —6B 34
Studley Est. SW4 —1J 93
Studley Grange Rd. W7 —2J 71
Studley Rd. E7 —6K 49
Studley Rd. SW4 —1J 93
Studley Rd. Dag —7D 52
Stukeley Rd. E7 —7K 49
Stukeley St. WC2 —6J 61 (7D 140)
Stumps Hill La. Beck —6C 112
Sturdy Rd. SE15 —2H 95
Sturge Av. E17 —2D 32
Sturgeon Rd. SE17 —5C 78
Sturges Field. Chst —6H 115
Sturgess Av. NW4 —7D 26
Sturge St. SE1 —2C 78 (4L 147)
Sturmer Way. N7 —5K 45
Sturminster Clo. Hay —6A 54
Sturrock Clo. N15 —4D 30
Sturry St. E14 —6D 64
Sturt St. N1 —2C 62
Stutfield St. E1 —6G 63
Styles Gdns. SW9 —3B 94
Styles Ho. SE1 —1B 78 (3J 147)
(off Eccles Pl.)
Styles Way. Beck —4E 126
Sudbourne Rd. SW2 —5J 93
Sudbrooke Rd. SW12 —6D 92
Sudbrook Gdns. Rich —3E 104
Sudbrook La. Rich —1E 104
Sudbury. E6 —6E 66
Sudbury Av. Wemb —3D 40
Sudbury Ct. E5 —4A 48
Sudbury Ct. SW8 —1J 93
Sudbury Ct. Dri. Harr —3K 39
Sudbury Ct. Rd. Harr —3K 39
Sudbury Cres. Brom —6J 113
Sudbury Cres. Wemb —5B 40
Sudbury Croft. Wemb —4A 40
Sudbury Gdns. Croy —4E 134
Sudbury Heights Av. Gnfd —5K 39
Sudbury Hill. Harr —2J 39
Sudbury Hill Clo. Wemb —4K 39
Sudbury Rd. Bark —5K 51
Sudbury Towers. Gnfd —5J 39
Sudeley St. N1 —2B 62
Sudlow Rd. SW18 —5J 91
Sudrey St. SE1 —2C 78 (5L 147)
Suez Av. Gnfd —2K 55
Suez Rd. Enf —4F 9
Suffield Rd. E4 —4J 19
Suffield Rd. N15 —5F 31
Suffield Rd. SE20 —2J 125
Suffolk Ct. E10 —7C 32
Suffolk Ho. SE20 —7K 111
(off Croydon Rd.)
Suffolk La. EC4 —7D 62 (9A 142)
Suffolk Pk. Rd. E17 —4A 32

Suffolk Pl. SW1 —1H 77 (2B 146)
Suffolk Rd. E13 —3J 65
Suffolk Rd. N15 —5D 30
Suffolk Rd. NW10 —7A 42
Suffolk Rd. SE25 —4F 125
Suffolk Rd. SW13 —7B 74
Suffolk Rd. Bark —7H 51
Suffolk Rd. Dag —5J 53
Suffolk Rd. Enf —5C 8
Suffolk Rd. Harr —6D 22
Suffolk Rd. Ilf —6J 35
Suffolk Rd. Sidc —6C 116
Suffolk Rd. Wor Pk —2B 130
Suffolk St. E7 —4J 49
Suffolk St. SW1 —7H 61 (1B 146)
Sugar Bakers Ct. EC3
     —6E 62 (8D 142)
(off Creechurch La.)
Sugar Ho. La. E15 —2E 64
Sugar Loaf Wlk. E2 —3J 63
Sugar Quay. EC3 —7E 62 (1D 148)
(off Lwr. Thames St.)
Sugar Quay Wlk. EC3
     —7E 62 (1D 148)
Sugden Rd. SW11 —3F 92
Sugden Rd. Th Dit —7B 118
Sugden Way. Bark —2K 67
Sulgrave Gdns. W6 —2E 74
Sulgrave Rd. W6 —3E 74
Sulina Rd. SW2 —7J 93
Sulivan Ct. SW6 —2J 91
Sulivan Enterprise Cen. SW6 —3J 91
Sulivan Rd. SW6 —3J 91
Sullivan Av. E16 —5B 66
Sullivan Clo. SW11 —3C 92
Sullivan Ct. N16 —7F 31
Sullivan Rd. SE11 —4B 78 (8J 147)
Sultan Rd. E11 —4K 33
Sultan St. SE5 —7C 78
Sultan St. Beck —2K 125
Sumatra Rd. NW6 —5J 43
Sumburg Rd. SW12 —6E 92
Summercourt Rd. E1 —6J 63
Summerdene Clo. SW16 —7G 109
Summerfield Av. NW6 —2G 59
Summerfield Rd. W5 —4B 56
Summerfield St. SE12 —7H 97
Summer Hill. Chst —2E 128
Summerhill Gro. Enf —6K 7
Summerhill Rd. N15 —4D 30
Summerhill Vs. Chst —1E 128
Summerhouse Av. Houn —1C 86
Summerhouse Dri. Bex & Dart
     —4K 117
Summerhouse Rd. N16 —2E 46
Summerland Gdns. N10 —3F 29
Summerland Grange. N10 —3F 29
Summerlands Av. W3 —7J 57
Summerlee Av. N2 —4D 28
Summerlee Gdns. N2 —4D 28
Summerley St. SW18 —2K 107
Summersby Rd. N6 —6F 29
Summers Clo. Sutt —7J 131
Summers Clo. Wemb —1H 41
Summers La. N12 —7G 15
Summers Row. N12 —6H 15
Summers St. EC1 —4A 62 (4G 141)
Summerstown. SW17 —3A 108
Summerton Way. SE28 —6D 68
Summer Trees. Sun —7A 102
Summerville Gdns. Sutt —6H 131
Summerwood Rd. Iswth —5K 87
Summit Av. NW9 —5K 25
Summit Clo. N14 —2B 16
Summit Clo. NW2 —6G 43
Summit Clo. NW9 —4K 25
Summit Clo. Edgw —7B 12
Summit Dri. Wfd G —2B 34

Summit Est. N16 —7G 31
Summit Rd. E17 —4D 32
Summit Rd. N'holt —7E 38
Summit Way. N14 —2A 16
Summit Way. SE19 —7E 110
Sumner Av. SE15 —1F 95
Sumner Bldgs. SE1 —1C 78 (2L 147)
(off Sumner St.)
Sumner Ct. SW8 —1J 93
Sumner Est. SE15 —7F 79
Sumner Gdns. Croy —1B 134
Sumner Pl. SW7 —4B 76 (9B 144)
Sumner Pl. M. SW7
     —4B 76 (9B 144)
Sumner Rd. SE15 —6F 79
     (in two parts)
Sumner Rd. Croy —1A 134
Sumner Rd. Harr —7G 23
Sumner Rd. S. Croy —1A 134
Sumner St. SE1 —1B 78 (2K 147)
Sumpter Clo. NW3 —6A 44
Sun All. Rich —4E 88
Sunbeam Rd. NW10 —4J 57
Sunbury Av. NW7 —5E 12
Sunbury Av. SW14 —4K 89
Sunbury Ct. Barn —4B 4
(off Manor Rd.)
Sunbury Gdns. NW7 —5E 12
Sunbury La. SW11 —1B 92
Sunbury Rd. Sutt —3G 131
Sunbury St. SE18 —3D 82
Sunbury Way. Felt —5A 102
Sun Ct. EC3 —6D 62 (8B 142)
(off Cornhill)
Suncroft Pl. SE26 —3J 111
Sunderland Rd. SE23 —1K 111
Sunderland Rd. W5 —3D 72
Sunderland Ter. W2 —6K 59
Sunderland Way. E12 —2B 50
Sundew Av. W12 —7C 58
Sundew Ct. Wemb —2E 56
(off Elmore Clo.)
Sundial Av. SE25 —3F 125
Sundorne Rd. SE7 —5A 82
Sundra Wlk. E1 —4K 63
Sundridge Av. Brom & Chst
     —1B 128
Sundridge Av. Well —2H 99
Sundridge Pde. Brom —7K 113
Sundridge Pl. Croy —1G 135
Sundridge Rd. Croy —7F 125
Sunfields Pl. SE3 —7K 81
Sungate Cotts. Romf —1F 37
Sunkist Way. Wall —7J 133
Sunland Av. Bexh —4E 100
Sun La. SE3 —7K 81
Sunleigh Rd. Wemb —1E 56
Sunley Gdns. Grnfd —1A 56
Sunnindale Av. Felt —2C 102
Sunningdale. N14 —5C 16
Sunningdale Av. W3 —7A 58
Sunningdale Av. Bark —1H 67
Sunningdale Av. Felt —3C 102
Sunningdale Av. Ruis —1A 38
Sunningdale Clo. Stan —6F 11
Sunningdale Ct. Houn —6H 87
(off Whitton Dene)
Sunningdale Gdns. NW9 —5J 25
Sunningdale Rd. Brom —4C 128
Sunningdale Rd. Sutt —1H 131
Sunningfields Cres. NW4 —2D 26
Sunningfields Rd. NW4 —2D 26
Sunninghill Ct. W3 —2J 73
Sunninghill Rd. SE13 —2D 96
Sunny Bank. SE25 —3G 125
Sunny Cres. NW10 —7J 41
Sunnycroft Rd. SE25 —4G 125
Sunnycroft Rd. Houn —2F 87
Sunnycroft Rd. S'hall —5E 54

Sunnydale Gdns. NW7 —6E 12
Sunnydale Rd. SE12 —5K 97
Sunnydene Av. E4 —5A 20
Sunnydene Gdns. Wemb —6C 40
Sunnydene St. SE26 —4A 112
Sunnyfield. NW7 —4G 13
Sunnyfield Rd. Chst —3K 129
Sunny Gdns. Pde. NW4 —2D 26
Sunny Gdns. Rd. NW4 —2D 26
Sunny Hill. NW4 —3D 26
Sunnyhill Rd. SW16 —4J 109
Sunnyhurst Clo. Sutt —3J 131
Sunnymead Av. Mitc —3H 123
Sunnymead Rd. NW9 —7K 25
Sunnymead Rd. SW15 —5D 90
Sunnymede Av. Eps —7A 130
Sunnyside Houses. NW2 —3H 43
(off Sunnyside)
Sunnyside Pas. SW19 —6G 107
Sunnyside Rd. E10 —1C 48
Sunnyside Rd. N19 —7H 29
Sunnyside Rd. W5 —1D 72
Sunnyside Rd. Ilf —3G 51
Sunnyside Rd. Tedd —4H 103
Sunnyside Rd. E. N9 —3B 18
Sunnyside Rd. N. N9 —3A 18
Sunnyside Rd. S. N9 —3A 18
Sunnyside Ter. NW9 —3K 25
Sunny View. NW9 —5K 25
Sunny Way. N12 —7H 15
Sunray Av. SE24 —4D 94
Sunray Av. Brom —6G 128
Sunrise Clo. Felt —3D 102
Sunrise View. NW7 —6G 13
Sun Rd. W14 —5H 75
Sunset Av. E4 —1J 19
Sunset Av. Wfd G —4C 20
Sunset Gdns. SE25 —2F 125
Sunset Rd. SE5 —4C 94
Sunset View. Barn —2B 4
Sun St. EC2 —5D 62 (5B 142)
Sun St. Pas. EC2 —5E 62 (6C 142)
Sunwell Clo. SE15 —1H 95
Surbiton Ct. Surb —6C 118
Surbiton Cres. King T —4E 118
Surbiton Hall Clo. King T —4E 118
Surbiton Hill Pk. Surb —5F 119
Surbiton Hill Rd. Surb —5E 118
Surbiton Pde. Surb —6E 118
Surbiton Rd. King T —4D 118
Surlingham Clo. SE28 —7D 68
Surma Clo. E1 —4H 63
Surrendale Pl. W9 —4J 59
Surrey Canal Rd. SE15 & SE14
     —6J 79
Surrey Ct. N3 —3G 27
Surrey Cres. W4 —5G 73
Surrey Gdns. N4 —6C 30
Surrey Gro. SE17 —5E 78
Surrey Gro. Sutt —3B 132
Surrey La. SW11 —1C 92
Surrey La. Est. SW11 —1C 92
Surrey M. SE27 —4E 110
Surrey Mt. SE23 —1H 111
Surrey Quays Rd. SE16 —3J 79
Surrey Quays Shopping Cen. SE16
     —3K 79
Surrey Rd. SE15 —5K 95
Surrey Rd. Bark —7J 51
Surrey Rd. Dag —5H 53
Surrey Rd. Harr —5G 23

Surrey Rd. W Wick —1D 136
Surrey Row. SE1 —2B 78 (4J 147)
Surrey Sq. SE17 —5E 78
Surrey St. E13 —3K 65
Surrey St. SE17 —5E 78
Surrey St. WC2 —7K 61 (9F 140)
Surrey St. Croy —3C 134
Surrey Ter. SE17 —5E 78
Surrey Water Rd. SE16 —1K 79
Surridge Ct. SW9 —2J 93
(off Clapham Rd.)
Surridge Gdns. SE19 —6D 110
Surr St. N7 —5J 45
Susan Clo. Romf —3J 37
Susan Lawrence Ho. E12 —4E 50
(off Walton Rd.)
Susannah St. E14 —6D 64
Susan Rd. SE3 —2K 97
Susan Wood. Chst —1E 128
Sussex Av. Iswth —3J 87
Sussex Clo. N19 —2J 45
Sussex Clo. Ilf —5D 34
Sussex Clo. N Mald —4A 120
Sussex Clo. Twic —6B 88
Sussex Cres. N'holt —6E 38
Sussex Gdns. N4 —5C 30
Sussex Gdns. N6 —5D 28
Sussex Gdns. W2 —7B 60 (9A 138)
Sussex Ga. N6 —5D 28
Sussex M. E. W2 —6B 60 (8B 138)
(off Clifton Pl.)
Sussex M. W. W2 —7B 60 (9B 138)
Sussex Pl. NW1 —4D 60 (3E 138)
Sussex Pl. W2 —6B 60 (8B 138)
Sussex Pl. W6 —5E 74
Sussex Pl. Eri —7H 85
Sussex Pl. N Mald —4A 120
Sussex Ring. N12 —5D 14
Sussex Rd. E6 —1E 66
Sussex Rd. Eri —7H 85
Sussex Rd. Harr —5G 23
Sussex Rd. Mitc —5J 123
Sussex Rd. N Mald —4A 120
Sussex Rd. Sidc —5B 116
Sussex Rd. S'hall —3B 70
Sussex Rd. S Croy —6D 134
Sussex Rd. W Wick —1D 136
Sussex Sq. W2 —7B 60 (9B 138)
Sussex St. E13 —3K 65
Sussex St. SW1 —5F 77
Sussex Wlk. SW9 —4B 94
Sussex Way. N19 & N7 —1J 45
Sussex Way. Barn —5A 6
Sutcliffe Clo. NW11 —5K 27
Sutcliffe Rd. SE18 —6J 83
Sutcliffe Rd. Well —2C 100
Sutherland Av. W9 —4J 59
Sutherland Av. W13 —6B 56
Sutherland Av. Orp —6K 129
Sutherland Av. Well —4J 99
Sutherland Clo. Barn —4B 4
Sutherland Ct. NW9 —5H 25
Sutherland Dri. SW19 —1B 122
Sutherland Gdns. SW14 —3A 90
Sutherland Gdns. Wor Pk —1D 130
Sutherland Gro. SW18 —6G 91
Sutherland Gro. Tedd —5J 103
Sutherland Ho. W8 —3K 75
Sutherland Pl. W2 —6J 59
Sutherland Point. E5 —4H 47
(off Tiger Way)
Sutherland Rd. E17 —3K 31
Sutherland Rd. N9 —1C 18
Sutherland Rd. N17 —1G 31
Sutherland Rd. SW1 —5F 77
Sutherland Rd. W4 —6A 74
Sutherland Rd. W13 —4A 56

Sutherland Rd. Belv —3G 85
Sutherland Rd. Croy —7A 124
Sutherland Rd. Enf —6E 8
Sutherland Rd. S'hall —6D 54
Sutherland Rd. Path. E17 —3K 31
Sutherland Row. SW1 —5F 77
Sutherland Sq. SE17 —5C 78
Sutherland St. SW1 —5F 77
Sutherland Wlk. SE17 —5C 78
Sutlej Rd. SE7 —7A 82
Sutterton St. N7 —6K 45
Sutton Arc. Sutt —5K 131
Sutton Clo. Beck —1D 126
Sutton Clo. Lou —1H 21
Sutton Comn. Rd. Sutt —7H 121
Sutton Ct. W4 —6J 73
Sutton Ct. Sutt —6A 132
Sutton Ct. Rd. E13 —3A 66
Sutton Ct. Rd. W4 —7J 73
Sutton Ct. Rd. Sutt —6A 132
Sutton Cres. Barn —5A 4
Sutton Dene. Houn —1F 87
Sutton Est. EC1 —3D 62 (2B 142)
(off City Rd.)
Sutton Est. W10 —5E 58
Sutton Est., The. N1 —7B 46
Sutton Est., The. SW3 —5C 76
Sutton Gdns. SE25 —5F 125
Sutton Gdns. Bark —1J 67
Sutton Gdns. Croy —5F 125
Sutton Grn. Bark —1K 67
Sutton Gro. Sutt —4B 132
Sutton Hall Rd. Houn —7E 70
Sutton La. Houn —3D 86
Sutton La. N. W4 —5J 73
Sutton La. S. W4 —6J 73
Sutton Pde. NW4 —4E 26
(off Church Rd.)
Sutton Pk. Rd. Sutt —6K 131
Sutton Pl. E9 —5J 47
Sutton Rd. E13 —4H 65
Sutton Rd. E17 —1K 31
Sutton Rd. N10 —1E 28
Sutton Rd. Bark —1J 67
Sutton Rd. Houn —1E 86
Sutton Row. N1 —6H 61 (7B 140)
Sutton Sq. E9 —5J 47
Sutton Sq. Houn —1D 86
Sutton St. E1 —7J 63
Sutton's Way. EC1 —4C 62 (4M 141)
Sutton Way. W10 —4E 58
Sutton Way. Houn —1D 86
Swaby Rd. SW18 —1A 108
Swaffham Way. N17 —7G 17
Swaffield Rd. SW18 —7K 91
Swain Clo. SW16 —6F 109
Swain Rd. T Hth —5C 124
Swains La. N6 —1E 44
Swainson Rd. W3 —2B 74
Swains Rd. SW17 —7D 108
Swalecliffe Rd. Belv —5H 85
Swallands Rd. SE6 —3C 112
     (in two parts)
Swallowbrook Bus. Cen. Hay —1B 70
Swallow Clo. SE14 —1K 95
Swallow Clo. Bush —1A 10
Swallow Ct. Ilf —5F 35
Swallow Ct. Ruis —1A 38
Swallow Dri. NW10 —6K 41
Swallow Dri. N'holt —2E 54
Swallowfield Rd. SE7 —5K 81
Swallow Pas. W1 —6F 61 (8K 139)
(off Swallow Pl.)
Swallow Pl. W1 —6F 61 (8K 139)
Swallow St. E6 —5C 66
Swallow St. W1 —7G 61 (1M 145)
Swanage Rd. E4 —7K 19

Swanage Rd. SW18 —6A **92**
Swanage Waye. Hay —6A **54**
Swan App. E6 —5C **66**
Swanbridge Rd. Bexh —1G **101**
Swan Clo. E17 —1A **32**
Swan Clo. Croy —7E **124**
Swan Clo. Felt —4C **102**
Swan Ct. SW3 —5C **76**
Swan Ct. Iswth —3B 88
(off Swan St.)
Swandon Way. SW18 —5K **91**
Swan Dri. NW9 —2A **26**
Swanfield St. E2 —3F **63** (2E 142)
Swan La. EC4 —7D **62** (1B 148)
Swan La. N20 —3F **15**
Swanley By-Pass. Swan —7H **117**
Swanley Rd. Well —1C **100**
Swan Mead. SE1 —3E **78** (7C 148)
Swan M. SW9 —1K **93**
Swan Pas. E1 —7G 63
(off Royal Mint St.)
Swan & Pike Rd. Enf —1H **9**
Swan Pl. SW13 —2B **90**
Swan Rd. SE16 —2J **79**
Swan Rd. SE18 —3B **82**
Swan Rd. Felt —5C **102**
Swan Rd. S'hall —6F **55**
Swanscombe Ho. W11 —1F 75
(off St Ann's Rd.)
Swanscombe Point. E16 —5H 65
(off Clarkson Rd.)
Swanscombe Rd. W4 —5A **74**
Swanscombe Rd. W11 —1F **75**
Swansea Rd. Enf —4D **8**
Swansland Gdns. E17 —1A **32**
Swan St. SE1 —3C **78** (6M 148)
Swan St. Iswth —3B **88**
Swanton Gdns. SW19 —1F **107**
Swanton Rd. Eri —7H **85**
Swan Wlk. SW3 —6D **76**
Swan Way. Enf —2C **8**
Swan Yd. N1 —6B **46**
Sward Rd. Orp —6K **129**
Swaton Rd. E3 —4C **64**
Swaylands Rd. Belv —6G **85**
Swaythling Clo. N18 —4C **18**
Swedenborg Gdns. E1 —7H **63**
Sweden Ga. SE16 —3A **80**
Swedish Quays Development. SE16
—3A 80
Sweeney Cres. SE1 —2F **79** (5F **148**)
Sweet Briar Grn. N9 —3A **18**
Sweet Briar Gro. N9 —3A **18**
Sweet Briar Wlk. N18 —4A **18**
Sweetland Ct. Dag —6B **52**
Sweetmans Av. Pinn —3B **22**
Sweets Way. N20 —2G **15**
Swell Ct. E17 —6D **32**
Swetenham Wlk. SE18 —5G **83**
Swete St. E13 —2J **65**
Sweyn Pl. SE3 —2J **97**
Swift Clo. E17 —7F **19**
Swift Clo. Harr —2F **39**
Swift Ct. Sutt —7K **131**
Swift Rd. Felt —4B **102**
Swift Rd. S'hall —3E **70**
Swiftsden Way. Brom —6G **113**
Swift St. SW6 —1H **91**
Swinbrook Rd. W10 —5G **59**
Swinburne Ct. SE5 —4D 94
(off Basingdon Way)
Swinburne Cres. Croy —6J **125**
Swinburne Rd. SW15 —4C **90**
Swinderby Rd. Wemb —6E **40**
Swindon Clo. Ilf —2J **51**
Swindon St. W12 —1E **74**
Swinfield Clo. Felt —3C **102**
Swinford Gdns. SW9 —3B **94**

Swingate La. SE18 —6J **83**
Swinnerton St. E9 —5A **48**
Swinton Clo. Wemb —1H **41**
Swinton Pl. WC1 —3K **61** (1E **140**)
Swinton St. WC1 —3K **61** (1E **140**)
Swiss Ct. WC2 —7H 61 (1B 146)
(off Panton St.)
Swiss Ter. NW6 —7B **44**
Swithland Gdns. SE9 —4E **114**
Swynford Gdns. NW4 —4C **26**
Sybil M. N4 —6B **30**
Sybil Phoenix Clo. SE8 —5K **79**
Sybourn St. E17 —7B **32**
Sycamore Av. W5 —3D **72**
Sycamore Av. Sidc —6K **99**
Sycamore Clo. E16 —4G **65**
Sycamore Clo. N9 —4B **18**
Sycamore Clo. SE9 —2C **114**
Sycamore Clo. W3 —1A **74**
Sycamore Clo. Barn —6G **5**
Sycamore Clo. Cars —4D **132**
Sycamore Clo. N'holt —1C **54**
Sycamore Ct. E4 —6G **19**
Sycamore Ct. E7 —6J **49**
Sycamore Ct. Eri —5K **85**
Sycamore Ct. Houn —4C **86**
Sycamore Ct. N Mald —3A **120**
Sycamore Gdns. Mitc —2B **122**
Sycamore Gro. NW9 —7J **25**
Sycamore Gro. SE6 —6E **96**
Sycamore Gro. SE20 —1G **125**
Sycamore Gro. N Mald —3K **119**
Sycamore Hill. N11 —6A **16**
Sycamore Ho. W6 —2D **74**
Sycamore Ho. Brom —2G **127**
Sycamore M. Eri —5K **85**
Sycamore Rd. SW19 —6E **106**
Sycamore Rd. EC1 —4C **62** (4L **141**)
Sycamore St. SW1 —2D **78**
Sycamore Wlk. W10 —4G **59**
Sycamore Wlk. Ilf —4G **35**
Sycamore Way. Tedd —6C **104**
Sycamore Way. T Hth —5A **124**
Sydcote. SE21 —1C **110**
Sydenham Av. SE26 —5H **111**
Sydenham Cotts. SE12 —2A **114**
Sydenham Hill. SE26 & SE23
—4F **111**
Sydenham Pk. SE26 —3J **111**
Sydenham Pk. Rd. SE26 —3J **111**
Sydenham Pl. SE27 —3B **110**
Sydenham Rise. SE23 —2H **111**
Sydenham Rd. SE26 —4J **111**
Sydenham Rd. Croy —1C **134**
Sydmons Ct. SE23 —7J **95**
Sydner M. N16 —4F **47**
Sydner Rd. N16 —4F **47**
Sydney Clo. SW3 —4B **76** (9B **144**)
Sydney Ct. N Mald —5B **120**
Sydney Elson Way. E6 —2E **66**
Sydney Gro. NW4 —5E **26**
Sydney M. SW3 —4B **76** (9B **144**)
Sydney Pl. SW7 —4B **76** (9B **144**)
Sydney Rd. E11 —6K **33**
Sydney Rd. N8 —4A **30**
Sydney Rd. N10 —1F **29**
Sydney Rd. SE2 —3C **84**
Sydney Rd. SW20 —2F **121**
Sydney Rd. W13 —1A **72**
Sydney Rd. Bexh —4D **100**
Sydney Rd. Enf —4J **7**
(in two parts)
Sydney Rd. Ilf —2G **35**
Sydney Rd. Rich —4E **88**
Sydney Rd. Sidc —4J **115**
Sydney Rd. Sutt —4J **131**
Sydney Rd. Tedd —5K **103**
Sydney Rd. Wfd G —4D **20**
Sydney St. SW3 —5C **76** (9C **144**)

Sylvan Av. N3 —2J **27**
Sylvan Av. N22 —7E **16**
Sylvan Av. NW7 —6F **13**
Sylvan Av. Romf —6F **37**
Sylvan Ct. N12 —3E **14**
Sylvan Est. SE19 —1F **125**
Sylvan Gdns. Surb —7D **118**
Sylvan Gro. SE15 —6H **79**
Sylvan Hill. SE19 —1E **124**
Sylvan Rd. E7 —6J **49**
Sylvan Rd. E11 —5J **33**
Sylvan Rd. E17 —5C **32**
Sylvan Rd. SE19 —1F **125**
Sylvan Wlk. Brom —3C **128**
Sylvan Way. Dag —4B **52**
Sylvan Way. W Wick —4G **137**
Sylverdale Rd. Croy —3B **134**
Sylvester Av. Chst —6D **114**
Sylvester Path. E8 —6H **47**
Sylvester Rd. E8 —6H **47**
Sylvester Rd. E17 —7B **32**
Sylvester Rd. N2 —2B **28**
Sylvester Rd. Wemb —5C **40**
Sylvestrus Clo. King T —1G **119**
Sylvia Ct. Wemb —7H **41**
Sylvia Gdns. Wemb —7H **41**
Sylvia Pankhurst Ho. Dag —3G 53
(off Wythenshawe Rd.)
Symes M. NW1 —2G **61**
Symons St. SW3 —4D **76** (9F **144**)
Syndey Pl. SW7 —4B **76**
Syon Ga. Way. Bren —7A **72**
Syon La. Iswth —6J **71**
Syon Pk. Gdns. Iswth —7K **71**

Tabard Garden Est. SE1
—3D **78** (5A **148**)
Tabard St. SE1 —2D **78** (4A **148**)
Tabard St. SW1 —2D **78**
Tabernacle Av. E13 —4J **65**
Tabernacle St. EC2 —4D **62** (4B **142**)
Tableer Av. SW4 —5H **93**
Tabley Rd. N7 —4J **45**
Tabor Ct. Sutt —6G **131**
Tabor Gdns. Sutt —7H **131**
Tabor Gro. SW19 —7G **107**
Tabor Rd. W6 —3D **74**
Tachbrook Est. SW1 —5H **77**
Tachbrook M. SW1
—4G **77** (8L **145**)
Tachbrook Rd. S'hall —4B **70**
Tachbrook St. SW1
—4G **77** (9M **145**)
Tack M. SE4 —3C **96**
Tadema Rd. SW10 —7A **76**
Tadmor St. W12 —1F **75**
Tadworth Av. N Mald —5B **120**
Tadworth Ho. SE1 —2B 78 (5J 147)
(off Webber St.)
Tadworth Rd. NW2 —2C **42**
Taeping St. E14 —4D **80**
Taffy's Row. Mitc —3C **122**
Taft Way. E3 —3E **64**
Tailworth St. E1 —5G 63
(off Chicksand St.)
Tait Ct. SW8 —1J 93
(off Allen Edwards Dri.)
Tait Rd. Croy —7E **125**
Takeley Clo. Romf —2K **37**
Talacre Rd. NW5 —6E **44**
Talbot Av. N2 —3B **28**
Talbot Clo. N15 —4F **31**
Talbot Ct. EC3 —7D 62 (9B 142)
(off Gracechurch St.)
Talbot Ct. NW9 —3K **41**
Talbot Cres. NW4 —5C **26**
Talbot Gdns. Ilf —2A **52**

Talbot Pl. SE3 —2G **97**
Talbot Rd. E6 —2E **66**
Talbot Rd. E7 —4J **49**
Talbot Rd. N6 —6E **28**
Talbot Rd. N15 —4F **31**
Talbot Rd. N22 —2G **29**
Talbot Rd. W11 & W2 —6H **59**
(in two parts)
Talbot Rd. W13 —1A **72**
Talbot Rd. Brom —3K **127**
Talbot Rd. Cars —5E **132**
Talbot Rd. Dag —6F **53**
Talbot Rd. Harr —2K **23**
Talbot Rd. Iswth —4A **88**
Talbot Rd. S'hall —4C **70**
Talbot Rd. Wemb —6D **40**
Talbot Sq. W2 —6B **60** (8B **138**)
Talbot Wlk. NW10 —6A **42**
Talbot Wlk. W11 —6G **59**
Talbot Way. NW10 —6A **42**
Talbot Yd. SE1 —1D 78 (3A 148)
(off Borough High St.)
Talbot Yd. SW1 —1D **78**
Talcott Path. SW2 —1A **110**
Talfourd Pl. SE15 —1F **95**
Talfourd Rd. SE15 —1F **95**
Talgarth Mans. W14 —5G 75
(off Talgarth Rd.)
Talgarth Rd. W6 & W14 —5F **75**
Talgarth Wlk. NW9 —5A **26**
Talisman Clo. Ilf —1B **52**
Talisman Sq. SE26 —4G **111**
Talisman Way. Wemb —3F **41**
Tallack Clo. Harr —7D **10**
Tallack Rd. E10 —1B **48**
Tall Elms Clo. Brom —5H **127**
Tallis Gro. SE7 —6K **81**
Tallis St. EC4 —7A **62** (9H **141**)
Tallis View. NW10 —6K **41**
Tall Trees. SW16 —4K **123**
Talma Gdns. Twic —6J **87**
Talmage Clo. SE23 —7J **95**
Talman Gro. Stan —6J **11**
Talma Rd. SW2 —4A **94**
Talwin St. E3 —3D **64**
Tamar Ho. SE11 —5A 78
(off Kennington La.)
Tamarind Yd. E1 —1G **79**
Tamarisk Sq. W12 —7B **58**
Tamar Sq. Wfd G —6E **20**
Tamar St. SE7 —4C **82**
Tamar Way. N17 —3G **31**
Tamesis Gdns. Wor Pk —2A **130**
Tamian Way. Houn —4A **86**
Tamworth. N7 —6J **45**
Tamworth Av. Wfd G —6B **20**
Tamworth La. Mitc —2F **123**
Tamworth Pk. Mitc —3F **123**
Tamworth Pl. Croy —2C **134**
Tamworth Rd. Croy —2B **134**
Tamworth St. SW6 —6J **75**
Tamworth Vs. Mitc —4G **123**
Tancred Rd. N4 —7B **30**
Tandridge Dri. Orp —7H **129**
Tandridge Pl. Orp —7H **129**
Tanfield Av. NW2 —4B **42**
Tanfield Rd. Croy —4C **134**
Tangier Rd. Rich —4G **89**
Tangleberry Clo. Brom —4D **128**
Tanglewood Clo. Croy —3J **135**
Tanglewood Clo. Stan —2D **10**
Tangley Gro. SW15 —6B **90**
Tangley Pk. Rd. Hamp —5D **102**
Tangmere. N17 —2D 30
(off Willan Rd.)
Tangmere Gdns. N'holt —2A **54**
Tangmere Way. NW9 —2A **26**

Tanhurst Ho. SW2 —7J 93
(off Redlands Way)
Tanhurst Wlk. SE2 —3D **84**
Tankerton St. WC1 —3J **61** (2D **140**)
Tankerton Ter. Croy —6K **123**
Tankerville Rd. SW16 —7H **109**
Tankridge Rd. NW2 —2D **42**
Tanner Point. E13 —1J 65
(off Brooks Rd.)
Tanners End La. N18 —4K **17**
Tanner's Hill. SE8 —1B **96**
Tanners La. Ilf —3G **35**
Tanner St. SE1 —2E **78** (5D **148**)
Tanner St. Bark —6G **51**
Tannery Clo. Beck —4K **125**
Tannery Clo. Dag —3H **53**
Tannington Ter. N5 —3A **46**
Tannsfeld Rd. SE26 —5K **111**
Tansley Clo. N7 —5H **45**
Tanswell St. SE1 —2A **78** (5G **147**)
Tansy Clo. E6 —6E **66**
Tantallon Rd. SW12 —1E **108**
Tant Av. E16 —6H **65**
Tantony Gro. Romf —3D **36**
Tanworth Gdns. Pinn —2A **22**
Tanyard La. Bex —7G **101**
Tanza Rd. NW3 —4D **44**
Tapestry Clo. Sutt —7K **131**
Taplow. Rd. N13 —4G **17**
Taplow St. N1 —2C **62**
Tappesfield Rd. SE15 —3J **95**
Tapp St. E1 —4H **63**
Tapster St. Barn —3C **4**
Tara Ct. Beck —2D **126**
Tarbert Rd. SE22 —5E **94**
Tarbert Wlk. E1 —7J **63**
Tariff Cres. SE8 —4B **80**
Tariff Rd. N17 —6B **18**
Tarleton Ct. N22 —2A **30**
Tarleton Gdns. SE23 —2H **111**
Tarling Clo. Sidc —3B **116**
Tarling Rd. E16 —6H **65**
Tarling Rd. N2 —2A **28**
Tarling St. E1 —6J **63**
Tarling St. Est. E1 —6J **63**
Tarn Bank. Enf —5D **6**
Tarn St. SE1 —3C **78** (7L **147**)
Tarnwood Pk. SE9 —1D **114**
Tarragon Clo. SE14 —7A **80**
Tarragon Gro. SE26 —6K **111**
Tarrant Pl. W1 —5D **60** (6E **138**)
Tarrington Clo. SW16 —3H **109**
Tarry La. SE8 —4A **80**
Tarver Rd. SE17 —5B **78**
Tarves Way. SE10 —7D **80**
Tash Pl. N11 —5A **16**
Tasker Ho. Bark —2H **67**
Tasker Rd. NW3 —5D **44**
Tasmania Ter. N18 —6H **17**
Tasman Rd. SW9 —3J **93**
Tasman Wlk. E16 —6B **66**
Tasso Rd. W6 —6G **75**
Tasso Yd. W6 —6G 75
(off Tasso Rd.)
Tatam Rd. NW10 —7K **41**
Tate Rd. E16 —1D **82**
(in two parts)
Tate Rd. Sutt —5J **131**
Tatnell Rd. SE23 —6A **96**
Tattersall Clo. SE9 —5C **98**
Tatton Cres. N16 —7F **31**
Tatum St. SE17 —4D **78** (9B **148**)
Taunton Av. SW20 —2D **120**
Taunton Av. Houn —2G **87**
Taunton Clo. Bexh —2K **101**
Taunton Clo. Sutt —1J **131**
Taunton Dri. Enf —3F **7**
Taunton M. NW1 —4D **60** (4E **138**)

Taunton Pl. NW1 —4D 60 (3E 138)
Taunton Rd. SE12 —5G 97
Taunton Way. Stan —2E 24
Taverners Clo. W11 —1G 75
Taverner Sq. N5 —4C 46
Taverners Way. E4 —1B 20
Tavern La. SW9 —2A 94
Tavistock Av. E17 —3K 31
Tavistock Av. Gnfd —2A 56
Tavistock Clo. N16 —5E 46
Tavistock Cres. W11 —5H 59
Tavistock Cres. Mitc —4J 123
Tavistock Gdns. Ilf —4J 51
Tavistock Ga. Croy —1D 134
Tavistock Gro. Croy —7D 124
Tavistock Ho. WC1 —4H 61
Tavistock Ho. Croy —1D 134
Tavistock M. E18 —4J 33
Tavistock M. W11 —6H 59
Tavistock Pl. E18 —3J 33
Tavistock Pl. N14 —6A 6
Tavistock Pl. WC1 —4J 61 (3C 140)
Tavistock Rd. E7 —4H 49
Tavistock Rd. E15 —6H 49
Tavistock Rd. E18 —3J 33
Tavistock Rd. N4 —6D 30
Tavistock Rd. NW10 —2B 58
Tavistock Rd. W11 —6H 59
Tavistock Rd. Brom —4H 127
Tavistock Rd. Cars —1B 132
Tavistock Rd. Croy —1D 134
Tavistock Rd. Edgw —1G 25
Tavistock Rd. Well —1C 100
Tavistock Sq. WC1
　　　　　—4H 61 (3B 140)
Tavistock St. WC2 —7J 61 (9D 140)
　(in two parts)
Tavistock Ter. N19 —3H 45
Tavistock Tower. SE14 —3A 80
Tavistock Wlk. Cars —1B 132
Taviton St. WC1 —4H 61 (3A 140)
Tavy Bri. SE2 —2C 84
Tavy Bri. Cen. SE2 —2C 84
Tavy Clo. SE11 —5A 78
　(off White Hart St.)
Tawney Rd. SE28 —7B 68
Tawny Way. SE16 —4K 79
Tayben Av. Twic —6J 87
Taybridge Rd. SW11 —3E 92
Tay Bldgs. SE1 —3E 78 (6C 148)
　(off Long La.)
Tayburn Clo. E14 —6E 64
Taylor Av. Rich —2H 89
Taylor Clo. N17 —7B 18
Taylor Clo. Hamp —5G 103
Taylor Clo. Romf —1G 37
Taylor Ct. E15 —5E 48
Taylor Ct. SE20 —2J 125
　(off Elmers End Rd.)
Taylormead. NW7 —5H 13
Taylor Rd. Mitc —7C 106
Taylor Rd. Wall —5F 133
Taylors Bldgs. SE18 —4F 83
Taylors Clo. Sidc —3K 115
Taylors Grn. W3 —6A 58
Taylors La. NW10 —7A 42
Taylor's La. SE26 —4H 111
Taylors La. Barn —1C 4
Taymount Grange. SE23 —2J 111
Taymount Rise. SE23 —2J 111
Tayport Clo. N1 —7J 45
Tayside Clo. SE5 —4D 94
Tayside Dri. Edgw —3C 12
Taywood Rd. N'holt —3D 54
Teak Clo. SE16 —1A 80
Tealby Ct. N7 —6K 45
　(off Georges Rd.)

Teal Clo. E16 —5B 66
Teal Cl. NW10 —6K 41
Teale St. E2 —2G 63
Teasel Clo. Croy —1K 135
Teasel Way. E15 —3G 65
Tebworth Rd. N17 —7A 18
Tedder Rd. S Croy —7J 135
Teddington Pk. Tedd —5K 103
Teddington Pk. Rd. Tedd —4K 103
Ted Roberts Ho. E2 —2J 63
　(off Parmiter St.)
Tedworth Gdns. SW3 —5D 76
Tedworth Sq. SW3 —5D 76
Tees Av. Gnfd —2J 55
Teesdale Av. Iswth —1A 88
Teesdale Clo. E2 —2H 63
Teesdale Gdns. SE19 —1E 124
Teesdale Gdns. Iswth —1A 88
Teesdale Rd. E11 —7H 33
Teesdale St. E2 —2H 63
Teesdale Yd. E2 —2H 63
　(off Teesdale St.)
Teeswater Ct. Eri —3D 84
Tee, The. W3 —6A 58
Teevan Clo. Croy —7G 125
Teevan Rd. Croy —1G 135
Teignmouth Clo. SW4 —4H 93
Teignmouth Clo. Edgw —2F 25
Teignmouth Gdns. Gnfd —2A 56
Teignmouth Pde. Gnfd —2B 56
Teignmouth Rd. NW2 —5F 43
Teignmouth Rd. Well —2C 100
Telcote Way. Ruis —7A 22
Telegraph Hill. NW3 —3K 43
Telegraph M. Ilf —1A 52
Telegraph Pas. SW2 —7J 93
Telegraph Rd. SW15 —7D 90
Telegraph St. EC2 —6D 62 (7A 142)
Teleman Sq. SE3 —4K 97
Telephone Pl. SW6 —6H 75
Telfer Clo. W3 —2J 73
Telferscot Rd. SW12 —1H 109
Telford Av. SW2 —1H 109
Telford Clo. SE19 —6F 111
Telford Rd. N11 —5B 16
Telford Rd. NW9 —6C 26
Telford Rd. SE9 —2H 115
Telford Rd. W10 —5G 59
Telford Rd. S'hall —7F 55
Telfords Ter. E1 —7G 63
Telford Ter. SW1 —6G 77
Telford Way. W3 —5A 58
Telford Way. Hay —5C 54
Telham Rd. E6 —2E 66
Tell Gro. SE22 —4F 95
Tellson Av. SE18 —1B 98
Temeraire St. SE16 —2J 79
Temperley Rd. SW12 —7E 92
Templar Dri. SE28 —6D 68
Templar Ho. NW2 —6H 43
Templar Pl. Hamp —7E 102
Templars Av. NW11 —6H 27
Templars Cres. N3 —2J 27
Templars Dri. Harr —6C 10
Templars Ho. E15 —5D 48
Templar St. SE5 —2B 94
Temple. EC4 —7A 62 (9G 141)
　(off Middle Temple La.)
Temple Av. EC4 —7A 62 (9H 141)
Temple Av. N20 —7G 5
Temple Av. Croy —2B 136
Temple Av. Dag —1G 53
Temple Chambers. EC4
　(off Temple Av.) —7A 62 (9H 141)
Temple Clo. E11 —7G 33
Temple Clo. N3 —2H 27
Temple Clo. SE28 —3G 83

Templecombe Rd. E9 —1J 63
Templecombe Way. Mord —5G 121
Temple Ct. SW8 —7J 77
　(off Thorncroft St.)
Temple Dwellings. E2 —2H 63
　(off Temple St.)
Temple Fortune Hill. NW11 —5J 27
Temple Fortune La. NW11 —6H 27
Temple Fortune Pde. NW11 —5H 27
Temple Gdns. N21 —2G 17
Temple Gdns. NW11 —6H 27
Temple Gdns. Dag —3D 52
Temple Gro. NW11 —6J 27
Temple Gro. Enf —3G 7
Temple Hall Ct. E4 —2A 20
Templehof Av. NW4 —7E 26
Temple La. EC4 —6A 62 (8H 141)
Templeman Rd. W7 —5K 55
Templemead Clo. W3 —6A 58
Temple Mead Clo. Stan —6G 11
Templemead Ho. E9 —4A 48
Temple Mill La. E15 —4D 48
Temple Mills Rd. E15 —4C 48
Temple Pl. WC2 —7K 61 (9F 140)
Temple Rd. E6 —1C 66
Temple Rd. N8 —4K 29
Temple Rd. NW2 —4E 42
Temple Rd. W4 —3J 73
Temple Rd. W5 —3D 72
Temple Rd. Croy —4D 134
Temple Rd. Houn —4G 87
Temple Rd. Rich —2F 89
Temple Sheen. SW14 —5J 89
Temple Sheen Rd. SW14 —4H 89
Temple St. E2 —2H 63
Templeton Av. E4 —4H 19
Templeton Clo. N16 —5D 30
Templeton Clo. SE19 —1D 124
Templeton Pl. SW5 —4J 75
Templeton Rd. N15 —6D 30
Temple Way. Sutt —3B 132
Templewood. W13 —5B 56
Templewood Av. NW3 —3K 43
Templewood Gdns. NW3 —3K 43
Templewood Point. NW2 —2H 43
　(off Granville Rd.)
Tempsford Clo. Enf —3H 7
Tempsford Ct. Harr —6J 23
Temsford Clo. Harr —2G 23
Tenbury Clo. E7 —5B 50
Tenbury Ct. SW12 —1H 109
Tenby Av. Harr —2B 24
Tenby Clo. N15 —4F 31
Tenby Clo. Romf —6E 36
Tenby Ct. E17 —5K 31
Tenby Gdns. N'holt —6E 38
Tenby Rd. E17 —5A 32
Tenby Rd. Edgw —1F 25
Tenby Rd. Enf —4D 8
Tenby Rd. Romf —6E 36
Tenby Rd. Well —1D 100
Tench St. E1 —1H 79
Tenda Rd. SE16 —4H 79
Tendring Way. Romf —5C 36
Tenham Av. SW2 —2H 109
Tenison Ct. W1 —7G 61 (9L 139)
Tenison Way. SE1 —1A 78 (3F 146)
Tenniel Clo. W2 —7A 60
Tennison Rd. SE25 —4F 125
Tennis St. SE1 —2D 78 (4A 148)
Tennis St. SW1 —2D 78
Tenniswood Rd. Enf —1K 7
Tennyson Av. E11 —7J 33
Tennyson Av. E12 —7C 50
Tennyson Av. NW9 —3J 25

Tennyson Av. N Mald —5D 120
Tennyson Av. Twic —1K 103
Tennyson Clo. SW19 —6A 108
Tennyson Clo. Enf —6E 8
Tennyson Clo. Well —1J 99
Tennyson Ct. SW6 —1K 91
　(off Maltings Pl.)
Tennyson Ho. SE17 —5C 78
　(off Browning St.)
Tennyson Rd. E10 —1D 48
Tennyson Rd. E15 —7G 49
Tennyson Rd. E17 —6B 32
Tennyson Rd. NW6 —1H 59
Tennyson Rd. NW7 —5H 13
Tennyson Rd. SE20 —7K 111
Tennyson Rd. W7 —7K 55
Tennyson Rd. Houn —2G 87
Tennyson St. SW8 —2F 93
Tensing Rd. S'hall —3E 70
Tentelow La. S'hall —5E 70
Tenterden Clo. NW4 —3F 27
Tenterden Clo. SE9 —4D 114
Tenterden Clo. SE12 —4C 114
Tenterden Dri. NW4 —3F 27
Tenterden Gdns. NW4 —3F 27
Tenterden Gdns. Croy —7G 125
Tenterden Gro. NW4 —3F 27
Tenterden Rd. N17 —7A 18
Tenterden Rd. Croy —7G 125
Tenterden Rd. Dag —2F 53
Tenterden St. W1 —6F 61 (8K 139)
Tenter Ground. E1 —5F 63 (6E 142)
Tenter Pas. E1 —6F 63 (8F 142)
Tent Peg La. Pet W —5G 129
Tent St. E1 —4H 63
Terborch Way. SE22 —5E 94
Teredo St. SE16 —3K 79
Teresa M. E17 —4C 32
Teresa Wlk. N10 —5F 29
Terling Clo. E11 —3H 49
Terling Rd. Dag —2G 53
Terling Wlk. N1 —1C 62
　(off Popham St.)
Terminal Ho. Stan —5J 11
Terminus St. SW17 —3F 77 (7K 145)
Terrace Gdns. SW13 —2B 90
Terrace La. Rich —6E 88
Terrace Rd. E9 —7K 47
Terrace Rd. E13 —2J 65
Terrace, The. EC4 —6A 62 (8H 141)
　(off Crown Office Row)
Terrace, The. N3 —2H 27
Terrace, The. NW6 —1J 59
Terrace, The. SW1 —2J 77
Terrace, The. SW13 —2A 90
Terrace, The. Harr —7B 24
Terrace, The. Wfd G —6D 20
Terrace Wlk. SW11 —7D 76
　(off Albert Bri. Rd.)
Terrace Wlk. Dag —5E 52
Terrapin Rd. SW17 —3F 109
Terretts Pl. N1 —7B 46
Terrick Rd. N22 —1J 29
Terrick St. W12 —6D 58
Terrilands. Pinn —3D 22
Territorial Ho. SE11 —4A 78 (9H 147)
　(off Reedworth St.)
Terront Rd. N15 —4C 30
Tessa Sanderson Pl. SW8 —3F 93
　(off Daley Thompson Way)
Tessa Sanderson Way. Gnfd —5H 39
Testerton Wlk. W11 —7F 59
Testwood Ct. W7 —7J 55
Tetbury Pl. N1 —1B 62
Tetcott Rd. SW10 —7A 76
Tetherdown. N10 —3E 28
Tetterby Way. SE16 —5G 79

Tetty Way. Brom —2J 127
Teversham La. SW8 —1J 93
Teviot Clo. Well —1B 100
Teviot St. E14 —5E 64
Tewkesbury Av. SE23 —7H 95
Tewkesbury Av. Pinn —5C 22
Tewkesbury Clo. N15 —6D 30
Tewkesbury Gdns. NW9 —3H 25
Tewkesbury Rd. N15 —6D 30
Tewkesbury Rd. W13 —1A 72
Tewkesbury Rd. Cars —1B 132
Tewkesbury Ter. N11 —6B 16
Tewson Rd. SE18 —5J 83
Teynham Av. Enf —6J 7
Teynham Grn. Brom —5J 127
Teynton Ter. N17 —1C 30
Thackeray Av. N17 —2G 31
Thackeray Clo. SW19 —7F 107
Thackeray Clo. Harr —1E 38
Thackeray Ct. W14 —3G 75
　(off Blythe Rd.)
Thackeray Dri. Romf —7A 36
Thackeray Rd. E6 —2B 66
Thackeray Rd. SW8 —2F 93
Thackeray St. W8 —3K 75
Thackeray M. E8 —6G 47
Thackrah Clo. N2 —2A 28
Thakeham Clo. SE26 —4H 111
Thalia Clo. SE10 —6F 81
Thame Rd. SE16 —2K 79
Thames Av. SW10 —1A 92
Thames Av. Dag —4H 69
Thames Av. Gnfd —2K 55
Thames Bank. SW14 —2J 89
Thamesbank Pl. SE28 —6C 68
Thames Barrier Ind. Area. SE1
　(off Faraday Way) —3B 82
Thames Exchange Building. EC4
　　　　　—7C 62 (1M 147)
　(off Up. Thames St.)
Thamesgate Clo. Rich —4B 104
Thameshill Av. Romf —2J 37
Thames Ho. EC4 —7C 62 (1M 147)
　(off Up. Thames St.)
Thameside. Tedd —7D 104
Thameside Cen. Bren —6F 73
Thameside Ind. Est. E16 —2B 82
Thameside. SE1 —8E —6A 68
Thamesmere Dri. SE28 —7A 68
Thames Pl. SW15 —3F 91
　(in two parts)
Thames Quay. E14 —2D 80
Thames Quay. SW10 —1A 92
　(off Chelsea Harbour)
Thames Rd. E16 —1B 82
Thames Rd. W4 —6G 73
Thames Rd. Bark —3K 67
Thames Rd. Rich —6G 73
Thames Rd. Ind. Est. E16 —2B 82
Thames Side. King T —1D 118
Thames St. SE10 —6D 80
Thames St. King T —2D 118
Thames Vale Clo. Houn —2E 86
Thames Village. W4 —1J 89
Thanescroft Gdns. Croy —3E 134
Thanet Ct. W3 —6G 57
Thanet Pl. Croy —4C 134
Thanet Rd. Bex —7G 101
Thanet St. WC1 —3J 61 (2C 140)
Thane Vs. N7 —3K 45
Thane Works. N7 —3K 45
Thant Clo. E10 —3D 48
Tharp Rd. Wall —5H 133
Thatcham Ct. N20 —7F 5
Thatcham Gdns. N20 —7F 5
Thatchers Way. Iswth —5H 87
Thatches Gro. Romf —4E 36
Thavies Inn. EC1 —6A 62 (7H 141)

275

Thaxted Ct. N1 —2D 62
(off Fairbank Est.)
Thaxted Ho. Dag —7H 53
Thaxted Pl. SW20 —7F 107
Thaxted Rd. SE9 —2G 115
Thaxted Rd. Buck H —1H 21
Thayers Farm Rd. Beck —1A 126
Thayer St. W1 —6E 60 (6H 139)
Theatre St. SW11 —3D 92
Theberton St. N1 —1A 62
Theed St. SE1 —1A 78 (3G 147)
Thelma Gdns. SE3 —1B 98
Thelma Gro. Tedd —6A 104
Theobald Cres. Harr —1G 23
Theobald Rd. E17 —7C 32
Theobald Rd. Croy —2B 134
Theobalds Av. N12 —4F 15
Theobalds Ct. N4 —3C 46
Theobald's Rd. WC1
　　　　　—5K 61 (6D 140)
Theobald St. SE1 —3D 78 (7A 148)
(off New Kent Rd.)
Theodore Ct. SE13 —6F 97
Theodore Rd. SE13 —6F 97
Therapia La. Croy —7H 123
(in two parts)
Therapia Rd. SE22 —6J 95
Theresa Rd. W6 —4C 74
Therfield Ct. N4 —2C 46
Thermopylae Ga. E14 —4D 80
Theseus Wlk. N1 —2B 62
(off City Garden Row)
Thesiger Rd. SE20 —7K 111
Thessaly Rd. SW8 —7G 77
Thetford Clo. N13 —6G 17
Thetford Gdns. Dag —7E 52
Thetford Rd. Dag —7D 52
Thetford Rd. N Mald —6K 119
Thetis Ter. Rich —6G 73
Theydon Gro. Wfd G —6F 21
Theydon Rd. E5 —2J 47
Theydon St. E17 —7B 32
Thicket Cres. Sutt —4A 132
Thicket Gro. SE20 —7G 111
Thicket Gro. Dag —6C 52
Thicket Rd. SE20 —7G 111
Thicket Rd. Sutt —4A 132
Thickett Gro. Dag —6C 52
Third Av. E12 —4C 50
Third Av. E13 —3J 65
Third Av. E17 —5C 32
Third Av. W3 —1B 74
Third Av. W10 —3G 59
Third Av. Dag —1H 69
Third Av. Enf —5A 8
Third Av. Romf —6C 36
Third Av. Wemb —2D 40
Third Cross Rd. Twic —2H 103
Third Way. Wemb —4H 41
Thirleby Rd. SW1 —3G 77 (7M 145)
Thirleby Rd. Edgw —1K 25
Thirlmere Av. Gnfd —3C 56
Thirlestane Ct. N10 —2E 28
Thirlmere Gdns. Wemb —1C 40
Thirlmere Rise. Brom —6H 113
Thirlmere Rd. N10 —1F 29
Thirlmere Rd. SW16 —4H 109
Thirlmere Rd. Bexh —1J 101
Thirsk Clo. N'holt —6E 38
Thirsk Rd. SE25 —4D 124
Thirsk Rd. SW11 —3E 92
Thirsk Rd. Mitc —7E 108
Thistlebrook. SE2 —2C 84
Thistlecroft Gdns. Stan —1D 24
Thistledene Av. Harr —3C 38
Thistle Gro. SW10 —5A 76
Thistlemead. Chst —2F 129

Thistlewaite Rd. E5 —3H 47
Thistlewood Clo. N7 —2K 45
Thistleworth Clo. Iswth —7H 71
Thomas a' Beckett Clo. Wemb
　　　　　—4K 39
Thomas Baines Rd. SW11 —3B 92
Thomas Ct. E17 —5D 32
Thomas Doyle St. SE1
　　　　　—3B 78 (6K 147)
Thomas England Ho. Romf —6K 37
(off Waterloo Gdns.)
Thomas Hewlett Ho. Harr —4J 39
Thomas La. SE6 —7C 96
Thomas More Highwalk. EC2
(off Barbican)　—5C 62 (6L 141)
Thomas More Ho. EC2
(off Barbican)　—5C 62 (6L 141)
Thomas More Way. N2 —3A 28
Thomas Neals Shopping Mall. WC2
　　　　　—6J 61 (8C 140)
Thomas North Ter. E16 —5H 65
(off Barking Rd.)
Thomas Pl. W8 —3K 75
Thomas Rd. E14 —6B 64
Thomas Rd. Ind. Est. E14 —5C 64
Thomas St. SE18 —4E 83
Thomas Wall Clo. Sutt —5K 131
Thompson Av. Rich —3G 89
Thompson Clo. Ilf —2G 51
Thompson Rd. SE22 —6F 95
Thompson Rd. Dag —3F 53
Thompson's Av. SE5 —7C 78
Thomson Cres. Croy —1A 134
Thomson Ho. SW1 —5H 77
(off Bessborough Pl.)
Thomson Rd. Harr —3J 23
Thorburn Sq. SE1 —4G 79
Thorburn Way. SW19 —1B 122
Thoresby St. N1 —3C 62 (1M 141)
Thorkhill Gdns. Th Dit —7A 118
Thorkhill Rd. Th Dit —7A 118
Thornaby Gdns. N18 —6B 18
Thorn Av. Bush —1B 10
Thorn Bank. Edgw —6B 12
Thornbury. NW4 —4E 26
(off Prince Of Wales Clo.)
Thornbury Av. Iswth —7H 71
Thornbury Clo. N16 —5E 46
Thornbury Ct. Iswth —7J 71
Thornbury Rd. SW2 —6J 93
Thornbury Rd. Iswth —7H 71
Thornbury Sq. N6 —1G 45
Thornby Rd. E5 —3J 47
Thorncliffe Rd. SW2 —6J 93
Thorncliffe Rd. S'hall —5D 70
Thorn Clo. Brom —6E 128
Thorn Clo. N'holt —3D 54
Thorncombe Rd. SE22 —5E 94
Thorncroft St. SW8 —7J 77
Thorndean St. SW18 —2A 108
Thorndene. SE28 —7B 68
Thorndene Av. N11 —1K 15
Thorndike Av. N'holt —1B 54
Thorndike Clo. SW10 —7A 76
Thorndike Rd. N1 —6D 46
Thorndike St. SW1 —4H 77 (9A 146)
Thorndon Clo. Orp —2K 129
Thorndon Gdns. Eps —5A 130
Thorndon Rd. Orp —2K 129
Thorne Clo. E11 —4G 49
Thorne Clo. E16 —6J 65
Thorne Clo. Eri —6H 85
Thorne Pas. SW13 —2A 90
Thorne Rd. SW8 —7J 77
Thornes Clo. Beck —3E 126
Thorne St. SW13 —3A 90
Thornet Wood Rd. Brom —3E 128

Thorney Cres. SW11 —7B 76
Thorney Hedge Rd. W4 —4H 73
Thorney St. SW1 —4J 77 (8C 146)
Thornfield Av. NW7 —1G 27
Thornfield Ct. NW7 —1G 27
Thornfield Rd. W12 —2D 74
Thorngate Rd. W9 —4J 59
Thorngrove Rd. E13 —1K 65
Thornham Gro. E15 —5F 49
Thornham St. SE10 —6D 80
Thornhaugh M. WC1
　　　　　—4H 61 (4B 140)
Thornhaugh St. WC1
　　　　　—4H 61 (4B 140)
Thornhill Av. SE18 —7J 83
Thornhill Cres. N1 —7K 45
Thornhill Gdns. E10 —2D 48
Thornhill Gdns. Bark —7J 51
Thornhill Gro. N1 —7K 45
Thornhill Ho. N1 —7A 46
Thornhill Ho. W4 —5A 74
(off Wood St.)
Thornhill Point. E9 —7J 47
Thornhill Rd. E10 —2D 48
Thornhill Rd. N1 —7A 46
Thornhill Rd. Croy —7C 124
Thornhill Sq. N1 —7K 45
Thornicroft Ho. SW9 —2K 93
(off Stockwell Rd.)
Thornlaw Rd. SE27 —4A 110
Thornley Clo. N17 —7B 18
Thornley Dri. Harr —2F 39
Thornley Pl. SE10 —5G 81
Thornloe Gdns. Croy —5A 134
Thornsbeach Rd. SE6 —1E 112
Thornsett Pl. SE20 —2H 125
Thornsett Rd. SE20 —2H 125
Thornsett Rd. SW18 —1K 107
Thornsett Ter. SE20 —2H 125
(off Croydon Rd.)
Thornton Av. SW2 —1H 109
Thornton Av. W4 —4A 74
Thornton Av. Croy —6K 123
Thornton Dene. Beck —2C 126
Thornton Gdns. SW12 —1H 109
Thornton Hill. SW19 —7G 107
Thornton Pl. W1 —5D 60 (5F 138)
Thornton Rd. E11 —2F 49
Thornton Rd. N18 —4D 18
Thornton Rd. SW12 —7H 93
Thornton Rd. SW14 —4K 89
Thornton Rd. SW19 —6F 107
Thornton Rd. Barn —3B 4
Thornton Rd. Belv —4H 85
Thornton Rd. Brom —5J 113
Thornton Rd. Cars —1B 132
Thornton Rd. Croy & T Hith —7K 123
Thornton Rd. Ilf —4F 51
Thornton Rd. E. SW19 —6F 107
Thornton Row. T Hith —5A 124
Thorntons Farm Av. Romf —1J 53
Thornton St. SW9 —2A 94
Thornton Way. NW11 —5K 27
Thorntree Ct. W5 —5E 56
Thorntree Rd. SE7 —5B 82
Thornville St. SE8 —1C 96
Thornwood Clo. E18 —2K 33
Thornwood Rd. SE13 —5G 97
Thornycroft Ho. W4 —5A 74
(off Fraser St.)
Thorogood Gdns. E15 —5G 49
Thorogood Way. Rain —1K 69
Thorold Rd. N22 —7D 16
Thorold Rd. Ilf —2F 51
Thorparch Rd. SW8 —1H 93
Thorpebank Rd. W12 —1C 74
Thorpe Clo. W10 —6G 59

Thorpe Ct. Enf —3G 7
Thorpe Cres. E17 —2B 32
Thorpedale Gdns. Ilf —4E 34
Thorpedale Rd. N4 —2J 45
Thorpe Hall Rd. E17 —1E 32
Thorpe Ho. N1 —1K 61
(off Barnsbury Est.)
Thorpe Rd. E6 —1D 66
Thorpe Rd. E7 —4H 49
Thorpe Rd. E17 —2E 32
Thorpe Rd. N15 —6E 30
Thorpe Rd. Bark —7H 51
Thorpe Rd. King T —7E 104
Thorpewood Av. SE26 —2H 111
Thorsden Way. SE19 —5E 110
Thorverton Rd. NW2 —3G 43
Thoydon Rd. E3 —2A 64
Thrale Rd. SW16 —5G 109
Thrale St. SE1 —1C 78 (3M 147)
Thrasher Clo. E8 —1F 63
Thrawl St. E1 —5F 63 (6F 142)
Thrayle Ho. SW9 —3K 93
(off Benedict Rd.)
Threadgold Ho. N1 —6D 46
(off Dovercourt Est.)
Threadneedle St. EC2
　　　　　—6D 62 (8B 142)
Three Colts La. E2 —4H 63
Three Colt St. E14 —6B 64
Three Corners. Bexh —2H 101
Three Cranes Wlk. EC4
　　　　　—7C 62 (1M 147)
(off Bell Wharf La.)
Three Cups Yd. WC1
(off Sandland St.)　—5K 61 (6F 140)
Three Kings Yd. W1 —7F 61 (9J 139)
Three Mill La. E3 —3E 64
Three Oak La. SE1 —2F 79 (4E 148)
Three Quays. EC3 —7E 62 (1D 148)
(off Tower Hill)
Three Quays Wlk. EC3
　　　　　—7E 62 (1D 148)
Threshers Pl. W11 —7G 59
Thriftwood. SE26 —3J 111
Thring Ho. SW9 —2K 93
(off Stockwell Rd.)
Throckmorton Rd. E16 —6K 65
Throgmorton Av. EC2
　　　　　—6D 62 (7B 142)
Throgmorton St. EC2
　　　　　—6D 62 (7B 142)
Throwley Clo. SE2 —3C 84
Throwley Rd. Sutt —5K 131
Throwley Way. Sutt —4K 131
Thrupp Clo. Mitc —2F 123
Thrush Grn. Harr —4E 22
Thrush St. SE17 —5C 78
Thruxton Way. SE15 —7F 79
Thurbarn Rd. SE6 —5D 112
Thurland Rd. SE16 —3G 79
Thurlby Clo. Harr —6A 24
Thurlby Clo. Wfd G —5J 21
Thurlby Croft. NW4 —3E 26
(off Mulberry Clo.)
Thurlby Rd. SE27 —4A 110
Thurlby Rd. Wemb —6D 40
Thurleigh Av. SW12 —6E 92
Thurleigh Rd. SW12 —7D 92
Thurleston Av. Mord —5G 121
Thurlestone Av. N12 —6J 15
Thurlestone Av. Ilf —4K 51
Thurlestone Rd. SE27 —3A 110
Thurloe Clo. SW7 —4C 76 (8C 144)
Thurloe Clo. SW7 —4B 76 (8B 144)
Thurloe Pl. M. SW7 —4B 76 (8B 144)
(off Thurloe Pl.)
Thurloe Sq. SW7 —4C 76 (8B 144)
Thurloe St. SW7 —4B 76 (8B 144)

Thurlow Clo. E4 —6K 19
Thurlow Gdns. Wemb —5D 40
Thurlow Hill. SE21 —1C 110
Thurlow Pk. Rd. SE21 —2B 110
Thurlow Rd. NW3 —5B 44
Thurlow Rd. W7 —2A 72
Thurlow Rd. SE17 —5D 78
Thurlow Ter. NW5 —5E 44
Thurlow Wlk. SE17 —5E 78
Thurnby Ct. Twic —3J 103
Thursland Rd. Sidc —5E 116
Thursley Cres. New Ad —7F 137
Thursley Gdns. SW19 —2F 107
Thursley Ho. SW2 —7K 93
(off Holmewood Gdns.)
Thursley Rd. SE9 —3D 114
Thurso St. SW17 —4B 108
Thurston Rd. SE13 —2D 96
Thurston Rd. SW20 —7D 106
Thurston Rd. S'hall —6D 54
Thurston Rd. Ind. Est. SE13 —3D 96
Thurtle Rd. E2 —2F 63
Thwaite Clo. Eri —6J 85
Thyra Gro. N12 —6E 14
Tibbatts Rd. E3 —4D 64
Tibbenham Wlk. E13 —2H 65
Tibberton Sq. N1 —7C 46
Tibbet's Clo. SW19 —1F 107
Tibbet's Ride. SW15 —7F 91
Tiber Gdns. N1 —1J 61
Ticehurst Clo. Orp —7A 116
Ticehurst Rd. SE23 —2A 112
Tickford Clo. SE2 —2C 84
Tidal Basin Rd. E16 —7H 65
Tidenham Gdns. Croy —3E 134
Tideswell Rd. SW15 —4E 90
Tideswell Rd. Croy —3C 136
Tideway Clo. Rich —4B 104
Tideway Ind. Est. SW8 —6G 77
(off Tideway Wlk.)
Tideway Wlk. SW8 —6G 77
Tidey St. E3 —5C 64
Tidford Rd. Well —2K 99
Tidworth Rd. E3 —4C 64
Tiepigs La. W Wick & Brom
　　　　　—2G 137
Tierney Ct. Croy —2F 135
Tierney Rd. SW2 —1J 109
Tiger La. Brom —4K 127
Tiger Way. E5 —4H 47
Tilbrook Rd. SE3 —3A 98
Tilbury Clo. SE15 —7F 79
Tilbury Rd. E6 —2D 66
Tilbury Rd. E10 —7E 32
Tildesley Rd. SW15 —6E 90
Tilehurst Point. SE2 —2D 84
Tilehurst Rd. SW18 —1B 108
Tilehurst Rd. Sutt —5G 131
Tile Kiln La. N6 —1F 45
Tile Kiln La. N13 —5F 17
Tile Kiln La. Bex —2J 117
(in two parts)
Tile Kiln Studios. N6 —1G 45
Tile Yd. E14 —6B 64
Tileyard Rd. N7 —7J 45
Tilford Av. New Ad —7E 136
Tilford Gdns. SW19 —1F 107
Tilford Ho. SW2 —7K 93
(off Holmewood Gdns.)
Tilia Rd. E5 —4H 47
Tiller Rd. E14 —3C 80
Tillett Clo. NW10 —6J 41
Tillett Sq. SE16 —2A 80
Tillet Way. E2 —3G 63
Tillingbourne Gdns. N3 —3H 27
Tillingbourne Grn. Orp —4K 129
Tillingbourne Way. N3 —4H 27
Tillingham Way. N12 —4D 14

Tilling Rd. NW2 —1E **42**
Tilling Way. Wemb —3D **40**
Tillman St. E1 —6H **63**
Tilloch St. N1 —7K **45**
Tillotson Ct. SW8 —7H **77**
  (off Wandsworth Rd.)
Tillotson Rd. N9 —2A **18**
Tillotson Rd. Harr —7A **10**
Tillotson Rd. Ilf —7E **34**
Tilney Ct. EC1 —4C **62** (3M **141**)
Tilney Dri. Buck H —2D **20**
Tilney Gdns. N1 —6D **46**
Tilney Rd. Dag —6F **53**
Tilney Rd. S'hall —4A **70**
Tilney St. W1 —1E **76** (2H **145**)
Tilson Gdns. SW2 —7J **93**
Tilson Ho. SW2 —7J **93**
Tilson Rd. N17 —1G **31**
Tilston Clo. E11 —3H **49**
Tilton St. SW6 —6G **75**
Tiltwood, The. W3 —7J **57**
Tilt App. SE9 —6D **98**
Timber Clo. Chst —2E **128**
Timbercroft. Eps —4A **130**
Timbercroft La. SE18 —6J **83**
Timberdene. NW4 —2F **27**
Timberdene Av. Ilf —1F **35**
Timberland Rd. E1 —6H **63**
Timber Mill Way. SW4 —3H **93**
Timber Pond Rd. SE16 —1K **79**
Timberslip Dri. Wall —7H **133**
Timber St. EC1 —4C **62** (3L **141**)
Timberwharf Rd. N16 —6G **31**
Times Sq. Sutt —5K **131**
Timothy Clo. SW4 —5G **93**
Timothy Clo. Bexh —5E **100**
Timothy Ho. Eri —2E **84**
  (off Kale Rd.)
Timothy Rd. E3 —5B **64**
Timsbury Wlk. SW15 —1C **106**
Tindal St. SW9 —1B **94**
Tinderbox All. SW14 —3K **89**
Tinniswood Clo. N5 —5A **46**
Tinsley Rd. E1 —5J **63**
Tintagel Cres. SE22 —4F **95**
Tintagel Dri. Stan —4J **11**
Tintagel Gdns. SE22 —4F **95**
Tintern Av. NW9 —3H **25**
Tintern Clo. SW15 —5G **91**
Tintern Clo. SW19 —6A **108**
Tintern Gdns. N14 —7D **6**
Tintern Rd. N22 —1C **30**
Tintern Rd. Cars —1B **132**
Tintern St. SW4 —4J **93**
Tintern Way. Harr —1F **39**
Tinto Rd. E16 —4J **65**
Tinworth St. SE11 —5K **77**
Tippett Ct. E6 —2D **66**
Tippetts Clo. Enf —1H **7**
Tipthorpe Rd. SW11 —3E **92**
Tipton Dri. Croy —4E **134**
Tiptree Clo. E4 —3K **19**
Tiptree Cres. Ilf —3E **34**
Tiptree Dri. Enf —4J **7**
Tiptree Rd. Ruis —4A **38**
Tiree Clo. Rich —1D **104**
Tirlemont Rd. S Croy —7C **134**
Tirrell Rd. Croy —6C **124**
Tisbury Ct. W1 —7H **61** (9A **140**)
  (off Wardour St.)
Tisdall Pl. SE17 —4D **78** (9B **148**)
Titan Av. Bush —1D **10**
Titchborne Row. W2
       —6C **60** (8C **138**)
Titchfield Rd. NW8 —2D **60**
Titchfield Rd. Cars —1B **132**
Titchfield Wlk. Cars —7B **122**

Titchwell Rd. SW18 —1B **108**
Tite St. SW3 —5D **76**
Tithe Barn Clo. King T —1F **119**
Tithe Barn Way. N'holt —2A **54**
Tithe Clo. NW7 —1C **26**
Tithe Farm Av. Harr —3E **38**
Tithe Farm Clo. Harr —3E **38**
Tithe Wlk. NW7 —1C **26**
Titley Clo. E4 —5H **19**
Titmuss Av. SE28 —7B **68**
Titmuss St. W12 —2D **74**
Tivendale. N8 —3J **29**
Tiverton Av. Ilf —3E **34**
Tiverton Dri. SE9 —1G **115**
Tiverton Rd. N15 —6D **30**
Tiverton Rd. N18 —5K **17**
Tiverton Rd. NW10 —1F **59**
Tiverton Rd. Edgw —2F **25**
Tiverton Rd. Houn —2G **87**
Tiverton Rd. T Hth —5A **124**
Tiverton Rd. Wemb —2E **56**
Tiverton St. SE1 —3C **78** (7L **147**)
Tivoli Gdns. SE16 —1B **80**
Tivoli Gdns. SE18 —4C **82**
Tivoli Rd. N8 —5H **29**
Tivoli Rd. SE27 —5C **110**
Tivoli Rd. Houn —4C **86**
Tobacco Dock. E1 —7H **63**
Tobacco Quay. E1 —7H **63**
Tobago St. E14 —2C **80**
Tobin Clo. NW3 —7C **44**
Toby Ct. N9 —7D **8**
  (off Tramway Av.)
Toby La. E1 —4A **64**
Todd Ho. N2 —2B **28**
  (off Grange, The)
Todds Wlk. N7 —2K **45**
Tokenhouse Yd. EC2
       —6D **62** (7A **142**)
Token Yd. SW15 —4G **91**
Tokyngton Av. Wemb —6G **41**
Toland Sq. SW15 —5C **90**
Tolcarne Dri. Pinn —3A **22**
Toley Av. Wemb —7F **24**
Tolhurst Sq. SE4 —3A **96**
Toll Bar Ct. Sutt —7K **131**
Tollbridge Clo. W10 —4G **59**
Tollesbury Gdns. Ilf —3H **35**
Tollet St. E1 —4K **63**
Tollgate Dri. SE21 —2E **110**
Tollgate Gdns. NW6 —2K **59**
Tollgate Rd. E16 & E6 —5A **66**
Tollgate Sq. E6 —6D **66**
Tollhouse Way. N19 —2G **45**
Tollington Pk. N4 —2K **45**
Tollington Pl. N4 —2K **45**
Tollington Rd. N7 —4K **45**
Tollington Way. N7 —3J **45**
Tolmers Sq. NW1 —4G **61** (3L **139**)
Tolpaide Ho. SE11 —5A **78**
  (off Marylee Way)
Tolpuddle St. N1 —2A **62**
Tolsford Rd. E5 —5H **47**
Tolson Rd. Iswth —3A **88**
Tolverne Rd. SW20 —1E **120**
Tolworth Gdns. Romf —5D **36**
Tolworth Pde. Chad —5E **36**
Tolworth Rise N. Surb —7H **119**
Tolworth Rise S. Surb —7H **119**
Tomahawk Gdns. N'holt —3B **54**
Tom Coombs Clo. SE9 —4C **98**
Tom Cribb Rd. SE28 —3G **83**
Tom Hood Clo. E15 —5F **49**
Tomkyns Ho. SE11 —4A **78** (9G **147**)
  (off Distin St.)
Tomlins All. Twic —1A **104**
Tomlin's Gro. E3 —3C **64**
Tomlinson Clo. E2 —3F **63**

Tomlinson Clo. W4 —5H **73**
Tomlins Orchard. Bark —1G **67**
Tomlins Ter. E14 —6A **64**
Tomlins Wlk. N7 —2K **45**
Tom Mann Clo. Bark —1J **67**
Tom Nolan Clo. E15 —2G **65**
Tom Oakman Cen. E4 —3A **20**
Tompion St. EC1 —3B **62**
Tompton St. EC1 —3B **62** (2K **141**)
Tom Smith Clo. SE10 —6G **81**
Tomswood Ct. Ilf —1G **35**
Tomswood Hill. Ilf —6K **21**
Tomswood Rd. Chig —6K **21**
Tonbridge Cres. Harr —4E **24**
Tonbridge Rd. WC1 —3J **61** (1C **140**)
Tonbridge Wlk. WC1 —3J **61** (1C **140**)
  (off Tonbridge St.)
Tonfield Rd. Sutt —1H **131**
Tonge Clo. Beck —5C **126**
Tonge Vs. Beck —5C **126**
Tonsley Hill. SW18 —5K **91**
Tonsley Pl. SW18 —5K **91**
Tonsley Rd. SW18 —5K **91**
Tonsley St. SW18 —5K **91**
Tonstall Rd. Mitc —2E **122**
Tons Way. SW11 —3A **92**
Tony Cannell M. E3 —3B **64**
Tony Law Ho. SE20 —1H **125**
Tooke Clo. Pinn —1C **22**
Took's Ct. EC4 —6A **62** (7G **141**)
Tooley St. SE1 —1D **78** (2B **148**)
Toorack Rd. Harr —2H **23**
Tooting Bec Gdns. SW16 —4H **109**
  (in two parts)
Tooting Bec Rd. SW17 & SW16
       —3E **108**
Tooting B'way. SW17 —5C **108**
Tooting Gro. SW17 —5C **108**
Tooting High St. SW17 —5C **108**
Tootswood Rd. Brom —5G **127**
Topham Sq. N17 —1C **30**
Topham St. EC1 —4A **62** (3G **141**)
Top Ho. Rise. E4 —7K **9**
Topiary Sq. Rich —3F **89**
Topley St. SE9 —4A **98**
Topmast Point. E14 —2C **80**
Top Pk. Beck —5G **127**
Topp Wlk. NW2 —2E **42**
Topsfield Clo. SW8 —5H **29**
Topsfield Pde. N8 —5J **29**
Topsfield Rd. N8 —5J **29**
Topsham Rd. SW17 —3D **108**
Torbay Rd. NW6 —7H **43**
Torbay Rd. Harr —2C **38**
Torbay St. NW1 —7F **45**
Torbitt Way. Ilf —5K **35**
Torbridge Clo. Edgw —7K **11**
Torbrook Clo. Bex —6E **100**
Torcross Dri. SE23 —2J **111**
Torcross Rd. Ruis —3A **38**
Tor Gdns. W8 —2J **75**
Tor Ho. N6 —6F **29**
Tormead Clo. Sutt —6J **131**
Tormount Rd. SE18 —6J **83**
Torney Ho. E9 —7J **47**
Toronto Av. E12 —4D **50**
Toronto Rd. E11 —4F **49**
Toronto Rd. Ilf —1F **51**
Torquay Gdns. Ilf —4B **34**
Torquay St. W2 —5K **59**
Torrens Ct. SE5 —3D **94**
Torrens Rd. E15 —6H **49**
Torrens Rd. SW2 —5K **93**
Torrens Sq. E15 —6H **49**
Torrens St. EC1 —2A **62**
Torre Wlk. Cars —1C **132**

Torriano Av. NW5 —5H **45**
Torriano Cotts. NW5 —5H **45**
Torriano M. NW5 —5G **45**
Torridge Gdns. SE15 —4J **95**
Torridge Rd. T Hth —5B **124**
Torridon Rd. SE6 & SE13 —7F **97**
Torrington Av. N12 —5G **15**
Torrington Clo. N12 —4G **15**
Torrington Clo. SE10 —6G **81**
Torrington Dri. Harr —3F **39**
Torrington Gdns. N11 —6C **16**
Torrington Gdns. Grnfd —1C **56**
Torrington Gro. N12 —5H **15**
Torrington Pk. N12 —5F **15**
Torrington Pl. E1 —1G **79**
Torrington Pl. WC1 —5H **61** (5A **140**)
Torrington Rd. E18 —3J **33**
Torrington Rd. Dag —1F **53**
Torrington Rd. Grnfd —1C **56**
Torrington Sq. WC1
       —4H **61** (4B **140**)
Torrington Sq. Croy —7D **124**
Torrington Way. Mord —6J **121**
Tor Rd. Well —1C **100**
Torr Rd. SE20 —7K **111**
Torver Rd. Harr —4J **23**
Torwood Rd. SW15 —5C **90**
Tothill St. SW1 —2H **77** (5A **146**)
Totnes Rd. Well —7B **84**
Totnes Wlk. N2 —4B **28**
Tottenhall Rd. N13 —6F **17**
Tottenham Ct. Rd. W1
       —4G **61** (4M **139**)
Tottenham Grn. E. N15 —4F **31**
Tottenham Hale Retail Pk. N17
       —4G **31**
Tottenham La. N8 —6J **29**
Tottenham M. W1 —5G **61** (5M **139**)
Tottenham Rd. N1 —6E **46**
Tottenham St. W1 —5G **61** (6M **139**)
Totterdown St. SW17 —4D **108**
Totteridge Comn. N20 —2H **13**
Totteridge Grn. N20 —2D **14**
Totteridge La. N20 —2D **14**
Totteridge Village. N20 —1B **14**
Totternhoe Clo. Harr —5C **24**
Totton Rd. T Hth —3A **124**
Toulmin St. SE1 —2C **78** (5L **147**)
Toulon St. SE5 —7C **78**
Tournay Rd. SW6 —7H **75**
Toussaint Wlk. SE16 —3G **79**
Tovil Clo. SE20 —2H **125**
Towcester Rd. E3 —4D **64**
Tower Bri. SE1 & E1
       —1F **79** (3E **148**)
Tower Bri. App. E1 —7F **63** (2E **148**)
Tower Bri. Rd. SE1 —3E **78**
Tower Bri. Sq. SE1 —2F **79** (4E **148**)
  (off Queen Elizabeth St.)
Tower Bri. Wharf. E1 —1G **79**
Tower Bldgs. E1 —1H **79**
Tower Clo. NW3 —5B **44**
Tower Clo. SE20 —7H **111**
Tower Ct. E5 —7F **31**
Tower Ct. WC2 —6J **61** (8C **140**)
  (off Tower St.)
Tower Gdns. Rd. N17 —1C **30**
Tower Hamlets Rd. E7 —4H **49**
Tower Hamlets Rd. E17 —3C **32**
Tower Hill. EC3 —7E **62** (1D **148**)
Tower Hill Ter. EC3 —7E **62** (1D **148**)
Tower La. Wemb —3D **40**
Tower M. E17 —4C **32**
Tower Pl. EC3 —7E **62** (1D **148**)
  (off Lwr. Thames St.)
Tower Rise. Rich —3E **88**
Tower Rd. NW10 —7C **42**
Tower Rd. Belv —4J **85**
Tower Rd. Bexh —4G **101**

Tower Rd. Twic —3K **103**
Tower Royal. EC4 —7D **62** (9A **142**)
Towers Bus. Pk. Wemb —4H **41**
  (off Carey Way)
Towers Pl. Rich —5E **88**
Towers Rd. Pinn —1C **22**
Towers Rd. S'hall —4E **54**
Tower St. WC2 —6J **61** (88 **140**)
Tower Ter. N22 —2K **29**
Tower View. Croy —7A **126**
Tower Yd. Rich —5F **89**
Towfield Ct. Felt —2D **102**
Towfield Rd. Felt —2D **102**
Towgar Ct. N20 —7F **5**
Towncourt Cres. Orp —5G **129**
Towncourt La. Orp —6H **129**
Towncourt Path. N4 —1C **46**
Towney Mead. N'holt —2D **54**
Towney Mead Ct. N'holt —2D **54**
Town Hall App. N16 —4D **46**
  (off Albion Rd.)
Town Hall App. Rd. N15 —4F **31**
Town Hall Av. W4 —5K **73**
Town Hall Rd. SW11 —3D **92**
Townholm Cres. W7 —3K **71**
Townley Ct. E15 —6H **49**
Townley Rd. SE22 —5E **94**
Townley Rd. Bexh —5F **101**
Townley St. SE17 —5D **78**
  (in two parts)
Town Mead Bus. Cen. SW6 —3A **92**
Town Meadow. Bren —6D **72**
Town Meadow Rd. Bren —7D **72**
Townmead Rd. SW6 —3K **91**
Townmead Rd. Rich —2H **89**
Town Quay. Bark —1F **67**
Town Rd. N9 —2C **18**
Townsend. Sidc —6B **116**
Townsend Av. N14 —4C **16**
Townsend Ind. Est. NW10 —2J **57**
Townsend La. NW9 —7K **25**
Townsend Rd. N15 —5F **31**
Townsend Rd. S'hall —1C **70**
Townsend St. SE17 —4E **78**, **78** (9B **148**)
Townsend Yd. N6 —1F **45**
Townshend Clo. Sidc —6B **116**
Townshend Est. NW8 —2C **60**
Townshend Rd. NW8 —1C **60**
Townshend Rd. Chst —5F **115**
Townshend Rd. Rich —4F **89**
Townshend Ter. Rich —4F **89**
Town Sq. Iswth —3B **88**
  (off Swan St.)
Town, The. Enf —3J **7**
Town Wharf. Iswth —3B **88**
Towpath, The. SW10 —1B **92**
Towpath Way. Croy —6F **125**
Towton Rd. SE27 —2C **110**
Toynbec Clo. Chst —4F **115**
Toynbee Rd. SW20 —1G **121**
Toynbee St. E1 —5J **63** (6E **142**)
Toyne Way. N6 —6D **28**
Tracey Av. NW2 —5E **42**
Tracey St. SE11 —5A **78**
Tracy Ct. Stan —7H **11**
Trade Clo. N13 —4F **17**
Tradescant Rd. SW8 —7J **77**
Tradewinds Ct. E1 —7G **63**
Trading Est. Rd. NW10 —4J **57**
Trafalgar Av. N17 —6K **17**
Trafalgar Av. SE15 —5F **79**
Trafalgar Av. Wor Pk —1F **131**
Trafalgar Clo. SE16 —4A **80**
Trafalgar Gdns. E1 —5K **63**
Trafalgar Gro. SE10 —6F **81**
Trafalgar Pl. E11 —4J **33**
Trafalgar Pl. N18 —5B **18**
Trafalgar Rd. SE10 —6F **81**

Trafalgar Rd. SW19 —7K 107
Trafalgar Rd. Twic —2H 103
Trafalgar Sq. WC2 —1H 77 (2B 146)
Trafalgar St. SE17 —5D 78
Trafalgar Ter. Harr —1J 39
Trafalgar Trading Est. Enf —4F 9
Trafalgar Way. E14 —1E 80
Trafalgar Way. Croy —2A 134
Trafford Clo. E15 —5D 48
Trafford Ho. N1 —2D 62
(off Cranston Est.)
Trafford Rd. T Hth —5K 123
Tramway Av. E15 —7F 49
Tramway Av. N9 —7C 8
Tramway Path, Mitc —4C 122
(in two parts)
Tranley M. NW3 —4C 44
Tranmere Rd. N9 —7A 8
Tranmere Rd. SW18 —2A 108
Tranmere Rd. Twic —7F 87
Tranquil Pas. SE3 —2H 97
Tranquil Vale. SE3 —2G 97
Transay Wlk. N1 —6D 46
Transept St. NW1 —5C 60 (6D 138)
Transmere Clo. Orp —6G 129
Transmere Rd. Orp —6G 129
Transom Sq. E14 —5D 80
Transport Av. Bren —5A 72
Tranton Rd. SE16 —3G 79
Traps La. N Mald —1A 120
Trash Pl. N11 —5A 16
Travellers Way. Houn —2A 86
Travers Clo. E17 —1K 31
Travers Rd. N7 —3A 46
Travis Ho. SE10 —1E 96
Treacy Clo. Bush —2B 10
Treadgold St. W11 —7F 59
Treadway St. E2 —2H 63
Treasury Pas. SW1 —2J 77 (4C 146)
(off Downing St.)
Treaty Cen. Houn —3F 87
Treaty St. N1 —1K 61
Trebeck St. W1 —1F 77 (2J 145)
Trebovir Rd..SW5 —5J 75
Treby St. E3 —4B 64
Trecastle Way. N7 —4H 45
Tredegar M. E3 —3B 64
Tredegar Rd. E3 —2B 64
Tredegar Rd. N11 —7C 16
Tredegar Sq. E3 —3B 64
Tredegar Ter. E3 —3B 64
Trederwen Rd. E8 —1G 63
Tredown Rd. SE26 —5J 111
Tredwell Clo. Brom —4C 128
Tredwell Clo. SE27 —4B 110
Tree Clo. Rich —1D 104
Treen Av. SW13 —3B 90
Tree Rd. E16 —6A 66
Treetops Clo. SE2 —5E 84
Treeview Clo. SE19 —1E 124
Treewall Gdns. Brom —4K 113
Trefgarne Rd. Dag —2G 53
Trefil Wlk. N7 —4J 45
Trefoil Ho. Eri —2E 84
(off Kale Rd.)
Trefoil Rd. SW18 —5A 92
Trefusis Ct. Houn —1A 86
Tregaron Av. N8 —6J 29
Tregaron Gdns. N Mald —4A 120
Tregarvon Rd. SW11 —4E 92
Tregenna Av. Harr —4E 38
Tregenna Clo. N14 —5B 6
Tregenna Ct. S Harr —4E 38
Trego Rd. E9 —7C 48
Tregothnan Rd. SW9 —3J 93
Tregunter Rd. SW10 —6A 76
Trehearn Rd. Ilf —1H 35
Treherne Ct. SW9 —1B 94

Treherne Ct. SW17 —4E 108
Trehern Rd. SW14 —3K 89
Trehurst St. E5 —5A 48
Trelawney Est. E9 —6J 47
Trelawney Rd. Ilf —1H 35
Trelawn Rd. E10 —3E 48
Trelawn Rd. SW2 —5K 93
Trellis Sq. E3 —3B 64
Treloar Gdns. SE19 —6D 110
Tremadoc Rd. SW4 —4H 93
Tremaine Clo. SE4 —2C 96
Tremaine Rd. SE20 —2H 125
Trematon Ho. SE11 —5A 78
(off Kennings Way)
Trematon Pl. Tedd —7C 104
Tremlett Gro. N19 —3G 45
Tremlett M. N19 —3G 45
Trenance Gdns. Ilf —3A 52
Trenchard Clo. Stan —6F 11
Trenchard Ct. NW4 —5C 26
Trenchard Ct. SE10 —5F 81
Trenchold St. SW8 —6J 77
Trenholme Clo. SE20 —7H 111
Trenholme Rd. SE20 —7H 111
Trenholme Ter. SE20 —7H 111
Trenmar Gdns. NW10 —3D 58
Trent Av. W5 —3C 72
Trent Gdns. N14 —6A 6
Trentham St. SW18 —1J 107
Trent Ho. SE15 —4J 95
Trent Rd. SW2 —5K 93
Trent Rd. Buck H —1E 20
Trent Way. Wor Pk —3E 130
Trentwood Side. Enf —3E 6
Treport St. SW18 —7K 91
Tresco Clo. Brom —6G 113
Trescoe Gdns. Harr —7C 22
Tresco Gdns. Ilf —2A 52
Tresco Rd. SE15 —4H 95
Tresham Cres. NW8
                          —4C 60 (3C 138)
Tresham Rd. Bark —7K 51
Tresham Wlk. E9 —5J 47
Tressell Clo. N1 —7B 46
Tressider Ho. SW4 —7H 93
Tressillian Cres. SE4 —3C 96
Tressillian Rd. SE4 —4B 96
Trestis Clo. Hay —4B 54
Treswell Rd. Dag —1E 68
Tretawn Gdns. NW7 —4F 13
Tretawn Pk. NW7 —4F 13
Trevanion Rd. W14 —5G 75
Treve Av. Harr —7G 23
Trevelyan Av. E12 —4D 50
Trevelyan Cres. Harr —7D 24
Trevelyan Gdns. NW10 —1E 58
Trevelyan Rd. E15 —4H 49
Trevelyan Rd. SW17 —5C 108
Trevera Ct. Enf —5F 9
Treveris St. SE1 —1B 78 (3K 147)
Treverton St. W10 —5F 59
Treville St. SW15 —7D 90
Treviso Rd. SE23 —2K 111
Trevithick St. SE8 —6C 80
Trevone Ct. SW2 —7J 93
(off Doverfield Rd.)
Trevone Gdns. Pinn —6C 22
Trevor Clo. Barn —6G 5
Trevor Clo. Brom —7H 127
Trevor Clo. Harr —7E 10
Trevor Clo. Iswth —5K 87
Trevor Clo. N'holt —2A 54
Trevor Gdns. Edgw —1K 25
Trevor Gdns. N'holt —2A 54
Trevor Pl. SW7 —2C 76 (5D 144)
Trevor Rd. SW19 —7G 107
Trevor Rd. Edgw —1K 25

Trevor Rd. Wfd G —7D 20
Trevor Sq. SW7 —2D 76 (6D 144)
Trevor Sq. SW7 —2C 76 (5D 144)
Trevose Ho. SE11 —5K 77
(off Orsett St.)
Trevose Rd. E17 —1F 33
Trewince Rd. SW20 —1E 120
Trewint St. SW18 —2A 108
Trewsbury Ho. SE2 —1D 84
Trewsbury Rd. SE26 —5K 111
Triandra Way. Hay —5B 54
Triangle Ct. E16 —5B 66
Triangle Pas. New Bar —4F 5
Triangle Pl. SW4 —4H 93
Triangle Rd. E8 —1H 63
Triangle, The. EC1 —4B 62 (3K 141)
Triangle, The. N13 —4F 17
Triangle, The. Bark —6G 51
Triangle, The. King T —2J 119
Trickett Ho. Sutt —7K 131
Trident Bus. Cen. N'holt —3B 54
Trident St. SE16 —4K 79
Trident Way. S'hall —3A 70
Trig La. EC4 —7C 62 (9L 141)
Trigon Rd. SW8 —7K 77
Trilby Rd. SE23 —2K 111
Trillo Ct. Ilf —7J 35
Trimmer Wlk. Bren —6E 72
Trinder Gdns. N19 —1J 45
Trinder Rd. N19 —1J 45
Trinder Rd. Barn —5A 4
Tring Av. W5 —1F 73
Tring Av. S'hall —6D 54
Tring Av. Wemb —6G 41
Tring Clo. Ilf —5H 35
Tring Ct. Twic —4A 104
Trinidad Gdns. Dag —7K 53
Trinidad St. E14 —7B 64
Trinity Av. N2 —3B 28
Trinity Av. Enf —6A 8
Trinity Bus. Cen. SE16 —2B 80
Trinity Bus. Pk. E4 —6G 19
Trinity Chu. Pas. EC4
          (off Fetter La.)   —6A 62 (7H 141)
Trinity Chu. Pas. SW13 —6D 74
Trinity Chu. Rd. SW13 —6D 74
Trinity Chu. Sq. SE1
                          —3C 78 (5M 147)
Trinity Clo. E11 —2G 49
Trinity Clo. NW3 —4B 44
Trinity Clo. SE13 —4F 97
Trinity Clo. SW4 —4G 93
Trinity Clo. Houn —4C 86
Trinity Clo. S Croy —7E 134
Trinity Cotts. Rich —3F 89
Trinity Ct. N1 —1E 62
Trinity Ct. SE7 —4B 82
Trinity Ct. SE25 —6E 124
Trinity Ct. Croy —2C 134
Trinity Cres. SW17 —2D 108
Trinity Gdns. E16 —5H 65
Trinity Gdns. SW9 —4K 93
Trinity Gro. SE10 —1E 96
Trinity M. SE20 —1H 125
Trinity M. W10 —6F 59
Trinity Path. SE26 —3J 111
(in two parts)
Trinity Pier. E14 —7G 65
Trinity Pl. EC3 —7F 63 (1E 148)
Trinity Pl. Bexh —4F 101
Trinity Rise. SW2 —1A 110
Trinity Rd. N2 —3B 28
Trinity Rd. N22 —7D 16
Trinity Rd. SW18 & SW17 —4A 92
Trinity Rd. SW19 —6J 107
Trinity Rd. Ilf —3G 35
Trinity Rd. Rich —3F 89

Trinity Rd. S'hall —1C 70
Trinity Sq. EC3 —7E 62 (1D 148)
Trinity St. E16 —5H 65
Trinity St. SE1 —2C 78 (5M 147)
Trinity St. Enf —2H 7
Trinity Wlk. NW3 —6A 44
Trinity Way. E4 —6G 19
Trinity Way. W3 —7A 58
Trio Pl. SE1 —2C 78 (5M 147)
Tristan Sq. SE3 —3G 97
Tristram Clo. E17 —3F 33
Tristram Rd. Brom —4H 113
Triton Sq. NW1 —4G 61 (3L 139)
Tritton Av. Croy —4J 133
Tritton Rd. SE21 —3D 110
Triumph Ho. Bark —3A 68
Triumph Rd. E6 —6D 66
Trojan Way. Croy —3K 133
Troon St. E1 —6A 64
Trosley Rd. Belv —6G 85
Trossachs Rd. SE22 —5E 94
Trothy Rd. SE1 —4G 79
Trott Rd. N10 —7J 15
Trotts St. SW11 —1C 92
Troughton Rd. SE7 —5K 81
Troutbeck Ho. NW1 —3F 61 (2K 139)
(off Albany St.)
Troutbeck Rd. SE14 —1A 96
Trouville Rd. SW4 —6G 93
Trowbridge Rd. E9 —6B 48
Trowlock Av. Tedd —6C 104
Trowlock Way. Tedd —6D 104
Troy Ct. SE18 —4F 83
Troy Rd. SE19 —6D 110
Troy St. SE18 —4F 83
Troy Town. SE15 —3G 95
Truesdale Rd. E6 —6D 66
Trulock Ct. N17 —7B 18
Trulock Rd. N17 —7B 18
Truman Clo. Edgw —7D 12
Trumans Rd. N16 —5F 47
Trumble Gdns. T Hth —4B 124
Trumpers Way. W7 —3J 71
Trumpington Rd. E7 —4H 49
Trump St. EC2 —6C 62 (8M 141)
Trundleys Way. Bush —1D 10
Trundle St. SE1 —2C 78 (4L 147)
(off Weller St.)
Trundleys M. SE8 —5K 79
Trundley's Rd. SE8 —5K 79
Trundley's Ter. SE8 —4K 79
Truro Gdns. Ilf —7C 34
Truro Ho. Pinn —1D 22
Truro Rd. E17 —4B 32
Truro Rd. N22 —7D 16
Truro St. NW5 —6E 44
Truslove Rd. SE27 —5A 110
Trussley Rd. W6 —3E 74
Trust Wlk. SE21 —1B 110
Tryfan Clo. Ilf —5B 34
Tryon St. SW3 —5D 76
Tryon St. SW3 —5D 76
Tuam Rd. SE18 —6H 83
Tubbs Rd. NW10 —2B 58
Tucklow Wlk. SW15 —7B 90
Tudor Av. Hamp —7E 102
Tudor Av. Wor Pk —3D 130
Tudor Clo. N6 —7G 29
Tudor Clo. NW3 —5C 44
Tudor Clo. NW7 —6H 13
Tudor Clo. NW9 —2J 41
Tudor Clo. SW2 —6K 93
Tudor Clo. Chig —4K 21
Tudor Clo. Chst —1D 128
Tudor Clo. Sutt —5F 131
Tudor Clo. Wall —7G 133
Tudor Clo. Wfd G —5E 20
Tudor Ct. E17 —7B 32

Tudor Ct. N1 —6E 46
Tudor Ct. N22 —7D 16
Tudor Ct. W3 —2G 73
Tudor Ct. Felt —4A 102
Tudor Ct. Sidc —3A 116
Tudor Ct. Tedd —6K 103
Tudor Ct. N. Wemb —5G 41
Tudor Ct. S. Wemb —5G 41
Tudor Cres. Enf —1H 7
Tudor Dri. King T —5D 104
Tudor Dri. Mord —6F 121
Tudor Enterprise Pk. Harr —3H 23
Tudor Est. NW10 —2H 57
Tudor Gdns. NW9 —2J 41
Tudor Gdns. SW13 —3A 90
Tudor Gdns. W3 —5G 57
Tudor Gdns. Harr —2H 23
Tudor Gdns. Twic —1H 103
Tudor Gdns. W Wick —3E 136
Tudor Gro. E9 —7J 47
Tudor Ho. Pinn —2A 22
(off Pinner Hill Rd.)
Tudor Pde. Romf —7D 36
Tudor Pl. Mitc —7C 108
Tudor Rd. E4 —6J 19
Tudor Rd. E6 —1A 66
Tudor Rd. E9 —1H 63
Tudor Rd. N9 —7C 8
Tudor Rd. SE19 —7F 111
Tudor Rd. SE25 —5H 125
Tudor Rd. Bark —1K 67
Tudor Rd. Barn —3D 4
Tudor Rd. Beck —3E 126
Tudor Rd. Hamp —7E 102
Tudor Rd. Harr —2H 23
Tudor Rd. Houn —4H 87
Tudor Rd. King T —7G 105
Tudor Rd. Pinn —2A 22
Tudor Rd. S'hall —7C 54
Tudor Stacks. SE24 —4C 94
Tudor St. EC4 —7A 62 (9H 141)
Tudor Wlk. Bex —6E 100
Tudor Way. N14 —1C 16
Tudor Way. W3 —2G 73
Tudor Way. Orp —6H 129
Tudor Well Clo. Stan —5G 11
Tudway Rd. SE3 —3K 97
Tufnell Pk. Rd. N19 & N7 —4G 45
Tufton Rd. E4 —4H 19
Tufton St. SW1 —3J 77 (6C 146)
Tugela Rd. Croy —6D 124
Tugela St. SE6 —2B 112
Tulip Clo. Croy —1K 135
Tulip Clo. Hamp —6D 102
Tulip Dri. Ilf —5F 51
Tulip Gdns. E4 —3A 20
Tulse Clo. Beck —3E 126
Tulse Hill. SW2 —6A 94
Tulse Hill Est. SW2 —6A 94
Tulse Ho. SW2 —6A 94
Tulsemere Rd. SE27 —2C 110
Tummons Gdns. SE25 —2E 124
Tuncombe Rd. N18 —4K 17
Tunis Rd. W12 —1E 74
Tunley Grn. E14 —5B 64
Tunley Rd. NW10 —1A 58
Tunley Rd. SW17 —1E 108
Tunmarsh La. E13 —3A 66
Tunnanleys. E6 —6E 66
Tunnel App. E14 —7A 64
Tunnel App. SE10 —3G 81
Tunnel App. SE16 —2J 79
Tunnel Av. SE10 —2F 81
(in two parts)
Tunnel Gdns. N11 —7B 16
Tunnel Rd. SE16 —2J 79
Tunstall Rd. SW9 —4K 93
Tunstall Rd. Croy —1E 134

Tunstall Wlk. Bren —6E 72
Tunstock Way. Belv —4F 85
Tunworth Clo. NW9 —6J 25
Tunworth Cres. SW15 —6B 90
Turchapel M. SW4 —3F 93
Turenne Clo. SW18 —4A 92
Turin Rd. N9 —7D 8
Turin St. E2 —3G 63
Turkey Oak Clo. SE19 —1E 124
Turk's Head Yd. EC1
—5B 62 (5J 141)
Turks Row. SW3 —5D 76
Turle Rd. N4 —2K 45
Turle Rd. SW16 —2J 123
Turlewray Clo. N4 —1K 45
Turley Clo. E15 —1G 65
Turnagain La. EC4 —6B 62 (7J 141)
(off Farringdon St.)
Turnage Rd. Dag —1E 52
Turnberry Quay. E14 —3D 80
Turnberry Way. Orp —7H 129
Turner Av. N15 —4E 30
Turner Av. Mitc —1D 122
Turner Av. Twic —3G 103
Turner Clo. NW11 —6K 27
Turner Dri. NW11 —6K 27
Turner Rd. E17 —3E 32
Turner Rd. Edgw —2E 24
Turner Rd. N Mald —7K 119
Turner's All. EC3 —7E 62 (9C 142)
Turners Meadow Way. Beck
—1B 126
Turners Rd. E14 & E3 —5B 64
Turners Rd. N1 —2E 62
Turner St. E1 —5H 63
Turner St. E16 —6H 65
Turner's Way. Croy —2A 134
Turners Wood. NW11 —1A 44
Turneville Rd. W14 —6H 75
Turney Rd. SE21 —7C 94
Turnham Grn. Ter. W4 —4A 74
Turnham Grn. Ter. M. W4 —4A 74
Turnham Rd. SE4 —5A 96
Turnmill St. EC1 —4B 62 (4J 141)
Turnpike Clo. SE8 —7B 80
Turnpike Ct. Bexh —4D 100
Turnpike La. N8 —4K 29
Turnpike La. Sutt —5A 132
Turnpike Link. Croy —2E 134
Turnpike Pde. N15 —3B 30
(off Green Lanes)
Turnpin La. SE10 —6E 80
Turnstone Clo. E13 —3J 65
Turnstone Clo. NW9 —2A 26
Turnstone Ct. SE8 —6B 80
Turpentine La. SW1 —5F 77
Turpin Av. Romf —1G 37
Turpington Clo. Brom —6C 128
Turpington La. Brom —7C 128
Turpin's La. Wfd G —5J 21
Turpin Way. N19 —2H 45
Turpin Way. Wall —7F 133
Turquand St. SE17 —4C 78 (9M 147)
Turret Gro. SW4 —3G 93
Turtle Rd. SW16 —2J 123
Turton Rd. Wemb —5E 40
Turville St. E2 —4F 63 (3F 142)
Tuscan Rd. SE18 —5H 83
Tuskar St. SE10 —6G 81
Tustin Est. SE15 —6J 79
Tutshill Ct. SE15 —7E 78
(off Lynbrook Clo.)
Tuttlebee La. Buck H —2D 20
Tweedale Ct. E15 —5E 48
Tweeddale Rd. Cars —1B 132
Tweed Grn. Romf —1K 37
Tweedmouth Rd. E13 —2K 65

Tweed Way. Romf —1K 37
Tweedy Rd. Brom —1J 127
Tweezer's All. WC2 —7A 62 (9G 141)
(off Milford La.)
Twelvetrees Cres. E3 —4E 64
Twentyman Clo. Wfd G —5D 20
Twickenham Bri. Twic & Rich
—5C 88
Twickenham Clo. Croy —3K 133
Twickenham Gdns. Gnfd —5A 40
Twickenham Gdns. Harr —7D 10
Twickenham Rd. E11 —2F 49
Twickenham Rd. Felt —3D 102
Twickenham Rd. Iswth —5A 88
Twickenham Rd. Rich —4C 88
Twickenham Rd. Tedd —4A 104
Twickenham Trading Est. Iswth
—6K 87
Twigg Clo. Eri —7K 85
Twilley St. SW18 —7A 92
Twin Bridges Bus. Pk. S Croy
—6D 134
Twine Ct. E1 —7J 63
Twineham Grn. N12 —4D 14
Twining Av. Twic —3G 103
Twinn Rd. NW7 —6B 14
Twisden Rd. NW5 —4F 45
Twybridge Way. NW10 —7J 41
Twyford Abbey Rd. NW10 —3F 57
Twyford Av. N2 —3D 28
Twyford Av. W3 —7G 57
Twyford Ct. N10 —3E 28
Twyford Ct. Wemb —2E 56
(off Vicars Bri. Clo.)
Twyford Cres. W3 —1G 73
Twyford Ho. N5 —3B 46
Twyford Ho. N15 —6E 30
(off Chisley Rd.)
Twyford Pl. WC2 —6K 61 (7E 140)
Twyford Rd. Cars —1B 132
Twyford Rd. Harr —1F 39
Twyford Rd. Ilf —5G 51
Twyford St. N1 —1K 61
Tyas Rd. E16 —4H 65
Tybenham Rd. SW19 —3J 121
Tyberry Rd. Enf —3C 8
Tyburn La. Harr —7K 23
Tyburn Way. W1 —7D 60 (9F 138)
Tyers Est. SE1 —2E 78 (4C 148)
(off Bermondsey St.)
Tyers Ga. SE1 —2E 78 (5C 148)
Tyers Ga. SE11 —5K 77
Tyers Ter. SE11 —5K 77
Tyeshurst Clo. SE2 —5C 84
Tylecroft Rd. SW16 —2J 123
Tylehurst Gdns. Ilf —5G 51
Tyler Clo. E2 —2F 63
Tyler's Ct. W1 —6H 61 (8A 140)
(off Wardour St.)
Tylers Ct. Wemb —2E 56
Tylers Ga. Harr —6E 24
Tylers Path. Cars —4D 132
Tyler St. SE10 —5G 81
(in two parts)
Tylney Av. SE19 —5F 111
Tylney Rd. E7 —4A 50
Tylney Rd. Brom —2B 128
Tyndale La. N1 —7B 46
Tyndale Mans. N1 —7B 46
(off Upper St.)
Tyndale Ter. N1 —7B 46
Tyndall Gdns. E10 —2E 48
Tyndall Rd. E10 —2E 48
Tyndall Rd. Well —3K 99
Tyneham Clo. SW11 —3E 92
Tyneham Rd. SW11 —2E 92
Tynemouth Dri. Enf —1B 8
Tynemouth Rd. N15 —4F 31

Tynemouth Rd. Mitc —7E 108
Tynemouth St. SW6 —2A 92
Tyne St. E1 —6F 63 (7F 142)
Tynley Av. SE19 —5F 111
Tynwald Ho. SE26 —3G 111
Type St. E2 —2K 63
Tyrawley Rd. SW6 —1K 91
Tyrell Clo. Harr —4J 39
Tyrell Ct. Cars —4D 132
Tyrone Rd. E6 —2D 66
Tyron Way. Sidc —4J 115
Tyrrell Av. Well —5A 100
Tyrrell Rd. SE22 —4G 95
Tyrrell Sq. Mitc —1C 122
Tyrrel Way. NW9 —7B 26
Tyrwhitt Rd. SE4 —3C 96
Tysoe St. EC1 —3A 62 (2H 141)
Tyson Gdns. SE23 —7J 95
Tyson Rd. SE23 —7J 95
Tyssen Pas. E8 —6F 47
Tyssen Rd. N16 —3F 47
Tyssen St. E8 —6F 47
Tytherton Rd. N19 —3H 45

Uamvar St. E14 —5D 64
Uckfield Gro. Mitc —1E 122
Udall St. SW1 —4G 77 (9M 145)
Udney Pk. Rd. Tedd —6A 104
Uffington Rd. NW10 —1C 58
Uffington Rd. SE27 —4A 110
Ufford Clo. Harr —7A 10
Ufford Rd. Harr —7A 10
Ufford St. SE1 —2A 78 (4H 147)
Ufton Gro. N1 —7D 46
Ufton Rd. N1 —7D 46
Ujima Ct. SW16 —4J 109
Ullathorne Rd. SW16 —4G 109
Ulleswater Rd. N14 —3D 16
Ullin St. E14 —5E 64
Ullswater Clo. SW15 —4K 105
Ullswater Clo. Brom —7G 113
Ullswater Cres. SW15 —4K 105
Ullswater Rd. SE27 —2B 110
Ullswater Rd. SW13 —7C 74
Ulster Gdns. N13 —4H 17
Ulster Pl. NW1 —4F 61 (4J 139)
Ulster Ter. NW1 —4E 60 (4J 139)
Ulundi Rd. SE3 —6G 81
Ulva Rd. SW15 —5F 91
Ulverscroft Rd. SE22 —5F 95
Ulverstone Rd. SE27 —2B 110
Ulverston Rd. E17 —2F 33
Ulysses Rd. NW6 —5H 43
Umberston St. E1 —6G 63
Umbria St. SW15 —6C 90
Umfreville Rd. N4 —6B 30
Underbridge Way. Enf —3F 9
Undercliff Rd. SE13 —3C 96
Underhill. Barn —5D 4
Underhill Ct. Barn —5D 4
Underhill Pas. NW1 —1F 61
(off Camden High St.)
Underhill Rd. SE22 —5G 95
Underhill St. NW1 —1F 61
Underne Av. N14 —2A 16
Undershaft. EC3 —6E 62 (8C 142)
Undershaw Rd. Brom —3H 113
Underwood. New Ad —5E 136
Underwood Rd. E1 —4G 63
Underwood Rd. E4 —5J 19
Underwood Rd. Wfd G —7F 21
Underwood Row. N1
—3C 62 (1M 141)
Underwood St. N1 —3C 62 (1M 141)
Underwood, The. SE9 —3D 114
Undine Rd. E14 —4D 80
Undine St. SW17 —5D 108

Uneeda Dri. Gnfd —1H 55
Unicorn Building. E1 —7K 63
(off Jardine Rd.)
Unicorn Pas. SE1 —1E 78 (3D 148)
Union Cotts. E15 —7G 49
Union Ct. EC2 —6E 62 (7C 142)
(off Old Broad St.)
Union Ct. Rich —5E 88
Union Dri. E1 —4A 64
Union Gro. SW8 —2H 93
Union Rd. N11 —6C 16
Union Rd. SW8 & SW4 —2H 93
Union Rd. Brom —5B 128
Union Rd. Croy —7C 124
Union Rd. N'holt —2E 54
Union Rd. Wemb —6E 40
Union Sq. N1 —1C 62
Union St. E15 —1E 64
Union St. SE1 —1B 78 (4J 147)
Union St. Barn —3B 4
Union St. King T —2D 118
Union Wlk. E2 —3E 62 (1D 142)
Union Yd. W1 —6F 61 (8K 139)
Unity Clo. NW10 —7C 42
Unity Clo. SE27 —5C 110
Unity Clo. New Ad —7D 136
Unity Way. SE18 —3B 82
University Clo. NW7 —7G 13
University Pl. Eri —7J 85
University Rd. SW19 —6B 108
University St. WC1
—4G 61 (4M 139)
Unwin Clo. SE15 —6G 79
Unwin Rd. SW7 —3B 76 (6A 144)
Unwin Rd. Iswth —3J 87
Upbrook M. W2 —6A 60
Upcerne Rd. SW10 —7A 76
Upchurch Clo. SE20 —7H 111
Upcroft Av. Edgw —5D 12
Updale Rd. Sidc —4K 115
Upfield. Croy —3H 135
Upfield Rd. W7 —5K 55
Upgrove Mnr. Way. SW2 —7A 94
Uphall Rd. Ilf —5F 51
Upham Pk. Rd. W4 —4A 74
Uphill Dri. NW7 —5F 13
Uphill Dri. NW9 —5J 25
Uphill Gro. NW7 —4F 13
Uphill Rd. NW7 —4F 13
Upland M. E13 —4J 65
Upland Rd. SE22 —5G 95
Upland Rd. Bexh —3F 101
Upland Rd. S Croy —5D 134
Upland Rd. Sutt —7B 132
Uplands. Beck —2C 126
Uplands Av. E17 —2K 31
Uplands Bus. Pk. E17 —2K 31
Uplands Clo. SW14 —5H 89
Uplands End. Wfd G —7H 21
Uplands Pk. Rd. Enf —2F 7
Uplands Rd. N8 —5K 29
Uplands Rd. Barn —1K 15
Uplands Rd. Romf —3D 36
Uplands Rd. Wfd G —7H 21
Uplands Trading Est. E17 —3K 31
Uplands Way. N21 —5F 7
Upnall Ho. SE15 —6J 79
Upney La. Bark —6J 51
Upnor Way. SE17 —5E 78
Upark Dri. Ilf —6G 35
Up. Abbey Rd. Belv —4F 85
Up. Addison Gdns. W14 —2G 75
Up. Bardsey Wlk. N1 —6C 46
(off Bardsey Wlk.)
Up. Belgrave St. SW1

Up. Beulah Hill. SE19 —1E 124
Up. Brighton Rd. Surb —6D 118
Up. Brockley Rd. SE4 —3B 96
Up. Brook St. W1 —7E 60 (1G 145)
Up. Butts. Bren —6C 72
Up. Caldy Wlk. N1 —6C 46
(off Caldy Wlk.)
Up. Camelford Wlk. W11 —6G 59
(off St Mark's Rd.)
Up. Cavendish Av. N3 —3J 27
Up. Cheyne Row. SW3 —6C 76
Up. Clapton Rd. E5 —2H 47
Up. Clarendon Wlk. W11 —6G 59
(off Clarendon Rd.)
Up. Dengie Wlk. N1 —1C 62
(off Basire St.)
Up. Elmers End Rd. Beck —4A 126
Up. Fosters. NW4 —5E 26
(off New Brent St.)
Up. Green E. Mitc —2D 122
Up. Green W. Mitc —2D 122
Up. Grosvenor St. W1
—7E 60 (1G 145)
Up. Grotto Rd. Twic —2K 103
Up. Ground. SE1 —1A 78 (2H 147)
Upper Gro. SE25 —4F 125
Up. Grove Rd. Belv —6F 85
Up. Gulland Wlk. N1 —6C 46
(off Oronsay Wlk.)
Up. Ham Rd. Rich —4D 104
Up. Handa Wlk. N1 —6D 46
(off Handa Wlk.)
Up. Harley St. NW1 —4E 60 (4H 139)
Up. Hawkwell Wlk. N1 —1C 62
(off Maldon Clo.)
Up. Holly Hill Rd. Belv —5H 85
Up. James St. W1 —7G 61 (9M 139)
Up. John St. W1 —7G 61 (9M 139)
Up. Lismore Wlk. N1 —6C 46
(off Clephane Rd.)
Up. Mall. W6 —5C 74
(in two parts)
Up. Marsh. SE1 —3K 77 (6F 146)
Up. Montagu St. W1
—5D 60 (5E 138)
Up. Mulgrave Rd. Sutt —7G 131
Up. North St. E14 —5C 64
Up. Park. N11 —5A 16
Up. Park Rd. NW3 —5D 44
Up. Park Rd. Belv —4H 85
Up. Park Rd. Brom —1K 127
Up. Park Rd. King T —6G 105
Up. Phillimore Gdns. W8 —2J 75
Up. Ramsey Wlk. N1 —6D 46
(off Ramsey Wlk.)
Up. Rawreth Wlk. N1 —1C 62
(off Basire St.)
Up. Richmond Rd. SW15 —4B 90
Up. Richmond Rd. W. Rich & SW14
—4G 89
Upper Rd. E13 —3J 65
Upper Rd. Wall —5H 133
Up. St Martin's La. WC2
—7J 61 (9C 140)
Up. Selsdon Rd. S Croy —7E 134
Up. Sheppey Wlk. N1 —6C 46
(off Skomer Wlk.)
Up. Sheridan Rd. Belv —4G 85
Up. Shirley Rd. Croy —3J 135
Up. Square. Iswth —3A 88
Up. Stalthe. W4 —1J 89
Up. Sutton La. Houn —7E 70
Up. Tachbrook St. SW1
—4G 77 (8L 145)
Up. Teddington Rd. King T —7C 104
Upper Ter. NW3 —3A 44
Up. Thames St. EC4
—7B 62 (9K 141)

Up. Tollington Pk. N4 —1A 45
(in two parts)
Upperton Rd. Sidc —5K 115
Upperton Rd. E. E13 —3A 66
Upperton Rd. W. E13 —3A 66
Up. Tooting Pk. SW17 —2D 108
Up. Tooting Rd. SW17 —4D 108
Up. Town Rd. Gnfd —4F 55
Up. Tulse Hill. SW2 —7K 93
Up. Vernon Rd. Sutt —5B 132
Up. Walthamstow Rd. E17 —4E 32
Up. Wickham La. Well —3B 100
Up. Wimpole St. W1
—5E 60 (5H 139)
Up. Woburn Pl. WC1
—3H 61 (2B 140)
Uppingham Av. Stan —1B 24
Upsdell Av. N13 —6F 17
Upstall St. SE5 —1B 94
Upton Av. E7 —7J 49
Upton Clo. Bex —6F 101
Upton Ct. SE20 —7J 111
Upton Dene. Sutt —7K 131
Upton Gdns. Harr —5B 24
Upton La. E7 —7J 49
Upton Lodge. E7 —6J 49
Upton Lodge Clo. Bush —1B 10
Upton Pk. Rd. E7 —7K 49
Upton Rd. N18 —5B 18
Upton Rd. SE18 —6G 83
Upton Rd. Bexh —4E 100
Upton Rd. Houn —3E 86
Upton Rd. T. Hth —2D 124
Upton Rd. S. Bex —6F 101
Upton Vs. Bexh —4E 100
Upway. N12 —6H 15
Upwood Rd. SE12 —6J 97
Upwood Rd. SW16 —1J 123
Urlwin St. SE5 —6C 78
Urlwin Wlk. SW9 —1A 94
Urmston Dri. SW19 —1G 107
Urquhart Ct. Beck —7B 112
Ursula Lodges. Sidc —5B 116
Ursula St. SW11 —1C 92
Urswick Gdns. Dag —7E 52
Urswick Rd. E9 —5J 47
Urswick Rd. Dag —7D 52
Usborne M. SW8 —7K 77
Usher Rd. E3 —1B 64
Usk Rd. SW11 —4A 92
Usk St. E2 —3K 63
Uvedale Rd. Dag —3G 53
Uvedale Rd. Enf —5J 7
Uverdale Rd. SW10 —7A 76
Uxbridge Rd. W12 —1B 74
Uxbridge Rd. W13, W5 & W3
—1B 72
Uxbridge Rd. Felt —2A 102
Uxbridge Rd. Hamp —4E 102
Uxbridge Rd. Harr & Stan —7B 10
Uxbridge Rd. Hay —6A 54
Uxbridge Rd. King T —4D 118
Uxbridge Rd. Pinn —2A 22
Uxbridge Rd. Harr & Stan —7A 10
Uxbridge Rd. S'hall & W7 —1E 70
Uxbridge St. W8 —1J 75
Uxendon Cres. Wemb —1E 40
Uxendon Hill. Wemb —1F 41

Valance Av. E4 —1B 20
Valan Leas. Brom —3G 127
Vale Clo. N2 —3D 28
Vale Clo. NW8 —3A 60
Vale Clo. W9 —3A 60
Vale Ct. W3 —1B 74
Vale Ct. W9 —3A 60
(off Maida Vale)

Vale Ct. New Bar —4E 4
Vale Cres. SW15 —4A 106
Vale Croft. Pinn —5C 22
Vale Dri. Barn —4C 4
Vale End. SE22 —4F 95
Vale Est., The. W3 —1A 74
Vale Gro. N4 —7C 30
Vale Gro. W3 —2K 73
Vale La. W3 —5G 57
Vale Lodge. SE23 —2J 111
Valence Av. Dag —1D 52
Valence Cir. Dag —3D 52
Valence Rd. Eri —7K 85
Valence Wood Rd. Dag —3D 52
Valencia Rd. Stan —4H 11
Valentia Pl. SW9 —4A 94
Valentine Av. Bex —2E 116
Valentine Ct. SE23 —2K 111
Valentine Pl. SE1 —2B 78 (5J 147)
Valentine Rd. E9 —6K 47
Valentine Rd. Harr —3G 39
Valentine Row. SE1 —2B 78 (5J 147)
Valentines Rd. Ilf —1F 51
Valentine's Way. Romf —2K 53
Vale of Health. NW3 —3A 44
Valerian Way. E15 —3G 65
Valerie Ct. Sutt —7K 131
Vale Rise. NW11 —1H 43
Vale Rd. E7 —6K 49
Vale Rd. N4 —7C 30
Vale Rd. Brom —1E 128
Vale Rd. Eps —4B 130
Vale Rd. Mitc —4H 123
Vale Rd. Sutt —4K 131
Vale Rd. Wor Pk —3B 130
Vale Row. N5 —3B 46
Vale Royal. N7 —7J 45
Vale St. SE27 —3D 110
Valeswood Rd. Brom —5H 113
Vale Ter. N4 —6C 30
Vale, The. N10 —1E 28
Vale, The. N14 —6E 6
Vale, The. NW11 —2G 43
Vale, The. SW3 —6B 76
Vale, The. W3 —1B 74
Vale, The. Croy —2A 135
Vale, The. Felt —6A 86
Vale, The. Houn —6C 70
Vale, The. Ruis —4A 38
Vale, The. Wfd G —7D 20
Valetta Gro. E13 —2J 65
Valetta Rd. W3 —2A 74
Valette Ho. E9 —6J 47
Valette St. E9 —6J 47
Valiant Clo. N'holt —3B 54
Valiant Clo. Romf —2H 37
Valiant Way. E6 —5D 66
Vallance Rd. E2 & E1 —3G 63
Vallance Rd. N22 —2G 29
Vallentin Rd. E17 —4E 32
Valley Av. N12 —4G 15
Valley Dri. NW9 —6G 25
Valleyfield Rd. SW16 —5K 109
Valley Fields Cres. Enf —2F 7
Valley Gdns. SW19 —7B 108
Valley Gdns. Wemb —7F 41
Valley Gro. SE7 —5A 82
Valley M. Twic —2K 103
Valley Rd. SW16 —5K 109
Valley Rd. Belv —4H 85
Valley Rd. Eri —4K 85
Valley Rd. Orp —7B 106
Valley Rd. Short —2G 127
Valley Side. E4 —2H 19
Valley Side Pde. E4 —2H 19
Valley View. Barn —6B 4
Valley Wlk. Croy —2J 135

Valliere Rd. NW10 —3C 58
Valliers Wood Rd. Sidc —1H 115
Vallis Way. W13 —5A 56
Valmar Rd. SE5 —1C 94
Valmar Trading Est. SE5 —1C 94
Valnay St. SW17 —5D 108
Valognes Av. E11 —4A 32
Valonia Gdns. SW18 —6H 91
Vambery Rd. SE18 —6G 83
Vanbrough Cres. N'holt —1A 54
Vanbrugh Clo. E16 —5B 66
Vanbrugh Ct. SE11 —4A 78 (9H 147)
(off Wincott St.)
Vanbrugh Fields. SE3 —6H 81
Vanbrugh Hill. SE10 & SE3 —5H 81
Vanbrugh Pk. SE3 —7H 81
Vanbrugh Pk. Rd. SE3 —7H 81
Vanbrugh Pk. Rd. W. SE3 —7H 81
Vanbrugh Rd. W4 —3K 73
Vanbrugh Ter. SE3 —1H 81
Vanburgh Clo. Orp —7J 129
Vanburgh Ct. H Bar —3B 4
Vancouver Rd. SE23 —2A 112
Vancouver Rd. Edgw —1H 25
Vancouver Rd. Rich —4C 104
Vanderbilt Rd. SW18 —1K 107
Vandome Clo. E16 —6K 65
Vandon Pas. SW1 —3G 77 (6M 145)
Vandon Pl. SW1 —3G 77
Vandon St. SW1 —3G 77 (6M 145)
Van Dyck Av. N Mald —7K 119
Vandyke Clo. SW15 —7F 91
Vandyke Cross. SE9 —5C 98
Vandy St. EC2 —4E 62 (4C 142)
Vane Clo. NW3 —5B 44
Vane Clo. Harr —6F 25
Vanessa Clo. Belv —5G 85
Vanessa Way. Bex —3K 117
Vane St. SW1 —4G 77 (8M 145)
Van Gogh Ct. E14 —3F 81
Vanguard Clo. Croy —1B 134
Vanguard Clo. Romf —2G 37
Vanguard St. SE8 —1C 96
Vanguard Way. Wall —7J 133
Vanoc Gdns. Brom —4J 113
Vansittart Rd. E7 —4H 49
Vansittart St. SE14 —6A 80
Vanston Pl. SW6 —7J 75
Vantage W. W3 —4F 73
Vantrey Rd. SE11 —4A 78 (9G 147)
(off Marylee Way)
Vant Rd. SW17 —5D 108
Varcoe Rd. SE16 —5H 79
Vardens Rd. SW11 —4B 92
Varden St. E1 —6H 63
Vardon Clo. N3 —1G 27
Vardon Clo. W3 —6K 57
Vardon Ho. SE10 —1E 96
Varley Pde. NW9 —4A 26
Varley Rd. E16 —6K 65
Varley Way. Mitc —2B 122
Varna Rd. SW6 —7G 75
Varndell St. NW1 —3G 61 (1L 139)
Vartry Rd. N15 —6D 30
Vassall Rd. SW9 —7A 78
Vauban Est. SE16 —3F 79 (7F 148)
Vauban St. SE16 —3F 79 (7F 148)
Vaughan Av. NW4 —5C 26
Vaughan Av. W6 —4B 74
Vaughan Clo. Hamp —6C 102
Vaughan Gdns. Ilf —7D 34
Vaughan Ho. SW4 —7G 93
Vaughan Rd. E15 —6H 49
Vaughan Rd. SE5 —2C 94
Vaughan Rd. Harr —7G 23
Vaughan Rd. Th Dit —7B 118

Vaughan Rd. Well —2K 99
Vaughan St. SE16 —2B 80
Vaughan Way. E1 —7G 63
Vaughan Williams Clo. SE8 —7C 80
Vauxhall Bri. SW1 & SE1 —5J 77
Vauxhall Bri. Rd. SW1
—3G 77 (7L 145)
Vauxhall Cross. SE1 —5J 77
Vauxhall Gdns. S Croy —6C 134
Vauxhall Gro. SW8 —6K 77
Vauxhall St. SE11 —5K 77
Vauxhall Wlk. SE11 —5K 77
Vawdrey Clo. E1 —4J 63
Veals Mead. Mitc —1C 122
Vectis Gdns. SW17 —6F 109
Vectis Rd. SW17 —6F 109
Veda Rd. SE13 —4C 96
Vega Rd. Bush —1B 10
Veldene Way. Harr —3D 38
Velde Way. SE22 —5E 94
Vellum Dri. Cars —3E 132
Venables Clo. Dag —4H 53
Venables St. NW8 —5B 60 (4B 138)
Vencourt Pl. W6 —4C 74
Venetian Rd. SE5 —2C 94
Venetia Rd. N4 —6B 30
Venetia Rd. W5 —2D 72
Venner Rd. SE26 —6J 111
Venners Clo. Bexh —2K 101
Venn Ho. N1 —1K 61
(off Barnsbury Est.)
Venn St. SW4 —4G 93
Ventnor Av. Stan —1B 24
Ventnor Dri. N20 —3E 14
Ventnor Gdns. Bark —6J 51
Ventnor Rd. SE14 —7K 79
Ventnor Rd. Sutt —7K 131
Venture Clo. Bex —7E 100
Venue St. E14 —5E 64
Venus Rd. SE18 —3D 82
Vera Av. N21 —5F 7
Vera Lynn Clo. E7 —4J 49
Vera Rd. SW6 —1G 91
Verbena Clo. E16 —4H 65
Verbena Gdns. W6 —5C 74
Verdant La. SE6 —7G 97
Verdayne Av. Croy —2K 135
Verdun Rd. SE18 —6A 84
Verdun Rd. SW13 —6C 74
Vereker Rd. W14 —5G 75
Vere St. W1 —6F 61 (8J 139)
Verity Clo. W11 —6G 59
Ver Meer Ct. E14 —3F 81
Vermont Rd. SE19 —6E 110
Vermont Rd. SW18 —6K 91
Vermont Rd. Sutt —3K 131
Verney Gdns. Dag —4E 52
Verney Rd. SE16 —6G 79
Verney Rd. Dag —4E 52
(in two parts)
Verney St. NW10 —3K 41
Verney Way. SE16 —5H 79
Vernham Rd. SE18 —6G 83
Vernon Av. E12 —4D 50
Vernon Av. SW20 —2F 121
Vernon Av. Wfd G —7E 20
Vernon Ct. NW2 —3H 43
Vernon Ct. W5 —7C 56
Vernon Ct. Stan —1B 24
Vernon Cres. Barn —6K 5
Vernon Dri. Stan —1A 24
Vernon Ho. SE11 —5K 77
(off Vauxhall St.)
Vernon M. E17 —5B 32
Vernon Pl. WC1 —5J 61 (6D 140)
Vernon Rise. WC1 —3K 61 (1F 140)
Vernon Rise. Gnfd —5H 39
Vernon Rd. E3 —2B 64

Vernon Rd. E11 —1G 49
Vernon Rd. E15 —7G 49
Vernon Rd. E17 —5B 32
Vernon Rd. N8 —3A 30
Vernon Rd. SW14 —3K 89
Vernon Rd. WC1 —3K 61
Vernon Rd. Ilf —1K 51
Vernon Rd. Sutt —5A 132
Vernon Sq. WC1 —3K 61 (1F 140)
Vernon St. W14 —4G 75
Vernon Yd. W11 —7H 59
Veroan Rd. Bexh —2E 100
Verona Rd. E7 —7J 49
Veronica Gdns. SW16 —1G 123
Veronica Rd. SW17 —2F 109
Veronique Gdns. Ilf —5G 35
Verran Rd. SW12 —7F 93
Versailles Rd. SE20 —7G 111
Verulam Av. E17 —6B 32
Verulam Bldgs. WC1
(off Grays Inn) —5K 61 (5F 140)
Verulam Ct. NW9 —7C 26
Verulam Rd. Gnfd —4E 54
Verulam St. WC1 —5A 62 (5G 141)
Verwood Rd. Harr —2G 23
Veryan Ct. N8 —5H 29
Vesage Ct. EC1 —5A 62 (6H 141)
(off Leather La.)
Vesey Path. E14 —6D 64
Vespan Rd. W12 —2C 74
Vesta Rd. SE4 —2A 96
Vestris Rd. SE23 —2K 111
Vestry M. SE5 —1E 94
Vestry Rd. E17 —4D 32
Vestry Rd. SE5 —1E 94
Vestry St. N1 —3D 62 (1A 142)
Vevey St. SE6 —2B 112
Veysey Gdns. Dag —3G 53
Viaduct Bldgs. EC1 —5A 62 (6H 141)
Viaduct Pl. E2 —3H 63
Viaduct Rd. N2 —2B 28
Viaduct St. E2 —3H 63
Viaduct, The. E18 —2K 33
Viaduct, The. Wemb —1E 56
Vian St. SE13 —3D 96
Viant Ho. NW10 —7K 41
Vibart Gdns. SW2 —7K 93
Vibart Wlk. N1 —1J 61
(off Outram Pl.)
Vicarage Av. SE3 —7J 81
Vicarage Clo. Eri —6J 85
Vicarage Clo. N'holt —7D 38
Vicarage Ct. W8 —2K 75
Vicarage Ct. Beck —3A 126
Vicarage Ct. Ilf —5F 51
Vicarage Cres. SW11 —1B 92
Vicarage Dri. SW14 —5K 89
Vicarage Dri. Bark —6J 51
Vicarage Dri. Beck —1C 126
Vicarage Farm Ct. Houn —7D 70
Vicarage Farm Rd. Houn —2C 86
Vicarage Field Shopping Cen. Bark
—7G 51
Vicarage Gdns. W8 —1J 75
Vicarage Gdns. Mitc —3C 122
Vicarage Ga. W8 —1K 75
Vicarage Gro. SE5 —1D 94
Vicarage La. E6 —3D 66
Vicarage La. E15 —7G 49
Vicarage La. Eps —7C 130
Vicarage La. Ilf —1H 51
Vicarage M. NW9 —2K 41
Vicarage Pde. N15 —4C 30
Vicarage Pk. SE18 —5G 83
Vicarage Rd. E10 —7C 32
Vicarage Rd. E15 —7H 49
Vicarage Rd. N17 —1G 31
Vicarage Rd. NW4 —6C 26

Vicarage Rd. SE18 —5G 83
Vicarage Rd. SW14 —5K 89
Vicarage Rd. Bex —1H 117
Vicarage Rd. Croy —3A 134
Vicarage Rd. Dag —7H 53
Vicarage Rd. Hamp W —1C 118
Vicarage Rd. King T —2D 118
Vicarage Rd. Sutt —3K 131
Vicarage Rd. Tedd —5A 104
Vicarage Rd. Twic —2J 103
Vicarage Rd. Whit —6G 87
Vicarage Wlk. SW11 —1B 92
Vicarage Way. NW10 —3K 41
Vicarage Way. Harr —7E 22
Vicars Bri. Clo. Wemb —2E 56
Vicar's Clo. E9 —1J 63
Vicars Clo. E15 —1J 65
Vicars Clo. Enf —2K 7
Vicar's Hill. SE13 —4D 96
Vicars Moor La. N21 —7F 7
Vicars Oak Rd. SE19 —6E 110
Vicar's Rd. NW5 —5E 44
Vicars Wlk. Dag —3B 52
Viceroy Clo. N2 —4C 28
Viceroy Ct. Croy —2D 134
Viceroy Pde. N2 —4C 28
  (off High Rd.)
Viceroy Rd. SW8 —1J 93
Vicery Ct. EC1 —4C 62 (3M 141)
  (off Bartholomew Sq.)
Vickers La. Houn —5C 86
Vickers Rd. Eri —5K 85
Vickers Way. Houn —5C 86
Victor Gro. Wemb —7E 40
Victoria Arc. SW1 —3F 77 (7K 145)
  (off Victoria St.)
Victoria Av. E6 —1B 66
Victoria Av. EC2 —5E 62 (6D 142)
Victoria Av. N3 —1H 27
Victoria Av. Barn —4G 5
Victoria Av. Houn —5C 86
Victoria Av. Surb —6D 118
Victoria Av. Wall —3E 132
Victoria Av. Wemb —6H 41
Victoria Clo. Barn —4G 5
Victoria Cotts. N10 —2E 28
Victoria Cotts. Rich —1F 89
Victoria Ct. E18 —3K 33
Victoria Ct. SE26 —6J 111
Victoria Ct. W3 —2G 73
Victoria Ct. Wemb —6G 41
Victoria Cres. N15 —5E 30
Victoria Cres. SE19 —6E 110
Victoria Cres. SW19 —7H 107
Victoria Dock Rd. E16 —6G 65
Victoria Dri. SW19 —7F 91
Victoria Embkmt. SW1, WC2 & EC4
  —2J 77 (4D 146)
Victoria Gdns. W11 —1J 75
Victoria Gdns. Houn —1C 86
Victoria Gro. N12 —5G 15
Victoria Gro. W8 —3A 76
Victoria Gro. M. W2 —7J 59
Victoria Ho. N1 —1K 61
  (off Charlotte Ter.)
Victoria Ho. Edgw —6C 12
Victoria Ind. Est., The. NW10 & W3
  —4A 58
Victoria La. Barn —4C 4
Victoria Mans. NW10 —7D 42
Victoria M. NW1 —1J 59
Victoria M. SW4 —4F 93
Victorian Gro. N16 —4E 46
Victorian Rd. N16 —3F 47
Victoria Pk. Ind. Cen. E9 —7C 48
  (off Rothbury Rd.)
Victoria Pk. Rd. E2 & E9 —1J 63

Victoria Pk. Sq. E2 —3J 63
Victoria Pas. NW8 —4B 60 (3A 138)
  (off Fisherton St.)
Victoria Pl. SW1 —4F 77 (8K 145)
Victoria Pl. Rich —5D 88
Victoria Point. E13 —2J 65
  (off Victoria Rd.)
Victoria Rise. SW4 —3F 93
Victoria Rd. E4 —1B 20
Victoria Rd. E11 —4G 49
Victoria Rd. E13 —2J 65
Victoria Rd. E17 —2E 32
Victoria Rd. E18 —2K 33
Victoria Rd. N4 —7K 29
Victoria Rd. N15 —4G 31
Victoria Rd. N18 & N9 —4A 18
Victoria Rd. N22 —1G 29
Victoria Rd. NW4 —4E 26
Victoria Rd. NW6 —2H 59
Victoria Rd. NW7 —5G 13
Victoria Rd. NW10 —5K 57
Victoria Rd. SW14 —3K 89
Victoria Rd. W3 —5K 57
Victoria Rd. W5 —5B 56
Victoria Rd. W8 —3A 76
Victoria Rd. Bark —6F 51
Victoria Rd. Barn —4G 5
Victoria Rd. Brom —5B 128
Victoria Rd. Buck H —2G 21
Victoria Rd. Bush —1A 10
Victoria Rd. Chst —5E 114
Victoria Rd. Dag —5H 53
Victoria Rd. Eri —6K 85
  (in two parts)
Victoria Rd. Gnfd —5B 56
Victoria Rd. King T —2F 119
Victoria Rd. Mitc —7C 108
Victoria Rd. Ruis —4A 38
Victoria Rd. Sidc —3K 115
Victoria Rd. S'hall —3D 70
Victoria Rd. Surb —6D 118
Victoria Rd. Surb —5B 132
Victoria Rd. Tedd —6A 104
Victoria Rd. Twic —7B 88
Victoria Sq. SW1 —3F 77 (6K 145)
Victoria St. E15 —7G 49
Victoria St. SW1 —3G 77 (7K 145)
Victoria St. Belv —5F 85
Victoria Ter. N4 —1A 46
Victoria Ter. W5 —4B 58
Victoria Ter. Harr —1H 39
Victoria Vs. Rich —4F 89
Victoria Way. SE7 —5K 81
Victor Rd. NW10 —3D 58
Victor Rd. SE20 —7K 111
Victor Rd. Harr —3G 23
Victor Rd. Tedd —4J 103
Victors Dri. Hamp —6C 102
Victors Way. Barn —3C 4
Victor Vs. N9 —3J 17
Victory Av. Mord —5A 122
Victory Bus. Cen. Iswth —4K 87
Victory Pl. SE17 —4D 78 (8M 147)
Victory Pl. SE19 —7F 111
Victory Rd. SW19 —7A 108
Victory Rd. M. SW19 —7A 108
Victory Sq. SE5 —7D 78
Victory Wlk. SE8 —1C 96
Victory Way. SE16 —2A 80
Victory Way. Houn —5A 70
Victory Way. Romf —2H 37
Vienna Clo. Ilf —2B 34
View Clo. N6 —7D 28
View Clo. Harr —4H 23
View Cres. N8 —5H 29
Viewfield Clo. Harr —7E 24
Viewfield Rd. SW18 —6H 91

Viewfield Rd. Bex —1C 116
Viewland Rd. SE18 —5K 83
View Rd. N6 —7D 28
View, The. SE2 —5E 84
Viga M. SE21 —7H 53
Vigilant Clo. SE26 —4G 111
Vignoles Rd. Romf —7G 37
Vigo St. W1 —7G 61 (1L 145)
Viking Clo. E3 —2A 64
Viking Ct. SW6 —6J 75
Viking Pl. E10 —1B 48
Viking Rd. S'hall —7C 54
Viking Way. Eri —3J 85
Villacourt Rd. SE18 —7A 84
Village Clo. E4 —5K 19
Village Gdns. Eps —7B 130
Village M. NW9 —2K 41
Village Rd. N3 —2G 27
Village Rd. Enf —7J 7
Village Row. Sutt —7J 131
Village, The. SE7 —6B 82
Village Way. NW10 —4K 41
Village Way. SE21 —6D 94
Village Way. Beck —2C 126
Village Way. Pinn —7C 22
Village Way E. Harr —7E 22
Villa Rd. SW9 —3A 94
Villas on the Heath. NW3 —3A 44
Villas Rd. SE18 —5G 83
  (in two parts)
Villa St. SE17 —5D 78
Villa Wlk. SE17 —5D 78
Villiers Av. Twic —1D 102
Villiers Clo. E10 —2C 48
Villiers Clo. Surb —4F 119
Villiers Gro. Sutt —7F 131
Villiers Path. Surb —5E 118
Villiers Rd. NW2 —6C 42
Villiers Rd. Beck —2K 125
Villiers Rd. Iswth —2J 87
Villiers Rd. King T —4F 119
Villiers Rd. S'hall —1D 70
Villiers St. WC2 —1J 77 (1C 146)
Vincam Clo. Twic —7E 86
Vincent Clo. SE16 —2A 80
Vincent Clo. Barn —3E 4
Vincent Clo. Brom —4K 127
Vincent Clo. Sidc —1J 115
Vincent Ct. N4 —1J 45
Vincent Gdns. NW2 —3B 42
Vincent M. E3 —2C 64
Vincent Rd. E4 —6A 20
Vincent Rd. N15 —4C 30
Vincent Rd. N22 —2A 30
Vincent Rd. SE18 —4F 83
Vincent Rd. W3 —3J 73
Vincent Rd. Croy —7E 124
Vincent Rd. Dag —7E 52
Vincent Rd. Houn —3B 86
Vincent Rd. Iswth —1H 87
Vincent Rd. King T —3G 119
Vincent Rd. Wemb —7F 41
Vincent Row. Hamp —6G 103
Vincents Path. N'holt —6C 38
  (off Arnold Rd.)
Vincent Sq. N22 —2A 30
Vincent Sq. SW1 —4H 77 (8M 145)
Vincent St. E16 —5H 65
Vincent St. SW1 —4H 77 (8A 146)
Vincent Ter. N1 —2B 62
Vince St. EC1 —3D 62 (2B 142)
Vine Clo. Surb —6F 119
Vine Clo. Sutt —3A 132
Vine Ct. E1 —5G 63
Vine Ct. Harr —6E 24
Vinegar All. E17 —4D 32
Vine Gdns. Ilf —5G 51

Vinegar St. E1 —1H 79
Vinegar Yd. SE1 —2E 78 (4C 148)
  (off St Thomas St.)
Vine Hill. EC1 —4A 62 (4G 141)
Vine La. SE1 —1E 78 (3D 148)
Vine Pl. W5 —1E 72
  (off Grange Pk.)
Vine Pl. Houn —4F 87
Vineries Bank. NW7 —5J 13
Vineries Clo. Dag —6F 53
Vineries, The. N14 —6B 6
Vineries, The. SE6 —1C 112
Vineries, The. Enf —3K 7
Vine Rd. E15 —7H 49
Vine Rd. SW13 —3B 90
Vinery Way. W6 —3D 74
Vines Av. N3 —1K 27
Vine St. EC3 —6F 63 (8E 142)
Vine St. W1 —7G 61 (1M 145)
Vine St. Romf —4J 37
Vine St. Bri. EC1 —4A 62 (4H 141)
Vine Yd. SE1 —2C 78 (4M 147)
  (off Sanctuary St.)
Vineyard Av. NW7 —7B 14
Vineyard Clo. SE6 —1C 112
Vineyard Hill Rd. SW19 —4J 107
Vineyard M. EC1 —4A 62 (3G 141)
  (off Vineyard Wlk.)
Vineyard Pas. Rich —5E 88
Vineyard Path. SW14 —3K 89
Vineyard Row. King T —1C 118
Vineyard, The. Rich —5E 88
Vineyard Wlk. EC1 —4A 62 (3G 141)
Viney Bank. Croy —7B 136
Viney Rd. SE13 —3D 96
Vining St. SW9 —4A 94
Vinson Clo. Orp —7K 129
Vintners Ct. EC4 —7C 62 (1M 147)
Vintners Hall. EC4 —7C 62 (1M 147)
  (off Up. Thames St.)
Vintner's Pl. EC4 —7C 62 (1M 147)
Viola Av. SE2 —4B 84
Viola Av. Felt —6A 86
Viola Sq. W12 —7B 58
Violet Av. Enf —1J 7
Violet Clo. Wall —1E 132
Violet Gdns. Croy —5B 134
Violet Hill. NW8 —2A 60
Violet La. Croy —6B 134
Violet Rd. E3 —4D 64
Violet Rd. E17 —6C 32
Violet Rd. E18 —2K 33
Violet St. E2 —4H 63
Virgil Pl. W1 —5D 60 (6E 138)
Virgil St. SE1 —3K 77 (6F 146)
Virginia Clo. N Mald —4J 119
Virginia Gdns. Ilf —2G 35
Virginia Rd. E2 —3F 63 (2E 142)
Virginia Rd. T Hth —1B 124
Virginia St. E1 —7G 63
Virginia Wlk. SW2 —6K 93
Viscount Dri. E6 —5D 66
Viscount Gro. N'holt —3B 54
Viscount St. EC1 —4C 62 (4L 141)
Vista Av. Enf —2E 8
Vista Dri. Ilf —5B 34
Vista, The. SE9 —7C 98
Vista Way. Harr —6E 24
Vivian Av. NW4 —5D 26
Vivian Av. Wemb —5G 41
Vivian Clo. N12 —5E 14
Vivian Gdns. Wemb —5G 41
Vivian Mans. NW4 —5D 26
  (off Vivian Av.)
Vivian Rd. E3 —2A 64
Vivian Sq. SE15 —3H 95
Vivian Way. N2 —5B 28

Vivienne Clo. Twic —6D 88
Voce Rd. SE18 —7H 83
Voewood Clo. N Mald —6B 120
Vogans Wharf. SE1 —2F 79 (4F 148)
Voltaire Rd. SW4 —3H 93
Voluntary Pl. E11 —6J 33
Vorley Rd. N19 —2G 45
Voss St. E2 —3G 63
Voss St. SW16 —6J 109
Vulcan Clo. Wall —7K 133
Vulcan Ga. Enf —2F 7
Vulcan Rd. SE4 —2B 96
Vulcan Sq. E14 —4C 80
Vulcan Ter. SE4 —2B 96
Vulcan Way. N7 —6K 45
Vyner Rd. W3 —7K 57
Vyner St. E2 —1H 63
Vyne, The. Bexh —3H 101

Wadding St. SE17 —4D 78 (9A 148)
Waddington Clo. Enf —4K 7
Waddington Rd. E15 —5F 49
Waddington St. E15 —6F 49
Waddington Way. SE19 —7C 110
Waddon Clo. Croy —3A 134
Waddon Ct. Rd. Croy —4A 134
Waddon New Rd. Croy —3B 134
Waddon Pk. Av. Croy —4A 134
Waddon Rd. Croy —3A 134
Waddon Way. Croy —6A 134
Wade Ct. N10 —7A 16
Wade Ho. Enf —5J 7
Wade Rd. E16 —6A 66
Wades Gro. N21 —7F 7
Wades Hill. N21 —6F 7
Wades La. Tedd —5A 104
Wadeson St. E2 —2H 63
Wadeville Av. Romf —6E 36
Wadeville Clo. Belv —6G 85
Wadham Av. E17 —7J 19
Wadham Gdns. NW3 —1C 60
Wadham Gdns. Gnfd —6H 39
Wadham Rd. E17 —1D 32
Wadham Rd. SW15 —4G 91
Wadhurst Clo. SE20 —2H 125
Wadhurst Rd. SW8 —1G 93
Wadhurst Rd. W4 —3K 73
Wadley Rd. E11 —7G 33
Wausworth Bus. Cen. Gnfd —2C 56
Wadsworth Clo. Enf —5E 8
Wadsworth Clo. Gnfd —2C 56
Wadsworth Rd. Gnfd —2B 56
Wager St. E3 —4B 64
Waggon M. N14 —1B 16
Waghorn Rd. E13 —1A 66
Waghorn Rd. Harr —2D 24
Waghorn St. SE15 —3G 95
Wagner St. SE15 —7J 79
Wagtail Clo. NW9 —2A 26
Waight's Ct. King T —1E 118
Wainfleet Av. Romf —2J 37
Wainford Clo. SW19 —7F 91
Wainwright Gro. Iswth —4H 87
Waite Davies Rd. SE12 —7H 97
Waite St. SE15 —6F 79
Wakefield Ct. SE26 —6J 111
Wakefield Gdns. SE19 —7E 110
Wakefield Gdns. Ilf —6C 34
Wakefield M. WC1 —3J 61 (2D 140)
Wakefield Rd. N11 —5C 16
Wakefield Rd. N15 —5F 31
Wakefield Rd. Rich —5D 88
Wakefield St. E6 —1B 66
Wakefield St. N18 —5B 18
Wakefield St. WC1 —4J 61 (2D 140)
Wakehams Hill. Pinn —3D 22

Warndon St. SE16 —4K 79
Warneford Rd. Harr —3D 24
Warneford St. E9 —1H 63
Warne Pl. Sidc —6B 100
Warner Av. Sutt —2G 131
Warner Clo. E15 —5G 49
Warner Clo. NW9 —7B 26
Warner Pl. E2 —2G 63
Warner Rd. E17 —4A 32
Warner Rd. N8 —4H 29
Warner Rd. SE5 —1C 94
Warner Rd. Brom —7H 113
Warners Clo. Wfd G —5D 20
Warners La. Rich —4D 104
Warners Path. Wfd G —5D 20
Warner St. EC1 —4A 62 (4G 141)
Warner Yd. EC1 —4A 62 (4G 141)
(off Warner St.)
Warnham Ct. Rd. Cars —7D 132
Warnham Ho. SW2 —7K 93
(off Up. Tulse Hill)
Warnham Rd. N12 —5H 15
Warple Way. W3 —1A 74
Warren Av. E10 —3E 48
Warren Av. Brom —7G 113
Warren Av. Rich —4H 89
Warren Av. S Croy —7K 135
Warren Clo. N9 —7E 8
Warren Clo. SE21 —7C 94
Warren Clo. Bexh —5G 101
Warren Clo. Hay —5A 54
Warren Clo. Wemb —2D 40
Warren Ct. N17 —3G 31
(off High Cross Rd.)
Warren Ct. Beck —7C 112
Warren Ct. Croy —1E 134
Warren Cres. N9 —7A 8
Warren Cutting. King T —7K 105
Warrender Rd. N19 —4G 45
Warren Dri. Gnfd —4F 55
Warren Dri. Ruis —7B 22
Warren Dri. N. Surb —7H 119
Warren Dri. S. Surb —7J 119
Warren Dri., The. E11 —7A 34
Warren Farm Cotts. Romf —4F 37
Warren Fields. Stan —4J 11
Warren Footpath. Twic —1C 104
Warren Gdns. E15 —5F 49
Warren La. SE18 —3F 83
Warren La. Stan —2F 11
Warren M. W1 —4G 61 (4L 139)
Warren Pk. King T —6J 105
Warren Pk. Rd. Sutt —6C 132
Warren Pl. E1 —6K 63
(off Caroline St.)
Warren Pond Rd. E4 —1C 20
Warren Rise. N Mald —1K 119
Warren Rd. E4 —2K 19
Warren Rd. E10 —3E 48
Warren Rd. E11 —6A 34
Warren Rd. NW2 —2B 42
Warren Rd. SW19 —6C 108
Warren Rd. Bexh —5G 101
Warren Rd. Brom —2J 137
Warren Rd. Bush —1B 10
Warren Rd. Croy —1F 135
Warren Rd. Ilf —5H 35
Warren Rd. King T —6J 105
Warren Rd. Sidc —3C 116
Warren Rd. Twic —6G 87
Warrens Shawe La. Edgw —2C 12
Warren St. W1 —4F 61 (4L 139)
Warren Ter. Romf —4D 36
(in two parts)
Warren, The. E12 —4C 50
Warren, The. Houn —7D 70
Warren, The. Wor Pk —3A 130
Warren Wlk. SE7 —6A 82

Warren Way. NW7 —6B 14
Warren Wood Clo. Brom —2H 137
Warriner Gdns. SW11 —1D 92
Warrington Cres. W9 —4A 60
Warrington Gdns. W9 —4A 60
Warrington Rd. Croy —3B 134
Warrington Rd. Dag —2D 52
Warrington Rd. Harr —5J 23
Warrington Rd. Rich —5D 88
Warrington Sq. Dag —2D 52
Warrior Sq. E12 —4E 50
Warsaw Clo. Ruis —6A 38
Warspite Rd. SE18 —3C 82
Warton Rd. E15 —7E 48
Warwall. E6 —6F 67
Warwick. Sidc —5B 116
Warwick Av. W9 & W2 —4K 59
Warwick Av. Edgw —3C 12
Warwick Av. Harr —4D 38
Warwick Chambers. W8 —3J 75
(off Pater St.)
Warwick Clo. SW15 —7B 90
Warwick Clo. Barn —5G 5
Warwick Clo. Bex —7E 100
Warwick Clo. Bush —1D 10
Warwick Clo. Hamp —7G 103
Warwick Ct. WC1 —5K 61 (6F 140)
Warwick Ct. Brom —7G 137
Warwick Ct. Harr —3J 23
Warwick Ct. New Bar —5E 4
(off Station Rd.)
Warwick Cres. W2 —5A 60
Warwick Dene. W5 —1E 72
Warwick Dri. SW15 —3D 90
Warwick Est. W2 —5K 59
Warwick Gdns. N4 —5C 30
Warwick Gdns. W14 —3H 75
Warwick Gdns. Barn —1C 4
Warwick Gdns. Ilf —1F 51
Warwick Gdns. T Hth —3A 124
Warwick Gro. E5 —2H 47
Warwick Gro. Surb —7F 119
Warwick Ho. St. SW1
—1H 77 (2B 146)
Warwick La. EC4 —6B 62 (7K 141)
Warwick Lodge. Twic —3F 103
Warwick Pde. Harr —2B 24
Warwick Pl. W5 —2D 72
Warwick Pl. W9 —5A 60
Warwick Pl. N. SW1
—4G 77 (9L 145)
Warwick Rd. E4 —5H 19
Warwick Rd. E11 —5K 33
Warwick Rd. E12 —5C 50
Warwick Rd. E15 —6H 49
Warwick Rd. E17 —1B 32
Warwick Rd. N11 —6C 16
Warwick Rd. N18 —4K 17
Warwick Rd. SE20 —3H 125
Warwick Rd. W5 —2D 72
Warwick Rd. W14 & SW5 —4H 75
Warwick Rd. Barn —4E 4
Warwick Rd. Houn —3A 86
Warwick Rd. King T —1C 118
Warwick Rd. N Mald —3J 119
Warwick Rd. Sidc —5B 116
Warwick Rd. S'hall —3D 70
Warwick Rd. Sutt —4A 132
Warwick Rd. T Hth —3A 124
Warwick Rd. Twic —1J 103
Warwick Rd. Well —3C 100
Warwick Row. SW1
—3G 77 (7K 145)
Warwickshire Path. SE8 —7B 80
Warwickshire Rd. N16 —4E 46
Warwick Sq. EC4 —6B 62 (7K 141)
Warwick Sq. SW1 —5G 77

Warwick Sq. M. SW1
—4G 77 (9L 145)
Warwick St. W1 —7G 61 (9M 139)
Warwick Ter. SE18 —6H 83
Warwick Way. SW1 —5F 77
Warwick Yd. EC1 —4C 62 (4M 141)
Washington Av. E12 —4C 50
Washington Rd. E6 —7A 50
Washington Rd. E18 —2H 33
Washington Rd. SW13 —7C 74
Washington Rd. King T —2G 119
Washington Rd. Wor Pk —2D 130
Wastdale Rd. SE23 —1K 111
Watchfield Ct. W4 —5J 73
Watcombe Cotts. Rich —6G 73
Watcombe Pl. SE25 —4H 125
Watcombe Rd. SE25 —5H 125
Waterbank Rd. SE6 —3D 112
Waterbeach Rd. Dag —6C 52
Water Brook La. NW4 —5E 26
Waterdale Rd. SE2 —6A 84
Waterden Rd. E15 —5C 48
Waterer Ho. SE6 —4E 112
Waterer Rise. Wall —6H 133
Waterfall Clo. N14 —3B 16
Waterfall Cotts. SW19 —6B 108
Waterfall Rd. N11 & N14 —4A 16
Waterfall Rd. SW19 —6B 108
Waterfall Ter. SW17 —6C 108
Waterfield Clo. SE28 —1B 84
Waterfield Clo. Belv —3H 85
Waterfield Gdns. SE25 —4E 124
Waterfield Gdns. SE28 —1B 84
Waterford Rd. SW6 —7K 75
Water Gdns. Stan —6G 11
Watergardens, The. King T —6J 105
Watergate. EC4 —7B 62 (9J 141)
Watergate St. SE8 —6C 80
Watergate Wlk. WC2
—1J 77 (2D 146)
Water Glade Cen., The. W5 —7D 56
Waterhall Av. E4 —4B 20
Waterhall Clo. E17 —1K 31
Waterhouse Clo. E16 —5B 66
Waterhouse Clo. NW3 —5B 44
Waterhouse Clo. W6 —4F 75
Water La. E15 —6G 49
Water La. NW1 —7F 45
Water La. SE14 —7J 79
Water La. Ilf —3J 51
Water La. King T —1D 118
Water La. Rich —5D 88
Water La. Sidc —3F 117
(in two parts)
Water La. Twic —1A 104
Waterloo Bri. WC2 & SE1
—7K 61 (1E 146)
Waterloo Clo. E9 —5J 47
Waterloo Gdns. E2 —2J 63
Waterloo Gdns. Romf —6K 37
Waterloo Pas. NW6 —7H 43
Waterloo Pl. SW1 —1H 77 (2A 146)
Waterloo Pl. Rich —4E 88
Waterloo Rd. E6 —7A 50
Waterloo Rd. E7 —5H 49
Waterloo Rd. E10 —7C 32
Waterloo Rd. NW2 —1C 42
Waterloo Rd. SE1 —2A 78 (2F 146)
Waterloo Rd. Ilf —2G 35
Waterloo Rd. Romf —5K 37
Waterloo Rd. Sutt —5B 132
Waterloo Ter. N1 —7B 46
Waterlow Ct. NW11 —7K 27
Waterlow Rd. N19 —1G 45
Watermans Clo. King T —1E 104
Watermans Ct. Bren —6E 72
Waterman's Sq. SE20 —7J 111
Waterman St. SW15 —3F 91

Waterman's Wlk. EC4
—7D 62 (1A 148)
(off Allhallows La.)
Watermans Wlk. SE16 —2A 80
Waterman Way. E1 —1H 79
Watermead Ho. E9 —5A 48
Watermead La. Cars —7D 122
Watermeadow La. SW6 —2A 92
Watermead Rd. SE6 —4E 112
Watermead Way. N17 —2G 31
Watermen's Sq. SE20 —7J 111
Watermill Bus. Cen. Enf —2G 9
Watermill Clo. Rich —3C 104
Water Mill Ho. Felt —2E 102
Watermill La. N18 —5K 17
Watermill Way. SW19 —1B 122
Watermill Way. Felt —2D 102
Watermint Quay. N16 —7G 31
Water Rd. Wemb —1F 57
Watersfield Way. Edgw —7J 11
Waters Gdns. Dag —5G 53
Waterside. Beck —1B 126
Waterside Clo. Bark —4A 52
Waterside Clo. N'holt —3D 54
Waterside Pl. NW1 —1E 60
Waterside Point. SW11 —7C 76
Waterside Rd. S'hall —3E 70
Waterside Trading Cen. W7 —3J 71
Waterside Way. SW17 —4A 108
Watersmeet Way. SE28 —6C 68
Waterson St. E2 —3E 62 (1D 142)
Watersplash Clo. King T —3E 118
Waters Rd. SE6 —3G 113
Waters Rd. King T —2H 119
Waters Sq. King T —3H 119
Water St. WC2 —7A 62 (9G 141)
(off Maltravers St.)
Water Tower Hill. Croy —4D 134
Water Tower Pl. N1 —1B 62
Waterworks La. E5 —2K 47
Waterworks Rd. SW2 —6K 93
Waterworks Yd. Croy —3C 134
Watery La. SW20 —2H 121
Watery La. N'holt —2A 54
Watery La. Sidc —6B 116
Wates Way. Mitc —6D 122
Watford By-Pass. Stan & Edgw
—1G 11
Watford Clo. SW11 —1C 92
Watford Rd. E16 —5J 65
Watford Rd. Harr & Wemb —7A 24
Watford Way. NW7 & NW4 —4F 13
Watkin Rd. Wemb —3H 41
Watkins. Sidc —5B 116
Watkinson Rd. N7 —6K 45
Watling Av. Edgw —1J 25
Watling Ct. EC4 —6C 62 (8M 141)
(off Watling St.)
Watling Farm Clo. Stan —1H 11
Watling Gdns. NW2 —6G 43
Watling Ga. NW9 —4K 25
Watlings Clo. Croy —6A 126
Watling St. EC4 —6C 62 (8L 141)
Watling St. Bexh —4H 101
Watlington Gro. SE26 —5A 112
Watney Mkt. E1 —6H 63
Watney's Rd. Mitc —5H 123
Watson Av. E6 —7E 50
Watson Av. Sutt —2G 131
Watson Clo. N16 —5D 46
Watson Clo. SW19 —6C 108
Watson's M. W1 —5C 60 (6D 138)
Watsons Rd. N22 —1K 29
Watson's St. SE8 —7C 80
Watson St. E13 —2K 65
Watsons Wlk. NW2 —2C 42

Wattisfield Rd. E5 —3J 47
Watts Clo. N15 —5E 30
Watts Gro. E3 —5D 64
Watts La. Chst —1F 129
Watts La. Tedd —5A 104
Watts Point. E13 —1J 65
(off Brooks Rd.)
Watts Rd. Th Dit —7A 118
Watts St. E1 —1H 79
Wat Tyler Ho. N8 —3J 29
(off Boynton Rd.)
Wat Tyler Rd. SE3 & SE10 —2E 96
Wauthier Clo. N13 —5G 17
Wavell Dri. Sidc —6J 99
Wavel M. N8 —4H 29
Wavel M. NW6 —7K 43
Wavendon Av. W4 —5K 73
Waveney Av. SE15 —4H 95
Waveney Clo. E1 —1G 79
Waveney Ho. SE15 —4H 95
Waverley Av. E4 —4G 19
Waverley Av. E17 —3F 33
Waverley Av. Surb —6H 119
Waverley Av. Sutt —2K 131
Waverley Av. Twic —1D 102
Waverley Av. Wemb —5F 41
Waverley Clo. E18 —1A 34
Waverley Clo. Brom —5B 128
Waverley Clo. Hay —3F 54
Waverley Ct. SE26 —5J 111
Waverley Ct. Enf —3H 7
Waverley Cres. SE18 —5H 83
Waverley Gdns. E6 —5C 66
Waverley Gdns. NW10 —2F 57
Waverley Gdns. Bark —2J 67
Waverley Gdns. Ilf —2G 35
Waverley Gro. N3 —3G 27
Waverley Ind. Est. Harr —3H 23
Waverley Pl. N4 —2B 46
Waverley Pl. NW8 —2B 60
Waverley Rd. E17 —3E 32
Waverley Rd. E18 —1A 34
Waverley Rd. N8 —6J 29
Waverley Rd. N17 —7C 18
Waverley Rd. SE18 —5H 83
Waverley Rd. SE25 —4H 125
Waverley Rd. Enf —3G 7
Waverley Rd. Eps —5D 130
Waverley Rd. Harr —2C 38
Waverley Rd. S'hall —7E 54
Waverley Vs. N17 —2F 31
Waverley Way. Cars —6C 132
Waverton Rd. SW18 —7A 92
Waverton St. W1 —1E 76 (2H 145)
Wavertree Ct. SW2 —1J 109
Wavertree Rd. E18 —2J 33
Wavertree Rd. SW2 —1K 109
Waxlow Cres. S'hall —6E 54
Waxlow Ho. Hay —5B 54
Waxlow Rd. NW10 —2J 57
Waxwell Clo. Pinn —2B 22
Waxwell Farm Ho. Pinn —2B 22
Waxwell La. Pinn —2B 22
Waxwell Ter. SE1 —2K 77 (5F 146)
Wayfarer Rd. N'holt —3B 54
Wayfield Link. SE9 —6H 99
Wayford St. SW11 —2C 92
Wayland Av. E8 —5G 47
Wayland Clo. E8 —5G 47
Wayland Ho. SW9 —2A 94
(off Robsart St.)
Waylands Mead. Beck —1D 126
Waylett Ho. SE11 —5K 77
(off Loughborough St.)
Waylett Pl. SE27 —3B 110
Waylett Pl. Wemb —4D 40
Wayneflete Av. Croy —3B 134
Wayneflete Sq. W10 —7F 59

Waynflete St. SW18 —2A 108
Wayside. NW11 —1G 43
Wayside. SW14 —5J 89
Wayside. New Ad —6D 136
Wayside Clo. N14 —6B 6
Wayside Ct. Twic —6C 88
Wayside Ct. Wemb —3G 41
Wayside Gdns. SE9 —4D 114
Wayside Gdns. Dag —5G 53
Wayside Gro. SE9 —4D 114
Wayside M. Ilf —5E 34
Weald Clo. SE16 —5H 79
Weald La. Harr —2H 23
Weald Rise. Harr —7E 10
Weald Sq. E5 —2G 47
Wealdstone Rd. Sutt —2H 131
Weald, The. Chst —6D 114
Weald Way. Romf —6H 37
Weale Rd. E4 —3A 20
Weall Ct. Pinn —4C 22
Weardale Gdns. Enf —1J 7
Weardale Rd. SE13 —4F 97
Wear Pl. E2 —3H 63
Wearside Rd. SE13 —4D 96
Weatherbury Ho. N19 —3H 45
(off Wedmore St.)
Weatherley Clo. E3 —5B 64
Weavers Clo. Iswth —4J 87

—5E 108
Weavers La. SE1 —1E 78 (3D 148)
Weaver St. E1 —4G 63
Weavers Way. NW1 —1H 61
Weaver Wlk. SE27 —4C 110
Webber Row. SE1 —2B 78 (5H 147)
Webber St. SE1 —1A 78 (4H 147)
Webb Est. E5 —7G 31
Webb Gdns. E13 —4J 65
Webb Ho. SW8 —7H 77
Webb Ho. Dag —3G 53
(off Kershaw Rd.)
Webb Ho. Felt —3C 102
Webb Pl. NW10 —3B 58
Webb Rd. SE3 —6H 81
Webbscroft Rd. Dag —4H 53
Webb's Rd. SW11 —4D 92
Webb St. SE1 —3E 78 (7C 148)
Webster Gdns. W5 —1D 72
Webster Rd. E11 —3E 48
Webster Rd. SE16 —3G 79
Wedderburn Rd. NW3 —5B 44
Wedderburn Rd. Bark —1J 67
Wedgewood Way. SE19 —7C 110
Wedgwood M. W1 —6H 61 (8B 140)
Wedgwood Wlk. NW6 —5K 43
(off Lymington Rd.)
Wedlake St. W10 —4G 59
Wedmore Av. Ilf —1E 34
Wedmore Gdns. N19 —2H 45
Wedmore M. N19 —3H 45
Wedmore Rd. Gnfd —3H 55
Wedmore St. N19 —3H 45
Weech Rd. NW6 —4J 43
Weedan Ho. W12 —6C 58
Weedington Rd. NW5 —5E 44
Weekley Sq. SW11 —3B 92
Weigall Rd. SE12 —5J 97
Weighhouse St. W1

—6E 60 (9H 139)
Weighton M. SE20 —2H 125
Weighton Rd. SE20 —2H 125
Weighton Rd. Harr —1C 23
Weihurst Ct. Sutt —5C 132
Weihurst Gdns. Sutt —5B 132
Weimar St. SW15 —3G 91
Weirdale Av. N20 —2J 15
Weir Hall Av. N18 —6J 17
Weir Hall Gdns. N18 —5J 17
Weir Hall Rd. N18 & N17 —5J 17

Weir Rd. SW12 —1G 109
Weir Rd. SW19 —3K 107
Weir Rd. Bex —7H 101
Weir's Pas. NW1 —3H 61 (1B 140)
Weiss Rd. SW15 —3F 91
Welbeck Av. Brom —4J 113
Welbeck Av. Sidc —1A 116
Welbeck Clo. N12 —5G 15
Welbeck Clo. Eps —7C 130
Welbeck Clo. N Mald —5B 120
Welbeck Rd. E6 —3B 66
Welbeck Rd. Barn —6H 5
Welbeck Rd. Harr —1F 39
Welbeck Rd. Sutt & Cars —2B 132
Welbeck St. W1 —5E 60 (6H 139)
Welbeck Wlk. Cars —1C 132
Welbeck Way. W1 —6F 61 (7J 139)
Welbourne Rd. N17 —3F 31
Welby Ho. N19 —7H 29
Welby St. SE5 —1B 94
Welch Pl. Pinn —1A 22
Weldon Clo. Ruis —6A 38
Weldon Ct. N21 —5E 6
Weld Pl. N11 —5A 16
Welfare Rd. E15 —7G 49
Welford Clo. E5 —3K 47
Welford Pl. SW19 —4G 107
Welham Rd. SW17 & SW16

—5E 108
Welhouse Rd. Cars —1C 132
Wellacre Rd. Harr —6B 24
Welland Clo. Sidc —5B 100
Welland Gdns. Gnfd —2K 55
Welland Ho. SE15 —4J 95
Welland M. E1 —1G 79
Wellands Clo. Brom —2D 128
Welland St. SE10 —6E 80
Well App. Barn —5A 4
Well Clo. SW16 —4K 109
Well Clo. Ruis —3C 38
Wellclose Sq. E1 —7G 63
Well Cottage Clo. E11 —6A 34
Well Ct. EC4 —6C 62 (8M 141)
Welldon Ct. Harr —5J 23
Welldon Cres. Harr —5J 23
Weller Ho. SE16 —2G 79
(off George Row)
Wellers Ct. NW1 —2J 61
Weller St. SE1 —2C 78 (4L 147)
Wellesley Av. W6 —3D 74
Wellesley Ct. NW2 —2C 42
Wellesley Ct. W9 —3A 60
(off Maida Vale)
Wellesley Ct. Sutt —1G 131
Wellesley Ct. Rd. Croy —2D 134
Wellesley Cres. Twic —2J 103
Wellesley Gro. Croy —2D 134
Wellesley Lodge. Sutt —7K 131
(off Worcester Rd.)
Wellesley Pde. Twic —3K 103
Wellesley Pl. NW1 —3H 61 (2A 140)
Wellesley Pl. NW5 —5E 44
Wellesley Rd. E11 —5J 33
Wellesley Rd. E17 —6C 32
Wellesley Rd. N22 —2A 30
Wellesley Rd. NW5 —5E 44
Wellesley Rd. W4 —5G 73
Wellesley Rd. Croy —1C 134
Wellesley Rd. Harr —5J 23
Wellesley Rd. Ilf —2F 51
Wellesley Rd. Sutt —6A 132
Wellesley Rd. Twic —3H 103
Wellesley St. E1 —5K 63
Wellesley Ter. N1 —3C 62 (1M 141)
Wellfield Av. N10 —3F 29
Wellfield Rd. SW16 —4J 109

Wellfield Wlk. SW16 —5K 109
Wellfit St. SE24 —3B 94
Wellgarth. Gnfd —6B 40
Wellgarth Rd. NW11 —1K 43
Well Gro. N20 —1F 15
Well Hall Rd. SE9 —3C 98
Wellhouse La. Barn —4A 4
Wellhouse Rd. Beck —4C 126
Welling High St. Well —3B 100
Wellington. N8 —4J 29
Wellington Av. E4 —2H 19
Wellington Av. N9 —3C 18
Wellington Av. N15 —6F 31
Wellington Av. Houn —5E 86
Wellington Av. Pinn —1D 22
Wellington Av. Sidc —6A 100
Wellington Av. Wor Pk —3E 130
Wellington Bldgs. SW1 —5F 77
Wellington Clo. SE14 —1K 95
Wellington Clo. W11 —6J 59
Wellington Clo. Dag —7J 53
Wellington Ct. NW8 —2B 60
(off Wellington Rd.)
Wellington Ct. SW6 —1K 91
(off Maltings Pl.)
Wellington Ct. Pinn —1D 22
Wellington Ct. Hamp —5H 103
Wellington Cres. N Mald —3J 119
Wellington Dri. Dag —7J 53
Wellington Est. E2 —2J 63
Wellington Gdns. SE7 —6A 82
Wellington Gdns. Twic —4H 103
Wellington Gro. SE10 —7F 81
Wellington Ho. W5 —3E 56
Wellington Mans. E11 —1E 48
Wellington M. SE7 —6A 82
Wellington M. SE22 —4G 95
Wellington Pde. Sidc —5A 100
Wellington Pk. Est. NW2 —2C 42
Wellington Pl. N2 —6C 28
Wellington Pl. NW8

—3B 60 (1B 138)
Wellington Rd. E6 —1D 66
Wellington Rd. E7 —4H 49
Wellington Rd. E10 —1A 48
Wellington Rd. E11 —5J 33
Wellington Rd. E17 —4A 32
Wellington Rd. NW8 —2B 60
Wellington Rd. NW10 —3F 59
Wellington Rd. SW19 —2J 107
Wellington Rd. W5 —3C 72
Wellington Rd. Belv —5F 85
Wellington Rd. Bex —5D 100
Wellington Rd. Brom —4A 128
Wellington Rd. Croy —7B 124
Wellington Rd. Enf —5K 7
Wellington Rd. Hamp & Twic

—5H 103
Wellington Rd. Harr —3J 23
Wellington Rd. Pinn —1D 22
Wellington Rd. N. Houn —3D 86
Wellington Rd. S. Houn —4D 86
Wellington Row. E2 —3F 63
Wellington Sq. SW3 —5D 76
Wellington St. SE18 —4E 82
Wellington St. WC2 —7J 61 (9D 140)
Wellington St. Bark —1G 67
Wellington Ter. E1 —1H 79
Wellington Ter. N7 —7J 59
Wellington Ter. Harr —1H 39
Wellington Way. E3 —3C 64
Welling Way. SE9 & Well —3G 99
Wellow Wlk. Cars —1B 132

Well Pl. NW3 —3B 44
Well Rd. NW3 —3B 44
Well Rd. Barn —5A 4
Wells Clo. N'holt —3A 54
Wells Dri. NW9 —1K 41
Wells Gdns. Dag —5H 53
Wells Gdns. Ilf —7C 34
Wells Ho. Rd. NW10 —5A 58
Wellside Clo. Barn —4A 4
Wellside Gdns. SW14 —4J 89
Wells M. W1 —5G 61 (6M 139)
Wellsmoor Gdns. Brom —3E 128
Wells Pk. Rd. SE26 —3G 111
Wellsprings Cres. Wemb —3H 41
Wells Rise. NW8 —1D 60
Wells Rd. W12 —2E 74
Wells Rd. Brom —2D 128
Wells Sq. WC1 —3K 61 (2E 140)
Wells St. W1 —5G 61 (6L 139)
Wellstead Av. N9 —7E 8
Wellstead Rd. E6 —2E 66
Wells Ter. N4 —2A 46
Wells, The. N14 —1C 16
Well St. E9 —7J 47
Well St. E15 —6G 49
Wells Way. SE5 —6D 78
Wells Way. SW7 —3B 76 (6A 144)
Wells Yd. N7 —5A 46
Well Wlk. NW3 —4B 44
Wellwood Rd. Ilf —1A 52
Welsford St. SE1 —5G 79
Welsh Clo. E13 —3J 65
Welshpool St. E8 —1G 63
Welshside. NW9 —5A 26
(off Goldsmith Av.)
Welsingham Lodge. SW13 —1C 90
Weltje Rd. W6 —4C 74
Welton Ct. SE5 —1E 94
Welton Rd. SE18 —7J 83
Welwyn St. E2 —3J 63
Wembley Commercial Cen. Wemb

—2D 40
Wembley Hill Rd. Wemb —5F 41
Wembley Pk. Bus. Cen. Wemb

—3H 41
Wembley Pk. Dri. Wemb —4F 41
Wembley Rd. Hamp —7E 102
Wembley Stadium Ind. Est. Wemb

—4H 41
Wembley Way. Wemb —6H 41
Wemborough Rd. Stan —1B 24
Wembury Rd. N6 —7F 29
Wemyss Rd. SE3 —2H 97
Wendela Ct. Harr —2J 39
Wendell Rd. W12 —3B 74
Wendle Ct. SW8 —6J 77
Wendling Rd. Sutt —1B 132
Wendon St. E3 —1B 64
Wendover. SE17 —5E 78
(in two parts)
Wendover Clo. Hay —4C 54
Wendover Ct. NW2 —3J 43
Wendover Dri. N Mald —6B 120
Wendover Rd. NW10 —2B 58
Wendover Rd. SE9 —3B 98
Wendover Rd. Brom —3K 127
Wendover Way. Well —5A 100
Wendy Clo. Enf —6A 8
Wendy Way. Wemb —1E 56
Wenlock Barn Est. N1 —2D 62
(off Wenlock St.)
Wenlock Ct. N1 —2D 62
Wenlock Gdns. NW4 —4C 26
Wenlock Rd. N1 —2C 62
Wenlock Rd. Edgw —7C 12
Wenlock St. N1 —2C 62

Wennington Rd. E3 —2K 63
Wensdale Ho. E5 —2G 47
Wensley Av. Wfd G —7C 20
Wensley Clo. SE9 —6D 98
Wensleydale Av. Ilf —2C 34
Wensleydale Gdns. Hamp —7F 103
Wensleydale Pas. Hamp —7E 102
Wensleydale Rd. Hamp —7E 102
Wensley Rd. N18 —6C 18
Wentland Clo. SE6 —2F 113
Wentland Rd. SE6 —2F 113
Wentworth Av. N3 —7D 14
Wentworth Clo. N3 —7E 14
Wentworth Clo. Hayes —2J 137
Wentworth Clo. Mord —7J 121
Wentworth Ct. Twic —3J 103
Wentworth Cres. SE15 —7G 79
Wentworth Gdns. N13 —3G 17
Wentworth Hill. Wemb —1F 41
Wentworth M. E3 —4A 64
Wentworth Pk. N3 —7D 14
Wentworth Pl. Stan —6G 11
Wentworth Rd. E12 —4B 50
Wentworth Rd. NW11 —6H 27
Wentworth Rd. Barn —3A 4
Wentworth Rd. Croy —7A 124
Wentworth Rd. S'hall —4A 70
Wentworth St. E1 —6F 63 (7E 142)
Wentworth Way. Pinn —4C 22
Wenvoe Av. Bexh —2H 101
Wernbrook St. SE18 —6G 83
Werndee Rd. SE25 —4G 125
Werneth Hall Rd. Ilf —3D 34
Werrington St. NW1 —2G 61
Werter Rd. SW15 —4G 91
Wesleyan Pl. NW5 —4F 45
Wesley Av. NW10 —3K 57
Wesley Av. Houn —2C 86
Wesley Clo. N7 —2K 45
Wesley Clo. SE17 —4B 78 (9K 147)
Wesley Clo. Harr —2G 39
Wesley Rd. E10 —7E 32
Wesley Rd. N2 —1C 28
Wesley Rd. NW10 —1J 57
Wesley Sq. W11 —6G 59
Wesley St. W1 —5E 60 (6H 139)
Wessex Av. SW19 —2J 121
Wessex Clo. Ilf —6J 35
Wessex Clo. King T —1H 119
Wessex Ct. Barn —4A 4
Wessex Ct. Beck —1A 126
Wessex Dri. Pinn —1C 22
Wessex Gdns. NW11 —1G 43
Wessex Ho. SE1 —5F 79
Wessex La. Gnfd —2H 55
Wessex St. E2 —3J 63
Wessex Way. NW11 —1G 43
Westacott Clo. N19 —1H 45
West App. Orp —5G 129
W. Arbour St. E1 —6K 63
West Av. E17 —4D 32
West Av. N2 —4K 27
West Av. N3 —6D 14
West Av. NW4 —5F 27
West Av. Pinn —6D 22
West Av. S'hall —7D 54
West Av. Wall —5J 133
West Av. Rd. E17 —4C 32
W. Bank. N16 —7E 30
W. Bank. Bark —1F 67
West Bank. Enf —2H 7
Westbank Rd. Hamp —6G 103
W. Barnes La. N Mald & SW20

—3D 120
Westbeech Rd. N22 —3A 30
Westbere Dri. Stan —5J 11
Westbere Rd. NW2 —4G 43
Westbourne Av. W3 —6K 57

Westbourne Av. Sutt —2G 131
Westbourne Bri. W2 —5A 60
Westbourne Clo. Hay —4A 54
Westbourne Cres. W2
　　　　—7B 60 (9A 138)
Westbourne Cres. M. W2
　　　　—7B 60 (9A 138)
(off Westbourne Cres.)
Westbourne Dri. SE23 —2K 111
Westbourne Gdns. W2 —6K 59
Westbourne Gro. W11 & W2 —7H 59
Westbourne Gro. M. W11 —6J 59
Westbourne Gro. Ter. W2 —6K 59
Westbourne Ho. Houn —6E 70
Westbourne Pk. M. W2 —6K 59
Westbourne Pk. Pas. W2 —5J 59
Westbourne Pk. Rd. W11 & W2
　　　　—6G 59
Westbourne Pk. Vs. W2 —5J 59
Westbourne Pl. N9 —3C 18
Westbourne Rd. N7 —6K 45
Westbourne Rd. SE26 —6K 111
Westbourne Rd. Bexh —7E 84
Westbourne Rd. Croy —6F 125
Westbourne St. W2
　　　　—7B 60 (9A 138)
Westbourne Ter. W2 —6A 60
Westbourne Ter. M. W2 —6A 60
Westbourne Ter. Rd. W2 —5K 59
Westbridge Rd. SW11 —1B 92
Westbrook Av. Hamp —7D 102
Westbrook Clo. Barn —3G 5
Westbrook Cres. Barn —3G 5
Westbrooke Rd. Sidc —2H 115
Westbrooke Rd. Well —3B 100
Westbrook Rd. SE3 —1K 97
Westbrook Rd. Houn —7D 70
Westbrook Rd. T Hth —1D 124
Westbrook Sq. Barn —3G 5
Westbury Av. N22 —3B 30
Westbury Av. S'hall —4E 54
Westbury Av. Wemb —7D 40
Westbury Ct. Bark —1H 67
(off Westbury Rd.)
Westbury Gro. N12 —6D 14
Westbury Ho. E17 —4B 32
Westbury La. Buck H —2F 21
Westbury Lodge Clo. Pinn —3B 22
Westbury Pl. Bren —6D 72
Westbury Rd. E7 —6K 49
Westbury Rd. E17 —4C 32
Westbury Rd. N11 —6D 16
Westbury Rd. N12 —6D 14
Westbury Rd. SE20 —1K 125
Westbury Rd. W5 —6E 56
Westbury Rd. Bark —1H 67
Westbury Rd. Beck —3A 126
Westbury Rd. Brom —1B 128
Westbury Rd. Buck H —2F 21
Westbury Rd. Croy —6D 124
Westbury Rd. Felt —1B 102
Westbury Rd. Ilf —2E 50
Westbury Rd. N Mald —4K 119
Westbury Rd. Wemb —7E 40
Westbury St. SW8 —2G 93
Westbury Ter. E7 —6K 49
W. Carriage Dri. W2
　　　　—7C 60 (1C 144)
W. Central St. WC1 —6J 61 (7C 140)
W. Centre Av. NW10 —4D 58
W. Chantry. Harr —1F 23
Westchester Dri. NW4 —3F 27
West Clo. N9 —3A 18
West Clo. Cockf —4K 5
West Clo. Gnfd —2G 55
West Clo. Hamp —6C 102
West Clo. Wemb —1F 41

Westcombe Av. Croy —7J 123
Westcombe Dri. Barn —5D 4
Westcombe Hill. SE3 —7J 81
Westcombe Pk. Rd. SE3 —6G 81
W. Common Rd. Hayes —2J 137
Westcoombe Av. SW20 —1B 120
W. Coombe La. SW20 —7A 106
Westcote Rd. SW16 —5G 109
West Cotts. NW6 —5J 43
Westcott Clo. N15 —6F 31
Westcott Clo. Brom —5C 128
Westcott Clo. New Ad —7D 136
Westcott Cres. W7 —6J 55
Westcott Ho. E14 —7C 64
Westcott Rd. SE17 —6B 78
West Ct. E17 —4D 32
West Ct. Houn —7G 71
West Ct. Wemb —2C 40
Westcroft Clo. NW2 —4G 43
Westcroft Clo. Enf —1D 8
Westcroft Gdns. Mord —4H 121
Westcroft Rd. Cars & Wall —4E 132
Westcroft Sq. W6 —4C 74
Westcroft Way. NW2 —4G 43
W. Cromwell Rd. W14 & SW5
　　　　—5H 75
W. Cross Cen. Bren —6A 72
W. Cross Route. W10, W11 & W12
　　　　—7F 59
W. Cross Way. Bren —6B 72
Westdale Pas. SE18 —6F 83
Westdale Rd. SE18 —6F 83
Westdean Av. SE12 —1K 113
W. Dean Clo. SW18 —6K 91
W. Dene. Sutt —6G 131
Westdown Rd. E15 —4E 48
Westdown Rd. SE6 —7C 96
West Dri. SW16 —4G 109
West Dri. Harr —6C 10
West Dri. Sutt —7F 131
West Dri. Gdns. Harr —6C 10
W. Eaton Pl. SW1 —4E 76 (8G 145)
W. Eaton Pl. M. SW1
(off W. Eaton Pl.) —4E 76 (8G 145)
W. Ella Rd. NW10 —7A 42
W. End Av. E10 —5F 33
W. End Av. Pinn —4B 22
W. End Ct. Pinn —4B 22
W. End Gdns. N'holt —2A 54
W. End La. NW6 —5J 43
W. End La. Barn —4A 4
W. End La. Pinn —3B 22
W. End Rd. Ruis & N'holt —6A 38
W. End Rd. S'hall —1C 70
Westerdale Rd. SE10 —5J 81
Westerfield Rd. N15 —5E 31
Westergate Rd. SE2 —6E 84
Westerham Av. N9 —3J 17
Westerham Dri. Sidc —8B 100
Westerham Ho. SE1
(off Law St.) —3D 78 (6B 148)
Westerham Lodge. Beck —7C 112
(off Park Rd.)
Westerham Rd. E10 —7D 32
Westerley Cres. SE26 —5B 112
Western Av. NW11 —6F 27
Western Av. Dag —6J 53
Western Av. Gnfd & W3 —3C 56
Western Ct. N3 —6D 14
Western Gdns. W5 —7G 57
Western Gateway. E16 —7J 65
Western International Mkt. S'hall
　　　　—4A 70
Western La. SW12 —7E 92
Western M. W9 —4H 59
Western Pde. New Bar —5D 4
Western Pl. SE16 —2J 79
Western Rd. E13 —2A 66

Western Rd. E17 —5E 32
Western Rd. N2 —4D 28
Western Rd. N22 —2K 29
Western Rd. NW10 —4J 57
Western Rd. SW9 —3A 94
Western Rd. SW19 & Mitc —1B 122
Western Rd. W5 —7D 56
Western Rd. S'hall —4A 70
Western Rd. Sutt —5J 131
Westernville Gdns. Ilf —7G 35
Western Way. SE28 —2J 83
Western Way. Barn —6D 4
Westferry Cir. E14 —1B 80
Westferry Rd. E14 —7C 64
Westfield Clo. Enf —3F 9
Westfield Clo. Sutt —4H 131
Westfield Dri. Harr —4D 24
Westfield Gdns. Harr —4D 24
Westfield La. Harr —4D 24
(in two parts)
Westfield Pk. Pinn —1D 22
Westfield Rd. NW7 —3E 12
Westfield Rd. W13 —1A 72
Westfield Rd. Beck —2B 126
Westfield Rd. Bexh —3J 101
Westfield Rd. Croy —2B 134
Westfield Rd. Dag —4E 52
Westfield Rd. Mitc —2D 122
Westfield Rd. Surb —5D 118
Westfield Rd. Sutt —4H 131
Westfields. SW13 —3B 90
Westfields Av. SW13 —3A 90
Westfields Rd. W3 —5H 57
Westfield St. SE18 —3B 82
Westfield Way. E1 —3A 64
W. Garden Pl. W2 —6C 60 (8D 138)
West Gdns. E1 —7H 63
West Gdns. SW17 —6C 108
W. Gate. W5 —3E 56
Westgate Ct. SW9 —3A 94
(off Canterbury Cres.)
Westgate Rd. SE25 —4H 125
Westgate Rd. Beck —1E 126
Westgate St. E8 —1H 63
Westgate Ter. SW10 —5K 75
Westglade Ct. Kent —5D 24
West Grn. Pl. Gnfd —1H 55
W. Green Rd. N15 —4B 30
West Gro. SE10 —1E 96
Westgrove La. SE10 —1E 96
W. Halkin St. SW1 —3E 76 (6G 145)
W. Hallowes. SE9 —1B 114
W. Hall Rd. Rich —1H 89
W.Hampstead M. NW6 —6K 43
W. Harding St. EC4 —6A 62 (7H 141)
Westhay Gdns. SW14 —5H 89
W. Heath Av. NW11 —1J 43
W. Heath Clo. NW3 —3J 43
W. Heath Ct. NW11 —1J 43
W. Heath Dri. NW11 —1J 43
W. Heath Gdns. NW3 —3J 43
W. Heath Rd. NW3 —2J 43
W. Heath Rd. SE2 —6D 84
W. Hill. SW15 & SW18 —7F 91
W. Hill. Harr —2J 39
W. Hill. S Croy —7E 134
W. Hill. Wemb —1F 41
W. Hill Ct. N6 —3E 44
Westhill Pk. N6 —2D 44
(in two parts)
W. Hill Rd. SW18 —6H 91
W. Hill Way. N20 —1E 14
Westholm. NW11 —4K 27
West Holme. Eri —1J 101
Westholme. Orp —7J 129
Westhorne Av. SE12 & SE9 —7J 97

Westthorpe Gdns. NW4 —3E 26
Westthorpe Rd. SW15 —3E 90
West Ho. Clo. SW19 —1G 107
West Ho. Cotts. Pinn —4B 22
Westhurst Dri. Chst —5F 115
W. India Av. E14 —1C 80
W. India Dock Rd. E14 —7B 64
W. Kensington Ct. W14 —5H 75
(off Edith Vs.)
W. Kensington Mans. W14 —5H 75
(off Beaumont Cres.)
Westlake Clo. N13 —3F 17
Westlake Clo. Hay —4C 54
Westlake Rd. Wemb —2D 40
Westland Dri. Brom —2H 137
Westland Ho. E16 —1E 82
(off Rymill St.)
Westland Pl. N1 —3D 62 (1A 142)
Westlands Ter. SW12 —6G 93
West La. SE16 —2H 79
Westlea Rd. W7 —3A 72
Westleigh Av. SW15 —5D 90
Westleigh Ct. E11 —5J 33
Westleigh Dri. Brom —1C 128
Westleigh Gdns. Edgw —1G 25
W. Lodge Av. W3 —1G 73
W. Mead. Eps —6A 130
W. Mead. Ruis —4A 38
Westmead Corner. Cars —4C 132
Westmead Rd. Sutt —4B 132
Westmere Dri. NW7 —3E 12
West M. N17 —6C 18
West M. SW1 —4G 77 (9L 145)
(off W. Warwick Pl.)
Westmill Ct. N4 —2C 46
(off Brownswood Rd.)
Westminster Av. T Hth —2B 124
Westminster Bri. SW1 & SE1
　　　　—2J 77 (5D 145)
Westminster Bri. Rd. SE1
　　　　—2K 77 (5E 146)
Westminster Bus. Sq. SE11 —5K 77
Westminster Clo. Ilf —2H 35
Westminster Clo. Tedd —5A 104
Westminster Ct. E11 —6J 33
(off Cambridge Pk.)
Westminster Dri. N13 —5D 16
Westminster Gdns. E4 —1B 20
Westminster Gdns. Bark —2J 67
Westminster Gdns. Ilf —2G 35
Westminster Ho. Har W —7E 10
Westminster Ind. Est. SE18 —3B 82
Westminster Rd. N9 —1C 18
Westminster Rd. W7 —1J 71
Westminster Rd. Sutt —2B 132
Westmoat Clo. Beck —7E 112
Westmoor Gdns. Enf —2E 8
Westmoor Rd. Enf —2E 8
Westmoor St. SE7 —3A 82
Westmoreland Av. Well —4J 99
Westmoreland Pl. SW1 —5F 77
Westmoreland Pl. W5 —5D 56
Westmoreland Pl. Brom —3J 127
Westmoreland Rd. NW9 —3F 25
Westmoreland Rd. SE17 —6D 78
Westmoreland Rd. SW13 —1B 90
Westmoreland Rd. Brom —5G 127
Westmoreland St. W1
　　　　—5E 60 (6H 139)
Westmoreland Ter. SW1 —5F 77
Westmoreland Wlk. SE17 —6D 78
Westmoreland Clo. E12 —2B 50
Westmoreland Clo. Twic —6B 88
Westmoreland Ct. Surb —7D 118
Westmorland Dri. Sutt —7K 131
Westmorland Rd. E17 —6C 32
Westmorland Rd. Harr —5F 23

Westmorland St. W1 —5E 60
Westmorland Ter. SE20 —7H 111
Westmorland Way. Mitc —5H 123
Westmount Rd. SE9 —2D 98
W. Oak. Beck —1F 127
Westoe Rd. N9 —2C 18
Westonbirt Ct. SE15 —6F 79
(off Ebley Clo.)
Weston Ct. N4 —3C 46
Weston Dri. Stan —1B 24
Westone Mans. Bark —7K 51
(off Upney La.)
Weston Gdns. Iswth —1J 87
Weston Grn. Dag —4F 53
Weston Gro. Brom —1H 127
Weston Rd. Dag —4E 52
Weston Rd. Enf —1J 7
Weston St. SE1 —2E 78 (6B 148)
(in three parts)
Weston Wlk. E8 —7H 47
Westover Clo. Sutt —7K 131
Westover Hill. NW3 —2J 43
Westover Rd. SW18 —7A 92
Westow Hill. SE19 —6E 110
Westow St. SE19 —6E 110
West Pk. SE9 —2C 114
West Pk. Av. Rich —1H 89
West Pk. Clo. Houn —6D 70
West Pk. Clo. Romf —5D 36
West Pk. Rd. Rich —1G 89
West Pk. Rd. S'hall —1G 71
West Pier. E1 —1H 79
West Row. W10 —4G 59
Westrow. SW15 —6E 90
W. Row. W10 —4G 59
Westrow Dri. Bark —6K 51
Westrow Gdns. Ilf —2K 51
Westport St. E1 —6K 63
W. Poultry Av. EC1 —5B 62 (6J 141)
W. Quarters. W12 —6C 58
W. Quay. SE10 —1A 92
W. Quay Dri. Hay —5C 54
W. Ridge Gdns. Gnfd —2G 55
West Rd. E15 —1H 65
West Rd. N2 —2B 28
West Rd. N17 —6C 18
West Rd. SW3 —5D 76
West Rd. SW4 —5H 93
West Rd. W5 —5E 56
West Rd. Barn —1K 15
West Rd. Chad —6D 36
West Rd. King T —1J 119
West Rd. Rush —7K 37
Westrow. SW15 —6E 90
W. Row. W10 —4G 59
Westrow Dri. Bark —6K 51
Westrow Gdns. Ilf —2K 51
W. Sheen Vale. Rich —4F 89
Westside. N2 —3D 28
W. Side Comn. SW19 —5E 106
W. Smithfield. EC1 —5B 62 (6J 141)
W. Spur Rd. SE11 —3B 78 (7J 147)
West St. E2 —2H 63
West St. E11 —3G 49
West St. WC2 —6H 61 (8B 140)
West St. Bexh —3F 101
West St. Bren —4C 72
West St. Brom —1J 127
West St. Cars —3D 132
West St. Croy —4C 134
West St. Eri —4K 85

West St. Harr —1H **39**
West St. Sutt —5K **131**
West St. La. Cars —4D **132**
W. Temple Sheen. SW14 —5H **89**
W. Tenter St. E1 —6F **63**
West Ter. Sidc —1J **115**
W. Towers. Pinn —6B **22**
W. View. NW4 —4E **26**
W. View Clo. NW10 —5B **42**
Westview Clo. W7 —6J **55**
Westview Clo. W10 —6E **58**
Westview Cres. N9 —7K **7**
Westview Dri. Wfd G —2B **34**
Westville Rd. W12 —2C **74**
Westville Rd. Th Dit —7A **118**
West Wlk. Barn —7K **5**
Westward Rd. E4 —5G **19**
Westward Way. Harr —6E **24**
W. Warwick Pl. SW1
 —4G **77** (3J **145**)
Westway. N18 —4J **17**
West Way. NW10 —3K **41**
Westway. SW20 —4D **120**
Westway. W2 —5K **59**
West Way. Croy —2A **136**
West Way. Edgw —6C **12**
West Way. Houn —1D **86**
Westway. Orp —5H **129**
West Way. Pinn —4B **22**
West Way. W Wick —6F **127**
Westway Clo. SW20 —3D **120**
Westway Ct. N'holt —1E **54**
W. Way Gdns. Croy —2K **135**
Westways. Eps —4B **130**
Westwell M. SW16 —6J **109**
Westwell Rd. SW16 —6J **109**
Westwell Rd. App. SW16 —6J **109**
Westwick Gdns. W14 —2F **75**
Westwood Av. SE19 —1D **124**
Westwood Av. Harr —4F **39**
Westwood Clo. Brom —3B **128**
Westwood Ct. Gnfd —5H **39**
Westwood Ct. Wemb —4B **40**
Westwood Gdns. SW13 —3B **90**
Westwood Hill. SE26 —5G **111**
Westwood La. Sidc —5A **100**
Westwood La. Well —3K **99**
Westwood Pk. SE23 —7H **95**
Westwood Pk. Trading Est. W3
 —5H **57**
Westwood Rd. E16 —1K **81**
Westwood Rd. SW13 —3B **90**
Westwood Rd. Ilf —1K **51**
W. Woodside. Bex —1E **116**
Wetheral Dri. Stan —1B **24**
Wetherby Clo. N'holt —6F **39**
Wetherby Gdns. SW5 —4A **76**
Wetherby Mans. SW5 —5K **75**
 (off Earl's Ct. Sq.)
Wetherby M. SW5 —5K **75**
Wetherby Pl. SW7 —4A **76**
Wetherby Rd. Enf —1H **7**
Wetherden St. E17 —6B **32**
Wetherell Rd. E9 —1K **63**
Wetherill Rd. N10 —1E **28**
Wevell Ho. N6 —7E **28**
 (off Hillcrest)
Wexford Rd. SW12 —7D **92**
Weybourne St. SW18 —2A **108**
Weybridge Rd. T Hth —4A **124**
Weydown Clo. SW19 —1G **107**
Weyland Rd. Dag —3F **53**
Weyman Rd. SE3 —1A **98**
Weymarks, The. N17 —6J **17**
Weymouth Av. NW7 —5F **13**
Weymouth Av. W5 —3C **72**
Weymouth Ct. Sutt —7J **131**

Weymouth M. W1 —5F **61** (5J **139**)
Weymouth St. W1 —5E **60** (6H **139**)
Weymouth Ter. E2 —2F **63**
Weymouth Wlk. Stan —6F **11**
Whadcoat St. N4 —2A **46**
Whalebone Av. Romf —6F **37**
Whalebone Ct. EC2 —6D **62** *(7A* **142***)*
 (off Telegraph St.)
Whalebone Gro. Romf —6F **37**
Whalebone La. E15 —7G **49**
Whalebone La. N. Romf —1E **36**
Whalebone La. S. Romf & Dag
 —7F **37**
Whales Yd. E15 —7G **49**
 (off W. Ham La.)
Wharfdale Rd. N1 —2J **61**
Wharfdale Ct. E5 —4A **48**
Wharfedale Gdns. T Hth —4K **123**
Wharfedale St. SW10 —5K **75**
Wharf La. Twic —1A **104**
Wharf. Pl. E2 —1H **63**
Wharf Rd. E15 —1F **65**
Wharf Rd. N1 —2C **62**
Wharf Rd. Enf —6F **9**
Wharf Rd. Ind. Est. Enf —6F **9**
Wharfside Rd. E16 —5G **65**
Wharf St. E16 —5G **65**
Wharncliffe Dri. S'hall —1H **71**
Wharncliffe Gdns. SE25 —2E **124**
Wharncliffe Rd. SE25 —2E **124**
Wharton Clo. NW10 —6A **42**
Wharton Cotts. WC1
 —3A **62** (2G **141**)
Wharton Rd. Brom —1K **127**
Wharton St. WC1 —3K **61** (2F **140**)
Whateley Rd. SE20 —7K **111**
Whateley Rd. SE22 —5F **95**
Whatley Av. SW20 —3F **121**
Whatman Rd. SE23 —7K **95**
Wheatfields. E6 —6F **67**
Wheatfields. Enf —1F **9**
Wheatfield Way. King T —2E **118**
Wheathill Rd. SE20 —2H **125**
Wheatlands. Houn —6E **70**
Wheatlands Rd. SW17 —3E **108**
Wheatley Clo. NW4 —2C **26**
Wheatley Gdns. N9 —2K **17**
Wheatley Mans. Bark —7A **52**
 (off Bevan Av.)
Wheatley Rd. Iswth —3K **87**
Wheatley St. W1 —5E **60** (6H **139**)
Wheatsheaf Clo. N'holt —5C **38**
Wheatsheaf La. SW6 —7E **74**
Wheatsheaf La. SW8 —7J **77**
Wheatsheaf Ter. SW6 —7H **75**
Wheatstone Clo. Mitc —1C **122**
Wheatstone Rd. W10 —5G **59**
Wheeler Gdns. N1 —1J **61**
 (off Outram Pl.)
Wheelers Cross. Bark —2H **67**
Wheel Farm Dri. Dag —3J **53**
Wheelwright St. N7 —7K **45**
Whelan Way. Wall —3H **133**
Wheler St. E1 —4F **63** (4E **142**)
Whellock Rd. W4 —3A **74**
Whenman Av. Bex —2J **117**
Whernside Clo. SE28 —7C **68**
Whetstone Clo. N20 —2G **15**
Whetstone Pk. WC2
 —6K **61** (7E **140**)
Whetstone Rd. SE3 —2A **98**
Whewell Rd. N19 —2J **45**
Whichcote St. SE1 —1A **78** *(3G* **147***)*
 (off Mepham St.)
Whidborne Clo. SE8 —2C **96**
Whidborne St. WC1
 —3J **61** (2D **140**)
Whimbrel Clo. SE28 —7C **68**

Whimbrel Way. Hay —5B **54**
Whinchat Rd. SE28 —3H **83**
Whinfell Clo. SW16 —5H **109**
Whinyates Rd. SE9 —3C **98**
Whippendell Way. Orp —7B **116**
Whipps Cross. E17 —5F **33**
Whipps Cross Ho. E17 —4F **33**
 (off Wood St.)
Whipps Cross Rd. E11 —5F **33**
Whiskin St. EC1 —3B **62** (2J **141**)
Whisperwood Clo. Har W —1J **23**
Whistler Gdns. Edgw —2F **25**
Whistlers Av. SW11 —7B **76**
Whistler St. N5 —5B **46**
Whistler Tower. SW10 —7A **76**
 (off Worlds End Est.)
Whistler Wlk. SW10 —7B **76**
Whiston Rd. E2 —2F **63**
Whitbread Clo. N17 —1G **31**
Whitbread Rd. SE4 —4A **96**
Whitburn Rd. SE13 —4D **96**
Whitby Av. NW10 —3H **57**
Whitby Ct. N7 —4J **45**
Whitby Gdns. NW9 —3G **25**
Whitby Gdns. Sutt —2B **132**
Whitby Rd. SE18 —4D **82**
Whitby Rd. Harr —3G **39**
Whitby Rd. Ruis —3A **38**
Whitby Rd. Sutt —2B **132**
Whitby St. E1 —4F **63** (3E **142**)
Whitcher Clo. SE14 —6A **80**
Whitcher Pl. NW1 —6G **45**
Whitchurch Av. Edgw —7A **12**
Whitchurch Clo. Edgw —6A **12**
Whitchurch Gdns. Edgw —6A **12**
Whitchurch La. Edgw —7J **11**
Whitchurch Pde. Edgw —7B **12**
Whitchurch Rd. W11 —7F **59**
Whitcomb Ct. WC2 —7H **61** *(1B* **146***)*
 (off Whitcomb St.)
Whitcomb St. WC2 —7H **61** (1B **146**)
White Acre. NW9 —2A **26**
Whiteadder Way. E14 —4D **80**
Whitear Wlk. E15 —6F **49**
Whitebarn La. Dag —1G **69**
Whitebeam Av. Brom —7E **128**
Whitebeam Clo. SW9 —7K **77**
White Bear Pl. NW3 —4B **44**
White Butts Rd. Ruis —3B **38**
Whitechapel High St. E1
 —6F **63** (7F **142**)
Whitechapel Rd. E1 —5G **63**
Whitechurch La. E1 —6G **63**
White City Clo. W12 —7E **58**
White City Est. W12 —7D **58**
White City Rd. W12 —7D **58**
White Conduit St. N1 —2A **62**
Whitecote Rd. S'hall —6G **55**
Whitecroft Clo. Beck —4F **127**
Whitecroft Way. Beck —5E **126**
Whitecross Pl. EC2 —5D **62** (5B **142**)
Whitecross St. EC1
 —4C **62** (3M **141**)
Whitecross St. EC2
 —5C **62** (5M **141**)
Whitefield Av. NW2 —1E **42**
Whitefield Clo. SW15 —6G **91**
Whitefoot La. Brom —4E **112**
Whitefoot Ter. Brom —3H **113**
Whitefriars Av. Harr —2J **23**
Whitefriars Ct. N12 —5G **15**
Whitefriars Dri. Harr —2H **23**
Whitefriars St. EC4 —6A **62** (8H **141**)
Whitefriars Trading Est. Harr —3H **23**
White Gdns. Dag —6G **53**
Whitegate Gdns. Harr —7E **10**
Whitehall. SW1 —1J **77** (2C **145**)
Whitehall Ct. SW1 —1J **77** (3C **145**)

Whitehall Gdns. E4 —1B **20**
Whitehall Gdns. SW1
 —1J **77** (3C **146**)
 (off Horseguards Av.)
Whitehall Gdns. W3 —1G **73**
Whitehall Gdns. W4 —6H **73**
Whitehall La. Buck H —2D **20**
Whitehall Pk. N19 —1G **45**
Whitehall Pk. Rd. W4 —6H **73**
Whitehall Pl. E7 —5J **49**
Whitehall Pl. SW1 —1J **77** (3C **146**)
Whitehall Pl. Wall —4F **133**
Whitehall Rd. E4 & Wfd G —2B **20**
Whitehall Rd. W7 —2A **72**
Whitehall Rd. Brom —5B **128**
Whitehall Rd. Harr —7J **23**
Whitehall Rd. T Hth —5A **124**
Whitehall St. N17 —7A **18**
White Hart Ct. EC2 —5E **62** *(6C* **142***)*
 (off Bishopsgate)
White Hart La. N22 & N17 —1K **29**
White Hart La. NW10 —6B **42**
White Hart La. SW13 —2A **90**
White Hart La. Romf —1G **37**
White Hart Rd. SE18 —4J **83**
White Hart Rd. Orp —7K **129**
White Hart Slip. Brom —2J **127**
White Hart Yd. SE11 —5A **78**
White Hart Yd. SE1 —1D **78** (3A **148**)
Whitehaven Clo. Brom —4J **127**
Whitehaven St. NW8
 —4C **60** (4C **138**)
Whitehead Clo. N18 —5J **17**
Whitehead Clo. SW18 —7A **92**
Whitehead's Gro. SW3 —5C **76**
White Heron M. Tedd —6K **103**
Whitehorn Gdns. Croy —2H **135**
Whitehorn St. E3 —5C **64**
White Horse All. EC1
 —5B **62** (5J **141**)
 (off Cowcross St.)
White Horse Hill. Chst —4E **114**
White Horse La. E1 —5K **63**
Whitehorse La. SE25 —4D **124**
Whitehorse M. SE1 —3A **78** (6H **147**)
White Horse Rd. E1 —6A **64**
White Horse Rd. E6 —3D **66**
Whitehorse Rd. Croy & T Hth
 —7C **124**
White Horse St. W1 —1F **77** (3K **145**)
White Horse Yd. EC2
 —6D **62** (7A **142**)
White Ho. SW4 —7H **93**
 (off Clapham Pk. Est.)
White Ho. Dri. Stan —4H **11**
White Ho. Dri. Wfd G —6C **20**
Whitehouse Est. E10 —6E **32**
Whitehouse La. Enf —1H **7**
Whitehouse Way. N14 —2A **16**
White Kennett St. E1
 —6E **62** (7D **142**)
Whiteledges. W13 —6C **56**
Whitelegg Rd. E13 —2H **65**
Whiteley Rd. SE19 —5D **110**
Whiteleys. W2 —6K **59**
Whiteley's Cotts. W14 —4H **75**
Whiteley's Way. Felt —3E **102**
White Lion Ct. EC3 —6E **62** *(8C* **142***)*
 (off Cornhill)
White Lion Ct. SE15 —6J **79**
White Lion La. Iswth —3B **88**
White Lion Hill. EC4
 —7B **62** (9K **141**)
White Lion St. N1 —2A **62**
White Lodge. SE19 —7B **110**
White Lodge Clo. N2 —6B **28**
White Lodge Clo. Sutt —7A **132**
White Lyon Ct. EC2 —5C **62** *(5L* **141***)*
 (off Fann St.)

Whiteoak Ct. Chst —6E **114**
White Oak Dri. Beck —2E **126**
White Oak Gdns. Sidc —7K **99**
Whiteoaks La. Gnfd —3H **55**
White Orchards. N20 —7C **4**
White Orchards. Stan —5F **11**
White Post La. E9 —6C **48**
Whitepost La. SE13 —3C **96**
White Post St. SE15 —7J **79**
White Rd. E15 —7G **49**
Whites Av. Ilf —6J **35**
Whites Dri. Brom —6H **127**
White's Grounds. SE1
 —2E **78** (5D **148**)
White's Grounds Est. SE1
 —2E **78** (4D **148**)
 (off White's Gronds)
White's Meadow. Brom —4E **128**
White's Row. E1 —5F **63** (6E **142**)
Whites Sq. SW4 —4H **93**
Whitestile Rd. Bren —5C **72**
Whitestone La. NW3 —3A **44**
Whitestone Wlk. NW3 —3A **44**
White St. S'hall —2B **70**
Whiteswan M. W4 —5A **74**
Whitethorn Gdns. Croy —2H **135**
Whitethorn Gdns. Enf —5J **7**
Whitewebbs Way. Orp —1K **129**
Whitfield Pl. W1 —4G **61** (4L **139**)
Whitfield Pl. W1 —4G **61** *(4L* **139***)*
 (off Whitfield St.)
Whitfield Rd. E6 —7A **50**
Whitfield Rd. SE3 —2F **97**
Whitfield Rd. Bexh —7F **85**
Whitfield St. W1 —4G **61** (4L **139**)
Whitford Gdns. Mitc —3D **122**
Whitgift Av. S Croy —5C **134**
Whitgift Cen. Croy —2C **134**
Whitgift Sq. Croy —2C **134**
Whitgift St. SE11 —4K **77** (8E **146**)
Whitgift St. Croy —3D **134**
Whiting Av. Bark —7F **51**
Whitings Rd. Barn —5A **4**
Whitings Way. E6 —5E **66**
Whitland Rd. Cars —1B **132**
Whitley Rd. N17 —2E **30**
Whitlock Dri. SW19 —1G **107**
Whitman Rd. E3 —4A **64**
Whitmead Clo. S Croy —6E **134**
Whitminster Ct. SE15 —6E **78**
 (off Brockworth Clo.)
Whitmore Clo. N11 —5A **16**
Whitmore Est. N1 —1E **62**
Whitmore Gdns. NW10 —2E **58**
Whitmore Ho. N1 —1E **62**
 (off Whitmore Est.)
Whitmore Rd. N1 —1E **62**
Whitmore Rd. Beck —3B **126**
Whitmore Rd. Harr —7G **23**
Whitnell Way. SW15 —5E **90**
Whitney Av. Ilf —4B **34**
Whitney Rd. E10 —7D **32**
Whitney Wlk. Sidc —6E **116**
Whitstable Clo. Beck —1B **126**
Whitstable Ho. W10 —6F **59**
 (off Walmer Rd.)
Whittaker Av. Rich —5D **88**
Whittaker Ct. Rich —5D **88**
 (off Whittaker Av.)
Whittaker Rd. E6 —7A **50**
Whittaker Rd. Sutt —3H **131**
Whittaker St. SW1 —4E **76** (9G **145**)
Whittaker Way. SE1 —4G **79**
Whitta Rd. E12 —4B **50**
Whittell Gdns. SE26 —3J **111**
Whittingham. N17 —7C **18**
Whittingham Ct. W4 —7A **74**
Whittingstall Rd. SW6 —1H **91**
Whittington Av. EC3 —6E **62** (8C **142**)

Whittington Ct. N2 —5D **28**
Whittington Rd. N22 —7D **16**
Whittington Way. Pinn —5C **22**
Whittlebury Clo. Cars —7D **132**
Whittle Clo. S'hall —6F **55**
Whittle Rd. Houn —7A **70**
Whittlesea Clo. Harr —2B **10**
Whittlesea Path. Harr —1G **23**
Whittlesea Rd. Harr —7B **10**
Whittlesey St. SE1 —1A **78** (3H **147**)
Whitton Av. E. Gnfd —5J **39**
Whitton Av. W. N'holt & Gnfd
—5F **39**
Whitton Clo. Gnfd —6B **40**
Whitton Dene. Houn & Iswth —5G **87**
Whitton Dri. Gnfd —6A **40**
Whitton Mnr. Rd. Iswth —6G **87**
Whitton Rd. Houn —4F **87**
Whitton Rd. Twic —6J **87**
Whitton Wlk. E3 —3C **64**
Whitton Waye. Houn —6E **86**
Whitwell Rd. E13 —3J **65**
Whitworth Ho. SE1
—3C **78** (7M **147**)
Whitworth Rd. SE18 —7E **82**
Whitworth St. SE25 —3E **124**
Whitworth St. SE10 —5G **81**
Whorlton Rd. SE15 —3H **95**
Whymark Av. N22 —3A **30**
Whytecroft. Houn —7B **70**
Whyteville Rd. E7 —6K **49**
Wickersley Rd. SW11 —2E **92**
Wickers Oake. SE19 —4F **111**
Wicker St. E1 —6H **63**
Wicket Rd. Gnfd —3A **56**
Wicket, The. Croy —5C **136**
Wickford St. E1 —4J **63**
Wickford Way. E17 —4K **31**
Wickham Av. Croy —2A **136**
Wickham Av. Sutt —5E **130**
Wickham Chase. W Wick —1F **137**
Wickham Clo. Enf —3C **8**
Wickham Clo. N Mald —6B **120**
Wickham Ct. Rd. W Wick —2E **136**
Wickham Cres. W Wick —2E **136**
Wickham Gdns. SE4 —3B **96**
Wickham La. SE2 & Well —5A **84**
Wickham M. SE4 —2B **96**
Wickham Rd. E4 —7K **19**
Wickham Rd. SE4 —4B **96**
Wickham Rd. Beck —2D **126**
Wickham Rd. Croy —2K **135**
Wickham Rd. Harr —2H **23**
Wickham St. SE11 —5K **77**
Wickham Way. Beck —4E **126**
Wick La. E3 —1C **64**
(in two parts)
Wickliffe Av. N3 —2G **27**
Wickliffe Gdns. Wemb —2H **41**
Wicklow Ho. N16 —1F **47**
Wicklow St. WC1 —3K **61** (1E **140**)
Wick M. E9 —6A **48**
Wick Rd. E9 —6K **47**
Wick Rd. Tedd —7B **104**
Wicks Clo. SE9 —4B **114**
Wick Sq. E9 —6B **48**
Wickstead Ho. SE1 —3C **78**
Wicksteed Clo. Bex —3K **117**
Wicksteed Ho. SE1
—3C **78** (7M **147**)
Wicksteed Ho. Bren —5F **73**
Wickway Ct. SE15 —6F 79
(off Cator St.)
Wickwood St. SE5 —2B **94**
Widdecombe Av. S Harr —2C **38**
Widdenham Rd. N7 —4K **45**
Widdin St. E15 —7F **49**

Widecombe Gdns. Ilf —4C **34**
Widecombe Rd. SE9 —3C **114**
Widecombe Way. N2 —5B **28**
Widegate St. E1 —5E **62** (6D **142**)
Widenham Clo. Pinn —5A **22**
Wide Way. Mitc —3H **123**
Widgeon Clo. E16 —6K **65**
Widley Rd. W9 —3J **59**
Widmore Lodge Rd. Brom —2B **128**
Widmore Rd. Brom —2J **127**
Wigan Ho. E5 —1H **47**
Wigan Pl. SE11 —5A **78**
Wigeon Path. SE28 —3H **83**
Wigeon Way. Hay —6C **54**
Wiggins Mead. NW9 —7G **13**
Wigginton Av. Wemb —6H **41**
Wightman Rd. N8 & N4 —4A **30**
Wigley Rd. Felt —2B **102**
Wigmore Pl. W1 —6F **61** (7J **139**)
Wigmore Rd. Cars —2B **132**
Wigmore St. W1 —6E **60** (8G **139**)
Wigmore Wlk. Cars —2B **132**
Wigram Rd. E11 —6A **34**
Wigram Sq. E17 —3E **32**
Wigstan Clo. N18 —5K **17**
Wigston Rd. E13 —4K **65**
Wigton Gdns. Stan —1E **24**
Wigton Pl. SE11 —5A 78
(off Cator St.)
Wigton Rd. E17 —1B **32**
Wilberforce Rd. N4 —2B **46**
Wilberforce Rd. NW9 —6C **26**
Wilberforce Way. SW19 —6F **107**
Wilbraham Pl. SW1 —4D **76** (8F **144**)
Wilbury Way. N18 —5J **17**
Wilby M. W11 —1H **75**
Wilcox Clo. SW8 —7J **77**
Wilcox Pl. SW1 —3G **77** (7M **145**)
Wilcox Rd. SW8 —7J **77**
Wilcox Rd. Sutt —4K **131**
Wilcox Rd. Tedd —4H **103**
Wild Ct. WC2 —6K **61** (8E **140**)
Wildcroft Gdns. Edgw —6J **11**
Wildcroft Mnr. SW15 —7E **90**
Wildcroft Rd. SW15 —7E **90**
Wilde Clo. E8 —1G **63**
Wilde Pl. N13 —6G **17**
Wilde Pl. SW18 —1B **108**
Wilderness Rd. Chst —7F **115**
Wilderness, The. Hamp —4F **103**
Wilderton Rd. N16 —7E **30**
Wildfell Rd. SE6 —7D **96**
Wild Goose Dri. SE14 —1J **95**
Wild Hatch. NW11 —6J **27**
Wilds Rents. SE1 —3E **78** (6C **148**)
Wild St. WC2 —6J **61** (8D **140**)
Wildwood Clo. SE12 —7H **97**
Wildwood Gro. NW3 —1A **44**
Wildwood Rise. NW11 —1A **44**
Wildwood Rd. NW11 —6K **27**
Wildwood Rd. NW3 —1A **44**
Wilford Clo. Enf —3J **7**
Wilfred Owen Clo. SW19 —6A **108**
Wilfred St. SW1 —3G **77** (6L **145**)
Wilfrid Gdns. W3 —5J **57**
Wilkes St. E1 —5F **63** (5F **142**)
Wilkie Way. SE22 —1G **111**
Wilkins Clo. Mitc —1C **122**
Wilkinson Ho. N1 —2D **62**
(off Cranston St.)
Wilkinson Rd. E16 —6A **66**
Wilkinson St. SW8 —7K **77**
Wilkinson Way. W4 —2K **73**
Wilkin St. NW5 —6E **44**
Wilkin St. M. NW5 —6F **45**
Wilks Gdns. Croy —1A **136**
Wilks Pl. N1 —2E **62**

Willan Rd. N17 —2D **30**
Willan Wall. E16 —7H **65**
Willard St. SW8 —3F **93**
Willcott Rd. W3 —1H **73**
Will Crooks Gdns. SE9 —4B **98**
Willenhall Av. Barn —6F **5**
Willenhall Ct. New Bar —6F **5**
Willenhall Rd. SE18 —5F **83**
Willersley Av. Sidc —1K **115**
Willersley Clo. Sidc —1K **115**
Willesden La. NW2 & NW6 —6E **42**
Willes Rd. NW5 —6F **45**
Willett Clo. N'holt —3A **54**
Willett Clo. Orp —6J **129**
Willett Ho. E13 —2K 65
(off Queens Rd. W.)
Willett Pl. T Hth —5A **124**
Willett Rd. T Hth —5A **124**
Willett Way. Orp —5H **129**
Willet Way. SE16 —5H **79**
William Allen Ho. Edgw —7A **12**
William Banfield Ho. SW6 —2H 91
(off Munster Rd.)
William Barefoot Dri. SE9 —4E **114**
William Bonney Est. SW4 —4H **93**
William Booth Rd. SE20 —1G **125**
William Carey Way. Harr —6J **23**
William Clo. Romf —1J **37**
William Cobbett Ho. W8 —3K 75
(off Scarsdale Pl.)
William Ct. Gnfd —5C **56**
William Covell Clo. Enf —1E **6**
William Ellis Way. SE16 —3G **79**
William Evans Ho. SE8 —4K 79
(off Haddonfield)
William IV St. WC2 —7J **61** (1C **146**)
William Gdns. SW15 —5D **90**
William Gunn Ho. NW3 —5C **44**
William Guy Gdns. E3 —3D **64**
William Henry Wlk. SW8 —6H **77**
William Margrie Clo. SE15 —2G **95**
William M. SW1 —2D **76** (5F **144**)
William Morley Clo. E6 —1B **66**
William Morris Clo. E17 —3B **32**
William Morris Ho. W6 —6F 75
(off Margravine Rd.)
William Morris Way. SW6 —3A **92**
William Paton Ho. E16 —6K **65**
William Pike Ho. Romf —6K 37
(off Waterloo Gdns.)
William Pl. E3 —2B **64**
William Rd. NW1 —3F **61** (2K **139**)
William Rd. SW19 —7G **107**
William Rd. Sutt —5A **132**
Williams Av. E17 —1B **32**
Williams Clo. N8 —6H **29**
Williams Gro. N22 —1A **30**
Williams Ho. NW2 —3E 42
(off Stoll Clo.)
William's La. SW14 —3J **89**
Williams La. Mord —5A **122**
William Smith Ho. Belv —3G **85**
Williamson Clo. SE10 —5H **81**
Williamson Ct. SE17 —5C **78**
Williamson Rd. N4 —6B **30**
Williamson St. N7 —4J **45**
Williamson Way. NW7 —6B **14**
Williams Rd. W13 —1A **72**
Williams Rd. S'hall —4C **70**
Williams Ter. Croy —6A **134**
William St. E10 —6D **32**
William St. N17 —7A **18**
William St. SW1 —2D **76** (5F **144**)
William St. Bark —7G **51**
William St. Cars —3C **132**
William White Ct. E13 —1A 66
(off Green St.)
Willifield Way. NW11 —4H **27**

Willingale Clo. Wfd G —6F **21**
Willingdon Rd. N22 —2B **30**
Willingham Clo. NW5 —5G **45**
Willingham Ter. NW5 —5G **45**
Willingham Way. King T —3G **119**
Willington Rd. SW9 —3J **93**
Willis Av. Sutt —6C **132**
Willis Rd. E15 —2H **65**
Willis Rd. Croy —7C **124**
Willis Rd. Eri —4K **85**
Willis St. E14 —6D **64**
Will Miles Ct. SW19 —7A **108**
Willmore End. SW19 —1K **121**
Willoughby Av. Croy —4K **133**
Willoughby Dri. Rain —7K **53**
Willoughby Gro. N17 —7C **18**
Willoughby Highwalk. EC2
(off Barbican) —5D 62 (6A 142)
Willoughby Ho. EC2
(off Barbican) —5D 62 (6A 142)
Willoughby La. N17 —6C **18**
Willoughby Pk. Rd. N17 —7C **18**
(in two parts)
Willoughby Rd. N8 —3A **30**
Willoughby Rd. NW3 —4B **44**
Willoughby Rd. King T —1F **119**
Willoughby Rd. Twic —5C **88**
Willoughbys, The. SW14 —3A **90**
Willoughby St. WC1 —5J 61 (6C 140)
(off Gt. Russell St.)
Willoughby Way. SE7 —4K **81**
Willow Av. SW13 —2B **90**
Willow Av. Sidc —6A **100**
Willow Bank. SW6 —3G **91**
Willow Bank. Rich —3B **104**
Willow Bri. Rd. N1 —6C **46**
Willow Brook Rd. SE15 —7F **79**
Willowbrook Rd. S'hall —3E **70**
Willow Bus. Pk. SE26 —3J **111**
Willow Clo. Bex —6F **101**
Willow Clo. Bren —6C **72**
Willow Clo. Brom —5D **128**
Willow Clo. Buck H —3G **21**
Willow Cotts. Rich —6G **73**
Willow Ct. E11 —2G 49
(off Trinity Clo.)
Willow Ct. EC2 —4E 62 (3C 142)
(off Willow St.)
Willow Ct. Edgw —4K **11**
Willowcourt Av. Harr —5B **24**
Willowdene. N6 —7D **28**
Willowdene. SE15 —1H **95**
Willow Dene. Bush —1D **10**
Willow Dene. Pinn —2B **22**
Willowdene Clo. Twic —7G **87**
Willowdene Ct. N20 —7F 5
(off High Rd.)
Willow Dri. Barn —4B **4**
Willow End. N20 —2D **14**
Willow End. Surb —7E **118**
Willow Farm La. SW15 —3D **90**
Willow Gdns. Houn —1E **86**
Willow Grange. Sidc —3B **116**
Willow Grn. NW9 —1A **26**
Willow Gro. E13 —2J **65**
Willow Gro. Chst —6E **114**
Willowhayne Gdns. Wor Pk —3E **130**
Willow Ho. Brom —2G **127**
Willow Ho. Mitc —5D **122**
Willow La. Ind. Est. Mitc —6D **122**
Willow Lodge. SW6 —1E **90**
Willowmead Clo. W5 —5D **56**
Willow Mt. Croy —3E **134**
Willow Pl. SW1 —4G **77** (8M **145**)
Willow Rd. E12 —3D **50**
Willow Rd. NW3 —4B **44**
Willow Rd. W5 —2E **72**
Willow Rd. Enf —3K **7**

Willow Rd. N Mald —4J **119**
Willow Rd. Romf —6C **36**
Willow Rd. Wall —7F **133**
Willows Av. Mord —5K **121**
Willows Clo. Pinn —2A **22**
Willowside Ct. Enf —3G **7**
Willows, The. E6 —7E **50**
Willow St. E4 —1A **20**
Willow St. EC2 —4E **62** (3C **142**)
Willow St. Romf —4J **37**
Willow Tree Clo. E3 —1B **64**
Willow Tree Clo. SW18 —1K **107**
Willow Tree Clo. Hay —4A **54**
Willow Tree Ct. Sidc —5K **115**
Willow Tree La. Hay —4A **54**
Willow Tree Wlk. Brom —1K **127**
Willow Vale. W12 —1C **74**
Willow Vale. Chst —6F **115**
Willow View. SW19 —1B **122**
Willow Wlk. N2 —2B **28**
Willow Wlk. N15 —4B **30**
Willow Wlk. N21 —6E **6**
Willow Wlk. SE1 —4E **78** (8D **148**)
Willow Wlk. Sutt —3H **131**
Willow Way. N3 —7E **14**
Willow Way. SE26 —3J **111**
Willow Way. W11 —7F **59**
Willow Way. Eps —6A **130**
Willow Way. Twic —2F **103**
Willow Way. Wemb —3A **40**
Willow Wood Cres. SE25 —6E **124**
Willrose Cres. SE2 —5B **84**
Willsbridge Ct. SE15 —6F 79
(off Bibury Clo.)
Wills Cres. Houn —6F **87**
Wills Gro. NW7 —5H **13**
Wilman Gro. E8 —7G **47**
Wilmar Gdns. W Wick —1D **136**
Wilmer Clo. King T —5F **105**
Wilmer Cres. King T —5F **105**
Wilmer Gdns. N1 —1E **62**
Wilmer Lea Clo. E15 —7F **49**
Wilmer Pl. N16 —2F **47**
Wilmer Way. N14 —5C **16**
Wilmington Av. W4 —7K **73**
Wilmington Gdns. Bark —6H **51**
Wilmington Sq. WC1
—3A **62** (2G **141**)
Wilmington St. WC1
—3A **62** (2G **141**)
Wilmot Clo. N2 —2A **28**
Wilmot Clo. SE15 —7G **79**
Wilmot Pl. NW1 —7G **45**
Wilmot Pl. W7 —1J **71**
Wilmot Rd. E10 —2D **48**
Wilmot Rd. N17 —3D **30**
Wilmot Rd. Cars —5D **132**
Wilmot St. E2 —4H **63**
Wilmount St. SE18 —4E **82**
Wilna Rd. SW18 —7A **92**
Wilsham St. W11 —1F **75**
Wilshaw St. SE14 —1C **96**
Wilsmere Dri. Har W —7D **10**
Wilsmere Dri. N'holt —6C **38**
Wilson Av. Mitc —7C **108**
Wilson Gro. Wemb —7F **25**
Wilson Dri. Wemb —7F **25**
Wilson Gdns. Harr —7G **23**
Wilson Gro. SE16 —2H **79**
Wilson Rd. E6 —3B **66**
Wilson Rd. SE5 —1E **94**
Wilson Rd. Ilf —7D **34**
Wilson's Av. N17 —2F **31**
Wilson's Pl. E14 —6B **64**
Wilson's Rd. W6 —5F **75**
Wilson St. E17 —5E **32**
Wilson St. EC2 —5D **62** (6B **142**)

Wilson St. N21 —7F **7**
Wilson Wlk. W4 —4B **74**
  (off Prebend Gdns.)
Wilstone Clo. Hay —4C **54**
Wilthorne Gdns. Dag —7H **53**
Wilton Av. W4 —5A **74**
Wilton Cres. SW1 —2E **76** (5G **145**)
Wilton Cres. SW19 —7H **107**
Wilton Dri. Romf —1J **37**
Wilton Est. E8 —6G **47**
Wilton Gro. SW19 —7H **107**
Wilton Gro. N Mald —6B **120**
Wilton M. SW1 —3E **76** (6H **145**)
Wilton Pl. SW1 —2E **76** (5G **145**)
Wilton Pl. Harr —EX **23**
Wilton Rd. N10 —2E **28**
Wilton Rd. SE2 —4C **84**
Wilton Rd. SW1 —3G **77** (7L **145**)
Wilton Rd. SW19 —7C **108**
Wilton Rd. Barn —4J **5**
Wilton Rd. Houn —3B **86**
Wilton Row. SW1 —2E **76** (5G **145**)
Wilton Row. SW6 —7G **75**
Wilton Sq. N1 —1D **62**
Wilton St. SW1 —3F **77** (6J **145**)
Wilton Ter. SW1 —3E **76** (6G **145**)
Wilton Vs. N1 —1D **62**
  (off Wilton Sq.)
Wilton Way. E8 —6G **47**
Wiltshire Clo. NW7 —5G **13**
Wiltshire Clo. SW3 —4D **76** (9E **144**)
Wiltshire Ct. N4 —1K **45**
  (off Marquis Rd.)
Wiltshire Ct. Ilf —6G **51**
Wiltshire Gdns. N4 —6C **30**
Wiltshire Gdns. Twic —1G **103**
Wiltshire Rd. N1 —1D **62**
Wiltshire Rd. SW9 —3A **94**
Wiltshire Rd. Orp —7K **129**
Wiltshire Rd. T Hth —3A **124**
Wiltshire Row. N1 —1D **62**
  (off Bridport Pl.)
Wilverley Cres. N Mald —6A **120**
Wimbart Rd. SW2 —7K **93**
Wimbledon Bri. SW19 —6H **107**
Wimbledon Hill Rd. SW19 —6G **107**
Wimbledon Pk. Rd. SW19 & SW18
  —2G **107**
Wimbledon Pk. Side. SW19 —3F **107**
Wimbledon Rd. SW17 —4A **108**
Wimbledon Stadium Bus. Cen. SW17
  —3K **107**
Wimbolt St. E2 —3G **63**
Wimborne Av. Hay —6A **54**
Wimborne Av. Orp & Chst —4K **129**
Wimborne Av. S'hall —4E **70**
Wimborne Clo. SE12 —5H **97**
Wimborne Clo. Buck H —2E **20**
Wimborne Clo. Wor Pk —1E **130**
Wimborne Dri. NW9 —3G **25**
Wimborne Dri. Pinn —7B **22**
Wimborne Gdns. W13 —5B **56**
Wimborne Ho. SW8 —7K **77**
  (off Dorset Rd.)
Wimborne Rd. SW12 —3G **109**
Wimborne Rd. N9 —2B **18**
Wimborne Rd. N17 —2E **30**
Wimborne Way. Beck —3K **125**
Wimbourne Ct. SW12 —3G **109**
Wimbourne St. N1 —2D **62**
Wimpole Clo. Brom —4A **128**
Wimpole Clo. King T —2F **119**
Wimpole M. W1 —5F **61** (5J **139**)
Wimpole St. W1 —5F **61** (5J **139**)
Winans Wlk. SW9 —2A **94**
Wincanton Cres. N'holt —5E **38**
Wincanton Gdns. Ilf —3F **35**
Wincanton Rd. SW18 —7H **91**

Winchcombe Ct. SE15 —6E **78**
  (off Lydney Clo.)
Winchcombe Rd. Cars —7B **122**
Winchcomb Gdns. SE9 —3B **98**
Winchelsea Av. Bexh —7F **85**
Winchelsea Clo. SW15 —5F **91**
Winchelsea Rd. E7 —3J **49**
Winchelsea Rd. N17 —3E **30**
Winchelsea Rd. NW10 —1K **57**
Winchelsey Rise. S Croy —6F **135**
Winchendon Rd. SW6 —1H **91**
Winchendon Rd. Tedd —4H **103**
Winchester Av. NW6 —1G **59**
Winchester Av. NW9 —3G **25**
Winchester Av. Houn —6D **70**
Winchester Clo. E6 —6D **66**
Winchester Clo. SE17
  —4B **78** (9K **147**)
Winchester Clo. Brom —3H **127**
Winchester Clo. Enf —5K **7**
Winchester Clo. King T —7H **105**
Winchester Dri. Pinn —5B **22**
Winchester Ho. SW9 —7A **78**
Winchester Ho. Bark —7A **52**
  (off Keir Hardie Way)
Winchester Pk. Brom —3H **127**
Winchester Pl. E8 —5F **47**
Winchester Pl. N6 —1F **45**
Winchester Rd. E4 —7K **19**
Winchester Rd. N6 —7F **29**
Winchester Rd. N9 —1A **18**
Winchester Rd. NW3 —7B **44**
Winchester Rd. Bexh —2D **100**
Winchester Rd. Brom —3H **127**
Winchester Rd. Felt —3D **102**
Winchester Rd. Harr —4E **24**
Winchester Rd. Ilf —3H **51**
Winchester Rd. Twic —6B **88**
Winchester Sq. SE1 —1D **78** (2A **148**)
  (off Winchester Wlk.)
Winchester St. SW1 —5F **77**
Winchester St. W3 —1J **73**
Winchester Wlk. SE1
  —1D **78** (2A **148**)
Winchet Wlk. Croy —6J **125**
Winchfield Clo. Harr —6C **24**
Winchfield Rd. SE26 —5A **112**
Winchmore Hill Rd. N14 & N21
  —1C **16**
Winckley Clo. Harr —5F **25**
Wincott St. SE11 —4A **78** (8H **147**)
Wincrofts Dri. SE9 —4H **99**
Windborough Rd. Cars —7E **132**
Windermere Av. N3 —3J **27**
Windermere Av. NW6 —1G **59**
Windermere Av. SW19 —3K **121**
Windermere Av. Ruis —7A **22**
Windermere Av. Wemb —7C **24**
Windermere Ct. SW13 —6B **74**
Windermere Ct. Wemb —7C **24**
Windermere Gdns. Ilf —5C **34**
Windermere Gro. Wemb —1C **40**
Windermere Hall. Edgw —5A **12**
Windermere Ho. New Bar —4E **4**
Windermere Point. SE15 —7J **79**
  (off Old Kent Rd.)
Windermere Rd. N10 —1F **29**
Windermere Rd. N19 —2G **45**
Windermere Rd. SW15 —4A **106**
Windermere Rd. SW16 —1G **123**
Windermere Rd. W5 —3C **72**
Windermere Rd. Bexh —2J **101**
Windermere Rd. Croy —1F **135**
Windermere Rd. S'hall —5D **54**
Windermere Rd. W Wick —2G **137**
Winders Rd. SW11 —2C **92**
Windfield Clo. SE26 —4K **111**
Windham Rd. Rich —3F **89**

Winding Way. Dag —3C **52**
Winding Way. Harr —4J **39**
Windlass Pl. SE8 —4A **80**
Windlesham Gro. SW19 —1F **107**
Windley Clo. SE23 —2J **111**
Windmill Av. S'hall —2G **71**
Windmill Cen. S'hall —2G **71**
Windmill Clo. SE1 —4G **79**
Windmill Clo. SE13 —2E **96**
Windmill Clo. Surb —7C **118**
Windmill Ct. NW2 —6G **43**
Windmill Dri. SW4 —5F **93**
Windmill Gdns. Enf —3F **7**
Windmill Gro. Croy —6C **124**
Windmill Hill. NW3 —3A **44**
Windmill Hill. Enf —3G **7**
Windmill La. E15 —6F **49**
Windmill La. Bush —1D **10**
Windmill La. Gnfd —5G **55**
Windmill La. S'hall & Iswth —1G **71**
Windmill La. Surb —6B **118**
Windmill M. W4 —4A **74**
Windmill Pas. W4 —4A **74**
Windmill Rise. King T —7H **105**
Windmill Rd. N18 —4J **17**
Windmill Rd. SW18 —6B **92**
Windmill Rd. SW19 —4D **106**
Windmill Rd. W4 —4A **74**
Windmill Rd. W5 & Bren —4C **72**
Windmill Rd. Croy —7C **124**
Windmill Rd. Hamp —5F **103**
Windmill Rd. Mitc —5G **123**
Windmill Row. SE11 —5A **78**
Windmill St. W1 —5H **61** (6A **140**)
Windmill St. Bush —1D **10**
Windmill Wlk. SE1 —1A **78** (3H **147**)
Windover Av. NW9 —4K **25**
Windrush. SE26 —2K **79**
Windrush. SE28 —1B **84**
Windrush Clo. SW11 —4B **92**
Windrush Clo. W4 —1J **89**
Windrush La. SE23 —3K **111**
Windsor Av. E17 —2A **32**
Windsor Av. SW19 —1A **122**
Windsor Av. Edgw —4C **12**
Windsor Av. N Mald —5J **119**
Windsor Av. Sutt —3G **131**
Windsor Cen., The. N1 —1B **62**
  (off Windsor St.)
Windsor Clo. N3 —2G **27**
Windsor Clo. SE27 —4C **110**
Windsor Clo. Bren —6B **72**
Windsor Clo. Chst —5F **115**
Windsor Clo. Harr —3E **38**
Windsor Ct. N14 —7B **6**
Windsor Ct. NW11 —6G **27**
  (off Golders Grn. Rd.)
Windsor Ct. SW11 —2B **92**
Windsor Ct. W10 —6F **59**
  (off Darfield Way)
Windsor Ct. Pinn —3B **22**
Windsor Cres. Harr —3E **38**
Windsor Cres. Wemb —3H **41**
Windsor Dri. Barn —6J **5**
Windsor Gdns. W9 —5J **59**
Windsor Gdns. Croy —3J **133**
Windsor Gdns. Hay —1F **69**
Windsor Gro. SE27 —4C **110**
Windsor Ho. N1 —2C **62**
Windsor M. SW18 —7A **92**
  (off Wilna Rd.)
Windsor Pl. SW1 —4G **77** (8M **145**)
Windsor Rd. E4 —4J **19**
Windsor Rd. E7 —5K **49**
Windsor Rd. E10 —2D **48**
Windsor Rd. E11 —1J **49**
Windsor Rd. N3 —2G **27**
Windsor Rd. N7 —3J **45**
Windsor Rd. N13 —3F **17**

Windsor Rd. N17 —2G **31**
Windsor Rd. NW2 —6D **42**
Windsor Rd. W5 —7E **56**
Windsor Rd. Barn —6A **4**
Windsor Rd. Bexh —4E **100**
Windsor Rd. Dag —3E **52**
Windsor Rd. Harr —1G **23**
Windsor Rd. Houn —2A **86**
Windsor Rd. Ilf —4F **51**
Windsor Rd. King T —7E **104**
Windsor Rd. Rich —2F **89**
Windsor Rd. S'hall —3D **70**
Windsor Rd. Tedd —5H **103**
Windsor Rd. T Hth —2B **124**
Windsor Rd. Wor Pk —2C **130**
Windsors, The. Buck H —2H **21**
Windsor St. N1 —1B **62**
Windsor Ter. N1 —3C **62** (1M **141**)
Windsor Wlk. SE5 —2D **94**
Windsor Way. W14 —4F **75**
Windspoint Dri. SE15 —6H **79**
Windus Rd. N16 —1F **47**
Windus Wlk. N16 —1F **47**
Windy Ridge. Brom —1C **128**
Windy Ridge Clo. SW19 —5F **107**
Wine Clo. E1 —7J **63**
Wine Office Ct. EC4
  —6A **62** (8H **141**)
Winford Pde. S'hall —6F **55**
  (off Brunel Pl.)
Winforton St. SE10 —1E **96**
Winfrith Rd. SW18 —7A **92**
Wingate Cres. Croy —6J **123**
Wingate Rd. W6 —3D **74**
Wingate Rd. Ilf —5F **51**
Wingate Rd. Sidc —6C **116**
Wingate Trading Est. N17 —7B **18**
Wingfield Ct. Sidc —2K **115**
Wingfield Rd. E15 —4G **49**
Wingfield Rd. E17 —5D **32**
Wingfield Rd. King T —6F **105**
Wingfield St. SE15 —3G **95**
Wingfield Way. Ruis —6A **38**
Wingford Rd. SW2 —6J **93**
Wingmore Rd. SE24 —3C **94**
Wingrave Rd. W6 —6E **74**
Wingrove. E4 —7J **9**
Wingrove Ct. Romf —5J **37**
Wingrove Rd. SE6 —2G **113**
Wings Clo. Sutt —4J **131**
Winifred Gro. SW11 —4D **92**
Winifred Rd. SW19 —1J **121**
Winifred Rd. Dag —2E **52**
Winifred Rd. Eri —5K **85**
Winifred Rd. Hamp —4E **102**
Winifred St. E16 —1D **82**
Winifred Ter. E13 —2J **65**
  (off Victoria Rd.)
Winifred Ter. Enf —7A **8**
Winkfield Rd. E13 —2K **65**
Winkfield Rd. N22 —1A **30**
Winkley St. E2 —2H **63**
Winlaton Rd. Brom —4F **113**
Winmill Rd. Dag —3F **53**
Winnett St. W1 —7H **61** (9A **140**)
Winnifred Mandela Ho. Wemb
  —7F **25**
Winningales Ct. Ilf —3C **34**
Winnings Wlk. N'holt —6C **38**
Winnington Clo. N2 —6B **28**
Winnington Rd. N2 —6B **28**
Winnington Rd. Enf —1D **8**
Winn Rd. SE12 —1J **113**
Winns Av. E17 —3B **32**
Winns Comn. Rd. SE18 —6J **83**
Winns M. N15 —4E **30**
Winns Ter. E17 —3C **32**

Winscombe Cres. W5 —4D **56**
Winscombe St. N19 —3F **45**
Winscombe Way. Stan —5F **11**
Winsford Rd. SE6 —3B **112**
Winsford Ter. N18 —5J **17**
Winsham Gro. SW11 —5E **92**
Winslade Rd. SW2 —5J **93**
Winslade Way. SE6 —7D **96**
Winsland M. W2 —6B **60** (7A **138**)
Winsland St. W2 —6B **60** (7A **138**)
Winsley St. W1 —6G **61** (7M **139**)
Winslow. SE17 —5E **78**
  (off Kinglake St.)
Winslow Clo. NW10 —3A **42**
Winslow Clo. Pinn —6A **22**
Winslow Gro. E4 —2B **20**
Winslow Rd. W6 —6E **74**
Winslow Way. Felt —3C **102**
Winsmoor Ct. Enf —3G **7**
Winsor Ter. E6 —5E **66**
Winstanley Est. SW11 —3B **92**
Winstanley Rd. SW11 —3B **92**
Winstead Gdns. Dag —5J **53**
Winston Av. NW9 —7A **26**
Winston Clo. Harr —6E **10**
Winston Clo. Romf —4H **37**
Winston Ct. Harr —7A **10**
Winston Ho. N1 —2D **62**
  (off Cherbury St.)
Winston Ho. W13 —2A **72**
Winston Rd. N16 —4D **46**
Winston Wlk. W4 —3K **73**
Winston Way. Ilf —3F **51**
Winter Av. E6 —1C **66**
Winterbourne Rd. SE6 —1B **112**
Winterbourne Rd. Dag —2C **52**
Winterbourne Rd. T Hth —4A **124**
Winter Box Wlk. Rich —5F **89**
Winterbrook Rd. SE24 —6C **94**
Winterfold Clo. SW19 —2G **107**
Wintergreen Clo. E6 —5C **66**
Winter's Ct. E4 —3J **19**
Winters Rd. Th Dit —7B **118**
Winterstoke Gdns. NW7 —5H **13**
Winterstoke Rd. SE6 —1B **112**
Winterton Ct. SE20 —2G **125**
Winterton Pl. SW10 —6A **76**
Winterwell Rd. SW2 —5J **93**
Winthorpe Rd. SW15 —4G **91**
Winthrop St. E1 —5H **63**
Winthrop Wlk. Wemb —3E **40**
Winton Av. N11 —7B **16**
Winton Clo. N9 —7E **8**
Winton Gdns. Edgw —7A **12**
Winton Way. SW16 —5A **110**
Wirrall Ho. SE26 —3G **111**
Wisbeach Rd. Croy —5D **124**
Wisborough Rd. S Croy —7F **135**
Wisden Ho. SW8 —6K **77**
Wisdons Clo. Dag —1H **53**
Wise La. NW7 —5H **13**
Wiseman Rd. E10 —2C **48**
Wise Rd. E15 —1F **65**
Wiseton Rd. SW17 —1C **108**
Wishart Rd. SE3 —2B **98**
Wisley Rd. SW11 —5E **92**
Wisley Rd. Orp —7A **116**
Wisteria Clo. Ilf —5F **51**
Wisteria Rd. SE13 —4F **97**
Witan St. E2 —3H **63**
Witham Ct. E10 —4D **48**
Witham Rd. SE20 —3J **125**
Witham Rd. W13 —1A **72**
Witham Rd. Dag —6G **53**
Witham Rd. Iswth —1H **87**
Witherby Clo. Croy —4E **134**
Witherby Clo. S Croy —5E **134**
Witherfield Way. SE16 —5H **79**

288

Witherington Rd. N5 —5A 46
Withers Mead. NW9 —1B 26
Withers Pl. EC1 —4C 62 (3M 141)
Witherston Way. SE9 —2E 114
Withington Ct. SE15 —6E 78
(off Brockworth Clo.)
Withycombe Rd. SW19 —7F 91
Withy Mead. E4 —3A 20
Witley Cres. New Ad —6E 136
Witley Gdns. S'hall —4D 70
Witley Ho. SW2 —7K 93
Witley Ind. Est. S'hall —4C 70
Witley Rd. N19 —2G 45
Witney Path. SE23 —3K 111
Wittenham Way. E4 —3A 20
Wittersham Rd. Brom —5H 113
Wivenhoe Clo. SE15 —3H 95
Wivenhoe Ct. Houn —4D 86
Wivenhoe Rd. Bark —2A 68
Wiverton Rd. SE26 —6J 111
Wix Rd. Dag —1D 68
Wix's La. SW4 —3F 93
Woburn. W13 —5B 56
(off Clivedon Ct.)
Woburn Clo. SW19 —6A 108
Woburn M. WC1 —4H 61
Woburn Pl. WC1 —4H 61 (3B 140)
Woburn Rd. Cars —1C 132
Woburn Rd. Croy —1C 134
Woburn Sq. WC1 —4H 61 (4B 140)
Woburn Wlk. WC1 —3H 61 (2B 140)
Woffington Clo. King T —1C 118
Woking Clo. SW15 —4B 90
Woldham Rd. Brom —4A 128
Wolfe Clo. Brom —6J 127
Wolfe Cres. SE7 —5B 82
Wolfe Cres. SE16 —2K 79
Wolfe Ho. W12 —7D 58
(off White City Est.)
Wolferton Rd. E12 —4D 50
Wolffe Gdns. E15 —6H 49
Wolffram Clo. SE13 —5G 97
Wolftencroft Clo. SW11 —3C 92
Wollaston Clo. SE1 —4C 78 (8L 147)
Wolmer Clo. Edgw —4B 12
Wolmer Gdns. Edgw —3B 12
Wolseley Av. SW19 —2J 107
Wolseley Gdns. W4 —6H 73
Wolseley Rd. E7 —7K 49
Wolseley Rd. N8 —6H 29
Wolseley Rd. N22 —1K 29
Wolseley Rd. W4 —4J 73
Wolseley Rd. Mitc —7E 122
Wolseley Rd. Romf —7K 37
Wolseley Rd. W'stone —3J 23
Wolseley St. SE1 —2F 79
Wolsey Av. E6 —3E 66
Wolsey Av. E17 —3B 32
Wolsey Clo. SW20 —7D 106
Wolsey Clo. Houn —4G 87
Wolsey Clo. King T —1H 119
Wolsey Clo. S'hall —3G 71
Wolsey Clo. Wor Pk —4C 130
Wolsey Cres. Mord —7G 121
Wolsey Cres. New Ad —7E 136
Wolsey Dri. King T —5E 104
Wolsey Gro. Edgw —7E 12
Wolsey M. NW5 —6G 45
Wolsey Rd. N1 —5E 46
Wolsey Rd. Enf —2C 8
Wolsey Rd. Hamp —6F 103
Wolsey St. E1 —5J 63
Wolsley Clo. Dart —5K 101
Wolstonbury. N12 —5D 14
Wolvercote Rd. SE2 —2D 84
Wolverley St. E2 —3H 63
Wolverton. SE17 —5E 78

Wolverton Av. King T —1G 119
Wolverton Gdns. W5 —7F 57
Wolverton Gdns. W6 —4F 75
Wolverton Rd. Stan —6G 11
Wolverton Way. N14 —5B 6
Wolves La. N22 & N13 —7F 17
Womersley Rd. N8 —6K 29
Wonersh Way. Sutt —7F 131
Wontner Clo. N1 —7C 46
Wontner Rd. SW17 —2D 108
Woodall Clo. E14 —7D 64
Woodall Ho. N22 —1A 30
Woodall Rd. Enf —6E 8
Woodbank Rd. Brom —3H 113
Woodbastwick Rd. SE26 —5K 111
Woodberry Av. N21 —2F 17
Woodberry Av. Harr —4F 23
Woodberry Cres. N10 —3F 29
Woodberry Down. N4 —7C 30
Woodberry Down Est. N4 —7C 30
Woodberry Gdns. N12 —6F 15
Woodberry Gro. N4 —7C 30
Woodberry Gro. N12 —6F 15
Woodberry Gro. Bex —3K 117
Woodberry Way. E4 —7K 9
Woodberry Way. N12 —6F 15
Woodbine Clo. Twic —2H 103
Woodbine Gro. SE20 —7H 111
Woodbine Gro. Enf —1J 7
Woodbine La. Wor Pk —3E 130
Woodbine Pl. E11 —6J 33
Woodbine Rd. Sidc —1J 115
Woodbines Av. King T —3D 118
Woodbine Ter. E9 —6J 47
Woodborough Rd. SW15 —4D 90
Woodbourne Av. SW16 —3H 109
Woodbourne Clo. SW16 —3J 109
Woodbourne Gdns. Wall —7F 133
Woodbridge Clo. N7 —2K 45
Woodbridge Ct. Wfd G —7H 21
Woodbridge Ho. E11 —1H 49
Woodbridge Rd. Bark —5K 51
Woodbridge St. EC1
                   —4B 62 (3J 141)
Woodbrook Rd. SE2 —6A 84
Woodburn Clo. NW4 —5F 27
Woodbury Clo. E11 —4K 33
Woodbury Clo. Croy —2F 135
Woodbury Ho. SE26 —3G 111
Woodbury Pk. Rd. W13 —4B 56
Woodbury Rd. E17 —4D 32
Woodbury St. SW17 —5C 108
Woodchester Sq. W2 —5K 59
Woodchurch Clo. Sidc —3H 115
Woodchurch Dri. Brom —7B 114
Woodchurch Rd. NW6 —7J 43
Wood Clo. E2 —4G 63
Wood Clo. NW9 —7K 25
Wood Clo. Bex —3K 117
Wood Clo. Harr —7H 23
Woodclyffe Dri. Chst —2E 128
Woodcock Ct. Harr —7E 24
Woodcock Dell Av. Harr —7D 24
Woodcock Hill. Harr —5C 24
Woodcocks. E16 —5A 66
Woodcombe Cres. SE23 —1J 111
Woodcote Av. NW7 —6K 13
Woodcote Av. T Hth —4B 124
Woodcote Av. Wall —7F 133
Woodcote Clo. Enf —6D 8
Woodcote Clo. King T —5F 105
Woodcote Ct. Sutt —6J 131
Woodcote Dri. Orp —7H 129
Woodcote Grn. Wall —7G 133
Woodcote M. Wall —6F 133
Woodcote Pl. SE27 —5B 110
Woodcote Rd. E11 —7J 33

Woodcote Rd. Wall & Purl —6F 133
Wood Crest. Sutt —7A 132
(off Christchurch Pk.)
Woodcroft. N21 —1F 17
Woodcroft. SE9 —3D 114
Woodcroft. Gnfd —6A 40
Woodcroft Av. NW7 —6F 13
Woodcroft Av. Stan —1K 23
Woodcroft Rd. T Hth —5B 124
Wood Dri. Chst —6C 114
Woodedge Clo. E4 —1C 20
Woodend. SE19 —6C 110
Woodend. Sutt —2A 132
Wood End Av. Harr —4F 39
Wood End Clo. N'holt —5H 39
Woodend Gdns. Enf —4D 6
Wood End Gdns. N'holt —5G 39
Wood End La. N'holt —5H 39
(in two parts)
Woodend Rd. E17 —2E 32
Wood End Rd. Harr —4H 39
Woodend, The. Wall —7F 133
Wood End Way. N'holt —5G 39
Wooder Gdns. E7 —4J 49
Wooderson Clo. SE25 —4E 124
Woodfall Av. Barn —5C 4
Woodfall Rd. N4 —2A 46
Woodfall St. SW3 —5D 76
Woodfarrs. SE5 —4D 94
Wood Field. NW3 —5D 44
Woodfield Av. NW9 —4A 26
Woodfield Av. SW16 —3H 109
Woodfield Av. W5 —4C 56
Woodfield Av. Cars —6E 132
Woodfield Av. Wemb —3C 40
Woodfield Clo. SE19 —7C 110
Woodfield Clo. Enf —3K 7
Woodfield Cres. W5 —4C 56
Woodfield Dri. Barn —1K 15
Woodfield Gdns. N Mald —5B 120
Woodfield Gro. SW16 —3H 109
Woodfield La. SW16 —3H 109
Woodfield Pl. W9 —4H 59
Woodfield Rise. Bush —1C 10
Woodfield Rd. W5 —4C 56
Woodfield Rd. W9 —5H 59
Woodfield Rd. Houn —2A 86
Woodfield Way. N11 —7C 16
Woodford Av. Ilf —3B 34
Woodford Bri. Rd. Ilf —3B 34
Woodford Ct. W12 —2F 75
(off Shepherd's Bush Grn.)
Woodford Cres. Pinn —2A 22
Woodford New Rd. E18 & Wfd G
                   —4G 33
Woodford Pl. Wemb —1E 40
Woodford Rd. E7 —3K 49
Woodford Rd. E18 —4J 33
Woodford Trading Est. Wfd G
                   —3B 34
Woodger Rd. W12 —2E 74
Woodget Clo. E6 —6C 66
Woodgrange Av. N12 —6G 15
Woodgrange Av. W5 —1G 73
Woodgrange Av. Enf —6B 8
Woodgrange Av. Harr —5C 24
Woodgrange Clo. Harr —5D 24
Woodgrange Gdns. Enf —6B 8
Woodgrange Rd. E7 —4K 49
Woodgrange Ter. Enf —6B 8
Wood Green Shopping City N22
                   —2A 30
Woodhall Av. SE21 —3F 111
Woodhall Av. Pinn —1C 22
Woodhall Dri. SE21 —3F 111
Woodhall Dri. Pinn —1B 22
Woodhall Ga. Pinn —1B 22

Woodham Ct. E18 —4H 33
Woodham Rd. SE6 —3E 112
Woodhatch Clo. E6 —5C 66
Woodhaven Gdns. Ilf —4G 35
Woodhayes Rd. SW19 —7E 106
Woodheyes Rd. NW10 —5K 41
Woodhill. SE18 —4C 82
Woodhill Cres. Harr —6D 24
Woodhouse Av. Gnfd —2K 55
Woodhouse Clo. Gnfd —2K 55
Woodhouse Gro. E12 —6C 50
Woodhouse Rd. E11 —3H 49
Woodhouse Rd. N12 —6G 15
Woodhurst Av. Orp —6G 129
Woodhurst Rd. SE2 —5A 84
Woodhurst Rd. W3 —7J 57
Woodington Clo. SE9 —6E 98
Woodin St. E14 —5D 64
Woodison St. E3 —4A 64
Woodknoll Dri. Chst —1D 128
Woodland App. Gnfd —6A 40
Woodland Clo. NW9 —6J 25
Woodland Clo. SE19 —6E 110
Woodland Clo. Eps —6A 130
Woodland Clo. Wfd G —3E 20
Woodland Cres. SE10 —6G 81
Woodland Cres. SE16 —2J 79
Woodland Dri. Felt —2B 102
Woodland Gdns. N10 —5F 29
Woodland Gdns. Iswth —3J 87
Woodland Hill. SE19 —6E 110
Woodland Rise. N10 —4F 29
Woodland Rise. Gnfd —6A 40
Woodland Rd. E4 —1K 19
Woodland Rd. N11 —5A 16
Woodland Rd. SE19 —5E 110
Woodland Rd. T Hth —4A 124
Woodlands. NW11 —5G 27
Woodlands. SW20 —4E 120
Woodlands. Harr —4E 22
Woodlands. Short —4H 127
Woodlands Av. E11 —1K 49
Woodlands Av. N3 —7F 15
Woodlands Av. W3 —1H 73
Woodlands Av. N Mald —1J 119
Woodlands Av. Romf —7E 36
Woodlands Av. Ruis —4A 22
Woodlands Av. Sidc —1J 115
Woodlands Av. Wor Pk —2B 130
Woodlands Clo. NW11 —5G 27
Woodlands Clo. Brom —2D 128
Woodlands Ct. SE22 —7H 95
Woodlands Ct. Brom —1H 127
Woodlands Ct. Harr —5K 23
Woodlands Dri. Stan —6E 10
Woodlands Ga. SW15 —5H 91
Woodlands Gro. Iswth —2J 87
Woodlands Pk. Bex —4K 117
Woodlands Pk. Rd. N15 —5B 30
Woodlands Pk. Rd. SE10 —6G 81
Woodlands Rd. E11 —2G 49
Woodlands Rd. E17 —3E 32
Woodlands Rd. N9 —1D 18
Woodlands Rd. SW13 —3B 90
Woodlands Rd. Bexh —3E 100
Woodlands Rd. Brom —2C 128
Woodlands Rd. Enf —1J 7
Woodlands Rd. Harr —5K 23
Woodlands Rd. Ilf —3G 51
Woodlands Rd. Iswth —3H 87
Woodlands Rd. S'hall —1B 70
Woodlands Rd. Surb —7D 118
Woodlands St. SE13 —7F 97
Woodlands, The. N12 —6F 15
Woodlands, The. N14 —1A 16
Woodlands, The. SE13 —7F 97
Woodlands, The. SE19 —7C 110
Woodlands, The. Harr —2J 39

Woodlands, The. Iswth —2K 87
Woodlands, The. Stan —5G 11
Woodlands, The. Wall —7F 133
Woodland St. E8 —6F 47
Woodlands Way. SW15 —5H 91
Woodland Ter. SE7 —4C 82
Woodland Wlk. NW3 —5C 44
Woodland Wlk. SE10 —5G 81
Woodland Wlk. Brom —4G 113
(in two parts)
Woodland Way. N21 —2F 17
Woodland Way. NW7 —6F 13
Woodland Way. SE2 —4D 84
Woodland Way. Croy —1A 136
Woodland Way. Mitc —7E 108
Woodland Way. Mord —4H 121
Woodland Way. Orp —4G 129
Woodland Way. Wfd G —3E 20
Woodland Way. W Wick —4D 136
Wood La. N6 —6F 29
Wood La. NW9 —7K 25
Wood La. W12 —6E 58
Wood La. Dag —4D 52
Wood La. Iswth —6J 71
Wood La. Stan —3F 11
Wood La. Wfd G —4C 20
Woodlawn Clo. SW15 —5H 91
Woodlawn Cres. Twic —2F 103
Woodlawn Rd. SW6 —7F 75
Woodlea Dri. Brom —5G 127
Woodlea Rd. N16 —3E 46
Woodleigh. E18 —1J 33
Woodleigh Av. N12 —6H 15
Woodleigh Gdns. SW16 —3J 109
Woodley Clo. SW17 —7D 108
Woodley La. Cars —3C 132
Wood Lodge Gdns. Brom —7C 114
Wood Lodge La. W Wick —3E 136
Woodman Pde. E16 —1E 82
(off Woodman St.)
Woodmans Gro. NW10 —5B 42
Woodman's M. W12 —5D 58
Woodmansterne Rd. SW16 —7G 109
Woodman St. E16 —1E 82
(in two parts)
Wood Mead. N17 —6B 18
Woodmere. SE9 —1D 114
Woodmere Av. Croy —7J 125
Woodmere Clo. SW11 —3E 92
Woodmere Clo. Croy —7K 125
Woodmere Ct. N14 —7A 6
Woodmere Gdns. Croy —7K 125
Woodmere Way. Beck —5E 127
Woodnook Rd. SW16 —5F 109
Woodpecker Clo. N9 —6C 8
Woodpecker Clo. Bush —1B 10
Woodpecker Mt. Croy —7A 136
Woodpecker Rd. SE14 —6A 80
Woodpecker Rd. SE28 —7C 68
Woodquest Av. SE24 —5C 94
Wood Retreat. SE18 —7H 83
Wood Ride. Barn —1G 5
Wood Ride. Orp —4H 129
Woodridge Clo. NW2 —3D 42
Woodridge Clo. Enf —2F 7
Woodridings Av. Pinn —1D 22
Woodridings Clo. Pinn —1C 22
Woodridings Ct. N22 —1H 29
Woodriffe Rd. E11 —7F 33
Woodrow. SE18 —4D 82
Woodrow Clo. Gnfd —7B 40
Woodrow Ct. N17 —7C 18
Woodrush Clo. SE14 —7A 80
Woodrush Way. Romf —4D 36
Woodseer St. E1 —5F 63
Woodsford Sq. W14 —2G 75
Woodshire Rd. Dag —3H 53
Woodside. N10 —3E 28

Wood Side. NW11 —5J 27
Woodside. SW19 —6H 107
Woodside. Buck H —2F 21
Woodside Av. N6 & N10 —5D 28
Woodside Av. N12 —4F 15
Woodside Av. SE25 —6H 125
Woodside Av. Chst —5G 115
Woodside Av. Wemb —1E 56
Woodside Clo. Bexh —4K 101
Woodside Clo. Stan —5G 11
Woodside Clo. Surb —7J 119
Woodside Clo. Wemb —1E 56
Woodside Ct. E12 —1A 50
Woodside Ct. N12 —4E 14
Woodside Ct. W5 —1E 72
Woodside Ct. Rd. Croy —7G 125
Woodside Cres. Sidc —3J 115
Woodside Dri. Dart —4K 117
Woodside End. Wemb —1E 56
Woodside Gdns. E4 —5J 19
Woodside Gdns. N17 —2E 30
Woodside Grange. N12 —4E 14
Woodside Grange Rd. N12 —4E 14
Woodside Grn. SE25 —6G 125
(in two parts)
Woodside Gro. N12 —3F 15
Woodside La. N12 —3F 15
Woodside La. Bex —6D 100
Woodside Pk. SE25 —6H 125
Woodside Pk. Av. E17 —4F 33
Woodside Pk. Rd. N12 —4E 14
Woodside Pl. Wemb —1E 56
Woodside Rd. E13 —4A 66
Woodside Rd. N22 —7E 16
Woodside Rd. SE25 —6H 125
Woodside Rd. Bexh —4K 101
Woodside Rd. Brom —5C 128
Woodside Rd. King T —7E 104
Woodside Rd. N Mald —2K 119
Woodside Rd. Sidc —3J 115
Woodside Rd. Sutt —3A 132
Woodside Rd. Wfd G —4D 20
Woodside Way. Croy —6J 125
Woodside Way. Mitc —1F 123
Woods M. W1 —7E 60 (9F 138)
Woodsome Rd. NW5 —3E 44
Wood's Pl. SE1 —3E 78 (7D 148)
Woodspring Rd. SW19 —2G 107
Woods Rd. SE15 —1H 95
Woodstead Gro. Edgw —6K 11
Woodstock Av. NW11 —7G 27
Woodstock Av. W13 —3A 72
Woodstock Av. Iswth —5A 88
Woodstock Av. S'hall —3D 54
Woodstock Av. Sutt —7H 121
Woodstock Clo. Bex —7F 101
Woodstock Clo. Stan —2E 24
Woodstock Ct. SE11 —5K 77
Woodstock Ct. SE12 —6J 97
Woodstock Cres. N9 —6C 8
Woodstock Gdns. Beck —1D 126
Woodstock Gdns. Ilf —2A 52
Woodstock Gro. W12 —2F 75
Woodstock M. W1 —5E 60 (6H 139)
(off Westmoreland St.)
Woodstock Rise. Sutt —7H 121
Woodstock Rd. E7 —7A 50
Woodstock Rd. E17 —2F 33
Woodstock Rd. N4 —1A 46
Woodstock Rd. NW11 —7H 27
Woodstock Rd. W4 —4A 74
Woodstock Rd. Cars —5E 132
Woodstock Rd. Croy —3D 134
Woodstock Rd. Wemb —1F 57
Woodstock St. E16 —6G 65
Woodstock Ter. E14 —7D 64
Woodstock Way. Mitc —1F 123

Woodstone Av. Eps —5C 130
Wood St. E16 —7K 65
Wood St. E17 —3E 32
Wood St. EC2 —6C 62 (8M 141)
Wood St. W4 —5A 74
Wood St. Barn —4A 4
Wood St. King T —2D 118
Wood St. Mitc —7E 122
Woodsyre. SE26 —4F 111
Woodthorpe Rd. SW15 —4D 90
Woodtree Clo. NW4 —2F 27
Wood Vale. N10 —5G 29
Wood Vale. SE23 —1H 111
Woodvale Av. SE25 —3F 125
Wood Vale Est. SE23 —7H 95
Woodvale Wlk. SE27 —5C 110
Woodville. SE3 —1K 97
Woodville Clo. SE12 —5J 97
Woodville Clo. Tedd —4A 104
Woodville Ct. SE19 —1F 125
Woodville Gdns. NW11 —7F 27
Woodville Gdns. W5 —6E 56
Woodville Gdns. Ilf —3F 35
Woodville Gro. Well —3A 100
Woodville Rd. E11 —1H 49
Woodville Rd. E17 —4B 32
Woodville Rd. E18 —2K 33
Woodville Rd. N16 —5E 46
Woodville Rd. NW6 —2H 59
Woodville Rd. NW11 —7F 27
Woodville Rd. W5 —6D 56
Woodville Rd. Barn —3E 4
Woodville Rd. Mord —4J 121
Woodville Rd. Rich —3B 104
Woodville Rd. T Hth —4C 124
Woodville St. SE18 —4C 82
Woodward Av. NW4 —5C 26
Woodwarde Rd. SE22 —6E 94
Woodward Gdns. Dag —7C 52
Woodward Gdns. Stan —7E 10
Woodward Rd. Dag —7B 52
Woodward's Footpath. Twic —6H 87
Woodway Cres. Harr —6A 24
Woodwell St. SW18 —5A 92
Wood Wharf Bus. Pk. E14 —1D 80
Woodyard Clo. NW5 —5E 44
Woodyard La. SE21 —7E 94
Woodyates Rd. SE12 —6J 97
Woolacombe Rd. SE3 —2A 98
Wooler St. SE17 —5D 78
Woolf Clo. SE28 —1B 84
Woolgar M. N16 —4E 46
(off Gillett St.)
Woollaston Rd. N4 —6B 30
Woolley Ho. SW9 —3B 94
(off Loughborough Rd.)
Woolmead Av. NW9 —7C 26
Woolmer Gdns. N18 —5B 18
Woolmer Rd. N18 —5B 18
Woolmore St. E14 —7E 64
Woolneigh St. SW6 —3K 91
Woolridge Way. E9 —7J 47
Wool Rd. SW20 —6D 106
Woolstaplers Way. SE16 —3G 79
Woolston Clo. E17 —2K 31
Woolstone Rd. SE23 —2A 112
Woolwich Chu. St. SE18 —3C 82
Woolwich Comn. SE18 —6E 82
Woolwich Dockyard Ind. Est. SE18
—3C 82
Woolwich Ind. Est. SE28 —3J 83
(in two parts)
Woolwich Mnr. Way. E6 & E16
—4D 66

Woolwich New Rd. SE18 —5E 82
Woolwich Rd. SE2 & Belv —6D 84
Woolwich Rd. SE10 & SE7 —5H 81
Woolwich Rd. Bexh —3G 101
Wooster Gdns. E14 —6F 65
Wooster M. Harr —3G 23
Wootton Gro. N3 —1J 27
Wootton St. SE1 —1A 78 (4H 147)
Worbeck Rd. SE20 —2H 125
Worcester Av. N17 —7B 18
Worcester Clo. Croy —2C 136
Worcester Clo. Mitc —3F 123
Worcester Ct. N12 —5E 14
Worcester Ct. Harr —3J 23
Worcester Ct. Wor Pk —3A 130
Worcester Cres. NW7 —3F 13
Worcester Cres. Wfd G —5E 20
Worcester Dri. W4 —2A 74
Worcester Gdns. Gnfd —6H 39
Worcester Gdns. Ilf —7C 34
Worcester Gdns. Wor Pk —3A 130
Worcester M. NW6 —6K 43
Worcester Pk. Rd. Wor Pk —3A 130
Worcester Rd. E12 —3D 50
Worcester Rd. E17 —2K 31
Worcester Rd. SW19 —5H 107
Worcester Rd. Sutt —7J 131
Worcesters Av. Enf —1B 8
Wordsworth Av. E12 —7C 50
Wordsworth Av. E18 —3H 33
Wordsworth Av. Gnfd —3H 55
Wordsworth Ct. Harr —7J 23
Wordsworth Dri. Sutt —4E 130
Wordsworth Pde. N8 —4B 30
Wordsworth Rd. N16 —4E 46
Wordsworth Rd. SE1
—4F 79 (9F 148)
Wordsworth Rd. SE20 —7K 111
Wordsworth Rd. Hamp —4D 102
Wordsworth Rd. Wall —6G 133
Wordsworth Rd. Well —1J 99
Wordsworth Wlk. NW11 —4J 27
Worfield St. SW11 —7C 76
Worgan St. SE11 —5K 77
Worland Rd. E15 —7G 49
Worlds End St. SW10 —7B 76
World's End La. N21 & Enf —5E 6
World's End Pas. SW10 —7B 76
World's End Pl. SW10 —7B 76
Worleys Dri. Orp —4H 137
Worlidge St. W6 —5E 74
Worlingham Rd. SE22 —4F 95
Wormholt Rd. W12 —7C 58
Wormwood St. EC2
—6E 62 (7C 142)
Wornington Rd. W10 —4G 59
Woronzow Rd. NW8 —1B 60
Worple Av. SW19 —7F 107
Worple Av. Iswth —5A 88
Worple Clo. Harr —1D 38
Worple Rd. SW20 & SW19 —2E 120
Worple Rd. Iswth —4A 88
Worple Rd. M. SW19 —6H 107
Worple Way. Harr —1D 38
Worple Way. Rich —5E 88
Worship St. EC2 —4D 62 (4B 142)
Worslade Rd. SW17 —4B 108
Worsley Bri. Rd. SE26 & Beck
—4B 112
Worsley Ho. SE23 —2H 111
Worsley Rd. E11 —4G 49
Worsopp Dri. SW4 —5G 93
Worthfield Clo. Eps —7A 130
Worth Gro. SE17 —5D 78
(off Liverpool Gro.)
Worthing Clo. E15 —1G 65

Worthing Rd. Houn —6D 70
Worthington Clo. Mitc —3F 123
Worthington Rd. Surb —7F 119
Wortley Rd. E6 —7B 50
Wortley Rd. Croy —7A 124
Worton Ct. Iswth —4J 87
Worton Gdns. Iswth —2H 87
Worton Hall Ind. Est. Iswth —4J 87
Worton Rd. Iswth —4J 87
Worton Way. Houn & Iswth —2H 87
Wotton Rd. NW2 —3E 42
Wotton Rd. SE8 —6B 80
Wouldham Rd. E16 —6H 65
Wragby Rd. E11 —3G 49
Wrampling Pl. N9 —1B 18
Wrangthorn Wlk. Croy —4A 134
Wray Av. Ilf —3E 34
Wrayburn Ho. SE16 —2G 79
(off Llewellyn St.)
Wray Cres. N4 —2J 45
Wrayfield Rd. Sutt —3F 131
Wray Rd. Sutt —7H 131
Wraysbury Clo. Houn —5C 86
Wrekin Rd. SE18 —7G 83
Wren Av. NW2 —4E 42
Wren Av. S'hall —4D 70
Wren Clo. E16 —6H 65
Wren Clo. N9 —1E 18
Wren Cres. Bush —1B 10
Wren Gdns. Dag —5D 52
Wren Landing. E14 —1C 80
Wren Path. SE28 —3H 83
Wren Rd. SE5 —1D 94
Wren Rd. Dag —5D 52
Wren Rd. Sidc —4C 116
Wren's Pk. Ho. E5 —2H 47
Wren St. WC1 —4K 61 (3F 140)
Wrentham Av. NW10 —2F 59
Wrenthorpe Rd. Brom —4G 113
Wrenwood Way. Pinn —4A 22
Wrestlers Ct. EC3 —6E 62 (7C 142)
(off Clark's Pl.)
Wrexham Rd. E3 —2C 64
Wricklemarsh Rd. SE3 —1K 97
(in two parts)
Wrigglesworth St. SE14 —7K 79
Wright Rd. N1 —6E 46
Wright Rd. Houn —7A 70
Wrights All. SW19 —6E 106
Wrights Clo. SE13 —4F 97
Wrights Clo. Dag —4H 53
Wrights Gro. SW4 —4H 93
Wrights La. W8 —3K 75
Wrights Pl. NW10 —6J 41
Wright's Rd. E3 —2B 64
Wrights Rd. SE25 —3C 124
Wrights Row. Wall —4F 133
Wrights Wlk. SW14 —3K 89
Wrigley Clo. E4 —5A 20
Wrotham Ho. Beck —7B 112
(off Sellindge Clo.)
Wrotham Rd. NW1 —7G 45
Wrotham Rd. W13 —1C 72
Wrotham Rd. Barn —2B 4
Wrotham Rd. Well —1C 100
Wrottesley Rd. NW10 —2C 58
Wrottesley Rd. SE18 —6G 83
Wroughton Rd. SW11 —6D 92
Wroughton Ter. NW4 —4D 26
Wroxall Rd. Dag —6C 52
Wroxham Gdns. N11 —7C 16
Wroxham Rd. SE28 —7D 68
Wroxton Rd. SE15 —2J 95
Wrythe Grn. Cars —3D 132
Wrythe Grn. Rd. Cars —3D 132
Wrythe La. Cars —1A 132
Wulfstan St. W12 —5B 58
Wyatt Clo. SE16 —2B 80

Wyatt Clo. Bush —1D 10
Wyatt Pk. Rd. SW2 —2J 109
Wyatt Rd. E7 —6J 49
Wyatt Rd. N5 —3C 46
Wyatts La. E17 —3E 32
Wybert St. NW1 —4G 61 (3K 139)
Wyborne Ho. NW10 —7J 41
Wyborne Way. NW10 —7J 41
Wyburn Av. Barn —3C 4
Wyche Gro. S Croy —7D 134
Wych Elm Lodge. Brom —7H 113
Wych Elm Pas. King T —7F 105
Wycherley Clo. SE3 —7H 81
Wycherley Cres. Barn —6E 4
Wychwood Av. Edgw —6J 11
Wychwood Av. T Hth —3C 124
Wychwood Clo. Edgw —6J 11
Wychwood End. N6 —7G 29
Wychwood Way. SE19 —6D 110
Wycliffe Clo. Well —1K 99
Wycliffe Rd. SW11 —2E 92
Wycliffe Rd. SW19 —6K 107
Wyclif St. EC1 —3B 62 (2J 141)
Wycombe Gdns. NW11 —2J 43
Wycombe Pl. SW18 —6A 92
Wycombe Rd. N17 —1G 31
Wycombe Rd. Ilf —5D 34
Wycombe Rd. Wemb —1G 57
Wydehurst Rd. Croy —7G 125
Wydell Clo. Mord —6F 121
Wydenhurst Rd. Croy —7G 125
Wydeville Mnr. Rd. SE12 —4K 113
Wye Clo. Orp —7K 129
Wyemead Cres. E4 —2B 20
Wye St. SW11 —2B 92
Wyfields. Ilf —1F 35
Wyfold Ho. SE2 —2D 84
(off Wolvercote Rd.)
Wyfold Rd. SW6 —7G 75
Wyhill Wlk. Dag —7J 53
Wyke Clo. Iswth —6K 71
Wyke Gdns. W7 —3A 72
Wykeham Av. Dag —6C 52
Wykeham Grn. Dag —6C 52
Wykeham Hill. Wemb —1F 41
Wykeham Rise. N20 —1B 14
Wykeham Rd. NW4 —4E 26
Wykeham Rd. Harr —4B 24
Wyke Rd. E3 —7C 48
Wyke Rd. SW20 —2E 120
Wyldes Clo. NW11 —1A 44
Wyldfield Gdns. N9 —2A 18
Wyld Way. Wemb —6H 41
Wyleu St. SE23 —7A 96
Wylie Rd. S'hall —3E 70
Wylien Clo. E1 —4J 63
Wymans Way. E7 —4A 50
Wymering Rd. W9 —3J 59
Wymond St. SW15 —3E 90
Wynan Rd. E14 —5D 80
Wynash Gdns. Cars —5C 132
Wynaud Ct. N22 —6E 16
Wyncham Av. Sidc —1J 115
Wynchgate. N14 & N21 —1C 16
Wynchgate. Harr —7D 10
Wynchgate. N'holt —5D 38
Wyncombe Av. W5 —4B 72
Wyncroft Clo. Brom —3D 128
Wyndale Av. NW9 —6G 25
Wyndcliffe Rd. SE7 —6A 81
Wyndcroft Clo. Enf —3G 7
Wyndham Clo. Sutt —7J 131
Wyndham Cres. N19 —3G 45
Wyndham Cres. Houn —6E 86
Wyndham Est. SE5 —7C 78
Wyndham M. W1 —5D 60 (6E 138)
Wyndham Pl. W1 —5D 60 (6E 138)

Wyndham Rd. E6 —7B 50
Wyndham Rd. SE5 —7C 78
Wyndham Rd. W13 —3B 72
Wyndham Rd. Barn —1J 15
Wyndham Rd. King T —7F 105
Wyndham St. W1 —5D 60 (5E 138)
Wyndham Yd. W1 —5D 60 (6E 138)
Wyneham Rd. SE24 —5D 94
Wynell Rd. SE23 —3K 111
Wynford Pl. Belv —6G 85
Wynford Rd. N1 —2K 61
Wynford Way. SE9 —3D 114
Wynlie Gdns. Pinn —2A 22
Wynndale Rd. E18 —1K 33
Wynne Rd. SW9 —2A 94
Wynnstay Gdns. W8 —3J 75
Wynter St. SW11 —4A 92
Wynton Gdns. SE25 —5F 125
Wynton Pl. W3 —6H 57
Wynyard Ho. SE11 —5K 77
(off Newburn St.)
Wynyard Ter. SE11 —5K 77
Wynyatt St. EC1 —3B 62 (2J 141)
Wyre Gro. Edgw —3C 12
Wyresdale Cres. Gnfd —3K 55
Wythburn Pl. W1 —6D 60 (8E 138)
Wythenshawe Rd. Dag —3G 53
Wythens Wlk. SE9 —6F 99
Wythes Clo. Brom —2D 128
Wythes Rd. E16 —1C 82
Wythfield Rd. SE9 —6D 98
Wyvenhoe Rd. Harr —3G 39
Wyvil Rd. SW8 —6J 77
Wyvis St. E14 —5D 64

Xylon Ho. Wor Pk —2D 130

Yabsley St. E14 —1E 80
Yalding Rd. SE16 —3G 79
Yale Clo. Houn —5D 86
Yale Ct. NW6 —5K 43
Yaohan Plaza. NW9 —3K 25

Yarborough Rd. SW19 —1B 122
Yardley Clo. E4 —5J 9
Yardley Ct. Sutt —4E 130
Yardley La. E4 —5J 9
Yardley St. WC1 —3A 62 (2G 141)
Yarmouth Cres. N17 —5H 31
Yarmouth Pl. W1 —1F 77 (3J 146)
Yarnfield Sq. SE15 —1G 95
Yarnton Way. SE2 & Eri —2C 84
Yarrow Cres. E6 —5C 66
Yateley Rd. SE18 —3B 82
Yeading Av. Harr —2C 38
Yeading Fork. Hay —5A 54
Yeading Ho. Hay —5B 54
Yeading La. Hay & N'holt —6A 54
Yeading Wlk. N Har —5D 22
Yeames Clo. W13 —6A 56
Yeate St. N1 —7D 46
Yeatman Rd. N6 —6D 28
Yeats Clo. SE13 —2F 97
Yeldham Rd. W6 —5F 75
Yelverton Lodge. Twic —7C 88
Yelverton Rd. SW11 —2B 92
Yenston Clo. Mord —6J 121
Yeoman Clo. SE27 —3B 110
Yeoman Ct. Houn —7D 70
Yeoman Rd. N'holt —7C 38
Yeomans M. Iswth —6H 87
Yeoman's Row. SW3
—3C 76 (7D 144)
Yeoman St. SE8 —4A 80
Yeomans Way. Enf —2D 8
Yeo St. E3 —5D 64
Yerbury Rd. N19 —3H 45
Yester Dri. Chst —7C 114
Yester Pk. Chst —7D 114
Yester Rd. Chst —7C 114
Yew Clo. Buck H —2G 21
Yew Ct. E4 —6G 19
Yewdale Clo. Brom —6G 113
Yewfield Rd. NW10 —6B 42
Yew Gro. NW2 —4F 43
Yew Tree Clo. N21 —7F 7
Yewtree Clo. N22 —1G 29

Yewtree Clo. N Har —4F 23
Yewtree Clo. Well —1A 100
Yew Tree Clo. Wor Pk —1A 130
Yew Tree Clo. N'wd —5H 27
(off Bridge La.)
Yew Tree Ct. Sutt —7A 132
(off Walnut M.)
Yew Tree Gdns. Chad —5E 36
Yew Tree Gdns. Romf —5K 37
Yew Tree Lodge. SW16 —4G 109
Yew Tree Lodge. Romf —5K 37
(off Yew Tree Gdns.)
Yew Tree Rd. W12 —7B 58
Yewtree Rd. Beck —3B 126
Yew Tree Wlk. Houn —5D 86
Yew Wlk. Harr —1J 39
Yoakley Rd. N16 —2E 46
Yoke Clo. N7 —6J 45
Yolande Gdns. SE9 —5C 98
Yonge Pk. N4 —3A 46
York Av. SE17 —5C 78
York Av. SW14 —5J 89
York Av. W7 —1J 71
York Av. Sidc —2J 115
York Av. Stan —1B 24
York Bri. NW1 —4E 60 (3G 139)
York Bldgs. WC2 —7J 61 (1D 146)
York Clo. E6 —6D 66
York Clo. W7 —1J 71
York Clo. Mord —4K 121
York Ct. N13 —3D 16
York Ga. N14 —7D 6
York Ga. NW1 —4E 60 (4G 139)
York Gro. SE15 —1J 95
York Hill. SE27 —3B 110
York Ho. SE1 —3K 77 (7F 146)
York Ho. Enf —1J 7
York Ho. Wemb —5G 41
York Ho. Pl. W8 —2K 75
Yorkland Av. Well —3K 99
York Mans. SW5 —5K 75
(off Earl's Ct. Rd.)
York Mans. SW11 —1E 92
(off Prince Of Wales Dri.)

York M. NW5 —5F 45
York M. Ilf —3E 50
York Pde. Bren —5D 72
York Pl. SW11 —3B 92
York Pl. WC2 —7J 61 (1D 146)
(off Villiers St.)
York Pl. Dag —6J 53
York Pl. Ilf —2F 51
York Rise. NW5 —3F 45
York Rd. E4 —4H 19
York Rd. E7 —6J 49
York Rd. E10 —3E 48
York Rd. E17 —5K 31
York Rd. N11 —6C 16
York Rd. N18 —6C 18
York Rd. N21 —7J 7
York Rd. SE1 —2A 77 (5F 146)
York Rd. SW18 & SW1 —4A 92
York Rd. SW19 —6A 108
York Rd. W3 —6J 57
York Rd. W5 —3C 72
York Rd. Barn —5F 5
York Rd. Bren —5D 72
York Rd. Croy —7A 124
York Rd. Houn —3F 87
York Rd. Ilf —3E 50
York Rd. King T —7F 105
York Rd. Rain —7K 53
York Rd. Rich —5F 89
York Rd. Sutt —6J 131
York Rd. Tedd —4J 103
Yorkshire Clo. N16 —3E 46
Yorkshire Gdns. N18 —5C 18
Yorkshire Grey Pl. NW3 —3A 44
Yorkshire Grey Yd. WC1
—5K 61 (6E 142)
Yorkshire Pl. E14 —6A 64
Yorkshire Rd. E14 —6A 64
Yorkshire Rd. Mitc —5J 123
York Sq. E14 —6A 64
York St. W1 —5D 60 (6E 138)
York St. Bark —1G 67
York St. Mitc —7E 122
York St. Twic —1A 104

York Ter. Enf —1H 7
York Ter. Eri —1J 101
York Ter. E. NW1 —4E 60 (4H 139)
York Ter. W. NW1 —4E 60 (4G 139)
Yorkton St. E2 —2G 63
York Way. N1 —1J 61
(off Tiber Gdns.)
York Way. N7 —6H 45
York Way. N20 —3J 15
York Way. Felt —3D 102
(in two parts)
York Way Est. N7 —6J 45
Young Clo. NW6 —7G 43
Youngmans Clo. Enf —1H 7
Young Rd. E16 —6A 66
Youngs Bldgs. EC1 —4C 62 (3M 141)
(off Old St.)
Youngs Rd. Ilf —5H 35
Young St. W8 —2K 75
Yoxley App. Ilf —6G 35
Yoxley Dri. Ilf —6G 35
Yukon Rd. SW12 —7F 93
Yuletide Clo. NW10 —6A 42
Yunus Khan Clo. E17 —5C 32

Zampa Rd. SE16 —5J 79
Zander Ct. E2 —3G 63
Zangwill Rd. SE3 —1B 98
Zealand Rd. E3 —2A 64
Zenith Lodge. N3 —7E 14
Zennor Rd. SW12 —1G 109
Zenoria St. SE22 —4F 95
Zermatt Rd. T Hth —4C 124
Zetland Ho. W8 —3K 75
(off Marloes Rd.)
Zetland St. E14 —5D 64
Zion Pl. T Hth —4D 124
Zion Rd. T Hth —4D 124
Zoar St. SE1 —1C 78 (2L 147)
Zoffany St. N19 —2H 45

AREAS COVERED BY THIS ATLAS

with their map square reference

Names in this index shown in CAPITAL LETTERS, followed by their Postcode area, are Postal addresses (Postal Districts in London)

ABBEY WOOD. (SE2) —4C 84
Acton Green. —4K 73
ACTON. (W3) —1J 73
ADDINGTON. (CR0) —5C 136
ADDISCOMBE. (CR0) —1G 135
Aldborough Hatch. —4K 35
Aldersbrook. —2K 49
Alperton. —1E 56
ANERLEY.(SE20) —2H 125
Angell Town. —1A 94
Avery Hill. —6H 99

BALHAM. (SW12) —1F 109
Bandonhill. —4H 133
BARKING. (IG11) —1G 51
BARKINGSIDE. (IG6) —3G 35
BARNEHURST. (DA7) —3J 101
BARNES. (SW13) —2B 90
BARNET. (EN4 & EN5) —4B 4
Barnet Vale. —5E 4
Barnsbury. —7K 45
Barons Court. —5G 75
BATTERSEA. (SW11) —1B 92
Bayswater. —7A 60
Beacontree Heath. —2G 53

BECKENHAM. (BR3) —1C 126
Beckton. —5D 66
Beckton Park. —6D 66
Becontree. —2E 52
Beddington Corner. —7E 122
BEDDINGTON. (CR0 & SM6)
—3J 133
Bedford Park. —3K 73
Belgravia. —3E 76 (7H 145)
Bell Green. —4B 112
Bellingham. —3D 112
Belmont. —1B 24
(Harrow)
BELVEDERE. (DA17) —3G 85
Benhilton. —2K 131
BERMONDSEY. (SE1 & SE16)
—2F 79 (5F 148)
BERRYLANDS. (KT5) —6G 119
BETHNAL GREEN. (E2)
—3H 63 (2J 143)
BEXLEY. (DA5) —7H 101
BEXLEYHEATH. (DA4 & DA7)
—4G 101
BICKLEY. (BR1) —3C 128
Blackfen. —6A 100
Blackheath Park. —4H 97

BLACKHEATH. (SE3) —2H 97
Blackheath Vale. —2H 97
Blackwall. —7E 64
Blendon. —6D 100
Bloomsbury. —5J 61 (5C 140)
Blythe Hill. —7B 96
Borough, The. —2D 78 (4A 148)
Boston Manor. —5B 72
Bounds Green. —6C 16
Bow Common. —5C 64
BOW. (E3) —3C 64
Bowes Park. —7D 16
Brent Cross. —7E 26
Brentford End. —7B 72
BRENTFORD. (TW8) —6D 72
BRIMSDOWN. (EN3) —2F 9
BRIXTON. (SW2) —4K 93
Broadgate. —5E 62 (5C 142)
Broad Green. —7B 124
BROCKLEY. (SE4) —4B 96
Bromley. —3D 64
(Bow)
BROMLEY. (BR1 & BR2) —2J 127
(Kent)
Bromley Park. —1G 127
Brompton. —2D 76 (7D 144)

Brondesbury. —7H 43
Brondesbury Park. —1G 59
Brook Green. —4F 75
Broom Hill. —7K 129
Brownswood Park. —2B 46
Brunswick Park. —3K 15
BUCKHURST HILL. (IG9) —2G 21
Buckingham Palace.
—2G 77 (5L 145)
Burnt Oak. —1J 25
Bushey Heath. —1C 10
Bushey Mead. —3F 121
BUSHEY. (WD2) —1A 10
Bush Hill Park. —6A 8

CAMBERWELL. (SE5) —1D 94
CAMDEN TOWN. (NW1) —1F 61
Cann Hall. —4G 49
Canning Town. —6H 65
Canonbury. —6C 46
Canons Park. —7K 11
Carshalton Beeches. —7C 132
Carshalton on the Hill. —7E 132
CARSHALTON. (SM5) —4E 132
Castelnau. —6D 74

CATFORD. (SE6) —7D 96
CHADWELL HEATH. (RM6) —7D 36
Chalk Farm. —7E 44
Chapel End. —1C 32
CHARLTON. (SE7) —6B 82
Chase Side. —1J 7
CHEAM. (SM2 & SM3) —6G 131
CHELSEA. (SW3) —5C 76
CHIGWELL. (IG7) —3K 21
Child's Hill. —3J 43
CHINGFORD. (E4) —1K 19
Chingford Green. —1A 20
Chingford Hatch. —4A 20
Chingford Mount. —4H 19
Chipping Barnet. —4B 4
CHISLEHURST. (BR7) —7G 115
Chislehurst West. —5E 114
CHISWICK. (W4) —6K 73
Church End. —6A 42
(Willesden)
CHURCH END. (N3) —1H 27
(Finchley)
CITY OF LONDON. (EC1 to EC4)
—6D 62 (8A 142)
Clapham Common. —5F 93
Clapham Junction. —4C 92

Clapham Park. —6H 93
CLAPHAM. (SW4) —4G 93
Clapton Park. —4K 47
Clayhall. —2D 34
Clerkenwell. —4A 62 (4J 141)
COCKFOSTERS. (EN4) —4K 5
Coldblow. —1J 117
Cole Park. —6A 88
Colindale. —3A 26
College Park. 3D 58
COLLIER ROW. (RM5) —1H 37
Collier's Wood. —7B 108
Colney Hatch. —6J 15
Coney Hall. —3G 137
Coombe. —7K 105
Copse Hill. —7D 106
Cottenham Park. —1D 120
Covent Garden. —1D 50
Cranbrook. —1D 50
Cranley Gardens. —4F 29
Creekmouth. —4A 68
CRICKLEWOOD. (NW2) —4F 43
Crofton Park. —5B 96
Crouch End. —7H 29
CROYDON. (CR0) —2C 134
Crystal Palace. —6F 111
Crystal Palace National Recreation
    Cen. —6G 111
Cubitt Town. —4E 80
Custom House. —6A 64
Cyprus. —7E 66

DAGENHAM. (RM8 to RM10)
    —6G 53
Dalston. —6F 47
Dartmouth Park. —3F 45
De Beauvoir Town. —7E 46
DEPTFORD. (SE8) —7C 80
Dollis Hill. —3C 42
Dormer's Wells. —7F 55
Downham. —5F 113
Ducks Island. —6A 4
Dudden Hill. —5D 42
DULWICH. (SE21) —2E 110
Dulwich Village. —7E 94

EALING. (W5) —7D 56
EARL'S COURT. (SW5) —5J 75
Earlsfield. —1A 108
East Acton. —7A 58
East Barnet. —6H 5
Eastcote. —7A 22
EAST DULWICH. (SE22) —4F 95
EAST FINCHLEY. (N2) —4C 28
EAST HAM. (E6) —1D 66
East Sheen. —4J 89
East Village. —5A 22
East Wickham. —1C 100
EDEN PARK. (BR3) —5C 126
Edgware Bury. —1A 12
EDGWARE. (HA8) —6B 12
Edmonton. —4B 18
ELMERS END. (BR3) —4K 125
ELMSTEAD. (BR7) —6D 114
Eltham Park. —4E 98
ELTHAM. (SE9) —6D 98
Elthorne Heights. —5H 55
ENFIELD. (EN1 to EN3) —3J 7
Enfield Highway. —2E 8
Enfield Town. —3J 7
EWELL. (KT17) —7B 130

Fair Cross. —5J 51
Fairlop. —1K 35
Falconwood. —4J 99

Fallow Corner. —7F 15
FINCHLEY. (N3) —1J 27
Finsbury. —3A 62 (2H 141)
FINSBURY PARK. (N4) —2A 46
Fitzrovia. —5G 61 (5L 139)
Foots Cray. —6C 116
Forestdale. —7A 136
FOREST GATE. (E7) —5K 49
FOREST HILL. (SE23) —2J 111
Fortis Green. —3E 28
Fortune Green. —4J 43
Forty Hill. —1A 8
Friday Hill. —2B 20
Friern Barnet. —5J 15
FULHAM. (SW6) —2G 91
Fulwell. —4H 103
Fulwell Cross. —2G 35
Furzedown. —5F 109

Gants Hill. —6E 34
Giggshill. —7A 118
Globe Town. —3K 63
GOLDERS GREEN. (NW11) —6G 27
Goodmayes. —1A 52
Gospel Oak. —4E 44
Grahame Park. —1B 26
Grange Park. —6G 7
Greenford Green. —6J 39
GREENFORD. (UB6) —3G 55
Greenhill. —5K 23
GREENWICH. (SE10) —7E 80
Grove Park. —1J 89
    (Chiswick)
Grove Park. —3K 113
    (Lee)
Gunnersbury. —4H 73

HACKBRIDGE. (SM6) —1E 132
HACKNEY. (E8) —6H 47
Hackney Wick. —6C 48
Hadley. —3C 4
Hadley Wood. —1F 5
Haggerston. —2F 63
Hale End. —6A 20
Hale, The. —5E 12
HAMMERSMITH. (W6) —4E 74
Hampstead Garden Suburb. —5A 28
HAMPSTEAD. (NW3) —4A 44
Hampton Court. —3A 118
HAMPTON HILL. (TW12) —5G 103
HAMPTON. (TW12) —7F 103
HAMPTON WICK. (KT1) —1C 118
HAM. (TW10) —3C 104
Hanger Hill. —4F 57
HANWELL. (W7) —1K 71
HANWORTH. (TW13) —4B 102
Harlesden. —2A 58
Harringay. —5B 30
HARROW. (HA1 to HA3) —6J 23
Harrow on the Hill. —1J 39
HARROW WEALD. (HA3) —7D 10
HATCH END. (HA5) —1D 22
HAYES. (BR2) —1K 137
    (Kent)
Headstone. —4G 23
HENDON. (NW4) —5D 26
HERNE HILL. (SE24) —6C 94
Heston. —7E 70
Higham Hill. —2A 32
Highams Park. —6A 20
HIGH BARNET. (EN5) —3B 4
HIGHBURY. (N5) —4B 46
HIGHGATE. (N6) —1F 45
Highwood Hill. —3G 13
Hither Green. —6G 97
Holborn. —5A 62 (6G 141)

Holders Hill. —2F 27
Holland Park. —1H 75
HOLLOWAY. (N7) —3J 45
HOMERTON. (E9) —5A 48
Honor Oak. —6K 95
Honor Oak Park. —7A 96
Horn Park. —5K 97
HORNSEY. (N8) —4J 29
Hornsey Vale. —5K 29
HOUNSLOW. (TW3 to TW6) —3F 87
Hounslow West. —2C 86
Houses of Parliament.
    —2J 77 (5D 146)
Hoxton. —2E 62
Hurlingham. —3K 91
Hyde Park. —1D 76 (2E 144)
HYDE, THE. (NW9) —5B 26

ILFORD. (IG1 to IG6) —3F 51
ISLEWORTH. (TW7) —3A 88
ISLINGTON. (N1) —7B 46

Joydens Wood. —4K 117

Kempton Park Race Course. —7A 102
KENNINGTON. (SE11) —6A 78
Kensal Green. —3E 58
Kensal Rise. —2F 59
Kensal Town. —4G 59
KENSINGTON. (W8) —2K 75
KENTISH TOWN. (NW5) —5F 45
KENTON. (HA3) —5C 24
Kew Gardens. —7F 73
KEW. (TW9) —7G 73
Kidbrooke. —2K 97
KILBURN. (NW6) —1J 59
Kingsbury. —6J 25
Kingsbury Green. —5J 25
King's Cross. —2J 61
Kingsland. —6E 46
KINGSTON UPON THAMES.
    (KT1 & KT2) —2E 118
Kingston Vale. —4A 106
Knightsbridge. —2D 76 (6E 144)

Ladywell. —5D 96
LAMBETH. (SE1 & SE11)
    —3K 77 (7E 146)
Lamorbey. —1K 115
Lampton. —1F 87
Lea Bridge. —3K 47
Leamouth. —7G 65
LEE. (SE12) —5H 97
Lessness Heath. —5G 85
LEWISHAM. (SE13) —3E 96
LEYTON. (E10) —3E 48
LEYTONSTONE. (E11) —1G 49
Limehouse. —6B 64
Lisson Grove. —5C 60 (5D 138)
Little Ealing. —4D 72
LITTLE HEATH. (RM6) —4B 36
    (Romford)
Little Ilford. —4E 50
Little Stanmore. —7A 12
London City Airport. —1C 82
LONDON, CITY OF. (EC1 to EC4)
    —6D 62 (8A 142)
London Zoo. —2E 60
Lonesome. —1G 123
LONG DITTON. (KT6) —7C 118
Longlands. —3H 115
Lords Cricket Ground.
    —3B 60 (2B 138)
LOWER CLAPTON. (E5) —4H 47

LOWER EDMONTON. (N9) —3B 18
Lower Holloway. —5K 45
Lower Place. —2J 57
Lower Sydenham. —4A 112
Loxford. —5G 51
Lyonsdown. —5F 5

MAIDA HILL. (W9) —4H 59
Maida Vale. —3K 59
Malden Green. —1C 130
MANOR PARK. (E12) —4C 50
    (Newham)
Marks Gate. —2E 36
Marling Park. —7D 102
Marylebone. —5E 60 (5H 139)
Maswell Park. —5G 87
Mawney. —3H 37
Mayfair. —7F 61 (1J 145)
Maypole. —1K 117
    (Bexley)
Merry Hill. —1A 10
Merton. —7K 107
Merton Park. —2J 121
Mid Beckton. —5D 66
Mile End. —3A 64
MILL HILL. (NW7) —5G 13
Mill Meads. —2F 65
Millwall. —4D 80
MITCHAM. (CR4) —3D 122
Monken Hadley. —2C 4
Monks Orchard. —7A 126
Morden Park. —6C 120
MORDEN. (SM4) —3K 121
MORTLAKE. (SW14) —3K 89
Motspur Park. —6C 120
Mottingham. —2C 114
MUSWELL HILL. (N10) —3F 29

Nash. —6J 137
Neasden. —3A 42
NEW BARNET. (EN4 & EN5) —4F 5
New Beckenham. —6B 112
Newbury Park. —6H 35
New Charlton. —4A 82
New Cross Gate. —1K 95
NEW CROSS. (SE14) —7B 80
New Eltham. —2G 115
Newington. —3C 78 (7L 147)
Newlands. —3K 11
    (Edgware)
Newlands. —5K 95
    (SE23)
NEW MALDEN. (KT3) —4A 120
NEW SOUTHGATE. (N11) —5A 16
Nine Elms. —7G 77
Noel Park. —2B 30
NORBITON. (KT1 & KT2) —2G 119
Norbury. —2K 123
North Acton. —4K 57
North Beckton. —5C 66
NORTH CHEAM. (SM3) —4F 131
North Cray. —5E 116
North End. —2A 44
    (Hampstead)
Northfields. —3B 72
NORTH FINCHLEY. (N12) —5F 15
NORTH HARROW. (HA2) —6F 23
NORTH KENSINGTON. (W10) —5F 59
NORTHOLT. (UB5) —7E 38
North Sheen. —3G 89
NORTHUMBERLAND HEATH. (DA8)
    —7J 85
North Wembley. —2B 40
North Woolwich. —2E 82
Norwood Green. —4E 70
Norwood New Town. —6C 110

NORWOOD. (SE19) —6E 110
NOTTING HILL. (W11) —7H 59
Nunhead. —3H 95

Oakleigh Park. —1G 15
Oakwood. —6C 6
Old Bexley. —7H 101
Old Brentford. —7D 72
Old Ford. —2B 64
Old Isleworth. —3B 88
Old Malden. —1B 130
Old Oak Common. —5A 58
ORPINGTON. (BR5 & BR6) —7K 129
Osidge. —1A 16
Osterley. —7H 71
Oval Cricket Ground, The. —6K 77

PADDINGTON. (W2) —6B 60 (8A 138)
PALMERS GREEN. (N13) —4F 17
PARK LANGLEY. (BR3) —4E 126
Park Royal. —3H 57
Parson's Green. —1J 91
PECKHAM. (SE15) —1G 95
Penge. —7J 111
Pentonville. —2K 61
Perivale. —1C 56
Petersham. —1E 104
PETTS WOOD. (BR5) —5G 129
Pimlico. —4G 77
Pinner Green. —2A 22
PINNER. (HA5) —3C 22
Pinnerwood Park. —1A 22
Plaistow. —7J 113
    (Bromley)
PLAISTOW. (E13) —3K 65
    (Newham)
Plashet. —6C 50
Plumstead. —4J 83
Plumstead Common. —6H 83
Ponders End. —5D 8
POPLAR. (E14) —7D 64
Poverest. —4K 129
Preston. —1E 40
Primrose Hill. —1E 60
Putney Heath. —6E 90
PUTNEY. (SW15) —4G 91
Putney Vale. —3C 106

Queensbury. —3F 25

Ratcliff. —6A 64
Rayners Lane. —1E 38
Raynes Park. —4E 120
Redbridge. —6C 34
Regent's Park. —2F 61 (1K 139)
Richmond Park. —1J 105
RICHMOND. (TW9 & TW10) —5D 88
Rippleside. —1B 68
Rise Park. —1K 37
Roe Green. —4J 25
Roehampton. —7C 90
Rosehill. —1A 132
ROTHERHITHE. (SE16)
    —2J 79 (5L 149)
Roundshaw. —7J 133
Roxeth. —2H 39
RUSH GREEN. (RM7) —1K 53
Ruxley. —7E 116

St Helier. —7C 122
St James's. —1H 77 (3A 146)
St John's. —2C 96
    (Deptford)

ST JOHN'S WOOD. (NW8) —2B 60
St Luke's. —4C 62 (3M 141)
St Margarets. —6B 88
  (Twickenham)
St Pancras. —3J 61 (1C 140)
Sands End. —1A 92
Seething Wells. —6C 118
Selhurst. —6D 124
Seven Kings. —1J 51
Sewardstone. —1K 9
Shacklewell. 4F 47
Shadwell. —7J 63 (9L 143)
SHEPHERD'S BUSH. (W12) —2E 74
SHIRLEY. (CR0) —2K 135
Shirley Oaks. —1K 135
Shooters Hill. —1E 98
Shoreditch. —3E 62 (2D 142)
SHORTLANDS. (BR2) —2G 127
SIDCUP. (DA14 & DA15) —4A 116
Silvertown. —1B 82
Snaresbrook. —5J 33
Soho. —6H 61 (8A 140)
Somers Town. —3H 61 (1A 140)
South Acton. —2H 73
Southall Green. —3C 70
SOUTHALL. (UB1 & UB2) —1D 70
South Barnet. —1K 15
South Beddington. —6H 133
Southborough. —7E 118
  (Surbiton)
SOUTHBOROUGH. (BR1 & BR2)
  (Bromley) —6C 128
South Bromley. —6F 65
South Chingford. —6G 19
SOUTH CROYDON. (CR2) —5D 134
Southend. —4E 112
Southfields. —1J 107
SOUTHGATE. (N14) 1C 16
South Hackney. —1J 63
South Hampstead. —7A 44
SOUTH HARROW. (HA2) —3G 39
SOUTH KENSINGTON. (SW7)
  —4B 76 (8B 144)

SOUTH LAMBETH. (SW8) —7J 77
SOUTH NORWOOD. (SE25)
  —4F 125
SOUTH RUISLIP. (HA4) —4A 38
South Teddington. —7A 104
SOUTH TOTTENHAM. (N15) —5F 31
SOUTHWARK. (SE1)
  —1D 78 (2A 148)
South Wimbledon. —6K 107
SOUTH WOODFORD. (E18) —2J 33
Spencer Park. —5B 92
Spitalfields. —5F 63 (5E 142)
Spring Grove. —2J 87
Spring Park. —3C 136
Stamford Hill. —1F 47
STANMORE. (HA7) —5G 11
STEPNEY. (E1) —5K 63
STOCKWELL. (SW9) —2K 93
STOKE NEWINGTON. (N16) —3F 47
Stonegrove. —4A 12
STONELEIGH. (KT19) —5C 130
Stoneybridge. —1K 57
Strand on the Green. —6H 73
STRATFORD. (E15) —7F 49
Stratford Marsh. —7D 48
Stratford New Town. —5F 49
Strawberry Hill. —3K 103
Streatham Common. —6J 109
Streatham Hill. —1J 109
Streatham Park. —4G 109
STREATHAM. (SW16) —4J 109
Streatham Vale. —7G 109
Stroud Green. —7K 29
Sudbury. —5B 40
Suffield Hatch. —4K 19
Summerstown. —3A 108
Sundridge. —6A 114
  (Bromley)
SUNDRIDGE PARK. (BR1) —7A 114
SURBITON. (KT5 & KT6) —6D 118
SUTTON. (SM1 to SM3) —5K 131
  (Surrey)
SYDENHAM. (SE26) —4J 111

TEDDINGTON. (TW11) —5A 104
Temple Fortune. —5H 27
Temple Mills. —5D 48
THAMES DITTON. (KT7) —6A 118
Thames Flood Barrier. —2B 82
Thamesmead Central. —1A 84
Thamesmead East. —6G 85
Thamesmead North. —6C 68
THAMESMEAD. (SE28) —2A 84
Thamesmead South. —2D 84
Thamesmead South West. —2K 83
Thamesmead West. —3H 83
THORNTON HEATH. (CR7) —4B 124
Tokyngton. —6H 41
Tooting Bec. —3E 108
Tooting Graveney. —6D 108
TOOTING. (SW17) —5C 108
Tottenham Hale. —3G 31
TOTTENHAM. (N17) —2F 31
Totteridge. —1B 14
Tower of London, The.
  —7F 63 (1E 148)
Tufnell Park. —4G 45
Tulse Hill. —1B 110
Turnham Green. —5K 73
Twickenham Rugby Football Ground.
  —6J 87
TWICKENHAM. (TW1 & TW2)
  —1A 104

Underhill. —5D 4
UPPER CLAPTON. (E5) —2H 47
UPPER EDMONTON. (N18) —5C 18
UPPER ELMERS END. (BR3)
  —5B 126
UPPER HOLLOWAY. (N19) —2G 45
Upper Norwood. —1E 124
Upper Ruxley. —7G 117
Upper Shirley. —4K 135
Upper Sydenham. —3H 111
Upper Tooting. —3D 108
Upper Walthamstow. —4F 33

Upton. —5D 100
  (Bexleyheath)
Upton. —7J 49
  (Plaistow E13)
Upton Park. —2B 66
  (E6)

Vale of Health. —2A 44
Vauxhall. —5J 77

Waddon. —3A 134
Walham Green. —7K 75
Wallend. —1E 66
WALLINGTON. (SM6) —6F 133
WALTHAMSTOW. (E17) —4C 32
WALWORTH. (SE17) —5C 78
Wandsworth Common. —1D 108
WANDSWORTH. (SW18) —5K 91
Wanstead. —7K 33
Wapping. —1H 79 (3K 149)
Watling. —7E 12
WEALDSTONE. (HA3) —3J 23
WELLING. (DA16) —3B 100
WEMBLEY. (HA9 & HA0) —5E 40
Wembley Park. —5G 41
Wembley Stadium. —5G 41
West Acton. —6G 57
West Barnes. —4D 120
West Beckton. —6B 66
Westbourne Green. —6H 59
WEST BROMPTON. (SW10) —6A 76
West Dulwich. —2D 110
WEST EALING. (W13) —7B 56
West End. —2B 54
  (Northolt)
WEST EWELL. (KT19) —7A 130
West Green. —4B 30
West Ham. —1J 65
West Hampstead. —6K 43
West Harrow. —7G 23
West Heath. —7D 84

West Hendon. —7C 26
West Hill. —6H 91
WEST KENSINGTON. (W14) —4H 75
West Kilburn. —3H 59
WESTMINSTER. (SW1)
  —2J 77 (5C 146)
WEST NORWOOD. (SE27) —4C 110
WEST WICKHAM. (BR4) —1E 136
WHETSTONE. (N20) —2F 15
Whitechapel. —6G 63 (7G 143)
White City. —7D 58
WHITTON. (TW2) —7G 87
Widmore. —3B 128
Willesden Green. —6D 42
WILLESDEN. (NW10) —6C 42
Wimbledon, All England Tennis Club.
  —3G 107
Wimbledon Park. —3J 107
WIMBLEDON. (SW19) —6G 107
WINCHMORE HILL. (N21) —7F 7
Windsor Park. —5F 67
Woodcote Green. —7G 133
Wood End. —5H 39
  (Northolt)
Woodford. —6E 20
Woodford Bridge. —6H 21
WOODFORD GREEN. (IG8) —6D 20
Woodford Side. —5C 20
Woodford Wells. —3E 20
WOOD GREEN. (N22) —2A 30
Woodlands. —2J 87
  (Isleworth)
Woodside. —6G 125
  (SE25)
Woodside Park. —4D 14
WOOLWICH. (SE18) —3E 82
WORCESTER PARK. (KT4) —1C 130
World's End. —4F 7
Wrythe, The. —3D 132

Yeading. —4A 54

BRITISH RAIL, DOCKLANDS LIGHT RAILWAY AND LONDON UNDERGROUND STATIONS
with their map square reference

ABBEY WOOD, British Rail —4C 84
ACTON CENTRAL, British Rail —1K 73
ACTON MAIN LINE, British Rail —6J 57
ACTON TOWN, District & Piccadilly —2G 73
ADDISCOMBE, British Rail —1F 135
ALBANY PARK, British Rail —2D 116
ALDGATE, Circle & Hammersmith & City —6F 63 (8E 142)
ALDGATE EAST, District & Hammersmith & City
  —6F 63 (7F 142)
ALDWYCH, Piccadilly —7K 61 (9F 140)
ALEXANDRA PALACE, British Rail —2J 29
ALL SAINTS, Dockland Light Railway —7D 64
ALPERTON, Piccadilly —1D 56
ANERLEY, British Rail —1H 125
ANGEL, Northern —2A 62
ANGEL ROAD, British Rail —5D 18
ARCHWAY, Northern —2G 45
ARNOS GROVE, Piccadilly —5B 16
ARSENAL, Piccadilly —3A 46

BAKER STREET, Bakerloo, Circle, Hammersmith & City & Jubilee
  —4D 60 (4F 138)
BALHAM, British Rail & Northern —1F 109
BANK, British Rail, Central & Northern —6D 62 (8A 142)

BANK, Docklands Light Railway —7D 62 (9B 142)
BARBICAN, British Rail, Circle & Hammersmith & City
  —5C 62 (5L 141)
BARKING, British Rail, District & Hammersmith & City —7G 51
BARKINGSIDE, Central —3H 35
BARNEHURST, British Rail —2J 101
BARNES BRIDGE, Brtish Rail —2B 90
BARNES, British Rail —3C 90
BARONS COURT, District & Piccadilly —5G 75
BATTERSEA PARK, British Rail —7F 77
BAYSWATER, Circle & District —7K 59
BECKENHAM HILL, British Rail —5E 112
BECKENHAM JUNCTION, British Rail —1C 126
BECKTON, Docklands Light Railway —5E 66
BECKTON PARK, Docklands Light Railway —7D 66
BECONTREE, District —6D 52
BEDDINGTON LANE, British Rail —6G 123
BELLINGHAM, British Rail —3D 112
BELSIZE PARK, Northern —5C 44
BELVEDERE, British Rail —3H 85
BERMONDSEY, Jubilee —3G 79 (6G 149)
  (Open 1998)
BERRYLANDS, British Rail —4H 119
BETHNAL GREEN, British Rail —4H 63 (3J 143)
BETHNAL GREEN, Central —3J 63 (2L 143)

BEXLEY, British Rail —1G 117
BEXLEYHEATH, British Rail —2E 100
BICKLEY, British Rail —3C 128
BIRKBECK, British Rail —3J 125
BLACKFRIARS, British Rail, Circle & District —7B 62 (9J 141)
BLACKHEATH, British Rail —3H 97
BLACKHORSE ROAD, British Rail & Victoria —4K 31
BOND STREET, Central & Jubilee —6F 61 (8J 139)
BOROUGH, Northern —2C 78 (5M 147)
BOSTON MANOR, Piccadilly —4A 72
BOUNDS GREEN, Piccadilly —6C 16
BOW CHURCH, Docklands Light Railway —3C 64
BOWES PARK, British Rail —7D 16
BOW ROAD, District & Hammersmith & City —3C 64
BRENT CROSS, Northern —7F 27
BRENTFORD, British Rail —6C 72
BRIMSDOWN, British Rail —2F 9
BRIXTON, British Rail & Victoria —4A 94
BROCKLEY, British Rail —3A 96
BROMLEY-BY-BOW, District & Hammersmith & City —3E 64
BROMLEY NORTH, British Rail —1J 127
BROMLEY SOUTH, British Rail —3J 127
BRONDESBURY, British Rail —7H 43
BRONDESBURY PARK, British Rail —1G 59
BRUCE GROVE, British Rail —2F 31

MALDEN MANOR, British Rail —7A **120**
MANOR HOUSE, Piccadilly —7C **30**
MANOR PARK, British Rail —4B **50**
MANSION HOUSE, Circle & District —7C **62** (9M **141**)
MARBLE ARCH, Central —6D **60** (8F **138**)
MARYLAND, British Rail —6G **49**
MARYLEBONE, British Rail & Bakerloo —5D **60** (5E **138**)
MAZE HILL, British Rail —6G **81**
MERTON PARK, British Rail —1J **121**
MILE END, Central, District & Hammersmith & City —3B **64**
MILL HILL BROADWAY, British Rail —6F **13**
MILL HILL EAST, Northern —7B **14**
MITCHAM, British Rail —4C **122**
MITCHAM JUNCTION, British Rail —5E **122**
MONUMENT, Circle & District —7D **62** (9B **142**)
MOORGATE, British Rail, Circle, Hammersmith & City & Northern
—5D **62** (6A **142**)

MORDEN, Northern —3K **121**
MORDEN ROAD, British Rail —2K **121**
MORDEN SOUTH, British Rail —5J **121**
MORNINGTON CRESCENT, Northern —2G **61**
MORTLAKE, British Rail —3J **89**
MOTSPUR PARK, British Rail —5D **120**
MOTTINGHAM, British Rail —1D **114**
MUDCHUTE, Dockslands Light Railway —4D **80**

NEASDEN, Jubilee —5A **42**
NEW BARNET, British Rail —5G **5**
NEW BECKENHAM, British Rail —7B **112**
NEWBURY PARK, Central —6H **35**
NEW CROSS, British Rail & Metropolitan —7B **80**
NEW CROSS GATE, British Rail & Metropolitan —7A **80**
NEW ELTHAM, British Rail —1G **115**
NEW MALDEN, British Rail —3A **120**
NEW SOUTHGATE, British Rail —5A **16**
NORBITON, British Rail —1G **119**
NORBURY, British Rail —1K **123**
NORTH ACTON, Central —5K **57**
NORTH DULWICH, British Rail —5D **94**
NORTH EALING, Piccadilly —6F **57**
NORTHFIELDS, Piccadilly —3C **72**
NORTH GREENWICH, Jubilee Line —2G **81**
  (Open 1998)
NORTH HARROW, Metropolitan —5F **23**
NORTHOLT, Central —6E **38**
NORTHOLT PARK, British Rail —4F **39**
NORTH SHEEN, British Rail —4G **89**
NORTHUMBERLAND PARK, British Rail —7C **18**
NORTH WEMBLEY, British Rail & Bakerloo —3D **40**
NORTHWICK PARK, Metropolitan —7B **24**
NORTH WOOLWICH, British Rail —2E **82**
NORWOOD JUNCTION, British Rail —4G **125**
NOTTING HILL GATE, Central, Circle & District —1J **75**
NUNHEAD, British Rail —2J **95**

OAKLEIGH PARK, British Rail —7G **5**
OAKWOOD, Piccadilly —5B **6**
OLD STREET, British Rail & Northern —4D **62** (3B **142**)
OSTERLEY, Piccadilly —7H **71**
OVAL, Northern —6A **78**
OXFORD CIRCUS, Bakerloo, Central & Victoria —6G **61** (8L **139**)

PADDINGTON, Bakerloo, British Rail, Circle, District &
  Hammersmith & City —6B **60** (8A **138**)
PALMERS GREEN, British Rail —4E **16**
PARK ROYAL, Piccadilly —4G **57**
PARSONS GREEN, District —1J **91**
PECKHAM RYE, British Rail —2G **95**
PENGE EAST, British Rail —6J **111**
PENGE WEST, British Rail —6H **111**
PERIVALE, Central —2A **56**
PETTS WOOD, British Rail —5G **129**
PICCADILLY CIRCUS, Bakerloo & Piccadilly —7H **61** (1A **146**)
PIMLICO, Victoria —5H **77**
PINNER, Metropolitan —4C **22**

PLAISTOW, District & Hammersmith & City —2H **65**
PLUMSTEAD, British Rail —4H **83**
PONDERS END, British Rail —5F **9**
POPLAR, Docklands Light Railway —7D **64**
PRESTON ROAD, Metropolitan —1E **40**
PRIMROSE HILL, British Rail —7E **44**
PRINCE REGENT, Docklands Light Railway —7A **66**
PUTNEY BRIDGE, District —3H **91**
PUTNEY, British Rail —4G **91**

QUEENSBURY, Jubilee —3F **25**
QUEENS PARK, British Rail & Bakerloo —2H **59**
QUEEN'S ROAD (PECKHAM), British Rail —1J **95**
QUEENSTOWN ROAD (BATTERSEA), British Rail —1F **93**
QUEENSWAY, Central —7K **59**

RAVENSBOURNE, British Rail —7F **113**
RAVENSCOURT PARK, District —4D **74**
RAYNERS LANE, Metropolitan & Piccadilly —7D **22**
RAYNES PARK, British Rail —2E **120**
RECTORY ROAD, British Rail —3F **47**
REDBRIDGE, Central —6B **34**
REGENT'S PARK, Bakerloo —4F **61** (4J **139**)
RICHMOND, British Rail & District —4E **88**
RODING VALLEY, Central —4G **21**
ROTHERHITHE, Metropolitan —2J **79** (4M **149**)
ROYAL ALBERT, Docklands Light Railway —7C **66**
ROYAL OAK, Hammersmith & City —5K **59**
ROYAL VICTORIA, Docklands Light Railway —7J **65**
RUSSELL SQUARE, Piccadilly —4J **61** (4C **140**)

SAINT HELIER, British Rail —6J **121**
SAINT JAMES'S PARK, Circle & District —3H **77** (6A **146**)
SAINT JAMES STREET, WALTHAMSTOW, British Rail —5A **32**
SAINT JOHNS, British Rail —2C **96**
SAINT JOHN'S WOOD, Jubilee —2B **60**
SAINT MARGARETS, British Rail —6B **88**
SAINT PANCRAS, British Rail, Circle, Hammersmith & City,
  Northern, Piccadilly & Victoria —3J **61** (1C **140**)
SAINT PAUL'S, Central —6C **62** (7L **141**)
SANDERSTEAD, British Rail —7D **134**
SELHURST, British Rail —5E **124**
SEVEN KINGS, British Rail —1J **51**
SEVEN SISTERS, British Rail & Victoria —5E **30**
SHADWELL, Docklands Light Railway & Metropolitan
  —7H **63** (9K **143**)
SHEPHERD'S BUSH, Central —2F **75**
SHEPHERD'S BUSH, Hammersmith & City —1E **74**
SHOREDITCH, Metropolitan —4F **63** (4F **142**)
SHORTLANDS, British Rail —2G **127**
SIDCUP, British Rail —2A **116**
SILVER STREET, British Rail —4A **18**
SILVERTOWN & CITY AIRPORT, British Rail —1B **82**
SLOANE SQUARE, Circle & District —4E **76** (9G **145**)
SNARESBROOK, Central —5J **33**
SOUTH ACTON, British Rail —3J **73**
SOUTHALL, British Rail —2D **70**
SOUTH BERMONDSEY, British Rail —5J **79**
SOUTHBURY, British Rail —4C **8**
SOUTH CROYDON, British Rail —5D **134**
SOUTH EALING, Piccadilly —3D **72**
SOUTHFIELDS, District —1H **107**
SOUTHGATE, Piccadilly —1C **16**
SOUTH GREENFORD, British Rail —3J **55**
SOUTH HAMPSTEAD, British Rail —7A **44**
SOUTH HARROW, Piccadilly —3G **39**
SOUTH KENSINGTON, Circle, District & Piccadilly
  —4B **76** (8B **144**)
SOUTH KENTON, British Rail & Bakerloo —1C **40**
SOUTH MERTON, British Rail —3H **121**
SOUTH QUAY, Docklands Light Railway —2D **80**
SOUTH RUISLIP, British Rail & Central —5A **38**
SOUTH TOTTENHAM, British Rail —5F **31**
SOUTHWARK, Jubilee Line —1B **78** (3J **147**)
  (Open 1998)

SOUTH WIMBLEDON, Northern —7K **107**
SOUTH WOODFORD, Central —2K **33**
STAMFORD BROOK, District —4B **74**
STAMFORD HILL, British Rail —7E **30**
STANMORE, Jubilee —4J **11**
STEPNEY GREEN, District & Hammersmith & City —4K **63**
STOCKWELL, Northern & Victoria —2J **93**
STOKE NEWINGTON, British Rail —2F **47**
STONEBRIDGE PARK, British Rail & Bakerloo —7H **41**
STONELEIGH, British Rail —5C **130**
STRATFORD, British Rail, Central & Docklands Light Railway
  —7F **49**
STRATFORD, Jubilee Line —7F **49**
  (Open 1998)
STRATFORD (LOW LEVEL), British Rail —7F **49**
STRAWBERRY HILL, British Rail —3K **103**
STREATHAM, British Rail —5H **109**
STREATHAM COMMON, British Rail —7H **109**
STREATHAM HILL, British Rail —2J **109**
SUDBURY & HARROW ROAD, British Rail —5B **40**
SUDBURY HILL, HARROW, British Rail —4J **39**
SUDBURY HILL, Piccadilly —4J **39**
SUDBURY TOWN, Piccadilly —6B **40**
SUNDRIDGE PARK, British Rail —7K **113**
SURBITON, British Rail —6E **118**
SURREY QUAYS, Metropolitan —4K **79**
SUTTON, British Rail —6A **132**
SUTTON COMMON, British Rail —2K **131**
SWISS COTTAGE, Jubilee —7B **44**
SYDENHAM, British Rail —4J **111**
SYDENHAM HILL, British Rail —3F **111**
SYON LANE, British Rail —7A **72**

TEDDINGTON, British Rail —6A **104**
TEMPLE, Circle & District —7K **61** (9F **140**)
THORNTON HEATH, British Rail —4C **124**
TOOTING BEC, Northern —3E **108**
TOOTING, British Rail —6D **108**
TOOTING BROADWAY, Northern —5C **108**
TOTTENHAM COURT ROAD, Central & Northern
  —6H **61** (7B **140**)
TOTTENHAM HALE, British Rail & Victoria —3H **31**
TOTTERIDGE & WHETSTONE, Northern —2F **15**
TOWER GATEWAY, Docklands Light Railway —7F **63** (9E **142**)
TOWER HILL, Circle & District —7F **63** (9E **142**)
TUFNELL PARK, Northern —4G **45**
TULSE HILL, British Rail —2B **110**
TURNHAM GREEN, District —4A **74**
TURNPIKE LANE, Piccadilly —3B **30**
TWICKENHAM, British Rail —7A **88**

UPNEY, District —7K **51**
UPPER HOLLOWAY, British Rail —2H **45**
UPTON PARK, District & Hammersmith & City —1A **66**

VAUXHALL, British Rail & Victoria —5J **77**
VICTORIA, British Rail, Circle, District & Victoria
  —4F **77** (8K **145**)
VICTORIA, Coach Station —4F **77** (9J **145**)

WADDON, British Rail —4^ **134**
WADDON MARSH, British Rail —1K **133**
WALLINGTON, British Rail —6F **133**
WALTHAMSTOW CENTRAL, British Rail & Victoria —5C **32**
WALTHAMSTOW QUEENS ROAD, British Rail —5C **32**
WANDSWORTH COMMON, British Rail —1D **108**
WANDSWORTH ROAD, British Rail —2G **93**
WANDSWORTH TOWN, British Rail —4K **91**
WANSTEAD, Central —6K **33**
WANSTEAD PARK, British Rail —4K **49**
WAPPING, Metropolitan —1J **79** (3L **149**)
WARREN STREET, Northern & Victoria —4G **61** (3L **139**)
WARWICK AVENUE, Bakerloo —4A **60**
WATERLOO, British Rail, Bakerloo & Northern —2A **78** (4G **147**)

Every possible care has been taken to ensure that the information given in this publication is accurate and
whilst the publishers would be grateful to learn of any errors, they regret they cannot accept any responsibility
for loss thereby caused.

The representation on the maps of a road, track or footpath is no evidence of the existence of a right of way.

The Grid on this map is the National Grid taken from the Ordnance Survey map with the permission of the
Controller of Her Majesty's Stationery Office.

Copyright of Geographers' A-Z Map Co. Ltd.

No reproduction by any method whatsoever of any part of this publication is permitted without the prior consent of
the copyright owners.

Printed and bound in Great Britain by
BPC Hazell Books Ltd
A member of
The British Printing Company Ltd